The Principles of JEWISH LAW

The Principles of JEWISH LAW

Edited by

Menachem Elon
Professor of Jewish Law
The Hebrew University of Jerusalem

ENCYCLOPAEDIA JUDAICA

KETER PUBLISHING HOUSE JERUSALEM LTD.
P.O. Box 7145, Jerusalem, Israel

ISBN 0-7065-1415-7
Catalog No. 25079

THE HEBREW UNIVERSITY OF JERUSALEM
The Faculty of Law The Institute for Jewish Studies
THE INSTITUTE FOR RESEARCH IN JEWISH LAW
Publication No. 6

Set by Isratypset Ltd., Jerusalem
Printed and bound by Keterpress Enterprises, Jerusalem
Printed in Israel

CONTENTS

PREFACE

The publishers and editorial board of the *Encyclopaedia Judaica* undertook a task of major significance when they decided to include a special division for Jewish law *(Mishpat Ivri)* in the Encyclopaedia. This important discipline within the general field of Judaica is described in something close to 150 separate entries, which embrace all aspects of the subject: sources of law; general part; the laws of property, obligations, torts, family and inheritance; criminal law; evidence, procedure and execution; public and administrative law; and conflict of laws. In each entry the principle or institution of the law involved is discussed and the main details of that law or institution are given in a clear and concise fashion. The description and the discussion are from two aspects; the first from the internal point of view of Jewish law, and the second in comparison with the accepted discipline in general law, showing the points of similarity and difference. The source for each item in every entry is indicated and at the end of each entry there is appended a detailed bibliography of research material which deals with the various issues discussed in the entry.

The various Jewish law entries in the Encyclopaedia have been received very favorably. We suggested to Keter Publishers that it would be a worthwhile project to publish all the Jewish law material in a separate volume in order to make it easier to use and in order to make it available for as wide an audience as possible. The sum total of the Jewish law articles in the Encyclopaedia form a complete unit which offers the reader a true and methodical description of the principles and institutions of Jewish law in all its areas. In my book *Ha-mishpat ha-Ivri* (Hebrew; Magnes Press, the Hebrew University, Jerusalem, 1973), I discussed at length and in detail the history of Jewish law and its basic principles, the legal sources through which Jewish law continued to grow and develop throughout the ages, as well as the literary sources which contain the enormous amount of material regarding Jewish law in all the various periods. In the introduction to that book I have drawn the attention of the reader who wishes to find a systematic description of each institution in the Jewish legal system according to its various areas – public, criminal and civil – to the entries in the *Encyclopaedia Judaica.* The collection of these entries which is now presented to the reader therefore fills a definite need even for the Hebrew reader, and how much more so for the English reader.

Most of the entries were written by myself, by Justice of the Supreme Court, Professor Hayyim Cohn, by the president of the District Court of Jerusalem, Dr. B. Schereschewsky and by Professor Shalom Albeck. Other entries were written by various scholars, a full list of whom appears at the end of this volume. It goes without saying that the actual method of presentation in the various articles is not the same; each author presented his material in his own way and according to his own research. In many articles the treatment is dogmatic-historical, i.e., a description of the content of the particular law as it was manifested during various periods and in various centers with particular attention to its development. In other entries the description is primarily dogmatic. The common denominator of the overwhelming majority of the articles is that they present a comprehensive description of the subject not only as it is to be found in the Bible and in talmudic literature but also from the point of view of the enormous and varied volume of legal material which accumulated after the closing of the Talmud. The judicial autonomy which Jewish centers enjoyed until close to the Emancipation in the 18th century (and in the Orient even after that date) and the strong social and religious discipline of the organized Jewish community which saw in its Jewish courts and in a day-to-day life according to Jewish law an exalted value, made Jewish law into a living and dynamic legal system relevant in all places where Jews lived – into a system of law which listened to the reverberations of the age and which understood the needs of the generation. Throughout all these periods, Jewish law was both theoretically and practically active in all the various areas of civil law, in many and varied areas of public and administrative law and, to a not inconsiderable degree, even in the area of criminal law. An examination of the contents of each legal institution as it is reflected in the legal literature of the commentaries and novellae, the codes, the collections of documents and *takkanot* clearly verifies this fact. First and foremost among those silent witnesses is the huge and practically inexhaustible literature of the responsa which is, in fact, the case law of Jewish law. This verity will also, I hope, be quite clear to the reader of this present volume. In addition, in many of the entries special attention has been given to the place of Jewish law in the legal system in the State of Israel.

This book is not only intended for Jewish law students, nor even for legal scholars. We hope that every person to whom the world of the *halakhah* is dear and every person who wishes to study various areas in Jewish history and Judaism will find material of relevance to him here.

I believe that the appearance of this volume in this day and age of the return of the Jewish people to political sovereignty, which also involves legal sovereignty, is of special significance. Frequently both within Israel and outside it, the problems of religion and state, as they are reflected in the legal system, are discussed as well as the question of the reception of the principles of Jewish law into the legal system of the Jewish State. All too frequently these discussions take place – and even among the intelligentsia – against a background of ignorance of the scope and detail of Jewish law. This book can be a true aid in this matter.

In order not to delay the publication of the book, we decided to publish the various articles as they were written by their authors for the *Encyclopaedia.* Only changes necessitated by the fact that all the entries appearing in one collection were made. The classification into sections was not always made according to the accepted principles of other legal systems. In fact there is no unified system of classification and very often the principles of classification are quite different from one legal system to another. While fixing criteria in this matter one must take into account the special nature of certain legal institutions in Jewish law. A good example of this is *Ḥazakah* which appears in the section on Procedure because of the procedural character of that subject in Jewish law. Occasionally we included an article in a specific division because of its special connection with the preceding article. A good example of this is the entries Sales, *Ona'ah* and *Hafka'at She'arim* which have been included one after the other in the Laws of Property division. Certain articles appear under their Hebrew names; some of these are: *Ones, Minhag, Takkanot, Ha'anakah* and *Ye'ush.* The reason for this is that some Hebrew concepts do not allow a precise and brief translation into another language. A further consideration is that we feel it to be entirely fittting that basic Hebrew legal concepts should become known in their accepted legal terminology just like the many concepts which are known by their original Latin names even in other legal systems. The reader will easily find the English equivalent of these aspects both in the actual entry and by means of the index.

For the purpose of publishing this volume, all the sources in the text were re-checked and those mistakes which crept in were corrected. Where the reader is referred from one article to another, we have indicated the exact page number in those cases where we felt that it was important. At the end of the volume there is a list of all the bibliographical abbreviations as well as a detailed subject index which will surely help the interested reader to find a specific subject.

It is my pleasant duty to thank all those who helped in the publication of this book. Keter Publishers willingly and enthusiastically accepted the suggestion to produce this separate volume and did much to facilitate its early appearance. Dr. Raphael Posner devoted a great deal of time to help solve the various problems involved in this book, and supervised the preparation of the appendices and index. Rabbi Hayyim Schneid aided him and saw the book through all its stages. Mr. Hillel Wiseberg took an active part in the preparation of the index. Most of the articles were written originally in Hebrew and were translated by Mr. Julius Kopelowitz, B.A., LL.B. And, finally, Rabbi B.D. Klein checked the sources and the bibliographies and contributed in no small manner in correcting the errors. His constructive remarks were always welcome and helpful.

We hope that this book will be an important contribution to the study and knowledge of this important aspect of Judaism and Jewish History and that it will also be of some help in bringing more of the principles of Jewish law into the legal system of the Jewish State.

MENACHEM ELON

Tishrei, 5735 – October, 1974.
The Hebrew University,
Mount Scopus,
Jerusalem.

INTRODUCTION

Contents

DEFINITION AND TERMINOLOGY

Jewish Law in its equivalence to the term *halakhah* comprises all the normative rules of Judaism, both the laws applicable between man and man and the precepts concerning man and God. However, it is now generally accepted that the term *mishpat Ivri* משפט עברי be used for those matters of the *halakhah* whose equivalent is customarily dealt with in other present-day legal systems, that is, matters pertaining to relations between man and man and not the precepts governing the relationship between man and his Maker. This use of the term *mishpat Ivri* diverges from the original meaning of the Hebrew term *mishpat* or *mishpatim*. Used in the sense of a system of laws – like the English term "law," or the German term *"Recht"* – the term refers not only to matters between man and man (in the sense of *jus, ius humanum*), but also to the precepts between man and his Maker (in the sense of *fas, ius divinum*). Thus for instance in Exodus 21:1 the words *ve-elleh ha-mishpatim* are stated by way of introduction to chapters 21, 22 and 23, which deal not only with matters of civil and criminal law but also with the laws of the sabbatical year, the Sabbath, first fruits, and so on.

Another Hebrew term for law is the word *dinim* (sing. *din*), used to designate matters included in the fourth mishnaic order, *Nezikin* (see Deut. 17:8; Ḥag. 1:8; *Ramban* Gen. 34:13). The term comprises two main classes of laws, namely *dinei mamonot* and *dinei nefashot*. The concept of *dinei mamonot* corresponds to but is not identical with "civil law," since it is wider than the latter in some respects (see Sanh. 2:2 and see below) and narrower in others, excluding, for instance, that part of family law dealing with what is ritually permitted and prohibited, the laws of usury, and so on. (Subject to this qualification, the term civil law will be used below and in the other articles on Jewish law as the equivalent of *dinei mamonot*.) The concept *dinei nefashot* takes in that part of the criminal law dealing with matters that call for capital and certain other forms of corporal punishment. (The term *dinei kenasot* relates to matters which are part of *dinei mamonot;* see Obligation, Law of[1].) However, even the term *dinim* does not exclude matters concerning the precepts between man and God, as is evident from the concept of *dinei issur ve-hetter* – ritual prohibitions and permissions.

The reason for the absence in Hebrew sources of an accepted term describing legal norms pertaining exclusively to relations between man and man – for instance in the sense of "English law" or "Swiss law" – lies in the basic fact that both the laws applicable between man and man and the precepts concerning man and God have a single and common source, namely the Written and the Oral Law. This fact further asserts itself in the phenomenon that all parts of the entire halakhic system share and are subject to common modes of creation, thought and expression, as well as principles and rules (see below). This, however, constitutes no hindrance to the acceptance of the term *mishpat ivri* in the sense here described. The term first came to be used in this sense around the beginning of the 20th century, when the Jewish national awakening – which to some extent stimulated also the desire for a return to Jewish law – prompted a search for a Hebrew term to designate that part of the *halakhah* whose subject matter paralleled that which normally comprises other legal systems. What was sought was a suitable term that would circumscribe the bounds of the legal research and preparatory work to be undertaken. Thus there was accepted the term *mishpat "Ivri,"* in the same way as *safah "Ivrit"* and later also *medinah "Ivrit."* Today the term *mishpat Ivri,* as defined above, is generally accepted in all fields of practical legal life and research in the sense here described. Throughout this work Jewish Law is used as synonymous with *mishpat Ivri* as explained above. In the Knesset legislation use is made of the term *din Torah* (authorized Eng. translation, "Jewish religious law": see, e.g., sec. 2, "Rabbinical Courts Jurisdiction (Marriage and Divorce) Law," 1953); this Hebrew term is inaccurate as far as the distinction between *de-oraita* and *de-rabbanan* (see below) is concerned.

"RELIGIOUS" HALAKHAH AND "LEGAL" HALAKHAH

Common Features. The "religious" and the "legal" norms of the *halakhah* share certain common features, a fact that finds expression in a number of ways (and accounts for our use of quotation marks since the *halakhah* does not recognize the concept of special "religious" law, which is used here in its modern sense). In the talmudic discussions the same theoretical argumentation, terminology, and modes of interpretation that are applied to a matter of civil law are applied also to matters concerning, for instance, the Sabbath, the sacrificial cult and ritual purity and impurity. Many legal principles are common to both parts of the *halakhah*. Thus for instance the laws of agency apply in the same way to matters of *hekdesh, terumah,* and the slaughter of the paschal sacrifice, as they do to matters of marriage, divorce, recovery of debt, and so on. Moreover, the essential legal principle underlying the principal-agent relationship – that "a person's agent is as himself" – was derived by the scholars from the scriptural passages dealing with matters of the pascal sacrifice and *terumah* (Kid. 41b. et al.), and it is in relation to the laws of prayer that the solitary mishnaic reference to the above principle is made (Ber. 5:5). "Religious" directives are often found to be based on "legal" directives. This is illustrated in the discussions on the question of whether a person who has acquired the right to no more than the fruits of his neighbor's field, may, when bringing the first fruit, read the *Bikkurim* portion which includes the passage, "And now, behold, I have brought the first fruit of the land, which Thou, O Lord, hast given me" (Deut. 26:10), since this involves a declaration that the land is his. The answer is made dependent on the elucidation of a question of legal principle, whether acquisition of the fruits *(kinyan perot)* is as acquisition of the body (*kinyan ha-guf;* Git. 47b) – an elucidation which has important consequences in all fields of Jewish law.

To their common origin must also be attributed a mutual interaction between the two parts of the *halakhah,* with directions pertaining to the "religious" field supplementing lacunae in the "legal" field. This is illustrated in the law concerning the father's duty to maintain his children. In the *takkanah* of Usha, as finally accepted, it was laid down that the duty extended to children until the age of six years. In practice it sometimes happened that a father failed to maintain his minor children above the age of six and in such an event the court compelled the father to do so by applying two rules pertaining to the laws of charity: first, that a person who has sufficient for his own needs may be compelled to give charity if there is a poor man in need; secondly, that as regards the giving of charity, "the poor of a person's own household take precedence over the poor of his town, and the poor of his town over those of another town," and of all the poor the father's children are the nearest to him (Ket. 49b; Sh. Ar., YD 251:3, EH 71:1). Another illustration is found in the post-talmudic development regarding the establishment of an obligation by way of the promisor's vow or oath or undertaking on pain of ban to give or do according to his promise – whose fulfillment is imposed on him as a religious duty. This method was employed especially in the case of obligations which were incapable of being established in terms of the "legal" rules of the *halakhah,* such as an obligation relating to something not yet in existence (Rema ḤM 209:4), or one tainted

1. page 242.

with the defect of *asmakhta* (Sh. Ar., ḤM 207:19) and so on (see Contract[1]).

Distinguishing Between "Religious" and "Legal"Halakhah – Ritual and Civil Law. A study of the halakhic sources reveals that the *halakhah,* notwithstanding its overall unity, distinguishes materially between the two main fields of its subject matter, between "matters of *mamon*" or *"mamona"* and "matters not of *mamon*" or *"issura"* (lit. "prohibitions," i.e., ritual law). Although the concepts of *issura* and *mamona* are not coextensive with the modern concepts of "religious" and "legal" law (see above), the material distinction made between them exerted a decisive influence on the evolutionary path taken by that large part of the *halakhah* embraced in the term *mishpat Ivri.* The first manifestations of the distinction date back to the time of Bet Shammai and Bet Hillel (Yev. 15:3; Eduy. 1:12 – "If you have permitted in a matter relating to the stringent prohibition of incest, shall you not permit in civil matters *(mamon)* which are less stringent? ") and in the course of time it became entrenched in many fields of the *halakhah,* as illustrated in the following examples: As regards the freedom of stipulation, the principle was laid down that "when a person contracts out of the law contained in the Torah, a stipulation which relates to a matter of *mamon* is valid but one that relates to a matter not of *mamon* is invalid" (Tosef., Kid. 3:8). The explanation is that the legal order prescribed by the Torah in civil matters was not enjoined in the form of a binding obligation (i.e., *jus cogens*), but as conditional on the will of the parties (i.e., *jus dispositivum; Ramban,* Nov. BB 126b) except in cases of a stipulation inimical to personal freedom or the public weal (for details see Contract[2]). In case of an illegal contract the rule is that a contract whose fulfillment involves the transgression of law shall not be enforced, but transgression of a "religious" prohibition does not deprive the contract of legal validity and it will be enforced by the court; hence, "if a person sells or gives on the Sabbath, and certainly on festivals, even though he should be flogged, his act is effective" and an obligation undertaken on the Sabbath is similarly valid, "and a *kinyan* performed on the Sabbath (i.e., *kinyan sudar,* see Acquisition[3]) is valid, and the writing and handing over take place after the Sabbath" (Yad, Mekhirah 30:7).

The distinction between *issura* and *mamona* also has an important bearing on the question of legislative authority in Jewish law. While such authority was to some extent limited in matters of *issura,* it remained fully effective in matters of *mamona* (see *Takkanot*[4]). So far as the legislative authority conferred on the public and its leaders was concerned, this never extended beyond matters pertaining to the civil law and criminal offenses (see *Takkanot ha-Kahal*[5]). The distinction is also an important factor in the binding force of custom, particularly as regards the basic principle that "custom overrides the law," which is applicable in matters of the civil law exclusively (see *Minhag*[6]). Similarly, different rules and principles of decision were laid down for civil and for ritual matters. A basic principle is that matters of ritual law are not to be learned from matters of civil law and vice versa, for the reason that on the one hand ritual matters are by their very nature of greater stringency than matters of the civil law, while on the other hand the rule that "the burden of proof rests on the person seeking to recover from his fellow" applies to civil but not to ritual law. Flowing therefrom are a number of rules applicable to matters of the ritual law only (for instance, that in certain circumstances "the majority is not followed in civil law matters"; BK 46b). It was likewise accepted by all scholars that the rule of *dina de-malkhuta dina* has no application to matters of ritual law (*Tashbeẓ,* 1:158, and see below), since all the reasons given for the adoption of the doctrine are relevant only to matters of the civil law. Thus the *halakhah* represents a unitary system of law with both its "religious" precepts and "legal" directions sharing a common origin and theoretical propagation as well as mutual principles and rules, the one part supplementing the other. At the same time the *halakhah,* as crystallized during its different periods, evolved a clear distinction between matters of *issura* and those of *mamona,* the latter being the counterpart of a substantial part of the subject matter of modern legal systems. This material distinction lent the legal part of the *halakhah,* which was the more sensitive and subject to the influence of changing social and economic realities, a wide flexibility and capacity for development.

LAW AND MORALS

Jewish law, like other legal systems, distinguishes between legal norms enforced by sanction of the courts and moral and ethical norms lacking such sanction. However, Jewish law also recognizes the existence of a special reciprocal tie between law and morality, a tie that stems from the common origin of both concepts in Judaic sources. The Pentateuchal commands, "Thou shalt not kill" and "Thou shalt not steal" (Ex. 20:13), are enjoined with the same finality as "Thou shalt love thy neighbor as thyself: I am the Lord" (Lev. 19:18), and the common origin of the concepts of law and morality remained a guideline for Judaism in all periods and generations (see, e.g., Bertinoro Avot 1:1). The stated tie finds expression in the fact that from time to time Jewish law, functioning as a legal system, itself impels recourse to a moral imperative for which there is no court sanction, and in so doing sometimes prepares the way to conversion of the moral imperative into a fully sanctioned norm. An illustration is to be found in the law of tort, where there are cases in which the tortfeasor is legally exempt from the payment of compensation – whether for lack of necessary causality between his act and the resultant damage, or because he acted with license, or for other reasons – yet with reference to many of these cases the rule was laid down that the person occasioning damage to another "is exempt according to the laws of man but liable according to the law of Heaven" (BK 6:4; BK 55b; and codes), or "he is exempt according to the law of man but his judgment is entrusted to Heaven" (Tosef., BK 6:16-17). Liability according to the law of Heaven means, according to some scholars, that although the court should not compel compliance by regular sanction it "should bring pressure to bear on him, verbally, without compulsion" (*Yam shel Shelomo,* BK 6:6); others held that the court should exercise no constraint – not even verbal – but should inform the individual: "We do not compel you, but you shall have to fulfill your duty to Heaven" *(ibid.).* Hence even the adjuration that the duty to Heaven must be fulfilled is addressed to the individual concerned by the court.

An instance of the conversion of a moral imperative into a legally sanctioned norm is to be found in the direction to act *li-fenim mi-shurat ha-din* (i.e., leniently, beyond the requirements of the law). In the Talmud this direction does not generally carry the import of a norm fortified by some form of sanction, and means only that it is fitting for the person who has a concern for his manner of conduct not to base his deeds on the strict letter of the law but to act leniently beyond the requirements of the law (as in the matter of restoring lost property or that of paying compensation for damage resulting from an erroneous opinion: BM 24b and 30b; BK 99b). As regards the talmudic matter concerning the exemption of workers from liability for damage caused by them – even though they are unable to prove the absence of negligence on their part – the *posekim* were divided on whether or not this involved an enforceable duty to act beyond the requirements of the law

1. page 298; 2. page 251; 3. page 208; 4. page 77; 5. page 656; 6. page 97.

(*Mordekhai* and others; see *Baḥ* ḤM 12:4). In the post-talmudic period the direction to act *li-fenim mi-shurat ha-din* became, according to the majority of scholars, a full-fledged legal norm enforced in certain instances by the court (for instance in the case of a wealthy litigant; *Baḥ* loc. cit. and Rema ḤM 12:2). See also Law and Morality.

DE-ORAITA AND DE-RABBANAN

Jewish law, in fact the entire *halakhah,* distinguishes between two categories of law, expressed in the two Aramaic terms *de-oraita* ("of the Torah") and *de-rabbanan* ("of the scholars"). The second category is sometimes also termed *mi-divrei soferim* (a term which has an additional meaning, see Sanh. 88b, but is normally used as the equivalent of *de-rabbanan*) or *takkanat ḥakhamim.*

Distinguishing Between the Two Categories. Classification of the halakhic rules into these two categories is beset with many difficulties and has been the subject of much scholarly discussion and research (see Z. H. Ḥayyut (Chajes), *Torat ha-Nevi'im,* s.v. *"Torah she be-al peh";* Ḥ. Albeck, *Mavo ha-Mishnah* (1959), 49–53). Certainly the rules expressly stated in the Pentateuch are *de-oraita,* while those clearly originating from the enactments or decrees of scholars are *de-rabbanan.* More difficult is classification of the rules deriving from one of the different modes of Pentateuchal Midrash (exegesis, see Interpretation). Maimonides held that any such rule was not to be considered *de-oraita* unless the interpretation accorded with a tradition from Moses at Sinai and the Talmud specifically lays down that the rule is *de-oraita* (*Sefer ha-Mitzvot,* rule no. 2). Naḥmanides held that such rules were *de-oraita* except when the Talmud specifically determines that the midrashic derivation of a particular rule amounts to no more than *asmakhta,* in which event the rule is *de-rabbanan* (*Hassagot ha-Ramban le-Sefer ha-Mitzvot,* ad loc.). Naḥmanides' opinion was accepted by a majority of the scholars (many of whom interpret Maimonides' view in a manner which tends to reconcile it with that of Naḥmanides). This, however, still does not constitute an adequate distinction, since there are *halakhot* which are regarded as *de-oraita* even though they are linked to particular scriptural passages by way of *asmakhta* alone, and there are also many *halakhot* which are regarded as *de-oraita* even though they do not originate from the legal source of Midrash (but from some other legal source, such as *sevarah*). Nor does classification of the *halakhah* into *de-oraita* and *de-rabbanan* necessarily have a bearing on the antiquity of a particular law, since it is possible that a law classified as *de-rabbanan* had its origin in a particularly ancient *takkanah,* whereas a later law may be classified as *de-oraita* because of its derivation from the interpretation of Pentateuchal passages. There are many institutions whose classification into one or other of the two stated categories occasioned doubt to the scholars of different periods, for instance, in the following matters: *ketubbah* (Ket. 10a; 110b); the husband's right to inherit his wife's property (Ket. 83a; Bek. 52b; and see Succession); the husband's duty to maintain his wife (Ket. 47b; and see Maintenance); *kinyan meshikhah* (BM 47b); and modes of acquisition deriving from trade custom (*Kesef ha-Kedoshim,* Sh. Ar., ḤM, 201:1) and other matters. There is accordingly no absolute and exhaustive classification of the *halakhah* into *de-oraita* and *de-rabbanan* and the only method of determining the class to which a particular law belongs is an examination of the Talmudic and post-talmudic literature to determine the manner in which such law was classified by the sages of the Talmud and scholars who decided and codified the *halakhah.*

Legal Consequences of the Classification. A basic divergence between the two categories of law occurs when there is doubt or dispute as to the applicability or scope of a particular rule in certain circumstances: in a *de-oraita* matter a stringent approach is required, whereas a lenient approach is indicated in a *de-rabbanan* matter (Beẓah 3b; Av. Zar. 7a). In some cases the scholars laid down alleviations of the law as regards a *de-rabbanan* legal obligation, even in the absence of any doubt as to the existence of such an obligation (for instance as regards recovery of the *ketubbah* money; Tosef., Ket. 13 (12):3 and Ket. 110b; see also Conflict of Laws[1]) when special circumstances justified such leniency (Ket. 86a; Rashbam BB 132b). In general however the scholars "imparted to their enactments the force of rules of the Torah" (see Git. 64b–65a; Ket. 84a). When the scholars saw the need for introducing a basic legal institution into daily life, they sometimes even enforced a rule of the rabbinical law more restrictively than a rule of the Torah. For this reason it was laid down that the parties may not stipulate for the payment of a lesser *ketubbah* amount than that determined by the scholars, notwithstanding the rule of freedom of stipulation in civil matters, even those pertaining to the *de-oraita* law (Ket. 56a). The rule that a legal obligation classified as part of the rabbinical law has the same legal efficacy as a *de-oraita* obligation is of special importance in view of the fact that so many of the rules in all the different branches of Jewish law belong to the *de-rabbanan* category (particularly those concerning the modes of acquisition, and the laws of obligation and tort). Any diminished regard for the standing and validity of a rule of the rabbinical law would have entailed the possibility of a far-reaching effect on the manner of execution and enforcement of such rules (see detailed discussion in Radbaz, 1,503).

THE BASIC NORM AND THE SOURCES OF JEWISH LAW

Three Meanings of the Expression "Source of Law." Every legal system gives occasion for inquiry into the sources of its law *(fontes juris, Die Quellen des Rechts).* The expression "source of law" has three principal meanings, which may be distinguished as literary, historical, and legal sources of law.

The literary sources of law (in German, *Die Erkenntnisquellen des Rechts*) are those sources which serve as the recognized and authentic literary repository of the various rules and directions of a particular legal system for purpose of ascertaining their content.

The historical sources are those sources which constitute the historical-factual origin of particular legal norms. Legal research is largely concerned with an investigation of the historical sources of the directions comprising a particular legal system, of the various influences of one legal system on another, and other similar questions. The historical sources of law, in the wide sense of the expression, may also include any economic, social, moral, or other factor that led to the creation of a particular legal norm and there are many instances of laws which were enacted in answer to particular economic or social needs.

The legal sources (in German *Die Entstehungsquellen des Rechts*) are the sources of law and means of creating law recognized by a legal system itself as conferring binding force on the norms of that system (see J. W. Salmond, *Jurisprudence* (1966), 109ff.).

The distinction between a legal and a historical source of law is of a material nature. The quest for the legal source of a particular norm is aimed at ascertaining the source from which the latter derives the force of law, that is, the principle within the relevant legal system which serves to confer binding validity on such a norm. Thus it is possible to ascertain that a norm has its legal source in statute or precedent and so on, without any need to be concerned with the factual background or historical origin

1. page 720.

of such a norm. Salmond states: "This is an important distinction which calls for careful consideration. In respect of its origin a rule of law is often of long descent. The immediate source of a rule of English law may be the decision of an English court of justice. But that court may have drawn the matter of its decision from the writings of some lawyer, let us say the celebrated Frenchman, Pothier; and Pothier in his turn may have taken it from the compilations of the emperor Justinian, who may have obtained it from the praetorian edict. In such a case all these things – the decision, the works of Pothier, the *corpus juris civilis,* and the *edictum perpetuum* – are the successive material sources of the rule of English law. But there is a difference between them for the precedent is the legal source of the rule, and the others are merely its historical sources. The precedent is its source, not merely in fact, but in law also. The others are its sources in fact, but obtain no legal recognition as such" (op. cit., p. 109).

The historical sources of law play only an indirect role in the evolution of a legal system, as factors which either offer a possible course to follow by way of imitation (as in the absorption of a principle from a different legal system) or create a need for the further developement of such a legal system (as in the case of particular economic or social conditions). On the other hand, the legal sources play a direct role in the evolution of a legal system, serving as the sole means to add to, subtract from, or vary in any other way the existing norms of that system. This division of the sources of law into three classes is valid also for the Jewish legal system.

The Literary Sources of Jewish Law. Various Classes of Informative Sources of Law. The literary sources of a legal system constitute, as already mentioned, authentic sources for the ascertainment of its legal norms. Thus, for instance, the laws of a country may be ascertained from its official Statute Books. Similarly, knowledge of the law may also be gathered from what is called "the literature of the law." This includes the literature in which the law is discussed or interpreted, although that literature itself is not recognized as an authoritative and authentic source from which binding legal norms may be ascertained (e.g., legal textbooks and articles: see Salmond, op. cit. 112, n. c). From a certain standpoint even general literature may contribute greatly toward a better knowledge of a legal system. Thus, if an author gives a historical-economic description of a particular period and mentions bankruptcies and the imprisonment of debtors, it may be possible to learn from this that it was customary at that time to imprison a debtor for the nonpayment of his debt; this may be deduced from the contents of a book even though the author dealt only incidentally with the legal aspects of that subject. In this regard, both the literature of the law and general literature must be approached with caution and the degree of the author's accuracy and objectivity carefully examined in each case. These informative sources avail also in Jewish law. While its authoritative literary sources are the most important informative class, both literature of the law and general literature serve the important function of filling in the social and economic background to many legal norms. They are of added importance – subject to the above cautionary remarks – in relation to those periods when there were few authoritative literary sources, as was the position in Jewish law until the literary redactions undertaken in the tannaitic period. The different literary sources of the *halakhah* are briefly reviewed below in a general manner. (These are separately discussed in great detail in M. Elon, *Ha-Mishpat Ha-Ivri,* III.)

From the Written Law Until the Period of the Tannaim. The Bible is not only the source of authority of the whole of the Jewish legal system (see below), it is also its first and foremost authoritative literary source. It contains legal directions which date from patriarchal times onward and are dispersed in specific books and chapters of the Pentateuch (Gen. 23:3–20; 31:41–43; Ex. 20–23; Lev. 5; 18–21; 24–25; 27; Num. 27:35–36; Deut. 1; 4–5; 15–17; 19–25). The next authoritative literary source is represented by the Books of the Prophets and the Hagiographa. From these information may be gained on the laws concerning the modes of acquisition (Ruth 4; Jer. 32 and see TJ, Kid. 1:5; 60c), the monarchy (I Sam. 8; I Kings 21), suretyship (Prov. 6: 1–5; 11–15, et al.), the laws confining criminal responsibility to the transgressor (II Kings 14:6), and so on. It may be noted that the Prophets and Hagiographa contain scant material of a legal nature. The attention of the prophets and chroniclers was mainly directed to the numerous internal and external wars of their times, to moral, social, and religious problems. Therefore the silence of these sources on different matters of the law cannot be interpreted as pointing to the absence of a legal order on such matters.

Much of the accumulated knowledge of Jewish law in the above period and for some time after can be found in the informative sources termed literature of the law and general literature. These include the papyri (such as the Elephantine papyri of the fifth century b.c.e.), the Septuagint (end of the third century b.c.e.), the writings of Philo (first half of the first century), the writings of Josephus (the period of the Temple destruction), the Apocrypha (from the fourth century b.c.e. until the year 200), and other works. This literature contains some *halakhot* which are identical to those quoted in talmudic literature and others which are sometimes contrary to it. This may indicate a possible development in certain norms of Jewish law or it may also be that this literature preserved *halakhot* that appeared in talmudic sources which are no longer extant. Great care is needed in deducing conclusions from this literature: sometimes it represents the viewpoint of small sects or even of a single individual; sometimes it may show the influence of a surrounding legal system (as in the case of the Elephantine papyri); sometimes the particular author gathered a rule of Jewish law from a translation and not in its original form (as did Philo in making use of Greek translations); and sometimes the description of certain matters reveals a blatant tendentiousness (see, for instance, Jos., Ant. 4:279 (ed. Schalit) note 174; ed. Shor, note 3; for details see Elon, *Ha-Mishpat Ha-Ivri,* III, p. 834).

From the Tannaitic Period Until the Redaction of the Talmud. This period, spanning the lives of the *tannaim* and *amoraim* gave rise to literary creations which constitute the classical sources of Jewish law and the starting point, until this day, for the study or discussion of any matter in it. Extant from tannaitic times are the following: compilations of halakhic Midrashim (see Interpretation); the Mishnah – compiled by Judah ha-Nasi and constituting the post-Mosaic "Corpus Juris" of Jewish law – and the Tosefta (see Codification of Law[1]); other authoritative tannaitic literary sources are the *Beraitot* included in the two Talmuds, and *Megillat Ta'anit* which includes, besides descriptions of political and military events, halakhic and legal material. Authoritative amoraic literary sources are the Jerusalem Talmud and the Babylonian Talmud, which include commentaries and expositions on the Mishnah, *memrot* (new *halakhot* of the *amoraim*), *ma'asim* (i.e., cases, see *Ma'aseh*), questions and answers, *takkanot,* and *gezerot* as well as rules of decision (see Codification of Law;[2] Elon, *Ha-Mishpat Ha-Ivri,* III, p.849 ff.).

The Post-Talmudic Period. The following are the three main branches of the post-talmudic literary sources of Jewish law commencing from the geonic period:

(1) The *Perushim* and *Ḥiddushim* – commentaries and

1. page 122; 2. page 124.

novellae – to the Mishnah and Talmud (as well as the other talmudic literary sources). The commentary literature represents the efforts of the scholars to elucidate the earlier literary sources with a view to facilitating the study and understanding of them; the classic commentary is that of Rashi on the Babylonian Talmud (11th century). The novellae literature is a product of the study and comparison by the scholars of different sources and their reconciliation of contradictory statements within the talmudic literature, in the course of which new interpretations and *halakhot* were derived; the classic novellae are those of the tosafists to the Babylonian Talmud (12th and 13th centuries). Of these two literary branches the commentaries represent the earlier development, which reached its peak in the 11th century (i.e., as regards commentaries on the TB; the commentaries on the TJ date from the 16th century onward), only then to be followed by the novellae, which have continued to be written until the present day (see Elon, *Ha-Mishpat Ha-Ivri,* III, 908ff.).

(2) *She'elot u-Teshuvot* – the *responsa prudentium* of Jewish law. The responsa literature represents the decisions and conclusions written down by halakhic scholars in answer to written questions submitted to them. For the major part of the post-talmudic period these questions came either from *dayyanim* who sat in judgment over the litigants in their own community and found it necessary to turn to the outstanding halakhic scholars in the area for the solution to difficult problems, or they arose from disputes between the individual and the community, or between different communities, which came directly before the competent scholars of the particular area. The responsa represent legal decisions on concrete questions arising in daily life and served as the main vehicle for the creativity and evolution of Jewish law in post-talmudic times. This body of literature is the case law of the Jewish legal system, estimated to include a total of approximately 300,000 judgments and decisions (see also *Ma'aseh*[1] and Elon, *Ha-Mishpat Ha-Ivri,* III, p. 1213ff.).

(3) *The Codes* (see in detail under Codification of Law). Besides these three main sources two other classes of literary sources belonging to this period may be mentioned: first, the collections of bonds and deeds (see *Shetar*), i.e., forms of written documents in use at various times during this period and serving to order the legal relations between parties in different fields of the law – such as deeds of sale, indebtedness, lease, marriage, and *ketubah;* secondly, the collections of *takkanot,* particularly the *takkanot* enacted by the community and its leadership, namely *takkanot ha-kahal.* In addition, there is the auxiliary literature of Jewish law consisting of various works of aid and reference, which may conveniently be classified into five categories: (1) works of introduction to the Talmud or to the *halakhah* in general (such as the *Iggeret R. Sherira Ga'on;* the *Sefer ha-Keritot* of Samson b. Isaac of Chinon; et al.); (2) encyclopedias of the *halakhah* (such as *Paḥad Yiẓḥak* by Isaac Lampronti and, more recently, the *Enẓiklopedyah Talmudit,* etc); (3) biographies of the halakhic scholars (such as the *Sefer ha-Kabbalah* of Abraham ibn Daud; first part of *Shem ha-Gedolim* by H. J. D. Azulai); (4) bibliographies of halakhic works (such as the Oẓar ha-Sefarim by Benjacob, the second part of Shem ha-Gedolim by H. J. D. Azulai); and (5) lexicons and dictionaries (such as *He-Arukh* by Nathan b. Jehiel of Rome; the *Arukh Completum* by A. Kohut; Levi's *Wörterbuch;* Jastrow's *Aramaic Dictionary of the Talmud;* Elon, *Ha-Mishpat Ha-Ivri,* III, 1278ff.) The main literary source in the post-talmudic period, however, remained the Talmud while around it and in continuation thereof there grew up a vast and profound literature in the form of all the aforementioned branches sources and auxiliary works.

The Historical Sources of Jewish Law. It is possible to point to the historical background of many norms of Jewish law – to the economic, social, and moral conditions leading to their creation (particularly in the case of the norms originating from *takkanot*), or to the influence of a different legal system (see below) and similar historical influences. General research on such historical sources is to be found in various works dealing with the history of the *halakhah* and some special research has been done on this subject (latterly, for instance, Y. Baer, *Yisrael ba-Ammim;* idem, in: *Zion,* 17 (1951/52), 1–55; 27 (1961/62), 117–55). Ascertaining the precise historical sources of a particular legal norm is often a formidable task which offers no assurance that the correct answer will be found. Some proffered answers lie in the realm of mere conjecture and are unacceptable without adequate further investigation and proof (see for instance the strictures of G. Alon in his *Meḥkarim,* 2 (1958), 181–247).

The Legal Sources of Jewish Law. There are six legal sources of Jewish law (as regards the Written Law see below) (1) *kabbalah* ("tradition"), based on "tradition transmitted from person to person" back to Moses from God (Avot 1:1; ARN *ibid.;* Yad, Mamrim, 1:2; Maim., Introd. to Comm. Mishnah); it is materially different from the other legal sources of Jewish law, since it is not subject to change or development but is, by its very nature, static and immutable, whereas the other legal sources are dynamic by nature and mainly serve as the means toward the continued creativity and evolution of Jewish law; (2) Midrash ("exegesis" and "interpretation"), embracing the norms derived from interpretation of the Written Law and of the *halakhah* in all periods, and to a certain extent also taking in other principles relating to interpretation of deeds, communal enactments, and so on; (3) *takkanah* and *gezerah,* representing the legislative activities of the competent halakhic authorities and public bodies in every generation; (4) *minhag,* representing the legal norms derived from custom in all its different forms; (5) *ma'aseh,* representing the legal norms derived from judicial decision or the conduct of a halakhic scholar in a particular concrete case; (6) *sevarah,* reprsenting the legal norms originating directly from the legal-human logic of the halakhic scholars.

The last five of these are recognized in Jewish law as being capable of both solving new legal and social problems and changing existing legal norms, when this need arises from the prevailing economic, social, and moral realities. In making use of these legal sources the halakhic scholars continued to shape and develop the Jewish legal system, which gave direction to the daily realities of life while being itself directed by them. This task the halakhic scholars carried out with a constant concern for the continued creativity and evolution of the *halakhah,* tempered at the same time by the heavy responsibility of preserving its spirit, objective, and continuity. This twofold assignment is entrusted in Jewish law to the halakhic scholars in every generation: "the judge that shall be in those days" (Deut. 17:9 and Sif. Deut. 153), in accordance with the fundamental principle that "the court of Jephthah is as that of Samuel . . . for the contemporary judge is in his generation as the judge who was in earlier generations" (Eccles. R. 1:4, no. 4; Tosef., RH 2 (1):3; RH 25b). No supra-human power – such as a heavenly voice or the prophet acting as bearer of the divine vision – has ever had any authority or influence in the determination and decision of the *halakhah* (Sifra, Be-Ḥukkotai 13:7–8; BM 59b; TJ, MK 3:1, 81d; for other opinions see Authority, Rabbinical[2]).

The Basic Norm of Jewish Law. As already mentioned, by the legal sources of a legal system is meant those sources which that legal system itself recognizes as valid sources from which its legal norms derive their binding force. Whence do these legal sources themselves derive their authority and validity? How and

1. page 114; 2. page 54.

by whom have they been recognized as having the efficacy to determine and introduce legal norms into the legal system concerned? Salmond (loc. cit.) states (111–2): "There must be found in every legal system certain ultimate principles, from which all others are derived, but which are themselves self-existent. Before there can be any talk of legal sources, there must be already in existence some law which establishes them and gives them their authority . . . These ultimate principles are the grundnorm or basic rules of recognition of the legal system." Thus the direct legal source of a municipal bylaw is the authority of the municipality to make bylaws; the bylaw has legal validity because parliament has delegated power to the municipality to make bylaws, while there exists a further rule – the grundnorm – which determines that an act of parliament has binding authority in the English legal system.

So in any legal system there is to be found a chain of delegation of power extending from the ultimate legal value – the grundnorm – to lower ones. The source of authority of the ultimate legal principle must be sought beyond the concepts of law and within the confines of history, religious faith, and beliefs, and the like: "But whence comes the rule that Acts of Parliament have the force of law? This is legally ultimate; its source is historical only, not legal. The historians of the constitution know its origin, but lawyers must accept it as self-existent. It is the law because it is the law, and for no other reason than that it is possible for the law itself to take notice of" (Salmond, op. cit., p. 111).

In the above-mentioned sense the basic norm of the Jewish legal system is the rule that everything stated in the Written Law is of binding authority for the Jewish legal system. The basic norm of Jewish law therefore not only expresses the concept of the delegation of power, but it is actually woven into the substantive content of the Written Law, the latter constituting the eternal and immutable constitution of Jewish law. This norm is the fountain of authority and starting point for the entire halakhic system with all its changes and evolution throughout the generations, and it is this norm that delegates authority to the legal sources of Jewish law rendering them valid means toward the continuing creativity and evolution of the latter. The source of authority of this basic norm itself is the basic tenet of Judaism that the source of authority of the Torah is divine command. In considering the matter from the aspect of Judaism as a whole it has to be said that there cannot be seen in it a system of legal norms isolated from and independent of other constellations of norms. All these constellations of norms have a single and uniform ultimate value, namely divine command as expressed in the Torah given to Moses at Sinai. Hence even the pre-Mosaic laws mentioned in the Written Torah – for instance concerning circumcision and the prohibition on flesh torn from a living animal, robbery, incest and so on – have binding force "because the Holy One commanded us through Moses" (Maim. Comm. Ḥul. 7:6) and because at the time the Torah was given "Israel entered into a covenant to observe them" (Rashbam Gen. 26:5).

The exclusive authority to interpret the Written Law and ensure its continuing evolution was found by the halakhic scholars to be delegated, in the Written Torah itself, to the halakhic scholars of every succeeding generation. Such authority they derived from a number of Pentateuchal passages, particularly Deuteronomy 17:8–11, in which the resolution of problems and disputes arising from time to time is entrusted to the teachers and judges in every generation (see also Authority, Rabbinical). In this and in other passages the halakhic scholars found not only their general authority to resolve problems but also the appointed means, that is the legal sources, wherewith to reach this goal (see Yad, Mamrim, 1:2; Maim., Introd. to Comm. Mishnah). Further particulars of Pentateuchal passages as a basis for the various legal sources of Jewish law are given elsewhere under the heading of each legal source.

THE DIFFERENT PERIODS OF JEWISH LAW

Jewish law has a history extending over a period of more than 3,000 years. For reasons of convenience and, to a certain extent, for historical and substantive reasons, this may be divided into two general periods, each with its own further sub-divisions; the first covering the time from the Written Law until the closing of the Talmud, the second from the post-talmudic period until the present day. This division between talmudic and post-talmudic *halakhah* has no bearing on the matter of the continuing creativity and evolution of Jewish law. Such creativity not only continued uninterruptedly after the closing of the Talmud but, as regards volume and literary output, even gathered momentum in certain fields of law. The significance of the closing of the Talmud as a historical dividing line finds expression in the degree of authenticity attributed to talmudic *halakhah,* the latter having been accepted in Judaism as the authoritative expression and rendering of the Oral Law: "All matters stated in the *Gemara* . . . must be followed . . . and have been agreed to by all Israel" (Maim., Introd. to *Mishneh Torah*). Until the redaction of the tannaitic literary sources – and to some extent even of the amoraic – the Written Law was the direct source according to which the law was applied by the *dayyan.* After the redaction of the talmudic literary sources the Written Law still remained the constitution of Jewish law, but the Mishnah, the halakhic Midrashim *(midreshei halakhah),* the two Talmuds, and the remaining talmudic literature became the direct sources according to which all matters of Jewish law were decided. The talmudic literature became the starting point for any study or discussion of Jewish law, and retained this status even after Jewish law was enriched – in the course of some 1,500 years – by many additional literary creations which, in comprehensiveness, orderly arrangement, and convenience of use, overtake the talmudic literature. The first great period of Jewish law is further distinguished by the fact that in this period Jewish law acquired its characteristic lines and forms of legal thought and expression, and the fact that in this period there were evolved and consolidated the legal sources which served as the vehicle for the creativity and development of Jewish law in this and in the post-talmudic period.

The first general period can be subdived in six eras: (1) the biblical age (up to the time of Ezra and Nehemiah, about the middle of the fifth century b.c.e.); (2) the period from Ezra and Nehemiah until the age of the *zugot* (up to 160 b.c.e. approximately), the greater part of which is customarily described as the age of the *soferim* ("the scribes"; see N. Krochmal, *Moreh Nevukhei ha-Zeman,* ed. Rawidowicz, 56, 194), but latterly the use of the term as descriptive of the scholars of this period only has been criticized (see Kaufmann, Y., Toledot, 4 pt. 1 (1960), 481–5); (3) the age of the *zugot* ("the pairs"; from 160 b.c.e. up to the beginning of the Common Era), which takes its name from the five pairs of leading scholars who headed the *battei din* during this period. (The names of the *zugot,* of whom the last pair were Hillel and Shammai, are given in Ḥag. 2 and Avot 1); (4) the age of the *tannaim* (up to 220 c.e.) which spans the activities of six generations of *tannaim,* from Gamaliel the Elder (grandson of Ḥillel) and his contemporaries to Judah ha-Nasi (redactor of the Mishnah). The generation succeeding R. Judah (that of R. Ḥiyya Rabbah and his contemporaries) saw the transition from the tannaitic age to that of the *amoraim.* Besides the Mishnah, there are extant from the end of this period also collections of halakhic Midrashim, the Tosefta, and other tannaitic literary sources; (5) the age of the *amoraim* embracing the activities of five generations of *amoraim* in Ereẓ Israel (until the end of the fourth century c.e.) and seven generations of *amoraim* in Babylon (up to the end of the fifth century). Extant from this period are the Jerusalem and Babylonian Talmuds; (6) the age of the *savoraim* (up to the end of the sixth century or, according to some scholars, the middle of the seventh century). This age must be regarded as the closing part of the talmudic period since the *savoraim* were mainly occupied with completing the redaction of the Babylonian Talmud and determining rules of decision (see Codification of Law).

In the second period there are two main subdivisions, the age of the *geonim* and the rabbinic age, but the latter may be subdivided into further categories. (1) The age of the *geonim* (from the end of the age of the *savoraim* until approximately the middle of the 11th century). The name is derived from the official title by which the heads of the academies of Sura and Pumbedita were known during this period. For most of this period the Babylonian academies remained the spiritual center of Jewry as a whole and most Jewish communities assigned absolute legal validity to the decisions and responsa of the *geonim.* For internal Jewish and external political reasons, the ties of the Babylonian *geonim* with the centers of learning that had arisen in North Africa and Spain became loosened towards the end of this period and, commencing from the middle of the 11th century, the phenomenon of a single spiritual center for the various centers of Jewish life came to an end and each of the latter began to rely on its leaders and teachers. This new reality was to exercise a great deal of influence on the subsequent modes of development of Jewish law, evidenced, for instance, in the proliferation of local custom and legislation (see Minhag; *Takkanot; Takkanot ha-Kahal;* Conflict of Laws). The *geonim* were instrumental in converting the Babylonian Talmud into the source according to which the *halakhah* was decided for all Jewry. In addition, this period saw the first flowering of the division of the post-talmudic literary sources of Jewish law into its three branches which exist until the present day – namely the commentaries and novellae, the responsa, and the codes (see above). Among the better-known *geonim* are R. Yehudai, R. Amram, R. Saadiah, R. Samuel b. Hophni, R. Sherira, and Sherira's son, R. Hai. Of the well-known figures of this period who did not officially hold the title of *gaon,* mention may be made of R. Aḥa (Aḥai) of Shabḥa, author of the *Sefer ha-She'iltot,* and R. Simeon Kayyara, author of the *Halakhot Gedolot* (see Codification of Law[1]). (2) The rabbinic age, which followed, was itself divided into three periods: (a) The period of the *rishonim* (the "early" scholars), from the middle of the 11th century (the time of Isaac Alfasi) until the 16th century (the time of Joseph Caro and Moses Isserles). This was the golden period of the rabbinic age in which were compiled the classic creation in all three branches of the post-talmudic literary sources of Jewish law: Rashi's commentary on the Talmud and the novellae of the tosafists; the codes of Isaac Alfasi, Maimonides, Jacob b. Asher, Joseph Caro, Moses Isserles, and others; the responsa collections of Solomon b. Abraham Adret (Rashba), Meir (Maharam) of Rothenburg, Asher b. Jehiel (Rosh), Isaac b. Sheshet Perfet (Ribash), Simeon b. Ẓemah Duran (Tashbeẓ), Joseph b. Solomon Colon (Maharik), and others. This was also the period in which the main part of the communal enactments was produced. It embraces the rise and decline of Spanish Jewry, and its close saw the initial flowering of several other Jewish centers – particularly in Ereẓ Israel and Poland-Lithuania – whose outstanding scholars were to make a great contribution to Jewish law, especially to its codification and to its responsa literature.

(b) The period of the *aḥaronim* (the "later" scholars), from the time of Joseph Caro and Moses Isserles until the coming of emancipation around the end of the 18th century. The legal creativity reflected in the three above-mentioned literary sources of Jewish law was continued in this period, particularly in the field of the responsa, which reached a peak of activity. From this period there have also come down numerous collections of communal enactments (such as the *Pinkas Va'ad Arba Araẓot, Pinkas Medinat Lita, Takkanot Mehrin,* and others).

(c) The period of the abrogation of Jewish judicial autonomy. The era of emancipation, which brought in its train the abrogation of Jewish judicial autonomy, represents a turning point in the evolution of Jewish law. This period may be further subdivided: from the end of the 18th century until the beginning of the 20th century, i.e., until the period of Jewish national awakening; from the beginning of the 20th century until the establishment of the State of Israel in 1948; from the establishment of the State of Israel onward.

JEWISH LAW – A LAW OF LIFE AND PRACTICE

For the greater part of its history of over 3,000 years, Jewish law has served the Jewish people while they not only lacked political independence but were for a considerable part of this period deprived of their own homeland – Ereẓ Israel – and dispersed throughout the various countries of the Diaspora. The legal systems of other ancient peoples went into decline as soon as they lost their political sovereignty, eventually ceasing to exist except in scattered archaeological remains. Even Roman law, which has left an imprint upon – and still nourishes – many other legal systems, ceased to exist as a creative law of life and practice after the fall of the Roman Empire in the West in the 5th century, and in the East with the fall of the Byzantine Empire about 1000 years later. In the case of Jewish law, the position is otherwise. Despite loss of political independence and lack of physical tie with the homeland, the Jewish people retained judicial autonomy and Jewish law not only did not decline, but it experienced most of its creativity and structural evolution – the Babylonian Talmud and all the other post-talmudic creativity – after the exile. Two factors explain this unique phenomenon: an internal one resting on the substance and nature of Jewish law and its place in the cultural life of the Jewish people, and an external one resting on the general juridical-political outlook that was common in the political history of the nations among whom the Jews lived up to the 18th century.

The Religious and National Character of Jewish Law. Of the two above factors, the internal one is the more important, based as it is on the character of Jewish law which is both religious and national. It is a basic tenet of the Jewish faith that the source of Jewish law – like that of the entire edifice of the *halakhah* – is divine revelation; in the same way as the Jew is commanded in the Written Law to uphold the "religious" precepts – those pertaining to man's relations with the Almighty, such as the laws of the Sabbath and the festivals, the laws of *kashrut* and the like – so he is commanded in the Torah itself to uphold the "legal" precepts – those pertaining to man's relations with his fellows, for instance in matters concerning the law of labor, tort, property, and different matters of the criminal law. The Ten Commandments enjoin observance of the Sabbath and "Thou shalt not steal," or "Thou shalt not murder," equally – as it were in the same breath. Hence, just as the vitality of the "religious" life remained unaffected by the people's exile, so the "legal" life continued to have unabated validity, and questions

1. page 126.

arising in both fields were brought before the same court or halakhic scholar for decision.

In addition to its religious character Jewish law has also been the national law of the Jewish people and its entire development has been the creative invention of this people. In this regard Jewish law differs from other legal systems, such as the Canon law or Muslim law, which were created and developed by followers of the faith – Catholic or Muslim – among many different nations. Notwithstanding its dispersion, the Jewish people continued to exist as a nation – not only as a religious sect – and constantly sought recourse to Jewish law, which it regarded as a part of its national assets through which to give expression to its essential being and character in all fields of its internal social and economic life.

The Jewish Judicial System – The Scope of its Jurisdiction. A precondition for the practical application of a legal system is the existence of an effective judicial machinery to administer and carry out the law. The Pentateuchal law provides express and detailed instructions for the maintenance of a judicial system (Ex. 18:21–27; Deut. 16:18; for particulars see also *Bet Din*) and a Jewish judicial system has always existed, even in the absence of Jewish political sovereignty and in all countries of the Diaspora. The Jewish court *(bet din)*, alongside the various institutions of Jewish autonomy (the exilarch, the community, inter-communal organizations), provided the mainstay of Jewish internal autonomy from the destruction of the Temple until the period of emancipation. The scope of Jewish judicial autonomy underwent change from time to time depending mainly on the attitude of the ruling power under whose protection the Jews lived.

After the destruction of the Temple, Jewish judicial autonomy was restricted for a short period in Ereẓ Israel (according to talmudic tradition jurisdiction over capital punishment *(dinei nefashot)* was abolished 40 years before the destruction (Shab. 15a; TJ, Sanh. 1:1, 18a; 7:2, 24b), but in practice the Jewish courts apparently did deal with such cases at least until the destruction). Soon, however, autonomy was fully restored and the time of R. Gamaliel, R. Akiva, and their contemporaries was one of the most creative periods in the history of Jewish law. Later, with the decrees of Hadrian and the revolt of Bar Kokhba, Jewish judicial autonomy was faced with another crisis (TJ, Sanh. 7:2, 24b), but by the end of the second century C.E., autonomy had already been fully restored (see Alon, *Toledot*, 1 (1958[3]), 129f.). The Babylonian Jewish center enjoyed wide judicial autonomy from an early period, and one of its main institutions was the Jewish court. After the decline of the Babylonian center the Jewish courts in all other centers continued to exercise the judicial function in matters between Jews. The halakhic scholars and communal leaders sought to impose a strict internal discipline in order to insure that all disputes between Jews would be aired before the Jewish judicial institutions. At the same time, they made every effort to obtain charters of privileges from the various rulers under whom they lived in order to insure the independence of Jewish law and the grant of powers of compulsion to the Jewish courts and internal authorities (see below).

The jurisdiction of the Jewish courts extended first and foremost to most civil law matters such as property, obligations, tort, family and succession law, and also to matters concerning the administration of local Jewish government at the hands of the representative communal and intercommunal institutions – such as election to the latter bodies, tax imposition and collection, relations between the individual and the community, and the like (see below). This measure of judicial autonomy was generally extended (up to the 18th century), even in times and places of restriction of the rights of Jews. In many centers such autonomy extended even to criminal matters, varying from place to place in its scope and modes of execution. In certain places it also extended to capital offenses, particularly with reference to informers (e.g., in Spain, see Resp. Rashba, 1:181; 5:290; Resp. Rosh, 17:1, 8: *Zikhron Yehudah*, 58 and 79; Resp. Ritba, 131; Resp. Ribash, 251; in Poland – see Resp. Maharam of Lublin, 138, etc.; see also Capital Punishment); in other places it extended merely to religious offenses, offenses against property, and police administrative offenses.

The wide range of matters over which the Jews enjoyed autonomous jurisdiction may be gathered from a study of the responsa literature containing decisions given by the leading halakhic scholars of different periods on concrete questions arising from the daily realities. Thus, out of some 1,050 responsa of Asher b. Jehiel – one of the leading scholars of German and Spanish Jewry in the second half of the 13th century and the beginning of the 14th – one-fifth (about 200) deal with precepts concerning man and God (such as the laws of prayer, festivals, forbidden food, and the like) and the remaining four-fifths with Jewish law (i.e., matters for the greater part included in Sh. Ar., EH and ḤM). Of the latter group, some 170 questions deal with matters of Jewish family law (marriage and divorce, parent and child, and the like) and the rest, more than 600, are concerned with all other "legal" branches of Jewish law (civil, criminal, and public-administrative; see Elon, Mafte'aḥ, introd. (Heb. and Eng.)). A similar ratio of subject matter is found to be more or less constant in all the responsa literature up to the 16th century, and slightly different in that of the 17th and 18th centuries, where the percentage of matters concerning religious law is somewhat higher. A material change can be detected in the responsa literature from the 18th century onward – following the era of emancipation, which saw the abrogation of Jewish judicial autonomy – and by far the greater part of these responsa deal with matters of religious precepts and family law, with a modest and minor place reserved for the remaining branches of Jewish law.

The Available Sanctions of the Jewish Judicial System. Within the framework of judicial autonomy described above the Jewish courts and competent authorities of the self-ruling bodies had the power to impose sanctions. These too varied from place to place and from period to period. The ordinary means of compulsion were attachment of property, monetary fines, and corporal punishment. In certain centers there were even Jewish prisons under the control of Jewish institutions and supervised by Jewish wardens (see Imprisonment[1]). At times the autonomous Jewish authorities had to seek the assistance of the central authorities in carrying out the sanctions imposed by the Jewish courts, especially so in case of the death sentence. A common and most effective sanction was the *ḥerem*, the quality and severity of which varied from place to place and also according to the nature of the offense and the degree of compulsion required. The use of this sanction was essential in circumstances where the Jewish authorities lacked the normal attributes of sovereignty, and it served as a most effective deterrent and means of compulsion in view of the self-centered living and residential conditions of the Jewish collectivity as an autonomous group. A person on whom the ban was pronounced was to a greater or lesser extent removed from the religious and social life of the community, and the stringent consequences of this sanction induced many halakhic scholars to refrain from its imposition except in the most difficult and serious cases.

The Prohibition on Litigation in the Gentile Courts. A striking expression of the religious and national character of Jewish law is to be found in the prohibition on litigation in the

1. page 537.

gentile courts *(arka'ot shel goyim),* to which the halakhic scholars and communal leaders attached the utmost importance. The first mention of this prohibition was made soon after the destruction of the Temple, when Jewish judicial autonomy was for a short period restricted by the authority of Rome (see above). It was laid down that there was to be no resort to the gentile courts not only when the material law applied in the latter courts differed from Jewish law but even when their law on a particular matter was the same as that applied in the Jewish courts (Git. 88b). Resort to the gentile courts was regarded as prejudicial to the existence of Jewish judicial autonomy and the prohibition served as a protective shield insuring the uninterrupted existence of such autonomy throughout the period of Exile; any person transgressing the prohibition was "deemed to have reviled and blasphemed and rebelled against the Torah of Moses our teacher" (Yad, Sanhedrin 26:7, based on Tanḥ. *Mishpatim,* 3). Contrary to the general principle that every rule of the civil law *(mamonot)* is *jus dispositivum,* so that in respect of it a man may contract out of the law of the Torah, it was laid down by a majority of halakhic scholars that the parties to a transaction may not mutually agree to submit their dispute to the jurisdiction of a gentile court, and also that resort to the gentile courts is not justifiable on the principle of *dina de-malkhuta dina* ("the law of the land is law"; Ramban Ex. 21:1; Resp. Rashba, vol. 6, no. 254; Tur and Sh. Ar., ḤM 26:1,3).

In the political and social realities of the different centers of the dispersion it was not always fully possible to enforce this prohibition. As early as the middle of the ninth century Paltoi Gaon laid down that it was permissible to institute proceedings in a gentile court against a party aggressively and obdurately refusing to appear in a Jewish court (B. M. Levin (ed.), *Oẓar ha-Ge'onim,* BK, Resp. no. 227). It was decided that in such a case the plaintiff, after first obtaining leave of the Jewish court, might prosecute his claim in the gentile court, "in order not to strengthen the hands of the powerful and violent who do not obey the law" (Yad, Sanhedrin 26:7 and Radbaz thereto; Tur and Sh. Ar., ḤM 26:2, 4). At times resort to the gentile courts was permitted in certain matters in which the central authorities had a special interest, such as disputes over land (Resp. Rema, no. 109), governmental taxes and currency (Finkelstein, *Middle Ages* pp. 361f.). Some of the halakhic scholars permitted recourse to the gentile courts when this was agreed on by both parties (Resp. Maharam of Rothenburg, ed. Cremona, no. 78; Finkelstein, op. cit., pp. 153, 156 and n. 1; *Sma* ḤM 26 n. 11 and *Taz* thereto; see also *Siftei Kohen,* ḤM 22, n. 15). In different periods there were communities and places where Jews scorned the prohibition, but in general the halakhic scholars and communal leaders firmly stood guard over the authority of the Jewish courts by enacting special *takkanot* and adopting sharp countervailing measures against those who thus undermined the autonomy of Jewish jurisdiction (see Assaf, *Battei ha-Din* . . ., 11, 17–18, 24, 109–13; Elon, in: ILR 2 (1967), 524–7; as regards recourse to the gentile courts from the period of the emancipation onwards see below).

Arbitration and the Jurisdiction of Lay Jewish Tribunals. The aim of preventing recourse to the gentile courts as a means of preserving Jewish judicial autonomy induced the halakhic scholars to maintain judicial institutions composed of Jewish judges, even if the judgments of the latter were not based on Jewish law, or were based on this law in slight measure only. Institutions of this kind were arbitral bodies and lay tribunals in their various forms.

The arbitral body had its origin in the second half of the second century (R. Meir and other *tannaim:* Sanh. 3:1–3), when Jewish judicial autonomy was restricted, as we have already noted, by the decrees of Roman imperial rule following on the Bar Kokhba revolt. The courts were destroyed and those which remained were deprived of the power of compulsion. In these circumstances the scholars directed the people to the institution of arbitration, in which *ro'ei bakar* ("herdsmen," simple folk untutored in the law) could also sit and adjudicate in accordance with their own good sense and understanding. In order to give such adjudication a Jewish form, the scholars laid down that the arbitral body should be composed of three arbitrators (Sanh. 3:1), like the Jewish court which was always composed of at least three *dayyanim (ibid.* 1:1; and see *Bet Din)* and unlike the position in Roman law where there was generally a single arbitrator. Even after the restoration of judicial autonomy, arbitration continued to fulfill an important function alongside the regular judicial institutions, and its rules and procedures were prescribed by the halakhic scholars (see Arbitration; Compromise).

Of interest is the evolution of the institution of adjudication by lay judges (*hedyotot,* i.e., persons untutored in Jewish law; the term also has the meaning of judges tutored in the *halakhah* but lacking *semikhah* ("ordination"; see, e.g., Git. 88b), a distinction that must be borne in mind). The precise origin of this institution is disputed by scholars; one opinion is that it dates from before the destruction of the Temple, while others hold that it too developed after the Bar Kokhba revolt and the withdrawal of autonomous jurisdiction from the Jewish courts (see Elon, op. cit., p. 529). Lay jurisdiction was likewise designed to ensure that the people would bring their disputes before Jewish judges – even if the latter were not versed in the law – rather than resort to the gentile courts. These tribunals were composed of three members, one of whom had to be *gamir* – i.e., to have acquired some knowledge of the *halakhah* – while the other two had to be persons fit at least to understand any matter explained to them (Sanh. 3a, Rashi and Nov. Ran ad loc.). The scholars bestowed on the lay tribunal authority to deal with all matters of civil law, to the exclusion of criminal matters (Sanh. 3a and *Piskei Rosh* thereto, 1) along with power to compel the appearance of the parties (*Piskei Rosh* thereto, 2; Tos. to Sanh. 5a; Tur ḤM 3:2; Sh. Ar., ḤM 3:1). In order to prevent resort to the gentile courts at all costs in post-talmudic times the scholars laid down that in any community where not even one *gamir* was to be found, three laymen could make up the tribunal even if none of them possessed this minimal qualification, provided that they were "fit and God-fearing persons, spurning corruption and equipped with sense and understanding"; such tribunals could deal also with criminal matters, in cases of great need and after much prior forethought and consultation (Resp. Rashba, vol. 2, no. 290). The existence of tribunals composed entirely of lay judges is confirmed in other historical sources (see, e.g., the Valladolid *takkanot* of 1432, in Finkelstein, *Middle Ages,* pp. 356–7), and the validity of such courts was halakhically recognized (Rema ḤM 8:1).

In general, the major part of the legal hearings, in disputes between individual Jews and between the individual and the communal authorities, took place before a court composed of three *dayyanim* expert in Jewish law and deciding in accordance therewith (a court of this kind called simply, *bet din;* Resp. Rashba, vol. 1, no. 1010); however, in most Jewish centers there were also lay tribunals functioning alongside these courts as a permanent judicial institution (a court of this nature being referred to as *bet din shel hedyotot;* Rashba loc. cit.). Many factors – social, economic, standards of knowledge and education – determined the measure of resort to lay tribunals. Their judges (known by different names: *tovei ha-ir, berurei tevi'ot, berurei averot, piskei ba'alei battim, parnasim, zekenim,* etc.)

generally based their decisions on communal enactments (see *Takkanot ha-Kahal*), trade usages (see *Minhag*), appraisal, justice, and equity (see e.g. Resp. Rashba, vol. 2, no. 290; vol. 3, no. 393 et al.; Resp. Maharshal, no. 93; Resp. Rema no. 33) and at times even upon a particular branch of a foreign legal system (*Beit ha-Beḥirah,* Sanh. 23a concerning "courts in Syria"; see also *takkanot* of the Leghorn community: S. Toaff in: *Sefunot,* 9 (1964/65), 190f.). Sometimes lay tribunals turned to halakhic scholars for their opinion and advice (*Zikhron Yehudah,* no. 58). In some places the limits of their jurisdiction were clearly defined. Mention is made of a tribunal composed of *tovei ha-ir* which dealt with tax matters (Resp. Rosh no. 7:11). At times there was a predetermined division of matters over which the different courts were to have jurisdiction; thus a *takkanah* of the Lithuanian community prescribed that the courts of the communal leaders were to deal with matters of monopolies as well as certain tax and penal matters, and the *dayyanim* of the community with matters of civil law (*Pinkas ha-Medinah* [*Lita*], no. 364); in a *takkanah* of the Leghorn community it was laid down that all matters of trade, insurance, and the like were to be dealt with by the communal leaders *(adonei ha-ma'amad)* judging in accordance with the general law as regards trade customs, but that matters of marriage and divorce, inheritance, mortgage, interest, and the like were to be dealt with according to Jewish law (Toaff, in: *Sefunot* loc. cit.).

The lay tribunals were originally and primarily instituted for the purpose of preventing resort to the gentile courts and also so as to enable certain matters of trade and the like, which were dependent on local custom, to come before a tribunal of merchants and professional experts. These tribunals tended, however, to gain in influence and to assume jurisdiction in additional matters, notwithstanding the existence of courts composed of *dayyanim* learned in the law. The halakhic scholars regarded this development as posing a threat to the ordered evolution of Jewish jurisdiction and application of Jewish law (see, e.g., Resp. Maharyu, no. 146). The fact that these tribunals tried matters according to appraisal and a subjective feel for justice, rather than according to any fixed legal rules, led the scholars to apprehend the danger of possible partiality and perversion of justice, especially since the tribunals were generally composed of the leaders and wealthy members of the community with the poorer and less influential members of society almost completely unrepresented. Strong criticism to this effect was often expressed by the scholars (see, e.g., *Keneh Ḥokhmah, Derush ha-Dayyanim,* pp. 25f.; *Derushei ha-Ẓelaḥ,* 3:12–14). However, such criticism never challenged the basic existence and positive merits of an institution which served as a vital additional means of preventing recourse to the gentile courts. For this reason adjudication by lay tribunals was also held to "accord with the Torah," even if it had not always the same merit as adjudication by the courts of *dayyanim,* and only "the practice in a few places to turn without hesitation to the gentile courts is actually contrary to the Torah and amounts to a public profanation of the Divine Name for which those who act in this way will have to account" (*Sefer ha-Zikhronot,* 10:3). To do so was to undermine Jewish judicial autonomy. (In Sh. Ar., ḤM the matter of lay tribunals (ch. 8) is clearly distinguished from the stringent prohibition on recourse to the gentile courts (ch. 26); see also M. Elon, in: ILR, 2 (1967), 529–37.)

The Judicial-Political Position and Social-Fiscal Relations. The national-religious character of Jewish law, and the profound awareness that a zealous watch over this inalienable asset would ensure the continued existence and unity of the Jewish people, thus constituted the primary element in the application of Jewish law in the daily life of the Jewish people even when dispersed in exile. Yet it may be asked how it proved possible for the Jews to maintain judicial autonomy under the political sovereignty of the governments under whose rule they lived, and what motivated the state authorities to respond to the demand of the Jewish collectivity for its own autonomy. The answer lies in the second of the two factors mentioned above, that is the judicial-political concepts of government and jurisdiction as these were common up to the 18th century, and the fiscal and social relations between the central authorities and the different strata, including foreigners, who dwelt under their rule. The judicial system was based on the individual's adherence to one of a number of distinctive groups with different legal systems, which were recognized by the state. Unlike modern centralistic states, the medieval state was corporative in nature and comprised of a series of autonomous strata and bodies, such as the nobility, the burghers, the guilds, etc. The latter frequently competed with one another and some of them with the central authority, and the Jewish community was often the object of rivalry among these different strata, bodies, and the central authority. This political-legal reality rendered possible the existence of an autonomous Jewish group with its own judicial autonomy. Readiness to grant such autonomy to the Jews arose for many reasons; some degree of tolerance towards other religions; considerations from the sphere of religious faith and belief; and particularly fiscal interests. The central authority, as well as the different strata and bodies amidst whom the Jews lived, regarded it as their "duty" and right to impose on the Jews heavy taxes in return for the privileges of settlement and residence. The collection of such taxation from each individual involved many difficulties, especially as the Jews were counted as members of a separate and foreign national group. The authorities accordingly found it convenient to impose an aggregate tax on the Jewish collectivity as a whole and for this purpose to enable the latter to be a unitary autonomous body, functioning in such manner that its leaders would bear the responsibility of producing the total amount of the tax apportioned and collected by each community from among its individual members. The existence of an autonomous public Jewish body also made it possible to give directions and conduct negotiations on other state rights and obligations through the recognized leaders of this body.

In this manner a zealously pursued desire of the Jewish people coincided with the existence of external historical conditions and factors to enable this people to preserve its religious and national law as a law of life and practice, faithfully served and interpreted by Jewish courts throughout the dispersion. The preservation by the Jews of their national law has been the main factor in the preservation of Jewish national existence. In the words of Y. Kaufmann *(Golah ve-Nekhar),* "It was judicial autonomy which truly made of the Jewish nation in exile 'a state within a state' " (1 (1929), 518) and "This autonomy derived from the striving of the nation to embody in its life the ideal of the Torah to the utmost limits. It derived especially from the striving to uphold the Jewish legal system, the Law of the Torah, and to base thereon the order of internal life. For this reason the ancient autonomy was fundamentally a judicial autonomy" (*ibid.,* 2 (1930), 312).

THE EVOLUTION OF JEWISH LAW

A material feature of Jewish law is the fact of its ever-continuing evolution. This is the logical and necessary outcome of the fact of Jewish law's being a living and practical law, since constant evolution is a characteristic feature of every living thing whether it is discernible during the passage from one state to another or only clearly distinguishable in the perspective of history. It will be clear to anyone taking up the *halakhah* that he has before him one large unit in which the earlier and later, the basis and the construction, are all interwoven and arranged according to subject matter with no particular regard shown for historical-epochal distinctions. The halakhic scholars rightly considered that Jewish law was of a nature which required them to unite and integrate the various periods of the *halakhah* into a single, all-embracing epoch of unitary *halakhah,* and not to divide and differentiate between different stages and periods. This is a legitimate and accepted conception in any system of legal thought, especially in a legal system which, by its very nature, deems the existing body of laws to be the starting point for its own renewal and further development. This is also largely true, as regards, for instance, the development of most of English law. However, this conception does not in any way bar the scholar from examining each and every one of the institutions of Jewish law in historical perspective, with a view to determining the different stages of development they may have undergone. Morever, an examination of such different stages of development and of the legal sources through which these stages were integrated into the fabric of Jewish law will reveal that the halakhic scholars themselves frequently emphasized the changes and development through which one or other institution of Jewish law had passed. This is evidenced in their resort not only to *takkanah* – a means of expressly adding to or changing the existing law – but also to Midrash and the other legal sources of Jewish law (see M. Elon, *Ḥerut ha-Perat* . . . 12 (introd.), 261–4).

Submission to Jewish law and the Jewish courts brought in its wake an unending creative development of the Jewish legal system. Social realities and economic exigencies change from period to period, and among the special conditions of the Jewish people must be included the social and economic variations that marked the different centers of the dispersion. Even when the Jewish people had possessed a single political center – and later on a spiritual center – there had existed a various and widely scattered Diaspora; however, geographical dispersion really began to impress its mark more critically at the end of the tenth and the beginning of the 11th century when the one center, the Babylonian, which had until then held sway over the entire Diaspora, declined and a number of centers made their appearance side by side and successively in North Africa, in Spain and Germany, in France and Italy, in Turkey, Egypt, and the Balkan countries, in Poland-Lithuania, and elsewhere. It is certainly true that despite the geographical scattering, Jewish scholars everywhere dealt with the same talmudic and rabbinic sources and that very often contact, personal and by correspondence, was also maintained among the different centers. But the variations in the social, commercial, and economic life of the Jews in each center, their communal organization and representative institutions in each locality, their relationship with the gentile environment and the state authorities – all these from time to time gave rise to problems for some of which the existing Jewish law provided no express solution and for some of which it was necessary to find solutions which differed from those provided by the existing law. At times the influence of local conditions led to the absorption of undesirable legal principles which were contrary to the spirit of Jewish law and did not serve to advance the system of law as a whole. To the extent that such foreign principles deviated from the fundamental doctrines of Jewish law they generally came to be rejected in the course of time (see, e.g., Imprisonment,[1] Imprisonment for Debt[2]).

Thus Jewish law continued to evolve as a law of life and practice, giving direction to the daily realities while being itself directed thereby. The phenomenon of a legal system which demands that the determination of its law and its solutions to legal problems be founded on the past while answering the manifold needs of every succeeding generation is found to be true of Jewish law in all periods of its history, both in the time of Jewish political sovereignty and during the long period when this was absent but the Jewish people enjoyed judicial autonomy in Ereẓ Israel, in Babylonia, and in all the other countries of the dispersion. This demand was satisfied through the ever-continuing evolutionary development of the institutions of Jewish law and through preservation of the central concept of each institution which constituted the common factor of all the different stages and changes through which it passed. (For illustrations of such development, see Authority, Rabbinical; Capital Punishment; Contract; *Ha'anakah; Hassagat Gevul;* Imprisonment for Debt; Lien; Limitation of Actions; Obligation, Law of; Surety; Taxation. See also Interpretation; *Ma'aseh; Minhag; Sevarah; Takkanot; Takkanot ha-Kahal;* and see M. Elon, *Ha-Mishpat Ha-Ivri,* I Intro. and 129ff.

Since the development of Jewish law was the outcome of the practical application of the latter in daily life, it follows that in places where there was diminished submission to Jewish law and its courts system there was a corresponding falling off in the creative development of this legal system, as is evidenced, for instance, in the case of Italian Jewry in certain periods (Resp. Rambam (ed. Leipzig), pt. 1, no. 140, p. 26; *Sefer ha-Zikhronot,* 10:3). This was, however, an uncommon phenomenon until the 18th century and the era of emancipation. Thereafter, with the abrogation of Jewish judicial autonomy, Jewish law was to a far lesser extent a law of practice and this was to lead to a far-reaching diminution in the creativity of Jewish law (see below).

THE EVOLUTION OF JEWISH LAW REFLECTED IN ITS LITERARY SOURCES

Sefer ha-Zikhronot (loc. cit.) emphasizes that recourse to the Jewish courts is of importance not only for the continuance of the creative development of Jewish law itself but also for the enlargement of its literature. A study of the various matters with which halakhic literature has dealt at different times shows that the part of the *halakhah* which was of practical application came to occupy an increasingly and incomparably larger place than the part that was not of such application.

The Mishnah as compiled by Judah ha-Nasi contains six orders, each of which treats of one basic branch of the *halakhah,* and together they embrace the whole halakhic system. In the two Talmuds, the literary creations following immediately upon the Mishnah, the following phenomenon is apparent: the Babylonian Talmud, unlike the Jerusalem Talmud, contains no Talmud on the order of *Zera'im* (apart from the tractate *Berakhot* dealing with prayers and benedictions). There is no doubt that the Babylonian *amoraim,* like those of Ereẓ Israel, studied all the six orders of the Mishnah and their deliberations on *Zera'im* are largely scattered throughout the tractates of the other orders. That no Babylonian Talmud was edited for this order is due to the fact that the rules therein stated – "precepts which are dependent on the land" (these being applicable only in Ereẓ Israel), such as the laws of *shevi'it* (the Sabbatical Year) and *pe'ah* (the corner of the field) – were not of practical concern in Babylonia, whereas in Ereẓ Israel itself, where these rules were actually applied, a Talmud on this order was compiled and edited. In the post-talmudic period the overwhelming part of the halakhic literary creativity was also concentrated on the "precepts contemporaneously in use," that is on the branches of the *halakhah* which were of everyday use and not on the laws connected with the "precepts dependent on the land" with the Temple, ritual purity, and the like. It is found that sometimes even theoretical study itself was centered around the practical

1. page 539; 2. page 637.

orders – *Mo'ed, Nashim,* and *Nezikin* – and those tractates of the other orders containing precepts in contemporaneous use – such as *Berakhot, Ḥullin* (concerning the laws of ritual slaughter and *kashrut*), and *Niddah* (concerning ritual purity of women) – were arranged together with these three orders (see *Beit ha-Beḥirah* (ed. Jerusalem, 1965[2]), Introd. to Ber., p. 32). In geonic times many monographs were written on various halakhic subjects, most of them on strictly legal topics and part on matters of ritual law, the majority of both kinds dealing exclusively with the laws of everyday use. These monographs were primarily compiled for practical use in the *battei din.*

This phenomenon recurs in two branches of the post-talmudic literature – in the responsa and in the codifications – and to a certain extent also in the third branch, the commentaries and novellae. Thus Alfasi included in his code only those laws then operative and not, for instance, the laws of the order of *Kodashim* (except the tractate *Ḥullin* in which the topics discussed remained of contemporaneous significance). The only one to deviate from this path was Maimonides in his code, *Mishneh Torah.* He sought to restore the *halakhah* to its original dimensions and included in his code even matters of faith and belief, which he formulated in legal style. However, this undertaking was unique and in all subsequent codifications, such as *Piskei Rosh, Arba'ah Turim,* and Shulḥan Arukh, the example set by Alfasi was followed and only the rules in current application were included. The responsa literature also deals overwhelmingly with practical questions of the law and not with matters of ritual purity and defilement or sacrifices. This is obviously due to the fact that problems arose, and were referred to the leading halakhic scholars for solution, only in the area of the practical day-to-day application of the law. In the commentaries and novellae alone is there found any more extensive discussion of the "theoretical" branches of the *halakhah,* but even here the greater part is devoted to practical halakhic matters. This is one explanation for the fact that commentaries and novellae to the Jerusalem Talmud were written only from the 16th century onward, following the renewal of the Jewish settlement in Ereẓ Israel in this period. (It is noteworthy that in latter times – before and since the establishment of the State of Israel – there has been greatly increased creativity in the field of the laws pertaining to the order of *Zera'im,* in all three literary branches of the *halakhah,* clearly because these laws have once more come to be of practical significance.) While it is true that at all periods Jewish law was frequently studied in a purely theoretical manner, as Torah for its own sake, and an appreciable literature was created to this end, yet such study and literary creativity represent no more than embellishments of the main core, aids to the knowledge of Jewish law for everyday use in practical life.

THE DIFFERENT BRANCHES OF JEWISH LAW

Illustrations of Development and Change in the Different Branches of Jewish Law. In the different periods of its history Jewish law has comprised all the branches of law customary in other legal systems although from time to time changes of a structural nature took place. The institutions of Jewish law in all its different branches underwent, as already mentioned, an ever-continuing process of creative development. In some fields – for instance property, family and inheritance, procedure and evidence – this process was of no material consequence as regards the framework or content of a particular branch of the law, notwithstanding any changes in its principles. In other fields the process had a more material effect as regards the content and classification of an entire branch of the law.

Laws of Obligation. A change of this nature took place, for instance, in the field of the laws of obligation. The original Jewish law fundamentally and unequivocally rejected any form of enslavement of the debtor's person as a means towards realizing the creditor's rights (see Execution, Civil[1]). Consequently there arose the need to find a strong alternative means of ensuring the fulfillment of an obligation in the form of an encumbrance on the debtor's property, which found expression in a right of lien over the debtor's property automatically conferred on the creditor upon creation of the obligation. For this reason an obligation in Jewish law had essentially a real character because the creditor was afforded a right of a real nature in the debtor's property, and in consequence of this many rules belonging to the field of property law came to be applied also to the laws of obligation (see Lien;[2] Contract[3]). In the course of time, the nature of the contractual obligation in Jewish law underwent a substantive change, one that found expression in a series of basic innovations introduced and given recognition in successive stages; these included the possibility, contrary to the laws of property, of establishing an obligation with regard to something not yet in existence; the possiblity of establishing an obligation whether or not the property in the debtor's possession at such a time was capable of satisfying the debt, and a long series of further developments (see Contract[4]). Such a substantive change in the subject matter of a legal institution is an important factor in its classification or reclassification as belonging, for instance, to the field of the laws of obligation rather than the laws of property.

Administrative Law. A different phenomenon is evidenced in the field of administrative law, for the central subjects of this branch changed almost completely in consequence of the material changes in the nature of public Jewish leadership and administration in different periods. Whereas in ancient times the institutions of public law determined relations between the individual leader – whether it be the king, the *nasi* or the exilarch – and the people (see M. Elon, *Ha-Mishpat Ha-Ivri,* I, p. 42ff. and II, 558 ff.), new social realities spurred the development of a pervasive system of administrative law based on collective leadership, elected or appointed. The representative and elective institutions of local Jewish government and intercommunal organization were built up on the principles of Jewish law, and the halakhic scholars as well as the communal leaders were called upon to resolve (the latter by way of communal enactments) the numerous problems arising in the field of administrative law. These related, among others, to the determination of relations between the individual and the public authority, between the latter and its servants; to the composition of the communal institutions and the methods of election and appointment to the latter and to other public positions (see Public Authority); to the modes of legislation of the community and to the legal administration of its institutions (see *Hekdesh; Takkanot ha-Kahal*); to the imposition and collection of taxes (see Taxation[5]), and to many additional problems concerning economic and fiscal relations in the community. This wide range of problems was dealt with in a very large number of responsa and communal enactments, in the course of which the halakhic scholars and public leaders developed a new and complete system of public law within the framework of the *halakhah.*

Conflict of Laws. In the field of the conflict of laws development came mainly in consequence of periodic migratory movements and social changes in the life of the Jewish people. The conflict of laws is not usually regarded as a distinct branch of Jewish law, because of the substantive nature of Jewish law as a personal law purporting to apply to each and every Jew wherever he may be – even beyond the territorial limits of Jewish sovereignty or autonomy. From this it naturally follows that in

1. page 621; 2. page 287; 3. page 247; 4. page 248; 5. page 666.

Jewish law no importance attaches to the fact, as such, that a contract between two Jews is scheduled to mature in a different country than that in which it was concluded – a fact that is normally the staple source of problems arising in the area of the conflict of laws. Nevertheless, the fact that for the greater part of their history, the Jews enjoyed their judicial autonomy under the political sovereignty of a foreign ruler with his own legal system, and especially the fact of the geographical dispersion of the various Jewish centers, inevitably caused the Jewish legal system to be confronted with many fundamental problems relating to the conflict of laws. There developed in Jewish law the phenomenon of a multiplicity of *takkanot* and customs relating to the same legal subject but varying in content from place to place. To some extent this phenomenon was also present in talmudic times, but it assumed significant proportions only from the tenth century onward when there ceased to be a single Jewish center exercising hegemony over the other centers of the Diaspora. The result of the rise of many centers was the proliferation of local *takkanot,* customs, and legal decisions, which brought in train the problem of the choice between different laws – not between Jewish law and any other law, but between the rules deriving from differing customs and *takkanot* within the Jewish legal system itself. Similarly, as a result of the close contact between Jewish law and the various legal systems of the nations amidst whom the Jewish collectivity lived, there evolved the principle of *dina de-malkhuta dina* and, flowing from this, various rules pertaining to the field of the conflict of laws.

Criminal Law. A different and completely opposite trend is evidenced in the field of criminal law. During those periods when the Jewish people enjoyed full judicial authority, it is possible to point to the existence of important principles and great creativity extending also to the criminal law (see Penal Law; Punishment). However, the scope of application of this branch of the law was already substantially narrowed around the time of the Temple destruction, and in consequence it reflects a diminished creative continuity and a smaller framework. It is true, as already mentioned, that in some places Jewish judicial jurisdiction extended even to capital offenses but in most centers the criminal jurisdiction of the Jewish courts was confined to offenses against property, administrative offenses, and the like. On the whole the lack of sovereignty deprived the Jewish people of the media required for the proper implementation of criminal jurisdiction and of suitable conditions for its organic development. All these factors therefore stunted the growth of the functional framework and content of this branch of Jewish law.

Classification of the Different Branches of Jewish Law. Like other legal systems, Jewish law has its own distinctive basic principles pertaining to each of the different branches of the system. Sometimes these principles are unique to Jewish law and characterize its approach to matters such as personal freedom and the rights of the individual, the substance and nature of legal and moral obligations, the concept of ownership of property, the essential nature of judicial jurisdiction, modes of proof, and other fundamental questions. In other cases the principles of Jewish law correspond to parallel principles in other legal systems. Such differences and similarities are dealt with elsewhere under the heading of the subject to which they pertain.

It may be added that classification of the subjects comprising a legal system is a task beset with difficulties, particularly so in the case of the Jewish law, and calls for the exercise of much care. Thus, for instance, certain institutions of Jewish law are classified both under the laws of property and the laws of obligation because of the close connection between these two branches of the law. This is true also as regards the classification of criminal matters, which in Jewish law do not always conform to those customarily classified in other legal systems as part of criminal law. It is questionable whether the classification of subject matter in one legal system is appropriate for another and any automatic application to Jewish law of the classification adopted in another legal system is especially liable to be misleading. To a certain extent the special legal terminology of Jewish law also influences the manner of classification of its subject matter (see for instance the definitions above of the terms *mishpat Ivri, issura, mamona,* and others). The difficulties entailed in the classification of Jewish law into defined legal branches derive in part from the fact that during the periods when the foundations of the various rules of Jewish law were laid, the system knew only a classification of a most general nature. This is reflected in the Mishnah and in the remaining halakhic literature of the tannaitic period and also in the two Talmuds. A more definitive and detailed classification of Jewish law came only with the compilation of Maimonides' code, the *Mishneh Torah,* and some of the subsequent codes. A classification of the subject matter of Jewish law in keeping with the character and spirit of this legal system is possible only after deep and careful study of its different institutions. For these reasons the classification made in the present volume is not to be regarded as final and absolute.

PUBLIC JEWISH LEADERSHIP IN THE DEVELOPMENT OF JEWISH LAW

The halakhic scholars and the *battei din* filled the central role in the development of the Jewish legal system. In addition, an important creative role was filled by the public leadership and representation of the Jewish people in all the different institutional forms it assumed throughout the history of the Jews: from the kings, the *nesi'im,* and exilarchs down to the elected or appointed representatives of the community.

The King's Law. The fundamentals of the laws concerning the king and his kingdom are enjoined in the Pentateuch (Deut. 17:14–20, dealing mainly with the duties of the king and his modes of conduct), in the first Book of Samuel (ch. 8, in which the prerogatives of the king and the duties owed him by the people are defined), and in other biblical passages (see for instance I Kings 21, concerning the matter of Naboth's vineyard). The scholars also learned about the powers of the king from certain biblical statements concerning leaders of the people other than the kings (see for instance Josh. 1:18 concerning rebellion against the kingdom; cf. Sanh. 49a). The king was vested with wide powers in the legislative (see *Takkanot*), judicial, and executive fields, with authority to deviate in various matters from the rules as laid down in the *halakhah.* His authority was not confined solely to fiscal and economic matters relating directly to the rule of the kingdom, such as taxation and the mobilization of manpower or property, but extended also to the field of criminal law. In the latter field he had authority, for instance, to impose the death sentence on a murderer, despite the existence of formal defects in the evidence against him, when this was required "for the sake of good order in accordance with the needs of the hour" (Yad, Melakhim 3:10; 5:1–3 *ibid.,* Roẓe'aḥ 2:4 and Sanhedrin 14:2, 18:6).

The king's law represents the earliest determination in Jewish law of a creative factor not directly attributable to halakhic scholars, and the *halakhah* conferred similar creative authority on the various other post-monarchic institutions of central Jewish government. Thus for instance it was said of the exilarchs who headed the internal Jewish government in the Babylonian exile that "they take the place of the king" (Yad, Sanhedrin 4:13, based on Sanh. 5a and Rashi ad loc.) and that the king's law applies "in every generation . . . in favor of the leaders of each generation" (*Beit ha-Beḥirah,* Sanh. 52b; see also *Mishpat Kohen,* no. 144). The question of the relationship between the regular law and the king's law is often the subject of discussion in halakhic literature, particularly of the post-talmudic period. R. Nissim b. Reuben Gerondi explains the parallel existence of the two systems on the basis that justice administered according to law, while correct and ideal, does not always answer the social and other needs of the hour, and that this function is filled by administration of the king's law; for this reason Scripture enjoins the king to have the Torah with him always, "that his heart be not lifted up above his brethren" (Deut. 17:14–20), because inasmuch as he is not always subject to the law he must at all times, when making use of his powers, take particular care to ensure that he does not deviate from the general object of the Torah and its principles of justice and equity (*Derashot Ran.* Derush no. 11). All subsequent creative authority permitted in Jewish law to deviate, in certain cases, from the rules of the *halakhah* was subject to this above basic requirement (see *Minhag,*[1] *Takkanot ha-Kahal*[2]). In later periods different scholars found a legal basis for the authority of the king's law in the idea of an agreement between the king and the people in terms of which the latter allows the king his prerogatives in all matters falling within the king's law in return for his undertaking to guard and protect them (see Z.H. Ḥayyut (Chajes) *Torat ha-Nevi'im,* ch. 7 *"Melekh Yisrael"*). This idea was apparently the influence of the commonly accepted medieval theory which based the validity of the king's law on a consensus of the people, a theory which different halakhic scholars also adopted as a basis for the doctrine of *dina de-malkhuta dina.*

Local Jewish Government. Creativity in the legislative field of Jewish law is also evidenced at the local governmental level. The halakhic sources relating to the early part of the Second Temple period already mention certain legislative powers entrusted to the townspeople (*Benei ha-Ir,* see Tosef., BM 11:23, BB 8b). From this modest beginning there developed, at a much later stage, a wide legislative creativity at the hands of the autonomous governmental institutions of the Jewish community and intercommunal organizations. This was expressed in the *takkanot ha-kahal,* enacted, particularly from the tenth century onward, in all fields of the civil, criminal, and administrative law. As in the case of the king's law, it was possible for these enactments to be contrary to a particular rule of the *halakhah,* and the scholars determined ways to ensure that such enactments remained an integral part of the overall Jewish legal system. One of their principal means was to check that the enactments did not conflict with the Jewish law principles of justice and equity. Another contribution to Jewish law, not directly attributable to the halakhic scholars, was that which resulted from participation of the public in some of the institutions of Jewish jurisdiction, such as arbitration and the lay tribunals (see above). Although at times these jurisdictional institutions were prejudicial to the orderly evolution of Jewish law, it may nevertheless be accepted that the generally harmonious cooperation that existed between these institutions and the halakhic scholars enabled the public leaders to make a significant contribution toward the forging of a stronger link between Jewish law and the realities and problems of everyday life. This in turn was a spur to the further development of Jewish law.

THE RELATIONSHIP BETWEEN JEWISH LAW AND FOREIGN LAW

The question of the relationship between Jewish law and foreign law has two aspects. First, the extent – if any – of reciprocal relations and influence of the one on the other in a manner leading to the integration into the one legal system of legal directives deriving from the other; secondly, the extent of the recognition – if any – given to a directive of a foreign legal system, without such recognition involving any integration of the directive into the host system. These are two separate but related aspects, for recognition by the host system of the validity of a foreign legal principle entails, in certain cases, some measure of recognition – witting or unwitting – of the correctness of the foreign principle and of the possibility that the contents of the host legal system may be influenced in a manner leading to the integration of a foreign legal principle into its own framework.

Reciprocal Influences. From the 17th century onward a great deal of research in Jewish law has been devoted to the subject of mutual influence between Jewish law and other legal systems (latterly see B. Cohen, bibl., Introd. and ch. 1). More than any other, this field of research has been particularly conducive to the adoption of an apologetic approach – in the form of both an over-emphasis on the influence of foreign law on the Jewish legal system and exaggeration of the influence of Jewish law on other legal systems. Moreover, the influence of one legal system on another is no easy matter to prove because of the possibility that similar circumstances may have led to the evolution of like institutions in different legal systems, uninfluenced by each other. However, in general it may be said that there were reciprocal relations and influences between Jewish law and the surrounding legal systems or that of the nation under whose political sovereignty Jewish law functioned in any particular period of its history. The fact that the Jewish collectivity lived its social and economic life in accordance with its own law, yet all the while was under the patronage of many different nations with their own legal systems, inevitably left the mark of Jewish law on the other legal systems. The reverse process applied equally: the halakhic scholars were familiar with the law applied in the general courts of the land and sometimes even recommended the adoption of a foreign legal practice which commended itself to them (see, e.g., Elon, Mafte'aḥ 425; *Terumat ha-Deshen, Pesakim u-Khetavim* no. 83; Resp. Israel of Bruna no. 132). In certain cases the halakhic scholars recognized the particular social efficacy of certain aspects of the foreign law (see *Derashot Ran,* Derush no. 11) and sometimes they were not even deterred from lauding the gentile administration of justice when they found this superior to that of the Jews (*Sefer ha-Ḥasidim* no.1301). To some extent directives of the foreign law were absorbed by Jewish law by means of the legal source of custom (see *Minhag*). When absorption of a foreign principle did take place, such a principle underwent a process of internal "digestion" designed to accommodate it to the general principles and objectives of Jewish law. If in particular social circumstances a foreign principle was occasionally absorbed which conflicted with the fundamental doctrines of Jewish law, such a principle was usually rejected in the end by the Jewish legal system (see, e.g., M. Elon, *Ḥerut ha-Perat . . . ,* pp. 238–54; 259f.).

Recognition of Foreign Legal Rules. The much-discussed subject of the validity in Jewish law of the provisions of a foreign legal system centers around the doctrine of *dina de-malkhuta dina,* which holds that the law of the land is law and must be followed. The earliest formulation of the doctrine was made in the Babylonian Exile by the *amora* Samuel as appears from some of the legal explanations given for its entrenchment. An unqualified recognition of the provisions of the foreign law pertaining to civil matters – *dinei mamonot* (in matters of ritual law the doctrine of *dina de-malkhuta dina* never applied; *Tashbeẓ,* 1:158 and see above) – would have constituted a serious danger to the orderly evolution of the Jewish legal system and may well have rendered it of theoretical interest only. As the main means of averting this danger many halakhic scholars

1. page 109; 2. page 660.

restricted the scope of the above doctrine – contrary to the plain meaning of some talmudic *halakhot* – by holding it applicable solely to certain matters falling within the sphere of relations between the central authorities and the public, such as taxation, expropriation of property for governmental purposes, and the like. Such restriction was expressly justified on the ground that extension of the doctrine to all matters of civil law would lead to "nullification of all the laws of Israel" *Beit ha-Beḥirah,* BK 113b). Even the scholars who in principle extended the doctrine beyond matters concerning relations between the authorities and the public (see Resp. Rashba, vol. 1, no. 895; Nov. Ramban, BB 55a; Nov. Ran and *Nimmukei Yosef ibid., Sefer ha-Terumot* 46:8, 5), did not always carry this out in practice (see Resp. Rashba, vol. 6, no. 254) and some scholars restricted the scope of the doctrine in other ways (see *Teshuvot Ḥakhmei Provinẓyah* (ed. A. Sofer), pp. 426f.; *Siftei Kohen,* ḤM 73, n. 39). The *halakhah* was decided according to the view that restricted the application of the doctrine solely to certain matters concerning relations between the authorities and the public (Rema ḤM 369:11).

The proliferous and ever-continuing creativity evidenced in talmudic and post-talmudic Jewish law offers eloquent proof of the fact that the doctrine of *dina de-malkhuta dina* remained only a marginal aspect of the Jewish legal system. Indeed, by their judicious use of the doctrine, the scholars rendered it a contributory factor toward the preservation of Jewish judicial jurisdiction, since qualified recognition of certain matters of foreign law enabled the Jewish collectivity to adapt itself, in the required and necessary manner, to the conditions of the gentile environment. The attitude of Jewish law toward a different legal system is determined, first and foremost, by its basic objective of safeguarding its own continued existence and, flowing therefrom, autonomous Jewish jurisdiction with all that it entails. As long as the realization of this objective is not endangered, no obstacle presents itself in Jewish law to resorting in certain cases, as the need arises, to a rule deriving from foreign law. Even then, however, such recognition is given only to the extent that the rule of the foreign law is not in conflict with any of the fundamental Jewish law principles of justice and equity. For this reason Jewish law attributes no validity to the law of the land with regard to a directive which does not apply equally to all but discriminates between different citizens, since any directive of this nature "is robbery" (Yad, Gezelah 5:14). Similarly, Jewish law holds the imposition of a monetary fine on the whole public, on account of the transgression of a few individuals, to be "absolute robbery" because such conduct contraverts the principle which prohibits the imposition of a collective fine and vicarious criminal responsibility (Resp. Ribash Ha-Ḥadashot no. 9; in support the following biblical references are cited: Gen. 18:25; Num. 16:22; Pes. 113b; see also Deut. 24:15 and II Kings 14:6).

THE ERA OF EMANCIPATION

Inner Spiritual and External Political Changes. On the eve of emancipation and the end of Jewish autonomy, substantial changes began to manifest themselves in Jewish law which were crucial to its development. As already indicated, two basic factors account for the survival of Jewish law as an operative law, even when it was deprived of its single territorial center and political sovereignty: the first the internal discipline of traditional Jewish society which regarded itself enjoined from a national-religious point of view to preserve Jewish law as a living force, and the second the political circumstances of the corporative medieval state. Both these elements now underwent a decisive change. At the same time as the rise of pressures for equality of rights for all, including Jews, the governments of Europe in turn deprived the Jewish community of the mandatory jurisdictional rights of the Jewish courts, even in matters of civil law; the use of the *ḥerem* as well as other means of execution were forbidden. But the main factor for the progressive ending of the living practice of Jewish law was the social-spiritual change that began to assert itself among the Jewish people. The Jewish community, which had hitherto regarded the *halakhah* as the supreme value of its existence, split into a society part of which remained traditional while part no longer regarded itself as bound to the observance of the Torah and its precepts, and this decisively weakened the internal factor of a religious imperative to order daily practical life in accordance with Jewish law. This substantive change in the spiritual outlook of the Jewish world carried with it also a disregard for the national element in Jewish law and not only did the leaders of the community not oppose the abolition of Jewish judicial autonomy but a good number of them welcomed the ending of the "separation" between the Jewish and the general public, regarding it as promising achievement of the hoped-for freedoms and equality of rights as well as organic integration into the vibrant Europe of the emancipation era.

The Abrogation of Jewish Judicial Autonomy. With the beginning of this transformation relating to the continued existence of Jewish judicial autonomy, a number of the leading halakhic scholars gave voice to their concern and warned about the religious and national dangers inherent in yielding up this autonomy. Thus R. Ezekiel Landau railed against the frequent recourse to the gentile courts, a practice so prevalent that "all three pillars of the world are shaken: the Law, Truth and Peace" (*Derushei ha-Ẓelaḥ,* 8:14; 22:24). R. Raphael Cohn, spiritual leader of various communities in Poland-Lithuania and Germany in the 18th century, devoted much effort in the latter years of his life toward the preservation of an autonomous Jewish legal system and all it entailed. Acknowledging the new reality of a laxity in Torah observance by a section of the Jewish public, he emphasized that the neglect of recourse to Jewish judicial jurisdiction was the most serious defect in non-observance of the laws of the Torah, and he particularly criticized those members of the Jewish public who saw the abrogation of such Jewish jurisdiction as a step toward equality of rights and duties (see *Zekher Ẓaddik,* pp. 7, 8, 20).

These political and spiritual changes, which were increasingly manifest in the course of the 19th century, left their impress upon that part of Jewry that continued to preserve the religious tradition. As regards Western and Central European Jewry, recourse to the general courts rapidly became widespread and common to all Jewish circles. Traditional Jewry of Eastern Europe still preserved for some considerable time its connection with Jewish law and brought its disputes to the rabbi and his *bet din* for *din Torah.* However, the decisions of the rabbinical courts became more and more arbitral awards and compromise settlements, lacking the semblance of judgments under a living and organic law, and in the course of time, here also, resort to the general courts grew increasingly. Even the halakhic scholars reconciled themselves with the new situation of the lack of judicial autonomy and justified it on the principle of *dina de-malkhuta dina* – quite contrary to the attitude taken by the scholars in earlier periods (see, e.g., *Kelei Ḥemdah,* Mishpatim, no. 1, and see above). The main and greater part of Jewish law in civil and criminal, administrative and public matters, came to be treated as if it were rules "not contemporaneously applied" and now studied merely theoretically. The only sphere of Jewish law that continued to be practiced was a part of family law, the arrangement of marriage and divorce in accordance therewith. In this field, involving the laws of prohibitions and permissions, a powerful internal discipline continued to govern traditional Jewry and to some extent also those who did not observe religious precepts. However, recognition by the central authorities of such marriage and divorce varied from country to country in the Diaspora.

Continuance of Judicial Autonomy in the Eastern Jewish Centers. An interesting phenomenon is the fact that to some extent Jewish law continued to develop as a living law among oriental Jewish communities in Turkey, North Africa, and elsewhere. This phenomenon is partly explained by the different political circumstances of the Ottoman Empire in the 19th and 20th centuries, but was also an outcome of the determined struggle waged by oriental Jewish communities, as in Algeria for instance, to retain their judicial independence in the face of efforts by the central authorities to impose on them the general law of the land. A demonstrative expression of this reality is the fact that even in the 19th century the responsa literature of this Jewry continued to occupy itself to a very large extent with matters of the *Ḥoshen Mishpat* arising from actual events in everyday life, while the responsa literature of European Jewry of this period is very poor in this respect and even then is more of a theoretical study than a consideration of practical problems.

Consequences of the Abrogation of Judicial Autonomy. The abrogation of Jewish judicial autonomy carried with it two far-reaching consequences with regard to the world of Jewish law. In the first place, Jewish law's dynamism as a living law of practice was greatly inhibited and its organic development suffered a marked curtailment. It was unfortunate for Jewish law that this development occurred in the course of the 19th century, a period which saw a revolution in social, economic, and industrial life that left a decisive imprint on different legal fields. The other consequence was the loss, by the greater part of the 19th-century Diaspora communities, of the former deep national and religious awareness that daily practical life, ordered in accordance with Jewish law, in all fields, had made an integral part of the way of life of the Jewish people. This consequence, as was later to become apparent, carried even more fateful implications for Jewish law than those flowing from the first-mentioned consequence.

THE PERIOD OF JEWISH NATIONAL AWAKENING

Ha-Mishpat ha-Ivri Society and Mishpat ha-Shalom ha-Ivri. The Jewish national awakening and the rise of Zionism also evoked a change in the mental attitude of the Jewish people toward Jewish law. Soon after the Balfour Declaration the Ha-Mishpat ha-Ivri Society was founded in Moscow. Its members – drawn from all sections of the Jewish public – regarded the return of Jewish society to Jewish law as an aspect of national renaissance parallel to the building of the Jewish homeland and revival of the Hebrew language. Among the goals set by the society was the preparation of suitable literature on Jewish law and the establishment in Jerusalem of an institute – within the framework of a university – for research into that law preparatory to its adoption in the future Jewish state. In the editorial introduction to the first number of the journal *Ha-Mishpat ha-Ivri* (Moscow, 1918) it is noted that "the 'legal' *halakhah* has been integrally bound up with the 'religious' *halakhah* . . . [yet] . . . over the last decades a process has begun of separating out our law from its religion and ethics and we intend to continue this process in order to prepare our law for a secular existence." The pursuit of this object was and still is a controversial one and its desirability as well as manner of achievement remain central problems relating to the integration of Jewish law into the legal system of the State of Israel (see below).

In 1909–10, on the initiative of the head of the Palestine office of the Zionist Organization, Mishpat ha-Shalom ha-Ivri was established in Jaffa as a judicial institution for the adjudication of disputes between Jews in Ereẓ Israel. In the course of time district tribunals were established in a number of places and over them a supreme tribunal. Between the years 1918 and 1936 rules and regulations were issued containing directives as to judicial organs, procedure, evidence, and so on. The first head of Mishpat ha-Shalom ha-Ivri was Arthur Ruppin and the writer S. Y. Agnon served as its first secretary. Mishpat ha-Shalom ha-Ivri functioned as an arbitral body and its work was facilitated by the enactment of the Arbitration Ordinance in 1926, which recognized the submission of disputes not only to individual arbitrators but also to an existing "arbitration tribunal" (see Arbitration[1]). It worked alongside the official bodies, first of the Ottoman Imperial government and later of the Mandatory power, and alongside the rabbinical courts. Mishpat ha-Shalom ha-Ivri did not, however, achieve its goal. Its main activities were confined to the years 1920–30 and after this date the number of cases brought before it began to wane. All in all it cannot be said to have produced any real harvest of Jewish law in consequence of its deliberations and decisions. Some of the reasons for this were objective, such as the tribunal's lack of powers of compulsion and the fact that it provoked sharp criticism from the rabbinical courts, the leaders of national religious Jewry, and respected scholars such as S. Assaf who were opposed to the existence of fixed judicial bodies outside the framework of the rabbinical courts and in opposition to them. Mainly, however, its lack of success was due to the fact that not only did it not assume to decide according to the existing *halakhah* as set out in the Shulḥan Arukh *Ḥoshen Mishpat* and the subsequent halakhic literature, but it possessed no system of norms, either of Jewish law or generally, upon which to act. In fact, proceedings before this tribunal were much like inquiries by laymen based on generally conceived principles of justice and equity, ethics and public good, since the judges were for the larger part persons of general education only, without any legal training or specific knowledge of law (see P. Daikan, *Toledot Mishpat ha-Shalom ha-Ivri,* and bibl. there cited; J. Yonovitz, Introd. to S. Assaf, *Ha-Onshin* . . . (1922), 5–6).

Jewish Law in the Rabbinical Courts. At the beginning of the 20th century the rabbinical courts in Ereẓ Israel displayed a total lack of central organization. With the establishment of the Chief Rabbinate in 1921, most of the rabbinical courts came to organize themselves within the framework of this institution. In matters of personal status, the rabbinical courts were assigned exclusive jurisdiction as regards marriage, divorce, and "probate" of wills, and concurrent jurisdiction as regards maintenance, succession, etc. (all other areas of the law remained within the jurisdiction of the general Mandatory courts). The task of this supreme halakhic institution was pictured by its first head, Rabbi Kook. After outlining the important creative role played by the *battei din* in all periods, through the enactment of *takkanot,* he went on to add that "in our renewed national life in Ereẓ Israel there will certainly sometimes be great need to make important *takkanot* which, as long as they are consented to by the majority of the competent scholars and are then accepted by the community, will carry the force of a law of the Torah" (*Ha-Tor,* 1 (1921), nos. 18, 21–22). To some extent the rabbinical courts were equal to this important task in matters of procedure and personal status, but in all other areas of Jewish law almost nothing was achieved.

Matters of Procedure and Personal Status. An important *takkanah* enacted immediately in 1921 established the Rabbinical Supreme Court of Appeal, thus introducing a regular

1. page 570.

appellate tribunal which had not previously existed in Jewish law (see Practice and Procedure). That this *takkanah* rendered the appellate court an integral part of the Jewish legal system was made clear in a judgment of the Rabbinical High Court of Appeal of Jerusalem which rejected the contention that no right of appeal existed in Jewish law, holding that "the right of appeal has been enacted by a rabbinical *takkanah*, the force of which is as that of a rule of our Holy Torah" (OPD, p.71).

At first the rules of procedure in the rabbinical court left much to be desired, but improvement followed upon the publication in 1943 of procedural regulations by the Chief Rabbinate Council. These included detailed provisions on the initiation of proceedings, on procedure during the hearing, rules of evidence, modes of appeal, and on other matters. A series of forms were also appended, among them statements of claim, summonses of parties and witnesses, applications for appeal and so on. In part these regulations were based on Jewish law and in part they showed the influence of existing practice in the general legal system. An innovation in Jewish law were the detailed rules laid down concerning the payment of various court fees and the adoption of children. The most radical innovation introduced by the above regulations involved an engagement by the rabbinical courts to distribute the estate of a deceased person in accordance with the provisions of the Succession Ordinance of 1923, which prescribed an order of distribution treating husband and wife and son and daughter in terms of equality. In 1944 a number of *takkanot* were enacted introducing further important changes: the customary minimum sum of the *ketubbah* was increased; the levir refusing to grant the widow of his brother *ḥaliẓah* was rendered obliged to maintain her until releasing her (see Levirate Marriage and *Ḥaliẓah*[1]); an important *takkanah* imposed on the father the legal duty to maintain his sons and daughters up to the age of 15 years and not merely until the age of six years in accordance with talmudic law (see Parent and Child;[2] M. Elon *Ha-Mishpat Ha-Ivri,* II, 667 ff.).

After 1944, however, creativity by way of *takkanot* ceased almost entirely, except for three additional *takkanot* enacted by the Chief Rabbinate in 1950 (the principal one involving a prohibition on the marriage of children under the age of 16 years; see Child Marriage[3]). This may be regarded as a matter for great regret since a number of urgent problems in the area of personal status still await solution by way of *takkanah* (such as certain cases of hardship for the *agunah,* problems relating to the joint property of the spouses, and other matters; see M. Elon, *Ha-Mishpat Ha-Ivri,* II, p. 686 ff.). On the other hand, there has since the 1940s been halakhic creativity in the area of personal status by means of interpretation as applied in actual cases. In this manner, for instance, there was innovated the substantive principle giving a woman, upon divorce, the right to receive over and above her *ketubbah* a certain additional sum, called "compensation." The amount thereof varies with the circumstances, one of the important considerations in its determination being the need to award the woman part of the property acquired in the course of the marriage through the joint efforts of the spouses (see M. Elon, *Ḥakikah Datit . . .,* 165ff.).

Other Fields of the Law. In fields of the law other than personal status the rabbinical courts were assigned no jurisdiction under the general law of the land, and the bearers of the *halakhah* initiated no real effort toward adaption of the Jewish legal system to the contemporary social and economic needs of Ereẓ Israel Jewry. The call to the people to submit their disputes in civil matters to the rabbinical courts by way of arbitration brought a very restricted response, even from the religious section of the community. Hence, except in a few exceptional cases, no evidence is to be found in the judgments of the rabbinical courts of any creative activity in the overwhelming part of the civil law. One notable exception is represented by a leading judgment given in 1946, in a matter concerning the laws of evidence. A marriage was entered into before two witnesses in the absence of a rabbi. As violators of the Sabbath both witnesses were incompetent (Sh. Ar., ḤM 34:2, 24) and since they were the only witnesses the marriage stood to be regarded invalid according to Jewish law. On the man's death, this was the contention raised by the remaining heirs of the deceased in opposition to the woman's claim to the widow's share in the estate of the deceased. The court, however, recognized the validity of the marriage, holding the witnesses to have been competent: "For reasons of religious transgression . . . and bearing in mind the fact . . . that libertarianism has increasingly spread for general and universal reasons, transgressions of this kind are not likely to affect the credibility of witnesses . . . who act almost unwittingly. The disqualification of transgressors as witnesses arises from the fear that their evidence will be false . . . and therefore in such cases the credibility of a witness is largely determined by reasons of time and place. If it is clear to the court that the person is not one who is likely to lie for the sake of deriving a benefit, he is to be admitted as a competent witness" (OPD, p. 137). This decision of principle was essential to the proper administration of justice under present day social realities in which a substantial part of the public is not religiously observant, and it is carried out in practice by the rabbinical courts. (A stringent conflicting view was given by the Rabbinical Supreme Court of Appeal; see Elon, *Ha-Mishpat Ha-Ivri,* I, p. 115, No. 158).

Jewish Law and the Hebrew Language. It is appropriate that the quest for the restoration of Jewish law as a law of practice be compared with the struggle for the revival of Hebrew as a spoken language. From one aspect the latter represented the more difficult task. Ever since the beginning of the Diaspora, Hebrew had served almost exclusively as a literary language, not spoken in the common pursuits of everyday life, and as a result of emancipation it came to be further and further removed from life – even the spiritual and cultural – of the Jewish people. Many of the faithful followers of the Zionist movement in its early stages entertained doubt about the possibility of using Hebrew in modern conditions: "Who among us knows sufficient Hebrew to ask for a train ticket in this language? " asked Herzl, who contemplated a Jewish state without Hebrew as its commonly spoken language (*The Jewish State,* ch. 5). Yet an inner awareness that the use of Hebrew in the social, economic, and cultural life of the people was a prime requisite without which there could be no complete national revival led eventually to Hebrew becoming not merely a holy tongue, but the national language, written and spoken, of the Jewish people returning to its homeland. As a result of the untiring efforts of individuals and public bodies expressions and terms were coined and style and forms created, largely drawn from the ancient treasure houses of the language, and in this manner there flowered a modern living language, based on and preserving continuity with the ancient holy tongue.

In other respects the possibility of restoring Jewish law was more limited than the revival of Hebrew, which is not so dependent on political sovereignty or assistance from the ruling authorities and is more closely connected with individual inclination and the wishes of interested bodies; legal norms encroach more on the realm of philosophy and ideological outlook than do the byways of a language and the task of restoring Jewish law demanded more comprehensive study and preparation than did the revival of Hebrew. Yet it is conceivable that these obstacles to the restoration of Jewish law could have been overcome by a

1. page 408; 2. page 426; 3. page 365.

determined effort. To a large extent the political autonomy of the Jews in Ereẓ Israel in the pre-state period was similar to that enjoyed by the Jewish people in the Diaspora until emancipation, an autonomy which also allowed for judicial independence. Moreover, by far the greater part of the subject matter with which Jewish law deals – such as obligations, property, public administration, and so on – is free of fundamental religious or ideological dispute. However, emancipation had produced a weakened religious and national consciousness of the need for daily life to be ordered in accordance with Jewish law, and all sections of the population displayed an irresolute apathy toward the preparation of Jewish law for its historic task. It is true that research was undertaken and books were written by scholars such as A. Gulak, S. Assaf, and A. Freimann, which were of importance for the scientific research of Jewish law. But the required auxiliary literature of the law, written in convenient form with the law phrased and classified in accordance with modern legal concepts and terminology, was not prepared, nor were possible solutions to modern legal problems for which Jewish law has no ready or adequate existing answer, although it allows for one to be found by way of *takkanah* or any other of its recognized creative legal sources.

The Legal System in Ereẓ Israel Preceding the Establishment of the State of Israel. The unique legal system in force in Ereẓ Israel under the British mandatory regime was a factor which might have served as a strong stimulus toward the integration of Jewish law into the legal system of the State about to be established. The principles which governed the mandatory legal system were set out in Article 46 of the Palestine Order in Council of 1922. In accordance with this, on the eve of the establishment of the State of Israel there was crystallized a legal system nourished by a number of legal systems: the *Mejelle,* based on Muslim religious law; various Ottoman laws embracing principles of French law and other legal systems; mandatory ordinances based on English law; law based on the English common law and doctrines of equity introduced into the mandatory legal system, in cases where the existing system provided no solutions to concrete problems. In addition, matters of personal status were to a considerable extent dealt with under the religious law of the different communities recognized by the general law. This was a legal system composed of a number of disparate elements and created a situation inviting its own replacement by a homogeneous legal system.

JEWISH LAW IN THE STATE OF ISRAEL

The Official Position Assigned to Jewish Law. On the establishment of the State of Israel, Jewish law continued to occupy the same official position in the legal structure of the state as it had done in the pre-State period. The Law and Administration Ordinance of 1948 prescribed that the law in existence on the eve of establishment of the state should remain in force (sec. 11), with the practical result that officially Jewish law was incorporated in the area of personal status only. At the same time the Hebrew language celebrated its final victory, even in a formal sense, and section 15b of the above ordinance repealed any provision in any law requiring the use of English, thus making Hebrew the language of the state, of its law, and of its everyday life.

Matters of Personal Status. The jurisdiction of the rabbinical courts was defined in a Knesset law of 1953 which, save for one or two changes, entailed no substantial departure from the existing situation. It gave the rabbinical courts exclusive jurisdiction in matters of marriage, divorce, and *ḥaliẓah;* as regards the wife's claim for maintenance, jurisdiction is given to the court to which the wife applies – the rabbinical or the district court. In this and in other laws there were also prescribed the circumstances in which the rabbinical courts have concurrent jurisdiction in other matters of personal status (see Adoption; *Apotropos;* Maintenance; Succession).

The Rabbinical Courts. Matters entrusted to the jurisdiction of the rabbinical courts are naturally dealt with in accordance with Jewish law. In the course of their activities these courts have given decisions introducing a number of important innovations in Jewish law, such as a married woman's right to the income deriving from the pursuit of her own profession, and recognition of the existence of mutual pecuniary rights between spouses married abroad in a civil ceremony only, and so on (see M. Elon, *Ḥakikah Datit . . . ,* 166–72). In certain matters the law prescribes that the rabbinical courts too must decide in accordance with the general law. In the Succession Ordinance of 1923 provision was made for the treatment of son and daughter, husband and wife, on terms of equality as regards the division of certain kinds of property on succession, and the Women's Equal Rights Law, 1951, extended the directive to all other property. Some of the other main provisions of this law are the following: men and women are equated as regards all legal acts; the father and mother are given natural guardianship of their children; a married woman is given full capacity of acquisition during marriage and retention of her rights to property acquired by her prior to the marriage. In addition this law allows the litigants, if they are above the age of 18 years, to consent to having their case tried according to the laws of their community. It also states that its provisions shall not affect any halakhic prohibition or permission relating to marriage or divorce. In the main its provisions accord with the position under Jewish law as it has evolved (for instance as regards equal rights on succession), a notable exception relating to the husband's right to the fruits of his wife's *melog* property (see Husband and Wife). A law of 1955 prescribes the status and manner of appointment of rabbinical court *dayyanim* and, except for two variations, its provisions correspond closely to those laid down in the Judges Law, 1953. (As regards two variations see M. Elon, *Ḥakikah Datit . . . ,* 47–49.)

The General Courts. In matters of personal status concerning Jewish parties the general courts are also required to decide according to Jewish law, except when a law of the state makes express provision on the matter. As already mentioned, the general courts have jurisdiction in all matters not entrusted to the exclusive jurisdiction of the rabbinical courts. Matters of marriage and divorce may also be pronounced on by the general courts, either when the problem arises incidentally to the matter before the court (for instance in a claim by the wife for maintenance there may arise incidentally thereto the question of the validity of her marriage), or in a matter brought before the Supreme Court sitting as a High Court of Justice. Possibly a rabbinical court and a general court, even though both apply Jewish law, may arrive at entirely different conclusions. Thus, for instance, the general courts first resort to the principles of private international law before applying Jewish law and therefore may recognize a marriage entered into abroad as valid in accordance with the law of the country concerned, even when it is invalid according to Jewish law. In addition the general courts apply only substantive Jewish law and not its laws of evidence and procedure, thus for instance admitting the testimony of the parties themselves and that of their relatives.

Legislative Provisions Contrary to Jewish Law. Legislation in the area of personal status contrary to Jewish law is reflected in a number of provisions, scattered in various Knesset laws, which confer on the commonly reputed spouse ("wife" as well as "husband") numerous rights. These provisions relate to rights of a social-economic nature (pensions, tenants' protection, and so on), rights under the Succession Law, and include also the right conferred on a woman to give her child born of the man reputed to be her husband the latter's family name, even without his consent. These rights were held by the Supreme Court to extend to the commonly reputed spouse even though the latter (or even both parties) be validly married to another (except with regard to the right of succession, which is only available if, upon the death of one of the parties who have lived together as husband and wife in a common household, neither is then married to another). The explanation that the above enactments were made in order to alleviate the hardship which is sometimes suffered by a couple who are unable to marry on account of Jewish law prohibition (for instance in certain cases of the *agunah*) is indeed weighty and hope may be expressed that the Chief Rabbinate will speedily find solutions to these problems. Nevertheless, it does not seem to justify the institution of the reputed spouse with its threat to the orderly existence of the family unit. This institution is the subject of controversy in Israel society and there are recent indications of a tendency by the Supreme Court to limit its scope (see M. Elon, *Ḥakikah Datit . . .*, 119–54).

"Who is a Jew? " – Answered According to Jewish Law. In March 1970 an amendment to the Law of Return of 1950 incorporated into this law a most material principle of Jewish law. This law, which ensures for every Jew the right to come to Israel as an *oleh* and automatic citizenship from the moment of his arrival, was amended to define the term "Jew" as a person born of a Jewish mother or converted to Judaism, who is not a member of a different religious faith. This definition, including the latter part, is entirely in accord with Jewish law. A Jew converted to a different faith remains a Jew as regards his personal status and all this entails – such as the need for him to grant a divorce to his Jewish wife – but he is deprived of various religio-social rights and is not numbered as a member of the Jewish community (i.e., he cannot be counted toward *minyan* and so on); for this reason he is also deprived of the rights of a Jew under the Law of Return. The stated definition applies also for purposes of registering an individual's Jewish nationality *(le'om)* in the population register and related documents, including the identity card.

Legislation Conforming With Ritual Law. In addition to the already mentioned cases, Israel law is also based on the *halakhah* – in the wide sense of the term – in a number of different matters. Thus in 1948 the Provisional Council of State enacted that the supply of *kasher* food be ensured to all Jewish soldiers of the Defense Army of Israel; a law of 1962 prohibits the raising, keeping, or slaughtering of pigs in Israel except in specified areas (populated mainly by non-Jews) and for certain other limited purposes; the provisions of the Law and Administration Ordinance of 1948 (as amended) lay down that the Sabbath and the Jewish festivals shall be prescribed days of rest in the state (but do not prohibit labor on such days, such matters being ordered in certain respects in the Hours of Work and Rest Law of 1951) and allows non-Jews the right to observe their own Sabbath and festivals as days of rest.

The "Unofficial" Application of Jewish Law in the State. Independence of the Israel Legal System. As already mentioned, Jewish law is reserved no official place in the Israel legal system save in matters of personal status. The proposal (made by P. Daikan on the eve of the state's establishment and subsequently raised again by others) that Israel law be freed from its dependence on the English common law and principles of equity and that Jewish law be resorted to in any case of lacuna in the law of the state (see above, Art. 46 of the Palestine Order in Council) was not accepted. Until the present time there is to be found in four Laws only, the Succession Law of 1965, the Land Law of 1969, the Law of Contract (Remedies for Breach of Contract) 1970 and the Law of Contract (General Part) 1973, a provision (entitled "Autarky of this Law") which excludes the operation of the aforementioned article 46 in all matters with which the relevant law is concerned. None of the other laws so far passed by the Knesset proclaims its own independent operation. To some extent such independence has been established in the case law in consequence of decisions by the Supreme Court to the effect that the post-1948 English case law does not have binding force in Israel law as does that of the pre-1948 period, and even reliance on the pre-1948 English case law is also gradually diminishing.

Legislation Based on Jewish Law Principles. In some measure law in the State of Israel follows the principles of Jewish law even in areas where the latter system has not officially been rendered applicable. In the introduction to a draft bill for one of the early comprehensive laws there were set out the general legislative guidelines adopted for the entire area of the civil law. The legislative policy thus enunciated assigned to Jewish law the status of "the main but not the only or binding source" and enumerated the existing legal and factual position in Israel as well as the laws of other countries as additional sources (Draft Bill for a Succession Law, published by the Ministry of Justice in 1952). To some extent this policy has been adhered to in practice and some of the matters enacted in accordance with the principles of Jewish law are the following: the possibility of separate ownership of dwellings in a cooperative house (see Ownership); the prohibition of delay in the payment of wages (see Labor Law); the right of the dismissed employee to severance pay (see *Ha'anakah*); the legal arrangement concerning imprisonment for debt; the laws of bailment (see Bailment), and so on. Particular reliance on Jewish law is to be found in the provisions of various Knesset laws in the area of family law, relating among others to the following matters: the duty of a person to maintain, besides his wife and children, also his other relatives (on the Jewish law principle of obliging a person to uphold the *mitzvah* of *ẓedakah;* see Maintenance); in matters of guardianship that the minor's own good is the primary consideration and that "the court is the father of all orphans" and a complete departure – expressed in various provisions – from the Roman law concept of *patria potestas* (see *Apotropos*); in matters of succession Jewish law is followed in the conferment of equal rights on all children of the deceased whether born in or out of wedlock, in the solution provided to the problem which arises in the case of commorientes (see Succession), in acceptance of the Jewish law institution of a *shekhiv mera* will (see Wills) and in the provision made for maintenance out of the estate of the deceased (see Widow).

Legislation Contrary to Jewish Law. In contrast, there are Knesset laws containing provisions which are – without any real justification – contrary to the position taken by Jewish law. Some of the matters so enacted are the following: the right of the creditor to turn directly to the surety even without initial agreement to this effect (see Surety); the right of a party to plead prescription of a claim along with an admission as to the existence of the debt (see Limitation of Actions); the automatic administration of an oath to all witnesses whereas Jewish law leaves the matter to the discretion of the court (Resp. Ribash no. 170; *Tashbeẓ*, 3:15; Rema ḤM 28:2; for further illustrations see Elon, in: ILR, 4 (1969), 80–140).

Jewish Law in the Case Law of the General Courts. The decisions of the courts, particularly of the Supreme Court, represent a further channel through which the influence of Jewish law is brought to bear on the Israel legal system. In numerous decisions of the Supreme Court diverse legal matters have been dealt with by way of a comparison between the position under the general law and Jewish law respectively, the two systems sometimes leading the judges to the same conclusion and sometimes otherwise. In some cases Jewish law has been quoted for the purpose of construing legal terms and definitions and on occasion Jewish law has constituted the primary legal source relied on by the Supreme Court, even in areas in which Jewish law is not expressly rendered applicable. This integration of Jewish law through the case law of the general courts is of great practical significance from the aspect of the confrontation between Jewish law and the legal problems that have arisen before the courts in the 1950s and 1960s.

Jewish Law in the Case Law of the Rabbinical Courts. A noteworthy phenomenon is the existence of a proliferous case law of the rabbinical courts, in diverse areas of the civil law, in matters coming before these courts as arbitral bodies. Some 30% of the judgments of these courts published since the middle of the 1960s deal with matters unrelated to personal status and concern, for instance, labor law, contracts, copyright, partnership, pledge, administrative law, and so on. These offer an instructive insight into the manner in which concrete questions of everyday life are dealt with in accordance with Jewish law and represent an important contribution to the solution of modern social and economic problems (see, e.g., Contract; *Ha'anakah;* Labor Law; Public Authority).

Attitudes Toward Jewish Law in the Law of the State. Integration of Jewish law into the legal system of Israel is sometimes opposed because it entails a "secularization" of the *halakhah* since the acceptance by the state of a Jewish law principle does not stem from recognition of the binding validity of such a principle from the religious point of view, but is dictated by purely human and national interests. The argument views that by such integration the Knesset's own binding authority substitutes itself as the source of authority of any Jewish law principle it has adopted, and that neither the Knesset nor the general courts possess the necessary qualifications postulated by the halakhic system for deciding any of its rules. This view is decried by a decisive majority of religious Jewry and its spiritual leaders, who consider that the *halakhah* does not become secularized for the mere reason that the theory of the general law may hold a change to have taken place as regards the basic norm of a particular halakhic rule. It is argued that neither the Knesset nor the courts purport – nor indeed is it possible for them to do so – to decide the *halakhah* within the religious meaning of such activity; that not only is the *halakhah* not prejudiced by its integration into the legal system of the state, but the halakhic system itself commends that the legal order in the Jewish state shall, even if not based on religious faith, correspond with the substance of Jewish law and its principles of justice and equity rather than be founded on other legal systems. For some generations now this middle path has been followed by a decisive majority of religious Jewry, also with regard to other fundamental Jewish values, as with the revived use of the holy tongue in everyday secular life and with the settlement of the holy land even without observance of the religious precepts. The declared attitude of non-observant Jewry also favors the assignment of first priority to the reception of Jewish law principles when these are in keeping with present-day social and economic needs (see, e.g., the statement made in the session of Nov. 29, 1965, by Knesset members belonging to almost all political parties with reference to the Gift Law and Pledge Law Bills (*Divrei ha-Keneset,* v. 44, pp. 24–36)). It should be borne in mind that except in the area of family law, Jewish law is generally free of fundamental public dispute of a religious or ideological nature.

The integration of Jewish law into the legal system of Israel is of importance to the former since it has a vital need to contend with the problems of practical everyday life as the only means toward the restoration of its former, almost unbroken, creative and evolutionary function, and this in its natural environment – the Jewish state and its legal system. Such an integration of Jewish law is no less important for the legal system of the State. Israel legislation is of an eclectic nature, the legislator choosing as he sees fit from many different legal systems. There is well-founded apprehension that this must necessarily result in a lack of homogeneity and lead to contradictions in Israel law due to the absence of a common axis around which the entire legal structure may revolve. A legal system so constructed moreover lacks roots and a past. If, as the revival of Hebrew proved, a people's language has to lean on history and foundations, then a priori a people's legal system requires roots and a past on which to draw for sustenance and growth. The absence of these requisites in Israel law accounts for the large number of Supreme Court decisions evidencing resort to numerous legal systems in a search for solutions to legal problems. The appointed way for the emerging legal system of the Jewish state to take root, to find the common denominator for its laws as well as the homogeneity it requires, is for it to become linked and integrated in the proper way with historical Jewish legal thinking and creativity.

Modes of Integration. Achievement of the desired integration of Jewish law with the Israel legal system demands strict observance of the rule that in all legislative activity preference be given to every principle of Jewish law which is in keeping with the existing social and economic exigencies. It is also necessary to ensure that all principles of Jewish law adopted in the laws of the state shall be construed within the spirit of the Jewish sources of law from which they were derived. Finally, it is necessary to lay down a "Jewish version" of the controversial Article 46, to the effect that the Jewish sources of law shall be resorted to in the event of any lacuna in the existing law. The decisions of the Supreme Court and of the rabbinical courts in matters involving Jewish law – not only in the area of personal status but in all its different fields – and a long series of varied research studies undertaken in recent years, point to the fact that it is within the power of Jewish law to contend successfully with the overall range of new problems that arise. In addition, Jewish law occupies a substantial part of the law faculty study curriculum at different universities in Israel and to the new generation of Israel lawyers and jurists Jewish law is no longer a remote and unfamiliar subject. Accelerated research activity in the different fields of Jewish law and the preparation of an auxiliary literature to facilitate study of and resort to the latter will be invaluable aids to the process of integrating the legal system of the State of Israel and Jewish law.

Legal Creativity. During various periods of its history Jewish law has experienced the reality of jurisdiction and legislation existing alongside the jurisdictional and legislative system of the halakhic authority itself – as illustrated by the king's law, jurisdiction of the public leadership, lay jurisdiction, and communal enactments. In numerous matters such jurisdiction and legislation of the Jewish leadership diverged from the rules of Jewish law, but the halakhic system evolved a series of rules and principles which ensured that such jurisdiction and legislation of the public leadership became an integral part of the overall system (see *Takkanot ha-Kahal*[1]). It is true that during all the abovementioned periods the entire Jewish people looked upon Jewish law as the ultimate and binding value, whereas the same cannot be said of the present-day Jewish public, which, in the existing socio-cultural realities, finds itself divided on matters of religious

1. page 659.

faith and ideological outlook. Yet in this society there have developed certain cultural and social values – such as the restored language and homeland – which exist as the undisputed assets of all. Consequently the hope may be expressed that the acceptance of Jewish law principles into the legal system of Israel in a proper and consistent manner, along with the latter's formation of a tie with Jewish law for purposes of its own supplementation, will ensure that at some time in the future unity and integrity – and thereby continuity as well – will also be restored to this precious cultural and spiritual asset of the Jewish nation, that is, to Jewish law.

Menachem Elon

Literature on the subjects discussed in the Introduction: Gulak, Yesodei, 1 (1922), 3–31; 4 (1922), 3–45; S. Assaf, *Ha-Onshin Aḥarei Ḥatimat ha-Talmud* (1922); idem, *Battei ha-Din ve-Sidreihem Aḥarei Ḥatimat ha-Talmud* (1924); M. Elon, *Ḥerut ha-Perat be-Darkhei Geviyyat Ḥov* . . . (1964), 11–14 (intro.), 255–69; idem, in: ILR, 2 (1967), 515–65; 3 (1968), 88–126; 416–57; 4 (1969), 80–140; idem, in: *Ha-Peraklit,* 25 (1968/69), 27–53; idem, *Ḥakikah Datit* . . . (1968); idem, *Ha-Mishpat Ha-Ivri* I, (1973); idem, *Mi-Bayot ha-Halakhah ve-ha-Mishpat bi-Medinat Yisrael,* Institute of Contemporary Jewry, Hebrew University (1973); A.H. Freimann, in *Lu'aḥ ha-Areẓ* (1945/46), 110–25; H. Cohen, in: *Ha-Peraklit,* 3 (1946), 38ff; idem, Secularization of Divine Law *Scripta Hierosolymitana,* xvi), 1966; Baron, Community; Hebrew Law and the State of Israel: a *Symposium,* in: Sura, 3 (1957/58), 457–518; Alon, Toledot[2]; Alon, Meḥkarim; M. Silberg, *Kakh Darko Shel Talmud* (1961), 66ff.; Finkelstein, Middle Ages; B. Cohen, *Jewish and Roman Law,* 2 vols. (1966); J.I. Englard, in: ILR, 3 (1968), 254–78; S. Eisenstadt, *Ein Mishpat,* Jerusalem (1931); J. Bazak (ed.), *Ha-Mishpat Ha-Ivri u-Medinat Yisrael* (1969; collection of articles); G. Tedeschi, On Reception and on the Legislative Policy of Israel (Scripta Hierosolymitana, xvi) 1966; J. Herzog, *The Main Institutions of Jewish Law* (1965/72) Pt. I, ch. 1.

I. THE SOURCES OF LAW

Contents

This section contains no detailed articles on the other literary sources of Jewish Law: the Bible, Mishnah, Tosefta, and two Talmuds, Perushim (Commentaries) and Ḥiddushim (Novellae), responsa literature etc. The reason for this is that no separate articles on these topics appeared in the Encyclopaedia Judaica as part of the section on Jewish Law. Detailed discussion of these can be found in the recently published work, M. Elon, *Ha-Mishpat Ha-Ivri,* vol. 3, Magnes Press; Hebrew University, Jerusalem.

AUTHORITY, RABBINICAL. The authority of the halakhic scholars in maintaining the creativeness and development of Jewish law, by means of its legal sources.

Development of the Law. An important tenet of Judaism and a guiding principle of the halakhists is that, together with the Written Law *(Torah she-bi-khetav)* Moses received also the Oral Law *(Torah she-be-al peh)* (Meg. 19b), the latter, within its wider meaning, embracing all the *halakhah* not explicit in the Written Law (Sifra, Beḥukkotai 8:12). However, the talmudic sages themselves clearly distinguished between that part of the Oral Law based on a tradition handed down from generation to generation, from the time of Moses who received it from God Himself (Avot 1:1; ARN[1] 1:1; *ibid.*, Maim. Yad, Mamrim, 1:1–2), and the other parts of the Oral Law, created and developed by the halakhic scholars. The sages of the Midrash in answer to the question whether Moses learned the whole Torah in forty days while he was on Mt. Sinai, answered that "God taught Moses the principles" (Ex. R. 41:6). These words are interpreted by Joseph Albo to mean that "the law of God cannot be (given) in complete form so as to be adequate for all times . . . and therefore at Sinai Moses was given general principles . . . by means of which the sages in every generation may formulate the details as they present themselves" (*Ikkarim,* 3:23). A study of the statements of the halakhic scholars reveals that just as they emphasized in unequivocal terms the supra-human and divine nature of the source of *halakhah,* so too – and with the same degree of emphasis – they insisted upon the human element, the exclusive authority of the halakhic scholars to continue to develop and shape the *halakhah.* This dual image of *halakhah* finds expression in two basic and apparently contradictory dicta: on the one hand, the basic tenet that "the Torah is from Heaven" *(Torah min ha-Shamayim)* – on the other, the principle that "the Torah is not in Heaven" (*Torah lo ba-Shamayim;* BM 59b based on Deut. 30:12; Maim. Yad, Yesodei ha-Torah, 9:4). In other words, the source of the *halakhah* is divine, but its place, its life, development, and formation, is with mankind, in the life of society. The halakhic scholars saw no inconsistency in these two principles, believing as they did that in their exegesis, enactments, innovations, and creativeness, they were merely giving practical expression to a further unfolding of the revelation at Sinai, destined from the beginning for the needs of each particular generation (Ex. R. 28:6; Tanḥ. Yitro, 11).

Authority of the Halakhic Scholars. Even in the written law problems are encountered to which no solutions are given within the framework of the existing law – such as the case of the blasphemer (Lev. 24:10–16), the gatherer of sticks on the Sabbath (Num. 15:32–36), and the inheritance of the daughters of Zelophehad (Num. 27:1–11; 36:1–10) – but are explicitly made known by God to Moses. On the other hand, a number of biblical passages, particularly Deuteronomy 17:8–13, enjoin that a decision for every future problem, whether arising from a precept governing man's relationship with the Divine, or with his fellowman, must be sought at the hands of "the priest, the levite, and the judge," sitting at the particular time in the midst of the people in judgment over them. This combination of priest, levite, and judge was designed to ensure, according to the halakhic interpretation, that the law should be determined by teachers and judges deciding according to their human knowledge and understanding, since the function of the priest and levite was to instruct and teach the people (cf. Deut. 33:10; Ezek. 44:23–24; Mal. 2:7; Josephus' reference to the prophet (Ant., 4:218) within the context of Deuteronomy 17:9, is contrary to the plain meaning of the text). Hence, when in the course of time the teaching of the law ceased to be the exclusive function of the priests and levites, it was decided that while it was proper for priests and levites to be members of the *bet din,* their absence would not affect its competence (Sif. Deut. 153).

Authority in Deciding the Halakhah. The prophet in his function as a bearer of the divine vision is assigned no part in determining the *halakhah.* " 'These are the commandments' – henceforth a prophet may no longer make any innovations" (Sifra, Beḥukkotai 13:7). A halakhic rule that is forgotten may not be recalled by means of "divine spirit," but by way of study and logical reasoning (Tem. 16a; see Maim., intro. to Comm. to the Mishnah).

The sages of the Talmud carried this basic conception concerning the exclusive authority to interpret the Torah and continue its development, to an extreme but inevitable conclusion – "even if they tell you that left is right and right is left – hearken unto their words" (Comm. on Deut. 17:10, 11; Mid. Tan. p. 102–3, Sif. Deut. 154 et al.; cf. the version in TJ, Hor. 1:1, 45d: "until they tell you that right is right and left is left." For a reconciliation between the texts see Abrabanel to Deut., *ibid.; Divrei David* (of David b. Samuel ha-Levi, author of the *Turei Zahav*) ad loc.; D. Hoffman, in Bibliography. (It is possible that the two versions are related to the conflicting views between R. Kahana and R. Eliezer concerning the *Zaken Mamre* (Sanh. 88a))). Thus the *halakhah* is so identified with its scholars and tradents that even their errors are binding as *halakhah* – a notion clearly expressed by Naḥmanides (Comm. on Deut. *ibid.;* see also Nissim Girondi, *Derashot ha-Ran,* nos. 7 and 11). This twofold principle of the exclusive authority of the halakhic scholars and of excluding any supra-human influence on the determination of the *halakhah* is vividly exemplified in the well-known *aggadah* of the dispute between R. Eliezer b. Hyrcanus and R. Joshua b. Hananiah and his colleagues concerning the "oven of Aknai" (BM 59b). Although a heavenly voice *(bat kol)* came forth to confirm the correctness of the former's minority opinion, R. Joshua refused to concede, countering with the argument that the Torah "is not in Heaven" "the Torah has already been given . . . embracing the rule that the majority must be followed" (Ex. 23:2). The *aggadah* concludes that even God accepted the majority view, and "rejoiced that His children had vanquished Him." Thus, the absolute truth may be according to the opinion of an individual and the majority may err, but the halakhic truth lies with the majority opinion, since the *halakhah* was entrusted to the scholars, whose decision is accepted, as it were, by the Lawgiver Himself. It is true that some scholars took a contrary view, attributing a certain influence to supra-human authority in the determination of the *halakhah,* particularly with regard to the visions of the prophets, whose halakhic statements were interpreted as the Torah itself. Even after prophecy had ceased there were scholars who attached significance to supra-human influence, as illustrated in the *aggadot* of the *bat kol* intervening in the above-mentioned dispute and in that between Bet Hillel and Bet Shammai (Er. 13b). These must be seen, however, as the opinion of individual scholars, and it is clear that the opinion of Joshua prevailed, that "no attention is paid to a *bat kol*" (Ber. 52a; Pes. 114a). Maimonides (introd. to Yad.) assigns to the prophets and their courts an honorable place as links in the chain of tradition of halakhic transmission, stressing however that this was by virtue of the prophets, functioning as scholars and not in the role of prophets, and he explains that "the prophet does not come to make law but to command about the precepts of the Torah, to warn people that they shall not transgress them." A prophet who claimed divine instruction as to what was law or the *halakhah*, was to be branded "a false prophet" (Yad., Yesodei ha-Torah, 9:1–4), from which it follows that "even if a thousand prophets, all of them equal to Elijah and Elisha, should hold to a reasoned opinion, and a thousand and one scholars reason otherwise, the majority must yet be followed" and the *halakhah* decided according to the words of the latter (Yad. introd.). Some seven centuries later Aryeh Leib b. Joseph ha-Kohen succinctly summarized the matter, stating: "the Torah was not given to the angels, but to man who possesses human intelligence . . . the Torah was given to be determined by human intelligence, even if human intelligence errs . . . and the truth is determined by the agreement of the sages by using human intelligence" (introd. to *Keẓot ha-Ḥoshen* to Sh. Ar., ḤM).

Authority in Every Generation. This guiding principle in the *Weltanschauung* of the halakhists dictated the development of the *halakhah* in all its history. From time to time there emerged new spiritual centers of the Jewish people. When Jabneh became such a center, after the destruction of the Temple, it was laid down that the court there was to be the central determining authority (Sif. Deut. 153) and Yose ha-Gelili explains the words "in those days" in that verse (Deut. 17:9), as referring to "a competent judge functioning at the particular time" (Sif. Deut. 153). The possibility is recognized that future scholars might not be as wise as their predecessors; nevertheless contemporary scholars and judges should be regarded with the same esteem as those of past generations and "whoever is appointed leader of the community, even if he be the least worthy, is to be regarded with the same esteem as the mightiest of earlier generations." Moreover, "Say not, 'How was it that the former days were better than these? ' for it is not out of wisdom that you enquire concerning this" (R.H. 25b based on Eccles. 7:10; Tosef. R.H. 2:3). The enduring continuity and vitality of the *halakhah* dictate that the scholars of each generation exercise the authority conferred on them in the cause of its continued creativity and development, and to refrain from using such authority or to question it, on the grounds that the wisdom of later scholars does not match that of their precursors, would show lack of understanding.

Evolution of the Halakhah. The halakhic scholars exercised the authority given them by the basic norm of the *halakhah* – i.e., the Written Torah, in certain established ways, recognized by the halakhic system itself for the purpose of its own evolution, i.e., by utilizing *halakhah*'s legal sources. The primary legal source is Midrash (i.e., interpretation and construction), various modes of which were employed to find solutions to new problems, first by interpretation of the written law and thereafter of the Mishnah and successive halakhic sources (see Interpretation). When interpretation offered no means of a solution, or the proffered solution provided no answer to contemporary requirements, a second legal source was used: namely, legislation or enactment by way of the *takkanah* and *gezerah* (see *Takkanot*). Other legal sources employed were *minhag* ("custom"), *ma'aseh* ("case and precedent"), and *sevarah* ("legal logic"). In pursuing, by means of the above-mentioned legal sources, their task of fashioning the *halakhah* – which gave order to daily vicissitudes of life, while itself being shaped by them – the halakhic scholars clung to a two-fold objective. On the one hand they maintained an unswerving concern for the continued evolution and development of the *halakhah*, and, on the other, for the great and onerous responsibility of preserving its spirit, orientation and continuity.

The Rule of "Hilkheta Ke-Vatra'ei" (i.e., that "the law is according to later halakhic scholars"). This substantive rule was a development of the post-talmudic period, endorsed by the fundamental principle of the halakhic scholars' authority. In the history of the *halakhah*, the terms *"rishonim"* and *"aḥaronim"* are commonly accepted as signifying the scholars from the middle of the 11th to the 16th centuries and those from the 16th century onward, respectively. These terms, however, are also applied to halakhic scholars prior to the 11th century to indicate not only their chronological order but also the greater authority halakhically attributed to earlier scholars as compared with later ones. R. Johanan stated: "The hearts of the *rishonim* were like the door of the *ulam* ("the larger hall of the Temple") and those of the *aḥaronim* like the door of the *heikhal* ("the smaller hall") but ours are like the eye of a fine needle." Abbaye, Rava, and Rav Ashi compared with even more modesty their own standing with that of earlier scholars (Er. 53a). *Amoraim* were not permitted to dispute statements of the *tannaim*, a relationship of deference preserved in turn by the *geonim* and the *rishonim* and *aḥaronim* of the rabbinic period toward their respective predecessors.

The high regard paid to the statements of earlier scholars did not prevent Jewish law from developing in the course of time an important rule, essential for the purpose of bestowing authority on contemporary scholars to decide the *halakhah* according to the prevailing circumstances and problems of their time. This rule – that the law is according to later scholars – dates from the geonic period. It laid down that until the time of Abbaye and Rava, i.e., the middle of the fourth century C.E., the *halakhah* – in case of any difference of opinion among the scholars – was to be decided according to the views of the earlier scholars rather than those of later dissenting scholars; from the time of Abbaye and Rava onward and also in case of disputes among the post-talmudic scholars, the opinions of later scholars would prevail over the contrary opinions of an earlier generation in deciding the *halakhah* (Asher b. Jehiel, *Piskei ha-Rosh,* BM 3:10; 4:21; Shab. 23:1). Certain sources render this rule applicable also to the period preceding Abbaye and Rava (see L. Ginzberg, *Geonica,* 2 (1909), 21–22, 32). The principle of *hilkhata ke-vatra'ei* is applicable also when a pupil dissents from his teacher (Resp. Maharik, 84; Malachi b. Jacob ha-Kohen, *Yad Malakhi,* no. 17) and even when an individual disputes the views of a number of earlier scholars (*Yad Malakhi,* no. 169; *Pitḥei Teshuvah* no. 8, Sh. Ar., ḤM 25).

Among the reasons advanced for this rule are those of Asher ben Jehiel. "All matters not elucidated in the Talmud, as compiled by Rav Ashi and Ravina, may be controverted and reconstructed even when the statements of the *geonim* are dissented from . . . The statements of later scholars carry primary authority because they knew the reasoning of earlier scholars as well as their own, and took it into consideration in making their decision" (*Piskei ha-Rosh,* Sanh. 4:6; Resp. Rosh, 55:9); Joseph Colon gives the somewhat similar reason that since the later scholars knew of the statements of earlier scholars and deliberated them, yet did not heed them, "it is a sign that they knew that the statements of earlier scholars were not to be relied upon in the particular matter" (Resp. Maharik 84). So, too, various reasons were given as to why this rule was only relevant from the time of Abbaye and Rava onward; one view being that from their time onward pupils learned not only the system of their own teacher but other systems as well, and therefore the pupils' decision was to be preferred (Colon, *ibid.*); in the *tosafot* (Kid. 45b) the view is given that later scholars "took greater pains to present the *halakhah* in a sound form."

It follows from the above-mentioned reasons that the rule of *hilkheta ke-vatra'ei* only applied when the later scholar had considered the statements of his predecessor, and, after weighing them, was able to prove the correctness of his opposing view in ways acceptable to his contemporaries (*Piskei ha-Rosh, ibid.;* Resp. Maharik, 94). Thus, too, the rule was accepted by Isserles as a guiding principle in deciding Jewish law (to Sh. Ar., ḤM 25:2). Some of the scholars, particularly among the *aḥaronim,* laid down several additional reservations concerning the operation of the rule. The rule should not be understood as diminishing in any way the esteem in which scholars of an earlier generation were held by later ones, but rather as inspiring the later *posek* ("decider") to reach his decision with a sense of responsibility, awe, and humility; once having reached his conclusion, the *halakhah* was as he and not as earlier scholars had decided.

On the meaning of the rule that "a *bet din* may not set aside the ruling of another *bet din* unless it exceeds the latter in wisdom and standing," and the resultant conclusions, see *Takkanot.*[1]

Bibliography: Z. H. Chajes, *Torat ha-Nevi'im* (1836), ch. 1 = his: *Kol Sifrei Mahariz Ḥayyut,* 1 (1958); D. Hoffmann, *Der Oberste Gerichtshof* . . . (1878), 9–13; M. Tchernowitz, *Toledot ha-Halakhah,* 1 pt. 1 (1934), 67–111; ET, 9 (1959), 341–5; Urbach, in: *Tarbiz,* 18 (1946/47), 1–27; Elon, in: ILR, 2 (1967), 550–61; idem, *Ha-Mishpat Ha-Ivri,* I, p. 223ff.

Menachem Elon

INTERPRETATION. This article is arranged according to the following outline:

Definition of Terms
Bible Exegesis
- Substance of Bible Exegesis in Jewish Law: Creative Interpretation and Integrative Interpretation
- Halakhic Creativity by Means of Interpretation (Midrash)
- Evidence of Creative Interpretation in Ancient *Halakhah*
- Midrash and Roman Law *Interpretatio*
- Different Literary Forms for Creative and Integrative Interpretation
- Development of Bible Exegesis
  - Until Hillel the Elder
  - R. Neḥunyah b. ha-Kanah and R. Nahum of Gimzo
  - R. Ishmael and R. Akiva and their Academies
  - R. Eliezer b. Yose ha-Gelili
  - In the Amoraic Period
  - In the Post-Talmudic Period
- Thirteen *Middot* of R. Ishmael
- Elucidative Interpretation
  - *Kelal u-Ferat*
  - *Davar she-Hayah ba-Kelal ve-Yaẓa min ha-Kelal*
  - *Davar ha-Lamed me-Inyano, Davar ha-Lamed mi-Sofo*
  - *Shenei Ketuvim ha-Makhḥishim Zeh et Zeh*
  - Interpretation of Words and Phrases
- Analogical Interpretation
  - *Kal va-Ḥomer*
  - *Gezerah Shavah*
  - *Binyan Av*
  - *Hekkesh ha-Katuv*
- Logical Interpretation
- Restrictive Interpretation

Interpretation of the *Halakhah*
- Use of the Principles of Bible Exegesis for Interpretation of the *Halakhah*
- Restrictive and Expansive Interpretation
- Interpretation of the *Halakhah* in Post-Talmudic Times
- Interpretation of Documents
  - *Doreshin Leshon Hedyot*
  - *Ha-Kol Holekh Aḥar ha-Taḥton*
  - *Yad Ba'al ha-Shetar al ha-Taḥtonah*
  - Interpretation *le-Fi Leshon Benei Adam*
- Interpretation of *Takkanot ha-Kahal*
  - Entrustment of Interpretative Authority
  - Interpretation of *Takkanot le-Fi Leshon Benei Adam*
  - Interpretation in Accordance with the Language of the *Takkanah*
  - Circumstances in Which the Background to a *Takkanah* and Its motivating Factors May Be Taken into Account
  - Conflicting Provisions and Ambiguity in the Text

DEFINITION OF TERMS

In Jewish law interpretation is called Midrash – a word deriving from the verb *darosh,* meaning study and investigation of the inner and logical meaning of a particular text as opposed to its plain and literal reading. The word *darosh* is also used in the same sense to denote investigation of the true and "unrevealed" position as regards a particular factual event (Deut. 13:15; *"Ve-darashta ve-ḥakarta ve-sha'alta heitev"* – "you shall investigate and inquire and interrogate thoroughly" – hence the term *derishah va-ḥakirah* with reference to the interrogation of witnesses). For the act of interpretation the word *talmud* is sometimes used (e.g., Sanh. 11:2; cf. Avot 4:13), and also the word *din* (e.g., Mak. 5b). In the field of the *halakhah,* the concept of Midrash has a meaning similar to *interpretatio* in Roman law and to "interpretation" in English law. The term *parshanut* was originally used in the sense of commentary (i.e., elucidation), generally amounting to a rephrasing or translation of the text into simpler and more easily understood terms; however, in the course of time the term *parshanut* also came to be employed in Jewish law in the sense of interpretation, and at the present time has both meanings. The interpretative process is often executed with the aid of fixed rules by which the exegete is guided; these are "the *middot* by means of which the Torah is interpreted" (see below). The process of interpretation began with Midrash of the Torah (i.e.; Bible exegesis) and was followed by Midrash of the *halakhah,* i.e., of the Mishnah, both Talmuds, and post-talmudic halakhic literature (see below). In addition there evolved, from very early days, a system for the interpretation of various legal documents (see below), and after the redaction of the Talmud for the interpretation of communal enactments also (*takkanot ha-kahal;* see below).

BIBLE EXEGESIS

Substance of Bible Exegesis in Jewish Law: Creative Interpretation and Integrative Interpretation. A reading of halakhic literature reveals that very many *halakhot* are stated in midrashic form, i.e., the particular *halakhah* is integrated into and interwoven with a biblical passage (this is the form adopted in the *Midreshei Halakhah,* halakhic literature on biblical passages, some details of which are mentioned below) and is not stated in the form of an abstract *halakhah* which stands by itself (as is the accepted and general form in the Mishnah). Scholars have expressed different opinions on the substanstive nature of this form of interpretation. According to some, it is merely a literary device for a manner of studying the *halakhot,* i.e., the essential halakhic rule was not created in consequence of the interpretation of a particular scriptural passage but had already been in existence (having originated from other legal sources of the *halakhah,* such as *kabbalah* ("tradition"), *takkanah* ("enactment"), *minhag* ("custom"), etc.) and the scholars merely found support for the existing halakhic rule through allusion to a biblical passage. Such allusion was made for two reasons: (a) in order to facilitate recall of a rule which, in ancient times, had never been reduced to writing but studied orally and hence had to be studied together with the relevant biblical passage; (b) in order to stress the integral connection between the Oral and the Written Law, since the latter constituted the basic norm of the entire halakhic system. Another view is that Bible exegesis is much more than a mere

1. page 81.

literary device for studying the *halakhah;* on the contrary, the biblical passage into which the halakhic rule is integrated constitutes at the same time the source of the rule; i.e., the rule was created out of the study and examination of the particular passage and without such an interpretation of the passage the rule would never have existed at all. Some scholars suggest that at first Midrash served as a source for the evolution of the law and that in later times it ceased to serve this purpose, while other scholars take the contrary view.

It is clear that even the scholars who hold that Bible exegesis served as a source for the evolution of the law do not regard that fact as meaning that in every case of Bible exegesis the halakhic rule in question necessarily evolved from such exegesis. Thus as regards a certain section of the biblical expositions, it is specifically stated that they are in the nature of *asmakhta be-alma* (i.e., simply allusion to a particular passage; see, e.g., Ber. 41b; Er. 4b: "They are but traditional laws for which the rabbis have found allusions in Scripture," cf. Tosef. Ket. 12:2; TJ, Git. 5:1, 46c). Thus the scholars emphasize that the *halakhot* do not derive from the Bible exegesis, but from some other legal source of the *halakhah,* and are merely supported by allusions to particular biblical passages. This is also so in the case of numerous other *halakhot* arrived at by way of interpretation; even though they are not said to be in the nature of *asmakhta* alone, it cannot be determined with certainty whether in each case they derived from the particular interpretation of the biblical passages concerned, or whether they evolved from some other legal source and were merely integrated into the relevant biblical passages.

Halakhic Creativity by Means of Interpretation (Midrash). It appears that from the inception of the *halakhah* and throughout its history, Midrash has served as a creative source of Jewish law and as an instrument in its evolution and development (see Yad, introd. and Mamrim 1:2). In point of time and importance, it constitutes the primary legal source of Jewish law (see Introduction[1]). Throughout the history of the *halakhah,* scholars had to face the twofold problem of (a) reconciling difficulties emerging from the study of biblical passages, and (b) resolving new problems arising in daily life, particularly in consequence of changed economic and social realities. The evolution of new *halakhot* was a natural outcome of the use of Midrash by the scholars in their efforts to overcome difficulties in the elucidation of Scripture, and Midrash led to great creativity, especially when applied to the solution of new problems. Although other means of solving such new problems were available (e.g., through the enactment of *takkanot*), the scholars nevertheless first and above all sought to find the solutions in Scripture itself, by endeavoring to penetrate to its inner or "concealed" content. In the eyes of the scholars Midrash was also to be preferred over the *takkanah* as a means of resolving new problems; the *takkanah* represented intentional and explicit lawmaking, designed to add to, detract from, or otherwise change the existing and sanctified *halakhah,* whereas in the case of Midrash the new *halakhah* derived from the scriptural passage concerned was not designed to add to the latter and certainly did not stand in contradiction to it. The link between the new *halakhah* and the Written Law was seen as a natural one of father and offspring, and the *halakhah* evolved from Scripture was, as it were, embedded in the latter from the beginning. Hence it may reasonably be assumed that the halakhic scholars would first have turned to Midrash in their search for solutions to the new problems that arose, and only when this offered no adequate or satisfactory answer would they turn to other legal sources of the *halakhah.*

Evidence of Creative Interpretation in Ancient Halakhah. From early tannaitic sources it may be inferred that Midrash already served as a creative legal source of the *halakhah.* Thus the description is given of how the judges would deliberate the relevant scriptural passage in each case before they gave judgment: "And if he had committed murder, they deliberated the passage dealing with murder; if he had committed incest, they deliberated the passage dealing with incest" (Tosef. Sanh. 9:1); similarly as regards the legal order of succession. The Pentateuch prescribes the order as son, daughter, brother, brothers of the father, and then the nearest kin of the deceased (Num. 27:6–11); the father is not mentioned as an heir but this omission is rectified in the Mishnah, where his place in the order is determined as falling after the children of the deceased and before the latter's brothers (BB 8:1). The scholars arrived at this result by interpreting the above-mentioned pentateuchal passage in this manner: "Ye shall give his inheritance unto his kinsman that is next to him of his family, 'that is next to him' – the nearest relative takes preference." Even though the above is only enjoined after the brothers of the deceased and his father's brothers are mentioned as heirs, the scholars nevertheless ranked the father above the latter since "the Torah has authorized the scholars to interpret and say: 'whoever is nearest in kinship takes preference in inheritance' " (Sif. Num. 134). At times differences of opinion amongst the scholars regarding the manner of interpreting the verse naturally also led to different legal conclusions (e.g., Git. 9:10 and Mid. Tan. to Deut. 23:15, p. 148, concerning the grounds for divorce; also, as regards the taking of a pledge from a rich widow, see BM 9:13 and BM 115a; and see below).

Midrash and Roman Law Interpretatio. In Roman law also and by a similar process in other legal systems – at the beginning and after the Twelve Tables – *interpretatio* fulfilled an eminently creative function which, according to R. Sohm (*The Institutes* (1970[3]), 54f.), evolved and even changed the law without affecting the written letter of it. The purpose of *interpretatio* in Roman law has been described by Dernburg: "It is true that the content of a law should be expressed in the document wherein it is contained, but it is not necessary that this content must be derived directly from the words of the law; often the general wording of a law leads one to conclusions that are not expressed in so many words in this law, but which nevertheless are undoubtedly the correct conclusions to be drawn therefrom; *interpretatio* must therefore recognize as an authoritative conclusion from the law, not only that which derives from what is explicitly and directly stated in the law but also that deriving from what is indirectly stated therein; this may be referred to as the 'concealed content' of the law" (H. Dernburg, *Pandekten,* 1, pt. 1 (1900[6]), 73ff.).

Different Literary Forms for Creative and Integrative Interpretation. The existence of the two forms of Midrash, differing in function and objective, also led to a differentiation in their literary expression. When the object of the interpretation was not to create *halakhah* but simply to integrate existing *halakhah* into a scriptural verse, this could be achieved even by means of forced and symbolic modes of interpretation – such as analysis of seemingly superfluous words and letters – since this sufficed for the integrative purpose. Such artificial associations also represented an accepted literary device in other ancient civilizations (see S. Lieberman, in bibl., p. 62f., 77f.; in recent generations efforts have been made to explain these symbolic modes of interpretation in an orderly and systematic manner and much was done in this field by Meir Loeb Malbim). On the other hand, when the interpretation was made in order to evolve a particular *halakhah,* this was generally effected solely through rational modes of interpretation in the wider sense of the term, i.e., within the framework of the "concealed content" of the scriptural verse (although there are also instances in which *halakhot* were evolved through symbolic modes of interpretation, and this

1. page 14.

was particularly the case in the academy of R. Akiva; see, e.g., Sanh. 51b and see below).

Development of Bible Exegesis. Until Hillel The Elder. The process of exegesis began immediately after the law-giving, since in turning to the Written Law the halakhic scholars necessarily had to have recourse to various modes of interpretation for the purposes of its elucidation and application to the new problems that arose. However, the earliest clear literary references to exegetical activity only date back to the time of Ezra and Nehemiah. With reference to Ezra's efforts to direct the returned exiles back to the law of the Torah, its is stated: "For Ezra had set his heart to interpret *(lidrosh)* the law of the Lord, and to do it, and to teach in Israel statutes and ordinances" (Ezra 7:10). The people were taught the law: "And they read in the book, in the law of God, distinctly; and they gave the sense, and caused them to understand the reading" (Neh. 8:8), i.e., they interpreted the Torah by way of deep study, in order to understand its contents and laws. Ezra is called *ha-sofer* ("the scribe"; Ezra 7:11), a name which has also adhered to his contemporaries and to the succeeding scholars and which has been explained thus: "Therefore the *rishonim* were called *soferim* because they used to count all the letters of the Torah" (Ḥag. 15b; Kid. 30a). The Midrash of the scribes, or *soferim,* was not mere *interpretatio doctrinalis,* with no legal and binding validity attaching to the conclusions derived from it, but was in the nature of *interpretatio authentica,* and the conclusions derived from it constituted an integral and binding part of the *halakhah* itself. This was so even though it was derived outside the context of the law's being decided in a concrete case (see *Ma'aseh*[1]).

Evidence of the interpretative process can be found in the Septuagint Bible translation and in the Book of Ben Sira (e.g., 39:1–3); the process received a sharp impetus in the time of the *zugot* (pairs of scholars), when the Pharisees, in their struggle against the Sadducees, sought to prove the correctness of the Oral Law with the aid of interpretation. Thus, for instance, of the fourth scholarly pair it was said, "the two greatest men of our generation, Shemaiah and Avtalyon . . . are great sages and great interpreters" (*darshanim;* Pes. 70b), and of Hillel, a member of the fifth scholarly pair, it was said that he "expounded seven *middot* [rules of interpretation] before the elders of the sons of Bathyra" (introd. to Sifra, *Baraita* of R. Ishmael, concl.; see also Tosef. Sanh. 7:11; ARN[1] 37:10). These *middot,* or rules, were not innovations of Hillel; he simply crystallized them, although he may have provided some of the names which adhere to them (Sifra, loc. cit.)

R. Neḥunyah B. Ha-Kanah and R. Nahum of Gimzo. Toward the end of the first century a difference of approach to Bible exegesis was asserted by two of Johanan b. Zakkai's pupils. Neḥunyah b. ha-Kanah took the view that a rational standard (by way of the rule of *kelal u-ferat,* i.e., the general and the particular: see below) had to be maintained in the conclusions drawn from the modes of interpretation; while Nahum of Gimzo favored drawing wide conclusions from the modes of interpretation (by way of *ribbui u-mi'ut,* i.e., inclusion and exclusion), even when the conclusion was not altogether in keeping with the general meaning of the verse (Tosef. Shevu. 1:7; Shevu. 26a).

R. Ishmael and R. Akiva and Their Academies. These two different approaches to the interpretative method were fully developed by the pupils of each of these scholars. Both R. Ishmael – a pupil of R. Neḥunyah – and R. Akiva – a pupil of R. Nahum – followed his teacher's method and founded his own academy. These established two different schools of Bible exegesis and complete works containing the Midrashim of each are extant. From the academy of R. Ishmael there remains the *Mekhilta* to Exodus (*mekhilta* meaning *middot,* i.e., measures; see Isa. 40:12), *Sifrei* to Numbers, *Sifrei* to Deuteronomy (until 11:26), etc.; and from the academy of R. Akiva, the *Mekhilta* of R. Simeon b. Yoḥai to Exodus, *Sifra* to Leviticus *(Torat Kohanim), Sifrei Zuta* to Numbers, *Sifrei* to Deuteronomy from 11:26 on), etc. R. Ishmael and his academy endeavored to uphold modes of interpretation that would maintain the legal and logical meaning of the scriptural passages concerned. Thus, for instance, they laid down the rule that "the Torah speaks in the language of men" (Sif. Num. 112; Sanh. 64b, etc.; in the TJ, "a language of synonym, employed by the Torah"; Shab. 19:2, 17a). That is to say, just as the language of synonym occurs in the narrative part of Scripture for purposes of reinforcement and emphasis – because this is the phraseology adopted by men in their discussions (e.g., Gen. 31:30; 40:15) – so in the legal part of the Torah there ought to be no interpretation of such repetition (e.g., Lev. 19:20). R. Akiva and his academy took a different approach and adopted modes of interpretation that widened the meaning of Scripture far beyond the terms of the written text, expounding every seemingly superfluous word or phrase (see BK 41b), and the occurrence of every synonym or repetition of a word or even letter (see Yev. 68b). Often the dispute between the two schools is found to relate not to the actual legal principle involved, but to the question of how to integrate such a principle with the scriptural verse (from this period onward this type of Midrash continued to expand). R. Ishmael's method was to integrate the *halakhah* with the scriptural verse by means of interpretation that remained within the meaning of the text, while R. Akiva integrated the same halakhic ruling by interpretative devices based on the apparent redundancy of words, or even a single letter, such as *vav.* For an example of the two respective methods compare R. Ishmael and R. Akiva on the rule that a bill of divorcement need not be delivered into the hands of the wife personally, but is valid if placed within her *reshut* ("domain"; cf. Git. 8:1, 77a, with Sif. Deut. 269, TJ. Git. 8:1, 49b). Similarly, in a case where R. Ishmael found no suitable interpretative device to aid him in his integration of an existing *halakhah* with the appropriate verse, he would forego such midrashic integration ("in three places the *halakhah* bypasses Scripture": TJ, Kid. 1:2, 59d; Sot. 16a; etc.), in the same circumstances R. Akiva nevertheless effected the integrative process by enlisting the method of "redundancy" (Sif. Deut. 122 and 269; Sifra, Aḥarei Mot, 11:10, 84d).

There are even instances in which R. Akiva and his academy also created *halakhah* through the interpretative method based on the analysis of redundancy, a fact that met with strong opposition from R. Ishmael and his academy (see, e.g., Sanh. 51b, concerning the case of adultery committed by a priest's daughter). On more than one occasion such symbolic mode of interpretation from Akiva's academy provoked sharp scholarly reaction (see Sifra, *Va-Yikra,* 4:5; *Ẓav,* 11:6, 34df.; *Tazri'a* 13:2; Sif. Num. 75; cf. Men. 29b). Although opposed to modes of interpretation that departed from the logical sense of the scriptural text, R. Ishmael expanded the *middot* of Hillel and fixed their number, thereby establishing the 13 well-known hermeneutical rules (see below). In principle the 13 rules of R. Ishmael are contained within Hillel's seven, except that the former are further subdivided and amplified (thus, e.g., R. Ishmael subdivided Hillel's rule of *kelal u-ferat* (see above) into four *middot*).

R. Eliezer B. Yose Ha-Gelili. To R. Eliezer, one of the generation succeeding R. Ishmael and R. Akiva, is attributed the *baraita* of the 32 rules of Bible exegesis. However, this subdivision was made primarily for the purpose of aggadic and not halakhic Midrash (the *baraita* is printed in TB, after Ber.). The accepted number of hermeneutical rules remained at 13, but

1. page 110.

other exegetical principles were stated, also in the field of the *halakhah*, which are not embraced in the 13 *middot*.

In the Amoraic Period. For the *amoraim*, Bible exegesis generally served as interpretation intended to integrate already known *halakhot* with the relevant scriptural texts. They too regarded themselves as competent to engage in Bible exegesis in order to decide the *halakhah* in accordance with their own interpretation, but in practice during this period Bible exegesis had ceased to serve as a source for the continued creativity of the law. The change came about because Scripture no longer constituted the sole authoritative source within the halakhic system for the deduction of legal conclusions, since meanwhile collections of Mishnayot and halakhic Midrashim *(Midreshei Halakhah)* had been compiled. In particular the Mishnah – since its redaction by R. Judah and its acceptance at the end of the tannaitic period and the beginning of the amoraic period – had become the legal codex to be studied and interpreted and serve as the basis and starting point for the creation and continued evolution of the *halakhah*. Of course the Written Law remained the primary source of the *halakhah*, occupying the highest rung on its scale of values and authority, yet the Mishnah and other tannaitic works now became the immediate source for purposes of study and adjudication in daily life. For the same reason there was a decline in interpretation aimed at integrating existing *halakhah* with scriptural texts; once the Mishnah had become an authoritative book of *halakhah* there was no longer a need for such integration in order to lend validity to a particular halakhic ruling, since the very inclusion of the latter in the Mishnah, and its integration into this authoritative compilation, sufficed to invest it with full legal-halakhic recognition and authority. Thus it is found that at times one *amora* was surprised by the efforts of another to integrate a known *halakhah* with a scriptural verse, when such *halakhah* could equally have been founded on logical deduction (see *Sevarah*[1]); "Do we need Scripture to tell us this? It stands to reason" (BK 46b; Ket. 22a), a question never asked in tannaitic times even when the aim was merely to integrate a particular *halakhah* with a scriptural verse.

In the Post-Talmudic Period. The redaction of the Talmud was followed by a general decline in Bible exegesis, even in the form of the integrative interpretation of existing *halakhah*. The link with the Written Law became a spiritual one, whereas in practical life adjudication was based on the talmudic *halakhah* as crystallized in the halakhic Midrashim, the Mishnah, the Tosefta, and both Talmuds. At the same time, it may be noted that sometimes the statements of the *geonim* and *rishonim* contain various interpretations of scriptural verses which are not recorded in the extant halakhic Midrashim. In some cases it transpires that such interpretations were taken from midrashic compilations available to the *rishonim* which are no longer extant (see e.g., Yad, Avadim, 2:12, concerning the matter of a slave who falls ill, where the origin of an interpretation mentioned there remained unknown until the publication of the Mekh. SbY to 21:2). However, sometimes it also happened that the post-talmudic scholars had recourse to Bible exegesis in seeking support for a new law derived from *sevarah* or enactment *(takkanah)*; "Whenever it is known that a certain matter has been truly stated, but without ascertainment of the scriptural support, then everyone is free to interpret and advance such support" (Aaron ha-Levi of Barcelona, quoted in *Nimmukei Yosef*, BK, commencement of *Ha-Ḥovel*). The practical application of this procedure is illustrated in a number of instances (see, e.g., Yad, Arakhin 6:31–33 and Ravad, ad loc.; Resp. Maharshal no. 89; Resp. Radbaz no. 1049).

Thirteen Middot of R. Ishmael. The 13 hermeneutical rules of R. Ishmael (for a detailed enumeration see Sifra introd. and Ravad ad loc.; Elon, *Ha-Mishpat Ha-Ivri*, II, p. 270 ff.) belong mainly to two general categories of interpretations: one of elucidative interpretation *(midrash ha-meva'er)* – i.e., that which is concerned with the explanation and elucidation of scriptural passages; and the other of analogical interpretation *(midrash ha-mekish)* – i.e., that which is concerned with the drawing of analogous conclusions from one matter to another with a view to widening the law and solving new problems. The first category is akin to *interpretatio grammatica* in Roman law, but is much wider and more comprehensive, while the second is akin to *analogia*.

Elucidative Interpretation. This category includes the last ten of R. Ishmael's 13 hermeneutical rules, which are further subdivisible into four groups.

Kelal U-Ferat ("the general and the particular"; *middot* 4–7). The central problem dealt with by the first three rules in this group may be stated as follows: when a law lays down a certain direction, which such a law renders operative both in particular and in general and the general includes the particular, must the direction be held to apply only to the particular expressly mentioned and the general be interpreted as including only such a particular and no more, or must it be held that the direction applies to everything embraced by the general and that the particular is quoted only in illustration of the general and not in exhaustion of it? This question is answered by the said three rules in different ways depending on the juxtaposition of the general and the particular (for illustration of each of these rules, see Sifra introd.; BK 62b). The fourth rule deals with the case in which the general and the particular serve neither to amplify nor to limit, but the one is merely in elucidation of the other, i.e., the two are mutually interdependent (see Sifra introd.; Bek. 19a).

Davar she-Hayah Ba-Kelal ve-Yaẓa Min ha-Kelal (*middot* 8–11: "the particular stated separately after forming part of the general"). The central problem to which the rules of this group provide help in finding an answer is: when there are two separate directions on a common matter (and not a simple direction with a generality and a particularity, as in the previous group) – the one a general direction *(lex generalis)* and the other a special direction *(lex specialis)* – what is the relationship between the two classes of directions and for what reason has the special direction been stated separately from the general one? The main and most commonly applied rule in this group is the eighth (see Mekh. Shabbata 1; Shab. 70a).

Davar ha-Lamed me-Inyano, Davar ha-Lamed mi-Sofo (*middah* 12; "inference from the context"). This rule prescribes that a doubtful direction is to be determined from the context in which it occurs, either from other parts of the same subject matter, or from the adjacent subject (see Mekh. ba-Ḥodesh 8, Sanh. 86a).

Shenei Ketuvim ha-Makhḥishim Zeh et Zeh (*middah* 13; "two passages which contradict each other"). This rule is applied in case of a contradiction between two passages dealing with the same subject: whether between two verses in different *parashot* (e.g., Sif. Deut. 279; BM 110b); between two passages in the same *parashah* (e.g., Mekh. Mishpatim 20); or even between two different parts of the same verse (Mekh. Mishpatim, 7, p. 274). Such contradiction, the rule prescribes, must be reconciled by reference to a third passage which will determine the issue, or, when this is impossible, by the decision of the halakhic scholars according to their understanding of the matter (Sifra, introd.; TJ, Ḥag. 1:1, 76a).

Interpretation of Words and Phrases. Also belonging to the category of elucidative interpretation are many Midrashim purporting to explain various terms and concepts appearing in scriptural verses, and as an outcome also the content and scope

1. page 119.

of the scriptural direction (e.g., Mekh., Mishpatim, 1, p. 249, explanation of the term *shevi'it;* Ber. 1:3, dispute between Bet Shammai and Bet Hillel concerning interpretation of the words *be-shokhbekha u-ve-kumekha* in the context of *keri'at Shema*). Similarly there are various exegetical rules dealing with matters such as the construction of conjunctive words and letters (e.g., Sanh. 66a, dispute between R. Joshia and R. Jonathan), the question of whether or not mention of the masculine gender includes the feminine (e.g., BK 15a; Tos. to Kid. 2b; Yad, Edut 9:2; and *Kesef Mishneh* thereto), and similar grammatical and syntactical constructions.

Analogical Interpretation *(midrash ha-mekish).* This category of interpretation is the subject matter of the first three of the 13 *middot* enumerated by R. Ishmael.

Kal va-Ḥomer (an a fortiori inference, *a minori ad majus* or *a majori ad minus*). The basis of this *middah* is found in Scripture itself (Gen. 44:8; Deut. 31:27) and the scholars enumerated ten pentateuchal *kallin va-ḥomarim* (Gen. R., 92:7). The rule of *kal va-ḥomer* (for correct reading of the term, see Bacher, *Erkhei Midrash* (1923), 118) is a process of reasoning by analogy whereby an inference is drawn in both directions from one matter to another, when the two have a common premise – i.e., it can be drawn either from the minor to the major in order to apply the stringent aspect of the minor premise also (BM 95a), or from the major to the minor in order to apply the lighter aspect of the major premise to the minor premise (Beẓah 20b). Material to this rule is the principle *dayo la-vo min ha-din lihyot ka-niddon* (Sifra, loc. cit.; BK 25a, etc.), i.e., it suffices when the inference drawn from the argument *(ha-ba min ha-din)* is equal in stringency to the premise from which it is derived (the *niddon*), but not more so, not even when it might be argued that logically the inference should be even more stringent than the premise from which it is derived.

Gezerah Shavah ("inference from the analogy of words"). Scholars have given much thought to the etymology as well as the scope and content of this hermeneutic rule (see Lieberman in bibl.; Albeck, Mishnah, Kod., pp. 403f.). Lieberman translates the term as "a comparison with the equal" (*ibid.*, p. 59; in Scripture and halakhic literature the meaning of the term *gezerah* is "decision" or "decree"; cf. the meaning of the parallel Greek term, Lieberman, *ibid.*). Originally, *gezerah shavah* meant the analogy and comparison of two equal or similar matters, but later this rule came to refer "not to analogy of content but to identity of words" (i.e., verbal congruities in the text, Lieberman, *ibid.*, p. 61), even in the absence of any connection in content between the two matters. Some scholars held that an analogy was not to be drawn from one matter to another by way of a *gezerah shavah* unless the term in question was *mufneh* ("vacant," empty of content) in either of the matters (Nid. 22b; Sif. Deut. 249). This mode of interpretation – involving the deduction of halakhic inferences from analogous words only without regard for similarity of content between two separate matters – was likely to lead to comparisons for which there were no logical foundations and to strange and unusual halakhic conclusions (e.g., TJ, Pes. 6:1). However, this was avoided by the determination in talmudic tradition of the rule that "no one may infer by *gezerah shavah* on his own authority," i.e., this exegetical rule was to be applied only in cases where a scholar received a tradition from his teacher that the particular word or phrase might be interpreted by that method (TJ, Pes. 6:1; Nid. 19b and Rashi thereto; see also Naḥmanides Commentary to *Sefer ha-Mitzvot,* 2nd *shoresh*).

Binyan Av (a principle "built up" from biblical passages). This *middah* is enumerated by R. Ishmael in two parts: *binyan av mi-katuv eḥad* (e.g., Sanh. 30a; Sot. 2a) and *binyan av mi-shenei ketuvim* (e.g., Mekh. Mishpatim 9). It appears from the halakhic literature that the application of this rule was also extended to derivation of a principle from three passages (e.g., Sif. Num. 160) and even from four passages (e.g., BK 1:1). By this rule, a principle is constructed from one passage, or a characteristic common to several passages; the *av* is the basic premise, and the *binyan* is the principle constructed.

Hekkesh ha-Katuv (analogy drawn in the Bible itself). To the category of exegetical principles by analogy must be added a further rule, which often appears in talmudic literature although it is not included in the 13 *middot* enumerated by R. Ishmael. This is known as *hekkesh ha-katuv,* or simply *hekkesh* (Zev. 49b; Sanh. 73a), and also as *(hishvah) ha-katuv* (Kid. 35a), etc. It is distinguished from the other three analogic *middot* by the fact that in their case it is the halakhic scholars who draw the analogy whereas *hekkesh ha-katuv* represents an analogy drawn in the Bible itself. From this point of view the rule has been of fundamental importance to the process of Bible exegesis, since it enabled halakhic scholars to find in the Bible itself the basis for reasoning by analogy for purposes of drawing legal conclusions. A classic example of this form of analogy is found in the scriptural passage dealing with the violation of a betrothed maiden (*na'arah me'orasah,* see Marriage) which enjoins that the maiden, even though she is betrothed, must suffer no punishment: "But unto the damsel thou shalt do nothing; there is in the damsel no sin worthy of death – for as when a man riseth against his neighbor, and slayeth him, even so is this matter" (Deut. 22:26). Here, through analogy with the murderer's victim, Scripture holds the violated girl blameless, and the halakhic scholars pursued the analogic argument from the two cases, deriving additional *halakhot* from them (Sanh.74a). Sometimes *hekkesh ha-katuv* occurs in implicit rather than in explicit form (Sif. Deut. 208). For further particulars concerning the 13 *middot* see Elon, *Ha-Mishpat Ha-Ivri.*

Logical Interpretation. This third category of Midrash (i.e., in addition to the elucidative and analogic) plays an important role in the modes of interpretation in Jewish Law, although it is not enumerated among the 13 *middot.* Known as *midrash ha-higgayon,* it is similar to the Roman law *interpretatio logica.* In substance and objective, it is akin to the elucidative category, since its main purpose is to explain and contribute toward logical understanding of Scripture, and its application often led to the determination of new *halakhot* and legal principles. Thus, for instance, in the matter of the violation of a betrothed girl, the statement that nothing should be done to her, "For he found her in the field; the betrothed damsel cried, and there was none to save her" (Deut. 22:25–27), was interpreted in this way: the word field is not to be understood literally, but the measure of the damsel's innocence or guilt must be determined by her resistance or lack of it. "Shall it be said, in the city she is liable, in the field she is exempt? We are taught: 'she cried . . . and there was none to save her'; if there was none to save her whether in the city or in the field, she is exempt, and if there was someone to save her whether in the city or in the field, she is liable" (Sif. Deut. 243). Similarly, the enjoinder, "No man shall take the mill or the upper millstone to pledge; for he taketh a man's life to pledge" (Deut. 24:6) was interpreted as follows: "They spoke not only of the mill and the upper millstone, but of aught wherewith is prepared necessary food, as it is written 'For he taketh a man's life to pledge'" (BM 9:13, Sif. Deut. 272).

In this form of interpretation reliance is sometimes placed on logical reasoning which is circumscribed by factors of practical reality. Thus, from the enjoinder concerning the paschal sacrifice – "and the whole assembly of the congregation of Israel shall kill it" (Ex. 12:6) – R. Joshua b. Karḥa deduced the following legal principle: "Does then the whole assembly really slaughter? Surely only one person slaughters? Hence it follows that a man's agent is as himself" (Mekh. Pisḥa 5; Kid. 41b). In other words, as the verse cannot be literally interpreted since such would be physically impossible, it may be inferred that the act of one person can be attributed to another and regarded as his act and the same is true even of an entire assembly; this constitutes the principle of principal and agent. The mode of interpretation thus exemplified is akin to the *rerum natura* in Roman law.

Restrictive Interpretation. Just as Midrash served to extend the scope of the *halakhah* by the addition of new laws, so it sometimes served to narrow, to a varying extent, the operation of a particular law through a process of restrictive interpretation. Thus, for instance, the prohibition, "An Ammonite or a Moabite shall not enter into the assembly of the Lord; even to the tenth generation shall none of them enter into the assembly of the Lord forever" (Deut. 23:4), was restrictively interpreted by the scholars as applying to men only, thus rendering women acceptable immediately after they converted. Some scholars explained this law on the basis that the prohibition was enjoined "because they met you not with bread and with water on the way, when you came forth out of Egypt" (Deut. 23:5), a reason which was inapplicable to women because, for reasons of modesty, they are not in the habit of going out to meet other men; other scholars reasoned that the prohibition reads "an Ammonite but not an Ammonitess, a Moabite but not a Moabitess" (Yev. 8:3; Sif. Deut. 249; Yev. 77a). The scholars dated this interpretation to the time of the prophet Samuel, who anointed David king over Israel (I Sam. 16:13), and held it to be the explanation for David's entry "into the assembly of the Lord," even though he was descended from Ruth the Moabitess (Yev. 77a).

At times the text was so restrictively interpreted as to make any practical application of the law impossible from the start. This is illustrated in the matter of the stubborn and rebellious son, of whom it was said that he must be brought before the city elders and stoned to death (Deut. 21:18–21). The relevant verses were interpreted as meaning that the law only applied if the son committed the transgression within three months of his reaching the age of 13 years – and even then he was to be held exempt, unless the proceedings against him were completed within the same period (Sanh. 8:1; Sanh. 68b–69a). In addition, the passage was interpreted as requiring the existence of various preconditions relating to the qualities of the parents *(ibid.)*. The practical impossibility of having all these conditions fulfilled is recognized in tannaitic tradition: "There never has been a stubborn and rebellious son, and never will be. Why then was the law written? That you may study it and receive reward" (Tosef. Sanh. 11:6; Sanh. 71a). A similar interpretation was given by the scholars to the passage concerning the destruction of a city condemned for idolatry (Deut. 13:13–17; Sif. Deut. 92; Sanh. 16b; 71a; 111b; 113a; Tosef. Sanh. 14:1).

INTERPRETATION OF THE HALAKHAH

Use of the Principles of Bible Exegesis for Interpretation of the Halakhah. Just as the *middot* and other rules for Bible exegesis served the scholars as a source for the shaping of the *halakhah* and its continued creativity and development, so the scholars engaged in the same interpretative activity – and with the same objective – with regard to the available halakhic material. This activity may be referred to as *Midrash Halakhah* as opposed to Midrash Torah which has been dealt with so far. Interpretation of the *halakhah* continued to be engaged in throughout the history of Jewish law, and at times, for purposes of a particular exegetical rule, the scholars distinguished between modes of interpreting the Bible and those of interpeting the *halakhah*. The term Midrash was even used by the scholars to describe the latter. Thus, for instance, in early *halakhah* – until the middle of the second century – the duty of a father to maintain his children was in the nature of a religio-moral obligation only and not a legal one (Ket. 49a–b); the question arose whether the absence of a legal obligation applied to sons only, and whether such a duty did not in fact exist in respect of daughters, in the same way as they were entitled to be maintained out of the estate of their deceased father. The answer was arrived at in this way: "The father is not liable for the maintenance of his daughter. R. Eleazar b. Azariah gave this exposition *(zeh midrash darash)* at Kerem de-Yavneh. 'The sons shall be heirs and the daughters shall be maintained.' As the sons only inherit after the death of their father, so the daughters are not entitled to maintenance except after the death of their father" (Ket. 4:6). The dictum that "the sons shall be heirs and the daughters shall be maintained" derived from an ancient rabbinical enactment relating to the laws of succession (BB 9:1, 131b) and R. Eleazar, reasoning that the two component *halakhot* of the dictum were analogous, concluded that both were applicable at a common stage namely after the death of the father.

Restrictive and Expansive Interpretation. Many *halakhot* were derived from both restrictive and expansive interpretation. Thus for instance the Mishnah records a dispute between Bet Hillel and Bet Shammai on whether the then existing *halakhah* concerning the trustworthiness of a woman's declaration of her husband's death (so as to enable her to remarry) had to be narrowly or widely interpreted (Yev. 15:1–2). Similarly, as regards the legal capacity of a minor to acquire lost property he found himself, the *amora* Samuel gives the term *katan* ("minor"), which appears in the Mishnah (BM 1:5), a restrictive interpretation referring to biological minority, holding that no minor is capable of acquiring for himself lost property; R. Johanan, on the other hand, gives the same term the liberal interpretation of referring only to those who are maintained by their fathers, and therefore "a minor who is not maintained by his father is regarded as a major" (BM 12a–b). A further illustration is to be found in the different interpretations given by the *amoraim* of Ereẓ Israel and of Babylonia to the Mishnah, BK 3:1 (see BK 27b).

Interpretation of the Halakhah in Post-Talmudic Times. In post-talmudic times the scholars of every generation continued to apply all the different modes of interpretation to the existing *halakhah*. For this purpose they even resorted to some of the 13 *middot* (see, e.g., Resp. Abraham, son of Maimonides, nos. 78 and 97; Resp. Ramban (in Assaf, *Sifran shel Rishonim*), no. 3; Resp. Rashba vol. 2, no. 14; Resp. Maharam of Rothenburg, ed. Prague, no. 85; Resp. Rosh, 78:1, 3). In one instance a 15th-century scholar expounded the responsum of an earlier scholar by the rule of *kelal u-ferat* in order to solve a basic legal problem in the field of the public law, one concerning the power of the communal representatives (Resp. Judah Mintz no. 7).

INTERPRETATION OF DOCUMENTS

In early times there had already evolved a further category of Midrash – that concerning the interpretation of the text of various legal documents in daily use, such as the *ketubbah* deed and deeds of acquisition *(kinyan)*, indebtedness, testamentary disposition, and the like. The documents, the text of which was sometimes determined by the scholars and sometimes by popular usage, became integrated into the overall Jewish legal system, extending and developing it. In their study of such documents, whether theoretically or for the practical purpose of deciding the law, the scholars were faced with the need to elucidate and understand their contents, and to this end, they had recourse to interpretative norms used in the exegesis of the Bible and the *halakhah,* and, in the course of time, developed additional – and sometimes different – interpretative norms.

Doreshin Leshon Hedyot ("interpreting human speech"). Interpretation of documents was originally referred to as *doreshin leshon hedyot* (Tosef. Ket. 4:9ff.; TJ, Ket. 4:8, 28d; TJ, Yev. 15:3, 14d; BM 104a), since the scholars "used to analyze and interpret the language used by men in writing their deeds, as they would do with Scripture . . . and not according to the literal meaning" (quoted in the name of Hai in Nov. Ramban to BM 104a and in commentary of Zechariah b. Judah Agamati to BM loc. cit., p. 143 – a photographic reprint of the Ms. published by Jacob Leveen, London, 1961). The term *leshon hedyot* came to be used in contradistinction to *leshon Torah* (in a similar manner to *mammon hedyot* ("property of human beings") and *mammon gavohah* ("sacred property"), in Kid. 1:6; see Agamati, loc. cit.), since even documents formulated by the scholars, such as the *ketubbah* deed, fall within the rule's applicability. In the Talmud, various examples are quoted of documents interpreted in accordance with *leshon hedyot,* for instance deeds of *ketubbah,* lease of a field, pledge, etc. (Tosef., TJ, and TB, loc. cit.), and in this manner problems of principle were sometimes solved. Thus it is recorded that in Alexandria, Egypt, there occurred cases of women who entered into *kiddushin* with a particular man but prior to completion of the marriage (the *nissu'in*) married another man; in these circumstances the children born of the latter marriage had to be regarded as *mamzerim,* since their mother was already an *eshet ish,* a woman already married (see Marriage; *Mamzer*). However, Hillel the Elder studied the *ketubbah* deeds of the women in Alexandria and interpreted *"leshon hedyot,"* finding it written in the *ketubbah* that the *kiddushin* was to be regarded as valid only if followed by a marriage *(ḥuppah)* between the parties – and since the condition remained unfulfilled in the case of the first *kiddushin* it followed that the latter was no *kiddushin* at all and therefore the children born of the husband to whom she was actually married were not to be regarded as having any blemish of status (Tosef., TJ, and TB, loc. cit.). The concept of *doreshin leshon hedyot* was also held to be a principle applicable to the laws of custom (see *Minhag*).

Ha-Kol Holekh Aḥar ha-Taḥton ("all according to the latter reference"). There has also been extensive discussion in Jewish law of various problems relating to the interpretation of legal documents, aimed at the elucidation of the text and of various terms which appear in them as well as the reconciliation of conflicting passages in the same document. The following are some of the rules of principle derived for this purpose. If there are two conflicting references to the same subject, for instance first a figure of 100 is mentioned and thereafter a figure of 200, then the rule is, "all according to the latter reference," since it is to be assumed that what is first stated has been retracted (BB 10:2; Yad, Malveh 27:14; Sh. Ar., ḤM 42:5; see also Nov. Ri Migash BB 166b). It was laid down that if there is a possibility of reconciling a divergence between two different parts of a deed, "we must endeavor, in whatever way possible, to uphold both as being in agreement with each other . . . even if the possibility is somewhat strained" (Resp. Ribash no. 249; Sh. Ar., ḤM 42:5 and *Sma* thereto, n.10). Sometimes the first reference is to be followed as the decisive one. Thus, for instance, if at the beginning of a deed there is a detailed enumeration of the items composing the total amount and at the end the total amount is set out and it is at variance with the enumerated details, it has to be assumed that an error was made in the calculation of the total amount and the detailed enumeration must be regarded as decisive – i.e., the first reference is the one which is followed (R. Isaiah, quoted in Tur, HM 42:8 and in Sh.Ar., HM 42:5).

Yad Ba'al ha-Shetar al ha-Taḥtonah ("the holder of a deed is at a disadvantage"). Another rule is that in case of doubt about the correct interpretation of a document "the holder of a deed is at a disadvantage," i.e., the interpretation that is less onerous for the person in possession must be followed, since the burden of proof rests on the claimant – who is the holder of the deed (Ket. 83b; BB 166a; Yad, Malveh 27:16; Sh. Ar., ḤM 42:8). This rule also applies when the doubt arises from conflicting references in different parts of the deed if in the particular circumstances the rule of "all in accordance with the latter reference" has no reasonable application in the matter. Thus, for example, if the words "100 which are 200" are written in a deed, there will be no possibility of saying that the second reference (200) is a retraction of the first (100), and therefore the holder of the deed will be at a disadvantage and entitled to recover 100 only (BB 10:2; Yad, Malveh 27:14). However, the rule is applied only if it does not have the effect of prejudicing the validity of the deed even when it is interpreted in accordance with the statement of particulars which is less onerous for the person in possession. If the choice is between upholding the deed or invalidating it entirely, the holder of the deed must not be deemed to be at a disadvantage, but, on the contrary, at an advantage, "for we must at all times seek all possible ways of upholding the validity of a deed, even if in a circuitous manner" (Resp. Ribash no. 345). For this reason it was held by Asher b. Jehiel that in a deed in which A undertook to give B 15 *zehuvim* "after Passover" – and not "after next Passover" – the undertaking must be interpreted as intended to mean "after next Passover," otherwise it would have to be said that the reference was to the last Passover before the end of the world, an interpretation that would deprive the deed of all meaning and validity (Resp. Rosh, no. 68:14; Sh. Ar., ḤM 42:9). Clearly, in the case of a legal error in the formulation of a deed – for instance mention of an inappropriate *kinyan* (see Acquisition) – the deed will be invalid (Resp. Maharik no. 94; Rema ḤM 42:9).

Interpretation le-Fi Leshon Benei-Adam ("According to the common usage of the people"). The terms which appear in a deed are to be given their ordinary meaning as used by people in their everyday speech and not interpreted according to their meaning in the language of the Torah or of the scholars. Thus it was laid down that a person who bequeathed his property to his sons thereby excluded his grandsons from the estate, since it was not customary for people to refer to a grandson as a "son" *(ben)* even though the word had this meaning in biblical language (BB 143b and Rashbam ad loc.; Yad, Zekhiyyah 11:1; Sh. Ar., ḤM 247:3). The scholars drew a parallel between the interpretation of terms in documents and those used by a person in making a vow (BB 143b; Ned. 63a) – since in each case the meaning which the person attaches to the document he has prepared or the vow he has made is of decisive importance. In the case of a vow the rule is: "the speech of men is followed" (*aḥar leshon benei adam;* Ned. 51b, et al.). This rule was interpreted to mean the speech of men "in the place, in the language, and at the time the vow was made" (Yad, Nedarim 9:1, 13; Sh. Ar., YD 217:1), i.e., according to the meaning normally given to the term by the person taking the vow, so as to take into account any possible change in the meaning of a particular term – even in the same locality – from time to time (see Yad, Nedarim 9; Sh. Ar., YD 217). In the responsa literature this rule is discussed extensively, along with its influence in bringing about differences between certain rules relating to the exegesis of the Bible and the *halakhah* and those relating to the interpretation of documents (see, e.g., Resp. Maharik no. 10; Resp. Rashba, vol. 3, no. 26; vol. 5, no. 260; Resp. Maharashdam EH no. 48; see also Wills[1]).

1. page 459.

INTERPRETATION OF TAKKANOT HA-KAHAL
("Communal Enactments")

The interpretation of communal enactments, i.e., *takkanot* enacted by the community or its representatives in the fields of civil and criminal law (see *Takkanot ha-Kahal*) constitutes a category which is related to the interpretation of documents. Communal enactments appeared in Jewish law mainly from the tenth century onward, with the increasing importance of the Jewish community in the various centers of the Diaspora, and are parallel to legislative activities by the public and its representatives in other legal systems. As in the case of statutes, regulations, etc. in any other legal system, in the course of their practical application in daily life the Jewish communal enactments also led to the development of an imposing system of norms for their interpretation.

Entrustment of Interpretative Authority. In the main, authority to interpret communal enactments was entrusted to the halakhic scholars before whom an issue between parties would be aired. The issue was sometimes between individuals, sometimes between an individual and the community, and sometimes between different communities. In a considerable proportion of the responsa literature dealing with matters of public, civil, and criminal law, there are detailed discussions by the scholars on the interpretation of the communal enactments at issue. At times – in the *takkanah* itself – authority to interpret a *takkanah* was vested in the halakhic scholars (see, e.g., *Takkanot Medinat Mehrin,* no. 292), and at others in the communal leaders (see Resp. Rashba, vol. 3, no. 409; vol. 5, nos. 221, 289). However, interpretative authority would be vested in the communal leaders only if doubt existed about the meaning of any particular term, but the leaders would have no authority to depart from the reasonable meaning of the term; the authority to determine the existence, or otherwise, of any doubt concerning the meaning of the term would once again be entrusted to the halakhic scholars (see Resp. Ritba, no. 134).

Interpretation of Takkanot le-Fi Leshon Benei Adam (in accordance with their common usage). In dealing with the interpretation of communal enactments, the halakhic scholars laid down many rules for the interpretation of statutes. For the interpretation of both communal enactments and documents, there was a common rule, requiring that they be interpreted according to the speech of men," i.e., in accordance with the common usage of the terms employed (Ritba, loc. cit.). Thus it was decided that a reference in a *takkanah* to the term *shetar* ("deed") could not be interpreted as embracing a wife's *get* ("bill of divorce"), even though this was sometimes the case in the language of the scholars (e.g., Git. 10b; Kid. 5a–b), since "in common usage the term *get* is particularly and solely applied to bills of divorcement for women, and other *shetarot* are never called by the name of *get,* nor is a woman's *get* ever called a *shetar*" (Resp. Ribash, no. 304). Clearly, there was not always necessarily a variation between common usage and that of the scholars and sometimes there may exist a continuing identity of meaning in the language of Scripture, that of the scholars, and the common usage of the people (Resp. Rashba, vol. 4, no. 312). Since the communal enactments were of far more substantive and general significance and validity than were the documents of individuals, it follows that more fundamental and comprehensive norms came to be determined for the interpretation of the former. Some of these are outlined below.

Interpretation in Accordance with the Language of the Takkanah. It was laid down that a *takkanah* must be interpreted according to the view and understanding of those qualified to do so, in accordance with the ordinary meaning of the text (Resp. Rashba, vol. 4, no. 308; vol. 5, no. 247), and not according to the intention of those who enacted it (*ibid.*, vol. 3, no. 409), nor to the supposed motivating reasons of the latter (*ibid.*, vol. 4, no. 268). This rule is much discussed in the interpretation of *takkanot* in various legal fields, particularly family law (Resp. Rosh, no. 50:10), the law of hire (*Tashbez*. 2:61) and tax law (Rashba, vol. 5, no. 282, see also Taxation[1]). However, the text of the *takkanot* may be contradicted if it may reasonably be assumed that a scribal error was made when it was drafted (Resp. Rosh, no. 6:8).

Circumstances in Which the Background to a Takkanah and Its Motivating Factors May Be Taken into Account. In circumstances where the intention of a *takkanah* may be presumed as a matter of "common cause" *(kavvanot muskamot la-kol),* the *takkanah* may be interpreted accordingly (Resp. Rashba, vol. 3, no. 409). Thus where it was enacted that the taxpayers had to submit their declarations at "the synagogue" – which served as the central gathering place for the community – it was held that not the synagogue itself was intended, but areas such as the courtyard or the upper floor, even though these had distinctive names, since the matter at issue was not one of prayer (Resp. Rashba, vol. 5, no. 222). It was also laid down that rigid formalism was to be avoided in the interpretation of a *takkanah* (*ibid.*, vol. 3, nos. 407, 408).

For purposes of understanding the objective of a *takkanah,* its preamble was also sometimes relied on even though it was not an integral part of the enactment (Rashba, vol. 5, no. 287; Resp. Ribash, no. 331). Similarly, it was held that in cases where the text allows for two possible interpretations, the one beneficial to the public and the other prejudicial to it, the former must be adopted since the general objective of every *takkanah* is to increase the public good and not the contrary (Resp. Rashba, vol. 5, no. 287). Hence it was decided that a certain *takkanah* purporting to prohibit public worship in all but certain places could not be assumed to have intended the prohibition of public worship in a synagogue to be erected in the future. It must be interpreted only as prohibiting such worship in the homes of individuals – even though such an interpretation was a strain on the text – for otherwise the *takkanah* would "prevent many from fulfilling a *mitzvah*" and amount to something "distorted and improper" (Resp. Ribash, no. 331). In such a case it was held permissible to consult the community about its intention in enacting the *takkanah,* but the explanatory remarks should only be accepted if it was stated that at the time of enactment of the *takkanah* it was thought that the relevant intention was actually expressed in the text. If at that time it was known that the meaning of the text varied from the avowed intention of those who enacted it, the explanation would not avail and the *takkanah* must be interpreted within the ordinary meaning of the text *(ibid.)*.

Conflicting Provisions and Ambiguity in the Text. Conflicting provisions in the text of a *takkanah* must be interpreted, in the case of a suit between two parties, in favor of the defendant (Resp. Rashba, vol. 3, no. 397; vol. 5, no. 281). In other cases, for instance a *takkanah* dealing with the authority of the trustees of the community chest to make expenditures, it was held that the rule of "all according to the latter reference" (see above) must be followed, but the attempt should be made to reconcile, as far as possible, conflicting references to the same matter, as in the interpretation of documents (see above; Resp. Rashba, vol. 3, no. 386). At times such conflicts were held to be completely irreconcilable and it was decided that perhaps they had to be ascribed to error (Resp. Rashba, loc. cit.). In case of doubt about the meaning of the text, an interpretation must be preferred which excludes any matter of halakhic controversy from the area of the application of the *takkanah,* and in interpreting the mean-

1. page 694.

ing of a *takkanah* it is permissible to be guided by the manner of its practical application in daily life for a certain period after its enactment (Resp. Ribash, no. 304). In their interpretation of communal enactments, the halakhic scholars were much guided by a comprehensive study of the entire collection of *takkanot* in which the enactment in question appeared, in order to draw analogies from one provision to another, either to distinguish between them or to apply to the one the terms of the other. Not only the analogic modes of interpretation were applied to communal enactments but also those of elucidative interpretation (see above; for an illustration of the interpretation of a *takkanah* by the rule of *kelal u-ferat,* see Resp. Rashba, vol. 3, no. 396) dealing also in detail with interpretation of words and phrases. In the course of these discussions by halakhic scholars, the Jewish legal system was enriched by the addition of many and varied canons of interpretation (see further Resp. Rashba, vol. 5, nos. 126, 277, 279, 284, 285, 288, 290; vol. 6, no. 7; Resp. Rosh, no. 55:9; Resp. Ritba, no. 50; Resp. Ribash, no. 249). These offer profitable jurisprudential sources concerning interpretation of laws and statutes.

Bibliography: Samson b. Isaac of Chinon, *Sefer Keritut;* Z.H. Chajes, *The Student's Guide through the Talmud* (1960[2]); D.Z. Hoffmann, *Zur Einleitung in die halachischen Midrashim* (1887); Hebrew translation, and additional notes by H.S. Horowitz in: *Mesillot le-Torat ha-Tanna'im* (1928), ed. by A.Z. Rabinowitz, 1–91; A. Schwarz, *Die hermeneutische Analogie in der talmudischen Litteratur* (1897); idem, *Der hermeneutische Syllogismus in der talmudischen Litteratur* (1901); idem, *Die hermeneutische Induktion in der talmudischen Litteratur* (1909); idem, *Die hermeneutische Antinomie in der talmudischen Literatur* (1913); idem, *Die hermeneutische Quantitaetsrelation in der talmudischen Literatur* (1916); idem, *Der hermeneutische Kontext in der talmudischen Literatur* (1921); idem, in: MGWJ, 72 (1928), 61–66; Bacher, *Erkhei Midrash* (1923); Weiss, Dor, 1 (1904[4]), 76–78, 132–6, 144–6, 155–61; 2 (1904[4]), 39–49; Frankel, Mishnah, 17–21, 106–9, 112–4; J.M. Guttmann, in: *Ha-Ẓofeh le-Ḥokhmat Yisrael,* 5 (1921), 17–34, 113–29; idem, Mafte'aḥ 3, pt. I (1924), appendix; also published separately; idem, *Beḥinat Kiyyum ha-Mitzvot* (1931), 19–29; M. Ostrowski, *Ha-Middot she-ha-Torah nidreshet bahem* (1924); H.G. Enelow (ed.), *The Mishnah of Rabbi Eliezer . . .* (1933); Ch. Tchernowitz, *Toledot ha-Halakhah,* 1, pt. 1 (1934), 37–66; 4 (1950), 68–97; J. Neubauer, in: *Sinai,* 22 (1947/48), 49–80; D. Daube, in: HUCA, 22 (1949), 239–64; S. Lieberman, *Hellenism in Jewish Palestine* (1950), 47–82; A. Karlin, in: *Sinai,* 29 (1951), 133–45; 31 (1952), 163–76; ET, 4 (1952), 1–12; 5 (1953), 546–64; 6 (1954), 553–60; 728–48; 7 (1956), 77–82; 10 (1961), 557–75; J.N. Epstein, *Mevo'ot le-Sifrut ha-Tanna'im* (1957), 501–44; E. E. Urbach, in: *Tarbiz,* 27 (1957/58), 166–82; Ḥ. Albeck, *Mavo la-Mishnah* (1959), 40–62, 88–98; L. Finkelstein, in: *Sefer ha-Yovel le-Yiẓḥak Baer* (1960), 28–47; B. de Vries, *Toledot ha-Halakhah ha-Talmudit* (1962), 9–36; idem, *Meḥkarim be-Sifrut ha-Talmud* (1968), 161–4; B. Cohen, in: HTR, 47 (1954), 197–203; reprinted in his: *Jewish and Roman Law* (1966), 58–64; addenda, *ibid.,* 767f.; M. Elon, *Ha-Mishpat Ha-Ivri,* II (1973), 239–390; idem, Mafte'aḥ, 23–41; idem, in: ILR, 2 (1967), 542–4.

Menachem Elon

TAKKANOT (Legislation) (Heb. תקנות pl.; sing. תקנה). This article is arranged according to the following outline.

Definition and Substance
Legislation in the Halakhah
Nature of Halakhic Legislation
Rules of Legislation
Role of the Public
Annulment of Takkanot
Takkanot until the End of the Tannaitic Period
In the Amoraic Period
In the Geonic Period
In Post-Geonic Times
Legislation in Different Centers
Post-Geonic Legislation in Family Law
Takkanot of the Chief Rabbinate of Ereẓ Israel

Definition and Substance. A *takkanah* is a directive enacted by the halakhic scholars, or other competent body (see *Takkanot ha-Kahal*), enjoying the force of law. It constitutes one of the legal sources of Jewish law (see Introduction[1]). A law which has its creative source in *takkanah* serves as the motivated addition of a new norm to the overall halakhic system, whereas a law originating from the legal source of *midrash* (exegesis, i.e., from construing a biblical passage or other existing law; see Interpretation) serves to reveal the concealed content of existing law within the aforementioned system. The consequence of this substantive difference between these two legal sources of Jewish law is that a law created by means of Bible exegesis mostly belongs to the category of laws called *de-oraita,* whereas a law deriving from *takkanah* always belongs to the category called *de-rabbanan* (see Introduction[2]). The *takkanah* in Jewish law is akin to that part of legislation which in other legal systems is termed subordinate. The Written Torah is the constitution – the supreme legislation – of Jewish law, and in the Torah itself power is delegated to the halakhic scholars to enact *takkanot.* Similarly, in the primary legislation of other legal systems authority is delegated to certain bodies to be subordinate legislators (e.g., to cabinet ministers by way of regulations, to municipal councils by way of by-laws, etc. – see Salmond, 12th ed., 116–124). The authority of the halakhic scholars to enact *takkanot* is said to derive from the Pentateuchal enjoinder, "According to the law which they shall teach thee and according to the judgment which they shall tell thee, thou shalt do; thou shalt not turn aside from the sentence which they shall declare unto thee, to the right hand, nor to the left" (Deut. 17:11), or, according to another opinion, to the enjoinder, "Ask thy father and he will declare unto thee, thine elders, and they will tell thee" (*ibid.,* 32:7; Shab. 23a; Yad, Mamrim 1:1–2; *Hassagot Ramban le-Sefer ha-Mitzvot,* Principle 1). The authority of the scholars to impose *gezerot* (decrees, see below) is held to have been entrusted to them in the enjoinder, "Therefore shall ye keep My charge" (Lev. 18:30), interpreted to mean, "Make a safeguard to keep My charge" (Sifra, Aḥarei Mot 10:22; Yev. 21a).

The legislative activity of the halakhic scholars is sometimes termed *takkanah* and sometimes *gezerah.* The term *gezerah* is generally applied to the determination of directives aimed at deterring man from the prohibited, at making "a fence around the Torah" – i.e., directives of a negative nature prohibiting the performance of a particular act. The term *takkanah,* on the other hand, generally refers to directives aimed at imposing a duty to perform a particular act, i.e., directives of a positive nature enjoining the doing of a particular matter (Maim., Comm. to Mishnah, Intr.). This distinction is not, however, consistently observed in the use of the two terms (see, e.g., Git. 4:2; Shab. 15b). Sometimes a *takkanah* is termed a *tenai bet din* or simply *tenai* (Ket. 4:12; BK 80b), because the *bet din* (court) circumscribes – "conditions" as it were – a particular directive in the manner of a *takkanah* and because sometimes the creation of a *takkanah* is preceded by a condition imposed between the parties to a matter. Sometimes a *takkanah* is also termed *minhag*

1. page 14; 2. page 9.

(see RH 4:1, and cf. Tosef., RH 4:3; Beẓah 4b, etc.). The two terms share in common the factor of legislation save that in the case of *takkanah* the legislative activity is deliberate and open whereas in *minhag* it is anonymous and undirected (see *Minhag*).

Legislation in the Halakhah. Halakhic legislation generally functions with two principal objectives: (1) to fill a lacuna in the law created in consequence of changed social and economic realities and the emergence of problems which find no answer in the existing *halakhah;* in this event the *takkanah* generally serves to add to the existing *halakhah;* (2) to amend and vary the existing *halakhah* to the extent that this is dictated by the needs of the hour; in this event it cannot be said that the existing law fails to provide guidance but, on account of changed circumstances, the law as it stands creates difficulties of a social, economic, or moral nature, which the *takkanah* seeks to rectify and resolve. These two objectives are pursued by legislation, whether *takkanah* or *gezerah,* in all the different fields of the *halakhah* – certain areas whereof are wholly founded on such legislation while in other areas its influence is felt to a greater or lesser degree. The latter phenomenon is largely a reflection of the extent to which it proved possible to resort to interpretation *(midrash)* for a solution to the problems that arose. In seeking the solution to a problem that arose the scholars had recourse, first and above all, to the legal source of interpretation, since by so doing the solution would be forthcoming from scriptural passages or from existing *halakhah.* Only when interpretation was not a means to a solution did the scholars resort to *takkanah* – which represented an innovation in the world of the *halakhah.* Thus a substantial part of the laws of tort, of unlawful possession *(gezelot),* and bodily injury *(ḥavalot),* originate from *midrash,* since these matters are extensively dealt with in the Torah. On the other hand, the laws of property and obligations – which are scantily dealt with in the Torah – developed mainly through the legal source of legislation. At times exegesis and legislation functioned with more or less equal efficacy in the development of a particular field of the law, as for instance in the area of family law.

The scholars dealt extensively with the question how to reconcile the aforementioned objectives of legislation with the fundamental norm of the Torah that "ye shall not add unto the word which I command you, neither shall ye diminish from it" (Deut. 4:2 and 13:1). Did not a rule derived by means of a *takkanah* or *gezerah* in some manner add to or detract from the laws of the Torah? Two of the principal answers given by the scholars to this question may be mentioned. In Solomon b. Abraham Adret's opinion, the enjoinder against adding to or subtracting from the Torah law is directed against any addition to the precepts of the Torah on the part of an individual acting without due authority, but not against the halakhic scholars acting under the authority entrusted to them as regards the interpretation and continued creativity of the *halakhah;* that, as regards the latter, they are expressly enjoined (Deut. 17:8–11) to solve new problems, also by way of legislation, and once they have done so the individual must not depart from their enactments (Nov., Rashba, RH 16a). A different answer was given by Maimonides, and other scholars sharing his view, in holding that the aforementioned Pentateuchal prohibition is directed against the individual as well as the halakhic scholars and the courts, and that the solution to the problem posed lies in the strict care taken by the halakhic scholars as regards their manner of exercising the legislative function. According to these scholars, the enjoinder against addition to, or subtraction from, the law of the Torah applies to circumstances in which it is sought to hold that a particular law is one which also has its origin in the Torah and is equal in standing to a law of the Torah; however, when the scholars expressly state that according to the Torah the law is so, and that they, by virtue of the authority entrusted to them are enacting or decreeing such and such as a law of the rabbis, the matter is permissible (Yad, Mamrim 2:9; Intr. to *Mishneh Torah*) – "for 'ye shall not add' only applies to an addition to the Torah meant to be equal therewith, but making fences and restrictions is not an addition, for these are not to be equated with the Torah" Ramban, Deut. 4:2). Thus in making their enactments the scholars are prohibited from acting within the sphere of primary legislation since this is the domain of Pentateuchal enactment alone, which is everlasting and stands for all time. The legislative activity of the scholars is operative only in the area of subordinate legislation, in which area they are authorized and enjoined to make enactments and decrees of a transient nature – "as a temporary measure" (*le-fi sha'ah; hora'at sha'ah,* etc.) – but not to lay down immutable directives (although this distinction is theoretical only, having regard to the very many *takkanot* which have become transformed into an integral part of the laws comprising the halakhic system and have been accepted as decided law in the Talmud and codificatory literature).

Nature of Halakhic Legislation. The basic principle underlying the legislative activities of the halakhic scholars also serves as the basis for the other legal sources of the *halakhah,* namely, that the Torah and its continuing creativity was entrusted to the authority of the halakhic scholars (Ramban, Deut. 17:11; see also Interpretation; *Ma'aseh;* Authority, Rabbinical; *Sevarah*). This exclusive authority led the halakhic scholars to a complete identification with the spirit and purpose of the Torah. Such an identification at once obliged them to act with great care and responsibility in their exercise of the legislative function, while also rendering possible their enactment of daring and decisive *takkanot* when persuaded that these indeed reflected the spirit and purpose of the Torah. With the sense of responsibility of a physician, entrusted with the well-being and perfection of the *halakhah* (Yad, Mamrim 2:4), the halakhic scholars made penetrating and far-reaching statements which have become well-known maxims of the *halakhah.* An illustration is their interpretation of the verse, "It is time for the Lord to work; they have made void Thy law" (Ps. 119:126), as meaning: "it is better that one letter of the Torah should be uprooted than the entire Torah become forgotten to Israel" (Tem. 14b; see also Ber. 9:5, Yoma 69a, and Rashi, ad loc.); similarly, "there are times when the disregard of the Torah may be its foundation" (Men. 99a/b), and – "that he shall live by them and not die because of them" (Sanh. 74a; Yoma 85b), and so on.

No discussion concerning the measure of the scholars' legislative authority, or the determination of rules for their exercise of the legislative function, is to be found until the end of tannaitic times. The sole explanation accompanying many *takkanot* is the factual background and circumstances leading to their enactment. Thus the defilement of oil by the Greeks is the background to the *takkanah* relating to the festival of Ḥanukkah (Shab. 21b). Natural disasters and war are the background to the *takkanot* of the *agunot* ("deserted wives"; Yev. 16:7). Abstention from giving credit explains the institution of the prosbul (Shev. 10:3–4). "For the sake of good order" *(tikkun olam)* or "for the sake of peace" *(darkhei shalom)* is the general explanation for many other *takkanot* (e.g., Git. 4:2–7; 5:3 and 8–9). When the halakhic scholars were persuaded of the need of the hour they enacted and decreed accordingly, in order that the Torah, its ways and precepts, should not become strange to the Jewish people.

Rules of Legislation. Besides the above mentioned basic principle, the *amoraim* laid down a number of rules and guidelines which determined the scope and authoritative force of the legislative activities of the halakhic scholars.

(1) Abstention from Fulfilling a Mitzvah. The rule was established that the court may determine by *takkanah* that a (positive) precept prescribed by the law of the Torah shall not be fulfilled, i.e., that it may direct to abstain from performing an act – "sit and do not do" *(shev ve-al ta'aseh)*. A commonly quoted example is the *takkanah* to abstain from blowing the *shofar* on Rosh Ha-Shanah falling on a Saturday (RH 29b, and see Yev. 89a–90b for other examples). In R. Ḥisda's opinion the court is even entitled to enact a *takkanah* which entails the uprooting *(akirah)* of a Pentateuchal prohibition, i.e., that the scholars may direct to "arise and do" *(kum va-aseh)* an act the doing whereof is prohibited in the Torah. Rabbah expressed a contrary opinion and the *halakhah* was decided that "the court may not make a provision uprooting a matter in the Torah by way of a direction to "arise and do." In the talmudic discussion centering around the above difference of opinion a number of exceptions to the stated rule are laid down, each of which constitutes a self-standing rule of legislation (Yev. loc. cit.).

(2) Hefker Bet Din Hefker. This rule lays down that in matters of the civil law *(dinei mamonot)*, and in every other matter – even in the field of ritual prohibitions and permissions – which is based on the ownership of property, the scholars have authority to enact even such *takkanot* as involve the uprooting of a law of the Torah by directing to "arise and do." The scholars deduced from the passage, "and that whosoever came not within three days, according to the counsel of the princes and elders, all his substance should be forfeited, and himself separated from the congregation of the captivity" (Ezra 10:8), that the court has authority to divest the individual of his rights of ownership in property (TJ, Shek, 1:2, 46a; TJ Pe'ah 5:1, 18d). This authority was interpreted to extend not merely to a divestment of proprietary rights but also to the transfer of such rights to new owners of the same property – a conclusion based also on Joshua 19:51 (Yev. 89b; Nov. Rashba, Git. 36b). The principle was the basis for the enactment of very many *takkanot* in different fields of civil law – property, tort, succession, and wills – in terms whereof the ownership of property due to a person according to the law of the Torah was shorn from the latter and vested in favor of another. Thus by virtue of the rule of *hefker bet din hefker* the scholars enacted that a woman validly married in accordance with *de-rabbanan* enactment, but not the strict law, is inherited by her surviving husband – thereby divesting her father's kin, her legal heirs under the strict law in the absence of a valid marriage, of their ownership of the estate in favor of the husband (Yev. loc. cit.). This is likewise the explanation for the validity of all those modes of acquisition instituted in the enactments of the scholars. According to the strict law such a mode of acquisition would not avail to extinguish the transferor's title, but the scholars enacted that ownership should nevertheless pass to the transferee by the use of such mode – the authority for such transfer of ownership deriving from the rule of *hefker bet din hefker*.

This rule is also the basis on which the *amoraim* explained the institution of the prosbul. The Torah enjoins the remission *(shemittah)* of monetary debts in the seventh year, forbids the lender from claiming his debt thereafter, and expressly adjures him not to refrain from lending money for fear that the debt will be wiped out in the seventh year (Deut. 15:1–6). Hillel the Elder, when he saw that the people transgressed the law by refraining from lending to each other, enacted that the lender should write out a prosbul, whereupon the debt would not be wiped out in the seventh year and the lender remain entitled to recover it even thereafter (Shev. 10:3–4). In the Talmud it is asked how it was possible for Hillel to enact a *takkanah* contravening a law of the Torah by prescribing permission to do that which was prohibited. One of the given answers is that Hillel had authority to ordain thus by virtue of the rule of *hefker bet din hefker*, that is the scholars laid down that the money of the debt in the ownership of the borrower passes into the ownership of the lender so that the question of claiming a debt exposed to the Sabbatical year does not arise because the lender seeks to do no more than claim money of which he has already acquired ownership (Git. 36b, Rashi and Nov. Rashba thereto). The latter example is an illustration of the use of the said rule in relation to a matter of ritual prohibition – i.e., the lender's claim for the money – based on the factor of property ownership. Another example of a *takkanah* of this kind is the annulment of a woman's marriage in certain circumstances on the basis of a retrospective change in the husband's ownership of the *kiddushin* ("marriage") money (see Marriage; Yev. 90b and Rashi ad loc.; BB 48b and Rashbam ad loc.).

(3) In Criminal Law. The halakhic scholars are entitled to enact *takkanot* in the area of the criminal law even though they involve the uprooting of a law in the Torah by way of "arise and do", when this need is dictated by the exigencies of the time, that is when such enactment amounts, in the words of the Babylonian *amoraim*, to making a safeguard for the Torah *(migdar milta)*. The rule is transmitted in the name of Eleazar b. Jacob: "I have heard that the *bet din* imposes flogging and punishment not prescribed in the Torah *(bet din makkin ve-onshin she-lo min ha-Torah)*; not to transgress the law of the Torah but to make a fence for the Torah" (Yev. loc. cit.; Sanh. 46a). By virtue of this rule it was held permissible to lay down punishment by flogging, and even the capital sentence, when rendered necessary by the prevailing social and moral realities (Sanh. loc. cit.). This was so despite the fact that the Torah law prohibits the flogging of any person for whom such punishment was not reserved (Yad, Sanhedrin 16:12) and that certainly it is prohibited to kill a person not liable to the death sentence according to Torah law since it involves a transgression of "Thou shalt not murder" (Radbaz, Mamrim 2:4). Thus in terms of this rule there were prescribed special punishments (such as incarceration – Sanh. 9:5; see Imprisonment[1]) and procedural rules (for instance, admitting circumstantial evidence and dispensing with the need for prior warning – see TJ Ḥag. 2:2, 78a), when this was necessary for the preservation of good order and the public weal. This legislative guideline served the halakhic scholars throughout the ages as a valuable means toward the ordering of Jewish society. It was instrumental in the development – insofar as the judicial autonomy extended to the different Jewish centers allowed for it – of a proliferous legislation in different fields of the Jewish criminal law and procedure answering the social needs of the time (see, e.g., the statements of Judah b. Asher in *Zikhron Yehudah*, no. 79). At the same time the scholars stressed the need to guard, in the exercise of such wide legislative authority, against doing undue injury to man's image and dignity: "all these matters apply to the extent that the *dayyan* shall find them proper in the particular case and necessitated by the prevailing circumstances; in all matters he shall act for the sake of Heaven and he shall not lightly regard the dignity of man . . . " (Yad, Sanhedrin 24:10; see also Resp. Rashba, vol. 5, no.238).

(4) Emergency Measures to Restore the People to the Faith. This legislatory guideline, operative also in the area of ritual prohibitions and permissions even as regards enactments involving the uprooting of a law of the Torah by directing to "arise and do," is derived from the act of Elijah in offering a sacrifice on the Mount of Carmel in order to bring back the

1. page 537.

people from the worship of Baal to worship of the Lord (I Kings 18:19–46), notwithstanding that the Torah prohibits such sacrificial offerings except at the Temple in Jerusalem and that sacrificial slaughter elsewhere is a transgression of two Pentateuchal prohibitions (Yev. 90b, Rashi and Tos. ad loc.). Legislative authority of this kind is summarized by Maimonides as follows (Yad, Mamrim 2:4): "And if they (the *bet din*) have seen fit for the time being to abrogate a positive precept or to transgress a negative precept so as to bring back the public to worship of the faith, or to save many in Israel from stumbling in other matters – they do according to the need of the hour. Just as the physician severs a person's hand, or foot, so that he shall survive at all, so the *bet din* at times instructs temporarily to transgress some of the precepts in order that all of them shall be fulfilled, as it was laid down by the early scholars (Yoma 85b); 'Profane on his account one Sabbath so that many Sabbaths shall be observed'."

(5) Enactments for which "There is Reason and Justification" (In Matters of Ritual Permissions and Prohibitions). A study of the rabbinical enactments reveals that the rules of legislation enumerated above do not exhaust the full measure of the halakhic scholars' legislative authority. From time to time there is found a *takkanah* which the former were unable to relate to any of the stated rules and they explained them on special legal and social grounds. Classic examples thereof are the *takkanot* of the *agunot* ("deserted wives") – some of the most important *takkanot* in Jewish law, from the aspect both of their social and humanitarian implications and of the conclusions deriving therefrom as regards the substance of legislation in the *halakhah*. The *takkanot* concern the matter of a married woman whose husband is missing and cannot be traced, and there is lacking sufficient evidence as required by the Torah – two witnesses at least (Deut. 19:15; Git. 26b) – to establish the husband's death, so as to permit her to remarry. In ancient times this legal situation had already created many practical difficulties since it happened more than once that a married man lost his life in circumstances of natural disaster or war but the fact could not be confirmed by the testimony of two witnesses, thus leaving the wife an *agunah* for the rest of her life. The halakhic scholars sought the answer to the problem by resorting to the different legal sources of the *halakhah*, above all through the institution of a series of *takkanot*.

The earliest of the series appears to be the one laying down that the wife is believed – and permitted to remarry – if after having gone abroad with her husband she returns alone and declares his death (Yev. 15:1; Eduy. 1:12). Quoted as the factual background to the enactment of this *takkanah* is the case of a woman who returned reporting the death of her husband, it being mentioned that the court investigated the facts finding her report to be true (Yev. and Eduy. *ibid.;* Yev. 116b and Tos.). This *takkanah* failed to meet the existing exigencies, since often, and particularly in times of war, the wife did not accompany her husband and therefore was not in a position to testify to the circumstances of his death. Hence a further *takkanah* was enacted – dating to the time of Gamaliel the Elder in the first half of the first century c.e. – prescribing the testimony of a single witness to the husband's death to suffice in order to permit the wife's remarriage. This *takkanah* apparently was not generally accepted, and even two generations later – in the time of Gamaliel of Jabneh, grandson of Gamaliel the Elder – the *tannaim* were still divided on the matter of permitting the wife's remarriage on the testimony of a single witness to her husband's death. Yet the increasing number of *agunot* left behind by the frequent wars led in the end to the general acceptance of this *takkanah* (Yev. 16:7; Eduy. 6:1 and 8:5).

The *amoraim* were much occupied with the legal substantiation of these *takkanot* which directed to "arise and do" in disregard of the law of the Torah on a matter of ritual prohibition – by permitting a woman, regarded in strict law as still married to her first husband, to marry another. The general explanation of the *amoraim* is that the rabbis relaxed the law in favor of an *agunah* (Yev. 88a). The legal explanations offered are that a woman is presumed to be careful herself to make sure that her husband is dead before remarrying (Yev. 25a; 93b; 115a; 116b), and that it need not be feared that people will lie about a matter the truth whereof is bound to be discovered *(ibid.)*. These explanations nevertheless do not suffice in themselves to render permissible the remarriage of an *agunah,* i.e., in accordance, with the law of the Torah. The halakhic reason given for the authority of the scholars to so enact concerning *agunot* is this: "For even if the scholars lack authority to uproot a law of the Torah by way of 'arise and do' – certainly all agree that there is such authority to uproot when there is reason and justification for the matter" (Tos. to Naz. 43b; Tos. to Yev. 88a; some of the *rishonim* base their explanation of the *takkanah* on the principle that anyone who married does so subject to the consent of the scholars and the scholars annulled the marriage of a missing husband (see below), but this does not appear to be correct in view of the opinion that the *agunah* who has remarried must be divorced from her second husband if the first should reappear – Rashba, quoted in *Shitah Mekubbeẓet,* Ket. 3a). The laws concerning *agunot* were added to in many other enactments. In tannaitic times, and later in amoraic and post-talmudic times, numerous other relaxations of the law were laid down, such as the admission of hearsay evidence, of the testimony of various kinds of disqualified witnesses, and so on (Yev. 16:6–7; Tosef., Yev. 14:7–8; TJ, Yev. 16:1, 15c; RH 22a And Codes; see also *agunah*) – "so that the daughters of Israel shall not remain fettered (agunot)" (Yad, Gerushin 13:29; for further instances of *takkanot* of this kind, see Av. Zar. 13a and Tos. thereto; Yad, Nedarim 3:9 and *Kessef Mishneh* thereto)).

Role of the Public. The main legislative factor in Jewish law is the authority exercised by the courts and the halakhic scholars in all succeeding generations. Another factor is the legislative authority of the public and its representatives. The source of legislative authority other than that of the halakhic scholars is to be found in the powers conferred on the king (Deut. 17:14–20; I Sam. 8; see also Ramban, Lev. 27:29), which, among others, embrace also legislative activity in different fields of civil and criminal law (Sanh. 20b; Yad, Melakhim, 3 and 4; Gezelah, 5:9–18, Roẓe'ah 2:4, Sanhedrin 4:2, and 18:6; see also Introduction). The earliest manifestations of legislative activity on the part of the public and its representatives are to be found in ancient *halakhot* relating to "the townspeople" *(benei ha-ir)*. With the rise of the Jewish community from the tenth century onward and the enactment of *Takkanot ha-Kahal,* this legislative activity became a factor of wide scope and importance in Jewish law. Its field of operation extended to the residents of a particular community or federation of communities, or particular districts, and it functioned in the areas of civil, criminal, and public law, but not in that of ritual prohibitions and permissions (see *Takkanot ha-Kahal*[1]).

It is true that the public also exercises a decisive influence on legislation emanating from the halakhic scholars. However, in this case the influence is exercised after the legislative act, whereas in the case of communal enactments – and legislation in other legal systems – the public initiative precedes the the legislative act. This conception finds expression in the two Talmuds in different versions: in the Babylonian Talmud – "no decree *(gezerah)* is imposed on the public unless the majority is able to

1. page 656.

abide thereby" (Av. Zar. 36a); in the Jerusalem Talmud (Av. Zar. 2:9, 41d) – "any decree *(gezerah)* which is imposed by the *bet din* and not taken upon themselves by the majority of the public is not a decree." In a combination of the two versions the principle is summarized by Maimonides thus: "A court which sees fit to institute a decree or enact a *takkanah* or introduce a practice must consider the matter and know beforehand whether or not the public is able to abide thereby . . . If the court has instituted a decree believing the majority of the public able to abide thereby, and thereafter it is found to be scorned by the people and not followed by a majority of the public – it will be void, and it will not be permissible to compel the people to its observance" (Mamrim 2:5–6, and see commentaries thereto).

Annulment of Takkanot. In the Mishnah the rule was laid down that "one *bet din* may not overrule the statements of another unless it exceeds the other in wisdom and number" (Eduy. 1:5). This rule was construed as applying to a court in its exercise of the legislative function, but in its exercise of the interpretative function the second court has authority to arrive at a different conclusion through an alternative interpretation of a biblical passage or ancient *halakhah* (Yad, Mamrim 2:1). However, a number of exceptions were laid down in terms whereof one court may annul the *takkanah* of an earlier court even though lacking the attributes specified in the above rule. The main exceptions are the following: (1) if at the time of making its enactment the court expressly prescribed that it could be annulled by any court wishing to do so (Ma'as. Sh. 5:2; MK 3b; see also Tos. to BK 82b); (2) when an enactment believed to have spread among all of Jewry is later found not to have spread among the majority of the Jewish people (Yad, Mamrim 2:7); (3) when the original reason and justification for the enactment have ceased to be valid (Beẓah 5a/b; *Hassagot Rabad* on Yad, Mamrim 2:2; Rashi and *Beit ha-Beḥirah,* cf. the contrary opinion of Maimonides, loc. cit.). The rule precluding one court from overruling another has the effect of lending the enactments of the scholars a stability and validity equaling, but not exceeding, that of the laws of the Torah itself. Hence, all the rules and guidelines concerning the authority of the halakhic scholars as regards legislating in connection with a law of the Torah obviously apply also as regards their authority to legislate in connection with a rule originating from earlier enactment by the halakhic scholars: "And if circumstances require it is seeming for the *bet din* to uproot even such matters (enactments and decrees of other courts) – even though it be of lower standing than the earlier *(battei din)* – so that such decrees shall not be of greater stringency than the laws of the Torah itself, since even the latter may be uprooted by any *bet din* as an emergency measure" (Yad, Mamrim 2:4).

Takkanot Until the End of the Tannaitic Period. Jewish law has experienced legislative activity in all periods of its history, although in varying degrees of intensity. It should be stressed that the actual number of laws originating from legislative activity by the scholars greatly exceeds the number of laws expressly stated to have been derived from *takkanah.* When a particular law is quoted without designation of its legal source, it is only rarely possible to ascertain such a source – by comparing the statement of the same law in other literary sources – and it may reasonably be assumed that *takkanah* is the legal source of a substantial proportion of such laws. It is possible that even laws construed by way of *midrash Torah* (Bible exegesis) had their creative source in *takkanah,* and that such *midrash* served only to integrate such laws with the relevant Pentateuchal passages (see Interpretation). Sometimes the halakhic scholars themselves mentioned this possibility (see, e.g., TJ, Shev. 10:1–2, 39c, concerning the prosbul); at other times it may be gathered from comparison with other sources dealing with the same subject matter. It is likewise possible that laws presented as having their legal source in *minhag, ma'aseh* or *sevarah* may have had their original source in *takkanah.*

(1) In the Scriptural Period. Talmudic tradition attributes various *takkanot* to most ancient times, for instance to the Patriarchs (their institution of prayers – Ber. 26b); to Moses and Joshua (various enactments concerning relations between the individual and the public in matters of property – BK 80b–81b and cf. Joshua 24:25); to Samuel, Boaz, David, Solomon, Jehoshaphat, Haggai, Zechariah, Malachi, and others. Certain *takkanot* are expressly designated in the Books of the Prophets and the Writings (see, e.g., the ordinance of King David in the area of military law – I Sam. 30:24–25).

(2) The Knesset ha-Gedolah ("Great Assembly"). One of the principal tasks of the men of the Great Assembly was to make legislation ". . . and make a fence around the Torah" (Avot 1:1). Talmudic tradition attributes to the times of Keneset ha-Gedolah numerous *takkanot* in different fields of *halakhah* – benedictions and prayers (Ber. 33a; cf. BB 15a), family law (incest in the second degree – Yev. 2:4; Yev. 21a). *Takkanot* pertaining to procedural rules and other fields of the *halakhah* are attributed to Ezra the Scribe (BK 82a; TJ, Meg. 4:1, 75a).

(3) The Sanhedrin and the Period of the Tannaim. The Great Sanhedrin fulfilled the function of a legislative body. The *takkanot* it enacted in the Temple period, as well as those enacted by the *nasi* and his *bet din* after the destruction of the Temple, are of material importance and served to prescribe the modes for the development of the *halakhah,* fashioning its character and evolutionary path for generations to come. A very substantial part of these *takkanot* are embraced in the different fields of Jewish law – civil, criminal, and public. The overwhelming majority of the *takkanot* of the Sanhedrin have come down anonymously, having been ordained by the Sanhedrin as a legislative body. In restricted cases the name of the halakhic scholar heading the Sanhedrin is recalled – for instance Simeon b. Shetaḥ (in *takkanot* concerning family and criminal law, etc. – Shab. 14b–16b; Ket. 82b; TJ, Ket. 8:11, 32c), Hillel the Elder (concerning the prosbul – see above, and others), Gamaliel the Elder (particularly in the area of family law – Git. 4:2–3, and concerning the *agunot,* see above), Johanan b. Zakkai, Gamaliel of Jabneh, and so on. The aforementioned *takkanot* were also enacted by the Sanhedrin as a body, but they have been traditionally transmitted in the name of the contemporary head of this body. Around the middle of the second century the Sanhedrin sitting at Usha in Galilee enacted a number of *takkanot* known as the *"Takkanot Usha."* This was a time of warfare and hardship following on the decrees of the emperor Hadrian, and it brought in its train a certain disintegration of family life. A large number of the Usha *takkanot* are concerned with the determination of different family law directives in the area of rights and obligations between spouses and between parent and child (Ket. 49bf.; BK 88b; BB 139b). There are also *takkanot* dating from the end of the tannaitic period attributed to particular scholars, such as Yose b. Ḥalafta of Sepphoris and Judah ha-Nasi.

A decisive majority of the *takkanot* known to have been enacted until the end of tannaitic times have not come down in the names of the bodies or scholars who enacted them. Consequently it is difficult, as regards a large proportion of the *takkanot,* to establish their exact stage of enactment during this long and significant period. These anonymous *takkanot* embrace whole areas of Jewish law, such as family law, property and obligations, labor law, tort, procedure and evidence – in which fields the directives thus laid down constitute basic principles of the aforesaid legal system (see Bloch, bibliography).

In the Amoraic Period. In addition to the already mentioned rules of legislation laid down by the *amoraim,* in which they circumscribed the legislative authority of the halakhic scholars, they also enacted many *takkanot* in all fields of the *halakhah,* laying down additional legislative guidelines in this connection. An illustration is their adoption of the enjoinder to "do that which is right and good" (Deut. 6:17–18) as a legislative guideline decreeing the need, at times, to supplement the law – "His testimonies and His statutes" *(ibid.)* – through the enactment of directives answering the demands of social and economic justice (cf. Ramban, Deut. 6:18). On this principle the *amoraim* based their institution of the law of the abutter's preemptive right (BM 108a), which gives the abutter the right of not only preempting neighboring land put up for sale, but also of claiming such land from a third party purchaser in return for the amount paid by the latter to the seller: ". . . even if the purchaser is a scholar or a neighbor or relative of the seller and the abutter is an ignorant person and not related to the seller, the latter nevertheless takes priority and evicts the purchaser; this because it is said, 'thou shalt do that which is right and good' and the scholars have held that since the sale is the same, it is right and good that the owner of the abutting land rather than an outsider should buy this place" (Yad, Shekhenim 12:5). It was laid down that for the very reason of doing "right and good," constituting the foundation of the abutter's right, the latter right is not available in certain cases. This applies, for instance, when the purchaser is an orphan – "because greater right and good is done by kindness to these rather than the abutter" – or a woman – "because she is not in the habit of constantly exerting herself to buy and therefore once she has bought the land, it is a kindness to let the land remain with her" (Yad, Shekhenim 12:13–14, based on BM *ibid.*). The principle of "right and good" is also the basis of the *takkanah* (concerning matters of execution (civil)) laying down that property assessed in satisfaction of a debt is always returnable to the debtor against payment (BM 35a; Yad, Malveh 22:15–16).

Another legislative principle of the *amoraim* is that stated by them in matters of marriage and divorce that "a man who marries a woman does so subject to the conditions laid down by the rabbis and his marriage is annulled by the rabbis." The meaning of this is that since every marriage takes place according to "the law of Moses and Israel," it takes place subject to the consent of the scholars who laid down the relevant laws and therefore the scholars have the power, in circumstances deemed proper, to annul the marriage and hold it to have been invalid *ab initio.* The *amoraim* relied on this principle in explaining an earlier *takkanah* of Gamaliel the Elder. According to the strict law, the husband who dispatches a bill of divorcement to his wife may cancel it any time before actual delivery thereof to the wife – it being permissible for him to do so before the court even in the absence of his wife. However, Gamaliel the Elder enacted, "for the general good," that there should be no cancellation of the *get* ("bill of divorcement") in the wife's absence (Git. 4:1–2), because the wife might receive the bill without learning of its cancellation and perhaps marry again, at a time when she is in fact still a married woman so that the children of her second marriage will be *mamzerim* (Git 33a). Simeon b. Gamaliel held the husband's act of cancelling a *get* in the wife's absence contrary to the *takkanah* of R. Gamaliel to be ineffective, i.e., that the divorce is valid and the wife free to remarry. In the talmudic discussion on the matter it is asked how the scholars could possibly rule that a *get* ineffective according to the strict law (because of its valid cancellation as aforesaid) should nevertheless be effective and thereby render the wife free to remarry. In answer to this question the Babylonian Talmud states that "a man who marries a woman does so subject to the conditions laid down by the rabbis, and his marriage is annulled by the rabbis" – i.e., since in such case the husband has disregarded the enactments of the scholars by cancelling the *get* contrary to their directives, therefore they retrospectively annul the *kiddushin* so as to obviate any need at all for the wife to receive a *get* (Git. loc. cit.). Basing themselves on this principle the scholars laid down various rules in the area of marriage and divorce (see, e.g., Ket. 2b–3a). The Jerusalem Talmud has no reference to the principle that a man who marries does so subject to the conditions laid down by the rabbis. It explains the words of R. Simeon b. Gamaliel – that even if the husband cancels the *get* this is ineffective as stemming from the authority of the sages to uproot even a law of the Torah (TJ, Git. 4:2, 20b). In the opinion of the Babylonian Talmud too, the rabbis possess authority to cancel a valid *kiddushin* even without relying upon the aforementioned rule that the marriage is dependent upon their agreement, as in the case of *kiddushin* celebrated between a man and a woman forcefully "snatched" by him (Yev. 110a and Tos.; BB 48b and Tos.).

In the Geonic Period. In geonic times Jewish life in Babylonia was overtaken by significant social and economic changes. The central authorities imposed heavy taxes on land held by Jews, often even expropriating such land, with the result that cultivation was steadily abandoned by Jews in favor of commerce and the trades. This in turn gave rise to many new problems in different fields of Jewish law, the answers to which – when they were not forthcoming by way of interpretation – were found by the *geonim* through resorting to the legal source of *takkanah.* Thus the *geonim* enacted that a debt is recoverable out of the debtor's personal as well as his real estate – contrary to the talmudic law that it is recoverable out of the real estate only, "since here most of the people (i.e., Jews) have no land and the later scholars made a *takkanah* so that the door should not be bolted before borrowers" (*Ḥemdah Genuzah,* no. 65). With the development of commercial life it was found expedient to enact a *takkanah* creating the possibility of the plaintiff's giving a power of attorney extending to litigation with the defendent on all manner of claims – a possibility which is restricted under the talmudic law (Yad, Sheluḥin 3:7). Many other *takkanot* were enacted in different fields of the law, such as property, obligations, family law, evidence, and civil execution (for particulars see Tykocinski and Schipansky, bibliography, see also Execution (civil)). *Takkanot* were also enacted on matters affecting the validity of a marriage or divorce. At the beginning of the tenth century, Judah Gaon enacted a *takkanah* requiring the *kiddushin* ceremony to be performed in public along with the recital of the *erusin* ("betrothal") benediction (see Marriage) and signing of the *ketubbah* ("marriage deed") by witness. The enactment was designed to avoid the doubtful validity of marriages which were hastily contracted on festive occasions by placing a ring on the woman's finger with the object of *kiddushin.* This *takkanah* quoted the amoraic principle that a marriage takes place subject to the conditions laid down by the rabbis (see above), in laying down that a marriage not celebrated in the manner prescribed by the takkanah need not give rise to any apprehension (of possibly being valid), since any such marriage contradicted the requirements of the contemporary scholars.

In the 12th century, Jacob Tam expressed the opinion that the halakhic scholars of the post talmudic period have no authority to enact a *takkanah* which could affect the validity of marriage or divorce. In an early geonic *takkanah* it had been laid down, contrary to the talmudic *halakhah,* that the husband could be compelled to give his wife an immediate *get* when the latter claimed such on a plea of *ma'us alai* ("he is repulsive to me"). The background to this *takkanah* was caused by the socio-moral realities of the time, since the wife would invoke the aid of the gentile courts toward compelling her husband to grant her a *get* the effect whereof was to render such a divorce invalid in Jewish law as an unlawful *get me'usseh* ("coerced" *get* – i.e., not falling within one of the halakhically recognized cases of *get* by coercion, see Divorce). The *geonim* consequently enacted that the case of *ma'us alai* should also be included among the cases of lawful *get* by coercion. R. Tam negated the validity of this *takkanah* because, in his opinion, no authority had been carried over to the post-talmudic scholars to enact a *takkanah* serving to validate a *get* invalid according to talmudic *halakhah,* the post-talmudic legislative authority in the area of family law being confined solely to the pecuniary aspects such as the manner of recovering the *ketubbah* and the like (*Sefer ha-Yashar,* Resp. no. 24). However, the majority of the other *rishonim* – including Naḥmanides and Asher b. Jehiel – did not question the stated legislative authority in matters of marriage and divorce as a matter of principle. They held the *geonim* to have relied on the principle that a marriage is subject to the requirements of the halakhic scholars and the latter consented to annul a marriage on a plea of *ma'us alai* (Resp. Rosh, 43:8). Yet the former too were opposed to applying the above *takkanah* in their own times – but for different reasons. The special background giving rise to enactment of the *takkanah* by the *geonim* had ceased to exist, and its application had not spread among the majority of the Jewish people (Nov. Ramban (Rashba), Ket. 63; Resp. Rosh loc. cit.; cf. also Yad, Ishut 14:8).

In Post-Geonic Times. A material change in the historical reality of the Jewish dispersion asserted itself from the tenth century onward. A Diaspora had existed even in most ancient times, but there had always been one predominant Jewish center exercising spiritual hegemony over all the other centers of Jewish life. Its first location was Ereẓ Israel. Afterward Babylonia enjoyed this standing until the close of the geonic period. The close of this period saw the decline of the Babylonian Jewish center with no other center assuming its predominant influence. Instead there had come into being, and there continued to develop, a number of small centers existing and functioning alongside each other. Beside the North African Jewish centers there arose in the course of time centers of Jewish life in Spain, Germany, France, Italy, Turkey, the Balkan countries, Poland, Lithuania, and elsewhere. From time to time outstanding scholars were still able, by force of their personal standing and influence, to link one center with another or more, but there was no longer one single center recognized by all the others as exercising authoritative influence. This new historical reality found expression in different fields of Jewish life, also as regards the substantive nature of law-making in the *halakhah.* Whereas legislation until this time – whether in Ereẓ Israel or in Babylonia – had enjoyed a national dimension as being applicable to the whole of the Jewish people, it was now to assume a local character and extend only to the particular center of activity of the halakhic scholar or court enacting the *takkanah.* This phenomenon is classically illustrated through the well-known *takkanah* of R. Gershom b. Judah (and see below), prohibiting polygamy (see Bigamy[1]), which although introducing a decisive change in Jewish family law was not accepted – until comparatively recent times – in a number of sizeable oriental Jewish centers. The post-geonic enactments, despite their local character, nevertheless became, like the decree of R. Gershom, an integral part of the overall system of Jewish law. This body of local legislation is at the same time indicative of the vitality of Jewish law, of its sensitivity and adaptation to the changing needs of the place and hour. This too can be learned from the enactment of R. Gershom, which was influenced by the prevailing conditions in Germany and the surrounding countries and the fact that in these countries polygamy was prohibited under the general law, whereas the prevailing conditions and outlook in the Muslim countries of the East were different, and there polygamy was a customary and lawful practice. Another material phenomenon in post-geonic Jewish legislation was the gradual consolidation of the view that the legal source of *takkanah* should not be resorted to in order to affect, in any manner contrary to the existing *halakhah,* the validity of a marriage or divorce. The already mentioned isolated opinion to this effect was reinforced, from the 14th century onward, by numerous other opinions holding that the operation of the guiding principle stated by the *amoraim* (on marriage subject to rabbinical requirements and its retrospective annulment) should be confined to the cases of its application in talmudic times. Also, this phenomenon is largely attributed to the fact that the *takkanot* of this period were of a local character, obliging only a limited and defined public, a fact fostering the apprehension that this sensitive area of Jewish family law might come to be governed by many different laws lacking in uniformity.

Legislation in Different Centers. Commencing from the 11th century it is possible to distinguish two main legislative directions in Jewish law: (a) legislation invested with halakhic authority, i.e., enactments by the courts or halakhic scholars; and (b) legislation by the public, i.e., communal enactments *(Takkanot ha-Kahal).* Often there was close cooperation between the two legislative bodies – the halakhic scholars and the public – and many *takkanot* were jointly enacted by them. This was a natural and understandable phenomenon considering that Jewry as a whole represented a traditional society which looked upon the *halakhah* as the supreme value governing its way of life.

A brief outline of legislative activity on the part of the two stated bodies, acting either separately or in cooperation, is given below.

(1) In Germany and France. Among the earliest *takkanot* enacted in the above centers are those of the late 10th- and early 11th-century German scholar, Rabbenu Gershom b. Judah – known as the "Light of the Exile" *(Me'or ha-Golah),* because "he brought light to the eyes of the exile through his enactments." To him are attributed many *takkanot* which have left a lasting imprint on Jewish law, particularly in the area of family law. Whether all the *takkanot* attributed to R. Gershom were in fact enacted by him is a matter of dispute among research scholars. It would appear that there is no reason to doubt the early tradition ascribing many *takkanot* to Rabbenu Gershom. Two of these are of substantive importance. One is the *takkanah* prohibiting a married man from taking another wife. In talmudic times it had already been hinted that polygamy was an undesirable phenomenon in Jewish life, and some scholars of this period even made the husband's right to take a second wife conditional on the consent of his first wife. However, the prohibition of polygamy as a matter of law was first instituted by R. Gershom – on pain of ban, hence the *Ḥerem de-Rabbenu Gershom,* by which name the *takkanah* is known. In so doing he put the stamp of monogamy on the Jewish family save, as already mentioned, in certain oriental communities where the *takkanah* was not accepted. The second *takkanah* is that in which R. Gershom, contrary to the ancient *halakhah,* prohibited the husband from divorcing the wife against her will.

Some time after R. Gershom's death there were enacted various *takkanot* which are attributed to Rashi. Later, in the 12th century, two great rabbinical conferences took place in Troyes, each headed by Rabbenu Tam (the first also by his

1. page 367.

brother, Samuel b. Meir (Rashbam)) – at which were enacted important *takkanot* in different fields of Jewish law. At the commencement of the 13th century the outstanding scholars of the generation participated in a number of synods held in Germany at which were again promulgated *takkanot* on matters of basic principle in different areas of the law. These *takkanot* known as the "*Takkanot Shum*" שו"ם = Speyer, Worms, Mainz), were accepted by all the Jewish communities of France and Germany, and later also by those of Poland and other Eastern European countries. Thereafter many more *takkanot* were enacted at various other synods, for instance, at Mainz toward the end of the 14th century, and by individual scholars – among others Meir of Rothenburg and Perez of Corbeil in the 13th century, Jacob Weil and Israel Bruna in the 15th century, and others. Various *takkanot* were also enacted by the great synod at Frankfort at the beginning of the 17th century, the last of its kind held in Germany. From then on Poland replaced Germany as the main center of Ashkenazi Jewry.

(2) In Spain, Italy, etc. From the 11th to the 13th centuries legislative activity in the Spanish Jewish center was mainly initiated by the outstanding contemporary scholars or by individual communities, and not – for various political and social reasons – at inter-regional or wider synods as with Ashkenazi Jewry (see Finkelstein, bibliography, pp. 99ff.). The *takkanot* thus enacted also laid down important matters of principle, and among others may be mentioned those of Toledo and Molina relating to family law. Toward the middle of the 14th century numerous *takkanot* were adopted at a conference attended – apparently in Barcelona – by representatives of the communities in Aragon. A complete collection of *takkanot* resulted from a conference of Castilian communal representatives held at Valladolid in 1432, initiated and headed by the Castilian court rabbi, Don Abraham Benveniste. The collection is divided into five parts, approximately one-half consisting of *takkanot* having an important bearing on different legal matters. Extant too is a collection of *takkanot* of the Spanish exiles in Fez, North Africa, enacted during the period from the end of the 15th century until the end of the 17th century in connection with different aspects of Jewish law (the collection is to be found in *Kerem Ḥamar*, vol. 2).

In Italy many *takkanot* were enacted at different national Jewish conferences called during the 15th century (Forli, Florence, etc.) and the 16th (Ferrara). *Takkanot* were also enacted in other smaller centers such as Crete (see Artom and Cassuto, bibliography), Corfu (see Finkelstein, bibliography, p.96), and others.

(3) In Poland, Lithuania, etc. Toward the end of the 16th century there came into being the Council of Four Lands *(Va'ad Arba Araẓot)* the central communal and legislative body of the Polish Jewish center for some 200 years (for details, see Halpern, Pinkas, bibliography). The meetings of the council were attended by delegates and leading scholars representing the Jewish communities in each of the participating regions or lands. As such the Council was, among its other functions, the supreme legislative body of Jewish autonomy in Poland.

The central body of Jewish autonomy in Lithuania was the *Va'ad Medinat Lita,* from early in the 17th century. Whereas very few of the *takkanot* of the Polish council are extant, there has come down a full collection of *takkanot* of the *Va'ad Medinat Lita,* covering the period from 1623 to 1761 and constituting a detailed repository of laws and decisions embracing the different fields of Jewish law (see Dubnow, bibliography). A similar central body of Jewish autonomy, though of smaller scope compared with the other two, was that representing the Jewish communities of Moravia. This body too engaged in a ramified legislative activity of which there is extant a collection of *takkanot* over the period 1650–1748 (see Halpern, bibl.).

Over and above the aforementioned central legislation, there was also legislative activity on the part of the local courts and individual communities (inter alia, the *takkanot* of the communities of Cracow, Nikolsburg (Mikulov), Tiktin (Tykocin), etc., see, e.g., M. Elon, *Ḥerut ha-Perat . . .* (1964), 280). Much of this great mass of material is scattered, and recalled in various ways, in the different branches of halakhic literature, particularly in the literature of the responsa and in historical material. It still awaits thorough assembly and classification. In this connection it may be mentioned that special attention to this matter is devoted in the indices to the responsa literature now being published by the Hebrew University's Institute for Research in Jewish Law.

Post-Geonic Legislation in Family Law. (1) Different Branches of the Law. The post-geonic legislative activity comprehended the civil law, family law and succession, administrative law, and evidence and procedure. There was also wide legislative activity, though in lesser measure, in criminal law, its scope having greatly depended on the measure of judicial autonomy enjoyed by the different communities in criminal matters. (For particulars of enactments in various branches of the law, see bibliography, and see under the relevant branch in this book.)

(2) Special Trend in Family and Succession Law. Legislation in the area of family and succession law reflects a special trend. On the one hand a very wide legislative activity is evidenced as regards the pecuniary aspects of these legal branches, including the enactment of *takkanot* contradicting existing law. On the other, scholars came to restrict authority to make enactments contradicting existing law on matters affecting the validity of a marriage or divorce.

The position is illustrated in the following examples: according to talmudic law the husband inherits his wife's entire estate in preference to all other heirs. In answer to the prevailing social realities in different centers, the husband's rights to his deceased wife's estate were restricted in a long series of *takkanot* of Troyes. The *takkanot "Shum"* (see above) laid down that the property brought by the wife at the time of her marriage should be returned by her husband to the person who gave her the property, or to her heirs, in the event of her dying childless within a year of the marriage – if within the second year, the husband to return half of such property. In the Spanish *takkanot,* as expressed in the *takkanot* of Toledo and Molina, the husband's right was restricted to one-half of the estate of his deceased wife, regardless of how long after the marriage she died, the other half to go to the children of the marriage – and if none, to the wife's relatives. In dealing with the substance of these *takkanot* Simeon b. Zemah Duran held as follows: "By this *takkanah* the husband's right of inheritance, which is *de-oraita,* is infringed, yet they are entitled to do so for it is found that the scholars instituted the *ketubbat benin dikhrin* [Ket. 52b; see Succession[1]], so as to encourage a person to give to his daughter as to his son, and since it has been the custom to be generous in giving a dowry, they made the enactment infringing somewhat the husband's right of inheritance" (*Tashbeẓ* 2:292). A variety of *takkanot* exist which give the daughter equal rights with the son for succession (Resp. Ritba 180; *Kerem Hamar,* Takkanah 8).

A different trend is evidenced as regards legislative authority to annul a marriage. By the commencement of the rabbinical period some scholars held that the principle, already mentioned, of the authority of the scholars of the talmudic period to annul a marriage should not be applied in relation to a marriage valid

1. page 448.

according to the talmudic law but not conforming to requirements laid down by the scholars in post-talmudic times: "if the rabbis (in the talmudic period) had authority to annul a marriage, we for our part have no authority to do so" (opinion of the Mainz scholars, see *Raban (= Even ha-Ezer)*, part 3, p. 47b ed. Jerusalem; see also the opinion of R. Tam, above). However, the majority of the scholars held that the post-talmudic scholars also enjoyed such authority (opinion of the scholars of Worms and Speyer, see *Raban*, loc. cit., see also the opinions of Naḥmanides and Asher b. Jehiel, under the Geonic Period, above). Later the opinion was expressed that while the authority of the post-talmudic scholars to annul a marriage was not the same as in the talmudic period, yet if the manner of celebrating a marriage be prescribed in a *takkanah* specially enacted for this purpose – for instance with a view to the prevention of deceit and bad faith, by requiring the presence of at least ten persons and the consent of the bride's parents – in which it is expressly provided that a marriage not celebrated in the prescribed manner shall be invalid, then a marriage so celebrated will be invalid (*Sefer Teshuvot ha-Rashba ha-Meyuḥasot le-ha-Ramban*, 125, 142; Resp. Rashba, vol. 1, nos. 551, 1162, 1185; Resp. Rosh, 35:1–3). It was added that a marriage would be invalid not only when celebrated contrary to a *takkanah* of the court but also when contrary to a communal enactment (Rosh and Rashba, loc. cit.; *Toledot Adam ve-Ḥavvah*, Ḥavvah 22:4). This was in fact the practice in different communities. Some 100 years after the above opinion was expressed, it was held by Isaac b. Sheshet Perfet that though this was the law in theory, "in practice I would tend toward greater stringency and because of the stringency of the matter I would not rely on my own authority alone to hold her unmarried without a prior *get*, but do so only if all the scholars of the regions consent thereto and share the responsibility" (Resp. Ribash, no. 399). This distinction between the theoretical statement of the law and decision in a practical case came increasingly to be accepted by the halakhic scholars (see, e.g., Resp. *Yakhin u-Vo'az*, Pt. 2, no. 20). The *halakhah* was decided in this special way: "If a community has made assent and enacted that no person shall marry save in the presence of ten, or the like, and a person nevertheless marries in transgression thereof – it is apprehended that his marriage is valid and the wife requires a *get;* even though the community may expressly have provided that the marriage shall be invalid and have nullified [ownership of] his money [i.e., with retrospective effect so that the *kiddushin* money was not that of the bridegroom and the marriage therefore invalid – see above], nevertheless it is necessary that the greatest stringency be applied in a practical case" (Rema, EH 28:21). After this ruling *takkanot* decreeing a marriage to be invalid unless celebrated in a prescribed manner were still enacted from time to time in the oriental Jewish centers, but there too it was generally decided that the marriage was not invalid.

It appears that the development of the trend toward restriction of legislative authority as regards marriage annulment is connected with the substantive nature of legislation in the post-geonic period. The fact that legislation had a mere local scope led to a proliferation of laws on the same legal subject, enacted by each Jewish center – and even community – acting independently of the others. In general this variety of laws created no insurmountable difficulties, and even greatly stimulated the development of the Jewish law rules of the conflict of laws. The position was different, however, in the case of laws affecting matters of marriage and divorce. The possibility that a woman regarded in one place as married could be regarded elsewhere as unmarried – in terms of a local *takkanah* – entailed an inherent serious threat to the upholding of a uniform law in one of the most sensitive spheres of the *halakhah*, that of the *eshet ish*. The only way for its prevention was through a restriction of legislative authority in this area (see Resp. Ribash, loc. cit.; Resp. Maharam Alashkar, no. 48).

Takkanot of the Chief Rabbinate of Ereẓ Israel. The spread of the Emancipation and the abrogation of Jewish judicial autonomy, from the end of the 18th century onward, saw a sharp decline – almost to the point of complete cessation – in the resort to the legal source of *takkanah*. This was a natural outcome of the new Jewish historical reality following on the Emancipation. Since the legislative function is a natural accompaniment to governmental organization and judicial autonomy the loss of the one obviated the need for the other (see Introduction[1]).

A certain change took place as from the 1930s, coinciding with the establishment of the organizational institutions of the Jewish settlement in Ereẓ Israel, notably the Chief Rabbinate Council. The Jewish judicial authority in matters of family and succession introduced a period of legislative activity on the part of the halakhic institutions. The Rabbinical Supreme Court of Appeal had been established in 1921. When it was later contended before this body that the *halakhah* did not allow for lodging an appeal against the judgment of a court, it was held that "the matter of an appeal has been accepted as an enactment of the scholars, the validity whereof is as that of the law of our holy Torah" (OPD, 71). In 1943 procedural *takkanot* were enacted, most of them based on the *halakhah* and "some of them enacted by the Chief Rabbinate Council for the purpose of ordering procedure in the courts of Ereẓ Israel and for the public good" (introductory note to the *takkanot*). Thus payment of court fees was imposed in connection with litigation – contrary to the existing *halakhah*. Similarly, the introduction of adoption as a legal institution represented an innovation in Jewish law (see Adoption). Another important innovation introduced by *takkanah* was the engagement by the rabbinical courts to hold equal the rights of sons and daughters and those of husband and wife for purposes of intestate succession. In 1944 the following three matters were enacted in different *takkanot:* the minimal amount of the *ketubbah* was increased, "having regard to the standard of living in the *yishuv* and economic considerations"; the levir refusing to grant the widow of his deceased brother *ḥaliẓah* was rendered obliged to maintain her until releasing her; the legal duty was imposed on the father to maintain his children until reaching the age of 15 – not merely until the age of six years as prescribed by talmudic law. Included in the matters laid down by *takkanah* in 1950 was the prohibition against the marriage of a girl below the age of 16. The introductory remarks to the *takkanot* of 1944 emphasize the twofold basis of their enactment, halakhic authority and the assent of the communities of the *yishuv* and their representatives.

Since then there has been no further legislative activity on the part of the bearers of the *halakhah* in the State of Israel. This may be regarded as regrettable since there still remain diverse halakhic problems awaiting solution by means of the legal source of *takkanah*. There is particular need to give attention to a number of problems concerning the *agunah* and other cases involving hardship to women – among others, of the married woman whose husband is unable to give her a *get* on account of his mental illness and cases in which difficulties arise in connection with the granting of *ḥaliẓah*. Solutions to these problems are capable of being found through the enactment of *takkanot* leading to an annulment of marriage in special cases, in the manner and by virtue of the talmudic principle described above in some detail. The already mentioned threat of a proliferation of laws and lack of uniformity on a matter of great halakhic

1. page 33.

sensitivity, which inhibited past generations from acting on the stated principle, has much abated in modern times in the light of the central spiritual standing which may be allocated to the halakhic authority in Israel in its relations with other centers of Jewry in the Diaspora.

Bibliography: Z.H. Chajes, *Torat Nevi'im . . .* (1958); idem, *The Student's Guide through the Talmud* (1960²), 35–110; Weiss, Dor, 2 (1904⁴), 49–65; Halevy, Dorot, 1, pt. 3 (1923), 46ff.; M. Bloch, *Sefer Sha'arei Torat ha-Takkanot,* 3 vols. (1879–1905); Ch. Tchernowitz, *Toledot ha-Halakhah,* 1 (1934), 174–88; Ḥ. Albeck, in: *Zion,* 8 (1942/43), 165–78; I.Z. Kahana, *Sefer ha-Agunot* (1954), passim; J.M. Ginzburg, *Mishpatim le-Yisra'el* (1956), 45–55; *Pinkas ha-Medinah* (Lita), ed. by S. Dubnow (1925); *Takkanot Kandia ve-Zikhronoteha,* ed. by A.S. Artom and M.D. Cassuto (1943); *Takkanot Medinat Mehrin,* ed. by I. Halpern (1951); Halpern, Pinkas; A.H. Freimann, *Seder Kiddushin ve-Nissu'in . . .* (1945); I. Schipansky, in: *Hadorom,* 24 (1966, 135–97; 26 (1967), 173–97; 28 (1968), 145–59; I.D. Gilat, in: *Sefer Bar-Ilan,* 7/8 (1970), 117–32; M. Elon, *Ha-Mishpat ha-Ivri;* II, p. 391–712; idem, *Ḥakikah Datit . . .* (1968), 158–65, 182–4; ET, 1 (1951³), 279–82; 3 (1951), 325–30; 5 (1953), 529–46; 10 (1961), 95–110; Finkelstein, Middle Ages; Ḥ. Tykocinski, *Takkanot ha-Ge'onim* (1959). See also bibliography of *Takkanot ha-Kahal.*

Menachem Elon

MINHAG (Hebrew מנהג "custom," "usage") from the verb "to lead." This entry is arranged according to the following outline:

Definition
Minhag as a Source of Law
Elucidation of Terms
Scriptural Support for the Validity of *Minhag* as a Legal Source
Functions and Categories of *Minhag*
Minhag as Deciding the *Halakhah*
Minhag as Adding to Existing *Halakhah*
"Custom Overrides the Law" – *Minhag Mevattel Halakhah*
Proof of the Existence of a Custom
Custom *(Minhag)* and Usage *(Nohag)*
General and Local Custom
Minhag and the Conflict of Laws (within Jewish Law)
Control over *Minhag* by the Halakhic Scholars

Definition. Minhag (custom) indicates a particular normative act, occurring constantly, and whose existence can be demonstrated without doubt. Minhag is one of the sources of Jewish Law.

Minhag as a Source of Law. Three possible meanings may be attributed to the term "source of law": a historical source of the law, i.e., a source which factually and historically speaking constitutes the origin of a particular legal norm; a legal source of the law; i.e., the source which lends the particular normative direction legal recognition and validity as part of the entire body of legal rules comprising the relevant legal system; and a literary source of the law, i.e., the informative source constituting the authentic repository for purposes of ascertaining the content of a particular legal direction (see Introduction[1]). *Minhag,* as does custom in other legal systems, sometimes serves as the historical source of a particular legal norm and sometimes as the legal source.

As a Historical Source. A study of the formative stages of any legal system will reveal that to some extent its directions originated from customs evolved in the practical life of the society concerned, and that only at a later stage was legal recognition conferred on such customs – by way of legislation or decision on the part of the legislator or judge. This phenomenon is also evidenced in Jewish law. Thus, for instance, certain legal usages which had been prevalent in pre-Mosaic Hebrew society later came to be affirmed in the Torah, as, for example, the law of the bailees' liability (see Bailment), and sometimes also with material modifications, as with regard to the laws of *yibbum* (see Levirate Marriage and *Ḥaliẓah*). The historical source of such directions is the pre-Mosaic usage, but their legal source is the Written Law, which gave them recognition and validity. Custom has fulfilled this historical function in all stages of the development of Jewish law, by serving to prepare a particular normative direction for acceptance into this legal system.

As a Legal Source. In Jewish law *minhag,* like custom in any other legal system, has also fulfilled an important function as a legal source, and it is with custom in this capacity that this article is concerned. Custom constitutes a legal source when the legal system, in certain circumstances and upon fulfillment of certain requirements, recognizes a consistently followed course of conduct as a binding legal norm. When custom serves merely as a historical source, it is only capable of preparing the normative course of conduct toward acquisition of legal recognition by means of a law-creating source, such as *takkanah;* however, when custom is a legal source, the normative usage already has legal force by virtue of such usage alone, without the affirmation of any law-creating source. As a legal source, the primary purpose of custom is like that of legislation (see *Takkanot*), namely to fill a void in the existing *halakhah* when the latter offers no solution to new problems that arise, or in order to rectify or vary existing legal rules if and when the need arises. There is, however, a formal difference – which, as will be seen below, is also of substantive importance – between these two legal sources: legislation functions demonstratively and directly, at the direction of the competent authority, such as the halakhic scholars or the leaders of the people and of the community; custom, on the other hand, functions without preconceived intent and anonymously – at the hands of all or part of the people at large – and in order to ascertain it, it is necessary to "go and see what is the practice of the people" (Ber. 45a; Pes. 54a; in the TJ the version is, "go and see what is the practice of the public, and follow it" (TJ, Pe'ah 7:6, 20c; Ma'as. Sh. 5:3, 56b; Yev. 7:2, 8a). It is true that even in the case of a normative direction originating from custom there is the indirect influence of the halakhic scholars, by virtue of a certain control which they exercise over it (see below; see also Yad, Mamrim, 1:2–3); nevertheless it is the public as a whole that is the direct creative source of the legal direction. The public is invested with such creative authority on the presumption that, since its conduct is founded on the Torah, its creative authority will be directed in the spirit of the Torah, in accordance with the statement of Hillel the Elder made in affirmation of the binding force of a public custom in determining the *halakhah:* "Leave it to Israel. If they are not prophets, they are still the children of prophets" (Pes. 66a).

Substantiating the Validity of Minhag as a Legal Source. Some of the scholars apparently sought to explain the validity of a custom by saying that it had to be assumed that the earliest source of such a norm – now appearing in the form of custom – was ancient *halakhah* founded on transmitted tradition, *takkanah,* or other legal sources, but that the latter had become forgotten in the course of time, leaving the norm in the form of a custom only. This opinion finds expression in the Jerusalem Talmud: "Any Torah which has no source *(bet av)* is no Torah" (TJ, Shab. 19:1, 17a stated in relation to the *baraita* (Pes. 66a) in which Hillel recalls that the custom followed by the people

1. page 10.

concerning the paschal sacrifice on a Sabbath day he had heard mentioned by Shemaiah and Avtalyon (see below); the term *torah* is here used in the sense of custom). Elsewhere it is stated: "a custom which has no support in the Torah, is like the erroneous exercise of discretion" (Sof. 14:18; see also *Mordekhai* BM 366). According to this view custom has no independent creative force, but merely offers testimony to the existence of a rule created by one of the legal sources of the *halakhah.* In post-talmudic times some halakhic scholars expressly adopted this attitude toward custom (Resp. Rif no. 13; Nov. Ramban BB 144b s.v. *Ha de-Amrinan*). Some scholars explained the decisive power of custom, even when this was called forth only to decide between disputing scholarly opinions (see below), on the basis that a custom proves the existence of an ancient, deliberate determination of the law which has become forgotten, being preserved in this form only (Resp. Rosh 55:10). The source of authority of custom remained a matter of dispute among the *aḥaronim* (for particulars, see *Pitḥei Teshuvah* ḤM, 163, n. 16).

Certainly there are customs which have their source in ancient *halakhah,* as is evidenced by the Jerusalem Talmud in the matter of the paschal sacrifice on a Sabbath day (see above) and in other instances (see, e.g., Tosef., MK 2:14–15; see also Pes. 51a and TJ, Pes. 4:1, 30d). However, it transpires that the distinguishing feature of custom as a legal source lies not in its probative efficacy but in the law-creating authority of the public, whether the custom serves to decide between disputing opinions or to add to the existing *halakhah.* This is undoubtedly so as regards the validity of custom in matters of the civil law *(dinei mamonot),* where it is within the power of custom to operate even contrary to the existing law, in terms of the general principle of Jewish law which permits the parties to a transaction – and all the more so the public as a whole – to contract out of the Law of the Torah (see below). This is accepted by the majority of halakhic scholars as the explanation for the rule that custom overrides the law in matters of the civil law, which is certainly a classic illustration of the creative activity of custom.

Elucidation of Terms. At times, a particular halakhic direction which has its source in custom is also called *dat* (Beẓ. 25b and Rashi thereto) or *dat yehudit* (Ket. 7:6 and Rashi to Ket. 72a; Tosef., Ket. 7:7). At other times the term *minhag* is used by the halakhic scholars to describe a normative direction having its source in *takkanah* (e.g., TJ, Ket. 1:5, 25c; Mid. Prov. to 22:28) and even the verb הנהיג is sometimes used to describe the enactment of a *takkanah* (cf. Tosef., RH 4:3 with RH 4:1 and Suk. 3:12). The use of a common term to describe both *takkanah* and custom (cf. further Yad, Mamrim 1:2–3; Resp. Rashba, vol. 2, no. 268) is attributable to their common function, namely legislative activity (each in its own different way, as already mentioned). Sometimes the term *minhag* is also used to describe *halakhah* which has its source in the Bible itself (see Sifra, Emor, 17:8, the law concerning habitation of a *sukkah* etc., described as *minhag le-dorot;* in Suk. 43a/b, the phrase is *mitzvah le-dorot*). Contrariwise, a normative direction having its source in custom is sometimes called *halakhah* (BM 7:8; Kid. 38b and see Samuel's interpretation, in TJ, Or. 3:8, 63b of the term *halakhah* appearing in Or. 3:9). Such use of common labels of *minhag, takkanah,* and *halakhah* for differing concepts not only calls for the exercise of great care in distinguishing the correct identity of each law appearing under such a name, but also offers proof of the legal efficacy of normative directions which have their source in custom and are integrated into the general halakhic system as a substantive part of it (even though there is a variance at times between the force of a direction originating from *takkanah* and one originating from custom; see below). Transgression against a direction decreed by custom is punishable by sanction: "Just as a fine is imposed in matters of *halakhah,* so a fine is imposed in matters of *minhag*" (TJ, Pes. 4:3, 30d) and R. Abbahu even sought to have punishment by flogging imposed on a person who transgressed a prohibition decreed by custom (TJ, Kid. 4:6, 66b; see also Kid. 77a).

At the same time, the scholars occasionally distinguished, primarily in the field of the ritual law, between a rule originating from custom and one originating from another legal source. Such distinctions, particularly from the amoraic period onward, are illustrated by the following examples: the majority of the *amoraim* held that the prohibition of *orlah* (eating the fruit of young trees) outside of Ereẓ Israel had its source in custom, and therefore they sought various legal ways in which to permit the fruit of *orlah* outside of Ereẓ Israel – something they would not have done had the prohibition belonged to the category of *halakhah le-Moshe mi-Sinai* (Kid. 38b–39a and see above). Similarly, there is recorded the talmudic dispute between R. Johanan and R. Joshua b. Levi as to whether the rite of taking the willow-branch on Sukkot (the branch that is raised and beaten on Hoshana Rabba) was an enactment of the prophets or a custom of the latter – i.e., a usage of the prophets but not enacted as a *takkanah* (Suk. 44a and Rashi ad loc.; see also *Sha'arei Teshuvah* no. 307); the answer to this question was relevant to the need (i.e., if it was an enactment) or otherwise (if it was a custom) for recital of a benediction at the time of beating the willow-branch (see Suk. 44a and see *takkanot*[1] concerning benedictions in respect of matters instituted by the halakhic scholars). Even as regards deciding the *halakhah* in a matter under dispute, the *amoraim* distinguished between *halakhah* determined by way of open and deliberate decision, *halakhah* determined by custom introduced by the scholars, and *halakhah* determined by mere anonymous undirect custom (see TJ, Shek. 1:1, 46a, Meg. 1:6, 70d, Nid. 3:1, 50c, and Pes. 4:6, 31a; Av. Zar. 14b; Yev. 13b; Nid. 66a; et al.). Some of the Babylonian *amoraim* even laid down a further distinction, one relating to the nature of the custom. Thus three possibilities are distinguished: *nahagu ha-am* ("the practice followed by the people") was apparently interpreted by the Babylonian *amoraim* as referring to a usage not yet fully crystallized into an established custom, and therefore "we do not teach in this way initially, but should a person have done so, we allow the matter to stand"; *minhag,* to crystallized custom which, although it has sufficient authority for the people to be taught to act from the start in accordance with it, nevertheless does not have the same force as a rule openly and expressly decided by the halakhic scholars – "we do not teach to act in this way in public, but we may teach (those who ask, to act according to the rule embodied in the custom)"; and that which is decided as *halakhah,* which must be published and made known to the public (Ta'an. 26b and see also Er. 62b and 72a). These distinctions relate primarily to the field of ritual law and not the creative function of custom as it relates to civil law matters (see below, "Custom overrides the law").

Scriptural Support for the Validity of Minhag as a Legal Source. Halakhic scholars sought to rely on various scriptural passages as the source of the validity of custom. Simeon b. Yoḥai's statement, "Change not the custom set by your fathers! " is supported in the Midrash (Mid. Prov. 22:28, and see annotation there), by allusion to the scriptural injunction, "Remove not the ancient landmark, which thy fathers have set" (Prov. 22:28). R. Johanan found support for the validity of custom in another passage from the Book of Proverbs (1:8), "Hear, my son, the instruction of thy father, and forsake not the

1. page 74.

teaching of thy mother" (see Pes. 50b; Ḥul. 93b; cf. also *She'iltot,* Va-Yakhel, Sh. 67; *Halakhot Gedolot* end of Hil. Megillah). Sherira Gaon quotes the following tradition, which is not extant in the Talmuds: "Whence is it said that custom obliges? As it is said, 'Thou shalt not remove thy neighbor's landmark, which they of old time have set' " (Deut. 19:14; *Sha'arei Ẓedek,* 1:4, 20; Tur, ḤM 368). The discussion concerns an article stolen from its owner and sold to another; in law, if the owner has "despaired" (see *Ye'ush*[1]), the purchaser will not be required to return the article to him, but Sherira Gaon decided that there was in operation a custom to restore the article in such circumstance, from which there could be no departure. The factor which is common to all legal sources is that a norm which has been followed for some considerable time (see below) acquires for itself a fixed place in the *halakhah* and may not be overlooked nor "trespassed" upon (cf. the comment of Philo on the above scriptural passage, Spec. 4:149).

Functions and Categories of Minhag. Just as *takkanah* – the directed legislation of the halakhic scholars – has functioned in all fields of the *halakhah,* so custom – anonymous legislation – has also functioned in all its fields, although in some of them the measure of authority of custom is limited as compared with that of *takkanah.* Custom fulfills a number of functions in *halakhah* and is also divisible into several further *categories.*

Functions. Custom serves three possible functions: (1) as the decisive factor in the case of disputing opinions as to a particular halakhic rule; in this event the custom operates even where the *halakhah,* but for such a custom, would be decided differently in accordance with the accepted rules of decision; (2) as adding to the existing *halakhah,* whenever the practical realities give rise to new problems to which the former has no available answer; and (3) as establishing new norms which stand in contradiction to the existing *halakhah,* i.e., norms which serve to vary the latter, or derogate therefrom. The latter two functions of custom parallel that of legislation (see *Takkanot*), save that the last one (abrogation of an existing law) is of lesser efficacy than is the case with legislation (see below).

Categories of Minhag. *Custom (Minhag) and Usage (Nohag).* At times *minhag* functions of its own inherent power, independently and directly, just as does a direction by express *takkanah;* at other times it functions by way of an inference that the parties to a particular matter acted as they did on the assumption that the decree of the *minhag* concerned would determine their relationship. This distinction is developed in other legal systems too, and in English law *minhag* of the first kind is termed "legal custom" or simply "custom," and *minhag* of the second kind "conventional custom" or "usage." In current Hebrew the latter is customarily termed *nohag.*

General Custom and Local Custom. A custom may be general in the sense of obliging the whole of the people or the public, or it may be local and obligatory only for the people of a particular place, in which case it is termed local custom, *mores civitatis* in Roman law. In the same way the operation of a custom may be confined to people of a particular class, occupation, etc., and further like subdivisions of custom may be made (see below).

Minhag as Deciding the Halakhah. In case of dispute between halakhic scholars as to the law, custom decides the issue – whether in circumstances where there are no established rules of decision concerning the particular matter, or in circumstances where the custom stands in contradiction to the accepted rules of decision. The matter is illustrated by the following examples: It is recorded that R. Tarfon differed from the majority opinion of the scholars with regard to the blessing to be recited over water (Ber. 6:8) and the *amoraim,* when asked how to decide the *halakhah,* replied: "go and see what is the practice of the people" (Ber. 45a; Eruv. 14b); this was also stated with regard to a similar question concerning the eating of *terumah* (TJ, Pe'ah 7:6, 20c, Ma'as. Sh. 5:3, 56b, and Yev. 7:2, 8a). In another case R. Judah and R. Yose held the view that just as the priests generally did not lift their hands when reciting the priestly benediction at the *Minḥah* (afternoon) service – because of the proximity of the service to the meal and the apprehension that a priest might lift his hands while intoxicated – so this was forbidden at the *Minḥah* service on the Day of Atonement (even though the above apprehension would not exist) lest this lead the priests to the erroneous practice of lifting their hands during weekday *Minḥah* services; however, R. Meir differed, holding that such lifting of the hands was permissible at the *Minḥah* service on the Day of Atonement (Ta'an. 26b). Although the accepted rules of decision required that the *halakhah* on the matter be decided according to R. Yose (see Eruv. 46b) – who in this case represented the stringent view – it was nevertheless decided according to the view of R. Meir – representing in this case the lenient view – for the reason that "the people followed the view of R. Meir" (Ta'an. 26b; see also Resp. Maharik no. 171).

According to some of the Babylonian *amoraim,* the power of determining the *halakhah* contrary to the accepted rules of decision was to be withheld from custom in matters concerning the ritual law *(dinei hetter ve-issur).* Thus in response to R. Johanan's statement, "In regard to carob trees, it has become the custom of the people to follow the rule of R. Nehemiah" (RH 15b) – i.e., contrary to the majority of the scholars – the question is asked: "In a matter of prohibition, shall it be permitted to follow a custom? " *(ibid.).* On the other hand, the *amoraim* of Ereẓ Israel – along with some Babylonian *amoraim* – conferred on custom the power of deciding the law in any case of dispute, even in matters of ritual law and even when it was contrary to the accepted rules of decision, for instance when decreeing in favor of an individual opinion against the majority opinion (TJ, Shev. 5:1, 35d, the opinion of R. Johanan quoted in RH 15b; cf. the statement of Rava, "The custom accords with the view of R. Meir" Ta'an. 26b; see also Pes. 103a and Ber. 52b, contrary to the unqualified statement of the law in the Mishnah).

In the 13th century, Meir b. Baruch of Rothenburg stated, "For in all matters on which the great halakhic scholars are in dispute, I hold that a stringent approach must be followed, save . . . when the permissibility of a matter has spread in accordance with the custom of the scholars by whom we have been preceded" (Resp. Maharam of Rothenburg, ed. Berlin, no. 386 p.294). At this time too the dispute concerning the extent to which it was within the power of custom to determine the *halakhah* was continued. Thus Jacob Moellin justified the custom of lending the money of orphans at fixed interest (*ribbit keẓuẓah,* see Usury[2]), contrary to the opinion of the majority of scholars, who held this to be prohibited; Moellin based his view on a solitary opinion (Resp. Maharil no. 37), which in fact only permitted such interest in respect of loans given from charitable funds (*Or Zaru'a,* Hil. Ẓedakah, no. 30), but Moellin extended the opinion to embrace also money lent by orphans, "for all matters concerning orphans are deemed to be matters of *mitzvah,* and this is truly so because they are alone and meek" (Maharil, loc. cit.). Other scholars contested this view: "There are places where it is customary for an *apotropos* [guardian] to lend orphans' money at fixed interest, but this is an erroneous custom and should not be followed" (Rema to YD 160:18; see also *Siftei Kohen* thereto, n. 27).

Minhag as Adding to Existing Halakhah. In its previously described function, custom serves to decide between two

1. page 228; 3. page 502.

existing disputing opinions rather than to create a new rule. The latter effect is achieved by custom in fulfillment of its second function, namely that of establishing a new rule in relation to a question to which the existing *halakhah* offers no solution. For instance, as regards the paschal sacrifice, it is enjoined that it shall be brought on the 14th day of the month of Nisan (Num. 9:3), even when this falls on a Sabbath day (Pes. 6:1); when Hillel the Elder was asked what the law was in the event that it had been forgotten to prepare the knife on the eve of the Sabbath – i.e., whether it was also permissible to have the knife fetched on the Sabbath – he replied: "Leave it to Israel! If they are not prophets, they are still the children of prophets" (i.e., to await the morrow and see how the people would act); on the morrow, "he whose sacrifice was a lamb, stuck it [the knife] in its wool, and he whose sacrifice was a goat, stuck it between its horns; he [Hillel] saw the act and recalled the *halakhah*, saying, 'thus have I received the tradition from Shemaiah and Avtalyon'" (Pes. 66a). Hillel thus left the solution to the custom of the people, only later recalling that this custom had its source in ancient *halakhah*. A further illustration is to be found in the reply given in the Jerusalem Talmud to the question whether it was necessary or not to set aside tithes from the fruit of trees in their fourth year: "when there is no clearly established *halakhah* on any matter before the court and you do not know what its true nature is – go and ascertain the custom of the public and act accordingly, and we see that the public does not set aside tithes in this case" (TJ, Pe'ah 7:6, 20c and see Ma'as. Sh. 5:3, 56b). In this way custom served to decide the *halakhah* in a lenient manner (in TJ, Yev. 7:2, 8a – the above rule is quoted in connection with the function of custom as deciding between disputing opinions; see also Resp. Rosh 55:10).

"Custom Overrides the Law" – Minhag Mevattel Halakhah. Many halakhic scholars devoted a great deal of attention and research to the question whether it was within the power of custom, "concealed legislation," not only to add to existing *halakhah* but also to vary the latter and set aside any of its rules in certain circumstances – as it was within the power of *takkanah*, "open legislation," to do. This function, which in talmudic sources is termed *minhag mevattel halakhah* ("custom overrides the law"), has been the subject of much dispute – as in other legal systems in which custom is a recognized legal source. In Roman law, for instance, disputing opinions are found on the question whether custom *(mores, consuetudo)* has the power to create also a rule that is contrary to existing law (*contra legem*, see J. Salmond, *Jurisprudence* (1966[12]), 189–212; C. K. Allen, *Law in the Making* (1964[7]), 82f.).

Distinction between Civil and Ritual Law. Jewish law distinguishes between civil and ritual law for purposes of the instant function of custom, recognizing the power of the latter to set aside the law in civil law matters but not in matters of the ritual law, where it cannot operate contrary to existing law in permitting that which has been prohibited. The explanation for this distinction lies in one of the substantive differences between these two fields of the law – one that relates to the freedom of stipulation (see Introduction;[1] Contract[2]). In matters of the civil law the rule is, "a person may contract out of the law of the Torah" – i.e., the law is *jus dispositivum*, since the premise is that halakhic rules of the civil law are laid down as a binding arrangement only as long as the parties do not disclose their preference for an alternative arrangement. On the other hand, the directions of the ritual law are *jus cogens*, obligatory and not variable at the will of the parties concerned. The logical conclusion is that just as the order in civil law matters is variable at the instance of the parties to a particular transaction, so it may be varied by the public as a whole, which, as it were, stipulates in advance that such and such an order, contrary to that laid down in the Torah, is convenient and desirable for each and every one of its members (see Resp. Rosh 64:4; Resp. Rashbash no. 562; Resp. Maharashdam ḤM no. 380). Thus custom, in expressing the collective will of the public, functions with power to change the *halakhah* in the civil law field – where the will to change the law has recognized authority – but not in the field of ritual law, in which a prohibition is obligatory and unchangeable whether at the will of the instant parties or of the public as a whole. In this function there is accordingly an important distinction between open legislation by way of *takkanah* and concealed legislation by way of custom. The Torah, in all fields, was entrusted to the authority of the halakhic scholars (see Authority, Rabbinical), authority being delegated to them in the Torah itself to make legislation, whether to add to or derogate from the existing *halakhah* (see *Takkanot*[3]). This is not the case as regards the authority of the public in relation to concealed legislation; the public may decide, by way of *minhag*, between disputing opinions of the halakhic scholars within the existing *halakhah*, may add to the *halakhah*, but may not set aside any rule of the existing *halakhah* – except when the abrogation of such a rule is rendered possible at the hands of individual members of that public by way of express stipulation, i.e., in the field of civil law.

Coinage of the Phrase Minhag Mevattel Halakhah. The essential principle that in the field of civil law custom overrides the law is mentioned in various parts of talmudic and post-talmudic halakhic literature (see below). However, the characteristic phrase for this principle, *minhag mevattel halakhah*, is quoted in the Jerusalem Talmud in connection with the following two matters: The first relates to the determination in the Mishnah (BM 7:1) of the laborer's working hours in two different ways: one whereby he goes to work early in the morning and returns home late, these being the hours of work according to law (BM 83a–b); the other, whereby the laborer goes to work at a later hour and returns home earlier. The Mishnah lays down that local custom determines the hours of work even if this is contrary to the hours laid down by law; the comment of R. Hoshaiah is, "that is to say the custom overrides the *halakhah*" (TJ, BM 7:1, 11b), so that the employer may not withhold the wages of the worker by requiring that he abide by the legally prescribed working hours, but will himself have to abide by the working-hours decreed by custom – this without need for any proof that the parties had so intended (TJ, *ibid.*). The second matter in which the phrase is quoted relates to the laws of *ḥaliẓah* (see Levirate Marriage); the fact that this forms part of ritual law does not affect the premise that in the latter field of the law the doctrine of *minhag mevattel halakhah* does not operate. In the Mishnah (Yev. 12:1) it is stated that the *ḥaliẓah* rite may be performed with a shoe or sandal (both of leather) but not with *anpilya* (sock or shoe made of cloth) since only the first two are included in the Pentateuchal term *na'al* (Deut. 25:9). In the Jerusalem Talmud (Yev. 12:1, 12c) it is stated: "If Elijah should come and state that *ḥaliẓah* may be performed with a shoe he would be obeyed; that *ḥaliẓah* may not be performed with a sandal he would not be obeyed, for it has been the practice of the public to perform *ḥaliẓah* with a sandal, and custom overrides the law." In this particular case custom supports the existing *halakhah*, since the Mishnah permits *ḥaliẓah* with a sandal and this is not prohibited by any extant talmudic source; accordingly, if Elijah were to come and forbid performance of *ḥaliẓah* with a sandal he would be determining a new rule, contradicting the existing *halakhah*, and in such an event custom – in supporting the existing *halakhah* – would serve to override the new *halakhah* being laid down by Elijah, a

1. page 7; 2. page 251; 3. page 75.

function of custom effective in the field of the ritual law. (It is also possible that the phrase *minhag mevattel halakhah* was originally stated in relation to the laborer's hours of work and its application extended to the case of *ḥaliẓah* by the redactor of the talmudic discussion. It may be noted that the above version of the doctrine does not occur in Yev. 102a, where the rule, "if Elijah should come . . . " is also found, nor in BM 83a–b; see also Men. 31b–32a).

The rule that it is not within the power of custom to render permissible an undisputed prohibition is stressed by the use, on several occasions, of the phrase, "Does the matter then depend on custom? " (Ḥul. 63a; BM 69b–70a). On the other hand, custom does have the power, even in the field of the ritual law, to render prohibited something that has been permitted, since the law is not abrogated thereby but only rendered more stringent: "Custom cannot set aside a prohibition, it can only prohibit that which has been permitted" (Yad, Shevitat Asor, 3:3; see also Resp. Rosh 55:10). According to some scholars, custom – even in civil law matters – only overrides *halakhah* when it has been accepted by way of a communal enactment (see *Takkanot ha-Kahal;* and see *Nimmukei Yosef* BB 144b; Nov. Ritba to Ket. 100a and *Shittah Mekubbeẓet* ad loc.; *Bedek ha-Bayit* ḤM 368: 6, commentary on the statement of Sherira Gaon). This view seems to be in conflict with the plain meaning of a number of talmudic discussions, particularly as regards the rule of *sitomta* (affixing of a mark; see below), and was not accepted by the majority of the scholars. The matter was succinctly summarized by Solomon b. Simeon Duran – after a detailed discussion of the two relevant talmudic references – as follows: "It will be seen that the doctrine of 'custom overrides *halakhah*' is true in matters of civil law, but erroneous when applied to a matter in which it has been the practice to permit something that is prohibited, for custom only has the power to prohibit something that has been permitted, and not to render permissible something that has been prohibited" (Resp. Rashbash no. 562).

Minhag as Varying the Law in Various Fields. The facility of custom to override the law in civil matters has lent Jewish law great flexibility in adapting to changing economic realities, and many rules – sometimes even entire branches of the law – have come to be based on the legal source of custom.

In the Talmudic Period. The following are some of the rules that were laid down: deeds that are not signed as required by law are valid if prepared in accordance with local custom (BB 10:1; BB 165a; Kid. 49a); debts which according to law may only be recovered from the debtor's immovable property (Ket. 51a, 69b) may also be recovered from his movable property when it is local custom to recover them in this way (TJ, Git. 5:3, 46d; in geonic times a special *takkanah* was enacted permitting the recovery of debts from the debtor's movable property since at that time most Jews had ceased to be landowners (see Execution, Civil[1]); this is an illustration of *halakhah* received first by way of custom and later by expressly enacted *takkanah*). Similarly, many illustrations of the rule that custom overrides the law are to be found in matters of the financial relationship between husband and wife (see Ket. 6:3–4; Tosef., Ket. 6:5–6; see also *Beit ha-Beḥirah,* Nov. Rashba, and *Shitah Mekubbeẓet* to Ket. 68b).

In the Post-Talmudic Period. In this period too custom actively fulfilled the far-reaching function of changing the law, this phenomenon sometimes leading to sharp dispute – even in the case of one specific matter only – and at other times accepted by all scholars in relation to an entire branch of the law. Thus, as regards the authentication of deeds (see *Shetar*[2]) – which according to law must be done by three judges and is ineffective if done by a single judge (Ket. 22a) – it was stated in the 15th century: "For the scholars of the yeshivot it is the accepted custom for deeds to be authenticated by the signature of one [judge], and this is a possible application of the doctrine that custom overrides the law in matters of the civil law" (*Terumat ha-Deshen,* Resp. no. 332). This custom was accepted by Moses Isserles (Rema ḤM 46:4), but others differed (see *Yam shel Shelomo,* BK 10:11; *Siftei Kohen* ḤM 46, n. 8). On the other hand, it is generally accepted that the extensive field of tax law is largely founded on the legal source of custom. This is due to the fact that halakhic principles stated in the Talmud in this field (including also the rule of *dina de-malkhuta dina* and the laws of partnership) were unable to offer adequate solutions to the multiple legal problem that had arisen – commencing from the tenth century onward – in this field of the law (see Taxation[3]). At first a certain hesitation was expressed concerning the extent to which it was within the power of custom to create an obligation even when it was contrary to "established and known *halakhah*" of the Talmud concerning tax law matters (see statement of Baruch of Mainz, 12th-century author of the *Sefer ha-Ḥokhmah,* quoted in *Mordekhai* BB no. 477); later, however, this hesitation gave way to full recognition of the validity of any legal rule or usage sanctioned by custom, even when it was contrary to the existing *halakhah:*

> Nowhere are the tax laws founded on talmudic sanctity and everywhere there are to be found variations of such laws deriving from local usage and the consent of earlier scholars; and the town residents are entitled to establish fixed *takkanot* and uphold recognized customs as they please, even if these are not according to *halakhah,* this being a matter of civil law. Therefore if in this matter they have an established custom, it should be followed, since custom overrides the *halakhah* in matters of this kind (Resp. Rashba, vol. 4, nos. 177, 260 and see Taxation[4] for further particulars).

The preference for flexible custom above rule of *halakhah* as regards the legal order in all public matters was emphasized by Israel Isserlein:

> In all matters affecting the public, their custom shall be followed in accordance with the order they set for themselves as dictated by their needs and the matter under consideration, for if they be required to follow the strict law in every matter, there will always be strife among themselves; furthermore, at the outset they allow each other to waive the strict law and make up their minds to follow the decree of their own custom (*Terumat ha-Deshen,* Resp. no. 342).

At the same time, the halakhic scholars made every effort to integrate the legal norm originating from custom into the pattern and spirit of the rules within the Jewish legal system, and in this regard Isserlein adds *(ibid.):*

> Even though it has been said that in tax matters custom overrides the law, it is at any rate desirable and proper to examine carefully whether we can reconcile all customs with the strict law and even if not entirely so, it is yet preferable that we find support and authority in the statements of the scholars and substantiate them with the aid of reason and legal logic *(ibid.).*

In this and in other ways – for instance by means of the control exercised by the halakhic scholars to ensure that rules originating from custom should not depart from the Jewish law principles of justice and equity – the rules of tax law, largely derived from custom, became an integral part of the Jewish legal system.

In Jewish Law in the State of Israel. The stated power of custom continues even in present times actively to assert itself in Jewish law, a fact that finds expression particularly in the decisions of the rabbinical courts in Israel. A notable example

1. page 627; 2. page 185; 3. page 167; 4. page 668.

concerns the matter of severance pay, payable to the employee on his dismissal. The rabbinical courts have sought various legal ways of conferring binding legal force on the employer's duty to pay this (see *Ha'anakah*[1]) and one of the principal ways has been reliance on the legal source of custom. Thus it was held, "since in our times there has spread this custom of paying compensation to employees . . . we have to enforce this as an obligation according to the law of the Torah, in terms of the rule stated in regard to the hire of workers: 'all in accordance with local custom' " (PDR, 1:330f); moreover, by virtue of custom the claim for severance pay "is not a matter of grace, but a claim founded on law," for which the employer, even if a charitable institution, is liable (PDR, 3:286f.). Particular importance was held to attach to custom in this case, since "we have found support for it in the Torah and *halakhah* . . . this custom being based on the Pentateuchal law of the grant payable by the master to his Hebrew bound servant" (*ha'anakat eved Ivri,* PDR, 4:129; *Yam ha-Gadol* no. 22), and as such represented "a proper and just custom" (PDR, 1:330f.; cf. *Terumat ha-Deshen,* Resp. no. 342 concerning reliance on the Pentateuchal law on tax matters).

Minhag in the Development of the Modes of Acquisition and of Establishing Obligation. In the above field – one that is particularly sensitive to changing trends in commercial life, the nature and scope of which is subject to constant fluctuation – custom was destined to exercise a decisive influence. A transaction executed in a verbal manner alone attains no legal validity in Jewish law, which provides for the transfer of ownership and establishment of an obligation in prescribed ways, generally requiring much formality, as by way of *kinyan meshikhah* or *hagbahah,* etc. ("acquisition by pulling or lifting," etc.; see Contract; Acquisition). Such formality was not in keeping with the demands of developing commerce, which called for more convenient and flexible modes of acquisition. Custom, in the form of mercantile or trade usage, was instrumental in providing a large part of the forthcoming answer to the stated demands.

As early as talmudic times (BM 74a), it was laid down that where it was the custom of the merchants for a sale of wine to be concluded by the purchaser affixing a mark (*sitomta,* Rashi ad loc. and Targ. Jon., Gen. 38:18) on the barrel of wine this action would complete the sale even though the purchaser had not yet "pulled" the barrel and it remained in the seller's possession. This is an illustration of law overridden by custom, since in law acquisition was not complete until the purchaser had "pulled" the barrel, and until then both the seller and the purchaser remained free to retract; thus, in law the barrel would still have remained in the ownership of the seller but custom decreed that ownership of the chattel would pass to the purchaser after it was marked in the customary manner and after this the parties might no longer retract. From this *halakhah* Solomon b. Abraham Adret concluded: "From this we learn that custom overrides the law in all matters of the civil law, in which everything is acquired and transferred in accordance with custom; hence the merchants effect *kinyan* in any mode according with their own usage" (Nov. Rashba BM 73b; see also *Nimmukei Yosef* BM, loc. cit.; *Maggid Mishneh* Mekhirah 7:6; *Sma* ḤM 201, n. 2). In the course of time and on the basis of this principle, Jewish law came to recognize new modes of acquisition and of establishing obligation. Thus the fact that it was the trade custom to conclude a transaction by shaking hands, by making an advance on the purchase price (*Piskei ha-Rosh,* BM 5:72), or by delivering a key to the place where the goods were stored was held to be sufficient to confer full legal validity on a transaction concluded in any of these ways (Sh. Ar., ḤM 201:2).

1. page 317; 2. page 247.

The extent of the creative power of custom in relation to the modes of acquisition has been the subject of much discussion founded on halakhic and economic considerations. R. Joel Sirkes held that custom served to create new modes of acquisition in respect of transactions of movables only, "as there is much trade in these and he [the purchaser] has not the time to pull all the goods into his possession" (*Baḥ* ḤM 201:2), but the majority of scholars took the view that custom also served to do so as regards various transactions of immovable property (*Yam shel Shelomo,* BK 5:36; *Sma* ḤM 201, n. 6; *Siftei Kohen* thereto, n. 1). Similarly, many scholars held that custom served to lend full legal validity to an acquisition of something not yet in existence (see Acquisition, Modes of; Contract; Resp. Rosh 13:20; other scholars differed – see *Keẓot ha-Ḥoshen* 201, n. 1; *Netivot ha-Mishpat, Mishpat ha-Urim,* 201, n. 1). At times custom operated with such far-reaching effect that not only were new modes of acquisition added to those halakhically recognized but even certain substantive elements of the existing acquisitory modes as determined by the halakhic scholars were changed (see, e.g., Resp. Ribash no. 345 on the custom concerning acquisition incidental to four cubits of land (*kinyan aggav arba ammot karka*), without specification of the land, contrary to the opinion of Maimonides, when locally the latter's statement of the law was otherwise followed; similarly, in Resp. Rosh 79:4).

In the 13th century a question of principle arose whose answer was to be of great significance as regards the measure of the creative power attaching to custom in general. The fundamental idea underlying the need in Jewish law for acquisitory formalities in the formation of legal transaction is that in such a manner the parties demonstrate their absolute *gemirut ha-da'at* ("making up of their minds") to close the transaction (see Contract[2]). The modes of acquisition that came to be decreed by custom also served to demonstrate such *gemirut ha-da'at,* since these represented accepted trade customs; however, the question arose whether local custom to close a transaction in a verbal manner alone was capable, from the standpoint of Jewish law, of conferring full legal validity on such transaction. Asher b. Jehiel took the view that no affirmative conclusion could be drawn from the rule of *sitomta* (see above), except with regard to the validity of a custom requiring the performance of some act such as those mentioned above (handshake, etc.), "but never by mere speech alone, and even when this is the practice it is a bad custom which is not to be followed" (Resp. Rosh 12:3). This view denied custom the power of contraverting the basic requirement of Jewish law for the performance of some act indicating the absolute *gemirut ha-da'at;* a custom of this kind was therefore not proper except when it served only to change the substance of the act, but when it was aimed at eliminating the need for any act at all it was a "bad custom" from which the scholars would withhold validity (see below).

Another view was that whenever custom decreed mere speech alone as sufficient for the conclusion of a legal transaction it had to be assumed that absolute *gemirut ha-da'at* would come about in such a way too (opinion of Meir of Rothenburg and of R. Jehiel, quoted in *Mordekhai,* Shab. nos. 472–3), and this was the opinion accepted by the majority of the *posekim.* Thus it was decided that a person who had promised his neighbor to be the *ba'al berit* (*sandek;* i.e., the person who holds the baby) at a circumcision ceremony was not free to retract from such an undertaking and assign it to another "since it has long been the practice among all Israelites for the privilege of performing such a *mitzvah* to be conferred in mere verbal manner and it is already established that custom is an important tenet in all matters of this kind" (Resp. Radbaz no. 278). This is also the position as regards the formation of partnership. According to talmudic law a partnership is formed by performance on the part of each partner of an act of acquisition in relation to the share of the other partners (Ket. 10:4; Yad, Sheluḥin 4:1; and see Partnership). However, it was held that "where it is local custom to become a partner even by speech alone – there will be a partnership; such is the custom in this country too . . . and so we decide in every case, for custom is an important matter in the field of the civil law" (Resp. Radbaz no.380). This opinion came to be accepted as *halakhah* by the later *posekim*, "reason inclines to the view that whenever it is the custom to rely on speech alone, it is like the custom of *sitomta*" (*Kesef ha-Kedoshim* ḤM 201:1), in terms of which full recognition according to Jewish law was given to public sales (*Mishpat u-Ẓedakah be-Ya'akov*, no. 33), to sales on the exchanges (Resp. Maharsham, pt. 3, no. 18), and to like legal transactions customarily concluded in mere verbal manner (see *Ohel Moshe* pt. 2, no. 138).

In cases before the rabbinical courts in the State of Israel reliance on custom (see above) is particularly evident in the field of the modes of *kinyan*. In several cases acquisition by way of registration in the registry in accordance with the state law is recognized as a valid *kinyan* according to Jewish law, by the force of custom (see, e.g., PDR 4:81). In another leading decision it was laid down that "in our times a signed contract between purchaser and seller constitutes a *kinyan* by virtue of the rule of *sitomta*, whether relating to immovable or to movable property, since this is a trade custom" (PDR 6:216, and see also the distinction drawn with regard to the text of the contract).

The Rule of Minhag Mevattel Halakhah – in the Case of Local Custom. Custom overrides the law even when it is not general but customary with part of the public only. Thus in talmudic law it is laid down that when a desert caravan is attacked by robbers who demand a price for the release of the travelers, each must pay according to the amount of the property he carries and not on a per capita basis; in the case where a guide is taken to avert danger to life, payment of the guide is made according to a calculation based both on the amount of property carried by each and per capita; however, "the custom of caravan travelers must not be departed from" (i.e., if the custom decrees that the participation always be according to property and not per capita, it must be followed, Tosef., BM 7:13–14; see also BK 116b; TJ, BM 6:4, 11a). Similarly, it is laid down that "a shippers' custom [*minhag sappanin*] must not be departed from" in the case where cargo has to be jettisoned to lighten the load (Tosef., loc. cit.). Hence it follows that a local custom or trade usage overrides the *halakhah* for the people governed by such custom: "In matters of the civil law custom is followed, even the custom of ass drivers and shippers, for even if the strict law requires that participation must be according to money and the load carried, nevertheless the custom of ass drivers and of shippers overrides the law" (Resp. Maharik, no. 102).

Proof of the Existence of a Custom. Jewish law sets three requirements for the validity of a custom:

(1) It must be widespread over the whole country, or in the whole of a particular locality, or amidst the whole of a particular class of people, according to its purported field of operation: "In all such matters [of the financial relationship between spouses] custom is an important tenet and must be followed in deciding the law, provided, however, that the custom be widespread *(pashut)* over the whole country" (Yad, Ishut 23:12 and cf. with the matter of *takkanah*, *ibid.* 16:7–9). A custom which exists in most parts of a particular district must be presumed to exist in the whole of such a district (Resp. Rosh 79:4; *Beit Yosef* ḤM 42:21).

(2) A custom must be of frequent application: "It must be known that the custom is established and widespread, that the townspeople have followed it at least three times, for often the public adopt for themselves a practice to suit their immediate needs [i.e., in regard to a particular matter only] without intending to establish a custom at all" (*Terumat ha-Deshen*, Resp. no. 342; Resp. Maharashdam, ḤM no. 436). The time required for the evolution of a custom depends on the nature of the matter in each case: "This matter [whether or not there was a custom to exempt the communal cantor from tax payment] is not like a custom relating to the hire of workers, which happens every day so that everyone can see what the custom is; but as regards the cantor's tax immunity, since there is only one cantor in the town, how shall the fact that tax was not demanded from one or two cantors be called a custom unless it be public knowledge in the town that cantors had been exempted there on account of local custom to exempt them" (Resp. Ribash no. 475).

(3) The custom must be clear: "The custom must be clearly to exempt" (Resp. Ribash, loc. cit.). In another matter Samuel b. Moses Medina held that the rule of custom overrides *halakhah* was applicable to that case, provided only that the instant custom was sufficiently clear, "there are two approaches to this matter: one according to the law of our holy Torah, the other according to the trade custom; for there is no doubt that in such matters custom is decisive, provided that the import of the custom be clear, but if there be any doubt about this then we have to revert to what is decreed by the law of the Torah" (Resp. Maharashdam, ḤM no. 33).

Jewish law dispenses with the formality of the laws of evidence for purposes of proving the establishment of a custom – a fact that has provided custom with wide creative opportunity. Thus hearsay evidence suffices and the testimony of normally disqualified witnesses is admitted (*Terumat ha-Deshen*, Resp. no. 342). The wide latitude which Jewish law allows to the creative power of custom is evidenced in a decision given by the rabbinical court in the State of Israel concerning the matter of severance pay due to an employee upon his dismissal (see above). In 1945 R. Ouziel (in a responsum quoted in M. Findling, *Teḥukat ha-Avodah*, p. 133f.) refrained from basing the law of severance pay on the legal source of custom (relying instead on an ethical-halakhic principle: see *Ha'anakah*[1]), for the reasons that a custom had no validity unless it was widespread, of frequent application, and clear: "and as far as I am aware this custom [of severance pay] is not widespread in the whole country nor of common application, but only followed in certain specific cases, and therefore the court is not ordering severance pay to be paid in terms thereof" *(ibid.)*. A mere ten years later the rabbinical court – seeking a full legal justification for the obligation of severance pay – held: "Now that this custom has spread and become accepted in the whole country, and is popular and of common, daily application, it must be followed and the statements mentioned above (i.e., of R. Ouziel), made in the year 1945, are no longer applicable or valid because the custom has become widespread and established." Recognition of such an accelerated spread of a custom within the short period of ten years is indicative of the special readiness of Jewish law to enrich itself by means of the legal source of custom.

Custom (Minhag) and Usage (Nohag). The customs so far discussed belong mainly to those in the category of a legal norm functioning of its own power and independently of the consent of the parties to a particular transaction. Thus, for instance, the validity of a mode of acquisition sanctioned by custom is not to be explained on the ground that the parties to a particular transaction intended, by implication, to confer legal validity thereon – since it is beyond the authority of the parties to pass on the

1. page 317.

validity of a *kinyan* even if they should expressly say so. In this case the new mode of acquisition draws its validity from the efficacy of custom to create new legal norms of selfstanding force. On the other hand, many customs operate in the *halakhah* – as in other legal systems – not from their own independent force but by virtue of a presumption that the parties intended, by implication, to introduce a particular usage as part of the transaction between themselves. An agreement between two parties is generally composed of two kinds of terms, those expressly stipulated and those imported by implication as an integral part of the agreement. Such implied terms may be inferred in two ways: either because they are judged logical and reasonable factors, or because they are usual and customary, since it may be presumed that the parties intended to include in the terms of their agreement the dictates of all the former factors (see J. Salmond, *Jurisprudence* (1966[12]), 193–7). The matter may be illustrated as follows: The Mishnah (BM 9:1) lays down that a transaction of *arisut* or *ḥakhirah* (land tenancy and cultivation in return for a share of the crop, see Lease and Hire) includes implied terms concerning cultivation of the land in accordance with local usage – *keminhag ha-medinah* – and that neither party to the transaction may contend, for instance, that he intended the crop to be reaped by scythe when it was local custom to reap by hand (BM 9:1). The Talmud adds that a party's plea that he had not intended to abide by local custom will not be accepted even if it is supported by circumstantial evidence, such as higher or lower rental than usual (see BM 103b), because in the absence of any express stipulation to the contrary it will be presumed that both parties intended to embrace local custom in their agreement (see also Yad, Sekhirut 8:6; Sh. Ar., ḤM 320:4–5). Talmudic *halakhah* offers abundant examples, in most branches of the civil law, of usages which are imported by implication as part of the terms agreed upon between the parties to a transaction, e.g., in the laws of joint ownership (BB 1:1 and 4a; TJ, BB 1:2, 12d) and partnership (BM 68b; 69b; Tosef., BM 5:6–7; TJ, BM 5:6, 10b; see also Yad, Sheluḥin 5:1 and 8:4; and see Partnership); in the laws of pledge (e.g., BM 67b–68a; Yad, Malveh 7:2–3); in the laws of master and servant (BM 7:1:BM 83a concerning the hours of work; 86a concerning the worker's sustenance; 87a concerning the worker's wages; and see Labor Law); in the laws concerning the pecuniary relationship between spouses (see above; see also Husband and Wife), etc. Usages of the above kind also fulfill an important role as regards the interpretation of various deeds and documents, in which local usage in the particular matter is of decisive importance (BB 166b; Yad, Malveh 27:15; and see Interpretation[1]).

The Rule of Doreshin Leshon Hedyot. This rule (Tosef., Ket. 4:9ff.; TJ, Ket. 4:8, 28d, TJ, Yev. 15:3, 14d; BM 104a) is of application in the interpretation of documents (for details, see Interpretation[2]). Many halakhic scholars regarded this rule as serving to give recognition to the implicit importation into the terms of a document of a usage followed by the people, on the presumption that the parties intended their transaction to be subject to such usage: "For whatever is customarily written by the people is deemed to have been written by the parties, even if they have not done so . . . and this is as if provided by an enactment" (*tenai bet din;* Resp. Rashba vol. 1, no. 662; vol. 3, nos. 17, 433, et al.; this is also the view of Hai Gaon and Ramban, in Nov. Ramban, Tos., *Beit ha-Beḥirah,* Nov. Ritba and *Shitah Mekubbeẓet* BM 104a; Resp. Ran no. 54; Resp. Ritba no. 53). Just as scholars saw the need in matters of marriage and *ketubbah* to enact essential conditions for the good of all, these being applicable, *setaman ke-furshan,* i.e., binding even if not expressly stipulated between the parties – so there are matters "which the scholars did not enact and which have not been accepted by all, but are usages which have been followed by the people in certain places, simply of their own accord without [communal] enactment, and this too is a matter of *setaman ke-ferushan,* which the scholars refer to as *derishat hedyotot*" (Resp. Rashba, vol. 4, no. 186). In this sense the rule of *derishat leshon hedyot* served the halakhic scholars as a means of solving many legal problems relating to the laws of marriage, property, and obligations (see Resp. Rashba, Ritba and Ran as cited above; for an interesting example in the field of obligations see Resp. Rashba, vol. 4, no. 125).

General and Local Custom. A general custom is created at the hands of the public as a whole and as such applies to the whole of that public, whereas a local custom is created at the hands of the people of a certain place, class, or some other group, and as such its application and validity is confined to the people of that place or group. Already mentioned above are the customs of various trade associations like those of shipper and caravan drivers, and the talmudic sources also mention customs relating to priests (Kid. 78b; TJ, Bik. 1:5, 64a and Kid. 4:6, 66b), women (Pes. 48b; TJ, Pes. 4:1, 30c), *ḥavurot* in Jerusalem (Tosef., 4:15; TJ, Meg. 4:10, 75c), the fair-minded *(nekiyyei ha-da'at)* of Jerusalem (Sanh. 30a), etc. Often a custom is referred to as *minhag ha-medinah* (i.e., custom of a particular area or district: BM 7:1 and 9:1; BB 1:1 and 10:1; Suk. 3:11, et al.). Sometimes a custom is quoted as followed in Judea (Ket.; 1:5 and 4:12; Tosef. Ket. 1:4, BB 100b, et al.) in Galilee (Tosef. and Mishnah, *ibid.*), or in particular settlements, e.g., Tiberias, Acre, Kabul, (TJ, Pes. 4:1, 30d, TJ, Ta'an. 1:6, 64c), also Jabneh, Sepphoris, etc. Such local or group customs relate to diverse fields of the *halakhah,* both the civil and the ritual law.

Many local customs render the law more severe by prohibiting matters which are permitted (see e.g., Pes. 4:1–4). Thus although the law permitted the performance of all labor on the 14th day of Nisan – i.e., on the eve of Passover – it became the general custom to refrain from labor from noon onward, since from that time the paschal sacrifice could properly be brought, so that the rest of the day was treated as a festival day; the Mishnah records that there were places where it was customary to perform labor until noon, and other places where it was customary not to do so lest the need for burning the leaven and other requirements of the festival be forgotten, and the Mishnah prescribes that the local inhabitants should follow their own custom. The halakhic validity of a custom that prohibited what was legally permissible was justified by regarding this as a form of vow undertaken by the public, and the sanction against breaking such a custom as akin to that of the prohibition against breaking a vow: "Matters which are permitted [in law] but prohibited by others by virtue of their custom may not be rendered permissible to the latter, as it is said (Num. 30:3), 'he shall not break his word' " (Ned. 15a; see also Ḥ. Albeck, *Shishah Sidrei Mishnah,* Nashim, p. 137f.). It seems however that the Babylonian *amoraim* restricted the operation of the prohibition deriving from the above rule, holding it as applicable only to a custom of the Cuthites (non-Jews), or of Jews amidst whom there were no scholars – out of apprehension that if the latter persons were permitted matters which their own custom prohibited, even though these were permissible in law, they would make light also of other prohibitions stemming from the law itself (Pes. 50b–51a).

These local customs were also discussed in relation to the biblical injunction, "you shall not cut yourselves" (Deut. 14:1), interpreted by the halakhic scholars as a stringent prohibition against the formation of separate "societies" in relation to the rules of *halakhah* so that the Torah "should not become like several Torot." In R. Johanan's opinion this prohibition only

1. page 68; 2. page 68.

applied in circumstances where in one place a decision is given according to one opinion – for instance according to Bet Hillel, and in another place according to another opinion – for instance according to Bet Shammai, for in this way the *halakhah* itself would be divided; however, if from the standpoint of the law all decide according to the same opinion but part of the public renders the law additionally stringent for itself, this does not amount to a division of the *halakhah,* and it is permissible in the same way as any individual may take a vow and render prohibited for himself that which is permissible in law (TJ, Pes. 4:1, 30d; Yev. 13b; see also L. Ginzberg, *Perushim ve-Ḥiddushim ba-Yerushalmi,* 1 (1941), 152–60). Despite this theoretical distinction, the halakhic scholars maintained that in practice the diversity of customs might lead to division and strife and therefore laid down that a person should follow no custom but that of the place where he finds himself at any given time, if to do otherwise might lead to dispute (pes. 4:1 and 51a; Yad, Yom Tov, 8:20; see also in detail *Peri Ḥadash,* OḤ 468 and 496).

Minhag and the Conflict of Laws (within Jewish Law). The multiplicity of customs, particularly local customs, inevitably gave rise to the phenomenon of varying laws on the same legal subject. At times it transpired that the law on the same subject differed in different places, and in this event – when the different stages of a legal obligation required performance in different places, in each of which there prevailed a different law concerning such an obligation – there arose the question of whether to apply the customary law at the time and place of establishment of the obligation, or the customary law at the time and place of its performance, or some other law. This and like questions, relating to the field of the conflict of laws, frequently arose in many fields of Jewish law against the background of differing customs on the same subject: e.g., as regards the laws of marriage, divorce, labor, partnership, and land tenancy. The result was the evolution of a proliferous body of case law on the subject of the conflict of laws, constituting one of the important contributions made by custom to the development and creativity of Jewish law.

Control over Minhag by the Halakhic Scholars. Custom, because of its spontaneous and undirected nature, sometimes calls for a measure of supervision and control. At times a custom may be founded on error, or develop unreasonably or illogically in a certain direction, or may even be in conflict with substantive and fundamental principles of Jewish law in a manner leaving no room for its integration into this system. From time to time the halakhic scholars exercised such control in order to contain or discredit entirely a particular custom.

Custom Founded on Error. The Mishnah (Er. 10:10) mentions the case of a certain usage observed in Tiberias until the scholars came and set it aside; according to one opinion the usage of the people of Tiberias involved a prohibition which the scholars later permitted; according to another opinion, it involved a permission which the scholars later forbade *(ibid.).* Some commentators held that the usage was set aside because it was based on error (Tos. to Eruv. 101b, s.v. *R. Yose omer";* for a further illustration, see Ḥul. 6b concerning Rabbi's permissiveness regarding the eating of untithed fruit from Beth-Shean). In the Jerusalem Talmud a rule is laid down by R. Abun that a custom founded on error may be set aside: if the custom prohibits when it is clearly known that the relevant matter is permitted in law, the custom is valid and the matter must not be rendered permissible; however, if the custom prohibits as an outcome of an erroneous belief that the relevant matter is prohibited in law, when the error is discovered, the matter may be rendered permissible and the custom discredited (TJ, Pes. 4:1, 30d).

In post-talmudic literature frequent reference is made to customs discredited by the halakhic scholars on the ground of error. Thus Rabbenu Tam censured those who counted a minor as helping to make up a *minyan* as long as he held a Pentateuch in his hand: "This is a nonsensical custom . . . is a Pentateuchal to be regarded as a man?" (Tos to Ber. 48a). In another case Asher b. Jehiel examined the source of a custom concerning the testamentary disposition of property by a woman, concluding that "this is certainly an erroneous custom" and even if widespread, "it is not a custom that may properly be relied upon for purposes of the disposition of property . . . the custom is wrong and it must be invalidated" (Resp. Rosh 55:10). Similarly Mordecai Jaffe opposed the custom of not reciting *birkat ha-mazon* (Grace after Meals) in the home of a gentile, holding that the spread of "this nonsensical custom" originated from an erroneous understanding of a talmudic statement completely unconnected with such a custom (*Levush ha-Tekhelet,* 193:6). In another instance it became customary to take a stringent view and regard a woman as married in circumstances where – in the opinion of all scholars – there was no *kiddushin* at all in law; Simeon Duran strongly condemned this custom: "In circumstances where the whole world holds that there is no *kiddushin,* some people wish to impose on themselves such a stringent rendering of the law – this is a custom born in ignorance which the public must not be compelled to uphold" (*Tashbeẓ,* 1:154).

Unreasonable or Illogical Custom. At times the scholars examined a custom from the aspect of its reasonableness. Thus it was determined that a custom of the women not to do any work during the whole of the evening following the Sabbath was unreasonable and of no validity except insofar as it was restricted to the time of prayer on that evening (TJ, Pes. 4:1, 30d; Ta'an. 1:6, 64c); similarly invalid was a custom of the women not to do any work on Mondays and Thursdays, but their custom to do no work on a public fast-day or on Rosh Ḥodesh was reasonable and proper *(ibid.).* Some customs were condemned as imposing hardship on the public and contrary to the purpose of the actual law concerned. Thus the custom of those who prepared grits in Sepphoris and of the crushers of wheat in Acre not to work on *ḥol ha-mo'ed* was held to be a good custom since it was not likely to detract from the joy of the festival; however, the custom of the fishermen of Tiberias not to work on *ḥol ha-mo'ed* was opposed by the scholars, since it was impossible to prepare in advance fresh fish for the whole festival, and the custom was therefore likely to detract from the joy of the festival (TJ, *ibid.*).

Bad Custom. In post-talmudic times there was disputed the question of the extent to which a custom concerning a matter of civil law had to be accepted even when it appeared to be a "bad custom." On the dispute over a custom concerning the erection of a partition between two joint holders so that one might not observe the other (see below), Rabbenu Tam held that a custom of erecting a partition which fell short of the talmudic requirements was a bad custom and was not to be followed: "it may be concluded that some customs are not to be relied upon, even though it has been said, 'all in accordance with custom' " (Tos. to BB 2a). This opinion was followed by many scholars but others held that in civil law matters even a custom of this kind had to be followed when locally accepted (see *Piskei ha-Rosh* BB 1:1 and 5; Tur, ḤM 157:3–4, 16; Sh. Ar., ḤM 157:1 and commentaries; *Haggahot Maimuniyyot,* Shekhenim 2:20; *Mordekhai,* BM no. 366). Even those who took the former view conceded that in certain matters even a bad custom had to be followed – for instance in tax matters – if it was necessary for the good order of the public (*Terumat ha-Deshen,* Resp. no. 342; Sh. Ar., ḤM 163:3, Rema and commentaries).

Custom Contrary to Fundamental Rules and the Principles of Equity and Justice. The halakhic scholars were also at pains to ensure that custom did not contravert basic general rules as well as the principles of equity and justice in Jewish law. In so doing they rendered possible the integration of legal norms originating from custom into the general framework of the law, in the same way as their similar close control over communal enactments (see *Takkanot ha-Kahal*[1]) rendered possible their integration. The matter is illustrated by the following examples:

(1) When Asher b. Jehiel decided that the custom of closing a transaction by verbal agreement alone contraverted the basic rule requiring demonstration of the absolute *gemirut ha-da'at* of the parties to a transaction, he laid down that this amounted to a bad custom which was not to be followed (see above).

(2) In law, on division of a courtyard between joint owners, "a partition must be built by both of them in the middle, so that neither may observe his neighbor in the enjoyment of his portions, since the injury of being observed is a real injury" (Yad, Shekhenim 2:14, based on BB 3a); the width of the partition is determined by local custom "even when the custom is to build the partition of reeds and palm fronds" (BB 4a; Yad, Shekhenim 2:15). In this regard, Rashba decided that a custom not to erect any partition at all – leaving each neighbor free to observe the other – was of no legal validity, so that either partner could oblige the other to erect the partition: "If it has been the custom, as regards houses and courtyards, not to pay heed at all to the injury of observing one's neighbor, the custom is a bad one and no custom at all; for waiver may only be made in matters of civil law in which event a person may give of his own or tolerate damage to his property, but he is not free to breach the fences of Israel and to act immodestly in a manner causing the Divine Presence [*Shekhinah*] to depart from this people, as it is said, 'a person shall not make his windows to open onto his joint owner's courtyard' (BB 3:7) . . . Scripture relates, 'And Balaam lifted up his eyes, and he saw Israel abiding in his tents according to their tribes' (Num. 24:2). What did he see? That the openings to their tents were not made to face each other, and he said, 'These are worthy that the Divine Presence abide with them' " (BB 60a; Resp. Rashba, vol. 2, no. 268). Thus the custom in question stood in conflict with what must be considered a material feature of the *halakhah* and therefore could be given no legal recognition.

(3) A custom may not conflict with the Jewish law principles of justice and equity. Hence even in cases where a bad custom is given legal recognition, as in tax matters (see above), some way must be found for anchoring it within the general spirit of the *halakhah*. Hence a tax custom which did not adequately distinguish between rich and poor was held to have no legal validity: "The contention of the rich has no justification, for certainly according to the law of the Torah taxes must be shared according to financial means and there can be no greater injustice than to make the rich and the poor bear the tax burden in virtually equal measure, and even if the custom has been in existence for some years it must not be upheld" (Moses Rothenburg, quoted in *Pithei Teshuvah*, ḤM 163, n. 16).

Bibliography: S. Eisenstadt, *Ein Mishpat* (1931), 45–49; M. Higger, *Massekhet Soferim* (1937), 270–1; Weiss, Dor, index s.v. *Minhag;* Guedemann, Gesch Erz, index s.v.; Urbach, in: *Tarbiz*, 27 (1957/58), 169; B. De Vries, *Toledot ha-Halakhah ha-Talmudit* (1966[2]), 157–68; Dinary, in: *Benjamin De Vries Memorial Volume* (1968), 168–98; *Nahalat Shivah* no. 27, notes 6–16; S.A. Horodezky, in: *Ha-Shilo'ah*, 6(1899), 417–20; Weiss, Dor, 2 (1904[4]), 62–65; Ha-Toseftai, in: *Ha-Shilo'ah*, 25 (1911), 600–8; A. Perls, in: *Festschrift . . . Israel Lewy* (1911), 66–75; J. Unna, in: *Jeschurun*, 10 (1923), 463–78; J. Carlebach, *ibid.*, 14 (1927), 329–51; Ch. Tchernowitz, *Toledot ha-Halakhah*, 1 pt. 1 (1934), 144–50; A. Guttmann, in: MGWJ, 83 (1939, repr. 1963), 226–38; J.L. Fischmann, in: *Sefer ha-Yovel . . . B.M. Lewin* (1939), 132–59; M. Vogelmann, in: *Ha-Zikkaron . . . le-ha-Rav . . . Cook* (1945), 366–77; Z.H. Chajes, *Darkhei ha-Hora'ah*, in his collected works: *Kol Sifrei Mahariz Hayyot*, 1 (1958), 207–80; T.Z. Kahana, in: *Mazkeret Kovez Torani . . . la-Rav Herzog* (1962), 554–64; M. Havatzelet, in: *Sinai*, 54 (1963/64), 155–63; idem, in: *Talpioth*, 9 (1964), 261–76; B.Z. Katz, *Mi-Zekenim Etbonen* (1964); Elon, Mafte'ah, 131f., 418–24; idem, in: ILR, 2 (1967), 547f.; idem, *Ha Mishpat Ha-Ivri*, II(1973), 713–767.

Menachem Elon

MA'ASEH (Heb. מעשה ; case) **AND PRECEDENT**; the factual circumstances from which a halakhic rule or principle is derived; as such it constitutes one of the legal sources of Jewish law. A legal principle originating from *ma'aseh* is formally distinguished from those originating from one of the other legal sources of Jewish law – such as Midrash (see Interpretation), *takkanah*, *minhag*, and *severah* (see Introduction[2]) – by the fact that in the latter cases the legal principle appears in selfstanding form, whereas in *Ma'aseh* it is integrated with and bound to a particular set of concrete facts, from which it must be separated and abstracted if it is to be enunciated. As will be seen below, this formal distinction is also of substantive importance. The term *ma'aseh* is customarily used in tannaitic sources (Shab. 24:5; BB 10:8; Eduy. 2:3); in the Babylonian Talmud the equivalent term is *uvda* and in the Jerusalem Talmud sometimes *dilma* (see, e.g., TJ, Ber. 1:1, 2c, Pe'ah 3:9, 17d; et al.).

Substance of Ma'aseh. Ma'aseh constitutes a legal source in two ways: one is represented by the judgment given in a concrete "case" before the court or competent adjudicator (halakhic scholar) – as in other legal systems; the other, by the specific act or conduct of a competent halakhic scholar, not necessarily in his capacity as judge or *posek*. In either case *ma'aseh* serves as a source for the determination of a halakhic principle as regards both civil law *(dinei mamonot)* and ritual law *(dinei issur ve-hetter)*.

Citation of a halakhic principle by way of *ma'aseh* does not in every case warrant the conclusion that such *ma'aseh* is necessarily the source from which the principle was evolved – since the principle may possibly have been in existence before and the halakhic scholar only have applied it in such case. In this event, the *ma'aseh* is not constitutive but only declarative of the existence of the particular halakhic rule (see below). However, *ma'aseh* – even when only declarative – lends the particular halakhic principle a special validity, as *ma'aseh rav* ("an act is weightier," Shab. 21a) or *ma'aseh adif* ("an act is preferred," BB 83a), since a rule tested in the crucible of practical life is regarded by the scholars as having a different force from one for which there is no evidence of its practical application. Hence, once a particular halakhic principle has been followed in practice – even though its application is subject to dispute – it may no longer be varied, since "what has been done is no longer open to discussion" (RH 29b, concerning blowing of the *shofar* on Rosh Ha-Shanah when it falls on a Sabbath).

The particular force of a halakhic principle originating from *ma'aseh* is tied to the substantive principle underlying the entire halakhic system, namely that the Torah was entrusted to the authority *(al da'atan)* of the halakhic scholars (see Authority, Rabbinical; Introduction[3]), it being presumed that the judicial decision and conduct in daily life of the competent halakhic scholar are the outcome of his penetration and correct under-

1. page 659; 2. page 14; 3. page 14.

standing of the *halakhah*. The scholars were fully aware of the power attaching to an act of deciding the law and for this reason exercised great care before doing so (Git. 19a, 37a, and Rashi thereto). In particular, the halakhic scholar is held to reveal, by his conduct, the active image of the *halakhah* and therefore "the service of the Torah is greater than the study of it" (Ber. 7b); one of the ways by virtue of which the Torah is acquired is "attendance on the sages" (Avot 6:6), since practical application of the Torah leads to appreciation of the living and active *halakhah*, its correctness and creative force. For this reason it was required of the halakhic scholars to act with much forethought in their day-to-day conduct of halakhic matters (Tosef., Dem. 5:24 concerning the discussion between R. Gamaliel and R. Akiva); R. Ishmael explained his particularly careful approach toward a certain rule concerning the *Keri'at Shema* in these words: "lest the pupils see and lay down *halakhah* for generations" (Ber. 11a; Tosef., Ber. 1:6).

In Jewish law, *ma'aseh* constitutes a legal source, not because it has the force of binding precedent which (as will be seen below, the Jewish legal system generally does not recognize as a principle), but because the scholars recognized it as a lawmaking source from which to derive halakhic principles becoming part of the general halakhic system. The fact that it remained permissible to dispute a halakhic principle derived from *ma'aseh* did not serve to deprive it of its substantive character as one of the legal sources of Jewish law – just as, for instance, Midrash remained such notwithstanding the fact that different and contradictory halakhic principles were often derived from it by the use of different methods of Bible exegesis.

An Act of Deciding the Law. The laws derived from *ma'aseh* form a very substantial part of the general system of Jewish law – the latter representing, in its nature and path of development, a classic example of a legal system founded on a series of legal acts or "cases," adding up to a comprehensive system of case law (see also Codification of Law[1]). This character was already stamped on the *halakhah* in the Torah, in which there are many laws enjoined in consequence of a particular act or event, as, for instance, in the matter of the blasphemy of the Name (Lev. 24:10–23), the gathering of sticks on the Sabbath (Num. 15:32–36), the law of inheritance concerning the daughters of Zelophehad (Num. 27:1–11), and the law of the second Passover (Num. 9: 6–14).

Talmudic sources are replete with *halakhot*, in all fields of the law, quoted in the form of an act of legal decision or in the form of an independent ruling which is, however, either preceded or followed by the facts of the relevant case. The case described does not always form the original source of the halakhic rule, but frequently, and in various ways, it is possible to prove that the rule was actually created as an outcome of the case. Sometimes this fact is expressly stated. Thus, with reference to the law that a bill of divorce must be prepared by the husband for delivery to his wife, the Mishnah states that it suffices if the bill be prepared by the wife provided that the husband procures the signature of witnesses to it since what matters is the signature and not the person by whom the bill is drawn up (Git. 2:5). This principle was learned from a case that occurred in a small village near Jerusalem, a case in which the scholars decided that it was only necessary for a bond of indebtedness to be signed, and not drawn up, by the witnesses (Eduy. 2:3). Similarly, the *amoraim* derived from earlier cases a number of halakhic principles concerning the laws of proselytization (Yev. 46b) and the laws of restoring a loss *hashavat avedah:* cf. BM 25b with TJ, BM 2:4, 8c – the rule of Abba b. Zavda).

Sometimes derivation of a halakhic principle from the *ma'aseh* is not expressly acknowledged, but from the content it may be deduced that the principle was derived from the adjacent case description. Thus, according to ancient *halakhah*, suretyship for a loan undertaking was valid only if made prior to establishment of the principal debt, i.e., the creditor as it were agreeing to grant the loan on the strength of such suretyship. However, R. Ishmael, in a case that came before him, extended the scope of suretyship by holding it valid in certain circumstances, even if made after grant of the loan, i.e., if the person standing surety signed after signature by the witnesses of the deed of loan. Ben Nanas differed, maintaining that the suretyship had to precede grant of the loan. The new principle enunciated by R. Ishmael is earlier stated in the Mishnah, in the form of a selfstanding legal rule (BB 10:8; for further examples, see Ned. 9:5; BM 30a).

Conduct of a Halakhic Scholar. Talmudic sources also contain a great number of *halakhot*, in all fields of the law, stated in the form of a description of the conduct of a halakhic scholar and in like manner to the statement of acts of legal decision. Thus in one instance the Mishnah (Shab. 24:5) first quotes several *halakhot* concerning permissible labors on the Sabbath in the form of independent rules: "they may stop up a light-hole or measure a piece of stuff or a *mikveh*"; in continuation, it is stated that in the time of R. Zadok's father and in the time of Abba Saul b. Botnit there occurred a case in which such labors were done on the Sabbath and in conclusion it is stated that from such occurrence the permissibility of these labors on the Sabbath was learned. An analysis of the *halakhot* thus stated offers proof that even when the selfstanding halakhic ruling is stated in the Mishnah before the *ma'aseh*, it does not exclude the possibility that chronologically speaking the *ma'aseh* preceded such a ruling and that the former is the source of the latter – except that the compiler of the Mishnah saw fit to state first the ruling and then the *ma'aseh*. At times disputes concerning a tradition entertained by the halakhic scholars and relating to the conduct of a particular halakhic scholar led in turn to disputing opinions as regards the halakhic principle to be derived from the aforesaid conduct (see, e.g., Suk. 2:7 concerning the dispute between Bet Shammai and Bet Hillel, arising in connection with the *ma'aseh* of R. Johanan b. ha-Ḥorani).

Distinguishing Ma'aseh. Just as a halakhic principle acquires special force and significance from the fact that it has been applied in a practical case, so the latter fact entails the risk of possible error in the manner of deduction of the principle from the practical case. Hence, in deduction of the principle it is required that two important distinctions be made: first, the factual aspect of the case must be precisely distinguished from the legal aspect; secondly – and more difficult – the part that is not material and has no bearing on the halakhic conclusion must be distinguished from the material part which leads to the halakhic conclusion. This distinguishing process is sometimes directed toward a specific purpose, for instance toward restriction of the halakhic principle derived from a case when the need for it arises in a concrete matter for decision. In English law – which has the system of case law – the process of distinguishing is also greatly developed, and here too one of the main functions of the process is to distinguish between the *ratio decidendi* and mere *obiter dictum*. The distinguishing process has been of primary importance to the development of both legal systems.

The phrase commonly employed in the Mishnah for the act of distinguishing is *einah hi ha-middah*, "that is not the inference" (Pes. 1:6–7), and in the Talmud, "This was not stated explicitly but by implication" (BM 36a, et al.; see also BB 130b and Rashbam thereto s.v. *halakhah adifah*), or "Tell me what actually transpired!" (BM 70a, et al.). The process of distinguishing is well illustrated in Bava Meẓia 36a. Rav is quoted as holding

1. pages 124, 130.

that a bailee who entrusted a bailment to another bailee is not liable – i.e., for any more than he would have been liable had he kept the bailment himself – since he entrusted it to a person having understanding *(ben da'at);* however, R. Johanan is recorded as holding the first bailee liable for all damage occasioned to the bailment while it is deposited with the second bailee, since the owner might say to the former that he entrusted the bailment to his personal care and did not wish it entrusted to another (see Bailment). In the continuation of the discussion it is stated, "R. Ḥisda said: this was not stated by Rav explicitly but by implication," i.e., that Rav's rule was deduced by implication from a legal decision he gave in a practical case, but that the rule was deduced in error because no proper distinction had been made. The facts of the case decided by Rav were as follows: Gardeners used to deposit their spades every day, on completion of their work, with an old woman; one day they deposited their spades with one of their members and the latter, wishing to join in some festivity, deposited them with the old woman, from whom they were stolen; when the other gardeners sought compensation from the bailee gardener for the loss of their spades, Rav held the latter exempt from liability. From his decision it had been erroneously concluded that the latter held in favor of exempting a first bailee from liability for damage occasioned to a bailment he had entrusted to a second bailee, for Rav had only exempted the first bailee in that particular case because of the fact that the gardeners had generally been accustomed to deposit their spades with the old woman, and were therefore precluded from saying that they wanted their spades entrusted to the gardener only. Generally, however, if the facts were different, a bailee would be liable if damage resulted to the bailment he entrusted to another, even in Rav's opinion. In this manner the Talmud records how the deduction of an erroneous legal conclusion from a particular case is illuminated by the process of distinguishing.

The Talmud (BB 130b) provides basic guidance on the manner of deriving a legal conclusion from a case without apprehension of error: "The *halakhah* may not be derived either from a theoretical conclusion or from a practical decision (without knowing the facts of the case) unless one has been told that the rule is to be taken as a rule for practical decisions; once a person has asked and been informed that a *halakhah* was to be taken as a guide for practical decisions (and therefore knows the facts), he may continue to give practical decisions accordingly" (see Rashbam, ad loc.). In the 13th century the approach to *ma'aseh* and the distinguishing process was expressed in these terms: "Not in vain were the many practical cases embracing various rules written into the Talmud, not so that the law concerning the relevant matter be applied in accordance with what is stated there, but so that the scholar, by having frequent reference to them, shall acquire the art of weighing his opinion and a sound approach in giving practical decisions" (Resp. Abraham b. Moses b. Maimon no. 97).

In Post-Talmudic Times. *Ma'aseh,* both as an act of legal decision and as conduct of a halakhic scholar, continued to serve as an important legal source in post-talmudic times. The halakhic scholars of this period derived many legal conclusions from practical cases in talmudic literature. Thus Maimonides decided that a person engaged in study of the Torah shall stop studying and recite the *Keri'at Shema* whenever it is the time to do so; however, a person engaged in public matters shall not desist from such activity, even if meanwhile the time for *Keri'at Shema* passes (Yad, Keri'at Shema, 2:5). Maimonides derived this *halakhah* from an account in the Tosefta stating that R. Akiva and R. Eleazar b. Azariah omitted the recitation of the *Keri'at Shema* because they were preoccupied with public matters (Tosef., Ber. 1:4; see comment of Elijah Gaon to Sh. Ar., OḤ 70:4).

In like manner, *ma'asim* of the post-talmudic scholars, in the form of both practical decisions (see below) and conduct, served as a legal source for the deduction of *halakhot* by subsequent scholars. *Ma'asim* of the latter kind are frequently quoted in post-talmudic halakhic literature in the form of testimony by pupils to the conduct of their teachers in different matters of the *halakhah.* Special books of *halakhah* were even compiled in which a considerable part of the material was based on the author's observation of the conduct of his eminent teacher, for he had not only acquired the latter's teachings but also served him in daily life. An example of such a work is the *Sefer Tashbeẓ* of Simeon b. Ẓemaḥ Duran, a pupil of Meir b. Baruch of Rothenburg, which deals mainly with the laws in the Shulḥan Arukh's *Oraḥ Ḥayyim* and *Yoreh De'ah,* and to some extent also with matters of family and civil law, largely quoted by the author as the manner in which he had seen his teacher conduct himself (see, e.g., sections 1, 7, 18-23, et al.).

The Responsa Literature. With the development in post-talmudic times of one of the main branches of the literary sources of Jewish law, namely the responsa literature, *ma'aseh* came to fulfill an important role as a lawmaking source. The responsa literature represents the case law of the Jewish legal system. A concrete problem that arose in daily life – whether in matters between individuals or in matters of man's relationship to the Almighty, in matters of civil or ritual law – was brought before the local *dayyan* or halakhic scholar, and they, whenever they experienced any doubt or difficulty in reaching a solution to the problem at hand, turned to the distinguished halakhic scholars of their generation. Certain matters, particularly disputes between the individual and the public or its representative bodies, came directly before the most prominent halakhic scholars. They deliberated all the factual and legal aspects of the case and submitted their findings and conclusion in a written responsum to the questioner. The *she'elah u-teshuvah* – question and response – accordingly represents a classic example of an act of legal decision, and answers to all the requirements set by the talmudic sages for recognition of *ma'aseh* as a legal source, since this procedure is a true application of "having asked and been informed that a *halakhah* is to be taken as a guide for practical decisions. . ." (above; BB 130b). This character of the responsa literature has served to lend the legal principle emerging from it a particular standing and force exceeding that of a principle derived from the commentaries and novellae and even, in the opinion of the majority of halakhic scholars, exceeding that of a principle derived from the books of *halakhot* and *pesakim* (see Codification of Law) in cases of inconsistency between the two. Hence, "more is to be learned from the conclusions stated in the responsa than from those stated by the *posekim* [in the codes], since the latter did not write their conclusions in the course of deciding the law in a concrete instance" (Resp. Maharil no. 72). Similarly, "when *halakhah* is laid down in practice there is greater penetration to the heart of the matter than in the course of theoretical study; there is also greater divine guidance *(sayata di-shemaya)* in a practical case . . . for a conclusion that comes in answer to a practical case is preferable and more directed to the real truth than what is forthcoming from mere theoretical study" (*Meshiv Davar,* pt. 1, no. 24).

Jewish Law and Binding Precedent. Recognition in Jewish law of *ma'aseh* as a legal source from which may be derived the principles that emerge from it is unconnected with the question of whether any conclusion so derived has the force of binding precedent for the purpose of deciding the law in a similar case. In fact, as will be seen below, Jewish law does not recognize the principle of binding precedent.

Precedent in Other Legal Systems. The legal "case" occupies a very modest place in the source hierarchy of the Roman legal system; certainly the latter does not recognize at all the principle of binding precedent. Justinian expressly laid down tha judgments be given according to laws and not precedents: *"non exemplis, sed legibus iudicandum est"* (C. 7.45.13; see J. Salmond, *Jurisprudence* (1966[12]), 14lf.; C.K. Allen, *Law in the Making* (1964[7]), 172f.). Most continental legal systems, following that of Rome, exemplify the codificatory system of law, and in these the decisions of the courts represent no more than material of a theoretical and persuasive nature, without binding force (Salmond, *ibid.*). The position is different in English law: "The importance of judicial precedents has always been a distinguishing characteristic of English law. The great body of the common or unwritten law is almost entirely the product of decided cases, accumulated in an immense series of reports extending backward with scarcely a break to the reign of Edward I at the close of the 13th century . . . A judicial precedent speaks in England with authority; it is not merely evidence of the law but a source of it" (Salmond, p. 141). As regards the extent to which the courts are bound by precedent, Salmond goes on to say: "It is necessary to point out that the phrase 'the doctrine of precedent' has two meanings. In the first, which may be called the loose meaning, the phrase means merely that precedents are reported, may be cited, and will probably be followed by the courts. This was the doctrine that prevailed in England until the 19th century, and it is still the only sense in which a doctrine of precedent prevails on the continent. In the second, the strict meaning, the phrase means that precedents not only have great authority but must (in certain circumstances) be followed. This was the rule developed during the 19th century and completed in some respects during the 20th" (p. 142). The merits of this development toward the strict meaning of precedent have not remained unquestioned, and in recent times there has been increasing discussion of the correctness and efficacy of this approach (*ibid.*, p. 143 and see note, p. ix, concerning the extra-judicial statement made in the House of Lords in 1966, relaxing the rule of being bound to follow its own previous decisions "when it appears right to do so").

Comparison of Precedent in English and in Jewish Law. At their respective starting points the two legal systems have much in common in their approach to precedent but they diverge in their manner of development. In both "case" constitutes a source of law; both are, to a large extent, built up around case law, and have developed in consequence of concrete legal decisions in daily life; the basic material at the heart of most Jewish law codifications is likewise the product of legal principles derived from day-to-day legal decisions (see Codification of Law[1]), and from this point of view the main difference between the two legal systems is that the Jewish law equivalent of the "immense series of reports," namely the responsa literature, dates from the geonic period onward, i.e., from the middle of the eighth century and not, as in England, from the end of the 13th century (see Elon, *Ha-Mishpat Ha-Ivri,* III, 1213ff.). On the other hand, Jewish law has not accepted the doctrine of precedent in the strict meaning of the term – as has English law, commencing from the 19th century – and the power of *ma'aseh* in Jewish law has been confined to that of precedent in the loose meaning of the term, as described by Salmond, "precedents are reported, may be cited, and will probably be followed by the courts." For two reasons, each of which will be dealt with below, Jewish law has been unable to adopt the doctrine of a binding precedent which imposes its inherent halakhic conclusion on the *dayyan* when deciding the matter before him: first, because of this legal system's conception of the substantive nature of a judgment given between the two parties to a suit; secondly, because of the method and approach of Jewish law toward deciding of the *halakhah* in general.

Substantive Nature of a Judgment in Jewish Law and the Problem of Precedent. In Jewish law, the finality of a judgment is subject to many reservations, even in relation to the instant parties themselves. According to the original Jewish law, no judgment is absolute and final in the sense of *res judicata* in Roman law, except in so far as it accords with the true objective state of affairs as regards both the facts and the law. Hence, it always remained possible for a judgment given by the court on the available facts to be set aside, and for the matter to be heard afresh when either of the parties was able to produce new evidence. Since this possibility posed a serious obstacle to the due administration of justice and to orderly economic life, which demand an end to litigation, the practice was introduced of having the parties acknowledge – in court and prior to judgment – that they had no further evidence whatever to adduce, thereby annulling in advance the efficacy of any further evidence they might later wish to bring (see Sanh. 31a; Yad, Sanhedrin, 7:6–8; Sh. Ar., ḤM 20). Similarly, the original law held that any judgment which transpires to be wrong in law – i.e., in case of error as regards decided and clear *halakhah* – is inherently invalid, although not so in case of an erroneous exercise of discretion. Here again the way was found to ensure the stability and finality of a judgment (Sanh. 33a; Yad, Sanhedrin 6:1; Sh. Ar., ḤM 25:1–3 and Rema thereto; see also Gulak, Yesodei, 4 (1922), 175-83, 201–3; and see Practice and Procedure (Civil)).

A judgment in Jewish law accordingly has a dual nature: theoretically it is not final until the truth has been fully explored; in practice reservations were laid down – which would be accepted by the parties and normally would apply automatically – aimed at ensuring an end to litigation between the parties to a dispute and at acceptance of the judgment as decisive and as determining the respective rights of the parties.

The stated theoretical nature of a judgment, which applies even as regards determination of the law for the instant parties themselves, has necessarily entailed the conclusion that a judgment shall not have the force of a binding precedent in relation to a similar problem arising between different parties; hence "if another case comes before him even if it be a like case in all respects – he may deal with it as he sees fit, since the *dayyan* need only act according to what his own eyes see" (Nov. Ran to BB 130b; Nov. Ritba, BB *ibid.*).

Methods and Approach of Jewish Law Concerning Deciding of the Halakhah and the Problem of Precedent. The doctrine of binding precedent also conflicts with the very method and approach of Jewish law concerning deciding the *halakhah* (see Introduction; Authority, Rabbinical;[2] Codification of Law[3]). The fact of halakhic difference of opinion, as the latter developed in the course of time, is regarded as a phenomenon that is not only legitimate but also desirable and indicative of the vitality of the *halakhah* and of the possibility of different approaches, based on common general principles, in the search for solutions to new problems that arise. The decisive yardstick in a case of halakhic dispute, is the correctness of each opinion "in accordance only with the Talmud of R. Ashi" (i.e., the Babylonian Talmud: *Piskei ha-Rosh,* Sanh. 4:6) and based "with definite proof on the Talmud, as well as the Jerusalem Talmud and Tosefta, when there is no definite decision in the Talmud" (*Yam shel Shelomo,* introd. to BK). For this reason no codification of Jewish law was accepted which laid before the *dayyan* deciding the law one single, arbitrary, and final opinion on any given matter. For the same reason Jewish law accepted the doctrine of *hilkheta ke-Vatra'ei* ("the law is according to the later scholars"), which was

1. page 124, 130; 2. page 56; 3. page 124, 131 et. al.

designed to ensure freedom of decision for later scholars – albeit with due reference to and regard for the decisions of earlier scholars. The basic rule applicable is that the judgment of a person who has erred because he was unaware of the decisions of earlier scholars shall be of no force as soon as that person gains such knowledge and realises his error; however, "if he does not find their statements correct and sustains his own view with evidence that is acceptable to his contemporaries – the authority of Jephthah in his generation was as that of Samuel in his, and there is only the judge that 'shall be in those days' – he may contradict their statements, since all matters which are not clarified in the Talmud of R. Ashi and Ravina may be questioned and restated by any person, and even the statements of the *geonim* may be differed from . . . just as the later *amoraim* differed from the earlier ones; on the contrary, we regard the statements of the later scholars to be more authoritative since the latter knew not only the legal thinking of their contemporaries but also that of the earlier scholars, and in deciding between the different views they reached the heart of a matter" (*Piskei ha-Rosh*, loc. cit.).

This conception of a flexible and dynamic legal order naturally left no room for the doctrine that especially a conclusion springing from a practical decision should impose itself on the judicial process. The court which is apprised of a matter has the task of referring to, and taking into proper consideration, all the available relevant laws and certainly the rules emerging from earlier practical decisions, particularly when the halakhic principle emerging from the practical decision has been accepted without exception in a series of legal decisions ("daily practical acts of decision," Ket. 68b; BB 173b; etc). However, if after such study the judge should, in reasonable manner and in reliance on the halakhic system itself, come to a different legal conclusion from that reached by earlier scholars, he will have not only the right but also the duty to decide as he sees fit; such decision will take precedence over an earlier decision in a like matter, since the judge will also have known the legal thinking of earlier scholars and have decided as he did by going to the root of the matter.

Thus *ma'aseh* constitutes one of the significant lawmaking sources of the Jewish legal system, and every principle emerging from it becomes part of the accumulated body of laws comprising this system, in accordance with which the judge must decide. In standing and validity such principles are like any others deriving from the statements of *posekim* and halakhic scholars, and embraced by the common rule that the judge must consider every law on its substantive merits and decide, in the concrete case before him, according to his own knowledge and understanding deriving from due examination of all the relevant rules of Jewish law.

Bibliography: Epstein, Mishnah, 598–608; J. M. Guttmann, in: *Devir,* 1 (1922/23), 40–44; Ch. Tchernowitz, *Toledot ha-Halakhah,* 1 pt. 1 (1934), 189–96; A. Kaminka, *Meḥkarim ba Mikra u-va-Talmud* . . . (1951), 1–41; A. Weiss, *Le-Ḥeker ha-Talmud* (1954), 111–67; Ḥ. Cohn, in: *Mishpat Ve-Khalkalah,* 3 (1956/57), 129–41; Ḥ. Albeck, *Mavo la-Mishnah* (1959), 92f.; E.Ẓ. Melamed, in: *Sinai,* 46 (1959/60), 152–65; B. de Vries, *Toledot ha-Halakhah ha-Talmudit* (1962), 169–78; M. Elon, in: ILR, 2 (1967), 548–50; idem, *Ha-Mishpat Ha-Ivri,* II, (1973), 768–804.

Menachem Elon

SEVARAH (Legal Logic), the legal logic employed by halakhic scholars in their reasoning. This logic is founded on observation of the characteristics of human beings as they are disclosed in their social relations with one another and on a study of the practical realities of daily life. *Sevarah* may serve both as a historical source of law – a source which factually and indirectly leads to the creation of a particular legal rule – and as legal source of law – a source recognized by the particular legal system as a direct means for the acceptance of a legal rule into that system. (On the different sources of law, see Introduction.[1]) Logic may also serve as a historical source in the functioning of the other legal sources of Jewish law. Thus, for instance, when a particular legal rule is created by means of the legal source of Midrash (see Interpretation), the interpretative activity constitutes the direct creative source of that rule; however, the interpreter is guided along his interpretative path by logic and reasoning, which therefore form the historical-factual source of the rule. The same is true of rules created by means of legal sources of legislature, that is *takkanah, ma'aseh,* and *minhag,* where the rules are naturally created and fashioned in outcome of certain needs as dictated by logic and practical exigencies. It is as a historical source in the aforementioned sense that *sevarah* is quoted as a basis for the study and understanding of the *halakhah* (see, e.g., Git. 6b; Shab. 63a; Suk. 29a, et al.). On the other hand, *sevarah* functions as a legal source whenever it serves as the direct source of a particular rule, that is whenever such rule is created by virtue of logic and reasoning alone, outside the framework of and without assistance from any other legal source such as *Midrash, minhag,* or *ma'aseh.*

An important place is assigned to *sevarah* as the creative source of halakhic norms in all fields of the *halakhah* – whether in relation to the precepts between man and his Maker or the laws pertaining to relations between man and his fellow men either in matters of ritual law or civil law. The high regard in which *sevarah* was held also finds expression in the manner of classification of the laws originating from this legal source. Thus a law having its creative source in *takkanah* or *minhag* is numbered among the category of laws known as *de-rabbanan* (see Introduction[2]), whereas a law having its direct source in *sevarah* is generally numbered among the category known as *de-oraita* (Chajes, in bibl., and see below). The honorable status thus lent a rule originating from *sevarah* is attributable to the fundamental principle which underlies the whole of the halakhic system, namely, that the Torah was given on the authority *(al da'at)* of the halakhic scholars (see Authority, Rabbinical); hence every rule founded on the logical reasoning of the halakhic scholars originates, as it were, from the Torah itself, because the logic of the halakhic scholars corresponds with the logic embodied in the Torah.

Sevarah as the Creative Source of General Legal Principles. It is an important principle of Judaism that a person who is told to transgress or else suffer death should transgress rather than be killed (Sanh. 74a), since the laws of the Torah were given so that man could live by them and not die because of them (Yoma 85b; Yad, Yesodei ha-Torah 5:1). However, in three cases a person given the choice between transgression or death should choose the latter; idolatry, incest (including adultery), or murder (Sanh. 74a; Pes. 25a–b; et al.). As regards idolatry and incest the rule was established by way of biblical exegesis (Sanh. 74a), but with regard to murder the rule was derived logically, and not by way of exegesis, as follows: "The *sevarah* is . . . who shall say that your blood is redder? Perhaps the blood of the other is redder! " (Sanh. 74a); for "as far as the murderer is concerned, since in the end man is anyhow destined to die, why should it be permissible for him to transgress? Who knows that the Creator holds his life to be of greater worth than that of his fellow? " (Rashi, ad loc.). Thus the rule that as regards the shedding of blood a person shall choose death rather than transgression has its legal source in *sevarah.*

1. page 10; 2. page 9.

There is a long series of general legal principles operating in the field of both ritual and civil law which similarly originate from the legal source of *sevarah.* The rule that the burden of proof is on the claimant is derived from logic on the reasoning that just as the person who has a pain seeks out a doctor and recites his symptoms (and it is not the doctor who runs around to find out who is ill), so too the person who has a claim against another must first bring proof to substantiate his claim and the defendant need not first prove that he is not liable on such claim (BK 46b). So too a woman's statement that she was married and became divorced – there being no witnesses to the fact that she was married – is believed as regards her becoming divorced, in terms of the rule pertaining to the laws of evidence that "the mouth which has rendered prohibited is the mouth which has rendered permissible"; this rule is derived from the logical reasoning that since she prohibited her own self (to others) she may also permit her own self (Ket. 2:5; Ket. 22a; from this rule there was derived in amoraic times the rule of *miggo;* see Pleas; Evidence).

The two aforementioned rules are expressly stated as having their legal source in *sevarah* and this also appears to be the case with reference to a number of further rules and principles, for instance as regards the principle of *ḥazakah* as a legal presumption – such as the presumption that a person is alive (Git. 3:3), the presumption of legal competence (*ḥezkat kashrut;* BB 31b), the presumption of bodily fitness (Ket. 7:8), and numerous other kinds of presumptions. Logic is also the source of the rule regarding reliance on the majority, even when the majority is not a factual one (such as a majority of the judges hearing a particular case), but is based on surmise alone [Ḥul. 11a; the biblical passages cited there with regard to several kinds of majority and *ḥazakah* are in the nature of *asmakhta* ("mere allusion") alone; see also Interpretation[1]]. These presumptions have validity in all fields of the *halakhah,* in matters of the civil law as well as matters of ritual prohibitions and permissions, and even in matters which are *de-oraita:* "For matters learned by way of *sevarah* are of the same value as the actual statements of the Torah itself . . . since the power of observation deriving from experience is of precisely the same value to them [the halakhic scholars] as a matter learned through application of the exegetical *middot*" (see Interpretation; Chajes, in bibl., 118–30).

Sevarah in the Amoraic Period. A substantial proportion of the laws and principles deriving from *sevarah* are attributable to an early period of the *halakhah.* From talmudic sources it is also possible to conclude that the use of *sevarah* as a legal source of the *halakhah* was particularly resorted to during amoraic times – just as the *amoraim* laid down rational rules with regard to the use of other legal sources and the modes of studying the *halakhah* (see *Takkanot;*[2] *Asmakhta*). Thus in regard to forbidden food and drink R. Johanan laid down that the taking of even half of the determined measure was also forbidden by the pentateuchal law – since one half-measure may combine with another half-measure to constitute a full measure, it follows that he will be eating that which is forbidden (Yoma 74a). The *amoraim* stated that in respect of various laws it may be said that they have their source either in a biblical passage or in *sevarah,* for instance as regards certain matters relating to the laws of evidence (Sanh. 30a), the laws of *ḥaliẓah* (Yev. 35b) and in other fields (see, e.g., Shevu. 22b and Tos. loc. cit.).

In other cases the *amoraim* searched for the legal source of a particular rule and came to the conclusion that such a rule had its origin in the legal source of *sevarah.* An interesting illustration of this is to be found in the discussions of the *amoraim* concerning the legal source of the rule that three years' possession of real property confers presumptive rights of ownership (i.e., upon a claim of lawful acquisition with subsequent loss of the title deed, but with possession for the said period without protest from the former owner; see *Ḥazakah*). The *amoraim* confronted difficulties in attributing the source of the rule to Midrash (see Interpretation) and to Kabbalah (see Introduction[3]) in turn, and then Rabba determined the legal source of the rule thus: "The first year a person guards his title deed and so he does the second and third years; thereafter he guards it no longer" (BB 28a–29a). That is to say, logic – which is founded on the observation of daily practical life – teaches that a person who purchases property takes care to guard his title deed for a period of three years as proof against any challenge to his right in such property; however, after three years have elapsed without any such challenge, he no longer sees need to guard the material evidence of his ownership since he is already sure that he is fully in possession of the property and does not contemplate the possibility that his right to it will any more be challenged. This *sevarah* was accepted as the legal source of the rule that three years' possession of property suffices to prove the possessor's acquisition thereof according to law, even when the latter cannot produce his title deed or any other proof (for additional substantiation of the rule, see *Ḥazakah*).

Sevarah continued to be a creative legal source in the post-talmudic period. For examples, see Elon, *Ha-Mishpat Ha-Ivri,* II (1973), 820f. However, the halakhic literary sources of this period, unlike those of the talmudic period, do not generally specially emphasize the fact that certain rules have their source in *sevarah,* as is generally done in the case of *minhag, takkanah,* and other legal sources. Hence painstaking research is required in order to distinguish the post-talmudic halakhic literary principles which originate from *sevarah.*

Bibliography: Weiss, Dor, 2 (1904[4]), 48f.; J. M. Guttmann, in: *Devir,* 2 (1924), 128–30; Ch. Tchernowitz, *Toledot ha-Halakhah,* 1 (1934), 151–63; Z. H. Chajes, *The Student's Guide Through the Talmud* (1960[2]), 29–31, 118–30; M. Elon, in: ILR, 2 (1967), 550; idem, *Ha-Mishpat Ha-Ivri,* II (1973), 805–828.

Menachem Elon

CODIFICATION OF LAW. This article is arranged according to the following outline:

The Concept and Its Prevalence in Other Legal Systems
In Jewish Law
In the Mishnah
  Format and Style of the Mishnah
The Talmud and Post-Talmudic Halakhic Literary Forms
Variety of Literary Forms in the Codes
In the Geonic Period
The Rif (Alfasi)
Maimonides' Method
Reactions to Maimonides' Approach
  "Arms-Bearers"
Codification until the Compilation of the Arba'ah Turim
The System of the "Ba'al ha-Turim"
  Structure of the Turim
  "Arms-Bearers" to the Turim
the Method of Joseph Caro
Structure and Arrangement of the Shulḥan Arukh
The Rule of Moses Isserles (Rema) in Halakhic Codification
Reactions to the Shulḥan Arukh
Acceptance of the Shulḥan Arukh as the Authoritative Halakhic Code
After the Shulḥan Arukh

1. page 59; 2. page 76; 3. page 14.

The Concept and Its Prevalence in Other Legal System. The term codification, within its historical meaning, is the reduction to writing of a law previously only extant in oral form. In this sense the concept of codification does not differ substantially from legislation. In time, however, the concept of codification came to acquire a different meaning; namely, that whereas legislation serves to lay down a specific normative instruction – with the object either of innovating a legal norm where none had previously existed or of varying and amending an already existing legal norm (in the halakhic system this function is carried out by way of the *takkanah* or *gezerah*, see *Takkanot*) – codification is concerned with circumscribing a whole legal system, or at least a branch of it. The background to codification and its motivation is the realization of the need to eliminate the shortcomings stemming from diverse and universal juridical and historical phenomena, such as the proliferation of legal provisions scattered in different literary sources, the awkward and heterogeneous style of legal directives, and the gradual accumulation of conflicting legal norms within a particular legal system. Furthermore, a codification constitutes the authoritative source for locating any law forming part of a particular legal branch, its directives having the effect of abrogating any other provision of the said branch of the law preceding the codification and inconsistent with it. The hope of the initiators of the great codifications (beginning from the middle of the 18th century, such as the Prussian and Napoleonic Codes) was that such codification would simplify the law and make it understandable and readily available to every citizen. This hope soon proved to be unfounded when it was realized that the interpretation and understanding of the legal profession was still indispensable.

Unlike the great codifying movements which originated and developed in continental Europe, the Anglo-Saxon systems of law have rejected the move to codification because of a difference in approach to the substantive and fundamental problem of providing for the continued development and creativity of the legal system. Whereas continental legal systems deferred to the principle that the continued development of the law, with its amendments and refinement, should be entrusted to the legislator, Anglo-Saxon law has looked upon the doctrine of precedent – i.e., decisions of the courts on actual problems arising in daily life – as the principal medium for the continued shaping of the law, a process in which the courts consequently play an honorable role. The problem of the proliferation and unwieldy nature of the material accumulating from statutory legislation is solved in Anglo-Saxon law by the devices of "Compilation" and "Revision." A Compilation, i.e., a collection of the texts of various statutes arranged according to subject matter, merely provides prima facie evidence of the original version of the statute, to which reference must be made for an authoritative statement of the enacted law. On the other hand, a Revision or Consolidation – which is also a collection of statutes arranged according to subject matter – is deliberately and authoritatively published by the relevant legislative powers, and therefore represents the binding version with regard to variations from the original wording of the statutes. Both a Compilation and a Revision are concerned exclusively with statutes and not with the provisions of Common Law. Only in isolated fields of English law, for example, do codifications exist which include all existing provisions – whether statutory or of Common Law – and which have the binding force of parliamentary enactment. In the United States partial codifications of this kind are more frequently encountered, but even there, except in isolated states, the greater part of the law is still enshrined in Common Law and in regular legislative enactments, whereas in continental Europe all the law is to be found in various codes embracing the separate branches.

In Jewish Law. In Jewish law the question of codification is bound up with the particular problems innate in its substance and history. The principle that a code abrogates any inconsistent rule of earlier date has never been tenable – nor even propagated – within the halakhic system. The determining factor of the *halakhah,* i.e., the basis of its binding force and authority, has been its continuity; and the validity of every rule or norm added to the body of the *halakhah* during the course of its development, through its legal sources (such as Interpretation, *Takkanot, Minhag, Ma'aseh,* and *Sevarah*), rests on its stemming from the basic norm of the *halakhah,* i.e., the Written Law, and from the accumulation of *halakhot* throughout the generations. Not even Maimonides, who compiled the *Mishneh Torah,* the greatest and most comprehensive halakhic code of all, with the stated purpose that "a person shall not need to have recourse to any other work in the world concerning any of the laws of Israel . . . that a person shall first read the Written Law and then this work and learn therefrom all of the Oral Law and shall not require to read any other work" (Yad. introd.) – not even he sought to establish his work as the source of halakhic authority, nullifying all of the previously determined *halakhah.* Nor did he envisage introducing any change in the *halakhah* through his work, since he emphasized (in his introduction) the unbroken chain of transmission stretching back to Moses at Sinai and the validity of the laws of the Babylonian Talmud as being "incumbent on all Israel." He made his position clear in a letter to Phinehas b. Meshullam, *dayyan* of Alexandria: "Have I commanded or had in mind the burning of all books written before me on account of my own work? " (*Kovez Teshuvot ha-Rambam ve-Iggerotav,* ed. Leipzig (1859), pt. 1, no. 140, 25a–27a). He intended no more – and even this aim was to meet with vigorous opposition as a daring and revolutionary one – than that the law was henceforth to be ascertained and the *halakhah* to be decided only according to his codification, because of his conviction that his work included all the rules of the *halakhah* and any conflict between his work and the preceding and binding halakhic literature was inconceivable. Hence, it is clear that in view of the inseparable link between the *halakhah* and its sources, it cannot tolerate expression in the form of a Codex or a "Revision," but only that of a "Compilation." However, from the standpoint of the validity attaching to such compilatory work and the possibility of deciding in terms of it, it has been regarded not merely as constituting presumptive evidence, but as carrying also the authority of a proper codex.

Despite the intolerance engendered by the very substance of the halakhic system, and the fact that Jewish law has evolved pragmatically through providing solutions to the problems of daily existence as they arise and not by way of the prior determination of rules of principle (see Introduction; Authority, Rabbinical, and Ma'aseh), it has nevertheless been influenced by factors and incentives similar to those operating in other legal systems. In the context of the particular history of the Jewish people and the practical reality of the *halakhah*, these and other special factors at times rendered some form of codification of the body of halakhic rules imperative. Codification of the halakhic system confronted those who undertook the task with a search for suitable ways of overcoming the substantive problems involved, and in the process, throughout the long history of the *halakhah,* there were evolved different literary genres, until a form was arrived at which could be reconciled with the halakhic system.

In the Mishnah. The first halakhic code to be compiled after the Written Law, which constitutes not only the basic norm of the entire halakhic system but also its first, and founding codification, was the Mishnah. Compiled by Judah ha-Nasi in about 200 c.e., it embraces within its six orders the whole framework of Jewish law (the *Sefer Gezerata,* known to have been in existence prior to the Mishnah, was a Sadducean code, apparently mainly a criminal one). Some scholars are of the opinion that Judah ha-Nasi merely sought to assemble in the Mishnah the accepted *halakhot* of his time and to arrange them according to their subject matter so that each law could readily and conveniently be ascertained, and that it was not his intention to decide the *halakhah* in the Mishnah. Prima facie support for this view is to be found in the fact that for the greater part the Mishnah does not give only one single halakhic ruling, clear and unequivocal, but instead cites different opinions on a particular ruling, without any explicit statement as to the decision on the matter. Notwithstanding this, most scholars are of the opinion – and this indeed appears to be the case – that Judah ha-Nasi's purpose was to compile a halakhic code in accordance with which the law was to be decided. This may be concluded from an examination of the transmitted texts, comparing the wording of *halakhot* in the Mishnah and the wording of the same *halakhot* in the Tosefta and *beraitot*; and in particular from the fact of Judah ha-Nasi's quotation, in an anonymous way *(stam)*, of the opinion in accordance with which he sought to decide the law (see Ḥul. 85a).

Further evidence that Judah ha-Nasi was engaged in a task of codifying in compiling the Mishnah may be adduced from the theory and history of the *halakhah*. Anonymity and uniformity were features of the ancient *halakhah*. Commencing from the time of the first pair of scholars, Yose b. Joezer and Yose b. Johanan, only one instance of a disputed halakhic rule is known (Ḥag. 2:2) and in all, until the time of the last pair, Shammai and Hillel, only four matters were the subject of disputed *halakhot* (TJ, Ḥag. 2:2, 77d). The reason for the almost complete uniformity of the *halakhah* until the beginning of the tannaitic period is that every problem was decided, in the final analysis, by the Sanhedrin – the supreme judicial and legislative body of the people – and a rule decided by a majority opinion simply became the law of the Sanhedrin as a body, leaving no room for mention to be made of the names of the scholars who supported either the majority or the minority opinion. From the start of the tannaitic period, the cases of dispute increased in all fields of the *halakhah*, and numerous differing opinions have come down with the names of the scholars who expressed them. This substantive change in the image of the *halakhah* was caused by the undermining of the Sanhedrin's powers of decision and its weakened authority. This was brought about by the influence of various external political factors in Ereẓ Israel in the half century preceding the destruction of the Temple and the operation of internal factors such as the intensification of the dispute between the Pharisees and the Sadducees, and between the scholars of Bet Shammai and Bet Hillel (see R. Yose, Tosef., Sanh. 7:1; Sanh. 88b; TJ, Sanh. 1:4, 19c). The destruction of the Temple, the disruption of the halakhic center deprived of its traditional location, and the migration of the scholars and their courts gave rise to an increase in halakhic disputes in which no decision was reached.

At the beginning of the second century, following the consolidation of Jabneh as the new center of the law under the presidency of Gamaliel II, a determined effort was made to restore uniformity to the *halakhah* (Tosef., Eduy. 1:1; cf. Sif. Deut., 48, p. 113, and Shab. 138b). At that time it was laid down that in general, in a dispute between Bet Shammai and Bet Hillel, the view of the latter was to prevail (TJ, Ber. 1:7, 3b). At the same time many traditions and laws, based on various "testimonies" *(eduyyot),* were assembled and arranged in the tractate *Eduyyot.* The flowering and development of the *halakhah* at the academies of Akiva and Ishmael, and particularly the numerous disputes later waged by the former's pupils, confronted the scholars of Judah ha-Nasi's generation with the need to reduce once more this abundant halakhic material to uniform law. Hence it may reasonably be assumed that Judah ha-Nasi's object in compiling the Mishnah was the same as that of his grandfather, Gamaliel of Jabneh; namely, to avert the danger of proliferating dispute by undertaking the compilation of a code that would decide and determine the law. Another historical reason explaining the need for a code of Jewish law at that time was expressed thus: "the number of scholars is on the decrease, new troubles on the increase . . . a work should be written to be available to all, so that it can speedily be learned and not be forgotten" (Maim., Yad, introd.). It may be asked why Judah ha-Nasi chose such an indirect method in his determination of the *halakhah;* i.e. by stating the opinion with which he was in agreement in an anonymous manner, as opposed to the simpler method of stating only the opinion according to which he decided, to the complete exclusion of other opinions. It appears that he did so in order to preserve the element of continuity possessed by the *halakhah,* since deletion of the names of the scholars and their opinions would have severed the chain of transmission from scholar to scholar (see N. Krochmal, *Moreh Nevukhei ha-Zeman;* ch. 13). A thousand years later the fact that Maimonides chose the opposite path in his *Mishneh Torah* was one of the main reasons for the vigorous criticism with which his work was received.

Format and Style of the Mishnah. The laws in the Mishnah are mostly formulated in a casuistic, rather than normative, manner, i.e., a particular legal rule is expressed in the form of a factual case and not by a bare statement of the legal principle without embodiment in a concrete example. Thus, for instance, the normative principle that a person – even when acting in his own domain – must guard against causing harm to his neighbor, is expressed by way of a long series of practical instances of prohibitions or injunctions: that a man must not dig a pit near his neighbor's property, or that he must remove his salt or lime from his neighbor's wall, etc. (BB 2:1ff.). This casuistic method is characteristic of the *halakhah* which developed and kept pace with everyday realities and in this manner was transmitted throughout the generations. Occasionally Mishnayot are rendered in combined casuistic-normative manner (BB 1:6; 3:1; Git. 2:5–6) and there are some rare cases of a purely normative formulation (BK 1:2). This form, adopted for the first halakhic code compiled after the Written Law, put its imprint on all subsequent codifications and was retained even in Maimonides' *Mishneh Torah.* From the point of view of the possible development of the law, this method commends itself since it allows for a large measure of differentiation between one matter and another. An important quality of the Mishnah as a code is its style, which is a concise yet clear and lucid Hebrew, that served as the basis of Maimonides' style in the *Mishneh Torah* (see *Sefer ha-Mitzvot,* introd.) and is still a general and rewarding source of Hebrew style, particularly in legal usage.

The Talmud and Post-Talmudic Halakhic Literary Forms. The Talmud *(Gemara)*, which includes deliberations of the sages, halakhic commentaries of the early *tannaim* and *amoraim,* decisions, epistles, responsa, and decisory rules, has been accepted in the halakhic world as authentic and binding material constituting the starting point for the deliberation of any halakhic subject whatsoever. Yet, from the viewpoint of literary classification, it does not bear the character of a codex. The codificatory form reappears in halakhic literature in the post-talmudic period, in a branch known as the literature of the *posekim* (i.e., codifiers or simply "the Codes") representing one of the three main literary forms in which the *halakhah* has been stated, commencing from the geonic period. Of the other two forms the first is represented by the commentaries and novellae (*perushim* and *ḥiddushim*), which have as their object the interpretation of the Mishnah, the two Talmuds and the remaining halakhic literature, and innovation by way of comparison between the different sources and reconciliation of the emerging contradictions (see Elon, *Ha-Mishpat Ha-Ivri,* III (1973), 908–937). The third form is represented in the literature of the Responsa Prudentium, which is the Jewish "Common Law," a great storehouse of decisions given on concrete matters arising throughout the generations in all countries of the Jewish Diaspora (see Elon, *Ibid,* p. 1213–1277). The literature of the Codes and that of the responsa had the common purpose of deciding the law; however, in the case of a responsum the decision is arrived at after deliberation of the specific case before the halakhic scholar, whereas the *posek,* apart from embracing the entire field of the *halakhah,* or at least a particular branch of it, arrives at his decision after an abstract consideration of the existing halakhic material pertaining to each particular subject. Hence the literature of the Codes corresponds in form to the codificatory literature found in other legal systems.

Variety of Literary Forms in the Codes. The problems of codifying the *halakhah* were responsible for the adoption of the different literary forms found in the Codes. These may be classified into three main categories: (1) "books of *halakhot,*" i.e., books having the avowed purpose of collecting the conclusions from the halakhic rules pertaining to either the whole or a particular branch of the *halakhah,* the conclusion being preceded in each case by a brief discussion and précis of the talmudic sources on which it is founded; (2) "books of *pesakim*" ("decisions"), having the purpose of stating the conclusions from the halakhic rules – in their entirety or in a particular branch of the law – without any preceding discussion of the underlying sources; and (3) a combination of the first two, which assumed different forms at different times. In addition to an intrinsic literary difference between categories (1) and (2) there is also, generally speaking, an extrinsic divergence stemming from this intrinsic difference. A "book of decisions" is arranged according to halakhic subject matter, even though the various rules pertaining to each subject are dispersed throughout the different literary sources, and this is the most convenient and helpful form for both *dayyan* and student; on the other hand the author of a "book of *halakhot*" – who preceded his conclusion with a discussion and quotation of sources – was compelled by logic to tie the arrangement of his work to that of the literary source in which the relevant halakhic discussion is to be found, i.e., generally the appropriate talmudic tractate.

In the Geonic Period. From the eighth century onward, i.e., the earliest period from which considerable geonic halakhic literature has come down, increasing activity in the field of halakhic codification becomes noticeable and, although they appear in different literary forms, the codes of this period may all be classified as belonging to the category of "books of *halakhot.*"

The first book to be written after the closing of the Talmud was the *Sefer ha-She'iltot* of Aḥa(i) of Shabḥa, Babylonia, in the first half of the eighth century. Mainly a collection of homiletic discussions *(derashot)* usually starting with a question (hence *she'iltot*) formulated in accordance with the type of exposition set in talmudic times by the leading scholars, this work nonetheless displays a clear decisory element. Soon after the work appeared the author's statements were quoted for the purpose of deciding in accordance with them (see Assaf, Geonim, 155ff.), so that it may be classified as forming part of the literature of the Codes. It displays the unusual feature of being arranged according to neither subject matter nor the talmudic tractates, but according to the order of the weekly portions of the Pentateuch, as in the case of midrashic literature; the halakhic subject with which the *she'ilta* deals is often linked with the particular portion of the Pentateuch in which the subject is treated in narrative form; e.g., the laws of theft and robbery dealt with in *she'ilta* no. 4 relate to the weekly portion *Noah* (with reference to Gen. 6:13), the laws of bailment in *she'ilta* no. 20 relate to the portion *Va-Yeẓe* (with reference to Jacob taking care of the sheep of Laban); and the laws of suretyship in *she'ilta* no. 33 relate to the portion *Mi-Keẓ* (with reference to Judah acting as the guarantor of Benjamin's welfare).

At about the same time, Yehudai b. Naḥman Gaon wrote *Halakhot Pesukot,* the earliest classic example of the "books of *halakhot,*" which was to exercise a decisive influence on the literature of the Codes. This work was arranged according to both subject matter – *hilkhot Eruvin, Halva'ah, Ketubbot,* etc. – and the talmudic tractates, the halakhic conclusion generally being preceded by a brief synopsis of the underlying talmudic sources. No laws were included that were not relevant at the time *(mitzvot she-einan nohagot be-zeman ha-zeh),* such as precepts pertaining to the land of Israel *(mitzvot ha-teluyot ba-areẓ)* not observed in Babylonia, and the laws of *Kodashim* (Temple cult) and *Tohorot* (ritual purity). In so doing, Yehudai Gaon established a precedent followed by practically all subsequent *posekim,* who from then on confined themselves to the codification only of the *halakhah* in practice at the particular time. This work soon became known in all countries of the Diaspora and others compiled various abridgments of it, known as *Halakhot Ketu'ot,* or *Halakhot Keẓuvot* etc., while a Hebrew translation is known as the *Hilkhot Re'u* (based on the first word in Exodus 16:29, with which the work commences). About a hundred years later there appeared the *Halakhot Gedolot,* the greatest halakhic work of the geonic period in scope and content. In the opinion of most scholars the author was Simeon Kayyara of Basra (Bassora), Babylonia. Here, too, the conclusions are preceded by a brief review of the sources, the arrangement following the order of the talmudic tractates.

In this period the scholars are known to have been concerned about various questions relating to the codification of Jewish law. Several factors operated to promote the codifying trend: from one source it appears that the *Halakhot Pesukot* was compiled because of the difficulty in finding a way through the proliferous material in the orders and tractates of the Talmud (*Seder Olam Zuta,* in Neubauer, Chronicles, I (1887), 178); elsewhere it is mentioned that Aḥa compiled the *Sefer ha-She'iltot* for the sake of his son, "in order that every Sabbath when the order is read, he shall be able to clarify for himself familiar *halakhot* from the Talmud" (Ha-Meiri, *Beit ha-Beḥirah* to *Avot,* introd.). Subsequently both reasons were frequently mentioned as the background to many "books of *halakhot*" and *"pesakim."* It seems that a historical factor in the internal life of the Jewish people was also a contributing factor. In the middle of the eighth century Karaism emerged in Babylonia. For approximately the next 200 years the *geonim,* commencing with Yehudai Gaon waged a persistent and relentless struggle against the Karaites who disavowed the rabbinic Law in terms of the statement attributed to Anan: "Abandon the words of the Mishnah and Talmud and I shall make for you a Talmud of my own" (*Seder*

Rav Amram, ed. Warsaw, 38a). In the course of this conflict the *geonim* and other halakhic scholars produced a proliferation of halakhic and philosophical works and it appears that an important instrument toward crystallization of the traditional Jewish attitude, founded on the rules of the Oral Law, was the compilation of books which would elucidate and summarize the latter in convenient synoptic form.

On the other hand, the compilation of codes gave rise to the fear that any neglect in the study of the talmudic literature itself would tend to alienate the *halakhah* from its sources. In the middle of the ninth century Paltoi b. Abbaye Gaon was told: "The majority of the people incline after *Halakhot Ketu'ot*, saying: Why should we be occupied with the complexity of the Talmud? " Paltoi replied condemning this attitude stating that it would cause study of the Law to be forgotten and adding that "*Halakhot Ketu'ot* have been compiled not in order to be studied intensively, but rather so that they may be referred to by those who have studied the whole of the Talmud and experience doubt as to the proper interpretation of anything therein" (*Ḥemdah Genuzah*, no. 110; S. Assaf, *Teshuvot ha-Geonim Mi-Tokh ha-Genizah* (1928), 81, no. 158). It is possible that such a negative attitude toward codification by such a prominent scholar was responsible for the fact that almost no other "books of *halakhot*" were written during the remainder of the geonic period. From then on halakhic creativity mainly found expression in the form of responsa and, commencing from the first half of the tenth century, in a new literary form: that of full and summarizing monographs, written mostly in the fields of civil and family law and the laws of evidence and procedure, and in terms of which the law was applied in the Jewish communities and in their courts (e.g. *Sefer ha-Yerushot, Sefer ha-Pikkadon*, etc. of Saadiah Gaon; *Sefer ha-Shuttafut, Sefer ha-Arevut ve-ha-Kabblanut*, etc. of Samuel b. Hophni Gaon; *Sefer Shevu'ot, Sefer ha-Mikkaḥ ve-ha-Mimkar*, of Hai Gaon; See also *Beit ha-Beḥirah* to *Avot*, introd.).

The Rif (Alfasi). The geonic period was one of growing literary activity in the field of commentaries and responsa. Many *takkanot* were also framed in various fields of the law. At the close of this period the need for codification of the *halakhah* once more came to the fore, prompted by the historical factor that Babylonia had ceased to be the dominant center of the Jewish Diaspora, new centers of Jewish life having emerged in North Africa and in Europe, by which it was gradually supplanted. The proliferation of centers of Jewish life created the familiar phenomenon of varying customs and rules in different halakhic fields, a phenomenon present also in geonic and earlier times, but one that became increasingly manifest with the widening dispersion of the Jewish people. The outcome was the compilation, in the middle of the 11th century, of one of the most important "books of *halakhot*" in Jewish law, namely the *Sefer ha-Halakhot* of Isaac b. Jacob ha-Kohen Alfasi, known as the "Rif." In general form, this work is arranged along the lines of the *Halakhot Gedolot* although differing from it in several material respects. Like earlier "books of *halakhot*," it is arranged in the order of the talmudic tractates, and embraces only the laws in practice at the time (the relevant laws dispersed in the orders of *Kodashim* and *Tohorot*, and current at the time – such as *hilkhot Sefer Torah, mezuzah, tefillin, ẓiẓit*, etc. – were compiled by Alfasi in a separate work called *Halakhot Ketannot*). The brief talmudic discussion with which the author precedes each halakhic conclusion is far more extensive than in similar geonic works; in synoptic form the Rif outlines the talmudic problem and includes also aggadic statements of halakhic relevance (see Rif to BK 93a). Hence the work is also known as *Talmud Katan* (the small Talmud). Alfasi also undertook the great task of deciding many halakhic problems which had been the subject of dispute and he frequently quotes from the Jerusalem Talmud; in cases of dispute between the Jerusalem and Babylonian Talmuds on a particular matter, Alfasi decided according to the latter, following the rule of *Hilkheta ke-Vatra'ei* ("the law is according to the later scholars" – see Rabbinical Authority), since the redaction of the Babylonian Talmud was the later of the two (idem, Er., concl.). Alfasi's work was accepted by later generations as decisive and binding (see Menahem b. Zerah, introduction to *Ẓeidah la-Derekh*), and it prevailed over "books of *halakhot*" written during the next 100 years (such as the *Halakhot Kelulot* of Isaac ibn Ghayyat; the *Sefer ha-Ittim, Yiḥus She'ar Basar*, and *Sefer ha-Din* of Judah Barzillai, the *Even ha-Ezer* of Eliezer b. Nathan). Maimonides later noted that he differed from Alfasi in some ten cases only (Introduction to his commentary on the Mishnah; in his responsa collection, ed. by J. Blau, no. 251, the figure mentioned is 30). Five hundred years later Joseph Caro described Alfasi as "one of the three pillars of halakhic decision [*ammudei hora'ah*] supporting the House of Israel," and in this way part of Alfasi's conclusions found their way into Caro's code which has remained the authoritative codex of Jewish law until the present day.

The *Sefer ha-Halakhot* became the focal point of a prolific literature, partly in disagreement with it, partly in its defense, and partly in interpretation of its contents. This literature, which later accompanied the main Jewish law codifications, is termed *nosei kelim* ("arms-bearers"); the principal works are: Zerahiah ha-Levi Gerondi's *Ma'or;* Abraham b. David of Posquières' *Katuv Sham;* Naḥmanides' *Milḥemet ha-Shem* and *Ha-Zekhut;* and the commentaries of Nissim Gerondi and Joseph Ḥabiba (the latter called *Nimmukei Yosef*).

Maimonides' Method. In the 12th century Maimonides created a new literary form for the Codes, that of a "book of *pesakim*," of which his own work, the *Mishneh Torah*, was the peak. This new type of codifying appears to have asserted itself at the beginning of the 12th century, shortly after Alfasi's death, as is evidenced in a responsum of Joseph ibn Migash. Asked whether a *dayyan* – even when not sufficiently familiar with the methodology of the Talmud or understanding of the source of a law in the Talmud itself – was entitled to adjudicate in accordance with a "book of *halakhot*" and whether a decision of this kind could properly be relied upon, Ibn Migash replied that such conduct was not only fit and proper but preferable to a decision based on examination of the Talmud only, from which error could result, since "in our times there is no person whose knowledge of the Talmud attains a level which is reliable enough for him to decide from it"; the danger of error would be averted if the *dayyan* found good support for his decision in the statements of a great halakhic scholar as expressed in a "book of *halakhot*" (Ri Migash, Resp. no. 114). According to this approach, therefore, a "book of *halakhot*" was not to be regarded simply as an aid, to be referred to when the solution was not to be found in the Talmud itself – as was the opinion of Paltoi Gaon – but rather as a work in its own right and one to which reference should be made in preference to the Talmud in order to ascertain the law. It may be surmised that this opinion by a scholar greatly admired by Maimonides (see Introduction to his commentary on the Mishnah), influenced the latter's decision to undertake the great and laborious task of creating a code of Jewish law, which alone would serve as the basis for deciding the *halakhah*.

In the introduction to both his *Sefer Mitzvot* and *Mishneh Torah*, and elsewhere, Maimonides clearly explained his motivation, and the object and method of compiling his *Mishneh*

Torah. Factors such as the proliferation of halakhic material and the difficulty in ascertaining and understanding it "so that all the laws shall stand revealed to great and small," are known to have had a bearing on other halakhic codifications too, but Maimonides' great innovation lay in his objective and in the manner in which this objective was pursued. While his book never purported to be the source of authority of the *halakhah* – a status previously assigned only to the Written Law together with the Oral Law – it was nevertheless designed as the authoritative compilation in accordance with which the *halakhah* should be decided, since Maimonides was convinced that no contradiction between his book and earlier binding halakhic literature was conceivable. To attain his objective, Maimonides observed four guiding criteria in the preparation of his codification, criteria which are still observed in the compilation of a code:

(1) Location and concentration of all the material of Jewish law, from the Written Law until his time, and the scientific and systematic processing of this. This criterion, extensively discussed by Maimonides, was expressed in his unequivocal statement that anyone who referred to the Written Law and to his own book would know each and every detail of the *halakhah* and have no need for any other book. To this end Maimonides wrote a commentary on the Mishnah and the Jerusalem and Palestinian Talmuds, as well as his *Sefer Mitzvot,* before writing the *Mishneh Torah,* which he started in 1177 and worked on for ten years. In furtherance of this purpose he not only examined various versions of different *halakhot,* determining their exact wording (see Yad, Yom Tov, 2:12; Ishut, 11:13; Malveh etc., 15:2; etc.), but also included in his codification items of non-halakhic learning and scientific material necessary for the elucidation of the *halakhah* (see Yad, Kiddush ha-Ḥodesh, 17:24; 19:16). In this work, he embraced the whole spectrum of the *halakhah* and included laws not in practice at the time as well as bodies of rules in Jewish philosophy, principles of faith and religious dogma, and ethical and moral guidance, sometimes blended with halakhic matters (see Yad, Megillah 3:1–3; 4:12–14).

(2) Subdivision and classification of the material according to the subject matter. On Maimonides' own admission this criterion was a most difficult one to fulfill and in certain chapters the laws were collected from "ten or more places." As a model for his work Maimonides took the Mishnah, which itself is far from strictly classified according to subject matter (e.g., in the tractate *Kiddushin* there are many laws of property and likewise in *Gittin* there are many laws of agency, and so on). Similar subdivisions in earlier halakhic works, including the monographs of the geonic period, had hardly exhausted all the relevant material. Maimonides divided his work into 14 books (for this reason it is also called *Ha-Yad ha-Ḥazakah* – i.e., the letters "י" and "ד" representing 14 – based on Deut. 34:12), each subdivided into several parts (called *halakhot* – construct form: *hilkhot*) totaling 83 in all; the parts were further subdivided into a total of 1,000 chapters *(perakim)* consisting of some 15,000 paragraphs (each called a *"halakhah"*). Maimonides' efforts enabled later scholars, such as the authors of *Turim* and the Shulḥan Arukh, to continue with the classification of halakhic material.

(3) Deciding upon and designation of a single halakhic rule, without reference to disputing opinions or designation of sources. If Maimonides achieved his first two aims with a rare talent for assembling and classifying the material, his third was accomplished with a masterly daring and willingness to depart from custom in keeping with a man of his stature. Until his time there had been no halakhic work prescribing the rules of Jewish law without mention of the names of those who handed them down, or their sources in talmudic literature. If, in principle, Maimonides recognized as axiomatic the fact of the continuity of the *halakhah,* he nevertheless did not consider it necessary that such continuity should be outwardly emphasized. He realized that the quoting of differing opinions and the designation of talmudic sources were likely to confuse and limit the usefulness of a code. Accordingly, he introduced a new form into the literature of the Codes, that of a "book of *pesakim*" which gives a single statement of a rule of law – unqualified, final, and with no designation of sources, except in the case of some 120 halakhic rules added by Maimonides himself and prefaced with remarks such as "it seems to me" and a further 50 rules in which he decided between the opinions of *geonim* and other *rishonim.*

(4) Style and formulation. Maimonides chose for his code the language of the Mishnah in preference to that of the Pentateuch which he considered too limited for the adequate expression of all the rules, and also in preference to that of the Talmud, which he considered insufficiently understood in his time (introduction to *Sefer ha-Mitzvot*). In fact this disclosure is eloquent testimony to Maimonides' modesty, for even though he took the style of the Mishnah as his basis, the overall stylistic structure of his work is nonetheless an original creation marked by two qualities: a clear and mellifluous Hebrew and a lucid legal formulation which is precise and can be read and understood without difficulty. The creation of a Hebrew legal style is one of the highlights of Maimonides' work, which has not been emulated until the present day. The various sources from which Maimonides assembled his halakhic material – the Mishnah, midrashic works, the two Talmuds, the Tosefta and the literature of the *geonim* and other *rishonim* – had all been written in different languages or different idioms. Maimonides molded this linguistic and stylistic medley into a harmonious and uniform style with no obtrusive reminders of its past. It has been the good fortune of the Hebrew language that in this regard he departed from his practice of writing in Arabic, thus bequeathing to the Hebrew language the precious asset of a legal style, which is still drawn upon at the present time. (His reply to a pupil's request that the *Mishneh Torah* be translated into Arabic was "it would lose all its appeal"; *Kovez Teshuvot ha-Rambam ve-Iggerotav* pt. 2 (1859), 15b.)

Notwithstanding all his innovations in the codification of Jewish law, Maimonides left virtually unchanged the casuistic method of formulation that had been customary until his time, except that he rendered the casuistic exposition in a clear and concentrated manner and sometimes added also a normative principle (see e.g., Yad, To'en, etc. 9:7–8). In doing so Maimonides was apparently influenced by three considerations: (1) he feared that the omission of the casuistic exposition and the statement of a normative legal principle in its place would fail to ensure inclusion of all the pertinent legal facts embraced by the rule, whereas his basic aim was to cover the entire existing body of the *halakhah*; (2) since outwardly he severed his book from talmudic law, Maimonides' adherence to the casuistic method enabled him to preserve an inherent connection between the two, as anyone reading the *Mishneh Torah* inevitably senses the spirit and atmosphere of talmudic literature; and (3) the casuistic method, being substantive to the development of Jewish law, dictated itself as the chosen method for codification, so as to facilitate development of the law by way of distinguishing between earlier legal precedents.

Reactions to Maimonides' Approach. As may have been anticipated, Maimonides' far-reaching innovation in the form of a code of Jewish law gave rise to acrimonious debate and strong criticism – centering mainly around his failure to mention the names of the scholars and their different opinions, or to give any indication of talmudic sources. Maimonides justified his omission of the scholars' names on the grounds that this was in answer to the Karaites whose complaint against the Oral Law was that "you rely on the statements of individuals"; therefore he had taken note of the chain of transmission in his introduction but simply stated the halakhic rule in the body of the work in order to make known that "the law was transmitted by way of the many to the many and not from a single individual to another individual" (Letter to R. Phinehas, *dayyan* of Alexandria, in *Kovez Teshuvot* . . . pt. 1, p. 26, no. 140). However, he did recognize the validity of one contention, and admitted that he should have indicated the source from which a particular law was taken, not in the codification itself but in a separate work (a task which he contemplated undertaking but was apparently unable to accomplish; *ibid.*). In the style of a great master, confident of the essential validity of his creation, Maimonides wrote: "In time to come, when the envy and stormy passions have subsided, all of Israel will rest content with it alone and will not seize on any other [halakhic work]" (*Iggerot ha-Rambam,* ed. by D. H. Baneth, no. 6). To some extent his prophecy was fulfilled and even in his lifetime the law was decided in accordance with his codification in most of the academies in Babylonia (*Teshuvot ha-Rambam,* ed. A. Freimann (1934), 69), Sicily Yemen (*Kovez Teshuvot ha-Rambam ve-Iggerotav* (1859), pt. 2, 24ff.), and elsewhere; in a number of countries, particularly in the Oriental ones, special *takkanot* were enacted to lay down that all matters were to be decided in accordance with this work (Ran, Resp. no 62).

However, many other scholars strongly criticized Maimonides for these omissions, even though they admired and were awed by the greatness of his labors (see e.g., *Hassagot Rabad,* Kelayim, 6:2). His sharpest critic in his own lifetime was the Provençal scholar Abraham b. David of Posquières (Rabad), who feared that the convenient use of Maimonides' work would inhibit study of the talmudic sources and deprive the *dayyan* of a choice between different opinions in making his decision *(ibid.)*. Accordingly, when Maimonides' work reached him he studied it in its entirety, writing strictures of exemplary brevity on a substantial proportion of its laws, often sharply worded so as to oblige the reader to refer to the talmudic sources in ascertaining the correctness of Maimonides' statements, so that the link between the law and its sources would be restored. Approximately 100 years later Maimonides' basic notion concerning the place of a "book of *pesakim*" in Jewish law was sharply criticized by the distinguished halakhist of Germany and Spain, Asher b. Jehiel (the Rosh). Dealing with the decision of a *dayyan* based on a rule in the *Mishneh Torah,* Asher b. Jehiel determined that the *dayyan* had erred as a result of not properly understanding Maimonides' statements as could be proved by examination of the talmudic source of the rule in question. He concluded that "all teachers err if they instruct from the statements of Maimonides without being sufficiently familiar with the *Gemara* so as to know where they were taken from . . . therefore no person should be relied upon to judge and instruct on the strength of his book without finding supporting evidence in the *Gemara*" (Rosh, Resp. 31:9). Asher's attitude was in keeping with his general view of the *dayyan*'s freedom to decide and his authority to dissent from an instruction not originating from the Talmud itself, provided that this could be established in a clear and convincing manner (*Piskei ha-Rosh,* Sanh. 4:6 and see Rabbinical Authority). In his opinion, any undefined codification that did not link a rule with its talmudic source served to deprive the *dayyan* of his decisory authority and for this reason the halakhic system could not condone the existence of such a codification. As a result, it was once more laid down that a "book of *halakhot*" possessed no independent standing but was to serve only as an aid to finding the law in talmudic literature itself. If Maimonides' original purpose was not accepted, his *Mishneh Torah* nevertheless exerted a significant influence on the future codification of Jewish law, not only because Maimonides was the "second pillar" on which Joseph Caro rested his Shulḥan Arukh, but because the latter even accepted the basic premise of Maimonides' method, although with a different approach and in a changed form.

"Arms-Bearers" *(Nosei Kelim)*. The bitter controversy which the *Mishneh Torah* evoked was the spur to the creation of a proliferous literature and a large camp of "arms-bearers," whose central purpose was to uncover Maimonides' sources, and also to comment on, qualify, and defend him – the *hassagot* of Abraham b. David serving as their primary starting point. The best-known of these, appearing in virtually all the editions of Maimonides, are the commentaries *Migdal Oz* and *Maggid Mishneh* of Shem Tov b. Abraham ibn Gaon and Vidal Yom Tov of Tolosa respectively, both 14th-century Spanish scholars; the *Kesef Mishneh* of Joseph Caro, author of the Shulḥan Arukh, and the *Yekar Tiferet* of David b. Solomon ibn Abi Zimra, leading Egyptian scholar of the 16th century; the *Leḥem Mishneh* of Abraham b. Moses de Boton, a late 16th-century scholar of Salonika; and the *Mishneh le-Melekh* of Judah Rosanes, a leading Turkish scholar at the beginning of the 18th century. Also noteworthy is a work called *Haggahot Maimuniyyot,* apparently written by a pupil of Meir b. Baruch of Rothenburg at the end of the 13th century, with the object of supplementing the laws in the *Mishneh Torah* with the rules of the German and French scholars. It would be difficult to find in all of halakhic literature another instance of a work that produced results so contrary to the avowed purpose of its author. Far from restoring to the *halakhah* its uniformity and anonymity, "without polemics or dissection . . . but in clear and accurate statements" (Yad, introd.), Maimonides' pursuit of that very aim became the reason for the compilation of hundreds of books on his work, all of them dissecting, complicating, and increasing halakhic problems, resulting in a lack of uniformity far greater than before.

Codification until the Compilation of the Arba'ah Turim. The polemic surrounding Maimonides' work resulted in the adoption of many literary forms for codification of the *halakhah,* all aimed at compressing and classifying the material in an assimilable manner while preserving at the same time the link with the talmudic sources. Many scholars adopted the familiar form of the "book of *halakhot*" arranged in the order of the talmudic tractates, partially divided in accordance with the subject matter; most noteworthy are: *Sefer Avi ha-Ezri* and *Sefer Avi Asaf* by Eliezer b. Joel ha-Levi (Ravyah), a late 12th-century German scholar; *Or Zaru'a* by Isaac b. Moses of Vienna (Riaz), first half of the 13th century; and the *Mordekhai* of Mordecai b. Hillel ha-Kohen, a late 13th-century German scholar. A work written at the beginning of the 14th century, in classic "book of *halakhot*" form, was Asher b. Jehiel's *Piskei ha-Rosh* (also known as *Sefer Asheri*). In pursuit of his fundamental approach toward the codification of Jewish law and the *dayyan*'s freedom to decide, Asher compiled his work to resemble Alfasi's *Sefer ha-Halakhot* (it has been suggested that his work was compiled as an addendum to the latter), adopting both the outer arrangement following the order of the talmudic tractates, and the inner structure of a synoptic statement (though wider than Alfasi's) of the talmudic discussion, leading to determination of the halakhic rule. Asher, who at first was the leader of German Jewry after the death of his eminent teacher, Meir of Rothenburg, and later became one of the leading scholars of Spain, included the opinions of both schools in his work and decided between them. His work was acknowledged as a recognized and binding "book of *halakhot*," its stated conclusions often being preferred to those in the *Mishneh Torah.* Asher was the "third pillar" on which Joseph Caro founded his Shulḥan Arukh 200 years later.

Another form of "book of *halakhot*" in this period was that arranged according to subject matter, of which a classic example is the *Sefer ha-Terumot* of Samuel b. Isaac ha-Sardi, a contemporary of Naḥmanides. His work is divided into 70 gates *(she'arim)* – each dealing with a particular subject – in turn subdivided into chapters (*inyanim* or *ḥalakim*) and paragraphs *(peratim)*, a subdivision similar to that of the *Mishneh Torah.* From the point of view of its contents, this work is a "book of *halakhot*" proper and not a "book of *pesakim*," since in each case the conclusion is preceded by a discussion of the talmudic source, and different opinions are quoted and a decision taken. The entire work is devoted to the civil law *(dinei mamonot)*, the first codification to deal exclusively with this field of Jewish law. Some writers adopted the form of a "book of *halakhot*" arranged according to the order of the *mitzvot*. Maimonides had written his *Sefer ha-Mitzvot* with the object of enumerating all the precepts so as to avoid omitting any of them later in the compilation of his code, but in this later period "books of *mitzvot*" were written with the object of deciding the law. In the mid-13th century the *Sefer Mitzvot Gadol* (known as the SeMaG) was compiled by Moses of Coucy, a French tosafist. It is divided into two parts, consisting of the negative and positive precepts, and each precept is accompanied by a quotation of the talmudic sources in which the rules of the precept are discussed as well as the opinions of other scholars, followed by the halakhic conclusion. When faced with differences of opinion between Maimonides and distinguished Franco-German scholars – such as Rashi and Rabbenu Tam – Moses of Coucy generally decided in accordance with the later scholars. One of the contributing factors to the spread of this work appears to have been the decree of Pope Gregory IX (1242) banning the Talmud and its study, Moses' work being designed to serve as a means of study and decision until the ban was lifted. For some considerable time it remained one of the best known and most acknowledged halakhic textbooks. Some time later Isaac b. Joseph of Corbeil wrote his *Ammudei ha-Golah,* known also as the *Sefer Mitzvot Katan* or SeMaK. Here too the laws, accompanied by a very brief statement of their talmudic sources, are arranged in the order of the precepts, and the work is divided into seven parts corresponding to the seven days of the week, with the various precepts quoted in relation to particular days of the week on the strength of various hints and homilies (e.g., the laws of marriage on Wednesday since "a virgin marries on a Wednesday," (Ket. 2a); procedural laws on Thursday, since the *battei din* were in session on this day according to the *Takkanat Ezra*).

Other "books of *halakhot*" were arranged according to the individual criteria of their authors; for example, Isaac b. Abba Mari, the 12th-century Provençal scholar, partly arranged his *Ittur Soferim* (also known as the *Sefer ha-Ittur*) according to the order of appearance of the letters in a certain passage. Zedekiah ben Abraham Anav (13th century, Italy) composed the *Shibbolei Ha-Lekket* and the *Sefer Issur ve-Heter* in an order not too different from that later to be adopted by the Tur. A classic codification, in two parts, was compiled in the 14th century by another Provençal scholar, Jeroham b. Meshullam. The first part, called *Mesharim,* is devoted exclusively to the civil law, including associated family law (maintenance, the *ketubbah,* etc.); the second part, *Adam ve-Ḥavvah,* deals with ritual law *(issur ve-hetter)* including that part of family law concerned with the nonpecuniary relationships between spouses, such as the laws of marriage and divorce; it is further divided into two parts, and arranged in the order of application of the various laws at separate stages in a man's lifetime – *Adam* covers from birth to marriage, and *Ḥavvah* from marriage to death. The whole codification is divided into parts called *netivot,* with further subdivision. In this period a new type of codification emerged which in the course of time played a decisive role in the codification of the *halakhah,* the *Torat ha-Bayit* of Solomon b. Abraham Adret (Rashba), spiritual leader of Spanish Jewry in mid-13th century. This work comprises two separate books: the first, *Torat ha-Bayit ha-Arokh,* may properly be classified as a "book of *halakhot*" as the author deals with the talmudic sources and the different opinions of the *geonim* and *rishonim* in relation to each halakhic matter, reaching the halakhic conclusion after full discussion of the sources; however the second, *Torat ha-Bayit ha-Kaẓar,* falls into the category of a "book of *pesakim,*" since in each case the author merely states the halakhic conclusion which he reached in the first part of his work. In this manner Adret sought to overcome the major stumbling block to codification of the *halakhah*: in the one book he preserved a close link with all the halakhic sources, in the second – based on the discussion and sources in the former – he provided a classic codification presenting a single opinion only, final and decisive. The work as a whole is divided into seven *battim* ("houses") subdivided into *she'arim* ("gates"), and deals with only a part of the ritual law, such as the dietary laws. Adret apparently intended to prepare such a twofold codification to cover the entire field of *halakhah* but succeeded in compiling works in only a few spheres of the *halakhah; Avodat ha-Kodesh* on the festival laws, *Shaar ha-Mayim* on the laws of *mikveh,* and *Piskei Ḥallah* on the laws of *ḥallah.* This may have been the reason why Adret's novel and original method failed to make any great impact on his contemporaries and it was only about 200 years later that its proper worth was recognized.

The System of the "Ba'al ha-Turim." While most of the forms of codification so far discussed were able to sustain the link with the halakhic sources, they failed to produce a work that was convenient to use, easily assimilable, and clearly decisive. Furthermore, in the 12th and 13th centuries a rich and extensive halakhic literature – over and above the halakhic manuals already described – was created in the main centers of Jewish life. In Germany, France, and other Western European countries there was the impressive literary output of the tosafists which, even if expressed mainly in the form of novellae, was obviously not to be overlooked by the *dayyan* when deciding the law. Numbered among the tosafists were some of the most distinguished scholars, such as Rabbenu Tam and Meir of Rothenburg (MaHaRaM), whose thousands of responsa constituted a decided law which was binding on the courts. Equally important was the halakhic literature, in the form of commentaries, novellae, and responsa, of the contemporaneous scholars of the Spanish school, such as Meir ha-Levi Abulafia (RaMah), Naḥmanides, and Solomon b. Abraham Adret. This flowering of halakhic literature not only made necessary the compilation of a suitable codification to assemble and classify the whole, but was also responsible for growing differences of opinion and custom in the various Jewish centers: "and there remains no halakhic decision which is not subject to disputing opinions so that many will search in vain to find the word of the Lord" (introd. to *Tur,* YD; cf. Tosef. Eduy. 1:1 and see also compilation of the Mishnah, above). This phenomenon caused particular difficulty in the wide field of civil law *(Dinei Mamonot)* in relation to the plea of *Kim li,* a plea which had become particularly prevalent, in the view of many halakhic scholars, from the time of Meir of Rothenburg onward and one which tended to undermine the existence of proper and ordered judicial authority. In terms of this plea, based on the principle that the onus of proof rests on the party seeking to recover from his neighbor *(ha-moẓi me-ḥavero alav ha-re'ayah)*, the defendant was able to avail himself of the existence of disputing halakhic opinions to contend that the opinion which favored his position was the correct one, and that no *mamon* was to be recovered from his possession until the contrary had been proved (introd. to *Tur*, ḤM; see also introd. to *Yam shel Shelomo*, BK).

Against this background Jacob b. Asher, third son of Asher b. Jehiel and *dayyan* in Toledo in the first half of the 14th century, compiled his code in the form of four *Turim* (lit. "rows" or "columns"). In his work he observed two criteria. Firstly, he decided in accordance with the opinion of Alfasi, and, whenever this was disputed by Maimonides or other *posekim*, accepted the opinions of his father, as they are expressed in Asher b. Jehiel's responsa or in his decisions (Introd. to Tur, ḤM). To this end he compiled an abridgment of the *Piskei ha-Rosh*, called *Sefer ha-Remazim* or *Simanei Asheri*. Jacob's acceptance of his father's decisions was based on the rule of *Hilkheta ke-Vatra'ei*, since Asher was the last *posek* to know of and decide between the opinions of the German and Spanish scholars. Secondly, with regard to form, Jacob – unlike Solomon b. Adret – produced his codification in a single work combining the qualities of a "book of *halakhot*" with those of a "book of *pesakim*." He states the essence of the individual rules briefly, without indicating the talmudic sources or the names of scholars (except at the beginning of a *Tur* or a particular group of rules), thus giving his work the quality of a "book of *pesakim*." A statement of each individual rule is followed by a brief quotation of the different opinions expressed on it by the post-talmudic scholars, the *geonim* or other *rishonim* and on these the author makes his decision, sometimes explicitly and sometimes by implication (see introd. to Tur, OḤ, YD, and ḤM); in this way the work is also a "book of *halakhot*." In this manner Jacob b. Asher struck a balance by finding a format that was convenient and concise yet preserved the link with the halakhic sources.

Structure of the Turim. Jacob b. Asher's codification, like Alfasi's but unlike that of Maimonides, includes only the laws in practice in his time and is divided into four parts *(turim)*, each further subdivided into *halakhot* and *simanim* (the latter now further subdivided into *se'ifim* or subsections). The first *Tur*, *Tur Oraḥ Ḥayyim*, includes all the rules relating to man's day-to-day conduct, such as the laws of prayer, blessings etc., as well as those relating to the Sabbath and festivals; the second *Tur Yoreh De'ah* deals with the dietary laws, laws of ritual purity, circumcision, visiting the sick, mourning, and the like, and also with laws at present treated as part of the "civil" law, such as the law of interest (in the *Mishneh Torah* dealt with as part of the law of lender and borrower); the third, *Tur Even ha-Ezer*, covers all matters of family law such as the laws of marriage and divorce and the pecuniary relationship between spouses; the last, the *Tur Ḥoshen Mishpat* covers by far the greater part of civil law as well as certain portions of criminal law, beginning with the laws relating to composition of the courts and judicial authority, followed by the laws of evidence, the civil law (loans, partnership, property, etc.), and concluding with the laws of theft and robbery and tort. This arrangement of the material differed from that of the *Mishneh Torah*, where Maimonides was influenced by the order in which the material is treated in the Talmud. (Thus in the *Mishneh Torah* Maimonides first deals with the laws of tort in the 11th book and in his last book with the laws of composition of the courts, evidence, etc., in a similar manner to the order in the Talmud in which the laws of tort are opened with the tractate *Bava Kamma* and the laws of court composition, evidence, etc. are dealt with in the tractate *Sanhedrin*.) Similarly, the various halakhic subjects are subdivided into smaller and more clearly defined units than in Maimonides' code. Like Maimonides, however, Jacob b. Asher combines his introduction or conclusion to the various halakhic subjects with statements of an ethical and moral nature, especially at the beginning of each *Tur* or of particular parts of them. In these statements he deals at length with aggadic sayings, their authors, and talmudic sources (see e.g., the introduction to OḤ and ḤM and to *hilkhot* Shabbat, OḤ 242). Although the *Mishneh Torah* crystallizes the subject matter of the *halakhah* into more self-contained and complete divisions and is written in a more attractive and lucid style, in the *Turim* Jacob b. Asher not only assembled and classified the entire *halakhah* of his time in a convenient and orderly form but was also successful in finding a form of codification suited to the special nature of the *halakhah*. Although some Oriental communities continued to regard the *Mishneh Torah* as the binding "book of *pesakim*," the communities of the West – particularly those of Germany, Italy, and Poland – decided in accordance with the *Turim*, which became the second Hebrew book to appear in print (in 1475).

At the same time and in the following generations several other "books of *halakhot*" and *"pesakim"* were compiled, mostly dealing with the subject matter of the *Tur Oraḥ Ḥayyim* and *Yoreh De'ah*. These include: the *Abudarham* of David b. Joseph Abudarham, a 14th-century Spanish scholar; the *Agur* of Jacob b. Judah Landau, a 15th-century Italian scholar; and the 14th-century German scholar Isaac b. Meir of Dueren's *Sha'arei Dura*, which deals only with the ritual laws and may be classified as a "book of *pesakim*," since the opinions of the *rishonim* are scantily quoted and talmudic sources not at all. Other similar works from this period deal with family law also, as in the *Orḥot Ḥayyim* of Aaron b. Jacob ha-Kohen of Lunel, an early 14th-century French scholar, and the *Ẓeidah la-Derekh* of the contemporary Spanish scholar, Menahem b. Zerah. During this period a few halakhic works dealt also with the topics of civil law *(dinei mamanot)* and matrimony. In Ashkenaz in the first half of the 14th century the *Aggudah*, comprising *pesakim* and novellae, was compiled by Alexander Suslin ha-Kohen, on all the tractates of the Talmud, arranged in the order of the latter. In Spain several halakhic works were compiled. Of special interest is the *Ḥukot ha-Dayyanim* of Abraham b. Solomon Ibn Tazarti, a pupil of Solomon ben Adret, published only in recent years. The whole work deals with civil law *(dinei mamanot)* and matrimony in the sphere of *halakhah*. In many respects his method of codification is similar to that of the *Turim*. The above-mentioned works remained in use alongside Jacob b. Asher's *Turim*, which for some 200 years was the accepted and central "book of *pesakim*," and in due course formed a basis for the compilation of Joseph Caro's Shulḥan Arukh, the foremost codification of Jewish law.

"Arms-Bearers" to the Turim. Works on the *Turim* were written in the 15th century by Spanish scholars (see Introd. *Beit Yosef* to Tur OḤ, mentioning the commentaries of Isaac Aboab, Jacob ibn Ḥabib, etc.), but the classic "arms-bearers" of the *Turim* were composed in the 16th and early 17th centuries, most of them by German scholars. Two of the best known are the *Beit Yosef* and *Darkhei Moshe*. In the second half of the 16th century Joshua Falk b. Alexander Katz of Poland compiled his *Beit Yisrael*, a work in three parts: the first, *Perishah*, is a commentary on the *Turim;* the second, *Derishah*, deals with the different opinions of other halakhic scholars; and the last, *Be'urim*, consists of glosses on *Darkhei Moshe*. The classic work on the *Turim* is the *Bayit Ḥadash ("Baḥ")*, a commentary by Joel b. Samuel Sirkes, the 17th-century Polish scholar, in which the sources of the *Turim* are indicated, and differing opinions quoted in the *Turim, Beit Yosef,* and *Darkhei Moshe* discussed, and the law decided. In addition, Sirkes made a critical examination of the text of the *Turim.*

The Method of Joseph Caro. In the period from Jacob b. Asher until Joseph Caro a series of decisive historical events profoundly influenced Jewish life. The outbreak of the Black Death (1348–50), followed by intensified persecution of German Jewry, and that of Spanish Jewry, commencing from the middle of the 14th century and ending with the expulsion from Spain in 1492, resulted in the mass migration of Jewish communities and the establishment of new centers. Thus Polish Jewry was built up from German migrants while Spanish Jews settled mainly in Oriental countries, especially Turkey, Ereẓ Israel, Egypt, and North Africa. One such migrant was Joseph Caro, who was born in Spain in 1488 and settled at Safed in Ereẓ Israel where he became a member of the Great Rabbinical Court, the foremost halakhic tribunal of his time.

This process of uprooting and resettlement of whole Jewish communities brought many halakhic problems in its wake and many conflicts between established communities and new arrivals, with the result that "... the Law has come to consist of innumerable *torot*" (*Beit Yosef* to Tur OḤ, introd.) and "everyone builds a platform unto himself" (S. Luria, *Yam shel Shelomo* to BK, introd.). This state of affairs was accompanied by considerable creativity in the field of halakhic literature, particularly in the form of responsa, with which the *dayyan* could not easily keep abreast. At this time, too, the longing of the Jews to return to their ancient homeland, to restore their life "as in the days of yore," once more came to the fore. One of the ways in which this longing was expressed was Jacob Berab's efforts to renew ordination (*semikhah;* Caro was one of the first to be ordained by him), in order to restore supreme halakhic authority over the nation. A codification that would assemble, summarize, and reduce the *halakhah* therefore became necessary; the task was undertaken by Joseph Caro, who envisaged the compilation of a single work consisting of two parts, differing from each other in form and content but supplementing each other in their common purpose. Maimonides too hinted at this method when he planned to supplement his *Mishneh Torah* with a separate book on its sources, and Solomon b. Abraham Adret actually adopted this method (supra), but it was Caro who succeeded in bringing the method to fruition and converting it into the principal and appointed codificatory receptacle of the *halakhah.*

Of the two parts of his code, the *Beit Yosef* and the Shulḥan Arukh, the former takes precedence, not only chronologically but also in scope and content. Caro set himself two principal objectives in *Beit Yosef.* He aimed at including all the halakhic material in use at the time, with the talmudic sources and the different opinions expressed in post-talmudic literature up to his day; here Caro linked himself to the *Turim,* avoiding the need to quote the halakhic material already stated there (*Beit Yosef* to Tur OḤ, introd.). Apart from talmudic literature itself, *Beit Yosef* includes material from the works of 32 of the most distinguished halakhic scholars, who are mentioned by name *(ibid.),* including a few "sayings from the Zohar" (although he stresses that in cases of contradiction the Talmud is to be preferred to the Zohar; *Beit Yosef,* OḤ, 25). Caro's second objective was to decide the law, "since this is the purpose that we shall have one Torah and uniform law" *(ibid.).* For this purpose he chose an original method of calculating the rule: whenever Alfasi, Maimonides, and Asher b. Jehiel had dealt with a particular matter, the law was decided according to their majority opinion (except if a majority of halakhic scholars held a different opinion and there was a contrary custom); if a matter had been discussed by only two of these three and their opinions differed, five additional authorities were considered (Naḥmanides, Solomon b. Abraham Adret, Nissim Gerondi, Mordecai b. Hillel, and Moses b. Jacob of Coucy) and the law decided according to their majority opinion; if none of the first three had dealt with a matter, the law was decided according to the opinion of the majority of the "famous scholars *(mefursamim, ibid.).* Caro admitted that the proper method of deciding the law would have been by a substantive examination of the correctness of each rule in terms of the talmudic sources, but added that this would have made the task of deciding between the great halakhic scholars extremely laborious and protracted, considering the large number of rules quiring decision *(ibid.).*

Caro realized that the *Beit Yosef* as it stood, in essence a "book of *halakhot,*" would not answer the main requirements and that only a book embracing the *halakhah* in undefined and summarized form, in the manner of the *Mishneh Torah,* was capable of being "a regulation for the benefit of the world" (*tikkun ha-olam; Kesef Mishneh* on Introd. to *Mishneh Torah*). He accordingly decided to compile an additional book, the Shulḥan Arukh (a name already appearing in Mekh., Mishpatim, 1), in which conclusions from his *Beit Yosef* were to be stated "briefly in clear language ... so that every rule [that the *dayyan* shall be asked to deal with] shall be clear in practice" (introd. to Sh. Ar., ḤM). Caro's aim was that the Shulḥan Arukh should serve not only the *talmidei ḥakhamim,* but all of the people; that "the *talmidim ketannim* shall constantly have reference thereto" – as was the wish of earlier codifiers of the *halakhah,* just as it had been the codificatory objective in other legal systems (supra). He therefore divided the Shulḥan Arukh into 30 parts, one to be read each day so that the whole work could be covered every month *(ibid.).*

If the motivation and aims of Maimonides and Caro in codifying the *halakhah* were the same, their choice of method differed, since the former sought to obviate any subsequent need for a book other than his own in deciding the *halakhah,* whereas the latter realized that this was "a short and a long road, because no rule would ever be known according to its proper derivation" (*Beit Yosef,* introd. to OḤ – on the subject of summaries such as the *Semak, Aggur,* and *Kol Bo*). Therefore a brief, synoptic "book of *pesakim*" would be a useful supplement to a separate "book of *halakhot*" embracing the sources and different opinions. Thus it was that Maimonides regarded the *Mishneh Torah* as his main creation and his other halakhic works as preparatory and secondary thereto, whereas Caro regarded the *Beit Yosef* as his primary creation; he devoted 20 years to compiling it and a further 12 to annotating it (see also introd. to his *Bedek ha-Bayit*), calling it his *Ḥibbur ha-Gadol* ("great work," introd. to Sh. Ar.), compared with *Beit Yosef,* the Shulḥan Arukh was no more than a "collection from the flowery crown of this large and thick tree" *(ibid.).* Two books, separate yet supplementary – the one a "book of *halakhot*" in which the conclusion is tied to the sources, the other a "book of *pesakim*" containing the same conclusion, in most cases stated briefly and standing alone – were the final form adopted for codification of the *halakhah.*

Structure and Arrangement of the Shulḥan Arukh. Caro's use of the *Turim* as the basis for his work accounts for their similar subdivision and structure; the Shulḥan Arukh is also divided into four parts with the same titles as those of the four *turim,* in turn subdivided into some 120 *halakhot* 1,700 *simanim* and 13,350 *se'ifim.* There are, however, a number of differences between the two codifications. Thus Jacob b. Asher's subdivision of large units into smaller ones is not followed in the Shulḥan Arukh, where the material is to some extent more concentrated, Caro in this sense having chosen a middle way between Maimonides and Jacob b. Asher (cf. e.g., the subdivision in the Tur and Sh. Ar., ḤM, 39–74 and 190–226; so too the four books of *Nezikim, Kinyan, Mishpatim,* and *Shofetim* are divided in the *Mishneh Torah* into 19 *halakhot* and the same material is divided in the Tur and Sh. Ar., ḤM, into 58 and 42 *halakhot* respectively; on rare occasions the Sh. Ar. is subdivided to a greater extent: see e.g., ḤM, 303–6 and 157–75). Caro also provided each *siman* with a heading (see introd. to *Sma,* conclusion), at times shortening the names of *halakhot* when they were unduly long (cf. Tur and Sh. Ar., ḤM, 241–9 and 273–5) or adding to them when they were inadequate descriptions of their contents (*ibid.,* 272 and 388). At times Caro added an entire topic that does not appear in the *Turim* (*ibid.,* 427; cf. Maim.Yad, Roẓe'aḥ 11) and occasionally he deleted some *halakhot* (Sh. Ar., ḤM 247).

The Shulḥan Arukh omits not only the halakhic sources and the names of the scholars – as is the case in the *Mishneh Torah* – but also anything additional that is not essential to the rule itself, such as moral and ethical statements, scriptural authority, and substantiation of the rule. Hence Caro's work is far briefer than that of Jacob b. Asher or even of Maimonides (compare, e.g., Yad, Tefillah, 11:1–2, with Sh. Ar., OḤ, 150:1–2; Yad, To'en 12:5 with Sh. Ar., ḤM 144:1, Tur, OḤ 1 with Sh. Ar., OḤ 1:1). In its uniform and integral creation as well as clarity and beauty of style, the *Mishneh Torah* has retained its position of supremacy; yet, from the standpoint of brevity and decisiveness the Shulḥan Arukh stands supreme, a factor undoubtedly contributing toward its acceptance as the standard "book of *pesakim*" of the *halakhah.* The Mishnah, the first halakhic codification after the biblical law, was completed in Lower Galilee at the end of the second century; about 1350 years later, in 1563, the last authoritative codification was completed in Upper Galilee and once again "the Law went forth from Zion" to the whole Diaspora. In 1565 all four parts of the Shulḥan Arukh were printed for the first time in Venice and Caro lived to see his work reprinted several times and disseminated among all the communities of Israel.

The Role of Moses Isserles ("Rema") in Halakhic Codification. Moses Isserles was one of the leading scholars of Polish Jewry at the time Caro's code reached that country. His teacher Shalom Sakhna was utterly opposed to the idea of codifying the *halakhah,* as he believed that the decision of the *dayyan* must be made on the strength of an individual study of the halakhic sources and that the very fact of the law's redaction sufficed to deprive him of his decisory discretion in any concrete case before him. This followed from the doctrine of *Hilkheta ke-Vatra'ei* (see Authority, Rabbinical[1]) which would constrain the *dayyan* to consider himself bound by the decision contained in the code. Consequently he would refrain from following other canons of decision, namely that the *dayyan* must act "only according to what he sees with his own eyes" and that he must decide "according to the present exigencies and the dictates of his own heart" (see the statement of Israel, son of Shalom Shakhna, quoted in Rema, Resp. no. 25; this had also been the attitude of Jacob Pollak, teacher of Shalom Shakhna, *ibid.*). At first Isserles sought to compile his book, the *Darkhei Moshe,* to follow the *Turim* and merely to assemble all the halakhic material until his time in brief and synoptic form – including the different opinions but without deciding between them – for the sole purpose of making it easier for the *dayyan* to find the material (introd. to *Darkhei Moshe*). However, while he was writing his book, Caro's *Beit Yosef* reached him and when he realized that Caro had already assembled all the halakhic material his first reaction was not to continue with his own book. In the end he decided to complete it, for two main reasons: firstly, because Caro had not incorporated a substantial portion of halakhic literature, particularly the contribution of the Ashkenazi scholars; secondly, because he disputed Caro's main decisory canon, namely that Alfasi, Maimonides, and Asher b. Jehiel were the "pillars of halakhic decision," since it conflicted with the principle of *Hilkheta ke-Vatra'ei,* that the law was to be decided in accordance with the opinions of later distinguished scholars. Isserles accordingly changed the direction of his book to decide the law in accordance with this latter principle, noting specifically, moreover, that it would be permissible for the *dayyan* to differ even from this determination since "he must act only in accordance with what he sees with his own eyes" (*ibid.;* the *Darkhei Moshe* printed in the regular editions of the *Tur* and called *Darkhei Moshe Kaẓar* is apparently an abridgment of *Darkhei Moshe ha-Arokh*). Isserles pursued these objectives in his second codifying work, the *Torah Ḥattat,* embracing a substantial part of the ritual, mainly dietary laws, and compiled in the wake of the *Sha'arei Dura* (above). Later, when the Shulḥan Arukh also came to hand, Isserles decided to add his own glosses to it, which he "spread like a cloth" (i.e., *mappah,* by which name his glosses are known), on Caro's "prepared table" (the meaning of *shulḥan arukh*) of the *halakhah.*

In his glosses, representing the conclusions arrived at in his *Darkhei Moshe* (Rema, Resp. nos. 35 and 131), Isserles quoted the different Ashkenazi opinions and customs in order to decide between them according to the *Hilkheta ke-Vatra'ei* rule (*ibid.,* introduction), all in the brief and decisive style of the Shulḥan Arukh. If his glosses served to interrupt the element of uniform law imparted by the Shulḥan Arukh, this was nevertheless in keeping with Isserles' purpose: "That students shall not follow thereafter to drink from it without dispute," but that the *dayyan* should know of the existence of differing opinions, even if briefly stated, and decide according to the rule of *Hilketa ke-Vatr'ei* and "what he sees with his own eyes" *(ibid.)*. His glosses also make changes in the wording of the *meḥabber's* statements (i.e., "the author," as Caro is referred to in the Sh. Ar.; see e.g., Sh. Ar., ḤM 121:9, Isserles and *Sma* 20); sometimes Caro's statements are explained (Isserles, Sh. Ar., ḤM 131:4 concl.) or contradictions between different decisions pointed out; at times a particular rule is added, so as to refine the structure of the main work (e.g., Sh. Ar., ḤM 182:1; cf. also the statements of Caro and Jacob b. Asher, mentioned above and Yad, *Sheluḥin* etc., 1:1). Isserles' glosses rounded off the Shulḥan Arukh into a codification embracing all the nuances of the *halakhah* in use in the various Jewish centers. Whereas Abraham b. David's strictures on the *Mishneh Torah* resulted in a strong movement against Maimonides and the ultimate non-acceptance of his work as the codex of the *halakhah,* the glosses of Isserles – who called Caro "Light of Israel" and *Rosh ha-Golah"* (introd. to *Darkhei Moshe*) and accepted the basic pattern of a "book of *pesakim*" alongside a "book of *halakhot*" – actually paved the way for the acceptance of the Shulḥan Arukh, in due course, as the authoritative and binding code of the masses of Israel.

Reactions to the Shulḥan Arukh. As was the case with earlier codifications, appreciation of the Shulḥan Arukh along with Isserles' glosses was mingled in the initial stages with a great deal of criticism, often severe, from the Oriental communities as well as those of Germany and Poland (see e.g., the criticism – later retracted – of Joseph ibn Lev of Turkey in *Shem ha-Gedolim* s.v. *Beit Yosef;* cf. the statements of Paltoi Gaon). Many halakhic scholars noted occasional contradictions between the *Beit*

1. page 55

Yosef and Shulḥan Arukh; Jacob de Castro, Caro's younger contemporary, attributed these to the author's infirmity since the latter wrote the Shulḥan Arukh toward the end of his life (*Oholei Ya'akov,* 20), and accordingly wrote his own annotations, *Erekh Leḥem.* Samuel Aboab, an Italian scholar of the mid-17th century, circulated the rumor that Caro had entrusted the compilation of the Shulḥan Arukh to his pupils (*Devar Shemu'el,* no. 255). Yom Tov Ẓahalon, an early 17th-century scholar of Ereẓ Israel, ventured the sweeping opinion that the Shulḥan Arukh was compiled by Caro for "minors and ignoramuses *(Ammei ha-Areẓ)*" (Maharitaẓ, Resp. no. 67). These speculations contradicted Caro's own explicit statements on the subject (introd. to Sh. Ar.), except that he envisaged that pupils too should study his work, as was the hope of other codifiers (see also, in explanation of the above-mentioned contradictions, Azulai, *Shem ha-Gedolim,* s.v. *Shulḥan Arukh;* idem, *Maḥzik Berakhah,* YD 47:4; idem, *Birkei Yosef,* OḤ, 188:12). Scholars of the Oriental communities were very hesitant to accept Caro's canon of deciding according to the majority opinion of Alfasi, Maimonides, and Asher b. Jehiel, since it conflicted with the *Hilkheta ke-Vatra'ei* rule (Reshakh, Resp. pt. 1 no. 134; *Birkei Yosef,* ḤM 25, 29). To some extent this difficutly was overcome by the aid of a tradition that 200 rabbis of Caro's generation had accepted his decisory canon *(Birkei Yosef, ibid.),* so that a majority of later scholars had in effect agreed to decide according to the "three pillars of halakhic decision." Despite these doubts, Caro's decisions and directives were accepted by the majority of Oriental scholars in his own lifetime (Ranaḥ, resp. pt. 1, no. 109; *Yad Malakhi, Kelalei Sh. Ar.* 2).

In Poland and Germany criticism of the Shulḥan Arukh was far more severe and fundamental. The very concept of codifying the *halakhah* had already been rejected by the spiritual founders of Polish Jewry, Jacob Pollak and his pupil Shalom Shakhna, and this path was followed by the latter's pupils, Judah Loeb b. Bezalel and his brother Ḥayyim. In Judah's opinion, once the already-decided law could be ascertained from a code without any mental effort, such effort would inevitably be channeled in the undesirable direction of *pilpul* ("hairsplitting") for its own sake, and proper study – in the order of Scripture, Mishnah, and Talmud – would become neglected (*Derekh Ḥayyim, Avot* 6:6). Moreover, study and understanding of the law were prerequisites for deciding it; making decisions from a study of the talmudic and post-talmudic discussions – even if error were occasionally to result – was to be preferred to "decision based on a single work without knowledge of the underlying reasoning, in a blind manner" (*ibid.,* and his *Netivot Olam, Netiv ha-Torah,* 15). In pursuing this approach, Judah Loeb b. Bezalel remarked that Maimonides and Jacob b. Asher had also intended no more than that the law should only be decided according to their codifications after the talmudic source of a rule was known to the *dayyan (ibid.),* a puzzling remark, particularly in the light of Maimonides' own unequivocal statements (introd. to *Mishneh Torah*). Judah's brother Ḥayyim was opposed to the compilation of halakhic summaries, since "these lead to tardiness in studying the ancient works . . . progressively so the more they ease study" (introd. to *Vikku'aḥ Mayim Ḥayyim,* ed. Amsterdam (1711/12); moreover he fundamentally rejected the idea of reducing the *halakhah* to uniformity, the idea at the root of any codification, since "it may be believed that just as it is the nature of creation for the face of mankind to differ, so wisdom remains yet divided in its heart." Not only was it wrong to call lack of uniformity "a shortcoming rendering the Torah two *Torot,* Heaven forbid! "; on the contrary, "this is the way of the Torah, and these statements and those represent the words of the living God" *("Ellu ve-Ellu Divrei Elohim Ḥayyim").* Hence dispute was vital to the substance of the *halakhah* and offered increased possibilities for deciding the law according to the *dayyan*'s own lights and existing circumstances *(ibid.).*

Other scholars of this generation took a less extreme attitude toward codifying in itself but criticized the method and form adopted by Caro and Isserles. Solomon Luria also raised his voice against the proliferation of halakhic dispute in his time, but vigorously opposed Caro's method of deciding the law – which he termed "compromise" – holding that a decision had to be made after examination of all opinions against the background of talmudic sources only, for "ever since the days of Ravina and Rav Ashi it has not been customary to decide according to one of the *geonim* or *aḥaronim,* but . . . according to the Talmud only and also – where a matter has been left undecided in the Talmud – according to the Jerusalem Talmud and Tosefta" (introd. to *Yam shel Shelomo,* BK; cf. Asher b. Jehiel's opinion, above). In this spirit he compiled his own "book of *halakhot,*" *Yam shel Shelomo* (which he too began writing before Caro's works had reached him, altering it in the light of the latter). In this work the talmudic sources and different opinions of the halakhic scholars are quoted alongside each rule, arranged in the order of the talmudic tractates. Although originally covering 16 tractates (according to his pupil, Eleazar Altschul in *Yam shel Shelomo* to BK, ed. Prague, 1622/3), only a part, covering seven tractates, is extant, in which his decisions on the law are given at the conclusion of the discussions.

A different approach was taken by Mordecai b. Abraham Jaffe – younger contemporary of Solomon Luria and Isserles – in his book *Levush Malkhut* (a title derived from Esth. 8:15). He too protested vigorously against the exaggerated *pilpul* marking study of the Torah in his time, but, unlike Judah Loeb b. Bezalel, he sought to restore the study method which had as its objective the ascertainment of the halakhic truth through the medium and study of a "book of *halakhot.*" He regarded *Beit Yosef* as unsuitable for this purpose because of its lengthy deliberations, and when the Shulḥan Arukh with Isserles' glosses reached him he considered it equally unsuitable, because the statements were unduly brief and decisive. He therefore sought to compile a work that would "strike a balance between the two extremes . . . expanding when explanation is called for and abridging when proper" (introd. to his *Levush*). In addition to its instructional purpose, he intended his work to serve as a code *(ibid.),* containing in one and the same book the final conclusion without the talmudic discussions, but substantiated in each case in a brief and convenient manner. He divided his work into eight parts (actually ten) called *Levushim* (such as *Levush ha-Tekhelet, ha-Hur, Ir-Shushan,* etc. all derived from Esth. 8:15), and in the first five "tailored" (as he described it himself in his introduction) the entire body of the *halakhah* practiced in his time; the remaining *Levushim* were devoted to biblical exegesis, philosophy, etc.

In Mordecai Jaffe's generation and in the succeeding one protest increased against deciding the *halakhah* according to the Shulḥan Arukh. Thus Samuel Eliezer Edels, the early 17th-century Polish scholar, considered that those who laid down the *halakhah* without having studied the talmudic sources were deserving of censure (in his *Ḥiddushei Halakhot ve-Aggadot,* Sot. 22a) and in order to promote general study of the Talmud he wrote a classic supercommentary on the Talmud, Rashi's commentary, and the *tosafot.* Meir b. Gedaliah (the MaHaRaM of Lublin), who also wrote a supercommentary on the Talmud and its commentaries noted that he would base no decision of his own on the Shulḥan Arukh and the *Levushim,* "which are like head-notes and unclear and many are led astray by their statements to wrongly permit what is prohibited or exempt from liability" (his Responsum no. 135). He recognized Caro's stature and sometimes even relied on his rulings (e.g., Resp. no. 118), but sought to prevent the Shulḥan Arukh or any other similar work from constituting an authoritative code of the *halakhah.* The contemporary scholar Yom Tov Lipmann Heller, author of the *Tosafot Yom Tov* on the Mishnah, also criticized the codifying efforts of Maimonides and Jacob b. Asher as well as Caro and Isserles. Like his teacher, Judah Loeb b. Bezalel, Heller too was satisfied that in any event none of them had envisaged that the law should be decided in accordance with his own work except "after having already labored to find and know the problems in the *Gemara*" (intro. to *Ma'adanei Yom Tov* and *Divrei Ḥamudot* on *Piskei ha-Rosh*). Even when this condition was satisfied, a proper codification should adopt the method of Alfasi and Asher b. Jehiel who precede the halakhic conclusion with the relevant talmudic discussion *(ibid.).* Since Heller regarded Asher b. Jehiel's *Piskei ha-Rosh* as the halakhic code, he wrote his commentaries *(Ma'adanei Yom Tov* and *Divrei Ḥamudot)* to explain this work and resolve the problems emerging from it and he also corrected errors and added rules elaborated since Asher's time, even differing occasionally from Asher's decisions (*ibid.* introd.).

Acceptance of the Shulḥan Arukh as the Authoritative Halakhic Code. This attitude to Caro's and Isserles' codification was apparently shared by most of the succeeding generation of scholars and for some time it seemed that their combined creation, like all similar earlier works, would fall short of providing an overall solution to the problem of an acceptable code. In the end, however, two factors were instrumental in bringing about the desired result. The first was the contribution of Joshua b. Alexander Ha-Kohen Falk, pupil of both Solomon Luria and Isserles. In the form it adopted he found no fault with the *Beit Yosef* (although he criticized it for other reasons), but he took a different view with regard to the Shulḥan Arukh and Isserles' glosses. In his opinion Caro and Isserles had only intended the law to be decided according to the Shulḥan Arukh when the talmudic sources were known from a study of the *Tur* and *Beit Yosef* (cf. the views of Judah Loeb b. Bezalel and of Heller, above). He added that in his time "people decide according to the Shulḥan Arukh [only] and render themselves a disservice . . . since they do not properly understand the substance of the statements" (in his introd. to *Beit Yisrael* and *Sma*). In order that Caro's original purpose should be fulfilled, Falk wrote (in addition to his commentaries on the *Turim* and *Beit Yosef*) a commentary on the Shulḥan Arukh itself, intended not only to explain the latter but to constitute an integral part of it: "without this commentary it shall be forbidden to decide the law according thereto" (i.e., to the Sh. Ar.; *ibid.*). In this way, he believed, the Shulḥan Arukh – with its brief and decisive rules – would become the "book of *pesakim,*" but decision in accordance with it would be permissible only after study of the corresponding comment alongside each paragraph, so that possible error resulting from misunderstanding of the main work would be eliminated. Falk found experience to have shown that Caro's method of compiling two separate types of books to supplement each other did not suffice to link a synoptic and determinative statement of the *halakhah* with its sources, and therefore this link had to be established in the "book of *pesakim*" itself – not, however, by fusing the substantiation into the final conclusion, but by separately adducing the former alongside the latter (*ibid.* and in this connection see also his remarks concerning Jaffe's *Levushim*). His commentary, *Sefer Me'irat Einayim* (known as the *"Sma"*) quotes the sources of each law and the different opinions expressed, as well as new rules and resolved problems. It is confined to the part on *Ḥoshen Mishpat,* "which is an occupation of Torah and to which all turn their eyes to decide in accordance therewith" *(ibid,* interesting evidence of the practice in Jewish civil law), the author apparently having been unable to complete his intended commentary on all parts of the Shulḥan Arukh *(ibid.).*

Joel Sirkes (author of *Bayit Ḥadash,* "a commentary on the *Turim*"), who was opposed to deciding the law from the Shulḥan Arukh for very similar reasons (Baḥ, Resp. Yeshanot no. 80; also Baḥ, Resp. Ḥadashot no. 42), apparently sought to follow in the footsteps of Falk. In addition to commenting on the *Turim* and the *Beit Yosef,* he began a commentary on the Shulḥan Arukh (Baḥ to ḤM, introd.), presumably with the same object in mind as Falk. The *Sma* rounded off the final form of the halakhic code that had been prepared by Caro and Isserles. The brevity and finality of a "book of *pesakim*" ensured convenient use and easy reference; the extended scope of a "book of *halakhot,*" with commentary alongside the former within the same book, provided the link between the *halakhah* and its sources. Distinguished scholars of the post-*Sma* generation were soon to adorn all parts of the Shulḥan Arukh with their commentaries. The following became its classic and acknowledged "arms-bearers," in whose terms and directives of the Shulḥan Arukh have been rendered authoritative and binding: the *Turei Zahav* or "Taz" of David b. Samuel ha-Levi (on all four parts, but mainly on OḤ and YD); the *Siftei Kohen* or *"Shakh"* of Shabbetai b. Meir ha-Kohen (on YD and ḤM); the *Ḥelkat Meḥokek* of Moses Lima; the *Beit Shemu'el* of Samuel b. Uri Shraga Phoebus (both on EH); and Abraham Abele Gombiner's *Magen Avraham* (on OḤ).

It is more than likely that this eventual resolution of the problem of codifying would have been further delayed but for the fateful historical events overtaking the Jewish world at this time. The generation of the "arms-bearing" commentators on the Shulḥan Arukh saw Jewish life in central Europe disrupted once more, this time by the upheavals of the mid-17th century, when the Chmielnicki massacres of 1648 resulted in the liquidation of many Jewish communities and halakhic centers. Once more such disruption stimulated the trend to codification, but this time there was a code complete and ready, waiting only for endorsement by the leading scholars of the generation. Thus Menahem Mendel Krochmal, the distinguished 17th-century German scholar, stated that "upon publication of the *Beit Yosef* and Shulḥan Arukh followed by Isserles' glosses, and the dispersal of these among all Israel . . . we have nothing but their statements" (*Ẓemaḥ Ẓedek* no. 9). In the course of time it was further emphasized that, with the addition of its abovementioned commentaries, the Shulḥan Arukh had become the authoritative and binding halakhic code (*Pitḥei Teshuvah,* YD 242:8).

After the Shulḥan Arukh. A study of the codificatory trend in Jewish law reveals the interesting historical phenomenon of a recurring revival of activity at regular intervals of 100–200 years: in the eighth and ninth centuries – the geonic "books of *Halakhot*"; in the 11th century – Alfasi's *Sefer ha-Halakhot;* in the 12th century – Maimonides' *Mishneh Torah;* in the 14th century – Jacob b. Asher's *Turim* and finally, Caro's Shulḥan Arukh with Isserles' glosses in the 16th century. This historical pattern has stood interrupted since then and for some four centuries there has been no further recognized and authoritative code that embraces the entire field of the *halakhah.* The reason for this is bound up with the coming of emancipation at the end of the 18th century, an event that fundamentally changed the face of Jewish society. One of its consequences was the abrogation of Jewish organizational and, gradually, judicial autonomy, leading to the division of Jewish society into traditional and non-traditional elements. All this weakened the authority of the *halakhah* and deprived it of much of its dynamism, just as it reduced the need for any additional "book of *pesakim*." As the fields of halakhic interest and influence narrowed, so the scope of halakhic works from the middle of the 18th century onward became more and more limited to matters of actual moment in daily life – in the same way as the overwhelming majority of earlier "books of *halakhot*" and "*pesakim*" had dealt only with the laws customary at the time of their compilation. Thus works such as the *Shulḥan Arukh* of Shneur Zalman of Lyady (1747–1812, the founder of Ḥabad Ḥasidism), the *Ḥayyei Adam* and *Ḥokhmat Adam* of Abraham Danzig (1748–1820), and the well-known *Kiẓẓur Shulḥan Arukh* of Solomon Ganzfried (1804–1886) are confined in effect to matters discussed in *Oraḥ Ḥayyim, Yoreh De'ah,* and part of *Even ha-Ezer* (in the Sh. Ar.) and virtually do not deal at all with matters in the *Ḥoshen Mishpat,* the latter continuing to be a subject of academic study only. (A notable exception is the *Arukh ha-Shulḥan* compiled by Jehiel Michael Epstein (d. 1908) on all four parts of the Shulḥan Arukh; additional portions of this work have been published under the title *Arukh ha-Shulḥan he-Atid,* dealing with matters not discussed in the Shulḥan Arukh, such as the laws of *Pe'ah, Terumah, Sanhedrin, Melakhim,* etc.) None of these works, however, has been able to disturb the status of the Shulḥan Arukh as the authoritative "book of *pesakim*" in Jewish law, not even with reference to the matters actually dealt with in them, and they may be described as merely forming part of the great commentative literature surrounding the Shulḥan Arukh.

Of course, apart from the above-mentioned works of the post-Shulḥan Arukh period, the literature of the *halakhah* has been further increased by a rich contribution of supplementary "arms-bearers" to the Shulḥan Arukh: commentaries, novellae, and responsa, as well as *takkanot* and customs; all of which the present-day *dayyan* must take into consideration when deciding the law – subject still to the overriding authority of the Shulḥan Arukh with its acknowledged commentaries. With the return of the Jewish people to their homeland, all the past factors and imperatives of codification have reasserted themselves – perhaps with greater vigor. To the usual array of factors necessitating elucidation of the law – halakhic dispute, profusion of material (particularly since compilation of the Shulḥan Arukh), and the more recent phenomenon of a religiously divided Jewry – must now be added a large variety of questions arising from the social, economic, and technological realities of the present time.

Bibliography: P. Buchholz, in: MGWJ, 13 (1864), 201–17, 241–59; C. P. Ilbert, *The Mechanics of Law Making* (1914), 150–80; J. Guttmann (ed.), *Moses Ben Maimon, sein Leben, seine Werke und sein Einfluss,* 2 vols. (1908–14); E. Freund, *Legislative Regulation* (1932), 3–17; A. Gulak, in: *Tarbiz,* 6 (1934/35), no. 2, 139–51; J. A. Seidmann, in: *Sinai,* 12 (1942/43), 428–38; H. Tchernowitz, *Toledot ha-Posekim,* 3 vols. (1946–47); Z. J. Cahana, in: *Sinai,* 36 (1954/55), 391–411, 530–7; 37 (1955), 51–61, 157–64, 220–7, 381–5; 38 (1955/56), 46–53, 114–7, 243–6; L. Ginzberg, *On Jewish Law and Lore* (1955) 153–84, 257; Assaf, Ge'onim, 133–320; J. N. Epstein, *Mevo'ot le-Sifrut ha-Tanna'im* (1957), 225f. J. Nissim, in: *Sefer ha-Yovel . . . Sinai* (1958), 29–39; idem, in: *Sefunot,* 2 (1958), 89–102; J. M. Toledano, in: *Sinai,* 44 (1958/59), 25–30; Ch. Albeck, *Mavo ha-Mishnah* (1959), 105–11, 270–83; M. Havazelet, in: *Sinai,* 56 (1964/65), 149–58; M. Elon, *Ha-Mishpat Ha-Ivri,* III (1973), 865–884 and 938–1212; idem. in: *Hagut ve-Halakhah* (1968), 75–119; J. Twersky, in: *Judaism,* 16 (1967), 141–58.

Menachem Elon

II. GENERAL

Contents

LAW AND MORALITY.

In the Bible. In the Pentateuch, legal and moral norms are not distinguished by any definitional criteria. The manner of presentation of both is via revelation – moral norms are not presented as wisdom but rather as prophetic revelation. Thus the two remain indistinguishable as to authority. The basis of adherence to the system as a whole is the fact that it constitutes divine command. Even in the form of presentation, no distinction is made between the two types. The apodictic form, for example, is used both for the prohibition on murder (Ex. 20:13) and the command to love one's neighbor (Lev. 19:18). On the critical issue of enforcement, no textual distinction exists on which to base enforced and nonenforced forms or between humanly enforced and divinely enforced ones. The premise of the pentateuchal code is that no propounded norm of human behavior is either optional or lacking in enforcement. Indeed the sanction system is one in which human punishment and divine retribution function as equal components of a single scheme.

This single corpus of legal-moral behavioral norms was distinct from Ancient Near-Eastern legal-moral systems in a number of significant respects. First, the very unity of morality and law in the Pentateuch created a new basis of authority for the behavioral precepts of Hebrew civilization. Secondly, in the Torah individualistic morality gave way to national morality which was addressed to the people of Israel as a corporate moral entity. Thus the national entity was made party to the maintenance of the mandated standards of behavior and could be held responsible for the breach of such norms by individual citizens. Thirdly, despite the exclusivity of the covenantal relationship between God and the Jewish people, God's role in the enforcement of legal-moral behavioral norms is clearly pictured as universal. Thus Cain, the generation of the flood, Sodom, the seven Canaanite nations, and others, are all pictured as subjects of divine retribution for illegal-immoral behavior though they were not parties to the covenent.

In the prophetic literature, no new realm of purely moral concern was created. The breaches of social morality which play such a prominent part in the prophetic critique of the Jewish people were all premised on the identical legal-moral behavioral norms. The "immorality" of the people was in reality their "illegal" behavior. The major shift which distinguishes the literary prophets from their predecessors was that the notion of corporate legal-moral responsibility was given a vital new component. In the Pentateuch, national doom was threatened for cultic sins in particular and for neglect of the divine commandments in general. The prophets introduced the notion that the most decisive factor in the corporate fate of the nation was that aspect of mandated legal-moral behavioral norms which encompassed social relations. Thus when Amos threatens national doom and exile, he speaks of the sins of the normal life context, of social, economic, and political behavior, but maintains complete silence with regard to the sin of idolatry. In Isaiah and Micah too, the threat of national destruction is created by social corruption – the violation of the legal-ethical behavioral norms of everyday life. Failure to observe the divine command results in the corporate punishment of the nation whether the sin is cultic or legal-moral in nature.

The Talmudic Period. There was not yet any development of a specific moral order as distinct from the legal system in the talmudic period. However, it is already clearly recognized in tannaitic literature that legal sanctions could not enforce every form of behavior which was morally desirable. Indeed Mishnah and Tosefta make occasional references to situations where, despite justification, one party lacks any legal recourse against the other and "... he has noting but resentment [*taromet*] against him" (e.g., BM 4:6, 6:1; Tosef., Git., 3:1, BM 4:22). This recognition of a gap between sanctionable behavior and behavior which though desirable is not enforceable produced three types of relationships between the two realms: morality as a direct source of law; morality as a source of private, higher standards of legal liability; and morality in legal form.

Morality as a Direct Source of Law. The tannaitic period was particularly rich in social legislation motivated by the desire to expand the scope of enforcement in order to encompass as broad as possible a range of morally desirable behavior. Two terms in particular were often used to indicate the presence of a moral interest as the basis for tannaitic legislation:

(1) "In the interest of peace" *(mi-penei darkhei shalom)*. This term is a composite, indicating that the legislative purpose of the statute is the prevention of communal conflict which would result from some immoral practice not otherwise limited by law. The specific forms of immoral behavior viewed by the *tannaim* as likely to produce communal conflict included: unequal distribution of religious honors, threat to the good reputation of a group or an individual, taking by force where property rights are uncertain, unearned benefit from the labor or initiative of another, and the exclusion of groups from societal privileges and responsibilities. In all of these instances, the methods used to avoid the conflict were either to legalize a status quo which was both orderly and fair, or to extend legal rights to situations or persons otherwise excluded (e.g. Git. 5:8–9; Tosef., Pe'ah 3:1, Hul. 10:13, Git. 5 (3): 4–5).

(2) "For the benefit of society" *(mi-penei tikkun ha-olam)*. This tannaitic term is also a composite, reflecting the presence of a moral interest being translated into an enforceable legal norm. The Mishnah (Git. 4:3–5:3) contains an entire codex of such statutes. The unique character of the situations governed "for the benefit of society" is that the moral interest involved, while produced by an existing or incipient legal relationship, affects primarily persons outside the relationship itself. The legislation affecting that relationship is thus primarily designed to have general communal benefit. Some of the moral interests dealt with in this type of legislation are the prevention of bastardy (see *Mamzer*) and of abandoned wives (see *Agunah*), the deterrence of theft and of non-punishable injurious behavior, the encouragement of lending and of returning lost property, the encouragement of care for orphans and destitute children, and the encouragement of public service in the area of law and medicine (e.g., Git. 4:2–5:3, 9:4; Tosef., Ter. 1:12–13, Git. 4(3):5–7, 8 (6):9).

The *amoraim* did not themselves use *darkhei shalom* or *tikkun ha-olam* as bases for further translation of morality into law. However, their awareness that in tannaitic legislation morality was being used as a source of law is clearly indicated through their use of the notion of the prevention of hostility *(mi-shum eivah)* as a legislative end. While no legislation in tannaitic literature is described as having been designed to prevent hostility, the *amoraim* often ascribe that very purpose to tannaitic legislation. Thus tannaitic legislation giving a husband the right to his wife's earnings is viewed by the *amoraim* as motivated by the desire to prevent ill-feeling or hostility *(eivah)* between them (Ket. 58b). The source of the ill-feeling would be the inequality resulting from the husband being obliged to support his wife without being entitled to ownership of whatever she earns. This recognition that legislation based on the tendency of ill-feeling to undermine an existing relationship was an attempt to cure legislatively the underlying inequality led the *amoraim* to limit the application of the statute to those situations where its motivating moral interest was relevant. Thus where the marital relationship is in any case about to be terminated, ill-feeling may be a matter of indifference (BM 12b), and further, where the relationship must be terminated by law, ill-feelings between the parties may actually be functional (Yev. 90b) and therefore the law designed to prevent such hostility is inapplicable.

The role of morality as a source of law continued into the legal work of the *amoraim* themselves, although it shifted from the realm of legislation to that of juridical interpretation. Two standards of moral behavior, one positive and one negative, predominate in this amoraic process:

(1) "And thou shalt do that which is right and good" (Deut. 6:18; *ve-asita ha-yashar ve-ha-tov*). Two amoraic laws are based on this verse: (a) Property taken by a creditor in payment of a debt may be redeemed at any time (i.e., absence of injury to the creditor; BM 35a; see Execution, Civil[1]); and (b) Right of an abutting property owner to first purchase is preserved despite sale of the property (i.e., absence of injury to the original owner; BM 108a; see *Maẓranut*). In both cases doing the "right and good" involves the restoration of a legal right which a person had lost through no fault of his own.

(2) "Her ways are ways of pleasantness" (Prov. 3:17; *darkhei no'am*). The fact that "pleasantness" was viewed as a basic characteristic of biblical law dictated to the *amoraim* the rejection of any juridical interpretation which could lead to the establishment of a law that could cause either the loss of personal dignity or injury to a marital relationship (e.g., Suk. 32b; Yev. 15a). The principle, however, operated in a negative fashion only, to preclude any particular juridical alternative which contravened the moral qualities of "pleasantness" (see also *Takkanot*).

Morality as a Source of Private, Higher Standards of Legal Liability. There are occasions which arise in any legal system where, despite the existence of a law prohibiting certain action, the hands of the court are tied because of evidentiary or procedural principles. The absence of enforcement in such instances, while producing an inequity in that particular case, could only be remedied by the abandonment of a principle which on balance is of value to the legal system. In the attempt to minimize such injustice, the *tannaim*, and subsequently the *amoraim* also, attempted to use the threat of divine retribution as a means of inducing the wrongdoer to remedy the injury of his own free choice, rejecting the exemption which the system allows him (see Divine Punishment). It was in this specific context that the rabbis often asserted that while the defendant was "exempt by human law, he is liable by divine law" (*ḥayyav be-dinei shamayim;* e.g., BK 6:4. An entire codex of such situations where "his case is passed on for divine judgment" is found in Tosef. BK 6: 16–17). A similar case of moral pressure being brought to bear to emphasize the need for voluntary rectification where the judiciary is unable to act is reflected in the phrase "the sages are greatly pleased with him" (*ru'aḥ ḥakhamin noḥah heimenno;* e.g., Shev. 10:9. For the reverse formulation, see BB 8:5). The moral pressure for this type of behavior led the *amoraim* to use similar formulations to urge self-judgment even in cases where the initial liability itself was in doubt (BM 37a; see Extraordinary Remedies). In such cases the *amoraim* suggest that a man assume liability upon himself if "he wishes to fulfill his duty in the sight of heaven."

Two uniquely amoraic devices supplement the above as moral means of urging an individual to accept higher standards of civil liability where he has indeed been the cause of injury to another. Both are literary legal fictions in that they attempt to explain tannaitic statements or actions which in reality might have been based on completely different reasons. (a) Pious behavior *(middat ḥasidut)*. Each time that the *amora* Rav Ḥisda suggests that a particular tannaitic statement constituted a suggestion of especially righteous behavior it is part of an attempt to resolve an inner contradiction in a Mishnah (e.g., BM 52b; Shab. 120a; Ḥul. 130b). While the Talmud on one occasion rejects R. Ḥisda's suggestion for some alternative resolution (Shab. 120a), the device itself, and its frequent acceptance by the *amoraim*, gives recognition to their use of moral persuasion to encourage private adoption of the highest possible standards of civil liability. Indeed R. Hisda may well have been pointing out a more general phenomenon, that of recording dissenting opinions in the Mishnah in order that such higher standards remain as a personal option. (b) Beyond the limit of the law *(li-fenim mi-shurat ha-din)*. This device too, emerging from the school of Rav, is used consistently to resolve the disparity between existing law and the behavior of some earlier scholar (e.g., BK 99b; BM 30b; et. al.). While it may be the case that in each instance the scholar behaved in full accord with the law of his own time, the exemption from liability not yet having become applicable, the significance of the amoraic suggestion lies in its openness to the acceptance and desirability of such private assumption of higher standards of legal liability. Indeed, by eradicating the time difference between the existing law and earlier behavior, the *amoraim* in effect maintain the viability of the entire history of legal development as a source of rules devised to produce the result most morally desirable in any particular case. While in their talmudic usage none of these devices leads to enforceable law, many *rishonim* and *aḥaronim* insist on the partial or total enforceability of a good number of the laws denominated as *dinei shamayim, middat ḥasidut* and *li-fenim mi-shurat ha-din* (e.g., Rema HM 12:2; PDR 5: 132–153, 151). Thus, while formal legislation was basically absent and no admission would be made that juridical interpretation really involved the creation of new law, such reinterpretations to create higher standards of enforceability were in fact part of the continuity of the process of the use of morality as a source of new law. In this way the use of morality to create private, higher standards of liability has often led to the eventual adoption of those new standards as law for everyone.

Morality in Legal Form. The impact of morality on Jewish law has been felt in a third way, as a result of rabbinic formulation of moral principles in legal form. The unwillingness of the rabbinic mind to accept seriously any substantial gap between the two realms is evidenced by the gradual assimilation into the realm of law, of forms of behavior which were not initially enforceable but were formulated in the terminology of illegal behavior. The two prime categories in this pattern are where immoral behavior is compared to illegal action and where the seriousness of the behavior is indicated by a disproportionate penalty.

(1) "As if . . ." *(ke-illu)*. The term *ke-illu*, in its legal usage (like *na'asah ke*), usually introduces a legal fiction (BM 34a; Yev. 13:3). In its usage in the process of grading the moral significance of behavior it creates fictional analogies to legal or illegal behavior. Thus a person who conducts himself with humility is as one who offers all the sacrifices (Sot. 5b), while one who honors an evil person is as one who worships idols (Tosef. Av. Zar. 6(7):16). In tannaitic usage, this device is used almost exclusively to encourage behavior which is not legally mandatory (except where it is used in exegesis in the form, "Scripture considers him as if . . ."; e.g., Sanh. 4:5). In such instances, the weight of the divine legal prohibition is used to bolster moral pronouncements which otherwise lack any authority. The fact that *amoraim* began to extend this comparative device to add the weight of divine law to the authority of rabbinic law (e.g., Ber. 35a) introduced the possibility that the first half of the formula was not merely unenforceable moral teaching, but was itself

1. page 627.

legally binding in its own right. It was then only a short step to the frequent conclusions of *rishonim* that behavior which is compared to illegal action must itself be illicit (e.g., Sot. 3:4; cf. Yad, Talmud Torah 1:13).

(2) Disproportionate penalty, such as "liable to the death penalty" *(ḥayyav mitah)*. While the Bible lays down the penalty of death at the hands of the court for a variety of crimes, the *tannaim* had already begun using the ascription of the death penalty to crimes for which clearly no court would prescribe such punishment. This exaggerated penalty was an effective way of communicating rabbinic feelings about the enormity of misbehavior. The *amoraim* made extensive use of this device to indicate their indignation at immoral behavior. Thus, in a passage which makes manifestly clear that it is aimed at emphasis rather than true legal liability, the Talmud says, "A mourner who does not let his hair grow long and does not rend his clothes is liable to death" (MK 24a). Similarly the rabbis asserted that, "Any scholar upon whose garment a [grease] stain is found is liable to death" (Shab. 114a). Again, however, the very use of legal terminology in formulating the moral position led to the conclusion that the behavior so described was indeed legally prohibited, and it was therefore often considered as this by the *rishonim* (cf. instances in Sanh. 58b, 59a, and codes). Thus in the constant growth of the scope of the law the morality of one generation frequently became the law of the next.

See also Contract; *Ha'anakah; Hassagat ha-Gevul;* Mishpat Ivri; Noachide Laws; Obligation, Law of; Punishment; *Takkanot;* Torts; and Unjust Enrichment.

Bibliography: H.B. Fassel, *Tugend- und Rechtslehre . . . des Talmuds . . .* (1848, 1862²); M. Bloch, *Die Ethik in der Halacha* (1886); S. Schaffer, *Das Recht und seine Stellung zur Moral nach talmudischer Sitten- und Rechtslehre* (1889); M. Lazarus, *Die Ethik des Judentums,* 2 vols. (1904–11); I. S. Zuri, *Mishpat ha-Talmud,* 1 (1921), 86f.; S. Federbusch, *Ha-Musar ve-ha-Mishpat be-Yisrael* (1947); S. Pines, *Musar ha-Mikra ve-ha-Talmud* (1948); J. Z. Lauterbach, *Rabbinic Essays* (1951), 259–96; ET, 1 (1951³), 228–30, 334f.; 7 (1956), 382–96; E. Rackman, in: *Judaism,* 1 (1952), 158–63; Y. Kaufmann, *The Religion of Israel* (1960), 122–211, 291–340; M. Silberg, *Kakh Darko shel Talmud* (1961); M. Elon, *Ha-Mishpat Ha-Ivri* I(1973) 171–180; idem., in: *De'ot,* 20 (1962), 62–67; Z. J. Melzer, in: *Mazkeret . . . le-Zekher . . . ha-Rav Herzog* (1962), 310–5; B. Cohen, in: *Jewish and Roman Law,* 1 (1966), 65–121; 2 (1966), 768–70; E. Urbach, *Ḥazal–Pirkei Emunot ve-De'ot* (1969), 254–347.

Saul Berman

LEGAL MAXIMS, concise statements of the law as it is or, often, succinct statements embodying a guiding principle established in law. The word *kelal,* in one of its varied meanings, is the Hebrew equivalent of a legal maxim. "The burden of proof is on the plaintiff" (BK 3:11), for example, is referred to as "a great maxim of jurisprudence" *(kelal gadol ba-din;* BK 46a; see also Evidence).

Historical Periods. The wealth of Jewish legal maxims is essentially talmudic. The great corpus of tannaitic and amoraic literature contains hundreds of maxims, i.e., legal rules and principles of jurisprudence stated in brief form and summary fashion.

Of Biblical Origin. Even maxims which can be traced back to the Bible owe their epigrammatic popularity to the Talmud. These "biblical" maxims are of three types: a literal quotation of a verse or of a part thereof, "At the mouth of two witnesses . . . shall a matter be established" (Deut. 19:15, cited very frequently in talmudic literature); a condensation of a biblical verse: "Do not place a wicked man as a witness" (Sanh. 27a; cf. Ex. 23:1); and a standardized, non-literal interpretation of a verse: "According to the majority [of judges] must the case be decided" (Sanh. 1:6; cf. Ex. 23:2).

Tannaitic Times. A great number of maxims were developed in post-biblical and tannaitic times. They are cited in tannaitic literature, often anonymously and without their validity being challenged: "A man's agent is like the man himself" (Mekh. Pisḥa 5); "Local custom decides everything" (BM 7:1); and "A condition made contrary to an express biblical law is void" (Ket. 9:1; see Contract). A number of tannaitic rules and maxims, on the other hand, represent minority opinions and are not binding: "Marriage takes no effect when there is a prohibitory law against it" (Akiva, Ket. 29b). Other tannaitic *kelalim,* although accepted, were disputed (cf., e.g., L. Ginzberg, *Perushim ve-Ḥiddushim ba-Yerushalmi,* 2 (1941), 159–64, on the rule, "Women are exempt from positive commandments which have a time limit"; Kid. 34a).

Amoraic Period. A significant increase in the wealth of legal maxims was accomplished by the *amoraim.* Many are recorded in the Jerusalem Talmud; for example: "No price can be put on a Sefer Torah" TJ, BM, 4:9 and "Unless otherwise stipulated, partners are to divide equally" (TJ, Ket. 10:4, 34a). A great wealth of maxims is found in the Babylonian Talmud; for example: "There is no agent in wrongful acts," a maxim explained by the following one: "If the Master's [God's] words conflict with the pupil's [the principal's] words, whose words shall we [who are called upon to act as agent] obey?" (Kid. 42b.); and "Any acquisition made in error is voidable" (Git. 14a). All these are cited anonymously; many others are quoted in the name of the *amora* who first formulated them. "Less than the legal quantity is forbidden by the law of the Torah" (Johanan, Yoma 73b); "No man is presumed to have paid his debt before the time due" (Simeon b. Lakish, BB 5 a-b); and "A man is a kinsman unto himself, hence no man may incriminate himself" (Rava, Sanh. 9b; see Confession). The *amoraim* succeeded in introducing numerous Aramaic legal maxims: "The law of the state is law" *(Dina de-Malkhuta Dina;* Git. 10b); "Force majeure *(Ones)* is excused by the law" (BK 28b), and "The stronger wins" (Git. 60b; see Extraordinary Remedies). There appears to be no correlation between language and geography; Aramaic and Hebrew maxims were formulated by Babylonian and Palestinian *amoraim* equally.

Legal maxims may also be gleaned from midrashic and medieval works: "One makes a festive meal to celebrate the conclusion of the Torah reading" (Song R. 1: 1, no. 9). They usually contain moral overtones: "As long as advocacy for the accused has not ceased, the trial is not over" *(Midrash Sekhel Tov,* Gen. 19:1); "One cannot serve two masters" (Israel Davidson, *Oẓar ha-Meshalim ve-ha-Pitgamim,* 2, no. 126).

The Mishnaic Kelal. Of special interest is the mishnaic *kelal.* The Mishnah often formulates a general statement which summarizes numerous particulars. Sometimes the general statement is found at the beginning of a bill of particulars; sometimes it is found at the end. In the former case, the general statement is introduced by the expression "A general rule have they [the rabbis] stated" *(kelal ameru,* e.g., Pe'ah 1:4), or "A great rule have they stated" *(kelal gadol ameru;* e.g., Shab 7:1). In the latter, the general statement is introduced by the expression, "This is the general rule" *(zeh ha-kelal;* e.g., Ket. 3:9. For details cf. Frankel, Mishnah, 306f.; see also Codification of the Law). Like the Roman *regula,* the mishnaic *kelal* summarizes the law without being an authentic or complete expression of the law. The Roman jurist proclaims, "The law is not derived from the *regula,* rather the *regula* is deduced from the law" (Paulus, D. 50:17, 1). Similarly, a basic rule of mishnaic exegesis is enunciated by the Babylonian Talmud, "We deduce nothing from general statements" *Ein lemedin min ha-Kelalot* (Kid. 34a). The Jerusalem Talmud expressed the same idea as follows, "The general statements made by Rabbi [Judah ha-Nasi, editor of the Mishnah] are not general statements" (*Leit kelalin de-Rabbi kelalan;* TJ, Ter. 1:2, 40c).

A good illustration of the nonauthoritative nature of the mishnaic *kelal* is found in the talmudic analysis of Mishnah Kiddushin 1:7. The Mishnah reads: "(a) With regard to all positive commandments which have a time limit – men are obligated and women are exempt; (b) With regard to all positive commandments which have no time limit – men and women are equally obligated; (c) With regard to negative commandments, regardless of whether they have or do not have a time limit – men and women are equally obligated except for the prohibitions of shaving [with a razor, Lev. 19:27], of removing sidelocks [*ibid.*], and of *kohanim* defiling themselves by contact with a human corpse [Lev. 21:1]. These three exceptions apply to men, not to women."

The Talmud (Kid. 34a-36a) records that, in "violation" of paragraph (a), women are obligated to observe the commandments of *mazzah* (Ex. 12:18), rejoicing on festivals (Deut. 16:14), and participation in the public assembly on Sukkot every seventh year (Deut. 31:12), although these commandments are positive and have a time limit. In "violation" of paragraph (b), women are exempt from the commandments of Torah study (Deut. 11:19), procreation (Gen. 1:28), and the redemption of the firstborn son (Ex. 13:13). Paragraph (c), however, admits of no exceptions. This would lead one to assume that a general statement which limits itself by adding "except for" is indeed authoritative, for the very concern for exceptions would appear to indicate the accuracy of the general statement in non-excepted instances. R. Johanan, a Palestinian *amora* of the third century, was therefore careful to point out, "We cannot learn from general principles, even where exceptions are stated" (see his proof from Er. 3:1). Thus, even where exceptions are specified, the *kelal* is not a truly general statement. As a result, Maimonides (Commentary on the Mishnah, Kid. 1:7) states that the word *kol* ("all," "every") in a *kelal*-statement must be understood as meaning nothing more than *rov* ("most").

Some would limit the rule, "We cannot learn from general principles," to general statements introduced by the world *kol,* as, for example, the *mishnayot* from *Kiddushin* and *Eruvin* cited in the previous two paragraphs (R. Jacob Berab, Nov. Kid. 34a, in: *Sefer ha-Yovel . . . B. M. Lewin,* 222f.). Other authorities are of the opinion that the rule applies to statements formulated as a *kelal* as well (Nov. Ran, Meg. 19b). The rule is limited in application, however, only to those statements whose general nature is challenged by facts adduced from authoritative sources: "We on our own may not reject a general *kelal* which we have as a tradition from the rabbis; for if we do so, there is no limit and we can no longer depend upon our Talmud as edited, for it consists mainly of general statements" (*kelalot;* Rosh, Shevu. 6, para. 5). The Talmud itself never rejected a *kelal* except out of necessity or in deference to an oral tradition regarding the exception to the *kelal;* without such necessity or in the absence of an oral tradition, the accuracy of the general statement is to be accepted (Pseudo-Rashba, Men. 6b). Although the rule, "We cannot learn from *kelalot,*" was formuated by the *amoraim* concerning general statements found in the tannaitic sources, the matter is disputed whether the rule holds true regarding amoraic *kalalim* as well (cf. *Yad Malakhi,* Kelalei Alef, 23). A similar dispute exists as to whether the rule applies equally to general statements found in the codes (R. Ẓevi Hirsch Ashkenazi, *Ḥakham Ẓevi,* 55 says that the rule does not apply; R. Jacob Reicher, *Ḥok Ya'akov,* 429, no. 8, and R. Alexander Schorr, *Tevu'ot Shor,* 32, n. 6, maintain that the rule does apply).

Compilations of Maxims. A bibliography of Hebrew works containing legal maxims, rules, and general principles is found in P. Jacob Kohn, *Oẓar ha-Be'urim ve-ha-Perushim* (1952), 448–62. Other books (published after 1952 and therefore not included in Kohn's bibliography) containing lists of maxims and rules are: ET (as titles of individual articles); Elon, Mafte'ah, 405–412; Y. Y. Ḥasidah, *Oẓar Ma'amrei Halakhah* (3 vols., 1959–60); Joseph Schechter, *Oẓar ha-Talmud;* David Etrog, *Peri Eẓ Hadar* (1952). The following works contain lists of Hebrew legal maxims, translated and explained in English: Lewis N. Dembitz, s.v. *Maxims, Legal,* in: *Jewish Encyclopedia,* vol. 8 (1904); George Horowitz, *The Spirit of Jewish Law* (1953), 99–104; M. Mielziner, *Legal Maxims and Fundamental Laws* (1898).

Bibliography: ET, 1 (1951^3), 295f., and the works mentioned above.

Aaron Kirschenbaum

LEGAL PERSON, a body of men or of property which the law, in imitation of the personality of human beings, treats artificially as subject of rights and duties independent of its component parts. The classic example of a legal person is the corporation. Although the most familiar type of corporation is that engaged in business activities, history has witnessed corporations formed as the vehicle for charitable enterprises, cooperative nonprofit-making enterprises, municipal and governmental operations, and religious and social activities. For example, in the classical Roman legal system, the *universitates* – corporate groups which possessed common treasuries and were endowed with a legal personality separate and distinct from that of their individual members – included various municipal and religious, as well as industrial and trading, associations. The corporation has usually featured the following characteristics: a name common to the aggregate of its component individuals or properties; a life independent of the lives of its components; the possession of privileges or rights, liabilities or duties, which do not inhere in its membership as individuals; and the divorce of ownership and management, with the authority of the managers to act as the agents and representatives of the corporation being conferred, limited, and determined not by the consent of the owners but by the law itself.

Talmudic and Post-Talmudic Law. Traditional Jewish law apparently did not recognize the type of ownership implied in the idea of the corporation. Common ownership is ordinarily expressed in terms of partnership (*shuttafut;* Maim. Yad, Sheluḥin ve-Shuttafin 4–10; Tur. and Sh. Ar., ḤM 157–81). The salient differences whereby partnership may be distinguished from the corporation are: the continued existence of a partnership is dependent upon the lives of the partners or their respective heirs; the privileges, rights, liabilities, and duties associated with a partnership inhere almost directly in the individual members of the association; the manager of a partnership enterprise is construed as the agent of the component members. Although the corporation is not a juristic category in the classical sources of Jewish law, scholars have attempted, with various degrees of success, to find types of associations and proprietal arrangements in Jewish history which parallel or approximate the corporation and which may be regarded as embodiments of the concept of the legal or artificial person. The fruits of these attempts may be summarized as follows:

Hekdesh, the term for objects, animals and money consecrated for the upkeep of the Temple precincts and for the sacrificial service therein. The administrator of this corporate body was the Temple treasurer *(gizbar)*. All Temple properties were placed under the jurisdiction of the *gizbar,* at whose discretion acquisitions and sales of these properties were controlled and who was empowered to represent the interests of the Temple in litigation (Ḥag. 11a; BM 58a). Thus the typical feature of the modern corporation, the divorce of ownership and management, was the salient characteristic of *hekdesh* – for God was viewed as the "owner" and the *gizbar* the manager thereof.

On the other hand, the Temple corporation was unique in the world of commerce. Its acquisition of property was by consecration and its sales were by redemption; thus its transactions were governed by special rules. Moreover, there were numerous regulations that were inapplicable to *hekdesh* possessions, e.g., the rules of overreaching *(ona'ah)* did not apply to Temple property so that valuable properties could be redeemed at the cost of a perutah, the smallest coin; theft of *hekdesh* property was not punishable by the normal legal sanctions; construction of *hekdesh* appurtenances was accomplished while the materials were still unsanctified, and their consecration to the Temple took place only after the construction was completed (BM 57b; BK 62b; Me'il. 14b). Hence the corporate body of Temple properties may not be regarded as a typical legal person, subject to the normal rights and duties attributed to human beings.

Benei ha-ir, the name given to the municipal community in talmudic parlance. In the Talmud, the community is regarded as an aggregate of the individuals who comprise its membership. The legal definition of this aggregate is that of a partnership. Thus, no member of the community could act as a witness in matters which affected communal property; he was disqualified as an interested party. The governing body of the community, known as the "seven notables of the city" *(shivah tovei ha-ir,)* was regarded as an agent of the citizenry, and its acts had to be ratified by the citizenry meeting as a body *(be-ma'amad benei ha-ir;* Meg. 26a).

In post-talmudic jurispurdence, the community was converted from a juridic partnership to a corporate body with numerous features characteristic of a legal person. Communal transactions were no longer regarded as those of its constituent members. Municipal ordinances *(takkanot ha-kahal)* could no longer be vetoed by individual citizens; the ruling of the majority members of the governing body was binding on all members of the community. Members of the community, no longer regarded as interested parties, were accepted as witnesses in matters affecting the municipality (see *Beit Yosef,* ḤM 37, notes 12 and 14; *Sma,* ḤM 156, note 6). Thus the body politic came to be clothed with an existence juridically independent of the citizens who comprised it.

Ḥavurat Ẓedakah, the communal charity fund, which eventually evolved into a legal person. In the Talmud, the poor were construed as owners of the monies deposited in the charity fund, and the communal collectors were viewed as their agents (BK 36b). This created disadvantages for the poor, for the rule of procedure in the Talmud was that interests of indeterminate plaintiffs were not actionable *(mamon she-ein lo tovin,* Rashi, BK 93a). As in the case of *benei ha-ir,* here, too, post-talmudic jurisprudence endowed charity funds with the character of an artificial person. An association *(ḥavurah)* founded for charitable purposes was regarded as somewhat akin to the modern corporation, i.e., an aggregate of property earmarked for specific purpose with the *ḥavurah* construed as the means created for the advancement of this purpose. The collectors and administrators of the charitable *ḥavurah* were henceforth classed as its managerial staff fully authorized to conduct its affairs. This authorization included the power to bring suit in court to protect the interests of the funds under its supervision (see *Beit Yosef,* ḤM 149, note 37; *Netivot ha-Mishpat,* ḤM 149, *Mishpat ha-Kohanim,* note 46). It is quite possible that an additional example of a legal person in Jewish history may be found among the Qumran and Essene sects which were based upon the renunciation of private property on the part of their members (cf. E. Koffmahn, in *Biblica,* 42 (1961), 433–42, and 44 (1963), 46–61).

In Modern Rabbinic Law. The problem of the corporation and its application to Jewish law has arisen in the following areas:

Interest on Loans. Inasmuch as Jewish law forbids lending and borrowing money on interest to or from Jews (see Usury), the question has arisen whether (or how) Jewish people may conduct the normal transactions involved in banking, insurance, and the like, and whether (or how) they may invest in such companies without violating the religious restrictions created by the participation of other Jewish people therein.

Sabbath Law. The religious restriction on labor on the Sabbath includes the prohibition of aiding and abetting as well as deriving benefit from the labor of others, non-Jews and, more so, Jews. How may a Jew be a stockholder in a company whose operations include Sabbath labor?

Passover Restrictions. A Jew may not eat, derive benefit from, or possess *ḥameẓ* during the Passover season. How do these restrictions affect the permissibility to invest in companies which do business with *ḥameẓ?*

The response of the rabbinic authorities of the past 100 years has been divided. The controversy may be summarized in the following manner. One school of rabbis is of the opinion that, inasmuch as the traditional sources do not recognize the concept of legal personality in normal commerce and trade, the corporation is, halakhically, nothing more than the conventional partnership. Hence, the rules of partnership are to be applied to the questions of loans on interest, Sabbath labor, and *ḥameẓ,* and only the dispensations traditionally allowed within the framework of partnerships may be allowed with regard to corporations. These, it must be added, are highly circumscribed (e.g., Solomon Ganzfried, *Kiẓẓur Shulḥan Arukh* 65:28 and Isaac Wasserman, in: *No'am,* 3 (1960), 195–203, regarding loans; Moses Feinstein, *Iggerot Moshe,* vol. 1, OḤ 90, regarding the Sabbath; Israel Be'eri, in: *Ha-Torah ve-ha-Medinah,* 11–13 (1960–62), 454–62, regarding all three questions). Another group of authorities, although in agreement with the first group in refusing to recognize the corporation as a unique and novel halakhic category, has nevertheless, through involved reasoning, found ways of avoiding the traditional restrictions and has been able to permit Orthodox Jews to invest in and conduct transactions with corporations (e.g., Ẓevi Hirsch Shapiro, *Darkhei Teshuvah,* YD,-160, 16, note 121, and M. N. Lemberger, in: *No'am,* 2 (1959), 33–37; 4 (1961), 251–7. Both these authorities address themselves to the problem of loans. Moses Feinstein, *Iggerot Moshe,* EH 7, places great stress on the extent to which management is divorced from ownership).

There is, however, a third group of modern talmudists who have taken full cognizance of the divorce of ownership from management in the corporation and of the artificiality of the corporate personality. This school of rabbis has come to the resultant conclusion that the traditional restrictions placed upon individual businessmen or partnerships with regard to the laws of usury, Sabbath rest, and *ḥameẓ,* are inapplicable to the corporation (e.g., Aryeh Leib Horowitz, *Harei Besamin,* Pt. 2, 115; Moses Sternbuch, *Mo'adim u-Zemannim,* vol 1, p. 203f.; Joseph Rosin, *Ẓafenat Pa'ne'aḥ,* 184, regarding loans; David Ẓvi Hoffmann, *Melammed le-Ho'il*, OḤ 91, regarding *ḥameẓ*). Permission has also been granted to buy and sell shares in companies that do business in non-kosher foods, although an individual is forbidden by the *halakhah* to engage in regular transactions involving such foods (Gedaliah Felder, in: *Kol Torah*, 6 (1959), nos. 7–11).

In connection with the ritual requirement that one who "takes" the *lulav* and *etrog* on the holiday of Sukkot must have title in it in order to fulfill the commandment properly, an interesting discussion arose in the circles of the religious kibbutzim in Israel whether and to what extent the kibbutzim constituted a legal person and what their status was in the eyes of Jewish traditional law (cf. A. Nachlon, in: *Ammudim* (Ha-Kibbutz ha-Dati, 1956), nos. 123, 124 and (1957), nos. 126, 128).

For further particulars on the problem of legal person in Jewish law see *Hekdesh;* Partnership; *Takkanot ha-Kahal;* Taxation.

Bibliography: L. Loew, in: *Ben Chananja*, 8 (1965), 77–83, 92–99, 108–15, 124–9; reprinted in his *Gesammelte Schriften*, 2 (1890), 133–64; Gulak, Yesodei, 1 (1922), 50–54; 2 (1922), 84 n. 2; 4 (1922), 63f.; Gulak, Oẓar, 345ff.; idem, *Le-Ḥeker Toledot ha-Mishpat ha-Ivri bi-Tekufat ha-Talmud*, 1 (*Dinei Karka'ot*, 1929), 124; idem, *Toledot ha-Mishpat be-Yisrael bi-Tekufat ha-Talmud*, 1 (*Ha-Ḥiyyuv ve-Shi'budav*, 1939), 90, 95n. 37a, 112; B. Safra, in: *Ha-Mishpat ha-Ivri*, 2 (1927), 45f.; P.W. Duff, *Personality in Roman Private Law* (1938); A. Karlin, in: *Sinai*, 4 (1938/39), 445–52; D. Weinreb, in: PAAJR, 19 (1950), 225–9 (Eng. summ. 100–2); ET, 3 (1951), 374–9; 5 (1953), 435–8; 10 (1961), 342–442; S. Huebner, in: *Hadorom*, 24 (1966), 108–16; S. Miron, in: *Sinai*, 59 (1966), 228–45; Elon, *Ha-Mishpat ha-Ivri*, II (1973), p. 626.

Aaron Kirschenbaum

MAJORITY RULE, deciding a matter according to the majority opinion. In the field of the *halakhah* this rule is applied in three principal instances: (a) determination of the binding law according to (the view of) the majority of halakhic scholars; (b) adjudication of dispute by the majority decision of the courts' judges; and (c) imposition by majority decision of the community, or its representatives, of a communal enactment (see *Takkanot ha-Kahal*), binding on all members of the community. The basis for the majority rule is to be found in the exegesis of the scriptural phrase, *aḥarei rabbim lehattot* (to "follow a multitude . . . " Ex. 23:2).

In Deciding the Halahkah. In the Talmud the phrase *aḥarei rabbim lehattot* was converted into a decisory canon: "where there is a controversy between an individual and the many, the *halakhah* follows the many" (Ber. 9a). The sages of the Talmud explained the existence of this rule as a practical neccessity, for if the Torah had been given in the form of an exhaustive code, "the world could not have existed" (TJ, Sanh. 4:2, 22a; cf. Mid. Ps. 82:3). The halakhic opinion that has prevailed is that the law is decided in accordance with the view expressed by a majority of the scholars, and this is so even if in a particular matter a heavenly voice *(Bat-Kol)* should declare that the law is according to the minority opinion (BM 59a).

The individual may continue to express his opinion that the majority has erred, but may not instruct to practice according to the minority opinion; if he actually instructs others to follow the minority opinion, he becomes (when there is a Sanhedrin) a *zaken mamre* (i.e., a "rebellious scholar"; Maim. Yad, Mamrim, 3:5–6). If a majority of scholars should arrive at the same conclusion but each for a different reason, some scholars hold this to be a majority opinion which is binding while other scholars hold the contrary view (*Maggid Mishneh*, Ishut 7:12; Maharik, resp. nos. 41, 52, 94, 102).

Some of the *geonim* and *rishonim* took the view that a minority opinion is to be preferred above a majority opinion of scholars of lesser wisdom. This question first arose in a responsum of Hai Gaon concerning a court decision on the concrete matter in issue, and not as concerns deciding of the *halakhah* in general (*Ge'onim Kadmoniyyim*, resp. no. 144; Ramban nov. Sanh. 23a; *Sefer ha-Ḥinnukh*, no. 77). Some of the scholars opposed this opinion, holding that the law is always as decided by the majority (*Haggahot Asheri*, Av. Zar. 1:3; *Siftei Kohen*, supplementary note to YD 242), while other scholars laid down that whenever the minority opinion is qualitatively superior to the majority opinion, the position is as if opinions are divided equally and either may be followed (Ramban nov. Sanh. 23a; Ritba, RH 14b). In the Shulḥan Arukh, the most authoritative code of Jewish law, determination of the *halakhah* is generally made by application of the majority rule, the author (Joseph Caro) having adopted for himself the principle that the binding *halakhah* was to accord with the opinion held in common by any two of three great halakhists preceding him, namely Alfasi, Maimonides, and Asher b. Jehiel – or with the majority opinion selected on a different basis if a particular matter had not been dealt with by the three above-mentioned scholars. See Elon, *Ha-Mishpat Ha-Ivri* III (1973), p. 1093ff.; Law, Codification of.

Decision by the Court. Within its plain meaning and read within its context, the above-mentioned scriptural passage (Ex. 23:2) has reference to a judgment of the court. The sages of the Talmud derived therefrom an additional interpretation relating to the field of criminal law – in which there is need for a specific majority, i.e., of two at least: "Thou shalt not follow after the many to do evil – I conclude that I must be with them to do well. Then why is it written [To follow] after the many to change judgment? [It means that] thy verdict of condemnation shall not be like thy verdict of acquittal, for thy verdict of acquittal is reached by the decision of a majority of one, but thy verdict of condemnation must be reached by the decision of a majority of two" (Sanh. 1:6 and cf. Mekh., Kaspa 20). Some scholars explain the need for a specific majority in matters of the criminal law on the basis that in matters of the civil law no judgment solely condemns or solely absolves, since any suit involves two litigants and what is to the one's benefit is to the other's detriment; whereas in criminal law matters the judgment is condemnatory, i.e., to the detriment of the accused (Tos. to Sanh. 3b).

A majority is only required in the event that a judicial decision has to be made in a concrete case before the court, whereas in deciding the *halakhah* in the criminal law field – outside the context of instant litigation – a simple majority of one suffices as it does in all other cases (Resp. Radbaz, *Li-Leshonot ha-Rambam*, no. 1690).

The *amoraim* question how a judgment in a civil law matter, arrived at by majority decision, should be worded. It was decided, in accordance with the opinion of R. Eleazar, that the judgment must be written in the name of the court without mention being made of the names of the judges favoring one view or the other (Sanh. 30a; Maim. Yad, Sanh. 22:8); similarly, that a judgment given by a majority decision must be signed also by the judge dissenting therefrom (TJ, Sanh. 3:10, 21d; *Avkat Rokhel*, no. 19; *Mabit*, vol. 2, pt. 1, resp. no. 173; ḤM 19–*Urim*, n.4). Hai Gaon's opinion (see above) that a preponderance of wisdom should be preferred above numerical majority, also with reference to court decisions, and even that the opinion of one individual may prevail against that of the many, remained generally unaccepted in later generations. Even those who favored wisdom above a numerical majority as the basis for deciding the *halakhah,* agreed that the majority opinion was to be preferred as the basis for a judgment by the court in the concrete matter before it (*Sefer ha-Ḥinnukh,* no. 77; Ramban nov. Sanh. 23a).

Communal Decisions and Enactments. The view that has prevailed in Jewish law is that communal resolutions and enactments are passed by a decision of the majority and bind the minority.

This general view was dissented from by Rabbenu Jacob Tam, who held that only after an enactment had been passed by the whole community might the majority lay down fines for transgression thereof, and that the minority could not be compelled by the community to comply with a decision of the majority to which it had been opposed (*Mordekhai,* BK 179 and BB 480). The doctrine of *aḥarei rabbim lehattot* has been relied upon by the scholars in support of the right to pass a communal enactment by majority decision (Rosh, resp. no. 6:5).

According to some of the scholars, the ordinances of a guild or an association – as distinguished from communal enactments – must be passed with the consent of all members in order to be binding (Ramban, nov. BB 9a; *Nimmukei Yosef,* BB 9a; *Leḥem Rav,* no. 216).

In the case of a judicial tribunal, it was laid down that a majority decision is not binding unless all the judges have participated in the proceedings and the judgment is that of the majority of the full complement (Sanh. 5:5). Some scholars deduced therefrom that also a communal enactment passed by majority decision is not binding unless the minority has participated in the proceedings (Rashba, vol. 2, resp. no. 104; Maharik, resp. no. 180; Maharit, vol. 1, resp. no. 58). Since this ruling, if followed, might enable the minority to impose its will on the majority by absenting itself from the discussions of the community, it came to be laid down in the course of time that the decision of the majority shall be binding despite the minority's nonparticipation in the discussions leading thereto. The scholars supported the conclusion either on the basis of a presumption that the absentee minority impliedly agrees to accept the decision of the majority which exerts itself to participate (*Mishpat Shalom,* no. 231; *ibid., Kunteres Tikkun Olam,* "vav"), or on the basis that the minority impliedly delegates authority to the majority (*Ḥatam Sofer,* ḤM, resp. no. 116); custom too is relied upon by some scholars in support of the majority rule of those participating in the proceedings in communal legislation (Mabit, vol. 1, resp. no. 264). If the community has delegated authority to its representatives, the latter decide by majority decision, but only if the minority too is present (*Penei Moshe,* vol. 2, resp. no. 110; *Kirkei Yosef,* ḤM 13:7; see Elon, *Ha-Mishpat Ha-Ivri,* II, 580ff.).

Bibliography: A. H. Freimann, in: *Yavneh,* 2 (1947/48), 1–6; I. A. Agus, in: *Talpioth,* 5 (1950), 176–95; 6 (1953), 305–20; B. Reicher, in: *Sinai,* 33 (1953), 174–7, 244–6, 383f.; A. I. Zaslanski, *ibid.,* 36 (1954/55), 451–4; I. A. Agus, in: JQR, 45 (1954/55), 120–9; ET, 9 (1959), 241–339; B. Lipkin, in: *Ha Torah ve-ha-Medinah,* 2 (1960), 41–54; S. Federbusch, in: *Mazkeret . . . T.H. Herzog* (1962), 575–81; M. Elon, *Ha-Mishpat Ha-Ivri* III, (1973), index of subjects: *Rov;* M. P. Golding, in: JSOS, 28 (1966), 67–78; A. J. Blau, in: *Torah she-be-al Peh,* 10 (1968), 128–34.

Shmuel Shilo

DOMICILE.

Definitions. In contrast to "residence," which is the place of physical abode, domicile is that place where a man has his true, fixed, and permanent home and principal establishment and to which whenever he is absent he has the intention of returning. For example, in matters governed by local custom, a man is bound to follow the practices of his place of domicile *(lex loci domicilii)* if they conflict with those of the locality in which he happens to be residing (Pes. 51a; Maim. Yad, Yom Tov, 8:20; see also *Minhag*). There is also a distinction between "resident" and "inhabitant," the latter term implying a more fixed and permanent abode than the former and imposing privileges and duties to which a mere resident would not be subject. Thus, one who uttered a vow not to derive any benefit from the "inhabitants" of a certain city *(anshei ha-ir, benei ha-ir)* is forbidden to do so from those who have resided there more than 12 months, but is permitted to derive benefit from anyone residing there less than that. If, however, his vow was not to derive any benefit from the "residents" of the city *(yoshevei ha-ir),* he is forbidden to do so from anyone who has lived there for more than 30 days (BB 8a; Maim. Yad, Nedarim, 9:17).

Intention to establish domicile. Intention in the matter of establishing domicile may be avowed, implied, or construed. Occasionally, these types are in conflict with one another, and authorities have disagreed as to the relative strength of each type. A famous case is that of the observance of the second day of a festival. Inhabitants of Ereẓ Israel keep one day; those of the Diaspora keep two. The settled law is that people traveling between Ereẓ Israel and the Diaspora follow the practice of the place to which they have arrived if their avowed intention is to establish domicile there (Sh. Ar., OḤ 496:3, and commentaries). But the following geonic responsum illustrates how implied intention or circumstantial factors modify the settled law:

> African Jews who have married in Ereẓ Israel and reside there: if 12 months have as yet not elapsed since they took up residence, they are obligated to keep two days following their place of origin; for this have the rabbis (BB 7b) taught, "How long must one reside in a city in order to be considered as one of its inhabitants? – 12 months." If, however, 12 months have elapsed, then thereafter – even if their avowed intention is to return – they follow the practice of the inhabitants of Jerusalem until they actually return to their homes.

The foregoing refers to people going to Ereẓ Israel from Africa. As for people, however, who go to Ereẓ Israel from Babylonia which has two talmudic academies:

> If their avowed intention is to return – even though many years have elapsed – they keep the more stringent practices of both localities. If, however, they do not have the avowed intention of returning, they follow the practices of Ereẓ Israel whether this will make for more stringent or for more lenient observance. *(Oẓar ha-Ge'onim* ed. by B. M. Lewin, Pes. (1930) 72, no. 175).

Domicile as a source of obligations. The Talmud has a series of rules according to which the length of residence in a place determines the extent to which one becomes obligated to participate in local activities and to perform communal duties. Thirty days' residence carries with it the obligation to contribute to the communal soup kitchen maintained for the poor *(tamḥui).* It also renders one subject to the rules of the apostate city (*ir ha-niddaḥat*; Sanh. 112a). Three months' residence carries with it the additional obligation to contribute to the general charity fund of the community; six months' to the fund which provided clothing for the poor; nine months' to the fund which covered the funeral expenses of the poor. Twelve months' residence changes one's status to that of inhabitant and subjects one to all communal expenses, taxes, and imposts; in this respect, the purchase of a home has the equivalent effect of 12 months' residence (BB 7b–8a; Maim. Yad, Mattenot Aniyyim, 9:12, Shekhenim, 6:5). See also Taxation.

Domicile of a married woman. According to the tannaitic sources, the domicile of a married woman is established by her husband. She could, with a few specified exceptions calculated to avoid undue hardship for her, be compelled to follow him on pain of divorce and loss of alimony rights *(ketubbah)*. Thus, if they have been living in the country he may not compel her to move to the city, and if they have been living in the city he may not compel her to move to the country, "for in certain respects living in the country is preferable and in other respects living in the city is preferable." Another one of the exceptions to the general rule is taking up residence in the Holy Land. If a woman insists upon emigrating to Ereẓ Israel or, in Israel, to Jerusalem, and her husband is adamant in his refusal, a divorce must be granted, and she retains her rights to alimony (Ket. 110b; Maim. Yad, Ishut, 13:17–20).

The problem of domicile arises also in connection with the laws of *eruv teḥumin* concerning the distance one might be permitted to walk outside the city limits on the Sabbath, as well as regards the problem of *ḥerem ha-yishuv* in medieval Jewish communities. Great importance attaches to it in regard to Conflict of Laws, which see.

Bibliography: I. S. Zuri, in: *Ha-Mishpat Ha-Ivri* (1926) vol. 1, 95–103.

Aaron Kirschenbaum

AGENCY. Agency is a legal doctrine enabling a person (the principal) to perform a legal act through another (the agent), in such a manner that it will be recognized as the legal act of the principal, whereby a person's possible field of legal activity is extended beyond the normal physical and other limitations.

The concept of agency was not recognized in ancient legal systems. Only in the later stages of Roman law did agency achieve a limited form of recognition – a phenomenon ascribed to the powerful status of the Roman *pater-familias* ("family head") on whose behalf all acquisitions by his kinsmen or servants were made in any event, thus obviating any urgent need for developing a doctrine of agency. In Jewish law the principle of agency was, however, already recognized in ancient times. While there is no express scriptural provision for it, the *tannaim* applied the doctrine of agency in various halakhic fields, i.e., to the laws of *mamonot* ("civil law"), *terumah* ("heave offering"), sacrifices, divorce, and betrothal, and established the rule that "a man's agent is as himself" *(Sheliḥo shel adam kemoto)*.

Acording to the Tosefta (Kid. 4:1), Bet Shammai and Bet Hillel agreed that a person appointed to carry out a specific mandate is disqualified from acting as a witness in a case involving such mandate, whereas amoraic sources quote a tannaitic tradition to the opposite effect. (Kid. 43a) and the tamudic *halakhah* was decided accordingly. The agent is not regarded as the principal, in the full sense of the term "as himself," since the agent is competent to testify with regard to the subject matter of his mandate in circumstances where the principal is disqualified from being a witness.

Criminal Law. In this field a contrary rule was laid down, namely, that "there can be no agent to do a wrong" (*Ein shali'aḥ li-devar averah;* Kid. 42b). The reasoning behind the rule is derived in answer to the hypothetical question: "Whose words does one obey? Those of the master" (i.e., the Almighty) "or of the pupil" (i.e., the mandator)? The legal import of the rule is that the agent himself is the transgressor, and liable, whereas the principal is exempt in respect of any transgression committed by the agent in execution of the former's mandate. There is, on the other hand, a tradition that a person who says to his agent, "Go forth and kill that soul!" (Kid. 43a), is personally liable, but the *halakhah* was decided to the effect that "in all matters a person's agent is 'as himself' except with regard to wrongdoing . . ." (Isserles to Sh. Ar., ḤM 182:1). However, the scholars laid down that in three fields the doctrine of agency applied also to transgression: (1) misappropriation of a deposit *(sheliḥut yad);* (2) slaughtering and selling (of stolen animals – see Theft and Robbery); and (3) conversion of consecrated property (see *Hekdesh*) to profane use *(me'ilah)*. In addition to these three specifically excepted cases, there are also a number of general exceptions to the rule that there can be no agent to do a wrongful act. According to the *amora* Ravina, the rule does not apply if the prohibition does not extend to the agent himself, e.g., where a priest commissions an Israelite to celebrate *kiddushin* with a divorcee on the priest's behalf (a marriage prohibited to a priest). Similarly, the *amora* Samma is of the opinion that an agency is constituted when the agent, in committing transgression, fails to act of his own free will; e.g., when he is unaware that his act amounts to a transgression (BM 10b; Isserles to Sh. Ar., ḤM 182:1 and 348:8). Furthermore, an agency to do a wrong is constituted whenever an agent delegated to commit a wrong must be presumed likely to execute his assignment because he is is known to commit such wrongs (Sh. Ar., ḤM 388:15, gloss; see also *Siftei Kohen, ibid.,* 67 for a contrary opinion). Whenever the law recognizes agency in the commission of a wrong, the agent himself will be liable (*Siftei Kohen* sub. sec. 4 to Sh. Ar., ḤM 292; see also *Netivot ha-Mishpat* to Sh. Ar., ḤM 348, n. 4).

Limitations. The rabbis of the Talmud, relying on the scriptural text, excluded the operation of the maxim that a person's agent is as himself in certain instances (TJ, Kid. 2:1, 62a; Yev. 101b). Some of the *posekim* exclude agency when the mandate cannot be carried out at the time of the agent's appointment (*Darkhei Moshe* to Tur, ḤM 182:1, based on Naz. 12b); but others differ (Responsa Maharit 2:22; *Arukh ha-Shulḥan* to Sh. Ar., ḤM *ibid.*). On the question of the husband's competence to annul the vows of his wife on the day of hearing them (Num. 30:9), the rabbis decided that it would not be the same if the vows were heard by an agent, and that the latter was not competent to annul them since "the appointment of an agent is not appropriate to a passive act" (*be-midi de-mi-meila;* Rosh to Ned. 72b). Similarly, there can be no agency with regard to a precept *(mitzvah)* which one is personally obligated to perform, such as laying *tefillin* or sitting in a *sukkah* (Tos. Rid. to Kid. 42b). So, too, the rabbinical enactment permitting assignment of debt by way of *ma'amad sheloshtan,* has been interpreted as requiring the participation of the parties themselves and the assignor could not appoint an agent for this purpose (Sh. Ar., ḤM 126:20). Some scholars hold that an agent cannot deliver an oath on behalf of his principal (Responsa, *Noda bi-Yhudah,* first series, YD 67 and last series YD 147).

It is not a requirement of agency that the manner of carrying out the mandate should be specifically detailed; the principal may grant his agent a degree of discretion, e.g., in celebrating *kiddushin* on his principal's behalf, an agent may be authorized to treat either with a specific woman or with one of a larger group (Maim., Yad, Ishut 3:14). Or, the principal can instruct his agent, "Go and purchase for me a field which you consider suitable," in which case the choice of the field is left to the full discretion of the agent. To be properly constituted, agency requires that the parties thereto are both legally competent and it was laid down that *einam benei da'at* ("persons who lack proper understanding," i.e., *ḥeresh, shoteh, ve-katan* ("deaf-mutes, idiots, and minors")) were disqualified from acting as either principal or agent (Git. 23a; Sh. Ar., ḤM 188:2).

Appointment and Powers. It appears from tannaitic and amoraic sources, neither of which discuss specifically the manner of appointing an agent, that such appointment may be done orally. The *halakhah* was so decided, it being held that there was no need for a formal *kinyan* (see Acquisition). In various places it nevertheless became the practice to assign by way of a formal *kinyan*. This was partly due to the influence of an analogous procedure in certain matters where an act of *kinyan* was required by law, such as the appointment of an agent in a lawsuit or for the purposes of agency in divorce – although the *kinyan* is not essential to the underlying agency itself but rather for the purpose of *bittul moda'ah* (see *Ones*[1]). It was also due in part to the desire of the parties to express in a formal act that the decision to conclude an agency was a serious one, and not one undertaken irresponsibly (Maim., Mekhirah, 5:12–13).

The agent is required to act strictly within the scope of his mandate, and if he exceeds his authority, all his actions are rendered null and void. The same result follows if the agent errs in any detail of his mandate, since the latter is appointed "to uphold and not to depart from the mandate" (Maim., Yad, Sheluḥin 1:3, Sh. Ar., ḤM 182:2). The possible consequences of a complete nullification can, however, be averted by especially stipulating for such a contingency (Maim. and Sh. Ar., *ibid.*). Thus it became the practice for a condition of this kind to be inserted in written instruments (see Hai Gaon, *Sefer ha-Shetarot*, 65–67).

Some authorities went so far as to hold that even in the absence of such a condition, there was a presumption – if the mandate were carried out – that the principal had authorized the agent to "uphold and to depart from the mandate," unless the contrary could be proved by the principal (Sh. Ar., ḤM 182:4). An agent who departs from the terms of his mandate and deals with a third party without disclosing that he is acting as an agent, will be liable for his actions (Maim., Sheluḥin 2:4; Sh. Ar., ḤM 182:2 and 6).

Revocation. The mandate of the agent may be revoked by the principal. The Talmud records a dispute between the Palestinian *amoraim*, Johanan and Resh Lakish, as to whether or not revocation can be done orally (TJ, Ter. 3:4, 42a and Git 4:1, 45c; see also Kid. 59a), and the *halakhah* was decided in favor of such revocation. Where a formal *kinyan* accompanies the agent's appointment, some take the view that the "act" of *kinyan* cannot be revoked orally, but the general opinion is in favor of it. In order to prevent the principal from withdrawing his agent's mandate, it became customary to submit the former to an oath to this effect. This procedure normally served as an effective deterrent, but if, despite the oath, the principal revoked it, the revocation is effective. Agency is also terminated upon the death of the principal.

It was recognized that a revocable mandate could prejudice a third party who was unaware of it, e.g., a debtor who paid his debt to the creditor's agent would continue to be indebted to the creditor or his heirs if it subsequently transpired that the agent's mandate had previously been revoked. It was determined, on various grounds, that in such circumstances the debtor would be released from his obligation. Isaac b. Abba Mari expressed the opinion that a defendant who received a deed of authorization from the agent, would suffer no damage even if it later transpired that the mandate had been revoked *(Sefer ha-Ittur, harsha'ah)*. Abraham b. David of Posquières justified the debtors release on the ground that the creditor's revocation of the mandate was tantamount to negligence. Later the above rule was justified on the further ground that, even if by the laws of agency the defendant had dealt with a person who was no agent, the transaction was nevertheless afforded legal validity by virtue of the laws of suretyship (*Arukh ha-Shulhan* to Sh. Ar., ḤM 122:2).

Brokerage. On the question of the agent's failure to observe the terms of his mandate, Jewish law distinguishes between an agent who acts in a voluntary capacity *(shali'aḥ)* and one who does so for payment called a *sarsur* ("broker" or "factor,") e.g., one who receives property for the purposes of sale, the latter being required to make good any consequent loss to the principal. Maimonides adds that in a case where the broker sells property at less than the authorized price, the purchaser must restore the goods to the owner if he knows that it was being sold by a broker on behalf of the true owner (*ibid.*, 2:6; and see Sh. Ar., ḤM 185:1). Similarly, in case of theft or loss the liability of the broker is equal to that of a bailee for reward (Maim. and Sh. Ar., *ibid.*). An agent may not purchase for himself the property which he has been authorized to sell, even at the authorized selling price (Sh. Ar., *ibid*).

Non- or Improper Performance by the Agent. The principal has no claim for pecuniary compensation against an agent who relinguishes his appointment without fulfilling his mandate (Sh. Ar., *ibid.*, 183:1). However, one opinion says that the principal has a claim for "loss of profits" against an agent who acts for payment, e.g., for the profits likely to have been earned by the principal had the mandate been properly carried out (*Netivot ha-Mishpat* to Sh. Ar., *ibid. Be'urim*, 1).

When the agent is given money by his principal in order to purchase property, and such property is purchased by the agent for himself with his own money the transaction is valid, "although the agent is a rascal," but the transaction will be for the benefit of the principal if the agent purchased for himself with the money of the principal (Sh. Ar., *ibid.*, and Isserles).

Agency for the Recovery of Debts (See Attorney). The appointment of an agent for the recovery at law of a debt owing to a claimant, is the subject of particular problems. The rabbis of Nehardea decided (BK 70a) that the claimant's representative must be equipped with an "instrument of permission" (*ketav harsha'ah*, "power of attorney"), bearing the following written instruction by the claimant: "Go and take legal action to acquire title and secure for yourself." Unless this is done the defendant may plead that the representative has no standing in the matter. The possibility of a plea of this nature arises from the talmudic principle that a creditor's representative cannot seize property in settlement of a debt owing to his principal, if there are additional creditors (Ket. 84b). The principle was construed at the commencement of the geonic period as applying whether the action of the agent is likely to prejudice other creditors, or merely the debtor himself (*She'iltot de-Rav Aḥai Ga'on*, 150). Another explanation offered for the aforesaid plea is the possible suspicion that the mandate was no longer in force, because of the principal's death or because it had been revoked by him. The aforesaid wording of the authorizing instrument rendered the agent a party to the legal proceedings, which in turn gave rise to the fear that the agent would keep whatever he recovered for himself. It therefore became customary at first to supplement the authorization with a further formality such as the principal's declaration before witnesses that he was appointing the agent as his representative (*Hal. Gedolot*, BK 70a, col. 3), and in other ways. Gradually these additional measures were abandoned and the instrument of authorization itself was accepted – without further formality – as constituting the agent a party, along with the defendant, to the proceedings and at the same time as safeguarding the rights of the principal (*Temim De'im*, 61; *Or*

1. page 180.

Zaru'a BK 7:300). Since, according to the above-mentioned wording of the authorization, or power of attorney, the principal in effect assigned *(hakna'ah)* to the agent the subject matter of the power of attorney, it was impossible – according to talmudic *halakhah* – for such power of attorney to relate to matters which could not validly be assigned. Thus the rabbis of Nehardea decided that no power of attorney could be written relating to movables, in respect of which the defendant denied the claim. In the post-talmudic period these restrictions were removed – by way of interpretation, custom and rabbinical enactment – and Jacob b. Asher records the practice of giving a power of attorney unrestricted as to subject matter (Tur., ḤM 123:2). A convenient act of *kinyan* employed to accompany the authorization, was assignment of the subject matter of the claim *aggav karka* (incidental to land; see Acquisition[1]).

In the geonic period, when most Jews had ceased to be landowners, it became necessary to find ways of employing the method of *kinyan aggav karka,* making it applicable to those who possessed no landed property. Thus arose the custom of assignment by way of *arba ammot be-Ereẓ Israel* ("four cubits of land" which every Jew was considered to own in Ereẓ Israel; Responsum Nahshon Gaon, Asaf; Responsa Geonica, ed. 1929, p. 31; see Acquisition). In post-geonic times, diminishing reliance was placed on this method, and Maimonides was of the opinion that an assignment (i.e., power of attorney) so effected was not binding on the debtor (Yad, Sheluḥin 3:7). In Germany and France it became customary to rely on *hoda'ah* (i.e., an admission by the principal that he owned land; see Admission; Acquisition). Naḥmanides suggested *kinyan* or assignment incidental to a synagogue seat or a place in the cemetery, common to all (Novellae to BB 44b) and further modes of assignment are discussed by other scholars.

<u>Aquisition of Property Through a Third Party Other than an Appointed Agent</u>. This may arise through an application of the rule that " a benefit may be conferred on a person in his absence" (Eruv. 7:11). Thus *A* may acquire property from *B* on behalf of *C* without the latter's knowledge, if this is to his benefit – for instance, a gift. *C* becomes the owner of the property as soon as *A*'s acquisition thereof is complete, unless *C*, upon hearing of the matter, rejects such ownership, in which event the transaction is void *ab initio* (Maim., Yad, Zekhiyyah, 4:2; Sh. Ar., ḤM 243:1; see also Acquisition).

In the State of Israel the laws of agency are governed by the "Agency Law, 5725–1965," which confirms the doctrine that "a man's agent is as himself" and further provides that the actions of the agent, including his knowledge and intention, are binding on and benefit the principal – as the case may be (sec. 2).

Bibliography: Simmons, in: JQR, 8 (1896), 614–31; M. Cohn, in: *Zeitschrift fuer vergleichende Rechtswissenschaft,* 36 (1920), 124–213, 354–460; Gulak, Yesodei, 1 (1922), 42–50; 2 (1922), 198–9; 4 (1922), 54–60; Gulak, Oẓar, 191–2, 272–9; I. H. Levinthal, *Jewish Law of Agency* (1923); Herzog, Institutions, 2 (1939), 141–53; ET, 1 (1951^3), 338–42; 12 (1967), 135–98; Rakover, *Ha-Sheliḥut ve-ha-Harsha'ah ba-Mishpat ha-Ivri* (1972); idem., in; *Sinai,* 63 (1968), 56–80; H. E. Baker, *Legal System of Israel* (1968), 118–21; 65 (1969), 117–138; Elon, *Ha-Mishpat Ha-Ivri* (1973) II, p. 462ff, III, p. 1135ff; and index of subjects, *Sheliḥut, Dinai.*

Nahum Rakover

ASMAKHTA (Aram. אסמכתא "Support," "reliance"), legal term with two connotations in the Talmud.

(1) In rabbinical exegesis it denotes the use of a biblical text merely as a "support" for a *halakhah* without suggesting that the *halakhah* is thus actually derived from this exegesis. Thus for the institution of the prosbul (see Usury) by Hillel for reasons which are explicitly given, the Talmud in addition gives Deuteronomy 15:9 as an *asmakhta* (TJ, Shev. 10:3, 39c). Its purpose was to give as much pentateuchal authority as possible to a purely rabbinic enactment but it was also used as a mnemotechnical aid (see: Herzog, Instit, 1 (1936), 2; Elon, *Ha-Mishpat Ha-Ivri,* II, p. 256ff; see also Interpretation).

(2) In civil law *asmakhta* is an important concept with regard to contracts and acquisition. It applies to such contracts in which one of the parties binds himself to an unreasonable penalty, which presumes that there was a lack of deliberate intention *(gemirat da'at)* on the part of the person entering into it. As a result the general rule is laid down that "an *asmakhta* does not give title" (BB, 168a). It is only valid if it can be proved that the contract was regarded as binding *(semikhat da'at).*

Maimonides is of the opinion that every contract, even in writing, introduced by the conditional "if" constitutes an *asmakhta* and takes effect only from the time that the condition is fulfilled, since the person entering into the condition hopes that its nonfulfillment will nullify it. There is a difference of opinion as to the extent to which *asmakhta* applied to gambling and other games which depend upon chance. *Asmakhta* as a legal term is inherently connected with *semikhat da'at* ("mental reliance") and *gemirat da'at* ("perfect intention"), both highly significant concepts in the Jewish law of contract and acquisition. The underlying idea is that the validity of an obligation or a transaction depends on the confidence of one party that the other party's intention is serious, deliberate, and final. *Semikhat da'at* and *gemirat da'at* are complementary terms not only because most transactions impose reciprocal obligations, but also because, logically, no finality of intention can be presumed on either side as long as there might be reason that confident reliance is lacking on the part of one or the other. The connotation of "reliance" is evident in the word *asmakhta* from סמך "to lean," (but see Gulak, Yesodei, 1 (1922), 68, especially n. 1) and, in the context of obligations or conveyance, it must originally have meant that in respect of that "reliance" the transaction was somehow problematic; eventually it came to be associated with transactions which were definitely defective in respect of reliance. It is clear that *asmakhta,* as a legal term, implies the absence of reliance. Thus, Gulak describes it as the absence of *gemirat da'at* and *semikhat da'at* (Gulak, loc. cit.). This description is much too wide as an exact definition of *asmakhta.* Firstly, the lack of *gemirat da'at* and *semikhat da'at* would undoubtedly invalidate the transaction, whereas there is a controversy in the Talmud as to whether or not *asmakhta* invalidates the transaction. *Asmakhta* must be seen as restricted, therefore, to cases where the question of finality of intention and reliance is debatable. Secondly, the cases in which the Talmud raises the question of *asmakhta* are all associated with conditional transactions (BM 48b, 66a-b, 109a-b, et al.). More precisely, the conditions visualized are suspensive conditions (conditions precedent) usually introduced simply by the word *im* ("if") which project the finalization of the obligation into the future in such a way that the obligation is not operative unless and until the condition is fulfilled, in contradiction to resolutive conditions (conditions subsequent) which allow for the immediate operation of the obligation *(me-akhshav,* "from now"), though the obligation may be reverted if the condition was not fulfilled. In fact, according to Jewish law, an obligation (or conveyance) would, as a rule, be valid only if it was immediately effective, by explicitly stipulating "from now," i.e., by letting

1. page 208.

the person obligated to take possession of the property in question actually or symbolically perform an act of acquisition *(kinyan)*, or the like. Maimonides (Yad, Mekhirah, 11, esp. para. 2 and 6) consequently draws the conclusion that all conditional transactions (i.e., not using the standard formulae of a condition such as *me-akhshav* (from the present moment) and *al-menat* (on condition that) but merely *im* (if)) are invalid on account of *asmakhta*, because the person obligating himself may be relying *(samkhah da'ato)* on the fact that the condition may not be fulfilled so that he will not be obligated. Since there has been no perfect intention of obligating oneself, the obligation is invalid *ab initio*, even if the condition were to be fulfilled.

Linking *asmakhta* with the rule of condition made the post-talmudic authorities introduce the whole range of the theory of condition into the discussion of *asmakhta*. There are, for example, fine distinctions between different conditions, the fulfillment of which is dependent on the person binding himself, on the other party or on both parties mutually, on a third person or on accident. Rabbinic literature is replete with arguments showing how these and other distinctions may be of consequence in considering whether or not a certain transaction is defective on account of *asmakhta* (cf. glosses to Maim. Yad, Mekhirah and to Sh. Ar., ḤM 207). The linking of *asmakhta* with the problem of conventional penalties is particularly significant – this is emphasized by Solomon b. Abraham Adret (Resp. 1:933). Accordingly, the term *asmakhta* would be applicable to cases where a person promises to pay a conventional amount as a penalty, should there be a breach of a primary obligation. The validity of such a promise would be dependent on whether or not the penalty was "extravagant and unreasonable" and whether the fulfillment of the condition was dependent on the person binding himself, or on accident, etc. The points involved here can be illustrated by the case presented in Bava Batra 168a. The Mishnah there speaks of a debtor who, while paying a part of his debt, allows the *shetar* ("bill of indebtedness") to be left in trust with a third person, with the instruction that the *shetar* for the full amount be handed to the creditor, in the event of the nonpayment of the balance at a time stipulated. The transaction comprises, in effect, two obligations, one relating to the actual debt (or rather to the outstanding balance) and the second to the payment of the penalty (the full amount of the *shetar* instead of the balance). It is clear that the minds of the parties were primarily set on the original obligation, whereas reliance and finality of intention may be in doubt over the matter of the penalty. The fulfillment of the condition is dependent on the person binding himself, which is to be viewed as diminishing reliance on the part of the person he is obligated to. In addition, the extravagance of the penalty is a relevant factor, unlike a case discussed in Bava Meẓia 104a-b, where in respect of land farmed on a percentage basis, the tenant obligates himself to pay a penalty if he lets the land lie fallow. Here the penalty is seen as justified, since it compensates the owner of the land for his damage (see: BM 109a, also Tos., Sanh. 24b-25a). There is a striking similarity to the differentiation in English law between "liquidated damages" and "penalty" proper (*in terrorem*, or extravagant and unconscionable). From the discussion in the Talmud (BB 168a) in the above quoted passage it would appear that such a penalty arrangement is invalid on account of *asmakhta*; on the other hand, from Nedarim 27b it appears that, if the arrangements were concluded with the due formalities of a *kinyan* before a recognized court, it is valid.

Thus already in talmudic times, remedies were sought to secure the validity of penalty clauses in practice, even though on principle they were defective because of *asmakhta*; this problem continued to occupy the post-talmudic authorities. The authorities in medieval Spain devised the following method to evade the pitfalls of *asmakhta*. *A* obligates himself to *B* to pay a penalty of 100 dinars if he does not fulfill a certain obligation on a stipulated day. A document is drawn up whereby *A* undertakes in absolute terms without a penalty clause to pay *B* 100 dinars. A separate document is then drawn up whereby *B* waives his claim to the 100 dinars, on condition that *A* fulfills his primary obligation on the stipulated day. Both documents are given to a third person to be handed over to *A* after he fulfills his primary obligation as stipulated, otherwise they are to be handed to *B*, who can then enforce his claim for 100 dinars on the strength of the first document (Maim. *ibid.*, 18, and see Isserles to Sh. Ar., ḤM 207:16).

It would appear that such arrangements were current in medieval England, at a time when finance was largely controlled by Jews, but later, the obligation to pay a certain amount and the conditional waiver came to be included in one document, now designated as a "conditional bond" (see: J. J. Rabinowitz, EH, *s.v.*, *asmakhta* and the literature indicated there).

It appears that this device was applied particularly to *shiddukhin* ("marriage contracts" – see Betrothal) in which were included very heavy penalties against breach of promise. The Ashkenazi authorities however tend to the opinion that the rule of *asmakhta* does not apply at all in this context, since the penalties may justifiably be considered as fair compensation for the damage, insult, and shame caused by a breach of promise (see: Tos. to BM 66a; Sanh. 24b–25a and Sh. Ar., ḤM 207; 16). In the discussion whether and under what circumstances *asmakhta* applied to gambling contracts, the fact that the conditions are mutual and reciprocal is of significance (see: Sanh. 24b and Tos. in loc.). *Asmakhta* does not apply to a vow to *hekdesh* (Sh. Ar., YD 258:10); nor to any transaction strengthened by vow, oath, or handshake, even if it would otherwise be defective on account of *asmakhta* (ḤM 207:19). If *A* obligates himself unconditionally to *B*, there can be no question of *asmakhta*, and the obligation is valid, even if there was no actual justification for the obligation, as "*B* owed him nothing" (*ibid.*, 20). The implication of this statement is twofold: (a) *asmakhta* relates to conditional transactions; and (b) although the defect of penalty arrangement is primarily that it is unjustified, lack of justification does not invalidate a promise, if it was absolute and unconditional. In the Jerusalem Talmud *asmakhta* is designated as *iẓẓumin* (TJ, BB 10, 17c; Git. 5, 47b).

Bibliography: Gulak, Yesodei, 1 (1922), 67–75; N. Wahrmann, *Die Bedingung (Tenai und Asmakhta) im juedischen Recht* (1938); ET, *s.v.*; B. Cohen, in: *H. A. Wolfson Jubilee Volume* (1965), 203–32; M. Elon, in: *Divrei ha-Congress ha-Olami ha-Revi'i le-Madda'ei ha-Yahadut*, 1 (1967), 201ff.; 268–9 (Eng. summ.); idem, *Ha-Mishpat Ha-Ivri* (1973), I, p. 158, II, p. 256ff, 573ff, III, p. 895, index of subjects: *Asmakhta*.

A. Zvi Ehrman

CONDITIONS תנאים tena'im).

Definition. Conditions is an ambiguous word inasmuch as it refers not only to the external factors upon which the existence of an agreement is made to depend, but also to the actual terms of the contract itself. Thus, one speaks of *tana'ei ha-ketubbah*, which really means the terms of the *ketubbah*. Similar ambiguities exist in English law (see G. C. Cheshire and C. H. S. Fifoot, *The Law of Contract* (1960[5]), 118ff.). In Jewish law, there is a further contingency; *tenai* consists not only of the stipulations of the contracting parties but also refers to legislative provisions, as evident in the expression *tenai bet-din* (see Takkanot[1]). As to conditions proper, i.e., stipulations (qualifications or limitations)

1. page 74.

attaching to a principal agreement, the basic concept in Jewish law seems to be very much the same as that in other systems of law. For example, distinctions between conditions precedent and conditions subsequent, differentiations between affirmative and negative conditions, between authoritative, casual, and mutual conditions or between expressed and implied conditions, and much besides, are found in all legal systems, although in Jewish law they may not be so clear-cut terminologically.

A vital characteristic of conditions in Jewish law is the provision referred to as *tenai benei Gad u-venei Re'uven,* based on Numbers 32. This was the occasion when Moses allocated land to the tribes of Gad and Reuben (and to half the tribe of Manasseh) on the east side of the Jordan River on condition that they crossed the Jordan and assisted the other tribes in the conquest of the Holy Land. The Mishnah notes (Kid. 3:4) that when Moses made this stipulation he used a *tenai kaful* ("double condition"), expressing himself, that is, both in the affirmative and the negative: if they fulfill the condition, they shall be entitled to the allocation; if they do not, they shall not. Significance is here attached to the fact that the affirmative precedes the negative *(hen kodem le-lav).* Moreover, it is required that the conditions be stipulated prior to the actual transactions – which means, according to some authorities, that, as a matter of formality, conditions should be referred to before mentioning the main transaction *(tenai kodem le-ma'aseh).* A fourth requirement, usually listed in the context, is that the condition must be *davar she-efshar lekayyemo,* i.e., something objectively capable or possible of fulfillment (Maim. Yad, Ishut, 6:1–13; Sh. Ar., EH 38: 1–4).

It is remarkable that the codes just referred to cite these rules in the context of matrimonial law, but it is the express opinion of Maimonides (*ibid.,* 6:14) that they apply equally to other provinces of the law, e.g., to sale and gift, and he persists in his ruling, despite the fact that later *Geonim* (to whom he explicitly refers) would have the formal requirements of *tenai kaful* and *hen kodem le-lav* apply to *kiddushin* (see Marriage) and *gittin* (see Divorce) only, and not to matters of *mamon* (see Introduction). Maimonides aptly argues that the biblical "precedent," from which the present law is derived, concerned *mamon* ("acquisition of property"), and it would therefore be illogical to consider it as applicable only to matrimony rather than to matters of *mamon.* Nevertheless, in the light of the glosses and commentaries to Maimonides (Maim. Yad, Ishut 6:14, and Zekhiah u-Mattanah 3:8) there is good authority for restricting the said requirements to *kiddushin* and *gittin;* and there is logic, too, in freeing everyday transactions from unreasonable formal requirements, since the predominant factor should be the will of the parties – and if they want a certain condition to be fulfilled, it should stand even if formalities like *tenai kaful* have not been observed (Rabad ad loc). Moreover, custom, which is a powerful agent in *Dinei Mamonot,* may have regarded such a requirement in the field of commercial transactions as obsolete (Haggahot Maimoniyyot to Ishut 6:14). Yet, even if the *halakhah* were to be decided as suggested by Maimonides, there still exist various means of evading the problems arising out of the formalistic requirements of *tenai kaful* and *hen kodem le-lav.* Maimonides himself notes (Ishut 6:17) that if the word *me-akhshav* ("from now") was used in the stipulation, which would seem to turn a suspensive condition into a resolutive one, the requirement of *tenai kaful* may be ignored. Equally, the use of the words *al menat* ("provided that"), as distinct from the simple *im* ("if"), has the same effect as *me-akhshav* (Sh. Ar., EH 38:3). Furthermore, if the condition is contained in a written document, the date of the document could have the effect of *me-akhshav* (Git. 77a).

Already in the Middle Ages, when most of the transactions among Jews were in chattel, there seems to have been a tendency to consider the *tenai benei Gad u-venei Re'uven,* if applicable at all, as being restricted to the transfer of landed property (as was the case, in fact, in the original "deal" with the tribes of Gad and Reuben); pure obligations *(in personam),* not involving the transfer of property, would then certainly be exempt from those rules (see Gulak, Yesodei, 1 (1922), 80). It may be mentioned in this context that some "reservations" *(shi'ur)* do not fall under the term "condition." For example, if one sells his house, but reserves the right to a certain part of it, this is not construed as the vendor having said that he would sell the house "on condition that " . . . therefore the requirement of *tenai kaful,* etc., does not apply (Sh. Ar., ḤM 212:3).

The requirement that the conditions should be capable of fulfillment, which is the most reasonable requirement and applies regardless of the form of the stipulation, needs some elaboration. The consequence of stipulating an impossible condition is that the principal transaction remains valid, despite the "nonfulfillment" of the condition (Maim. Yad, Ishut 6:7). By contrast, in Roman law the whole transaction would be voided by the defect of the condition (for a further discussion of this point see Gulak, loc. cit., 81). It should be said at once that this is not the case of a person being prevented from fulfilling a condition by reason of *force majeure* (see *Ones*), but with conditions stipulating something which according to all human experience is a priori impossible. The example usually given in the sources is "if you climb to the sky." Moreover, only physical and not moral or legal impossibility is visualized in this context. For example, if one promises to give his horse to another on condition that the prospective donee commits a sin, the condition would stand, and if he committed the sin he would have the horse, if not he would not (Maim. Yad, Ishut 6:8; Rema to EH 38:4). For a discussion of the problems of *jus dispositivum jus cogens,* and illegal contract, see Contract.[1]

Implied Conditions. A last category, widely discussed, is that of implied conditions. The classical case is that of a man who sold his possessions because he intended to emigrate to the Holy Land, but made no mention of his intentions during the negotiations. His plans having been foiled, he then wanted to renege on the transaction, arguing that he only sold his possessions on condition that his plans would be realized. The ruling here is that such mental reservations have no effect ("words which are in the heart are not words," Kid. 49b–50a). This does not mean that only explicit conditions are valid; in fact, it is sufficient if in the circumstances, the dependency of the transaction on certain events was clearly apparent. For example, if a person, in contemplation of death, donated all his property, it is assumed that he did so on the premise that his death was imminent (especially if the donation was made during a particular illness). Accordingly, if he survived, the donation is ineffective (BB 9:6; see also Wills[2]). On the general question as to whether and to what extent the parties are bound by the transaction before the condition is fulfilled (Maim. Yad, Ishut 6: 15–16; Sh. Ar., EH 38: 6–7), it should be noted that, here again, conditions introduced by the simple *im* would lack forcefulness, which can be remedied by the addition of *me-akhshav* or by using the formula of *al menat,* a differentiation discussed above in connection with *tenai kaful* (see also *Asmakhta*). Special problems of conditions attaching to specific transactions are further discussed in the respective articles on Bethothal, Sale, Wills, etc.

See also Acquisitions; Contract; Obligations, Law of.

Bibliography: Gulak, Yesodei, index; N. Wahrmann, *Die Entwickung der Bedingungsformen im biblisch-talmudischen Recht* (1929); idem, in: *Zeitschrift fuer vergleichende Rechts-*

1. page 251; 2. page 453.

wissenschaft, 45 (1930), 219–39; idem, *Die Bedingung* תנאי *und* אסמכתא *im juedischen Recht* (1938); Herzog, Instit, 2 (1939), 217ff.; B. Cohen, in: *H. A. Wolfson Jubilee Volume* (1965), 203–32; also separately; *Conditions in Jewish and Roman Law;* S. Albeck, *Ha-Tenaim Bedinei ha-Talmud, in: Mishpatim* 4 (1972) 77–104; B. Lipschutz, *Ha-Yesod Ha-Iyyunei Shel Ha-Tenai Be-Mishpat Ha-Ivri,* in: *Mishpatim* 4 (1973) 636–652; M. Elon, *Ha-Mishpat Ha-Ivri* (1973), II, p. 518ff, 754ff, III, p. 1104ff, 1281ff, index of subjects: *Tenaim, dinei.*

A. Zvi Ehrman

MISTAKE. A legal transaction requires that the "making up of the mind" (or the conclusive intention of the parties to close the bargain – *gemirat ha-da'at*) be demonstrated (see Acquisition). When it is apparent that one of the parties lacked such conclusive intention, the transaction may be voided, but only at the instance of that party. One of the factors showing that the required conclusive intention was missing is mistake, whether caused by the mistaken party himself or by the other party, whether willfully or unintentionally or whether relating to the subject matter of the transaction, its price, or any other aspect of the transaction. In all these cases the mistaken party is allowed to withdraw from the transaction, provided that the mistake is outwardly and objectively revealed, and not of a subjective nature only, even if it can be proved.

The contracts of sale and marriage exemplify the rules of mistake in Jewish law. An error as to price is generally termed *ona'ah* (overreaching), but when relating to the subject matter or any other aspect of the transaction it is termed *mikkaḥ ta'ut* (mistake). If the mistake is common to both parties the contract is voidable at the instance of either of them, otherwise it is voidable only at the instance of the mistaken party (Maim. Yad, Mekhirah 17: 1–2). If however the latter consented to the transaction as actually carried out, such consent being demonstrated by him either explicitly or by his subsequent use of the subject matter of the transaction with knowledge of the mistake (*ibid.* 15:3), he may not withdraw from the transaction, even though it does not accord with his original intention. Since the test for mistake is an objective one, the transaction will be voidable only if the average person of a particular place and time would consider it material, so that one would generally be expected to refuse to accept the property sold if the true position were made known (*ibid.* 15:5). Thus, if bad wheat is sold as good, the purchaser may withdraw. Similarly the seller may withdraw if he purported to sell bad wheat, which is in fact found to be good. When a person sells dark-colored wheat which is found to be white, or olive wood that turns out to be sycamore, both parties may withdraw since this is not what was agreed upon (*ibid.* 17: 1–2). Similarly, the discovery of a defect in the property sold entitles the purchaser to void the transaction, provided that he has not waived such right by his interim use of the property (*ibid.* 15:3). The purchaser retains this right even if the seller mentioned the defect at the time the transaction was negotiated, but did so in a manner that would not normally be taken as revealing the true existence of the defect. An example of this kind of mistake would be if the seller declares, "this cow is blind, lame, given to biting and to lying down under a load" and it is found to have one or other of these latter two defects but is neither blind nor lame, since the purchaser naturally assumed that the latter defects were as nonexistent as the two former ones (*ibid.* 15:7–8).

Generally speaking, mistake is established when the subject matter of the transaction suffers from a defect rendering it unfit for the known purpose for which it is acquired. Thus the purchaser of a slave may withdraw from the transaction if the slave is found to be ill or to have committed armed robbery, but not if he merely has a scar or a bad odor, which do not interfere with his work (*ibid.* 12–13). Similarly, it is a mistake if an ox is purchased for ploughing purposes and is found to be given to goring (*ibid.* 16:5). When the mistake is discovered only through use of the subject matter, which is of such a nature that on account of such use it can no longer be returned to the seller, the seller must refund the money – an example being if seeds bought for sowing fail to grow or if an animal bought for slaughtering is found to be ritually unclean (*ibid.* 16:1, 6). So too, the seller must refund the money if the subject matter is lost on account of a latent defect, as for instance where an ox is sold and is left with the purchaser's cattle but is unable to eat and starves to death on account of defective teeth (*ibid.* 9). However, it is the purchaser's own responsibility if the subject matter is stolen or lost after the discovery of a defect therein (*ibid.* 4).

In the State of Israel, the rules of mistake are governed by English law in the field of contract, and by the Law of Sale (1968) in the field of property which follows the draft of the uniform international sale of goods law. The problem of mistake arises also in other legal fields. On mistake in criminal law, see Penal Law; on error in judgment, see M. Elon, *Ha-Mishpat Ha-Ivri* (1973), II, p. 498, 801ff; on error in the language of a *takkanah,* see *ibid.* p. 373, 378, 383ff. on error in the drafting of a deed, see *ibid.* p. 358ff.; on custom founded on error, see *ibid.* p. 760ff.

Bibliography: Gulak, Yesodei, 1 (1922), 63f.; 2 (1922), 156; Herzog, Instit, 2 (1939), 116–29.

Shalom Albeck

ONES (Heb. אנס), either (1) compelling a person to act against his will, or (2) the occurrence of an unavoidable event that prevents or obstructs the performance of certain acts, or causes them to occur. Both categories on *ones* are derived exegetically from the verse in the Pentateuch dealing with *ones* in the sense of compulsion. With regard to the rape of a bethrothed maiden, it states (Deut. 22:26): "But unto the damsel thou shalt do nothing." From this the sages inferred that in all cases of "*ones* the merciful [Torah] exempts." (Ned. 27a; BK 28b).

Compelling a Person to Act Against his Will. Categories of Ones of Compulsion. *Ones* of compulsion comprises three categories: the threat of death; physical torture; and financial loss. Compulsion by threat of death or as a result of physical torture is adjudged as *ones* in all cases (Ket. 33b; see Tos. ad loc.). Financial pressure is not considered as *ones* in cases of transgression or *issur* (acts forbidden by the Torah), but as regards money matters, divorce, or an oath the authorities differ (see below). The threat of duress *(le'enos)* counts as *ones* if the threatener possesses the power to execute the threat himself or through the agency of others (Sh. Ar., ḤM 205:7), but some scholars do not permit the extension of *ones* to such a threat (Rema ad loc.). If the threat is made to a kinsman, for example, it is generally counted as *ones* of compulsion (Resp. Rashbash no. 339; *Haggahot Mordekhai* Git. no. 467; Resp. Bezalel Ashkenazi no. 15), but other scholars differ (*Tashbeẓ* 1:1; Rema, EH 134:4).

In Compulsion to Wrongdoing. Anyone who commits a transgression through *ones* is exempt (Tos. to Yev. 53b–54a; Yad, Yesodei ha-Torah 5:4) even from the judgment of heaven (Resp. Ribash 4 and 11). Even though a person commits one of the three transgressions of which it is said that he should choose death rather than commit them, he will not be punished if he acted under duress. He is obliged, however, to expend money to enable himself to escape from a situation where otherwise he would be forced to transgress (Resp. Ribash 387; and see Penal Law).

In Kiddushin. If a man was compelled under duress to betroth a woman, some authorities hold that the *kiddushin* (see Marriage) is valid (Yad, Ishut 4:1 and *Maggid Mishnah* ad loc. in the name of Rashba), but others maintain that it is of no effect (Sh. Ar., EH 42:1). Those who hold that the *kiddushin* is valid base their opinion on the fact that a man can divorce his wife without her consent (*Maggid Mishneh* loc. cit.; *Beit Shemu'el* 42, n. 1) – even after the ban of Rabbenu Gershom prohibiting divorce against the woman's will – should he have been compelled to betroth her under duress (*Beit Shemu'el* loc. cit.). If a woman is compelled under duress to be betrothed, the *kiddushin* is as valid as if she had acted willingly (BB 48b), but nevertheless the rabbis nullified it because of her partner's improper behavior (*ibid.;* see Marriage).

In Divorce. A husband divorcing his wife must act freely (Yad, Gerushin 1:1–2), and a divorce given by the husband against his will is divorce under duress and therefore invalid. There are, however, cases in which the court may compel the husband to grant a divorce and in such cases it is valid (Git. 9:8; see Divorce). Some authorities are of the opinion that in such cases the husband may say, "I am willing" (*Netivot ha-Mishpat, Mishpat ha-Urim* 205, n. 1), but others say that if he gives the divorce without making any remark then this is tantamount to saying, "I am willing" (*Havvot Ya'ir* nos. 55 and 56). Various explanations are given for the validity of this divorce despite its being given under duress. Some explain that just as in a sale under duress the sale is valid because of the assumption that in the end the seller made up his mind to sell (under certain conditions; see below), this is also the case in a divorce given under duress when compulsion is legally permitted (Tos. to BB 49a); others say that as it is a religious precept to obey the sages, the husband is reconciled to divorce (*Rashbam* BB 48a); while others hold that the laws of *ones* are not applicable to one legally bound to act in a particular way, even though his act results from compulsion (Yad, Gerushin 2:20). Financial duress counts as *ones* with regard to compulsion to divorce (Resp. Rashba vol. 4 no. 40; Nov. Ritba Kid. 50a s.v. *ve-ha*), but some authorites disagree and do not regard it as *ones* (*Toledot Adam ve-Ḥavvah,* Ḥavvah 24:1).

In Sale. If a purchaser snatches the property of the seller through giving him the purchase price against his will then this is an invalid sale. In this case the purchaser is treated as a predator, and he is obliged to restore the article he took as if he were a robber (BK 62a; Yad, Gezelah 1:9; see Theft and Robbery). In certain circumstances, however, though the seller sells under duress, it is assumed that in the end he agreed to the sale for he accepted money in consideration of the transferred property. Therefore if he was given the monetary value of the property for sale and took it into his hands, the sale stands (Sh. Ar., ḤM 205:1). Some hold the sale to be valid only if he took the money at the time of the actual transaction (Yad, Mekhirah 10:1, see *Mishneh le-Melekh*), while others hold it to be valid even if the money was taken afterward *(ibid.)*. If he was compelled to reduce the price, the sale is void (Sh. Ar., ḤM 205:4), but some scholars disagree (Resp. Maharik 185). If a man is compelled to purchase, the transaction is void and the purchaser may withdraw (Rema ḤM 205:12), but here too there are dissident opinions (*Ha-Gra ibid.*, n. 32). In the event of the purchaser's becoming reconciled to the sale, the seller is unable to withdraw (*Netivot ha-Mishpat,* Mishpat ha-Urim 205, n. 18). In the case of a business transaction that resembles sale, such as a compromise when it is uncertain where the legal right lies, if the parties become reconciled to it under duress then the same ruling applies as for sale and the compromise prevails (*Beit Yosef* ḤM 205:16).

In Gifts. If a man is compelled to assign a gift, the gift is void (Rashbam BB 47b). A transaction that resembles a gift, such as a compromise when the litigant would have succeeded at law but was forced to compromise, counts as a gift and the compromise is void (*Beit Yosef* loc. cit.). Similarly, an obligation undertaken through an acknowledgement of liability where none exists rates as a gift in regard to *ones* and the obligation cannot be enforced (*Beit Yosef* loc. cit.).

Moda'ah ("Notification"). If the person under duress discloses in advance that the transaction he is about to acquiesce to will be effected against his will and that he has no intention of executing it, the subsequent transaction is void through lack of intent. Such a declaration to witnesses is termed *mesirat moda'ah* ("making a notification"). The witnesses usually wrote a deed of *moda'ah,* but this was not imperative (BB 40a–b; ḤM 205). If the seller makes a *moda'ah* the sale is void even though he accepts the purchase price (ḤM 205:1). A *moda'ah* made before a single witness is ineffective even if the compeller admits the duress, for since the person under duress knows that he cannot prove that he made a *moda'ah* he acquiesces in the transaction (*Sha'ar Mishpat* 46, n. 21). If, however, he made the *moda'ah* in the presence of two witnesses separately, it is effective (*Keneset ha-Gedolah,* ḤM 205, Tur no. 36). Where the sale is void because a *moda'ah* has been made, the purchaser too has the right to withdraw on becoming aware that the seller made a *moda'ah* prior to the sale (*Ḥavvot Ya'ir* no. 40).

A deed of *moda'ah* may not be written in the first instance unless the witnesses know the duress (Sh. Ar., ḤM 205:5), and the witnesses must write "we the witnesses know the *ones*" (Sh. Ar., ḤM 205:1). If they write that the person concerned made a *moda'ah* in their presence, although they were unaware of the duress, the transaction will be void if he subsequently proves that there was *ones.* If witnesses testify to, or write, the *moda'ah* without knowing the *ones,* and other witnesses testify to the *ones,* these are combined and the transaction is void *(ibid.)*. In a case where there is duress but the man under it is not able to make the *moda'ah,* if witnesses know of the *ones,* this has the same effect as a *moda'ah,* (*Tashbeẓ* 2:169; *Matteh Shimon,* ḤM 205, Tur no. 39). The deed of *moda'ah* may be written before or after the transaction, providing the one under duress makes the notification before the transaction (*Netivot ha-Mishpat,* Mishpat ha-Urim 205 n. 6; *Keẓot ha-Ḥoshen* 205, n. 1; *Haggahot Maimuniyyot,* Mekhirah 10:2). If the deed of *moda'ah* is undated and it is not known whether notification was made before or after the transaction because the witnesses are not available, it is valid and the transaction is void (Rema ḤM 205:9), for since the witnesses knew of the *ones* it is to be assumed, unless there is evidence to the contrary, that the notification was made beforehand *(ibid.)*. In the case of gifts and similar dealings, such as remission of debt, the witnesses may write the *moda'ah* without knowing the *ones;* the *moda'ah* will then testify to lack of intent (Tur ḤM 205:12 and *Beit Yosef* thereto). The authorities differ as to why this should be so, some holding that the *moda'ah* is effective as regards a gift even without the witnesses' knowledge of the *ones,* because if there is no *ones,* why should anyone confer a gift and make a *moda'ah*? It is therefore assumed that there must be *ones.* Accordingly if it is known with certainty that there is no *ones,* the *moda'ah* may not be written. Others hold, however, that in the case of a gift manifestation of lack of proper intent is effective even without *ones* (see Gulak, Yesodei, 1 (1922), 61).

If after making the *moda'ah* the one under duress decides to effect the transaction and cancels his *moda'ah,* the transaction prevails (Sh. Ar., ḤM 205:11 and *Sma* thereto). It is possible, however, to make a *moda'ah* cancelling ab initio such a *moda'ah* and declaring that the cancellation all the time of the transaction will result from *ones* and lack of intent. Such a notification, called *"moda'ah de-moda'ah,"* cancels the transaction. To make certain that an action was not voided through a *moda'ah,* it became customary at the time of the transaction to cancel every *moda'ah* and every *moda'ah* cancelling a *moda'ah ad infinitum,* or alternatively for the party involved to disqualify the witnesses before whom he made any *moda'ah* with regard to the transaction at hand, thus making them unfit to testify on his behalf. By these methods the previous *moda'ot* are voided and the act subsists (*ibid.; Beit Yosef* ḤM 205:15).

Acts Counting as Ones. A man who performs an act under an erroneous impression of the facts is described as "forced by his heart"; since his understanding of the case was in error it is included in *ones.* This *halakhah* occurs especially in connection with an oath pledged under a mistaken impression. The one who swore the oath is delivered from it and exempted from offering a sacrifice, since he swore in error (Shevu. 26a; Ned. 25b; Maim. Yad, Shevuot 1:10; see Mistake). Forgetting rates as *ones* (BK 26b and *Nimmukei Yosef* ad loc.), as does an act performed as the result of an overpowering impulse. Hence, for example, a woman who is forced to have sexual intercourse is regarded as having been raped even though she yielded willingly during the final stages of the act, since she had not the power to resist to the end because her natural impulse compelled her desire (Yad, Sanhedrin 20:3, Issurei Bi'ah 1:9; Resp. Hatam Sofer, EH pt. 1, no. 18). A minor girl who commits adultery even willingly is regarded as acting under duress since "the seduction of a minor is deemed *ones*" because she has no will of her own (Yev. 33b), 61b; TJ, Sot. 1:2, 16c). Some hold that a deranged woman who commits adultery also counts as *ones* (*Mishneh le-Melekh,* Ishut 11:8), but others are doubtful about this (see Rape).

Acts Counting as Voluntary. A man compelled to incestuous or adulterous intercourse (see Incest) is guilty of a capital offense, since "an erection can only take place voluntarily" (Yad, Issurei Bi'ah 1:9), but some hold that he is not liable for the death penalty (*Maggid Mishneh* ad loc.). Duress arising from the person's own situation, as in the case of a man who sells his property because of financial distress, does not count as *ones* (Sh. Ar., ḤM 205:12). Similarly, if the duress was related to some other action and he was compelled to act as a cause of this – e.g., if he was compelled to give money and because he did not have it was compelled to sell – this is not *ones (ibid.).*

Unavoidable Causes. Categories of Causes Counting as Ones. The scholars developed a threefold division of the types of *ones,* a classification which was made especially in connection with the laws of divorce; a somewhat similar one was made in connection with the law of obligation, particularly with reference to torts. The three categories relating to divorce (see below) are: (1) an *ones* of common occurence; (2) an *ones* neither common nor uncommon; and (3) an uncommon *ones.* The classical examples of these are: (1) if a man returning home was delayed because the ferry was on the opposite bank of the river and so he could not cross it; (2) illness; and (3) if a man was killed when a house collapsed, or he was bitten by a snake, or devoured by a lion (Tos., *Piskei ha-Rosh* and *Mordekhai* to Ket. 2b and 3a and to Git. 73a; Sh. Ar., EH 144:1). A general *ones* not arising from human agency is termed *makkat medinah* ("regional mishap"; BM 9:6). As regards liability in the laws of obligation the division is made between an absolute *ones* and one which is relative. In the words of *rishonim* the distinction is between an *ones* "like theft" and one "like loss." The Talmud (BM 94b) has a dictum that "loss is close to negligence" while "theft is near to *ones*" (Tos. to BK 27b and to BM 82b).

Nonfulfillment of Obligation Resulting from Ones. A man bears no liability for the nonfulfillment of his obligations if he is prevented from doing so by *ones* (BK 28b; Ned. 28a), with the exception of the borrower (BM 93a; see Bailment). It is possible that a tortfeasor too is excluded from this rule, since "man is always liable, whether acting inadvertently or willingly, whether awake or asleep" (BK 2:6), or in another version "whether acting inadvertently or willingly, accidently or deliberately" (Sanh. 72a). It has, however, been ruled that there are kinds of *ones* which exempt even tortfeasors (Tos. to Sanh. 76b). A man accepting liability for every *ones* is not liable for an uncommon one (Resp. Ribash no. 250; Resp. Maharik no. 7; Sh. Ar., ḤM 225:4).

Nonfulfillment of Obligation by Reason of Ones. If a man was to execute an act on certain conditions and his nonfulfillment of these conditions was due to *ones,* the *amoraim* differ as to whether the act counts as not having been executed because the condition was not fulfilled although the nonfulfillment was caused by *ones,* or whether the act stands since it was *ones* that prevented fulfillment of the condition (TJ, Git. 7:6, 49a; see *Beit Yosef* and *Baḥ* ḤM 21; *Siftei Kohen* HM 21). Some explain the former opinion as follows: The rule is that "the merciful [Torah] exempts in cases of *ones*" and not that "in cases of *ones* the merciful [Torah] obligates" the other person. For in what way is he concerned with the *ones* of the other? His obligation was dependent on the other's fulfillment of the condition, which in fact was not done (*Siftei Kohen* loc. cit.; Resp. Ḥatam Sofer, ḤM no. 1; for other explanations see the ḤM and *Malbushei Yom Tov, Kuntres Mishpetei ha-Tanna'im 2*). The *halakhah* follows the first view (*Avnei Millu'im,* EH 38:1).

Ones in Divorce. Contrary to the principle: "the merciful [Torah] exempts in cases of *ones*" the rabbinic regulation lays down "accident is no plea in divorce." Hence, if a man says to his wife: 'This is your bill of divorce if I do not return by such a date," and he does not come back in time because of *ones,* the divorce is effective and he is unable to have it set aside on the plea that he was delayed by *ones.* There were two considerations behind this regulation. If the divorce was regarded as ineffective in a case of *ones,* a chaste woman, when her husband did not arrive on the stated day, would always consider that an accident might have befallen him, even when his absence was deliberate, and thus would remain unable to remarry. A loose woman, on the other hand, would always claim that her husband's failure to return was not due to *ones* and would contract a second marriage; then when subsequently his nonreturn was found to be due to *ones,* the divorce would be invalid and her children *mamzerim.* As a result the rabbis enacted that the divorce must always take effect, even though the husband's failure to return is due to *ones,* and even though he stands on the other bank of the river and cries aloud, "See I have returned and am not responsible because of *ones*" (Ket. 2b–3a; Tos. to Ket. 3a; Sh. Ar., EH 144: 1). The *rishonim* ruled that this *halakhah* applies to *ones* of common occurrence and to *ones* neither common nor uncommon, but not at all to uncommon *ones* (Tos., *Piskei ha-Rosh,* and *Mordekhai* to Ket. 2b–3a and to Git. 73a and codes).

Ones on the Due Date. A man who was obliged to perform an action within a certain period of time and relied on the fact that he still had the time to do it until the end of the period, who was then overtaken by *ones* at the very end of the period, is regarded as subject to *ones* (Sh. Ar., OḤ 108:8 and *Magen Avraham* thereto n. 11), but others do not consider this *ones* (Rema YD 232:12).

Bibliography: Gulak, Yesodei, 1 (1922), 57–62; 2 (1922),

70f.; M. Higger, *Intention in Talmudic Law* (1927); Herzog, Instit, 1 (19), 101–7; 2 (1939), 130–2, 240–3, 248–75; ET, 1 (1951[3]), 162–72; 5 (1953), 698–707; Z. Karl, in: *Mazkeret Levi... Freund* (1953), 29, 45f.; B. Rabinovitz-Teomim, *Ḥukkat Mishpat* (1957), 182–91; B. Lipkin, in: *Sinai – Sefer Yovel* (1958), 394–402; S. Albeck, *Pesher Dinei ha-Nezikin ba-Talmud* (1965), 175–82; Elon, *Ha-Mishpat Ha-Ivri* (1973), I, p. 133, 186, II, p. 287 ff, 293ff, 520ff, 790ff, 808ff, III, p. 842, index of subjects: *Ones;* Sh. Warhaftig, *Dinei Avodah ba-Mishpat ha-Ivri,* 2 (1969), 721–96, 829–66.

Shmuel Shilo

SHETAR (Heb. שטר), Formal legal document, or deed, derived from the Akkadian *satāru,* meaning writing.

Early Examples. The term *shetar* is not found in the Bible, where the term *sefer* is used to denote a legal document such as *sefer keritut* in Deuteronomy 24:1 for bill of divorce, or *sefer ha-miknah* in Jeremiah 32:11 for bill of sale. In tannaitic literature the terms *iggeret, get,* and *shetar* are commonly used to designate various types of legal documents. Subsequently, the word *get* acquired a more limited meaning, restricted to a document expressing legal separation such as divorce or manumission of a slave. In geonic times, the term *ketav* was frequently used to designate a legal document. The only legal document whose execution is elaborately described in the Bible is the one referred to in Jeremiah, which seems to have been written in duplicate, and was subscribed to by witnesses. One copy was sealed; a second copy was left unsealed for ready access. The sealed document is the antecedent of the "tied deed" known as a *Doppelurkunde.* Such documents were in wide use in the Near East during the period of the First and Second Temples.

The earliest known and extant collection of legal documents of Jewish origin is one from the Jewish garrison in Yeb of the fifth century b.c.e. written in Aramaic, known as the Elephantine Papyri. It is a collection of 33 complete legal documents of various kinds, including a *ketubbah.* They resemble the basic forms of Jewish documents as used in talmudic and post-talmudic times. In the Book of Tobit (probably composed in the second century b.c.e.) 5:3 there is a reference to a deed of deposit as well as to a marriage document. There is sufficient evidence to conclude that forms of legal documents were already standardized during the last two centuries of the Second Temple. Recently there have been discovered, among the Dead Sea Scrolls, legal documents dating from the first century c.e., which conform to the standards referred to in tannaitic literature. It is noteworthy that despite the large number of references to legal documents in tannaitic and amoraic literature, no complete form of legal contract or bill of indebtedness is recorded in the Talmud. There are, however, references to individual clauses and expressions, and their legal effects. It is evident that formalities were strictly adhered to, and that formularies, i.e., prototype standard forms, were available to the scribes, who would either copy the forms or merely fill in the particular information (Git. 3:2). These formularies related to every area of human relationship. Professional scribes were generally employed, and during the period of the Second Temple bonds of indebtedness were deposited in special archives for safekeeping (Jos., Wars, 2:427).

From the geonic period there are preserved a number of forms from the collection of Saadiah Gaon (882–942; see bibl.), as well as a collection of 28 formularies attributed to Hai Gaon, who died in 1038 c.e. (see bibl.). Many later collections are extant containing different types of forms, some including additional provisions to meet the demands of new exigencies. Asher Gulak edited a thesaurus of such formularies (*Oẓar ha-Shetarot,* 1926), containing 403 different forms, each representing a particular type of deed. Among these forms are private documents such as family and commercial agreements, as well as judicial and communal *shetarot.* The Institute for Research in Jewish Law of the Hebrew University in Jerusalem is preparing, in connection with the project of indexing responsa, a collection of *shetarot* which will include the formularies of *shetarot* as cited in the responsa literature whether quoted in full or in part. See M. Elon, *Ha-Mishpat Ha-Ivri* III (1973), 1286ff.

One of the earliest forms of documents was the "tied deed," *get mekushar,* which is described in the Mishnah (BB 10:2) and Tosefta (BB 11:1). It was a formal legal document wherein the agreement was written on one side and the document was then folded. The parchment was cut at the top in strips which were tied together, and three witnesses then signed between the knots on the reverse side. Such documents have been found among the Dead Sea Scrolls. The Talmud relates that this type of document was instituted by the rabbis to make it more time-consuming and more difficult for priests who might on impulse divorce their wives and are prohibited from remarrying even their former spouses (*Yad Ramah* to BB 160a; see Divorce; Marriage, Prohibited[1]). In contradistinction to the *get mekushar* is the *get pashut* ("plain deed"), which is not folded and tied and requires only two witnesses. This is the form in use today.

Format of the Shetar. Every *shetar,* as a formal document, requires the signatures of witnesses. It does not require the signature of the obligor. Credence is given, however, to documents either signed or written by the obligor, but unwitnessed, and which otherwise do not comply with the formalities of a *shetar.* Such a document is called *ketav yad* ("his own handwriting"; equivalent to a memorandum), and has the status of an oral understanding with all its legal consequences and without creating a lien on reality (Tur, ḤM 69; see Lien; Obligation, Law of). The *shetar* is somewhat different from modern western forms of contract which recite the facts of an agreement. The *shetar* records the testimony of the witnesses who state that on a given day the named obligors appeared before them and said such and such. For many centuries documents written in Israel and the countries of the Middle East and Africa would usually refer to the date according to the Seleucid calendar ("Era of the Documents"). Documents written in Europe usually referred to the year since creation ("Era of the Creation").

For the purpose of analysis, a *shetar* may be divided into two parts. The first part is the *tofes* (*typos,* "frame"), which is the general section of the instrument. A stereotyped copy may be used, not prepared specifically for the contract being undertaken. It contains the standard words of the preamble and the close of the the document, as well as the words of obligation and additional clauses which protect the obligee in every conceivable way permitted. The *toref* contains the names of the parties, the date, the nature and amount of the obligation. During the centuries in which Jewish civil law governed the internal economic relations between Jews there developed additional clauses and provisions, which were inserted into *shetarot* mainly for the protection of the obligee. These clauses include the following:

(1) A credence clause *(ne'emanut)* in which the obligor under the agreement asserts that he relieves the claimant of any oath which may be necessary, and that he considers the claimant's testimony that he has not been repaid sufficient to preclude the obligor from raising such a defense. The basis for this clause is to be found in *Shevu'ot* 42a. There are, of course, variants in the wording of such clauses which may strengthen the position of the claimant (Tur, ḤM 61).

(2) The right to collect from the best of the obligor's property *(shefer ereg nekhasin).* Though according to the

1. pages 421, 361.

Talmud a creditor can recover first from the average quality real estate of the debtor, and a woman for her *ketubbah* first from the least desirable land of her husband (see Execution), this clause, which is found in the usual *ketubbah* and bill of indebtedness, improved the claimant's position, so as to recover from best quality realty.

(3) A clause allowing the claimant to recover costs of litigation (see Execution).

(4) The obligor must sell his property to pay his obligation, rather than await a court sale (see Execution).

(5) In some isolated cases there were even incorporated undertakings by the obligor of personal servitude or imprisonment in case of his default (see Execution; Imprisonment for Debt).

(6) A common clause allowing the claimant to render the document effective through the use of a non-Jewish court, and in some cases by personal force (see Introduction). The end of the *shetar* usually included the statement that it was not a mere form but an actual document, and concluded with the words, *sharir ve-kayyam* ("firm and established"). Any provisions added after this phrase (other than corrections) are of no effect.

A legal instrument may not be written on a material which is susceptible to forgery. In the event of a correction, a mark must be made next to the corrected word or clause, and a reference to it must be added at the foot of the document, which must be witnessed (Tur, ḤM 42; see Forgery).

To enforce a claim based on a *shetar,* the claimant must submit the document to a court of at least three persons to establish the authenticity of the witnesses' signatures. This may be accomplished either by the witnesses themselves identifying their own signatures, or by others testifying that they are familiar with the signatures of the witnesses, or by a handwriting analysis. Once the signatures are authenticated, the court appends a validation certificate, *henpek* (or *hanpek*) or *asharta,* which precludes any future challenge to the validity of the document. This proceeding before the court may take place without the obligor being present and even over his objection. Such certification is referred to in the Talmud (BM 7b) and appears among the Elephantine documents of the fifth century b.c.e.

The language of a document does not affect its validity. Indeed, in addition to Aramaic or Hebrew, legal instruments were written in Persian, Arabic, Latin, Greek, English, Spanish, and all other languages used by Jews. Bills of divorce, however, were subject to special rules.

Shetarot Written before Gentile Courts. The general rule, as stated in the Mishnah, is that all legal instruments written by non-Jewish courts and witnessed by non-Jews are valid, except for bills of divorce and manumissions of slaves (Git. 1:5). Although there existed differences of interpretation and application between various rabbinic authorities on this point, it was generally agreed that where there was a basis for holding that the non-Jewish court was not totally corrupt, credence would be given to legal instruments such as contracts, deeds, and bills of indebtedness. A distinction is made between documents which evidence a business transaction, or at least state consideration, and which under the rule of *dina de-malkhuta dina* ("the law of the land is the law") required recognition, and deeds of gift which take on different legal incidents (Maim. Yad, Malveh ve-Loveh, 27:1). The medieval rabbis distinguished between deeds written in gentile courts and those written before notaries outside the court. Maimonides ruled the latter invalid, while Nahmanides upheld their validity.

Types of Document. A review of the various types of documents assembled in Gulak's *Oẓar ha-Shetarot* is sufficient to indicate the wide scope of relationships covered by such documents. These may be divided into the following five categories:

(1) *Family Documents:* These include betrothal agreements, marriage contracts (see *Ketubbah*), antenuptial agreements, releases between husband and wife, divorce documents, *ḥaliẓah* and *yibbum* (see Levirate Marriage), wills, deeds of trust (see *Shalish;* Consecration and Endowment) and guardianship (see *Apotropos*), and support contracts. It is evident that these documents cover the entire range of family relationships and evidence a sophisticated legal development. One of the more interesting documents is the *shetar shiddukhin* (see Betrothal, a contract between two sets of parents in which both parties undertake to betroth their children to each other, and promise to contribute whatever dowry is involved. The difference between this and a *shetar erusin* ("contract of betrothal") is that the latter document deals with promises made to and by the prospective couple, while the *shetar shiddukhin* involves promises exchanged by their parents or guardians. The *get* ("divorce") contains specific formulas which are dealt with elsewhere (see Divorce[1]).

(2) *Business Documents:* These documents relate to economic relations between Jews and include bills of sale, gifts, leases, partnerships, *Iska* (see Partnership), mortgages (see Lien), bonds, receipts, assignments, letters of attorney, employment contracts (see Labor Law), and escrow agreements. Each of these deeds had its own historical development. Thus, there exist many copies of partnership agreements in the Cairo *Genizah* which represent the frequent use of partnership, even on an international scale, during the period between the middle of the tenth to the middle of the 13th century.

(a) *Shetar Ḥov,* bond, bill of indebtedness. This is probably the most frequently used private legal document besides the *ketubbah.* In fact, when the term *shetar* is used without modification it refers to a *shetar ḥov.* It should be noted that a *shetar ḥov* may result from any type of credit or obligation transaction and need not be the result of a loan of money (see Loans; Obligation, Law of). A unique and important feature of the *shetar ḥov* (as well as of the *ketubbah*) is the fact that the *shetar ḥov* itself creates a lien on the debtor's real property, *aḥarayut nekhasim* or *shi'bud nekhasim,* which is an effective claim against that property even when it is sold to a third party. In other words, the *shetar ḥov* creates a mortgage on all the real property owned by the debtor on the date of the execution of the document. This provision was inserted into the *ketubbah* by Simeon b. Shetaḥ (Tosef., Ket. 12:1) in the first quarter of the second century b.c.e. The Talmud records a difference of opinion as to whether we do or do not imply the existence of such a lien when the phrase stating it is omitted. The final decision is that we attribute its omission to a scribal error, and assume the intention to create the lien. As a result of the creation of this lien, predated bonds are invalid because they prejudice the rights of other creditors, while postdated bonds are valid. During the geonic period the lien was extended by appropriate clauses in the document to movable property and even to property to be acquired later than the time of the contract. The rabbinic courts, however, would not enforce the claim of a creditor against the movables sold by a defaulting debtor.

The Torah prohibits the taking of interest for a loan (Ex. 22:24; Lev. 25:36–38; Deut. 23:20–21), and indeed a document which states that interest is to be paid is invalid (see Usury). The Elephantine documents do, however, contain penalty clauses which become operative if the debt is not repaid when due. Such a clause is prohibited by the majority of rabbinic opinion, but was widely used with approval in medieval England (during the 12th and 13th centuries), when a certain

1. page 420.

formal clause was included which stated that on default of repayment, the loan was reloaned to the debtor via a gentile intermediary. This legal fiction permitted the acceptance of the interest. A *shetar ḥov* which does not state when the debt is due is repayable not earlier than 30 days from the date of the loan.

During the Second Temple period assignment of debts by the obligee was permitted. In fact the innovation of prosbul was predicated on this assumption. In amoraic times, restrictions were placed on this right of assignment by permitting the assigner to forgive the debt after assignment (Kid. 48a). The Talmud also refers to bonds made out to the order of the holder. This type of document would be considered by modern standards as bearer paper. The question as to whether or not an assignee could claim under such a document is left unresolved in the Talmud. In post-talmudic times, however, it was the custom to insert a phrase in the bond allowing the named creditor or his agent to claim on the bond. Subsequently, there developed a document which named no creditor, but merely evidenced indebtedness to holder *mukaz* מוכ״ז *moẓi ketav zeh*). In order to assign a debt from a named creditor to another, it was necessary to write a deed of transfer which together with the original bond had to be physically conveyed to the assignee. This procedure is called *ketivah u-mesirah* (see Acquisition). There is some question whether this would be effective as against the debtor. Another method employed was to write a letter of attorney, *harsha'ah,* which provided for the transfer of four ells of land together with the indebtedness. From the tenth century on these four ells were the ones theoretically owned by every Jew in Israel (see Agency).

(b) *Shetar Iska,* a type of limited partnership agreement wherein the active partner borrows from a passive partner. Half the money is considered loan and half is investment in the business. This enables the active partner to pay a return to the passive partner, usually one third, without its being considered as usury. This type of agreement, which is referred to in the Talmud (BM 104b), was also called *shetar kis* and became very popular in the Middle Ages when the Jews were very active in the moneylending business and would borrow additional capital from fellow Jews. Originally, the passive partner bore part of the risk of loss. Later amendments to the standard text of such a document included undertakings by the active partner which amounted to a guarantee to the passive partner against any loss (see Gulak, Oẓar, nos. 234 and 235). The *shetar iska* resembles the medieval Latin document known as *commenda* (see Partnership; Usury).

(c) *Suftaja* or *Diokne,* bills of exchange. This type of document was in use during the geonic period in the countries involved in the Mediterranean trade centering around Egypt. As a rule these documents were drawn on well-known bands in another city or country, which charged a fee for their issue. In this way they facilitated international trade and functioned very much like the modern bill of exchange or check. These documents did not conform to Jewish law, but were, nevertheless, enforceable in rabbinic courts, where mercantile law was applied to protect the businessmen who relied on these documents (A. Harkavy (ed.), *Zikhron Kammah Ge'onim* (1887), no. 423; see *Minhag*).

(d) *Mimram,* also *mimrane,* a note of indebtedness which was widely used among Jews in Eastern Europe between the 16th and 19th centuries. The form of the document consisted of the signature of the debtor on one side of the note, and on the reverse side exactly opposite the signature, a statement as to the amount owed, the terms of payment (date due), and sometimes the place of payment (*Sifrei Kohen,* ḤM 48 end of n. 2). The origin of the term is not clear. It is probably derived from the Latin, *membrana* ("parchment"). Some suggest that it is a derivative from the document of remembrance referred to in the responsa of Asher b. Jehiel (Rosh, resp. no. 68:5) and corresponds to the Latin, *in memoriam.* The significant innovation of this document is the omission of the name of the creditor, which results in its being completely negotiable without any further requirements. The Jewish community councils of Poland passed special regulations protecting the holder of such notes, and implying, as a matter of law, waiver of defenses which the defendant may interpose. In fact, the *shetar mimram* does not conform to halakhic principle; nevertheless, it was granted rabbinic sanction as a result of its wide use (Baḥ Yeshanot, resp. no. 35). During the trade fairs in Poland there also developed the practice of having these notes signed in blank. Afterward the sum and terms of payment would be completed. This obviously involved the element of trust on the part of the purchaser (debtor) and a close relationship between the merchants. The use of *mimranot* was so widespread in 17th- and 18th-century Poland that a very substantial trade existed in the discounting and sale of such documents.

(3) *Court Documents.* Each stage of the rabbinic judicial process was recorded, and appropriate legal documents were issued by the court. These included summons *(hazmanah le-din),* decision *(pesak din),* appraisal of the debtor's property *(shuma),* writ of execution against the property *(shetar adrakhta),* and writ of execution against transferred realty *(shetar tirfa).*

See Execution; Practice and Procedure.

(4) *Communal Documents.* From the time of the destruction of the Second Temple to modern times the Jewish community was self-governed as to its internal affairs. Thus it had its own system of taxation and means of enforcing compliance in accordance with the decisions of the rabbinic court and community councils. The decree of *ḥerem* ("excommunication") was its most powerful weapon. Other examples of community documents are ordination *(semi khah),* letters of appointment of rabbis, community loan bonds, right of settlement, and *ḥazakah.*

(5) *Miscellaneous Documents.* There are many other documents extant which cannot be classified under any of the above categories. Some of these are of historical interest. Among them are deeds of manumission of slaves and bills of sale for slaves. One interesting document recorded by Gulak (*Oẓar* no. 399) is an order for anyone who had a claim against the overlord of Vienna in 1387 to come forward with his claim within 30 days or be forever barred.

Bibliography: L. Auerbach, *Das juedische Obligationenrecht* (1870), 199–505; Ph. Bloch, in: *Festschrift . . . A. Berliner* (1903), 50–64; L. Fischer, in: JJLG, 9 (1911), 45–197; V. Aptowitzer, in: JQR, 4 (1913/14), 23–51; I. S. Zuri, *Mishpat ha-Talmud,* 5 (1921), 43–59; Gulak, Yesodei, passim; Gulak, Oẓar (incl. bibl.); idem, in: *Etudes de papyrologie,* 1 (1932), 97–104 (Ger.); idem, *Das Urkundenwesen im Talmud . . .* (1935); Hai Gaon, *Sefer ha-Shetarot,* ed. by S. Assaf, in: *Musaf ha-Tarbiz,* 1 (1930), 5–77; I. Abrahams (ed.), *Starrs and Jewish Charters . . .* 3 vols. (1930–32); Z. Karl, in: *Ha-Mishpat ha-Ivri,* 5 (1936/37), 105–87; Herzog, Instit, 2 (1939), 314 (index), *s.v.;* H. Albeck, in: *Kovez Madda'i le-Zekher Moshe Schorr* (1944), 12–24; ET, 1 (1951^3), 218–20; 5 (1953), 717–42; J. J. Rabinowitz, *Jewish Law* (1956), passim; C. Roth, in: *Oxoniensia,* 22 (1957), 63–77; N. Golb, in: *Jewish Social Studies,* 20 (1958), 17–46; R. Yaron, *Introduction to the Law of the Aramaic Papyri* (1961); E. Koffmahn, *Die Doppelurkunden aus der Wueste Juda* (1968); Elon, Mafte'aḥ, 341–75; idem, *Ha-Mishpat Ha-Ivri* (1973), II, 386ff, 487ff, 501ff, 598ff, 739ff, 773ff, III, 1280ff; A. M. Fuss, *Dine Israel* 4 (1973); H. Soloveitchik, *Tarbiz* XLI (1972), p. 313; E. Strauss-Astor, *His-*

tory of the Jews in Egypt and Syria, vol. 3 (1970); S. Assaf in *Rav Saadya Gaon,* Ed. by R.J.L. Fishman (1943), p. 65ff; Y. Baer, *Die Juden Im Christlichen Spanien,* vol. 1 (1929), p. 1044; S. M. Davis, *Hebrew Deeds of English Jews Before 1920* (1888).

Abraham M. Fuss

III. LAWS OF PROPERTY

Contents

PROPERTY. Classification. Property may be divided into different classes in accordance with the various legal principles applicable thereto. One common division is between immovable property and movables, distinguished from each other in the following respects among others: in their different modes of acquisition, since there cannot be a "lifting" *(hagbahah)* or "pulling" *(meshikhah)* etc., of land; the law of overreaching (see *Ona'ah*) applies to the sale of movables but not land, apparently because land is always distinctive by virtue of its quality and situation and frequently it is of varying value for different people (see *Sefer ha-Ḥinnukh,* no. 340); in the case of land a rival claim to ownership may be resisted upon proof of three-year possession (see *Ḥazakah*), whereas movables which are in a person's possession for any period of time are presumed to belong to him; litigants are only required to swear an oath if the dispute concerns movables and not land; unlike movables, land can never be stolen (see Theft and Robbery) since it cannot be removed or carried away – and it is for this reason that originally only the debtor's land and not his movables became subjected to the creditor's lien (although later, as a result of changed economic circumstances, the lien was extended by the Babylonian *geonim* to both categories, probably because the majority of Jews had ceased to be landowners at that time). The laws relating to slaves resemble those applicable to land in some respects – for instance as regards overreaching – and in other respects resemble the laws applicable to movables – for instance as regards incidental acquisition (*kinyan aggav,* Tos. to BK 12a).

For the purposes of debt recovery, land is divided into best, median, and poorest quality (*iddit, beinonit,* and *zibburit,* respectively). A claim arising from tort is recovered from land of the best quality, the creditor's claim from the median, and the wife's *ketubbah* from the poorest (Git. 5:1; see also Execution). In biblical times land was further classified according to location, thus, "a dwelling house in a walled city," "land of one's holding," "land that is purchased" (Lev. 25:25ff; 27:16ff).

Movables may be classified by a number of criteria: (1) *perot* ("fruits" or produce") and *kelim* ("vessels" or "utensils"), the one for consumption and the other for use respectively; the latter serve for the purpose of acquiring by barter by way of *kinyan sudar,* the former not (see Acquisition[1]); (2) animals and other movables, the former requiring three-year possession for establishment of title whereas *ḥazakah* of the latter is immediately acquired (Sh. Ar., HM 133–5); (3) coins which are legal tender constitute a special category of movables which cannot be acquired or alienated by barter and can only be given as a loan for consumption but not for use and return (i.e., the borrower need not return the very coins of the loan); (4) deeds are another separate category of movables since these are not in themselves property but only serve as evidence of their contents, and they differ from other movables in their modes of acquisiton (see *Shetar;* Assignment).

A criterion unrelated to physical differences is one between property that is owned and ownerless property *(hefker),* for which there are different modes of acquisition. Owned property is further subdivisible into public property (see Meg. 26a; BB 23a and *Tosafot*) and private property (including joint ownership; see Partnership); and into consecrated property *(hekdesh)* as distinct from property of the common man *(nikhsei hedyot).* It is forbidden for the common man to derive a benefit from consecrated property as long as it retains its sanctity of which there are different categories (see *Hekdesh*[2]).

Consecrated property is further distinguished from property of the common man as regards the modes of acquisition and the applicable laws of overreaching, tort, etc. Land which is owned may be classifed into free, unencumbered property *(nekhasim benei ḥorin)* and encumbered and mortgaged property *(nekhasim meshu'badim),* the latter being land sold by the debtor to others but remaining charged in favor of his creditors for the repayment of debts which cannot be recovered out of his free property (see Lien[3]).

Another separate category is property from which no enjoyment may be derived, such as *ḥameẓ* ("leaven") on Passover, the ox that is condemned to death by stoning, fruit of the *orlah* (i.e., the first three years), etc. Such property is not considered to be in the possession of its owner, nor apparently does the latter have a full proprietary right thereto since it not only cannot be enjoyed but may not even be purchased or sold (see Lien).

Property is further divisible into capital, fruits or profits, and improvements (*keren, perot,* and *shevaḥ,* respectively). The capital is the property as it is at any given time; the fruits are the profits derived therefrom; and the improvement is the increase in market value of the property – whether deriving from actual improvement, natural or effected, or from increase in market price without such.

Proprietary Rights. Ownership. This is the most common proprietary right and is closely connected with possession. A person is the owner of property if he has possession thereof for an unlimited period, or if it is out of his possession for a limited period only and thereafter is due to be restored to him for an unlimited period – for instance when it had been let, lent, or even when it has been lost or stolen or robbed from the owner in circumstances where it may be surmised that he will regain possession of the property; if not, his ownership of the property will likewise terminate. Since the same property may be in the possession of different people – for instance, one in possession of a dwelling and another of its upper floor – it follows that ownership may be shared by different people with each owning a defined part of the property. The owner does not have unrestricted freedom to deal as he pleases with his property. In biblical times for instance it was not possible to sell a field in perpetuity, but only until the Jubilee Year. Other restrictions have applied at all times, including the following: a person may not use his land in such a manner as to disturb his neighbors in the normal use of their land (see Nuisance); in certain special circumstances a person is obligated to allow others the use of his land (BK 81a).

Rights in the Property of Others. Short of ownership, a person may have proprietary rights in the property of others *(jura in re aliena).* Such rights are not exhausted by the recognized legal categories thereof, but may be freely created by the parties thereto in a form and on conditions suited to their needs, without restriction. Broadly, however, these rights may be classified as falling into one of the following three categories: a right to the use of another's property along with its possession as in the case of hire (see Lease and Hire), loan, and bailment; a right to the enjoyment of another's property without its possession – such as the right to project a bracket into the space of the neighboring courtyard; a right in the form of a charge on another's property, such as a mortgage, and the abutter's rights (see *Maẓranut;* Execution). All the above proprietary rights have in common the fact that they avail against the whole world, including the owner of the property concerned, continue to attach to the property even if it be sold to a third party, and cannot be cancelled without the rightholder's consent. Hence these rights are like a form of limited or partial ownership for a specific purpose – their acquisiton being a "transfer of the body for its fruits," such as transfer of a tree for its fruit, a dovecote for the fledglings, or land for a road or thoroughfare (see Servitudes). Similarly, hire is like a sale for a limited period and loan

1. page 208; 2. page 703; 3. page 287.

like a gift for a limited period (Yad, She'elah 1:5; Sekhirut 7:1). However, this does not really amount to full, nor even limited ownership (*Nimmukei Yosef,* BM 56b, in the name of Ran), but only to a real right in the property, available against the whole world.

The most common of the first of the above-mentioned categories of *jura in re aliena,* i.e., with possession, is hire or lease. The lessor, like the lender or bailor, may not withdraw during the subsistence of the contract and the lessee's rights are protected against all comers, including the lessor. A contract of lease may take various forms and, in the case of land, may be for monetary remuneration or the right to work the land for a proportional part of the produce (Yad, Sekhirut 8:1) – the latter right either for a fixed period or passing on inheritance; the lease may even take the form of a sale of the land for return after a number of years. The "sale for the fruit" is so close to the transfer of ownership that the *amoraim* disputed whether acquisition for the fruits was an acquisition of the land itself (*kinyan ha-guf;* Git. 47b), i.e., whether the sale of a field for its fruits involved transfer of the field's onwership or not. When the law of Jubilee Year was observed, any sale of a field was in fact no more than a sale for its fruits.

The proprietary rights attaching to the above relationships carry also corresponding personal rights or obligations. Thus in the case of movables it is the duty of the hirer to take care of the hired property and he assumes liability for damage arising from his negligence, or from the loss or theft of the property, and – in the case of loan – even from inevitable accident. These obligations are separate from the proprietary right in question and the two may even come into effect at different times (see Tos. to BM 99a). Thus an unpaid bailee who has mere custody or detention, but not possession, of the deposit – since it may be removed by the owner at any time – apparently has not proprietary right in the deposit but only the obligation to take proper care thereof and to compensate for his neglect to do so. Other similar obligations may be circumscribed by agreement in the same way as are the terms of the real rights, since both may be created by the parties in a manner they think fit.

The second of the above-mentioned categories of proprietary rights are those which allow a person the enjoyment of another's property without its possession. These include a man's right to cause a nuisance to his neighbor or to project an abuttment into the airspace of his neighbor's court (see Servitudes). Similarly, a man buying a tree has the right of having it stand in the land of the seller (BB 81b), or the owner of a vine or shrub to have it cling to the tree of his neighbor (BM 116b). These too are proprietary rights which are transferable to others and available against purchasers of or heirs to the servient property, the owner whereof may not withdraw from or cancel the said rights.

Acquisition and Transfer of Proprietary Rights. The usual transfer of proprietary rights is by the parties' will. There are two categories of voluntary acquisition of ownership, the first involving the acquisition of ownerless property, and the second acquisition of property from its former owner. For acquisition of the former, i.e., original acquisition, it is necessarily required that the person becoming entitled thereto have possession of the property together with the intention of acquiring its ownership. Hence in this case the formality of acquisition is satisfied by way of a "lifting" or "pulling" of the property, or by its presence within his "premises which are guarded for him" or his "four cubits" *(arba ammot),* or, in the case of land, by acts revealing his control thereover (i.e., *ḥazakah*).

For the acquisition of property from its former owner, it is not necessary that the acquirer have possession of the property, which may be at any place whatever. In this case acquisition takes place by consent of the parties and their making up their minds to the transaction so as to exclude withdrawal therefrom. Here too it is not sufficient that the parties make up their minds, but this fact must also be revealed in a manner that is recognized by all. In general it is customary for the parties to make up their minds and complete the formal acquisition by the same modes as those applicable to the acquisition of ownerless property; additional modes of acquisition in this case are those which naturally reveal that the parties have made up their minds – including by way of money, deed, delivery *(mesirah),* barter, or by way of an act or formality which for historical reasons had become recognized as an act of acquisition, such as *kinyan sudar* (acquisition by means of the "kerchief") and *kinyan aggav* (incidental acquisition). These acts are not symbolic of anything else, but are acts bringing about the making up of the parties' minds and its revelation. Hence if in a particular locality some other act is customary in the closing of a transaction, it will be of equal legal validity (as, e.g., in the case of *kinyan sitomta,* i.e., affixing of a mark). For details, see Acquisition.[1]

Extinction of Ownership. A person's ownership of property is extinguished when he is reconciled (makes up his mind) to the fact that he no longer has permanent possession of the property or that it will no more return to his permanent possession. Here too his state of mind must be revealed and recognizable to all, save that no formal act is required and it may be indicated by speech or conduct alone. Thus ownership terminates upon: (1) *ye'ush* ("despair"), i.e., when the owner abandons hope of recovering possession of property of which he has been deprived, for example through loss or theft; (2) abandonment or renunciation whereby the owner reveals his intention to terminate his ownership, whether or not the property be in his possession (see *Hefker*); (3) transfer or alienation of property to another, whereby the owner reveals his intention to terminate ownership thereof but only through its acquisition by a specific person and only from the moment of such acquisition. Transfer of ownership other than by the will of the parties concerned, takes place on a person's death (see Succession), or upon forfeiture by order of the court, or by the operation of law (see Confiscation, Expropriation, Forfeiture). Ownership is also extinguished upon the destruction of property or its transmutation *(shinnui, specificatio).*

In the State of Israel. Property law in the State of Israel is governed mainly by Knesset laws, such as the Water Law, 5719–1959; the Pledges Law, 5727–1967; the Bailee's Law, 5727–1967; the Sale Law, 5728–1968; the Gift Law, 5728–1968, the Land Law, 5729–1969; etc. Some of the provisions of the above laws are in accordance with Jewish law on the particular subject.

Bibliography: T. S. Zuri, *Mishpat ha-Talmud,* 4 (1921); Gulak, Yesodei, 2 (1922), 172–6; idem, *Le-Ḥeker Toledot ha-Mishpat ha-Ivri bi-Tekufat ha-Talmud,* (*Dinei Karka'ot,* 1929); G. Webber, in: *Journal of Comparative Legislation,* 10 (1928), 82–93; Herzog, Instit, 1 (1936); Elon, in ILR, 4 (1969), 84f., 90–98, 104f; S. Albeck. -Sinai 68 (1971) 8–31.

Shalom Albeck

OWNERSHIP (Heb. בעלות , *ba'alut*). As a proprietary right, ownership is the most important of all rights in property, all other rights being inferior to it. The distinction between ownership and other proprietary rights is apparent not only in matters of civil law but is especially significant in other halakhic matters. Thus, the *etrog* ("citron") and other three species prescribed for the festival of Sukkot must be one's own property and not borrowed or stolen (Sh. Ar., OH 649: 1–2). This principle of

1. page 209.

ownership applies also to the first fruits of one's own field which have to be brought to the Temple and over which the scriptural recital (Deut. 26:1–11) is to be made (Bik. 1:1–2; Git. 47b).

The Talmud indicates that a person is the owner of property if it is in his possession for an unlimited period, or if possession thereof is due to revert to him for an unlimited period after he has temporarily parted with the property in question. At first glance, the distinctive feature of ownership appears to be the fact that a person is free to deal as he pleases with the property he owns, a power not available to the holder of any other proprietary right. It will be seen, however, that this feature is not in itself sufficient to define ownership, since it does not always apply. For instance, an owner must not use his land in a manner that interferes with a neighbor's use of his land (see Nuisance) nor may he use his property in such manner as to commit an offense. Furthermore, a person who has agreed to encumber or submit to any restraint whatsoever on the use of his land nevertheless remains the owner. A person who lets his property, for instance, even for a long-term period continues to be the owner. It is therefore apparent that the rights of ownership may adhere even to those who are not free to deal as they please with their property. Nor does the suggestion that ownership is characterized by a person's right to sell or alienate his property prove to be sufficiently distinctive. Thus the usufructuary may also transfer his right to another (Maim. Yad, Mekhirah, 23:8) and the borrower or lessee may also do so – with the owner's permission – yet these parties do not become owners of the property to which their rights extend. On the other hand, at the time when the laws of the Jubilee Year were operative, the owner could not sell his land forever, yet he was its owner. Moreover, sometimes a right in property other than ownership exceeds the owner's rights therein, such as the case of a tenant who holds a 100-year lease.

Possession (reshut). The distinctive quality of ownership is closely connected with the concept of *reshut* ("possession"); so much so that the commentators do not always descriminate betweeen the two and sometimes use the term *reshut* to denote ownership. *Reshut* (see also Acquisition) is a person's control over property, established by the existence of three requirements: (1) his ability and (2) intention to use the property (3) at any time he may wish to do so – even if only for a period of limited duration. All three requirements must be satisfied and operate simultaneously for the possession to be effective; hence coins which are in a place that cannot be reached are not in a person's *reshut,* even if they are his own (Tosef. Ma'as. Sh. 1:6). If such place is accessible to him, however, because "the way is open" and caravans pass there, the coins are said to be in his *reshut,* but not otherwise (TJ, Ma'as. Sh. 1:2, 52d). Similarly, chattels which have been stolen are in the *reshut* of the thief, since the latter is able to use the property at his pleasure and the owner is unable to prevent him from doing so or to use the property himself. Land cannot be stolen and is therefore always in possession of its owner, and since it cannot be carried away or hidden the owner can always have it restored to his use through the mediation of the court. He therefore remains free to use the land whenever he pleases, unlike a purported robber. Similarly, an object which is deposited remains in the *reshut* of its owner, not that of the bailee, from whom the owner can demand its return at any time. If, however, the bailee should refuse to return the property and denies the existence of a bailment, he will be deemed a robber and the property will thus be in his *reshut* (BM 7a and Alfasi ad loc.). Property on hire or loan for a fixed period, which the owner may not revoke, is in the *reshut* of the hirer or borrower for the duration of the stated period. In the same way, when a person sells the usufruct of his field, the field will be in the *reshut* of the usufructuary (BB 8:7), since the latter, not the owner, may use the field at his pleasure (Maim. Yad, Mekhirah, 23:7).

For the same reason, an object which is found on premises which are kept or reserved for the owner is in the latter's possession. This is so even if the premises are kept for him because people keep away from there of their own accord and not because of his own ability and power to guard his field (BM 102a); if however he is unable to use a thing which is on his premises, for instance when it is hidden and nobody expects to find it there, it will not be in his *reshut.* Property which is on a person's premises when they are not kept for him will not be in his *reshut,* as it is deemed certain to be lost or taken by others and is therefore not freely at his disposal (see Acquisition[1]).

Ownership and Possession. These are by no means identical concepts. The *amora,* R. Johanan states that stolen property is in the *reshut* of the thief, but the person robbed remains the owner (BM 7a). The same may be said with regard to hired property. *Reshut* nevertheless appears to be an essential element in the determination of ownership, for, as indicated, a person is held to be the owner if the property is permanently in his possession for an unlimited period – even if it passes out of his *reshut* for a limited period but is due to revert to him permanently (cf. Ran, Ned. 29a). Thus the law that a swarm of bees and doves of a dovecote may be owned has rabbinic authority only – for the sake of keeping the peace (BK 114b; Ḥul. 141b) – as in strict law these cannot be owned because they cannot be permanently kept in a person's *reshut.* Similarly, geese and fowl which have escaped are ownerless because they cannot be restored to the owner's *reshut* (Tos. to Ḥul. 139a). This is also the case in respect of lost property which the owner has despaired of finding and having restored to his *reshut* (see *Ye'ush*).

Permanent *reshut* is not the only requirement of ownership, however. Ownership may cease when a person makes up his mind that the property is to pass permanently out of his *reshut,* or that it shall not return permanently into his *reshut,* as by way of *ye'ush,* or when he renounces the property (see *Hefker*), or when he conveys it to another. Consequently a deafmute, idiot, or minor, none of whom has legal understanding, cannot lose ownership in any of these ways (BM 22b; Git. 59a). Hence it may be said that the right of ownership is characterized by two basic attributes: a positive one, that the property is in the *reshut* of the claimant for a period of unlimited duration; and a negative one, that such person shall not have resolved to remove the property permanently from his *reshut.*

Ownership of Limited Duration. Despite the general principles outlined above, it is possible for ownership to be limited in point of time. The outstanding example of this is a returnable gift, which, in the opinion of Rava, is a proper gift making the donee the owner as long as the gift is with him (Suk. 41b). The comment of the *rishonim* (Asheri *ibid.* 30; Ritba, Nov. r, Git. 83a, Kid. 6b) is that such a gift is a complete and full conveyance, and the return of the gift requires a fresh conveyance. Since it is a condition of the gift that it must be returned to the original donor, such a gift in fact only confers title for a limited period (cf. *Kezot ha-Ḥoshen,* HM 241 n. 4). Another example of ownership of limited duration is that cited by R. Isaac of the creditor acquiring a pledge for a debt (BM 82a). In this case it may also be said that this is a complete and full acquisition and the return of the pledge to the debtor requires an assignment thereof by the creditor. The Talmud discusses the question of such an assignment being involved even in the case of hire (Av. Zar. 15a).

The most important example of ownership for a limited period is to be found in the sale of land at the time that the

1. page 206.

Jubilee Year was customary, for in the Jubilee Year land reverted to the vendor. This is also the case when land is sold for any period of limited duration. In this case the acquisition is called *kinyan perot* (i.e., usufruct) in the Babylonian Talmud (Git. 47b) and *kinyan nekhasim* in the Jerusalem Talmud (Git. 4:9, 46b). It is stated in the latter that the purchaser may not dig any wells while the field is in his possession (*Mishneh la-Melekh,* to Maim. Shemittah, 11:1). According to the Babylonian Talmud *(ibid), kinyan perot* – before the occurence of the first jubilee – was like an acquisition of the land itself, since people had not yet been accustomed to the restoration of the land and looked upon a sale as leading to a permanent and irrevocable acquisition. However, in the opinion of Simeon b. Lakish, from the second jubilee onward *kinyan perot* was not like the acquisition of the land itself and the seller remained the owner because at the end of the stipulated period the land would revert permanently to his possession. R. Johanan is of the opinion that *kinyan perot* is like a *kinyan* of the land itself and that the Pentateuch provided for the termination of such ownership in the Jubilee Year and the restoration thereof to the owner of the land. The dispute also extends to land which is sold for a fixed period. The *halakhah* was decided in accordance with the view of Simeon b. Lakish.

Because of the element of possession in the concept of ownership, it is possible for a person to own only part of a thing, provided that it is possible for such part to be in his separate possession. Thus, it can sometimes happen that one person may own land and another the trees on it (BB 37a–b), or one person may own a house and another the top story (BM 117b).

In the State of Israel, the Cooperative Houses Law, 5713–1952, in keeping with Jewish law and contrary to the law in force until then, makes provision for the separate ownership of each apartment in a cooperative house.

See also Acquisition.

Bibliography: Gulak, Yesodei, 1 (1922), 131–4; Herzog, Instit; 1 (1936), 69–75; S. Albeck, in: *Sefer Bar-Ilan,* 7–8 (1970), 85–94; idem., Sinai (1971) 15–18.

Shalom Albeck

SERVITUDES (Heb. שעבודים, *shi'budim*). Generally a person is prohibited from using his land in such manner as to cause an interference with his neighbor's quiet use or enjoyment of his own land. A man may therefore restrain his neighbor from such use and compel him to remove the cause of the disturbance. However, this right is not always available and the use of land in certain ways – even if disturbing to the neighbor – must sometimes be suffered by him (see Nuisance). A person may agree with his neighbor to refrain from a particular use of his land, injurious to the latter, even if permitted by law; or to use his land in a manner injurious to his neighbor, even if such use is not permitted by law. In such event a proprietary right over the land is respectively granted to and extracted from the adjoining landowners. This right, called a *shi'bud* in the codes, is comparable to an "easement" in English law and serves to encumber land in favor of an adjacent owner, without the land being in the latter's possession.

Halakhic sources mention two categories of servitudes of this nature: (1) use of land, which, without involving the use or employment of neighboring land, causes injury to the neighbor, such as the emanation of noise, smoke, noxious odors, moisture, and so on, to the adjacent land, or when the latter is made to vibrate, or when the crops thereon are damaged; (2) an act which involves an encroachment on and the use or enjoyment of neighboring land, such as erecting projecting brackets on which chattels can be hung, affixing beams onto a neighboring wall, diverting the flow of rainwater onto a neighboring courtyard, or placing a ladder on neighboring premises in order to reach one's own roof (*Sma,* HM 153:16 and *Netivot ha-Mishpat, Mishpat ha-Kohanim, ibid.*). These servitudes are distinct in two ways; firstly the encumbered land is not in the possession of the rightholder, and secondly, they may be exploited only by the use of the adjoining land. Hence it may be said that the servitude is one of land to neighboring land. The right may be acquired for a specific period or for good.

The term *shi'budim* also has a wider meaning including all rights in the property of another *(jura in re aliena).* These include rights which are not specifically tied to the use of or encroachment on neighboring land and which may extend to both movable and immovable property, whether or not the rightholder is in possession of the encumbered property. Such *shi'budim* are rights to use and enjoyment of the property itself and are a kind of limited form of ownership in the encumbered property, being a kind of *kinyan perot* and not a servitude only (usufruct; see Ownership). These property rights are governed by laws which are entirely different from those applicable to the above-mentioned servitudes (easements). Instances thereof are: the acquisition of "a tree for its fruit, a dwelling for its occupation, sheep for its wool, a dovecote for the doves that will hatch therein, a hive for the honey that will accumulate there, an animal for its young, a slave for his handwork" (Maim. Yad, Mekhirah, 22:14; 23:2). These rights are a form of *kinyan perot* (usufruct), i.e., acquisition of the right to enjoy the use of the property itself (Maim., *ibid.,* 23:1). After *kinyan perot,* the most important servitude of this class is the right of way over the servient land (BB 99b), whether a private path or public road. It is considered a propriety right in the land and not an encumbrance (see Resp. Rashba, cited in *Beit Yosef;* HM 153, no 12, cf. his Nov. BB 23a, 28b). The Talmud discusses the applicable laws in detail – including such matters as the measure of the width of private and public roads, the respective rights of the parties, the modes of acquisition, and the circumstances in which the landowner may change the route of a public road passing over his field.

Easements are acquired in the same way as other legal rights, i.e., by an act of *kinyan* (see Acquisition). In the opinion of the *geonim* and the scholars of Spain (Nov. Ramban, BB 59a; HM 155:35), they may also be acquired in a tacit manner, by the adverse use of the servient land without protest from its owner, who is aware of such use; but other proprietary rights mentioned above can be acquired in express manner only, like the acquisition of ownership (Nov. Rashba, BB 23a, 28b). The scholars of France differ, holding that all servitudes must be expressly acquired (*Maggid Mishneh,* to Yad, Shekhenim, 11:4; Tur, HM 154). Consequently, a servitude exercised for three years, accompanied by the holder's plea that it was acquired from the neighbor, is evidence of title, as in the case of a plea of ownership to land. Other scholars are of the opinion that a servitude may be acquired by exercise of the right for a period of three years, without the need for any such plea (Tos. to BB 23a; *s.v.* והא; see also *Hazakah*). All the scholars agree that easements of a particularly onerous nature are not customarily agreed to in a tacit manner and therefore have to be expressly acquired by purchase or gift with an accompanying *kinyan.* Instances thereof are the encroachment of smoke, noxious odors, etc. onto neighboring land, even if existing for a number of years (Sh. Ar., HM 155:36). Some scholars are of the opinion that such servitudes, even when expressly consented to and assigned by way of sale or gift, cannot be validly acquired, and the assigner may withdraw his consent on a plea of mistaken *kinyan,* i.e., the mistaken belief that he would be able to bear the relevant harm (Tos. to BB 23a). Many of the *posekim* are of the opinion that insufferable harm in this context includes any interference with the neighbor's person, but not mere interference with his use of his property (Nov. Ramban, *ibid.* 59a). Easements are terminated in the same manner in which they are created. Thus the obligation may be extinguished if the servient owner repurchases the servitude, or if the dominant owner has ceased to exploit the servitude in a manner indicating his abandonment and waiver of its use, when it cannot be revived by renewed use (Resp. Rashba, vol. 1, no. 1133).

In the State of Israel, servitudes are governed by an original Israel law, the Land Law, 1969, which recognizes all kinds of *jura in re aliena.* Most of them can be acquired, in addition to the usual modes of acquisition, also by prescriptive use followed by registration in the Land Registry.

Bibliography: M. Bloch, *Das mosaisch-talmudische Besitzrecht* (1897), 49–59; Gulak, Yesodei, 1 (1922), 134, 141f., 146–8; Herzog, Instit, 1 (1936), 365–70; ET, (1956), 664–7; 10 (1961), 628–96 Z. Warhaftig, *Ha-Ḥazakah ba-Mishpat ha-Ivri* (1964), 241–60; Albeck, *Sinai,* 68 (1971), 18–24.

Shalom Albeck

ACQUISITION (Heb. קִנְיָן *Kinyan*), the act whereby a person voluntarily obtains legal rights.

In Jewish law almost all kinds of rights, whether proprietary *(jus in rem)* or contractual (*jus in personam;* see Obligations, Law of), can be voluntarily acquired only by way of *kinyan.* Acquisition of rights by way of *kinyan* can be divided into three groups: (1) Acquiring ownership over ownerless property *(hefker)* such as animals, fish in river or ocean, and lost property which the owner has abandoned hope of finding; (2) rights over property which has an owner, acquisition being by way of sale or gift. Acquisition of ownerless property (original acquisition) is called in the Talmud, *ein da'at aḥeret maknah* (literally "when no other mind conveys title") and acquisition from a previous owner (derivative acquisition) is called *da'at aḥeret maknah* ("another mind conveys title"). In this latter group are also included lesser rights than ownership *(jura in re aliena)* such as a lease or an easement; (3) contractual or personal rights such as debts, or the hiring of workmen, the acquisition of which also depends upon "another mind conveying the right."

In the case of original acquisition the formalities of acquiring title are to demonstrate that the property is in unrestricted possession of the person acquiring it, meaning that he has the ability and intent to use it whenever he wishes to do so, which includes the power to prevent others from interfering with that use. The *halakhah* enumerates, according to objective tests, the acts by which people would usually recognize that the property is in the possession of the acquirer. Consequently, the list of recognized forms of original acquisition is a closed one.

With regard to derivative acquisition, however, the function of *kinyan* is not to demonstrate that it has passed into the possession of the person acquiring it, but that the alienator and the acquirer had determined to conclude the transaction. In fact, the party acquiring title performs the *kinyan,* and the alienator expresses his approval orally. The sole reason for a formal *kinyan* is that a mere oral agreement may not be taken seriously and might enable the parties to withdraw from the proposed transaction. For this reason derivative acquisition can be effected in a greater variety of ways than original acquisition; when the parties derive mutual benefit from the transaction showing that they have wholeheartedly reached an agreement to conclude it, no formal *kinyan* is even required (R. Johanan, BM 94a). For the same reason an acquisition is valid if done in a mode customary among local merchants even though different from the talmudic *kinyanim* (Sh. Ar., HM 201:2). Since in the case of derivative acquisition the *kinyan* serves not to show possession but to indicate that the parties made up their minds to conclude the transaction, it can also be used for creation of contractual rights, such as a duty to sell something which is not yet in existence *(davar she-lo ba la-olam)* – even though one cannot effect transfer of a non-existent object (see Assignment; Sh. Ar., HM 60:6). The acquisition of rights requires "intention" on the part of the acquirer. The statement in the Talmud (BM 11a) that "a person's premises acquire for him without his knowledge" (see below) must therefore be taken to refer to the acquisition of such an object as the owner of the premises would have desired to acquire had he known of its presence there, and it must, by the same token, be property which is usually found there (Tos. to BB 54a).

There are general modes of *kinyan* which apply to both original and derivative acquisition, and others which apply only to derivative acquisition by way of sale and gift. Under the first class come:

(1) Kinyan Ḥazer (acquisition through one's courtyard"). A person's premises "acquire" for him such movable property as comes into it. Since, as stated, the property must be within his possession and control, such premises, in order to "acquire" on his behalf, must be fenced in, or "he stands at the side thereof" guarding what is in it (BM 11a), or that others keep away from the premises for any other reason (*ibid.* 102a). Consequently a shopkeeper does not acquire property lost in his shop, if it is in a place to which customers have access (Maim. Yad, Gezelah, 16:4). Nor does a person acquire anything in premises to which the public has access (Novellae Rashba to BM 25b). Similarly, a man's premises do not acquire fledglings because they can fly away (BM 11a) or chattels which may be blown away (Git. 79a). Similarly, treasure hidden in the ground, even of guarded premises, belongs to the finder (BM 25b) and not to the owner of the ground because the owner is not likely to find it because it is hidden, and therefore he has no control of it. The *ḥazer* need not necessarily be immovable property; the same rule applied to utensils if their owner had the right to leave them in a certain place where they would not be removed (BB 85a). It follows that a person's animal cannot acquire for him since it is a "moving courtyard" (Git. 21a) and may wander beyond its owner's care. On the other hand, a boat would "acquire" for its owner fish which leap into it (BM 9b) since it is property guarded by its owner. With regard to derivative acquisition, since thre is no need to demonstrate that the property is in the possession of its acquirer, even an unguarded *ḥazer* can acquire according to one opinion (BM 11b).

(2) Arba Ammot ("four cubits"). The area round a person within a radius of four cubits is regarded as having the same properties as a *ḥazer,* providing that he is in a place where he has control over the article (BM 10b). There seems to be a difference between the Babylonian and the Jerusalem Talmuds with regard to *kinyan* by *arba ammot.* According to the former it acquires even without an express formula on the individual's part, unless he has clearly stated or indicated that he does not wish to acquire and the Talmud refers to it as applying only to original acquisitions. The Jerusalem Talmud, on the other hand, requires an express declaration on his part that his *arba ammot* shall acquire the article for him (Elijah of Vilna to TJ, Pe'ah 4:2) and makes this rule apply also to derivative acquisition. Opinions differ as to the capacity of minors to acquire by *kinyan ḥazer* or *arba ammot* (BM 11a).

(3) Hagbahah ("lifting"), **Meshikhah** ("pulling"), and

Mesirah ("transfer"). Movable objects are acquired by *hagbahah* in the case of articles which can be lifted without difficulty; where they are too heavy, or can be raised only with difficulty, *meshikhah* takes its place (BB 86a). Both serve to demonstrate that the article thereby comes into the acquirer's possession, and is guarded for him as in his *ḥazer.* The article may be raised merely by the force of his body (Tos. to BK 98a). There is a difference of opinion as to whether it must be lifted one handsbreadth or three (Tos. to Kid., 26a). *Meshikhah,* applying to an animal, can be effected by striking or calling it so that it comes to one (BB 75b) or by leading or riding it (BM 8b). The prevailing opinion is that *meshikhah* applies only in premises owned by both parties or in a side street (BB 76b), but not in a public place. According to one opinion, however, it is effective in a public thoroughfare as well (TJ, Kid. 1:4, 60b; Tos. to BK 79a). The above-mentioned methods of *kinyan* apply both to original and derivative acquisition, but in cases of derivative acquisition the express permission of the alienator to the acquirer to perform *kinyan* is an indispensable element in the *kinyan* (BK 52a; BB 53a). These methods of *kinyan* apply also to personal obligations, such as those of a bailee (Tos. to BK 79a) or an artisan for his work (BM 48a; see Labor Law). *Mesirah* consists of grasping at the object to be acquired (BB 75b) and the term *mesirah* indicates that it is done at the behest of the transferor (Tos. to *ibid.*). Since it does not demonstrate intention to control the subject matter which is a necessary element of possession, it applies only to derivative acquisition. It is employed where *meshikhah* is ineffective, i.e., in a public place or in a *ḥazer* not belonging to either party.

(4) **Ḥazakah.** Whereas all the foregoing modes of acquisition apply to movables only, in the case of immovable property acquisition is by an act of *ḥazakah* (Kid. 26a) which consists of any act usually done by an owner, such as fencing, opening a gateway or locking the premises (BB 42a), or weeding or hoeing (*ibid.,* 54a), or putting down a mattress to sleep there (*ibid.,* 53b). In general, any improvement of the land is regarded as an act usually done by the owner (Maim. Yad, Mekhirah, 1:8). Such an act as preventing floodwaters from inundating a field, however, would not constitute a *ḥazakah* as it could be regarded simply as a voluntary neighborly act (BB 53a). There is a difference of opinion as to whether merely traversing the land is acquiring as it constitutes an act usually done by the owner (BB 100a). With regard to a sale or gift, the land acquired by the *ḥazakah* includes everything stipulated by the parties (Sh. Ar., HM 192:12); with regard to ownerless property, it includes only such part as is patently seen to be in his possession (*ibid.* 275:3–9). As with *meshikhah,* in the case of derivative acquisition the alienator must specifically instruct the acquirer to take possession, or otherwise indicate his consent (BK 52a; BB 53a). There are forms of acquisition by *ḥazakah* which apply either to original or to derivative acquisition, but not to both (Sh. Ar., HM 275:12–13). (For the *ḥazakah* established by three years' possession which is a method of proof and does not come within the category of *kinyan,* see *Ḥazakah*).

The following methods of *kinyan* apply to derivative acquisitions only because they do not demonstrate possession but rather the intention of the parties to conclude the transaction:

(5) **Kinyan Kesef** ("acquisition by money"). The transfer by the purchaser to the seller of the agreed monetary price of the article. R. Johanan is of the view that in strict law this mode of *kinyan* applies both to movables and immovables, and with regard to derivative acquisition the *kinyan* was done by paying money only and not by *hagbahah* and *meshikhah.* But it was enacted that instead of paying money *meshikhah* should be necessary, since if the object remains in the possesion of the transferor he may not guard it against being destroyed by fire or other dangers (BM 47a). Similarly, the need for a deed *(shetar)* was added in the case of immovables (Kid. 26a). The Jerusalem Talmud (Kid. 1:5, 60c) indicates other modes of *kinyan* with regard to immovables, one based on the removal of a shoe as mentioned in Ruth 4:7, and the other being *keẓaẓah,* without any indication of the period when those modes were practiced. But *kesef, shetar,* and *ḥazakah* alone remained. However, even though, since tannaitic times, neither movables nor immovables were acquired solely by *kinyan kesef,* the sale of immovables was not regarded as completed until the money had passed, though it could be paid to a third party according to the seller's instructions (Kid. 7a). Where only part of the purchase money is paid, the balance being postponed by the transferor in the form of a loan, even if only implicitly and without the loan being expressly stated, the part payment concludes the transaction, unless it is clear from the conduct of the transferor that this part payment did not complete the transaction, even if *kinyan* took place (BM 77b). *Kinyan kesef* is already mentioned in the Bible (Gen. 23; Jer. 32:6–15).

(6) **Kinyan Shetar** ("acquisition by deed"). In *kinyan shetar* the deed is not just evidence of the act of acquisition but constitutes the act of acquisition itself (*shetar kinyan,* Sh.Ar., HM 191:1). The vendor writes on paper or other material "my field is given (or sold) to you" and the receipt of that deed by the purchaser establishes his title even in the absence of witnesses (*ibid.,* 1). Movables cannot be acquired by *shetar. Kinyan shetar* is already mentioned in the Bible (Jer.32). See also *Shetar.*

(7) **Halifin** ("barter"), **Kinyan Sudar** ("*kinyan* of the kerchief"). The exchange of property is as effective as the payment of money in establishing acquisition, even if the two objects exchanged are not of equal value. Thus, if the alienator draws to him an article owned by the acquirer the transaction is effected. *Ḥalifin* cannot however be effected by current coinage since this would constitute *kinyan kesef,* which depends upon the monetary value (see BM 45b). Out of this there developed the act of acquisition called *kinyan sudar,* which is therefore also called *kinyan ḥalifin* (Kid. 6b; et al.). The kerchief *(sudar)* is merely pulled by the acquirer and can then be returned to the owner (*ibid.,* Ned. 48b). This mode of acquisition being very easy to perform in all kinds of situations, it became so prevalent that it is referred to simply as *kinyan* (cf. Git. 14a; BM 94a; BB 3a). The origin of *kinyan sudar* may be traced to Ruth 4:7. Throughout the tannaitic period it is never expressly mentioned. It is first mentioned at the beginning of the amoraic period in the dispute as to whether, as in the case of barter proper, the *sudar* must belong to the acquirer, or to the alienator (BM 47a); the former view prevailed. Apparently, because of the simplicity of this mode of acquisition, this *kinyan* is not regarded as completed even after the ceremony, as long as the parties are still talking about the deal (BB 114a).

(8) **Aggav Karka** ("the acquisition of movables incidental to land"). Movables may be acquired as an adjunct to land, the act of *kinyan* being performed only with regard to the land (Kid. 26a). It probably originated in the acquisition of a courtyard with everything contained therein (cf. Tosef., BB 2:13) or similar cases as field, olive press, etc. subsequently being extended to apply to everything belonging to them (cf. BB 78a), even if not actually there at the time of the transaction, and finally to all movables of unlimited amount being sold incidentally to any immovable property, even if they do not have any connection whatever with it (Kid. 26b). Thus the movables did not have to be assembled (*ibid.* 26a–b) except in the case of slaves (BK 12a). The final development was to acquire movables as an adjunct to an unspecified piece of land (Sh.Ar., HM 202:7 gloss) and the

land could be acquired by sale and the movables as a gift, and conversely. As a facile mode of acquiring movables, not necessitating the presence of the parties on the site, it was in operation for long periods. In the geonic period the "four cubits in Ereẓ Israel" which every Jew theoretically owns, was made the basis of a practice whereby an agent could be appointed to recover a deposit or a debt, *aggav karka,* of these four cubits (Maim. Yad, Sheluḥin, 3:7). See also Attorney.

(9) Usage and Custom. Generally speaking, any custom adopted by the local merchants as a mode of acquisition is valid according to Jewish law (Sh. Ar., HM 201:2), since it fulfills the principle that the purpose of the *kinyan* is to bring about the decision of the parties to conclude the transaction. Conversely, when a once accepted mode of acquisition fell into desuetude it could no longer be employed (cf. C. Albeck, *Shishah Sidrei Mishnah, Seder Nashim* (1958), 410–12; addenda to Kid. 1:4–5). The Babylonian Talmud mentions the custom of wine-merchants marking the barrels they had purchased (BM 74a), and in post-talmudic times three such customs prevalent among Christians were adopted since they fulfilled the same function as "affixing a mark" (Sh. Ar., HM 201:2). They are (a) the handshake *(Teki'at kaf)* mentioned in Proverbs 6:1 as a form of giving surety (*Piskei ha-Rosh,* BM 74a in the name of "R.H.," probably the tosafist Ḥayyim Cohen and not R. Hananel, who expressed a contrary view; see *Or Zaru'a,* BM 231). Some authorities even regarded a handshake as the equivalent of an oath (*Mordekhai* to Shevu. 757) but others regarded it as an act of acquisition (for further details see Suretyship); (b) the handing over of a coin by the purchaser to the vendor, which was originally a medieval Christian custom (Arrha, earnest money); and (c) handing over a key – the vendor hands to the purchaser the key of the premises where the merchandise is housed. Handing over a key is mentioned in the Babylonian Talmud (BK 52a; Tos. to *ibid.*), but only as the authorization by the alienator for the acquirer to make the *kinyan ḥazakah* and in the Jerusalem Talmud as a mode of derivative acquisition of the building (*Mareh ha-Panim* to Kid. 1:4). As a mode of acquiring movables it was a Christian custom (*Traditio clavium;* see B. Cohen, *Jewish and Roman Law,* 2 (1966), 538–56). Present day rabbinical courts have applied the principle of regarding local custom as valid; thus the transfer of immovable property through registration in the Land Registry is a valid *kinyan* in Jewish Law (PDR, 1:283). See also *Minhag.*

(10) Acquisition with No Formal Act. Where it is clear that the parties concerned decide to complete a transaction to their mutual benefit and satisfaction a formal *kinyan* is not essential (see Ket. 102b; Git 14a; BM 94a; BB 176b; cf. Maim. Yad, Mekhirah, 5:11). This rule obtains generally with regard to personal obligations but can include rights *in rem* (see BB 106b and *Haggahot ha-Rashash* on Tos. Bek. 18b). This principle was extended in the post-talmudic period (Hai Gaon, in *Ḥemdah Genuzah,* no. 135; responsa Meir of Rothenburg, ed. Prague, 941; responsa Ribash 476; Sh. Ar., HM 176:4). For other modes of acquisition see Admission, Assignment, Confiscation, Expropriation and Forfeiture, *Hefker, Hekdesh,* Succession, Theft and Robbery. See also Contract and Obligations, Law of.

In the state of Israel, sale is governed by the Law of Sale, 1968, based on the uniform international draft (Hague, 1964); gift is governed by the Law of Gift, 1968; and the acquisition of immovables by the Land Law, 1969. Ownership, in the case of sale, passes by way of offer and acceptance and, in case of gift, by delivery of the property. Transfer of title to land becomes valid only on registration in the Land Registry. Contractual obligations are created by agreement between the parties in any manner whatever. Legislation vests ownership of all unowned property in the state, which cannot therefore be originally acquired.

Bibliography: Maim. Yad, Mekhirah, 1–9; Sh. Ar., HM 189–203; Gulak, Yesodei, 1 (1922), 102–27; 2 (1922), 32–57; Gulak, *Le-Ḥeker Toledot ha-Mishpat ha-Ivri,* 1 (1929), 41–86; Herzog, Instit. 1 (1936), 137–200; S. Albeck, *Sinai,* 62 (1967/68), 229–61: idem, Tarbiz 40 (1971) 158–177, idem., Bar Ilan 9 (1972) 249–278; ET. *s.v. Aggav, Arba Ammot, Da'at Aḥeret Maknah, Hagbahah, Hithayyevut* M. Elon, *Ha-Mishpat Ha-Ivri* (1973), I, 130ff, II, 476ff, 533ff, 571ff, 741ff, III, 835ff, 1106ff.

Shalom Albeck

SALE (Heb. מכירה *mekhirah*). Sale may be defined as the permanent transfer for consideration of existing legal rights from one person to another. The consideration may be in money or in kind. By extension the term "sale" is also used to denote a transfer of rights for a lengthy (but predetermined) period, such as the sale of land for a period of many years (BM 79a; BB 136b; cf. Yad, She'elah, 1:5). When sale is mentioned, however, it primarily refers to the transfer of real or proprietary rights and not to mere personal rights, i.e., obligations or debts, since it was at first legally impossible to transfer such rights (see Assignment). The *geonim* already laid down that rights *in rem* applied only to corporeal or tangible things (Hai Gaon, *Sefer ha-Mikkah ve-ha-Mimkar,* ch. 2 cf. Resp. Maharashdam, HM 271), and therefore anything having neither length, breadth, nor depth – such as the smell of an apple or the taste of honey or the glitter of a precious stone – was incapable of being conveyed (Yad, Mekhirah, 22:14; cf. also TJ, BB 3:1, 13d and *Ha-Ittur,* vol 1, introd., ch. 2, *"Kinyan"*). This is probably the reason why it is impossible to convey title in something which is not yet in existence – since, being intangible, it cannot be the subject matter of a real right – as also it is impossible to convey to someone who has not yet been born (see below).

In the biblical period the sale of real property was restricted. Thus, fields could only be sold until the Jubilee, in which year they would automatically revert to their owners (Lev. 25:13ff), whereas dwelling houses in walled cities – if not redeemed within a year of their sale – would rest irrevocably with their purchasers regardless of the Jubilee *(ibid.)*. In Jewish law the term sale does not mean an agreement to sell in the future, but an immediately effective transfer of ownership. Sale, nevertheless, raises many of the problems relating to the creation, interpretation, and execution of contractual obligations. In the Talmud, *mekhirah* is an example used for clarifying these problems, since the laws of sale are an application of the wider principles of property and contract. The transaction of a sale is concluded with the *gemirat ha-da'at* ("firm decision") of the parties to transfer the relevant rights irrevocably from one to the other – at which point neither may resile from the bargain. The parties rely on the sale if there has been a manifestation of their *gemirat ha-da'at* by such a way of speech or conduct as will be understood by most people as an agreement to conclude the transaction – whether or not this is in accordance with the subjective intention of either of the parties. Undisclosed thoughts are of no consequence, and the test of the conclusion of the sale is purely objective; if in the particular circumstances most people would express their intention to conclude the transaction in that particular and manifest manner, the transaction will accordingly be effective, and it is immaterial that either party did not really intend to conclude the transaction in that particular way, or that there was no *consensus ad idem* between one party and the other. A corollary of this test is the principle that the parties need not make up their minds to the identical thing, and there may sometimes be no actual consensus between the parties even if outwardly their conduct is so interpreted. Moreover, when it is manifest that one of the parties had not properly made up his mind to the transaction, he may withdraw from it but not the other party who had done so – as may happen in the case where one party is mistaken as to the quality of the subject sold (Yad, Mekhirah, 17:1), or he has been overcharged in respect of the price (*ibid.*, 12:4).

The Decision of the Parties. The decision of the parties to conclude a sale is finalized by the performance of one of the appropriate acts of *kinyan* ("acquisition") by one of the parties – generally the purchaser – after the other parties have expressed their agreement that this be done (Ned. 44a; BB 54b; see Acquisition). Ownership thereupon passes, regardless of the question of possession, since possession sometimes accompanies the passing of ownership and sometimes not (see, e.g., BM 46a–b). If the consideration for the sale is a monetary payment, the purchaser, upon the passing of ownership, undertakes to pay the purchase price and it becomes a debt for which he is liable (BM 45b, 77b).

Furthermore, if an act is performed that brings about the *gemirat ha-da'at* of one or all of the parties but is not concluded by one of the customary acts of *kinyan*, any of the parties may withdraw; ownership will not have passed and the seller will remain responsible for the object. Nevertheless, since some of the parties rely upon such a sale and believe that all have made up their minds not to resile from it, any party who does retract is subject to the curse of "He who exacted vengeance from the generation of the flood and the generation of the dispersion will find redress from one who does not stand by his word" (BM 4:2). Hence, if the purchaser pays the consideration money to the seller but does not obtain possession of the object sold (i.e., *meshikhah*), the party who retracts will be subject to the said curse, since the payment of money is not a method of concluding a transaction in movables (BM 44a). Similarly, the fact that the seller has marked the object sold so as to distinguish it as his own will suffice to submit a retracting party to the curse – even though it is not local custom to conclude a transaction by making such a mark (BM 74a) – since there is a presumption that in affixing his mark the party concerned made up his mind to the bargain. Wherever the affixing of a mark is the customary manner of concluding a transaction, however, the sale will be effective and the parties will no longer be able to retract (BM 74a; see *Minhag*[1]). The sages disapprove of a party who retracts, even where the transaction is only concluded verbally, without the performance of any act by any party. If, however, there was a verbal promise which was not relied upon, the promisor may withdraw (BM 49a).

When it is clear that one of the parties has not made his decision to conclude the transaction – i.e., when most people would not do so in the circumstances – he may retract even if it has been agreed that title be effected and the act of *kinyan* performed. This is illustrated in the case of overreaching (see *Ona'ah*), mistake, certain cases of duress (see *Ones*), the nonfulfillment of a condition of the sale, or when one of the parties lacks understanding, and whenever people for any other reason would not normally rely on the transaction. If a person under duress sells a part of his property, the sale will be effective, since he makes up his mind and agrees to the sale simply to rid himself of the duress. Some scholars, however, express the opinion that if he is under duress to sell a specific field the sale will be void (BB 48b). If, prior to the sale, the seller made a statement before witnesses to the effect that he was selling only because of duress – whether of a physical or monetary nature – and the witnesses know of the duress, it will be manifest that the seller had not made up his mind to the sale and the transaction will be void (BB 40a–b).

This is also the law in the case of mistake as to price, whether due to deceit, intentional or inadvertent, or whether the object was sold for more than its true value and the purchaser overcharged, or sold for less than its true value and the seller thus deceived (BM 51a). If the mistake as to price is within a discrepancy of less than one-sixth, the sale will still be effective, since such comparatively small margins are usually overlooked; if the rate is one-sixth exactly, the sale will be effective, but the difference must be refunded; if the rate exceeds one-sixth, the sale is voidable, and the party standing to lose may retract, since such a large mistake would not usually be tolerated. Refunding the difference or voiding the transaction is only permitted within a specified period, during which the party at disadvantage could have become aware of his mistake; thereafter it is presumed that he has waived the rights arising from the mistake in favor of the other party and made up his mind to uphold the transaction as it stands (BM 49b; Rashi on the Mishnah, *ibid.*). The rules of mistake as to price apply equally to mistake in respect of any other aspect of the sale. Whenever the property sold or any of the conditions of the sale vary from that which the purchaser relied upon – and the variation is so great that people in similar circumstances would normally be particular enough to look upon the transaction as being something other than the one upon which they relied – it will be a case of a purchase in error *(mikkaḥ ta'ut)* which voids the transaction (see Sh. Ar., HM 232:6 and glosses thereto). Generally, if as a result of a variation in the property sold it is unsuited for the use for which the purchaser wanted it, it will be a case of *mikkaḥ ta'ut* (see, e.g., Yad, Mekhirah, 15:12, 13).

If the parties conclude the transaction of a sale and perform an act of *kinyan*, but have failed to determine the price, the purchaser will not have acquired title since there was no reliance on the transaction by the parties, and both of them may retract; if, however, the purchase price was fixed and known, the sale will be effective (Yad, Mekhirah, 4:11–12). Maimonides also expressed the opinion that a person cannot acquire from another something that is undetermined even as to species (Yad, Mekhirah, 21:1–3). Thus a purchaser cannot acquire title to "everything that is in this house, or box or sack, which the owner is selling for so much," even if he has performed an act of *kinyan*, since he does not rely on this transaction; however, when the species is known, e.g., "this heap of wheat or cellar of wine at such and such a price," the sale will be effective even if the actual measure and weight are unknown at that moment.

A sale by a person lacking legal capacity – such as a deaf-mute, idiot, or minor – is void, since he lacks understanding and hence the absence of the element of *gemirat ha-da'at*. The sages prescribed, however, that certain sales by such parties would be valid "for the sake of his sustenance" (Git. 59a), i.e., in order to procure the necessities of life. It was laid down that the minimum required age in the case of a minor would depend on the degree of his understanding *(ibid.)* and this was detailed as follows: a minor aged six years and over, having sufficient understanding to appreciate the nature of the transaction, could sell and purchase movable property; from the age of 13, his sale or purchase would be effective in respect of movables, even if he could not appreciate the nature of the transaction, but ineffective in respect of land unless he could appreciate the nature of the transaction; a minor could not sell land inherited from his ancestors until he reached the age of 20 (Yad, Mekhirah, 29:6ff). In the post-talmudic period, too, the age of majority was varyingly determined in respect of different legal transactions,

1. page 101.

depending upon the social and economic circumstances of the time (see Elon, in bibliography).

Sale of a Thing not yet in Existence. The talmud records conflicting opinions as to whether or not a person can transfer title in respect of something not yet in existence. Some scholars answer in the negative, on the ground that the purchaser does not rely on the transaction, or for the reason that there is nothing to which ownership can apply and so ownership cannot be transferred. Another opinion in the Talmud is that a thing not yet in existence may be assigned and that the acquisition will take effect upon the thing's coming into existence, with the result that the parties may not retract. Even according to this opinion, however, only that which will come into existence in the ordinary course of events – such as the fruit of a tree – can be assigned; otherwise all the scholars agree that no transaction can be effected (BM 33b). The scholars who answer this point in the negative expressed the further opinion that a person could not transfer a thing which was not yet his, e.g., if he should say "let this field be acquired by you as of the moment that I shall have taken it for myself" and thus was the *halakhah* decided (Yad, Mekhirah, 22:5). The sages, however, prescribed that the sale by a poor hunter (lacking the necessities of life) of "everything that my hunt will produce today," would be effective, as would similar acquisitions in keeping with this rule (Yad, Mekhirah, 22:6). On the other hand, a person can undertake an obligation to transfer a thing not yet in existence (Sh. Ar., HM 60:6; see Obligations, Law of; Contract[1]). He can furthermore transfer a real right in property which is in existence, e.g., by transferring "the body for its fruits," and thereby confer title to a thing not yet in existence, such as a "tree for its fruit" or an "animal for its young" (Yad, Mekhirah, 23:1–2). An opinion is also expressed that if the thing which is sold is available on the market, the sale will be effective even though it is not yet the seller's, and the latter is obliged to deliver it to the purchaser (Yad, Mekhirah, 22:3 and *Kesef Mishneh* thereto).

With regard to a sale to a person as yet unborn, one opinion is that even if a person may transfer something that is not yet in existence, he cannot do so to a person as yet unborn; another opinion is that one can confer title in favor of a person as yet unborn even if he cannot do so with regard to a thing not yet in existence (Git. 13b and Tos. thereto). The *halakhah* was decided to the effect that a person could not confer title on a person as yet unborn, in the same way that he could not do so in respect of a thing not yet in existence (Sh. Ar., HM 210:1).

It is the accepted view that a person can neither consecrate nor confer title in respect of a thing which is not in his possession, even though it is his property (BK 70a and Tos. thereto); hence a person cannot do so in respect of property stolen from him, since the thief gains possession thereof *(ibid.)*. However, another opinion is that one may consecrate, renounce (see *Hefker*), and confer title even in respect to property which is not in one's possession (BK 68b).

The Conditions of the Sale. The decision of the parties to conclude a transaction is often made subject to various conditions, which must be fulfilled if the transaction is to be effective (see Conditions). Thus if a person sells a house to another on condition that the latter perform some specific act on a specified day, the purchaser acquires the house if and when he performs the act in the specified manner, but not otherwise; the same applies if property is sold to the purchaser on condition that the latter give it to a third party, or if the seller has stipulated that the property is to be returned after a specified period – in which event the transaction is effective and the property must be returned (Yad, Mekhirah, 11:1). Likewise, the sale will be effective where a person stipulates that if he sells his field, the purchaser shall acquire it as of that moment, at a price to be determined later by three valuers (Yad, Mekhirah, 8:8).

The seller's decision to impose a condition on the sale must be manifest and made clear to all, including the purchaser, in the manner in which people would normally do so. Failing this, the sale may be effective but not the condition, since it will be seen from the seller's conduct that he did not intend to impose a material condition capable of voiding the transaction but a mere condition at large, not seriously intended. Hence, he must phrase his statements in the form of a double condition, i.e., specify what will be if the condition is fulfilled and what if not – since Hebrew-language usage requires both the affirmative and the negative to be specified, and if he does not follow the manner in which Hebrew is spoken, he is apparently not particular about fulfillment of the condition. Some scholars expressed the opinion that the requirement of a double condition applies only in the cases of marriage and divorce but not of sale, where a condition is effective whether a double one or not (*Hassagot Rabad,* Zekhiyyah, 3:8). Moreover, the phraseology of the condition requires the affirmative sentence to be included before the negative one, as only thus is it manifest that the party seriously intends to be particular about the fulfillment of the condition (*Beit ha-Beḥirah,* Kid, 61a); he must first state the condition and thereafter the act which is contingent on it, and not vice versa, and the condition must be one which is capable of being fulfilled by the purchaser, lest it appear that it was not seriously intended and the sale be effective without the condition (BM 94a; Kid. 61a).

At times, when it is manifest from the circumstances that the fulfillment of a condition has been relied upon, such condition will be effective even if the above-mentioned phraseology has not been adopted. Moreover, if it is manifest from the circumstances that the seller has relied on a certain condition, the condition will be effective even if he has not given any verbal expression thereto, since everything is dependent upon what people normally imply from the circumstances (Tos. to Kid. 49b). Often the parties do not specify any conditions and may not even be thinking of any, but the presumption is that they intend to sell and purchase in accordance with local custom. Hence local customs relating to purchase and sale are superimposed to supplement the decision of the parties; furthermore, statements of conditions which are not clearly expressed are construed in accordance with local custom (Yad, Mekhirah, 17:6; 26:7–8; 27:11; also *Hassagot Rabad,* Mekhirah 24:12). If the parties wish to exclude the conditions of local custom, they must make express provisions to this effect. Thus a person who transfers ownership to another generally intends it to pass upon the performance of the *kinyan* by the transferee; however, if for example, he says, "perform the *kinyan* and acquire 30 days hereafter," the acquisition will only be complete after 30 days (Ket. 82a).

Of the customary conditions, the most important one is the warranty of authority. Thus, one who purchases something which is later taken from him for reasons connected with the seller – for instance, that the land was not his or that it was mortgaged to his creditor – may hold the seller liable and recover the cost of it from him. This warranty of ownership by the seller is implied in every sale, even if not expressly formulated (Yad, Mekhirah, 19:3). If the seller wishes to be absolved from all or any part of such responsibility, he must do so by express stipulation (*ibid.,* 19:8). Another opinion (BM 14a) is that in an ordinary sale the seller takes no responsibility upon himself unless a specific provision to the contrary is made.

The Mishnah, in listing various categories of sale, clarifies the different (implied) conditions that will be included unless

1. page 248.

otherwise provided for by the parties and if not contrary to local custom. Thus one who sells a field sells also the stones which serve the land, the unreaped grain, the watchman's booth, and the trees which have no intrinsic value, but not the stones that are not necessary to the land, or the grain that has been severed from the ground, and the like (BB 4:8). So too, one who sells a field for sowing does not include rifts in it or rocks which are more than ten handbreadths high (BB 7:1); one who buys two trees in another's field does not buy any land with them, but one who buys three trees, buys also the land on which they are growing (BB 5:4); one who has sold a wagon has not sold the mules; and if he has sold the mules he has not sold the wagon (BB 5:1); one who has sold the head of a large animal, has not sold its feet also, but in the case of sheep the feet are included in the sale of the head (BB 5:5). Similarly, the Mishnah enumerates that which is included or excluded in the sale of numerous items of property ranging from houses, buildings, and trees to slaves and animals (BB 4–7). Implied conditions also apply with regard to the price. Thus one who has sold wheat to another for a fixed amount of money without specifying the quantity, must deliver wheat according to the market price at the time of the sale (Yad, Mekhirah, 21:4).

In cases where there is difficulty in construing the parties' intention, their ultimate purpose may be arrived at with the aid of the rule that "he who sells, sells in a liberal spirit," i.e., a liberal interpretation of the agreement is made. Thus, one who sells a house but does not include the cistern in the sale must purchase from the buyer a right of way to it, since the terms of the sale are to be interpreted liberally and he did not retain a right of way (BB 64a–b). However, a person who has sold a field but retained two trees for himself will also retain the soil in which they grow, even though the purchaser of only two trees acquires no soil with them (BB 71a). There are conflicting views on the matter, some scholars stating that a restrictive interpretation is also possible, i.e., "one who sells, sells in an illiberal spirit." However, all scholars accept that the maxim of a liberal interpretation is applicable in the case of gifts (BB 65a).

In the State of Israel. The rules of sale are set out in the Sales Law, 5828/1968, which in general adopts the draft uniform law relating to international sales, submitted at The Hague International Conference in 1964. In certain matters this law takes cognizance of the attitude of Jewish law (see Elon, in bibliography).

Bibliography: J.S. Zuri, *Mishpat ha-Talmud,* 5 (1921), 60–88; Gulak, Yesodei, 1 (1922), 55–93; 2 (1922), 152–9; Gulak, Oẓar, 159–82, 238–42, 306–8, 345f.; idem, *Le-Ḥeker Toledot ha-Mishpat ha-Ivri bi Tekufat ha-Talmud,* 1 (*Dinei Karka'ot,* 1929), passim; idem, *Toledot ha-Misphat be-Yisrael bi-Tekufat ha-Talmud,* 1 (*Ha-Ḥiyyuv ve-Shi'budav,* 1939), 10, 33n. 12, 62–65, 74, 100–4, 106; Herzog, Instit, 2 (1939), 61–71, 107–39; ET, 1 (1951[3]), 153–60, 216–8; 6 (1954), 616–24, 625–31, 661–83; 7 (1956), 30–67; B. Rabinowitz–Te'omim, *Ḥukkat Mishpat* (1957); M. Elon, in: ILR, 4 (1969), 91 n. 49, 122.

Shalom Albeck

ONA'AH (Heb. אונאה "overreaching"), the act of wronging another by selling him an article for more than its real worth or by purchasing from him an article for less than its real worth. To distinguish between *ona'ah* and *hafka'at shearim,* see next article.

Origin and Nature of the Prohibition. The prohibition against *ona'ah* has its origin in the Pentateuch, "And if thou sell aught unto thy neighbor, or buy of thy neighbor's hand, ye shall not wrong one another" (Lev. 25:14). The passage was construed by the scholars as relating to overreaching in monetary matters and they distinguished three degrees of this, according to whether the discrepancy amounts to one-sixth, less than one-sixth, or more than one-sixth of the value of the article (see below). The law of *ona'ah* applies to undercharging as well as overcharging (Sh. Ar., ḤM 227:2). The prohibition against *ona'ah* is a separate one but is also embraced within the wider prohibition against robbery. Despite the express enjoinder of the prohibition as a negative command, transgression is not punished by flogging since the overreaching is remediable by restitution, and the person who has overreached – whether wittingly or unwittingly – is obligated to make good the discrepancy (Yad, Mekhirah 12:1; Sh. Ar., ḤM 227:2).

Three Degrees of Ona'ah. In the case where a person has overreached by one-sixth, the transaction is valid but he must make good the discrepancy to the injured party (BM 50b). The discrepancy of one-sixth is calculated on the market value. If the discrepancy amounts to less than one-sixth, the transaction is valid and the difference need not be made good (Yad, loc. cit. 12:3). As regards sales and purchases transacted by minors the scholars, having noted that their transactions shall be valid for the sake of insuring their vital needs, also laid down that even though minors have no legal capacity to waive their rights, their mistake shall nonetheless be treated in the same way as the mistake of an adult (Sh. Ar., ḤM 235:3) and they must be deemed to waive their right in respect of overreaching amounting to less than one-sixth. If the discrepancy amounts to more than one-sixth the transaction is void but the injured party may waive his right in respect of the overreaching and uphold the transaction (Yad, loc. cit. 12:4). Some scholars held that the party who has overreached may insist on voiding the transaction even though the injured party is willing to waive his rights in the matter (Tos. to BM 50b).

Contracting out of the Law of Overreaching. A stipulation between the parties stating, "on condition that there is no overreaching therein" (i.e., in the transaction), or "on condition that you have no claim of overreaching against me," is invalid (Sh. Ar., ḤM 227:21), since the language used implies a stipulation contrary to a prohibition laid down in the Torah and one may not stipulate to set aside the Pentateuchal law; however, when the amounts involved in the transaction are specified, a stipulation of this nature is valid, since the injured party knows the precise amount of the overreaching to which he waives his right, and all stipulations in monetary matters are valid (*ibid. (mamon)* see also Contract[1]). If the parties agreed that the purchase price be determined by the valuation of a third party the parties to the transaction will have a claim against each other for overreaching if it is later found that the valuer erred in his valuation (Sh. Ar., ḤM 227:25).

Property not Subject to the Law of Overreaching. Four items are not subject to the law of overreaching: land, slaves, deeds, and consecrated property (*hekdesh;* BM 56a). "Even though it is a decree of the Torah, yet the matter must to some extent be amplified by logical reasoning. For a person sometimes buys land for more than its worth and the scholars called land something that is always worth the money paid for it and, contrariwise, when a person is in need of money but finds no purchaser he sells it (land) for much less than its worth since it is impossible to carry land from place to place. Similarly, slaves are sometimes the source of trouble, yet a person who is in need of a slave may be prepared to pay a high price for him. As regards deeds which are due for payment, these are sometimes subject to depreciation because of the financial position of the debtor or his aggressiveness. Concerning consecrated property in the Temple period, it was decided that "if *hekdesh* worth a *maneh* had been redeemed for the equivalent of a *perutah,* the redemption was

1. page 251.

valid' – hence, in the sale of consecrated property also there is no law of overreaching, even though the Temple treasury be wronged, so that the buyer cannot retract since 'a verbal undertaking in favor of the Temple treasury is as a delivery to the common man' " (*Arukh ha-Shulḥan,* ḤM 227:34).

Land. The law of overreaching applies neither to the sale nor the leasing of land (Yad, Mekhirah 13:14). Anything which is attached to the land is subject to the same law as the land itself, provided that it is dependent on that land itself (Sh. Ar., ḤM 193). An opinion was also expressed that the same law applies to both, even when the article attached to the land is not dependent on that land itself (Rema, ad loc.). A very early opinion that land outside Ereẓ Israel is considered as movable property and subject to the law of overreaching, was rejected (Tur., ḤM, 95:4).

Slaves. There is no overreaching as regards slaves, since the law of slaves is analogous to the law of land (BM 56b. See Slavery). Hence it was laid down as *halakhah* that the law of overreaching does not apply to the hire of laborers because it is as if the employer buys the laborer for a limited time and the latter's position is assimilated to that of a slave required for a limited period (Yad, Mekhirah, 13:15). The opinion that the law of overreaching applies to a contractor (*kabbelan;* Yad, loc. cit. 13:18), is disagreed with by certain scholars (Nov. Ramban, BM 56b; *Maggid Mishneh,* Mekhirah 13:15). A minority opinion that the hire of a laborer is subject to the law of overreaching was rejected (Resp. Maharam of Rothenburg, ed. Prague, no. 749; see also Labor Law). There is no law of overreaching as regards a Hebrew slave (*Minḥat Ḥinnukh,* no. 337).

Deeds. There is no overreaching as regards bonds, but money bills issued in different countries at the instance of the government are treated as money in all respects since they are officially issued and are taken in payment; however, shares and the like which are not officially issued are apparently like deeds and not subject to the law of overreaching (*Pitḥei Teshuvah,* YD 305, n. 7 and HM 95, n. 1).

The scholars expressed differing opinions on the question of whether enormous overreaching gives ground for invalidating a transaction relating to land, slaves, or deeds; one view is that the transaction may be invalidated when the overreaching exceeds one-sixth of the price (*Halakhot,* Rif, BM 57a); another is that this may be done if the overreaching reaches one-half of the purchase price (Rif, loc. cit.); and a third is that the sale is only invalidated when the limit of one-half has been exceeded (Rema, HM 227:29; *Sma, Siftei Kohen* and *Ha-Gra,* ad loc.). However, the accepted opinion is that with regard to land, slaves, and deeds the law of overreaching never applies nor does it ever serve to invalidate the transaction (Sh. Ar., HM 227:29; *Siftei Kohen,* HM 66, n. 122).

Consecrated Property. In the Temple period the law of overreaching did not apply to consecrated property (BM 56a; Yad, Mekhirah 13:8) but "in these times" the law of overreaching does apply in respect of consecrated property and property dedicated to the poor (HM 227, *Sma,* n. 49; see *Hekdesh*). Although it was enjoined, "if you shall sell" the law of overreaching applies to coins (BM 51b) despite the fact that a coin is not something that is sold (HM 227, *Sma,* n. 26).

Further Cases of Exclusion from the Law of Overreaching. Barter. The accepted opinion is that the law of overreaching does not operate in a transaction of barter (see Acquisition;[1] Yad, Mekhirah, 13:1; Sh. Ar., HM 227:20). In the opinion of some scholars utensils and animals that are stock in trade are subject to the law of overreaching even when bartered, and the rule excluding overreaching in barter was laid down solely in respect of property traded by a layman (Resp. Radbaz, no. 1340, and see below).

"One who trades on trust." There is no overreaching as regards "one who trades on trust" (BM 51b). "How so? If the seller said to the purchaser 'I purchased this article for so and so much and I wish to earn thereon so and so much,' the purchaser will have no claim against him for overreaching" (*Arukh ha-Shulḥan* 227:28), "even if the overreaching amounts to more than one-sixth" (Yad, Mekhirah 14:1). On the other hand, the scholars laid down that raising the prices of commodities beyond the accepted level, or beyond those fixed by the competent authority, amounts to a transgression of the prohibition against profiteering.

Personal Apparel. The law of overreaching does not apply to the sale of a person's own apparel because he would not sell such articles except if he received the price he demanded (BM 51a), and this is so even when he is known to have sold these items on account of financial hardship (Resp. Rosh, no. 105:2). The scholars differed as to whether in such a case the seller has a claim in respect of overreaching (*Shitah Mekubbeẓet* loc. cit.; *Maggid Mishneh,* Mekhirah 13:2). It was held that if the articles sold are normally traded, there will be a claim in respect of overreaching (*Hananel,* BM 51a).

Agency. The law of *ona'ah* does not operate in respect of property sold through an agent. If the agent is overreached in any manner the sale is void since his principal may say, "I delegated you to act to my advantage and not to my detriment" (Kid. 42b; Yad, Mekhirah 13:9). If the purchaser is the injured party some scholars hold that the sale is void, as it is in the reverse case, but the accepted opinion is that in this case the law applies as if the agent were acting independently and the purchaser waives a discrepency of less than one-sixth (Rosh, loc. cit.; Sh. Ar., EH 104:6). When the fact that a party was acting as an agent remained undisclosed, the sale will be valid as long as the overreaching did not reach the stipulated measure (Yad, Sheluḥin, 2:4). The principal has the right to retract on account of overreaching even in matters which are not otherwise subject to the law of overreaching (Sh. Ar., ḤM, 227:30). He has the right either to void the sale or to uphold it but the purchaser is not entitled to seek its invalidation (*Netivot ha-Mishpat, Mishpat ha-Urim* 185, n. 8).

The same law of overreaching applies to a guardian (see *Apotropos*) as to a principal (Sh. Ar., HM 227:30), even when the former is appointed by the court (Mekhirah 13:9). A partner who has bought or sold is subject to the same law as a person who has bought or sold his own property, since this is not a case in which it may properly be said, "I have delegated you to act to my advantage and not to my detriment" (*Siftei Kohen,* HM 77, 19). A broker who has an interest in the property sold is held by some scholars to be in the same position as an agent (*Netivot ha-Mishpat, Mishpat ha-Urim,* 227, n.16), while another opinion is that his position is equated with that of a partner (HM 227, *Sma* n. 42; see also *Shalish*). The law of overreaching does not apply to transactions negotiated by the "seven senior citizens" (i.e., public representatives) on behalf of the community (Ran on Rif to Meg. 27a; Rema, OḤ 153:7; *Taz,* thereto, n. 8).

Division of Property by Brothers or Partners. The law of overreaching applies to the division of inherited property by brothers or partners, since their position is assimilated to that of purchasers. This rule applies to partners in respect of the partnership property only and not to a mere profit-sharing or business partnership (*Arukh ha-Shulḥan,* HM 227:38; see also Ownership).

Claim for Restitution or Invalidation of a Transaction. A purchaser who wishes to claim restitution or to invalidate a transaction on the grounds of overreaching must do so within the time it would take for him to show the article to a merchant

1. page 208.

or other person from whom he may ascertain its market price (Sh. Ar., HM 227:7). Longer delay entails forfeiture of his right, but he need not pay the price if he has not yet done so (*Siftei Kohen,* thereto). If the injured party is the seller he may retract at any time since he no longer holds the article and cannot show it to a merchant (BM 50b; Yad, Mekhirah 12:6; Sh. Ar., HM 227:8). However, if the seller should ascertain the value of the article and thereafter fail to claim restitution of the amount of the overreaching or invalidation of the sale, he will forfeit his right to do so (Yad and Sh. Ar., loc. cit.), but another opinion is that the seller retains this right at all times (*Maggid Mishneh,* Mekhirah 12:6).

Bibliography: J. S. Zuri, *Mishpat ha-Talmud,* 5 (1921), 70–76; Gulak, Yesodei, 1 (1922), 64–66; 2 (1922), 153–60; P. Dickstein, in: *Ha-Mishpat ha-Ivri,* 1 (1925/26), 15–55; Herzog, Instit, 1 (1936), 112–7; 2 (1939), 121–4; E. Z. Melamed, in: *Yavneh,* 3 (1942), 35–56; ET, 1 (1951[3]), 153–60; B. Rabinowitz-Teomim, *Ḥukkat Mishpat* (1957), 113–40, Elon, *Ha-Mishpat Ha-Ivri* (1973), III, p. 1101, 1106; D. Sperber, *Laesio Enormis* and *the Talmudic Law of Onaah,* in: *Israel Law Review,* vol. 8 (April 1973), p. 254–274.

Shmuel Shilo

HAFKA'AT SHE'ARIM (Heb. הפקעת שערים raising the price of a commodity beyond the accepted level, or that fixed by a competent authority.

Profiteering and Overreaching. The law of *Hafka'at She'arim* ("profiteering") is analogous to that of overreaching (*ona'ah,* "misrepresentation"), it being the object of the law in both cases to preserve a fair and just price. However, the law of overreaching – fraudulent or innocent (i.e., mistaken) – stems from a biblical prohibition (Lev. 25:14): the law was fixed that if the price exceeded the value by one-sixth, the seller must return this part to the purchaser; if the price was higher yet, the purchaser might demand cancellation of the transaction; conversely, if the price was too low, the law applies *mutatis mutandis* in favor of the seller. The law of profiteering on the other hand has its source in rabbinic enactment designed to prohibit the setting of prices in excess of the customarily accepted ones, even if the purchaser is aware of and agrees to the inflated price; ". . . even when he [the seller] says 'it cost me one *sela* and I want to earn two on it,' he has not transgressed the law of *ona'ah* but he is prohibited by rabbinic enactment from making a profit of more than one-sixth in essential commodities" (*Beit ha-Beḥirah,* BM 51b).

Price-fixing and Control; Prohibition against Profiteering. It would seem that in the mishnaic period there were fixed prices, apparently determined by a competent authority (BM 4:12, 5:7). There is evidence that in Jerusalem – prior to the destruction of the Temple – the market commissioners "did not supervise prices but measures only" (Tosef., BM 6:14); in Babylonia (at the commencement of the third century C.E.) there was supervision of prices at the instance of the exilarch (TJ, BB 5:11, 15a; TB, BB 89a). The sages of that period were divided, however, on this matter. Some expressed the opinion that "price inspectors do not need to be appointed" and that competition between merchants would suffice to stabilize the price while others were of the opinion that it was incumbent on the court to supervise the prices because of the "swindlers" who hoarded commodities toward a time when they might be in short supply in order to sell them at a high price (TJ and TB, BB 89a). In the course of time the view favoring price supervision apparently became generally accepted (BB 89a; Yoma 9a) and thus it was decided in the codes: "but the court is obliged to determine prices and to appoint commissioners for this purpose, to prevent everyone from charging what he likes . . . " (Yad, Mekhirah 14:1; Tur and Sh. Ar., HM 231:20).

The scholars compared profiteering to the transgressions of "giving short measure of the ephah" (deceit with regard to weights and measures) and to that of charging interest on loans (BB 90b; and see Usury). In their opinion, the profiteer transgresses the biblical injunction "that thy brother may live with thee" (Lev. 25:36; *Sma* HM 231 n. 43) and they regarded profiteers as "bandits who prey on the poor . . . on whom they concentrate their attention" (Meg. 17b and Rashi, *ibid,*). The prescribed punishment for them: "flagellation and they are compelled to sell at the market price" (Yad, Genevah, 8:20; Tur and Sh. Ar., HM 231:21). Authority to determine prices was given not only to the court, but also to local communal representatives: "and the townspeople are authorized to fix prices" (of wheat and wine, so as to maintain the price in a particular year – Rashi) "and measures and workers' wages, which they may enforce by means of punishment" (i.e., fines; cf. BB 89a and Rashi; Tosef. BM 11:23; BB 8b; see also *Takkanot ha-Kahal*[1]). It appears that already in the talmudic period, the law of profiteering was only applied to essential commodities such as wheat, oil, and wine, and this was confirmed in the codes: "prices [of nonessentials] are not determined but everyone may charge what he likes" Yad, Mekhirah 14:2 and standard commentaries ad loc.; Tur and Sh. Ar., HM 231:20).

The maximum profit generally permitted to the seller was one-sixth (BB 90a). Some of the authorities took the view that this rate applied to one selling his merchandise in bulk, without toil (a wholesaler); a shopkeeper, however, "selling his merchandise little by little, might have his toil and overheads accounted for in addition to a profit of one-sixth" (Tur and Sh. Ar., HM 231:20). They also decided that the rules concerning profiteering were only to take effect if imposed as measures of general application to all vendors, otherwise the individual could not be obliged to adhere to the permitted maximum rate of profit *(ibid).*

Stringent Supervision in Ereẓ Israel. Particular care was taken to maintain a cheap supply of essential products in Ereẓ Israel, where no middleman between producer and consumer was tolerated: "it is forbidden to speculate in essential commodities in Ereẓ Israel but everyone shall bring from his barn and sell so that these [commodities] may be sold cheaply"; however, it was decided that in the case of a commodity in free supply or where a middleman worked to prepare and process the product, such as baking bread from wheat, profit-making was permitted, even in Ereẓ Israel (Tosef. Av. Zar. 4(5):1; BB 91a and Rashbam, *Yad Ramah and Beit ha-Beḥirah ibid;* Yad, Mekhirah 14:4; Sh. Ar., HM 231:23).

Measures to Prevent Profiteering. The sages sought in various ways to eliminate the factors which made for a climate for profiteering. Thus it was forbidden to hoard produce bought on the market, lest this cause prices to rise and bring losses to the poor, and in a year of famine no hoarding at all was permitted (not as much as a "cab of carobs"), not even of the produce harvested from one's own field (BB 90b; Yad, Mekhirah 14:5–7). In later *halakhah* storing of produce from the producer's own field was permitted, even in a famine year, for the sustenance of his family (Tur., HM 231:29) for a period of one year (Sh. Ar., HM 231:24). Produce hoarders, like profiteers, were compared to those who charged interest on loans (BB, 90b). In order to prevent profiteering, it was not permitted to export essential products from Ereẓ Israel, since this might cause a shortage and a consequent rise in prices (BB 90b–91a, Yad, Mekhirah 14:8; Sh. Ar., HM 231:26). With the same object in mind the rabbis laid

1. page 655.

down that the proclamation of a public fast (on account of drought) should not be announced for the first time on a Thursday as this would cause panic (out of fear of famine) at a time when everyone was preparing for the Sabbath, and this might lead to profiteering (Ta'an. 2:9).

In their war against profiteers the scholars made use of a deliberate interpretation of the law. At a time when the numerous sacrifices required to be brought by a woman who had given birth caused the price of a pair of sacrificial birds (two doves) to be raised to a golden dinar (25 silver dinars), Simeon b. Gamaliel the Elder vowed: "I shall not sleep this night until a pair sells for a dinar" (i.e., silver; Ker. 1:7). He entered the court and taught that a woman who had had five definite births (and thus should bring five sacrifices) need bring one sacrifice only and might eat of the *zevaḥim* ("sacrificial animals"), i.e. is ritually pure, and that "the remainder is not obligatory upon her; that same day the price of sacrificial birds stood at a quarter [of a silver dinar per pair]." *(ibid.);* Rashi (Ker. 8a) comments: "though he interpreted the word of the law leniently, it was a time to campaign for the Lord *(et la'asot la-shem)* for if no remedy had been found, not even one [sacrifice] would have been brought." Some 1,600 years later, when the fishmongers of Nikolsburg, Moravia, greatly raised the price of fish, "having seen that the Jews were not deterred by expensive prices from buying fish for the Sabbath," the Nikolsburg community enacted a *takkanah* which prohibited everyone from buying fish for a period of two months. Asked whether this *takkanah* did not in some measure slight the honor of the Sabbath, M. M. Krochmal, chief rabbi of Moravia, replied that in order to enable also the poor "to honor the Sabbath by [eating] fish" it were better not to buy fish for a few Sabbaths so as to bring down the prices, and he quoted the statements of Simeon b. Gamaliel (above), as a clear practical illustration of the saying: "it is well to desecrate one Sabbath, so that many Sabbaths be observed" (*Ẓemaḥ Ẓedek*, no. 28).

For the prohibition against profiteering in rent to protect tenants from eviction, see *Hassagat Gevul.*[1]

In the State of Israel. In the State of Israel there are a number of laws designed to combat profiteering in essential commodities. The Commodities and Services (Control) Law, 5718–1957, provides for various means of supervision over commodities declared to be subject to control by the minister charged with implementation of the law, enforcable on pain of imprisonment, fine, and closing down of a business, etc. The Tenants' Protection Laws, 5714–1954 and 5715–1955, control maximum rentals for residential and business premises and also limit the right of ejectment to grounds specified in these laws only. These laws are supplemented by the provisions of the Key Money Law, 5718–1958. The Restrictive Trade Practices Law, 5719–1959, restricts; amongst others, the artificial manipulation of price levels at the hands of a monopoly or cartel. In the Knesset debates preceding the passing of these laws, some members relied on Jewish law in support of their arguments (*Divrei ha-Keneset* vol. 7, p. 564; vol.14, p. 1822; vol. 18, p. 2176; vol. 21, p. 169; vol. 23, pp. 372, 374, 383; vol. 24, pp. 2478, 2514).

Bibliography: Gulak, Yesodei, 1 (1922), 64–66; P. Dickstein, in: *Ha-Mishpat ha-Ivri,* 1 (1925/26), 15–55; ET, 10 (1961), 41–49; M. Elon, *Ha-Mishpat Ha-Ivri* (1973) II, p. 310, III, p. 1078.

Menachem Elon

GIFT, the transfer of legal rights without any consideration or payment. It is essentially no more than a sale without payment and all the principles of the law of sale apply (see Sale).

The Da'at of the Parties. The decision *(gemirat ha-da'at)* of the parties to conclude a gift transaction – the intention of one to give and the other to receive – is established by means of an act of *kinyan,* i.e., by the performance of one of the recognized acts whereby property is acquired (see Acquisition). Upon performance of the *kinyan,* ownership of the property passses from the donor to the donee and neither may any longer withdraw from the transaction. The test as to whether or not the *gemirat ha-da'at* exists is an objective one, namely: if the parties performed an act customarily performed by people in order to conclude such a transaction and if in the particular circumstances of the case there existed no reason why most people would not conclude the transaction, the gift will be effective (Kid. 49b). A gift may be conferred on a person without his knowledge, because it is assumed that he agrees to get a benefit, the rule being that "a benefit may be conferred on a person in his absence, but an obligation may only be imposed on him in his presence" (Git. 11b). Similarly, the *gemirat ha-da'at* of the parties does not require a *consensus ad idem* between the parties. If it is manifest that the donor made up his mind to effect the gift, whereas the donee has not made up his mind to receive it, the latter may retract but the former may not, since the *gemirat ha-da'at* of a party to a transaction precludes him from retracting from it. Consequently, when a person confers a gift on another through a third party, the donee may refuse to accept it until it has reached his hands, even if he has heard of the intended gift – but the donor may not withdraw, since the person acquiring the gift on behalf of the donee performed a *kinyan* whereby the donor's decision to conclude the transaction was made (Yad, Zekhiyyah 4:2). If the donee should discover a defect in the gift, and it is of such nature that people would generally not want such a gift, the donee may retract even after the gift has come to his hands (*Kesef Mishneh,* Zekhiyyah 4:1, concl.).

When it is manifest to all that there was an absence of *gemirat ha-da'at* on the part of both parties, the transaction will be void. A person cannot transfer to another, by way of gift, something which is not yet in existence, or which is not his own; nor can a gift be conferred on someone who is not yet born; nor can a gift be conferred of something which one owns but which is not at the present time in his possession, such as where the owner has been robbed (see Theft and Robbery). According to some scholars, however, even these kinds of gifts may validly be conferred in certain circumstances (see Sale). Similarly, if a person promises a valuable gift to another verbally, but without a *kinyan,* so that the latter does not rely on the promise, there would not even be any moral sanction against him if he should withdraw (BM 49a).

If it is clear, notwithstanding an act of *kinyan,* that the donor did not really intend to effect the gift (for example, he was compelled to make the gift under duress), it will be void. Even if there was no duress, but prior to the gift the donor had declared before witnesses that he was not making it of his own free will, the transaction will also be void, even if the witnesses were not themselves aware of any duress exercised against him, because by his declaration he manifests an intention of not making the gift (Yad, Zekhiyyah, 5:4; see *Ones*). Moreover, as a gift must be made openly and publicly, an undisclosed gift is invalid,since "the donor is not presumed to have made up his mind to a gift, but is scheming for the loss of other people's property" (*ibid.* 5:1). Similarly, if a person makes a written disposition of all his property to one of his sons, the latter does not acquire it all since the assumption is that the father intended to do no more than appoint this son administrator so that his brothers should

1. page 342.

accept his authority. This is also the case if he made a disposition in favor of his wife. However, where he disposes of only part of his assets to his wife or son, or where he expressly states that an absolute gift is intended, the gift will be effective (*ibid.* 6:2–4). A gift by a woman before her marriage by way of a written disposition in favor of a person other than her prospective husband becomes ineffective if the latter should die or be divorced from her, since the disposition of her assets to another was made in order to keep these from her husband in the event of his inheriting her (*ibid.* 6:12). On the other hand, one who gives money for *kiddushin* (marriage) which is known to be invalid, e.g., to one's own sister, intends to do so for the sake of gift (Kid. 46b). According to another opinion he gives the money as bailment.

A deaf-mute, an idot, and a minor lack the legal capacity to make a gift, since they have no *da'at,* but the scholars prescribed that minors or deaf-mutes, depending on the degree of their understanding of the nature of the transaction, may effectively make certain gifts, by virtue of the rule of "for the sake of his sustenance" (Yad, Mekhirah 29; see Sale). According to many opinions, they may also receive gifts, even in terms of biblical law (Tos. Kid. 19a). The sages also prescribed that someone may acquire and receive a gift on behalf of a minor, even if the latter is no more than one day old (Rashbam to BB 156b).

Conditions of the Gift. The donor may make the gift conditional upon certain terms, failing which the gift will be void (see Conditions). As in the case of a sale, the stipulating party must impose his conditions in such a manner as to make it clear and known to all that he intends in all seriousness that the gift be considered void if the conditions should not be fulfilled and that he is not merely making a statement at large (Yad, Zekhiyyah 3:6–7). When it is apparent from the circumstances that he intends to make his gift subject to the happening of certain events, the condition will be operative even if not expressly stated and, at times, even if not stated at all (Tos. to Kid. 49b). Thus a gift would be void if made by a person who transfers all his assets to another on hearing of his son's death, but subsequently finds out that his son is still alive – since the circumstances show that he would not have given away all his assets if he had known that his son was really alive (BB 146b). Similarly, a gift made to the family of one's bride is returnable, if the marriage should fail to take place and the gift was not of a perishable kind *(ibid.).* So too, where it is customary for wedding gifts to be sent to a friend in order that the latter shall give his own similar gifts to the donor upon his marriage; the latter, i.e., the donor, may claim such from the former if they are not given, gifts of this kind being regarded as similar to loans (Yad, Zekhiyyah 7).

The donor may stipulate that the gift is to be returned, in which event the gift is valid but the recipient is obliged to return it after the expiry of the stipulated period. During this stipulated period, however, this gift is the property of the recipient, like all his other property; but after the stipulated period, the recipient must return the property to its former owner, and failure to do so will amount to the nonfulfillment of a condition, voiding the transaction of a gift *ab initio* (Sh. Ar., HM 241:6). Similarly, the donor may stipulate that he is making a gift, first for the benefit of one person and then for another (see Wills). Where the true intention of the donor is in doubt, his ultimate purpose may be deduced with the aid of the rule that "he who gives a gift gives in a liberal spirit." Thus if one says, "give to so-and-so a house capable of holding 100 barrels," and it is found to hold 120 barrels, the donee will have acquired the whole house (BB 71a). Generally, no responsibility is imposed in connection with the gift, and if it should be foreclosed, the donee will have no recourse against the donor, unless expressly provided for between the parties (Yad, Shekhenim 13:1).

In the State of Israel the rules of gift are ordered in terms of the Gift Law, 1968, consisting of six material paragraphs. On the question of the degree of its reliance on Jewish law, see Elon in bibliography.

See also Wills.

Bibliography: M. Bloch, *Das mosaisch-talmudische Erbrecht* (1890), 40 ff; idem, *Der Vertrag nach mosaisch-talmudischen Rechte* (1893), 87–90; Gulak, Yesodei, 1 (1922), 39, 76 n. 3, 118, 129ff; 2 (1922), 159–63; Gulak, Ozar, xxii, 38, 182–91, 346f.; Herzog, Instit, index; ET, 1 (1951[3]), 165f., 216f., 219, 291; 3 (1941), 203; 5 (1953), 400–3; 6 (1954), 89–92, 550f., 606f., 613f., 619, 625–31; 7 (1956), 30, 43f., 57, 170–3; 8 (1957), 435f.; 9 (1959), 161f.; 10 (1961), 64–66; 12 (1967), 140–6; B. Cohen, in: *Wolfson Jubilee Volume,* 1 (1965), 227f.; M. Elon, in: ILR, 4 (1969), 96–98; idem, *Ha-Mishpat ha-Ivri* (1973), I, p. 106ff, II, 480ff.

Shalom Albeck

HEFKER (Heb. הפקר), ownerless property and renunciation of ownership. *Hefker* is property that is ownerless and can therefore be legally acquired by the person who first takes possession of it. There are two categories of ownerless property: (1) property that has never been owned before – such as wild animals and birds, fish of the river and ocean, and wild or forest plants (Maim. Yad, Zekhi'ah, 1:1–2); and (2) property that has ceased to belong to its former owner.

Property becomes *hefker* in two different ways, just as ownership can generally cease in the same two ways: (1) When it is clear that the property can no more return permanently to an individual's possession – for example, birds which have escaped (Ran on Rif, Ḥul. beginning of Ch. 11) – provided that no other person has acquired it. Similarly, the property of a proselyte who leaves no Jewish heirs becomes *hefker,* since his gentile relatives do not inherit from him. (2) When the owner decides not to have it again in his possession, i.e., if he renounces it or if he gives up hope of recovering lost property. As in all other instances of termination of ownership, such as *ye'ush,* the only formality required in the case of renunciation is the manifestation of the owner's intention, whether by word or conduct, as when he declares "this is renounced in favor of anyone who wants it" (Ned. 43a) or by any conduct to this effect. Thus, for instance, if a Jew purchases land from a non-Jew, the latter may vacate it on receipt of the purchase money, whereas the purchaser may not wish to acquire the land except in the prescribed manner in which it would be acquired from another Jew, i.e., by *shetar* or *ḥazakah* (see Acquisition[1]). It is thus possible that in the interval the field becomes ownerless and may be acquired by anyone taking possession of it (BB 54b), although in practice the secular law of the land would usually prevail to make the transfer effective. Similarly, the circumstances in which property is found may indicate that ownership thereof has been renounced, as in the case of "intentional loss" *(avedah mi-da'at),* i.e., when the owner knowingly leaves the property in a place where he is likely to lose it, such as produce scattered on the threshing-floor (BM 21a), or open jars of wine or oil in a public domain (BM 23b). The fact that ownership is relinquished by mental decision means that minors, having no "mind" in law, cannot dispose of their property by renunciation (BM 22b). For the same reason *hefker* created through a mistake of fact (see Samson b. Abraham of Sens, Comm. Pe'ah, 6:1), or under duress (TJ, Suk. 4:2, 54b) is void.

There is a difference of opinion with regard to *hefker*

1. pages 207, 208.

between the schools of Shammai and Hillel. The former hold that a renunciation in favor of the poor only is valid, comparing it to *pe'ah* ("the corner of the field," Lev. 23:22), while the latter maintain that to be valid the renunciation must apply to rich and poor alike, as is the case with regard to *shemittah* ("the sabbatical year," Lev.25:1–7). In R. Johanan's view both schools agree that renunciation in favor of all human beings, but excluding animals, or to all Jews, but not non-Jews, is valid, while Simeon b. Lakish maintains that the school of Hillel would regard it as invalid (TJ, Pe'ah 6:1, 19b). It is possible that the difference of opinion centers around the principle that where the renunciation is not of universal application, the renouncer, by preventing the property from being acquired by certain categories excluded from the renunciation, thereby retains some possession of it which is a bar to renunciation. However, where the owner disregards the possibility of it being acquired by those whom he excludes, he thereupon ceases to guard it and it passes out of his possession. The school of Shammai opines that the owner who renounces his property in favor of the poor has no fear that the rich may take possession of it, while the school of Hillel disagrees.

Ownership of property that has been lost ceases from the moment the owner gives expression to his despair of recovering it (see *Ye'ush*). In the case of *hefker* there is a dispute as to whether it takes effect immediately upon renunciation, in which case the owner cannot retract, or upon the acquisition of the property by another (Ned. 43a; TJ, Pe'ah 6:1, 19b). A person may renounce his property for a fixed period, and if it is acquired by another within the stated period it becomes the latter's permanently. At the end of the stated period the renunciation is automatically annulled if the property has not so been acquired (Ned. 44a).

Hefker property is exempt from a number of commandments. It is free from the obligations of the gifts due to priests and levites, as from *terumah* ("heave offering"), tithes, and the giving of the firstborn of animals to the priest. Advantage was sometimes taken of this law to evade these obligations. The owners would renounce their property to evade their liability, subsequently reacquiring it before others could take possession of it. To prevent this an enactment was made restricting the ability to withdraw a renunciation to three days from the time it was made (Ned. 43b); within this period a renounced field remains subject to the various imposts, and owners would be afraid to make the renunciation apply for a longer period lest the field be acquired by someone else. However, there are different opinions as to the details of this enactment. Similarly, it was enacted that renunciation had to be made before three persons (Ned. 45a), so that it could be made public and people would be able to take advantage of it. Some scholars hold that the requirement of three witnesses is based on biblical law; others hold that in biblical law two witnesses suffice for this purpose, and that the need for three is a rabbinical enactment.

In the State of Israel, ownerless property belongs to the State, in accordance with the "State Property Law, 5711/1951." For acquisition of ownerless property, see Acquisition. For *hefker bet din hefker,* see Confiscation and Expropriation, *Takkanot*[1]).

Bibliography: Gulak, Yesodei, 1 (1922), 97 n. 1 and 4, 138–40; 3 (1922), 76 n. 8, 78 n. 4, 85f.; J. M. Guttmann, in: *Ve-Zot li-Yhudah . . . Aryeh Blau* (1926), 77–82; Herzog, Instit, 1 (1936), 287–96; S.S. Zeitlin, in: *Sefer ha-Yovel . . . Louis Ginzberg* (1945), 365–80; B. Cohen, in: *Israel* (Heb., 1950), 89–101; reprinted in his: *Jewish and Roman Law* (1966), 10–22 (Hebrew part); ET, 10 (1961), 49–95; S. Albeck, in: *Sefer ha-Shanah . . . Bar Ilan,* 7–8 (1970),94–116.

Shalom Albeck

1. page 548, 77.

LOST PROPERTY (Heb. *avedah u-meẓi'ah;* lit. "lost and found").

The Basis of the Law. Lost property, called *avedah,* is property which has passed out of its owner's possession and whose whereabouts are unknown to him. Both criteria must exist together for the property to be designated as an *avedah* (Rashi and Tos. to BM 30b, and see 31a). The Pentateuch enjoins that an *avedah* be returned to its rightful owner (Deut. 22:1–3). When the owner has clearly despaired of finding an *avedah* and of having it restored to his possession (see *Ye'ush*) his ownership in it ceases, and the finder is not obliged to return it but may retain it for himself (BM 21b). Even in the absence of the owner's *ye'ush,* the same consequence follows if there is no possibility of the *avedah* being restored to him (Tos. to BM 22b; Ran, Nov. Ḥul. 138b). The laws of *avedah u-meẓi'ah* comprise two categories: (1) laws forming part of property law, namely the determination of what constitutes an *avedah* and the point at which ownership thereof ceases so as to enable the property to be acquired by the finder *(zekhiyyah);* and (2) laws circumscribing the *mitzvah* of restoring the lost property, i.e., laws not appertaining to property law, since the finder who fails to return an *avedah* and who leaves it where it was found, transgresses the law but is not obliged to compensate the owner. However, the finder who takes an *avedah* and appropriates it for himself is considered a thief (BM 26b).

Avedah with Retention of Ownership. In accordance with the above definition, it may be noted that, for instance, an animal grazing on public land without the knowledge of the owner and where it is not kept from getting lost is considered an *avedah,* although not if it is grazing on a path when he is aware of its presence there (Ravad, in: Asheri BM 2:26). Similarly, a garment lying in a public thoroughfare is an *avedah,* but not one lying behind a fence (BM 31a). Nor would a vessel that is covered, even though found in a refuse heap, be deemed an *avedah* (BM 25b).

Restoration. The fact that an article has been lost does not in itself involve loss of ownership. Accordingly, a person who comes across property that appears to be lost is duty bound to take it into his custody and care until it can be restored to its owner. In certain circumstances, however, the finder is exempt from this duty. Thus a kohen is prohibited from entering a cemetery and therefore cannot be responsible for an *avedah* which he has seen there (BM 32a). Similarly a person is also exempt if he would not normally take the object, even if it were his own, such as an elderly person for whom such an action would be considered undignified (BM 30a). Furthermore, the finder of property which is of negligible value (i.e., less than a prutah; BM 27a), or a finder who would be involved in expense in restoring the property to its rightful owner (BM 30b), are also exempt. All other finders of lost property, however, must take charge thereof and seek out the owner, to whom it must be returned. Some scholars are of the opinion that the finder's degree of responsibility for an *avedah* – as long as it is in his care – must be the same as that of an unpaid bailee, while others equate the standard of care required to that of a paid bailee (BM 29a; see Bailment). In the case of an animal, if the expense of its upkeep should prove to be too high to make its return to the owner worthwhile, the finder may sell the animal after a certain period, but has to account for the proceeds to the owner (BM 28b). Inanimate property may not be used by the finder except to prevent its deterioration (BM 29b).

When the owner's identity is unknown to the finder, he must bring the *avedah* to the notice of the public, i.e., by announcing it. If the claimant owner offers notable identification marks *(simanim),* the property is returned to him, but if he is suspected of being an impostor he must also produce evidence of his ownership (BM 28b). Before the destruction of the Temple, the announcement was made from a stone platform in Jerusalem, during the three festivals when the people were gathered there. In later times the announcement was made in the synagogues and it was also enacted that, in places where the secular authorities expropriated all lost property, it would suffice if a finder made the matter known to his neighbors and acquaintances only (BM 28b). If no claimant responds to the announcement, the finder must retain the *avedah,* in trust for the owner, indefinitely (Sh. Ar., HM 267:15).

The *mitzvah* to restore lost articles to their owners is not limited to physical objects that are found, but it is extended to include the wider concept of preventing loss to one's fellow. Thus, if a man sees water flooding a neighbor's field and he is able to stop it he has a duty to do so; or if he sees an animal destroying a vineyard he has a duty to drive it away (BM 31a). Furthermore, this wider concept even extends to the person of an individual so that if anyone finds that another has lost his way, it is a *mitzvah* to set him right or to guide him as may be necessary (BK 81b).

Related to the *mitzvah* of returning an *avedah* is that of "loading and unloading" *(perikah u-te'inah),* which also involves saving one's neighbor from suffering losses. A person is required to come to the aid of a neighbor in the unloading and reloading of a heavily laden beast of burden (Ex. 23:5; Deut. 22:4; BM 32a–33a). In view of their common halakhic source, the laws of loading and unloading and of returning lost property are similar and interrelated (see Ḥ. Albeck, *Hashlamot* to *Mishnah,* BM 2:10).

Avedah with Loss of Ownership. When the owner despairs of having lost property restored to him, his ownership thereof ceases (see *Ye'ush*) and title to the property vests in the finder. *Ye'ush* may be inferred from speech or conduct, or may be assumed from the circumstances in which the lost property is found. For instance, an *avedah* which has no identification marks, or which is found in a public thoroughfare, or which appears to have been lost a long time before – factors which make it impossible for the property to be returned – are instances in which *ye'ush* would be inferred. Often it is doubtful whether under certain circumstances the owner is presumed to have despaired, and the sages disagree as to whether the finder has to restore the lost property or acquires ownership in it; e.g., where the lost property has identification marks but they are liable to be erased by being trodden upon, or when the property has marks which were not made intentionally, or whether the place in which the property was found can be an identification mark (BM 23a).

A second category of lost property which becomes ownerless and may therefore be appropriated by the finder, is that of *avedah mi-da'at* ("intentional loss"), i.e., when it appears from the circumstances that the property has been intentionally abandoned or thrown away by its owner and that he no longer desires it, e.g., scattered fruit on a threshing floor, figs which have dropped from a tree alongside a road, open jars of wine or oil left in a public place (BM 21a, 22b, 23b). Finally, lost property which can no longer be restored to its owner ceases to be owned by him and belongs to the finder, even if in the absence of the owner's *ye'ush.* Thus an *avedah* carried away by the river is lost to the owner and "to the whole world," even if the owner is unaware of his loss and even if he does not despair (Tos. to BM 22b). Some scholars nevertheless establish the owner's *ye'ush* in these circumstances, on which ground they justify the above rules (TJ, BM 2:1; 8b; Maim. Yad, Gezelah va-Avedah, 11:10). Similarly, geese and fowl which escaped from their owner and can no longer be restored to him belong to the finder (Ran on Rif Ḥul. ch. *Shillu'aḥ ha-Ken,* introd.).

In talmudic times it was already customary, as a matter of equitable law, to return certain classes of lost property, even if ownership thereof had already ceased, as in the case of an *avedah* dropped in a public thoroughfare (BM 24b). In post-talmudic times the communities of Europe adopted the practice of returning property carried away by a flood or similarly "lost to the world," either in terms of rabbinical enactments *(takkanot)* or in accordance with the principle of *dina de-malkhuta dina* (Mordecai, BM no. 257; Rema, ḤM 259:7; see also Bailment).

The laws of the State of Israel require all lost property to be handed over to the police, but the finder may claim it for himself if after a certain period the owner is not found.

Bibliography: T. Lampronti, *Paḥad Yiẓḥak,* s.v. *Avedah;* Gulak, Yesodai, 1 (1922), 137ff; 2 (1922), 190 n. 3; 3 (1922), 34, 40, 67f.; Herzog, Instit, 1 (1936), 299–317; ET, 1 (1951[3]), 11–15; 11 (1965), 53–100; H. E. Baker, *Legal System of Israel* (1968), 132–4; M. Elon, *Ha-Mishpat Ha-Ivri* (1973), II, 255ff, 281ff, 340ff, 564ff, 777ff.

Shalom Albeck

YE'USH (Heb. יאוש lit. "despair"), despair of property. A person's ownership of property ceases when it is apparent that he has made up his mind that the property will be out of his possession forever (see Ownership). This occurs (a) where he has indicated that he conveys the property to another in which case it ceases to be his the moment the latter acquires it (see Sale, Acquisition), (b) where he abandons it, or (c) where he despairs of it *(ye'ush),* thus ceasing to be the owner of it and no further act is required of him. *Ye'ush* means that under certain circumstances the owner indicates that he has lost all hope of recovering his property. *Ye'ush* is distinguished from acquisition and abandonment since it is only possible in respect of an object which is out of the "despairing" person's possession. Despair of an object still in the owner's possession is not considered *ye'ush.* Similarly, for property to be despaired of it must be against the owner's wish, for he despairs because the object has been lost or stolen; but if the owner gives up the object of his own free will, it is abandonment, and not *ye'ush. Ye'ush* may be apparent either from the owner's speech or behavior, or from the circumstances in which the right went out of his possession. In the first instance, if the owner has said: "What a misfortune that I have suffered a loss of money!" (BM 23a) he has indicated that he has despaired of recovering his money, and the same applies to any other expression having the same meaning. Similarly, if a river carries away logs and their owner does not pursue them, he has indicated his despair (BM 22a). In the second instance, if a lost object has no identification marks, it is presumed that the owner has despaired of it and that it has become ownerless *(hefker),* belonging to whoever finds it. This is also the case with an identifiable object which has been lost in a place frequented by the general public (BM 21b), or where a long time has passed since it was lost (Rashi, BM 23b). According to the Jerusalem Talmud (BM 2:1, 8b) and Maimonides (Yad, Gezelah 11:10), even property which is lost to its owner and to all persons, for instance if carried away by the river, may be kept by its finder, since the owner has given it up for lost. The circumstances in which the object is found create the presumption of *ye'ush* if most people would have despaired of the object in such circumstances; and it is immaterial that the owner protests that he had not given up hope, for it is presumed that surely in his heart he has, in fact, despaired. Even if he has not, the finder may disregard such an exceptional state of mind. If the circumstances are such, however, that most people would not usually despair, then *ye'ush* must be preceded by a specific act or speech by the owner (Maharik, no. 3).

Ye'ush does not require an act on the part of the despairer, only an indication of his state of mind, as is the case in all other cases whereby the ownership ceases by an indication of the owner's mind (abandonment and conveyance). Thus *ye'ush* cannot apply to the legally incompetent (BM 22b). The case where the owner cannot know that he has lost the object in circumstances that would usually result in *ye'ush*, is the subject of a dispute between Abbaye and Rava (BM 21b). According to Abbaye constructive *ye'ush* (i.e., if the owner does not know that he has a reason to despair) is not deemed to be *ye'ush* because, since the owner has not yet set his mind to the fact that the property is lost and irretrievable, the ownership thereof has not ceased. The finder will therefore gain ownership of the lost article only if he has found it after most people would have already known of its loss and despaired thereof. According to Rava constructive *ye'ush* is deemed to be *ye'ush* because, when the owner of the lost property learns of its loss, it is to be presumed that he will despair of it, and his reason for not yet despairing thereof is his ignorance of the true state of affairs. This dispute concerning *ye'ush* extends to acquisition as well, as in the case where a person confers property on another which does not belong to him without the knowledge of the owner, and the owner subsequently consents thereto; because acquisition, like *ye'ush*, is only the cessation of ownership by the owner's resolving that the property will never return permanently into his possession.

The concept of *ye'ush* is employed in the laws of lost property and in the laws of theft and robbery. In such cases the property goes out of the owner's possession and, accordingly, when it appears that the property will not be recovered by the owner, there is justification for *ye'ush*. Thereafter the finder or thief or robber acquired ownership of the property. According to Tosafot (BK 66a s.v. *Hakhi*) a finder who has taken lost property before any *ye'ush*, acquires it after there has been *ye'ush*, but has to pay the owner its value, in accordance with the laws of robbers. According to Naḥmanides (*Milḥamot ha-Shem*, BM 26b) if the finder takes the lost property with the intention of returning it, but subsequently changes his mind, the lost property never becomes his since the owner's *ye'ush* is, in fact, not *ye'ush;* but if the finder takes the lost property in order to keep it, he acquired it after there has been *ye'ush*. As to the laws of theft and robbery, various disputes are recorded in the Talmud, dating back to the day of the *tannaim*, as to when it was usual for a person to despair of converted property. There are some who think that only in the case of theft is there *ye'ush;* others contend that there is *ye'ush* only in the case of robbery; still others maintain that there is *ye'ush* in both cases. It is also disputed whether *ye'ush* is itself indicative of genuine despair in the owner's heart or whether a change of possession is also required (i.e., that the object pass into the hands of a third party), or a change of name (i.e., that the object becomes so transformed that people call it by another name) for the *ye'ush* to be genuine (see Theft and Robbery). In the law of the State of Israel *ye'ush* is of no consequence, and ownership does not cease as a result of despair.

Bibliography: J. S. Zuri, *Mishpat ha-Talmud,* 6 (1921), 57; S. S. Zeitlin, in: *Sefer ha-Yovel Levi Ginzberg* (1946), 365–80; B. Cohen, in: *Yisrael* (1950), ed. by A. R. Malachi, 89–101; reprinted Cohen's *Jewish and Roman Law* (1966), 10–22 (Heb. sect.; S. Albeck, in: *Sefer ha-Shanah Bar-Ilan,* 7–8 (1970), 94–116.

                                                                                                    Shalom Albeck

MAẒRANUT (Heb. מצרנות ,Abutter), the right of preemption available to the owner of land over the abutting land of his neighbor, when the latter is sold. The rule is not a provision of strict law but is derived from a rabbinical enactment to compel any prospective purchaser to yield to the abutting neighbor, in terms of the Pentateuchal injunction to "do that which is right and good in the eyes of the Lord" (Deut. 6:18; see also BM 108a and Rashi *ibid.*). For the other prospective purchaser does not sustain a great loss, since he will find land elsewhere, and should not burden the abutting neighbor with property in two separate localities. The right of the *maẓran* ("abutting neighbor") is a proprietary right *(in rem)* in the neighboring land itself *(Nimmukei Yosef* BM *ibid.*), similar to the right of a creditor in the case of lien or mortgage and other *jura in re aliena.* In applying this enactment, the scholars did not impose on the purchaser a duty to resell the land to the abutter, but rather endowed the abutter with the right to receive the land on the conclusion of the (putative) sale – without any additional act of acquisition being required – the purchaser thus becoming the agent of the abutter in regard to all the conditions of the sale to which the former agreed. Accordingly the purchaser is subject to all the laws governing an agent and holds the land in question on behalf of the abutter, the latter only acquiring actual title to it if and when he pays the price paid by the purchaser and fulfills the remaining terms agreed by the purchaser. As the abutter's right originates from the purchaser's obligation to "do what is right and good," if the latter is a non-Jew – to whom the obligation is not applicable – the corresponding right will also not accrue to the abutter (Rashi to BM 108b). The abutter also forfeits his preemptive right if he had indicated, by speech or conduct, that he does not wish to avail himself thereof (Sh. Ar., HM 175:32).

The abutter's right or preemption, being an application of the equitable principle to "do what is right and good," is a flexible right (Resp. Rashba vol. 1, no. 915) and does not prevail where it is not supported by the factors of "right and good." Thus the law of *maẓranut* does not apply if the exercise of the preemptive right would cause loss to the seller or purchaser or any loss to the public in general, or if the abutter were to derive no benefit therefrom. Consequently, the law of *maẓranut* is not applicable to a gift (BM 108b) as the recipient cannot get another gift in its stead and he would therefore suffer a loss (Ran, Kid. 59a). For the same reason the right of preemption is precluded when the purchaser is a woman since "it is not fitting for her to search in many places." Nor does the right exist in the following cases: when the purchaser is a co-owner of the land together with the seller, or if he is the mortgagee, for a sale of the land to such parties invokes the factors of "right and good" in their own cause; when the coins offered by the purchaser are of greater weight or more marketable than those offered by the abutter, for here the seller would lose; when all the seller's assets are sold to a single purchaser, lest the sale as a whole is prejudiced; when the landowner sells a distant field in order to purchase one that is nearer, or when the land is sold to defray funeral expenses or taxes or to provide maintenance for a widow, or when an orphan's land is sold, for in such cases the seller would suffer if he waited for the abutter. Furthermore, an abutter who wishes to cultivate the land must yield to a purchaser who wishes to build a house there, as public interest prefers habitation. Similarly, the preemptive right is excluded whenever its exercise would cause a loss in any other manner to the seller or purchaser, provided only that the judge is satisfied that there is no evasion of the abutter's right *(ibid.).*

The law of *maẓranut* is mentioned neither in the Mishnah nor in the Jerusalem Talmud, but only in the Babylonian Talmud by the *amoraim* of Babylonia. It may be assumed that in Ereẓ Israel conditions were not such as to justify the application of the preemptive right on the equitable ground of doing "right and good." The scriptural injunction teaches that the standards of proper conduct between man and his fellow are determined in accordance with the prevailing circumstances of the time and place and the scholars applying it created different rules accordingly (*Maggid Mishneh* to Maim. Yad, Shekhenim concl.). In post-talmudic times the right of preemption was customarily applied (in France, Germany, Spain, and in the Orient) and, in many places, also in relation to buildings even though it is doubtful whether the law was so extended in the talmudic period (*Piskei ha-Rosh* BM 9:34). In modern times the law of *mazranut* has been less and less frequently applied although the rabbinical courts of the State of Israel have given several decisions in which various problems have been determined in accordance with these laws.

In the State of Israel the law of *mazranut* was abolished by the Israel Land Law, 1969.

Bibliography: M. Bloch, *Das mosaisch-talmudische Besitzrecht* (1897), 59f.; ET, 4 (1952), 168–95; M. Silberg, *Kakh Darko shel Talmud* (1961), 105–110; M. Elon, *Ha-Mishpat Ha-Ivri* (1973), II, 513ff.

Shalom Albeck

SLAVERY.

BIBLICAL LAW

The Hebrew term for slave, *'eved* (pl. *'avadim*), is a direct derivation from the verb *'bd,* "to work"; thus the "slave" is only a worker or servant. The *eved* differs from the hired worker *(sakhir)* in three respects: he receives no wages for his work; he is a member of his master's household (cf. Gen. 24:2; Lev. 22:11; and see below); and his master exercises *patria potestas* over him; for example, the master may choose a wife for the slave and retains ownership of her (Ex. 21:4) and he has proprietary rights in him (see below).

Classification. The following classes of *'avadim* are to be distinguished:

Hebrew Slaves. A Hebrew could not become a slave unless by order of the court (for which see under Criminals, below) or by giving himself voluntarily into bondage (for which see under Paupers, etc., below; Yad, Avadim 1:1). Other slaves were always recruited from outside the nation. It has been opined that the epithet " *'eved 'ivri,"* and the laws relating to Hebrew slaves (Ex. 21:2–6) would apply also to such non-Jewish slaves as were born into the household as the offspring of alien slaves (see, for instance, Saalschuetz, *Das Mosaische Recht* (1853), Ch. 101).

Alien Slaves. "Of the nations that are round about you, of them shall ye buy bondmen and bondwomen. Moreover of the children of the strangers that do sojourn among you, of them may ye buy and of their families that are with you which they have begotten in your land; and they may be your possession" (Lev. 25:44–45).

Paupers and Debtors. A debtor who is unable to pay his debts may give himself in bondage to his creditor (cf. Lev. 25:39; Prov. 22:7; see also II Kings 4:1, Isa. 50:1; Amos 2:6, 8:6; Neh. 5:5). According to other opinions, the verse in Leviticus 25:39 deals with an ordinary pauper who sold himself and the debtor's bondage was against strict law, although it happened from time to time in practice (see Elon, *Ḥerut ha-Perat,* 1–10, and n. 9; Execution, Civil[1]).

Criminals. A thief who is unable to make restitution is "sold for his theft" (Ex. 22:2).

Prisoners of War. It would appear from Numbers 31:26–27 and Deuteronomy 20:10–11 that prisoners of war could be, and were, taken into bondage, though it has been contended that no prisoners of war were ever taken into private slavery (Kaufmann, Y., Toledot 1 (1937), 651).

Female Slaves. A father may sell his daughter into slavery (Ex. 21:7), usually apparently for household duties and eventual marriage (Ex. 21:7–11).

Children of Slaves. The Bible mentions "the son of thy handmaid" (Ex. 23:12), "he that is born in the house" (Gen. 17:12, 13; Lev. 22:11), indicating that the status of slaves devolved upon their children.

Termination of Bondage. Hebrew Slaves serve six years only and must be freed in the seventh (Ex. 21:2; Deut. 15:12). "And when thou lettest him go free from thee, thou shalt not let him go empty; thou shalt furnish him liberally out of thy flock, and out of thy threshing floor, and out of thy wine-press; of that wherewith the Lord thy God hath blessed thee" (Deut. 15:13–14; and see *Ha'anakah*). This short period of bondage conditioned the price of slaves. Whatever the master may have paid for the slave, "It shall not seem hard unto thee, when thou lettest him go free from thee; for to the double of the hire of a hireling hath he served thee six years" (Deut. 15:18). If the slave refuses to go free and wishes to stay on in his master's service, then the master pierces his ear with an awl and in this way the slave is bonded to him forever (Ex. 21:5–6; Deut. 15:16–17). If a Hebrew slave has been sold to an alien, he must be redeemed at once by a relative, failing which his servitude terminates with the Jubilee Year (Lev. 25:47–54).

Alien Slaves serve in perpetuity: "Ye may make them an inheritance for your children after you, to hold for a possession, of them ye may take your bondmen forever" (Lev. 25:46). The same rule would appear to apply to prisoners of war.

Debtors. Whatever the amount of debt for which the debtor sold himself he must be freed on the first ensuing Jubilee Year (Lev. 25:40). The same is true of a pauper. In that year he regains his lands and holdings (Lev. 25:10, 13) and can go back to his family and ancestral home (Lev. 25:41).

Female Slaves sold into bondage by their fathers go free if their master's sons deny them their matrimonial rights (Ex. 21:11).

Slaves must be released for grievous bodily injury caused to them: the master must let the slave go free "for his eye's sake" or "for his tooth's sake" (Ex. 21:26–27), if either be gouged out or knocked out by him.

Status of Slaves. Slaves are members of the master's household, and as such enjoy the benefit and are liable to the duty of keeping the Sabbath (Ex. 20:10, 23:12; Deut. 5:14–15) and holidays (Deut. 16:11–14, 12:18). They must be circumcised (Gen. 17:12–13); partake of Passover sacrifices when circumcised (Ex. 12:44), as distinguished from resident hirelings (Ex. 12:45); and may inherit the master's estate where there is no direct issue (Gen. 15:3) or perhaps even where there is (Prov. 17:2). Although slaves are the master's property (Lev. 22:11, etc.), they may acquire and hold property of their own; a slave who "prospers," i.e., can afford it, may redeem himself (Lev. 25:26; instances of property held by slaves are to be found in II Sam. 9:10; 16:4; 19:18, 30; cf. I Sam. 9:8). The killing of a slave is punishable in the same way as that of any freeman, even if the act is committed by the master (Ex. 21:20).

Treatment of Slaves. In the case of a pauper who sells himself into slavery or a man who is redeemed from bondage to a stranger, no distinction may be made between a slave and a hired laborer (Lev. 25:40, 53). A master may not rule ruthlessly over these slaves (Lev. 25:43, 46, 53). nor ill-treat them (Deut. 23:17); Ben Sira adds: "If thou treat him ill and he proceed to run away, in what way shalt thou find him?" (Ecclus. 33:31). A

1. page 621.

master may chastise his slave to a reasonable extent (Ecclus. 33:26) but not wound him (Ex. 21:26–27). The workload of a slave should never exceed his physical strength (Ecclus. 33:28–29). A fugitive slave must not be turned over to his master but given refuge (Deut. 23:16). There was no similar rule prevailing in neighboring countries (cf. I Kings 2:39–40). The abduction of a person for sale into bondage is a capital offense (Ex. 21:16; Deut. 24:7). In general, "thou shalt remember that thou wast a bondman in the land of Egypt" (Deut. 15:15), and that you are now the slaves of God Who redeemed you from Egypt (Lev. 25:55).

Implementation of Slavery Laws. From a report in Jeremiah (34:8–16) it would appear that the laws relating to the release of Hebrew slaves after six years' service were not implemented in practice: King Zedekiah had to make a "covenant" with the people that every man should let his slaves go free "at the end of seven years"; but hardly had the people released their slaves than they turned round and brought them back into subjection. In retribution for the failure to grant liberty to slaves, God would proclaim liberty "unto the sword, unto the pestilence, and unto the famine"; "and I will make you a horror unto all the kingdoms of the earth" (Jer. 34:17). According to Ezra (2:64–65) and Nehemiah (7:67), it would appear that in addition to the 42,360 people returning from Babylonia there were 7,337 slaves, male and female, and another 245 (or 200) musicians.

TALMUDIC LAW

Opinions are divided among modern scholars whether and to what extent slavery was practiced in post-biblical times. There is repeated mention of Tabi, the slave of Rabban Gamaliel (Ber. 2:7; Pes. 7:2; Suk. 2:1), and a freed slave formerly belonging to Tobiah the physician (RH 1:7) is also mentioned. In amoraic sources there are reports of cases of men selling themselves into slavery as gladiators (Git. 46b–47a), apparently from dire necessity (TJ, Git. 4:9, 46b). There is a strong talmudic tradition to the effect that all bondage of Hebrew slaves had ceased with the cessation of Jubilee Years (Git. 65a; Kid. 69a; Ar. 29a; Maim. Yad, Avadim 1:10), which would mean that from the period of the Second Temple the practice of slavery was at any rate confined to non-Hebrew slaves.

Classification. Hebrew Slaves. The term *eved Ivri* is reserved for, and identified with, a thief unable to make restitution who is sold for his theft or a pauper who sold himself into bondage (Kid. 14b; Yad, Avadim 1:1). This implies that a Hebrew slave may not be resold. The earlier Mishnah provides that a Hebrew slave may be acquired by the payment of money or the delivery of a deed of sale (Kid. 1:2).

Female Hebrew Slaves. Many provisions applying to slaves in general do not apply to female slaves. Thus, a woman may not sell herself into slavery (Mekh. Nezikin 3; Yad, Avadim 1:2), nor is a woman thief sold into slavery, even though she cannot make restitution (Sot. 3:8; Yad, Genevah 3:12). Contrary to an express scriptural provision (Deut. 15:17), a female slave's ear may not be pierced (Sif. Deut. 122; Kid. 17b; Yad, Avadim 3:13). The female Hebrew slave can only be a minor below the age of 12 years whom her father (not her mother: Sot. 3:8; Sot. 23b) has sold into bondage (Ex. 21:7; Ket. 3:8; Yad, Avadim 4:1); he may do so only when he has no other means of subsistence left (Tosef. Ar. 5:7; Yad, Avadim 4:2) and must redeem her as soon as he has the means (Kid. 18a; Yad, loc. cit.).

Non-Hebrew Slaves *(eved Kena'ani)* may be acquired by the payment of money, the delivery of a deed of sale, or three years' undisturbed possession (Kid. 1:3; BB 3:1) – to which were later added barter or exchange, and the physical taking into possession (Kid. 22b; Yad, Avadim 5:1; Sh. Ar., YD267:25).

Termination of Bondage. Hebrew Slaves. As well as release after six years' service or the beginning of the Jubilee Year, five more possibilities were added. The slave may redeem himself by paying his master part of the purchase price proportionate to the period served; for example, if he had been bought for 60 dinars and had served four years, he could redeem himself by paying 20 dinars, the whole period of service being six years. The redemption money is paid by a third person, either to the slave or to the master, on condition that it is used only for the redemption (Kid. 1:2; Yad, Avadim 2:8). A slave may be released by a deed of release delivered by his master (Kid. 16a; Yad, Avadim 2:12). He is released on the death of his master, provided the master left no male descendants (Kid. 17b; Yad, loc. cit.). Where the slave has had his ear pierced, he is released on the death of his master, irrespective of the master's surviving issue (Kid. 1:2; Kid. 17b; Yas, Avadim 3:7). Where the master is a non-Jew or a proselyte, the slave is released on his death (Kid. 17b; Yad, Avadim 2:12).

Female Hebrew Slaves. The provisions relating to release after six years' service, in the Jubilee Year, by payment, or by deed, also apply to female slaves. In addition, their bondage is terminated when the slave comes of age, i.e., shows "signs" of puberty (*simanim;* Kid. 1:2; Yad, Avadim 4:5), and by the death of the master, irrespective of the issue he left (Kid. 17b; Yad, Avadim 4:6).

Alien Slaves. For alien slaves the bondage is terminated in various fashions. Release may be by payment of money, the price demanded by the master being paid to him by a third party, either directly or through the slave (Kid. 1:3; Yad, Avadim 5:2). A deed of release may be delivered by the master (Kid. 1:3; Yad, Avadim 5:3). A verbal release, or a promise of release, is not sufficient in itself, but the court may enforce it by compelling the master to deliver a deed (Sh. Ar., YD 267:73–74). The slave is freed if the master causes him grievous bodily injury: the two biblical instances of gouging out the eye and knocking out the tooth are multiplied, and a long list of eligible injuries has been laid down (Kid. 24b–25a; Yad, Avadim 5:4–14; Sh. Ar., YD 267:27, 39). While the list in the codes was intended to be exhaustive, the better rule seems to be that all injuries leaving any permanent disfigurement are included (Kid. 24a). The rule is confined to non-Hebrew slaves only (Mekh. Nezikin 9); injuries inflicted on Hebrew slaves, male or female, are dealt with as injuries to freemen BK 8:3; Yad, Hovel 4:13 and Avadim 4:6). A slave may also be released if his master bequeaths him all his property (Pe'ah 3:8; Git. 8b–9a; Yad, Avadim 7:9; YD267:57). By marriage to a freewoman or by his de facto recognition in the presence of his master as a free Jew (e.g., using phylacteries and reading the Torah in public; Git. 39b–40a; Yad, Avadim 8:17; YD 267:70) a slave obtained his freedom. Marriage to the master's daughter may have been a not infrequent means of emancipation (Pes. 113a).

Status of Slaves. Discussions went on for centuries whether slaves, *qua* property, are to be regarded as belonging to the category of movables or immovables; Gulak (Yesodei 1 (1922), 92) held that originally they were likened to land and only much later to personal property. In effect, they were likened to land as regards modes of acquisition (money, deed, possession: Kid. 1:3), and in that they could not be the subject of theft or *ona'ah* or bailment (see Bailment; Sifra Be-Har 7:3; BM 4:9), but in other respects were treated as movables (cf. Tos. to BB 150a s.v. *avda;* Rashbam BB 68a s.v. *ella;* and see Herzog, Instit 1 (1936), 92–95. For the discussions on this question, see BK 12a; BB 68a, 150a; Yev. 99a; TJ, Kid. 1:3, 59df; etc.). Slaves may be mortgaged (Git. 4:4; BK 11b; HM 117:5; YD 267:68; and see Pledge). Slaves could be authorized to act as agents for their masters, and for certain purposes were so authorized by law or custom (Ma'as. Sh. 4:4; Er. 7:6; BM 8:3; Tosef. Pes. 7:4; BK 11:2–7; BK 119a; BM 96a, 99a; TJ, Er. 7:6, 246; etc.). Slaves could not act as agents for divorce (Git. 23b). Slaves could hold property of their own (Tosef. BK 11:1; Pes. 8:2; Shek. 1:5; Yev. 66a; TJ, Yev. 7:1; 8a; Tosef. Ar. 1:2; BB 51b–52a; Sanh. 91a, 105a; Ket. 28a; Meg. 16a; etc.), but they could not dispose of their property by will (Rashi and Tos. to Nazir 61b). A slave must be circumcised (Shab. 135b; Yad, Milah 1:3, YD 267:1).

A slave is not answerable for his torts, but when he comes into property after his release he may be held liable in damages for torts committed during bondage (BK 8:4). A slave has the right to stay in the Land of Israel, and may not be sold for export (Git. 4:6). If he is with his master abroad, he may compel him to take him to the Land of Israel (Ket. 110b; Yad, Avadim 8:9; YD 267:84), and he may flee with impunity to the Land of Israel, the prohibition on extradition (Deut. 23:16) being applicable to him (Git. 45a; Yad, Avadim 8:10; YD 267:85).

A slave may not be sold to a non-Jew: such sale is tantamount to the slave's release, and the vendor may be ordered by the court to repay the buyer not only the price he received but as much as tenfold of the price as a fine. When the slave is redeeemed in this way, he does not return to the vendor but goes free (Git. 4:6; Git. 44a–45a; Yad, Avadim 8:1; YD 267:80). Any slave – except a pauper who sold himself in bondage – can be married by his master to a non-Jewish female slave (Kid. 14b; Yad, Avadim 3:12). A bastard *(mamzer)* can legitimize his issue by marrying a female slave: her son would be a slave by birth and would become a pure freeman on his release (Kid. 3:13). A slave who has been jointly owned by two masters and is released by one becomes half-slave half-freeman; the remaining master may also be compelled by the court to release him (Git. 4:5; Yad, Avadim 7:7; YD 267:62–63).

Treatment of Slaves. The biblical "for to the double of the hire of a hireling hath he served thee six years" (Deut. 15:18) was interpreted as allowing slaves to be given double the work of hired laborers: while the latter work only during daytime, slaves may be required to work also at night (Sif. Deut. 123). The Talmud (Kid. 15a) states that this merely gives the master the right to give the slave a bondwoman in order to beget children. There is some early authority to the effect that a slave has no right to maintenance which can be enforced in law, notwithstanding his obligation to work (Git. 1:6; Git. 12a), the biblical "he fareth well with thee" (Deut. 15:16) being attributed to Hebrew slaves only (Kid. 22a). However, the predominant view, as expressed by Maimonides, is: "It is permissible to work the slave hard; but while this is the law, the ways of ethics and prudence are that the master should be just and merciful, not make the yoke too heavy on his slave, and not press him too hard; and that he should give him of all food and drink, and thus the early sages used to do – they gave their slaves of everything they ate and drank themselves, and had food served to their slaves even before partaking of it themselves . . . Slaves may not be maltreated or offended – the law destined them for service, not for humiliation. Do not shout at them or be angry with them, but hear them out, as it is written [Job 31:13–14]: "If I did despise the cause of my man-servant or maid-servant when they contended with me, what then shall I do when God riseth up? and when He remembereth what shall I answer?" (Yad, Avadim 9:8; and cf. YD 267:17). In another context, Maimonides says of the laws relating to slavery that they are all "mercy, compassion, and forbearance": "You are in duty bound to see that your slave makes progress; you must benefit him and must not hurt him with words. He ought to rise and advance with you, be with you in the place you chose for yourself, and when fortune is good to you, do not grudge him his portion" (*Guide* 3:39).

POST-TALMUDIC LAW.

Slavery became practically extinct in the Diaspora, and was prohibited except insofar as the secular laws allowed it, for instance, where rulers sold tax defaulters into bondage or offered prisoners of war for sale into slavery (Yad, Avadim 9:4; Tur and Sh. Ar., YD 267:18). However, it was laid down that even these "slaves" ought not to be treated as such, except if they did not conduct themselves properly (Yad, Avadim 1:8; YD 267:16). An incident related in the Talmud (BM 73b) was relied on as a precedent for the proposition that bondage may be imposed as punishment for misconduct (YD 267:15).

See also Execution (Civil); *Ha'anakah;* Labor Law.

Bibliography: Z. Kahn, *L'Esclavage selon la Bible et le Talmud* (1867; Ger. tr., 1888, Heb. tr., 1892); M. Olitzki, in: MWJ, 16 (1889), 73–83; M. Mielziener, *The Institution of Slavery Among the Ancient Hebrews* (1894); D. Farbstein, *Das Recht der unfreien und der freien Arbeiter nach juedisch-talmudischen Recht* (1896); S. Rubin, in: *Festschrift . . . Schwarz* (1917), 211–29; idem, *Das talmudische Recht auf den verschiedenen Stufen seiner Entwicklung mit dem roemischen verglichen und dargestellt,* 1 (*Die Slaverei,* 1920); J.L. Zuri, *Mishpat ha-Talmud,* 1 (1921), 29–31; 5 (1921), 122–33; Gulak, Yesodei, 1 (1922), 35, 38, 92; 3 (1922), 67; M. Lurje, *Studien zur Geschichte der wirtschaftlichen und sozialen Verhaeltnisse im israelitisch-juedischen Reiche* (1927), 49–55; A. Gulak, in: *Tarbiz,* 1 (1930), 20–26; 2 (1930–31), 246; Herzog, Instit, 1 (1936), 414 (index), s.v.; 2 (1939), 314 (index), s.v.; S. Assaf, *Be-Oholei Ya'akov* (1943), 223–56; J. Mendelsohn, *Slavery in the Ancient Near East* (1949); ET, 1 (1951^3), 74f., 77, 333f.; 2 (1949), 29–33, 320–2; 5 (1953), 727–42; 12 (1967), 720f., 738; M. Higger, in: *Mazkeret . . . Herzog* (1962), 520–3; S. Zeitlin, in: JQR, 53 (1962/63), 185–218; E.E. Urbach, *The Laws Regarding Slavery as a Source for the Social History of the Period of the Second Temple, the Mishnah and Talmud* (1964); M. Elon, *Ḥerut ha-Perat be-Darkhei Geviyyat Ḥov ba-Mishpat ha-Ivri* (1964), 1–17; B. Cohen, *Jewish and Roman Law,* 1 (1966), 159–278; 2 (1966), 772–7; K. E. R. Pickard, *The Kidnapped and the Ransomed* (1970).

Haim H. Cohn

IV. LAWS OF OBLIGATION; TORTS

Contents

Norms relative to various torts will be found in the section on Criminal Law, e.g. Theft and Robbery, et al.

OBLIGATIONS, LAW OF. This law is concerned with the rights of one person as against another *(jus in personam),* as distinguished from the law of property, which is concerned with a person's rights in a chattel or other property as against the world at large *(jus in rem).* Unlike Roman law, in Jewish law the mere existence of the obligation automatically creates in favor of the creditor a lien *(shi'bud)* over his debtor's property, a real right attaching to the obligation, which for a very long time was regarded as stronger than the personal right afforded by the obligation. The term *ḥiyyuv* originates in the word *ḥov,* meaning both the obligation which is imposed on the debtor (e.g., BB 10:6) and the right to which the creditor is entitled (Bik. 3:12; Git. 8:3). However, *ḥov* generally refers to a pecuniary obligation only, whereas *ḥiyyuv* has come to be used in a wider sense to include also the duty to perform an act, etc., comparable to the Roman law concept of *obligatio.*

The two parties to an obligation are the debtor (*ḥayyav,* BB 12b) – on whom the duty of fulfilling the obligation is imposed – and the creditor *(ba'al ḥov)* – who has the right to claim that the obligation be fulfilled. The term *ba'al ḥov* is sometimes used in the sources to describe the debtor as well (see Elon, *Ha-Mishpat Ha-Ivri* (1973), II, p. 483), which makes it necessary to exercise care in the use of these terms. It may be noted, too, that in Jewish law the term *malveh* ("lender") and *loveh* ("borrower") are not invariably used to denote an obligation arising from the transaction of a loan, but also to describe the parties to an obligation arising from any other transaction. This follows from the tendency in Jewish law to express a plain legal norm in concrete terms (e.g., *keren, shen, bor,* etc.; see *Avot Nezikin;* Introduction), and thus the transaction of loan *(halva'ah)* is used as a concrete illustration of a clear and common obligation (e.g., sections 97–107 of Sh. Ar., HM are grouped under the heading *Hilkhot Geviyyat Milveh,* even though they are not confined exclusively to the recovery of debts originating from loan). See Elon, *Ha-Mishpat Ha-Ivri* (1973); II, p. 483.

Creation of the Obligation. As in other legal systems, Jewish law recognizes the creation of obligations in two principal ways: (1) arising from contract, whereby one party acquires a claim of right against another which the latter is obliged to honor; and (2) arising from an act of tort (*nezek;* see Torts), whereby the conduct of one party causes another to suffer damage, so that the latter acquires a claim of right against the tortfeasor for indemnification in respect of the damage, which the law obliges the tortfeasor to honor. The first talmudic tractate of the order of *Nezikin,* namely *Bava Kamma,* deals mainly with the laws of obligations arising from tort, i.e., harm inflicted by one man on another's person (e.g., assault) or property (e.g., theft and robbery), as well as harm inflicted by means of one man's property *(mamon)* on the person or property of another. In this case the owner of the property is obliged to compensate the injured party for the damage suffered through his negligence in preventing harm arising by means of his property. The other two tractates, *Bava Meẓia* and *Bava Batra,* deal largely with obligations arising from contract. Jewish law distinguishes between the obligations arising from these two different sources, particularly from the point of view of the manner of recovery of the debt on the debtor's failure to make due payment of it in cash or chattels. Thus obligations arising from tort are recoverable from the best of the land *(idit),* whereas contractual obligations are recoverable only from land of average quality *(beinonit),* and the *ketubbah* obligation from the worst (*zibburit;* Git. 5:1; see also Execution, Civil[1]). Roman law in addition to a similar distinction between *obligationes ex contractu* and *obligationes ex delicto,* further subdivides the obligations into those which are quasi-delict and quasi-contract. Although Jewish law also recognizes quasi-contractual obligations, it does not employ the legal fiction of regarding these as arising, as it were, from a contract between the parties (as, e.g., in the case of the *negotiorum gestio*); the degree of liability imposed on the owner of a field toward one who "goes down to his field" and plants there without permission extends to the latter's expenses and, at most, to the value of the improvement from which the field has benefited (Tosef., Ket. 8:10, BK 10:7; Ket. 80a). See Unjust Enrichment.

Fines (kenasot). In the case of obligations arising from both contract and tort, the degree of liability is coextensive with the respective objective value of the contractual transaction or with the extent of the loss sustained as a result of the damage inflicted; this liability is called *mamon.* When the measure of liability does not correspond to the value or loss it is called *kenas* ("a fine"; e.g., BK 15 a–b and see Fines). Liability for such a fine may exist: (1) by the consent of the parties, i.e., their agreement to pay a certain liquidated sum upon breach of the contract; or (2) by operation of law, i.e., when the law provides for a measure of compensation that does not correspond to the actual loss caused by the act of tort (BK 15a–b). Such a fine by operation of law can take three possible forms: (1) the liability exceeds the actual damage (e.g., a thief being liable to pay double and four-or fivefold compensation: see Theft and Robbery); (2) the liability is less than the actual damage (e.g., where only half-damages are payable for a *shor tam* that has gored: see *Avot Nezikim*[2]); and (3) the liability is for a fixed and predetermined amount (e.g., in the case of defamation of a virgin: Deut. 22:19 and see also 29).

Imperfect (i.e., Unenforceable) Obligations. Jewish law recognizes the existence of two kinds of imperfect obligations. In the first category a legal obligation exists but the court will provide no remedy for the party seeking its enforcement. Thus in the case of fixed (direct) interest (*ribbit keẓuẓah;* e.g., 100 are lent so that 120 shall be repaid), which is prohibited by pentateuchal law, the lender is obliged to return the interest paid and it may even be reclaimed by the borrower through the court; if, however, the interest is indirect (*avak ribbit,* lit. "dust of interest"), which is forbidden by rabbinical law only, the borrower cannot reclaim the interest in court (BK 61b; Yad, Malveh 6:1; Sh. Ar., YD 161; and see Usury). Similarly, in all cases which are regarded as robbery according to rabbinical law only – e.g., when a person wins money in a game of chance (which is regarded as unjustified even if the loser consents) – the loser cannot reclaim the money in court (Sanh. 25b; Yad, Gezelah 6:6–16, and other *posekim,* see Elon, *Ha-Mishpat Ha-Ivri* (1973), I, 202ff). The second category of imperfect obligations derives from tort; regarding this it was prescribed that "the offender is exempt from the judgments of man but liable to the laws of heaven" (BK 55b), as for example, in the case of a man who bends his neighbor's standing grain toward a fire in such a way that the grain will catch fire if the wind changes or strengthens unexpectedly, although there is no such danger as long as the wind does not alter (BK 55b and codes; see further Law and Morality[3] and Elon, *Ha-Mishpat Ha-Ivri* (1973), I, 171ff for obligations carrying a moral or religious sanction only).

The Personal and Proprietary Aspects of Obligation in Jewish Law. Many ancient systems of law (e.g., Babylonian law, Assyrian law, the laws of Eshnunna) provided for the creditor's being able to secure repayment of his debt by enslaving the debtor or the members of his family (see Elon, *Herut ha-Perat* 3–8). According to the early Roman "XII Tables" and by means of the *legis actio per manus injectionem,* the creditor was even afforded the right, after certain preliminary procedures, of putting the defaulting debtor to death and taking his proportionate share of the body if there were several creditors. This "right"

1. page 627; 2. page 325; 3. page 155.

was abrogated by the *Lex Poetelia* and replaced by the possibility of imprisoning the debtor (see Imprisonment for Debt on the position in Jewish law).

On the other hand, Jewish law did not recognize any form of enslavement of the debtor's person (the bondsmanship referred to in the Bible is confined to two cases: one of the thief who lacks the means to make restitution (Ex. 22:2); the other of a person who voluntarily sells himself on account of utter poverty (Lev. 25:39)). The creditor is strongly adjured to act mercifully toward the borrower and not to take in pledge the latter's basic essentials nor to enter his house for the purpose of seizing a pledge (Ex. 22:24–26; Deut. 24:6, 10–13). If in practice the law was not always strictly observed and there were cases – due to the influence of surrounding legal customs – of enslavement for debt (II Kings 4:1; Isa. 50:1, etc.), such cases were roundly condemned by the prophets (Amos 2:6; 8:4–6) and it appears that after the sharp reaction of Nehemiah (Neh. 5:1–13) enslavement for debt was abolished in practice as well (Elon, *Herut ha-Perat,* 8–10).

The uncertain personal nature of an obligation in Jewish law led, in the second half of the fourth century, to fundamental differences of opinion on the substance of the borrower's personal liability to repay money to the lender. In the opinion of all scholars, restitution in the case of bailment or robbery constituted a clear legal obligation – since the bailor or the person robbed had a proprietary right in the property concerned. In the case of a loan of money, however, given in the first instance so that it could be used and expended by the borrower, in the opinion of R. Papa, the liability to repay the debt was no more than a religious duty (i.e., it was a *mitzvah* for a person to fulfill his promise and give effect to his statements (Rashi Ket. 86a)) and not a legal obligation. R. Huna, however, expressed the opinion – which was shared by the majority of the scholars and according to which the *halakhah* was decided – that the duty of repaying a debt was also a legal obligation. This personal aspect of the obligation is termed *shi'bud nafsheih* in the Talmud (i.e., pledging personal responsibility; see, e.g., Git. 13b, 49b; BK 40b; BM 94a; BB 173b). From the 11th century onward it seems, it was referred to as *shi'bud ha-guf* ("servitude of the person"), a term apparently mentioned for the first time in the statements of Alfasi (quoted in the Resp. Maharam of Rothenburg, ed. Cremona, no.146 and in greater detail in the statements of Jacob Tam cited in the commentary of Nissim Gerondi on Rif, to Ket. 85b; see also Contract).

The impossibility of securing repayment of a debt by enslaving the debtor created a need for the establishment of an adequate security, i.e., by charging the debtor's assets: land was well suited for this purpose since it could not be carried away and was not subject to loss or extinction. Hence the rule that, immediately a debt was created, the creditor acquired a lien over all the real estate possessed by the debtor in such a manner that the debt afforded the creditor not only a personal right of action against the debtor but also a right in the form of a lien over all his land. Land was accordingly termed "assets bearing responsibility" (*nekhasim she-yesh lahem aḥarayut;* i.e., guaranteeing the obligation of the debtor; Kid. 1:5; BM 1:6; BB 174a) and recovery therefrom was based on the creditor's charge and not on his right of recourse against the debtor personally. On the other hand, the debtor's chattels, being subject to loss and depreciation, were incapable of "bearing responsibility" for his obligation and were so termed (*nekahsim she-ein lahem aḥarayut;* Kid. 1:5), and the right of recovery from such assets was based on the creditor's personal right of recourse against the debtor (BK 11b; see also Lien[1]). The demands of developing commerce resulted in a substantive change in the concept of the contractual obligation in post-talmudic times; from an essentially real or property obligation it became an essentially personal one, with the property aspect subordinate to the personal. see Elon, *Ha-Mishpat Ha-Ivri,* I, 130ff.

Recovering Payment out of "Encumbered and Alienated" Assets (i.e., in the hands of a third party). The creditor's abovementioned lien over his debtor's property did not preclude the debtor from transferring the encumbered assets to a third party, except that any such transfer could be subject to the creditor's right to seize the assets from the transferee when seeking to enforce payment of the debt. At first this right did not extend to the debtor's chattels, since the creditor had no property right in them and his right of recovery from them derived merely from the debtor's personal obligation (see *Beit ha-Beḥirah,* BB 175b); thus they were beyond the creditor's reach once they had been transferred from the debtor's ownership (Ket. 92a). However, in the course of time and with the changes in the economic circumstances of Jewish life, this distinction between land and chattels underwent substantial changes. Similarly, the general lien on the debtor's assets gave rise to many problems, concerning both the need to protect trade *(takkanot ha-shuk)* and the rights of third party purchasers, as well as the question of securing debts for the benefit of creditors, concerning which various *takkanot* were enacted at different times (see Lien[2]).

Verbal and Written Obligations. Jewish law distinguishes between a verbal and a written obligation, termed in the Talmud a *milveh be-al peh* and a *milveh bi-shetar* respectively (BB 175a; see also Sh. Ar., HM 39:1, et al.). Although phrased in the language of loan, these terms are intended to embrace all obligations of whatever origin (see above). The distinction between the two forms of obligation relates to the weight of consequence accorded each one rather than to the substance of the obligation. This finds expression in two main respects: (1) a written obligation entitles the creditor to recover payment out of the debtor's encumbered assets which are in the hands of a third party, a right unavailable in the case of a mere verbal obligation, since here the obligation or debt has no *kol* ("voice") and does not provide notice that will put prospective purchasers on their guard; (2) in the case of a written obligation, a plea by the debtor that he has repaid the debt is not accepted without proof, whereas a plea of this kind is accepted without proof in the case of a verbal obligation (Shevu. 41b; Yad, Malveh 11:1, 15:1; Sh. Ar., HM 70:1, 82:1; see also Pleas).

The distinction between the two is not characterized by the mere fact of writing or its absence, and the fact that an obligation is recorded in a document does not of itself ensure the application of the special consequences attaching to a *milveh bi-shetar,* Thus, for example, an undertaking even in the debtor's own handwriting but not signed by witnesses will be treated as a *milveh be-al peh,* since only a properly written, witnessed, and signed obligation carries a "voice" and constitutes notice (BB 175b and codes). Similarly, since a written obligation affects the rights of the parties, it is not considered as such unless it has been drawn up and signed in accordance with the instructions of the parties (BB 40a and codes) and with the prior intention of constituting it a *milveh bi-shetar* and not simply an aide-memoire (Sh. Ar., HM 61:10). Contrariwise, it is possible that a wholly verbal obligation can be treated as a written one, as in the case of sale of land before witnesses when the purchaser from whom the land is seized may in turn exact the seller's responsibility to him out of encumbered and alienated assets sold by the latter (BB 41b). So too all verbal obligations claimed through, and upheld by, judgment of the court are treated as obligations by deed (BM 15a) which may be recovered out of encumbered and alienated assets, since in these circumstances they have a "voice" and

1. page 287; 2. page 290.

constitute notice even if they are not evidenced in writing.

The Parties to an Obligation. The capacity of the parties to an obligation or in any other legal act is dealt with separately in the appropriate article; see also Embryo and Legal Person.

From various scriptural sources it may be inferred that it is possible that an obligation may subsist toward a person unknown at the time (Josh. 15:16; I Sam. 17:25). This principle is also illustrated in this way: "he who says 'whoever shall bring me the tidings that my wife gave birth to a male child shall receive two hundred; that she gave birth to a female child a *maneh'*; [then] if she gives birth to a male he shall receive two hundred and if to a female child, he shall receive a *maneh*" (Tosef., BB 9:5; BB 141b). It was also followed in practice in the case of a deed granted by the community in respect of the right to collect a tax, in which the name of the grantee was not specified at the time of signature, it being provided that certain communal officials would determine the person to acquire the right (Resp. Rosh no. 13:20).

Plurality of Creditors and Debtors. Both possibilities are allowed for in Jewish law. Most sources indicate that each of the co-debtors is responsible for his proportionate share only; e.g., if they borrow in a common deed (Tosef., BM 1:21), or guarantee a single debt (Tosef., BB 11:15; but cf. Yad, Malveh 25:10 and Sh. Ar., HM 77:3 and commentators). In the same way a judgment of the court against one of the debtors does not of itself render the others liable (Rema, HM 176:25). Some scholars sought to infer from another source that each of the debtors is liable for the whole amount of the debt (R. Yose, TJ, Shevu. 5:1, 36a; *Piskei ha-Rosh,* Shevu. 5:2); but most of the *posekim* interpreted this source as prescribing that each of the debtors, in addition to the principal obligation for his proportionate share, is also liable as surety for the remainder of the debt upon default of the other debtors (Yad, Malveh 25:9; Tur and Sh. Ar., HM 77:1 and see also commentators); the *halakhah* was decided accordingly.

A similar rule prevails with regard to liability for damage jointly caused by several tortfeasors, namely the apportionment of liability according to the degree of participation of each (BK 10b and codes). Opinions are divided in the codes on the question of whether each of the tortfeasors is also liable as surety for the shares of the others (Tur, HM, 410:29 and Sh. Ar., HM 410:37). Similarly, when a debt is owed to a number of creditors jointly, each of them is entitled to his proportionate share. Any one of them may claim payment of the whole amount in circumstances where it can be presumed that he is acting as an agent for his fellow creditors with regard to their shares (Ket. 94a and codes). Where there is no room for this presumption and one creditor wishes to claim recovery of his share alone, two possibilities exist: if the share of each of the creditors is known, each may separately claim his own share, e.g., in the case where a creditor is survived by a number of heirs, each claiming his known share; if the proportionate share owing to each creditor is unknown, none may separately claim recovery but must be joined in his claim by the remaining creditors (Sh. Ar., HM 77:9–10 and *Siftei Kohen* ad loc., n. 25; Sh. Ar., HM 176:25). This is also the law when the debt derives from tort. See also Suretyship.[1]

Extinction of Obligation. An obligation is extinguished when it is fulfilled by the debtor, whether voluntarily or under compulsion by way of civil execution. (For the consequences of nonfulfillment of an obligation deriving from tort or contract see Damages; Torts; and Contract.) An obligation also becomes extinguished, even if unfulfilled, when a release is granted by the creditor to the debtor (see *Meḥilah*). According to pentateuchal law, a Jubilee year terminates certain obligations. Hillel the Elder and his court instituted the prosbul, whereby the obligation continues to exist and is not wiped out in the seventh year (see also Loans).

In the State of Israel. The law of obligations in the State of Israel is derived from numerous different sources: Ottoman and mandatory laws as well as Israel legislation. English common law and equity is a further source of the Israel law of obligation whenever there is a "lacuna" in the existing law (s. 46, Palestine Order in Council, 1922–47). In recent years there has been great and substantial legislation in this field, showing to a certain extent the influence of Jewish law. In some of these laws it is stated that the above section 46 no longer applies to them. See Contract[2] and Introduction.[3]

See further: Admission, Assignment; Bailment; Gifts; Labor Law; Lease and Hire; Maritime Law; Partnership; Sale; Servitude; *Shetar;* Suretyship.

Bibliography: L. Auerbach, *Das juedische Obligationsrecht,* 1 (1870), 159ff; I. S. Zuri, *Mishpat ha-Talmud,* 5 (1921); Gulak, Yesodei, 2 (1922), 3–30, 83–88; 105–18; idem, in: *Madda'ei ha-Yahadut,* 1 (1925/26), 46–48; idem, *Toledot ha-Mishpat be-Yisrael bi-Tekufat ha-Talmud,* 1 (*Ha-Ḥiyyuv ve-Shibudav,* 1939), 1–2, 15–52, 88–96; Herzog, Instit, 2 (1939); M. Silberg, *Kakh Darko shel Talmud* (1961), 71–75; M. Elon, *Ḥerut ha-Perat be-Darkhei Geviyyat Ḥov* (1964), 1–23; idem, *Ha-Mishpat Ha-Ivri* (1973), I, p. 130ff, II, 327ff, 476ff, 482ff, 741ff.

Menachem Elon

CONTRACT Heb. חוזה *ḥozeh*), in general law theory a legally binding agreement between two or more parties, in terms of which one party undertakes for the benefit of the other to perform or refrain from a certain act. As such, contract is the main source of the law of obligations. The scriptural term closest to this meaning is the word *berit* ("covenant"), although it occurs mainly in the sense of a covenant of love between man and his neighbor (I Sam. 18:3), or a perpetual covenant between the Almighty and man or the people of Israel (Gen. 9:9; 15:18; Ex. 31:16), as well as a covenant of peace between nations (Gen. 21:32; Judg. 2:2; II Sam. 5:3; Ezek. 30:5; Hos. 12:2). The word *ḥozeh* also occurs in Scripture, but not in any strict legal sense: e.g., ". . . with the nether-world are we at agreement" (Isa. 28:15). In the post-scriptural period no concrete legal significance was assigned to either of these terms, nor was there any embracing parallel term for contract in talmudic times (the word *kiẓa(h)* (Tosef. Ket. 4:7, et al.) is not a generic term for contract but represents a particular transaction only). In the rabbinical period (see Introduction), the term *hitkasherut* came into general use – a term rightly considered by Gulak to be a translation of the Latin *contractus* (from *contrahere,* "mutual binding together"), and one that aptly expresses the concept of contract. The term *ḥozeh* was used by I. S. Zuri (*Mishpat ha-Talmud,* 5 (1921), 1) as the equivalent of contract and this has come into general use in Hebrew legal parlance in the State of Israel.

The absence in Jewish law of a generic term for a concept paralleling that of contract in Roman law is apparently attributable to its preference for a concrete rather than abstract terminology (see Elon, *Ha-Mishpat Ha-Ivri* I, p. 132ff). The Jewish law principles of contract are to be gathered from the various laws of sale, lease, gift, loan, suretyship, etc. and from the additional special laws accruing in the course of time.

Creation of Contractual Ties. In ancient Jewish law it was possible for contractual ties to be created in various symbolic ways, such as by "removing and handing over the shoe" (Ruth 4:7; see also TJ, Kid. 1:5, 60c) and by handshake (*teki'at kaf,* Prov. 6:1; 11:15; 17:18; 22:26; Job 17:3; see also Ezra 10:19).

1. page 286; 2. page 255; 3. page 41.

The view of obligations as being of a concrete *(ḥefzi)* nature by giving the creditor a lien over the debtor's assets (see Obligations, Law of) resulted in the fact that the modes of creating contractual obligations came to be the same as those for the creation of ownership rights in property (see Acquisition). While Jewish law bases the conclusion of a contract on the *gemirut ha-da'at* (i.e., final intention or making up of the mind) of the parties to be bound, such intention may only be inferred from a formal and recognized *kinyan* ("mode of acquisition") executed by one of the parties. Hence, contrary to Roman law which allows for a contract to be concluded by the mere oral assent of the parties, Jewish law does not generally confer legal recognition on an obligation created merely orally (BM 94a; cf. Kid. 1:6; for exceptions to this rule, see below). Accordingly, the breach of a merely oral agreement involves "a breach of faith," carrying only moral sanction (BM 49a, opinion of R. Johanan, and Codes); and the obligation is not legally complete, even where the purchaser has paid the price but failed to observe the mode of acquisition proper to the transaction, and the sanction, if he should retract, is a "religious" one only: "He who punished the generation of the Flood and of the Dispersion will exact payment from one who does not stand by his word" (BM 4:2 and Codes). The reason for the existence of a religious or moral sanction in these circumstances is the underlying religio-moral duty of fulfilling a promise, i.e., an oral undertaking made without the execution of a formal *kinyan* (Ket. 86a; see also BM 9:7 and Pes. 91a).

Consideration. Jewish law attaches a great deal of importance to the existence of consideration in the creation of contractual ties, and in this respect shows an interesting similarity to English law (see Gulak, Yesodei, 2 (1922), 40ff). This requirement finds expression mainly in the fact that the contract is only concluded upon the actual passing of the consideration, such as the borrower's receipt of the loan money, or the performance of an act representing the receipt of the subject matter of the transaction by the purchaser, donee, hirer, or borrower. Even with regard to the creation of a bailment, which gives the bailee no right in the property itself or its fruits, it was laid down that an act of *meshikhah* (lit. "pulling," see Acquisition) of the subject matter established the obligation (BM 99a; see Bailment. Similarly, a contract of partnership for profit-making purposes is concluded when each of the partners performs an act of receiving part of the subject matter of the partnership belonging to the other partners – whether in money or chattels (Ket. 10:4) – the rule being: "partners acquire one from the other a common interest in the partnership capital in the same manners that the purchaser acquires [from the seller]" (Maim. Yad, Sheluḥin, 4:1). In the same way, a contract for the hire of a laborer is concluded upon the laborer commencing his work, the work being the contractual consideration (Tosef. BM, 7:1; BM 76b). None of the obligations normally deriving from any of the above-mentioned transactions, such as payment of the price by the purchaser and the seller's responsibility for the subject matter, or payment of the bailment money by the bailor and the obligation of the bailee to take care of the bailment, etc., will be legally binding on any of the parties, except upon their execution of the act of *kinyan* offering some exchange of consideration.

A number of contractual obligations were originally capable of being established merely orally – these cases being explained on the basis of a "spiritual" consideration. Thus, in the case of a dowry it was decided that the mutual promises of the parties achieved legal validity upon mere oral agreement ("matters concerning which *kinyan* is effected by a mere verbal arrangement," Ket. 102b); "owing to the pleasure in forming a mutual family tie, they finally make up their minds to allow one another the full rights of *kinyan.*" The distribution among the partners of partnership assets by lottery, even though effected orally only, was held to be legally binding for a similar reason (BB 106b). Similarly, the oral establishment of a suretyship obligation was justified because, "on account of the pleasure of being trusted [by the creditor, or court appointing him] he finally makes up his mind to undertake the obligation" (BB 173b, 176b).

The requirement of consideration for the creation of an obligation served to complicate the modes of formation of contractual ties, just as the need for real modes of acquisition complicated the manner of gaining a proprietary right. Beginning with the amoraic period, mention is made of "acquisition by the kerchief" *(kinyan sudar)* as a method both for the acquisition of a proprietary right and for the establishment of an obligation. This mode required that the promisee give the promisor some object belonging to him in return for which, as it were, the latter undertook the obligation; this procedure involved the handing over of a fictitious consideration – as the value of the object bore no relationship to the measure of the obligation and on completion of the formalities the object was returned to the promisee. Because it was convenient and easily executed, this procedure came to be widely followed from amoraic times onward as the mode of creation of different obligations (see BM 94a; BB 3a; etc.). In order to create mutual obligations between the parties, a *kinyan* would be effected by each in respect of his own undertaking.

Obligation by Admission (Hoda'ah) and by Deed. Admission offered a further means for the creation of an obligation without consideration. Originally admission was an aspect of the procedural law: i.e., a man's admission that he was indebted to another or that a specified object of his belonged to another was enough to establish liability without any further proof, in terms of the rule that "the admission of a litigant is as the evidence of a hundred witnesses" (Kid. 65b). Accordingly, admission created no new obligation but merely confirmed an already existing one. Out of the procedural form of admission, Jewish law developed an admission of a substantive nature capable of creating a new obligation, so that the mere admission of liability for an obligation established its existence without further investigation, even if it was known not to have existed previously (Ket. 101b). In the opinion of most commentators, obligation stemming from admission may be created orally (before witnesses) without any need for a formal *kinyan* even if it is known by both parties and the witnesses that there was not any debt in existence (Maim. Yad, Mekhirah, 11:15; Sh. Ar., HM 40:1). The scholars found a basis for the existence of a unilateral obligation in a suretyship undertaking (see Ket. 102b; Yad and Sh. Ar., loc. cit.; and Siftei Kohen, HM 40:1, n.7). Admission, like a formal *kinyan,* served not only to establish an obligation but was also a method of alienation *(hakna'ah)* of property (BB 149a); in both events it was required that an oral formula be adopted, making clear the fact of an admission (*kezot ha-ḥoshen,* HM 40:1). A written undertaking was also recognized by the majority of the commentators as a means of creating an obligation without consideration (Ket. 101b; BB 175b; Yad, Mekhirah 11:15; Sh. Ar., HM 40:1).

Obligations in Respect of Something Not Yet in Existence (Davar She-Lo Ba La-Olam). The tenet of Jewish law that a person cannot transfer title of something not yet in existence or not in his possession (*She-eino bi-reshuto;* see Acquisition), severely inhibited the development of trade. This problem was already referred to in tannaitic times in the statement: "one who declares, 'whatever I shall inherit from my father is sold to you, whatever my trap shall ensnare is sold to you,' has said nothing" (Tosef., Ned.6:7); if however he says: " 'whatever I shall inherit from my father to-day, whatever my trap shall ensnare to-day,' his statements are binding" *(ibid).* Although in both cases the subject matter of the transaction is not yet in existence, the rule in the latter case resulted from a rabbinical enactment aimed at providing the promisor with money for the burial of his dying father, or for his own sustenance on that day (BM 16a–b). Similarly, it may be inferred from the plain meaning of the statement: "whoever sells products to his neighbor believing them to be in his possession, and it is then found that they are not, the other [party] does not have to lose his right" (Tosef. BM 4:1), that the seller is still legally obliged to deliver products to the purchaser as undertaken (see also TJ, Ter. 6:3, 44b, statement of Abbahu). However, this *halakhah* was interpreted by the Babylonian *amoraim* as referring to the tradition of the moral sanction, "He who punished . . . " (BM 4:2) and not to a legal obligation (BM 63b; see also S. Lieberman, *Tosefot Rishonim,* 2 (1938), 111–2 on the wording of the Tosefta statement and attitude of the *rishonim* to it; cf. also BB 69b and Rashbam, ad loc.).

In the amoraic period an exception had already been stipulated to this general rule – something not yet in existence could be charged in a creditor's favor, even though no one could alienate it or transfer title to it; and the debtor could charge in favor of a creditor property which the former might acquire in the future (BB 157a and see Lien). Out of this proposition there developed, in relation to something not yet in existence, a basic and substantive distinction between a proprietary right and a right of obligation. Thus Solomon b. Abraham Adret (Rashba) made clear that a person who undertakes to give his neighbor all that he might earn in the following 30 days and charges all his property (whether existing or to be acquired in the future) to the latter is legally obliged to fulfill his undertaking, since this is not a case of transferring title of something not yet in existence, such as the fruit of the palm-tree, but a personal undertaking to give whatever the palm-tree shall produce during a specified period in the future; and "so far as obligations are concerned . . . the question of something that is not yet in existence is of no moment . . . because of the responsibility of the person himself" (Resp., vol. 3, no. 65; Rashba found a basis for the distinction in a man's undertaking to provide maintenance for a certain period which is valid even if he lacks the means for it at the time of the undertaking: Ket. 101b). The *halakhah* was also decided to the effect that the rule concerning something not yet in existence applied to a disposition couched in the language of sale or gift. If, however, it was couched in the language of obligation (e.g., "be witness that I oblige muself to *peloni* ["so-and-so"] for such-and-such," the obligation in question would be effective and binding (Tur. and Sh. Ar., HM 60:6), because "the obligation rests on his person and he is in existence" (*Sma*, HM 60:6, n. 18).

Substantive Change in the Nature of Contractual Obligation in Jewish Law. The distinction described above was a convenient way in which the contractual obligation could be used to meet the requirements of a developing commercial life. Although it had its roots in talmudic *halakhah* (Rashba, loc. cit. and see also *Sefer ha-Terumot,* no. 64:2), the distinction was apparently accepted as an explicit legal principle only from the 13th century onward (Maimonides, for instance, does not mention it at all). Until its acceptance, the main emphasis in regard to an obligation was placed on the real nature of the right of lien over the debtor's property, but recognition of the validity of an undertaking, even one relating to something not yet in existence, strengthened the personal aspect of the obligation, for it was founded on the actual existence of the debtor's person.

This concept was developed further during the same period. A corollary of the "real-right" aspect of an obligation had been the legal conclusion that an undertaking could not be legally created unless the promisor owned property at that time, which would become charged in favor of the promisee. The statements of the *amoraim* concerning the extension of the lien to include assets which would be acquired subsequent to creation of the debt meant that the lien would take in such assets in addition to those owned by the promisor at the time the debt was created. Arising from this, the tosafists discussed the validity of the then current practice of a bridegroom's written undertaking in favor of his bride, "for a hundred pounds even though he does not have a penny," and they confirmed this practice for the reason that, "the subjection of his person established the debt forthwith" (R. Elijah, Tos. to Ket. 54b; Rosh, *ibid.*). The result was to shift the emphasis in a contractual obligation to the personal aspect of the undertaking – "even for something he is not liable for and even if he has no assets, since he binds and holds responsible his own person" (*Beit Yosef,* HM 60, no. 15). This doctrine was even more explicitly enunciated by Moses Sofer in the 18th century (*Ḥatam Sofer,* nov. Ket. 54b). In this manner the contractual obligation underwent a substantial change, from being essentially real in nature to being essentially personal, with the property aspect subordinate to the personal.

The emphasis on the personal aspect brought in its train a series of additional halakhic rulings concerning contractual obligations. Thus, some of the *posekim* expressed the opinion that a person could validly give an undertaking in favor of someone not yet in existence – even though he was unable to transfer title in this manner – and hence it was decided, for example, that a stipulation in favor of a person yet unborn was binding "since the stipulator is at any rate in existence" (*Yad Malakhi, Kelalei ha-Dinim,* no. 127). Similarly, despite the rule that a person could not transfer title to an intangible thing, such as a right of usufruct or of occupation of a dwelling (Sh. Ar., HM 212:1 ff), some *posekim* expressed the view that a person could validly give an undertaking of this nature (Resp. *Naḥal Yizḥak,* 60:3). The majority of the *posekim* were of the opinion that a person could validly give an undertaking in regard to an unspecified amount, such as maintenance, to extend even for a period of unspecified duration (Resp. Rashba, pt. 2, no. 89; *Hassagot Rabad,* Yad, Mekhirah 11:16; Sh. Ar., HM 60:2; 207:21) and in the opinion of several *posekim* an undertaking could be given either to commit or to refrain from committing a certain act (Resp. Maharashdam, HM no. 370; Resp. Maharsham, pt. 2, no. 18).

Developments in the Formation of Contractual Ties by Way of Custom. As has already been stated, it has been a general principle of Jewish law that mere oral assent is not sufficient to constitute the *gemirat ha-da'at* of the parties, which is a fundamental requirement for the validity of any transaction involving a proprietary right or contractual obligation and is complete only when expressed in one of the recognized modes of acquisition or accompanied by the existence of some "spiritual" consideration, except for certain exceptions laid down in talmudic law (as in the case where the parties are husband and wife or parent and child, BK 102b and Nov. Rashba, ad loc.; also in other special cases, Bekh. 18b and Tos.; see also *Ḥazon Ish,* BK no. 21:5).

By means of the legal source of custom *(minhag),* Jewish law came to recognize a way of creating orally a legally valid transaction. According to talmudic law, the existence of a trade custom whereby a transaction was concluded by affixing a mark *(sitomta)* on a barrel of wine was sufficient to render the sale legally complete, despite the absence of a *meshikhah* – the recognized mode of acquiring movable property (BM 74a). This rule was justified on the grounds that "custom abrogates the law in all matters of *mamon*" (i.e., monetary matters or the civil law; see *Minhag*[1]) and therefore "acquisition is made in all manners customary among the merchants" (Rashba, nov. BM, 74a). In the course of time it was decided, in line with the above principle, that a transaction concluded by way of a handshake or the payment of earnest money (*demei kadimah,* Piskei Rosh BM 74a) or the delivery of the key to the place of storage of the goods, enjoyed full legal validity if based on a local mercantile custom (Sh. Ar., HM 201). From the 13th century on the question was discussed whether a transaction concluded merely orally on the strength of local custom could be afforded full legal validity. Asher b. Jehiel was of the opinion (Resp. 12:3) that an analogy could be made with the law of *sitomta* only so far as a custom provided for the performance of some act, like those mentioned above; but mere words alone could not suffice to conclude a transaction. In his opinion a custom of this nature could not override the basic attitude of Jewish law in requiring active formal expression of the *gemirat ha-da'at* of the parties, and custom could not only vary the essential nature of the formal act. An opposing opinion was expressed by Meir b. Baruch of Rothenburg (and R. Jehiel, quoted in *Mordekhai,* Shab., sec. 472–3) to the effect that the very existence of a custom to conclude a transaction orally justified the assumption that complete *gemirat ha-da'at* could also result from the use of words alone. This view was accepted in most of the Codes and confirmed, inter alia, in relation to an undertaking to perform a *mitzvah* (e.g., at a circumcision ceremony: Resp. Radbaz, pt. 1, no. 278) and to formation of a partnership, it having been decided that, despite the need for a formal *kinyan,* if there was a custom of establishing partnership by oral agreement, such agreement was sufficient, since "custom is a major factor in civil law" (*ibid.,* no. 380). This view was also accepted by the later *posekim* (see *Kesef ha-Kodoshim* 210:1), and in terms of this full validity was afforded to public sales (*Misphat u-Ẓedakah be-Ya'akov,* pt. 29 no. 33), to sales on the exchange (Resp. Maharsham, pt. 3 no. 18), and to similar transactions decreed by custom to be capable of being created in mere oral form.

Freedom of Stipulation. According to ancient *halakhah,* a condition stipulated by the parties that was contrary to the recognized provisions of the law was invalid: "any condition contrary to what is written in the Torah is void" (BM 7:11) – even in matters of civil law. For this reason a condition that the firstborn (see Firstborn) should not inherit a double portion or that a son should not inherit together with his brother was void (BB 126b and see Succession; the explanation given for a distinction in regard to matters of succession does not accord with the plain meaning of the Mishnah). This was still the view of Simeon b. Gamaliel (Ket. 9:1) and R. Meir (Ket. 56a) around the middle of the second century. At this time R. Judah expressed the view that only in matters of ritual law *(dinei issura,)* was it forbidden to contract out of the Pentateuchal law, such as a condition exempting a wife from the need to undergo a levirate marriage on her husband's death. In matters of *mamon,* however, such as a wife's right to maintenance, a condition would be valid: "this is the rule: any condition contrary to what is written in the Torah is valid if relating to a matter of *mamon;* if relating to a matter other than *mamon,* it is void" (Tosef. Kid. 3:7–8, Ket. 56a). This view was also followed by the scholars who stated that the husband's right of succession could properly be varied by contract (Ket. 9:1) and that a bailee could stipulate for a different measure of liability than that provided for in the Torah (BM 7:10).

The *amoraim* developed the view that regarded matters of ritual law as being in the nature of *jus cogens* and therefore not subject to contrary stipulation; unlike matters of civil law, which were regarded as being in the nature of *jus dispositivum* (Ket. 83b–84a; BM 51a–b; TJ, Ket. 9:1 32d; BB 8:5). The law was decided accordingly in the Codes (Yad, Ishut, 12:7–9; Shemittah, 9:10; Mekhirah, 13:3–4; Sh. Ar., EH 38:5, HM 67:9, 227:21) Hence the rule in Jewish law is that in matters falling within the purview of the civil law, the Torah itself prescribed no obligatory rules and therefore "a party may make a waiver [i.e., contract out] since the Torah does not require him to give an undertaking save of his own free will" (Nov. Ramban, BB 126b). A necessary requirement is that the condition be worded in the proper form; e.g., "on condition that *you* shall have no [complaint of] overreaching *[ona'ah]* against *me*" and not, "on condition that there shall not be any overreaching in the deal" (Mak. 3b, Rashi and Tos. *ibid.,* and Codes.)

Matters excluded, as a matter of principle, from being the subject of a stipulation include an agreement to submit to bodily injury or the curtailment of personal liberty. Hence an agreement to cut off another party's hand or put out his eye, even though they might be causing him pain, is void (BK 8:7 and TJ, BK 8:11, 6c; but cf. Tosef. BK 9:32). This applied even in the case of an ordinary beating – concerning which the opinion was expressed that as it did not amount to serious bodily harm no compensation was payable in respect of it (BK 93a; Resp. Ribash, no. 484 and see below Illegal Contracts). Similarly, a condition that the creditor shall have the right to imprison the debtor on his failure to repay the debt is invalid, since the imprisonment of an indigent debtor for non-payment is an infringement of his personal liberty (see Imprisonment for Debt). In this connection, the scholars disputed the validity of an agreement between husband and wife not to cohabit with one another: the opinion in the Jerusalem Talmud was in favor of it being upheld as valid (BM 7:10, 11c), and this was followed by some of the *rishonim* (see *Oẓar ha-Ge'onim,* 8 (1938), 168 (first pagination) and commentary of Rabbenu Hananel, *ibid.,* 45); other *rishonim,* however (Rashi to Ket. 56a) and the *posekim* (Yad, Ishut, 6:9–10; Sh. Ar., EH 38:5; 69:6) held such a condition to be invalid since it was a *tenai she-ba-guf* (i.e., a condition involving bodily suffering).

The scholars further restricted the freedom of stipulation in matters where they saw the need for enforcement and preservation. Thus it was decided that a stipulation between husband and wife that she should forego her *ketubbah* is void (Ket. 56b and Sh. Ar., EH 69:6). Similarly, a stipulation of the parties that they shall submit to the jurisdiction of a gentile court even in monetary matters was held to be invalid, as it was regarded as tending to undermine Jewish judicial institutions (see Tur, *Beit Yosef,* and Sh. Ar., HM 26). The scholars also expressed different opinions on freedom of stipulation in certain fields of the law such as suretyship and succession (Yad, Nahalot 6:1; cf. the sources of Maimonides' statements, which are contradictory to the plain meaning of the talmudic statements, in Meiri to BB 126b). A stipulation contrary to good public order and morals is also void. On this ground Ḥayyim Jair Bacharach decided that an agreement between local clothiers to refrain from suing each other on a complaint of unfair competition, trespass, etc., was void, since this could only lead to increased strife and disturbance of the public order (*Ḥavvat Ya'ir,* no. 163).

Illegal Contracts. Different systems reflect a varying approach to the question of illegal contracts, such as one involving the commission of a criminal offense or one made for an illegal purpose. Some European legal systems hold such contracts to be null and void *ab initio,* whereas English law does not void them initially but prescribes that the courts shall not enforce them or grant the parties any relief, all in terms of the two Roman Law

1. page 97.

maxims: *ex turpi causa non oritur actio* and *in pari delicto melior est pars possidentis.*

Jewish law reveals a materially different approach. Although fulfillment of a contract is not prescribed if this should involve the actual commission of an offense or transgression, the fact that it has been committed does not deprive the contract of its legal validity or preclude the court from granting relief in terms of it. Thus, in a transaction concerning lending at interest, prohibited by the Pentateuchal law to both lender and borrower (BM 61a and Codes; see Usury[1]), the lender cannot claim payment of the interest according to the agreement, since this involves the perpetration of the transgression itself, but the borrower may claim a refund of interest already paid by him, despite his transgression. Similarly, if the borrower has given the lender some object as a payment in lieu of interest money, the former may only claim the return of the amount of the interest but not the object itself, since "the transaction is binding and cannot be voided because it is in contravention of a prohibition" (BM 65a–b, Rashi and *Piskei ha-Rosh, ibid.*). In the opinion of R. Meir, the effect of a bond of indebtedness that includes interest is to fine the lender by precluding him not only from recovering the interest but also the principal (BM 72a); the *halakhah,* however, was decided according to the view of the other scholars, namely that the lender could recover the principal but not the interest (Yad, Malveh 4:6) except if in the bond an aggregate amount appears from which the separate amounts of principal and interest cannot be established (Sh. Ar., HM 52:1). The law was similarly decided with regard to any transaction prohibited in part; namely that the transaction is valid except that the illegal part must be severed from it (Sh. Ar., HM 208:1 and Rema thereto).

This basic approach was also followed in Maimonides' ruling that: "if a person sells or gives on the Sabbath, and certainly on festivals, even though he should be flogged, his act is effective" (Yad, Mekhira 30:7); so too with regard to an obligation contracted on the Sabbath: "if anyone performs a *kinyan* on the Sabbath, the *kinyan* is valid and the writing and handing over take place after the Sabbath" (Yad *ibid.;* Sh. Ar., HM 195:11; 235:28). This was held to be the case even with regard to a *kinyan* involving the desecration of the Sabbath according to Pentateuchal law (BK 70b).

This approach of Jewish law to the question of a contract involving a transgression illustrates its capacity to distinguish between the "legal" and the "religious" aspects of the *halakhah,* notwithstanding their common source and it is precisely because of the material link between law and morals that Jewish law deprives the transgressor of those addition "benefits" which result from the invalidation of the civil aspects of the contract. For the same reason the court will not grant relief to a party whenever enforcement of a transaction will, in the prevailing social circumstances, amount to an encouragement of criminal conduct. Thus the court will not order the refund of money paid for the procurement of false testimony, if the witness should fail to testify falsely (*Shevut Ya'akov,* vol. 1, no. 145; see also *Pitḥei Teshuvah,* HM 32:2, no. 1). A similar decision was given by the Great Rabbinical Court in a matter involving the contravention of the currency regulations in Ereẓ Israel (OPD, 63).

Stipulations in Favor of a Third Party. Unlike some legal systems, Jewish law shows no hesitation in recognizing the validity of a stipulation in favor of a person who is not party to the contract, provided that it confers a benefit and does not impose an obligation on him. In tannaitic times this rule was expressed in the doctrine that: "a benefit may be conferred on a person in his absence, but an obligation cannot be imposed on him in his absence" (Git. 1:6; BM 12a; etc.). The phrase "in his absence" *(she-lo be-fanav)* has been interpreted in the sense of *she-lo mi-da'ato* (i.e., without his knowledge or consent, Rashi to BM 12a). When the stipulation comes to the knowledge of the third party, he has the option either to accept it – in which case he may demand fulfillment by the promisor – or to reject it, since "a person cannot be compelled to accept a gift" (Yad, Zekhiah, 4:2 and *Maggid Mishneh;* Tur and Sh. Ar., HM 243:1–2; Sh. Ar. ḤM 190:4 in *Keẓot ha-Ḥoshen* 2. See also Agency.).

Specific Performance. Each party to a contract must fulfill his obligations under the contract, from which he is exempt only in the event of *ones* ("inevitable accident or duress") and the court will generally oblige the parties to render specific performance of their contractual obligations. Hence, the sale of an object to someone other than the party to whom the vendor had previously undertaken, in a valid contract, to sell the same object at a determined price, will be set aside and the object given to the party with whom the undertaking was originally made (Av. Zar. 72a and Codes; *Torat Emet,* no. 133). If, however, the vendor has worded his undertaking thus: "If I sell, I shall sell to you at such and such a price," and later sells the same object to someone else at a higher price, the sale to the latter will be valid, since the vendor made his prior undertaking conditional on his desire to sell, and "he did not desire to sell, but sold only because of the increment given by the other, placing him in the position of one who sold under duress" (Yad, Mekhirah, 8:7, Resp. Maharik, no. 20).

In the opinion of some of the *posekim,* specific performance is not ordered unless the claimant is in possession of the object which the vendor undertook to sell to him (Rashba and author of the *Ittur,* quoted in *Maggid Mishneh* to Yad, Mekhirah 8:7). However, the majority opinion in the Codes is that specific performance is granted even if the claimant is not in possession of the subject matter of the contract (see Tur, HM 206 and *Baḥ* thereto, no. 1). The opinion was also expressed that both Rashba and the author of the *Ittur* were in favor of compelling specific performance, even if the subject matter of the undertaking was not in the claimant's possession, in the case of an undertaking worded in the terms: "I bind myself to sell the object to you" (Resp. *Torat Emet,* no. 133). Specific performance is not dependent on the prior payment of the purchase price and the contract must be executed even if the parties have entrusted other persons, or the court, with the determination of the purchase price (Av. Zar. 72a and Codes, *ibid.*).

Specific performance is not granted on contracts for personal service, such as a contract of employment, since compelling a person to work against his will involves an infringement of his personal liberty and a form of disguised slavery (BM 10a). This is even more so because of the general attitude of Jewish law that any engagement of a laborer, even of his own free will, is a form of restraint on personal liberty; thus the laborer has special rights for his protection (BM 10a; 77a; see also Labor Law). Specific performance will be ordered, however, in the case of a contract of employment relating to a public service, if a breach of this would be harmful to the public. Thus, on the eve of a festival, if no other is available, a public bath-attendant, barber, or baker "may be restrained until he finds someone to replace him" (Tosef., BM 11:27; see also Resp. Maharam of Rothenburg, ed. Prague, no. 1016). Specific performance is accordingly recognized as a function of the law itself and not as a matter of equity, as in English law – from which Jewish law also differs in several other important respects on this subject.

Compensation and Penalty for Breach of Contract. Breach of contract renders the party in breach liable for the resulting damage, which, in talmudic times, generally included only

1. page 501.

compensation for the damage directly suffered by the other party and not for the loss of profit which, but for the breach, he would have earned. Since post-talmudic times, however, the tendency has been to extend liability in certain circumstances to cover also the loss of anticipated profits. Liability of this kind – i.e., consequential damages – is based on a category of damage known as *garmi* (see *Gerama*), or stems from an implied condition imputing an agreement between the parties to be liable to each other for the loss of profits in the event of either of them breaking the contract (see e.g., the statements of R. Jeroham, quoted in *Beit Yosef,* Tur, HM 176 no.21; HM 176:14). In order to bolster the effectiveness of contractual obligations, the practice was adopted from tannaitic times of specifying in the contract a fixed amount to be payable on breach of the contract by one of the parties (see e.g. Ned. 27b; BB 10:5). The question arose, however, whether such an undertaking was not to be regarded as defective on the grounds of *asmakhta* (an undertaking to forfeit an asset upon nonfulfillment of a condition). Since the founding basis of a contract in Jewish law is the *gemirat ha-da'at* of the parties to be bound, the scholars debated the validity of the additional undertaking to pay a fixed amount by way of a penalty, which they regarded as having been given solely on the strength of a "confident reliance" by the promisor on his ability to fulfill the principal contractual obligation, without his contemplating the possibility of having to fulfill the penalty obligation (BB 168a). The question was decided to the effect that in certain circumstances such an undertaking would be void for reasons of *asmakhta,* primarily if it appeared that the amount stipulated was exaggerated and beyond any reasonable estimate of the damage suffered by the other party and this would imply the lack of any serious intention by the promisor (BM 104b and Codes.).

The development of commercial life spurred on the search for a way of overcoming the invalidating effect of *asmakhta* on contractual stipulations. In talmudic times it had been decided that an undertaking effected by way of a formal *kinyan* before a court of standing excluded it from the operation of the law of *asmakhta* since in this manner the undertaking made with a complete *gemirat ha-da'at* would be clear (Ned. 27b and Codes). In the post-talmudic period the process of avoiding the invalidating effect of *asmakhta* on a penalty-undertaking was furthered by the enactment of a *takkanah* by the scholars of Spain. Thus the parties might undertake to pay each other, unconditionally, an amount specified in advance, each agreeing in advance to release the other from this undertaking in the event of the fulfillment of the principal obligation under the contract. Since, in terms of the *takkanah,* the undertaking to pay the amount fixed in advance is an unconditional one, it is valid and unaffected by the defect of *asmakhta* (Yad, Mekhirah 11:18; Tur and Sh. Ar., HM 207:16). Another way that was found to avoid the effect of *asmakhta* was by strengthening the penalty-undertaking with a vow, oath, or ban (Sh. Ar., HM 207:19). It was also decided that the law of *asmakhta* did not apply to certain obligations, such as an undertaking to pay a penalty for breach of a marriage promise (see Betrothal) or for breach of contract by a teacher without his finding a replacement, these being valid undertakings.

In the State of Israel. In Israel until recently the law of contract was based on various different sources – Ottoman and Mandatory law, as well as legislation after the foundation of the state. English Common Law and Equity represented an important source of the law of contract in Israel in all cases where the existing law provides no answer to the problems that arise (i.e., *lacunae;* cf. 46, Palestine Order in Council, 1922–1947). Various directions in the law of contract have been included in a number of laws of the Knesset and recently a substantial change took place through the passage of two laws in the Knesset: The Law of Contract (Remedies for Breach of Contract) 1970, and the Law of Contract (General Part) 1973. These deal with substantial parts of the general problems of the Law of Contract. Both these laws contain a direction which nullifies a considerable sector of the Ottoman Law in these fields, and also a special section directing that the above section 46 of the Palestine Order in Council which states that English Law is to be a source for any *lacunae,* does not apply to the subjects dealt with in these two laws (see section 24 of the first law and section 63 of the second law). Several of the principles in these two laws are influenced by Jewish Law.

See also Mistake and *Ones.* On specific contracts, see Admission; Bailment; Betrothal; Gift; Labor Law; Lease and Hire; Loan; *Meḥilah;* Obligations, Law of; Partnership; Sale; Suretyship; Unjust Enrichment.

Bibliography: M. Bloch, *Das Vertrag nach mosaisch talmudischem Rechte* (1893); Gulak, Yesodei, 2 (1922), 10–12, 31–82, 147–200; idem, *Toledot ha-Mishpat be Yisrael,* 1 (1939), 15ff; Herzog, Instit, 2 (1939), 19ff; A. Shaky, in: *Sugyot Nivḥarot be-Mishpat* (1958), 470–508; B.-Z. Schereschewsky, *Kenas ve-Pizzuyim Ekev Hafarat Ḥozim Lefi Dinei Yisrael* (1950), 3–12; ET, 7 (1956), 138–49; 11 (1965), 245–59; B. Rabinovitz-Teomim, *Ḥukkat Mishpat* (1957), 2–4, 247–56, 269–73; M. Silberg, *Kakh Darko shel Talmud* (1961), 82–88; M. Elon, *Ḥerut ha-Perat be-Darkhei Geviyyat Ḥov ha-Mishpat ha-Ivri* (1964), 68ff; idem, in: ILR, 4 (1969), 96, 98; idem, *Ha-Mishpat Ha-Ivri* (1973), I, 130ff, 159ff, 163ff, 171ff, II, 327ff, 476ff, 482ff, 575ff, 741ff; H. E. Baker, *Legal System of Israel* (1968), 101–9; I. S. Zuri, *Mishpat ha-Talmud,* 5 (1921); Sh. Warhaftig, *Dinei Ḥozim Ba-Mishpat Ha-Ivri* (9174).

Menachem Elon

BAILMENT. The law relating to a bailee (i.e., one who is entrusted with the money or chattels of another) is first given in the Torah (Ex. 22:6–14) in several statements of principle from which have been deduced the three categories of bailee, known as the *shomer ḥinnam;* the *shomer sakhar;* and the *sho'el.*

The Shomer Ḥinnam. The *shomer ḥinnam* (שומר חנם , lit. "an unpaid bailee") is based on the first case cited in the Torah of one who is given "money or stuff" to look after (Ex. 22:6–8). Such a bailee is not liable to the owner in the event of the goods being stolen (and the thief not apprehended), provided that he confirms on oath before the court that he had not embezzled or otherwise converted the goods to his own use (*lo shalaḥ yado,* lit. "not put forth his hand"). In fact, his duty of care is minimal and his liability is limited only to cases where loss resulted from his own negligence (cf. BM 3:10; Sh. Ar., HM 291:1). Thus, in the absence of proven negligence and subject to his taking the prescribed judicial oath, he would also not be liable for loss caused by inevitable accident or unforeseeable damage (i.e., *ones;* Yad, Sekhirut, 1:2 and 3:1ff; Sh. Ar., HM 291:6 and 9). It was such leniency which led to this particular portion of the text being construed as relating to the *shomer ḥinnam* (Yad, loc cit. 1:2) compared with the higher duty of care imposed on the *shomer sakhar* (cf. Laws of Hammurapi, 125, 263–7). On the other hand, any bailee, even a *shomer ḥinnam,* who meddles with the deposited article without the owner's authority is considered guilty of theft (i.e., larceny by conversion; see Theft and Robbery) and is consequently liable for any subsequent loss. Indeed, according to Bet Shammai the mere formulation of his intent to "put forth his hand," without his necessarily committing an actual act of conversion, suffices to render the bailee liable, but Bet Hillel does not extend the principle so far (BM 3:12; Yad, Gezelah, 3:11; Sh. Ar., HM 292).

The Shomer Sakhar. The *shomer sakhar* (שומר שכר , lit. "a paid bailee") is derived from the second case in the Torah of one who is entrusted with "an ass, or an ox, or a sheep, or any beast, to keep, and it be hurt, or driven away . . . " (Ex. 22:9–12). The fact that this case refers only to animals, whereas the previous case mentions "money or stuff," has been interpreted as drawing a distinction, not between the types of property deposited (cf. Philo, Spec. 4:35; Rashbam, Ex. 22:6), but between the types of bailment, since "the safekeeping of money or vessels is generally undertaken without payment [i.e., *shomer ḥinnam*], whereas that of animals is undertaken for reward [i.e., *shomer sakhar*]" (Naḥmanides to Ex. 22:6). In this case the bailee is liable in the event of the goods being stolen or lost (which is further authority for the conclusion that Scripture is here referring to a *shommer sakhar*) and he cannot be absolved even by taking the judicial oath, except in certain specific instances where accident was a contributory factor. However, liability could be avoided, on his taking the judicial oath, if loss resulted from the animal dying or being driven away (BM 7:8; Yad, Sekhirut, 1:2; Sh. Ar., HM 303:1–2). The term *"sakhar"* has been given a wide interpretation, so as to include the receipt by the bailee of any benefit whatsoever from the article deposited. Accordingly, an artisan who is entrusted with an article on which he is to exercise his craft for remuneration is deemed a *shomer sakhar* (BM 6:6; cf. BM 43a; *Shitah Mekubbeẓet* BM 94a; *Sefer ha-Ḥinnukh* no. 55). However, during the talmudic period a rabbinical enactment specifically exempted a carrier from liability arising through his transportation of barrels "even though imposed on him in strict law . . . lest no person be willing to transport his neighbors' barrel" (Yad, Sekhirut, 3:2).

The Sho'el. The *sho'el* (שואל , "borrower") is explicitly mentioned as the third type of bailee (Ex. 22:13–14), and on him is imposed the highest duty of care toward the owner of the article, since the bailee has borrowed it for his own benefit. He is therefore liable to make restitution in all cases of "damage or death," even though they are caused by inevitable accident or other unforeseeable circumstances, as well as in cases of theft or loss. Exceptionally, however, the *sho'el* may be able to avoid liability "if the owner of the article was with it at the time" – this being interpreted by the *tannaim* as referring to the case where the owner is borrowed or hired along with his animal or chattel (BM 8:1). The scope of this *halakhah* was extended to make it applicable in circumstances where the owner was with his property at the time the bailment was accepted, though not necessarily when the loss or damage later occurred, and also in circumstances where the owner was hired by the *sho'el* for purposes quite unconnected with the hiring of his property. Its application has even been extended to the other types of bailees (BM 95b; Yad, Sekhirut, 1:3 and She'elah, 2; Sh. Ar., HM 291:28). This exemption of the *sho'el* has been justified on the grounds that, in the circumstances mentioned, the owner would presumably take care to guard his own property (*Sefer ha-Ḥinnukh* no. 56; see also supplement to *Torah Shelemah,* 18 (1958), 187f.).

The cited text of the Torah concludes with the following statement: "If it be a hireling, he loseth his hire" (Ex. 22:14). This has been construed as a continuation of the provisions relating to the *sho'el.* However, the view of some scholars is that this phrase creates another category of bailee, distinguishable from the unpaying borrower, which is called the *sokher* ("hirer"; *Midrash ha-Gadol* to Ex. 22:14 and Rashi thereto; see also Ḥ. Albeck, in: *Sinai,* 50 (1961/62), 103f.). However, the laws of the *sokher* do not appear to be elucidated in Scripture (cf. Laws of Hammurapi, 249) and the *tannaim* disputed the question whether such a bailee is to be treated as a *shomer ḥinnam* or a *shomer sakhar* (BM 93a). Hence, "their laws [i.e., of bailees] . . . are three" (BM 93a; Yad, Sekhirut, 1:1). The *halakhah* was decided on the basis that the law of the *sokher* is that of the *shomer sakhar* (Yad, Sekhirut, 1:2; Sh. Ar., HM 307:1).

Measure of Damages. Generally, the degree of a bailee's liability in damages is proportionate to the degree of benefit he received from the bailment. Thus the *sho'el,* who enjoys full use of the article borrowed, is fully liable; the *shomer sakhar* (and the *sokher*), who derives partial or indirect benefit, may take the judicial oath for a part and compensate for a part; and the *shomer ḥinnam,* who receives no benefit, may simply take the judicial oath and escape all liability (TJ, Shevu. 8:1, 38b; Tos. to Ket. 56a–b).

The Torah lays down that a thief must compensate his victim by repaying either twice or four or five times the value of the stolen article (Ex. 22:3–8 and see Theft and Robbery). If a bailee chooses to compensate the owner for an article stolen during its bailment, rather than take the judicial oath, the thief, if later apprehended, must pay the stipulated double, four- or five-fold penalty directly to the bailee and not to the owner (BM 3:1; Yad, She'elah, 8:1; Sh. Ar., HM 295:2). This ruling is based variously on scriptural authority (see Mekh. SbY to 22:6; TJ, BM 3:1, 9a), on the principle of an assignment of rights by the owner to the bailee, and also on a rabbinical enactment (BM 34a; Ritba, Nov. BM 34a).

The fact that certain types of property are referred to specifically in the text (e.g., money, stuff, animals) led the sages to conclude that the laws of bailment are not intended to apply to slaves, deeds, immovable property, consecrated property *(hekdesh),* and the property of idolaters (BM 4:9; BM 57b, 58a; Yad, Sekhirut, 2:1; Sh. Ar., HM 301:1), although the rabbis especially provided for the bailee's judicial oath to be taken in respect of consecrated property, lest such property "be treated lightly" (Yad, Sekhirut, 2:2). Nevertheless, the laws of bailment may be rendered applicable to the above-mentioned classes of property by way of a special undertaking to that effect (BM 58a; Yad, Sekhirut, 2:1; Sh. Ar., HM 301:4).

Principles of Liability. The *posekim* are divided on the question of whether a bailee's obligations, and thus his consequent liability to the owner, commence immediately the agreement between the two parties is concluded, or only after a *meshikhah* (legal act of acquisition; see Acquisition[1] of the bailment (Sh. Ar., HM 291:5). A general rule, which is based on logical deduction, is that a bailee is not liable for damage caused to the bailment while it is being used for the purpose for which it was received, e.g., a cow borrowed as a beast of burden that dies of its labors (*metah meḥamat melakhah;* BM 96b; Yad, She'elah, 1:1; Sh. Ar., HM 340:1).

A bailee who is able to safeguard his bailment with the help of others and fails to do so is considered negligent – a distinction being drawn between the respective duties of care owed by a *shomer ḥinnam* and a *shomer sakhar* (Yad, Sekhirut, 3:6; Sh. Ar., HM 303:8). Any necessary expenses involved in safeguarding a bailment are recoverable even by the *shomer ḥinnam* from the owner, as there is no obligation to incur such expense.

The laws of bailment may be expressly varied or excluded by agreement between the parties (BM 7:10); this view is even held by R. Meir, who considers it inapplicable in other legal contexts (BM 94a). The freedom of the parties to vary or exclude the general principles of the law is recognized even though the result may be to impose more stringent obligations on the bailee (Yad, loc. cit. 2:9, Sh. Ar., HM 291:27, 296:5, and 305:4).

Rights and Duties of a Bailee. One bailee may not entrust his

1. page 206.

bailment to another (Tosef. BM 3:1). If he does so and the bailment is lost or damaged, Rav held that the first bailee can only escape liability to the same extent as he would have been able to do had he retained the bailment, but R. Johanan held that he is liable even in the case of force majeure (BM 36a and Rashi thereto). Subsequently, this dispute was interpreted by Abbaye to mean that according to Rav there would be no liability even though a *shomer sakhar* entrusted his bailment to a *shomer ḥinnam,* whereas according to R. Johanan liability would arise even though a *shomer ḥinnam* entrusted his bailment to a *shomer sakhar.* Rava ruled finally that the *halakhah* should be in accordance with the opinion of R. Johanan – as explained by Abbaye – on the grounds that, as no privity of contract existed between the owner and the second bailee, the former was not obliged to accept the latter's judicial oath (BM 36a–b). Furthermore, the first bailee can avoid liability only if "inevitable accident" can be proved by independent witnesses (Yad, Sekhirut, 1:4; Sh. Ar., HM 291:26).

If a bailment deteriorates while it is in the care of the bailee, he has a duty to inform the owner immediately, if the latter is available (Hai Gaon, *Sefer ha-Mikkaḥ ve-ha-Mimkar,* ch. 6; Sh. Ar., HM 292:15). There is a dispute in the Mishnah over the bailee's obligations when the owner is not available, some *tannaim* taking the view that "fruit, even if wasting, must not be touched," while Simeon b. Gamaliel states that the "fruit" must be sold and its value thus preserved, but only at the direction of the court, i.e., not on the bailee's own initiative (BM 3:6). In talmudic times this dispute was regarded as referring to a case where the rate of deterioration was normal for the type of article involved, but in a case where the rate of deterioration was excessive all scholars agreed that the bailee had a duty to sell the bailment (BM 38a; Yad, She'elah, 7:1; Sh. Ar., loc. cit.). Any such sale had to be to a third party and not by the bailee to himself, so as to avoid suspicion (Tosef., BM 3:8; Pes. 13a; Yad, She'elah, 7:5; Sh. Ar., HM 292:19).

A bailee may be relieved of his responsibility if the owner refuses to accept the return of his property. A statement in the Mishnah, that an artisan is a *shomer sakhar* who becomes a *shomer ḥinnam* upon his offering to return the article against payment, was later interpreted to mean that an artisan who expressly indicates to the owner that he wishes to be relieved of all responsibility for the article is thereafter exempted from any liability, even that imposed on a *shomer ḥinnam* (Rema, HM 306:1 and *Sma ibid.,* n. 4). In the event of the owner being abroad, the bailee may be relieved of his obligations by depositing the article with the court, who will then appoint a trustee for it until the owner's return (Yad, She'elah, 7:12; Sh. Ar., HM 293:3).

A bailee from whom a deposited article is stolen must take three judicial oaths, affirming: that he was not negligent as regards his bailment; that he did not "put forth his hand" to it (see above); and that it is no longer in his possession (BM 6a and Rashi; Yad, She'elah, 4:1; Sh. Ar., HM 295:2). However, it was prescribed that a bailee who is prepared to pay compensation must nevertheless take the third of these oaths, "lest he has set his eyes on the bailment" (BM 34b), although Maimonides limited the application of this ruling only to cases where the article was not normally available in the open market (Yad, loc. cit. 6:1; Sh. Ar., HM 305:1).

A bailee who denies the existence of a bailment and commits perjury concerning it, but later admits to the truth, is obliged to compensate the owner to the extent of the article's capital value plus a fifth, and must also bring a guilt offering (Lev. 5:20–26; Shevu. 5 and 8:3; and see Oath).

In the State of Israel. In the State of Israel the law of bailments is governed by the Bailees Law, 5727–1967, which closely follows the principles of Jewish law as described above (see *Divrei ha-Keneset,* 49 (1967), 2148f.). Thus, the three categories of bailee are similarly defined (sec. 1), each attracting a different (and increasing) degree of liability determined by the degree of benefit received by the bailee (sec. 2 and see explanatory remarks in: *Haẓa'ot Ḥok,* no. 676 (1965/66), p. 54). Also, the bailee is exempted from liability for damage or loss sustained while the article was being ordinarily used in accordance with the terms of the bailment (sec. 4). Yet further, the bailee is held liable if he knowingly fails to inform the owner that his property is likely to suffer damage (sec. 2(d)), and he is impliedly authorized to take such urgent steps as may be reasonably necessary to prevent such damage (sec. 6). The Bailees Law also deals with the question of a bailee who entrusts his bailment to another (sec. 3, 7), and makes detailed provision with regard to one who refuses to accept the return of his property from a bailee (sec. 11). Still following the principles of Jewish law, the freedom to contract out of the act is specifically allowed, namely: "The provisions of the act shall apply . . . where no different intention appears from the agreement between the parties" (sec.14). The Law of Hiring and Borrowing (1971) deals in sections 26–34 with the institution of borrowing. The definition of borrowing is given as: the right to hold property and to use it for a limited period, when the right is granted without consideration. See also Lease and Hire.

Bibliography: N. Hurewitsch, in: *Zeitschrift fuer vergleichende Rechtswissenschaft,* 27 (1912), 425–39; I. S. Zuri, *Mishpat ha-Talmud,* 5 (1921), 105–17; Gulak, Yesodei, 2 (1922), 65–68, 190–2; Z. Karl, in: *Tarbiz,* 7 (1935/36), 258–82; Herzog, Instit, 2 (1939), 175–96; H. Albeck, *Shishah Sidrei Mishnah,* introd. to BM; suppl. thereto, 3:1; Elon, Mafte'ah, 229–33, 308f., 376–9; idem in: ILR, 4 (1969), 91–94; idem, *Ha-Mishpat Ha-Ivri* (1973), I, 186, II, 276ff, 516ff, 785ff; U. Cassuto, *Commentary on the Book of Exodus* (1967), 285–8; N. Rakover, in: *ha-Peraklit,* 24 (1968), 208–25.

Nahum Rakover

SHALISH (Heb. שליש , one with whom an article or money is deposited and who has authority to dispose of it according to law or in accordance with stipulated conditions.

Types of Deposit. The deposit can be effected by a single person who deposits something with the *shalish* to give to another person or to buy some article, or by two people who have greater trust in a third party than in one another, as, for instance, where there is a difference of opinion between them and they deposit an object with the *shalish* until it is established who is entitled to it, or where a debtor has paid his creditor only part of the debt and they deposit the bill of debt with a *shalish* until the balance is paid (Ket. 5:8, 6:7; BB 10:5; Tosef., BM 1:10; cf. Rema, HM 56:2).

The conditions to which the *shalish* is subject may at times be affected by the defect of *asmakhta,* as in the following example: If a debtor repays part of his debt and gives his bond to a *shalish* saying: "If I do not give you [the balance] by such a date, give the creditor his bond, so that he can again claim that part of the debt already paid" (BB 10:5); the *tannaim* disagree on whether the *shalish* must act in accordance with this condition, and the Talmud explains that the dispute stems from the argument that the condition is defective because of *asmakhta* (BB 168a). The *halakhah* established that the condition is void and the *shalish* need not return the bond to the creditor, unless the appropriate procedure has been followed, such as an act of acquisition in the presence of an important *(ḥashuv) bet din* in order to rectify the defect of *asmakhta* (Sh. Ar., HM 55:1).

The status of *shalish* can arise without any specific act. For example, if a wife has been administering her husband's property, or an administrator has been appointed over a person's property in circumstances where the owner has given the administrator absolute authority over all his possessions and trusted him completely, and the owner then dies, the administrator has the credibility of a *shalish* (Sh. Ar., HM 56:7, and *Siftei Kohen* thereto, no. 34).

The Credibility of the Shalish. A *shalish* is, in general, accorded greater credibility than a single witness. "The admission of a litigant is as good as a hundred witnesses but the *shalish* is believed more than both. If one [litigant] says one thing, the other [litigant] another, and the *shalish* something else, the *shalish* is believed" (Tosef., BM 1:10). The reason for this special credibility of the *shalish* is that the depositor has reposed confidence in him (Git. 64a; and see in detail PDR 1:294–5). For this reason it has been concluded that even a *shalish* who is a relative also merits credibility, despite the fact that a relative is disqualified from giving evidence (Sh. Ar., HM 56:1). The *shalish* is believed in preference to the debtor or creditor. If two witnesses contradict him, however, he is not believed (Sh. Ar., HM 56:2, *Sma* and *Siftei Kohen* thereto).

If someone has in his possession another's property and claims that its owner handed it to him as a *shalish* and the owner denies this, one opinion is that the one possessing the property is believed (Sh. Ar., HM 56:1): "Even if the owner claims: You robbed me of it, and the other retorts: It is not so, but you appointed me a *shalish* between you and so and so, the other is believed" (*Sma,* HM 56:1 n. 7). On the other hand, some *posekim* argue that if this were so, anyone could seize his fellow's property and enter into a collusive agreement with another and say, I am a *shalish.* Accordingly, they hold that the *shalish* is not believed unless the depositor admits that the property was deposited with him as a *shalish* (*Siftei Kohen,* HM 56:1 n. 5).

The *shalish* is believed without an oath, since he is not a litigant and is backed by the presumption: "A man does not sin when he personally gains nothing by it" (Hai Gaon, in *Oẓar ha-Ge'onim,* ed. by B. M. Lewin, 10 (1941), 143, no. 352; Sh. Ar., HM 56:1). If the date fixed for the return of the deposit passes and the *shalish* has not returned it, he is still a *shalish* and is still believed (Sh. Ar., *ibid.*). The unique credibility of the *shalish* continues only as long as the deposit is still in his possession (Tosef., BM 1:10; Sh. Ar., HM 56:1; *Divrei Ge'onim,* 107:7). It is thus considered a sensible precaution to return the deposit in the presence of the *bet din* and clarify the facts in its presence, lest a dispute should arise between the parties, and, if the *shalish* has already parted with the deposit, he would not be believed (Sh. Ar., HM 56:3). One opinion is that it is possible to restore the deposit to the *shalish* so that he would again have credibility (*Siftei Kohen,* HM 56, no. 20; *Divrei Ge'onim,* 107, no. 6).

Liability of a Shalish. A *shalish* who acts contrary to the conditions made with him may become liable to compensate for any loss caused by his action. If he returns to the creditor a bond deposited with him, contrary to what was stipulated, he is subjected to a ban until he undertakes to compensate the debtor for any loss sustained as a result of the return of the bond. If the *shalish* does not undertake to compensate, and the creditor obtains payment unjustly by means of the bond returned to him, the *shalish* does not have to compensate the debtor, since this is only a case of damage caused indirectly by *gerama* and the rule is that there is no liability for damages caused by *gerama* (Rema HM 55:1; *Divrei Ge'onim,* 107, no. 10). If, on the other hand, contrary to the stipulation, the *shalish* returns the bond to the debtor, the *shalish* must compensate the creditor, for this is a case of *garmi* (as opposed to *gerama*), when the tort-feaser is liable to pay (*Siftei Kohen,* HM 55, no. 4; *Divrei Ge'onim* 107, nos. 11 and 12).

The *shalish* is at liberty to retract and restore the deposit to the parties. If the parties do not want to take it back, he can hand it over to the *bet din.* A *shalish* who is paid for his services, however, cannot retract (*Arukh ha-Shulḥan,* HM 56:17).

"The claimant pays the expenses of the *shalish* (Rema, HM 56:1), for it is always the one for whose benefit and advantage something is effected that has to pay the cost" (*Sma,* HM 56 n. 13; *Arukh ha-Shulḥan,* HM 56:23). It is customary to write a deed when something is deposited with a *shalish* (for the wording of such a deed, see *Sefer ha-Shetarot* no. 65, and see Bailment).

Bibliography: *Paḥad Yizhak,* s.v. *Shalish, Shelishut;* I. S. Zuri, *Mishpat ha-Talmud,* 7 (1921), 53; Gulak, Yesodei, 2 (1922), 191f.; 4 (1922), 161; Elon, *Mafte'aḥ,* 387–90.

Nahum Rakover

LOAN (Heb. הלואה , *halva'ah*), a transaction in which a thing, usually money, is given by one person, called the *malveh* ("lender"), to another, called the *loveh* ("borrower"), for the latter's use and enjoyment, and in order that such thing or its equivalent be returned by the borrower at some later date. In halakhic literature the term *halva'ah* is often used to describe an obligation or debt *(ḥov)* in general – i.e., not necessarily one originating from a transaction of loan – and many of the *halakhot* applying to debt in the wide sense of this term apply to loan, and vice versa (see Gulak, Yesodei, 2 (1922), 5f.; Elon, *Ha-Mishpat Ha-Ivri,* II, p.482ff; see also Obligations, Law of[1]). In this article loan is treated in the restricted sense of the term defined above.

Oral Loan (milveh be-al peh) and Loan in Writing (milveh bi-shetar). A loan established orally is distinguished from one established in writing in two main respects: (1) in the former case the borrower's plea that he has repaid the loan is believed, whereas in the latter case such a plea by the borrower is not believed when the bond of indebtedness is in the lender's possession; (2) in the case of a loan in writing, the creditor has the right to levy on the debtor's *nekhasim meshu'badim* ("alienated and encumbered" assets, see Lien; Obligations, Law of[2]), a right not available to him in the case of an oral loan. The term *milveh be-al peh* is apparently a post-talmudic creation, although the distinction between the two forms of loan was recognized as early as tannaitic times (Gulak, loc. cit.; Elon, *Ha-Mishpat Ha-Ivri;* II, p. 487ff; Herzog, Instit, 1 (1936), 352).

Mitzvah of Lending. The precept of lending to the poor of Israel is based on Exodus 22:24: "If thou lend money to any of my people that is poor by thee" (see Mekh., Mishpatim, s. 19), and is included in the enumeration of the *mitzvot* (*Sefer ha-Mitzvot,* Asayin no. 197; *Semag,* Asayin no. 93; *Sefer ha-Ḥinnukh* no. 66). Some scholars derived this precept from other biblical passages (*She'iltot* no. 114; *Semak* no. 248). The lender, if he apprehends that he may not be repaid, may make his loan conditional on the receipt of a pledge from the borrower (Tos. to BM 82b; *Ahavat Ḥesed,* 1:8, n. 13). The merit of fulfilling this precept was lavishly extolled by the scholars – even beyond the act of charity (Shab. 63a). The duty was held to cover also a loan to a rich man in his hour of need (Sh. Ar., HM 97:1, *Sma* thereto, n. 1), but some scholars restricted its application to the case of a poor man only (Yad, Malveh ve-Loveh 1:1). In certain circumstances a person is prohibited from lending money to

1. page 241; 2. page 287, 243.

another. This is so if there are no witnesses to a loan (BM 75b), lest the borrower is tempted to deny his indebtedness or the lender to forget that he gave the loan; it nevertheless became customary for a loan, even an oral one, to be given in the absence of witnesses, and the *aḥaronim* sought to explain the custom and reconcile it with the talmudic *halakhah* (*Pilpula Ḥarifta* to BM 75b; Resp. *Ben Yehudah,* 1:153). Similarly prohibited is a loan given to a poor man for the repayment of another debt, since – but for such loan – the creditor might come to his relief on account of his poverty (Tos. to Ḥag. 5a).

Nature of the Repayment Obligation. The nature of the borrower's obligation to repay the loan was a matter of dispute among the *amoraim.* R. Papa took the view that the duty of repayment was no more than a *mitzvah* – just as it was a *mitzvah* for the lender to give a loan – whereas R. Huna b. Joshua held that repayment was a legal duty (Ket. 86a; BB 174a; Nov. Ritba, Kid. 13b; Resp. Mabit, vol. 1, no. 51; *Semag,* Asayin 93). It seems that alongside the legal duty, R. Huna recognized also the existence of a religious duty to repay the debt (Resp. Ribash 484; M. Elon, *Ha-Mishpat Ha-Ivri,* I, 156ff; for an opinion that the duty was a *mitzvah* only, see Nov. Ramban BB 174b). Some scholars held this *mitzvah* to be of Pentateuchal origin (Ritba, loc. cit.; Resp. Mabit, loc. cit., *Pitḥei Teshuvah,* HM 97, n. 4), while others interpreted R. Papa's statement as relating only to oral loan (Rashbam BB 174a). A borrower who fails to repay the loan is described as *rasha* ("wicked"; Ps. 37:21; *Semag,* Asayin no. 93; see also Contract;[1] Obligations, Law of).

Halva'ah and She'elah. *She'elah* (loan for use and return) relates to "utensils" *(kelim),* and *halva'ah* (loan for consumption) to money or "produce" *(perot).* Utensils are things which are not counted by weight and measure, nor exchangeable one for the other; things which are counted and exchanged in this way are "produce" (Gulak, Yesodei, vol. 1, p. 95; vol.2, pp. 20, 171). The *sho'el* (borrower for use and return) must return the subject matter of the loan in specie, whereas the *loveh* need not do so. Unless otherwise stipulated, a loan is for consumption and the borrower will only be liable for payment of the equivalent in produce or other property (see also Bailment).

Establishment of Loan. A loan transaction is concluded upon handing over of the money (or "produce") to the borrower. In post-talmudic times the opinion was advanced that a contract of loan might be established upon performance of a formal *kinyan* alone (see Acquisition), without handing over of the money, and that thereupon the borrower would become obliged to repay the money (Tur, HM 39:19 and *Beit Yosef* ad loc.); however, this opinion was not accepted by scholars (*Beit Yosef* loc. cit.; HM 39:17). Once the money of the loan has been given to the borrower, the lender will no longer have any right to retract and demand its return, even if it is still intact in specie (*Baḥ,* HM 39:19; *Siftei Kohen,* HM 39, n. 49). Where the lender has undertaken to give a loan and the borrower has already written a deed on the former's instruction, some scholars hold that as long as the money has not yet passed to the borrower the lender remains free to retract from the loan (Resp. Rashba, vol. 1, no. 1054; Sh. Ar., HM 39:17), while others preclude him from so doing (*Sefer ha-Terumot* 48:1; *Maggid Mishneh,* Malveh, 23:5). In the case of an oral loan, the lender may withdraw at any time before handing over of the money (*Netivot ha-Mishpat, Mishpat ha-Urim,* 39, n. 17).

Repayment Date. When Specified. If a specified date was stipulated between the parties, the lender may not reclaim the loan prior to that date (Mak. 3b; Yad, Malveh, 13:5). Some scholars maintain that the lender – even in circumstances where he has reason to fear the borrower's imminent departure abroad, or is aware that the latter may be squandering his assets and therefore unable to repay the debt on due date – is not entitled to anticipate the day of repayment (*Teshuvat ha-Ge'onim* no. 45; *Sefer ha-Terumot* 16:3; Tur, HM 73:15); other scholars invest the court with discretion in the matter and the power to order distraint of the property in the borrower's possession (Resp. Rif. no. 113; Resp. Rashba, vol. 1, no. 1111). It was held that the court might do this only if the borrower is squandering his assets, otherwise – even though his financial position may be steadily deteriorating for other reasons – the court will not have the power to intervene prior to the due date of repayment (*Yam shel Shelomo* BK 1:20; *Siftei Kohen* HM 73, no. 34, see also below; Execution, Civil[2]).

When Unspecified. A loan for an unspecified period is given for 30 days (Yad, Malveh 13:5), and may not be reclaimed within this period. If it is customary in a locality to retain a loan of unspecified duration for a longer or a shorter period, that custom is followed (Sh. Ar., HM 73:1, *Sma* and *Siftei Kohen* ad loc.). Some scholars expressed the opinion that in this matter even the gentile custom is followed (*Sma,* loc. cit.) – but others disputed this (*Siftei Kohen,* loc. cit., n. 1 and 39).

Further Differences. (1) In the case of a loan for a specified period, the borrower's plea that he has made repayment within the term of the loan is not believed, since "a person is not likely to make payment before due date" (BB 5a), whereas in the case of a loan for an unspecified period the borrower's plea that he has paid within the 30 days as required is believed (Tos. to BB 5a). This distinction has been justified by the scholars on many grounds. Some hold that in the case of a specified repayment date, the borrower, for no particular reason, knows that he will have no money available until the due date, but not so in the case of an unspecified repayment date (Resp. Rosh, 76:3); others hold that when no date is specified, the borrower will feel ashamed if he should have money before the end of the 30 days and fail to make repayment – hence it is presumed that he will repay the loan, even within the said period, if he has the money (*Shitah Mekubbeẓet,* BB 5a); yet another view is that in the case of an unspecified repayment date, the borrower is liable for repayment of the loan before expiry of the 30 days – save that he cannot be obliged by the court to make payment before then – hence he is likely to repay earlier if he has the money (*Devar Avraham,* vol. 1, no. 32). A minority opinion holds that in the case of a loan for an unspecified period the borrower is not likely to anticipate payment, and his plea to this effect is not to be believed (Be'ur Ha-Gra to HM 78 n. 24). (2) Apparently even those who adhere to the opinion that the property of a borrower – even when it is being squandered by him – cannot be distrained until due date of payment of the loan agree with all other scholars that as regards a loan for an unspecified period, the court may distrain the property in the debtor's possession even before expiry of the 30 days (*Keneset ha-Gedolah,* HM 73; *Tur,* 20).

Anticipation of Payment by the Borrower. Since determination of the repayment date is for the borrower's benefit (Ran to Ket. 81a, s.v. *vergarsinan*), it is permissible for him to repay the loan before the due date, regardless of the lender's wishes (Ran. loc. cit.). He may not, however, anticipate payment without the lender's consent when there is a substantial apprehension of an imminent and official change in currency values (*Sefer ha-Terumot* 30:2; see also below).

Acceptance of Payment. Payment made to the lender against the latter's will is a valid payment; if the latter refuses to accept the money and the borrower throws it to him, he will be discharged (*Sefer ha-Terumot* 50:1; Tos. to Git. 75a). However, when the lender is prepared to accept payment, the borrower must make the payment into his hands and may not throw it to

1. page 243; 2. page 624.

him (Git. 78b; Yad, Malveh 16:1). Payment to the lender's wife is held by some scholars to discharge the borrower, provided that she is accustomed to transacting her husband's business (see Husband and Wife; Resp. Maharam of Rothenburg, ed. Prague, no. 225; Rema, HM 120:2), but other scholars dispute that this is a valid discharge (*Yam shel Shelomoh* BK 9:39).

Place of Payment. The lender may claim repayment at any place, even in the wilderness (BK 118a; Sh. Ar., HM 74:1). Upon due date the borrower may oblige the lender to accept payment at any settled place *(yishuv)*, even if this is not the place where the loan was transacted nor the place of residence of the lender or borrower (*Sefer ha-Terumot,* 30:1, Sh. Ar., loc. cit.). If the loan was transacted in the wilderness, the borrower may oblige the lender to accept payment there (Rema HM 74:1).

Method and Means of Payment. A debt not yet due may be repaid little by little (BM 77b; *Mordekhai* BM no. 352; *Ittur,* vol. 1, pt. 2, s.v. *iska*); according to some scholars payment in this manner, although initially forbidden, is valid in retrospect (*Bedek ha-Bayit* HM 74; *Siftei Kohen* HM 74, no. 17). After due date the lender may, in the opinion of all scholars, refuse to accept payment in the said manner (*Mordekhai,* loc. cit.). The borrower must repay in money, and if he has none, in land. The lender may refuse to accept the land and offer to wait until the borrower has money – even if this is after the due date (Resp. Rosh, 80:9; Sh. Ar., HM 74:6; 101:4). If the borrower has no money, the lender may not instruct him to sell his assets in order to receive money for them, but must either take the assets as payment or wait until the borrower has money (Tos. to BK 9a). If payment in money entails a loss for the borrower, he may repay the loan in land (Tos. Ket. 92a and Ran ad loc.). If the borrower has money, land, and chattels, and wishes to pay in money, while the lender asks for land or chattels, some scholars hold the law to favor the lender and others the borrower (*Sefer ha-Terumot* 4:2; see also Execution, Civil[1]).

Fluctuation in Currency Values. In case of official withdrawal and replacement of the existing currency, the position is as follows: If the new currency is of the same kind, the borrower pays in the currency in circulation at the time of payment (BK 97). If, however, the withdrawn currency is circulating in another country on the same terms as it formerly did in the country of its withdrawal, the lender – if he has the means of reaching such a country and there is no particular difficulty in transferring the old currency – will be obliged to accept the withdrawn currency in payment (BK 97; Sh. Ar., HM 74:7). If as a result of a change in the value of the currency there is a reduction in the price index of the commodities ("produce"), the borrower pays in accordance with the new currency value and deducts for himself the excess (BK 97b, 98a); if the reduction in prices result from factors unconnected with a currency revaluation, the borrower pays in the stipulated currency, without any deduction (Sh. Ar., YD 165). The view that the rules stated with reference to a currency revaluation must also be extended, by analogy, to the case of a currency devaluation *Ateret Zahar* no. 165) (*Levush,* YD 165 and HM 74) was accepted as *halakhah* (*Piskei ha-Rosh,* BK 9:12; *Ḥikrei Lev,* Mahadura Batra, HM 9) in preference to a contrary opinion (*Piskei ha-Rosh,* loc. cit.; Resp. Rashba, vol. 3, no. 34).

In many Jewish communities *takkanot* were enacted which were aimed at reaching a compromise in disputes between parties relating to the manner of debt-payment in case of a change in currency values, and a decisive majority of the *posekim* inclined toward adjudging and compromising between the parties in terms of these *takkanot* (see Kahana, bibl.; *Takkanot ha-Kahal*).

Plea of Repayment (*Parati;* "I have repaid"). An oral loan is repayable without witnesses; a loan in writing, before witnesses. In a claim for repayment of an oral loan, the borrower's plea that he has already made repayment is believed (Sh. Ar., HM 70:1); such a plea is regarded as a general denial of the claim, and – on taking a solemn oath *(shevu'at hesset)* – the borrower is exempted (Sh. Ar., HM 70:1). Where there is a bond of indebtedness, the borrower's plea that he has made repayment is not believed, and the lender – on swearing an oath that he has not been repaid – proceeds to recover the debt *(ibid.).* (As regards the borrower's plea of payment prior to the due date, see above.) As a means of protecting the lender against such a possible plea of repayment, it became customary to stipulate, at the time of the loan, that credence be given to the lender upon his denial of a repayment plea by the borrower – such stipulation availing to dismiss the latter plea (Sh. Ar., HM 71:1). For the similar protection of the lender, the practice was adopted of stipulating at the time of the loan that it be repayable only before witnesses – the borrower's plea of repayment being thus deprived of credibility unless attested by witnesses (*ibid.,* 70:3). In the latter case it still remained possible for the borrower to plead that he had repaid the debt before witnesses *A* and *B,* who had since gone abroad, and – upon making a solemn oath – become exempted; to forestall this possibility the practice was adopted of stipulating, "You shall not repay me except before witnesses so and so, or before the court" – thus precluding the borrower from pleading that he made repayment before some other witnesses (*ibid.,* 70:4).

Multiple Loans. If a lender has given the same borrower two separate loans and the latter seeks to repay on account of one of them, the lender may appropriate the payment toward whichever loan he pleases without any right on the borrower's part to protest or maintain that he intended otherwise (Tur., HM 83:2 and *Beit Yosef* ad, loc.; *Sefer ha-Terumot* 20:2). This rule only applies when both loans have already fallen due for payment (*Sefer ha-Terumot,* loc. cit.); if one loan has fallen due but not the other, the payment is deemed to have been made on account of the former (Resp. Radbaz, 1252 (181)); if neither has fallen due, the law is apparently the same as for two loans already due (Radbaz, loc. cit.; *Keẓot ha-Ḥoshen* 83, n. 1).

Conversion into Loan of Other Contractual Obligation. At times the practice was adopted, for various reasons, of converting an obligation originating from a transaction other than loan into an obligation of loan. This practice is referred to as *zekifat ḥov be-milveh* and was adopted – for instance in the case of a purchaser indebted to the seller for the purchase price – because of the restricted number of pleas possible against a claim for a loan-debt as compared to a claim for a debt originating from the sale of goods (BM 77b; HM 190:10). *Zekifat ḥov* takes place in one of the following ways: (1) by the writing of a special bond of indebtedness for an already existing debt; (2) by the stipulation of a date for the repayment of an existing debt; and (3) by the gradual accumulation of a debt, for instance by purchase on credit from a shop. In this way the original obligation is largely – or even entirely – extinguished and converted into a new obligation. From the time of such *zekifah* the debt is an obligation of loan only, the new obligation retaining none of the legal characteristics of the old (Gulak, Yesodei, vol. 2, pp. 116–8).

Minor as Party to a Loan. By pentateuchal law, a minor has no legal capacity to lend. As long as the subject matter of such a loan is still intact (in specie), it must be returned by the borrower; hence in case of loss resulting from *ones* (force majeure) the borrower is exempt from liability as the property is deemed to be in its owner's possession for purposes of loss arising from *ones.* The rabbis enacted that a loan given by a minor should be valid, the borrower being liable also for loss resulting from *ones*

1. page 627.

(Gulak, Yesodei, vol. 1, p. 40). A minor who has borrowed is exempt from returning the loan, even after reaching his majority. According to some scholars, a minor who has borrowed for his own maintenance can be recovered from even during his minority (Gulak, loc. cit).

Measures to Prevent "Bolting the Door" to Borrowers. Hillel the Elder instituted a Prosbul designed to overcome reluctance to lend to a borrower at the approach of the *shemittah* (sabbatical) year (Shev. 10:3; Rashi Git. 37a; see Elon, *Ha-Mishpat Ha-Ivri,* II, p. 418ff, and also *Takkanot*[1]). Although according to pentateuchal law the need for *derishah* and *ḥakirah* (examination of witnesses) extends also to civil law *(dinei mamonot)* matters, the scholars enacted for this procedure to be dispensed with in the latter cases, so as not to bolt the door before borrowers (Sanh. 3a; see Elon, *Ha-Mishpat Ha-Ivri,* II, 497ff, and also Practice and Procedure; Witness). Despite an opinion upholding the need, by the pentateuchal law, for three expert judges in matters of *hoda'ot* ("acknowledgements") and loans, the scholars enacted for the competence of a court of three laymen, lest the door be bolted before borrowers for fear that no expert judges be found to enforce the law (Sanh. 3a; see also *Bet Din*). The scholars enacted that in certain circumstances the judges, if they erred, were not to be exempted from liability, in order not to discourage people from lending to others (Sanh. 3a). According to pentateuchal law, the creditor recovers the debt out of the *zibburit* ("worst land") of the debtor, but the scholars enacted that he might do so from the *beinonit* ("medium land"), for the reason mentioned above (Git. 50a; see also Execution, Civil[2]). According to those who held that the doctrine of *shi'bud nekhasim* was non-pentateuchal, the scholars enacted for a lender on a bond to recover from the debtor's *nekhasim meshu'badim* ("encumbered and alienated property"; see Lien;[3] BB 175b).

Bibiography: Gulak, Yesodei, 1 (1922), 145f.; 2 (1922), 33–35, 42f., 83–88, 105–9, 113–8, 170–2; 3 (1922), 102–6; 4 (1922), 85–90; idem, Oẓar, 205f., 208; J. Rappaport, in: *Zeitschrift fuer vergleichende Rechtswissenschaft,* 47 (1932/33), 256–378; Herzog, Instit, 1 (1936), 121–4, 219f.; 359f.; 2 (1939), 57f., 186f., 215f.; J. S. Kahana, in: *Sinai,* 25 (1949), 129–48; ET, 1 (1951³), 263–6; 4 (1952), 110–4; 5 (1953), 92–132; 9 (1959), 215–40; M. Silberg, *Kakh Darko shel Talmud* (1961), 71–75; M. Elon, *Ḥerut ha-Perat . . .* (1964); idem, *Ha-Mishpat Ha-Ivri* (1973), I, 156ff, II, 482ff, 531ff, 626ff, III, 983ff.

Shmuel Shilo

LEASE AND HIRE. The Hebrew term *sekhirut* embraces the lease of immovable property (houses and fields) as well as the hire of movable property and personal services, and is a near parallel of *locatio-conductio rei* in Roman law. In this article the term "hire" is generally used as the equivalent of *sekhirut* in its wide sense and also with reference to movable property, whereas the term "lease" is used solely with reference to the hire of immovable property. For details concerning the hire of personal services, see Labor Law.

In hire, the owner (the *maskir*) alienates to the hirer (the *sokher*) a real right in the demised property, the fruits and use of the property, for a fixed period, in return for a rental payable by the hirer to the owner. The rule is that hire is deemed to be a sale for a fixed period. This *halakhah* was stated in the Talmud with reference to the law of *ona'ah* ("overreaching"); i.e., just as there is overreaching in sale so there is overreaching in hire, and just as there is no overreaching in the sale of land so there is no overreaching in the lease of land (see BM 56b and Tos., ad loc.; Sh. Ar., HM 315:1). Some scholars held that the application of the above rule extended to additional *halakhot:* "A man may make any stipulation he wishes with regard to hiring just as he may do with regard to purchase and sale, since hiring is but a sale for a specified time. He who may sell may also let" (Yad, Sekhirut 7:1; see also *She'elah,* 1:5; Sh. Ar., HM 315:2; PD 8 (1954), 577–81). Opinions are divided on the question of whether the owner may, within the period for which he has let his property, let such property to a third party (see *Pitḥei Teshuvah,* HM 315, n. 1).

Formation and Determination of Hire. Property is hired in the same way as it is bought and sold (see Acquisition; BK, 79a; Yad, Mekhirah 1:18; Sh. Ar., HM 315:1), and until the required formal act of *kinyan* is performed both parties are free to retract (Sh. Ar., HM 307:2). The view was expressed that as regards the hire of movables, as opposed to their sale, the scholars had not abolished *kinyan kesef* ("acquisition by money"), because the subject matter of the hire would continue to belong to its owner, which would eliminate the apprehension that the latter might refrain from rescuing the property from danger – as there was reason to fear in the case of sale. The *halakhah* was decided accordingly (see Sh. Ar., HM 198:6; *Pitḥei Teshuvah,* n. 8). Determination of hire, before expiry of the stipulated period, may be effected by an act of *kinyan,* i.e., by the hirer transferring his real right in the property back to its owner. A right of hire cannot be extinguished by way of waiver alone (see *Sma,* HM 189). Just as a person's courtyard acquires for him (*kinyan ḥaẓer;* see Acquisition[4]), so he may acquire through a courtyard he has hired, and in this way acquire movables which are on the hired property (Yad, Mekhirah 3:7; see also Sh. Ar., HM 198:5 and *Siftei Kohen,* n. 7). Similarly, movables may be transferred by the method of acquisition incidental to hired land (*kinyan aggav;* Kid. 27a).

Ambit of Contract. The ambit of hire is determined in accordance with the customary uses of the property concerned. Thus a person who hires a house also hires its surrounding garden and the like (Yad, Sekhirut 6:1), all subject to local custom (see *Minhag*) and the common usage of the terms employed by the parties in their contract (Yad, loc. cit.; see also Sh. Ar., HM 313:1).

Obligations of the Lessor. The lessor must let to the lessee property which is fit for the intended purpose. If a house is let, the lessor must supply one with doors and windows properly affixed, and he must further ensure that all the things "which are produced by the craftsman and are essential to the habitability of houses and courts" are done (BM 8:7; Yad, Sekhirut 6:3; Sh. Ar., HM 314:1). The fact that the lessee occupies the premises prior to the lessor's execution of all his required duties does not amount to a waiver of these on the part of the lessee, and the lessor remains responsible for their execution (Rema, HM 314:1). Where the parties agreed on the letting of "this" – i.e., specified – house, the lessor will not, during the subsistence of the lease, be responsible for repairs; otherwise (i.e., where an unspecified house is let) the lessor remains responsible for repairs (Rema, loc. cit.). The opinion was expressed that even in the case where a specified house is agreed on by the parties, the lessor will, in certain circumstances, if the house has fallen into disrepair and become too dangerous to live in, be responsible for its repair (Sh. Ar., HM 312:17 and *Sma,* n. 32).

In case of the destruction of the leased property (see below), the law as regards the lessor's need to make available alternative property to the lessee is as follows. "If a man let to another an unspecified house and after he delivered possession to the lessee the house collapsed, he is bound to rebuild it or to supply the lessee with another house. If the second house is smaller than the

1. page 77; 2. page 627; 3. page 287; 4. page 206.

one that collapsed the lessee cannot object, provided it may be classified as a house, for it was but an unspecified house that the lessor let to the lessee. If, however, the lessor said, 'I am letting to you a house like this one,' he must supply the lessee with a house of the length and width of the one he indicated to him"; in the latter event, the lessor cannot depart from the dimensions and qualities of the said house except by mutual consent (BM 103a; Yad, Sekhirut 5:7; Sh. Ar., HM 312:17).

Rental or Hire. Two views are expressed in the Talmud concerning the owner's right to payment of the rental or hire (Kid. 48a–b). One opinion is that the hire (i.e., wages) is "a liability from beginning to end" and that the hired worker becomes continuously entitled to this in accordance with the portion of the work done (Yad, Ishut 5:20; see also Akum 7:5 and Rashi Kid. 48a, s.v. *ella*). A different opinion is that "wages are a liability only at the end" (Kid. loc. cit.), that the lessor does not become entitled to the rental until determination of the lease or – in the event that property was handed over for improvement – until return of the property to its owner (Rashi Kid. 48b, s.v. *einah li-sekhirut;* but cf. *Beit ha-Beḥirah,* Kid. 48a). The *halakhah* was decided according to the first opinion (see Yad, loc. cit. and Sh. Ar., EH 28:7). However, the practical significance of the above dispute is confined to matters concerning the laws of *kiddushin* (see Marriage) and those concerning wages in cases involving idolatry, whereas it appears to have no relevance to relations between the lessor and lessee. Hence, as regards the time for the payment of the hire it was accepted as *halakhah* that "wages are a liability only at the end" (see Tos. to BK 99a to BM 65a; but cf. Nov. Ritba Kid., 48b). It is a positive precept to pay the worker's hire on time and failure to do so is a transgression of a pentateuchal prohibition *(halanat sakhar)* which was interpreted as extending to the hire of personal services and that of animals and utensils (see Labor Law). However, as regards the rental for land and houses, disputing opinions are expressed in the codes (see Yad, Sekhirut 11:1; Sh. Ar., HM 339:1 and *keẓot ha-Ḥoshen* n. 1).

Where property is hired for a fixed period at a stipulated remuneration, the latter may not be increased within the said period (Sh. Ar., HM 321:10; Rema, HM 312:9). In the case where a property is tacitly relet on expiry of the hire period, and in the absence of any express agreement regarding the amount of the hire for the renewal period, the hirer – according to Hai Gaon – will be at an advantage: If the amount of the hire stipulated for the first period is higher than the appropriate amount, the hirer pays only the latter amount; if the stipulated amount is lower than is appropriate, the hirer nevertheless pays no more than the lower amount (*Ittur* 1, pt. 1, s.v. *sekhirut*). On the other hand, from the Shulḥan Arukh it may be gathered that the hirer, in the above circumstances, always pays according to the stipulated amount for the first period, regardless of any increase or decrease in the customary rate (HM 312:9; see also Nov. Meir Simḥah ha-Kohen of Dvinsk, BM 101b, s.v. *va-agalleh*). If the hirer retracts during the term of the hire he remains liable for the whole amount of the hire (Yad, Sekhirut 5:4; Sh. Ar., HM 311:6).

Departure from the Object and Terms of the Hire. The hirer may not use the hired property for a more onerous purpose than that for which it was hired (Yad, Mekhirah 23:8, Sekhirut 4:1, 4–5; Sh. Ar., HM 212:6; 308), subject to any different local custom (Yad, Sekhirut 4:8; Sh. Ar., HM 308:3). If the hirer puts the property to any more onerous use, for which the customary hire is greater than the amount agreed upon, he must add to the hire accordingly (Rema HM 308:1). In certain circumstances it may be sought to safeguard that the property is put to its full stipulated use. Thus, for instance, the lessor of a shop may object to its being left vacant by the lessee lest the regular customers become accustomed to buying elsewhere, which would detract from the value of the premises (Resp. Maharsham, pt. 2, no. 198). Use of the property in a different but not more onerous manner than that agreed upon is held to be forbidden by some scholars but is permitted by others, who hold that to forbid this is "the practice of the Sodomites" (see Law and Morality; Tur., HM 308:3–4; 311:3–4; *Perishah, ibid.* 4; *Sma* HM 311, n. 2).

If a house is jointly hired (see Partnership) by two persons for their cotenancy, neither may transfer his rights in it to a third party – not even if the latter has a smaller household – except with the consent of the other partner. Similarly, one tenant cannot compel his cotenant to partition the tenancy, since the house is not their property but is only let to them for a term. However, it was held that joint lessees of a field can compel each other to a partition of the lease (Sh. Ar., HM 171:9 and Rema, ad loc.; HM 316:2 and *Sma* n. 6). The lessee may not, without the lessor's consent, take in any of his relatives or acquaintances to live with him in the house as one of its occupants, unless they are dependent on him (Yad, Shekhenim 5:9; Sh. Ar., HM 154:2). As regards the stipulated terms, the rule is that these may not be departed from except where their strict enforcement would amount to "following the practice of the Sodomites" (Yad, Sekhirut 7:8; Sh. Ar., HM 318).

Assignment and Subletting. The rule is that the hirer may not sublet to someone else (Tosef. BM 3:1; Git. 29a). To do so without authority will render the sublease voidable (*Maḥaneh Efrayim,* She'elah u-Pikadon no. 7). There are several qualifications to this rule: It was laid down that a person who hires a cargo boat and unloads the cargo in the middle of the voyage may let the boat to someone else (for the rest of the journey), and the owner will have "a grievance only" against the original hirer; similarly, if the hirer sells the cargo in the middle of the voyage, disembarks, and leaves the purchaser to embark, the owner takes one-half of the freightage from each of the other two and the owner has "but a grievance against the seller for causing him to endure the inclinations of another man to whom he is not accustomed;" and so too in other similar cases. (Yad, Sekhirut 5:4; Sh. Ar., HM 311:6). This *halakhah* was extended by way of analogy: "On the basis of the above rule [Yad, loc. cit] I hold that if the owner lets his house for a fixed period, the lessee may sublet it to another until the end of the said period . . . since the rule of the sages that the hirer may not let applies only to movables, where the owner may say 'I do not wish my property deposited with another'; but as regards land, or a boat on which its owner is present, the owner cannot say so" (Yad, loc. cit. 5:5). Other scholars expressed the view that the lessee may never sublet the house, "for there are people who ruin the house that they occupy" (Yad, loc. cit., *Hassagot Rabad* and *Maggid Mishneh,* ad loc.). According to some scholars, even "chattels which are not likely to be carried away and which are habitually hired out and lent by their owners" may in turn be hired out and lent to third parties (Resp. Rashba, vol. 1, no. 1145; see also *Maḥaneh Efrayim,* Sekhirut no. 19). The *halakhah* was decided thus: "A person who has hired an animal or chattels may not hire these out to anyone else" (Sh. Ar., HM 307:4 see also 316:1). Similarly, a field may not be sublet, since in this case it is apprehended that the sublessee may do with the field as he pleases (see *Sma* HM 212:16 and 316:1).

The permissibility of subletting in the case of a house is subject to a number of restrictions. It may only be done if the members of the subtenant's household do not number more than those of the existing tenant (Yad, Sekhirut 5:5). It is also a condition that the sublease shall not entail a more onerous use than did the original lease. In addition, the lessor always retains a preemptive right to demand the leased property for himself and release the lessee from further payment of the rental (Yad, loc. cit.; see also Sh. Ar., HM 316:1; *Divrei Ge'onim* 104:40). Similarly, the lessee may not sublet to a disreputable person (Rema HM 312:7), or to someone who is hateful to the lessor (*Taz* HM 312:7), or to someone who will fail to take proper care of the property (*Arukh ha-Shulḥan* HM 316:2). In the case of a lawful sublease, any reward the lessee derives from it will belong to him, otherwise to the owner of the property (see *Maḥaneh Efrayim,* Sekhirut no. 19).

Frustration of Hire. It was laid down that if a hired ass fell sick or was taken into the king's service, it would not have to be replaced by its owner; however, if the ass died, the owner would be so obliged (BM 6:3; BM 78b; Sh. Ar., HM 310:1). The owner's exemption from the need to replace an ass if it fell sick was interpreted to be specifically applicable to the case in which an ass is hired to carry a normal load, since it would still remain possible to put the ass to some use; however, an ass that is hired to be ridden, or to carry glass utensils, has to be replaced by its owner, since there is no possibility of using it for the purpose for which it was hired (BM 79a; Sh. Ar., loc. cit.). In the case where the ass dies, a distinction is made between the hire of a specified ("this") ass and the hire of an unspecified one. In the case of an unspecified ass, the owner must replace it with another, otherwise, if the worth of the carcass suffices for the purchase or hire of another ass, the hirer must apply the proceeds therefrom toward the purchase or hire of an ass for the original purpose (BM loc. cit.; Sh. Ar., HM 310:1–2; see also Tur., HM 310:2; *Beit Yosef* and *Darkhei Moshe,* ad loc.).

In the Talmud it is laid down that if a specified house is hired, the loss – in the event of its collapse – is that of the lessee, and no provision is made for him to apply the proceeds of the sale of the boards and bricks toward the purchase or hire of another house (BM 103a; Sh. Ar., HM 312:17). However, an opinion was expressed that the lessee should do so in the above circumstances (Ramah in Tur, HM 312:16), and some scholars distinguished between the hire of an ass and that of a house (see Tos. to BM 79a; *Shitah Mekubbeẓet* BM 79a, under *Ha de-Amrinan* in the name of Rabad). If a house is demolished by the lessor, he must make available a similar house to the lessee and he must do likewise if he has caused the lessee to vacate the house during the period of the lease (Yad, Sekhirut 5:6; Sh. Ar., HM 312:2).

Four possibilities are distinguished as regards payment of the rent upon frustration of the lease, all illustrated by the case of a ship hired for the transport of wine which sinks with all its cargo:

(1) If a specified ship was hired for transporting a cargo of unspecified wine, the hirer will be exempt from payment of the freightage and entitled to a refund if he has already paid; this is because the hirer is prepared to submit other wine for transportation but the owner is unable to offer him the ship hired (BM 79a; Sh. Ar., HM 311:2). When the hirer can benefit from part performance of the contract – for instance if the cargo is salvaged and the hirer is able to transport it in some other manner to its destination, or to sell it at the place to which it has been brought – the ship owner will be entitled to part payment of the freightage, pro rata to the measure of the contract executed (see Tos. to BM 79a; Rema, HM 310:2, 311:2).

(2) If an unspecified ship was hired for the transport of a cargo of specified wine, the hirer will be liable for the freightage, since he presents the obstacle, inasmuch as the shipowner is able to offer another ship whereas the hirer is unable to submit the same wine that was lost (BM 79a–b). There is an opinion that the hirer, in the above event, is only liable for part payment, pro rata to the measure of the hire executed (Tos. to BM 79b; Sh. Ar., HM 311:3 and Rema ad loc.). There is also an opinion that in circumstances where the cargo is lost even though the ship has not sunk, the hirer, in spite of the fact that he presents the obstacle, is exempt from payment of the hire since the obstacle has arisen from inevitable accident (see *Ones;* Tos. to BM 79a; *Sma* HM 311, n. 2; *Siftei Kohen, ibid.,* n. 2).

(3) If a specified ship was hired for transporting a cargo of specified wine, the rule is that since the obstacle is presented by both parties, the party in possession is at an advantage, if the hirer has not yet paid the freightage he need not do so, but if he has already done so he will not be entitled to any refund (BM 79b; Sh. Ar., HM 311:4).

(4) If an unspecified ship was hired for transporting a cargo of unspecified wine, the shipowner and the hirer share the freightage (BM 79b; Sh. Ar., HM 311:5).

In the case where the lessee of a house dies during the currency of the lease, according to one opinion the lessor will not be entitled to the full rental but only that for the period for which the house was occupied, unless it was otherwise stipulated by the lessor; another opinion is that the lessor remains entitled to the full rental (Rema, HM 334:1; see also *Divrei Ge'onim,* 104:16).

Termination of the Contract. A lease for a fixed period terminates on expiry thereof and may not be terminated by the lessor prior to this date (Yad, Sekhirut 6:6; Sh. Ar., HM 312:1, 8). At times, in the absence of a stipulated time for the termination of a lease, the expiry date will be determined in accordance with the surrounding circumstances. Thus, if the rental has been paid in advance, even for a lengthy period of time, the lessor will not be able to eject the lessee until expiry of the period for which the rent has been paid (Sh. Ar., HM 312:1 and Rema ad loc.). Sometimes the date of termination of a lease is governed by local custom relating to such a particular category of lease (Tosef. BM 8:28; see also Yad, loc. cit.; Sh. Ar., HM 312:4). The lessor's sale of the leased premises is valid but does not have the effect of terminating the lease, and the purchaser may not eject the lessee until expiry of the lease period; the same applies when the premises are transferred by gift or inheritance (Yad, Sekhirut 6:11; Sh. Ar., HM 312:1 and 13; see also I. S. Zuri, *Torat ha-Mishpat ha-Ezraḥi ha-Ivri: ha-Irurim,* 1 (1935), 105, n. 36).

In the case where premises are let for an unspecified period, the scholars laid down the need for advance notice of termination. The rule is as follows: "He who lets a house to another for an unspecified term may not dispossess the lessee from the house unless he notifies him 30 days in advance, so as to enable him to find a place and prevent his being thrown into the street. At the end of the 30 days the lessee must vacate the premises (Yad, Sekhirut 6:7, based on BM 8:6 and BM 101b; see also Sh. Ar., HM 312:5). In certain circumstances, depending on the nature of the premises and its location, longer periods of notice are required (BM and Yad, loc. cit.). The obligation to give notice is mutual and, as regards the lessee, he may not vacate the premises without prior notice, but must pay the rent (Yad, Sekhirut 6:8 and Sh. Ar., HM 312:7; see also *Pitḥei Teshuvah* thereto; PDR 3:281–3; 6:113). When a lease is tacitly renewed for lack of prior notice of termination, the rent for the renewal period must be paid at the new prevailing rate, whether higher or lower than before (Yad, Sekhirut 6:9 and Sh. Ar., HM 312:9). If the lessor requires the premises for himself, for instance when his own dwelling has collapsed, he may eject the lessee from the leased premises, saying to him: "It is not right that you should remain in my house until you find another dwelling place, while I am lying on the street; your right in this house is not greater than mine" (Yad, Sekhirut 6:9 and 10; Sh. Ar., HM 312:11; see also Resp. Radbaz, pt. 4, no. 1214; Nov. Akiva Eger to Sh. Ar., HM 312:13). The fact that relations between the lessor and lessee have deteriorated during the currency of the lease is no ground for its termination; however, if at the time of the letting the lessor declared that he was only doing so because of his friendship for the lessee, if the two become enemies in the meantime, then he is entitled to terminate the lease (Rema HM 312:9; see *Pitḥei Teshuvah* n. 6).

Laws of Evidence. Based on the rule that "the burden of proof rests on the person seeking to recover from another," it was laid down that in case of ambiguity in the terms of the lease the owner of the premises is the party in possession and holds the advantage until the lessee brings evidence to support his claim. Thus if it is unclear whether an intercalated (leap year) month is for the benefit of the lessor or the lessee, the benefit will accrue to the lessor (BM 102b; Yad, Sekhirut 7:2; Sh. Ar., HM 312:15). Similarly, in the case of dispute over whether the lease was for a fixed or for an unspecified period – which would have a bearing on the need or otherwise for prior notice of termination – the burden of proof will rest on the lessee (Yad, loc. cit.; Sh. Ar., HM 312:16 and Rema ad loc.) and likewise in the case of dispute as to the date of commencement of a lease for a fixed period (Yad, Sekhirut 7:4; Sh. Ar., HM 317:2; for additional rules see Yad, Sekhirut 7:6; Sh. Ar., HM 317:3). If there is a dispute between the lessor and the lessee over whether the rent has been paid or not, then – if the lease was for a term of 30 days and the lessor has claimed the rent within this period, or if there was a stipulated date of payment and the rent has been claimed prior to this date – the lessee will have the burden of proving that he paid the rent, since it is presumed that "a person does not pay prior to due date" and that "rent is payable only at the end"; if, however, the claim is made on the 30th day or on the stipulated date, the lessor will have to prove that he has not yet been paid (Yad, Sekhirut 7:3; Sh. Ar., HM 317:1).

Precepts Relating to Property. The letting of premises has a bearing on the question of whether the duty of fulfilling the precepts relating to such property falls on the lessor or lessee. As regards the precept of searching out leaven on Passover eve, it was laid down that the duty devolves on the lessor if he has not delivered the key to the lessee before the 14th day of Nisan; if he has delivered the keys before this date, the duty is the lessee's (Yad, Ḥameẓ 2:18). At the same time, the fact that the lessee finds that the house he has hired has not been searched for leaven – even though he has hired it on this assumption – does not entitle him to void the contract on the grounds of error, since it is every person's duty to perform a *mitzvah* personally (Yad, loc. cit.; see also Sh. Ar., OH 437:1, 3).

Ḥokher and Mekabbel. In two cases, in which the lessee is called a *ḥokher* and a *mekabbel* respectively (as defined below), the consideration is payable in a different manner to that of the *sokher.* If a produce-bearing field or vineyard is rented for money, the lessee is called a *sokher;* when it is rented for a stipulated amount of the produce the lessee is called a *ḥokher;* when a person hires a field or orchard with the obligation to cultivate it, to incur the necessary expenses, and to pay a stipulated portion of the product derived therefrom, he is called a *mekabbel* (Yad, Sekhirut 8:1, 2; Sh. Ar., ḤM 320:1–3). There is one law for the *sokher* and the *ḥokher* (loc. cit.). As regards the *mekabbel* and the *ḥokher* (the two cases are referred to as *kabbelanut* or *arisut*), "whatever is essential to the protection of the land is chargeable to the owner and whatever constitutes added precaution is chargeable to the farmer *(ḥokher)* or tenant on shares *(kablan).*" The utensils and instruments for cultivation of the land – such as a spade for digging the ground or the vessels in which the dirt is carried – are chargeable to the owner. There is an opinion that the aforesaid obligations of the owner relate only to the *mekabbel* and not the *ḥokher* (Yad, Sekhirut 8:2; Sh. Ar., ḤM 320:3).

The owner derives his share from whatever is produced by the land, whether good or bad. If the field yields bad produce, the *ḥokher* nevertheless pays with this, and if good wheat is produced he may not say to the owner, "I will buy wheat for you from the market," but must pay out of this crop (Yad, Sekhirut 8:7; Sh. Ar., ḤM 323; see *Sma* n. 3). The nature of the work which must be done by the *ḥokher* in cultivating the field is determined by local custom (BM 9:1; Yad, Sekhirut 8:6; Sh. Ar., ḤM 320:4; *Sma* n. 2). If a field is leased on the condition that it is sown with a particular crop, the *ḥokher* may only sow a different crop which is less and not more exhaustive of the soil. In case of deviation, the *ḥokher* will have to purchase produce on the market for delivery to the owner as stipulated between them (Sh. Ar., HM 324, *Sma* n. 2). As regards a *meakbbel,* one opinion holds that he may depart from the stipulated manner of cultivation, even if this is more burdensome on the land, and another opinion is that he may not do so even for a less burdensome result (Rema ḤM, loc. cit.).

If a field taken by a *mekabbel* fails to produce its anticipated yield, nevertheless, if there is a prospect of extracting a yield exceeding the expenditures by a minimal amount, the *mekabbel* will be obliged to cultivate the field against his will – since this is part of his undertaking whether or not it was expressly stipulated in writing (Yad, Sekhirut 8:12; Sh. Ar., ḤM 328:1 and *Rema* ad loc.). If a *mekabbel* lets a field lie fallow, an appraisal is made of how much the field would have been likely to yield and the former must pay the owner his estimated due share – since this is part of his undertaking to the lessor, whether or not expressly stipulated. Such an undertaking was held not to be defective on account of *asmakhta,* since here the *mekabbel* does not take upon himself an obligation for something that is fixed, but only to indemnify the owner in accordance with the loss caused the latter, and hence the *mekabbel* is deemed to have firmly made up his mind to bind himself to the obligation. If, however, the *mekabbel* undertook to pay the owner an amount that is found to exceed the estimated loss, this will amount to *asmakhta,* and he will be liable to pay only according to the actual loss (Yad, Sekhirut 8:13; Sh. Ar., ḤM 328:2).

Frustration of Ḥakhirah. A distinction is made between partial frustration – for instance, if the tributary spring feeding an irrigated field dries up, or if a tree on the plantation is felled – and frustration deriving from a widespread misfortune – for instance, if the river dries up leaving no possibility at all of irrigating the field. In the first case the lessee may not make any deduction from the rental since it is regarded as his own misfortune; in the second case he may make such deduction. If the owner to entrust the field to his further cultivation until expiry irrigated field, or this tree plantation to you," his statement will be interpreted to mean that the lease was made as though the owner was letting the field as it was then, without change, and therefore the lessee will be entitled to make a deduction from the rental (Yad, Sekhirut 8:4, 5; Sh. Ar., ḤM 321 and 322).

Termination of Ḥakhirah. If on termination of the lease unharvested produce remains on the field, or if the market day for the sale of already harvested produce has not yet arrived, an appraisal is made of the lessee's share therein (Tosef. BM 9:1; Yad, Sekhirut 8:10 Sh. Ar., ḤM 327:1). If the lessee dies within the term of the lease and is survived by his son, the position is as follows: If the father had already received everything due to him for the whole of the term and the owner of the field does not wish to entrust it to the son until completion of the term and for the agreed purpose, the son will not be required to return anything received by his father in excess of the measure of his cultivation – since the son may say that he will complete the cultivation of the field if it is left with him; if the father had not yet received any part of his due share and the son should ask the owner to entrust the field to his further cultivation until expiry of the agreed term and in return for the whole of his father's stipulated share, the owner – who in this case is in the favored position – may deny the existence of any business tie with the lessee and proffer him payment in accordance with the measure of the work done by his father (Sh. Ar., HM 329; *Sma* n. 1).

For the responsibility of the hirer for the hired property, see Bailment; for the preemptive right of the hirer and operation of the abutter's right against him, see *Maẓranut;* for the laws and rabbinical enactments concerning protection of the hirer, see *Hassagat Gevul;*[1] and see also Labor Law.

In the State of Israel. The law of Hiring and Borrowing (1971) applies both to hire of immovable and movable property as well as to the hire of rights. Sections 1–25 and 31–34 deal with the obligations of the owner and the hirer, the duration of the hire, and other topics. The definition of hire in the law is: the right granted for a consideration (i.e., the rental) to hold the property and to use it for a limited period. See also Bailment.

Bibliography: I. S. Zuri, *Mishpat ha-Talmud,* 5 (1921), 91–100; Gulak, Yesodei, 1 (1922), 142–5; 2 (1922), 163–7, 188f.; idem. Oẓar, 195–8; P. Dickstein, in: *Ha-Mishpat ha-Ivri,* 2 (1926/27), 109–90; Herzog, Instit, 1 (1936), 329–38; A. Karlin, in: *Sinai,* 6 (1939/40), 485–91; ET, 2 (1949), 186–92; 13 (1970), 75–103; Elon, Mafte'aḥ 376–9; idem, *Ha-Mishpat Ha-Ivri* (1973), II, 354ff, 374ff, 755, III, 1342ff.

Nahum Rakover

PARTNERSHIP.

Formation. The earliest form of commercial partnership in Jewish law was partnership in property, or joint ownership. Craftmen or tradesmen who wished to form a partnership were required to place money in a common bag and lift it or execute some other recognized form of *kinyan* for movables (Ket. 10:4; Yad, Sheluḥin 4:1). The need for executing a *kinyan* precluded an agreement concerning a future matter (Maim., *ibid.* 4:2), since there can be no acquisition of a thing that is not yet in existence (see Acquisition). In later times this difficulty was overcome when the *halakhot* concerning the need for acquisition formalities were interpreted as having reference only to the formation of the partnership and not to matters in continuation thereof (Maharik Resp. no. 20).

From the tenth century onward, new developments became acknowledged with regard to the manner of forming a partnership. Thus the German and French scholars recognized formation of a partnership by mere agreement between the contracting parties (*Ha-Ittur,* vol. 1, s.v. *Shittuf; Mordekhai* BK 176; Resp. Rosh no. 89:13). A second development was recognition of each partner as the agent of his other partners (*Haggahot Maimuniyyot,* Gezelah 17:3 n. 4), which offered the possibility of partnership formed solely by verbal agreement (see Agency). A further development, that of recognizing each partner as the hireling of his other partners (*Hassagot Rabad,* Sheluḥin, 4:2), facilitated partnership agreement with reference also to further activities. The drawback of partnership by way of agency or hire is that each partner has the power to dissolve the partnership at any time. Another method was formation of partnership by personal undertaking, each partner taking a solemn oath to perform certain acts on behalf of the partnership (Ribash Resp. no. 71).

Partnership formation by agreement alone was most prevalent from the 16th to the 19th centuries, particularly in the communities of the Spanish exiles, in reliance on the principle of accepted trade customs (e.g., *kinyan sitomta:* see BM 74a and Codes; see also *Minhag*[2]). It was on the basis of a trade custom that formation of a partnership through verbal agreement alone was recognized, even by the mere recital of the single word *"beinenu"* (*Rosh Mashbir,* HM no. 31; *Kerem Shelomo,* Ribbit, 8) or by implication (*Shemesh Ẓedakah,* HM 35); and see substantial differences of opinion on this subject in Elon, *Ha-Mishpat Ha-Ivri,* II, p. 744ff. Texts of the standard partnership deeds developed over the years indicate that, in general, formation of the partnership agreement rested on a number of elements, mainly *kinyan sudar* (acquisition by the kerchief), personal undertaking, and hire (see e.g., *Darkhei No'am,* HM, 54). In this way it was possible to form a partnership with a minimum of formalites, valid also in respect of future activities and not retractable from prior to expiry of the specified period (see Contract[3]).

It may be noted that the fraternal heirs are deemed to be partners until the inheritance is divided among them (see Succession).

Distribution of Profits and Losses. In the earliest discussions of partnership in Jewish law, the question of distribution of profits was treated in cases of an unequal capital investment by the individual partners (Ket. 10:4). In the first *halakhot* two conflicting opinions were expressed: in the Mishnah, distribution in proportion to the amount invested; in the Tosefta, equal distribution of the partnership profits. In the Talmud, application of the mishnaic *halakhah* was limited to cases of capital gain or those in which it was impossible to make a physical division (TJ, BK 4:1, 4a, and Ket. 10:4; Ket. 93). Talmudic sources reflect no hard and fast rule concerning the distribution of profit deriving from commercial activity. For a long period of time, from the geonic period until the 19th century, these *halakhot* were applied by the scholars in both fashions discussed above. In centers of Jewish life where there was a great deal of activity in commerce and the crafts, the tendency was to decide in favor of an equal distribution of profits in all cases; in centers where there were many loan transactions the tendency was to decide in favor of a distribution pro rata to investment. Thus in the 12th and 13th centuries the principle of an equal distribution was followed in Spain, whereas the German and French scholars took the view that in general the gain, whenever divisible, should be shared in proportion to the investment of each partner.

In general, profit earned by a partner in an unlawful manner, for example, through theft, has not been considered as belonging to the partnership (*Ha-Ittur,* vol. 1, s.v. *Shittuf; Siftei Kohen,* HM, 176 n. 27). A contrary ruling with regard to partnership gains from theft was laid down in Germany and France in the 14th century, as an outcome of the persecution of the Jews (*Haggahot Maimuniyyot,* Sheluḥin 5:9 no. 4; see also Contract, on the attitude of Jewish law to illegal contracts). From the 17th century onward the application of this *halakhah* came to be confined to cases of necessity on account of danger (*Siftei Kohen,* loc. cit.) or those in which an act, although illegal, falls within the scope of the partnership business (*Arukh ha-Shulḥan* HM 176:60).

A tax waiver in favor of one partner benefits the whole partnership, except when a waiver is granted at the taxing authority's own initiative (HM 178:1). A condition that all profits shall belong to the partnership has been interpreted in accordance with the *ejusdem generis* rule, so as to exclude therefrom all unusual or unforeseeable profits (Rosh, Resp. no.

1. page 342; 2. page 100; 3. page 248.

89:15). A partner who salvages part of the partnership assets from a robbery does so for the benefit of the partnership in the absence of his prior stipulation to the contrary (BK 116b and Codes). The partners may not deal in goods whose use is prohibited, for example, for reasons of ritual impurity (Maim. Yad, Sheluḥin 5:10).

Until the end of the 12th century, any loss attributable to a partner's personal fault had to be borne by the partner himself, on the principle that an agent is liable for the consequences of a departure from his mandate (Yad, Sheluḥin 5:2; see also Agency). From the 13th century onward, the general trend has been toward collective partnership responsibility for a loss occasioned by one of its members. At first it was laid down that the partnership bear such a loss as if the member's liability were that of bailee for reward (see Bailment; later it was ruled that a partner be regarded as a gratuitous bailee for this purpose; and later still that the partnership bear the loss occasioned by a member even if it was the result of his own negligence (Mordekhai BB 538). The partner himself must bear any loss occasioned through his own acquiescence or active participation (Mabit, Resp. vol. 2, pt. 2, no. 158).

Each partner is responsible as a surety for the undertakings made by his other partners in respect of a partnership matter (Yad, Malveh 25:9). This liability is secondary however, as is usual in simple suretyship in Jewish law, and effective only upon default of the principal debtor (*Sefer ha-Terumot,* 44). According to another opinion, one partner is a surety for the other only when he has expressly subjected his person and assets as a surety for the undertaking, in which event he becomes the principal debtor (Rosh, Resp. n. 89:3).

Powers and Duties of the Partners. The rule is that a partner may not deviate from the regular course of activities of the partnership, and his powers, if not defined by agreement, are governed by trade custom (*Ha-Ittur,* vol. 1, s.v. *Shittuf;* Yad, Sheluḥin 5:1; Rosh Resp. no. 89:14). When the intention of the partners cannot be ascertained, a number of activities have been recorded as constituting deviation from the partnership. In the course of time the early partnership *halakhot* came to be interpreted in favor of wider powers for the individual partner. Thus, with regard to the rule that a partner might not transact partnership business away from the place of the partnership (Yad, loc. cit.), it was decided that the restriction did not apply to a market place situated in the same area (*Netivot ha-Mishpat, Mishpat ha-Kohanim* 176 n. 35) nor to the case in which one partner provided the other partners with suitable indemnities against possible loss (*Arukh ha-Shulḥan* HM 176:46–47).

The question of whether a partnership member has power to execute credit transactions was already disputed in geonic times. One approach tended to recognize the power of a partner to sell on credit in all cases, because it was considered that he was bound to be careful about securing the repayment of money in which he had a personal stake (*Sha'arei Ẓedek,* 4:8, 4). A second approach denied a partner the power to sell on credit unless this accorded with a custom followed by all local traders (Rif., Resp. no. 191) and, by way of compromise, it was laid down that it sufficed if the custom was followed by a majority of local traders (Rosh. Resp. no. 89:14). It was also laid down that a partner is exempted from liability if an overall profit results from all his transactions (*Ḥokhmat Shelomo* HM 176:10).

A partner may not introduce outsiders into the partnership activities as partners (Yad, Sheluḥin 5:2), but may employ them on his own behalf and at his own responsibility (Maharashdam, HM, 190). It was ruled that a member of a partnership might not engage in private transactions *(ibid.),* but this was later permitted when the same kind of merchandise as the partnership dealt in was involved (*Matteh Yosef* vol. 1 HM no. 9) or in association with an outsider (*Sma,* HM 176 no. 32). Partnership merchandise may not be sold before the appointed season for its sale (Git. 31b and Codes).

In general, a partnership member is not entitled to remuneration for his services (Reshakh, Resp. pt. 1 no. 139), but some of the *posekim* allowed this in the case of unusually onerous services (*She'ilat Yavez* no. 6; *Simḥat Yom Tov* no. 23). Similarly, a partner is not entitled to a refund of the amount expended on his subsistence while on partnership business (HM 176:45), except for extraordinary expenses (*Taz,* ad loc.). A partner who is unable to participate in the partnership activities on account of illness, or for some other personal reason, is not entitled to share in the profits earned by the partnership during his absence and must also defray his medical expenses, etc., out of his own pocket, unless local custom decrees otherwise (BB 144b and Codes). If partnership property is later found in the possession of one of the partners, his possession will not avail against any of the other partners (Alfasi, BB 4a; see *Ḥazakah*). Each partner may compel the other to engage in the partnership activities and also in certain circumstances to invest additional amounts therein (*Netivot ha-Mishpat, Mishpat ha-Urim,* HM 176:32).

The act of a partner may be validated by subsequent ratification, which may also be implied from the silence of the remaining partners (Maharik, Resp. no. 24). Far-reaching powers are afforded a partnership member through application of the principle that an act may be "for the benefit of the partnership." In the opinion of a number of scholars, a partner may deviate from the customary framework of the partnership activities when he considers this to be necessary in the interests of the partnership, provided that the terms of the partnership agreement expressly permit him to trade in all kinds of merchandise and that there is no radical departure from the customary partnership practices (Resp. Maharashdam, HM 166; *Ne'eman Shemu'el* no. 100). One partner may oblige another who is suspected of an irregularity with regard to a partnership matter to deliver an oath in accordance with a rabbinical enactment (Shevu. 7:8). For this reason it was originally forbidden for a Jew to take a gentile as a partner, as the latter was likely to make an idolatrous reference in swearing his oath, but this is permissible now because of "their belief in the Maker of heaven and earth" (Ran on Rif, Git. 50b).

Representation of the Partnership by One of its Members. In talmudic law the principle was established that only when all the partners are in the same town can they be represented by the partner who is plaintiff in an action, this even without their express power of attorney (Ket. 94a and Codes). From the 13th century onward, the following guiding rules came to be laid down: one partner represents the others when there is an equal division of profits between them; partners who have not been joined as plaintiffs may not thereafter renew the action in their own names unless they plead new issues; one partner represents the others only when he makes a claim against the defendant and not a waiver in his favor (*Shitah Mekubbeẓet,* Ket. 94). Other scholars expressed opinions in favor of the reverse situation, i.e., that one partner represents the others only if there is no denial of liability on the defendant's part and there is no dispute between them (Maharit, Resp., vol. 2 HM no. 16); the plaintiff partner represents the remaining partners once the latter have knowledge of the suit, even if they are not all present in the same town (Resp. Solomon b. Isaac ha-Levi, HM no. 41); the partner who is on the scene may sue in all cases, but may not recover the shares of his absent partners (*Piskei ha-Rosh,* Ket. 10:12); the absent partners have the right to sue in their own names if they do so immediately after their return to the town in question, but lose this right after a certain period of delay (*Mikhtam le-David,* HM no. 31; *Edut bi-Yhosef* vol. 2 no. 38). The partners may each plead in turn, or empower one of them to represent all (Maharam of Rothenburg, Resp., ed. Prague, nos. 332, 333). A partner has authority to collect debts owing to the partnership in terms of a bond of indebtedness of which he is the holder (Rashba, Resp. vol. 1, no. 1137). One partner generally does not represent the remaining partners as defendant in an action unless empowered by them to do so (*Mordekhai,* Ket. 239). The defendant does, however, represent his absent partners if he is in possession of the subject matter of the claim (Tur, HM 176:31). See also Agency; Practice and Procedure.

Dissolution of Partnership. The activities of a partnership formed for an unspecified period of duration may be terminated at any time at the instance of any of its members, except if this is sought when it is not the season for the sale of its merchandise and provided there are no outstanding partnership debts for which all partners are liable. A partnership formed for a specified period may not – according to the majority of the *posekim* – be dissolved before the stipulated date (Yad, Sheluḥin 4:4). The existence of a partnership is also terminated when its capital has been exhausted, its defined tasks completed and on the death of any of its members. Improper conduct on the part of a member – such as theft – does not, in the opinion of the majority of the *posekim,* serve to terminate the partnership. On dissolution of a partnership, division of its monies – if in the same currency – may be made by the partner in possession thereof and this need not necessarily be done before the court. Division of the partnership assets must be made before three persons, who need only be knowledgeable in the matter (Yad, Sheluḥin 5:9).

Iska ("In Commendam" Transactions). Freedom to contract a partnership is limited to some extent in the case where one party provides the capital and the other the work. In order to avoid a situation in which the party furnishing the capital ultimately receives an increment on his investment which is in the nature of interest, there was evolved a form of transaction known as *iska,* i.e., "business," in which half of the furnished capital constitutes a loan to the "businessman," or active partner, and the other half is held by him in the form of a deposit (BM 104b and Codes). The parties to an *iska* are free to stipulate as they please, provided that they observe the principle that the "businessman," must enjoy some greater benefit than the "capitalist," by way of remuneration for his services (BM 5:4). It would seem that the profits from the loan part of the capital belong to the businessman and the profit from the deposit part, after deduction of the former's remuneration, belong to the capitalist. Unless otherwise agreed upon, the businessman is to receive wages as a regular worker if he devotes himself entirely to the affairs of the business, and if not, he may be paid a token amount. Another possibility, if nothing is stipulated, is that the businessman receives two-thirds of the profits, and bears one-third of the losses (Yad, Sheluḥin 6:3) or, according to another opinion, one-half of the losses (*Hassagot Rabad* thereto). The businessman's liability in respect of the loan half of the capital is absolute, whereas his liability in respect of the deposit half is that of a gratuitous bailee (Yad, Sheluḥin 6:2) or according to another opinion, that of a bailee for reward (*Hassagot Rabad, ibid.*).

According to one school, an *iska* is constituted whenever the partnership arrangement involves an active as well as an inactive partner, and it makes no difference whether the inactive partner alone or both of them contribute the capital (Yad, Sheluḥin, 6:1); according to another school, there is no *iska* unless the distinction between an investing but inactive and an active but noninvesting partner is clearly maintained in the partnership arrangement (*Beit Yosef,* YD 177). The capital-investing partner takes no share in the profits of a prohibited *iska* (*She'elot v-Teshuvot ha-Rosh* 88:8).

That an *iska* is essentially a legal device designed to avoid the prohibition against usury may be seen from the fact that a nominal remuneration may be agreed upon for the active partner and from the rule that the latter may not distinguish between the loan and the deposit parts but must put to work the whole amount of the capital invested (Yad, Sheluḥin 7:4). In most respects the law of *iska* follows the law of partnership but the following basic differences may be noted: the "businessman," unlike a partner in a regular partnership, may retract from the contract at any time, as in the case of a worker (Tur. HM 176:28) and he must receive remuneration for his services (*Mishpat Ẓedek,* vol. 2, no. 16, et al.).

Joint Ownership. As already indicated, the *halakhot* of partnership developed mainly from the law of joint ownership. Characteristic of this is the power of each part-owner to compel the others to carry out the usual and required activities with regard to the common property – such as the construction of a gate to the premises – or to refrain from any unusual use of the property, such as keeping an animal on the premises; similarly, each part owner may bring about a dissolution of the partnership by compelling a partition of the common property provided that thereupon each share still fits the original description of the property and, in the case of immovable property, that it is possible to erect a partition against exposure to the sight of neighbors. If the common property does not allow for proper subdivision, the interested partner may offer to sell his share to the remaining partners or to purchase their shares from them; if the matter cannot be settled in this manner, the property must be sold, or let to a third party, or an arrangement must be made for its joint use by the partners, simultaneously or successively, all in terms of detailed rules on the subject (BB 1–3, and Codes).

A Legal Persona. A cooperative body in modern legal systems is an entity with rights and obligations quite apart from those of its component members (see G. Procaccia, Ha-Ta'agid Mahuto . . . vi-Yẓirato (1965), p. 39). According to the law of the State of Israel, a registered partnership is a legal persona, capable of suing and being sued (The Partnerships Ordinance, 1930, sec. 61 (1)). However, this approach is foreign to Jewish law, the *halakhah* recognizing man alone – whether individually or in cooperation with others – as the subject-matter of the law, so that it does not accord an association a separate personality (see Gulak, Yesodei, 1 (1922), 50). It is for this reason that the word "partners" rather than "partnership" is the more commonly employed halakhic term. Thus a suit brought by the partners against one of their number, e.g., arising out of fraud (see *Ona'ah*), is not the suit of the partnership but of its individual members (Yad, Sheluḥin, 5:6; Sh. Ar., HM 176:4). Nevertheless, even though the partnership as such does not have the status of an independent legal persona, the moment a person is recognized as a partnership member his rights and obligations change and no longer correspond to those attaching to the individual or to an agent. Thus one partner represents his fellow partners vis-á-vis third parties, and unlike an agent, renders them bound by the consequences of his acts in certain circumstances, even without having been appointed as their representative (Yad, Sheluḥin, 3:3); Similarly, if jointly owned property is later found in the possession of one of the co-owners, the latter's possession will not be recognized, despite the rule that the onus of proof is on the person seeking to recover from the neighbor (BB 4a and Codes); subsequent ratification of a fellow partner's acts amounting to deviation from the customary partnership activities suffices to absolve the latter from liability for such deviation – according to some of the *posekim* even if they are only passed over in silence without protest (*Shenei ha-Me'orot ha-Gedolim* no. 26). Thus the special standing which the law affords a partner to some extent lends a partnership the coloring of a legal persona.

In the State of Israel. The laws of partnership are governed by the above-mentioned mandatory partnership ordinance, which is based on the British Partnership Act, 1890, but differs from it mainly in that it necessitates registration of a partnership to which it lends the character of a legal persona (sec. 61 (1)). Still unclear is the position as regards the standing of an unregistered partnership (PD 15:1246; Pesakim Meḥoziyyim, 56:362). Case law shows that the *halakhah* is sometimes quoted with regards to problems left unresolved within the framework of the Partnership Ordinance (e.g., on the questions of dissolution of partnership (PD 21:576) and the share of each of the spouses in the profits and losses deriving from their common enterprise (Pesakim Meḥoziyyim, 23:418)). In cases where the parties agree to submit their dispute to a rabbinical court, the issue will be decided in accordance with Jewish law (see PDR 2:376, 5:310).

Bibliography: J. S. Zuri, *Mishpat ha-Talmud,* 4 (1921), 55–59; 5 (1921), 154–6; idem, *Arikhat ha-Mishpat ha-Ivri . . . Ḥok Hevrat ha-Shutafut* (1940); Gulak, Yesodei, 1 (1922), 135–7; 2 (1922), 192–8; Gulak, Oẓar, 147f., 217–23; E. E. Hildesheimer, *Das juedische Gesellschaftsrecht . . .* (1930); Herzog, Instit, 1 (1936), 213–23; 2 (1939), 155–66; Elon, Mafte'aḥ, 328–41; idem, *Ha–Mishpat Ha-Ivri* (1973), II, 559ff, 586ff, 603ff, 626ff, 653, 745ff, 755ff, 764ff, III, 881ff, 1110ff.

Shmuel D. Revital

SURETYSHIP (Heb. ערבות), one person's undertaking to fulfill the obligation of another toward a third person (called the *arev, ḥayyav,* and *nosheh* respectively). In Jewish law fulfillment of an obligation is secured primarily through the assets of the debtor – "a man's possessions are his surety" (BB 174a; see Lien) – and it is in addition to this that a person may serve as a surety for the fulfillment of the debtor's obligation toward his creditor.

Suretyship in the Bible and the Talmud. The biblical term *'eravon* ("pledge"), although philologically related to the term *'arev* or *'arevut,* occurs in the sense of an obligation secured by property and not personally (Gen. 38:17ff.; and see Targ. Onk. and Rashi thereto; cf. Neh. 5:3). The form of personal pledge mentioned in the matter of Judah's undertaking to Jacob to be surety for Benjamin's safe return (Gen. 43:9) has no bearing on the present discussion, since Judah was at one and the same time surety and principal debtor (*ibid.,* 8; and see *She'iltot* 33 ed. Mirski). Detailed discussion of suretyship is to be found in Proverbs, where the surety's undertaking is described as given verbally and accompanied by a handshake (*teki'at kaf;* Prov. 6:1–5, 11:15; 17:18; 22:26; see also Job 17:3). It is likely that a handshake also served as the mode of establishing other kinds of obligations (see Ezra 10:19). In the Book of Proverbs there is a strong exhortation against undertaking a suretyship obligation because if it is unfulfilled, the creditor might levy payment even on the surety's garments and bedding (20:16; 22:27; 27:13). Since this is the extreme consequence with which the surety is threatened, it may be deduced that the creditor is forbidden to subject the surety to personal bondage, just as he is forbidden from so subjecting the debtor (see Obligations, Law of[1]). Suretyship involving the bodily subjection of an individual is to be found only in the field of military law, with reference to the taking of hostages in time of war (II Kings 14:14; II Chron. 25:24).

A guarantee to present the debtor before his creditor and the court (on due date) is described in the Talmud as "the law of the Persians" (BB 173b). The existence of this phenomenon in Jewish law was hinted at in geonic times (*She'elot u-Teshuvot ha-Ge'onim,* Constantinople 1575, last reprint Jerusalem, 1960, no. 213), but Maimonides denied the validity of this form of suretyship (Yad, Malveh, 25:14; also see *Hassagot Rabad* and *Maggid Mishneh* thereto). The unfavorable attitude expressed in Proverbs toward the very act of undertaking a suretyship obligation is reflected also, although to a lesser degree, in the apocryphal books (Ecclus. 8:13; 29:17–20). Even in talmudic times suretyship is mentioned as one of the things a man is advised to avoid (Yev. 109a).

Formation of Suretyship. At first Jewish law recognized suretyship only insofar as it was undertaken before or at the time of the creation of the debtor's principal obligation (BB 10:7: "If a man loaned his fellow money on a surety's security . . . "), because in such an event "he had lent him the money through his trust in the surety" (*ibid.,* 8). R. Ishmael decided that a written suretyship was valid even if it was given after creation of the principal obligation (*ibid.;* and cf. Ket. 101b–102b). Some of the early *amoraim* held that such a suretyship was valid even if it was undertaken verbally, but the *halakhah* was decided in accordance with the opinion of R. Naḥman, to the effect that a verbal suretyship is valid if given at the time of creation of the principal obligation ("at the time the money is handed over"); otherwise (i.e., "after the money has been handed over") it will only be valid if accompanied by a *kinyan sudar* (see Acquisition;[2] BB 176a–b and Codes). The distinction stems from the general principle in Jewish law that the promissor's "final making up of the mind" (*gemirat ha-da'at,* see Contract[3]) is an essential precondition of a valid undertaking. Hence it may be presumed that this requirement is satisfied on the part of the surety whenever the loan is given "on his security" – even if undertaken verbally – since he is aware that the very loan is given on the strength of his suretyship; the position is different, however, if the suretyship is given after the execution of the loan transaction, since then the surety's final decision is not manifest unless his verbal undertaking is accompanied by the formality of a *kinyan sudar.* According to the view of the Babylonian *amoraim,* which was accepted as the *halakhah,* the possible absence of a *gemirat ha-da'at* was to be feared more with a suretyship undertaking than with any other kind of undertaking, since the very essence of the suretyship undertaking is tainted with the defect of *asmakhta* – i.e., the surety's confident assumption that the borrower will pay the debt and the claim against him will never materialize. The invalidating effect of *asmakhta* on suretyship was overcome by the scholars through reasoning that the surety derives pleasure from being regarded as trustworthy and a man of means.

In the following cases a verbal suretyship without a *kinyan* is valid even if it is undertaken after establishment of the principal obligation: if it is given on the instructions of the court (BB 176b and Codes); if on the strength of the suretyship the lender has returned to the borrower the bond of indebtedness or pledge (Sh. Ar., HM 129:3); and if the surety is not an individual but the community or its representative (Resp. Maharam of Rothenburg, ed. Prague, no. 38; see also Public Authority[4]). Alternatives to a *kinyan sudar* also came into being. Thus, according to some of the *posekim,* a written suretyship obviates any need for a *kinyan* (Nov. Ramban, and *Beit ha-Beḥirah,* BB 176; Sh. Ar., HM 129:4). Suretyship may also be established by handshake whenever custom decrees that an obligation may be established in this way (*Darkhei Moshe,* HM 129:5; Rema, HM 129:5). It is interesting to note the historical changes concerning

1. page 242; 2. page 208; 3. page 247; 4. page 647.

the use of a handshake as a means of establishing a suretyship obligation. In biblical times it had this function; it fell into complete disuse during the talmudic period, and it appeared again in post-talmudic times under the influence of its use in other contemporary legal systems. According to some of the *posekim* even a verbal suretyship undertaken after the establishment of the principal obligation is valid if it is the custom to dispense with the need for a formal *kinyan* (see *Minhag*[1]).

Arev and Arev Kabbelan. The *tannaim* and the *amoraim* of Ereẓ Israel knew the regular form of surety *(arev)* in which the creditor must first sue and seek to recover payment from the debtor; only when the debt cannot be satisfied out of the debtor's property may the creditor turn to the surety for payment, because it is presumed that it was the surety's intention to become liable for the debt only in such an event. A creditor who wished to ensure effective recovery of the debt could stipulate with the surety that "I shall recover from whomever I choose," whereupon he could claim directly from the surety whether or not the debtor had sufficient property to satisfy the debt. R. Simeon b. Gamaliel's opinion, that as long as the debtor has property, payment must always be demanded from him first, was not accepted as *halakhah* (BB 10:7; TJ, BB 10:14, 17d, and see statements of R. Johanan, loc. cit.). The Babylonian *amoraim,* however, interpreted these mishnaic statements (in the light of R. Johanan's variant version) to mean that even when the creditor has stipulated with the surety as mentioned above, he may not, in the opinion of all, demand payment from the surety as long as the debtor's known assets, such as land, have not been exhausted. In their opinion, the only case in which the creditor may claim directly from the surety without first excusing the debtor (even if he has known assets) is when the surety is an *arev kabbelan,* that is, when he has carefully formulated his undertaking in a particular manner so as to avoid the use of terms such as "loan" or "suretyship," saying instead, e.g., "Give to him and I shall give to you." R. Simeon b. Gamaliel's contrary opinion, that the debtor must first be excused if he has any property even if the surety is an *arev kabbelan,* was not accepted as *halakhah* (BB 173b and Tos. ad. loc. s.v. *Hasurei Meḥasrei*).

An explanation for the restraint on the freedom of contract in suretyship, contrary to the general principle of Jewish law that "contracting out of the Torah" is permissible in matters of civil law, see Contract,[2] lies in the apprehension expressed by the Babylonian *amoraim* about the surety's lack of final resolve when making a suretyship undertaking, and the resulting inference that the surety does not seriously intend to be bound by his undertaking as long as the debt may be recovered from the principal debtor – even if he has expressly agreed to it (Rashba. Nov. BB 173b). In post-talmudic times the scholars sought ways in which to overcome the restriction on the freedom of stipulation in suretyship because of its limiting effect of the scope of credit transactions. Some scholars interpreted the statements of the Babylonian *amoraim* to mean that they, like the *amoraim* of Ereẓ Israel, held the opinion that the creditor might claim directly from the surety once he has stipulated with the latter to recover "from whomever I choose" (Ibn Miggash, quoted in *Sefer ha-Terumot,* 35:2; Yad, Malveh 25:4; and see Elon, *Divrei ha-Congress* 203ff). Other scholars considered the version "I shall recover from whomever I choose" to be ineffective and distinguished it from one worded "I shall recover first from whomever I choose," holding that this entitles the creditor to claim directly from the surety whether or not the debtor has any property (Ramban, Nov. BB 173b; Tur, HM 129:17, et al.). The *halakhah* was decided according to the former opinion (Sh. Ar., HM 129:14).

The post-talmudic socioeconomic realities spurred a number of further developments designed to enable the creditor to claim directly from the surety, including a regular surety, even without prior stipulation to this effect. Thus it was laid down that if the debtor is violent and does not comply with the judgment of the court, or if he is abroad and the suit against him involves many difficulties, or if he has died, the creditor may claim directly from the surety (Yad, Malveh 25:3; 26:3 and *Maggid Mishneh* thereto; Sh. Ar., HM 129:8–12). The creditor always retains the right to claim first from the debtor, even when he is entitled to claim directly from the surety, and the debtor is not entitled to refer him to the surety; however, if the surety is a *kabbelan* who has personally received the money of the loan from the lender and passed it on to the borrower, no legal tie will have been created between lender and borrower and the lender will be entitled to recover the debt from the surety alone (Yad, Malveh 26:3; Sh. Ar., HM 129:15, 19).

Substance and Scope of Suretyship. The surety's obligation is secondary to that of the principal debtor; hence the validity of the suretyship obligation is co-extensive with that of the principal obligation and extinction of the latter automatically terminates the suretyship: "if there is no debt, there is no suretyship" (Resp. Maharashdam, HM no. 218). Thus e.g., if the principal obligation is void because the debtor was acting under duress (see *Ones*), the suretyship will be equally ineffective – even though it was undertaken according to the law (*ibid.* and Resp. Reshakh, pt. 1, no. 44). Moreover, the same result follows even when the underlying principal obligation is essentially valid but cannot be realized against the debtor on account of a procedural defect, as may happen if the name of the debtor and other details mentioned in a bond of indebtedness fit two persons and do not allow for his proper identification, thus barring proceedings against him. In such an event the surety, too, cannot be called upon for payment, not even in the case where he is surety to two debtors who have identical names (Bek. 48a; Tur and Sh. Ar., HM 49:10; cf. also the contrary opinion of Rema, HM 129:8 and *Baḥ* thereon).

On the other hand, suretyship may be undertaken in respect of only a part of the principal obligation and the surety may also stipulate that his obligation shall only be in effect for a specified period after the debt has fallen due (Resp. Rashba, vol. 1, no. 1148; Rema and standard commentaries to Sh. Ar., HM 129:1 and Tur. *ibid.; Arukh ha-Shulḥan,* HM 129:7). Suretyship may be undertaken in respect of either an already existing principal obligation or one about to be established, the sole distinction between them being their two different modes of establishment (see above). The validity of suretyship in respect of a debt of an unfixed amount is a matter on which there is a division of opinion in the Codes. It was held by some scholars that if the surety has said, "I am surety for whatever amount you shall give." he is liable for the whole amount, "even if one hundred thousand" (Yad, Malveh 25:13; see Samuel b. Hophni, bibl., ch. 3). According to other *posekim,* the surety is not liable at all in such an event: "since he does not know what it is that he has bound himself for, he did not make a final resolve and did not bind himself" (Yad, loc. cit.). A third opinion is that the suretyship is binding to the extent of the amount for which the surety may reasonably be presumed to have bound himself, with attention given to his financial means (*Hassagot Rabad* and *Maggid Mishneh* loc. cit.). The *halakhah* was decided to the effect that a suretyship for an unspecified amount is valid (Sh. Ar., HM 131:13).

Scope of the Surety's Liability. The suretyship obligation includes liability for the expenses incurred by the creditor in claiming payment, such as the costs of a legal suit (Sh. Ar., HM

1. page 102; 2. page 251.

129:10 and *Sma* n. 29), and for any other reasonable loss suffered by the creditor (Tur, HM 131:7–10 and Maharik, quoted in *Beit Yosef, ibid.*, Sh. Ar., HM 131:7–8). According to the majority of the *posekim*, a regular surety is discharged from liability if the creditor, after due date of payment, neglects to recover the debt from the debtor when he has the possibility of doing so (Tur and Sh. Ar., HM 131:4; *Beit Yosef* and *Baḥ* thereto). Similarly, "if the debtor was present in the town when the debt fell due for payment and the creditor allowed him to depart the town, he cannot claim from the surety" (*Keneset ha-Gedolah*, HM 129; Tur. no. 58). The surety is likewise discharged from liability if the creditor releases any of the debtor's property which he holds as a pledge (Resp. Rashba, vol. 1, no. 892; Sh. Ar., HM 129:8 and Rema thereto; *Sma* HM 129–26; *Arukh ha-Shulḥan* HM 129:26).

Suretyship in Respect of Different Kinds of Obligations. In general, suretyship may validly be undertaken with reference to all kinds of obligations, regardless of the manner in which they arise (for instance from loan, the most common case, tort (Git. 49b), and so on). In certain cases, however, this has been a matter of halakhic dispute, particularly with reference to the husband's *ketubbah* obligation. Among the *tannaim* and *amoraim* of Ereẓ Israel, and for most of the period of the Babylonian *amoraim*, there was never any doubt that a person could be surety for the husband's obligations toward his wife in respect of her *ketubbah* (BB 9:8; BB 174b, in the matter of Moses bar Aẓri). However, in the sixth generation of the Babylonian *amoraim*, following on their raising the problem of the invalidating effect of *asmakhta* on suretyship (see above), they likewise called into question the measure of final resolve and seriousness with which the surety might undertake his obligation in respect of a *ketubbah* liability. There were two reasons for this: firstly, because it was considered that in such a case the surety intends no more than to perform a *mitzvah* and to bring about a matrimonial tie between the couple concerned; secondly, because in this case the husband undertakes to give his wife an amount which comes out of his own pocket and not one which the wife has initially expended – unlike the case of a loan, for instance, in which the creditor is made to incur an actual expenditure. Special requirements were accordingly laid down for the validity of suretyship as regards the *ketubbah*. Some scholars held regular suretyship to be entirely ineffective here, except if the surety is the groom's father (because of the kinship the existence of *gemirat ha-da'at* may be presumed), in which case it is valid if executed by *kinyan sudar;* other scholars held that regular suretyship is effective when executed by *kinyan sudar* and that this formality is unnecessary when the surety is the groom's father. If the suretyship is of the *kabbelan* type, the scholars agree that it is valid in all cases and there is no need for a *kinyan* (BB 174b; Yad, Malveh 25:6; Ishut 17:9 and *Hassagot Rabad* thereto).

With regard to a gift, the scholars are futher divided on the question of whether the suretyship undertaking in respect of this is to be treated like suretyship for the *ketubbah* (because in gift also the donee will suffer no actual loss if the transaction is not carried out) or whether it should be regarded otherwise since in the case of a gift it cannot be said that the surety's intention is the performance of a *mitzvah;* (Tur. HM 129 and *Beit Yosef* s.v. *beresh perek ha-nezakin*, Sh. Ar., EH 102:6 and Rema thereto).

A Surety's Right of Recourse Against Debtor. A surety has the right to recoup from the debtor whatever he has paid to the creditor in discharge of the principal obligation. In order for him to succeed in his claim against the debtor, it will not suffice for the surety to present the bond of indebtedness as holder thereof; he must prove by way of the creditor's certification or in some other equally persuasive manner that he has actually discharged the debt (Tosef. BB 11:15; Yad, Malveh, 26:7–8; Sh. Ar., HM 130:1, 3). The surety's right of reimbursement is to be explained either on the basis of an implied agreement between the debtor and the surety that the latter will be entitled to reimburse himself from the former if he discharges the principal obligation, or that upon receiving payment from the surety the creditor assigns to him (by way of subrogation) his right of recovery against the debtor (BB 32b and Rashbam thereto; *Maggid Mishneh*, Malveh 26:8; and see below).

The right of recourse against the debtor is available to the surety only when his suretyship has been solicited by the former and, in the case of a regular surety, only after the creditor has already proceeded against the debtor (Yad, loc. cit. 6; Sh. Ar., HM 131:2). For if he is a surety on his own initiative, "any person who wishes to avenge himself of his neighbor might do so by becoming surety for him in order to turn to the latter after discharging his debt" (Resp. Radbaz no. 2084); an unsolicited surety is in the position of a volunteer who pays another's debt without the latter's knowledge or approval and as such also has no right of action against the debtor (Ket. 107b–108a; Yad, loc. cit; Sh. Ar., HM 128:1; see also Unjust Enrichment[1]). Suretyship established in the debtor's presence will be presumed to have been undertaken with his approval (Resp. Radbaz, no. 2084; *Leḥem Mishneh* to Yad, Malveh 26:6). There is also an opinion that the surety has a right of recourse against the debtor even if he has not been solicited by him (*Maggid Mishneh*, relying on the opinion of Rabad to Yad, Malveh, 26:6; cf., however, Tur, HM 129 and Resp. Radbaz no. 2084, where this view is contested and Rabad's opinion interpreted differently). The surety's right of recourse extends not only to the amount of the principal obligation but also to the expenses he has incurred in the matter, because it is presumed that the debtor "takes upon himself . . . to compensate for and make good all loss . . . even without expressly stipulating to this effect" (Resp. Rosh 18:7; Tur and Sh. Ar., HM 131:7ff.), except for unreasonable expenses such as "interest much above the customary" (*Beit Yosef*, HM 131, n. 7; and see above with regard to the scope of the surety's liability).

Plurality of Sureties and Debtors. If there are several sureties the creditor may not claim more from each than his proportional share of the debt unless he has expressly contracted for the right to recover the whole amount of the debt from any of them (Tosef. BB 11:15). Maimonides, contrary to this *halakhah*, held that the creditor may recover the whole of the debt from any one of several sureties and Abraham b. David of Posquières was of the opinion that the matter is determined by local custom, but other *posekim* confirmed that a proportional share only may be recovered from each (Yad, Malveh 25:10 and *Hassagot Rabad* thereto; Sh. Ar., HM 132:3 and standard commentaries). Where several debtors are jointly involved in a single legal transaction – such as "two who borrow on the same bond . . . or a partner who borrows on behalf of the partnership" – some of the *posekim* hold that each is a principal debtor in respect of the whole debt, but the majority opinion is that each is liable as principal debtor in respect of his proportional share only and must be considered a regular surety as regards the rest of the debt; i.e., the creditor must first claim from each his proportional share, and only if one of them is unable to pay will the other be liable as surety for him (TJ, Shevu. 5:1, 36a; Yad, Malveh 25:9 and standard commentaries; Tur and Sh. Ar., HM 77:1–2; for further particulars see Obligations, Law of[2]).

In the State of Israel. In 1967 the Knesset enacted the Surety Law, which replaces the provisions of the *Mejelle* (Ottoman law) on this subject. Although largely based on Jewish law, it nevertheless deviates from it on one central matter. The law provides

1. page 337; 2. page 245.

that "the surety and debtor are jointly and severally liable to the creditor, but the creditor may not require of the surety fulfillment of his suretyship without first requiring the debtor to discharge his debt" (sec. 8). The creditor is not required to make prior demand of the debtor if this need is waived by the surety, or if it is clear that the debtor has no property, or if service of the demand against him involves special difficulties. The law accordingly allows the creditor to turn directly to the surety, even a regular one, since a demand from the debtor is a mere formality and it is not necessary that legal proceedings be instituted against him. This accords with the attitude of both the *Mejelle* (arts. 643, 644) and English law, both of which dispense even with the need for a prior demand from the debtor, a requirement which is indeed of little practical value (I. Jenks, *Digest of English Civil Law,* 1 (1938[1]), 277, no. 682). On the other hand, Swiss law (*Code des obligations.* para. 495.6) and the Nordic Draft Code of 1963 (see V. Kruse, *A Nordic Draft Code* (1963), para. 1301) accord with Jewish law in this respect and require the creditor, in the absence of an express agreement to the contrary, to claim first from the principal debtor and to exhaust execution proceedings against him before turning to the surety, except if there are special difficulties involved in suing the debtor. Swiss law furthermore recognizes the institution of *Solidarbuergschaft* (*ibid.* para. 496), which is akin to the *ạrev kabbelan* in Jewish law.

Bibliography: Samuel b. Hophni, *Sefer ha-Arevut ve-ha-Kabbelanut,* ed. by S. Assaf, in: *Zikhronot . . . shel ha-Rav Kook* (1945), 139–59; I. S. Zuri, *Mishpat ha-Talmud,* 5 (1921), 139–41; A. Abeles, in: MGWJ, 66 (1922), 279–94; 67 (1923), 35–53, 122–30, 170–86, 254–7; Gulak, Yesodei, 2 (1922), 88–95; idem, Oẓar, 59–65, 107–9, 152, 259–66; idem, *Toledot ha-Mishpat be-Yisrael bi-Tekufat ha-Talmud,* 1 (*Ha-Ḥiyyuv ve-Shi'budav,* 1939), 81–88; Herzog, Instit, 2 (1939), 197–208; ET, 7 (1956), 61–63; 12 (1967), 717–21; S. M. Stern, in: JJS, 15 (1964), 141–7; Elon, in: *Divrei ha-Congress ha-Olami ha-Revi'i le-Madda'ei ha-Yahadut,* 1 (1967), 197–208; Engl. abstract: *ibid.,* Engl. section, 268f.; idem, in: ILR, 4 (1969), 4–96; idem, *Ha-Mishpat Ha-Ivri* (1973), I, p. 104ff, II, 572, 775ff, III, 838ff, 900ff, 950ff, 960ff, 1345ff; A. Greenbaum, in: KS, 46 (1970/71), 154–69.

Menachem Elon

LIEN (Heb. שעבוד נכסים, *Shi'bud Nekhasim*). **The Concept.** Jewish law enables the creditor to exercise a lien over all the debtor's property, in addition to his remedies against the debtor personally. This lien automatically comes into existence on the creation to the obligation and is called *aḥarayut* or *shi'bud nekhasim* (i.e., "property bearing responsibility" or the "encumbrance of property"). Sometimes the parties may limit the application of the lien to a specified part of the debtor's property, in which event it may operate either in addition to the general charge on the debtor's property or so as to release the remaining property from any such encumbrance. A limitation of the lien to a specified asset may be effected in two ways: firstly, by the asset remaining in the debtor's possession, in which event the lien is called *apoteke* (see below); secondly, by the debtor surrendering possession of the asset to the creditor, this being called *mashkon,* i.e., pledge. The law relating to the latter is dealt with fully under pledge.

Import of the Term Aḥarayut Nekhasim. Originally, the general lien applied only to the real estate (*karka,* "land") of the debtor because land could not be carried away or spoiled and was therefore deemed "property bearing responsibility" (Kid 1:5). Chattels were regarded as incapable of being preserved and were therefore deemed property "not bearing responsibility" *(ibid.).* The special reasons for the availability in Jewish law of the automatic lien in respect of all obligations will be dealt with below and in the article on Obligation.

The concept of a charge on assets is already mentioned in a *takkanah* from the time of Simeon b. Shetaḥ, concerning a husband's written undertaking to his wife that all his property shall be charged in her favor to secure the repayment of her *ketubbah* (Ket. 82b); it may be assumed that a charge of this nature was known at that time in respect of other obligations as well. In the third century the *amoraim* Ulla and Rabbah disputed the question whether a charge of this nature originated from Pentateuchal law *(shi'buda de-oraita)* or from rabbinical enactment *(de-rabbanan).* According to some of the *rishonim,* this dispute related only to the question of seizing assets which had been alienated by the debtor to a third party, and that as long as the assets remained with the debtor all agreed that they were subject to the Pentateuchal lien (Tos. to BB 175b and *Bet ha-Beḥirah* thereto). Other *rishonim* were of the opinion that the dispute was one of principle, whether or not the encumbered assets had been alienated, namely: whether the right of recovery of the debt in this way flowed from the personal aspect of the obligation, as was the case when the creditor recovered payment out of the chattels of the debtor, or whether in relation to land the creditor acquired a lien also in the nature of a rent right, in addition to the personal obligation (Rashbam, Tos. to BB 175b; Nov. Rashba, *ibid.;* Nov. Ritba Kid. 13b; see also Elon, *Ha-Mishpat Ha-Ivri,* II, 485, 488ff and *Ḥerut ha-Perat . . .* 21). The *halakhah* was decided in accordance with the view of *shi'buda de-oraita* (Yad, Malveh, 11:4; Sh. Ar., HM 111; *Sma ibid.,* n. 1).

Substance of the Creditor's Right in the Debtor's Property. The creditor's general lien over the debtor's property does not allow him a full proprietary right *(zekhut kinyanit).* This finds expression mainly in two respects. Firstly, the right of lien does not preclude the debtor from validly transferring ownership of his property to another, albeit subject to the fact that the creditor, when seeking to recover payment, is entitled to seize the property from the party who acquired it (this right of seizure is known as *terifah,* from the *nekhasim meshu'badim,* i.e., the "encumbered and alienated property"). As will be seen below, special rules were laid down governing the right of seizure from any such transferee. Secondly, the lien is subordinate to and dependent on the debtor's own ownership in the property, and hence the latter, in certain circumstances, is able to oust or extinguish the creditor's lien over his property.

Recovery of the Debt out of Encumbered Assets. It is a substantive principle that a debt may not be satisfied out of the *nekhasim meshu'badim* (see above) as long as the debtor is possessed of other assets, i.e., *nekhasim benei ḥorin* ("free property"), even if the remaining assets are inferior to those to which the creditor is entitled (e.g., the free assets are *beinonit* or average, whereas the obligation is tortious and must therefore be satisfied from the *iddit,* or best). If the debtor has sold the encumbered property to several purchasers, the creditor must first recover from the last purchaser since the anterior one may plead: "I have left you room to recover from him." Similarly, the purchaser retains the right to pay in cash rather than surrender the encumbered property. Where there are several creditors, a preferential right of lien over the debtor's property will be enjoyed by the creditor to whom the debtor first became indebted (Git. 48b; BK 8a; Sh. Ar., HM 104; see also Execution, Civil[1]).

Creation of the Debt. As long as the debtor's property remained in his possession there would be no need to limit the creditor's lien therein, as mentioned above. However, there was

1. page 629.

good reason for limiting the right of seizure from the transferee of the encumbered assets only to cases where the debt was originally evidenced in writing (i.e., *milveh bi-shetar,* "loan by deed") and not orally *(milveh be-al peh).* The *amoraim* disputed the legal justification of this limitation (BB 175b). In the opinion of Ulla, the law entitled the creditor to seize encumbered land from the purchaser even for an orally established debt, except that the scholars had regulated against it in order not to cause loss to the purchaser of such land, since an "oral" debt had no *kol* ("publicity," lit. "voice") and the purchaser would therefore have no notice of the land's encumbrance in favor of the creditor. On the other hand, Rabbah was of the opinion that the law did not recognize the institution of *aḥarayut nekhasim* at all and the creditor's right to recover from the debtor's property, including land, derived from a personal liability only, which could not be enforced except against the debtor's free property (see above). However, the scholars enacted that, in the case of a debt evidenced in writing and constituting notice, the creditor could seize the debtor's property from the purchaser, for otherwise the creditor would have no security for the repayment of the debt and thus no borrower would ever be able to obtain a loan. The need to secure repayment of the debt in such a firm manner so as to forestall any reluctance to grant a loan most probably stemmed from the fact that in Jewish law the prohibition against interest precluded the earning of any profit from the actual loan, and accordingly the principal at least had to be adequately secured. From its application to a liability originating from loan, this rule was also extended to other obligations (L. Auerbach, *Das juedische Obligationenrecht,* 1 (1870), 172). Since the reason for precluding seizure from the purchaser in the case of an oral debt was to avoid loss because he had no notice of the debt's existence, R. Pappa decided that the creditor could seize the land of the debtor if the third party into whose hands it had passed was the heir of the debtor (BB 176a; but cf. the opinion of Rav, TJ, BK 10:1, 7b and BM 1:6, 8a; BB 175a and the opinion of Samuel there); the *halakhah* was decided accordingly in the codes (Yad, Malveh 11:4, Sh. Ar., HM 107:1).

In post-talmudic times various *takkanot* were enacted laying down that a debt was not to be considered a written one unless the deed was written and signed by a scribe and witnesses specially appointed for the purpose (see Sh. Ar., HM 61:1), whereby the maximum notice and warning were thus afforded to potential purchasers – in much the same way as mortgages are registered in land registry offices at the present time.

A debt established by deed provided the right of exacting payment out of encumbered property, even if not so expressly stipulated – the omission being attributed to "an error of the scribe" (BM 14a; 15b). With regard to an obligation stemming from the *ketubbah,* this rule was specifically endorsed in a special enactment (Ket. 4:7). An exception to the rule distinguishing between oral obligation and one by deed was recognized in the case of land sold with a guarantee (i.e., in respect of claims by third parties against the land) in the presence of witnesses, even without a deed. In this event the purchaser could exact the purchase price from the encumbered property, it being considered that a sale of land before witnesses would become known even in the absence of a written instrument (BB 41b and Codes). Similarly, and for the same reason, the creditor could exact payment from the debtor's encumbered property if there was an obligation established by way of a *kinyan* before witnesses (see Acquisition; BB, 40a; Sh. Ar., HM 39:1).

Seizure for a Debt of Fixed Amount Only. The scholars regulated "for the sake of good order" *(mi-penei tikkun olam)* that recovery could be made out of encumbered assets only for a debt of a fixed amount and not otherwise, e.g., in respect of maintenance for a wife and daughters (Git. 5:3, 50b and Codes).

Debts Stemming from Tort. According to tannaitic law, an injured party could recover all the various measures of compensation from *nekhasim meshu'badim* (even though not stipulated in the deed; Tosef., Ket. 2:2). However, the *amoraim* disputed the question of whether an obligation imposed by a law was subject to the same rules as one agreed upon in a deed (Bek. 49b et al.). In the light of the rule that a debt for an unspecified amount was not recoverable from encumbered assets, it would seem that there was room for extending the limitation also to a debt stemming from tort, for precisely the same reason. The matter remained a disputed one, however, even in the Codes (see e.g., Tos. To BK 8a s.v., כול *Beit Yosef,* Tur, HM 119 n. 4).

Any obligation not recoverable out of *nekhasim meshu'badim* becomes recoverable in this way in consequence of a judgment of the court on a claim submitted (BB 175b; BK 104b–105a).

Encumbrance of Assets. Originally, the law was that a lien extended only to assets in the possession of the debtor at the time the debt was created (cf. the ancient wording: "all the property that I have," Ket. 4:7; Tosef., Ket. 12:1), and property later acquired could not be seized by the creditor once it had been transferred to a third party (Yad, Malveh 18:1; Sh. Ar., HM 112:1). In order to increase the creditor's security, however, the scholars prescribed that if, at the time the debt was created, the debtor agreed that property he might acquire in the future would also be subjected to the lien, this would also form part of his encumbered assets, i.e., from the time it came into his possession (TJ, Ket. 4:8, 29a; BB 44b). This rule was discussed in the light of the principle that a person could not transfer ownership of something not in his possession (*reshut;* see Contract[1]), but the distinction was made that one could nevertheless encumber property in this manner (BB 157a/b; Yad, Malveh 18:1; Sh. Ar., HM 112:1). The opinion is expressed in the Codes that, in view of the rule of "the scribe's error" (see above), the lien also extended to assets acquired by the debtor after the creation of the debt, even if not expressly agreed to by him when the obligation came into being (Rema, HM 112:1).

Chattels as Encumbered Property. In the amoraic period the rule that a lien extended only to the debtor's land underwent a variation: it was laid down that if, at the time of creation of the debt and as security for it, the debtor expressly charged the chattels incidental to his land *agav karka;* see Acquisition[2]), the lien would also extend to such chattels, whether they were in his possession or acquired thereafter (BB 44b; Yad, Malveh 18:2; Sh. Ar., HM 113:1–2). The extension of the lien in this manner was due to the fact that the number of landowners had diminished and the lien, if limited to land alone, would have failed to provide adequate security for the repayment of a debt. With the intensification of this economic trend in geonic times, the practice was accepted of *kinyan* ("acquisition") incidental to land – even if the debtor owned none at all – involving the doctrine of the "four cubits *[arba ammot]* in Ereẓ Israel" said to be possessed by every Jew. For the same reason a special *takkanah* was enacted in the geonic period, making it possible – contrary to talmudic law (see Ket. 92a) – for the creditor also to exact payment out of the debtor's chattels acquired by his heirs (*Ḥemdah Genuzah* no. 65; cf. justification of the rule on similar grounds, Rashbam BB 174a; see also Yad, Malveh 11:11; Sh. Ar., HM 107:1).

This *takkanah* concerning the seizure of the debtor's chattels after they passed into the hands of his heirs was unlikely to create difficulty, since it was only proper that the heirs should fulfill the obligations of the deceased. However, so far as pur-

1. page 248; 2. page 208.

chasers were concerned, the growing practice whereby even one's chattels were charged on the creation of an obligation, caused the creditor's consequent right of seizure to be a serious obstacle to business transaction. Accordingly, the earlier practice was reverted to and it became accepted that the creditor would not recover from chattels sold to a third party, even though the debtor had expressly agreed in the deed to charge such of his chattels as were incidental to land – this being justified by the *takkanat ha-shuk* ("market overt") – for otherwise no person would be able to buy any chattel from his neighbor for fear that a lien existed in favor of his creditors (Resp. Rosh 79:5; also 4 and 6; Tur, and Sh. Ar., HM 60:1; but cf. also *Siftei Kohen* HM 60, n. 4, where the custom is contested).

To counter the fear of prospective purchasers that property acquired from a seller was subject to being seized by the latter's creditors, the practice was adopted – in terms of a *takkanah* enacted in the Middle Ages and observed in many communities – whereby at the time of the sale of land any person claiming a right or lien over the property in question was publicly called upon to come forward within a period of 15 days (Resp. Rashba, vol. 6, nos. 6–7) or 30 days (idem, vol. 2, no. 95) and establish his claim, failing which he would lose his right and thenceforth be precluded from raising any objection to the sale and from making any claim by way of lien or otherwise over the property (see also Resp. Rosh no. 18:16; Tur, HM 104:3; Resp. Ritba, no. 156).

Cancellation and Extinction of Lien. The creditor's lien over the debtor's property is extinguished by the cancellation of the underlying obligation – i.e., by the repayment of the debt or the debtor's release from it – and hence "a deed which has been borrowed on and repaid cannot be borrowed on again, since release has already been granted from its lien" (Ket. 85a). The creditor may, however, relinquish his lien in favor of one purchaser while retaining it in respect of other purchasers (Ket. 95a and Codes), and he may also release part of the encumbered assets from the operation of the lien, while retaining it in respect of other parts (Tur and Sh. Ar., HM 111:12). In both cases the release has no validity unless formally effected by way of *kinyan* (*ibid.;* also 118:1).

As mentioned above, the creditor's lien does not amount to an independent proprietary right, but is subject to the debtor's own ownership of the encumbered property. Hence, the termination of the latter's ownership of the property may, in certain circumstances, automatically extinguish the creditor's lien therein. The Talmud mentions three cases in which the creditor's lien is extinguished as a result of the debtor's loss of ownership of the encumbered property: when the proprietor has made an irredeemable consecration (*kedushat ha-guf;* see *Hekdesh*) of the property, in which event it is thereafter and for all time placed beyond the ownership of the common man (*hedyot;* Git. 40b; Tur and Sh. Ar., HM 117:7) – according to Maimonides a redeemable consecration *(kedushat dammim)* also extinguishes the lien, save that the creditor may seize the property if and when it is redeemed (Yad, Malveh 18:6–7; Arakhin 7:14–16); when there is a prohibition against deriving benefit from the property, e.g., *ḥameẓ* ("leaven") during Passover, which has the effect of nullifying ownership of the property; and when the property in question is a slave manumitted by his owner, since thereupon the right of ownership is totally extinguished (Git., Yad, Land Sh. Ar., *ibid.;* and see below).

A person who causes a lien over his property to be extinguished is nevertheless liable to the creditor for any loss resulting to the latter (see also *Gerama;* Torts).

Apoteke (אפותיקי) *Apoteke* is distinguished from the implied general lien by the fact that it is limited to a specific part of the property of the debtor, in whose possession it remains. The term is of Greek origin and in several tannaitic sources is rendered as "היפותיקי" (*hippoteke;* Tosef. Shev. 8:6, Ket. 11:8, BM 1:8). Despite this Greek origin, however, in its substance and legal rules *apoteke* is in Jewish law similar to the general lien, and in fact it differs from the Greek hypothec (υποθηκη) in essential principles (see below). In effect, *apoteke* does not create a new charge on the property in question since all the debtor's property is included in the implied, comprehensive charge that comes into existence upon creation of the obligation, but merely serves to restrict an already existing charge to particular assets. For this reason, Jewish law sources make no specific mention of the term *shi'bud apoteke,* but speak of "defining" or "setting aside" a field (Git. 37a; Ket. 54b, 55a, 81b; BB 50a; TJ, Shev. 10:1, 39b), i.e., singling out of a particular asset from the generally charged property. The *rishonim* interpreted the term *apoteke* as a notarikon (from אפה תהא קאי , i.e., "on this it shall stand": *Arukh ha-Shalem,* s.v. אפתק ; Rashi BK 11b; Rashbam BB 44b; or from פה תקנה – Maim., Comm. to Git. 4:4). The rule is that the creditor may only exact payment from the hypothecated property in respect of such obligations as would serve to create in his favor a general lien over the debtor's property, i.e., a debt by deed and not an oral one, etc. (*Beit Yosef,* HM 117, n. 3). Talmudic sources indicate that the *apoteke* itself had to be created by deed (Tosef., Shev. 8:6); but it was later laid down in the Codes that an *apoteke* could be created before witnesses without deed, although the underlying obligation itself had to be under deed (*Beit Yosef,* loc. cit.).

The hypothecated property generally consisted of land, but instances are also mentioned where the *apoteke* attached *(inter alia)* to slaves (Git. 4:4) and to a bond of indebtedness, e.g., the *ketubbah* (Tosef., Ket. 11:1; Rashi's interpretation, in commenting on Ket. 54a, that the *apoteke* is effected specifically in relation to the land of the wife included in the *ketubbah* does not accord with the plain meaning of the Tosefta statement, but shows the influence of Rava's ruling; see below); and to chattels collectively (to a *ḥavilah,* "bundle"; Tosef., Ket. 11:8). In the fourth century it was laid down by Rava in Babylonia that a hypothecated slave who had been sold could be seized by a creditor in recovery of his debt, since the sale of a slave carried a "voice" and purchasers would have warning, whereas the sale of a hypothecated ox or ass carried no "voice" and therefore these were not recoverable from a purchaser in settlement of the vendor's debt. Even then, however, a hypothecated slave afforded only limited security for the creditor, since already in the Mishnah it was prescribed that a slave manumitted by his owner, i.e., the debtor, could not be seized in recovery of the latter's debt (Git. 4:4) because his manumission extinguished the charge (TJ, Yev. 7:1, 8a and see above). This was in accordance with the fundamental doctrine of human liberty that "a slave, once liberated, does not return to servitude" (TJ, Pes. 2:2, 29a). Hence it was not common to execute *apoteke,* not even in respect of slaves, and *apoteke* came to be equaled with the general lien, attaching to land only and not to chattels. Later this was enshrined in the Codes in absolute manner, to the effect that no (alienated) hypothecated chattels of any kind were recoverable in payment of a debt since they carried no "voice," even if the *apoteke* was executed by deed and the purchaser had notice of it (Tur and Sh. Ar., HM 117:3; see also *Sma,* HM 117, n. 13).

Simple and Express Apoteke (apoteke setam and apoteke meforash). Jewish law recognizes hypothecation of a specific asset in two different ways, each having its own rules concerning the creditor's right of recovery from such an asset. In the first case, referred to in the Codes as *apoteke setam* (Tur, HM 117:1), the debtor gives a written undertaking to his creditor that if he should fail to repay the debt, "you may recover from this asset." As long as the debtor fails to repay the debt in cash and the asset remains in his possession, the creditor is entitled to exact payment out of such an asset and the debtor is not entitled to offer substitute assets. If the hypothecated asset should not suffice to repay the debt, or becomes spoiled, or ceases to exist, the creditor may recover payment out of the debtor's other asset (Git. 41a; Yad, Malveh 18:3; Sh. Ar., HM 117:1). Just as the general lien does not preclude the debtor from selling his assets, so he is also free to sell assets subject to a simple hypothecation. As long as he retains any free property, the creditor may not recover his debt out of such hypothecated assets alienated by the debtor (TJ, Yev. 7:1, 8a; Git. 41a). If the debtor has no free property, the creditor may recover from the hypothecated property in a purchaser's hands, even if other encumbered assets were alienated by the debtor after his alienation of the hypothecated property; in this respect *apoteke* gives the creditor a right that ranks in preference to that available to the creditor under the general lien (see above). However, the purchaser of hypothecated property – like the debtor himself – retains the right to repay the debt in cash (Yad, Malveh 18:4, 8, and *Maggid Mishneh,* ad. loc. *Sma,* HM 117 n. 8).

Simeon b. Gamaliel expressed the opinion that alienation was forbidden of assets hypothecated in favor of a woman's *ketubbah,* since "a woman is not in the habit of having recourse to the courts," and that she could recover her *ketubbah* from the hypothecated property only, and not from the remaining property in her husband's possession (Git. 41a). Apparently, however, he too was of the opinion that if the hypothecated property did not equal the value of the *ketubbah* or if it depreciated, the wife could recover from the remaining property of her husband (cf. Ket. 4:7; Tosef., Ket. 11:8; see Gulak, *Ha-Hiyyuv ve Shi'budav,* 55). The *halakhah* was decided in accordance with the opposing view of the scholars, so that no difference is recognized between the *ketubbah* obligation and any other obligation (Yad, and Sh. Ar., loc. cit.).

Express *apoteke* (termed *apoteke meforash* in the Codes is constituted when the debtor makes a written declaration to the creditor that "you shall not recover payment except out of this [asset]" (*lo yehe lekha pera'on ella mi-zo,* Git. 41a; BM 66b; TJ, Ket. 10:6, 34a). In this event no charge attaches to the debtor's remaining property and hence if the hypothecated property should be spoiled the creditor may not recover payment out of the debtor's free property nor out of other property alienated by him to a third party (Git. 41a). Expressly hypothecated property also does not provide the creditor with an absolute proprietary right therein. Thus, if its value exceeds the amount of the debt, the creditor must return the balance to the debtor. Furthermore, while the *amoraim* of Ereẓ Israel disputed the question of whether the debtor could alienate expressly hypothecated property (TJ, Shev. 10:1, 39b), it appears from the Babylonian Talmud that he may do so, except that the creditor can exact payment out of the hypothecated assets in the purchaser's possession even if the debtor has any free property, and except further that the purchaser is not entitled to pay in cash in lieu of the hypothecated property, as he may do in the case of simple hypothecation (BK 96a; the debtor himself retains the right to pay in cash in both cases). The *halakhah* was decided in the Codes in accordance with the latter view (Tur and Sh. Ar., HM 117:1; *Sma* HM 117, n. 5 and 6). Basically, therefore, express hypothecation afforded the creditor no greater rights than did simple hypothecation, whereas it did serve to deprive him of the general lien over all the other property of the debtor, and Gulak (*Ha-Ḥiyyuv* . . . p. 59f.) correctly surmises that its main purpose was to promote the free transaction of land sales by freeing all but a distinct part of the debtor's property from the creditor's lien.

In the State of Israel. The law in Israel recognizes no implied general lien of the kind known in Jewish law, but allows for the bonding of a specified asset in the creditor's favor by way of pledge or mortgage. A real estate mortgage is registered in the Land Registry Office, whereupon the mortgagor may not transfer ownership of the property without the consent of the mortgagee.

For further particulars see Pledge.

Bibliography: I. S. Zuri, *Mishpat ha-Talmud,* 4 (1921), 61–67; Gulak, Yesodei, 1 (1922), 141f., 149–65; 2 (1922), 8–10; idem, in: *Madda'ei ha-Yahadut,* 1 (1925/26), 46–48; idem, Oẓar, 235–8; idem, *Das Urkundenwesen im Talmud . . .* (1935), 114–25; idem, *Toledot ha-Mishpat be-Yisrael bi-Tekufat ha-Talmud,* 1 (*Ha-Ḥiyyuv ve-Shi'budav,* 1939), 31–61; Herzog, Instit, 1 (1936), 339–63; ET, 1 (1951^3), 216–20; 2 (1949), 130–4; 5 (1953), 121–32; M. Elon, *Ḥerut ha-Perat be-Darkhei Geviyyat Ḥov* (1964), 1–23; idem, Mafte'aḥ, 391–6; idem, *Ha-Mishpat Ha-Ivri* (1973), II, p. 354, 458ff, 482 – 493, 531ff, 601ff, 775ff.

Menachem Elon

PLEDGE

The Concept. In Jewish law, in addition to the personal right of action against the debtor, the creditor also has a right of lien on the latter's property. This lien automatically comes into being when the debt is created and is termed *aḥarayut* or *shi'bud nekhasim.* Sometimes the operation of the lien may be limited by the parties to a specified asset or part of the debtor's property, in one of two possible ways: either this distinct asset remains in the debtor's possession, in which case the lien is termed *apoteke,* or possession of the asset is surrendered to the creditor, which is termed *mashkon* ("pledge"). In both cases limitation of the lien to a distinct asset may be effected either so that it operates over and above the general lien on all the debtor's property, or so as to free all but the distinct asset from its operation; in the case of pledge, these two forms are referred to respectively as *mashkon stam* ("unconditional") and *mashkon meforash* ("express pledge"; Tur, HM 117:1).

Jewish law distinguishes between three types of pledge: a pledge taken when the debt is due for repayment, not in payment of it but as a security for its repayment; a pledge taken when the debt is established with the consent of both debtor and creditor, as security for repayment of the debt on the due date; and a pledge given by the debtor to the creditor for the latter's use and enjoyment of its fruits.

Taking a Pledge After Establishment of the Debt. There are various biblical enjoinders concerning taking a pledge from the debtor: "If thou lend money to any of My people, even to the poor with thee, thou shall not be to him as a creditor; neither shall ye lay upon him interest. If thou at all take thy neighbor's garment to pledge, thou shalt restore it unto him by that the sun goeth down; for that is his only covering, it is his garment for his skin; wherein shall he sleep?" (Ex. 22:24–26); similarly, "When thou dost lend thy neighbor any manner of loan, thou shalt not go into his house to fetch his pledge. Thou shalt stand without, and the man to whom thou dost lend shall bring forth the pledge without unto thee. And if he be a poor man, thou shalt not sleep with his pledge; thou shalt surely restore to him the pledge when the sun goeth down, that he may sleep in his garment, and bless thee; and it shall be righteousness unto thee before the Lord thy God" (Deut. 24:10–13); and, "No man shall take the mill or the upper millstone to pledge, for he taketh a man's life to pledge"

(Deut. 24:6). In their plain meaning, these passages refer to a debtor from whom a pledge is taken. These passages (which also lay down general principles concerning the creditor-debtor relationship; see Execution, Civil[1]) are the source of a threefold direction in matters of pledge and relate to articles which may never be taken in pledge, articles which may be taken in pledge but must be returned to a poor debtor when he needs them, and the prohibition against taking a pledge from a widow.

From the biblical prohibition on taking "the mill or upper millstone to pledge," the scholars deduced that it is forbidden to take in pledge "aught wherewith is prepared necessary food" (BM 9:13). They generally agree that the prohibition applies to utensils which are used in the actual preparation of "necessary food," such as a grain mill, certain cooking pots, an oven, and a sieve (Tur, HM 97:17), as well as water, wine, or oil jugs, "since this involves taking from a man a utensil which was fashioned for the actual preparation of necessary food for himself and his family, and this the Torah has forbidden, to save him hurt" (*Arukh ha-Shulḥan,* HM 97:11). In the case of things which do not meet this exact requirement but are used by a man to earn his livelihood, such as oxen for plowing and the like, some scholars hold that these may be taken in pledge, except for the essentials of his sustenance which must be left with the debtor, in terms of the rule of making an "arrangement" or assessment for the debtor (Rema, HM 97:8 and *Arukh ha-Shulḥan, ibid.*); other scholars hold that these things too fall into the category of "necessary food" and, therefore, may not be taken in pledge (Tur, HM 97:17 in name of *Ramah*; this opinion also conforms with the ordinary meaning of the statements in Tosef., BM 10:11 and those surrounding the discussion about a yoke of oxen and a pair of barber's shears, in BM 116a). With regard to articles which may be taken in pledge but must be returned to a needy debtor, Maimonides states "when a person takes a pledge from his neighbor [when the debt is due for payment] – whether through a court, or forcibly of his own accord, or with the debtor's consent – then if the debtor is poor it is a *mitzvah* to return the pledge to him if and when he be in need thereof; he must return to him the pillow at night to sleep thereon, and the plow by day to work therewith" (Yad, Malveh 3:5). Anyone who does not return a poor man's pledge when he needs it transgresses two prohibitions of the Torah and one positive precept.

It is in the interest of the creditor to take a pledge – notwithstanding his obligation to return it to the debtor when the latter is in need of it – in order that the debt shall not be wiped out in the Jubilee Year, just as a debt established against a pledge is not wiped out in order to recover payment of it on the death of the debtor, so that it should not be like movable property in the hands of orphans, which is not charged in the creditor's favor (Tosef., BM 10:9; BM 115a, Yad and Sh. Ar., loc. cit.). "Why then does he continue each day to take the pledge after he has returned it to the debtor whenever necessary? So that the debtor shall hurry to repay the debt because he is ashamed of having his pledge returned by the creditor day after day" (Tos. to BM 115a). In a dispute with R. Simeon b. Gamaliel, the scholars held that the creditor must return the debtor's pledge in this way as long as the debtor is alive; Gamaliel's opinion was that the creditor need only return the pledge during a period not exceeding 30 days; thereafter it must be sold through the court. All the scholars agree that if the creditor takes in pledge articles which are not essential to the debtor and therefore need not be returned to him from time to time, the creditor will be entitled to have the pledge sold through court, in similar manner to a pledge taken at the time of the establishment of the debt.

In the case of a widow, R. Judah held that the prohibition applies to all widows, rich or poor, giving to the word "widow" its ordinary meaning, since "he did not seek the reason for the scriptural law." R. Simeon, because "he sought the reason for the scriptural law," was of the opinion that the prohibition only applied to a poor widow, since the creditor would have to return her pledge if she needed it, and by entering and leaving her house from time to time would bring her into disrepute. The *halakhah* was decided according to R. Judah's opinion. Maimonides' opinion that the prohibition extends also to a pledge taken from a widow at the time the debt is established (Yad 3:1) is disputed in most of the Codes on the ground that the Torah deals solely with the question of a pledge taken when the debt is due for payment and that this is also to be deduced from the statements in the Talmud, even when the debtor is a widow (*Hassagot Rabad* and *Maggid Mishneh,* ad loc.).

The laws concerning a pledge of the debtor's property which the creditor takes after the debt is due as security for but not in payment of a debt are set out in detail in Scripture; although these laws were also dealt with in the Talmud and in the Codes, by then they had become of less practical importance in daily life. The result was that the relevant laws came to be interpreted as applying also to the matter of actually satisfying a debt out of the debtor's property (Maimonides, for instance, incorporates a number of matters pertaining to the *siddur le-va'al-ḥov* in his treatment of the above laws (Yad, Malveh 3:6) and this is done by other commentators also.) This process is particularly noticeable in the treatment of the prohibition against entering the debtor's home; the prohibition was interpreted in talmudic discussions and until the 12th century as applying also to the case of the creditor seeking to recover his debt, and only R. Tam interpreted the prohibition as applying solely to the case of entry for the purpose of taking a pledge.

In talmudic times, when the creditor came to take any of the debtor's assets after the debt was due, he generally did not do so in order to take a pledge, but rather as a means of recovering his debt. For this purpose too the scholars specified a number of articles which a debtor needed for the sustenance of himself and his family which might not be taken from him. From talmudic times onward it became most common for the pledge to be delivered by the debtor to the creditor at the time the debt was established.

Pledge Taken When the Debt is Established. The distinction drawn in Hebrew legal parlance in the State of Israel between the terms *mashkon* and *mashkanta,* pertaining to movables and to immovable property respectively, does not appear in the sources, where the term *mashkanta* is simply the Aramaic form of *mashkon* (although the distinction is already hinted at in earlier periods – see, e.g., Elon, Mafte'aḥ, note on p. 152).

Modes of Establishing a Pledge. The ancient form of pledge was apparently executed in the following manner: the debtor would sell one of his assets – land or movable property – to the creditor on the condition: "whenever I so desire I shall return the money and take it back." On receipt of the property the creditor would hand over the money; if, in the course of time, the money was returned by the debtor, the transaction constituted a loan and the property a pledge, otherwise the property would be forfeited to the creditor, presumably upon determination and expiry of a maximum period allowed the debtor for redemption of the property. This form of pledge also existed in other legal systems (Tosef., BM 4:4; Gulak, *Toledot ha-Mishpat be-Yisrael bi-Tekufot ha-Talmud,* 1 *(Ha-Ḥiyyuv ve-Shi'budav),* 62–65). A variation of this form of pledge was one in which the sale only came into effect upon the debtor's failure to make repayment on the date due (BM 63a). In the first case the creditor was entitled to sell the property after it had

1. page 621.

been delivered to him, although the debtor retained the right to redeem the property from a third party – i.e., within the period determined for this purpose; since the property had already been sold to the creditor, his usufruct thereof was not in conflict with the prohibition against interest (see below). In the second case, however, it was forbidden for the creditor to sell the property before the agreed date of repayment and, therefore, according to some scholars, the fruits of the property were forbidden to the creditor, as amounting to interest, since the property had not yet been effectively sold to the latter. Common to both the above forms of sale was forfeiture of the property to the creditor upon the debtor's failure to return the money within the determined period (Gulak, 65–66). Forfeiture of this kind, although likely to have resulted in the creditor gaining property whose value exceeded the amount of the debt, was not regarded by the scholars as prejudicial to the debtor since the latter retained the option of selling the pledged property to a third party before the due date for repayment of the debt and then paying the creditor the exact amount only (Tos. to BM 65b).

In the later form of the pledge that was customary in talmudic times, the creditor was only entitled to recover out of the pledge – when the debt matured – the exact amount owing to him, and the remainder belonged to the debtor; conversely, if the value of the pledge was less than the amount of the debt, the creditor was entitled to recover the shortfall from the debtor. (Nevertheless, from a number of *halakhot* it is discernible that later, as early as amoraic times, forfeiture of the whole of the pledge continued to be practiced; see Gulak, 69–71.) It was customary for the parties to stipulate that the whole of the pledge be forfeited to the creditor upon the debtor's failure to repay the debt within a prescribed period, even if the value of the pledge exceeded the amount of the debt. Some scholars upheld the validity of such express conditions, but R. Judah held a contrary opinion: "In what manner shall this party become entitled to that which is not his!" (Tosef. BM 1:17). For part of the amoraic period some scholars maintained that the above condition was valid, but later the *halakhah* was decided to the effect that this condition was invalid because of the defect of *asmakhta* (BM 66a–b). A similar decision was made in the codes; namely, that this condition was invalid unless imposed in a special manner so as to obviate the defect of *asmakhta* (Yad, Malveh 6:4; Sh. Ar., HM 73:17).

Ownership and Responsibility for the Pledge. Property pledged by the debtor remains in his ownership, but cannot be alienated by him to another since it is not in his possession (Rashi, Pes. 30b). The debtor may, however, alienate the pledge to another in such manner that the *kinyan,* i.e., transfer of ownership, shall take effect after he has redeemed the pledge from the creditor, and then retroactively to the time of alienation; in addition, the debtor may immediately alienate that portion of the pledge which is in excess of the amount of the debt (Ket. 59a–b, Tos. to BM 73b, s.v. *hashata;* Rema, YD 258:7).

The creditor acquires a limited proprietary interest in the pledge (Pes. 31b; et al.), hence a marriage contracted by him through the means of a pledge he holds is valid (according to Maimonides, the creditor has *mikẓat kinyan,* "a measure of *kinyan,*" in the pledge: Yad, Ishut 5:23). The creditor may assign to another the charge which he has on pledged property. According to the *posekim,* the creditor only has *mikẓat kinyan* in a pledge that is taken after the debt is established, and no *kinyan* whatever in a pledge taken at the time of establishment of the debt, so that a marriage contracted by the debtor through the means of pledged property of the latter kind will be invalid (Tos. to BM 82b, s.v. *emor;* Rema; *Siftei Kohen* HM 72, n. 9; R. Isaac's above statement is also based on a passage dealing with a pledge taken after establishment of the debt).

Opinions were divided on the question of the creditor's responsibility for the pledge in his possession, some holding him liable as a bailee for reward and others regarding him as an unpaid bailee (BM 6:7). The majority of the *posekim* decided according to the first view: "hence if the pledge was lost or stolen, he will be liable for its value; if the value of the pledge equaled the amount of the debt, the one party will have no claim against the other; if the debt exceeded the value of the pledge, the debtor must pay the difference; but if the value of the pledge exceeded the debt, the creditor must refund the difference to the debtor; if the loss of the pledge was due to *ones,* the creditor must swear that this was the case, whereupon the pledger must repay the debt to the last penny" (Yad, Sekhirut 10:1; *Hassagot Rabad,* ad loc.; Rema, HM 72:2).

Use of the Pledge. The use of the pledge is forbidden to the creditor, since this is tantamount to taking interest on the loan. In the case of a poor debtor, if the nature of the pledge is such that it suffers only slight deterioration upon use and the return for its hire is great – for instance a plowshare or spade – the creditor will be entitled to hire the pledge to others and to apply the proceeds in reduction of the debt, since this is assumed to be convenient for the debtor. It is precisely to others and not to himself that the creditor may hire the pledge in this manner, lest he be suspected of using the pledge without reducing the debt accordingly. If originally, however, the parties stipulate with each other that the creditor might use the pledge and apply the hire in reduction of the debt, then he will be entitled to use the pledge himself, since anyone who knows that he holds a pledge will also know what he stipulated with the debtor. When the pledge consists of books, the use of the pledge is permitted by some scholars because it is a *mitzvah* to lend books for study, but other scholars include books in the general prohibition against the use of the pledged property (Rema, HM 72:1; and YD 172:1).

Recovering Payment out of the Pledge. When the debt matures the creditor must notify the debtor, before two witnesses, that the debt must be repaid and the pledge redeemed or else he will seek leave from the court to sell the pledge in satisfaction of the amount owing to him. The debtor, according to some of the *posekim,* has 30 days in which to make payment, failing which the value of the pledge is assessed by three knowledgeable assessors and "he [the creditor] shall sell it at the assessment price allowed by the above three and he is given the advice to sell it before witnesses, lest the debtor say that it was sold for more than the assessment price" (Yad, Malveh 13:3; Sh. Ar., HM 73:12–15). The creditor himself may not purchase the pledge, but some scholars aver that he may do so if the pledge is sold through a court of experts.

Pledge (Mortgage) with a Right of Usufruct in the Creditor's Favor. Usufruct and the Probition against Interest. In the case of a long-term debt in a large amount, land was generally given in pledge, to remain in possession of the creditor until the debt matured; this practice is illustrated in Nehemiah 5:3–5. According to the Jewish laws of interest, any benefit derived by the lender over and above repayment of the original amount of the loan is regarded as interest and prohibited (BM 5:9). Strict observance of the minutiae of the prohibition posed no particular economic hardship in the case of small short-term loans, but when large credits were involved it was difficult to deny the creditor the right to derive any benefit from the mortgaged land in his possession. In other legal systems it was customary for the creditor to enjoy the fruits of the mortgaged property by way of interest and the existence of this phenomenon in Greco-Roman laws was mentioned in the Talmud. In order to ensure the availability of credit, the halakhic scholars sought to evolve special ways for the creation of a mortgage in a manner enabling the creditor to derive some usufructuary benefit from it without transgressing the prohibition against interest.

As already noted, the use and enjoyment of the pledge was permitted the creditor in case of a sale for return and – in the opinion of R. Judah – even in the case where the sale only came into effect upon the debtor's failure to make payment on the due date. This was because the property was regarded as sold to the creditor whereas the question of interest could only arise in the case of loan. The Babylonian *amoraim* regarded even the above cases as involving prohibited interest, since upon repayment of the debt the land would return to the debtor and the sale become voided retroactively (see BM 67a and Rif; Sh. Ar., HM 182:12; and *Ha-Gra*). A way of permitting the creditor a usufruct of the pledged property was found by the latter scholars on the principle of a reduction of the debt, at times until full liquidation thereof, by virtue of and in return for the usufruct. Even if such reduction bore no proportion to the actual value of the usufruct enjoyed by the creditor, yet this method – unlike the case of a sale of the body of the land – involved some real and not fictitious consideration for the usufruct. An important matter for the Babylonian *amoraim* in treating the permissibility of such usufruct was the distinction between a mortgage "in a place where it is customary to make the creditor give up possession" and a mortgage "in a place where it is not the custom . . . " In the former case the debtor could repay the debt at any time and recover possession of his land from the creditor and therewith regain the usufruct of his land; in the latter case the creditor could not be made to give up possession within a fixed period and thus the mortgage was akin to a sale for a specified period, whereby the suspicion of prohibited interest was reduced. In certain places it was laid down that, unless expressly stipulated between the parties, the debtor might not recover possession of the land from the creditor during the first year at least (BM 67a–b).

Three forms of usufruct of the mortgaged land were customarily recognized by the Babylonian *amoraim.*

Mortgage with a Fixed Deduction. With a mortgage of this kind the practice was to make a deduction from the amount of the debt against the creditor's enjoyment of the usufruct, as if the fruits were sold for the amount deducted. The rate of the deduction was fixed and amounted to far less than the value of the usufruct enjoyed, hence a *talmid ḥakham* was forbidden from enjoying the usufruct of the mortgaged property, even with the deduction (BM 67b).

Mortgage with a Stipulated Time Limit. The practice in this case was for the creditor to enjoy the usufruct of the mortgaged land against a deduction for the first five years – i.e., with a minimal reduction of the debt (and none at all according to another opinion) – and thereafter enjoyment of the usufruct would be assessed at its full value for purposes of repayment of the debt. Some of the scholars held this form of mortgage to be permissible also to a *talmid ḥakham* (BM 67b). During the first five years the creditor apparently could not be made to surrender possession of the land, the mortgage being akin to a sale and the suspicion of prohibited interest therefore reduced.

Mortgage "as Arranged in Sura." In this form of mortgage the parties would insert into the bond the condition: "on the expiry of so-and-so-many years, this estate reverts [to the debtor] without any payment." Here the creditor would enjoy the usufruct for a period stipulated in advance, at the end of which the land reverted to the debtor and the debt was considered as fully repaid. In this case too the value of the usufruct may have exceeded the amount of the debt, but this method was preferable to the "time limit" mortgage as regards the interest prohibition. In the "Sura" mortgage the creditor, as against his profits, also had to face a possible loss, since the land would revert to the debtor at the end of the stipulated period even though the creditor may not have enjoyed any profits during one or more years; on the other hand, in the "time limit" mortgage, repayment of the debt, after the first five years, would take place according to the measure of the profits enjoyed, and during the first five years the profits could be enjoyed without any risk of loss. With the "Sura" mortgage the suspicion of prohibited interest was entirely eliminated, since it in no way resembled a loan transaction, but rather one of "purchasing the fruits of these particular years against this particular payment" (Rashi, BM 67b). Hence all the scholars agreed that a "Sura" mortgage was permissible even to a *talmid ḥakham* (BM, loc. cit.).

In permitting a usufruct of the mortgaged property, both with reference to the ancient forms of mortgage and those sanctioned by the Babylonian *amoraim,* the scholars relied on the law of the redemption of dwellings in walled cities and fields of possession (Lev. 25:16, 27, 29; Tosef., BM 4:2; TJ, BM 5:3, 10b; BM 67b).

Disputing Opinions in the Codes. The problem of the creditor's enjoyment of a usufruct of the mortgaged property continued to engage halakhic scholars in post-talmudic times and became a subject of much controversial discussion in the Codes (*Ha-Gra,* YD 172, n. 1, enumerates six different methods entertained by the *posekim*). The main points of dispute may be briefly summarized as follows:

It was generally agreed that a "Sura" mortgage was permissible. As regards a mortgage "with deduction," Alfasi's opinion (to BM 67b) was that although enjoyment of the fruits is initially prohibited to the creditor, nevertheless the *post facto* value of this cannot be reclaimed from him, since no fixed or direct interest is involved, but only *avak ribbit* or indirect interest. The distinction between the two forms of interest, even as regards mortgage, was already discussed in the Talmud (BM 67b). In this case Maimonides permitted enjoyment of the usufruct from the start, but only with reference to a field, "since in the case of a field, the profits are not yet in existence at the time of the loan, and it is possible that the creditor may either derive fruits and profits therefrom or suffer loss in the sowing and cultivation of the field." In the case of a courtyard or a dwelling, Maimonides held the profits to be available at the time of loan and enjoyment of them, although prohibited initially, became permissible, *ex post facto* – because this entailed no more than *avak ribbit* by virtue of the reduction (Yad, Malveh 6:7). Rabad held that a mortgage "with deduction" is only permissible from the start where the local custom is not to make the creditor give up possession of the mortgaged property (against repayment of the debt) and that for this purpose no distinction should be made between a dwelling and a field (*Hassagot Rabad* to Malvah 6:7). Rashba, on the other hand, held all mortgages "with deduction" to be permissible from the start, whether relating to a field or dwelling and regardless of local custom on the question of the debtor regaining possession of the mortgaged property.

A great deal of difference of opinion is also expressed in the Codes concerning a mortgage with no deduction at all in return for the usufruct. Alfasi (to BM 67b) regarded this as amounting to fixed interest which could be reclaimed by action. Maimonides (Yad, Malveh 6;7) regarded this form of mortgage as entailing direct interest when relating to a courtyard or dwelling, and "dust of interest" when relating to a field or vineyard, and Rabad's view *(ibid.)* was that such a mortgage entailed direct interest or "dust of interest" depending respectively on whether it was local custom to make the creditor give up possession of the mortgaged property (against repayment of the debt) or not. Rashi (on BM 62a, 67a) was of the opinion that in the case of a field a mortgage, even without deduction, was permissible from the start wherever it was the custom not to make the creditor give up possession of the property, since by virtue of the latter fact, "all agree that all these years he holds the field as if purchased by him" (see also Tur, YD 172). However, in the case of a dwelling, such a mortgage (i.e., a usufruct without further deduction of the debt) entailed direct interest (see *Leḥem Mishneh* to Malveh 6:7). Although extremely liberal as regards the permissibility of a mortgage with deduction, Ibn Adret nevertheless held that where it was customary to make the creditor give up possession of the property, a mortgage without deduction entailed direct interest, and where it was customary not to make the creditor give up possession, it was "dust of interest" (*Nimmukei Yosef,* BM 67b; *Leḥem Mishneh,* loc. cit.).

The diversity of opinions made it difficult to decide the law in practice: "how shall we enter into the scholarly discussions . . . we have no power to decide the issue, but the court must act in accordance with its own understanding" (Resp. Abraham b. Isaac of Narbonne, no. 173). In one of his responsa Naḥmanides similarly expressed regret at the diversity of opinion, which left the *halakhah* on the subject uncertain and lacking in binding force. Therefore it had to be left for every community to act in this matter according to local custom. The opinions of the posekim were summarized by Isserles in a similar fashion: "Local custom is to be followed in this matter and in these countries the custom is to permit [enjoyment of usufruct] in the case of a mortgage with deduction, even when the debtor may reclaim possession [of the property from the creditor] and in this regard no distinction is drawn between a field and a dwelling or the different kinds of movables, since in all cases a mortgage with deduction is permissible" (Rema, YD 172:1).

In the State of Israel. The laws of pledge are ordered in two laws of the Knesset: the Pledge Law, 1967, and the Land Law, 1969. Sections 85–91 of the second law deal with a pledge of land, termed *mashkanta,* i.e., mortgage (sec. 4), to which all the provisions of the Pledge Law are applicable save as otherwise provided in the Land Law itself (sec. 91). The provisions of the Pledge Law are partially in accord with the attitude of Jewish law on the subject. The bill originally submitted to the Knesset (in 1964) included a provision entitling the creditor to enjoy the income of the pledge, with the debtor's consent and in return for an appropriate consideration to the latter, his waiver thereof to be of no validity (sec. 23). In the final version passed by the Knesset, the law provides that the creditor shall pay the debtor appropriate remuneration "unless otherwise agreed." This in effect means that upon the debtor's waiver of consideration the creditor becomes entitled to use and enjoy the income of the pledged property without making any reduction of the debt, which is contrary to Jewish law, where this amounts to prohibited interest.

Bibliography: F. Goldmann, in: *Zeitschrift fuer vergleichende Rechtswissenschaft,* 21 (1908), 197–241; N. A. Nobel, in: *Judaica . . . H. Cohen* (1912), 659–68; J. S. Zuri, *Mishpat ha-Talmud,* 4 (1921), 67–71; T. Ostersetzer, in: *Tarbiz,* 8 (1936/37), 301–15; 9 (1937/38), 395–7; J. N. Epstein, *ibid.,* 316–8; Herzog, Instit, 1 (1936), 339–44, 361–3; 2 (1939), 196; ET, 1 (1951³), 128f.; 2 (1949), 19f., 11 (1965), 100–12; T. Be'eri, in: *Mazkeret . . . Herzog* (1962), 113–9; M. Elon, *Ḥerut ha-Perat be-Darkhei Geviyyat Ḥov* (1964), 1f., 59–67; idem, Mafte'aḥ, 152–60; idem, *Ha-Mishpat Ha-Ivri* (1973), II, 252ff, 287ff, 756.

Menachem Elon

ANTICHRESIS (αντίχρησις) in Greco-Roman law an arrangement whereby a creditor may, under certain conditions, enjoy the use and fruits of property (land or chattels) given to him as security. In talmudic literature, such an arrangement appears under various designations such as *mashkanta di-Sura, nakhvata, kizuta* (see Loan, Pledge, Usury), while the word *antichresis* (אנטיכרסיס) itself appears only once in the Talmud (TJ BM 6:7, 11a; another passage in TJ Git. 4:6, 46a has אנטריס which might be a corruption of *antichresis* אנטיכרסיס see Epstein, in: *Tarbiz,* 8 (1937), 316–8). In Greco-Roman sources too, though antichretic transaction must have been widespread, the word antichresis appears only rarely, and it is difficult to ascertain its exact meaning. The glossator Cujacius (Observations 3:35) restricts the term to an arrangement whereby the usufruct is in lieu of interest *(in vicem usurarum).* A. Manigk, rejecting this narrow definition, argues that in Roman, Assyro-Babylonian, Greco-Egyptian, Syrian, and other laws, arrangements whereby usufruct was granted in partial or total amortization of the principal debt were also included in *antichresis:* hence Manigk speaks of "amortization-*antichresis*" as distinct from "interest-*antichresis*" (F. Stier-Somlo and A. Elster (eds). *Handwoerterbuch der Rechtswissenschaft,* 1 (1926), s.v.). By allowing a token deduction from a principal debt, actual interest-*antichresis* can be made to appear as amortization-*antichresis* (which is what *mashkanta di-Sura* or *nakhyata* really were). This was a means of evading the prohibition of usury. It is thus difficult to say whether the terse statement in the Talmud, which explicitly denounces *antichresis* as usury, refers to pure interest-*antichresis* or also to amortization-*antichresis* of the fictitious kind. The Mishnah discussing it deals with loans on pledge and quotes a saying of Abba Saul allowing amortization-*antichresis* under certain circumstances ("a poor man's pledge").

In Christian countries in the Middle Ages, when all interest on loans was forbidden, *antichresis* was linked with the evasion of usury (see C. F. Glueck, *Ausfuerliche Erlaeuterung der Pandecten,* 14 (1813), 47ff). Economically justified interest rates having become permissible, the significance of *antichresis* faded away and is not found in modern legislation.

Bibliography: A. Gulak, *Toledot ha-Mishpat be-Yisrael bi-Tekufat ha-Talmud,* 1 (1939); *Ha-Ḥiyyuv ve-Shi'bbudav,* 72, 76, 80, 121, 152; B. Cohen, in: *Alexander Marx Jubilee Volume* (1950), 179–202, reprinted in his *Jewish and Roman Law,* 2 (1966), 433–56, addenda 784–5; Ehrman, in: *Sinai,* 54 (1963/64), 177–84).

A. Zvi Ehrman

SHI'BUDA DE-RABBI NATHAN (Aram. "Rabbi Nathan's Lien"), a rule of law attributed to R. Nathan, a *tanna* of the second century, and cited in the Babylonian Talmud as follows: "Whence is the rule derived that if one man [A] claims a *maneh* [100 *zuz*] from his neighbor [B], and his neighbor [B] [claims a like sum] from another neighbor [C], that we collect from the one [C] and give it to the other [A]? From the verse, '. . . and he shall give it unto him to whom he is indebted' " (Num. 5:7–Pes. 31a). The Bible does not state, "unto him who lent him the money" [B], but rather "unto him to whom he is indebted," i.e., to whom the principal rightfully belongs now [A] (Rashi, ad loc.).

The Substantive Law. In the Shulhan Arukh the rule reads as follows: Reuben claims 100 from Simeon, and Simeon from Levi; we collect from Levi and give it to Reuben. No distinction is made as to whether Levi was already obligated to Simeon when the latter borrowed from Reuben or whether Levi had become obligated thereafter. Nor is any distinction made between a loan (see Loans) having documentary attestation and one having only oral attestation (about these definitions see Obligations, Law of[1]). As long as both debtors acknowledge indebtedness, each to his respective creditor, we collect from Levi and give it to Reuben. This holds true for every type of obligation which Levi incurs toward Simeon, whether it be through loan, sale, lease, or hiring (see Lease and Hire; HM 86:1). Indeed, the liabilities may have arisen from torts, damages, bailments (see Bailment), and larceny (see Theft and Robbery) as well. Nor need the two debts, i.e., of Simeon and Levi, have been of the same kind. For example, Simeon's indebtedness to Reuben may have arisen as the result of a loan, whereas Levi's indebtedness to Simeon may have been incurred through purchase. Similarly, Simeon's liability may be according to biblical law and Levi's according to rabbinic law (*Siftei Kohen,* HM 86:1). Reuben's ability to collect from Levi is limited to the circumstance that Simeon is insolvent (Sh. Ar., HM 86:2), although a dissenting opinion, which considers Levi virtually a debtor of Reuben, would extend the said liability even to those cases where Simeon was solvent (*Siftei Kohen,* HM 86:2).

According to most commentators, *Shi'buda de-Rabbi Nathan* differs from an ordinary lien in being essentially a procedural device for the collection of debts rather than a substantive incumbrance on the property of the debtor. Thus, an ordinary lien attaches only to those properties of the debtor which were in his possession at the time he incurred the debt. Moreover, the indebtedness created through an ordinary lien may be discharged by the payment of money even in the case where the indebtedness arose through the delivery of a deposit or a pledge. R. Nathan's Lien, however, attaches to those properties the debtor acquired after he had incurred the debt as well, and the debtor could be compelled to deliver the object itself to his creditor's creditor. Yet, in the case where a debtor subsequent to his loan sold his property, Rabbi Nathan's Lien is ineffectual, for inasmuch as the debtor himself has no claim against the purchaser, his creditor also may have no claim against the purchaser. Under such circumstances, however, an ordinary lien is effective, and in the case of nonpayment the creditor may seize the property from the purchaser for the satisfaction of his (earlier) claim (*Keẓot ha-Ḥoshen,* HM 86).

Legal Analysis. Privity of contract is expressed in talmudic literature in the form of the refusal of a debtor to enter into litigation with his opponent on the ground that *lav ba'al devarim didi at* ("You have no claim against me," or "You are not my plaintiff"). *Shi'buda de-Rabbi Nathan* is a method of assignment which Jewish law makes available in order to overcome, when necessary, the limitations created by the principle of privity. Rabbi Nathan's Lien differs from the other methods of assigning rights, such as: *ma'amad sheloshtan* (see Assignment; Obligations, Law of), which is a kind of assignment by substitution and requires the physical presence of the debtor, the assignor, and the assignee; *mesirat shetarot* (see Acquisition[2]), which effectuates assignment through the delivery of the bonds or notes of indebtedness to the assignee accompanied by a deed of assignment; and *harsha'ah* (see Agency), which creates a power of attorney under the form of assignment. These three methods of assignment depend upon the initiative and consent of the assignor, whereas *Shi'buda de-Rabbi Nathan* creates what is essentially an automatically transferred obligation. In contrast with the other methods, however, *Shi'buda de-Rabbi Nathan* is limited to circumstances in which the assignee is a creditor of or claimant against the assignor. *Shi'buda de-Rabbi Nathan* finds its closest parallel in the statutory proceeding of garnishment in American law (see Herzog, Instit, 2 (1939), 214, n. 2).

Historical Development. Asher Gulak (*Ha-Ḥiyyuv ve-Shi'budav,* bibl.) maintains that *Shi'buda de-Rabbi Nathan* underwent a series of developments in talmudic times whereby it received a progressively wider application. The original statement of R. Nathan is to be found in Sifrei Numbers 3, and merely provides for the right of a creditor to collect his debt from monies which have been awarded to the debtor in court but which the latter has as yet not collected. The text of R. Nathan's statement as it appears in the Babylonian Talmud (e.g., Pes. 31a) represents, according to Gulak, a further development whereby debts owed to the debtor are construed as property of the latter and subject to collection on behalf of his creditor even before they have been awarded to the debtor in court. Thus, at this point the assignment of rights has been created without any reference, however, to lien. The final development of R. Nathan's statement is to be seen in the construction placed upon it by the Babylonian Talmud, namely, that there is a lien that the creditor has on all the properties of his debtor's debtors. This construction is part of the general tendency which Gulak discerns in the Babylonian Talmud, i.e., to incorporate lien into the very concept of obligation.

Bibliography: N. A. Nobel, in: *Sefer . . . le-David Ẓevi . . . Hoffmann* (1914), 98–105; Gulak, Yesodei, 2 (1922), 101–3; 4 (1922), 193f.; Herzog, Instit, 1 (1936), 201–12; 2 (1939), 209–14; A. Gulak, *Toledot ha-Mishpat be-Yisrael bi-Tekufat ha-Talmud,* 1 (*Ha-Ḥiyyuv ve-Shi'budav,* 1939), 150f.; Elon, Mafte'aḥ, 396f.

Aaron Kirschenbaum

ASSIGNMENT (OF DEBT).

History and Development. Basically, Jewish law did not recognize the concept whereby personal rights or obligations (whether arising from contract or from a liability for damages in tort) could be legally assigned, either by the creditor or the debtor, to one who was not a party to the obligation itself. This was because a debt was considered intangible and therefore incapable of legal transfer (Rashi, Git. 13b; R. Gershom, BB 147b; Tos. to Ket. 55b). It was compared to the case of an object that was not yet in existence *(davar she-lo ba la-olam)* which also could not be transferred (see Tos. to BK 36b).

The development of commerce and its increasingly sophisticated requirements made it necessary however to overcome this difficulty in the law, and the assignment of debts, whether verbal or by deed, is already mentioned in the tannaitic period (Tosef., BM 4:3, et al.). Two principal methods of assignment were invented: (1) a form of novation, whereby an existing debt was canceled and an identical, but new debt created between the debtor and the creditor's assignee – all three parties consenting; and (2) a formula whereby the creditor appointed an agent to recover a debt on his behalf, but empowered the agent to retain the proceeds for himself. From these two methods were developed the two legal forms of assignment of debts dealt with in the Talmud, namely *Ma'amad Sheloshtan* (lit. "a meeting of the three") and *Mekhirat Shetarot* ("sale of bonds"). In addition, there was the *Shi'buda de-Rabbi Nathan* (see previous article) a process of legal execution entrusted to the court.

Ma'amad Sheloshtan, as an authorized legal transaction, is first mentioned by the early *amoraim* (Git. 13b). All three parties – the creditor, the debtor, and the assignee – being present together, the creditor would say to the debtor: "There is a debt owing to me by you; give it to – (the assignee)." On this simple oral declaration the assignee acquired good legal title to the debt and could claim it direct from the debtor. In the same way it was possible to transfer a pledge. The Talmud concludes

1. page 244; 2. page 208.

that there was no legal reason for this arrangement, it having been evolved merely to facilitate commercial dealings (Tos. to Git. 14a).

However, some *amoraim* do suggest a legal basis for it. For example, Amemar opines that its legal justification rests on the assumption that, when the obligation first arises, the debtor is deemed to render himself liable not only to the principal creditor but to anyone claiming through him. On the other hand, R. Ashi takes the view that the benefit which the debtor enjoys from the cancellation of the original obligation to the creditor and the creation of a new one to the assignee, with a different date of payment, is itself sufficient to demonstrate, without further act or formality, the debtor's firm intention to bind himself to the assignee, as his new creditor. Relying on R. Ashi's reasoning, some held that the debtor's actual consent was required to complete a *Ma'amad Sheloshtan,* but others held that only his presence was necessary (*Ran* on *Rif,* Git. 13b). Thus, according to R. Ashi, the institution of *Ma'amad Sheloshtan* would appear to be equivalent to novation and it may be assumed that before *Ma'amad Sheloshtan* was recognized the assignment of debt was done by canceling the old debt and creating a new one through the formal act of *kinyan* ("acquisition"), constituting, in effect, a novation (Git. 14a).

Mekhirat Shetarot ("sale of bonds") was a method whereby a debt, embodied in a bond, was assigned by selling the bond and was effective when the bond was delivered to the assignee (BB 76a). However, although one opinion of the *tannaim* was that physical delivery was sufficient in the case of a bond, another opinion (by which the *halakhah* was ultimately decided) held that a further deed was required in the assignee's name, because whereas the act of delivery validly assigned the bond itself, i.e., the actual paper on which it was written, the debt, and the creditor's rights to the debt were not an intrinsic part of the paper and therefore not assigned with it. Accordingly, in the ancillary deed the creditor would confirm that the assignee should "acquire [the bond] and any rights contained therein" (BB 76b).

As to the sale of bonds, the *amora* Samuel stated: "If one sells a bond of indebtedness to another and then releases the debtor from his liability, the release is valid [and therefore binding on the assignee], and such release can even be given by the creditor's heir [with the same third-party consequences]" (Ket. 86a). The basis for this ruling was that since the initial premise (stated above) was that a debt was intangible and thus incapable of legal transfer, the creditor is really doing no more than giving the assignee a power of attorney to recover the debt and keep the proceeds. This is, in fact, the second of the two earlier methods of assignment already referred to. As the assignee is, from the strictly legal point of view, no more than an agent of the creditor, the latter remains competent to release the debtor or even to recover the debt himself. In such a case, however, it was accepted as the *halakhah* that the creditor would be liable to compensate the frustrated assignee for any loss.

As the *Ma'amad Sheloshtan,* unlike the sale of bonds, was not based on the principle of agency, it would seem that after its completion the original creditor could no longer give a valid release to the debtor (Tos. to Git. 13b). Nor could a *Ma'amad Sheloshtan* be used as a means of selling a bond (*Siftei Kohen* no. 97 to Sh. Ar., HM 66:29), since being a form of novation whereby a new debt is substituted for an old one, the old debt ceases to exist and becomes valueless. The Talmud explains (Ket. 86a) that if a new bond is addressed to the assignee the original creditor is no longer competent to release the debtor – his debt having ceased to exist and there being no question of agency, as in the case of sale of bonds.

Other explanations have also been advanced to justify the validity of a release by the original creditor, even after he has sold his bond. One is that whereas the sale of bonds was *mi-de-rabbanan* ("instituted by the sages"), the legality of a release of a debt was *mi-de-oraita* ("stemming from biblical law"; Maim. Yad, Mekhirah, 6:12; Tos. to BB 76b). This explanation is, however, questionable as in other cases of sale instituted by rabbinical enactment (including the *Ma'amad Sheloshtan*) a subsequent release by the assignor was not recongized. Another explanation suggests that the original creditor has two rights from his debtor – one proprietary and the other personal, the latter being inalienable. This also presents difficulty since a debt itself is intangible and therefore inalienable; it is strange therefore that the idea of a personal right, which is not mentioned elsewhere, should be introduced here, when the general rule would be equally applicable. If the original creditor transferred a pledge he was holding to the purchaser he cannot then release the debtor (see Pledge).

It may be assumed that in tannaitic times the assignment of debts, whether verbal or under bond, was also effected by means of a power of attorney proper: known in the Babylonian Talmud as *urkhata* (BK 70a). However, although tannaitic sources mention powers of attorney with regard to the assignment of debts (Rashi, Kid. 47b), in the Babylonian Talmud – where such a device is not recognized as applying to intangibles (such as debts) – the references mentioned are interpreted differently (Kid. 47b; *Or Zaru'a.* BK 296). Presumably the formula "institute proceedings, acquire and take for yourself," forming part of the text of a power of attorney, was a relic from the tannaitic period when the assignee was appointed as attorney to recover the debt and then retain the proceeds. In Babylonia this form of attornment was only used for the recovery of movables, not debts, and certainly not for the assignment of debts (BK 70a and Tos.), leaving unanswered the question of why this device was necessary in view of the well-established rule that "a man's agent is like himself" (Yam shel Shelomo, BK 7:12).

Assignment by the Debtor. Although the Babylonian Talmud does not mention the case of a debtor assigning his liability to another, reference to this can be found in the Mishnah (BM 9:12) and in the Jerusalem Talmud (cf. BM 4:1, 9c,) but only in relation to a banker or shopkeeper, both commonly engaged in financial transactions (Gulak, in: *Tarbiz,* 2 (1930/31), 154–71). It is possible that assignments of this kind were effected by a means similar to the *Ma'amad Sheloshtan,* to which they are compared by the codifiers (Rif. to BM 112a). Details of such assignments are unknown, however, particularly as the *Ma'amad Sheloshtan* is not mentioned in the Jerusalem Talmud.

Post-Talmudic Developments. In post-talmudic times the power of attorney was used for the recovery of debts, but not for their assignment (Tos. to BK 70a; Maim., Yad, Sheluḥin ve-Shutafin 3:7; see also Attorney). Some authorities held that a bond of indebtedness, drawn in favor of the creditor and anyone claiming through him, enabled it to be assigned by mere delivery and thereafter precluded the original creditor from releasing the debtor; but others disagreed (Sh. Ar., HM 66:26). It was also customary to draw a bond in favor of "whomsoever may produce it"; this being assignable by mere delivery and precluding the debtor's release by the assignor (Responsa Rosh 68:9), and the bond thus became negotiable (cf. J. J. Rabinowitz, *Jewish Law* (1956), 342ff). In Poland, from the 16th century onward, a bond drawn in favor of "whomsoever may produce it," bearing only the debtor's signature, the amount of the debt, and the date of payment, became customary. Such a bond was known as a *"Memoram"* and was, in effect, a negotiable instrument like a promissory note (Ir Shushan 48: *Sma* to ḤM 48:1).

In the State of Israel. In the state of Israel the assignment of debts is governed by the Assignment of Obligations Law, 1969, under the provisions of which every obligation or any part of it can be assigned either by the creditor or by the debtor. The debtor's assignment can only be made with the agreement of the creditor. Promissory notes and checks are in common use and are governed by the Bills of Exchange Ordinance, 1929, which permits the assignment of a debt by the mere delivery of the relevant bill.

Bibliography: Gulak, Yesodei, 2 (1922), 96–104; A. Gulak, *Toledot ha-Mishpat be-Yisrael,* 1 (1939), *Ha-Hiyyuv ve-Shi'bud-av,* 96–104; Herzog, Instit, 1 (1936), 201–12; S. Albeck, in: *Tarbiz,* 26 (1956/57), 262–86; M. Elon, *Ha-Mishpat Ha-Ivri* (1973), I, 204ff, II, 479ff, 533.

Shalom Albeck

MEḤILAH (Heb. מחילה, "waiver"), the renunciation repudiation, abandonment, or surrender of some claim, right, or privilege. *Meḥilah* may be the waiver of a present right or lien or the waiver of the right to a future increment; in the latter case, it is usually referred to as *silluk* (TJ, Ket. 9:1, 32d; Ket. 82a).

Range of Applicability. *Meḥilah* cancels any debt, lien, or obligation regardless of origin. Thus, debts arising out of loans, sale, leasing and hiring, labor, partnership, and surety; lien on property put up as collateral; obligations originating in contract or tort – all are effectively cancelled by *meḥilah* on the part of the creditor. Nor is the effectiveness of *meḥilah* curtailed by the form of the obligation; it applies with equal vigor whether the obligation is an oral or written one, whether it is attested to by witnesses or not (Gulak, Yesodei, 2 (1922), 111–4, 162f.).

Silluk, i.e., the waiving of future accretions, however, is only of limited effectiveness. This is due to the general reluctance of Jewish law to grant effective control over things that have as yet not come into existence (*davar she-lo ba la-olam;* see Contract). Thus, if, on the one hand, a person possesses a present right, claim, or lien, *silluk* cannot dissolve it; only *meḥilah* can do so. If, on the other hand, the future right, claim, or lien is so remote as to have no specific relationship to this particular person, his *silluk* is equally ineffective since it pertains to *davar she-lo ba la-olam.* However, if the future right, claim, or lien, although not in existence, has by the operation of circumstances at least achieved a likelihood of accruing to a specific person, then his *silluk* is effective. Thus, the ability of a man to waive the rights of usufruct in his wife's property depends upon the status of his relationship with her; if he has already married her *(nissu'in),* his claim on her usufruct is a present one; hence his waiver must be in the form of *meḥilah,* and his *silluk* is no longer effective. If he has not entered into the first stage of marriage *(erusin),* the usufruct in her property has as yet not come into existence (it is a *davar she-lo ba la-olam*); hence it is sufficiently remote as to vitiate the effectiveness of either form of waiver, that of *meḥilah* and that of *silluk.* If, however, he has entered into the first stage of marriage *(erusin)* but has not yet consummated the marriage *(nissu'in),* the right of usufruct, although not yet in existence, has achieved sufficient likelihood of accruing to him as to have endowed him with the power, not of *meḥilah,* but of *silluk* (Ket. 83–84a, and Codes).

The effectiveness of *silluk* with regard to obligations which are *mi-de-rabbanan* (i.e., rabbinic origin) that have as yet not come into existence is undisputed among the early authorities (*rishonim;* see Introduction,[1] Authority, Rabbinical). Its effectiveness with regard to obligations which are *mi-de-oraita* (i.e., biblical origin; see Introduction[2]) that have as yet not come into existence presented these scholars with two major difficulties; (1) it is an established rule of law that conditions contrary to biblical law are void (BM 7:11). (2) The Talmud rules that biblical rights of succession, which are *mi-de-oraita,* such as those of a son to inherit his father's estate (in contradistinction to the right of a husband to inherit his wife, which is *mi-de-rabbanan*), cannot be waived (cf. Ket. 83a). The first difficulty was overcome by the limitation of the rule to non-monetary conditions on the one hand (see Contract[3]), and by the limitation of the power of waiver to monetary obligations on the other. The second limitation was overcome by construing *mi-de-oraita* rights of inheritance as being unique in that they inhere in the heirs even before the death of the owner of the estate; hence *silluk,* as the waiver of future rights, is impossible (*Keẓot ha-Ḥoshen* 209 n. 11).

Waiver is limited to rights; it is ineffective as a mode of transfer of real property or of chattel (Rema HM 241:2).

Legal Analysis. It has been pointed out that in the realm of rights, where it is effective, waiver does not constitute a transfer; rather it is mere withdrawal. A creditor who waives his claim does not transfer his right to the debtor and thereby extinguish the claim; on the contrary, he withdraws his right or removes his lien from the debtor and his estate. The effectiveness of *meḥilah*, therefore, is independent of the wishes of the debtor. Thus, if a creditor waives the debt due to him and the debtor refuses to avail himself of the waiver, the waiver nevertheless takes effect. Had *meḥilah* been viewed as a kind of transfer, it would have failed to take effect inasmuch as the debtor, as transferee, had declined (cf. Herzog, Instit, 2 (1939), 229). The juridic basis of waiver is the insistence of the law that the obligatory nature of monetary obligations is always dependent upon the will of the party to whom the obligation is due; the suspension of this will, e.g., by waiver, automatically extinguishes the obligation (Ramban, nov., BB 126b).

Formal Requirements. *Meḥilah* requires no formality (*meḥilah einah ẓerikhah kinyan;* Yad, Mekhirah 5:11 and Ishut 17:19; Tos. to Sanh. 6a s.v. *ẓerikhah*). It is effective by parole alone. Some authorities, however, do require a formal *kinyan* to validate the waiver of a creditor who retains possession of the debtor's promissory note (cf. commentaries to Sh. Ar., HM 12:8; see also Acquisition). There is no formal requirement that witnesses validate a waiver of indebtedness. The function of witnesses is evidentiary, preventing the creditor from subsequently denying his act of waiver or from alleging that the act was made in jest. For this purpose, the witnesses need not have been formally appointed; their mere presence suffices (Sh. Ar., HM 81:29).

Implied Waiver. Waiver may be express or implied. Thus, the mere declaration of the creditor that the debtor owes him nothing absolves the latter of all obligation; for although he knows that the creditor's statement is incorrect, it is nevertheless construed as an implied waiver (Sh. Ar., HM 75:11; Rema, HM 40:1; but cf. *Siftei Kohen*, HM 81, n. 72). Asher Gulak has pointed out the similarity between this waiver implied in the creditor's denial of the debtor's indebtedness with the *acceptilatio* in Roman law. This was an oral form of dissolving obligations by having the debtor ask the creditor, "What I have promised you, have you received it *(habesne acceptum)*?" and the creditor answering, "I have *(habeo).*" The effectiveness of the Roman *acceptilatio* was limited, however, to the dissolution of obligations created by verbal contracts *(verbis);* it was ineffective in dissolving obligations created by real *(re)* and written *(litteris)* contracts. This limitation does not exist in Jewish law where the creditor's declaration of receipt of payment dissolves all obligations, regardless of origin (cf. Gulak, Yesodei, 2 (1922), 112f.). Implied waiver serves as the operational rationale of a

1. page 17, 55; 2. page 9; 3. page 251.

number of legal rules. Thus, the rule that monetary conditions contrary to law are valid is justified on the grounds that the parties entering into the agreement governed by said conditions have implicitly waived their (monetary) rights (Rashi Kid. 19b; see also Contract[1]). Similarly, the rule that overreaching *(ona'ah)* that involves less than one-sixth of the fair price need not be returned to the injured party is explained on the basis of an implied waiver on the part of the latter (Yad, Mekhirah 12:3; cf. *Sma,* HM 227 n. 2). Again, the lapse of the right of a widow who no longer lives on her husband's estate to collect her *ketubbah* after 25 years, in localities where written *ketubbot* are not used, is based upon implied waiver (Ket. 104a; Yad, Ishut 16:23; see also Limitation of Actions[2]).

Legal Rules Limiting its Effectiveness. Some of the legal rules governing waiver may be summarized as follows:

(1) The power of waiver applies to claims estimable in money *(mamona ityahiv li-meḥilah);* it is thus inapplicable to modes of effectuating marriage and divorce (Kid. 7a; Git. 64a). (2) Waiver need not be made in the presence of the debtor, but the debt does not lapse until the waiver has come to his knowledge (*Arukh ha-Shulḥan,* HM 241:4; but cf. Herzog, Instit, 2 (1939), 231f.). (3) If co-debtors are named in one promissory note and the creditor waives the obligation of one of them, the other's obligation remains intact and is actionable (opinion of Sh. Ar., HM 77:6; disputed by Rema, ad loc.). If the debtors are correal, however, i.e., where each is bound severally to discharge the entire liability, the creditor's waive of the obligation to one of them cancels the liability of all *(ibid.).* (4) A waiver of the lien on an obligation, retaining, however, the obligation itself, must be accomplished by a *kinyan* in order to be effective (*Derishah,* HM 111, n. 10). (5) A creditor may effectively waive part of the obligation, or he may postpone the date of payment by waiving the time stipulated in the *shetar* (Sh. Ar., HM 66:24, and *Siftei Kohen, ibid.,* n. 83). (6) A waiver, in order to be effective, must be related to an object that is definite or to a quantity that is fixed; obligations that are vague, limitless, or unknown are unaffected by *meḥilah* (Yad, Mekhirah 13:3; Sh. Ar., HM 232:7). (7) Waiver is ineffective if made through error (see Mistake; Tos. to BM 66b, s.v. *hatam;* cf. Herzog, Instit, 2 (1939), 299); if made under duress (see *Ones,* Tos. to BB 48a, s.v. *amar*); if made in jest (Yad, Mekhirah 5:13 and Ishut 17:19); and if made by minors and, presumably, by deaf-mutes and mentally incompetents (BM 22b). (8) the effectiveness of *mehilah* is disputed in cases where the creditor retains possession of the debtor's promissory note or his pledge, some authorities requiring a formal *kinyan* to supplement the waiver by parole (Sh. Ar., HM 12:8; 241:2, and commentaries).

Bibliography: I. S. Zuri, *Mishpat ha-Talmud,* 5 (1921), 25; Gulak, Yesodei, 1 (1922), 159; 2 (1922), 111–4, 162f.; Herzog, Instit, 2 (1939), 115, 132ff., 229–33, 299f.; Elon, Mafte'aḥ, 123–9; idem, *Ha-Mishpat Ha-Ivri* (1973), II, p. 596ff, 765ff.

Aaron Kirschenbaum

LABOR LAW. In Scripture. Two fundamental principles relating to the laws of the hired servant are enjoined in the Pentateuch: firstly, the master's duty to pay the wages of his servant on time: "The wages of a laborer shall not remain with you until morning"; "You must pay him his wages on the same day, before the sun sets" (Lev. 19:13; Deut. 24:15); and secondly, the servant's right to eat from the produce of the field while he is working: "When you enter your neighbor's vineyard, you may, if you desire, eat your fill of the grapes . . . When you find yourself amid your neighbor's standing grain, you may pluck ears with your hand" (Deut. 23:25, 26). So too the liberal pentateuchal laws concerning the Hebrew bondsman (see Slavery) served as an important source for the development of labor law in later times. Other scriptural passages, even if not specifically related to the matter of master and servant, have also been relied upon by the scholars in support of labor laws, especially the enjoinder, "For it is to Me that the children of Israel are servants" (Lev. 25:55).

Hired Servant and Independent Contractor. The distinction between a hired servant and an independent contractor is one of principle: whereas the former is hired for a specific period, the latter is hired for a specific task (*Maggid Mishneh* Sekhirut, 9:4; cf. the Roman law distinction between *locatio conductio operarum* and *locatio conductio operis*). The time factor in the hire of a servant has the effect of tying him to his work for fixed hours during which he cannot choose not to work, whereas the independent contractor may work as and when it pleases him (Resp. Maharam of Rothenburg, ed. Prague, n. 477). Hence an element of slavery attaches to a hired servant, while a contractor "is not a slave except unto himself" (Rashi, BM 77a).

The Contract of Hired Service. The contractual tie in an agreement for the hire of personal services is effected through one of the recongized modes of acquisition, such as *kinyan sudar.* Typically, however, the tie is effected by commencement of the work (BM 76b; Nov. Ramban thereto) or by the master pulling *(meshikhah)* the servant's tool of trade (R. Tam, Tos. to BM 48a; see also Contract). When the master is a public body the contract requires no *kinyan* and a verbal agreement suffices (*Mordekhai* BM nos. 457, 458). A service contract is not susceptible to specific performance, i.e., the party in breach cannot be compelled to carry out his undertaking. The master cannot be compelled to employ the servant against his will, since only the master's property *(mamon)* and not his person becomes subjected in the servant's favor (Resp. Mahari'az Engil no. 15). The servant, on the other hand, cannot be compelled to work against his will, since the law is that a worker may withdraw from the employment even in the middle of the day (BM 10a; see also below); even if his withdrawal should involve irretrievable loss to his master (see below); he will not be compelled to work, but the loss may be recovered out of his property (*Ḥazon Ish,* BK no. 23:6). This is also the position with an independent contractor, who cannot be compelled to carry out his undertaken task (Maharih to *Piskei ha-Rosh,* BM 77a). In the circumstances, the tie between the parties to a service contract is a loose one in its legal consequences (TJ, BM 6:2, 11a), with the result that it became customary for such parties to bind themselves to each other in various ways aimed at precluding the possibility of withdrawal, e.g., by oath, handshake, or imposition of a fine upon the retracting party.

Personal Nature of the Service Contract. A service contract falls into the category of agreements of a personal nature. Therefore, if the master has engaged the servant to work in his field, he cannot compel him to work in a neighbor's field, even if the work there is lighter (Tosef. BM 7:6). Similarly, the servant is not entitled to substitute another worker for himself if the master should want his particular services (Resp. Maharit, vol. 2, YD no. 50). Generally, however, it will be presumed that the master is not particular about the matter, save as regards a position of a public nature which the holder cannot pass on to another without the consent of the public (*Mordekhai,* BK no. 108).

The master may change the nature of the servant's work except if the servant has been hired for a specific task, in which case it cannot be changed against the servant's will, whether for lighter or heavier work (Nov. Ramban, BM 77a). If the task for which the servant has been hired is completed before expiry of the hire period, his master may keep him engaged on some other

1. page 251; 2. page 596.

but not heavier labor (Tosef. BM 7:6; BM 77a); in the opinion of some scholars he may be given heavier labor than before but with an increase in remuneration (Maharam of Rothenburg, in: *Mordekhai,* BM no. 346, HM 335:1; Ramakh, in *Shitah Mekubbeẓet,* BM 76b). In similar circumstances the servant may not, however, in the absence of prior stipulation, demand that he be retained on some other labor (Tosef. BM 7:6) but only claim the wages of an "unemployed worker" *(sekhar po'el batel)* or the full stipulated wage until expiry of the period of his hire (see below).

Remuneration. In the absence of express agreement, it will be presumed that the parties intended a contract of service for remuneration, on the assumption that a person does not work for nothing, and the measure of remuneration will be determined in accordance with local custom (see *Minhag; Modekhai* loc. cit.); in a place where laborers are hired at different rates, remuneration will be according to the lowest, since people generally have in mind the cheapest possible rate (Alfasi to BM 76a).

Obligations of the Parties. It is the servant's duty to do his work in a faithful manner, hence he may not absent himself from work without adequate cause lest he become liable to dismissal as well as loss of remuneration for the period he has not worked. For the same reason he has to work with all his strength (Yad, Sekhirut, 13:7) and may not go hungry or otherwise afflict himself, nor engage in any additional work, whether inside or outside his original working hours (Tosef. BM 8:2). If he should do so without his master's authority, the latter may demand a refund of his earnings (Resp. Rashba, vol. 1, no. 1042). The prohibition against additional work is only applicable, apparently, to a servant obliged – by agreement or custom – to work a full day for his master (see below). The servant must furthermore comply with his master's instructions insofar as these do not deviate from their agreement or local custom (SER 15; Resp. Israel of Bruna, no. 242).

The master's main obligation is to pay the servant's wages on time, i.e., at the end of the day or month as the case may be, since "the hire is only payable at the end" (BM 65a), unless otherwise agreed upon by the parties or decreed by custom (*Mordekhai,* BB, no. 468). The duty to pay the servant's wages on time is a positive command and delay in payment also amounts to transgression of a negative command (see above). Wage delay *(halanat sakhar)* is constituted when payment has been withheld for more than 12 hours after it is due (BM 111a). The prohibition is not transgressed, nor is the master in default, unless and until the servant has demanded the payment of his wage (Sifra, Kedoshim 2:9–12) and the master has the ready cash to make it (BM 112a), or has chattels which he can sell without loss and fails to do so (Nov. Ritba, BM 111b). Here too the parties may contract out of the law with regard to the time of wage payment (Sif. Deut. 279), and they may also stipulate that the master shall not be in transgression of the prohibition against wage delay if he should fail to pay on time (*Sefer Ḥasidim,* no. 1066). According to some scholars, wage delay entitles the servant to claim compensation for what he could have earned from his wages if he had been paid on time, but this is prohibited by most scholars as tantamount to interest (*Or Zaru'a,* BM no. 181).

The servant must be paid in cash and not chattels (BM 118a), although there is an opinion that payment may be made in commodities (foodstuffs) which the servant is in need of (Maharam of Rothenburg, in: *Mordekhai* BK 1), and the latter may also waive his right to payment in cash. In case of dispute over whether or not the master has made payment of the servant's wages, the servant will be entitled to payment thereof upon delivering an oath – this is a rabbinical enactment in favor of the servant (Shev. 45a). The master is generally not obliged to provide his servant with food, save as otherwise agreed between them or decreed by custom (BM 83a), in which event the master may choose to provide an allowance instead of food (Resp. Maharsham, pt. 3, no. 54). So far as a servant working in the field is concerned, he is entitled to eat from the produce, but only while he is working (see above; BM 87a).

The master may not employ his servant outside lawful working hours, which – in the absence of an agreement between the parties – are determined by local custom (BM 83a; Nov. Ritba thereto). Scripture hints at the ancient custom of regarding a working day as lasting from sunrise until the appearance of the stars (Ps. 104: 19–23), and this is known in the Talmud as a workday of a worker – *de-oraita* (BM 83b).

Period of Service. If not explicitly agreed upon between the parties, the duration of the service period is determined by custom (*Divrei Malkiel,* pt. 3, no. 151), and in the absence of such this is a matter within the judges' discretion (*Ḥazon Ish,* BK, sec. 23:2). Cancellation of the service contract is subject to prior notice within a reasonable time in accordance with local custom and conditions (*Ḥazon Ish,* loc. cit.). In the case of certain public appointments it was the custom to regard an appointment without a fixed period as one for life (*Ḥatam Sofer,* Resp. OH no. 206).

When the service contract is for a specified period, it will terminate on the date specified without need for any prior notice. In the case of public appointments there is an opinion that the servant cannot be dismissed, notwithstanding stipulation on the duration of the appointment, unless this is in accordance with local custom or an express agreement between the parties (*Ḥatam Sofer,* Resp. loc. cit.; *Ḥemdat Shelomo,* OH no. 7); another opinion is that the continued employment of a public servant after the specified date for termination of his service must be regarded as an implied agreement to employ him for an additional period equal to that originally agreed upon (*Mishpat Ẓedek,* vol, 2, no. 76). A public servant who has grown old has the right to avail himself of an assistant *(mesayye'a)* at the public expense (Resp. Rashba, vol. 1, no. 300). There is also a custom that a public position passes through inheritance to the holder's son, if he is worthy of it, in order that the widow's existence may be secured (*Sho'el u-Meshiv,* vol. 3, pt. 1, no. 154; *Imrei Yosher,* vol. 1, no. 169). A service contract may be terminated at any time by mutual consent of the parties. According to some scholars, a formal act, such as the signing of a deed, is required for this purpose (Resp. Maharam of Rothenburg, ed. Prague, no. 77), while others hold that word of mouth alone suffices (Resp. Radbaz pt. 1, no. 88).

Withdrawal by the Master. Justifiable grounds for the master's withdrawal from the contract are: the servant's neglect, i.e., his failure to discharge his duties in a proper manner; his unfitness; and improper conduct on the servant's part, even outside his employment. If on account of the improper discharge of his duties or his unfitness the servant should cause or be likely to cause his master irretrievable loss, the latter may dismiss him without any prior warning (BM 109a). Circumstances amounting to improper conduct on the servant's part and warranting his dismissal – even if not directly related to his employment – include the fact that he is a reputed thief or under suspicion of committing theft (Rema HM 421:6) or an offense against morality (Hai Gaon, in: *Sha'arei Teshuvah* no. 51).

The master's withdrawal is not justified on the grounds that it is possible for him to find another worker who costs less (BM 76a and Rashi thereto) or a better one (Rosh Resp. no. 104:4), or because of the existence of enmity which is not attributable to the servant; nor is his withdrawal justified on the ground that from the beginning he had no need of the worker's service (BM 76b), or because he has completed his work prior to the termination of the contracted period of employment (BM 77a). In the latter case there is neglect on the master's part since he ought to have foreseen that he would not be in need of the worker's services.

If the master interrupts the employment without justifiable cause, he is liable for the full wages of the servant until the contracted period of service has expired (BM 76b and Rashi thereto). At the same time, however, a worker who sits idle after the master has retracted is only entitled to the remuneration of an "unemployed worker," since it is presumed that the worker himself prefers not to work and to receive less rather than to work and receive his stipulated wage. The wage of an "unemployed worker" is half his stipulated wage (Rashi Resp. no. 239). If the worker is the kind of person to whom idleness is a greater trial than doing his work, the master will be obliged to pay his full wage (BM 77a). Liability for the servant's wage in the event of the master retracting, as described above, is only imposed on the master if the servant is unable to find alternative employment (Nov. Ramban, BM 76b). In the event of the master retracting on account of inevitable accident (see *Ones*) affecting either himself or the work, he will not be liable to pay the servant for the period of his idleness, not even the wages due to an unemployed worker, unless the mishap is of a general, statewide nature (BM 77a and *Piskei ha-Rosh* thereto; Rema HM 321:1).

Compensation on Dismissal or Severance Pay. On dismissing his servant, even after the expiry of the contracted period, the master is obliged to pay him compensation. This law, based on the pentateuchal enjoinder of *ha'anakah* (i.e., the grant payable by the master to his Hebrew bond servant), began to evolve in the post-talmudic period and in recent decades has achieved full legal recognition, particularly in the decisions of the rabbinical courts of the State of Israel. (For full details see, *Ha'anakah*[1]).

Withdrawal by the Servant. In the event of the servant's withdrawal from the contract in the midst of his employment, it is necessary to distinguish between the case where this will not result in irretrievable loss – i.e., the master can afford a delay in the work until he is able to find another worker on the same terms – and the case where delay in the work will cause the master irretrievable loss. There is a tannaitic dispute concerning the case where the servant's withdrawal does not involve irretrievable loss but the master wishes to avoid delay and immediately hires other wokers at a higher wage; the general opinion is that the master must pay the servant for the work already done on a pro rata basis, and R. Dosa holds that the master may deduct from what the servant has so far earned the loss he has incurred through hiring a new worker at a higher wage (BM 76b). The *amora* Rav ruled that the *halakhah* followed Dosa in the case of a contractor and the sages in the case of a hired servant (BM 77a). For since a hired servant is to some degree a slave (see above) he may withdraw his labor even in the middle of the day, as it is written (Lev. 25:55): "For unto Me, the children of Israel are servants," and not the servants of servants (BM 10a). In this case too the hired servant may waive his right to withdraw his labor (*Zera Emet,* vol. 2, YD no. 97).

If the servant's withdrawal involves irretrievable loss, the master will be entitled to hire another worker to complete the work and to deduct from the servant's earnings the wage increment payable to the new worker; in this case it is also permissible for him to "mislead" *(lehatot)* the servant – i.e., to promise him an increased wage as an inducement to continue the work, yet remain liable only for the wage originally agreed upon (BM 76b). According to the original law, the master was entitled to hire workers against the servant "up to 40 or 50 *zuz,*" i.e., to recoup from the retracting servant several times his stipulated wages; but in order to limit the servant's liability, it was laid down by R. Naḥman that the master might only recoup an amount not exceeding his servant's wages (BM 78a), i.e., wages due to the servant for work done until his withdrawal (Rashi thereto); if the master is in possession of the servant's bundle, he will be able to recoup from it the total amount of the increment. A worker retracting on account of *ones* does not lose his wages for the period he has worked, even where his withdrawal has resulted in irretrievable loss (BM 77b).

The Servant's Liability to his Master. The servant's liability for pecuniary loss caused to his master is equivalent to that of a bailee for reward (see Bailment), whether in respect of theft and loss or any other kind of damage (BM 80b, 82b). His liability is greater than that of a tort-feasor, since the latter is only liable in the case of relative *ones* (which is like *avedah,* i.e., loss) and exempt as regards absolute *ones* (which is like theft), while the servant is liable in both cases (Tos. to BK 27b; see also Torts). The servant is liable for damage resulting from his departure from custom or the terms of his employment (BK 100b; Tosef. BK 10:29), from his failure to take proper care (BK 98b), and from his lack of familiarity with the work (BK 99b). The servant is also liable for damage caused in the course of his work to the chattels of his master, even unintentionally (BK 99b). As regards breakages in the transportation of goods by porters, R. Meir regulated that the servant be exempted from liability upon delivery of an oath that these were not intentionally caused by him (BM 82b). A servant causing his master damage not only has to pay for this, but also forfeits his remuneration (BM 58a).

The sages of the Talmud were at pains to modulate the severity of the servant's liability, and with reference to damage negligently caused by porters Rav decided that the latter should not only be exempt from liability but also entitled to payment of their hire – this in reliance on Proverbs 2:20 and the equitable rule of *li-fenim mi-shurat ha-din* (BM 83a and Rashi).

The Master's Liability to the Servant. The master's liability for damage suffered by the servant flows from a breach of agreement or custom, or from the general law of tort. Thus a master who burdens his servant to "carry on his shoulder" a heavier load than that agreed upon or customary will be liable for any resulting harm suffered by the latter (Tosef. BM 7:10; *Beit ha-Beḥirah* BM 80b).

As for the master's liability to his servant in tort, it will be necessary to distinguish whether the harm suffered by the servant is attributable directly to the master or not. Thus if the master causes harm to the person or property of the servant, e.g., damage suffered by an agent as a result of the sale of his principal's defective goods, the master will be liable therefor (*Tashbeẓ,* 4:2, 17; see also Resp. Mabit, vol. 2, pt. 2, no. 156); if, however, harm is suffered by the servant within the course of his employment which is not caused by the master, the latter will be exempt from liability for the damage done, whether to the servant's person or property, as happens, for example, when a spark flies from under a forger's hammer and sets alight his heap (*Sefer Teshuvot ha-Rashba ha-Meyuḥasot le-ha-Ramban* no. 20). Similarly, the principal is not obliged to ransom his paid agent when he is taken captive en route (Resp. Mabit, vol. 2, pt. 2, no. 156), nor is there any obligation in respect of an agent killed while he is on his master's business but not because of the latter. In the latter case, however, the *posekim* laid down that the master, because of his connection with the occurrence of such a disaster, should be obliged to take upon himself an expiation and

1. page 317.

to compensate the heirs of the deceased as a matter of equity (Resp. Maharyu no. 125).

In the State of Israel. Labor legislation in force in the State of Israel is a composite of three statutory sources:

(1) Ottoman: a number of paragraphs dealing with labor law are included under the chapter "Hire" in the Ottoman Civil Code (Mejelle);

(2) Mandatory: in particular the Safety at Work Ordinance (New Version 5730–1970);

(3) Legislation of the Knesset, replacing most of the Mandatory legislation on the subject with original laws, of which the following are the most important: Annual Leave Law, 1952; Hours of Work and Rest Law, 1951; Wage Protection Law, 1953; Apprenticeship Law, 1953; Youth Labor Law, 1953; Employment of Women Law, 1954; National Insurance Law, 1954; Collective Agreements Law, 1957; Settlement of Labor Disputes Law, 1957; Employment Service Law, 1959; Severance Pay Law, 1963; Male and Female Workers (Equal Pay) Law, 1964; Labor Courts Law, 1969. In addition, labor law in Israel has been further interpreted and evolved in the case law precedents of the Supreme Court. These, like the above Knesset laws, reflect the substantial influence of Jewish law, noticeable particularly in the Wage Protection Law, 1953 and Severance Pay Law, 1963 (see Elon, ILR, bibl.).

The Labor Courts Law sets up a special judicial hierarchy, at both regional and national levels, for airing disputes between master and servant, without right of appeal to the regular courts. The existence of a special judicial machinery in labor matters is also to be found in the history of Jewish law. In the European Jewish communities of the late Middle Ages, and within the framework of the various artisans' and traders' associations, special courts were elected in accordance with articles approved by the communal rabbis.

Bibliography: D. Farbstein, *Das Recht der unfreien und der freien Arbeiter nach juedisch-talmudischen Recht* . . . (1896); M. Hoffmann, in: *Jeschurun*, 4 (1917), 571–600 (Germ.); I. S. Zuri, *Mishpat ha-Talmud*, 5 (1921), 117–22; Gulak, Yesodei, 2 (1922), 180–8; M. Sulzberger, in: JQR, 13 (1922/23), 245–302, 390–459; Ch. W. Reines, *Ha-Po'el ba-Mikra u-va-Talmud* (1935); idem, in: *Israel of Tomorrow*, ed. by Leo Jung, 1 (1949), 130–61; idem, in: *Judaism*, 8 (1959), 329–37; Herzog, Instit, 2 (1939), 167–74; M. Findling, *Teḥukkat ha-Avodah* (1945); ET, 1 (1951³), 141–6; 3 (1951), 330–5; 6 (1954), 539–42; S. Federbush, *Mishpat ha-Melukhah be-Yisrael* (1952), 165–84; J. H. Heinemann, in: HUCA, 25 (1954), 263–325; J. Gross, in: *Ha-Peraklit*, 16 (1959/60), 72–86, 153–78; H. E. Baker, *Legal System of Israel* (1968), 182–196; Elon, Mafte'aḥ, 201–3; idem, in: ILR, 4 (1969), 85–89; idem, *Ha-Mishpat Ha-Ivri* (1973), I, p. 102, 176ff, II, 284ff, 504ff, 558ff, 571ff, 718ff, 734ff, 749ff; Sh. Warhaftig, *Dinei Avodah ba-Mishpat ha-Ivri*, 2 vols. (1969); contains bibliography (vol. 2, pp. 1207–10); idem, in: *Sinai*, 66 (1969/70), 195–9.

Shillem Warhaftig

HA'ANAKAH (Heb. הענקה), the gratuity which the master was enjoined to pay his Hebrew bond servant when the latter was set free. This institution is the source, in Jewish law, of the law of severance pay, i.e., payment of compensation to employees on their dismissal. The term *ha'anakah* has been interpreted as deriving from the word *anak* ענק in the sense of an ornament (around the neck, Prov. 1:9), i.e., that the bondsman must be "ornamented" with the gratuity, or in the sense of "loading on his neck" (Rashi and Ibn Ezra to Deut. 15:14).

Scriptural References. The duty of *ha'anakah* is enjoined in the Bible as both a negative and a positive precept – "when thou lettest him go free from thee, thou shalt not let him go empty," and "thou shalt furnish him liberally out of thy flock, and out of thy threshing floor, and out of thy winepress of that wherewith the Lord thy God hath blessed thee" (Deut. 15:13, 14) – and in this twofold manner has been included in the enumeration of the precepts (Maim., *Sefer ha-Mitzvot*, pos. comm. 196 and neg. comm. 233; *Semag, lavin* 178 and *asayin* 84; *Sefer ha-Ḥinnukh*, nos. 450, 484). The duty of *ha'anakah* arose upon completion of the six-year period of service (Deut. 15:12) and the grant was to be made out of the things with which the master's house had been blessed by virtue of the bondsman's service (Deut. 15:14; Kid. 17b; see statements of Eleazar b. Azariah). The duty of *ha'anakah* was enjoined as a reminder of the bondage in Egypt and exodus to freedom (Deut. 15:15), when the Israelites were "furnished" with property of their Egyptian masters (Sif. Deut. 120; Rashi and Rashbam, ad loc.). The institution of *ha'anakah*, unique to Jewish law as opposed to other ancient legal systems, was rooted in the special attitude toward a Hebrew bondsman, whose position was compared to that of a worker hired for a fixed term: ". . . for to the double of the hire of a hireling hath he served thee six years" (Deut. 15:18).

The Right to the Gratuity. It was laid down that the servant became entitled to the gratuity upon expiry of his term of service, or termination thereof on account of the Jubilee or his master's death, but not for reasons attributable to the servant himself, as, for example, when he gained his freedom by "deduction from the purchase price" (i.e., by refunding his master part of the price paid for himself, pro rata to the uncompleted term of his service): "you shall furnish to whomever you set free, but not to anyone who sets himself free" (Sif. Deut. 119; Kid. 16b). For this reason the gratuity right was forfeited by a runaway, notwithstanding intervention of the Jubilee. In the opinion of R. Meir, one who was freed by deduction from the purchase price remained entitled to the gratuity since it took place with the master's approval (Kid. 16b); on the other hand, some of the *tannaim* denied the gratuity right to one who was set free on account of his master's death (TJ, Kid. 1:2, 59c).

In the *Midrash Halakhah* the gratuity right was extended both to the one sold into bondage through the court on account of his theft (Ex. 22:2) and to one who sold himself into bondage on account of utter poverty (Lev. 25:39), nor were these cases distinguished in the Mishnah (see Ḥ. Albeck, *Shishah Sidrei Mishnah, Seder Nashim*, 409f.). In a *baraita* disputing opinions were expressed on this matter; some scholars holding that only one sold into bondage through the court and not one selling himself was entitled to gratuity, with R. Eliezer (Kid. 14b) holding that both were entitled thereto; this dispute was carried over into the Codes (Yad, Avadim, 3:12; Tos. Kid, 15a, s.v. *idakh;* and commentaries). One of the grounds for the view that one who sold himself into bondage was not entitled to the gratuity was that in doing so voluntarily, he transgressed the prohibition, "For unto Me the children of Israel are servants; they are My servants" (Lev. 25:55) "and not the servants of servants" (Kid. 22b; *Yam shel Shelomo*, Kid. 1:22).

Substance of the Gratuity Right. In tannaitic times the gratuity was looked upon as a personal right of the freed servant which was not transferable on death (Sif. Deut. 119), but the *amoraim* held it to be part of his remuneration and therefore transmissible ". . . just as the wages of a hired servant belong to his heirs, so here too . . . " (Kid. 15a; cf. also the version of Elijah Gaon, loc. cit. and see *Minḥat Ḥinnukh* no. 482). Contrary to the principle of "R. Nathan's Lien" (see *Shi'buda de-Rabbi Nathan*) with regard to the general right to recover a claim from a third party indebted to the debtor, the gratuity right was not attachable by the servant's creditor (Kid. 15a–16b) and, according to the majority of the *posekim,* the creditor could not recover his debt from the amount of the gratuity – not even when the servant was already released and in possession of the gratuity payment (Maim. comm. to Kid. 1:2; cf. Nov. *Penei Yehoshu'a* Kid., final collection).

The duty of furnishing a gratuity was, according to the majority view of the scholars, independent of the measure of gain derived by the master from his servant's labor (Sif. *ibid.;* Kid. 17a/b and cf. contrary opinion of Eleazar b. Azariah), but all the scholars accepted that a minimum was payable (although disagreeing on the amount: Kid. 17a), together with an increment according to the measure with which the master has been "blessed," such increment being payable by the master with a "generous hand" (Sif. Deut., 119–20).

Two opposing views concerning the legal substance of the gratuity were expressed in the Codes. According to some scholars it was not part of the servant's remuneration for his labor but derived from the institution of charity (*ẓedakah;* Shakh. to HM 86:3) or of waiver and gift (*Sma, ibid.,* 86:2 and see *Giddulei Terumah* to *Sefer ha-Terumot,* 51:1,5); other *posekim,* following the *halakhah* of the *amoraim* concerning transmissibility at death, of the gratuity, took the view that the gratuity was mainly to reward the servant for services rendered "beyond his wages" (Beit ha-Beḥirah, Kid. 15a) and therefore it had to be considered as part of his remuneration (*Penei Yehoshu'a* Kid. 16b; *Mishneh la-Melekh,* to Yad, *ibid.).*

Severance Pay. Adaptation of the gratuity institution to one of general compensation for employees upon dismissal was first mentioned toward the end of the 13th century, when it was stated that notwithstanding the abolition of Hebrew bond service, which was linked with observance of the Jubilee year, the employer still had to pay a gratuity to his departing worker regardless of the period of service (*Sefer ha-Ḥinnukh,* 450). Although this was phrased at that time as a moral obligation only, later scholars found it possible to recognize this duty of the employer as legally binding. In recent times this development has been acknowledged in the decisions of various scholars, and particularly in the judgments of the rabbinical courts in Israel, in three different ways:

(a) In accordance with the principle of the bond servant's gratuity, in pursuance of the statements in the *Sefer ha-Ḥinnukh (ibid.),* it was held that "... the intention of the Torah was to make it the employer's duty to be concerned about the worker's future so that the latter should not depart from his work empty-handed" (PDR, 3:286f.). Because Jewish law compared the position of a bond servant to that of a hired worker, it was concluded that the latter "certainly enjoys all the former's privileges ... the more so since he does not transgress a prohibition" (i.e., that of selling himself into bondage – see above; resp. Maharam of Rothenburg, ed. Prague, no. 85; see also *Yam Gadol,* no. 22).

(b) A different approach was adopted by Benzion Ouziel (see his responsum quoted in *Teḥukat Avodah* (see bibl.) 132f.). Holding that the law of the gratuity could not properly be relied upon to support the existence of a full legal duty to compensate an employee upon his dismissal, he preferred to base this duty on the scriptural admonition, "That thou mayest walk in the way of good men, and keep the paths of the righteous" (Prov. 2:20) in the same way as it was relied upon in the Talmud with reference to exempting the hired worker in certain circumstances from liability for damage negligently caused to his employer (BM 83a). Although conceding that this talmudic principle was a matter of equity *(li-fenim mi-shurat ha-din)* rather than binding law, R. Ouziel followed the opinion of numerous *posekim* that it was nevertheless enforceable by the court (*Mordekhai* BM 257; Sh. Ar., HM 12:2, and Rema *ibid.,* also *Baḥ* HM 12), and therefore decided that the court, "having due regard to the respective positions of the parties and reasons for the worker's dismissal or for his own departure," was empowered to order an employer to compensate his worker.

(c) Since it was not generally accepted that an obligation solely *li-fenim mi-shurat ha-din* is enforceable by the court, some scholars preferred to base the principle of severance pay on the Jewish legal source of custom (see *Minhag;* PDR, 1:330f.). Thus the rabbinical courts, applying the rule that "custom overrides the law" has special reference to labor law (TJ, BM 7:1; 11b) and recognizing "the spread in our time of a usage to pay severance pay," have laid down that severance pay "is not a matter of grace but a claim under law" which is payable even if the employer be a charitable institution; in arriving at this decision the rabbinical courts incorporate also the principle of the gratuity, holding that particular significance attaches to custom in this instance, since "we find a basis for it in the Torah and *halakhah,*" and this custom is founded on the Torah, the gratuity payable to the Hebrew bond servant "and therefore it is fit and proper" (PDR, 1:330f.; 3:286f.; 4:129).

It may be noted that R. Ouziel, in giving his above-mentioned decision (in 1945), specifically refrained from basing the severance pay obligation on custom – for the reason that such a usage was not yet sufficiently known and widespread. A mere ten years later the court, seeking a basis for full legal recognition of the severance pay duty, had reason to find as follows: "now that the custom has spread and become accepted in the whole country, and is common and practiced daily, it must be followed and the above-mentioned statements [of R. Ouziel] no longer apply." This is an illustration of great flexibility in recognizing the establishment of a custom. (see Elon, *Ha-Mishpat Ha-Ivri,* II, 752–754).

In the years since the establishment of the State of Israel, the rabbinical courts have laid down a number of rules concerning the matter of severance pay, including the following provisions: compensation is to be paid at the customarily accepted rate, or if this be uncertain, as determined by the court (PDR, 1:332f.); it is payable also to a temporary employee – if he has worked for a period approximating two years *(ibid.),,* and also to a part-time employee (4:129), but an independent contractor is not entitled to severance pay (3:272). An innovation was the rule that the employer is obliged to provide his worker with one month's prior notice of dismissal, or a month's remuneration in lieu thereof. This was deduced by the analogy of the landlord's duty, in Jewish law, to provide the tenant with a month's notice of eviction, in order that the latter be not deprived of a roof over his head; *a fortiori* in the case of a worker, so that he be given an opportunity to find an alternative source of livelihood. (Sh. Ar., HM 312:5; PDR, 4:130 and 3:281–3, where disputing opinions are quoted on the aptness of the analogy.)

In the State of Israel. In Mandatory times the obligation of severance pay was upheld in numerous judgments of the Mishpat ha-Shalom ha-Ivri. This fact contributed toward entrenchment of the usage, which came to be recognized as legally binding in a decision of the Mandatory High Court (Cohen v. Capun, in: *Palestine Law Reports* 7 (1940), 80, 88) and until 1963, custom alone formed the legal basis for the payment of severance pay under the general law. Thus the Supreme Court of Israel, in considering the antiquity of the above custom, stated: "It is common cause that the principle of severance pay is rooted in the scriptural duty of *ha'anakah*" (PD 5:275; 17, pt. 2:1255). The lack of statutory guidance led to many difficulties in the application of the custom. In 1963 the Severance Pay Law was enacted by the Knesset, with emphasis on the fact that the fundamental idea of this law derived from traditional Jewish law. The following are some of the law's main provisions:

A person dismissed by his employer after having been continuously employed for one year or – in the case of a seasonal employee – for two seasons in two consecutive years, is entitled to severance pay at the rate of a month's wages per year of employment for a "salaried employee" and two week's wages per year for employment for a "wage earner" (i.e., one whose remuneration is paid on the basis of a lesser period than one month; secs. 1, 12); in certain circumstances the employee is entitled to severance pay following his own resignation, i.e., by reason of an appreciable deterioration of his conditions of employment or on account of his or a member of his family's state of health, or the transfer of his residence (secs. 6–8, 11). The employee is also entitled to severance pay if his employment has ceased owing to the death of his employer, and for certain other reasons (sec. 4) and upon the employee's own death, severance pay is payable to his survivors (sec. 5). A person employed under a contract for a fixed period is entitled to severance pay at the end of the period, as if dismissed, unless the employer has offered to renew the contract (sec. 9). Severance pay is deemed to be wages payable in precedence to all other debts (sec. 27) and a composition and acknowledgment of discharge as to severance pay are invalid unless reduced to writing and expressly state that they relate to severance pay (sec. 29).

See also Labor Law; Slavery.

Bibliography: H. Baker, *Legal System of Israel* (1968), 189–94; M. Wager and P. Dickstein, *Piẓẓuyei Pitturin* (1940); S. B. Bar-Adon, *Dinei Avodah* (1942), 51–63; M. Findling, *Teḥukat ha-Avodah* (1945), 49f., 132f.; ET, 9 (1959), 673–87; Sh. Warhaftig, *Dinei Avodah ba-Mishpat ha-Ivri,* 2 (1969), 643–53, 1090–1100; M. Elon, in: ILR, 4 (1969), 87–89; idem, *Ha-Mishpat Ha-Ivri* (1973) I, p. 102, II, 749ff.

Menachem Elon

TORTS. The Principal Categories of Torts. The liability of various tortfeasors is discussed in relative detail in the Torah. Four principal cases are considered: (1) where someone opens a pit into which an animal falls and dies (Ex. 21:33–4); (2) where cattle trespass into the fields of others and do damage (Ex. 22:4); (3) where someone lights a fire which spreads to neighboring fields (Ex. 22:5); (4) where an ox gores man or beast (Ex. 21:28–32, 35–6). To those has to be added the case where a man injures his fellow or damages his property (Ex. 21:18–19, 22–5; Lev. 24:18–20). The Talmud calls the cases contained in the Torah primary categories of damage *(Avot Nezikin)* and these serve as archetypes for similar groups of torts. The principal categories of animal torts are: *shen* (tooth) – where the animal causes damage by consuming; *regel* (foot) – where the animal causes damage by walking in its normal manner; and *keren* (horn) – where the animal causes damage by goring with the intention of doing harm or does any other kind of unusual damage. The other principal categories of damage are: *bor* (pit) – any nuisance which ipso facto causes damage; *esh* (fire) – anything which causes damage when spread by the wind; and direct damage by man to another's person or property. These principal categories and their derivative rules were expanded to form a complete and homogeneous legal system embracing many other factual situations. As a result they were capable of dealing with any case of tortious liability which might arise.

The Basis of Liability – Negligence. The Talmud states that a man could be held liable only for damage caused by his negligence *(peshi'ah),* and not for damage through an accident *(ones).* Negligence is defined as conduct which the tortfeasor should have foreseen would cause damage (BK 21b; 52a/b; 99b), since this would be the normal result of such conduct. Thus liability would be incurred for a fire which spread in an ordinary wind (BK 56a) or for fencing a courtyard with thorns in a place frequented by the public who habitually lean against this fence (BK 29b).

The rabbis ruled that negligence was to be determined objectively. A man is liable for conduct which people would normally foresee as likely to cause damage (see R. Ulla's statement, BK 27b; Tosef. BK 10:29). On the other hand, if his conduct was such that most people would not normally foresee it as likely to cause damage, the damage is considered a mishap and not a consequence of his act and he is not liable (see Rif, *Halakhot* on BK 61b). Even if the defendant was of above-average intelligence and foresaw that damage would occur, he could not be held liable for conduct causing damage if most people would not have foreseen damage as resulting from such conduct. In such circumstances no liability would be incurred under human law for even wilful damage (see Ra'ah and Meiri in *Shitah Mekubbeẓet,* BK 56a, beginning *U-le-Rav Ashi*) unless the damage claimed was depredation (BK 27a). However, rabbinical enactments created liability for deliberate acts in certain cases in the interests of public policy (Git. 53a; Tosef. Git. 4 (3):6). The objective criterion of negligence was also applied where the tortfeasor was of below-average intelligence and incapable of foreseeing the possibility of damage. However, the deaf-mute, idiot, and minor are not liable for the damage they cause, since they have no understanding and cannot be expected to foresee the consequences of their actions. Indeed, since they frequently do cause damage, those encountering them should take suitable precautions, and if they fail to do so would themselves be liable for the resulting damage. In this respect damage caused by the deaf-mute, idiot, and minor can be compared to damage by cattle on public ground for which the owners are not liable since the injured party himself is bound to take precautions.

This test of negligence was applied to all the principal categories of damage mentioned in the Torah (see BK 55b and Rashi beginning *ke-ein*). Thus, if an animal was injured by falling into an inadequately covered pit, the owner of the pit was liable. On the other hand, if the pit were properly covered but the cover became decayed, he would not be liable (BK 52a). Similarly, the owner of the pit would be liable if a young ox, incapable of looking after itself, fell into an open pit, but not if the ox were fully grown and fell into the pit during the daytime (*Milḥamot ha-Shem* BK 52b ad finem). Likewise, liability would be incurred for a fire which spread in a normal wind but not where it spread in an unusual wind (BK 56a); and the owner of cattle which consumed and trampled on crops in another's field would be liable for the damage only if the control he exercised over his cattle was insufficient to prevent this kind of damage (BK 55b, 56a).

As to damage done by man directly, the Mishnah states: he is always *Mu'ad* (forewarned, and therefore liable for the consequences), whether he acted intentionally or inadvertently, "whether he was awake or asleep" (BK 26a). Nevertheless, many cases are mentioned where the man who did the damage was not liable and Tosafot (BK 27b) tried to solve the contradiction by distinguishing between cases of absolute *"ones,"* and qualified *"ones."* Only in the latter case would liability be incurred. There is no hint of this distinction in the sources and the better view seems to be that a tortfeasor is liable only if he caused damage by *ones* (compulsion) which could have been foreseen by him, as putting himself in the hands of robbers who forced him to do damage, or lying down to sleep next to objects which he should have foreseen he might break in his sleep, aliter, if the vessels were placed next to him after he went to sleep. Likewise a person who caused damage through his lack of expertise could only be held liable where he should have foreseen that expertise was required. However, a person who caused proprietary damage to his neighbor in order to save himself is not exempt because of *ones,* as he chose to act in a way which would damage his neighbor's property and did foresee the damage.

No Liability Where no Negligence Exists. Cases where the defendant is entirely exempt from liability because he was in no way negligent are of two kinds: (1) the plaintiff himself was negligent because he should have foreseen the possibility of damage i.e., where the defendant acted in the usual way and the plaintiff acted in an unusual way and the damage was therefore unforeseeable; (2) neither party could have foreseen the possibility of damage and therefore neither was negligent. An instance of the second kind is where an animal, kept under sufficient control, escaped in an unusual manner and did damage, and no liability would be incurred (BK 55b). Similarly, where an animal managed to start a fire or dig a pit which caused damage, no liability would be incurred since such an unusual eventuality could not have been foreseen (see the Ravad in the *Shitah Mekubbeẓet,* BK 48a beginning *"Mai";* BK 22a). The Talmud cites examples where no liability would be incurred, such as where an animal fell into a pit whose covering was originally adequate but which later became decayed (BK 52a); where a wall or tree unexpectedly fell onto the highway (BK 6b); where a fire spread further than could have been anticipated (BK 61b); where a burning coal was given to a deaf-mute, idiot, or minor who set fire to something (BK 59b); or experts such as physicians who acted in the usual professional manner and caused damage (Tosef. BK 9:11). As instances of the first kind the Talmud cites the case where a person running along the street collided with and was injured by another walking along the street; here the former alone would be liable since his conduct was unusual (BK 32a). Similarly, if a man broke his vessel against a beam carried by the man walking in front of him, the owner of the beam would not be liable. Aliter, however, if the owner of the beam stopped unexpectedly, thereby causing the vessel to strike the beam and break (loc. cit.). Likewise, a person who places his objects on public ground where they are damaged by animals walking or grazing in a normal manner has no claim against the owner of the animals, since animals are to be expected on public ground (BK 19b, 20a). However, the presence of a pit, fire, or a goring ox on public ground would cause liability for damage since they are not normally present and people do not expect them and take no precautions (BK 27b). It would also be unusual behavior and therefore negligence to enter another's premises or bring chattels or livestock therein, without permission. Since his presence was unexpected the owner of the premises would not be liable for damage caused to the trespasser or his property, but the trespasser would be liable for damage caused to the owner or his property (BK 47a–b, 48a).

Sometimes a person is injured even though both parties behaved in the usual manner, e.g., when both walk in the street or if one enters the premises of another with permission. In these cases the tortfeasor is not liable because the other party should have taken precautions as he ought to have foreseen the normal behavior of the tortfeasor. Likewise, damage may occur when both parties behave in an unusual manner as where both were running along the street or where both entered the premises of a third party without permission (*ibid.,* 32a; 48a/b); in these cases too, the tortfeasor is exempt, since the fact that he was behaving abnormally should have made him foresee that others may behave abnormally too (Tos. BK 48b, s.v. *"Sheneihem"*).

If without negligence a man creates a situation which is likely to cause damage, he will not be liable for damage caused before he had a reasonable opportunity to know about the situation and remove it. An objective test was laid down as to when a man should have known of the existence of the nuisance and acted to remove it. If he adequately covered his pit and through no fault of his own the pit was uncovered he would not be liable for damage during the period that most people would not have known that the pit had become open and required covering (BK 52a). Similarly, if his animal escaped from his courtyard through no fault of his own, and caused damage during the period in which he could not have been expected to realize that the animal had escaped and to recapture it, he would not be liable (see BK 58a and Meiri in the *Shitah Mekubbeẓet* on 55b beginning *"nifreẓah"*). Similarly if a man's vessels broke non-negligently on the highway and, without intending to abandon them, he left them there, he is liable, except for damage caused by them before they could have been removed (BK 29a). Similarly, the owner of a wall or a tree which fell onto the highway and caused damage would be liable only if he knew that they were in a bad condition or was warned that they might fall (BK 6b).

The foreseeability test as the basis of liability for damage led the rabbis to conclude that even where negligent the tortfeasor would only be liable for damage that he could foresee. He is not liable for additional or other damage, or damage greater than that foreseeable. Thus where a fire spread in an ordinary wind the tortfeasor would be liable for whatever could be seen to be within the path of the fire but not for what was hidden, unless he should have contemplated the existence of hidden objects (BK 61b). Similarly, if a man dug a pit and did not cover it he would be liable for injury to a young animal or to an animal who fell into it at night but would not be liable for injury to a grown animal who fell into it in daylight (BK 54b), or for a human being who fell into the pit (BK 28b). If the pit was less than ten handbreadths deep, he would be liable for injury only, since animals do not normally die when falling into such a small pit (BK 3a). Likewise, liability for injury is restricted to the extent of its original gravity. If the injury becomes worse than was originally estimated the tortfeasor is not liable for additional damage (BK 91a). However, where the degree of damage was foreseen but the way in which the damage occurred was unexpected the rabbis disagreed as to whether the defendant should be held liable, some arguing that the defendant was liable in negligence while others holding that the defendant could not be liable for what he could not foresee. This situation is known in the Talmud as *Teḥilato bi-Feshi'ah ve-Sofo be–Ones* (negligent conduct leading to accidental damage). Thus, if a man put his dog on a roof and the dog fell off and broke nearby objects (BK 21b), he would be liable in negligence for putting his dog on the roof (since a dog could be expected to jump off a roof) but not for the mode of damage, since he could not have foreseen that the dog would fall.

Indirect Damage. The foreseeability test would appear to determine liability for indirect damage *(gerama)* where the damage is the ultimate consequence of the defendant's act. Only if the defendant should have foreseen the damage occurring would he be held liable for indirect damage.

Unusual Damage by Cattle. Unusual animal torts, such as goring, lie between liability in negligence for foreseeable damage and exemption for accidental damage. In such cases the animal's owners are liable for half-damages (BK 14a). But if the animal was a habitual gorer, having gored three times, the owner would be liable for full damage, since the damage was neither unusual nor unforeseeable. On the other hand, the owner would be completely exempt if he was not negligent at all. Thus, if the defendant's animal gored the plaintiff on the defendant's premises, no liability would normally be incurred since the defendant could not have foreseen that the plaintiff would enter his premises.

Defenses to Negligence. A person who negligently causes damage is not liable for damages in three situations: (1) where he received permission from the plaintiff to cause damage (BK 92a, 93a), e.g., was allowed to feed his cattle in the plaintiff's field; (2) where the defendant, in his capacity as a court official was given permission by a court to harm the plaintiff, e.g., by administering punishment (Tosef. BK 9:11); (3) where the damage inflicted was nonphysical, e.g., distress and sorrow (where there is no physical pain), or economic or commercial damage (BK 98a); for liability for damage is restricted to physical damage.

Damage Committed by the Person and by his Property. A distinction is found in several places in the Talmud between damage by a person and damage by his property (BK 4a; 4b). The difference is that liability for damage by the person is confined to negligent acts of commission whereas liability for damage by his property can also be incurred by negligent acts of omission. Thus, a man who spilt another's wine must pay for the damage, whereas if he saw the other's wine spill and did nothing to help him recover it, he would not be liable. On the other hand, the defendant whose ox grazed in the plaintiff's field would be liable for damage caused by the animal either because he put the ox there or because he did not adequately prevent its escape. Similarly, a man who did nothing to prevent a stray fire from spreading onto the highway would not be liable even though he was able to prevent the fire's spreading. He would be liable, however, if he caused the fire negligently or if he did not prevent the spread of a fire from his own premises, even though he did not start it.

Joint Tortfeasors. Where damage was caused by the negligence of two or more persons, the parties are liable in equal proportions. If the plaintiff and the defendant were equally negligent, the plaintiff recovers half damages from the defendant and loses the remainder (see Tos. BK 23a, s.v. *"U-Leḥayyev"*). The negligence of each tortfeasor is one of two types: (1) where he should have foreseen that his negligence alone would cause damage; (2) where he should have foreseen that damage would result from his conduct, coupled with that of the other tortfeasor, even though his conduct alone would not be expected to lead to damage. Thus if two men dug a pit together, they would both be held liable in negligence for damage caused by the pit (BK 51a). However, if only one of them was negligent, he alone is liable. Thus, a man who concealed sharp pieces of glass in his neighbor's dilapidated wall which the latter was about to pull down onto public ground would be liable in negligence to anyone injured by the glass pieces, whereas the neighbor would incur no liability since he could not have anticipated the presence of glass pieces in his wall (BK 30a). Similarly, someone who put objects by the side of a man sleeping would be solely liable if the latter broke the objects in his sleep (TJ, BK 2:8, 3a).

Where damage was caused by two tortfeasors, the first leading the second to perform the act, the rabbis were divided as to the liability of the party performing the damage. Examples of such cases, which are known as *Garme* (see *Gerama* and *Garme*), include informing about another's property which leads to its seizure (BK 117a) and the hiring of false witnesses (BK 55b). In each case the party performing the damage had a choice as to whether to act tortiously or not. If he had no choice in the matter because of lack of intelligence or the required expertise, he is no more than a tool in the hand of the first tortfeasor and the latter is liable for all the damages. Thus a man who puts an idiot or minor in charge of fire and thorns is liable for all the damage if his neighbor's house is burnt down (BK 59b); and the defendant who tells his neighbor to bring him his animal from the premises of a third party is solely liable if it transpires that the animal does not belong to the defendant at all and that the latter attempted to steal it (Tos. *ibid.,* 79a).

In the State of Israel. The law of torts is covered by the Civil Wrongs Ordinance (1944, new version 1968), originally enacted by the British Mandatory authorities, which came into force in 1947, and several amendments enacted by the Knesset. The ordinance is modeled on English law and section 1 referred to English law for explanations of, and supplements to, the ordinance. This section was nullified by the Knesset through a special ordinance in March 1972. See Elon, *Ha-Mishpat Ha-Ivri* (1973), I, 113 no. 151.

See also *Avot Nezikin; Gerama* and *Garme;* Damages.

Bibliography: Ch. Tchernowitz, *Shi'urim ba-Talmud,* 1 (1913); Gulak, Yesodei, 2 (1922), 201–37; idem, in: *Tarbiz,* 6 (1935), 383–95; B. B. Lieberman, in: *Journal of Comparative Legislation,* 9 (1927), 231–40, I.S. Zuri, *Torat ha-Mishpat ha-Ezraḥi ha-Ivri,* 3, pt. 1 (1937); J. J. Weinberg, *Meḥkarim ba-Talmud,* 1 (1937/38), 180ff.; J. S. Ben-Meir, in: *Sinai,* 7 (1940), 295–308; G. Horowitz, *The Spirit of Jewish Law* (1953), 569–623; B. Cohen, in: *Studi in onore di Pietro de Francisci,* 1 (1954), 305–36; reprinted in his: *Jewish and Roman Law* (1966), 578–609, addenda; *ibid.* 788–92; S. J. Zevin, in: *Sinai,* 50 (1961/62), 88–95; idem, in: *Torah she-be-Al-Peh,* 4 (1962), 9–17; Sh. Albeck, *Pesher Dinei ha-Nezikin ba-Talmud* (1965); Elon, *Ha-Mishpat Ha-Ivri* (1973) I, 173ff, 177ff, II, 301ff, 341ff, 482ff, 495ff, 516ff, 750ff, 764ff, III, 882ff.

Shalom Albeck

AVOT NEZIKIN (Heb. אבות נזיקין, lit. "Fathers of Damage"), the classification of torts. Certain passages in the Pentateuch (Ex. 21–22) have been expounded in the Talmud to form the basis on which tortious liability in Jewish law can be classified. The Mishnah (BK 1:1) classifies the tortfeasors into four categories: ox, pit, grazing, fire. Basically, three sources of common danger – (1) animals, (2) pits, and (3) fire – have been developed as the principal categories of the talmudic law of torts.

(1) Animals. The Talmud distinguishes between two kinds of damage that an animal can cause – habitual or common damage, termed *shen,* (Heb. שן, "a tooth") and *regel* (Heb. רגל "a foot"); and unusual or uncommon damage, termed *keren* (Heb. קרן "a horn"). These terms are derived from instances of damage by animals referred to in the Torah *(ibid.).*

(a) Shen and Regel: the former refers to acts of damage caused by an animal while grazing, while the latter refers to acts of damage caused by an animal while walking, i.e., both occuring during the course of an animal's normal activities. The fact that *shen* and *regel* torts result from an animal's normal activities distinguishes them from *keren* – the abnormal, unexpected act of an animal, such as goring, biting, or kicking. In cases of *shen* and *regel* damage is presumed to be foreseeable and the owner is therefore required to take suitable precautions, and, if negligent, is held fully liable for the damage caused. However, such liability is limited in that it attaches only when the damage is caused on the premises of the injured party or in any other place not commonly frequented by the animal. When the damage occurs on the owner's premises, or in the public domain, or in any other place commonly frequented by animals, the owner is exempt from *shen* or *regel* liability on the grounds that he is entitled to expect that the injured party would take reasonable precautions to protect himself against such foreseeable risks. Furthermore, the owner is also exempt from liability where the damage occurs in a place which neither the animal nor the injured party commonly frequent, since the presence of either of them there (especially the injured party) was not foreseeable (BK 14a).

(b) Keren: this term covers an animal's unexpected, vicious acts; i.e., goring, biting, or kicking, as mentioned above. The ox was the popular beast of burden and thus was frequently encountered in public places. Its nature and propensities made it a common cause of damage and the term *keren* was extended to include all the unforeseeable acts of an animal. Unlike *shen* and *regel* acts, *keren* damage is not the result of an animal's normal behavior, and since it is accordingly unforeseeable the owner cannot be accused of negligence. On the other hand, *keren* is not so uncommon as to exclude negligence altogether and exempt the owner from liability entirely. In fact, *keren* was deemed to be midway between negligence and inevitable accident and the authorities differed as to whether it should be included as a tort of negligence or not. Whatever the viewpoint adopted, however, all agreed that the owner should be liable for half the cost of the damage caused this being regarded according to the accepted opinion as a fine to encourage the owner to take greater care in preventing his animal from causing even unusual *(keren)* damage. The owner is exempt from all liability, however, where the injury caused by a *keren* act was completely unforeseeable, e.g., where his ox gored a pregnant woman, causing her to miscarry – this being an unexpected degree of damage (as far as the miscarriage is concerned). Similarly, the owner is not liable for acts of *keren* committed on his own premises – there being no negligence on his part – but such acts committed anywhere else, including the public domain, result in his being liable for half the damage caused.

This "half-damages" liability was deemed a charge on the carcass of the offending animal, so that the owner did not have to make up any shortfall. This was not interpreted, however, as implying that the animal itself was "liable," since the law is that a person who acquired an animal that had committed an act of *keren* while it was ownerless was exempt from the charge. The *tannaim* disputed the question whether the injured party's right was a lien on the carcass or created a part-ownership therein.

The first two times an animal commits an act of *keren* the damage is called *keren tammah* (i.e., caused by an animal considered harmless), but after the third such act (witnesses having duly testified to the facts before the court so that the owner was made fully aware of the position), the animal becomes *mu'ad* ("forewarned") and the damage is called *keren mu'edet* – the owner thereafter being liable for all futher damage caused by similar acts of the animal, even if committed in the public domain. But the animal becomes a *mu'ad* only for the same kind of act, remaining a *tam* ("innocent") in respect of any other unusual act causing damage. For example, an ox *mu'ad* to gore other oxen is not *mu'ad* to bite a person; if he does, it is a *tam* with regard to that act unless and until it commits it three times as well. A *mu'ad* can be restored to the status of *tam* if it can be proved that it has ceased displaying the particular propensity that made it a *mu'ad* – although three further acts of the same kind would result in the status of *mu'ad* again. Wild animals are always regarded as *mu'ad* and their owners fully liable in all cases. After the talmudic period, *keren* liability, whether of the *tam* or *mu'ad* variety, was not enforced because of its rarity; instead, the owner of the offending animal was placed under a ban until he came to terms with the injured party (Maim. Yad, Sanhedrin, 5:17; see also Damages).

(c) Ẓerorot (צרורות "pebbles"): this is the talmudic term for damage caused by an animal without bodily contact – the term being derived from the most common form of this type of damage, namely when an animal dislodges pebbles or the like which fall and break something. This category was extended to cover the case of a cock shattering a glass with the resonance of its crowing. Where *ẓerorot* damage is common, it is treated as a form of *regel* and where it is uncommon, it is treated as a form of *keren.* It appears that the Palestinian Talmud rendered the owner fully liable in the former case *(regel)*, but only half liable in the latter case (*keren;* TJ, BK 2:1, 2d). The Babylonian Talmud discusses whether the owner is fully or only half liable, but the dispute seems to center on whether *ẓerorot* is as common as *regel.* The *halakhah* accords with the view of Rava that in the case of common damage the owner is liable for half, while in the case of uncommon *ẓerorot* damage there is doubt whether he pays half or only quarter damages (BK 17b–19b).

(d) Killing a Human Being: an animal which kills a human being, whether it is a *tam* or a *mu'ad,* is stoned to death. Some regard this as a punishment for the animal, while others are of the opinion that it is simply to eliminate a public menace. A third view is that, as an animal has no mind, it cannot be subjected to punishment and its execution is therefore a punishment for the owner. If the animal was *mu'ad* as a killer, its owner had to indemnify the victim's heirs (*ibid.,* 41a), since he was negligent in failing to guard his animal properly. It follows, therefore, that such liability would not result from a killing that occurred on the owner's premises, as presumably there was there no negligence on his part (*ibid.,* 23b; see also Compounding Offenses).

(2) Pit (בור Bor). This is the name given to another leading category of tort and covers cases where an obstacle is created by a person's negligence and left as a hazard by means of which another is injured. The prime example is that of a person who digs a pit, leaves it uncovered, and another person or an animal falls into it. Other major examples would be leaving stones or water unfenced and thus potentially hazardous. The common factor is the commission or omission of something which brings about a dangerous situation and the foreseeability of damage resulting. A person who fails to take adequate precautions to render harmless a hazard under his control is considered negligent, since he is presumed able to foresee that damage may result, and he is therefore liable for any such subsequent damage.

If the *bor* (i.e., the hazard) is adequately guarded or left in a place where persons or animals do not normally pass, such as one's private property, no negligence or presumed foreseeability can be ascribed and no liability would arise (BK 49b, 50a). Furthermore, no liability attaches to a person whose property became a public hazard through no fault of his and he had abandoned it, e.g., where by an inevitable accident a vessel breaks and the owner abandons the broken pieces, which subsequently cause damage (Rif. *Halakhot,* BK 29a, 31a) – just as a mere passerby is under no legal obligation to render harmless a hazard he happens to encounter. A person is not liable for a *bor* he creates if he could not have foreseen that it would not have been rendered harmless before it was likely to cause injury; e.g., where he digs a well in a public place and then entrusts it to the proper public authority (BK 50a), or where he is the part-owner of a well and he leaves it uncovered while it is still being used by his co-owner (51a–b). In these cases, the lack of any negligence absolves him.

One who commits the tort of *bor* is liable for foreseeable damage, but not for unusual or unforeseeable damage. Thus, if one digs a pit and leaves it uncovered in the daytime in a place where it is clearly visible, he would not be liable because persons or animals passing by are expected to be able to look where they are going. It is thought by most authorities that this rule also applies to cases where vessels are dropped into and damaged by the *bor,* since a similar standard of care is expected from those who carry such vessels (52a, 53b). Furthermore, no liability attaches in the case where a *bor* causes damage or injury to someone or something for whom or for which it would not normally be considered a hazard (48b). On the other hand, a *bor* that is not a hazard by day may become one at night, or may not be a hazard to big animals but one to young animals, who may not be so capable of guarding against such dangers. There would also be liability in respect of a *bor* that could only cause injury to human beings, but not death, as people do not usually pay much attention to such minor hazards (28b). If an animal dies from falling into a pit less than ten handbreadths deep there is no liability, for such a small pit is not normally expected to cause death (3a). Where two people create a *bor* jointly, or where one enlarges a *bor* created by another, each is liable for half the resulting damage – if liability attaches at all under the rules outlined above.

(3) Fire (**אש** Esh). The third leading category of tort covers damage caused by a hazard, such as fire, that can spread if not adequately contained or guarded. A person is liable for such damage if it is caused by his own negligence, but not otherwise. Accordingly, he is liable for damage caused by fire carried by a normal wind (which he should have foreseen), but not if the wind was exceptional (BK 60a). Similarly, he is liable if the fire spread over a foreseeable distance, but not if it spread further than could reasonably have been anticipated (61a–b). Yet another example given is the sending of fire or burning objects in the hands of an imbecile, for which the sender would be liable if damage resulted – but not if he sent a mere flickering coal, which is presumed harmless (59b). Thus the underlying rule is that the tortfeasor is liable for foreseeable damage – because he is negligent if he does not prevent it – but not where the damage was unforeseeable and thus no negligence was involved.

One who is negligent in guarding a fire created by him is only liable to the extent of foreseeable damage. For example, a fire that consumes hidden articles would not render the tortfeasor liable for them, whereas he would be liable in respect of exposed articles, damage to them being foreseeable. However, the *tanna* R. Judah extended the liability to cover hidden articles as well, on the grounds that it should have been foreseen that articles may have been hidden (61b). Some scholars interpret this discussion as being a question of evidence only, i.e., the acceptability of the plea that the articles have been there (*Siftei Kohen* to Sh. Ar., ḤM 388, n. 6).

The Talmud records a dispute over the substantive nature of damage caused by fire, i.e., whether it is to be considered as damage caused by a person's property *(ke-mamono)* like damage caused by his animal, or as damage caused by the person himself *(ke-gufo)* as if he had shot an arrow. The difference is relevant in determining the measure of compensation, since higher damages are payable for damage caused directly by one person to another *(ke-gufo).* The conclusion seems to be that even those who consider *esh* to be a tort *ke-gufo* concede that sometimes it can only justly be regarded as a tort *ke-mamono,* thus incurring a lower measure of damages (BK 22a–b, 23a).

State of Israel. The Civil Wrongs Ordinance, 1944, makes no substantive distinction between liability for damage caused by animals or obstacles or fire and damage caused in other ways; in all cases there is liability if there has been negligence. However, if damage is caused by a dangerous animal or by a dangerous explosion or fire, the onus is on the possessor to prove that there was no negligence on his part.

Bibliography: Maimonides, Yad, Nizkei Mammon; Sh. Ar., ḤM 389–418; Gulak, Yesodei, 2 (1922), 227–37; ET, s.v. *Avot Nezikin, Esh, Bor, Hefker;* S. Albeck, *Pesher Dinei ha-Nezikin ba-Talmud* (1965), 93–172; Elon, *Ha-Mishpat Ha-Ivri* (1973) I, 154, II, 288, 301ff, 341ff, 823ff.

Shalom Albeck

GERAMA AND GARME (Aram. גרמא , גרמי), terms variously used in the Talmud to describe tortious damage caused indirectly by the tortfeasor's person. The following acts are examples cited of *garme* damage: a judge delivering an erroneous decision resulting in damage to another; burning another's bond – thus preventing him from recovering his debt; a banker giving an erroneous valuation of coins – causing them to be acquired at a loss; damaging mortgaged property held by a creditor – thus reducing the value of his security; informing on another's property to bandits – thus causing them to take it away. Opinion is divided in the Talmud over the question of liability for this kind of tort (BK 98b, 110a; 117b); some of the sages maintain that liability does exist, while others exclude it. In other cases – similar to those cited above – the damage is termed *gerama* (BK 48b, 60a; BB 22b), but here liability is excluded. Examples of *gerama* damage are: placing a ladder by a pigeon loft, enabling a weasel to climb up and eat the pigeons; directing something towards a fire so that the wind causes the conflagration; allowing an animal to trespass onto another's land, where it falls into a well so that its corpse pollutes the water. Other cases which were later interpreted as *gerama* are: bending the stalks of grain in another's field toward an approaching fire so that they catch fire; placing poison in the path of another's animal, causing it to eat this and die; sending a burning object through a minor or an idiot, who is irresponsible and thus causes damage; inciting another's dog to bite a third person; frightening another to the extent that he suffers injury or damage from such fright; leaving a broken vessel on public ground so that the pieces cause injury (BK 24b; 55b–56a). Even the earliest of the post-talmudic commentators found difficulty in explaining the difference between *gerama* damage, for which the Talmud does not impose any liability, and *garme* damage, for which talmudic opinion differs as to whether there is liability or not. According to Rashi (to BB 22b, s.v. *gerama;* see Sh. Ar., ḤM 386:4), there is no difference between the two concepts – and that those sages who exclude liability for *garme* damage also exclude it in cases of *gerama* damage, and vice versa. Some of the tosafists maintain (BB 22b, s.v. *zot omeret*) that, indeed, in strict law there is no distinction and that there is no liability in either case – save that the more common injuries are called *garme* and that those sages who impose liability for *garme* damage do so in the sense of fining the tortfeasor for the sake of public order. However, according to the majority of the tosafists, all indirect damage that is an immediate result of the tortfeasor is termed *garme,* whereas all other acts of indirect damage are called *gerama* – in respect of which the sages are unanimous in excluding liability. There are also further distinctions between *gerama* and *garme* damage, which all present difficulties and which are all less acceptable. It appears that the two categories can be distinguished by using *gerama* to refer to indirect damage that is too remote to have been foreseeable, and *garme* to refer to indirect damage that should have been foreseeable – but which was caused solely by the independent act of a second person who acted negligently following the first person's act, while he could have refrained from doing that which resulted in the damage. In the latter situation, some sages maintain that the first person is exempt from liability, even though he could have foreseen that his act would result in the negligent act of the second person – who is held to be solely responsible. On the other hand, others hold the first person liable, just because he should have foreseen that his own act would result in the negligent act of the second person. According to this distinction, therefore, the loss sustained by someone acting on the advice of an expert is *garme* damage – because he should have realized that other experts should be consulted before he acted on one expert's advice and he was himself negligent in failing to take such second opinions. If, however, the matter is such that only one suitable expert is available and there is no choice but to rely exclusively on his advice, it is not a case of *garme* damage, and it is the unanimous opinion that the expert is liable for the consequences of his negligent advice. The *halakhah* is that a person is liable for *garme* damage, although it is disputed in the codes whether such liability stems from the strict law or is in the nature of a fine for the sake of public order, as mentioned above. The law applicable in the State of Israel is the Civil Wrongs Ordinance, 1947, which makes a person liable for the natural consequences of his conduct – but not if the decisive cause of the damage is the fault of another. An expert is held liable for giving negligent declarations and opinions.

Bibliography: Gulak, Yesodei, 1 (1922), 157; 2 (1922), 24, 182, 206–9; 4 (1922), 162f.; Herzog, Institutions, 2 (1939), 311 (index), s.v.; ET, 6 (1954), 461–97; 7 (1956), 382–96; S. Albeck, *Pesher Dinei ha-Nezikin ba-Talmud* (1965), 43–61; B. Cohen, *Jewish and Roman Law,* 2 (1966), 578–609, addenda 788–92; M. Elon, *Ha-Mishpat Ha-Ivri* (1973) I, 173ff, 204.

Shalom Albeck

NUISANCE. The owner or person in possession of land is not at liberty to use it as he pleases. Land, even if unencumbered, may not be used in such manner as to harm or disturb one's neighbors. Any neighbor can require the offending landowner to abate the nuisance or to have the cause thereof removed from their common boundary.

Among the restraints imposed on the use of land, the Mishnah (BB 2) makes mention of the following: A person may not dig a cistern near to his neighbor's cistern or wall, since they would thus be damaged, and he must remove lime from the vicinity of his neighbor's wall; he may not open a bakery or stable under his neighbor's barn, nor a shop on residential premises where the customers will disturb the neighbors; he may not build a wall so close to his neighbor's windows as to darken them; he must not keep his ladder near his neighbor's dovecote since it will enable a weasel to climb it and devour the pigeons; his threshing floor must not be too near a town or his neighbor's field lest the chaff harm the vegetation. There are further instances of the potentially harmful use of land enumerated in the Talmud.

The *tanna,* R. Yose, is of the opinion that the person creating a nuisance cannot be obliged to abate it and is free to act as he pleases and the injured party must keep his distance if he wishes to avoid suffering harm. The *halakhah* of the Talmud was decided in accordance with R. Yose's view, but the latter was interpreted as admitting that the tortfeasor must abate a nuisance if the interference with his neighbor's use of his property arises from his own harmful act (i.e., an act of his own body, as if he had "shot arrows" into his neighbor's domain; BB 22b). The scope of this qualification is not clear and some scholars hold that most of the injuries enumerated in the Mishnah (above) are of the kind qualified by R. Yose, which the latter concedes must be abated by the tortfeasor. Other scholars hold that R. Yose disagrees with the above-mentioned *mishnayot* and obliges the tortfeasor to abate a nuisance only when damage is actually (and directly) caused by his own act (see Rashi and Tos. *ibid.*). In fact, in the post-talmudic period, the instances in which R. Yose was considered to have conceded the existence of a tortfeasor's obligation to abate a nuisance were extended as far as possible (see Asher b. Jehiel (Rosh), quoted in Tur. ḤM 155:20–23). The Talmud (BB 17b) also records the dispute over the question whether the obligation – when it exists – of abating a nuisance applies even if the offender's particular use of his land preceded that of his neighbor – the latter suffering no damage until the time of such conflicting use by him – or whether prior use takes precedence. Thus if the injured party's particular use of his land preceded his neighbor's conflicting use of his land, the latter must curtail his use, but if the other way round the obligation rests upon the injured party. There is an opinion (Tos. *ibid.,* 18b), which holds that the rule of precedence by virtue of prior use is universally accepted and that there is no dispute save with regard to a single case, that of digging a cistern in the vicinity of a common boundary with a neighbor.

Which Nuisance Must Be Abated. An analysis of the cases of nuisance referred to in talmudic literature and the reasoning behind them suggests that all cases of nuisance may be divided into four categories: (1) An interference arising when land is used in a manner usual for that particular place and time, but the neighbor suffers injury in an unusual manner, either because of the unusual use of his own land or because he is uncommonly sensitive to the disturbance. It is unanimously agreed that in this event the alleged tortfeasor is at no time obliged to abate the so-called nuisance. (2) The tortfeasor uses his land in an unusual manner for that particular place and time, while the injured neighbor uses his land in the usual manner, in the same way as other people do, and is neither more sensitive nor anxious than most people. In this event all agree that the tortfeasor must always abate the nuisance he has created. (3) Both parties use their land in the usual manner and the injured party is not uncommonly sensitive. (4) The tortfeasor uses his land in an unusual manner, and the injured party does so too or is uncommonly sensitive. The latter two categories are the subject of the dispute mentioned above between R. Yose and the sages, as to whether the party causing the nuisance is obliged to abate it or whether it must be suffered by the injured neighbor; and of the dispute whether the injuring party must always abate the nuisance or whether it is a matter of prior use taking precedence. Most acts of nuisance referred to in the Talmud fall into the third of these categories (see Albeck, bibliography.).

The Rules of Nuisance as Part of the Law of Property. The prohibition against using land in a manner interfering with a neighbor's enjoyment of his own property is inherent in the proprietary rights over that immovable property, and the right to the undisturbed use of one's property may be sold like any other proprietary right. A person may sell or transfer part (or all) of his right to the undisturbed enjoyment of his property by agreeing to a particular use of his neighbor's property, whereupon the neighbor may make such use of his land regardless of any nuisance thereby caused to the former. Thus, for instance, a person may become entitled to erect a dovecote alongside his common boundary and may transfer this right, together with the land itself, to a new owner. Furthermore this right is retained by the owner of the disturbing property even when the adjacent land is sold to a new owner (see Sh. Ar., ḤM 155:24). A nuisance which is continued for a period of three years (or even from the outset, according to some scholars), if supported by a plea that the right was granted to him by the injured neighbor (or even without such a plea, according to some scholars), constitutes evidence of such right of user. However, these rules apply only when the nuisance is not so severe as to be insufferable (*ibid.*, 155:35–36).

See also Servitudes; *Ḥazakah.*

Relationship of Nuisance to the Laws of Tort. A person suffering a nuisance may oblige his neighbor to abate the nuisance and if physical damage results from the nuisance which itself was the result of the neighbor's negligence, he is also entitled to be compensated for such damage (BB 20b). If the nuisance is of a kind which the law does not require the tortfeasor to abate, the neighbor cannot oblige the tortfeasor to do so, nor, according to some scholars, can he recover compensation for damage of a physical nature even when caused by negligence, because he, in turn, is expected to take precautions. Other scholars, however, hold the tortfeasor liable for resulting damage. If a person's use of his land is such that it may cause his neighbor damage for which compensation is payable but it is not likely that such damage will result, the neighbor cannot demand the abatement of the nuisance because people are not normally afraid of or disturbed by an unlikely risk; but if in fact the damage does result from the landowner's negligence he is obliged to compensate his neighbor. If such use of the land habitually causes damage for which compensation is payable, people will usually be disturbed thereby and the neighbor can require the abatement thereof. If the damage is of a kind which is foreseeable, the landowner will be deemed negligent, but if the damage was unforeseeable, he is exempt from liability. The law of the State of Israel (Civil Wrongs Ordinance, 1947) defines private nuisance as any conduct which causes a material interference with the reasonable use and enjoyment of another's immovable property. The injured party is entitled to compensation and the court may order the abatement of the nuisance.

Bibliography: Gulak, Yesodei, 1 (1922), 134, 146.; ET, 8 (1957), 659–702; 10 (1961), 628–96; S. Albeck, in: *Sinai,* 60 (1967), 97–123; M. Elon, *Ha-Mishpat Ha-Ivri* (1973) III, 879ff.

Shalom Albeck

DAMAGES.

Assessment. In Jewish law, once the tortfeasor's liability for the damage has been established and he is ordered to compensate for the loss, the measure of damages requires determination. This is done by assessing the market price of the damaged object prior to and subsequent to sustained damage (see BK 84b on injury suffered by an animal or person); the difference is the amount which the tortfeasor has to pay (BK 11a). In this way, the party who has suffered damage is enabled to purchase on the market an object such as was his before it was damaged, which damage is thereby annulled. If the damaged object is not sold separately on the market but as part of a larger unit only, the difference between the assessed market price of the unit – i.e., undamaged and with the damaged part – is the measure of compensation. Thus, for example, the owner of an animal which has consumed a row of unripe fruit in another's field, does not pay according to the value of the fruit eaten by his animal – as no one buys unripe fruit, which is valueless. Instead – it being customary for merchants to buy a large field of yet unripened fruit – the market price of the fruit in a large field is assessed, with and without the row in question respectively, and the difference is the measure of damages. Another opinion maintains that the measure is the difference between the respective market values of the land itself when sold with and without the row of fruit (see *Yam shel Shelomo* BK 6:18). The sages of the Talmud are divided on the question of the size of the field to be taken as the standard for valuing the damaged row, i.e., whether it should be 60 times the size of the row, or larger (BK 58b, 59b). Similarly, if injury is caused to the embryo of an animal, the measure of damages is the difference between the market values of the animal, pregnant and otherwise respectively, but the embryo itself is not assessed, for it is valueless – nor is it assessed as if it were already born (*Shitah Mekubbeẓet* BK 47a, s.v. *amar rava*).

In terms of this assessment, the tortfeasor does not compensate the injured party for any future loss of profits which result from the injury (Tos. to BK 34a, s.v. *she'ilmale*), nor for the loss of any benefits which could have been derived from the use of the damaged object, except insofar as such may already be accounted for in reducing the market price of the damaged object, at the time the damage was sustained. This rule is consistent with the principle that the tortfeasor is liable only for such damage as he ought to have foreseen at the time of his wrongful conduct, but not for any other or more extensive damage (see Torts). The reason for this is that any loss of profits not reflected in the market price is a loss which is not foreseeable, and one which people accordingly do not make allowance for in the price they are prepared to pay on the market. For this reason too the tortfeasor does not compensate for any damage which the injured party could have avoided after suffering injury, since the former could not have foreseen that the latter would not do so. (Tos. to BK 10b, s.v. *lo;* BK 85b, on the failure to observe medical instructions in a case of personal injury.)

Where a person could not have foreseen that his conduct would cause damage, he is in the position of an *"anus"* (i.e., the consequences are caused by a mischance) and is absolved from liability (see Torts); however if he benefits from the damage caused to another, as in the case where his animal eats vegetables left by another on a public road so that he does not have to feed it, he is liable to the injured party to the extent of the benefit derived (BK 20a:55b).

Assessment of Damages for Personal Injuries. A person who willfully, or by gross negligence *(karov la-mezid),* inflicts bodily harm *(ḥabbalah)* on another, must pay compensation to the latter, not only for the *nezek* ("loss," "damage") but also under four additional headings: *ẓa'ar* ("pain and suffering"), *rippui* ("medical expenses"), *shevet* ("loss of earnings"), and *boshet* ("humiliation"; detailed in ḤM 420). *Nezek* is assessed as in the case of damage to property, i.e., by comparing the injured party to a slave and estimating the respective prices he would fetch if sold as such on the market before and after the injury, the difference being the measure of compensation. This estimate takes account of the difference between the remuneration that could be earned for the heavy work he would have done if healthy and that which he shall earn for the work he can do having a disability (compare Abbaye's words *"shevet gedolah,"* BK 86a; and R. Isaac in TJ, BK 8:3, 6b). *Ẓa'ar* is assessed by estimating what a person, like the injured, would be prepared to pay to avoid the pain resulting from the injury as by way of narcotics or a drug; *rippui* is an estimate of the medical expenses to be incurred by the injured in order to be cured; *shevet* is the estimated loss of remuneration which the injured could have earned during the period of his illness; *boshet* is assessed according to the social position of both parties (BK 8:1). Because of the difficulty in measuring *boshet* in monetary terms, the sages at various times determined fixed measures for various acts of *boshet,* thus, e.g., 200 *zuz* for a slap on the face, 400 *zuz* for pulling a man's hair or spitting on him – the *tannaim* already being in dispute as to whether these measures were for the rich or for the poor (BK 8:6). Where the injured party suffers damage under one or some of the five headings only, the injuring party compensates him accordingly: thus if the injured party suffers *boshet* or *rippui* only, the latter compensates him under these headings alone.

Compensation for damage under the above four headings, excluding *nezek,* is payable only in the case of bodily harm inflicted wilfully, or by gross negligence, caused by the wrongdoer's person (Rashi to BK end of 26a). There is no liability for *boshet* in the absence of an intention to harm or shame (BK 8:1). The interpretation of the commentators is that there is liability for *nezek* even when resulting from mischance *(ones),* and no liability under the other four headings except when resulting from negligent or wilful conduct. But it may also be argued that there is liability for *nezek* in the case of negligence only, while a man is not liable under the other four headings unless the conduct is wilful, or grossly negligent. It would seem that the reason for confining liability under the aforesaid four headings to the case where an injury is wilfully inflicted by one person on the body of another (and not by a person on an animal or by an animal on a person), whereas for *nezek* there is liability in all the above cases, stems from the principle that the tortfeasor's liability for compensation is confined to such damage only as he could have foreseen at the time of causing the injury. Hence, inasmuch as damage under the said four categories of compensation varies from one injured party to another, the tortfeasor cannot be required to have foreseen the measures of each relevant to the particular injured party except when he has wilfully inflicted a bodily injury by his own hand, because in such case, having seen the injured party to whom he was about to cause harm, he should have known the measure of *ẓa'ar, rippui, shevet,* and *boshet* peculiar to this particular injured person. Insofar as the said four categories of damage accompany every case of *ḥabbalah* and thus their scope should therefore be foreseen by the tortfeasor, they are apparently already included in the assessment of the *nezek.* Moreover, even where compensation is payable under all five headings specifically, payment is made to the extent of the foreseeable measure of each only and in no larger measure. Thus if an assessment of compensation for an injury has been made, this amount of damages only is payable, even if the health of the injured party should thereafter deterioate unexpectedly (BK 91a).

Already in the talmudic period – in Babylonia, and certainly in other countries – many judges would not give judgment for damages under one or more of these five categories. Some would not award compensation for *boshet,* or even *nezek;* it was not necessary as a deterrent because damage of this type was not common, and the judges outside Ereẓ Israel, not being ordained by the rabbis of Ereẓ Israel, did not feel themselves qualified to deal with such matters (BK 84b). Also in the post-talmudic period damages were not awarded under one or more of these categories according to law (Sh. Ar., ḤM 1:2), but rather the tortfeasor would be placed under a ban or punished in some other manner until he effected a reconciliation with the injured party and reached agreement with him on an equitable compensation (*Piskei ha-Rosh* BK 8:3).

Payment of damages may be made in money or in chattels having a monetary value and sold on the market; land, to serve as a means of payment, must be "of the best" (BK 7a). The damages are looked upon as a debt due to the injured party, in the same way as a loan or any other debt. However there are traces in the Talmud of a view that payment of damages is a penalty serving to punish the wrongdoer for his conduct and is not merely compensation (Albeck, *Hashlamot ve-Tosafot* to his edition of the Mishnah BK 1:3). Some sages hold the opinion that payment of "half-damages" in the case of *shor tam* (ox that has not gored before –see *Avot Nezikin*[1]) is a fine (BK 15a), and therefore payment of "half-damages" was not sanctioned in Babylonia and in other countries as from the talmudic period (BK 15b)

The law of the State of Israel determines that the damages due to the injured party are the amount required to restore him, subjectively speaking, to the position in which he would have been but for suffering the injury. The measure of damages varies therefore not only according to the damage actually incurred, but also in accordance with the individual circumstances of the injured party.

See also Assaults; Contract; Labor Law.

Bibliography: Gulak, Yesodei, 2 (1922), 14ff., 22f., 31ff., 211ff.; idem, *Le-Ḥeker Toledot ha-Mishpat ha–Ivri bi-Tekufat ha-Talmud,* 1 *(Dinei Karka'ot)* (1929), 28–30, 33n. 2, 34n. 2; idem, *Toledot ha-Mishpat be-Yisrael bi-Tekufat ha-Talmud,* 1 *(Ha-Ḥiyyuv ve-Shi'bbudav)* (1939), 43f., 95n. 35, 109–11, 124, 141f., Herzog, Instit, 1 (1936), 211, 359; ET, 1 (1951^3), 81f.; 2 (1949), 167; 3 (1951), 42–50, 161f.; 7 (1956), 376–82; Z. Karl, in: *Mazkeret Levi . . . Freund* (1953), 29–32, 46–52; S. Albeck, *Pesher Dinei ha-Nezikin ba-Talmud* (1965); Elon, *Ha-Mishpat Ha-Ivri* (1973) II, 258ff, 486ff, III, 885ff.

Shalom Albeck

MARITIME LAW. The Talmud discusses many laws concerning shipping, and sea and river journeys – such as the sale of ships, instances of shipwreck salvage and rescue, rules of passage at sea, lading and charter agreements, and also various details of the laws of the Sabbath and ritual purity applicable to ships. Such laws do not, however, serve to create a distinct branch of maritime law proper, since they are interwoven into the wider principles of the laws of contract and damages (contrary to the view expressed by J. Dauvillier, in: *Revue Internationale des Droits de l'Antiquité,* 6 (1959), 33–63). Although in this field special shipping customs, if any, are followed, this is no more than an application of the general principle of contract law relating to local or trade customs (Rashba, Resp., vol. 2, no. 268).

With regard to the sale of ships, as with other sales, reference is made to accessories which are customarily sold with the ship and others which are considered as being independent and must therefore be purchased separately (BB 5:1). It is also stated that it was the practice of shipowners to receive not only the hire for the ship but also payment for its loss if shipwrecked (BM 70a). On arrangements for sea traffic it is stated: "Where two boats sailing on a river meet; if both attempt to pass simultaneously, they will sink; whereas if one makes way for the other, both can pass [without mishap]. Likewise if two camels meet each other while on the ascent of Beth-Horon [which is a narrow pass; see Josh. 10:10 and 11] . . . if one is laden and the other unladen, the latter should give way to the former; if one is nearer [to its destination] than the other, the former should give way to the latter. If both are equally near or far, make a compromise between them, and the one [to go through] must compensate the other" (Tosef. BK 2:10; Sanh. 32b). If a person hires a ship for carriage of cargo and it sinks in mid-journey, he must pay for half the journey; if, however, he hires a specific ship for shipping a specific cargo, he loses the hire if he has already paid for it but is not obliged to pay if he has not already done so (BM 79b and Tos.) In a case where a man hired boatmen to deliver goods, stipulating that they guarantee against any accident (see *Ones*) occurring on the way, and the river dried up during the journey, it was held that the boatmen had not guaranteed against this possibility since such an accident was not foreseeable (Git. 73a).

Various *halakhot* were decided with regard to shipwrecks.

1. page 325.

Thus when a boat is in danger of sinking and part of the cargo is thrown overboard to lighten the vessel, the resulting loss is not apportioned equally amongst the cargo owners, nor is it calculated according to the value of the goods of each owner, but the loss is apportioned according to the weight of the cargo of each owner – provided that this does not conflict with local maritime customs (BK 116b). In one instance a donkey being transported threatened to sink the boat and was thrown overboard, whereupon it was decided that no compensation was payable to its owner, since the deed was justified on the grounds of self-defense, the donkey being considered as pursuing with intent to kill (BK 117b). An interesting *halakhah* concerning maritime insurance is related: "The sailors can stipulate that whoever loses a ship shall get another one, but if the boat was lost due to his own negligence or if he sailed to a place to which boats would not normally sail, he would not be provided with another boat." The same rule applies also to carriers on land (Tosef. BM 11:26; BK 116b).

In the post-talmudic period many responsa dealt with trade custom (see e.g., Rashba, Resp., vol. 2, no. 268), some of them marine customs. Solomon b. Abraham Adret (RaSHBa), who lived in Barcelona where the well-known collection of marine customs *Consulat de Mar* was compiled, records the custom of depositing goods with a merchant traveling by sea for the latter to trade therein at the risk of the depositor – leaving the sailor exempt from liability for accident (his resp. vol. 2, no. 325; vol. 1, no. 930 and cf. no. 924). Also mentioned is the custom of paying the full wages, even if the journey for which the employee was hired was not completed due to accident overtaking the employer (Rashba, Resp., vol. 6, no. 224).

In the State of Israel maritime law is based on Israel legislation, conforming with the law of the maritime nations in those matters and also with Ottoman-French laws and English law.

Bibliography: Krauss, Tal Arch, 2 (1911), 338–49; Herzog, Instit, 2 (1939), 252–4, 268–70; B. Eliash in: *Iyyunei Mishpat* 1 (1971) 359–367; Passameneck and Brown in: ILR 8 (1973) 538–549; M. Elon, *Ha-Mishpat Ha-Ivri* (1973), II, p. 452, 560, 752.

Shalom Albeck

UNJUST ENRICHMENT. The Concept. The law of obligations deals with obligations arising from both contract and tort, i.e., those undertaken by the party or parties concerned of their own free will and those imposed by law on a person – against his will – in consequence of damage resulting from an act or omission on his part. There is a further group of cases which fall under a branch of the law known as unjust enrichment and relate to a person's liability which arises neither from his undertaking nor delictual act, but from the fact that he has derived a benefit to which he is not entitled, at the expense of another.

A general exemplification of this class of obligations in Jewish law is the discussion in the Mishnah of the matter of a person who hires from his neighbor a cow, which dies of natural causes after the hirer has lent it to a third party (BM 3:2). One opinion is that the hirer is not liable to the owner for the value of the cow – since the death of the cow is attributable to *ones* and the hirer has no liability for loss resulting therefrom – but the borrower must compensate the hirer (i.e., the person from whom he received the animal) – since the borrower is liable for loss resulting from *ones* (see Bailment). However, R. Yose differs, questioning the hirer's right to "traffic with his neighbor's cow," i.e., it is inconceivable that the hirer shall enrich himself at the expense of the owner of the cow, who is the real loser, without any color of right thereto, and the hirer must therefore restore to the owner the value of the cow received from the borrower. R. Yose's opinion was accepted as *halakhah* (BM 36b; Yad, Sekhirut 1:6; Sh. Ar., HM 307:5). The same principle is enunciated by R. Johanan: "it is forbidden for a person to benefit [without authority] from another's property" (BM 117b), and the *halakhah* was decided as follows: "similarly, whenever a person performs an act or benefit in favor of another, the latter may not say, 'you have acted for me gratis since I did not authorize you' but he must give such person his reward" (Rema, HM 264:4; see also Ran on Rif, Ket. 107b). The problems of unjust enrichment are treated in Jewish law under the following five headings: 1) rescue of another's life; 2) rescue of another's property; 3) payment of another's debt; 4) improvement of another's property; 5) deriving benefit from another's property.

Rescue of Another's Life. The duty to rescue the life of another when endangered is enjoined in the Pentateuch: "Thou shalt not stand idly by the blood of thy neighbor" (Lev. 19:16). This duty includes the obligation to hire other persons against payment in order to rescue the person in danger (Sanh. 73a), who must refund to his rescuer all the expenses thus incurred by the latter: "For it is not a person's duty to save the life of his fellow with his own money when the person saved has money" (*Piskei ha-Rosh* 8:2; Sanh. 73a; Sh. Ar., HM 426:1, *Sma* and *Siftei Kohen* ad loc.). It was likewise decided that the heirs of the deceased must refund the expenses incurred by a third person in connection with the medical treatment of the deceased, even if not expended at the latter's request, since a person who of his own accord seeks a cure for the sick must not lose inasmuch as it is a matter of *pikku'aḥ nefesh* ("saving life") and whoever hurries to do so is praised (Resp. Rosh no. 85:2). This too is the law as regards the rescue and ransom of a Jewish prisoner in the hands of a gentile, and the latter – if he has the means thereto – must refund the ransom money to his rescuer (Rema, YD 252:12), since it is inconceivable that such a person "shall enrich his children while being a burden on the community" (Resp. Maharam of Rothenburg, ed. Cremona, no. 32; *Mordekhai* BK sec. 59).

Rescue of Another's Property. Under this heading are included cases in which a person knowingly, and without being requested to do so, acts to the benefit of another in a manner whereby the rescuer does not add to the other anything he did not have before but prevents the latter from suffering pecuniary loss. The basic laws concerning the duty to rescue another's property are expressed in two pentateuchal enjoinders, relating respectively to the duty of restoring lost property (Ex. 23:4; Deut. 22:1–3) and that of releasing an animal lying under its burden (Ex. 23:5; Deut. 22:4). In both cases the duty carries no return consideration (as regards restoring lost property, see Sh. Ar., HM 265:1; as regards releasing an animal, see BM 32a; Yad, Roẓe'aḥ 13:7; Sh. Ar., HM 272:6). However, the duty to provide aid gratuitously exists only as long as the rescue activities cause no loss to the rescuing party, but when he is likely to suffer loss therefrom he will not be obliged to act gratuitously (BM 2:9; Yad, Gezelah 12:4; Sh. Ar., HM 265:1; Tur. HM 272:2). The result is that even in cases where the very act of beneficence toward another is imposed as a duty of the Torah, the beneficiary will be obliged, whenever the benefactor has suffered pecuniary loss, to compensate the latter on account of the benefit derived by himself. It was similarly laid down (BM 93b) that a paid herdsman must take precautions against possible circumstances of *ones,* for instance by hiring others to guard against beasts of prey, and that the owner of the herd must pay the herdsman for such expenses. This too is the law as regards any person, who hires people to protect another's herd from the threat of harm, and even though he has acted without being requested to do so by the owner of the herd, he is entitled to receive from the latter his expenses and remuneration (Tos. BK 58a).

As regards the duty to compensate the rescuer for a loss he has suffered, a distinction is drawn as illustrated in the following two examples. The Mishnah mentions the case where one person has a jar of wine and another a jar of honey; because of a crack in the honey jar, the owner of the other jar spills his wine and rescues the honey by pouring it into his own jar (the honey being the more expensive) and the Mishnah holds the latter is entitled "to his remuneration *[sekharo]* alone" (BK 10:4, and the further example there cited). According to this Mishnah the beneficiary has to remunerate the rescuer for his efforts alone and is not obliged to refund the latter the cost of his wine. On the other hand, in the Talmud in like circumstances it is stated in the name of R. Ishmael, the son of R. Johanan b. Beroka, that the person pouring out the wine "receives his wine out of the honey of his fellow" (BK 81b; 114b), i.e., that the owner of the wine is entitled to payment of the value of the wine spilled in order to rescue his fellow's honey. The contradiction between the two cases was reconciled on the basis that in the former case the owner of the rescued property was present at the place and time of the rescue but the rescuer, not having sought express consent for his action, is not entitled to a full refund of his expenses or the value of his wine, but only to his remuneration; in the latter case, however, the owner of the rescued property was not present as aforementioned and therefore the rescuer is entitled to a full refund of his expenses (for an explanation of this distinction, see Tos. BM 31b; *Piskei ha-Rosh* BM no. 28; *Mordekhai* BK no. 57).

In contrast to the above cases, the Talmud quotes the case of rescue of another's property (*mavri'aḥ ari* – one who chases away a lion from another's property) without the knowledge of the beneficiary, in which the latter is exempt from making any payment whatever to the rescuer (Ned. 33a; BK 58a; BB 53a). The Talmud mentions two elements which characterize the category of *mavri'aḥ ari* cases in which the rescuer is not entitled to remuneration. First, that the rescuer acted as he did of his own initiative; secondly, that he suffered no loss whatever as a result of such action. Some of the *rishonim* were of the opinion that this category of *mavri'aḥ ari* includes only those cases in which both the above elements operate and that the absence of one of them renders the beneficiary liable to payment for the benefit derived by himself (Tos. Ket. 107b; *Mordekhai* BK no. 57). Others held that this category includes also cases in which only one of the two elements is present and that there is no need for both to operate together (Tos. BK 58a; Rosh, loc. cit.). The *rishonim* added a further requisite for the beneficiary's exemption from payment in *mavri'aḥ ari* cases, namely, that the loss which the rescuer sought to avoid was of doubtful contingency. That is, when it may reasonably be accepted that even without the rescuer's intervention no loss would have occurred, as for instance in the case where the lion was far from the beneficiary's herd. Hence the rescuer will be entitled to payment of his remuneration if the beneficiary, but for the intervention of the former, was certain to have suffered loss (Tos. BK 58a; Rosh and *Mordekhai,* loc. cit.). Yet another material requirement (for the beneficiary's exemption from liability) is that the rescuer's action was not calculated to enrich the beneficiary in any way but merely to have prevented him loss (Tos. Ket. 107b; Tos. BK 58a).

Payment of Another's Debt. This question is discussed in the Mishnah (Ket. 13:2) in relation to the obligation of maintenance, in the case of a person who supports a wife whose husband has gone abroad – without being requested to do so by either the wife or her husband. Some of the *tannaim* hold the benefactor to have "put his money on the horn of a deer" and to have no claim, neither against the wife nor her husband, since he acted as he did of his own accord. Other *tannaim* take the view that the benefactor may deliver an oath as to the exact amount expended on the wife and recover this amount from her husband. The *halakhah* was decided according to the former opinion (Yad, Ishut 12:19; Sh. Ar., EH 70:8).

As regards debts arising from other causes, there is a difference of opinion among the scholars. In the Jerusalem Talmud (Ket. 13:2; 35d) two opinions are quoted. One is that the dispute concerning a debt for maintenance extends also to the case of any other regular debt paid on behalf of another and without the latter's knowledge; the other opinion is that the dispute relates solely to payment of a debt owed by the husband for the maintenance of his wife, but with regard to a regular debt paid on behalf of the debtor, the opinion of all is that it may not be reclaimed from the debtor since it cannot be said that the latter received an absolute benefit because of the possibility that his creditor may have granted a waiver of the debt, and therefore the person who has paid it is in the position of a *mavri'aḥ ari* (see above). From the Babylonian Talmud (Ned. 33a–b; Ket. 108a) it may be concluded, according to most of the commentators, that the dispute relating to a maintenance debt extends also to regular debts. Some of the commentators (R. Hananel and R. Tam) interpreted the statements in the Babylonian Talmud to mean that a debt not arising from maintenance and paid by another may, in the opinion of all, be reclaimed from the debtor because of the certainty of the benefit caused the latter (Tos. Ket. 108a). The majority opinion of the *posekim* is that a person who has paid another's debt of any kind whatever may not recover payment from the debtor (Yad, Malveh 26:6; Sh. Ar., HM 128:1; some scholars also explain the debtor's exemption on the grounds that it is a matter of *gerama* – Tos. Ket. 108a).

Improvement of Another's Property. This category includes cases in which a person knowingly, and without being requested thereto, acts so as to confer an actual benefit on another by affording him a gain or increment which he did not previously have. The classic example is the case of a person who "goes down" to another's property to plant it or erect a building thereon, without any request from the owner to do the work or undertaking on his part to pay for it (analagous to the Roman law *negotiorum gestio*). Thus, for instance, if a hired worker should work in the field of a third party, whether in error or because he was directed thereto by his employer, the owner of the field will have to pay for the benefit derived, even though he did not request the work, for otherwise he will be in the position of having been enriched without right at another's expense (Tosef. BM 7:7; BM 76a).

In the case where a person plants another's land without permission, Rav's opinion is that "an assessment is made and he is at a disadvantage," whereas Samuel holds, "an estimate is made of what a person would pay to plant such a field." In the Talmud it is stated that there is no dispute between Rav and Samuel but that Rav refers to a field which is unsuitable for that which has been planted thereon, while Samuel refers to a field which is suitable for such planting (BM 101a). The scholars disputed the meaning of the expression "an assessment is made and he is at a disadvantage." R. Hai Gaon (*Sefer ha-Mikkaḥ ve-ha-Mimkar,* 7:33) and R. Zerahiah ha-Levi (*Ha-Ma'or ha-Gadol* to Rif BM 101a) held it to mean that the planter is only entitled to payment on the basis of the lowest price at which cheap workers can be hired to execute the same work; according to Rashi (BM 101a), Rosh (ad loc.), and others, the expression means that if the planter's expenses exceed the gain derived by the owner of the field then the former is only entitled to the value of such gain, but if the other way round then the planter is only entitled to the sum of his expenses. The *halakhah* was decided that a person who plants another's field without permission is at a disadvantage when the field is unsuitable for such planting, but if it is so suitable an estimate is made of how much one would be prepared to pay for planting that field (Yad, Gezelah 10:4).

Another example is the case where a person whose property surrounds the property of another on all sides fences the interior borders of his property, thereby enclosing at the same time also the surrounded property – without the authority of its owner. In the Mishnah (BB 1:3) there is a difference of opinion as regards the measure of liability of the owner of the surrounded property to pay toward the cost of the fence by which he too is served, and in the Talmud these divided opinions are interpreted in various ways (BB 4b and Codes; Rashi BK 20b; *Ha-Ma'or ha-Gadol* (see above) to Rif BB 4b; cf. Tos. BK 20b; Maim., Comm. to BB 1; *Yad Ramah* BB 4b; Ramban, Nov. BB 4b; *Milḥamot ha-Shem* thereto, etc.). All opinions agree that the owner of the surrounded property has liability for payment toward the costs of the fence from which he benefits, even though he has neither requested its erection nor undertaken to bear the costs thereof; the dispute – even among the *posekim* – centers around the varying measure of his liability, according to the factual circumstances. Liability for payment derives from the consideration that the "enclosing owner" (the *makkif*) is caused special expenses by the surrounded property since it causes a lengthening of the boundaries of the surrounding property and because the owner of the surrounded property benefits without right on account of the special expenses caused to the other (see BK 20b; for a further example, see BK 9:4; BK 101a; Yad, Sekhirut 10:4; Sh. Ar., HM 306:3, 6).

The *posekim* did not fail to observe that the consequence of the above law was to submit everyone to the constant danger of being placed in the position where he might be caused a benefit from and become obligated to pay for expenses incurred by his fellow in which he is not at all interested. Hence it was decided that such a beneficiary was to be exempted from liability if he had declared in advance that he had no interest in the proposed benefit and was not prepared to make any payment whatever in connection therewith (*Maggid Mishneh* Shekhenim 3:3; *Beit Yosef* HM 155:13).

Deriving Benefit from Another's Property. This category includes the cases in which a person benefits without authority from another's property, the benefit taking the form of a saving of expenses or the prevention of harm. The classical case discussed in the Talmud is the matter of a person who lives in another's property without the latter's knowledge or consent (BK 20a). Four possibilities are discussed: a) If the premises are anyhow not available for letting and, in addition thereto, it is clear that even without such premises the occupier, for whatever reason, would not have hired some other residence for himself, then the latter is absolved from payment; the explanation for this is that he has neither caused a loss to the owner of the premises nor enjoyed any benefit himself since a benefit is expressed in some measure of monetary gain – nonexistent in this case. b) If the premises are for hire and the occupier, but for his occupation thereof, would have hired some other residence, he will be liable for payment since he has derived a benefit at the cost of the owner's loss. c) If the premises are not for hire and the occupier, but for his occupation thereof, would have hired some other residence, he will be absolved from payment since the benefit he has derived is not at another's expense, the owner having lost nothing; however, if enjoyment of the benefit should involve any measure of loss to the owner, the benefit will be at another's expense and the occupier liable for the full value of his benefit (BK 20a–b; Yad, Gezelah 3:9; Sh. Ar., HM 363: 6–7). d) Opinions are divided as regards the case where the premises are for hire but the occupier, even without his occupation thereof, would not hire other premises. Some of the *rishonim* held that the occupier, because he derives no benefit, need make no payment at all on account of enrichment at another's expense and that the loss suffered by the owner is in the nature of *gerama* only, for which there is exemption (Tos. BK 20a, R. Perez, quoted in *Mordekhai* BK 16). The majority of the other *posekim* took the view that there is room for holding the occupier liable on account of causing a loss to the owner (Rif, *Halakhot* BK 21a; Yad, Gezelah 3:9; Sh. Ar., HM 363:6); that even if it be true that the occupier enjoys no benefit – since he might find some other residence free of charge – he is nevertheless the one who eats up that which is the loss of his fellow (*Piskei ha-Rosh*, BK 2:6).

A person who benefits unawares must pay for the benefit. The laws of tort prescribe that the owner of an animal is absolved from paying for the produce of another which the animal has eaten up while grazing in a public domain; however, "if you have benefited, you must pay for the benefit" (BK 2:2), i.e., if the owner should derive benefit from the fact that his animal has fed in the aforementioned manner (by saving himself the cost of the animal's feed for that day), he will be liable to the owner of the devoured produce for the value of the benefit, lest he enjoy an undue gain at another's expense (BK 20a and Codes, *Nimmukei Yosef* thereto, TJ, BK 2:4, 3a; see also the difference of opinion there quoted concerning the manner of assessing the value of the benefit; for a further illustration of this class of case, see BK 6:2).

Bibliography: Gulak, Yesodei, 2 (1922), 176f., 199f.; A. Karlin, in: *Ha-Mishpat*, 1 (1927), 214–21; Herzog, Instit, 2 (1939), 49–59; A. Goldberg, in: *Ha-Peraklit*, 8 (1951/52), 314–25; ET, 12 (1967), 1–16; S. Warhaftig, *Dinei Avodah ha-Mishpat ha-Ivri* (1969), 212–28, 279–86, 802ff.

Yechezkel Rottenberg

HASSAGAT GEVUL. (Heb. הסגת גבול), a concept which originally had specific reference to the unlawful taking of another's land; later it was extended to embrace encroachment on various economic, commercial, and incorporeal rights of others.

Encroachment on Land. In Scripture. The original meaning of the term *hassagat gevul* was the moving (cf. *nasogu aḥor*, Isa. 42:17) of boundary stones or other landmarks from their resting places into the bounds of another's adjoining area of land, for the purpose of annexing a portion of the latter to one's own land. Naḥmanides' comment on the passage, "Thou shalt not remove thy neighbor's landmark, which they of old time have set, in thine inheritance which thou shalt inherit in the land that the Lord thy God giveth thee to possess it" (Deut. 19:14), is that Scripture speaks here "in terms of the present," i.e., of the usual situation, since it is common for landmark removal to take place in respect of ancient landmarks set up "of old time" which are not generally known and familiar. The prohibition against removal of the landmark is repeated in the enumeration of curses for recital on Mount Ebal (Deut. 27:17). The exact marking of land boundaries was already emphasized in patriarchal times as may be gathered from the description of the field in Machpelah bought by Abraham from Ephron the Hittite (Gen. 23:17), and this was also the case in other countries of the ancient East.

Many boundary stones, engraved with invocations and curses against their removal, have been found in ancient Babylonia.

Removal of the landmark is exhorted against and castigated in the books of the prophets and the hagiographa (Hos. 5:10; Prov. 22:28, 23:10). In Proverbs too the reference is to the "present" and usual situation, namely removal of ancient landmarks set by earlier generations. In the Book of Hosea the castigation is directed against the princes, the strong, and in Proverbs it is hinted that the weak, the fatherless, were the main sufferers. In Job too removal of the landmark is mentioned among other injustices perpetrated on orphans, widows, and the poor (24:2–4).

In the Talmud. In the talmudic period the abovementioned passage from Deuteronomy 19:14 was given a literal interpretation and the special prohibition against landmark removal was held to be applicable to land in Ereẓ Israel only. The fact that the enjoinder, "Thou shalt not remove the landmark," appears after it is already stated that "Thou shalt not rob," was held to teach that anyone who uproots his neighbor's boundaries breaks two prohibitions, robbery and removal of the landmark, but that this was the case in Ereẓ Israel only, since it is written "... in thine inheritance which thou shalt inherit in the land ..." *(ibid.)*, and outside Ereẓ Israel only one prohibition (robbery) is transgressed (Sif. Deut. 188). The *halakhah* was likewise determined in later time (Maim. Yad, Genevah 7:11; Sh. Ar., HM 376:1).

Land robbery, even outside Ereẓ Israel, has been regarded with great severity in Jewish law. The Talmud speaks of persons specially engaged in land measuring and the fixing of precise boundaries; surveyors are specifically instructed to make accurate calculations – down to the last fingerbreadth – and not to measure for one in summer and for the other in winter, since the measuring cord shrinks in summer (and expands in winter; BM 107b and Rashi *ibid.;* 61b; BB 89a; Maim. Yad, Genevah 8:1–3; Sh. Ar., HM 231:16–18).

In the Codes. It is explained that the general distinction made in Jewish law between *genevah* and *gezelah* (see Theft and Robbery) – the former taking unlawfully by stealth and the latter openly with violence – applies also to the matter of trespass on land: "a person who removes his neighbor's landmark and encloses within his own domain even as much as a fingerbreadth from his neighbor's domain is a robber if he does so with violence and a thief if he does so stealthily" (Yad, Genevah 7:11; Sh. Ar., HM 376; from the *Semag, Lavin,* 153 it also appears that this was understood to be the version of Sif. Deut. 188). The opinion was expressed by some of the *posekim* that the prohibition against robbery or theft – in relation to trespass on land – forms part of the *de-rabbanan* and not the *de-oraita* law, since land is never stolen but always remains in its owner's possession; this opinion is however contrary to the plain meaning of the above-mentioned statements in *Sifrei* (Tur, HM 371: 10, 376; *Perishah, ibid., Sma.* to HM 371:2).

The great severity with which trespass on land has been regarded in Jewish law is illustrated in a responsum of Solomon b. Abraham Adret (Rashba) concerning the following matter: "A person trespassed and built a wall within his neighbor's yard, thereby appropriating therefrom a cubit of land to his own, and then built a big house supported on this wall; now the owner of the yard comes to demolish the other's whole building." Asked whether in terms of the *takkanat ha-shavim* ("*takkanah* of restitution," see Theft and Robbery) the trespasser might pay for the value of the land taken without having to demolish the building in order to restore the land to its owner, Rashba replied in the negative: "the *takkanat ha-shavim* was instituted in respect of movable property only, and in respect of land it was not stated that he [the injured party] should sell his property and break up his inheritance" (Resp. vol. 3, no. 188).

Widening of the Concept. The first manifestations of a widening in the doctrine of *hassagat gevul* are traceable back to talmudic times, when various halakhot were derived from the doctrine by way of *asmakhta.* Thus the doctrine was cited in support of the prohibition against withholding from the poor (all or anyone of them) their gleanings from the produce of the field (Pe'ah 5:6; on the meaning of the term *olim* and *al tasseg gevul olim,* see Albeck, *Mishnah, ibid.*). The prohibition against *hassagat gevul* was similarly invoked to lend a quasi-legal recognition to an individual's right (copyright) in respect of his own spiritual or intellectual creations: "Whence can it be said of one who interchanges the statements of Eliezer with those of Joshua and vice versa, so as to say of pure that it is unclean and of unclean that it is pure, that he transgresses a prohibition? It is taught: 'you shall not remove your neighbor's landmark' " (Sif. Deut. 188). Even the prohibition against marrying a pregnant woman or one weaning a child (i.e., by another man, for reasons of the possible threat to the welfare of the embryo or child), is supported by the doctrine of *hassagat gevul* (Tosef. Nid. 2:7; see also Mid. Tan., Deut. 19:14; Comm. R. Hillel, Sif. Deut. 188).

Trespass on Economic, Commercial, and Incorporeal Rights. Post-talmudic economic and social developments fostered the need to give legal recognition and protection to rights which had not become crystallized within any accepted legal framework during the talmudic period. Some of these rights found legal expression and protection through an extension of the prohibition against landmark removal, so as to embrace also encroachment on another's economic, commercial, and spiritual confines.

Tenancy Rights. Jewish places of settlement in the Middle Ages were restricted – at times voluntarily, at other times perforce – to particular streets or quarters. Hence the demand by Jews for dwellings in these particular places frequently exceeded the available supply, and sometimes a prospective Jewish tenant would offer a landlord a higher than customary rental in order to have the existing tenant evicted, the more so since the *halakhah* excluded neither an offer to pay a high rental nor eviction of a tenant upon termination of his lease. In order to fill the breach against this undesirable social phenomenon, various *takkanot* were enacted in the different centers of Jewish life. These *takkanot,* aimed at protecting tenants from eviction, were reconciled with the principles of Jewish law through a widening of the doctrine of *hassagat gevul* to take in also the tenant's right to remain in occupation of the premises hired by him. The earliest of these *takkanot,* akin in content to the tenant's protection laws found in many modern legal systems, are attributed to the time of Gershom b. Judah (tenth century; for the text, see Finkelstein, Middle Ages, 181).

In a 13th-century *takkanah* of the community of Crete (Candia) it was laid down that: "a person shall not encroach on his neighbor's boundaries by evicting him from his home ... from today onward no Jew shall be permitted ... to offer an excessive payment or rental to any landlord in order to gain occupation of his house ... and thereby cause him to evict the existing Jewish tenant, for this is a transgression against 'cursed be he that removes his neighbor's landmark' "; not only was the offender to be fined, but the *takkanah* also prohibited anyone to hire the house in question for a full year from the date of its being vacated (*Takkanot Kandyah,* ed. Mekiẓe Nirdamim, p. 16). Similar *takkanot* were customary in different Jewish centers during the Middle Ages which developed in different ways (see Elon, *Ha-Mishpat Ha-Ivri*; II, p. 374-377, 655–658).

Trespass in Matters of Commerce and the Crafts. In tannaitic times the opinions of most sages inclined in favor of free commercial and occupational competition (BM 4:12, 60a–b; BB 21b). In the third century c.e. moral censure of someone setting up in competition with a fellow-artisan was expressed by some of the Palestinian *amoraim,* although without any legal sanction (Kid. 59a; Mak. 24a; Sanh. 81a). In the same century, in Babylonia, Huna laid down the legal principle that a resident of a particular alley operating a handmill could stop a fellow-resident from setting up in competition next to him, because this involved an interference with his source of livelihood (BB 21b). This view was not, however, accepted as *halakhah,* and at the end of the fourth century it was decided by Huna b. Joshua that one craftsman could not restrain a fellow craftsman and resident of the same alley from setting up business (in the same alley), nor even the resident of another town from setting up in the same town, as long as the latter paid taxes to the town in which he sought to ply his craft (BB 21b). Even so, however, there was no definition of the legal nature and substance of even this limited right of restraint, nor was it enforced by any sanctions upon infringement, such as the payment of compensation.

With the restriction of Jewish sources of livelihood in the Middle Ages, and the resulting intensified competition, the whole question once more came to the fore. A Jew who with much effort and money had succeeded in acquiring a monopoly in a particular commercial field stood to lose his investment and livelihood through the competition of a fellow-Jew. From the tenth century onward, the question of a right of monopoly, its scope and sanctions, came to be widely discussed in the literature of the responsa and the Codes. This discussion took in the *ma'arufyah* (a form of private monopoly) *takkanah,* which prohibited encroachment on the *ma'arufyah* of a fellow-Jew (*Or Zaru'a,* BM 10a, no. 28). Legally, the *ma'arufyah* right was a full-fledged right, capable of being sold (Resp. *Ge'onim Kadmoniyyim* 151) and was even discussed in relation to whether it passed on inheritance (Resp. *Ḥakhmei Ẓarefat va-Loter* 87). The law of the *ma'arufyah* was not free of dispute, and as late as the 16th century Solomon Luria differed thereon in a number of material respects (Resp. Maharshal, 35, 36; *Yam shel Shelomo,* Kid. 3:2); yet he too recognized extension of the doctrine of *hassagat gevul* to include a prohibition against infringement of another's livelihood, and the majority of the *posekim* accepted the overall law of the *ma'arufyah* (Sh. Ar., HM 156:5 and standard commentaries; *Ir Shushan,* HM 156:5; *She'erit Yosef* 17).

Various *takkanot* have come down concerning the restriction of competition, particularly with reference to the acquisition of a right of lease or concession. In medieval times, particularly in Poland, a substantial proportion of the tax-collection concessions granted in respect of the wine trade, mints, border-customs, salt-mines, distilleries and saloons, etc., were concentrated in the hands of Jews, and various *takkanot* were enacted to restrict the competition in this field that had led to higher rentals and reduced profits (Halpern, Pinkas, 11f.; *Pinkas Medinat Lita,* nos. 46, 73, 87, 104; Resp. Baḥ., Yeshanot 60; *Masot Binyamin* 27; Resp. Maharam of Lublin 62; *Takkanot Medinat Mehrin,* p. 86, no. 259; *Ḥavvat Ya'ir,* 42).

Setting up in competition with a fellow-artisan or professional was similarly restricted in various fields. Thus a *melammed* ("teacher") was prohibited from encroaching on a colleague's confines by taking one of the latter's pupils into his own *ḥeder* (Takk. Cracow of 1551 and 1638, quoted by P.H. Wettstein, in: *Oẓar ha-Sifrut,* 4 (1892), 580 (2nd pagination) and it was likewise decided with reference to ritual slaughterers (*Ba'ei Ḥayyei,* HM pt. 2, 80; *Naḥalah li-Yhoshu'a,* 29; *Mishpat Ẓedek,* vol. 3, no. 14), the offender in this case being regarded as a robber who could be deprived of the remuneration received for such *sheḥitah* (Resp. *Divrei Ḥayyim,* pt. 2, YD 20) which might possibly even be declared ritually unfit (Resp. Shneur Zalman of Lyady, 9; see also Meshullam Roth, *Kol Mavasser,* pt. 1, no. 17).

An interesting development in this field is related to the office of rabbi. As late as the 15th century, it was decided by Israel Isserlein and Jacob Weil that a scholar holding the office of rabbi in a particular town could not restrain another from holding a similar office there, even though the latter would interfere with the former's prospects of earning remuneration in return for services such as arranging weddings, divorces, and the like. This decision was based on the reasoning that accepting a remuneration for such services was essentially contrary to the *halakhah* and its permissibility was not easily justifiable, and therefore it could hardly be recognized as an occupation or source of livelihood to be protected from the encroachment of competitors (*Terumat ha-Deshen, Pesakim u-Khetavim* 128; Resp. Maharyu, 151; Rema, YD 245:22). This *halakhah,* however, underwent a change in the light of new economic and social realities. Already in the mid-17th century it was stated that even if competition of this kind was not prohibited in law, "perhaps there is reason for protesting against it on the grounds of custom" (*Siftei Kohen* to Sh. Ar., YD 245:22, n.15); and at the commencement of the 19th century the change was also given legal recognition when Moses Sofer explained that the rule which held the law of *hassagat gevul* to be inappropriate to the rabbinate was only applicable "to that particular period when a rabbi was not engaged in the same way as a worker . . . but every scholar led the community in whose midst he lived and as such remuneration for *gittin* and *kiddushin* came to him naturally . . . but nowadays a rabbi is engaged – sometimes from another town – for remuneration, in the same way as any other worker and the community is obliged to provide him with his livelihood; we are not deterred from the acceptance of such reward, and therefore any one encroaching on the rabbi's confines is in the position of a craftsman setting up in competition with his neighbor, (Resp. *Ḥatam Sofer,* HM 21)". "A rabbi who does so is disqualified from acting as a judge" (Resp. *Shem Aryeh,* OH 7).

The legal basis for the restriction of competition, with imposition of sanctions, was found in an extension of the legal doctrine of *hassagat gevul* to include encroachment on the confines of another's trade and source of livelihood. An interesting insight into the manner in which the said extension was arrived at is offered in the method of interpretation adopted by Solomon Luria (despite his advocacy of greater freedom of competition). In the case of a person ousted by his neighbor from a concession to a customs post, Luria reasoned that the defendant might be held liable for the pecuniary loss suffered by the other party even though it was decided law that there is no liability for *gerama* (a form of indirect damage) in tort. Luria relied on Roke'aḥ's statement that anyone interfering with another's source of livelihood falls within the enjoinder, "cursed is he who removes his neighbor's landmark," a statement Luria explained on the basis that this passage seemed to be redundant in the light of the prior scriptural injunction, "you shall not remove your neighbor's landmark," unless it was accepted that this passage related to trespass in the field of bargaining. Luria's decision accordingly was that the customs post be restored to the first concessionary without cost, or the defendant compensate him for the damage caused (Resp. Maharshal 89). Other scholars regarded trespass on a neighbor's trading interests as an integral part of the prohibition against trespass on another's right of tenancy (see Resp. Maharam of Padua 41).

Copyright. The first hints at recognition in Jewish law of the ownership of incorporeal property were given as early as tannaitic times. Thus it was stated, "a person who eavesdrops on his neighbor to reproduce his teachings, even though he is called a thief, acquires for himself" (Tosef., BK 7:13), and support for the prohibition against interchanging one scholar's statements with another's was found (Sif. Deut. 188) in the passage, "Thou shalt not remove thy neighbor's landmark." At the end of the 12th century the same passage was quoted by Judah he-Ḥasid in warning an heir against complying with a direction in the will of his deceased father to inscribe the latter's name as the author of a book, even though it was known to have been written by someone else (*Sefer ha-Ḥasidim*, ed. Mekiẓe Nirdamim, no. 1732, ed. R. Margaliot, no. 586). It was nevertheless only from the 16th century onward that copyright became a defined legal right, protected by sanctions and partially based on the extended doctrine of *hassagat gevul.*

As in other legal systems, this development arose from the spread of printing and a need for the protection of printers' rights. As early as 1518 as approbation *(haskamah)* to the *Sefer ha-Baḥur* of Elijah Levita contained a warning, on pain of ban, against anyone reprinting the book within the following ten years. In the mid-15th century, when Meir Katzenellenbogen complained to Moses Isserles about the appearance of a rival edition of Maimonides' *Mishneh Torah* (shortly after his work had been printed by Katzenellenbogen), Isserles responded by imposing a ban on anyone purchasing the *Mishneh Torah* from Katzenellenbogen's competitor (Resp. Rema 10). Thereafter it became customary to preface books with approbations containing a warning against trespass in the form of any unauthorized reprint of the particular book within a specified period. Halakhic literature contains detailed discussions on various aspects of encroachment on printers' rights. Thus Isserles imposed his abovementioned ban on anyone purchasing the *Mishneh Torah,* because in that instance it would not have availed against the printer, a non-Jew. Other scholars held the opinion that the ban should be imposed, not on the purchasers of the book – as this would cause study of the Torah to be neglected – but on the printer instead, except if he be a non-Jew (*Zikhron Yosef,* HM 2; Resp. *Hatam Sofer,* HM 79). Unlike Isserles, who confined the operation of his ban (to purchasers) within the country concerned only, other scholars extended operation of the ban to printers everywhere (Resp. *Ḥatam Sofer,* HM 41 and 79). In most cases the period of the prohibition varied from three to 15 years, but was sometimes imposed for as long as 25 years. Some of the scholars held that a prohibition imposed against trespass on a printing right takes effect from the date of the approbation in which it has been formulated, but other scholars held the prohibition to come into effect upon commencement of the printing (Halpern, Pinkas 486; Resp. *Shem Aryeh,* HM, 20; *Mayim Ḥayyim,* YD 44; Resp. *Sho'el u-Meshiv,* pt. 1, no. 44).

The above prohibition was mainly justified on grounds of the printer's need for an opportunity to recover his heavy outlay through the subsequent sale of the printed product, since reluctance to undertake any printing in the absence of such protection was likely to send up the price of books and cause study of the Torah to be neglected by the public. In this regard there was a fundamental difference of opinion among scholars concerning the fate of the prohibition once the printer had sold the whole of his edition, i.e., prior to expiry of the period of his protection. According to some scholars the prohibition remained fully effective against all other printers, but others held that continuation of the printer's protection, after he had already obtained his remuneration, was itself likely to cause the price of books to rise and to contribute to the neglect of study (*Ḥatam Sofer,* HM 79; *ibid.* Addenda no. 57; *Parashat Mordekhai,* HM 7; *Tiferet Ẓevi,* YD 62; *Mayim Ḥayyim,* YD 44; *Pitḥei Teshuvah,* YD 236:1; *Ateret Ḥakhamim,* YD 25). This was the central halakhic issue in the dispute, at the beginning of the 19th century, between the respective printers of the Slavuta edition of the Talmud (the brothers Shapiro) and the Vilna-Grodno edition (the widow and brothers Romm).

Out of this discussion grew the recognition given, in later generations, of the existence in Jewish law of a full legal right in respect of one's own spiritual creation. Thus Joseph Saul Nathanson, rabbi of Lvov, distinguished between printing the work of others, e.g., the Talmud, and printing one's own work, stating that in the latter event "it is clear that he has the right thereto for all time . . . for with regard to his own [work] a person is entitled to decree that it shall never be printed without his permission or authority . . . and this right avails him against the world at large" (*Sho'el u-Meshiv,* pt. 1, no. 44). In support of this opinion, Nathanson had reference to the copyright offered the patent-holder of an invention under general Polish law, adding that the effect of an author's restriction against any reprint of his work within a specified period was not to prohibit what would otherwise be permissible, but, on the contrary, to authorize others to reprint his work upon expiry of the period specified because "even if no express restriction is imposed . . . this remains prohibited as *hassagat gevul* by the law of the Torah" *(ibid.).* A similar view was expressed by Naphtali Ẓevi Judah Berlin concerning the individual's right in respect of his own teachings; he held that the individual might treat these as he would his own property – save for its total destruction, because it was a *mitzvah* to study and to teach others *(Meshiv Davar,* pt. 1, no. 24).

This view was not, however, generally accepted by the halakhic scholars. Thus Isaac Schmelkes saw no reason why others might not reprint a book – even if first printed by the author himself – once the original edition had been completely sold; "everyone retains the right to study and to teach . . . why should another not be able to benefit his fellow men and print and sell cheaply?" (*Beit Yiẓḥak,* YD, pt. 2, no. 75). In his opinion Nathanson's analogy of a patent-right offered no real support for the correctness of his view, since in that case the perpetuity of the right derived from royal charter, without which others might freely copy the inventor's model, and furthermore, a work relating to the Torah was to be distinguished from any other work of the spirit inasmuch as "the Torah was given to all free of charge . . . not to be used with a view to gaining remuneration" *(ibid.).* At the same time Schmelkes conceded the validity of a restriction imposed against reprint of a book within a specified period, not as a matter of *halakhah,* but in pursuance of the general law of the land, by virtue of the rule of *dina de-malkhuta dina* ("the law of the land is law").

The doctrine of *hassagat gevul* strikingly illustrates one of the paths for the development of Jewish law, namely extension of the content of a legal principle beyond its original confines, in a search for solutions to problems arising through changes in social and economic conditions.

Bibliography: Gulak, Yesodei, 1 (1922), 172–5; Gulak, Ozar, 355, 359f.; S. Funk, in: JJLG, 18 (1927), 289–304; Z. Markon, in: *Ha-Mishpat,* 2 (1927), 192–201; Herzog, Instit, 1 (1936), 127–36; L. Rabinowitz, *Ḥerem Hayyishub* (Eng., 1945), 122–6; Z. Falk, *Ha-Kinyan ha-Ruḥani be-Dinei Yisrael* (1947); E. Rivlin; in: *Emet-le Ya'akov . . . Freimann* (1937), 149–62; F. Baer, in: *Zion,* 15 (1949/50), 35f.; ET, 9 (1959), 542–6; J. Katz, *Tradition and Crisis* (1961), 59f; M. Elon, *Ha-Mishpat Ha-Ivri* (1973), II, 329ff, 374ff, 553ff, 653, 656ff, 724ff.

Menachem Elon

V. FAMILY LAW AND INHERITANCE

Contents

BETROTHAL (Heb. שידוכין, *shiddukhin*).

Definition. In Jewish law *shiddukhin* is defined as the mutual promise between a man and a woman to contract a marriage at some future time and the formulations of the terms (*tena'im*, see below) on which it shall take place. In general parlance, as opposed to legal terminology, it is known as *erusin* (Kid. 63a, Tos.), which is in fact part of the marriage ceremony proper (see Marriage[1]). The concept of *shiddukhin* can entail either a promise by the intending parties themselves or one made by their respective parents or other relatives on their behalf (Kid. 9b; Sh. Ar., EH 50:4–6 and 51). The sages regarded *kiddushin* (consecration; see Marriage[2]) without prior *shiddukhin* as licentiousness and prescribed that "he who enters into a marriage without *shiddukhin* is liable to be flogged" (TJ, Kid. 3:10, 64; TB, Kid. 12b; Maim. Yad, Ishut, 3:22 and Issurei Bi'ah, 21:14; Sh. Ar., EH 26:4). *Shiddukhin* as such has no immediate effect on the personal status of the parties – it being only a promise to create a different personal status in the future (Resp. Rosh 34:1; *Beit Yosef* EH 55). Nor does the promise give either party the right to claim specific performance from the other – since a marriage celebrated in pursuance of a judgment requiring the defendant to marry the plaintiff is repugnant to the basic principle that a marriage requires the free will and consent of both the parties thereto.

Gifts (Heb. סבלונות, *sivlonot*). The Talmud (Kid. 50b) discusses the question whether the bride's acceptance of gifts from her bridegroom is to be regarded as an indication that *kiddushin* has already been celebrated between them – thus making it necessary for her to receive a divorce, on the grounds of "doubt," in the event she does not marry him and wishes to marry someone else. The *halakhah* was decided that the matter be left dependent on local custom – so that any "doubt" as to whether or not *kiddushin* had already taken place would depend on whether or not there was any custom in the particular place where the parties resided to send such gifts before or after *kiddushin*. From the time that it became the general custom for parties to initiate their intended ties with each other by way of *shiddukhin* (when the bridegroom would send gifts to his bride) and for the *kiddushin* and *nissu'in* (the marriage proper; see Marriage) to take place simultaneously at a later date, there would usually be no opportunity for the bridegroom to send such gifts to the bride after the *kiddushin* but before the *nissu'in*, the *halakhah* was then decided that the giving of gifts per se implied no suspicion of *kiddushin* as mentioned above (Sh. Ar., EH 45:2; *Arukh ha-Shulḥan* EH 45:16:18. See also *Minhag*.

Tena'im (Heb. תנאים, "conditions"). It is customary, but not generally or necessarily so, for the *tena'im*, or conditions of the *shiddukhin*, to be reduced to writing – whereby such matters would be prescribed as the date and place of the proposed marriage, the financial obligations of the parties, i.e., the dowry (Heb. נדוניה, *nedunyah*) to be brought by the bride, or the period for which her father undertakes to provide for the couple. All such obligations undertaken at the time of the *shiddukhin* are valid and binding, even without a formal symbolic *kinyan* (see Acquisition), as obligations of this nature are "in these matters effected by mere verbal arrangement" (Ket. 102a; Kid. 9b; See also Contract). It is also customary to stipulate a sum of money as a penalty to be paid in the event of a breach of promise without good cause. In the Talmud such written instruments are termed *shetarei pesikta* – abbreviated by the *posekim* to *"shetarei"* or *tena'ei shiddukhin"* or simply *"tena'im"* (Rashi, ad loc.; Sh. Ar., EH 51: *Arukh ha-Shulḥan*, EH 51:13; see also forms: A. A. Rudner *Mishpetei Ishut*, 178f. and Gulak, Oẓar 1–19 (nos. 1–4), 362 (no. 403); see also *Shetar*).

1. page 356; 2. page 356.

Breach of the Shiddukhin. Consequences of Breach. The party committing a breach of promise, i.e., by not marrying the other party, may be liable to compensate the other party for any actual damage sustained, such as the expenses of the preparations for the marriage, and may also be obliged to return the gifts he received on the occasion of the *shiddukhin*, whether from the other party or from relatives and friends (Sh. Ar., EH 50:3–4; Resp. Rosh, 35:8; *Arukh ha-Shulḥan*, EH 50:20). The offending party may further be liable to pay the penalty stipulated in the *tena'im* – or, if not so stipulated, such amount as a court may determine as proper in the circumstances – having particular regard to the degree of mental suffering, shame, and public degradation suffered by the other party as a result of the breach of promise (Tos. to BM 66a; Sh. Ar., EH 50, *Ba'er Heitev* 15). In cases where the sum stipulated in the *tena'im* to be paid by way of compensation exceeds the value of the actual damage caused, so as to make it a real penalty, the *posekim* debate the legal validity of such a condition on the grounds that the promise is tainted with *asmakhta*, i.e., that a promise to pay such a sum by way of compensation might possibly not have been meant seriously, since both parties would have been at the time so certain and confident of fulfilling their respective commitments. Some of the authorities, mainly Ashkenazi, took the view that the law requiring one who shamed another to compensate the latter should be strictly applied in these cases as well, and that the plea of *asmakhta* avails only if the stipulated sum is a highly exaggerated one (Tos. to BM 66a and to Kid. 8b; Resp. Rosh 34:2,4; Rema EH 50:6 and *Beit Shemu'el, ibid.*; *Arukh ha-Shulḥan*, EH 50:21f.; Rema ḤM 207:16 and *Siftei Kohen, ibid.*). Other sages, primarily Sephardi, held that the plea of *asmakhta* would avail the offending party even in a breach of promise case involving *shiddukhin* (Maim. Yad, Mekhirah 11:18; Sh. Ar., ḤM 207:16; *Beit Yosef* EH 50; see also PDR 3:131–154). In order to avoid any doubts, however, in the Middle Ages the Sephardi authorities introduced the practice of two separate agreements between the parties – one whereby each party unconditionally undertook to pay to the other a fixed sum in the event of breach of promise and another whereby each party released the other from the former undertaking upon the fulfillment of all the obligations stipulated in the *tena'im* (Sh. Ar., ḤM, *ibid.*, and EH 50:6; Resp. Maharit, 1:131). Even if the *tena'im* had not been reduced to writing the court would adjudge the offending party to pay such compensation as may seem proper in the circumstances, having regard to the standing of the parties, provided the terms of the *shiddukhin* had been evidenced by *kinyan* between the parties.

Defenses Against Liability. Any justifiable reason for withdrawing from the *shiddukhin* is a valid defense to a claim for compensation. Since the matter in issue is a promise to marry, involving a personal tie between the parties, the court will tend to regard any reasonable ground for not entering the marriage as justified, even if it is not directly attributable to the defendant. For example, if the *tena'im* were agreed by the parents and subsequently the son or the daughter involved refused to accept them, such refusal would be regarded as justified and would not involve him or her in any liability (Resp. Rosh 34:1; Tur and Sh. Ar., EH 50:5, *Arukh ha-Shulḥan* EH 50:29; PDR 5, 322–9). However, if the grounds on which the defendant bases his withdrawal were known to him prior to the *shiddukhin* or if they became known to him thereafter and he did not immediately withdraw, he will be regarded as having waived his objections and such grounds will not later avail him as a defence.

Validity of the Tena'im after Marriage (Nissu'in). Noncompliance with the terms of the *tena'im* after the marriage has taken place does not exempt the parties from the duties imposed on them by law vis-à-vis each other as husband and wife. Thus, the husband is not absolved from his duty to maintain and provide a home for his wife because she or her parents may have failed to honor their undertaking to provide a home for the couple – the husband's duty being imposed on him by law (see Marriage) and being unconnected with any rights deriving from the *shiddukhin* (*Bayit Ḥadash* EH 52; Rema EH 52:1, and *Ba'er Heitev* 5). On the other hand, the existence of the marriage is not necessarily to be regarded as constituting a waiver and cancellation of the obligations created by the *shiddukhin.* In order to avoid such a contention, it is customary for the parties to draw up "secondary" or "new" *tena'im* at the time of the *kiddushin,* whereby they reaffirm the original *tena'im* – or else stipulate specifically in the *ketubbah* that the marriage is based on the terms of the original *tena'im;* the latter form being the customary procedure in the *ketubbah* adopted in the State of Israel (A. A. Rudner, *Mishpetei Ishut,* 179). Such procedures provide either party with a clear cause of action for claiming the specific performance of all obligations undertaken in the *tena'im* after the marriage has taken place. According to some *posekim,* there is no need for the original *tena'im* to be specifically recalled at the time of the *kiddushin* – as it is presumed that the *kiddushin* was entered upon in accordance with the terms which were fixed for the *tena'im* that preceded the *kiddushin* (PDR 1:289–313; 4:193–9, 289–304).

Customs. The ceremony and the writing of the agreement is called in Yiddish *teno'im shrayben.* The term *knas-mahl* ("penalty meal") was also used because of the penalty (usually 50% of the promised dowry) stipulated in the document to be paid by the party guilty of breach of the promise to marry (Sh. Ar., EH 51).

Though of secondary importance from an halakhic point of view, the "betrothal" remains a significant ceremony in marriage arrangements. According to Elijah b. Solomon, the Gaon of Vilna, a bridegroom, rather than break the engagement, should marry and then divorce his bride. In certain Jewish circles, a marriage is not contracted with a person who was a party to a broken engagement.

Among the Oriental Jews, the engagement ceremony is a very elaborate affair. Kurdish Jews had the custom of *hatlabba* ("bidding the bride") and those of Djerba indulged in great festivities. After the engagement, bride and bridegroom would exchange presents, and on Passover, Shavuot, and Sukkot, the groom would sent his bride clothing, jewelry, and choice fruits. Similarly among Ashkenazi Jews, as *sivlonot* the groom usually sent the bride clothing or jewelry, and she reciprocated with a new *tallit* or a richly embroidered *tallit* bag she had made herself. At the Ashkenazi *tena'im* ceremony, it is customary to break a plate; the act is parallel to the crushing of the glass at the wedding ceremony, symbolizing the destruction of the Temple in Jerusalem.

Bibliography: Buechler, in: *Festschrift . . . Lewy* (1911), 110–44; Gulak, Yesodei, (1922), 82; 3 (1922), 14–19, 22, 29, 45; Gulak, Oẓar, 1–19 (nos. 1–14), 362 (no. 403); idem, in: *Tarbiz* 3 (1931–32), 361–76; 5 (1933–34), 126–33, Herzog, Instit, 1 (1936), index; Ch. Albeck, in: *Kovez . . . M. Schorr* (1944), 12–24; ET, 2 (1949), 114; 6 (1954), 610; 7 (1956), 138–49; PD 12:1121–204; 16:2737–40; B. Schereschewsky, *Dinei Mishpaḥah* (1967²), 22–31; idem, *Kenas u-Fiẓẓuyim Ekev Hafarat Ḥozim le-fi Dinei Yisrael* (1960); B. Cohen, in: PAAJR, 18 (1949), 67–135; republished in his *Jewish and Roman Law,* 1 (1966), 279–347, addenda 777–80; H. Schauss, *The Lifetime of a Jew* (1950), 129–31, 150–2, 158–61, 165–9, 182–6; M. Elon, *Ha-Mishpat Ha-Ivri* (1973), II, 371ff., 438, 533, 633.

Ben-Zion Schereschewsky

MARRIAGE.

In Jewish law, marriage consists of two separate acts, called *kiddushin* and *nissu'in* respectively. The *kiddushin* (also called *erusin*) is an act performed between a man and a woman which leads to a change in their personal status, i.e., from bachelorhood to a status which remains unchanged until the death of either party or their divorce from one another. However, the *kiddushin* alone does not bring about all the legal consequences of this change of status, as all those will follow only from a further act between the parties, namely the *nissu'in.* The common usage of the term *erusin,* which refers merely to *shiddukhin,* i.e., engagement (see Betrothal[1]), is therefore not identical with its legal meaning.

Modes of Effecting Kiddushin. There are three ways of effecting a *kiddushin,* namely by way of *kesef* ("money"), *shetar* ("deed"), or *bi'ah* ("cohabitation").

Kesef. The bridegroom, in the presence of two competent witnesses, transfers (see Acquisition) to his bride money or its equivalent – today normally an unadorned ring – to the value of at least one *perutah,* for the purposes of *kiddushin.* It is customary for the bridegroom – after the officiating rabbi has recited the *Birkat ha-Erusin* – to place the ring on the bride's right-hand forefinger while addressing her with the words: *Harei at mekuddeshet lit be tabba'at zo ke-dat Moshe ve-Yisrael* ("Behold, you are consecrated unto me by this ring, according to the law of Moses and of Israel"; Kid. 2a, 5b; Rema Sh. Ar., EH 27:1); i.e., by transferring the ring to the bride the groom signifies his intent to reserve her exclusively to himself and by accepting it she signifies her consent. Hence it is necessary that the ring belong to the bridegroom and not to the bride, since a person cannot alienate something that is not his own, nor can a person acquire something that already belongs to him (Kid. 5b; 6b; 47a; Sh. Ar., EH 27:1, 7; 28:2).

Shetar. In the presence of two competent witnesses, the bridegroom hands over to the bride a deed in which is written, besides the names of the parties and the other particulars required for the purposes of a *kiddushin* by *shetar,* the words, "Behold you are consecrated unto me with this deed according to the law of Moses and of Israel" and the bride accepts the deed with the intention of thereby becoming consecrated to the bridegroom (Kid. 9a; Sh. Ar., EH 32:1, 4). Delivery of the deed is therefore not merely evidence that the *kiddushin* has taken place before, but is the means whereby the tie is created, and in this respect it differs from the *ketubbah* deed which the bridegroom has to give to the bride after completion of the *kiddushin* (see also Civil Marriage).

Bi'ah. If a man in the presence of two competent witnesses, addresses to a woman the words, "Behold you are consecrated to me with this cohabitation according to the law of Moses and of Israel," and in their presence he takes her into a private place for the purpose of *kiddushin,* she will, upon their cohabitation, be reserved to him (Kid. 9b; Sh. Ar., EH 33:1). Although valid this mode of *kiddushin* was regarded by the scholars as tantamount to prostitution, and they decreed that any person employing it was punishable by flogging (Kid. 12b; Yad, Ishut 3:21; Sh. Ar., EH 26:4; 33:1). On the other hand, this mode of *kiddushin* has served as the basis for the halakhic presumption that a man does not cohabit with a woman for the sake of prostitution (Git. 81b; Rema EH 33:1), and for the various rules founded on that presumption (see Husband and Wife; Divorce).

In practice, in present times, only *kiddushei kesef* is observed since the other two modes of *kiddushin* have long become obsolete. The version "Behold you are reserved . . . according to the law of Moses and of Israel" (which does not appear in the TB and is only found in the Tosefta (Ket. 4:9) and in the TJ, where

1. page 353.

the version is "according to the law of Moses and of the Jews" (*Yehudai;* Ket. 4:8, 29a), means that the bridegroom reserves the bride unto himself "according to the law of Moses" – i.e., the law of the Torah – "and of Israel" – i.e., in accordance with the rules of the halakhic scholars as applied in Israel, so that the *kiddushin* shall be valid or void in accordance with the regulations laid down by the scholars (Yev. 90b; Ket. 3a; Git. 33a; Rashi and Tos. ad loc.; see also Rashbam and Tos. to BB 48b). The version thus formulated provided the basis for the *halakhah* which empowered and authorized the scholars, in certain circumstances, to invalidate a *kiddushin* retroactively in such a manner that even if it was not defective in principle it was deemed to be void *ab initio.* The question whether this power to make regulations for the annulment of the *kiddushin* is conferred also on the rabbis of the times after the redaction of the Talmud has remained in dispute. One opinion is that a *kiddushin* which is valid according to talmudic law, even though it is celebrated contrary to a *takkanah* which expressly prohibits the celebration of a *kiddushin* in any manner except as therein provided (e.g., in the presence of a rabbi and a quorum of ten), will not be declared void *ab initio* and the woman will not be free to marry another man unless she first obtains a divorce (out of precautionary stringency; Resp. Ribash no. 399; see also Resp. Rashba, vol. 1, nos. 1185 and 1206 where no absolute decision is arrived at; Resp. Ḥatam Sofer, EH 1:108; ET, 2 (1949), 137–40; for a detailed discussion of the different opinions and the grounds for not making a *takkanah* to void the *kiddushin ab initio,* see Elon, *Ha-Mishpat Ha-Ivri* II, p. 686–712; see also *Agunah, Takkanot*).

The Nissu'in. The act of *nissu'in* requires that the bride, after completion of the *kiddushin,* be brought to the bridegroom under the *ḥuppah* before two competent witnesses, for purposes of the marriage proper, i.e., the *nissu'in* "according to the law of Moses and of Israel." There are different opinions concerning the import of the term *ḥuppah.* One view is that the bride must be brought to the home of the groom for the *nissu'in* (Ran to Ket. 2a, *Beit Shemu'el* 55, no. 4), an interpretation forming the basis of the present custom of bringing the bride to a place symbolizing the domain *(reshut)* of the bridegroom, i.e., to the place where a canopy is spread across four poles and where the bridegroom is already waiting. According to another opinion *ḥuppah* embraces a private meeting יחוד between bridegroom and bride, at a place set aside for the purpose, as an indication of their marriage proper (Ket. 54b, 56a and Rosh 5:6; Yad, Ishut 10:1, 2; Isserles EH 55:1, 61:1; Sh. Ar., EH 55:2). In order to dispel doubt, custom requires that, in addition to *ḥuppah*, the couple also have the said private meeting.

Legal Consequences. As already indicated, the legal consequences of the act of *kiddushin* differ from those of the act of *nissu'in.* The *kiddushin* creates a legal-personal tie between the parties which can only be dissolved upon divorce or the death of either party, and the *arusah* ("affianced bride") is regarded as a married woman *(eshet ish)* for all purposes under the *de-oraita* law, which thus renders invalid a *kiddushin* between herself and any other man (Kid. 5; Yad, Ishut 1:3; Sh. Ar., EH 26:3). The *arus* too is prohibited, as is a married man proper, from taking an additional wife, and although in his case the prohibition stems not from the *de-oraita* law but from the *ḥerem de-Rabbenu Gershom* (see Bigamy[1]), the prohibition for the *arus* is as stringent as it is for a married man proper (Rema EH 1:10; *Oẓar ha-Posekim* EH 1, no. 65; other scholars differ, see *Taz* EH 1, n. 15). *Kiddushin* alone, however, does not serve to call into being the mutual rights and duties existing between husband and wife (see Husband and Wife), and, in particular, cohabitation between them is prohibited (Rashi, Ket. 7b; Sh. Ar., EH 55:1, 6). This prohibition is also contained in the Consecration Blessing in the words, "and has prohibited us the *arus* but has permitted us those who are married to us by *ḥuppah* and *kiddushin*" (see Ket. 7b and Sh. Ar., EH 34:1). The *arus* is also not liable for the maintenance of his bride except after the lapse of 12 months from the time of the *kiddushin,* or any lesser period of time agreed upon between them, and then only if he has failed to marry her notwithstanding her demand and readiness to be married to him (Ket. 2, 57a; Sh. Ar., EH 55:4; 56:1,3 and commentaries). The *arusah* also has no *ketubbah,* unless the bridegroom executed such a deed in her favor at the *kiddushin* stage (Ket. 54b; Sh. Ar., EH 55:6). The absolute change in their personal status, with all the rights and duties it entails is created by the *nissu'in.*

Manner of Celebrating Kiddushin and Nissu'in. In order to avoid irregularities which might possibly bring about complications, custom decrees that the *kiddushin* be solemnized by a rabbi who supervises that everything is done according to law. It is also the generally accepted custom that there shall be present a least a *minyan* (ten men). Custom further decrees that the bridegroom shall always recite the above-mentioned formulation in the precise words, "Behold, you are consecrated . . . etc.,"; although post-factum the *kiddushin* will not be invalidated if any like version with a similar content is used, any change in the recognized version should be avoided at the outset (Yad, Ishut 10:6; Resp. Rosh 37:1; Sh. Ar., EH 55:3 and Rema EH 61:1). The presence of two competent witnesses at both stages of the marriage ceremony is mandatory; as they do not merely serve as eyewitnesses but their presence is an essential part of the legal act, their absence will invalidate both the *kiddushin* and the *nissu'in.* Hence if a man and a woman acknowledge, that there were not two witnesses present at their marriage, their acknowledgement *(hoda'ah)* that they are married will not serve as a basis for determining that this is the case (Kid. 65a; Yad, Ishut 4:6; Sh. Ar., EH 42:2). Conversely, if two competent witnesses testify to the celebration of a marriage between a particular couple, they will be regarded as duly married notwithstanding their own denial of the fact (OPD 132, 139). For a full description see above. Theoretically, *kiddushin* being an act of legal effect, it may also be performed between the parties through an agent; i.e., the bridegroom may appoint an agent to enter, on his behalf, into a *kiddushin* with a particular woman and the woman may do likewise for the purpose of accepting *kiddushin.* However, it is a *mitzvah* for each personally to take and be taken in marriage (Yad, Ishut 3:19; Sh. Ar., EH 35, 36). Similarly, in principle, the couple may celebrate a conditional *kiddushin* in such a manner that, provided all the rules applicable to conditions are observed (Sh. Ar., EH 38:2) and the condition itself fulfilled, the *kiddushin* will be valid from the start, or from the time of fulfillment of the condition, in accordance with the stipulation of the parties, but will be invalid if the condition is not fulfilled (Sh. Ar., EH 38). However, on account of the possible complications arising therefrom, and the stringency of the laws concerning a married woman, no conditions are permitted in *kiddushin* or *nissu'in.*

Legal Capacity of the Parties. Since marriage is an act of legal effect, it can be celebrated only by parties who have legal capacity. Hence if one of the parties to a marriage is a minor, acting independently, it will be invalid. In Jewish law a male is a minor *(katan)* until the age of 13 years; from the age of 13 years and one day he is a major (called *gadol*) and only then may he contract a valid marriage (Kid. 50b; Yad, Ishut 2:10; 4:7; Sh. Ar., EH 43:1). A female is a minor *(ketannah)* until the age of 12 years; from the age of 12 years and one day until the age of 12½ years she is called a *na'arah* (Yad, Ishut 2:1). Although as a *na'arah* she is considered a major *(gedolah;* Yad, Ishut 2:6), her

1. page 367.

marriage (when she is acting independently) will only be valid if she is orphaned of her father, but if he is alive, since a *na'arah* remains under her father's tutelage *(reshut)*, her marriage, when she is acting independently will be valid only after the tutelage ceases to exist, namely when she becomes a *bogeret,* i.e., when she reaches the age of 12½ years and one day (Kid. 43b, 44b; Yad, Ishut 2:2, 3:11–13, 4:8 and Gerushin, 11:6; Sh. Ar., EH 37:11, 155:20, 21). As regards the validity of a marriage entered into by a minor represented by his parents, see Child Marriage.

For the same reason, i.e., lack of legal capacity, a marriage to which an idiot *(shoteh)* is party will be invalid when it is clear that such a party is a complete idiot (Yev. 69b; 96b; Sh. Ar., EH 44:2; 67:7). However, if such person be of sound, although weak, mind his marriage will be valid (*Beit Yosef,* Tur. EH 44; the statement attributed to Isserles, in Sh. Ar., EH 44:2 is apparently a printing error, see *Beit Shemu'el,* n. 4 and *Ḥelkat Meḥokek* n. 2). In case of doubt as to the soundness of a person's mind, as when he has lucid intervals, his *kiddushin* will, out of apprehension, be regarded as a doubtful *kiddushin* and the parties will not be permitted to marry anyone else except after their divorce (out of precautionary restriction גט מחומרא; Sh. Ar., loc. cit.). A deaf-mute (*ḥeresh*, Yad, Ishut 2:26) is precluded, by Pentateuchal law, from entering into a *kiddushin* since his/her legal capacity is the same as that of the minor or the idiot. However, the scholars regulated that a *kiddushin* entered into by a deaf-mute shall be valid (Yev. 112b; Yad, Ishut 4:9; Sh. Ar., EH 44:1), but they did so without creating any obligations between the parties to such a marriage. Hence if one of the parties is a deaf-mute, none of the legal obligations flowing from marriage will devolve on them – neither the obligation of *ketubbah* (i.e., in places where no *ketubbah* deed is written), nor of a *ketubbah* condition, nor of maintenance (Sh. Ar., EH 67:8–10), except possibly where a deaf-mute expressly undertakes these pecuniary obligations in the *ketubbah* deed (PDR 8:65, 69–71; 74–77). The *ḥerem de-Rabbenu Gershom* does not apply to a husband who was a deaf-mute at the time of his marriage, nor does a deaf-mute's express undertaking not to take an additional wife or not to divorce his wife against her free will have any binding force, since he is incapable of undertaking obligations – at any rate as regards matters of a non-pecuniary nature (PDR loc. cit.).

In the State of Israel. Matters of marriage in the State of Israel are governed by Jewish law, in accordance with the provisions of sections 1 and 2 of the Rabbinical Courts Jurisdiction (Marriage and Divorce) Law, 5713/1953. As regards the customs relating to the celebration of *kiddushin* and *nissu'in, takkanot* were issued at an Israeli rabbinical conference in 1950, imposing a strict ban on anyone solemnizing *kiddushin* and *nissu'in* contrary to the accepted customs.

By virtue of the Marriage Age Law 1950 (as amended in 1960) a woman may not be married before the age of 17 years. This law further renders it a punishable offense for any person to marry a woman under the age of 17 years (it is no offense for the bride), or to solemnize or assist in any capacity in the celebration of the marriage of such a woman, or for a father or guardian to give her away in marriage, unless prior permission of the competent district court has been obtained – the latter being empowered to give this on the grounds specified in the law (see Child Marriage[1]). No minimal age is specified for the bridegroom. This offense, although punishable, has no effect on the personal status of the parties; i.e., if the marriage is valid according to Jewish law, the fact that the offense has been committed will in no way affect the validity of the marriage, whether the question arises in relation to a matter of Jewish or of civil law, in the rabbinical or in the civil courts. However, in the event of a marriage with a woman below the said minimum age, the law provides that application may be made to the rabbinical court – by the persons and in the circumstances specified in the law – in order to oblige the husband to grant his wife a divorce. It must be emphasized that this provision does not create grounds for action for divorce under Jewish law, so that in fact it is a dead letter, for in matters of divorce the rabbinical courts apply Jewish law only

Bibliography: M. Mielziner, *The Jewish Law of Marriage and Divorce . . .* (1901); J. Neubauer, *Beitraege zur Geschichte des biblisch-talmudischen Eheschliessungsrechts* (1920); Gulak, Yesodei, 3 (1922), 19–22; Gulak, Oẓar, 17–58; idem, in: *Tarbiz,* 5 (1933/34), 384f.; L. M. Epstein, *Marriage Laws in the Bible and the Talmud* (1942); E. Neufeld, *Ancient Hebrew Marriage Laws . . .* (1944); A. Freimann, *Seder Kiddushin ve-Nissu'in Aḥarei Ḥatimat ha-Talmud ve-ad Yameinu* (1945); ET, 1 (1951[3]), 257–61; 2 (1949), 137–40, 182–6; 4 (1952), 420–7, 631–51; 5 (1953), 138–52, 168–79; 6 (1954), 710–2; 7 (1956), 43–46; 12 (1967), 154–8; M. Vogelmann, in: *Sinai,* 43 (1958), 49–55; N. Sachs, in: *No'am,* 1 (1958), 52–68; O. Joseph, in: *Sinai,* 48 (1960/61), 186–93; H. Albeck, *ibid.,* 145–51; M. Silberg, *Ha-Ma'amad ha-Ishi be Yisrael* (1965[4]); K. Kahana, *The Theory of Marriage in Jewish Law* (1966); E. Berkowitz, *Tenai ba-Nissu'in u-va-Get* (1966); Z. W. Falk, *Jewish Matrimonial Law in the Middle Ages* (1966); B. Schereschewsky, *Dinei Mishpaḥah* (1967[2]), 32–51; Elon, *Ḥakikah Datit . . .* (1968), 31–37, 164, 183f.; idem, *Ha-Mishpat Ha-Ivri* (1973) I, 81ff, 97ff, 151, 160ff, II, 351ff, 427ff, 473ff, 518–527, 539ff, 577ff, 647ff, 654ff, 661, 675, 686–712, 794ff, III, 846, 1104ff.

Ben-Zion Schereschewsky

MARRIAGE, PROHIBITED. A marriage is prohibited whenever there is a legal impediment to a *kiddushin* (see Marriage) between the particular parties. In some cases the prohibition has the effect of rendering the marriage, if it is celebrated nevertheless, null and void *ab initio;* in other cases it does not invalidate the marriage, but provides a ground for having it terminated by divorce.

Prohibited and Void. This category includes: (1) Marriages which are גלוי עריות *(gillui arayot)* according to pentateuchal law, i.e., punishable by *karet* or death, namely: (a) marriages between parties related to one another within the prohibited degrees of kinship: i.e., the marriage between a man and his mother, daughter, sister, and certain other relatives (Lev. 18:6ff.; Kid. 67b and codes); the marriage between a man and the sister of his wife is also void during the latter's lifetime (i.e., even after divorce), as is marriage with his brother's widow (except in the case of the levirate widow) or divorced wife: such marriages are punishable by *karet* (Yad, Issurei Bi'ah, 2:1, 9; Sh. Ar., EH 15:22, 26; 44:6; see also Levirate Marriage); and (b) marriage between a man and a married woman, such adultery being punishable by death (see also Bigamy); (2) A marriage with a non-Jewish partner (Sh. Ar., EH 44:8; see also Mixed Marriage); (3) Other cases enumerated in Shulḥan Arukh, *Even ha-Ezer* 15.

Prohibited but Valid. In this category are included marriages which, although prohibited, do not constitute *gillui arayot* according to pentateuchal law and therefore are valid and not terminable unless by the death of either party or by divorce (Sh. Ar., EH 15:1; 18; 44:7). Since these marriages are nevertheless prohibited and remain tainted with the prohibition during their subsistence, their dissolution by divorce is generally compelled, whether or not either or both of the parties consented to, or had prior knowledge of, the true situation. Marriage prohibitions of this kind derive either from the pentateuchal law imposed and

1. page 365.

punishable as a plain prohibition only (Yad, Ishut 1:7) or from the rules laid down by the scribes, i.e., marriage prohibited, as "incest of a secondary [minor] degree," not by the Torah but only by rabbinical enactment (*ibid.,* 1:6; Sh. Ar., loc. cit.). The following are examples of such prohibitions:

(1) A married woman who has sexual relations with anyone but her husband becomes prohibited to the latter as well, and also to her lover even after her divorce from her husband (Sot. 27b; Sh. Ar., EH 11:1; 178:17). If she has had sexual relations of her own free will, she is prohibited to her husband forever, i.e., he must never remarry her after divorce from him even if in the meantime she has not married anyone else (Sh. Ar., EH 11:1). If she has been raped (see Rape), she is prohibited to her husband only if he is a priest, but if he is an ordinary Israelite, she is permitted to him. He need not divorce her and, if he has done so, he may remarry her provided she has not married someone else in the meantime (Sh. Ar., EH 6:10, 11). Similarly, the adulteress is also prohibited for all time from marrying her lover, i.e., even after divorce from her husband or his death (Yev. 24b and Rashi ad loc.; Sh. Ar., EH 11:1). This is because her lover has destroyed her family life, inasmuch as, owing to the adultery, he has rendered her prohibited to her husband. By the same token, and because the wife of an ordinary Israelite does not become prohibited to her husband when someone else has sexual relations with her against her own free will, some scholars are of the opinion that although beforehand she is prohibited to such a lover in order to penalize him, if they have nevertheless married each other, he will not be compelled to divorce her (Sh. Ar., EH 11; *Ba'er Heitev* n. 5 and *Beit Shemu'el* n. 2; but cf. Rema, EH 159:3, and *Ba'er Heitev* n. 6; *Oẓar ha-Posekim,* EH 11:1, n. 44).

(2) A divorcee who has remarried and her second marriage has also been terminated (by divorce or death) is prohibited to her former husband, in terms of an express prohibition in pentateuchal law (Deut. 24:4).

(3) A priest is prohibited by an express prohibition in the pentateuchal law from marrying a divorcee, a *zonah,* or a *ḥalalah* (see *Yuḥasin;* Lev. 21:7; Sh. Ar., EH 6:1). This prohibition is still in force (Rema, EH 3:6; PDR 5, 219, 221) despite the lack of certainty that all those known as priests are in fact the descendants of Aaron, for all of them are merely presumed to be priests (Yad, Issurei Bi'ah, 20:1). A divorced woman remains prohibited to a priest even if after her divorce she has remarried and become a widow (*Ḥokhmat Shelomo,* EH 6:1; Rema Sh. Ar., EH 66:11, and *Ḥelkat Meḥokek*, n. 41). A priest is forbidden to remarry even his own former wife (Resp. Ribash no. 348; see also Divorce). For the purposes of the above prohibition, the term *zonah* is not to be interpreted in its ordinary sense – i.e., a woman who has sexual relations other than within matrimony (Yev. 61b). Here it refers to a woman who is not a Jewess by birth, such as a proselyte, and also to a woman who has cohabited with a man to whom she must not be married by virtue of a general prohibition (i.e., not one relating to the priesthood as such) e.g., if she has cohabited with a non-Jew or a *mamzer* (Yev. 61a and Rashi; Sh. Ar., EH 6:8).

(4) A Jewish man or woman must not marry a *mamzer.* For details see *Mamzer.*

(5) A married man is prohibited, according to the decree of Rabbenu Gershom, to marry another woman while his marriage still subsists. If contracted, the second marriage is valid but the parties will be compelled to a divorce (see Bigamy[1]).

(6) Marriage with a divorcee or widow is prohibited before the lapse of 90 days from the date of her acquiring her new status, in order to avoid doubt concerning the descent of her offspring; similarly, for the good of her child, it is forbidden to marry a pregnant woman or nursing mother until the child has reached the age of 24 months (Sh. Ar., EH 13:1, 11–14; for further instances of prohibited, but valid marriages, see Sh. Ar., EH 15).

Legal Consequences of Prohibited Marriages. Family Law Aspects. So far as the parties themselves are concerned, no legal consequences at all attach to the celebration of a marriage which is forbidden as ערוה (incestuous) according to pentateuchal law, and there is therefore no need for them to be divorced (Sh. Ar., EH 15:1, and Ha-Gra n. 3; Sh. Ar., EH 44:6); their children will be *mamzerim.* Only a marriage of a married woman to another man, although invalid, requires that the woman obtain a divorce not only from her husband but also from the paramour (see Divorce; Bigamy; *Agunah*).

In the case of prohibited but valid marriages either party is entitled to demand a divorce, whether or not either or both parties were aware of the impediment at the time of the marriage or at any time thereafter. In case of the other party's refusal, divorce may be compelled, except in the case of a marriage contracted within 90 days of dissolution of the wife's previous marriage (Rema, EH 13:10). The need for divorce is also relaxed with reference to marriage with a pregnant woman or nursing mother (PDR 4:60). On the status of children born of such marriages, see *Yuḥasin.*

Civil Law Aspects. Since the law requires that a prohibited marriage be dissolved, there is no place for the imposition of reciprocal marital rights and duties which are designed to sustain the marriage. In principle this is the position whenever the husband has married his wife without knowing that she is prohibited to him (לא הכיר בה, *lo hikkir bah*). However, if he has done so knowingly, there will be no justification for his release from a husband's marital duties, and these he must fulfill, with the exception of those likely to impede dissolution of the marriage. This distinction between the husband's knowledge or lack of it is drawn mainly in regard to the most important cases of prohibited but valid marriages, i.e., cases of plain prohibition איסורי לאו *issurei lav*); (for the prohibitions concerning other cases of prohibited marriage, see Sh. Ar., EH 116:2ff.) Since a man who marries without knowing that his wife is prohibited to him is released from all the marital duties of a husband, the wife will not be entitled to receive her "main" or minimal *ketubbah* and therefore also not to the fulfillment of the *ketubbah* conditions since "the *ketubbah* conditions are as the *ketubbah* itself" (Ket. 54b and Rashi ad. loc. s.v. *tena'ei ketubbah;* see also Husband and Wife). Similarly, the wife will not be entitled to maintenance, either during the husband's lifetime or as his widow (Yad, Ishut 24:2; Sh. Ar., EH 116:1). In the same way, the wife too will be released from all her matrimonial duties, since these are imposed on her by law only in return for her husband's actual fulfillment of his duties toward her (see *Ketubbah;* Husband and Wife; Dowry). The husband will, however, remain liable for her *ketubbah* "increment" *(tosefet ketubbah),* as this is not an obligation imposed on him by law but one that he has voluntarily undertaken to fulfill for as long as she is willing to remain his wife, and this the law has forbidden her to do, independently of her own will in the matter (Yad, Ishut 24:3; *Taz*, EH 116, n. 3).

In cases where the husband knowingly contracts a prohibited marriage, the scholars regulated that in principle he should not be released from any of the matrimonial duties imposed upon the husband by law. Hence, in these circumstances he, or his estate, will be liable to his wife or widow for her *ketubbah* (including the *tosefet*) as well as its conditions as in every regular marriage. However, since everything should be done in order to bring about the dissolution of such prohibited marriages, the

1. page 367.

scholars further ruled that the husband was exempt from maintaining his wife during his own lifetime, in order to discourage her from remaining his wife (Sh. Ar., loc. cit, and *Taz,* n. 1). He will consequently not be entitled to her handiwork, since he is entitled to this only in return for actually maintaining her. Divergent opinions are expressed in the codes concerning the husband's right to the usufruct of his wife's property. According to some of the *posekim* the husband does not have this right, since it is in return for the obligation to ransom her from captivity, a duty which does not hold in the case of a prohibited marriage (see Dowry) as marital life with her is forbidden to him; therefore the husband must return the equivalent of any benefit he may have derived from this source (see, e.g., Yad, Ishut 24:4 and *Maggid Mishneh* ad loc.). Other *posekim* are of the opinion that only when the wife is taken captive must the husband make available for purposes of her ransom, the equivalent of the fruits of her property that he has enjoyed, but otherwise he will be exempt from compensating her in this regard (see, e.g., *Ḥelkat Meḥokek* n. 4 and *Beit Shemu'el* n. 2 to EH 116). Since the marital rights afforded by law to the wife in respect of her husband are conditional on the existence of corresponding legal duties of her husband toward her and, in the same way, the wife's duties to her husband do not exist independently but are in return for her enjoyment of her rights against him (Yad, Ishut 12:1–4) – a position which depends on his knowledge or ignorance of the prohibited nature of the marriage – her knowledge or ignorance in this respect is of no legal significance.

In the State of Israel. Apart from rules of private international law, the problem of prohibited marriages is governed by Jewish law (see sects. 1, 2 of the Rabbinical Court Jurisdiction (Marriage and Divorce) Law, 5713/1953.

Bibliography: ET, 1 (1951^3), 206–9; 2 (1949), 20f., 65, 84f.; 6 (1954), 343–54; 12 (1967), 49–67; Elon, *Ha-Mishpat Ha-Ivri* (1973), II, 282ff., 296ff., 312, 396, 456ff., 720 ; B. Schereschewsky, *Dinei Mishpaḥah* (1967^2), 51f., 56–62, 203–6.

See also bibliography to Marriage.

Ben-Zion Schereschewsky

CHILD MARRIAGE; a marriage to which either or both the parties are legal minors. A male is legally a minor *(katan)* until the end of his 13th year; thereafter he is considered an adult (*gadol* or *ish;* Maim. Yad, Ishut, 2:10). A female is legally a minor (*ketannah)* until the end of her 12th year; thereafter she is considered an adult *gedolah)* – but with one additional distinction: for the first six months after her 12th birthday she is called a *na'arah* and from the age of 12½ plus one day she is called a *bogeret* (Maim. Yad, Ishut 2:1–2). A child marriage involves two considerations: first, the capacity of a minor to change his personal status by marriage contracted as his own independent act; and secondly, whether others – such as parents – may validly give a minor in marriage and the resulting effect on the minor's personal status.

Marriage of a Minor Acting by Himself. The rule is that "an act of marriage *[kiddushin]* by a minor is – as everyone knows – nugatory" (Kid. 50b) and thus no divorce is required for the dissolution (Yev. 112b; Sh. Ar., EH 43:1, *Ḥelkat Meḥokek, ibid.* 1). This is also the rule regarding a *ketannah* (Kid. 44b; Sh. Ar., EH 37:4, 11). After she has reached her 12th birthday, subject to her father being no longer alive, she may contract a marriage which is valid under biblical law (Yev. 109b and 110a; BB 156a; Maim. Yad, Ishut, 2:6; Gerushin 11:6). If her father is still alive and she is a *na'arah*, she requires her father's prior consent to her marriage (Kid. 79a; Sh. Ar., EH 37:1,2). Males and females, on reaching the age of 13 years and a day and 12 years and a day respectively – unless they do not show signs of physical maturity (i.e., puberty: Maim. Hil. Ishut, 2:1–20) – may contract a marriage which is valid in all respects.

Marriage of a Minor, Contracted by Parents. The rule in the case of a minor male is that neither his father nor anyone else may contract a marriage on his behalf, and the rabbis did not enact a special rule permitting such marriage as they did in the case of a female minor, since the reason in the latter case (namely, so that people should not treat her licentiously – *minhag hefker*) is not considered applicable to a male minor (Yev. 112b; Sh. Ar., EH 43:1). A talmudic statement commending a parent who gives his children in marriage when they are close to the age of puberty (*samukh le-firkan;* Sanh. 76b; Yev. 62b) was interpreted as meaning that a father may give his son in marriage even before the age of 13 (Rashi and Tos. *ibid.; Baḥ*, EH 1; *Taz* 1, n. 3). However, the *halakhah* rejected this and the statement was interpreted to mean that, in the case of a boy, *samukh le-firko* meant just after his reaching the full age of 13. Giving him in marriage before that age was tantamount to prostitution and forbidden (Sh. Ar, EH 1:3 and Commentaries, *ibid.* 43:1; Oẓar ha-Posekim EH 1 n. 14). Although it is a *mitzvah* to marry in order to be able to observe the *mitzvah* of procreation and generally one is obliged to observe the *mitzvot* from the age of 13 – this particular *mitzvah* of procreation only devolves on the male from the age of 18 (EH 1:3).

In the case of a girl, however, a different rule prevails. A father is entitled to arrange the *kiddushin* of his daughter, whether she is a *ketannah* or a *na'arah*, without her consent (Kid. 44b and Sh. Ar., EH 37:1, 3). Accordingly, if a father effects *kiddushin* for his daughter by, e.g., accepting *kesef-kiddushin* for her (see Marriage), she is considered a married woman and cannot remarry until the death of her husband or her divorce from him (Kid. 44b and Rashi; Tur and *Beit Yosef,* EH 37; Sh. Ar., EH 37:1, 3). However, by talmudic times some of the sages were opposed to child marriages of this kind and opined that "it is forbidden for a father to give his minor daughter in marriage until she has grown up and can say: 'I want so-and-so' " (Kid. 41a). In later times, the uncertainties of life in the Diaspora made parents reluctant to delay their daughters' marriages until they had grown up. The prohibition was therefore not accepted as *halakhah* (Tos., Kid. *ibid.;* Sh. Ar., EH 37:8) – its observance was seen as a *mitzvah* (Maim., Ishut, 3:19; Sh. Ar., EH 37:8).

On the other hand, if a father has, on the strength of the aforesaid *halakhah,* given his minor daughter in marriage she passes permanently out of his guardianship, and in order to give valid effect to any divorce she must receive the bill of divorce *(get)* herself. Her father is no longer authorized to contract another marriage for her, even if she has not reached her majority (Sh. Ar., EH 37:3). But, being a minor, she is prohibited by biblical law from contracting a marriage by herself in the same way as if she were an orphan (Sh. Ar., EH 155:1). Thus, a *ketannah* who has become a widow or divorced is regarded as an "orphan in her father's lifetime" (Yev. 109a). However, because of the fear that nobody would take care of her or that she might be treated licentiously, a rabbinical *takkanah* permitted her – provided she understood the meaning and implications of marriage – to contract another marriage, either by herself, or, with her consent, through her mother or brothers (Yev. 107b; 112b and Rashi; Kid. 44b and Rashi; Maim., Ishut, 11:6; Sh. Ar., EH 155:1,2). According to one opinion, her father is also empowered by this *takkanah* to contract another marriage for his daughter, with her consent, although he is no longer competent to do so under biblical law (commentaries to Sh. Ar., *ibid.*).

Me'un (Declaration of "Refusal" or Protest). Since, according to biblical law, a marriage by a *ketannah* has no validity but is based only on a rabbinical *takkanah,* a formal divorce is not required if the girl subsequently refuses to live with her husband (see Divorce). Such refusal can be expressed by an informal declaration before the court (and, in retrospect, it is sufficient if the declaration was made before two witnesses) – not necessarily in her husband's presence – to the effect that she no longer wishes to live with her husband. If she made no such declaration and she is subsequently widowed, she may make a similar declaration with regard to her *levir* (see Levirate Marriage). This declaration is called *me'un* and the girl making it is called *mema'enet* – meaning that she refuses to continue to be the wife or levirate widow of the man she married, on the strength of which she is granted a bill of divorce by *me'un,* i.e., a certification of her "refusal" (Yev. 107b and 108a; Sh. Ar., EH 155:1, 3,4,5,7). The effect of *me'un* is not divorce, i.e., dissolution of the marriage thenceforward, but annulment of the marriage *ab initio,* as if it had never taken place. Accordingly, *me'un* does not have the legal consequences of divorce and, thus, among other things, the relatives of one party are not the prohibited kin of the other party; nor is she prohibited to a kohen; and if, after *me'un,* she contracts a second marriage which is subsequently dissolved, she may thereafter remarry her first "husband." Furthermore, she does not have to wait 90 days after *me'un* before remarrying (Yev. 34b, EH 155:10; and see Prohibited Marriages).

The marriage of a female minor, as mentioned above, is not effective unless she understands the implications of the marriage and consents thereto. In the absence of either of these conditions at the time of the marriage, therefore, even *me'un* is not required to annul the "marriage" (Sh. Ar., EH 155:1). On the other hand, she is entitled to declare her "refusal" as long as she is a *ketannah*, i.e., until the age of 12 years and a day (provided she showed no signs of puberty and had not had sexual intercourse with her husband). Her failure to do so until then is regarded as a form of consent, as an adult, to the marriage – which is thereafter binding on her and can only be dissolved by divorce or the death of her husband (Nid. 52a, Sh. Ar., EH 155:12, 19, 20, 21).

In the State of Israel. Steps have been taken by both the legislature (Knesset) and the chief rabbinate to prevent child marriages. By a *takkanah* adopted by the National Rabbinical Conference held in Jerusalem in 1950, a man is forbidden to contract a marriage with a girl under the age of 16, nor may her father give her in marriage (see Schereschewsky, bibl. pp. 431f.). However, this prohibition does not nullify a marriage that has nonetheless been celebrated in defiance of it, since in Jewish law such a marriage may be valid. Under the Marriage Age Law, 5710-1950, as amended in 5720-1960, it is an offense punishable by imprisonment or fine or both for any person to marry a girl under the age of 17 or to celebrate or to assist in the celebration of such a marriage in any capacity (e.g., as rabbi or cantor) or for a father, guardian, or relative to give the girl away in marriage. However, the district courts have jurisdiction to permit the marriage of a girl under the prescribed age in two cases: (1) regardless of her age, her marriage may be permitted to a man by whom she has had a child or is already pregnant; and (2) if in the discretion of the court thre are special circumstances which justify such permission being granted, provided in this case that the girl is not under 16.

There is no minimum age for marriage in the case of males. The law provides that the celebration of a marriage in contravention of the law is grounds for the dissolution or annulment of the marriage in any legal manner – in accordance with the law applicable to matters of personal status with reference to the parties concerned. The law applicable in the case of Jews (citizens and residents of Israel) is Jewish law (Rabbinical Courts Jurisdiction (Marriage and Divorce) Law, 5713-1953 – sections 1,2). Thus, if a marriage is valid according to the law governing the personal status of the parties, the mere fact that the marriage was celebrated in breach of the state law cited is not, of itself, grounds for divorce or annulment – if such a course would not be justified under the personal status law.

Generally speaking, child marriages do not occur in Israel – although there have been cases, among immigrants, of child marriages contracted in their countries of origin, notably in Yemen. Such cases have been the subject of discussion in proceedings before the rabbinical courts (see PDR vol. 1, p. 33ff.; vol 3, p. 3; vol. 4, p. 244ff.).

Bibliography: Gulak, Oẓar, 88f.; ET, 1 (1951³), 5f., 344; 3 (1951), 159; 5 (1953), 138f.; 12 (1967), 51; B. Schereschewsky, *Dinei Mishpaḥah* (1967²), 44-51, 431f.; M. Elon, in: ILR, 4 (1969), 115f; idem, *Ha-Mishpat Ha-Ivri* (1973), II, 416, 524, 675, 688.

Ben-Zion Schereschewsky

BIGAMY AND POLYGAMY. In Jewish law the concept of bigamy (or polygamy) can involve either (1) a married woman *(eshet ish)* purporting to contract a second marriage to another man (or to other men) during the subsistence of her first marriage; or (2) a married man contracting marriages to other women during the subsistence of his first marriage. These two aspects must be considered separately.

(1) Relating to Women. The general principle is that "a woman cannot be the wife of two [men]" (Kid. 7a and Rashi). In relation to a wife the term *kiddushin* implies her exclusive dedication to her husband. There can therefore be no *kiddushin* between her and another man while the first *kiddushin* subsists, and a purported marriage to another man is thus totally invalid. Nevertheless, such a bigamous "marriage" does incur severe legal consequences – primarily because of the law that sexual intercourse between a married woman and a man other than her husband (i.e., adultery) results in her subsequently being prohibited to both men forever and she then requires a *get* ("divorce") from both of them (see Divorce, Adultery). She requires a divorce from her husband, *mi-de-Oraita* ("according to biblical law"), because, although her adultery renders her prohibited to him, her legal marriage to him continues to subsist. To resolve this paradox she needs a *get.* She also requires a divorce from her adulterous "husband," *mi-de-Rabbanan* ("according to rabbinical enactment") – even though her marriage to him is invalid – so that people, ignorant of the true facts and perhaps under the impression that her second "marriage" was a valid one, should not be misled into thinking that she is free of him without a proper divorce (Yev. 88b and Rashi; Maim. Yad, Gerushin 10:5; Sh. Ar., EH 17:56).

Notwithstanding her divorce by both men, on the death of either of them she continues prohibited to the survivor forever (Sot. 27b; Yev. 87b and 88b; Yad, Gerushin, 10:4–5; Sh. Ar., EH 17:56). The aforementioned consequences result whether the bigamous "marriage" was intentional or inadvertent; e.g., if the woman was incorrectly informed by two witnesses of her legal husband's death (Yev. 87b; Yad, Gerushin 10:4 and Sh. Ar., EH 17:56). If, in spite of the said prohibitions, she does subsequently contract a later marriage with either of the two men, such a later marriage is a prohibited one (see Marriage, Prohibited[1]) and must be dissolved (Maim. Yad, Gerushin 10:4). Further legal consequences of a woman's bigamous "marriage" are that her children of the second, adulterous, union are classed

1. page 361.

as *mamzerim* according to biblical law and also that her financial rights are affected (Yev. 87b).

(2) Relating to Men. The law is different in the case of a married man who takes a second wife while still married. According to Jewish law this second marriage (and any others) is valid and can therefore only be dissolved by death or divorce (Yev. 65a; *Piskei ha-Rosh, ibid.*, 17; Yad, Ishut, 14:3; Sh. Ar., EH 1:9; 76:7). Permitted according to biblical law, polygamy was practiced throughout the talmudic period and thereafter until the tenth century (*Piskei ha-Rosh* to Yev. 65a; Sh. Ar., EH 1:9). Already in amoraic times, however, the practice was frowned upon by the sages, who prescribed that polygamy was permissible only if the husband was capable of properly fulfilling his marital duties toward each of his wives (see Marriage). The opinion was also expressed that if a man takes a second wife, he must divorce his first wife, if the latter so demands, and pay her *ketubbah* (Yev. 65a; Alfasi, *Piskei ha-Rosh,* and Sh. Ar., EH 1:9). Similarly, according to talmudic law, a man may not take a second wife if he has specifically undertaken to his first wife, e.g., in the *ketubbah,* not to do so (Sh. Ar., EH 76:8). Taking a second wife is also forbidden wherever monogamy is the local custom since such custom is deemed an implied condition of the marriage, it being presumed that the wife only wishes to marry in accordance with local custom (Sh. Ar., EH 1:9, *Beit Shemu'el,* n. 20, *Ḥelkat Meḥokek,* n. 15; 76:8). Generally, the husband can only be released from this restriction with his wife's consent (Sh. Ar., EH 1:9 and commentaries, *Darkhei Moshe,* EH 1, n. 8.).

Ḥerem de-Rabbenu Gershom. Substance of the Ban. In the course of time and for varying reasons (*Oẓar ha-Posekim,* EH 1:10, n. 61:2), it became apparent that there was a need for the enactment of a general prohibition against polygamy, independent of the husband's undertaking to this effect. Accordingly, relying on the principle of endeavoring to prevent matrimonial strife (which principle had already been well developed in talmudic law) Rabbenu Gershom b. Judah and his court enacted the *takkanah* prohibiting a man from marrying an additional wife unless specifically permitted to do so on special grounds by at least 100 rabbis from three "countries" (i.e., districts; see below). This *takkanah,* known as the *Ḥerem de-Rabbenu Gershom,* also prohibited a husband from divorcing his wife against her will. Various versions of the *takkanah* exist (*Oẓar ha-Posekim,* EH 1:10, n. 61:1) and, indeed, scholars have even questioned the historical accuracy of ascribing its authorship to Rabbenu Gershom. This, however, does not in any way affect its validity. See Elon, *Ha-Mishpat Ha-Ivri,* II, p. 633ff.

Since the prohibition against polygamy is derived from this *takkanah* and not from any undertaking given by the husband to his wife, she is not competent to agree to a waiver of its application, lest she be subjected to undue influence by her husband (Sh. Ar., EH 1:10; *Oẓar ha-Posekim,* EH 1:10 n. 61:5). Nevertheless, if the husband does enter into a further marriage it will be considered legally valid (Tur, EH 44, *Darkhei Moshe* n. 1; Sh. Ar., EH 44, *Beit Shemu'el* n. 11), but since it is a prohibited marriage, the first wife can require the court to compel the husband to divorce the other woman. Since the first wife cannot be obliged to live with a *ẓarah* ("rival"), she may also ask that the court order (but not compel) the husband to give her (i.e., the first wife) a divorce (Sh. Ar., EH 154, *Pitḥei Teshuvah,* 5; PDR vol. 7, pp. 65–74, 201–6). The husband continues to be liable to maintain his wife until he complies with the court's order – even though they are living apart – because as long as he refuses to divorce her he is preventing her from remarrying and thus being supported by another husband (*Keneset ha-Gedolah,* EH 1, Tur 16–17; PDR vol. 7 p. 74). However, if the first wife and the husband agree on a divorce and this is carried out, he is then released from his obligation to divorce his second wife, although his marriage to her in the first place was in defiance of the prohibition (Sh. Ar., *Pitḥei Teshuvah,* 5; *Oẓar ha-Posekim,* EH 1:10 n. 80:1 and 2).

Applicability of the Ḥerem as to Time and Place. Many authorities were of the opinion that the validity of the *ḥerem* was, from its inception, restricted as to both time and place. Thus, it is stated: "He [Rabbenu Gershom] only imposed the ban until the end of the fifth millennium," i.e., until the year 1240 (Sh. Ar., EH 1:10); others, however, were of the opinion that no time limit was placed on its application. At any rate, even according to the first opinion the *ḥerem* remained in force after 1240, since later generations accepted it as a binding *takkanah.* Accordingly, the *ḥerem,* wherever it was accepted (see below), now has the force of law for all time (Resp. Rosh 43:8; Sh. Ar., EH 1:10; *Arukh ha-Shulḥan,* EH 1:23; *Oẓar ha-Posekim,* EH 1:10, n. 76). In modern times it is customary, in some communities, to insert in the *ketubbah* a clause against the husband's taking an additional wife "in accordance with the *takkanah* of Rabbenu Gershom . . . ." However, the prohibition is binding on the husband, even though omitted from the *ketubbah,* as such omission is regarded as a "scribal error" (*Keneset ha-Gedolah,* EH 1, Tur 17; *Arukh ha-Shulḥan,* EH 1:23).

The *ḥerem* did not extend to those countries where it was apparent that the *takkanah* had never been accepted (Sh. Ar., EH 1:10). In a country where the acceptance of the *takkanah* is in doubt, however, its provisions must be observed (*Arukh ha-Shulḥan,* EH 1:23). In general it can be said that the *ḥerem* has been accepted as binding among Ashkenazi communities, but not among the Sephardi and most of the Oriental communities. This is apparently because in those countries where Ashkenazim formed the main part of the Jewish community, as in Europe, America, or Australia where European Jews migrated, polygamy was also forbidden by the dominant religion, Christianity, and therefore by the secular law. This was not the case in Oriental countries, as in Yemem, Iraq, and North Africa, polygamy being permitted in Islam (*Arukh ha-Shulḥan* and *Oẓar ha-Posekim,* loc. cit.). Thus, Maimonides, who was a Sephardi, makes no reference at all to the *ḥerem.* In practice, therefore, to prohibit polygamy Oriental communities would customarily insert an express provision in the *ketubbah,* whereby the husband was precluded from taking an additional wife except with the consent of his first wife or with the permission of the *bet din.* As this provision was a condition of the marriage, any breach thereof entitled the wife to demand either that her husband complied with the provision, i.e., by divorcing the second wife, or that she be granted a divorce with payment of her *ketubbah* (*Sedei Ḥemed,* Asefat Dinim, Ishut 2; *Keneset ha-Gedolah,* EH 1, *Beit Yosef* 13, 16; *Oẓar ha-Posekim,* 1:10, n. 80:8; PDR 7:65).

People who move from a country where the *ḥerem* is binding to a country where it is not, or vice versa, are subject to the following rules: (1) the ban adheres to the individual, i.e., it accompanies him from place to place and he always remains subject to it (*Arukh ha-Shulḥan,* loc. cit.; *Oẓar ha-Posekim,* EH 1:10, n. 75:1; Sh. Ar., EH 1); (2) local custom is followed, so that if the *ḥerem* applies to a particular country it is binding on everyone, irrespective of their country of origin (*Arukh ha-Shulḥan, ibid.; Oẓar ha-Posekim, ibid.* and n. 75:3; *Keneset ha-Gedolah,* EH 1, *Beit Yosef,* 22). Both these rules are strictly applied with the intent of extending the operation of the *ḥerem* as widely as possible. On the other hand, if a man legally married two wives in a country where this was permitted, he is not obliged to divorce either of them on arriving in another country where the *ḥerem* is in force, as the law is only infringed by his taking an additional wife and not when a man already has two *(Arukh ha-Shulḥan, ibid.)*.

Release from the Prohibition. The object of prohibiting bigamy is to prevent a man from marrying a second wife as long as he is not legally entitled to dissolve his first marriage. Thus, in order to avoid any circumvention of the prohibition, the *ḥerem* also generally prohibits divorce against the will of the wife. This double prohibition may, however, result in the husband being unjustifiably fettered in circumstances where he would not otherwise be required by law to maintain his ties with his wife – and yet may not divorce her against her will. This can, therefore, be obviated by the availability of a *hetter* ("release") from the *ḥerem* against bigamy, which is granted by the *bet din* in the appropriate circumstances. This *hetter* does not mean that the first wife is divorced, but that the husband is granted exceptional permission to contract an additional marriage. Naturally, such a step is only taken if the court, after a full investigation of the relevant facts, is satisfied that a release is legally justified. Thus, for example, a release would be granted in a case where a wife becomes insane. Her husband cannot, therefore, maintain normal married life with her, a fact which would ordinarily entitle him to divorce her; this he cannot do because of her legal incapacity to consent. However, as the first marriage must continue to subsist, the husband remains liable to support his wife – including medical costs – but he is permitted by the court to take an additional wife (Baḥ, EH 119; Sh. Ar., EH 1, *Beit Shemu'el* n. 23 and 119, n. 6; *Ḥelkat Meḥokek,* 119, n. 10–12; *Oẓar ha-Posekim,* EH 1:10 n. 72:19). Should the first wife subsequently recover her sanity she cannot demand that her husband divorce his second wife, as he married her in accordance with the law. On the contrary, the husband would be entitled – and even obliged – to divorce his first wife, so as not to remain with two wives, and if she refuses to accept his *get* he would be free from any further marital obligations towards her, save for the payment of her *ketubbah* (Sh. Ar., EH 1; *Beit Shemu'el, ibid.; Oẓar ha-Posekim,* EH 1:10, n. 72:17–18; PDR 3:271). However, the *hetter* would be revoked if the first wife recovered her mental capacity before the second marriage took place (Sh. Ar., EH 1, *Pitḥei Teshuvah,* 16, concl.; *Oẓar ha-Posekim,* EH 1:10 n. 72:14).

On the strength of the aforementioned rule, a release from the *ḥerem* may also be obtained by a man whose wife refuses to accept a *get* from him, despite the court's order that she does so, e.g., in the case of her adultery or where the marriage is a prohibited one (Sh. Ar., EH 1:10; *Ḥelkat Meḥokek, ibid.,* 16; *Oẓar ha-Posekim,* EH 1:10, n. 63:7). Some authorities are of the opinion that in the event of the wife's adultery the husband only requires a *hetter* from a regular court and not from 100 rabbis, since the *ḥerem* was not meant for such a case (*Oẓar ha-Posekim,* EH 1:10; n. 73:2). A *hetter* would be justified where a wife who has had no children during a marriage which has subsisted for at least ten years – a fact which entitles the husband to divorce her – refuses to accept the *get* and thus prevents her husband from remarrying and fulfilling the *mitzvah* to "be fruitful and multiply." In such a case the husband is obliged to take another wife to fulfill the *mitzvah* and so he would be entitled to the *hetter* (Sh. Ar., EH 1:10; *Oẓar ha-Posekim,* EH 1:10 n. 68; *Arukh ha-Shulḥan,* EH 1:25).

As has already been stated, in Oriental communities for a husband to take a second wife requires either his first wife's consent or the court's permission. The wife is required to give her consent before a regular court (not 100 rabbis) and the court will permit the second marriage only if satisfied, after a thorough investigation of the facts, that the wife has consented wholeheartedly, without anger or under undue influence (*Oẓar ha-Posekim,* EH 1:10, n. 61:5, subsec. 3; *Sedei Ḥemed,* Asefat Dinim, Ishut 2). Without her consent, the court will generally only grant a release to the husband in such cases where it would do so were the *ḥerem* to apply *(Sedei Ḥemed; Oẓar ha-Posekim, ibid.)*, since it is presumed that the husband's undertaking in the *ketubbah* is given on the understanding that no circumstances shall exist which, if the *ḥerem* were to apply, would warrant his release from the prohibition (*Sedei Ḥemed, ibid.; Oẓar ha-Posekim,* EH 1:10 n. 72:9).

Procedure for Granting the Hetter. After the court has decided that a release from the *ḥerem* should be granted, the matter is referred to 100 rabbis of three "countries" (*Oẓar ha-Posekim,* EH 1:10, n. 61:9) for approval and, if so approved, the *hetter* takes effect. As a preliminary, the husband is required to deposit with the court a *get* for his first wife, together with an irrevocable authority for the court to have the *get* delivered to his first wife as soon as she is able and willing to receive it from an agent appointed by the husband at the request of the court. However, in the case where the *hetter* is given because of the first wife's insanity, it is customary to give her a new *get* when she recovers, rather than the one previously deposited with the court, as some doubt could be cast on the latter's validity, since it was the wife's insanity that made it impossible to deliver the *get* to her originally and there may therefore possibly be other legal objections to its validity. The deposited *get* is usually only delivered to her if she is in danger of becoming a deserted wife (see *Agunah; Arukh ha-Shulḥan,* EH 1:26; *Oẓar ha-Posekim,* EH 1:10, n. 72:30–31). Furthermore, the husband is also generally required to deposit with the court the amount of the wife's *ketubbah* in cash or provide adequate security (Baḥ, EH 119; Sh. Ar., EH 1, *Beit Shemu'el* n. 23; *Arukh ha-Shulḥan,* EH 1:25; *Oẓar ha-Posekim,* 1:10, n. 72:23–24). Some authorities are of the opinion that the husband must also deposit with the court, or adequately secure in like manner, such sum as the court may determine to cover the wife's maintenance and medical expenses (*Oẓar ha-Posekim,* EH 1:10, n. 72:29).

In the State of Israel. At a national rabbinic conference called in 1950 by the chief rabbis of Israel, an enactment was passed making monogamy (apart from the above-mentioned permissions) binding upon all Jews irrespective of their communal affiliations. This *takkanah,* however, does not render a second marriage invalid according to biblical law, and therefore, if such a marriage does take place, it can be dissolved only by divorce. The criminal law of the state, however, renders it an offense on pain of imprisonment for a married person to contract another marriage (Penal Law Amendment (Bigamy) Law, 5719-1959). Nevertheless, for Jewish citizens no offense is committed if permission to marry a second wife was given by a final judgment of a rabbinical court and approved by the two chief rabbis of Israel. The latter's approval is accepted as conclusive proof that the permission was given according to the law. Special provisions relating to the grant of this permission are laid down in the *Takkanot ha-Diyyun be-Vattei ha-Din ha-Rabbaniyyim be-Yisrael,* 5720–1960.

Bibliography: L. Loew, in: *Ben Chananja,* 3 (1860), 317–29, 529–39, 657–67; 4 (1861), 111–5, 257–9, 271–3 (reprinted in his *Gesammelte Schriften,* 3 (1893), 33–86); F. Rosenthal, in: *Jubelschrift . . . Hildesheimer* (1890), 37–53; Finkelstein, Middle Ages, 111–26, 205–15; A. H. Freimann, *Seder Kiddushin ve-Nissu'in* (1945), passim; M. Elon, in: *Hed ha-Mishpat* (1957), 233–5; S. Lowy, in: JJS, 9 (1958), 115–38; I. Glasner, in: *Ha-Peraklit,* 16 (1960), 274–80; Z. W. Falk, *Nissu'in ve-Gerushin . . .* (1961), passim; P. Tishbi, in: *Tarbiz,* 34 (1964/65), 49–55; S. Eidelberg, *ibid.,* 287f.; I. Schepansky, in: *Hadorom,* 22 (1965), 103–20; I. Ta-Shema, in: *Tarbiz,* 35 (1965/66), 193;

E. Berkovitz, *Tenai be-Nissu'in u-ve-Get* (1966), passim; B. Schereschewsky, *Dinei Mishpaḥah* (1967[2]), 61–80; M. Elon, *Ḥakikah Datit* (1968), 34–36, 104–16, 122–7; idem, *Ha-Mishpat Ha-Ivri* (1973), II, 473, 554ff., 633ff., 653, 655, 675.

Ben-Zion Schereschewsky

CIVIL MARRIAGE, a marriage ceremony between Jews, celebrated in accordance with the secular, and not the Jewish law.

The Problem in Jewish Law. Since in Jewish law a woman is not considered a wife (*eshet ish*), unless she has been married "properly," i.e., in one of the ways recognized by Jewish law (Yad, Ishut 1:3 Sh. Ar., EH 26:1), any marriage celebrated according to the secular law and not intended to be in accordance with the "Law of Moses and Israel" should prima facie not be a "proper" one in the above-mentioned sense. The authorities nevertheless discuss the question whether, according to Jewish law, the consequences of marriage may apply to a civil marriage. This question arises from the fact that the parties are living together with the intention to live as husband and wife and not licentiously, and also from the halakhic presumption – the application whereof is subject to differences of opinions (see below) – that "a Jew does not live licentiously when he is able to live according to the *mitzvah*" (Yad, Ishut 7:23). Therefore, in the absence of evidence to the contrary, a Jewish couple living together as husband and wife are presumed to be doing so for the purpose of marriage to be constituted by their intercourse (*kiddushei bi'ah* – see Marriage[1]), and such a marriage is to be regarded valid when there is no other impediment (Git. 81b; Ket. 73a; Yad, loc. cit. and Gerushin 10:17, 19; Sh. Ar., EH 149:1, 2). The question accordingly is whether a couple married in a civil ceremony only and living together with the intention to live as husband and wife, and regarded as such by the public, are to be considered as being married to each other according to *halakhah* by way of *kiddushei bi'ah,* which would necessitate a *get* (divorce in accordance with law) if they should want to marry other parties. The civil (or un-Jewish) ceremony may indicate that the parties do not want to be married according to Jewish law and the situation would thus be worse than if no ceremony at all had taken place.

Difference of Opinions of the Posekim. The above question, in all its implications, first arose at the end of the 15th century with regard to the *anusim* of the expulsion from Spain (1492) who were prevented from openly practicing the Jewish faith and thus compelled to marry not in accordance with the "Law of Moses and Israel" but in accordance with the customs of the Catholic Church only. The opinions of the *posekim* were divided on the matter and have remained unreconciled.

One view was that on the basis of *halakhah* no significance is to be attached to non-Jewish marriages and that cohabitation by virtue thereof does not amount to *kiddushei bi'ah,* inasmuch as the latter means sexual relations between the parties for the sake of *kiddushin,* in this manner to create between themselves the legal tie of husband and wife according to Jewish law – whereas cohabitation between the parties by virtue of a civil marriage takes place not in order to thereby establish the marriage but rather on the basis of a marriage already celebrated. Moreover, their very marriage in a civil ceremony is an indication that they specifically desire to have the marital status not in accordance with the Law of Moses and Israel but in accordance with secular law. Hence, according to this view, a woman married in a civil ceremony could at most be considered a concubine and therefore without the legal status in relation to the man which emanates from marriage according to the Law of Moses and Israel: "Having started with marriage in accordance with the laws of the gentiles, they are to be considered as if having declared explicitly their intention not to be married in accordance with the law of Moses and Israel but in the ways of the gentiles who are not subject to *gittin* and *kiddushin* and, if so, she is not as a wife to him but like a concubine without *ketubbah* and *kiddushin*" (Resp. Ribash nos. 5 and 6; see also *Beit Yosef,* EH 149 (concl.); Sh. Ar., EH 33:1; 149:6).

According to this view, the legal result of such cohabitation cannot be more favorable than if the man, even for the purpose of *kiddushin* in accordance with law, recites toward the woman words which, according to the *halakhah,* are incapable of bringing about their marriage; in a civil marriage, moreover, the words he recites not only are not intended for *kiddushin* according to the Law of Moses and of Israel but have as their express object marriage in accordance with the secular law (Resp. Ridbaz, cited in Freimann, *Seder Kiddushin . . .,* 365). Thus there is also no room for applying here the presumption against "licentious living" (see above), since that presumption only applies to "good" Jews *(kesherim)* – i.e., not to the licentious, such as those who willingly deny the Jewish faith (Resp. Ribash no. 6; see also Yad, Gerushin 10:19, *Maggid Mishneh* thereto and to Naḥalot 4:6; Tur, EH 149; Sh. Ar., EH 149:5; Resp. Radbaz pt. 1 no. 351; *Kol Mevasser,* pt. 1, no. 22). According to this opinion a civil marriage creates no rights or change of status, neither concerning family law nor the law of inheritance, and thus there is no need for divorce or for prior permission in order to enable the parties to marry other persons. This view rejects also the legal reasoning which would require the said parties – in order to obtain permission to remarry – to obtain a *get mi-ḥumra* (i.e., out of strictness), lest the public, being unaware of the true position and considering them to be husband and wife in accordance with Jewish law, conclude that any such husband and wife could each contract a further marriage with another party without first having been divorced from each other; on the contrary, the requirement of a *get mi-ḥumra* may create the mistaken impression that a civil marriage creates a matrimonial tie – since a *get* is only possible in respect of an existing marriage – and therefore even a *get mi-ḥumra* is to be refrained from. Accordingly, the problem of an *agunah* can also not arise in respect of a woman married in a civil ceremony only (see Freimann, op. cit., and sources there quoted, pp. 358–60, 364; *Mishpetei Uzi'el,* EH no. 57).

According to another opinion, upholding the requirement of *get mi-ḥumra* for parties married in a civil ceremony only, as a precondition to the marriage of either of them to another party in accordance with Jewish law, emphasizes the danger that the public be led astray and believe that husband and wife, although properly married, are permitted to contract a marriage with others before being divorced from each other (see Freimann, op. cit., 367, 370–5). This view is supported in various additional ways. Some scholars hold that a civil marriage may, possibly, be regarded as a form of *kiddushei shetar* (marriage by deed – see Marriage[1]), since in connection with civil marriage the parties thereto generally sign in a governmental marriage register, and on the strength of such marriage take upon themselves, by virtue of law, certain obligations resembling those imposed on husband and wife married in accordance with Jewish law (Freimann, 370–1). Nevertheless, the first opinion sees a fundamental difference between a marriage by *shetar* and the said signing of the register, to wit: in the former case the man delivers the *shetar* to the woman for the purpose of thereby bringing about the marriage – i.e., the delivery of the *shetar* concurrently with his recital of the words "Behold, you are consecrated unto me by this *shetar* according to the Law of Moses and of Israel," creates the matrimonial status between the parties – whereas

1. page 356; 2. page 356.

signing the register in connection with civil marriage is no more than proof that their marriage has already taken place.

Another reason advanced in upholding the requirement of *get mi-ḥumra* in the circumstances outlined above is that cohabitation following upon a civil marriage may possibly be seen as having an element of *kiddushei bi'ah,* since the parties live together not for the purpose of prostitution but because they regard themselves as married (although only by virtue of civil marriage) and are so regarded by the public. According to this opinion to such parties the above-mentioned presumption against licentious living may possibly be applied (*Ḥelkat Meḥokek* EH 26, n. 3; and see Freimann, 360). Other *posekim* see an element of *kiddushei kesef* ("marriage by money" – see Marriage[1]) in a civil marriage, at all events when celebrated in countries where the groom, in accordance with local custom, hands a wedding ring to his bride even though he does so in pursuance of the civil marriage and not for the sake of *kiddushin* in terms of Jewish law (see Freimann, 371ff.).

The Halakhah in Practice. The above dispute stems essentially from the fact that on the one hand a civil marriage is a prima facie indication by the parties of their disinterest in marriage according to Jewish law; yet on the other hand, the surrounding circumstances may sometimes leave room for doubt as to whether the requirements of a Jewish marriage had not been fulfilled nevertheless. Hence the legal status of the parties requires determination according to the circumstances of each case, with particular regard to the legal system, social background, and degree of freedom pertaining to the celebration of marriages prevailing in the country concerned. In countries with no restriction on the celebration of marriages in accordance with Jewish law, whether recognized – or allowed – by the state without or only after a civil marriage, the absence of the Jewish ceremony can be considered a clear expression of the parties' intention to be married only in accordance with the secular law, and therefore they are not to be considered married under Jewish law. Consequently neither Jewish family law or law of inheritance will be of application to the parties, nor any branch of Jewish law the operation whereof is dependent upon the existence of a valid Jewish marriage between them. In contrast, however, in countries where the celebration of a Jewish marriage is likely to bring the parties into danger – as may be the case in some communist states – and it can be assumed that, but for the danger, the parties would have celebrated their marriage according to Jewish law, there may be room for assuming by virtue of the presumption against "licentious living" (see above), that a valid *kiddushin* has taken place between them. In this event the parties will require a *get mi-ḥumra* before either is permitted to enter into another marriage (*Terumat ha-Deshen* no. 209; Sh. Ar., EH 26:1 and Rema, *Ḥelkat Meḥokek,* n. 3; *Mishpetei Uzi'el,* EH no. 57 and cf. nos. 54–57). It follows that even in such countries no element of *kiddushin* is recognized as attaching to the relationship between parties contracting a civil marriage if they are non-observant Jews who completely deny Jewish law (*Kol Mevasser,* pt. 1, no. 22).

It is accepted, however, that in cases where there would be danger of the woman becoming an *agunah,* the circumstances that gave rise to the need of a *get mi-ḥumra* will not be considered sufficient ground to bar her from remarrying and she will be granted permission to do without a *get* (*Kol Mevasser,* pt. 1, no. 22; *Melammed Leho'il,* EH 20). Either party to a civil marriage will be entitled from the start to demand that the *bet din* oblige the other party to grant or accept a *get* because the doubt arising from such marriage entails a risk, as abovementioned, for the claimant and there is no justification for the defending party to be permitted to prolong this situation of risk and all it entails for the claimant (*Keneset Gedolah,* EH 1, *Beit Yosef* 24; PDR 3:369, 373–80).

The claim by a wife for maintenance cannot be entertained against her husband on the strength of their civil marriage alone, since such a claim must be founded on a marriage contracted in accordance with Jewish law, while she cannot do any more than prove facts giving rise to a doubt only of the existence of *kiddushin,* a doubt which does not suffice to entitle the plaintiff to obtain a monetary judgment against the defendant (PDR 3:378f.; a recent decision of a local rabbinical court in Israel may be noted, however, in which it was held, in the case of a Jewish couple seeking a divorce after being married in 1942 in a civil ceremony in Russia that, on the basis of an agreement to be assumed, their common property was to be divided in accordance with the *lex loci celebrationis* with reference to the division of property in such circumstances; PDR, 5:124–8, and see Conflict of Laws[2]).

The Approach of the Courts in the State of Israel. Marriage and divorce in Israel between Jews can only take place in accordance with Jewish Law (sec. 2 of the "Rabbinical Courts Jurisdiction (Marriage and Divorce) Law, 5713–1953") and, thus, no civil marriage can be contracted in Israel between Jews. In the case of a Jewish couple married abroad in a civil ceremony, the civil courts – unlike the rabbinical courts – in dealing with matters such as maintenance and succession, decide in accordance with the principles of private international law and recognize the validity of a civil marriage for the aforesaid purposes, in accordance with the *lex loci celebrationis.*

Bibliography: A. Ch. Freimann, *Seder Kiddushin ve-Nissu'in . . .* (1945), 346–84; A. A. Rudner, *Mishpetei Ishut* (1949), 132–42; E. L. Globus, in: *Ha-Peraklit,* 8 (1951/52), 52–62, 344–51; Z. Domb, in: *No'am,* 2 (1959), 235–40; Ch. S. Harlap, *ibid.,* 241–5; M. Schreibmann, *ibid.,* 246f.; M. Silberg, *Ha-Ma'amad ha-Ishi be-Yisrael* (1965[4]), 222–51; B. Schereschewsky, *Dinei Mishpaḥah* (1967[2]), 83–95; M. Elon, *Ḥakikah Datit* (1968), 77–79, 169–72.

Ben-Zion Schereschewsky

CONCUBINE. A concubine may be defined as a woman dedicating herself to a particular man, with whom she cohabits without *kiddushin* (see Marriage) or *ketubbah.* "What is the difference between wives and concubines? R. Judah said in the name of Rav: Wives have *ketubbah* and *kiddushin,* concubines have neither" (Sanh. 21a; Maim. Yad, Melakhim 4:4; *Leḥem Mishneh* and Radbaz, ad loc.). Not all the scholars adopt this reading, however, and Rashi, for instance, comments: "wives with *kiddushin* and ketubbah, concubines with *kiddushin* but without *ketubbah*" (Comm. to Gen. 25:6; see also Comm. Hagra, EH 26, n. 7). This latter reading is apparently that of the Jerusalem Talmud too (TJ, Ket. 5:2, 29d and Hagra, *ibid.;* but see *Mareh ha-Panim* thereto). The majority of the *posekim* accept the former reading as the correct one (Radbaz to Yad, Melakhim 4:4; *Kesef Mishneh* and *Leḥem Mishneh,* as against the *Maggid Mishneh,* to Yad, Ishut, 1:4; Radbaz, Resp., vol. 4, no. 225; vol. 7, no. 33; Naḥmanides, commentary to Gen. 19:8; 25:6; Ralbag to Judg. 19:1; Resp. Rashba, vol. 4. no. 314). Hence a concubine is to be distinguished both, on the one hand from a married woman, i.e., by *ḥuppah* ("marriage ceremony"), *kiddushin,* and *ketubbah,* and on the other from a woman who does not dedicate herself to one particular man exclusively, but who prostitutes herself, i.e., the harlot (*Hassagot Rabad* to Ishut 1:4 and see also Rema to EH 26:1).

The Prohibition against Concubinage. There are divided opinions in the codes on the question of whether the taking of a

1. page 356; 2. page 718.

concubine is prohibited or permitted. Some of the *posekim* are of the opinion that neither pentateuchal nor rabbinical law forbids it, if the woman observes the rules concerning the *mikveh* so that the man should not cohabit with her during her period of menstruation (Rema in the name of Rabad, EH 26:1). Others are of the opinion that although it is not legally prohibited, one should refrain from taking a concubine, and they caution against her, "lest knowledge of the permissibility encourage licentiousness and sexual relations with her at a time when she is sexually unclean" (*Sefer Teshuvot ha-Rashba ha-Meyuḥasot le-ha-Ramban,* no. 284). The majority of the *posekim,* however, are of the opinion that it is forbidden to take a concubine, although they differ as to the substantive nature of the prohibition. Some are of the opinion that taking a concubine is a transgression of a prohibition of the pentateuchal law, based on the negative command: "There shall be no harlot of the daughters of Israel" (Deut. 23:18), to be punished with lashes (Rema to EH 26:1 in the name of Maimonides; Rosh, and Tur), while others expressed the opinion that the prohibition stems from a positive command of the pentateuchal law, the Torah saying, "when a man takes a wife" (Deut. 24:1) – i.e., he should take her by way of *kiddushin.* According to another view, the prohibition is rabbinical law only. (On the different views and their reasons, see *Ozar ha-Posekim,* EH 26:3–8.) All the foregoing applies only to a woman who is unmarried; a married woman is by pentateuchal law at all times prohibited to have sexual relations with any man but her husband (*issur eshet ish;* see Marriage, Prohibited; Bigamy; Marriage).

Since more recent times it is unanimously accepted that the taking of a concubine is prohibited: "At the present time a woman is permitted to no man except through *kiddushin, ḥuppah, sheva berakhot,* and *ketubbah*" (Radbaz, Resp., vol. 4, no. 225; vol. 7, no. 33). This applies even more in the case of a married man, in the same way as he is prohibited from taking an additional wife (see Bigamy[1]), both for the protection of his wife and because his taking a concubine – since he is aware that he must not take an additional wife – can only be for the purpose of prostituting, and this is forbidden in the opinion of all the *posekim* (Rashba, Resp., vol. 4, no. 314; *Ozar ha-Posekim,* EH 1, n. 4; 26, n. 5).

Personal Status and Pecuniary Rights of a Concubine. Inasmuch as a concubine does not acquire the personal status of a wife (*eshet ish;* Sh. Ar., EH 26:1), she has no *ketubbah;* therefore, in accordance with the rule providing that the "terms and conditions of the *ketubbah [tena'ei ketubbah]* follow the [prescribed] *ketubbah*" (Ket. 54b; Rashi *ibid.* s.v. *tena'ei ketubbah*) she does not acquire any of the wife's pecuniary rights – especially she is not entitled to maintenance – as all those rights stem from the *ketubbah.* Nor does living with a man as his concubine create a kinship as an impediment to marriage between herself and any of the man's relatives, or between the man and her relatives, as would be the case if she would be considered to be his wife (Resp. Rosh. no. 32:1; *Ozar ha-Posekim,* EH 26, n. 3). For the same reason there is no need in principle for her to obtain a *get* (see Divorce) in order to be permitted to marry any other man (*Ozar ha-Posekim,* loc. cit.; *Sefer ha-Tashbez* 3:47). However, in the opinion of some of the *posekim,* for the sake of appearances, in view of the parties having lived together, the matter should be approached stringently and the woman should not be permitted to marry another man without obtaining a prior "*get* out of stringency" *(get mi-ḥumrah)* from the man with whom she has lived; but whenever the latter's refusal to grant her the *get* is likely to entail the risk of her becoming an *agunah,* she may certainly be permitted to marry without getting such *get* (*Ozar ha-Posekim,* EH 26, n. 3). Moreover since the prohibition against concubinage is intended solely to prevent her connection with the person with whom she cohabits, this fact alone and as such does not impair the personal status of children born of the union, nor their rights of inheritance according to law (Resp. Rashba, vol. 4, no. 314).

For concubinage in the biblical period see *Encyclopaedia Judaica,* vol. 5, p. 862.

Legal Position in the State of Israel. Since the question of concubinage touches on the issue of the requirements necessary for conferring on a woman the status of a wife, the question is a matter of "marriage" – within the meaning of the Rabbinical Courts Jurisdiction (Marriage and Divorce) Law, no. 64 of 5713/1953 – and therefore in the case of Jews who are citizens of the State of Israel, governed by Jewish law (sec. 1). However, legislation enacted for the first time after the creation of the state has given recognition to the concept of the "common law wife," i.e., a woman living together with a man to whom she is not married, but is so regarded (erroneously) by the public *(yedu'ah ba-ẓibbur ke-ishto)* and in some laws the same applies, vice versa, to such a "husband" – granting her certain rights, mainly with regard to pension and tenant's protection. According to decisions of the courts, such a woman is entitled to the said rights even if she is lawfully married to another man (C. A. 384/61, in PD, 16 (1962), 102–12). As to the actual definition of the term "a woman known to the public as his wife" and the modes of proving the necessary facts, widely differing opinions have been expressed in decisions of the courts. It is generally accepted, however, that the said legislation does not entail any change in the personal status of the woman, whose position is to some extent similar to that of a concubine.

Bibliography: L. M. Epstein, in: PAAJR, 6 (1934/35), 153–88; B.-Z. Schereschewsky, *Dinei Mishpaḥah* (1967²), 92, n. 39; M. Elon, *Ḥakikah Datit* (1968), 119–54.

Ben-Zion Schereschewsky

MIXED MARRIAGE The Concept. A mixed marriage is a marriage of a non-Jew to a Jew, i.e., one born of Jewish parents, or whose mother alone was Jewish, or who has become a proselyte in accordance with Jewish law (see *Yuḥasin*). Conversion from the Jewish religion, both in the case of a Jew by birth and of a proselyte who reverts to his "evil" ways, has no halakhic significance in respect of the law on mixed marriages. For "an Israelite, even if he has sinned, is still an Israelite" (Sanh. 44a; Rashi thereto; see Apostate).

Mixed Marriages are Prohibited and Invalid. From the biblical passage (Deut. 7:3) "neither shalt thou make marriages with them: thy daughter thou shalt not give unto his son, nor his daughter shalt thou take unto thy son," the sages inferred that marriage with a non-Jew is forbidden as a negative precept by the Torah (Av. Zar. 36b; Yad, Issurei Bi'ah 12:1–2; Sh. Ar., EH 16:1). As the passage cited refers to the "seven nations" ("The Hittite, and the Girgashite, and the Amorite, and the Canaanite, and the Perizzite, and the Hivite, and the Jebusite," Deut. 7:1), according to one opinion, the prohibition applies only to intermarriage with those seven nations. Others maintain, however, that the prohibition applies to all gentiles because after the prohibition "neither shalt thou make marriages" the biblical passage continues: "For he will turn away thy son from following after Me" (Deut. 7:4), which serves "to include all who would turn [their children] away" (Av. Zar. 36b and codes). The prohibition against marrying a gentile is also explicitly stated in the period of the return to Zion: "And that we would not give our daughters unto the peoples of the land, nor take their daughters for our sons" (Neh. 10:31; see Maim, *ibid.*). It was also inferred

1. page 367.

from the passage in Deuteronomy that in a mixed marriage there is "no institution of marriage," i.e., mixed marriages are not legally valid and cause no change in personal status (Kid. 68b; Yev. 45a; and codes). Hence if the Jewish partner of such a marriage subsequently wishes to marry a Jew there is no need, according to the *halakhah,* for divorce from the previous "marriage." However, where one or even both of the parties to a marriage are apostate Jews who have married in a halakhically binding manner, neither can marry a Jew as long as the first marriage is not terminated by death or divorce, since a purported change of religion does not affect personal status (Yev. 47b; Bek. 30b; Sh. Ar., EH 44:9). Similarly if both parties (or only one of them) apostasize after a halakhically valid marriage and are then divorced by way of a civil divorce, neither party can marry a Jew until the previous marriage is terminated as above (Yad, Ishut 4:15; Rema, EH 154:1).

Mixed Marriages have no Legal Consequences. Since mixed marriages are not binding, such marriages entail no legal consequences (Yad loc. cit.). Hence, the prohibition of marriage (in respect of certain relations of the other spouse), which apply to a valid marriage, do not apply to the parties – even after the non-Jewish partner has become a proselyte (see Marriage, Prohibited). Similarly the wife has no halakhic right to be maintained by her "husband," since this right arises only if a valid marriage exists between them. For the same reason, in a mixed marriage none of the inheritance rights that flow from a valid marriage, such as the husband's right to inherit his wife's estate (see Succession), come into effect.

The State of Israel. It is impossible to contract a mixed marriage in the State of Israel, since according to section 2 of the Rabbinical Courts Jurisdiction (Marriage and Divorce) Law, 5713–1953, no marriages of Jews in Israel are valid unless contracted in accordance with the law of the Torah. However, the criminal code does not provide criminal punishment for contracting a mixed marriage in Israel. Where a mixed marriage is contracted in the Diaspora, proceedings regarding it cannot be brought directly before the Israel rabbinical courts inasmuch as such courts have jurisdiction only in the event of both parties being Jews. In 1969, however, a law was passed whereby such marriages can be dissolved at the discretion of the president of the Supreme Court. If a problem arises before the civil courts, such as a wife's claim for maintenance, the civil courts will act according to the general principles of private international law, and where such a marriage cannot be denied validity according to those principles, it will be sustained. The Succession Law, 5725–1965 provides that differences of religion do not affect rights of inheritance.

Bibliography: ET, 5 (1953), 286–93, 295–300; B. Shereshewsky, *Dinei Mishpaḥah* (1967^2), 80–87, 349–51; M. Elon, *Ḥakikah Datit* (1968), 77–79, 85–89.

Ben-Zion Schereschewsky

APOSTATE. An apostate (*mumar* or *meshumed*) is a Jew who denies the Torah and converts to another faith. In matters of his (objective) personal status, his position is governed by the rule, "An Israelite, although a sinner, is still an Israelite" (Sanh. 44a). For it is not within the power of a Jew, whether by birth or proselytization, to renounce his Jewishness (Bekh. 30b; Yev. 47b and Rashi thereto; Sh. Ar., EH 44:2, 5, 6). Nevertheless, a Jew who apostatizes of his own volition, or does so under compulsion, but does not avail himself of an opportunity to recant (see *Beit Yosef,* EH 140; Resp. Ribash 11), is considered a *rasha* who has transgressed all the injunctions of the Torah. Hence the fact of his apostasy will have a decisive bearing in all cases where a person's legal status is dependent upon his conduct. These rules form the basis of the ensuing discussion.

Marriage. A marriage, celebrated in accordance with Jewish law between two apostates or an apostate and a Jew, is valid and the parties are husband and wife according to Jewish law (Yev. 47b; Sh. Ar., EH 44:9; *Tashbeẓ* pt. 3, 47; see Mixed Marriage). Hence, neither of them can contract another marriage with a Jew until their said existing marriage is dissolved by divorce, valid under Jewish law, or death *(ibid.).* If their marriage was celebrated according to the tenets of another faith, they are not considered married in Jewish law (even if they live together as husband and wife), and consequently they do not require a divorce. Nor, in this case, is there any room for applying the presumption that a person does not have licentious sexual intercourse which is the usual basis for the assumption that the cohabitation *(bi'ah)* constituted an act of *kiddushin,* since that presumption applies only in circumstances where there is reason to assume that the parties, in cohabiting together, intended a *kiddushin* to come about thereby in accordance with Jewish law, a possibility excluded in this case in view of the apostate's denial of the Jewish faith and his contracting the marriage according to the tenets of another faith (for differing views on this point, see Resp. *Terumat ha-Deshen,* 209, 237; Resp. Ribash, 11; PDR, 7:35, 39–44 as against 54–56).

Status. A child born of an apostate mother is a Jew, regardless of the stage at which she became an apostate, and if he marries a Jewess, even if she is an apostate, the marriage is valid (Maim. Yad, Ishut, 4:15).

Divorce. Although generally divorce is considered to be to a woman's detriment, since she is deemed to prefer the married state (Yev. 118b), this factor is disregarded when one of the parties is an apostate. Since an apostate wife is suspected as transgressing all the commandments of the Torah, including adultery, she becomes prohibited to her husband (see Adultery); and, as a married woman, prohibited to any other man. It can therefore be only to her benefit to be released from the bonds of marriage. Similarly, when the husband becomes an apostate: his wife will prefer a divorce to living with an apostate (Rema, Sh. Ar., EH 140:5; 154:1; Resp. Rashba 1:1162). Hence, even though, generally, a divorce does not take effect until the *get* ("bill of divorcement") has been delivered to the wife personally, or to an agent appointed by her for this purpose, in accordance with the halakhic rule that "one cannot act to a person's disadvantage without his knowledge or consent" (lit., "in his absence"; Yev. 118b), in this case, however, once the *get* reaches the hands of the agent, appointed not by the wife, but by the court or by her husband, it takes immediate effect, on the grounds of the opposite rule that "one may confer a benefit upon a person without his knowledge or consent" (Sh. Ar., EH 140:5; Resp. *Terumat ha-Deshen,* 209, 237; for Levirate Marriage and *Ḥaliẓah* with regard to an apostate – see Levirate Marriage[1]).

Competency as a Witness. Jewish law holds the testimony of an apostate to be unreliable, since he disavows the whole of the Torah and is therefore liable to be untruthful, even though he is considered a Jew from the point of view of his personal status. However, in accordance with the regulations which aim at easing the lot of an *agunah* ("deserted wife"), who has to establish death of her husband in order to remarry, the *halakhah* provides that the testimony of an apostate is admissible for this purpose provided that he makes the relevant statement in the course of casual conversation *("mesi'aḥ lefi tummo")* and not as formal evidence.

Inheritance. In strict law, a son is heir to his father by the mere fact of a kinship (Num. 27:8; BB 108a and 111a; and Codes)

1. page 407.

and accordingly his right is retained by the apostate son and for the same reason his father inherits him. However, the apostate having sinned, the court is authorized, if it so sees fit, to penalize him, excluding him from his father's inheritance by way of his portion passing to heirs who have not apostatized on the strength of the rule of *Hefker bet din hefker* (i.e., the court has the power of expropriation) as well as in order to discourage apostasy (Kid. 18a; and Codes; *Piskei ha-Rosh* to Kid. 22). A contrary opinion quoted by Solomon b. Abraham Adret in the name of Hai Gaon (Resp. 7:292) has not been adopted by the majority of the *posekim.*

In the State of Israel. The foregoing rules are generally followed in the interpretation of laws with reference to the question of determining the legal status of an apostate, unless the context or the purpose of the law requires a different construction. The question of whether the term "Jew" in the "Law of Return, 1950," which entitled "every Jew" to enter Israel as an immigrant, included an apostate, or whether an apostate could be registered as being of Jewish nationality under the "Registration of Inhabitants Ordinance, No. 50 of 5709–1949" (replaced by the "Registration of Population Law, 5725–1965"), was decided in the negative by a majority opinion of the Supreme Court (sitting as the High Court of Justice, in the case of *Rufeisen* (Brother Daniel); High Court Case 72/62, PD 16:2428–55).

Bibliography: Levi, in: REJ, 38 (1899), 106–11, 114–6; Weinberg, in: *No'am,* 1 (1958), 1–51; Benedikt, *ibid.,* 3 (1960), 241–58; ET, 1 (1962³), 202; 8 (1957), 443–4; 12 (1967), 162–6; B. Schereschewsky, *Dinei Mishpaḥah* (1967²), 80, 229, 333; M. Elon, *Ḥakikah Datit* . . . (1968), 52–53; idem, in: ILR, 4 (1969), 128ff; idem, *Ha-Mishpat Ha-Ivri* (1973), I, 145ff, II, 633; Zeitlin, "Mumar and Meshummad" in JQR 54 (1963/4), 84–86.

Ben-Zion Schereschewsky

HUSBAND AND WIFE. The act of marriage creates certain rights and duties between husband and wife. In performing them, both parties have to conduct themselves according to the following rules, comprising the fundamental principles for the relationship between husband and wife in Jewish law: "Thus the sages laid down that a man shall honor his wife more than his own self and shall love her as he loves himself, and shall constantly seek to benefit her according to his means; that he shall not unduly impose his authority on her and shall speak gently with her; that he shall be neither sad nor irritable. Similarly they laid down that a wife shall honor her husband exceedingly and shall accept his authority and abide by his wishes in all her activities . . ." (Maim. Yad, Ishut 15:19–20).

General Rights and Duties. A husband has ten obligations toward his wife (or her descendants) and four rights in respect of her. The obligations are: (a) to provide her with sustenance or maintenance; (b) to supply her clothing and lodging; (c) to cohabit with her; (d) to provide the *ketubbah* (i.e., the sum fixed for the wife by law); (e) to procure medical attention and care during her illness; (f) to ransom her if she be taken captive; (g) to provide suitable burial upon her death; (h) to provide for her support after his death and ensure her right to live in his house as long as she remains a widow; (i) to provide for the support of the daughters of the marriage from his estate after his death, until they become betrothed (see Marriage) or reach the age of maturity; and (j) to provide that the sons of the marriage shall inherit their mother's *ketubbah,* in addition to their rightful portion of the estate of their father shared with his sons by other wives. The husband's rights are those entitling him: (a) to the benefit of his wife's handiwork; (b) to her chance gains or finds; (c) to the usufruct of her property; and (d) to inherit her estate (Yad, Ishut 12:1–4; Sh. Ar., EH 69:1–3).

These rights and duties both derive from the law and not from mere agreement between the parties: "a man, by marrying a woman, becomes obligated to her in ten matters and acquires rights against her in four matters, even if they have not been taken down in writing" (Yad, Ishut 12:5; Sh. Ar., EH 69:1), i.e., the said rights and duties devolve as a matter of law from the act of marriage, whether or not a *ketubbah* deed is written and "writing thereof does not add and the absence thereof does not detract" (Resp. Ribash no. 480).

The Wife's Rights. Sustenance, see Maintenance.

Clothing and Lodging. This inlcudes the right to household utensils and furniture and to a home of a reasonable standard in accordance with local custom (Yad, Ishut 13:3, 6; Sh. Ar., EH 73:1, 7). The scope of this right is governed by the rules pertaining to the law of maintenance, since, for the purpose of the legal rights of the wife, the concept of maintenance – in its wider meaning – embraces also the above-mentioned right (Tur, EH 73). By the same token the wife loses her right to claim raiment from her husband whenever she forfeits her right to maintenance (Rema, EH 69:4).

The place of residence (town or village) is determined by the husband, since it is presumed that they so agreed in advance and the wife cannot object to her husband changing their residence unless there was an agreement, express or implied, that they would not move to another place without her consent (Sh. Ar., EH 75:1; PDR 2:233, 3:161, 163, 5:20, 22, 57). However, the husband must have reasonable grounds for deciding on a change against the will of his wife, e.g., for reasons of health, or his livelihood, or the fact that the matrimonial peace at their existing home is disturbed by his or her relatives (Resp. Ribash nos. 81, 88; PDR 1:271, 274–5; 2:233, 237; 5:36, 54, 57). The wife is not obliged to agree to a change of residence if this should be detrimental to her position, e.g., because her relationship with her husband is such that she has reasonable grounds for her reluctance to move beyond the proximity of her relatives, or because the new home will be inferior to the old home, or if she can justify her refusal on the grounds that she does not wish to move from a town to a village or vice versa (Sh. Ar., EH 75:2; PDR 1, 2, loc. cit. 3:161, 163).

These rules do not apply in their entirety to Ereẓ Israel vis-à-vis other countries, nor to Jerusalem vis-à-vis other places in Ereẓ Israel. In such cases the rule is that a spouse who genuinely prefers as his place of residence Ereẓ Israel to any other country, or Jerusalem to any other place in Ereẓ Israel, need not bow to the wishes of the other spouse. In effect, therefore, the law favors the party genuinely seeking to settle in Ereẓ Israel or Jerusalem, or refusing to depart therefrom, even if, for example, this should entail the loss of better economic opportunites elsewhere, unless there is reason to fear that in Ereẓ Israel or in Jerusalem they might become in need of charity (Sh. Ar., EH 75:3, 4; *Pitḥei Teshuvah, ibid.,* 6; PDR, 5:20, 36, 66). However, if settling in Israel involves any danger for the parties, neither spouse may compel the other to do so (Tos. to Ket. 110b, s.v. "*hu omer la'alot:* Sh. Ar., EH 75:5; for a contrary opinion, cf. Tur, EH 75; see also PDR 5:20).

The husband likewise determines the place of the dwelling – within the town or village, but each of the parties must comply with the other's request to move to another dwelling and cannot refuse to do so on the ground that he or she is not particular about the matters complained of by the other spouse, provided only that the request is genuine and justified in the circumstances, e.g., on the grounds that neighbors are habitually insulting, or that they are given to prostitution, or to desecration of the Sabbath, and the like (Yad, Ishut 13:15; Sh. Ar., EH 74:11–12). If the wife refuses, in defiance of these rules, to accede to her husband's just demands concerning their place of residence, she is liable to forfeit her right to maintenance since she is only entitled thereto as long as she lives with him; moreover she is likely to be considered a *moredet* (see below) and may eventually be obliged to accept a bill of divorce (Sh. Ar., EH 75:4, PDR, 3:161, 163, 164; 5:20, 23–28; 6:5, 9). Similarly, upon the husband's unreasonable refusal to accede to his wife's just demand to continue living in Ereẓ Israel, he may be ordered to provide maintenance for her – even though they live apart – and eventually to grant her a divorce with payment of her *ketubbah;* and if necessary, she may also demand an injunction restraining him from going abroad (PDR 5:20, 24, 29, 36, 57–59, 66).

Cohabitation. The husband's duty to cohabit with his wife stems from biblical law (Ex. 21:10) and he is obliged to do so according to his physical abilities and in so far as it is possible for him, having regard to the requirements of his occupation (Yad, Ishut 14:1, 2; Sh. Ar., EH 76:1–3). If he is unable to fulfill this duty the wife is entitled to demand a divorce (Yad, Ishut 14:7; Sh. Ar., EH 76:11) unless there are reasonable prospects, on the strength of medical evidence, that he may be cured of his disability (PDR 1:85–89; 3:84–89; see also Divorce[1]).

Mored ("rebellious" husband). A husband who refuses without justifiable reason, to cohabit with his wife is called a *mored* (Ket. 63a; Yad, Ishut 14:15), but he is not so regarded if he refuses to fulfill his other obligations toward her (*ibid.* and *Maggid Mishneh,* Ishut 14:15; Baḥ, EH 77). Proof that her husband is a *mored* entitles the wife to demand that he be obliged to grant her a divorce, and if necessary, that he be compelled to do so (on the distinction, see Divorce[2]). As long as the husband persists in his refusal to cohabit with his wife, she is entitled to demand that the amount of her *ketubbah* be increased from week to week, as may be determined by the court and to receive the increased *ketubbah* upon the grant of the divorce (Ket., Yad, and *Maggid Mishneh, ibid;* Sh. Ar., EH 77:1). In such event the wife's remedy is not necessarily limited to seeking a divorce – lest the husband be enabled thus indirectly to compel his wife to a divorce – she may alternatively demand that her husband be obliged to pay her maintenance only without prejudicing thereby her right to receive the increased *ketubbah* when later seeking a divorce (Sh. Ar., EH 77:1; *Piskei ha-Rosh* Ket. 5:32). The husband will not be regarded as a *mored* when he can adduce facts in support of his plea that his wife is repulsive to him, and declares that he is ready and willing to give her a divorce forthwith, with payment of her *ketubbah;* the wife's refusal to accept a divorce in such circumstances relieves the husband of all his obligations toward her, including that of maintenance (Resp. Rosh 42:1; PDR 5:292, 296, 297).

Moredet ("rebellious" wife). The wife is similarly regarded as a *moredet* only when she persistently refuses to cohabit with her husband (Ket. 63a., Yad and *Maggid Mishneh,* Ishut 14:8; Sh. Ar., EH 77:2), but not when she refuses to fulfill any of her other marital duties (Sh. Ar., EH 77:2 and *Baḥ* EH 77). The *moredet* fall into two categories: firstly, that of a wife who refuses to cohabit with her husband because of anger or a quarrel or for other reasons offering no legal justification; secondly, that of a wife who refuses to cohabit with her husband because she cannot bring herself to have sexual relations with him and can satisfy the court that this is for genuine reasons, which impel her to seek a divorce – even with forfeiture of her *ketubbah.* In both cases the *moredet* immediately loses her right to maintenance (Sh. Ar., EH 77:2; PDR 6:33, 42) and, in consequence thereof, her husband loses the right to her handiwork (see below) since he is only entitled to this in consideration of her maintenance, i.e., only if she is actually maintained by him (Rema, EH 77:2; and see below). Ultimately, the *moredet* also stands to lose her *ketubbah* and the husband will be entitled to demand a divorce, but this depends on conditions that differ according to the category of *moredet* and in this regard the *halakhah* underwent various developments.

So far as the first category of *moredet* is concerned, it was laid down in the Mishnah that her *ketubbah* shall be diminished from week to week until nothing remains and that thereafter her husband shall be entitled to divorce her without *ketubbah* (Ket. 63a). Later, as a means of inducing the wife to desist from her "rebellion," it was provided that a procedure be adopted of having certain warnings issued by the court as well as public announcements made, and on the wife's disregarding a final warning that her continued "rebellion" would render her liable to forfeiture of her *ketubbah,* the court could declare her a *moredet,* entailing the immediate forfeiture of her *ketubbah* and the acquisition by her husband of the right to divorce her forthwith. In the period of the later *amoraim* it was further prescribed that only after persisting in her refusal to cohabit with her husband for not less than 12 months would the *moredet* finally lose her *ketubbah* and the husband become entitled to divorce her (Ket. 63b; Yad, Ishut 14:9–11; Tur and *Beit Yosef.* EH 77; Sh. Ar., EH 77:2). This appears to be the *halakhah* at the present time (see PDR 6:33, 325).

In the case of the other category of *moredet* (i.e., on a plea of incompatibility, when accepted by the court), the procedure of warnings and announcements was regarded as being inappropriate and inapplicable since "the wife should not be urged to have sexual relations with a person whom she finds repulsive" (Yad, Ishut 14:8; PDR 6:5, 12, 18). Hence, in this case, the husband was at first considered entitled, according to her own wish, to give his wife an immediate divorce, without payment of her *ketubbah,* because she herself had desired this by her waiver of the *ketubbah* and, as a *moredet,* she is anyhow not entitled to her *ketubbah* (Ket. 63b: Sh. Ar., EH 77:2). In later times, however, the scholars regulated that even concerning this category of *moredet* the husband is not entitled to divorce her immediately, but only after the lapse of 12 months after a warning by the court that she might forfeit her *ketubbah.* A regulation aimed at enabling the wife to reconsider her attitude in the event that her rebelliousness had been due to sudden anger which she later regretted (Ket. 63b). Her failure to repent within those 12 months would then entitle the husband to divorce her without *ketubbah* but the wife's plea that her husband is "repulsive" to her does not give her the right to demand that her husband be adjudged to grant her a divorce. Maimonides' opinion (Ishut 14:8) that on the strength of the aforesaid plea, the husband might even be compelled to divorce his wife without delay – since "she is not like a captive to have to submit to intercourse with someone repulsive to her" – was not accepted by the majority of the authorities and a *takkanah* to a similar effect from the geonic period (known as the *dina de-metivta,* i.e., "law of the academies") was regarded as an emergency measure intended only for those generations and not as established *halakhah* (Resp. Rosh no. 43:6; 8; *Sefer Teshuvot ha-Rashba ha-Meyaḥasot le ha-Ramban* no. 138; Rema, EH 77:2, 3).

Since the wife only forfeits her *ketubbah* in the event that she does not desist from her rebellion within the prescribed period of 12 months, all her rights and duties on the strength of the *ketubbah* – save with regard to her maintenance and her handiwork – remain valid during the same period, since "the *ketubbah* conditions are as the *ketubbah* itself." If in conse-

1. page 415; 2. page 415.

quence of the wife's rebellion she is divorced by her husband, she will anyway be entitled to receive her *nikhsei melog*(property which never ceases to remain in her ownership but the usufruct whereof is enjoyed by the husband (see Dowry)) but special *halakhot* exist concerning her *nikhsei ẓon u-varzel* (see *Beit Shemu'el* and *Ḥelkat Meḥokek* at concl. of 77).

The "Main (Ikkar) Ketubbah. See *Ketubbah.*

Medical Care. The medical expenses incurred in case of the wife's illness must be borne by her husband, since these form part of her maintenance: "medical care in time of illness is as necessary to a person as is sustenance" (Ket. 4:9 and Rashi Ket. 51a s.v. *"ḥayyav lerape'ot"*). Hence, questions such as the scope of this obligation of the husband and whether and to what extent he is obliged to defray debts incurred by the wife in seeking a cure for her illness are governed by the same laws as those pertaining to her maintenance.

Ransom from Captivity. The husband is obliged to provide the money to perform any other act required to redeem his wife from captivity (Ket. 4:9 and 52a; Sh. Ar., EH 78:1). "Captivity" in this context is not confined to the case of actual captivity of the wife in time of war, but embraces all circumstances in which she is prevented, as a result of the restriction of her freedom, from living with her husband, e.g., where husband and wife are separated as a result of persecution or war and thereafter the husband succeeds in reaching Ereẓ Israel while his wife is stranded in a country from which she is not free to depart. If in such circumstances the payment of money will enable the wife to leave that country and join her husband, it is his duty to pay the required amount, even if it should exceed the amount of her *ketubbah,* because in general the husband's duty is to ransom his wife with all the means at his disposal: "his wife is as his own self" (Yad, Ishut 14:19; Rema EH 78:3 and *Ha-Gra,* n. 4). In consideration of this duty the husband is entitled to the usufruct of his wife's property. The husband cannot be relieved of this duty by his wife's waiver of her right to be ransomed – even if the parties should so agree prior to their marriage – lest she become assimilated among the gentiles (Sh. Ar., EH 69:5).

Burial. It is the husband's duty to bear the costs of his wife's burial and all related expenses such as those necessary for erecting a tombstone, etc. (Sh. Ar., EH 89:1). Since this duty is imposed on the husband as one of the *ketubbah* conditions and not by virtue of the laws of succession, he must bear these costs out of his personal property without regard to the question whether, and to what extent, his deceased wife had contributed a dowry or left an estate in his favor (*Beit Shemu'el* EH 89, n.1). If such burial costs are defrayed by third parties, e.g., by the *ḥevra kaddisha,* in fulfilling the *mitzvah* of burying the dead, in the husband's absence or upon his own refusal to do so, the husband will be liable to refund the amount expended to the parties concerned (Sh. Ar., EH 89:2).

Support of the Widow from the Estate of her Deceased Husband. See Widow.

Support of the Minor Daughters of the Marriage from the Estate of Their Deceased Father. See Parent and Child and Succession.

Inheritance by the Sons of the Marriage of Their Mother's Ketubbah, Over and Above Their Portion in the Estate of Their Father. This *takkanah,* known as the *ketubbat benin dikhrin* (i.e., *ketubbah* of male children), refers to a condition of the *ketubbah* whereby the husband agrees that his wife's *ketubbah* and dowry, which he – as by law he is her only heir (see Succession; and see Right of Inheritance, below) – would inherit if she predeceased him, shall, upon his own death, pass to the sons of the marriage only and this over and above and separately from the share of these sons in the rest of their father's estate shared equally by them with the sons of any other marriage contracted by him (Ket. 4:10 and 52b; Sh. Ar., EH 111). This *takkanah,* designed to ensure that the wife's property would remain for her sons only, was aimed at influencing the bride's father to give her, upon her marriage, a share of his property equaling that which his sons would get; however, since it anyway became customary for fathers to give their daughters such a share of their property, the need for including a specific undertaking of this kind in the *ketubbah*-deed fell away, and therefore by geonic times it was already recognized that the *takkanah* had become obsolete (Rema, EH 111:16).

The Husband's Rights. Ma'aseh Yadeha ("the wife's handiwork"). It is the wife's duty to do all such household work as is normally performed by women enjoying a standard of living and social standing similar to that of the spouse all in accordance with local custom. Also applicable is the rule that "the wife goes up with him, but does not go down with him," i.e., she is not obliged to do the kind of work that was not customarily done by the woman in her family circle prior to her marriage, although according to the husband's standard women used to do it, while at the same time she is entitled to benefit from the fact that her husband enjoys a higher standard of living than that to which she was accustomed prior to the marriage, so that she is not obliged to do work which is not normally done by women enjoying the husband's (higher) standard of living even if she used to do it prior to her marriage (Ket. 59a–61b; Sh. Ar., EH 80:1, 10). The expenses incurred by the husband in hiring domestic help due to the fact that the wife, although able to perform them, willfully refuses to perform the duties devolving on her, as described, must be refunded by the wife and may also be deducted by the husband from her maintenance (Sh. Ar., *ibid and Ḥelkat Meḥokek* 27). According to these rules is also to be decided the question whether, and to what extent, the wife is obliged to suckle or look after the infant children of the marriage, since this duty is imposed on her not as the mother of the children but as the wife of their father (Sh. Ar., EH 80:6–8). Hence a divorced woman is exempt from this duty, with the result that her former husband – who as father always bears sole responsibility for the maintenance of their children (see Parent and Child) – must compensate her for her efforts, if she nevertheless looks after them, in addition to bearing the expenses involved (Sh. Ar., EH 82:5; PDR, 1:118, 119; 2:3–8).

The wife is not liable for damage caused by her in the home – e.g., in respect of broken utensils – whether or not occasioned in the course of fulfillment of her duties (Yad, Ishut 21:9, Sh. Ar., EH 80:17 and *Ḥelkat Meḥokek* n. 29). The purpose of this *halakhah* is to preserve matrimonial harmony, since otherwise "matrimonial harmony will cease, because the wife in taking excessive care will refrain from most of her duties and quarreling will result" (Yad, loc. cit.).

The question whether the earnings of the wife from her own exertions *(yegi'a kappeha),* in talmudic language *ha'adafah* ("surplus"), and, if she exerts herself more than usual, "surplus resulting from undue exertion," are in the nature of *ma'aseh yadeha* and so belong to her husband, is a disputed one – both in the Talmud (Ket. 65b and Rashi thereto s.v. *ha'adafah;* 66a) and in the codes (Yad, Ishut 21:2 and Sh. Ar., EH 80:1 as against the Tur, *ibid.,* and other codes; PDR, 1:81, 90–94). In the light of this dispute the husband has no right to demand that his wife should go out to earn, nor that she should make over any such earnings to him; on the other hand, since some of the authorities are of the opinion that the husband does have this right – thus possibly entitling him to set off such earnings against her maintenance – he will not be ordered to pay her maintenance in so far as her earnings suffice for this purpose (*Baḥ* EH 80; PDR, 1:94, 118; 2:220, 226).

The husband's right to his wife's handiwork is granted to him in return for his duty to maintain her and in consideration of this, and is only available to him upon his actually discharging this duty (Ket. 47b, 58b, 107b; Sh. Ar., EH 69:4). The rule is that the wife's right to maintenance is primary, taking precedence over his right to her handiwork and existing even when she is unable to work, e.g., on account of illness (Ket. 58b; Rashi ad loc. s.v. *mezonei ikkar*). On the other hand, the husband loses the right to his wife's handiwork if for any reason whatsoever she does not actually receive her maintenance from him, whether on account of his refusal to provide it or because according to law she has forfeited her right to such maintenance, e.g., because she is a *moredet* (Rema EH 77:2; *Ba'er Heitev*, EH 80, n. 1). On the strength of the above rule, the wife, by her independent will, is able, by waiving the right of maintenance, to deprive her husband of his right to her handiwork ("I am not maintained, nor shall I do any handiwork . . ." Ket. 58b), a worthwhile step for her if she should earn more than the amount of her maintenance. The husband, on the other hand, cannot deprive his wife of her right to maintenance by waiving his right to her handiwork, nor may he demand that she go out to earn the cost of her maintenance ("Spend your handiwork for your maintenance," Ket. 58b, Sh. Ar., EH 69:4 and *Beit Shemu'el* n. 4).

Finds of the Wife. The husband is entitled to the finds or chance gains of his wife (Ket. 65b–66a; Sh. Ar., EH 84).

Usufruct of the Wife's Property. See Dowry.

Right of Inheritance. Jewish law decrees that the husband is the sole heir of his wife – to the absolute exclusion of everyone else, including her children – as regards all property of whatever kind in her estate, including the part in respect whereof he had no usufruct during her lifetime. However, the wife is not an heir to her husband's estate (BB 8:1 and 111b; Yad, Naḥalot 1:8; Ishut 22:1; Sh. Ar., EH 90:1); instead she has the right to claim maintenance and lodging from his estate for as long as she remains a widow. The husband inherits only the property actually owned by his wife at her death but not the property which is only contingently then due to her in certain circumstances, e.g., if she had been a contingent heir to her father but predeceased him (BB 113a; Sh. Ar., loc. cit.). The inheritance of the husband also embraces property sold by the wife subsequent to their marriage, since his right of inheritance comes into existence upon their marriage and therefore any sale of her property is only valid to the extent that it is not prejudicial to his right, i.e., only if he should predecease her or if they become divorced and she retains ownership of her property (Maim. Yad, Ishut 22:7; Sh. Ar., EH 90:9; see also Dowry). The husband's right to inherit his wife's estate is coextensive with the existence of a valid marriage between them at the time of her death, and remains effective even if the marriage between them was prohibited, e.g., between a priest and a divorcee (see Marriage, Prohibited[1]), and even if the husband had wished to divorce his wife but was prevented from doing so, whether for lack of time or on account of the decree of Rabbenu Gershom (see Divorce; Main. Yad, Naḥalot 1:8; Ishut 22:4; Sh. Ar., EH 90:1 and *Ba'er Heitev* n. 1).

Contracting out of the Law. All the above-mentioned rights and duties of the parties flow from the law. There is, however, no obstacle to an agreement between the parties to regulate their legal relationship with regard to monetary matters to another effect, provided that this is not in conflict with any general principles of the *halakhah.*

The rule is that "in a matter of *mamon* one's stipulation is valid," i.e., in matters of civil law the law does not restrict the freedom of contract and one may even stipulate contrary to biblical law (R. Judah, Kid. 19b; Sh. Ar., EH 38:5; 69:6). Hence the parties may come to an agreement stipulating therein terms and conditions whereby they forego certain pecuniary rights and obligations they are entitled to against each other according to law, provided that the agreement is express and in compliance with the legal provisions concerning the making of such an agreement or condition. In particular, and by way of an express agreement for the renunciation *(silluk)* of their rights, a husband and wife may effect a complete separation of their rights as to their respective properties so as to deprive the husband of the usufruct of his wife's property and of the right to inherit from her. It should be noted that such an agreement will lack validity prior to the creation of any legal tie between the parties with reference to the rights in question, because until then such rights constitute "something that is not yet in existence" (*davar she-lo ba la-olam;* See Contract[2]) and therefore cannot be the subject of a legal disposition; nor is such an agreement possible after full acquisition of the said rights, since a right once acquired cannot be conferred on another by renunciation but only by way of its transfer or assignment. Hence the above-mentioned renunciation agreement must be effected after the *kiddushin* but prior to the *nissu'in* ceremony (see Marriage), since at this stage the pecuniary rights are considered already to be "something in existence" but they are not yet fully acquired by the parties (see PDR 1, 289–313; *Beit Ya'akov,* EH 92:7). Since the custom at the present time is for the *kiddushin* and *nissu'in* ceremonies to be united and performed one after the other without interruption, it is necessary, if the parties should wish to effect the said renunciation, that the marriage ceremony be interrupted upon completion of the *kiddushin* to enable the parties to sign the renunciation deed, and then only to proceed with the *nissu'in* ceremony.

As said above, only with regard to monetary matters is such agreement valid. Therefore, an agreement whereby the wife undertakes to waive her right to cohabitation is of no effect since the corresponding duty of the husband is imposed on him by biblical law and does not involve a matter of *mamon;* hence the wife may always repudiate such an agreement and demand that her husband fulfill his duty to cohabit with her (Yad, Ishut 12:2, 7; Sh. Ar., EH 69:6 and *Ḥelkat Meḥokek* n. 10). On the other hand, the wife's duty to cohabit with her husband is not imposed on her by biblical law as such, but is merely a consequence of the husband's right to cohabitation by virtue of the marriage, which right he may waive. Hence an agreement between the spouses whereby the wife is released from this duty but without any waiver of her rights is valid, and she will not be considered a *moredet* if, in reliance upon such agreement, she should refuse to cohabit with her husband; neither will her right to maintenance and other pecuniary rights be affected (*Pitḥei Teshuvah,* EH 134, n. 9).

Also invalid is a condition depriving the wife of her "main" *ketubbah* – even though her right to the *ketubbah* is a matter of *mamon* – since a marital life in which the wife remains without her "main" *ketubbah* is considered "cohabitation for the sake of prostitution" (Ket. 5:1) and "it is forbidden for a man to remain with his wife for even one hour if she has no *ketubbah*" (Yad, Ishut 10:10). Depriving the wife of her "main" *ketubbah,* or the diminution thereof below the statutory minimum, is prejudicial to the very existence of the marriage and cohabitation in such circumstances is considered as tantamount to prostitution; hence a condition of this kind relates to *davar she-be-issur* (a matter of a ritual law prohibition) and not to a *davar she-be-mamon,* and accordingly it is invalid (Yad, Ishut 12:8; Sh. Ar., EH 69:6).

The husband's right to inherit from his wife, which flows

1. page 361; 2. page 248.

from the law upon the celebration of the marriage, likewise cannot be stipulated away during the subsistence of the marriage. Upon the celebration of the marriage the husband forthwith acquires the status of heir designate to his wife's estate and although this is calculated eventually to afford the husband rights of a monetary *(mamon)* nature it creates a legal status and as such cannot be the subject matter of a waiver of stipulation aimed at annulling it (Yad, Ishut 12:9; Sh. Ar., *ibid.*). Any such waiver or stipulation, in order to be valid, has therefore to be effected after *kiddushin* and prior to *nissu'in* (Yad, Ishut 23:5–7, and *Maggid Mishneh* thereto; Sh. Ar., EH 69:5, 7; 92:7, 8). For further particulars concerning freedom of stipulation between husband and wife, see Contract.[1]

In the State of Israel. The *halakhah* is generally followed so far as the particulars of the marital rights and duties are concerned. However, the husband's right to inherit from his wife is governed by the Succession Law, 5725–1965, in terms whereof – as also formerly in terms of the Succession Ordinance, 1923–34 – one spouse inherits from the other along with the latter's descendants (in the case of intestate succession), in the prescribed proportions (sec. 11). The inheritance rights of the spouses are governed solely by the provisions of the above law and the rabbinical courts must also adjudicate in accordance therewith, save when all the interested parties agree, in writing, to the jurisdiction of the rabbinical court and provided that the rights of a minor or a person lacking legal capacity who is party to the estate shall not be less than those afforded him under the above law (sec. 148, 155).

See also Marriage.

Bibliography: I. S. Zuri, *Mishpat ha-Talmud,* 2 (1921), 79–87; Gulak, Yesodei, 1 (1922), 36f.; 4 (1922), 53, 59 n. 1, 116, 144; Gulak, Oẓar, 23–25, 53f., 59–67; A. Gulak, in: *Ha-Mishpat ha-Ivri,* 2 (1926/27), 266; idem, in: *Zeitschrift fuer vergleidhende Rechtswissenschaft,* 47 (1932/33), 241–55; J. Epstein, in: *Ha-Mishpat ha-Ivri,* 4 (1932/33), 125–34; S. Eliezri, in: *Sinai, Sefer Yovel* (1958), 338–43; ET, 1 (1951[3]), 224–6; 4 (1952), 69–78, 80–88, 91–95; 7 (1956), 61–63; Z. Warhaftig, in: *Divrei ha-Congress ha-Olami ha-Revi'i le Madda'ei ha-Yahadut,* 1 (1967), 189–94; abstract in Engl.: *ibid.*, Eng. Sect., 267f.; B. Schereschewsky, *Dinei Mishpaḥah* (1967[2]), 105–16, 140–52, 171–203; M. Elon, *Ḥakikah Datit...* (1967), 42–44, 161, 167–9; idem in: ILR, 4 (1969), 134f., 137; idem *Ha-Mishpat Ha-Ivri* (1973), I, 160ff., 199ff., II, 465–476, 516ff., 538–546, 635ff., 659, 677ff,. 682ff., 774ff.,

Ben-Zion Schereschewsky

KETUBBAH (Heb. כתבה), a document recording the financial obligations which the husband undertakes toward his wife in respect of, and consequent to, their marriage, obligations which in principle are imposed on him by law (see Husband and Wife). For the *ketubbah* of a betrothed woman *(arusah)* see Marriage.[2]

The Concept. In talmudic times in certain places it was customary to dispense with the writing of a *ketubbah* deed, relying on the fact that the said obligations are in any event imposed by law (Ket. 16b), but the *halakhah* was decided to the effect that a *ketubbah* deed must always be written, since it is forbidden for the bridegroom to cohabit with his bride until he has written and delivered the *ketubbah* to her (Maim. Yad, Ishut 10:7; Sh. Ar., EH 66:1). On the other hand, they are allowed to cohabit only when they are married, and so the *ketubbah* deed must be ready for delivery to the bride when the betrothal blessings *(berakhot ha-erusin)* are recited and before the recital of the marriage blessings (*berakhot ha-nissu'in;* see Marriage[3]). Since in modern times it is customary in practically all communities to celebrate the *kiddushin* and *nissu'in* at the same time, the deed must be ready at the commencement of the recital of the *berakhot ha-erusin.* At the present time a standard form of *ketubbah* deed is normally used, which is read before the bridegroom and the witnesses and signed by them (for a standard *ketubbah* deed, see A. A. Rodner, *Mishpetei Ishut,* 179f.).

The *ketubbah* was instituted for the purpose of protecting the woman, "so that he shall not regard it as easy to divorce her" (Ket. 11a; Yev. 89a; Maim. loc. cit.), i.e., in order to render it difficult for the husband to divorce his wife by obliging him to pay her, in the event of a divorce, the sum mentioned in the *ketubbah,* which generally exceeded the sum due to her according to law. As this is the object of the *ketubbah,* some authorities are of the opinion that since the *ḥerem* of Rabbenu Gershom, which prohibited the divorce of a wife against her will, the same object is achieved in any event; it is therefore argued – on the analogy of *Ketubbot* 54a concerning the ravished woman who is thereafter married by her ravisher and, according to pentateuchal law, cannot be divorced – that there is no longer any need for a *ketubbah* to be written. However it has remained the *halakhah* that a *ketubbah* is to be written (Rema EH 66:3, concl.).

The amounts specified in the *ketubbah* deed are those of the "main" *ketubbah* and its increment (*ikkar ketubbah* and *tosefet ketubbah*) and those of the dowry and its increment, which amounts the wife is entitled to receive upon divorce or the death of her husband (Sh. Ar., EH 93:1).

The "Main" Ketubbah and its Increment. The "main" *ketubbah* is the amount determined by law as the minimum that the wife is entitled to receive from her husband or his estate on the dissolution of the marriage (Sh. Ar., loc. cit.). According to some authorities the liability to pay the main *ketubbah* is pentateuchal law (Ex. 22:15–16 and Rashi thereto; Mekh. Nezikin 17; Ket. 10a and Rashi thereto), but the *halakhah* is that the *ketubbah* is rabbinical law (Ket. loc. cit; Yad, Ishut 10:7; *Ḥelkat Meḥokek,* EH 66 n. 26). The minimum amount, as laid down in the Talmud, is 200 *zuz* in the case of a virgin and 100 *zuz* in all other cases (Ket. 10b; Sh. Ar., EH 66:6). Since in all matters concerning the *ketubbah* local custom is followed, the equivalent of the main *ketubbah* is fixed in accordance with custom and with the kind and value of the currency prevailing at the respective place (Ket. 66b; Yad, Ishut 23:12; Sh. Ar., EH 66:6, Rema EH 66:11). The said minimum amount is an obligation imposed on the husband by virtue of a rabbinical regulation *(takkanat bet din),* i.e., he is liable to pay this even when a lesser amount has been fixed in the *ketubbah* or no deed at all has been written (Ket. 51a). The authorities were at pains to safeguard the woman's rights in this respect, condemning cohabitation as tantamount to prostitution if the amount fixed as the main *ketubbah* is less than the said legal minimum (R. Meir, Ket. 54b; Sh. Ar., EH 66:9). The only circumstances in which the husband is exempted from meeting his obligations under the *ketubbah* are those in which the wife forfeits her *ketubbah* according to law (see Divorce[4]).

If the husband so wishes, he may add to the minimum amount of the *ketubbah,* an increment known as the *tosefet ketubbah.* Here, too, local custom prevails: i.e., if by virtue of local custom or rabbinical regulation it is customary for an increment to be made, the husband will be bound by this and cannot stipulate for less (Sh. Ar., EH 66:9–11). The general custom at the present time is to grant the increment and this is also reflected in the standard form of the *ketubbah* deed. It is not required that the two amounts shall be separately stated in the deed; they may be fixed as an aggregate amount, provided that this is not less than the minimum locally determined for the

1. page 251; 2. page 357; 3. page 358; 4. page 418.

main *ketubbah* (Rema EH 66:7). In 1953 it was laid down by the chief rabbinate of the State of Israel that the minimum amount of the *ketubbah* – i.e., for the main *ketubbah* and its increment – must not be less than IL 200 for a virgin and IL 100 for a widow or divorcee. The law regarding the increment is generally the same as that regarding the main *ketubbah,* unless the *halakhah* expressly stipulates otherwise (Maim. Yad, Ishut 10:7; Sh. Ar., EH 66:7).

Dowry. (Aram. נדוניא, *nedunya*). In addition to the above-mentioned amounts, there is also fixed in the *ketubbah* deed the amount which the husband – of his own free will and by virtue of his undertaking under the *ketubbah* deed – renders himself liable to return to his wife, when he pays her the *ketubbah,* as the equivalent of her dowry (within the restricted meaning of term). This amount is called *nedunya* and the husband's liability to return it becomes a charge on his estate (Rema EH 66:11). The question of whether, in the event of a fluctuation in currency values, the wife is entitled to recover the dowry to the amount specified in the *ketubbah* deed or according to its actual equivalent at the time of the recovery is greatly influenced by local law and custom concerning the repayment of a regular debt in such circumstances (Resp. *Ḥatam Sofer,* EH 1:126). Since the husband is permitted by law to trade with the dowry, it is the accepted custom for him to undertake liability for an increment to the dowry, i.e., to pay his wife at the due time an additional amount over and above the amount specified as the dowry; this is known as the dowry increment *(tosefet nedunya),* and all laws of the dowry are applicable to it. The usual custom from early times is to fix this increment at one-half of the sum specified as the dowry. As in all matters concerning the *ketubbah* local custom is followed, this custom has become obligatory on the bridegroom; thus he undertakes in the *ketubbah* deed to pay the main *ketubbah* and the dowry, together with their increments (Sh. Ar., EH 66:11). For further particulars see Dowry.

The Custom Concerning Consolidation of all the Ketubbah Amounts. As it is not required that the component amounts of the *ketubbah* be stated separately, an aggregate amount may be fixed, but it is also customary in some countries to enumerate them first separately and then state the aggregate amount (for the custom in Israel see Rodner op. cit.). If, therefore, separate amounts for the component portions are not expressly stated, they are deemed to be included in the aggregate amount specified in the deed (Rema EH 66:7, concl.). Since, generally speaking, the possibility of divorcing a wife without her consent is precluded by the *ḥerem* of Rabbenu Gershom, and in practice she may make her consent conditional on the satisfaction of her pecuniary claims, it is customary in many countries of the Diaspora to specify a nominal amount only for each or all of the *ketubbah* components (e.g., 200 *zekukim kesef ẓaruf:* see *Baḥ* EH 66). If, however, the wife is able to establish that the amount was written as a mere formality and not with the intention of limiting her rights, and that in fact the value of the property brought by her to the marriage exceeded the amount specified in the *ketubbah* deed, there is no legal obstacle to her obtaining satisfaction of her claims as far as she may prove them due to her. In the State of Israel it is the custom to specify in the *ketubbah* a realistic amount according to the specific respective facts.

In cases where the wife "forfeits" her *ketubbah* (see Divorce[1]) the effect, in general, is that the husband is released from his liability to pay her those portions of the *ketubbah* which had to come out of his own pocket, i.e., the main *ketubbah* and its increment; in the absence of any express halakhic rule to the contrary, the wife does not forfeit the dowry or its equivalent, which is regarded as her own property, even when she is obliged to accept a bill of divorce with forfeiture of her *ketubbah* (see, e.g., Sh. Ar., EH 115:5).

The Ketubbah Conditions (Heb. תנאי כתבה The financial obligations imposed on the husband by law (see Husband and Wife) and specified in the *ketubbah* – in addition to the amount the wife is entitled to receive on divorce or the death of her husband – are called the *ketubbah* conditions" (Maim. Yad, Ishut 12:2). The rule is that "the *ketubbah* conditions follow the law applying to the *ketubbah,* itself" (Yev. 89a); i.e., insofar as the wife is entitled to the main *ketubbah,* she is also entitled to the rights due to her under the *ketubbah* conditions. On the other hand, her forfeiture of the right to the main *ketubbah* also carries with it the loss of her rights under the *ketubbah* conditions, such as her maintenance (Yev. loc. cit.; Rashi and Asheri thereto; see also Sh. Ar., 115:5).

Loss of the Ketubbah Deed. Just as the bridegroom is forbidden to cohabit with his bride after marriage unless he has written and delivered the *ketubbah* to her, so the husband is forbidden to live with his wife for even one hour if she has no main *ketubbah* deed. Therefore, in the case of loss or destruction of the deed the husband is obliged to write a new one, and since the loss of the original deed does not relieve the husband of his obligations under it the new deed must ensure the rights that the wife was entitled to under the original one (Sh. Ar., EH 66:3 and *Ḥelkat Meḥokek* no. 14; for an example of such a deed כתבה דאירכסא, see Tur, EH after 66). For the same reason, the wife's waiver of her *ketubbah* is of no effect in respect of the main *ketubbah* and in such an event the husband is also obliged to write a new deed for her, but here only in respect of the main *ketubbah* (Sh. Ar., loc. cit.; for an example of such a *ketubbah,* see Tur, loc. cit.).

For recovery of the *ketubbah,* see Divorce, Widow, and Limitation of Actions.

In the State of Israel. The wife's rights under the *ketubbah* are unaffected by the laws of the State of Israel. However, according to the Succession Law 5725/1965, whatever she receives on the strength of her *ketubbah* must be taken into account against her rights of inheritance or of maintenance from the estate of her deceased husband (see. 11 (c); 59).

Bibliography: A. Buechler, in: *Festschrift . . . Lewy* (1911), 118, 122–9; J. S. Zuri, *Mishpat ha-Talmud,* 2 (1921), 57–93; Gulak, Yesodei, 3 (1922), 35f., 46f., 60–63; idem, Oẓar, 28–30, 41–67, 93–109, 167–70; idem, in: *Tarbiz,* 3 (1932), 249–57; S. Zeitlin, in: JQR, 24 (1933–34), 1–7; L. M. Epstein, *The Jewish Marriage Contract* (1927); Ḥ. Albeck, in: *Koveẓ Madda'i le-Zekher Moshe Schorr* (1945), 12–24; ET, 2 (1949), 18, 183f.; N. Lamm, in: *Tradition,* 2 (1959/60), 93–113; S. Goren, in: *Maḥanayim,* no. 83 (1963), 5–14; B. and H. Goodman, *The Jewish Marriage Anthology* (1965); Elon, *Ha-Mishpat Ha-Ivri* (1973), I, 199ff., II, 351ff., 458ff., 531ff., 540, 639ff., 650ff., 672, 774ff., 794ff.

Ben-Zion Schereschewsky

DOWRY. Dowry or *nedunyah,* apparently from the word *neden, nedeh* (i.e., gift – Ezek. 16:33 and commentaries), means all property of whatever kind brought by the wife to the husband upon their marriage (Yad, Ishut, 16:1 and *Maggid Mishneh* thereto). In its restricted and common meaning, the term is intended to refer to those assets of the wife which she of her own free will entrusts to her husband's responsibility, the equivalent whereof the husband of his own free will undertakes in the *ketubbah,* and in a sum of money specified therein as the *nedunyah,* to restore to his wife upon dissolution of their marriage (*Maggid Mishneh,* Ishut 16:1; Tur, EH 85; Sh. Ar., EH 66:11 and Rema 85:2,

1. page 418.

88:2). Such property is also called *nikhsei ẓon barzel,* to be distinguished from another category of the wife's property, called *nikhsei melog* (see below). It is the practice for the husband to undertake in the *ketubbah* to restore to his wife the dowry with an increment (the *tosefet nedunyah*) of one third or one half of the amount specified, subject to local custom. Both parts of the total amount may be stipulated together in an inclusive sum and this is the customary practice; to this inclusive sum is added the sum of the *ketubbah,* as fixed by the *halakhah,* and its increments (see *Ketubbah*), so that an overall sum is mentioned, but it is stressed that this sum is the aggregate of all the above-mentioned components (Sh. Ar., EH 66:11, Rema). The said obligation of the husband is treated in the same manner as any other pecuniary obligation (*Maggid Mishneh,* Ishut 16:1).

Nikhsei Ẓon Barzel (lit. "the property of iron sheep") is a term derived from the name of a transaction in which one party entrusts property on certain terms to another, the latter undertaking responsibility therefor as he would for iron, i.e., for return of the capital value of the property as at the time of his receipt thereof, even if it should suffer loss or depreciation; since, generally, small cattle was the subject matter of such transactions, they came to be described by the above term (BM 69b and Rashi thereto). Hence the use of the term *ẓon barzel* for the property of the wife, to denote that part of her property given over to her husband's ownership but under his responsibility, i.e., subject to his undertaking to restore to her the value thereof as fixed in the *ketubbah* upon dissolution of the marriage. This obligation of the husband is governed by the rule that any appreciation of depreciation in the property is his, regardless of any change it may undergo, or even its loss (Tur and Sh. Ar., EH 85:2); on the other hand, this obligation remains constant despite any fluctuations in currency values (as distinguished from the fluctuations in the value of the property) and the husband remains liable for the sum specified in the *ketubbah* as the dowry equivalent at its value on the date of the marriage, but subject to calculation thereof in accordance with the local law prevailing at the time of its recovery (*Taz* EH 66, n. 6; Rema HM 74:7; Resp. *Ḥatam Sofer* EH 1:126). However, if at the time of its recovery, i.e., upon divorce or the husband's death (Sh. Ar., EH 66:11 and Rema EH 93:1), the actual property is still in existence and fit for the purpose assigned to it at the time of the marriage – generally the case in respect of real property – the wife is entitled to demand the return thereof in specie, as being "the luster of her father's home" *(shevaḥ beit aviha),* and neither the husband nor his heirs can compel her to accept money instead (Sh. Ar., EH 88:3, *Beit Shemu'el* n. 4, *Taz* n. 3).

Nikhsei Melog (lit. "plucked property," i.e., usufruct) is a term derived from the word *meligah,* e.g., *meligat ha-rosh,* i.e., plucking of hair from the head which remains intact. Similarly, *melog* property is property of which the principal remains in the wife's ownership but the fruits thereof are taken by the husband so that he has no responsibility or rights in respect of the principal, both its loss and gain being only hers (Rashbam BB 139b; *Haggahot Maimoniyyot* Ishut 16:1), and upon dissolution of the marriage such property returns to the wife as it stands, in specie. This category embraces all the property of the wife falling outside the category of *nikhsei ẓon barzel* – save for property of the kind described in the next section – whether brought by her at the time of entering the marriage, or acquired thereafter, e.g., by way of inheritance or gift (Yad, Ishut 16:2; Tur and Sh. Ar., EH 85:7).

Property Which is Neither Ẓon Barzel Nor Melog. A third category is property of the wife concerning which the husband has no rights at all, neither as to the principal nor the fruits thereof. This includes property acquired by her after the marriage by way of gift, the donor having expressly stipulated that it be used for a specific purpose (such as for her recuperation), or that it be used for any purpose of her choice without her husband having any authority thereover (Yad, Zekhi'ah 3:13, 14; Sh. Ar., EH 85:11), or property given to her as a gift by her husband, he being considered here to have waived his rights to the fruits thereof, in terms of the rule "whoever gives, gives with a generous mind" (BB 51b and Rashbam thereto; Sh. Ar., EH 85:7; see also Gifts).

The Husband's Rights to the Principal. Since the wife is entitled to the ownership of her property – *melog,* because it has never ceased to be in her ownership, and *ẓon barzel,* in terms of the halakhic rule concerning "the luster of her father's home" (see above) – the husband is not entitled to deal therewith in any manner prejudicial to her right, e.g., sale, etc., and any such act is invalid with reference to both movable and immovable property (Sh. Ar., EH 90:13, 14, Rema to 14, *Beit Shemu'el* n. 48; Resp. Ribash no. 150). In the case of money the position is different: if it falls within the category of *ẓon barzel* and therefore passes fully into the husband's ownership, he being responsible for returning the equivalent thereof as determined in the *ketubbah,* he is free to trade or otherwise deal therewith, as with his own money (*Ḥelkat Meḥokek,* EH 85, n. 4; Resp Ribash no. 150); if, however, the money is part of the *melog* property and therefore not in the husband's ownership, he is not entitled to trade therewith save with his wife's consent but may only – and even will be obliged to do so if so requested by his wife – invest the money in such manner that the principal is preserved for her, while the fruits will be his (Resp. Ribash no. 150; *Ḥelkat Meḥokek* 85 n. 42).

Income From the Wife's Property. All the fruits of the wife's property, i.e., all benefits derived from her property in a manner leaving intact the principal and its continued capacity to provide benefits – such as natural or legal fruits, e.g., rental or the right of occupation or stock dividends – belong to the husband (Sh. Ar., EH 69:3, 85:1, 2, 13). In accordance with the regulations of the sages he is entitled to these in return for his obligation to ransom her should she be taken captive, in order to avoid the ill-feeling that would arise between them if he received no help from her (Ket. 47a–b and Codes). The wife cannot forego her right to be ransomed at her husband's expense with the object of depriving him of his right to the fruits of her property, lest she remain unransomed and become absorbed among the Gentiles (Sh. Ar., EH 85:1); for the same reason, the husband does not escape the obligation to ransom his wife by renouncing the fruits from her property *(ibid.).*

By virtue of this right, the husband is entitled to receive the fruits and to take all steps necessary for the realization thereof – such as collecting rent or demanding the ejection of a tenant – in his own name and without being specifically authorized thereto by his wife (Sh. Ar., ḤM 122:8; EH 85:4 and commentaries; PDR 4:107); nor does he require any specific authority from his wife in order to recover and receive any money to which she is entitled, including the principal, in order that it may be available to him for its investment and his enjoyment of its fruits (Sh. Ar., ḤM 122:8, Rema, and *Siftei Kohen* n. 33). On the other hand, the husband, being entitled to the fruits, has the corresponding obligation to defray thereof the expenses of the property (Sh. Ar., EH 88:7), and if the fruits do not suffice for the purpose and he has to invest of his own money and labor on the property, he generally will not be entitled to compensation, not even upon divorce, since he is considered to have waived any claim therefor, having invested them with a view to enjoying the fruits ("what he has expended, he has expended and what he has consumed, he has consumed" – Ket. 79b; Sh. Ar., EH 88:7).

The husband's ownership of the fruits is not absolute, since the object of the halakhic rule whence his right to the fruits of the wife's property is derived is "for the comfort of the home" Ket. 80b), i.e., for their mutual comfort in their home and so as to ease the burden of maintaining the household (see Yad, Ishut 22:20 and *Maggid Mishneh* thereto). Consequently he is not entitled to use the fruits for his personal advantage, and if he should invest them in a way showing that he is not using them for the comfort of the home, the investment will be considered the wife's property as capital forming part of her *nikhsei melog,* of which the fruits only may be taken by him, to be used for the comfort of the home (Tur, EH 85, *Perishah* n. 51, *Derishah* n. 2) For the same reason the husband's creditors, i.e., in respect of debts unconnected with the upkeep of the household, may not seize the fruits and recover their debt from the proceeds thereof since this would preclude them from being used for their assigned purpose (Sh. Ar., ḤM 97:26; commentaries to EH 85:17). On the other hand, since the fruits belong to the husband, the wife must not do anything which may deprive him of his right of usufruct. Hence her sale of the principal without her husband's consent will be invalid with regard to the fruits, as a sale of something not belonging to her and therefore the husband's right of usufruct is unimpaired thereby and he continues to enjoy the benefits thereof even if the principal is in the hands of the purchaser: "the husband may seize the fruits from the purchasers" (Sh. Ar., EH 90:9, 13). This does not mean, however, that Jewish law denies a married woman legal capacity, like an idiot or a minor, for the sale, as mentioned above, is invalid only in respect of the fruits, as being a sale of something that is not hers (Rema EH 90:9, 13, and *Ḥelkat Meḥokek* n. 29); with reference to the principal, therefore, her ownership is not affected by the husband's usufruct and her sale is valid, to the extent that upon her divorce or the death of her husband, the purchaser will acquire, in addition to the principal, the fruits also of the property purchased by him without any need for novation or ratification of the sale. Upon the death of his wife the husband, indeed, is entitled to seize also the principal from the purchasers, not because the sale is regarded as invalid for reasons of legal incapacity of the wife, but because the sages regulated that when a wife predeceases her husband, he is considered – *mi-ta'am eivah,* i.e., in order to avoid ill feeling between them – upon entering the marriage as the earliest purchaser of her property and therefore takes preference over any other purchaser (*"Takkanat Usha"* – see Ket. 50a, Rashi and Codes). The rule that "whatever the wife acquires, she acquires for her husband," therefore means no more than that he acquires the fruits but the principal is and remains her own (Git. 77a and Rashi; Sh. Ar., ḤM 249:3; on the question of the husband's right to the fruits when he is a *mored* ("rebellious spouse") see Husband and Wife[1]).

Dowry and the Marriage Deed. The wife may only recover her dowry at the same time as she does the *ketubbah,* i.e., upon divorce or the death of her husband (Rema Sh. Ar., EH 66:11, and 93:1). The two are distinct, however, since the amount of the *ketubbah* is payable from the husband's own pocket whereas the dowry is her own property. Hence, even in the case where the wife forfeits her *ketubbah* according to law (see Divorce[2]), she does not lose her dowry, save in case of any express halakhic rule to the contrary (Yad, Ishut 16:1; *Maggid Mishneh, ibid.*; PD 12:1121, 1197–1201).

The Daughter's Right to a Dowry. See Parent and Child.

In the State of Israel. The Supreme Court has interpreted section 2 of the Women's Equal Rights Law, 5711/1951, as directing that Jewish law is not to be followed in matters concerning the husband's rights to the fruits of his wife's property (PD 12:1528ff.). According to this interpretation there is complete separation between the property of the respective spouses with reference to both the principal and the fruits, and the fact of their marriage in no way affects the rights of either party with regard to his or her own property or the fruits thereof.

See also Betrothal.

Bibliography: L. M. Epstein, *The Jewish Marriage Contract* (1927), 89–106; Tchernowitz, in: *Zeitschrift fuer vergleichende Rechtswissenschaft,* 29 (1913), 445–73. H. Tchernowitz, in: *Sefer Yovel . . . Naḥum Sokolow* (1904), 309–28; I. S. Zuri, *Mishpat ha-Talmud,* 2 (1921), 73–79; Gulak, Yesodei, 3 (1922), 44–60; Gulak, Oẓar, 56–65, 109f.; ET, 4 (1952), 88–91; B. Cohen, in: PAAJR, 20 (1951), 135–234; republished in his: *Jewish and Roman Law* (1966), 179–278; addenda *ibid.*, 775–7, idem, in: *Annuaire de l'Institut de Philologie et d'Histoire Orientales et Slaves,* 13 (1953), 57–85 (Eng.); republished in his *Jewish and Roman Law* (1966), 348–76; addenda *ibid.*, 780f.; M. Silberg, *Ha-Ma'amad ha-Ishi be-Yisrael* (1965[4]), 348ff.; Elon, *Ha-Mishpat Ha-Ivri* (1973), I, 201ff., II, 368ff., 465–476, 537ff., 635ff., 677ff., 723ff.; B.-Z. Schereschewsky, *Dinei Mishpaḥah* (1967[2]), 100–5, 153–70, 213–23.

Ben-Zion Schereschewsky

MAINTENANCE (Heb. מזונות , *mezonot*), generally speaking, refers to the supply of all the necessaries of the party entitled thereto, i.e., not only food, but other matters such as medical expenses, raiment, lodging, etc. (Sh. Ar., EH 73:7; see Husband and Wife). When, however, the maintenance obligation is based on a personal undertaking (see below) and not on the operation of law, it will not cover raiment and perhaps not even medical expenses, unless the contrary is indicated by the terms of the undertaking (Sh. Ar., EH 114:12; Rema, HM 60:3 and *Siftei Kohen* n. 14). The liability of maintenance exists generally by virtue of law, but in the absence of any legal duty it may also be based on a voluntary undertaking (e.g., by the husband toward his wife's daughter by a previous marriage). Even though it is normally for an unfixed amount, such an undertaking will be binding and be governed by the general law of obligations (Sh. Ar., ḤM 60:2, contrary to the opinion of Yad, Meḥirah 11:16; see also Contract; Obligations, Law of).

The liability of maintenance by virtue of law is imposed on (1) a husband toward his wife; (2) a father toward his small children; and (3) the heirs of the deceased toward his widow. A divorced wife is not entitled to maintenance from her former husband (Sh. Ar., EH 82:6; see Divorce[3]), nor, generally speaking, a betrothed woman from the bridegroom (Sh. Ar., EH 55:4 and Rema thereto). Only maintenance between husband and wife, as a liability by virtue of law, will be discussed below (see also Widow; Parent and Child).

Scope of the Maintenance Obligation. The husband's duty to maintain his wife is one of the duties imposed on him by virtue of his marriage as *obligatio ex lege* (Yad, Ishut 12:2; Sh. Ar., EH 69:2). He has to provide her with at least the minimal needs for her sustenance in accordance with local custom and social standards (Yad, Ishut 12:10; Sh. Ar., EH 70:3). In addition and subject to the aforesaid, the wife's right to maintenance is governed by the rule that she "goes up with him but does not go down with him" (Ket. 61a; Tur, EH 70), i.e., the wife, regardless of the standard of living she enjoyed prior to the marriage, is entitled to a standard of living which matches that of her husband and to be maintained in accordance with his means and social standing. At the same time, she is not obliged to suffer having her standard of living reduced to one below that which

1. page 381; 2. page 418; 3. page 422.

she enjoyed prior to her marriage, at any rate not as compared with the standard of living customary in her paternal home with regard to family members backed by means similar to those available to her husband, even if he should choose a lower standard of living than he can afford (Yad, Ishut 12:11; Sh. Ar., EH 70:1, 3 and *Ḥelkat Meḥokek* n. 1). In addition to providing for all the domestic needs of the common household and as part of his duty of maintenance in its wider sense, the husband must give his wife a weekly cash amount for her personal expenses, again in accordance with their standard of living and social custom (Sh. Ar., EH 70:3 and *Ḥelkat Meḥokek* n. 7). In return for this obligation, the husband is entitled to his wife's "surplus handiwork," i.e., to her earnings from work done beyond the call of her legal duty toward him *(Ma'aseh Yadeha).* The said obligation being imposed on the husband as part of his duty to maintain his wife, she may, of her own choice, waive her right to the weekly allowance in order to retain for herself such surplus earnings, just as she may waive her maintenance in order to acquire for herself the proceeds of her handiwork (*Ḥelkat Meḥokek* loc. cit.). The unspent balance of the money given the wife for her maintenance belongs to her husband, since he is only required to give her an amount sufficient for her needs (Ket. 65b; Yad, Ishut 12:13; *Pitḥei Teshuvah,* EH 70 n. 1). However, if such balance results from the wife's spending less than she requires for her own needs, it belongs to herself; she need not invest the amount of it and if she should do so, the fruits of such investment would belong to her alone (see Dowry). Another opinion is that money given by the husband for his wife's maintenance always remains his own, except insofar as she actually expends it on the household or on her own maintenance, and therefore any balance, even if saved, belongs to him (see Rema, EH 70:3 and *Pitḥei Teshuvah* n. 1; PDR 2:229 and 289).

The wife's right to be maintained in the manner described above is independent of the fact that she may be able to maintain herself out of her own property and the fact that her husband may be in financial difficulties. She will accordingly not be obliged to sell her property or to use the fruits thereof, to which her husband has no right, in order to facilitate his fulfillment of his obligation to maintain her, since he has undertaken the obligation on the marriage and it is also expressed in the *ketubbah* deed in the phrase, "I shall work and support you" (see below, Sh. Ar., loc. cit. *Pitḥei Teshuvah,* EH 70 n. 2; PDR 1:97, 101f.).

Separated Parties. In general, the husband is only obliged to maintain his wife as long as she lives with him or, at any rate, if he is not responsible for the fact that they are separated (Rema, EH 70:12). Hence in the case of separation of the parties, it is necessary to establish which of them has left the common home.

When the Husband Leaves the Home. In principle the wife's right is not affected: "She was given to live and not to suffer pain" (Ket. 61a) and the husband remains responsible for her maintenance (*Mordekhai,* Ket. no. 273). To frustrate her claim, the husband must prove a lawful reason for his absence and refusal to maintain her, e.g., her responsibility for a quarrel justifying his departure (Rema, EH 70:12). However, even in circumstances where the husband is responsible for maintaining his wife despite their separation, it will nevertheless be presumed that he has left her with sufficient means to support herself for a reasonable period during his absence and therefore, in general, she will not be awarded maintenance during the first three months following his departure (Ket. 107a; Sh. Ar., EH 70:5). For the wife to succeed in a claim brought within this period, she must prove that her husband has left her without any means at all, or will have to rebut the above assumption in some other manner, e.g., by proving that her husband left the home as a result of a quarrel or with the intention of returning after a short interval but for some reason failed to do so (Rema, EH 70:12 and *Beit Shemu'el* n. 11; *Ḥut ha-Meshullash.* 1:6, 4).

The husband is not entitled to demand that his wife should work and support herself out of her earnings during his absence unless she has expressly or by implication consented to do this (Yad, Ishut 12:20; *Maggid Mishneh* thereto; Sh. Ar., EH 70:9 and *Ḥelkat Meḥokek* n. 33). This is so regardless of whether or not she has been accustomed to working prior to his departure and making over her earnings to her husband, according to law. The court will not of its own initiative investigate the matter of the wife's earnings from her own handiwork, but will take this into account only if it emerges out of the wife's own arguments. However, if after his return the husband can prove that the wife has been working and earning during his absence, he will not be obliged to repay a loan his wife has taken for her maintenance (see below), to the extent that he proves that she was able to support herself from such earnings during his absence. In this event he will similarly be entitled to demand that she refund to him all amounts she has recovered out of his property for the purposes of her maintenance (Yad, Ishut 12:16; Sh. Ar., EH 70:5).

When the wife is entitled to maintenance but her husband leaves her without sufficient means and she does not maintain herself out of her own earnings, she has the right to borrow for her maintenance and to hold her husband liable for the repayment of such a loan (Ket. 107b; Yad, Ishut 12:19; Sh. Ar., EH 70:8). This is not the case if prior to his departure she was supporting herself by her own efforts and remained silent when he publicly disavowed responsibility for debts she might contract, thus seeming to have consented to this (Rema, EH 70:12 and *Beit Shemu'el* n. 32). The husband's duty to repay such a loan is toward his wife only and he is not directly liable to the creditor. If, however, the wife has no property of her own, or if for any other reason the creditor might have difficulty in recovering from the wife, he may claim repayment of the loan from the husband directly, in terms of the *Shi'buda de-Rabbi Nathan* (permitting the creditor to recover the debt directly from a third party who owes money to the principal debtor if the creditor has no other means of recovering from the latter; (Yad, Ishut 12:19; Rema, EH 70:8).

If the wife has sold some of her own property to support herself, she will be entitled to recover from her husband the equivalent of the amount realized, provided that the facts do not demonstrate any waiver of this right on her part, such as an express declaration to this effect made by her before witnesses at the time of the sale, or if at that time there was a suit for divorce pending between the parties. If proof to this effect is forthcoming, the wife will not be entitled to recover anything from her husband since it is presumed that as long as the marriage tie is in existence, she will not do anything which might bring about its complete severance and will therefore also be prepared to waive her pecuniary rights against her husband (Rema, EH 70:8 and *Beit Shemu'el* n. 29; PDR 2:289, 291f.). Whenever the wife is not entitled to a refund of the amounts she has expended, during the period of her husband's absence, the earnings from her handiwork will be loans to her (Rema, EH 70:8).

Third parties who of their own accord assist the wife in respect of her maintenance are not entitled to be refunded for their expenditure – neither from the wife since she has not borrowed from them, nor from her husband since he has not instructed them to do so – but they are in the position of one who "has put his money on the horns of a deer" (Rema, EH 70:8; see also Unjust Enrichment[1]). If the wife can prove that

1. page 338.

assistance was given her in the form of a loan, the question of repayment will be governed by the aforesaid ordinary rules concerning a loan for purposes of the wife's maintenance, even if the assistance was given by her own parents (*Mordekhai,* Ket. no. 273).

When the Wife Leaves the Home. In principle the husband is not obliged to maintain his wife unless she lives with him (see above). Hence the mere fact of her leaving him, or her refusal to return to him after she has left him lawfully, provides the husband with a *prima facie* defense against her claim for maintenance, since by living apart from him she precludes herself from carrying out her marital duties, on due fulfillment of which her right to maintenance is dependent. Therefore, to succeed in a claim for maintenance in these circumstances, the wife must discharge the onus of proving facts justifying her absence from the marital home (Rema, EH 70:12 and *Beit Shemu'el* n. 34; PDR 6:33, 52f.). These may arise either from the husband's bad conduct toward her – e.g., his responsibility for a quarrel justifying in law her refusal to continue living with him together in the marital home (*Beit Yosef,* EH 70, end; Sh. Ar., EH 70:12) – or from other circumstances which are independent of the husband's blameworthy conduct toward her, such as his refusal to comply with her justified demand to move to another dwelling or to live away from her husband's relatives who cause her distress (see Husband and Wife). In general it may be said that any reason sufficient to oblige the husband to grant his wife a divorce will entitle her to claim maintenance from him even though she may have left the home, since the fact that the husband is obliged to grant her a divorce means that he must acquiesce in their living apart; therefore her refusal to live with him entails no breach of her duties toward him. Moreover, by unlawfully withholding a divorce from his wife the husband prevents her from marrying someone else who could maintain her, and there is a rule that a husband who, contrary to law, prevents his wife from marrying another man renders himself liable to maintain her until he grants her a divorce (PDR 1:74, 77–80). If the wife leaves the home on account of a quarrel she has unjustifiably caused, and generally when she has no justifiable reason for living apart from her husband, she will not be entitled to maintenance from him.

For other cases in which the wife forfeits her right to maintenance, see Husband and Wife; Divorce.

Claim for Maintenance Cannot be Assigned or Set Off. The husband is not entitled to set off against her claim for maintenance any pecuniary claim he may have against his wife, such as one arising from her sale, contrary to law, of her husband's property for purposes of her maintenance during his absence. His duty to maintain his wife requires him to provide her with the necessities of life with him, i.e., entails responsibility for her daily needs with regard to food, raiment, lodging, etc. This affords the wife a right against which pecuniary debts cannot be set off, since those two differ in their legal nature and her daily needs cannot be satisfied by a reduction of the debt she owes him (PDR 1:333, 338; 2:97, 99). If, however, the wife's claim is based on a right whose legal nature is purely pecuniary, e.g., her claim for repayment of a loan she has taken for her maintenance, there will be no bar to the husband setting off against such claim any other pecuniary claim he may have against her, if, for instance, she is indebted to him for a loan she obtained from him for the purpose of supporting her relatives – he may also set off such pecuniary claim against her claim with regard to payment of her *ketubbah* at the time of their divorce (see PDR 1 loc. cit.). The same reason that entitles the wife to receive actual payment of her maintenance prevents her from assigning this right to others (*Beit Shemu'el* EH 93 n. 18).

Arrear Maintenance. If the wife, although entitled to maintenance, does not bring an action for it in the court, she will be unable to claim maintenance for any period preceding the date of bringing her suit, since it will be presumed that she preferred to suffer rather than unfold her troubles before the court and her silence will therefore be interpreted as a waiver of her right for such a period (Yad, Ishut 12:22; Sh. Ar., EH 70:11). This presumption may be rebutted by evidence showing that she insisted on her rights, e.g., that she demanded her maintenance from her husband and refrained from instituting action only because of his promise to comply without recourse to the court (Rema EH 80:18 and *Beit Shemu'el* n. 27); institution of action has the same effect for any period thereafter even if a considerable amount of time elapses before judgment is given (Rema EH 70:5 and *Beit Shemu'el* n. 12; see also Limitation of Actions).

Nonpayment of Maintenance: Consequences. On the husband's failure to maintain his wife in the manner to which she is entitled, the court – at her instance – will order him to do so, whether he refuses payment although he has the means to meet it or whether he lacks the means because he does not work although he is able to work and earn this amount. In other words, the husband will be ordered to pay maintenance in accordance with his potential working and earning abilities, and not necessarily his actual earnings, for he has undertaken in the *ketubbah* to work and to maintain his wife (Rema, EH 70:3 and *Ḥelkat Meḥokek* n. 12). If he has sufficient for his own needs only for a single day, he must still share this with his wife since he is liable to maintain her "with himself" (Rema, EH 70:3). On the other hand, as he has to maintain her "with him" only, i.e., to no greater extent than he is able in respect of himself, he will be exempt from maintaining her if he cannot afford it because he is in a position of utter poverty and unable to work and earn for reasons beyond his control (*Pitḥei Teshuvah*, EH 70 n. 2; *Perishah,* ḤM 97 n. 41). For the same reason, inability to pay maintenance is excused on grounds of the husband's need to repay regular debts, these taking preference over the former *(ibid.)*. If the wife should not wish to content herself with a claim for maintenance, she may possibly be entitled to demand a divorce.

In the State of Israel. Maintenance for the wife is a matter of personal status within the meaning of article 51 of the Palestine Order in Council, 1922, and is therefore governed by Jewish law (sec. 51 thereof) even when claimed in a civil court by virtue of section 4, Rabbinical Courts Jurisdiction (Marriage and Divorce) Law, 5713–1953. So far as a Jewish wife is concerned, the above position was left unchanged by the Family Law Amendment Maintenance Law, 5719–1959, which expressly provides that the question of her maintenance shall be governed solely by Jewish law (sec. 2; see Supr. PD 15 (1961), 1056, 1058). If the husband refuses to comply with a judgment of the court for the payment of maintenance, he may be imprisoned for a period not exceeding 21 days for every unpaid instalment (Executive Law 5727–1967, sec. 70ff.); see also Imprisonment for Debt.

Bibliography: Gulak, Yesodei, 1 (1922), 37; 2 (1922), 68–70; 3 (1922), 37–39; Gulak, Oẓar, 149–58; ET, 1 (1951^3), 324f.; 4 (1952), 80–83, 91f.; 6 (1954), 656; Regional Rabbinical Court, Tel Aviv, Judgment, in: *Ha-Torah ve-ha-Medinah,* 9–10 (1957/59), 185–99; B. Cohen, in: PAAJR, 20 (1951), 135–234; republished in his: *Jewish and Roman Law,* 1 (1966), 179–278; addenda: *ibid.,* 2 (1966), 775–7; B. Schereschewsky, *Dinei Mishpaḥah* (1967^2), 117–40; Elon, *Ḥakikah Datit . . .* (1968), 44–46, 60–62; idem, *Ha-Mishpat Ha-Ivri* (1973), I, 160ff, II, 467ff, 486ff, 516ff, 531ff, 637ff. H. Baker, *Legal System of Israel* (1968), index.

Ben-Zion Schereschewsky

WIDOW. A widow is a woman who was married in a valid marriage and whose husband has died; if any doubt arises as to her widowhood, she will have to prove that she was so married (for the origin of the word "widow," see Levy, J., Neuhebr Tal, s.v. *alman*). The rabbis of the Talmud exegetically explained the same *almanah* ("widow") as being derived from the words *al maneh* ("because of the *maneh*"), i.e., because her statutory *ketubbah* is a *maneh* (= 100 *zuz*) and not 200 as in the case of a virgin (Ket. 10b).

Personal Status. A widow is generally free to marry any man except a high priest (Lev. 21:14); if she marries the latter she becomes a *ḥalalah* (see *Yuḥasin*; Lev. 21:15; Kid. 77a; Sh. Ar., EH 7:12). For the prohibitions imposed upon her in consequence of her previous marriage, see Marriage, Prohibited, and for the law prohibiting the widow of a childless brother to marry without prior levirate marriage or *ḥaliẓah*, see Levirate Marriage.

Rights and Obligations. The widow is entitled to the return of all her property of whatever kind, since her ownership of it is not affected by marriage (see Husband and Wife; for the difference in this respect between the different kinds of her property, see Dowry). In Jewish law a widow does not inherit her husband (see Succession[1]), but she is entitled to her *ketubbah* and the rights due to her by virtue of its provisions, which the husband's heirs must satisfy out of the estate; the most important of these provisions relate to her maintenance. She is entitled to the said rights by virtue of her bieng the widow, and it is therefore unimportant whether and to what extent she possessed property during the marriage. Her said rights arise upon marriage by virtue of law: "a man, upon marrying a woman, becomes bound to her in respect of the statutory *ketubbah . . .* and her right to be maintained out of his property and to live in his house after his death throughout her widowhood" (Maim. Yad, Ishut 12:1; Sh. Ar., EH 69:1–2); but they become due only upon her husband's death, since the *ketubbah* is "like a debt payable at some future date and will be recoverable only after the husband's death . . ." (Maim. Yad, Ishut, 16:3; Sh. Ar., EH 93:1). Since the said rights accrue to the widow by virtue of her *ketubbah*, they do not exist if she has lost her right to the *ketubbah* (see Divorce[2]).

Inasmuch as the rights of the widow arise upon her marriage and not upon the husband's death, he cannot prejudice them by his will, and any testamentary disposition to the effect that the widow shall not be entitled to her *ketubbah* or maintenance out of his estate is void (Ket. 68b; Sh. Ar., EH 69:2; 93:3). No express reference need be made to these rights in the *ketubbah* deed since they arise upon the marriage as a condition laid down by the *bet din (tenai bet din)*, i.e,, by virtue of law, although they are based upon her being entitled to a *ketubbah* (Ket. 52b; Sh. Ar., loc. cit.).

Satisfaction of the Widow's Rights out of the Estate. According to talmudic law, a widow can enforce her *ketubbah* and its provisions, including maintenance, only against the immovable property which forms part of the estate (Ket. 81b; Sh. Ar., EH 100:1). However, since the development of trade and the decrease of landholding among Jews led creditors to rely also upon the movables of debtors for repayment of their debts, the *geonim* ordained that the movable property of the estate should also be attachable for the widow's rights (Tos. Ket. 51a; Rosh to Ket. ch. 6:5; Sh. Ar., EH 100:1). Since the time of Maimonides it has become customary to include in every *ketubbah* deed a provision rendering the husband's movable property so attachable, whether acquired at the date of the marriage or to be acquired by him thereafter (Maim. Yad, Ishut, 16:8; see Lien).

Satisfaction of the Widow's Rights Against Purchasers. The husband's property being subject to the *ketubbah*, the widow may, in the event of the estate being insufficient to cover it, follow the property in the hands of the purchasers, i.e., recover the amount of the *ketubbah* out of immovable property which the husband or his heirs have transferred to others. This remedy, however, is not available with regard to movables so transferred, since, contrary to the case of immovable property where the purchaser can be required first to find out whether the vendor can indeed transfer it free from all incumbrances, in the case of movables, owing to regulations of furthering commerce *(takkanot ha-shuk)*, that cannot be required lest commercial stability would thereby be impaired (Ket. 51a; Sh. Ar., EH 100:1). On the other hand, if the husband has transferred his property by way of *donatio mortis causa* (see Wills), the widow is entitled to be satisfied for her *ketubbah* out of the movable property also, inasmuch as in such a case the property has passed upon death, subject to her rights which accrued to her already in his lifetime (Sh. Ar., ḤM 252:1, EH 100:1, and Rema). The rabbis, however, also prescribed that for her maintenance the widow cannot proceed against purchasers (see above) even in respect of immovable property, since the amount to be recovered is not a determinate sum but may vary periodically with her requirements, and a purchaser cannot know the precise debt for which the property is charged (Git. 48b, 50b and Rashi ad loc.; Sh. Ar., EH 93:20). On the other hand, as in the case of the *ketubbah*, the widow here may also recover from property transferred by way of *donatio mortis causa* (Sh. Ar., ḤM 252:1, EH loc. cit.). The said limitations upon the right of the widow to receive her *ketubbah* and maintenance from the husband's property which has been transferred to others do not apply if it was transferred fraudulently in order to deprive the widow of it, as "the sages of the Talmud set themselves against anyone who intends to defraud and negate his act" (Resp. Rosh, 78:1 and 3). Accordingly, upon proof that the heirs intend as a means of evasion to dispose of the immovable property of the estate and that her maintenance rights will be prejudiced thereby, she may apply to the court for a prohibitory injunction against them; but she cannot do so in regard to movable property of the estate, since the above-mentioned geonic regulation does not extend to such property (Yad, Ishut, 18:11–13 and *Maggid Mishneh* thereto; Sh. Ar., EH 93:21).

The widow's Maintenance. The widow is generally entitled to receive the same maintenance as she was entitled to receive during the husband's lifetime. The same rules therefore apply, e.g., maintenance will include clothing, residence, medical expenses, use of household articles, and the like. Similarly, the principle also applies that "she rises with him but does not descend with him," i.e., that she is entitled to the same standard of maintenance she was entitled to during her late husband's lifetime (Ket. 48a and 103a; Sh. Ar., EH 94:1 and 5). To some extent her said right to maintenance is affected by the very fact of her widowhood, since the personal relationship upon which her rights were based during her husband's lifetime is now absent, and she is now alone, so that her requirements are reduced. For this reason, although entitled to reside in the same apartment in which she lived with her husband, she is no longer entitled to occupy the whole of it if she, being alone, is not in need of it even in order to maintain her social status (Sh. Ar., EH 94:1 and Rema and commentaries PD 19, pt. 2 (1965), 338). Similarly, she is not entitled to transfer ownership of the apartment to others nor to let the whole or part of it, since the right of residence is conferred upon her in order to enable her to maintain her social status but not to make a profit (Sh. Ar., loc. cit.). The right of the widow with regard to the apartment is merely to have the use of it; therefore, upon her death, it returns

1. page 449; 2. page 418.

to the heirs of the husband only, and does not form part of her estate (*Beit Shemu'el* EH 94, n. 4).

This right of residence is not affected by sale of the apartment by the heirs, and the new owner cannot evict the widow from it (Sh. Ar., EH 94:4). Where the widow is unable to live in the apartment, for instance, if it is destroyed, she is entitled to receive out of the estate an amount necessary for renting another suitable apartment (*Ḥelkat Meḥokek* EH 94, nos. 6, 7). If the widow survives with small children of the husband, both boys and girls, and the estate is insufficient to maintain all of them, her right prevails; if, however, the young children surviving with her are either all boys or all girls, they all take equally (Ket. 43a and Tos. ad loc.; note the alternative opinion in Sh. Ar., EH 93:4; see also EH 113:6 regarding the priority of the widow's maintenance to the right of the daughters to their dowry out of the estate, and for the reason for the aforesaid distinction, see *Beit Shemu'el* and *Ḥelkat Meḥokek* to Sh. Ar., EH 93 nos. 8–9).

The Widow's Claim for Past Maintenance. A widow is entitled to maintenance, also for the time prior to her claim, since there is no reason to assume that she has waived her right to it. This contrasts with the right to maintenance of a wife who is entitled to it only as from the date of claim onward. If the widow has not claimed for a long period – such as when, being a wealthy woman, she delays for three years or, being poor, she delays for two years – she is presumed to have waived the past maintenance unless the presumption is rebutted by the facts, such as by the fact of her right having been secured by a pledge or mortgage (EH 93:14 and see Limitation of Action[1]).

The Widow's Right to Her Earnings and the Income from Her Property. Parallel to the rule prevailing during the husband's lifetime concerning his right to the wife's earnings, the heirs are entitled to the widow's earnings in consideration of her maintenance (Sh. Ar., EH 95:1). On the other hand, they are not entitled to the income from her property, as is the husband to the income from the wife's property – since to the husband it is due in consideration of her redemption only, i.e., of his obligation to ransom her if she is taken captive so that she can return and live with him as his wife, a reason not applicable in respect of the heirs. Correspondingly, the heirs are under no obligation to ransom her either when she has fallen into captivity or finds herself in a similar situation, for instance, when she cannot return from abroad except upon payment of a considerable sum which she does not possess (Ket. 52a; Yad, Ishut, 18:5 and 8; Sh. Ar., EH 78:8; 94:7).

Expiration of the Widow's Right to Maintenance. Since the widow is entitled to maintenance by virtue of the provisions of the *ketubbah* (see above), i.e., only while entitled to the *ketubbah*, her right to maintenance will expire upon her no longer being entitled to the *ketubbah*, i.e., if she has lost her right to it by virtue of law or if she has actually received payment of it from the heirs. Likewise, since one of the conditions in law connected with her maintenance is that she shall not be "ashamed," i.e., to enable her to preserve the honor of her husband, she will lose such right upon her voluntarily claiming her *ketubbah* in court – for by doing so she implicitly declares herself no longer concerned with the honor of her husband or with his heirs (Ket. 54a; Sh. Ar., EH 93:5 and *Ḥelkat Meḥokek*, n. 13).

The widow's right to maintenance also ceases if she remarries (see Marriage), because under the *ketubbah*, which is the source of her right, she is entitled to maintenance during widowhood only. According to most of the authorities, she even loses her maintenance upon her engagement for a new marriage – although by it alone she does not create a new personal status – because by it she shows that she no longer wishes to preserve the honor of her first husband and remain his widow (Ket. 52b; 54a; Sh. Ar., EH 93:7 and Rema ad loc.).

The Problem of Denial of Maintenance by Involuntary Receipt of the Ketubbah. Since the widow – if she has not lost her right to maintenance otherwise (see above) – is entitled to maintenance only so long as she has not received or claimed her *ketubbah* by legal process, opinion was divided already in the time of the Mishnah as to whether the heirs may compel her to receive it and thereby be released from their obligation to maintain her. It was finally decided that this question depends upon custom, because maintenance of the widow is one of the provisions of the *ketubbah*, and in all matters relating to the *ketubbah*, "local custom," i.e., the custom of the place of marriage, applies, such custom being considered a condition of the marriage and therefore not to be varied but with the consent of both spouses (Sh. Ar., EH 93:3 and *Ḥelkat Meḥokek*, n. 5). According to the custom of the people of Jerusalem and Galilee, the choice lay with the widow alone, and therefore they inserted in the *ketubbah* deed a term, "You shall dwell in my house and be maintained in it out of my estate throughout the duration of your widowhood" (Ket. 52b; 54a and Tos. ad loc.). According to the custom of the people of Judea, however, the choice was left with the heirs and there the corresponding term in the *ketubbah* deed was therefore, "until the heirs shall wish to pay you your *ketubbah*" *(ibid.)*. As regards this difference in custom it was said that while the people of Jerusalem cared for their honor, the people of Judea cared for their money (TJ, Ket. 4:15, 29b). The *halakhah* was decided in accordance with the custom of Jerusalem and Galilee, i.e., whenever there is no other fixed custom or rabbinical *takkanah*, the choice lies solely with the widow and the heirs cannot deprive her of maintenance against her wishes (Ket. 54a and Tos. ad loc.; Yad, Ishut, 18:1; Sh. Ar., EH 93:3; and see Conflict of Laws[2]).

Inasmuch as economic conditions during marriage may so change that the estate might be insufficient to provide both for the maintenance of the widow and for inheritance for the heirs – a state of affairs which the husband certainly did not intend – many of the authorities were of the opinion that it is proper to make a *takkanah* permitting the heirs to deprive the widow of her maintenance by payment to her (against her will) of her *ketubbah* (Rema EH 93:3 and *Pitḥei Teshuvah* thereto, n. 5). Accordingly, various *takkanot* were made in the matter and the most well known, cited also in the Shulḥan Arukh, are those known as the *Takkanot* of Toledo, Spain, of the 13th century, which in their main provisions laid down that the heirs may discharge their obligation for the widow's maintenance by payment unto her of her *ketubbah*, which if it amounts to more than half the value of the estate, shall be deemed to be discharged by payment unto her of half such value (Resp. Rosh 55; Sh. Ar., EH 118 and commentaries).

In Ereẓ Israel there is a distinction between the Sephardi and Ashkenazi communities. The former follow the author of the Shulḥan Arukh, i.e., that the choice lies with the widow alone and the heirs cannot rid themselves of the obligation for her maintenance against her wishes (Sh. Ar., EH 93:3). The Ashkenazim permit the heirs to do so by payment unto the widow of the *ketubbah* even if she does not agree to it. That is certainly the situation when the widow was the second wife of the deceased, but it is also customary with a first wife, although the rabbinical courts endeavor to get the parties to agree to a fair arrangement under which the widow will not lose her maintenance. At any rate, the heirs are not entitled to evict the widow from the marital home, and she is to be provided with the household utensils and silverware forming part of the estate, the size of the estate being taken into account (*Pitḥei Teshuvah*, nos. 5

1. page 596; 2. page 716.

and 6 to Sh. Ar., EH 93; *Sha'arei Uzzi'el,* 2 (1946), 244, nos. 14, 15; *Beit Me'ir,* EH 93:3; 94:1).

In The State of Israel. As to the personal status of the widow in the State of Israel, the rules of the *halakhah* generally apply, both in the rabbinical courts and in the secular civil courts, in the latter except insofar as private international law imports other rules. With regard to the widow's financial rights, however, the Succession Law of 1965 provides that the *halakhah* shall apply in the rabbinical courts alone, and only if all the interested parties have expressed their consent to it in writing (sec. 155). Failing such consent, jurisdiction is in the civil courts alone, and these apply the provisions of the said law only (secs. 148 and 151). Under these provisions the widow is entitled to a part of the estate as an heir. In addition, if she is in need of it, she is also entitled to maintenance out of the estate; the amount of such maintenance is fixed by the court, taking into account all the circumstances and particularly to what she is entitled as an heir and the extent of her *ketubbah* (secs. 56–65).

Bibliography: Gulak, Yesodei, 3 (1922), 38–40, 88–91, 95f., 99; Gulak, Oẓar, 98, 156f.; ET, 2 (1949), 16–20; 4 (1952), 744; B. Schereschewsky, *Dinei Mishpahah* (1967²), 236–70; M. Elon, in: ILR, 4 (1969), 130–2; idem, *Ha-Mishpat Ha-Ivri,* (1973), II, 252ff., 373ff., 458ff., 470ff., 650ff., 670ff., 682ff.

Ben-Zion Schereschewsky

LEVIRATE MARRIAGE AND ḤALIẒAH.

Definition. Levirate marriage (Heb. יבום, *yibbum*) is the marriage between a widow whose husband died without offspring (the *yevamah*) and the brother of the deceased (the *yavam* or levir), as prescribed in Deuteronomy 25:5–6:

"If brethren dwell together, and one of them die, and have no child, the wife of the dead shall not marry without unto a stranger [the last words according to AV translation, which is correct]; her husband's brother shall go in unto her, and take her to him to wife, and perform the duty of a husband's brother unto her. And it shall be, that the firstborn that she beareth shall succeed in the name of his brother that is dead, that his name be not blotted out of Israel."

When the levir does not marry the *yevamah,* the ceremony of *ḥaliẓah* (Heb. חליצה) takes place, whereby the woman becomes released from the levirate tie *(zikkat ha-yibbum)* and free to marry someone else:

"If the man like not to take his brother's wife, then his brother's wife shall go up to the gate unto the elders, and say: 'My husband's brother refuseth to raise up unto his brother a name in Israel; he will not perform the duty of a husband's brother unto me.' Then the elders of his city shall call him, and speak unto him; and if he stand, and say: 'I like not to take her'; then shall his brother's wife draw nigh unto him in the presence of the elders, and loose his shoe from off his foot, and spit in his presence; and she shall answer and say: 'So shall it be done unto the man that doth not build up his brother's house.' And his name shall be called in Israel 'The house of him that had his shoe loosed' " (Deut. 25:7–10).

In the Bible. The events concerning Judah and Tamar (Gen. 38) indicate that the practice of levirate marriage preceded the Mosaic law (cf. Gen. R. 85:5). However, it appears that levirate marriage then differed from that of Mosaic law in that the obligation also appears to have been laid on the father of the deceased husband (Gen. 38:26) and no mention is made of a release by way of *ḥaliẓah.* Some scholars expressed the opinion, following the view of Josephus (Ant. 5:332–5) and several Karaite authorities (*Gan Eden,* Nashim, 13, 30; *Adderet Eliyahu,* Nashim 5), that the events concerning Ruth and Boaz (Ruth 4) also indicate a levirate marriage, but it appears that in this case the duty of the *go'el* to marry Ruth was incidental to the laws concerning the redemption of property of the deceased; hence the variation in a number of details from the prescribed levirate marriage laws (Ibn Ezra, Deut. 25:5; Naḥmanides, Gen. 38:8).

In the Talmud. Need for Levirate Marriage and Ḥaliẓah. The word *ben* ("son") in Deuteronomy 25:5 is interpreted in the Talmud, in the Septuagint, and by Josephus (Ant. 4:254) to mean "offspring" and not only a male child (cf. Gen. 3:16), so that a levirate marriage is only obligatory when the deceased husband leaves no offspring whatever, whether from the *yevamah* or another wife, including a child conceived during his lifetime but not born until after his death, even if that child subsequently died (Yev. 2:5, 22b; Nid. 5:3; and codes). The words, "if brothers dwell together" (Deut. 25:5) are interpreted as confining the application of levirate marriage to the brothers of the deceased who were born prior to his death (Yev. 2:1,2). Thus if the birth of the levir precedes his brother's death by as little as one day and there are no other brothers, the *yevamah* must wait until he reaches the age of 13 years and a day, when he becomes legally fit either to marry her or grant her *ḥaliẓah* (Nid. 5:3; Yev. 105b). The law of *yibbum* applies only to paternal not maternal brothers (Yev. 17b). If the deceased is survived by several brothers, the obligation of *yibbum* or *ḥaliẓah* devolves on the eldest but is nevertheless valid if performed by another brother (Yev. 24a; 39a). If the deceased brother had several wives, fulfillment of the obligation in respect of one wife suffices and exempts the other wives (Yev. 4:11, 44a; and codes).

The tie *(zikkah)* between the *yevamah* and the *yevam* arises immediately upon the husband's death. From this stage, until she undergoes levirate marriage or *ḥaliẓah,* the *yevamah* is known as a *shomeret yavam* ("awaiting the levir") and relations between the levir and her kin are prohibited (as incestuous), as if he were married to her. Only a putative marriage can be contracted between a *shomeret yavam* and an "outsider," who is obliged to divorce her, although their offspring are not considered *mamzerim* (Yev. 13b; et al.; Yad, Ishut 4:14).

The *shomeret yavam* may not undergo levirate marriage or *ḥaliẓah* until three months after the date of her husband's death (Yev. 4:10 and codes) as with any other widow, who must await this period before remarrying. She is therefore entitled to maintenance from her husband's estate during this period, but not thereafter, neither from her husband's estate nor from the levir. However, if the levir evaded her after she had sued him in court either to marry her or grant her *ḥaliẓah* the rabbis fined him to pay her maintenance (Yev. 41b; Rashi, and Tosafot thereto), and this was also the law if he became ill or went abroad (TJ, Ket. 5:4, 29d; Yad, Ishut, 18:16).

In biblical law the levir did not require a formal marriage *(kiddushin)* to the *yevamah.* since the personal status tie, the *zikkah* between them, arises automatically upon the death of the husband of the *yevamah.* However, the scholars prescribed that the *yevamah* should be married like all women, in this case by *kiddushei kesef* or *shetar,* these *kiddushin* called *"ma'amar"* (lit. "declaration"): "first he addresses to her a *ma'amar* and then they cohabit" (lit. "he takes her into his home"; Tosef. Yev. 7:2; Yev. 52a). The levir who marries the *yevamah* succeeds to the estate of his deceased brother (Yev. 4:7), the passage *"ve-hayah ha-bekhor asher teled"* (Deut. 25:6) being interpreted as referring to the firstborn of the brothers on whom the duty of levirate marriage devolved and hence that the continuation of this passage, i.e., "shall succeed in the name of his brother" (meaning "shall succeed to the inheritance") refers to the levir undergoing levirate marriage. This argument was described as "having entirely deprived the text of its ordinary meaning through a *gezerah shavah*" (Yev. 24a; see Interpretation[1]). According to R. Judah (Yev. 4:7), "where there is a father, he inherits the son's property," otherwise the brothers succeed to the estate (Tosef. Yev. 6:3) and the levir marrying the *yevamah* inherits only a brother's proportionate share. He interprets the above passage literally, as referring to the firstborn of the union between the levir and the *yevamah*, who succeeds to the estate of the deceased brother (interpreted similarly by Tar. Yer., Ibn Ezra, and Rashbam, Deut. 25:6, Rashi, Gen. 38:8 – from whom Ramban Gen. *ibid.* differs). The *amoraim* commented, however, that R. Judah did not differ from the scholars but merely excepted the case of the deceased who is survived by his father, for the levir is compared to the firstborn *("ve-hayah ha-bekhor asher teled")*, who does not inherit in his father's lifetime (Yev. 40a). Even according to the scholars whose opinion was accepted, the levir does not succeed to a contingent inheritance *(ra'ui)*, i.e., to property due to come to the deceased brother (such as the proportional share of his father's estate which the deceased, but for his death, would have inherited), but only to property already owned by the brother at the time of his death, as in the case of the firstborn (Bek. 8:9; see Succession[2]). The *ketubbah*, i.e., the widow's jointure, is a charge on the property which the levir inherits from the deceased and he is prohibited from alienating the latter by way of sale or gift – any such attempted alienation being void (Ket. 82a). In a case where the levir inherits no property from his brother, the widow must receive her *ketubbah* from the levir's property "so that he shall not consider it easy to divorce her" (Yev. 39a). A levir who chooses to perform *ḥaliẓah* receives no more than a brother's share of the deceased's estate (Yev. 4:7) and upon *ḥaliẓah* the widow becomes entitled to receive her *ketubbah* from her deceased husband's estate (Yev. 85a; Sh. Ar., EH 165:4).

The Duty of Ḥaliẓah. According to the Torah, the duty of *ḥaliẓah* is imposed only when the levir wilfully refuses to marry the *yevamah*, and not when he is unable to or prohibited from marrying her, for "whoever is subject [lit. "goes up"] to levirate marriage is subject to *ḥaliẓah*, and whoever is not subject to levirate marriage is not subject to *ḥaliẓah*" (Yev. 3a). Thus, for example, where a levirate marriage is precluded because the relationship would be incestuous, the widow (supposing she is the levir's daughter or his wife's sister) is also exempted from *ḥaliẓah*. According to Bet Hillel, if one of the deceased's several wives is prohibited from marrying the levir she also exempts her co-wives (*ẓarah*, "rival") and the "rivals of her rivals" (if the rival has married another man) from levirate marriage and *ḥaliẓah*, but Bet Shammai's opinion was that the rival is not thus exempted (Yev. 1:1; 1:4; cf. Yev. 16a and TJ, Yev. 1:6, 3a). On the other hand, it was determined that at times the duty of *ḥaliẓah* exists even where levirate marriage is forbidden – as between a priest and divorcee – by a "prohibition of holiness" *(issur kedushah)*; in such a case *ḥaliẓah* is still required for, as in all cases of negative precepts, the marriage, even if prohibited, is nevertheless valid once it has taken place (Yev. 2:3 and Rashi ad loc., TJ, Yev. 1:1, 2c; see Marriage, Prohibited). This rule also applies when doubt exists as to whether levirate marriage is incumbent on the widow, in which case *ḥaliẓah* is required (Git. 7:3, et al.). In cases where the levir is seriously ill or there is a big difference in their ages, or the levir is "not suitable" *(eino hagun)* for the widow, etc., efforts were made to arrange for *ḥaliẓah* rather than marriage.

Priority between Levirate Marriage and Ḥaliẓah. In the course of time some scholars accepted the view that the duty of the *ḥaliẓah* always took priority over that of levirate marriage, a view stemming from the attempt to reconcile the prohibition of a man marrying his brother's wife (Lev. 18:16) with the command of levirate marriage. These biblical commandments induced the Samaritans to confine the application of levirate marriage to a woman who had undergone *kiddushin* but not *nissu'in* (see Marriage) – in which case she would not be considered a relative with whom marriage was prohibited (Kid. 75b–76a; TJ, Yev. 1:6) – while some Karaite scholars were led to interpret the word "brothers" as relatives and not literally (*Gan Eden* Nashim, 13; *Adderet Eliyahu*, Nashim, 5). The two biblical provisions do not conflict, however, for the prohibition in Leviticus 18:16 applies only where the deceased brother is survived by descendants, whereas the *mitzvah* of levirate marriage applies only when the deceased brother dies without issue, in order that the levir shall "succeed in the name of his brother." The *mitzvah* of levirate marriage and the prohibition of marrying a brother's wife "were said as one" (Mekh. Ba-Ḥodesh 7; Sif. Deut., 233; TJ, Ned. 3:2, 37d). Hence in the beginning, when the parties carried out the precept for the sake of fulfilling a commandment, levirate marriage took priority over *ḥaliẓah;* but when the precept was carried out for other reasons, the scholars said that *ḥaliẓah* took priority over levirate marriage, and "a levir who marries the *yevamah* other than for the sake of fulfilling a commandment commits incest" (Bek. 1:7 and Rashi ad loc.); and ". . . I am inclined to think that the child of such a union is a *mamzer*" (Abba Saul, Tosef. Yev. 6:9; Yev. 39b). The question of priority was much disputed by the scholars. In the third generation of *tannaim*, levirate marriage was customarily upheld (Yev. 8:4), while the Babylonian *amoraim* left the choice between marriage and *ḥaliẓah* to the levir, although some "reenacted the priority of levirate marriage over *ḥaliẓah*" (Yev. 39a–b). The Palestinian *amoraim* apparently held that *ḥaliẓah* took priority (Bar Kappara in TB, Yev. 109a, makes no mention of the above "reenactment" of levirate marriage priority).

The Order of Ḥaliẓah. *Ḥaliẓah* which releases the widow from the obligation of levirate marriage enables her to marry freely, except that the scholars prohibited a priest from marrying her (Yev. 24a). The *ḥaliẓah* ceremony is designed to shame the levir for not "building up his brother's house" (Deut. 25:9). It has been seen as an act of *kinyan* (acquisition), whereby the widow buys from the levir the inheritance of his deceased brother (Rashbam *ibid.;* cf. Ruth 4:7–8), or as a form of mourning for the levir's brother "for he shall be forgotten now that no offspring shall be raised in his name" (Jehiel of Paris cited in *Seder Ḥaliẓah* to Sh. Ar., EH 169:57, no. 82; Responsum of Isaac Caro at the end of Responsa *Beit Yosef*). Although the formalities of *ḥaliẓah* are performed by the *yevamah*, the levir is called the *ḥoleẓ*, i.e., "loosener" (Yev. 4:1, 5–8; 5:6; et al.), for the levir "participates in *ḥaliẓah* in that his intention to loosen is required," hence a deaf-mute levir who lacks such intention is called the *neḥlaẓ* and not the *ḥoleẓ* (Yev. 12:4; *Nimmukei Yosef* 104b, and Maim. commentary ad loc.).

Many details are stipulated for the order of the *ḥaliẓah* ceremony (Yev. 12:6; Yad, Yibbum 4:1–23; Sh. Ar., EH 169); essentially they are as follows: The levir and the *yevamah* appear before the *bet din*, the levir wearing on his right foot a special shoe, the "*ḥaliẓah* shoe"; the *yevamah* recites a passage indicating the levir's refusal to perform his duty to marry her; the levir responds by affirming his refusal – all this in Hebrew in the words prescribed in the Bible (Deut. 25:7, 9); the *yevamah* then removes the shoe from the levir's foot, throws it to the ground, spits on the ground before the levir, and utters the final prescribed passage (Deut. 25:9); finally, those present repeat the words *"ḥaluẓ ha-na'al"* three times. The Boethusians held that the *yevamah* is required actually to spit in the levir's face and this is also stated in two manuscripts of the Septuagint, in

1. page 65; 2. page 447.

Josephus' *Antiquities,* and in some of the apocryphal books, but the talmudic scholars held it to be sufficient if the elders see her spitting (Sif., Deut. 291). At the completion of the ceremony, the *dayyanim* express the wish "that the daughters of Israel shall have no need to resort to either *ḥaliẓah* or levirate marriage" (Sh. Ar., EH, 169, "abridged order of *ḥaliẓah,*" 56). At first it was customary to issue a deed of *ḥaliẓah* as proof that the ceremony had taken place (Yev. 39b – as distinguished from a deed of divorce where the delivery of the deed constitutes the act of divorce), but in the course of time this practice was abandoned since "the ceremony was performed in public, before ten people, and she does not require documentary proof" (Sh. Ar., EH 169, "abridged order of *ḥaliẓah,*" 13; and end of commentary *Seder Ḥaliẓah,* no. 82).

In the Post-Talmudic Period. Priority. In the post-talmudic period, the dispute over the question of priority was continued. In the opinion of the Sura *geonim,* levirate marriage took priority, while those of Pumbedita thought otherwise, as did some of the Sura scholars (R. Hillai and R. Natronai). In the rabbinic period the Spanish scholars – particularly Alfasi (to Yev. 39b), Maimonides (Yad, Yibbum 1:2), and Joseph Caro (Sh. Ar., EH, 165:1) – gave priority to levirate marriage, contending that otherwise there is no reason to shame and to submit the levir to the prescribed indignities and that the kabbalistic scholars said that "levirate marriage is very beneficial for the soul of the dead," and that Abba Saul who held that *ḥaliẓah* took priority, "did not know this kabbalistic mystery," otherwise he would not have come to the conclusion he reached (Isaac Caro, quoted in Resp. *Beit Yosef,* loc. cit.). Such has actually been the custom, until the present day, of the Jews of Spain and of the oriental communities in North Africa from Morocco to Egypt – in Yemen, Babylonia, and Persia. This was also the case in Ereẓ Israel (even at the end of the 1940s; see *Mishpetei Uziel,* EH no. 119) until the matter was settled by a *takkanah* of the chief rabbinate of Israel (in 5710–1949/50, see below). The scholars of northern France and Germany – particularly Rashi, Rabbenu Tam, Asher b. Jehiel (Tur. EH 165), and Moses Isserles (Rema EH, 165:1) – held that *ḥaliẓah* takes priority though they did not all assign the same measure of priority to it. The acceptance of Rabbenu Gershom's decree (prohibiting polygamy) among Ashkenazi Jews (see Bigamy[1]) apparently contributed greatly toward the entrenchment of the rule that *ḥaliẓah* takes priority – in order not to distinguish between a married and an unmarried levir – and Ashkenazi communities gradually came to adopt the practice of *ḥaliẓah* to the exclusion of levirate marriage.

Problems of Levirate Marriage – The Apostate Levir. The scholars devote a great deal of discussion to the solution of problems centering around the laws of levirate marriage and *ḥaliẓah,* arising both from objective factors and from the levir's conduct. The Mishnah (Git. 7:3) relates the case of a childless husband who fell ill and wrote his wife a "conditional" bill of divorce, effected upon his death, so that on his death the divorce would take effect retroactively to the date of delivery of the bill, with the intention of absolving her from the obligations of a *yevamah.* In the case of an "unsuitable" levir, or one suffering from a serious illness, or whose age differed greatly from that of the widow, it was sought to influence the levir in various ways to forego marriage in favor of *ḥaliẓah.* From the geonic period, mention is made (first in the *Halakhot Gedolot,* end of Hilkh. Yevamot) of the problem of the *yevamah* and the apostate levir "in the land of the Berbers, among gentiles" or "who cannot be reached in a far land," which placed the *yevamah* in the position of an *agunah.* Some of the *geonim* decided that she retained this status until released by the apostate levir, but others ruled that she was exempted from *ḥaliẓah* if at the time of her marriage to the deceased his brother was already an apostate. It seems that the Babylonian academies were also divided on this question, Sura taking a lenient view and Pumbedita a strict one (L. Ginzberg, *Ginzei Schechter,* 2 (1929), 167f.). In later times the view that *ḥaliẓah* was obligatory for the widow in every case became increasingly stronger and a solution for the problem was sought by the imposition – at the time of the *kiddushin* ceremony – of a condition specifying that the wife "shall be considered as not having been married if it shall be her lot to require levirate marriage at the hands of an apostate" (Rema, EH 157:4).

Problems of Ḥaliẓah. In an effort to overcome the problem that arose when a levir refused to undergo *ḥaliẓah,* many French and German communities enacted *takkanot* awarding the levir a substantial share of the deceased brother's estate – financed partly at the widow's expense – although according to law the levir was entitled only to a brother's share upon *ḥaliẓah.* The varying terms of these *takkanot* gave rise to frequent disputes, so that in practice the courts sought to compromise between the parties (Sh. Ar., EH 163:2, 165:4). As this, in turn, frequently caused the widow to be left at the levir's mercy, it became increasingly customary for the husband's brothers to write – at the time of the marriage – a "deed of undertaking to grant *ḥaliẓah*" committing themselves to release the widow, whenever the need might arise, in a valid *ḥaliẓah* ceremony, without delay or demand for consideration; this undertaking was enforced by way of a biblical oath and a severe penalty or ban. Where the levir was a minor at the time of his brother's marriage and his undertaking consequently unenforceable, his father would write a deed guaranteeing that his minor son would, upon reaching maturity, provide the required undertaking to his sister-in-law. The father backed his guarantee – which was itself lacking in authority (see *Asmakhta*[2]) – by a monetary pledge to his daughter-in-law, which would be canceled on the production of the required undertaking (Gulak, Oẓar, 90–97). Many of the *aḥaronim* decided in favor of obliging the levir to maintain the widow to whom he refused to grant *ḥaliẓah,* despite the lack of unanimity among the *rishonim* on the circumstances and terms on which maintenance should be awarded, as otherwise "she may be kept an *agunah* forever" (*Arukh ha-Shulḥan,* EH 160:8).

In recent years the problem of *ḥaliẓah* arising from the levir being absent abroad has become more acute, particularly in the case of countries in the Soviet bloc. Several halakhic authorities, led by Shalom Mordecai ha-Kohen Schwadron, head of the Brezen *bet din,* have sought to avoid the widow's need to travel to the *levir* by permitting her to be represented at the *ḥaliẓah* ceremony by an agent (Resp. Maharsham, pt. 1, nos. 14, 135), a view based on confining the prohibition on agency in *ḥaliẓah* to the levir only (Ket. 74a); however, most of his contemporaries dissented from this. It has also been rejected by modern Ereẓ Israel scholars (e.g., *Mishpetei Uziel* 2 (1938), EH 88; *Kunteres Sheliḥut ba-Ḥaliẓah*) and this problem – like that which arises when the *levir* is a minor, placing the widow in a position of an *agunah* until he reaches the age of 13 years and a day – urgently awaits a solution, possibly along the lines already indicated.

Takkanah of the Chief Rabbinate of Ereẓ Israel. In 1944 the chief rabbinate of Ereẓ Israel enacted a *takkanah* obliging the levir to maintain the levirate widow until he released her by *ḥaliẓah,* according to "law and precept," if a rabbinical court had certified that he refused to comply with its decision ordering him to grant her *ḥaliẓah.* This *takkanah,* which gives expression to the view of those halakhic scholars who would oblige the recalcitrant levir to maintain the widow, has made this obligation part of the law of maintenance, rather than its being a fine for

1. page 367; 2. page 172.

noncompliance. It was prompted by the fact of "much difficulty and suffering arising from the regrettable prevalence of cases of Jewish women who are in need of levirate marriage and are placed in the position of *agunot* because *ḥaliẓah* has been withheld from them." A further *takkanah* of the chief rabbinate of the State of Israel (1950) completely prohibited the practice of levirate marriage in Israel while making *ḥaliẓah* obligatory. This *takkanah,* extending also to the Sephardi and oriental Jewish communities in Israel, was expressly justified on the grounds that "most levirs do not undergo levirate marriage for the sake of fulfilling a *mitzvah,* and also to preserve peace and harmony in the State of Israel by keeping the law of the Torah uniform for all."

In the State of Israel. The Rabbinical Courts Jurisdiction (Marriage and Divorce) Law, 5713–1953 of the State of Israel confers on the rabbinical court exclusive jurisdiction in a case where a woman sues her deceased husband's brother for *ḥaliẓah,* and also with regard to maintenance for the woman until the day on which *ḥaliẓah* is granted (sec. 5). Section 7 of the same law further provides that "Where a rabbinical court, by final judgment [i.e., when it can no longer be appealed against; sec. 8] has ordered that a man be compelled to give his brother's widow *ḥaliẓah,* a district court may, upon expiration of three months from the day of making the order, on application of the attorney general, compel compliance with the order by imprisonment." A judgment compelling a levir to grant *ḥaliẓah* will be given by the rabbinical court in similar circumstances to those in which it customarily sees fit to compel the grant of a divorce, and in certain additional cases, e.g., where the levir is already married (Tur and Sh. Ar., EH 165), but at all times only where compulsion is supported by halakhic authority so as not to bring about a prohibited "forced *ḥaliẓah*" (Yev. 106a; Yad, Yibbum 4:25–26; Sh. Ar., EH 169:13). This procedure, so far as halakhically permitted, offers an effective means of dealing with a recalcitrant levir.

Bibliography: A Geiger, in: *He-Ḥalutz,* 6 (1861), 26–28; I. I. Mattuck, in: *Studies... Kohler* (1913), 210–22; I. S. Zuri, *Mishpat ha-Talmud,* 2 (1921), 113–23; Gulak, Yesodei, 3 (1922), 30–33; idem, Oẓar, 90–97; Finkelstein, Middle Ages, 229f., 245–7, 253–6; M. Price, in: *Oriental Studies... Haupt* (1926), 268–71; A. A. Judelowitz, *Av be-Ḥokhmah* (1927); Z. Karl, in: *Ha-Mishpat,* 1 (1927), 266–79; L. Ginzberg, in: *Ginzei Schechter,* 2 (1929), 166–81, 270f.; H. Albeck, in: *Berichte der Hochschule fuer die Wissenschaft des Judentums,* 49 (1932), 66–72; idem (ed.), *Mishnah, Nashim,* 7–10; B. M. Lewin (ed.), *Oẓar ha-Ge'onim, Yevamot* (1936), 34–37, 67–80; H. Tchernowitz, *Toledot ha-Halakhah,* 3 (1943), 186–203; A. H. Freimann, in: *Sinai,* 14 (1943/44), 258–60; idem, *Seder Kiddushin ve-Nissu'in Aḥarei Ḥatimat ha-Talmud* (1945), 385–97; S. Assaf, *Tekufat ha-Ge'onim ve-Sifrutah* (1955), 275–7; M. Elon, in: *Sefer Yovel le-Pinḥas Rozen* (1962), 187f.; idem, *Ha-Mishpat Ha-Ivri* (1973), I, 160ff, 186ff, II, 325ff, 373ff, 636, 639, 672ff, 675, 711ff, 736ff, 818ff, III, 841ff.; idem, *Ḥakikah Datit...* (1968), 31, 162, 172f.; M. Silberg, *Ha-Ma'amad ha-Ishi be-Yisrael* (1965[4]), 381–6, 391; B. Schereschewsky, *Dinei Mishpaḥah* (1967[2]), 226–36.

Menachem Elon

AGUNAH (Heb. עגונה , lit. "tied," cf. Ruth 1:13), a married woman who for whatsoever reason is separated from her husband and cannot remarry, either because she cannot obtain a divorce from him (see Divorce), or because it is unknown whether he is still alive. The term is also applied to a *yevamah* ("a levirate widow;" see Levirate Marriage), if she cannot obtain *ḥaliẓah* from the levir or if it is unknown whether he is still alive (Git. 26b, 33a; Yev. 94a; and Posekim). The problem of the *agunah* is one of the most complex in halakhic discussions and is treated in great detail in halakhic literature (no less than six volumes of *Oẓar ha-Posekim* are devoted to it – see bibliography).

Essence of the Problem. The *halakhah* prescribes that a marriage can only be dissolved by divorce or the death of either spouse. According to Jewish law, divorce is effected not by decree of the court, but by the parties themselves, i.e., by the husband's delivery of a *get* ("bill of divorce") to his wife (see Divorce). Hence the absence of the husband or his wilful refusal to deliver the *get* precludes any possibility of a divorce. Similarly the mere disappearance of the husband, where there is no proof of his death, is not sufficient for a declaration by the court to the effect that a wife is a widow and her marriage thus dissolved. The husband, on the other hand, is unaffected by *aginut,* i.e., by his wife's refusal to accept the *get* or her disappearance without trace, since in such a case under certain conditions the law affords him the possibility of receiving *hetter nissu'in* ("permission to contract an additional marriage"; see Bigamy[1]). In most cases of *agunot* the question is whether or not the husband is still alive. Such cases, result, for instance, from uncertainty about the husband's fate caused by condition of war or persecution – particularly in recent times as a result of the Nazi Holocaust; but the problem can also arise, for example, if the husband suffers from chronic mental illness making him legally incapable of giving a *get* or simply if he wilfully refuses to do so.

Rabbinical scholars have permitted many relaxations in the general laws of evidence in order to relieve the hardships suffered by the *agunah.* On the other hand great care was always taken to avoid the risk that permission may inadvertently be given for a married woman to contract a second marriage that would be adulterous and result in any children from such a second marriage being *mamzerim* (see *Mamzer*). Achieving both these ends, i.e., to enable the *agunah* to remarry while ensuring that an adulterous union does not result, is the object of intensive discussion in the laws of the *agunah.*

Mode of Proof (of the husband's death). It is a basic rule of *halakhah* that facts are to be determined on the testimony of two witnesses (see Evidence). However, the Mishnah already attributes to R. Gamaliel the Elder the *takkanah* that when a husband is missing because of war, and his fate is unkown, the wife may be permitted to remarry on the testimony of only one witness to his death (Yev. 16:7). Although somewhat later R. Eliezer and R. Joshua disagreed with this ruling, at the time of R. Gamaliel of Jabneh it was again determined *(ibid.)* not only that one witness was sufficient but also that hearsay evidence might be admitted, as well as the evidence of a woman, a slave, a handmaiden, or a relative (which classes were otherwise legally incompetent as witnesses). The legal explanation given for these far-reaching rules is that it is to be presumed that a person will not give false testimony on a matter which is likely to come to light, since the husband, if still alive, will undoubtedly reappear sooner or later (Yev. 93b; Maim., Yad, Gerushin, 12:15). Moreover, it may be assumed that the wife herself will endeavor to make sure of her husband's death before remarrying, since she will become prohibited to both men if it later transpires that her first husband is still alive, and her other rights, especially pecuniary ones, will be affected too (v. infra; Yev. 87b; Sh. Ar., EH 17:3, 56). Another reason given is that a relaxation of the law is appropriate in times of danger, the possibility that a woman may remain an *agunah* being deemed to be such a time of danger (Yev. 88a, 122a and Rashi *ibid.;* see also *Takkanot*).

An *agunah* may also be permitted to remarry on the strength

1. page 370.

of her testimony alone as to her husband's death, when she is known to have lived in harmony with her first husband and his absence is not due to war-conditions, for the reason, already mentioned, that certainly she has made careful inquiries herself before seeking to contract another marriage (Yev. 93b, 114b–116, and Posekim). On the other hand, five categories of woman are incompetent to testify as to the husband's death, including his mother and his daughter by another marriage, since it is feared, in view of their customary hatred of the wife, that they are likely to deliver false evidence, so that she should remarry and thus become prohibited to her first husband if it should later transpire that he is still alive (Yev. 117a and Posekim).

Similarly, an *agunah* may be relieved of her disability on the unsolicited statement of an apostate Jew (see Apostate) or a non-Jew, as to her husband's death; for instance, if during a casual conversation they happened to say, "it is a pity that so and so is dead, he was a fine man," or, "as we were walking together, he suddenly dropped dead," or the like (Yev. 121b–122a; Maim.; *ibid.,* 13:11; Sh. Ar., EH 17:14). For the purpose of permitting an *agunah* to remarry it is sufficient if written documents exist that testify to the husband's death (Sh. Ar., EH 17:11). The *halakhah* originally considered documents emanating from non-Jewish authorities as insufficient to permit an *agunah* to remarry (Maim., Yad, Gerushin, 13:28; Sh. Ar., EH, 17:14), but according to the opinion of most *posekim,* this *halakhah* does not apply to present-day non-Jewish authorities, whose documents, such as death certificates, etc., may be relied on (see, e.g., Ḥatam Sofer, responsa EH, 1:43).

Subject-Matter of the Proof. The *halakhah,* while striving to be as lenient as possible in the method of proving the husband's death, imposes strict requirements concerning the nature of the evidence with regard to the husband's death, lest a woman still married may thus be permitted to marry another man (Maim. *ibid.,* 15: Sh. Ar., EH 17:29). The identity must be established of the person whose death it is sought to determine and there exist most detailed rules in order to establish it with the maximum amount of certainty under the circumstances. Thus evidence as to circumstances from which death would be likely to result in a majority of cases is not considered as sufficient proof of death itself since it may be merely the opinion of the witness that the husband is dead, but not testimony as to the fact of death. Hence, the wife will not be permitted to remarry on the strength of evidence to the effect that her husband was seen to fall into the sea and drown in "water having no end" (i.e., where one can see only the sea but not its surroundings) when his death was not actually seen to have taken place, since he may have been rescued. If, however, the witness testifies that he was later present at the funeral of the husband or some other clear evidence of death, for example, that an identifiable limb was found at the place of drowning, it is accepted as evidence of death. On the other hand the death of the husband will be accepted as having been sufficiently proved and the *agunah* will be permitted to remarry on the strength thereof if there is evidence that he drowned in water "having an end" (i.e., that one can see its surroundings); and the witness stayed long enough at the scene "for the victim's life to depart," without seeing him rise to the surface (Yev. 120–121; Maim. *ibid.,* 15–27; Sh. Ar., EH 17:1–42, esp. 32).

Agunah in the Case of a Civil Marriage. A deserted wife who, practically speaking, has no prospects of obtaining a *get* from her husband, but was married in a civil ceremony only (see Civil Marriage), may in certain circumstances be declared by the court to have never entered a marriage and thus be permitted to marry another man without need of a *get* from her first husband. The court will reach this conclusion particularly if the wife is able to prove that her first husband expressly refused to marry her in a religious ceremony, declaring thus by implication that he did not wish to create the status of a marriage according to Jewish law (Resp. Melammed Leho'il, EH 20).

Mitzvah to Permit Agunot to Remarry. Finding a way for permitting an *agunah* to remarry is deemed a great *mitzvah* (Responsa Asheri, 51:2). Indeed, an onerous application of the law, without justification, and in cases where there is no suspicion of deception, is regarded not only as a failure to perform a *mitzvah,* but even as a transgression (Responsa Maimonides, ed. Freiman, 159; Sh. Ar., EH 17:21, Isserles). However, in view of the danger of legalizing a possibly adulterous union, it is customary for an *agunah* to be permitted to remarry only after consultation with, and consent having been obtained from other leading scholars (Sh. Ar., *ibid.,* 34; Isserles and other commentators).

Consequences of Remarriage. An *agunah* who remarries, after permission is granted by the court, is generally entitled to the payment of her *ketubbah* (Yev. 116b; 117a; Maim. Yad, Ishut 16:31; Sh. Ar., *ibid.,* 43, 44). If an *agunah* remarries after permission has been given, and then her first husband reappears, her legal position is that of an *eshet ish* "a married woman" who has married another man, thus becoming prohibited to both men (see Adultery). Accordingly, she requires a *get* from both, and any children born to her of her second husband will be *mamzerim* according to biblical law. Any children born to her from a union with her first husband, after he takes her back but prior to her having received a *get* from her second husband, will also be *mamzerim,* but only according to rabbinical law. In such event she is not entitled to her *ketubbah* from either husband (Yev. 87b, Maim. Yad, Gerushin, 10:5, 7; Sh. Ar., EH 17:56).

Proposals for Precautions to Avoid a Woman Becoming an Agunah. In view of the unhappy straits in which an *agunah* is likely to find herself, ways were sought already in early times of taking precautions against such an eventuality. Thus it was customary for anyone "going to wars of the House of David, to write a bill of divorce for his wife" (Ket. 9b and Rashi and Tos. *ibid.*). This *get* was a conditional one, i.e., becoming effective only should the husband not return from war until a specified date, whereupon the wife would become a divorcee and be entitled to marry another man without having to undergo a levirate marriage or *Ḥaliẓah* (Sh. Ar., EH 143). In certain countries this practice is adopted even in present times by those going to war, but complications may ensue; since the rules and the consequences of a *get* of this nature are beset with *halakhic* problems (Sh. Ar., *ibid.*), particularly when the husband is a *kohen,* since his wife will be a divorcee if he fails to return by the specified date, and by law he must not thereafter remarry her (See Marriage, Prohibited[1]). One of the solutions suggested was for the husband to grant his wife an unconditional divorce, save that each promises to remarry the other upon the husband's return from war. This, however, would not avail a *kohen* for the reasons mentioned. Furthermore, in the event of the wife's refusal to keep her promise upon her husband's return, the question may arise whether on the strength of the *get* she is free to marry another man, because of the reasonable possibility that the husband intended that the *get* be conditional, i.e., to be of effect only in the event of his failure to return from the war (see above). On this question there is a wide difference of opinion on the part of the authorities without any unanimity being reached (see S. J. Zevin, in bibliography). Another solution proposed, has been the stipulation of a condition at the time of the marriage to the effect that in certain circumstances the marriage should be considered retroactively void, for instance if the husband should

1. page 361.

fail, without his wife's permission, to return to her after a long absence of specified duration and should refuse, despite her demand, to grant her a *get;* or if he should die childless, leaving a brother who refuses to fulfill the obligation of a levir, etc. (see, for instance, *Ḥatam Sofer,* EH 1:111). This approach also presents formidable halakhic difficulties and was not generally accepted by the majority of the *posekim* (see Freimann, Kahana, and Berkowitz, in bibliography). A wife who is on bad terms with her husband and can prove the likelihood of her becoming an *agunah,* may possibly obtain an injunction from the court restraining her husband from traveling abroad without granting her a conditional *get,* as mentioned above.

It was also sought to avoid the disability of an *agunah* by the enactment of a *takkanah* by halakhic scholars to the effect that the *kiddushin* should be deemed annulled retroactively upon the happening or non-fulfillment of certain specified conditions, such as the husband being missing or his wilful refusal to grant a *get.* But this *takkanah,* based on the rule that "a man takes a woman under the conditions laid down by the rabbis . . . and the rabbis may annul his marriage" (Git. 33a), has rarely been employed since the 14th century. In recent times it has been suggested that halakhic scholars should adopt one or other of these procedures in order to solve certain problems relating to *agunah* (see Freimann, Silberg (in the court decision cited in bibliography). According to another opinion the halakhic scholars from the 14th century on, were loathe to utilize their authority to enact a *takkanah* which would retrospectively annul the *kiddushin* because such a *takkanah* could be valid only in the district in which it was enacted, since, after the era of the geonim, *takkanot* were usually local and had no validity elsewhere (see *Takkanot*[1]). This factor was liable to endanger the unity of the validity of a marriage throughout the Jewish world. Hence, as a result of the establishment in recent times of a central halakhic authority in the State of Israel, there exists the possibility of enacting a *takkanah* agreed to by all, or most of, the halakhic scholars and which would be universally applicable (see Elon, *Ha-Mishpat Ha-Ivri,* II, 686–712).

See also *Takkanot.*

In the State of Israel. The question of permitting an *agunah* to remarry, being a matter of marriage and divorce, falls under the exclusive jurisdiction of the rabbinical courts with regard to Jews who are nationals or residents of the State, in terms of the Rabbinical Courts Jurisdiction (Marriage and Divorce) Law 5713/1953 (sec. 1), which courts deal with the matter in accordance with the *halakhah.* The provisions of the Declaration of Death Law, 5712/1952 (enacted to meet consequences of the Nazi Holocaust), empowering the Jerusalem District Court under certain conditions to make a declaration as to a person's death, has no bearing on the problem of an *agunah,* since "a declaration of death constituting evidence by virtue of this Law, shall not affect the provisions of law as to the dissolution of marriage" (see *ibid.,* 17).

Bibliography: Bernstein, in: *Festschrift . . . Schwarz* (1917), 557–70; Blau, *ibid.,* 193–209; Gulak, Yesodei, 3 (1922), 24; Zevin, in: *Sinai,* 10 (1942), 21–35; A. Ch. Freimann, *Seder Kiddushin ve-Nissu'in* (1945), 385–97; Uziel, in: *Talpioth,* 4 (1950), 692–711; ET, 3 (1951), 161; 6 (1954), 706ff.; 9 (1959), 101–2; I. Z. Kahana, *Sefer ha-Agunot* (1954); Weinberg in: *No'am,* 1 (1958), 1–51; Roth, in: *Sefer Zikharon Goldziher* 2 (1958), 59–82; Benedict in: *No'am,* 3 (1960), 241–58; Goren, in: *Mazkeret . . . Herzog* (1962), 162–94; Unterman, *ibid.,* 68–73; E. Berkovits, *Tenai be-Nissu'in u-ve-Get* (1967); B. Schereschewsky, *Dinei Mishpaḥah* (1967[2]), 64–65, 89, 93; PD, 22 pt. 1 (1968), 29–52 (Civil Appeals nos. 164–7 and 220–67); M. Elon, *Ḥakikah Datit . . .* (1968), 182–4; idem, *Ha-Mishpat Ha-Ivri* (1973), I, 115, II, 352ff., 428–434, 500, 518–527, 676, 686–712, 828; G. Horowitz, *Spirit of Jewish Law . . .* (1953); 95–96, 292–4; L. M. Epstein, *Marriage Laws in the Bible and the Talmud* (1942), index; *Mishpetei Ouziel, She'elot u-Teshuvot be-Dinei Even ha-Ezer* (1964), 33–49; *Oẓar ha-Posekim,* 3–8 (1954–63); S. Greenberg, in: *Conservative Judaism* xxiv, 3 (Spring, 1970), 73–141.

Ben-Zion Schereschewsky

DIVORCE (Heb. גרושין). This entry is arranged according to the following outline:

The Concept
Divorce by Mutual Consent
Divorce other than by Consent
Right of the Wife to Demand a Divorce
Physical Defects as Grounds for Divorce
Conduct of the Husband as a Ground for Divorce
Right of the Husband to Demand a Divorce
Defects (or Disabilities) of the Wife
Conduct of the Wife
Divorce in the Case of a Prohibited Marriage
The Will of the Parties
The Husband
The Wife
Execution of the Divorce
Agency in Divorce
Conditional Get
Consequences of Divorce
In the State of Israel

The Concept. Divorce (*Gerushin,* e.g., Lev. 21:7) – in Scripture and even in Talmudic literature use is also made of the terms *shaleaḥ*(שלח Deut. 21:14; 24:13) and *hoẓie* (הוציא Ezra 10:3; cf. Deut. 24:2) – means the dissolution henceforth of a *kiddushin* (see Marriage). Divorce must be distinguished from a declaration of nullity of marriage in which the court declares that no marriage ever came into existence so that all rights and duties flowing therefrom – personal or pecuniary – are rendered inoperative *ab initio* (i.e., in the case of a marriage prohibited on account of incest according to biblical law). It must also be distinguished from an annulment of marriage, i.e., the retroactive invalidation thereof by decree of the court (see *Agunah;* Marriage). The verse, "A man takes a wife and possesses her. She fails to please him because he finds something obnoxious about her, and he writes her a bill of divorcement, hands it to her, and sends her away from his house" (Deut. 24:1), stated in relation to the prohibition against a man remarrying his divorced wife after her marriage to another man (see Marriages, Prohibited), provides the basis for the system of divorce practiced according to Jewish law, i.e., there is no divorce other than by way of the husband delivering to his wife – and not vice versa – a bill of divorcement, in halakhic language called a *get pitturin* or simply *get* (a word having the meaning of *shetar,* or bill: see Maim. Comm. to Mishnah, Git. 2:5). The rabbis stated that "whosoever divorces his first wife, even the altar sheds tears" (Git. 90b; cf. Mal. 2:14–16), and therefore she should not be divorced unless "he found something obnoxious about her" – an expression whose exact meaning was the subject of a dispute between Bet Hillel, Bet Shammai, and Akiva (Yev. 112b; Git. 90a). However, in terms of a rabbinical enactment known as the *Ḥerem de-Rabbenu Gershom* (see also Bigamy) it became prohibited for the husband to divorce his wife against her will (Rema EH 119:6; for the text of the *ḥerem* in relation to divorce see PDR 1:198). In Jewish law divorce is an act of the parties to the marriage, whereby it is to be fundamentally distinguished from

1. page 85, 89.

divorce in many other systems of law, in which the essential divorce derives from a decree of the court. In Jewish law the function of the court – i.e., in the absence of agreement between the parties – is to decide the question whether and on what terms one party may be obliged to give, or the other receive, a *get*. Even after the court has thus decided, the parties nevertheless remain married until such time as the husband actually delivers the *get* to his wife. At the same time, it is the function of the court to ensure that all the formalities required for divorce are carried out according to law.

Divorce by Mutual Consent. Jewish law shows a further distinction from many other legal systems in that the mere consent of the parties to a divorce, without any need for the court to establish responsibility for the breakup of the marriage, suffices for its dissolution, i.e., for delivery of the *get*. It must be given or received by them, however, of their free will and not out of fear that they may be obliged to fulfill any obligations which they undertook in the agreement in the event of their not being divorced (*Pitḥei Teshuvah* EH 134, n. 9; PDR 3:322–4; 4:353f.). Hence, if either party withdraws from the agreement and satisfies the court of a genuine desire for matrimonial harmony, the other party will likewise continue to be subject to all the recognized matrimonial obligations. In this case, however, the pecuniary conditions which the parties may have stipulated in the event of either of them failing to uphold the agreement may nevertheless be valid and enforceable (*Pitḥei Teshuvah* loc. cit.; PDR 2:9; 6:97; PD, 20, pt. 2 (1966), 6, 12f.). It is also customary to make provision in the divorce agreement for matters such as custody of the children and their maintenance, and in principle there is no reason why such conditions should not have binding validity vis-à-vis the legal relationships between the parties themselves (PDR 4:275, 281). On the question whether and to what extent such conditions are binding in respect of the children, see Parent and Child.

Divorce other than by Consent. In the absence of an agreement between the parties to a divorce, the court is required to decide whether or not there is a basis for obliging or – in cases where this is permitted by law – for compelling the husband to give, or the wife to receive, a *get*. The decision of the court is dependent upon the existence of any of the grounds recognized as conferring a right on the wife or husband to demand a divorce.

Right of The Wife to Demand a Divorce. The wife is entitled to demand a divorce on the grounds of (a) physical defects *(mumim)* of her husband or (b) his conduct toward her.

Physical Defects as Grounds for Divorce. In order to obtain a divorce on the grounds of physical defects the wife must prove that these preclude him, or her, from the possibility of cohabiting with each other, e.g., because he suffers from a contagious and dangerous disease – "afflicted with boils and leprosy" – or because the defects are likely to arouse in her feelings of revulsion when in his proximity, and the like. In the case of the unreasonable refusal of the husband to comply with the judgment obliging him to give his wife a *get* of his free will in these circumstances, the court may compel his compliance (Ket. 77a and codes; PDR 3:126). The question whether judicial coercion is possible in the case of epilepsy is disputed, and the practice of the courts is to oblige – but not compel – a divorce on this ground (PDR 1:65, 73f.; 2:188, 193), save in exceptional cases, e.g., where there is the danger of the wife becoming an *agunah* (PDR 4:164, 171–3). The wife is also entitled to a divorce if she is childless and claims that she wishes to have a child but that her husband is incapable of begetting children (Yev. 65a/b and codes; Resp. Rosh 43:4; PDR 1:5, 8; 2:150). The wife must satisfy the court, as a precondition to divorce on this ground, that she is not seeking the divorce for pecuniary reasons or because she has "set her eyes on another" (Yev. 117a and codes; Resp. Rosh 43:2; PDR 1:364, 369). Similarly, she must prove her claim that her husband is the cause of her childlessness; the lapse of ten years from the time of her marriage without her having been made pregnant by her husband establishes a presumption that there are no longer any prospects of her bearing her husband any children (Yev. 64a and codes; PDR 1:5, 9, 10, 369). If the husband claims that the cause does not lie with him he may demand that the matter be clarified by submission of himself and his wife to a medical examination; if his claim is established, he is exempted from paying his wife's *ketubbah* (Yev. 65a; Resp. Rosh, 43:12; Sh. Ar., EH 154 and *Beit Shemu'el* n. 14). A comparable cause of action arises from the wife's claim that her husband is impotent (i.e., he lacks *ko'aḥ gavra;* see Marriage). The claim is grounded not on the wife's desire to raise a family but on her right to sexual relations as such, and it is therefore of no consequence that she already has children, nor is she required to wait for ten years (Yev. 65b and codes; PDR 1:5, 9, 55, 59, 82, 84, 5:154). If the evidence leaves room for the conclusion that medical treatment may possibly lead to the husband's recovery, the court will refrain from obliging the husband to give a *get* immediately (Yev. 65b and codes; PDR 1:81, 84–89; 5:239). In principle, the wife's claim as to her husband's impotence is accepted as trustworthy in terms of the rule that she is believed in matters between her husband and herself; however, corroboration of her statements is required (Rema EH 154:7, PDR loc. cit.). In the opinion of some authorities, a wife who succeeds in her claim would also be entitled to the sum mentioned in her *ketubbah,* since her trustworthiness extends also to the pecuniary aspect (*Pitḥei Teshuvah* EH 154:7; *Ha-Gra, ibid.,* n. 41); according to others, full proof is required with regard to the latter aspect (Tur and Sh. Ar., EH 154 and commentators thereto). However, should the wife have married her husband with knowledge of his defects, or if she acquired such knowledge after their marriage and nevertheless continued to live with him, she is considered to have waived her objections unless she is able to show that the defects became aggravated to an extent which she could not have foreseen (Ket. 77a and codes; PDR 1:5, 9, 10; 2:188, 192; 6:221, 223). If she is able to account for her delay on grounds which negate any waiver of rights on her part (such as failure to approach the court because of her embarassment) her right to a divorce is likely to remain unaffected even if considerable time has elapsed since she first became aware of her husband's defects (PDR 1:11–12). No claim can be based on defects or circumstances which, however serious they may be, do not preclude the wife from cohabiting with her husband – e.g., his loss of a hand, leg, or an eye, etc. – whether occurring after the marriage or before, unless she proves that she did not know or, despite investigation, could not have known of the existence of the defect, and provided that she claims a divorce within a reasonable period after becoming aware thereof (Ket. 77a and codes; Resp. Rosh 42:2; *Maggid Mishneh* Ishut 25:11; *Beit Shemu'el* EH, 154 n. 2; PDR 1:5, 11, 65, 71).

Conduct of the Husband as a Ground for Divorce. Unjustified refusal of conjugal rights on the part of the husband entitled his wife to claim a divorce (Sh. Ar., EH 76:11; for her ancillary or alternative rights in this case, see Husband and Wife). Similarly, the wife may claim a divorce on the ground of her husband's unjustified refusal to maintain her when he is in a position to do so, or could be if he was willing to work and earn an income. In this event she may also claim maintenance without seeking a divorce (Ket. 77a, according to Samuel, contrary to Rav). The court will not decree that a divorce should be given on the husband's first refusal, but only if he persists in his refusal after being warned and obliged by the court to pay her maintenance (PDR 5:329, 332). Were the husband totally unable to provide her with the minimum requirements ("even the bread she needs"), some authorities are of the opinion that he can even be compelled to divorce her, whereas others hold that there is no room for compulsion since his default is due to circumstances beyond his control (Yad, Ishut, 12:11; Sh. Ar., EH 70:3 and commentators; PDR, 4:164, 166–70). The husband will not however be obliged to grant his wife a divorce if he maintains her to the best of his ability, even if this be the measure of "a poor man in Israel" and not in accordance with the rule that "she rises with him but does not go down with him" (see Maintenance; Sh. Ar., and commentators, loc. cit., PDR loc. cit.). Unworthy conduct of the husband toward his wife with the result that she cannot any longer be expected to continue living with him as his wife constitutes a ground for her to claim a divorce ("a wife is given in order that she should live and not to suffer pain": Ket. 61a; Tashbeẓ, 2:8). The ground is established when his conduct amounts to a continued breach of the duties laid down as a basis for conjugal life, i.e., "let a man honor his wife more than he honors himself, love her as he loves himself, and if he has assets, seek to add to her benefits as he would deal with his assets, and not unduly impose fear on her, and speak to her gently and not be given to melancholy nor anger" (Yad, Ishut, 15:19, based on Yev. 62b; see also Marriage). Thus the wife will have a ground for divorce if, e.g., her husband habitually assaults or insults her, or is the cause of unceasing quarrels, so that she has no choice but to leave the common household (Rema EH 154:3; Ha-Gra, ibid., n. 10; Tashbeẓ, loc. cit.; PDR 6:221). The same applies if the husband is unfaithful to his wife (Sh. Ar., EH 154:1 and commentators; PDR 1:139, 141); similarly, if he "transgresses the Law of Moses" – for instance when he causes her to transgress the dietary laws knowing that she observes them, or if he has intercourse with her against her will during her menstrual period (Rema EH 154:1; PDR 4:342). If the husband is able to persuade the court that his wife has condoned his conduct (PDR 1:139, 142), or of his genuine repentance, the court will not immediately oblige the husband to grant a divorce. The court will direct the parties to attempt living together for an additional period in order to ascertain whether a divorce is the only answer for them, unless it is satisfied that no purpose will be served by such delay (Sh. Ar., and commentators, loc. cit.; PDR 1:87–89; 3:346, 351; 4:259)

Right of the Husband to Demand a Divorce. The grounds on which the husband may demand a divorce (i.e., since the ḥerem de-Rabbenu Gershom) are mainly similar to those which afford the wife this right against him, and previous awareness or condoning of these defects invalidates his claim (PDR 1:66).

Defects (or Disabilities) of the Wife. In addition, however, defects of the wife which provide the husband with grounds for a divorce are those which are peculiar to a woman as such, and which prevent the husband from cohabiting with her, or which render her unfit for or incapable of such cohabitation (Nid. 12b; Yad, Ishut, 25:7–9; Resp. Rosh 33:2; Sh. Ar., EH 39:4 and 117:1, 2, 4; PDR 4:321; 5:131, 193). Included in such defects, according to the majority of the authorities, is epilepsy (Resp. Rosh 42:1; PDR 2:129, 134–6; 5:131, 194). If the husband was aware of such defects prior to the marriage or later became aware – or could have become aware – that they had existed before the marriage but still continued to cohabit with her he will be considered to have condoned them and they will not avail him as grounds for divorce (Ket. 75 and codes; PDR 1:66; 5:193). Similarly a defect which becomes manifest in the wife only after the marriage does not provide the husband with a ground for divorce, unless she is afflicted with a disease carrying with it mortal danger, such as leprosy, or she has become incapable of cohabiting (Ket. loc. cit. and codes; PDR 2:129, 134–6; 5:131, 194). The husband may demand a divorce if his wife has failed to bear children within a period of ten years of their marriage, and he has no children (even from another woman), provided that he persuades the court of his sincere desire to have children (Rema EH 1:3; Sh. Ar., EH 154:1; see also Oẓar ha-Posekim EH 1, n. 13–60; PDR 4:353).

Conduct of the Wife. The husband will have ground for demanding a divorce if his wife knowingly misleads him into "transgressing the Law of Moses," as when she has sexual relations with him during her menstrual period and conceals this fact from him, or when she causes him to transgress the dietary laws, etc., knowing that he observes these laws (Ket. 72a and codes), but not if she acted inadvertently, or out of fear, or in ignorance of the law, or if the husband has by his own conduct shown that he is not particular about them (EH 115:1; PDR 3:346, 350). Similarly, the husband may claim a divorce if his wife shows habitual immodesty or deliberately slights her husband's honor, as when she curses or assaults him, and generally any conduct on her part tending to disrupt normal family life in such manner as to convince the court that no further condonation and continuation of the matrimonial relationship can be expected of the husband (Ket. 72; Sot. 25a; codes; PDR ibid.). Condonation of the above also deprives him of his cause of action for divorce. A similar ground for divorce arises when the husband is able to prove, on the testimony of two witnesses, conduct on the part of his wife which gives rise to the strong suspicion that she has committed adultery, even if there is no evidence of actual adultery (Yev. 24b, 25a; Yad, Ishut, 24:15; Sh. Ar., EH 11:1). Where such proof is forthcoming, the husband is entitled to a judgment compelling his wife to accept a divorce (Sh. Ar., loc. cit. and commentators, Rema EH 115:4; PDR 1:51, 54; 2:125–8). If it is proved that the wife has committed adultery, of her own free will, she becomes prohibited to her husband and she will be unable to raise a plea of condonation on her husband's part, since there can be no consent to do what is prohibited by the law (Sot. 18b and 27b; Ket. 9a and codes; PDR 1:13). The wife can be compelled to accept a *get* against her will since she is not protected by the Ḥerem de-Rabbenu Gershom in this case. By virtue of the said prohibition, the wife herself may claim a divorce if her husband refrains from instituting action against her since he does not have the right to render her an *agunah,* because on the one hand he is prohibited from living with her and on the other she may not marry another man until divorced from her husband. (Oẓar ha-Posekim EH 11, n. 1–54; PDR 5:154, 156); however, this is disputed by some authorities (PDR ibid.). In this case too the evidence of two witnesses is essential in terms of the rule that "in matters of incest *(ervah)* there cannot be less than two [witnesses]" (Yev. 24b; Kid. 66a; and codes). Thus generally speaking her confession alone will not suffice because of the suspicion that she has "set her eyes on another man" (Yev. 24b; Kid. 66a; PDR 3:260), nor will the evidence of one witness only, unless her husband states that he believes her or the single witness as he would two witnesses, and provided the court too is satisfied of the truth of the matter (Kid. 66a and codes). In this event the court will oblige but not compel the parties to a divorce (Maim. loc. cit.; Sh. Ar., loc. cit.; PDR 4:160). A divorce on the grounds of adultery precludes the wife from remarrying her former husband – to whom she is prohibited by the Pentateuchal law – and from marrying the man with whom she committed adultery – to whom she is prohibited by the rabbinical law (Sot. 27b and codes). Moreover, she forfeits her *ketubbah* (Ned. 90b; Sh. Ar., EH 115:5). In cases of rape, the wife does not become prohibited to her husband unless he is a kohen (Yev. 56b and codes), nor does she lose her *ketubbah* (Ned. 91a and codes).

Divorce in the Case of a Prohibited Marriage. The court will always compel a divorce at the instance of either party to a prohibited marriage of the sort in which the marriage is valid when performed (see Marriage, Prohibited), regardless of whether or not they had knowledge of the prohibition, as a matter of law or fact, and regardless of their continued cohabitation after becoming aware of the prohibition (Ket. 77a; Git. 88b; and codes).

The Will of the Parties. The Husband. To be valid, a *get* must be given by the husband of his free will and is therefore invalid if given while he is of unsound mind, or under duress contrary to law (Yev. 112b; Git. 67b, 88b; and codes). "Contrary to law" in this context means the exercise of compulsion against him when it is not permitted in any way by law, or its exercise in an invalid manner; for instance if he gives the *get* in order to escape a payment imposed on him contrary to law, even by judgment of the court. Such a case may be when he is ordered to pay maintenance to his wife or children without being at all liable for this, or when he is ordered to pay an excessive amount (PDR 2:9–14). However, if the law specifically authorizes that he be compelled to give a *get* – as in the cases mentioned above – or if he is lawfully obliged to make a payment to his wife – e.g., when ordered to pay interim maintenance in an amount due to his wife pending the grant of a *get* and he has the option of escaping this obligation by granting the *get* – then the *get* will not be considered to have been given by him under unlawful duress, since his own prior refusal to give it was contrary to law (Yad, Gerushin, 2:20; BB 48a; Sh. Ar., EH 134:5). In order to obviate any suspicion that the *get* may have been given under duress contrary to law, it is customary, before the *get* is written and before delivery therefore, for the husband to annul all *moda'ot,* i.e., declarations made by him before others in which he purported to have been compelled to give a *get* (*Beit Yosef* EH 134:1; Sh. Ar., EH 134:1–3).

The Wife. There must be free will on the part of the wife also to receive the *get* as laid down in the *Ḥerem de-Rabbenu Gershom,* in order to maintain the prohibition against polygamy (see Bigamy) lest the husband circumvent the prohibition by divorcing his wife against her will and thus become free to take another wife. The wife was therefore given a right similar to that of the husband and cannot be divorced except with her consent (Resp. Rosh 42:1; Rema EH 119:6). This applies even in those communities which did not accept the said *ḥerem* against polygamy (cf. *Oẓar ha-Posekim* 1, n. 68, 12). Already according to talmudic law, it was forbidden to divorce a woman who had become of unsound mind, even though it was not prohibited to divorce a wife against her will. If her condition is such that she is "unable to look after her bill of divorcement," the latter will be invalid according to biblical law since it is enjoined that "he shall give it in her hand" (Deut. 24:1) and such a woman has no "hand" in the legal sense (Yev. 113b and codes). Where she "knows how to look after her *get*" even though she "does not know how to look after herself," she still cannot be divorced, but in this case by rabbinical enactment, lest advantage be taken of her and the husband will remain liable for all pecuniary obligations to her even if he should take another wife *(ibid.).* This is all the more so in terms of the aforesaid *ḥerem,* since in both cases the wife is incapable of receiving the *get* of her free will. Whereas talmudic law did not require the husband to obtain permission of the court before taking another wife, the *ḥerem* had the effect of prohibiting the husband from doing so, save with the permission of 100 rabbis. (On the question of the first wife's legal status after the grant of permission as aforesaid, see Bigamy[1]).

Execution of the Divorce. Divorce is carried into effect by the bill of divorcement being written, signed, and delivered by the husband to his wife. It is written by a scribe upon the husband's instruction to write "for him, for her, and for the purpose of a divorce." The materials used in the writing must belong to the husband and the scribe formally presents them as an outright gift to the husband before writing the *get.* The strictest care must be taken with the formula of the *get,* most of it in Aramaic, and the text is, with minor differences, according to the wording given in the Talmud. To obviate errors, it is still the practice at the present day to write the bill in Aramaic, although writing in any other language is theoretically permissible (Git. 19b, 87b and codes; on the rules of writing a *get,* its form and language, and the effect of variations therein, see Sh. Ar., EH 120ff.; for the version customary in Ereẓ Israel, see ET, 5 (1953), 656; see also Yad, Gerushin, 4:12; Sh. Ar., EH 154, *"Seder ha-Get,"* Rema at end). The following is a translation of an Ashkenazi *get,* according to the general usage in the Diaspora:

> On the . . . day of the week, the . . . day of the month of . . ., in the year . . . from the creation of the world according to the calendar reckoning we are accustomed to count here, in the city . . . (which is also known as . . .), which is located on the river . . . (and on the river . . .), and situated near wells of water, I, . . . (also known as . . .), the son of . . . (also known as . . .), who today am present in the city . . . (which is also known as . . .), which is located on the river . . . (and on the river . . .), and situated near wells of water, do willingly consent, being under no restraint, to release, to set free, and put aside thee, my wife, . . . (also known as . . .), daughter of . . . (also known as . . .), who art today in the city of . . . (which is also known as . . .), which is located on the river . . . (and on the river . . .), and situated near wells of water, who has been my wife from before. Thus do I set free, release thee, and put thee aside, in order that thou may have permission and the authority over thyself to go and marry any man thou may desire. No person may hinder thee from this day onward, and thou art permitted to every man. This shall be for thee from me a bill of dismissal, a letter of release, and a document of freedom, in accordance with the laws of Moses and Israel.
>
> . . . the son of . . ., witness.
> . . . the son of . . ., witness.

The bill of divorcement is composed of the *tofes,* i.e., the formula common to all such bills, and the *toref,* i.e., the specific part containing the details of the particular case, concluding with the declaration that the woman is henceforth permitted to any man. Care must be taken to write the correct date on which the bill is written, signed and delivered, otherwise it can be invalidated as a bill which is "anticipatory" or "in arrear" of the true date of its writing or signature or delivery (Sh. Ar., EH 127). The husband should also be careful to avoid sexual relations with his wife between the time of writing and delivery of the bill since such a bill, called an "antiquated" one *(get yashan),* although valid in the final instance may not be used in the first instance (Git. 79b; Sh. Ar., EH 148:1). Once the witnesses sign the *get,* it is delivered by the husband to his wife in the presence of "witnesses to the delivery" (generally the same witnesses as sign; Sh. Ar., EH 133:1). Delivery of the *get* in accordance with the regulations renders the wife divorced from her husband and free to marry any man save those to whom she is prohibited by law, e.g., a kohen or paramour (see Marriage, Prohibited). It is customary that after the wife has received the *get* she gives it to

1. page 369.

the court, who present her with a document stating that she has been divorced according to law. The court then tears the *get* in order to avoid any later suspicion that it was not absolutely legal and files it away in its torn state (*Beit Shemu'el* EH 135, n.2; Sh. Ar., EH 154, *"Seder ha-Get"* n. 6; *Sedei Ḥemed, Asefat Dinim,* Get 1:23). The rules pertaining to the writing, signing and delivery of a *get* are very formal and exact in order to avoid mistakes or a wrongful exploitation of the *get,* and they must therefore be stringently observed. (The exact details are to be found in Sh. Ar., EH 124–39.) As a result it was laid down that "no one who is unfamiliar with the nature of divorce (and marriage) may deal with them" (Kid. 13a). The Mishnah mentions a particular form of *get* which was customary in the case of kohanim, who were regarded as pedantic and hot-tempered and therefore likely to be hasty in divorcing their wives. This form of *get* – called a "folded" or "knotted" one as opposed to a "plain" *get* – consisted of a series of folds, each of which (called a *kesher*) was stitched and required the signature of three witnesses (two in the case of a "plain" *get*) who signed on the reverse side and not on the face, between each fold. All this was done to draw out the writing and signing of the *get* so that the husband might reconsider and become reconciled with his wife (BB 160ff.). The "folded" *get* was customary in ancient times only and the rules pertaining to it are omitted from most of the codes (e.g., Maim., Tur, Sh. Ar.).

Agency in Divorce. Although divorce in Jewish law is the personal act of the husband and wife, their presence in person is not a necessary requirement for its execution. Delivery and receipt of the bill of divorcement, like any regular legal act, may be effected through an agent in terms of the rule that "a man's agent is as himself" (see Agency; Git. 62b and codes). Appointment of the agent is made before the court by way of a power of attorney *(harsha'ah),* i.e., a written document very carefully and formally prepared to include all the relevant details, in which the agent is empowered to delegate his authority to another, and the latter to another in turn, etc. (Sh. Ar., EH 140:3, 141:29–30). An agent appointed by the husband for the purpose of delivering the *get* to his wife is called "the agent of delivery" and the *get* takes effect only upon delivery thereof by the husband or his agent to the wife or her agent, the latter called "the agent of receipt" (Sh. Ar., *ibid.*). In the latter case the fact that the wife may not know exactly when the *get* takes effect is likely to result in complications and doubts and it has not therefore been customary to resort to agency of this kind (Rema EH 141:29). The wife may also appoint a "delivery" agent – i.e., to deliver the *get* to her (and not to receive it on her behalf) after receiving it from the husband or his agent – in such manner that she will become divorced only upon delivery thereof to herself. The latter agent is not an "agent of receipt" and is subject to the same rules as is an "agent of delivery" (Sh. Ar., EH 140:5). The rules of agency in divorce are of practical importance in cases where the parties live in different countries and wish to avoid the expense involved in the grant and delivery of a *get* in the presence of each other, or where they do not wish to confront one another. The same applies when one of the parties is an apostate. In these cases the husband is enabled to divorce his wife by way of "conferring" the *get* on her *(get zikkui),* i.e., by delivery thereof to an agent appointed by the court, the divorce taking effect upon the agent's receipt of the *get.* (According to some of the *posekim* the *get* must thereafter be delivered to the wife herself so as to avoid doubt.) This *halakhah* that the court can appoint an agent for the wife without her explicit consent or knowledge is based on the rule that "a benefit may be conferred on a person in his absence" (Yev. 118b; see Agency), on the following reasoning: if the husband becomes an apostate it is presumed that the Jewish woman will always prefer living as a divorcée to living with an apostate; if the wife becomes an apostate it can only be to her advantage if she no longer remains tied to her Jewish husband and will thus no longer be liable if she cohabits with another (see Rema EH 1:10 and 140:5; *Oẓar ha-Posekim* EH 1, n. 81, 1–9).

Conditional Get. A *get* may be written and delivered conditionally, that is so as not to take effect except on fulfillment of a stipulated condition, e.g., if the husband should fail to return to his wife within a specified period or that no word from, or concerning him, shall be forthcoming until then. The condition must not contradict the basis nature of divorce, i.e., the absolute severance of the marriage relationship between the husband and wife. To have validity it is necessary that all the complicated laws pertaining to conditions be observed at the time of its imposition. Similarly, it must later be carefully investigated whether all the facts required to establish fulfillment of the condition have been adequately proved, since there is at stake the random divorce of a married woman. The doubts and complications attaching to a conditional *get* are likely to be particularly severe in the light of a rabbinical enactment to the effect that a plea of accident (*force majeure,* see *Ones*) does not avail in divorce. Thus, contrary to the general rule that a person is not responsible for his act or omission resulting from accident, the husband cannot plead that the condition to which the validity of the *get* was subject was fulfilled only on account of accident – such as his failure to return in time due to an unforeseeable disruption of the means of transportation (Ket. 2b, 3a; Sh. Ar., EH 144:1; see also *Takkanot*). Hence in general the practice is not to permit a conditional *get* save in exceptional cases, and then the above-mentioned laws may be of great practical importance, e.g., in times of persecution or war when there is separation between husband and wife and the danger of her becoming an *agunah.* In such cases the practice is sometimes adopted of granting a *get* on condition, e.g., if the husband should fail to return from the war by a certain date the *get* shall be deemed to be effective, and the wife divorced and free to remarry without need for a levirate marriage or *ḥaliẓah.* Upon fulfillment of the condition, the *get* will take effect either immediately or retroactively to the time of its imposition, according to the terms thereof, and provided that everything had been done in strict conformity with all the requirements of the law (Sh. Ar., EH 143, 144, 147; see also *Agunah,* Levirate Marriage). This aim may also be achieved by the conditional appointment of an agent, e.g., the appointment by the husband, before going to war, of an agent given written authority to write a *get* in his (the husband's) name and to deliver such to his wife, on condition that the power of attorney is not acted upon unless the husband should fail to return home within a stated period (Sh. Ar., EH 144:5, 6). The court itself may be thus appointed and may in turn, in terms of authority generally granted in the power of attorney, delegate its authority to a third party. A deathbed divorce (see Wills[1]) is also a conditional *get,* i.e., one given by a husband on his deathbed so as to free his wife from the requirement of a levirate marriage or *ḥaliẓah.* In practice such a *get* will also have no validity except if the husband dies, whereupon it will take effect retroactively from the date of its delivery (see Sh. Ar., EH 145).

Consequences of Divorce. Upon divorce, the parties are generally free to remarry as they please save as prohibited by law. The wife becomes entitled to the return of her own property from the husband, in accordance with the rules of law pertaining to the husband's liability therefor (see Dowry). She is similarly entitled to payment of her *ketubbah* and dowry, save where she forfeits her *ketubbah,* e.g., because of her adultery.

1. page 453.

Divorce terminates the husband's legal obligation to maintain his wife, since this duty is imposed only during the subsistence of the marriage (Sh. Ar., EH 82:6). For charitable reasons however, it is considered a *mitzvah* to sustain one's divorced wife more extensively than the poor at large (Rema EH 119:8). Upon divorce the parties are not permitted to continue their joint occupation of the former common dwelling, lest this lead to promiscuity (Sh. Ar., EH 6:7; 119:7, 11). If the dwelling belonged to one of them, whether owned or hired, it must be vacated by the other party and if it belonged to both it must be vacated by the wife *(ibid.)*, as "the husband has greater difficulty in moving about than the wife" (Ket. 28a); although sometimes the courts, in order to settle financial matters between the parties, or in awarding compensation to the wife, will decide that the dwelling remain in her hands (see e.g., OPD, 158, 163 n. 6). If the divorced parties nevertheless continue to jointly occupy the dwelling, or later return thereto – as testified to by witnesses – they will be presumed to have cohabited together as husband and wife for the sake of a marriage constituted by their sexual intercourse (*kiddushei bi'ah:* see Marriage[1]). This follows from the rule that "a man does not have intercourse for the sake of promiscuity if he is able to do so in fulfillment of a precept," i.e., it will not be presumed that the parties wished to transgress since they were lawfully in a position to marry each other (Yad, Gerushin, 10:17; Sh. Ar., EH 149:1). Hence they will be required to divorce each other once again if they should wish to marry third parties, i.e., a "*get* out of stringency" *(get mi-ḥumra)* at least and possibly even out of an undoubted *kiddushin* between them (Sh. Ar., EH 149:1, 2; PDR, 7:35). If the wife marries another man without having first obtained a second *get* as aforesaid, this marriage will accordingly require dissolution, since she is regarded as being the wife of the first husband (Sh. Ar., loc. cit. *Beit Shemu'el* n. 4). Since the aforesaid presumption is founded on the premise that the parties were in a position to be lawfully wedded, it will not apply in the reverse situation, e.g., in the case of a kohen who is prohibited from remarrying his divorced wife, or when the wife has meanwhile become the widow of or divorced from another husband, or if the husband has meanwhile taken another wife and hence become prohibited by the *ḥerem* from being married at the same time to another, i.e., his former wife. Consequently, according to some of the codes, there will be no need for a second *get* to be given in any of the cases mentioned above (*Beit Shemu'el* n. 4 to Sh. Ar., EH 149; PDR loc. cit.).

In the State of Israel. In terms of the *Rabbinical Courts Jurisdiction (Marriage and Divorce) Law,* 5713–1953, matters of marriage and divorce between Jews, citizens or residents of the state, fall within the exclusive jurisdiction of the rabbinical courts, which jurisdiction extends to any matter connected with the suit for divorce, including maintenance for the wife and for the children of the couple (sec. 3(1)). Divorce for Jews is performed in accordance with Jewish law (sec. 2). In applying the *halakhah* the rabbinical courts have introduced an important innovation, namely the award of monetary compensation to a wife who is being divorced; this is done even when the divorce is not specifically attributable to the fault of the husband, but the court, after close scrutiny of all the facts, is persuaded that the situation prevailing between the parties does not, objectively speaking, allow for the continuation of their marriage. In this event, the court, upon the husband's demand that his wife be obliged to accept a *get,* will customarily oblige the former to pay a monetary or equivalent compensation to his wife – in addition to her *ketubbah* – in return for her willingness to accpet the *get* (OPD 51–55; PDR 1:137). The extent of the compensation is determined by the court, having regard to all the circumstances, including the financial position of the parties and their respective contributions to the state of their assets. With reference to the law in the State of Israel between parties not of the same religion see Mixed Marriage.

Bibliography: D. W. Amram, *The Jewish Law of Divorce . . .* (1896); L. Blau, *Die juedische Ehescheidung und der juedische Scheidbrief . . .* 2 vols. (1911–12); I. B. Zuri, *Mishpat ha-Talmud,* 2: (1921), 36–56; Gulak, Yesodei, 3 (1922), 24–30; B. Cohen, in: REJ, 92 (1932) 151–62; 93 (1934), 58–65; idem, in: PAAJR, 21 (1952), 3–34; republished in his: *Jewish and Roman Law* (1966), 377–408; addenda, *ibid.,* 781–3; ET, 5 (1953), 567–758; 6 (1954), 321–26; 8 (1957), 24–26; M. Silberg, *Ha-Ma'amad ha-Ishi be-Yisrael* (1965[4]), 365–75; Berkovits, *Tenai be-Nissu'in u-va-Get* (1966); B. Schereschewsky, *Dinei Mishpaḥah* (1967[2]), 271–342; M. Elon, Mafte'aḥ, 26–37; idem, *Ḥakikah Datit . . .* (1967), 165–7; idem in: ILR, 3 (1968), 432ff; idem, *Ha-Mishpat Ha-Ivri* (1973), I, 72, 81ff., 97ff., 123ff., 151ff., 189, II, 251ff., 255ff., 314ff., 322ff., 337, 365ff., 373ff., 386ff., 461–464, 518–527, 541–546, 633–635, 686ff., 711ff., 773ff., 812, III, 1213, 1258.

Ben-Zion Schereschewsky

PARENT AND CHILD

STATUS OF THE CHILD

In Jewish law, there is no discrimination against a child because of the mere fact that he is born out of lawful wedlock. While the said fact may complicate the question of establishing paternity, once the identity of the father is clearly known there is no distinction in law so far as the parent-child relationship is concerned, between such a child and one born in lawful wedlock. This is also the position with regard to a *mamzer.* On the status of a child with one non-Jewish parent, see below. For further details, see *Yuḥasin.*

PARENTAL RIGHTS

Except as detailed below, the principle in Jewish law is that parents have no legal rights in respect of their children, neither as to their person nor their property (Ket. 46b–47a; Sh. Ar., ḤM 424:7). So far as male children are concerned, the father is entitled to the finds of his son even if the latter is a *gadol* (i.e., beyond the age until which his father is obliged by law to maintain him), provided that the son is dependent on him (lit. "seated at his table"); this is "for the reason of enmity," i.e., in order to avoid the enmity which might arise between father and son if the former, who supports his son without even being obliged to by law, was not even entitled to the finds that come to the son without any effort or investment on his part (BM 12a–b; Sh. Ar., ḤM 270:2 and commentaries). For the same reason the father is entitled to the income of his dependent son (Rema, ḤM 270:2). Hence a father who is obliged by law to maintain his son – for example, because he has so undertaken in a divorce agreement – has no claim to the finds or income of the son and therefore he is not entitled to set them off against his liability to maintain him (*Taz,* ḤM 270:2; PDR 3:329). As regards his daughter, the father is entitled to everything mentioned above, even if she is not dependent on him, until she becomes a major *(bogeret),* since until then she remains under his authority. For the same reason, until she reaches her majority, the father will be entitled to her handiwork and to give her in marriage (Ket. 46a–47a; Yad, Ishut 3:11; see also Avadim 4:2). The mother has none of these rights in respect of her children since in law she has no pecuniary obligations toward them (see below).

1. page 356.

PARENTAL OBLIGATIONS

The general rule is that the legal obligations toward their children are imposed on the father alone and not on the mother (*Maggid Mishneh,* Ishut, 21:18).

Maintenance. Obligations of the Father. The father's duty to maintain his son embraces the responsibility of providing for all the child's needs, including his daily care (Yad, Ishut 13:6; Sh. Ar., EH 73:6, 7). The rules concerning the duty of maintenance also apply with regard to the father's duty to educate his son and to teach him Torah, to see that he learns a trade or profession, and to bear all the necessary expenses connected with this (Kid. 29a, ff.; Sh. Ar., YD 245:1, 4). Until the son reaches the age of six years (see below) these obligations must be borne by the father even if he has limited means and the son has independent means of his own, e.g., acquired by inheritance (Sh. Ar., EH 71:1). These obligations are imposed on the father by virtue of his paternity, whether or not he is married to the child's mother and therefore notwithstanding termination of the marriage between the child's parents, by death or divorce, or the fact that the child was born out of wedlock (Resp. Ribash no. 41; Resp. Rosh 17:7; contrary to Ran, on Rif at end of Ket. ch. 5, who is of the opinion that the father's obligation to support his children is linked with his obligation to maintain his wife).

Obligation of the Mother. The mother has no legal obligation to maintain her children even if she is able to do so out of her own property or income (*Ba'er Heitev,* EH 71, n.1). She may only be obliged to do so on the strength of the rules of *ẓedakah* ("charity") if, after providing in full for her own needs, she is able to satisfy the needs of her children when they have no property or income of their own and the father, being poor, is unable to support them (*Pitḥei Teshuvah,* EH 82 n. 3; PDR 2:3). The position is different, however, if the mother has undertaken to maintain her children, for example in a divorce agreement. In this event, if the mother has the means to support her children at a time when the father is not legally obliged to do so (i.e., because they are above the specified age), she alone will have to maintain them as she is obliged to do by virtue of law (her undertaking); the father's duty in this case is based on the rules of *ẓedakah* only, and since the children have property of their own (the right to be maintained by the mother) they are no longer in need of *ẓedakah* (PDR 3:170; 4:3, 7). On the wife's duty to take care of her children as part of her marital duties toward her husband, see Husband and Wife.

If the child's mother is not entitled to maintenance from the father – e.g., because the parties are divorced – and the child is in need of her care so that she can no longer continue to work and support herself, there will be legal grounds for obliging the father to maintain her to a certain extent, including payment of the rental for her dwelling. Because it is in the interests of the child to be with the mother, she must dwell with him, and because the expenses necessary for taking care of the child devolve on the father, he has to bear them within the limits of the remuneration he would otherwise be called upon to pay any other woman for taking care of the child. This would include the cost of the child's dwelling (with the mother) – notwithstanding the fact that the mother is in a position to defray all the said expenses out of her own means (PDR 1:118f.; 2:3, 5f.). After being divorced, the mother may also claim from the child's father any of the said expenses she incurred before she filed her claim for them, since, unlike the case of a married woman, there is no room for considering that she has waived this claim (PDR 1:230, 234; 2:164f.; Resp. Maharsham, pt. 2, n. 236).

The Standard of Maintenance. Unlike maintenance for a wife (see Maintenance), the standard of maintenance to which children are entitled is determined by their actual needs and not by the financial status of their father (Yad, Ishut 13:6; Sh. Ar., EH 73:6). For this purpose the needs of a child will not be limited to an essential minimum, but they may vary according to whether the child is from a rich or a poor family. Certainly under the laws of *ẓedakah* a wealthy father may be made liable to maintain his children as befits them and not merely as absolutely necessary, although in a case where a child has other sources of income, and thus is not in need of *ẓedakah,* he will not be entitled to maintenance (Sh. Ar., EH 82:7; PDR 2:3, 8; 4:3, 7). On the other hand, in determining the essential minimum attention will be paid to what the father is capable of earning and not merely to his actual income.

Additional Obligations Toward Daughters. In addition to maintaining his daughter, the father has to see to her marriage to a worthy husband, and, if the need arises, to provide her with a dowry sufficient at least – if his means permit – to cover a year's raiment (*Ḥelkat Meḥokek* EH 58, n. 1). Although the father is not legally obliged to give a dowry in accordance with his means, it is a *mitzvah* for him and he should do so (Ket. 68a; Sh. Ar., EH 58:1 and Rema 71:1). On the father's death, and in the absence of a testamentary disposition depriving his daughter of a dowry, his heirs are bound to give the daughter a dowry based on an assessment of what her father would have given her had he been alive; in the absence of data that might form the basis for such assessment, the heirs have to give her one-tenth of his estate for the purpose of her marriage (see Succession; Ket. 68a; Sh. Ar., EH 113:2, 10).

Children Entitled to Maintenance Until a Certain Age. An opinion that a *takkanah* of the Sanhedrin (i.e., the *Takkanat Usha*) laid down that the father must maintain his children as long as they are minors (sons until the age of 13 and daughters until 12) was not followed, and the *halakhah* was laid down to the effect that the father's legal obligation is only to maintain his children until they reach the age of six full years (Ket. 49b; 65b; Sh., Ar., EH 71:1); above this age the obligation flows merely from the laws of *ẓedakah,* and, insofar as they are applicable (see above), fulfillment of the obligation will be compulsory. Since it concerns a person's own children the charitable duty is more stringent in this case than it is with ordinary *ẓedakah,* and therefore the father will be required to exert himself to the utmost in order to satisfy his children's needs (Ket. and Sh. Ar., loc. cit.; Yad, Ishut 12:14, 15; 21:17, *Maggid Mishneh;* Sh. Ar., YD 251:4). In the course of time it became apparent that the legal position as described above did not adequately protect the interests of children above six years of age, as the father tried to evade his duty. Hence it was ordained in a *takkanah* of the Chief Rabbinate of Palestine (1944) that the father shall be bound to maintain his sons and daughters until they reach the age of 15 years, provided they have no independent means of support (see Freimann, bibl.).

Maintenance out of the Deceased's Estate. The father's obligation to maintain his children is imposed on him as father and terminates upon his death without being transmitted to his heirs as a charge on the estate. Hence the minor heirs cannot demand from the others that they should be maintained out of the estate in addition to their normal share of the legacy; the estate will therefore be divided amongst all the heirs, each of them, regardless of age, being given his rightful share (BB 139a; Sh. Ar., ḤM 286:1). The position is different, however, with regard to the maintenance of the daughters of the deceased. Jewish law excludes daughters from succession to their father's estate when he is survived by sons or their descendants (see Succession[1]), and instead, in such a case, entitles daughters to be maintained out of the estate until their majority or marriage – whichever comes first – to the same extent as they were entitled

1. page 449.

during their father's lifetime (i.e., in accordance with their needs; Ket. 52b, 53b; Sh. Ar., EH 112:1). This right of the daughter flows from the conditions of her mother's *ketubbah* as her independent right and therefore she cannot be deprived of it without her own consent, neither by her father's testamentary disposition nor by her mother's waiver of the respective condition of the *ketubbah* in an agreement with the father, and it remains in force notwithstanding the divorce of her parents (Ket. loc. cit., Yad, Ishut 12:2; 19:10; Rema, EH 112:1). If the assets of the estate are not sufficient to satisfy both the daughters' right of maintenance and the heirs' rights of succession *(nekhasim mu'atim)*, the daughters' right takes preference (Ket. 108b; Sh. Ar., EH 112:11); even if the assets of the estate should suffice for both *(nekhasim merubbim)* but there is established reason to fear that the sons might squander them and thus endanger the daughters' maintenance, the court will have power to take any steps it may deem fit for the preservation of the daughters' right (Rema loc. cit.).

Custody of Children. The law deals here with the determination of a child's abode, taking into account the responsibility of the parents for his physical and spiritual welfare, his raising, and his education. The rule is that the child's own interest is always the paramount consideration and his custody is a matter of a parental duty rather than a right, it being a right of the child vis-à-vis his parents.

Different Rules for Boys and Girls. In pursuance of this rule, the halakhic scholars laid down that children below the age of six years must be in the custody of their mother, since at this tender age they are mainly in need of physical care and attention. Above the age of six, boys must be with their father, since at this age they are in need of education and religious instruction, a task imposed by law upon the father, and girls with their mother ("the daughter must always be with her mother"), since they are in need of her instruction in the ways of modesty (Ket. 102b, 103a; Yad, Ishut, 21:17; Sh. Ar., EH 82:7). As these rules are directed at serving the welfare of the child, the court may diverge from them if in a proper case it considers it necessary in the interests of the child and even order that he be removed from both his parents and be kept in a place where, in the court's opinion, his interests are better served (Rema, EH 82:7 and *Pitḥei Teshuvah* n. 6, in the name of Radbaz). The custody of the child is a matter not of the rights of the parents but of the rights of the child in respect of his parents. The principle of the matter is that the rule establishing the right that the daughter be always with her mother establishes the daughter's right and not the mother's; similarly in the case of the son until the age of six, it is the son's right which is established and not the father's (Resp. Maharashdam, EH 123; see also Resp. Radbaz, no. 123). As Ereẓ Israel is looked upon as the best possible place for bringing up and educating a Jewish child, his removal abroad will generally not be approved, but the court may nevertheless permit this to the mother or father if it is satisfied that in the circumstances it is necessary in the better interests of the child (PDR 1:103–7, 173–8).

Relation Between Custody and Duty of Maintenance. The rules concerning the custody of children have no influence on the parental obligation to maintain them. Hence the fact that the children are with their mother in accordance with these rules does not relieve the father from his obligation to maintain them – whether this is based on law or the rules of *ẓedakah* (Sh. Ar., EH 82:7). Moreover, the mother is not obliged to accept the children inasmuch as, on principle, the duty to take care of them is imposed on the father only; should she therefore refuse to take them, she may send them to him and he will not be entitled to reject them (Yad, Ishut 21:18; Sh. Ar., EH 82:8). However, if a boy above the age of six should be with his mother contrary to law, i.e., without the consent of the father or permission of the court, the father will be entitled to refuse to pay for the boy's maintenance for any period he is not with him *(ibid)*.

Access of the Non-Custodian Parent. The custodian parent has no right to deprive the other of access to their child, nor the child of access to the other parent, since the child is entitled to derive education and care from both his parents and to maintain his natural tie with both of them so as not to grow up as if orphaned of one of them. For the purpose of realization of this right of the child, it is incumbent on the parents to come to an understanding between themselves, failing which the court will decide the question of access on the basis of the child's interest rather than those of his parents. Since for each of the parents it is a matter of a duty (not of a right) toward their child, they will not be entitled to make performance of the one's obligation dependent upon performance of the other's. Thus the fact that the mother refuses to allow her son to visit his father, or the father to have access to him, in defiance of an agreement or order of the court to this effect, will not entitle the father to withhold the son's maintenance for as long as the mother persists in her attitude; nor will the mother be entitled to refuse the father access to the child because the father withholds the latter's maintenance (PDR 1:113, 118, 158, 176).

Custody in Case of Death of Either or Both Parents. In this case too the decisive question is the welfare of the child. On the death of either parent, it is presumed to be best served by leaving the child with the surviving parent, while in principle no special right of custody exists in favor of the parents of the deceased. Only when clearly indicated in the interests of the child, having the regard for all the circumstances including the care of teaching him Torah, will the court order otherwise (PDR 1:65–77). On the death of both parents, custody of the child will generally be given to the grandparents on the side of the parent who would have been entitled to custody had both been alive (Rema, EH 82:7 and *Ḥelkat Meḥokek* n. 11; Resp. Radbaz n. 123).

AGREEMENTS BETWEEN PARENTS CONCERNING THEIR CHILDREN

An agreement between parents as to maintenance or custody of their child will not avail to affect his rights unless proved to be in his best interest, nor will it preclude him, since he is represented by one parent, from claiming their enforcement against the other. The child is not party to an agreement between the parents and the rule is that "no obligation can be imposed on a person in his absence" (BM 12a; PDR 2:3). Hence the father, in a claim against him by the child for maintenance, will not escape liability on a plea that he is free of such a liability by virtue of an agreement made with the mother in which she took this liability upon herself (PDR 2:171–7; 5:171, 173). The effect, if any, of such agreement is merely that it may possibly give the father the right to recover from the mother any amount he may have to expend on the child's maintenance, but toward the child it is of no effect (PDR 5:171). Similarly, a divorce agreement in which the mother waives the right to custody of her children below the age of six, or the father to custody of his sons above this age, will not preclude the children from claiming through the other parent that the court should disregard the terms of the agreement and decide the matter in their own best interest only, in the light of all the circumstances. For this purpose, the question of whether the change of his abode may detrimentally affect the child's mental well-being will be a weighty consideration (PDR 1:177) and, in a proper case, if the court considers it just to do so, it will also pay due regard to the child's own wishes (*Ḥelkat Meḥokek* EH 82, n. 10 and *Ba'er Heitev* n. 6). The court's approval of such an agreement will not preclude a fresh approach to the court owing to the fact that the circumstances have later changed, nor an application for the reconsideration of the case with regard to the child's best interests in the light of such a change (Resp. Radbaz no. 123; PDR 4:332–6).

CHILDREN OF PARENTS WHO ARE NOT BOTH JEWISH

Unless both parents are Jewish, the father has no legal standing in relation to the children, neither as regards maintenance nor custody. If the father is Jewish and the mother not, the child will be considered a non-Jew while, halakhically speaking, the non-Jewish father will not be considered his father (see *Yuḥasin*). Since the duty of maintenance, like all other paternal duties, is only imposed on the person halakhically recognized as the father – toward his halakhically recognized child – there is therefore no room for the imposition of any recognized legal obligation incumbent on the father of a child qua father except if he and the mother are both Jewish. A different, and so far apparently unsupported, opinion was expressed by R. Ben Zion Ouziel (*Mishpetei Uziel,* EH no. 4).

IN THE STATE OF ISRAEL

Matters of child maintenance by Jewish parents are governed by Jewish law (s.3 of the Family Law Amendment (Maintenance) Law, 1959; see also no. 507/61 in PD 16 (1962), 925, 928; no. 426/65, PD 20, pt. 2 (1966), 21). Other matters, including custody – in the case of Jewish parents – are also governed by Jewish law, except as otherwise provided in the Capacity and Guardianship Law, 1962. For their greater part both the abovementioned laws are based on principles of Jewish law (see Elon, bibl.), and they regulate the legal position of both parents as regards maintenance and custody of their children even where one parent is a non-Jew.

Bibliography: Gulak, Yesodei, 3 (1922), 66–70; A. Aptowitzer, in: *Ha-Mishpat ha-Ivri,* 2 (1926/27), 9–23; A. H. Freimann, in: *Sinai,* 14 (1943/44), 254–62; ET, 1 (1951^3), 5–7, 228; 2 (1949), 22f., 378; 4 (1952), 744f.; 6 (1954), 329–32; M. Elon, in: ILR, 3 (1968), 430–2; 4 (1969), 119–26; idem, *Ha-Mishpat Ha-Ivri* (1973), I, 155ff., II, 273ff., 336, 340ff., 354, 465, 471–476, 673ff., III, 1069; B. Schereschewsky, *Dinei Mishpaḥah* (1967^2), 359–94.

Ben-Zion Schereschewsky

YUḤASIN (Heb. יוחסין), laws dealing with the determination of an individual's personal status and its legal consequences insofar as such a status derives from a person's particular parentage. From the beginning of Jewish history, the ascertainment of an Israelite's *yiḥus,* i.e., genealogy or pedigree, was considered of utmost importance, as is evidenced in Scripture (Num. 1:2, 18 and Rashi ad. loc.; Ezra 2:59–63; 8:1). According to the Talmud, a person's *yiḥus* was also of importance with regard to the amount of the "main" (or statutory) *ketubbah,* as for a certain period of time it was ruled that it should be increased beyond the regular minimum in the case of the daughters of priests and of other distinguished families (Ket. 12a–b and Tos. ad loc. s.v. *bet din shel kohanim*).

Determination of Paternity. A person's *yiḥus* obviously cannot be established unless the identity of his parents is known. Identifying the mother generally presents no difficulties but to identify the father it is necessary to distinguish between the offspring of a married and an unmarried woman.

The offspring of a married woman is presumed to have been fathered by her husband, according to the rule that the majority of cases is to be followed, since for the most part a woman cohabits with her husband (Ḥul. 11b; Sh. Ar., EH 4:15). Therefore if the husband denies paternity the onus is on him to rebut this presumption; he will succeed in his claim if he can prove that factually the child cannot be his, for example, if he was away from his wife and never saw her for an unbroken period of at least 12 months prior to the birth of the child (Sh. Ar., EH 4:14). When a child is born less than 12 but more than 10 months after the husband's separation from the child's mother, the matter will depend on the facts in each case (although the matter is not undisputed in the codes; see Sh. Ar., *ibid.* and *Ḥelkat Meḥokek* nos. 10 and 11): if on the evidence of the mother's conduct there is reason to suspect that she has committed adultery, the court will not be bound by the usual presumption and may decide that the husband is not the father of the child (Rema, *ibid.*); if, however, there is no basis for any such suspicion, it may possibly be held – unless there is some evidence to the contrary – that the fetus tarried in its mother's womb beyond the normal pregnancy period (270 days) and the court may rule that the husband is the father of the child.

The presumption of paternity does not apply where the husband expressly denies it and there is no evidence that he has cohabited with his wife during the relevant period. It must be clear, however, that his denial is based on his own conviction and not on mere speculation, and is in no way contradicted by his own conduct, e.g., if hitherto he has admitted his paternity – expressly or by implication. This *halakhah,* known as *yakir* ("acknowledge"), is based on Deuteronomy 21:17, from which it is deduced that the husband may acknowledge and designate a particular son as his firstborn, in preference to other sons born to his wife after their marriage, even if such a son is younger than the others – the husband thus implicitly declaring that the other ones are not his, but are *mamzerim* born to his wife through adultery (Kid. 74a; Sh. Ar., 4:29; PDR 3:97–108). The husband's declaration of a son's bastardy, however, is not believed if the son already has sons of his own, since because of the rule that the son of a *mamzer* is also a *mamzer* this would taint them with bastardy as well, and the Torah has not conferred so wide a power upon the husband (Sh. Ar., EH 4:29). On the other hand, as long as the husband himself does not deny paternity, the wife's declaration that he is not the father of her child will not be accepted as sufficient to exclude the husband's paternity, and this is so even if a third party admits to being the father of the child (Sot. 27a; Rema, EH 4:15 and EH 4:26–29; see also PDR 7:281, 289). Various questions arise in the case of **a child born as a result of artificial insemination; this problem is discussed by several scholars.**

In the case of the offspring of an unmarried woman the onus is on the child to prove (through his mother) that the defendant is his father. This is so not only because here the presumption of paternity as in the case of a married woman is inapplicable, but also because the mere fact that the defendant and the child's mother had sexual relations does not necessarily warrant the inference that the defendant is its father (Yev. 69b; Resp. Ribash, nos. 40 and 41). Differing opinions are expressed in the codes on how paternity is to be proved. In the Shulḥan Arukh it is laid down as *halakhah* that the defendant's paternity may only be proved by his own admission (EH 4:26 and Rema thereto; Resp. Ribash, *ibid.*). Such an admission need not necessarily be express and it is sufficient if facts can be established concerning the defendant's conduct from which an admission of his being the father may be inferred: e.g., his taking the mother to a hospital for her confinement, or paying the hospital bill for the mother or the child, etc. (Resp. Rosh 82:1; *Ozar ha-Posekim* EH 4, no. 108, 4).

Rules of Yuḥasin. The following four categories of offspring are to be distinguished: offspring of parents married to each other; offspring of parents not married to each other; offspring of parents of whom only one is Jewish; and offspring of unknown parents.

Offspring of Parents Married to Each Other. A child born to a marriage which is valid and not originally prohibited between the parties (see Marriage, Prohibited), is *kasher* (of unimpaired status), i.e., his (or her) marriage is permitted to any *kasher* Jewess (or Jew; Kid. 69a; Sh. Ar., EH 8:1). Such a child takes the father's status, not that of the mother, in accordance with Numbers 1:2, 18 (and Rashi ad loc.; Sh. Ar., EH 8:1). Thus, the son of a priest and an Israelite woman will be a priest and one born of an ordinary Israelite and the daughter of a priest will be an ordinary Israelite. If the marriage of the parents is valid but originally prohibited, the child's status follows that of the tainted parent (Kid. 66b; Sh. Ar., EH 8:4). Hence the offspring of a marriage of which one party is a *mamzer(et)*, will also be a *mamzer* (Kid. 66b; Sh. Ar., EH 4:18); similarly, the son of a priest and a divorcée is called a *ḥalal* (חלל), i.e., profaned, and is unfit for the priesthood, while the daughter of such a marriage is called a *ḥalalah* חללה and cannot marry a priest (Lev. 21:7; Kid. 77a; Sh. Ar., EH 7:12 and 8:4). Since the laws of the priesthood apply only to priests of unimpaired status *(kesherim)* there is no prohibition against a *ḥalal* marrying a divorcée (Sh. Ar., EH 7:20). Except in matters of priesthood, the *ḥalal* suffers no defect in status and he or she is allowed to marry an Israelite woman or man of unimpaired status (Sh. Ar., EH 8:2). A marriage between such parties not being prohibited, their offspring follows the father's status; i.e., the daughter of an Israelite and a *ḥalalah* is not profane and is permitted to be married to a priest, but the daughter of a *ḥalal* and an Israelite woman is also a *ḥalalah* and so must not marry a priest (Kid. 77a; Sh. Ar., EH 7:16).

Offspring of Parents not Married to Each Other. The mere fact that a child is born out of wedlock does not taint his personal status, nor is he thereby rendered unfit for the priesthood (Yev. 59b–60a; Sh. Ar., EH 6:8). Even though it prohibits fornication, which is punishable with flogging (Yad, Ishut 1:4), Jewish law, unlike other legal systems, does not render a child illegitimate, with its rights affected, merely because it is the issue of an extramarital union. The sole legal difference – in the present context – between such a child and one born of parents married to each other concerns the question of proving paternity (see above). Upon proof of paternity, the status of a child born out of wedlock is determined in the same manner as if it were born to parents married to each other. This applies only if (at the time of conception) there existed no legal impediment to a marriage between the parents of the child. However, if the parents were not in a position to contract a valid marriage with each other even if they had wished to do so, because their cohabitation would have amounted to incest (including adultery) according to the Torah (i.e., a union between parties prohibited to each other according to biblical law and for whom the punishment is *karet* or death), the child will be a *mamzer* and his status thus impaired (Kid. 66b; see Marriage, Prohibited).

Offspring of Parents of Whom Only One is Jewish. Here the rule is that the child takes his mother's status (Kid. 66b; Sh. Ar., EH 4:19). Accordingly, the offspring of a non-Jew and a Jewess is a Jew and is legitimate, subject to the limitation that a priest should not marry such a daughter, or unless the mother is herself a *mamzeret;* in this case the child is a *mamzer,* and this is so even if the Jewess is a married woman whose adulterous relations with a Jew would have made the child a *mamzer* (Sh. Ar., EH 4:19 and 4:5 with commentaries). On the other hand, the offspring of a Jew and a non-Jewish mother is not a Jew, regardless of the will of the parents, since the matter is determined by the objective facts alone. The child therefore can become Jewish only by first being a proselyte, in the same way as any other non-Jew. Here the status of the father is totally irrelevant and the child, after proselytizing according to Jewish law, will assume the status of a legitimate Israelite like all other proselytes; even if his father is a *mamzer* this will not affect the status of the proselyte child (Kid. 66b, Rashi ad loc.; Sh. Ar., EH 4:20). For the case of a child when either one or both of its parents is unknown see *Mamzer.*

The State of Israel. Questions of *yuḥasin* and paternity are apparently regarded as matters of personal status within the meaning of Act 51 of the Palestine Order in Council (1922), and therefore are governed by the personal law of the parties concerned – Jewish law in the case of Jews. The Supreme Court of Israel, however, has so far refrained from adopting a clear stand on the matter and has left it as a *quaere* (PD 5 (1951), 1341ff., 17 (1963), 2751, 2755). On the question of under what circumstances the offspring of a Jew and a non-Jewish mother can be registered as a Jew for the purposes of the population registration law – registration which in itself does not serve as proof that the person registered is a Jew – the Supreme Court has held, by a majority of five judges to four, that the subjective declaration of the parents should suffice unless it is obviously incorrect (PD 23, pt. 2 (1969), 477–608). An amendment in 1970 to the Law of Return states that the term Jew in the said law means a person born of a Jewish mother or converted to Judaism who is not a member of a different religious faith. The same amendment states that this definition applies also for purposes of registering an individual's Jewish nationality *(le'om)* in the population register and related documents, including the identity card (see also Introduction: Jewish Law in the State of Israel). With regard to the modes of proof of paternity of a child born of an unmarried mother, the Supreme Court has decided that the general rules of evidence and not the rules of Jewish law shall apply (PD 5 (1951), 1341ff.).

Bibliography: A. Buechler, in: *Festschrift Adolf Schwarz* (1917), 133–62, 572; L. Freund, *ibid.*, 163–92; Gulak, Yesodei, 3 (1922), 10; A. Buechler, in: MGWJ, 78 (1934), 126–64; ET, 1 (1951[3]), 3–5, 276f.; 2 (1949), 21f.; 3 (1951), 346; 4 (1952), 741f.; *No'am,* 1 (1958), 111–66; M. Silberg, *Ha-Ma'amad ha-Ishi be-Yisrael* (1965[4]); B. Schereschewsky, *Dinei Mishpaḥah* (1967[2]), 343–61; M. Elon, *Ha-Mishpat Ha-Ivri* (1973), I, 115, II, 304, 720.

Ben-Zion Schereschewsky

EMBRYO (Heb. עבר *,ubbar*), a child in the womb of its mother before its head emerges (Sanh. 72b; Sh. Ar., ḤM 425:2), the Hebrew *ubbar* meaning the unborn child in both the embryonic and fetal stages. Generally speaking, an embryo is incapable of having legal rights or duties, although there are various rules intended to protect its rights when born, and to prevent uncertainty with regard to its status.

Determining the Identity of the Embryo. A widow or divorced woman must not remarry until 90 days after the death of her husband or after her divorce (Sh. Ar., EH 13:1, see **Marriage, Prohibited**[1]). The reason for this prohibition is to ascertain whether or not she is pregnant, and thus to distinguish between the offspring of her first husband and of her second – lest a doubt arise whether the child she bears is a nine-month child of the first, or a seven-month child of the second, a doubt

1. page 361.

which might seriously affect its personal status (Yev. 41a–42a; and Codes).

Mother or Embryo – Who Takes Precedence? On the question of whether an embryo may be killed in order to save its mother in the case of a difficult confinement, see Abortion.

Parentage. Generally, the same laws that apply in determining the parentage of a born child and the capacity of the mother or her husband to deprive it of its status apply to the embryo; see *Mamzer;* Parent and Child.

Levirate Marriage or Ḥaliẓah of a Pregnant Woman. If a woman was pregnant when her husband died and the child is subsequently born alive, she is exempt from levirate marriage or *ḥaliẓah* (Sh. Ar., EH 156:4; see Levirate Marriage and *Ḥaliẓah*).

Succession. An embryo is incapable of acquiring rights, for only a person born can possess rights. Accordingly, if an embryo dies in its mother's womb, it does not leave the right of succession, to which it would have been entitled had it been alive when the deceased died, to those who would have been its heirs had it been born alive when the deceased died. Instead, such right of succession passes to the heirs of the deceased as if the embryo had never existed (BB 142a; Nid. 44a; and Codes, Rif to Yev. 67a). There is a contrary opinion, however, to the effect that intestate succession being automatic, the embryo does acquire it (*Piskei ha-Rosh* Yev. 67a; see Tur, ḤM 210). All agree, however, that a child born alive after the death of its father inherits its father as though it had been alive when he died (Rif, Ritba, to Yev. 67a, *Beit Yosef* and *Baḥ* to Tur and Sh. Ar., loc. cit.; see *Ḥiddushei Ḥayyim ha-Levi* to Yad, Terumot 8:4). Hence, an embryo that is born after the death of the deceased, even if it dies the day it is born, leaves the right of succession (after its mother) to its heirs on its father's side, but not to those on its mother's side – who would have inherited had the embryo died in her womb (Tur and Sh. Ar., ḤM 276:5). Only in respect of the special rights due to a firstborn son is a child born after the death of his father not of equal status with one already born when the father dies. Thus, if twins are born, the first one will not be entitled to the additional share in the father's estate due to the firstborn (see Firstborn), since the Torah states of the primogenitary right, "If they have borne him children..." (Deut. 21:15), i.e., only a firstborn alive when the father dies, but not an embryo, is entitled to the (additional) primogenitary share (BB 142b, and Codes).

A will in favor of the embryo of another has no validity, even if the embryo is born alive, since no rights can be conferred upon one not yet born (BB 141b–142; *Piskei ha-Rosh* to Yev. 67a; Sh. Ar., ḤM 210:1). However, when a man whose wife is pregnant makes a will in favor of his own embryo whether it be a will of a person being on his deathbed *(shekhiv me-ra)* or of a person regarded as being in health *(bari)* see Wills[1] – it is valid, because a person is favorably disposed toward his own child and wholeheartedly wishes to transfer ownership to him (Sh. Ar., ḤM 253:26–27). Some are of the opinion that this law applies only to a will made by a person on his deathbed and not to one made by a healthy person (*Beit Yosef* to Tur ḤM 210:3; Sh. Ar., ḤM 210:1).

Contractual Obligations to an Embryo. According to some authorities although transfer of rights cannot be made to an embryo, a contractual obligation can be undertaken in his favor (see Contract[2]). A guardian can be appointed to protect the rights of an embryo (Sh. Ar., ḤM 290:1).

The State of Israel. In general, Jewish law is followed. With regard to succession, however, section 3 of the Succession Law (1965) provides that a person born within 300 days after the death of the deceased is deemed to have been living when the deceased died, unless it is proved that he was conceived thereafter. In terms of section 33(b) of the Capacity and Guardianship Law, 5722–1962, the Court may appoint a guardian for a child *en ventre sa mère.*

Bibliography: Gulak, Yesodei, 1 (1922), 33; 3 (1922), 82, 116, 147; ET, 7 (1956), 50–53; 8 (1957), 102–20; 11 (1965), 255f.; Miklishanski, in: *Sefer ha-Yovel... Federbush* (1960), 251–60; G. Ellinson, in: *Sinai,* 66 (1969/70), 20–49; M. Elon, *Ha-Mishpat Ha-Ivri* (1973), II, p. 496.

Ben-Zion Schereschewsky

FIRSTBORN. The difference in the status of the firstborn son as compared with that of his brothers, from the legal aspect of Jewish law, is his right to a greater share in their father's inheritance. This status is known as *bekhor le-naḥalah* (firstborn or primogeniture as to inheritance) and derives from the verse "he must acknowledge the firstborn the son of the unloved one, and allot to him a double portion of all he possesses; since he is the first of his vigor, the birthright is his due" (Deut. 21:15–17). The firstborn in this context is the first son born to the father, even if not so to the mother, since it is written, "the first fruits of his vigor" (Bek. 8:1 and see commentators). Even if such son is born of a prohibited union, e.g., the son of a priest and a divorced woman, or a *mamzer* born as first son to his father – he is included, on the strength of the words "he must acknowledge the firstborn, the son of the unloved one" (Deut., loc. cit.), the term a "loved" or an "unloved" wife being interpreted as relating only to the question whether the wife's marriage was "loved" or "unloved," i.e., permitted or prohibited (Yev. 23a and see Rashi and *Posekim* ad loc.). The prerogative of the firstborn never extends to a daughter, not even in a case where she has a right of inheritance (Sif. Deut. 215; see Succession). A son born to a proselyte to Judaism, who had sons before he became a proselyte, does not enjoy the prerogative of a *bekhor le-naḥalah,* since he is not "the first fruits of his vigor" (Yev. 62a; Bek. 47a; *Posekim* ad loc.); on the other hand, if an Israelite had a son by a non-Jewish woman and thereafter has a son by a Jewish woman, the latter son does enjoy the prerogative, since the former is called her, and not his, son (Maim. Yad, Naḥalot 2:12). A first son who is born after his father's death, viz., if the mother gives birth to twins, is not considered a *bekhor le-naḥalah* since it is written "he must acknowledge (Deut. 21:17) and the father is no longer alive to do so (BB 142b; Rashbam and *Posekim* ad loc.).

Proof of Primogeniture. In determining the fact of primogeniture reliance is placed upon the statements of three persons – the midwife, the mother, and the father. That the midwife is relied upon immediately after the son's birth (where twins are born) is derived from Genesis 38:28 (see TJ, Kid. 4:2, 65d); the mother is relied on during the first seven days after childbirth, since the father has not yet succeeded in "accepting" or recognizing the child, as he does not pass out of his mother's hands until the circumcision; thereafter the father's determination is accepted at all times, since he "must acknowledge his son" – i.e., recognize the child as his firstborn son personally and before others. The father's determination is relied upon even if he thereby assails the status of his other sons, as may happen if he acknowledges as his firstborn the youngest of several sons borne by his wife after they married each other – thus characterizing the other sons as *mamzerim* (Yev. 47a; Kid. 74a and *Posekim* ad loc.; see also *Mamzer*). However, the father is not believed in this last-mentioned case if the disqualified son already has children of his own, as the disqualification would also affect their status – for which purpose the law does not authorize reliance on his words (Yev. 47a and *Posekim; Oẓar ha-Posekim,* EH 4 n. 137).

1. page 453; 2. page 248.

The Birthright Prerogative. The firstborn is entitled to a "double portion," that is, he takes twice the portion due to each of his brothers from their father's inheritance. Thus if the father has left a firstborn and two other sons, the former takes one-half and the latter one-quarter each of the estate (BB 122b–123a and *Posekim*). The prerogative does not extend to the mother's estate (BB 111b, 122b and Codes).

The firstborn takes a double portion only of the present and not of the contingent assets, i.e., only of the assets in the father's possession at the time of his death and not such as were due to come into his possession thereafter. Thus, if the father predeceased any of his own legators, the father's share in their estate passes through him to his own heirs, the firstborn taking only the share of an ordinary heir. This rule embraces a debt still owing to the father at his death, even if under deed or bond, since the debt is considered an asset still to fall due and not yet in possession. If, however, the loan was secured by a pledge, or mortgage, the firstborn takes a double portion since in Jewish law the creditor acquires a right over the pledged property (Git. 37a) and a loan thus secured is therefore considered as an asset in possession (see generally Bek. 51b–52a; BB 125b; commentators and *Posekim* ad loc.). For the same reasons the firstborn does not take a double portion of improvements or increments from which the father's estate has benefited after his death, except with regard to natural increments – as for instance in the case of a sapling which has become full-grown *(ibid.)*.

Observance of Prerogative – Peremptory on the Father. The above-mentioned underlying biblical injunction precludes the father from depriving the firstborn of his particular right of inheritance. Consequently, any form of testamentary disposition (see Wills) by a father purporting to bequeath to the firstborn less than his prescribed double portion of the inheritance is null and void. This rule only applies, however, where the father has clearly adopted the language of a testator, since a father cannot change the laws of inheritance as such (Maim., Yad, Naḥalot 6:1). Consequently, if the father has expressed himself in terms of making a gift, his disposition will stand (although "the spirit of the sages takes no delight therein," BB 133b and see *Posekim*), since he may freely dispose of his assets by way of gift. Since the exercise of the birthright involves a corresponding greater liability for the debts of the estate, the firstborn may escape such additional liability by way of renouncing his prerogative before the division of the estate (BB 124a; Sh. Ar., ḤM 278:10).

State of Israel Law. The Law of Inheritance 5725–1965 of the State of Israel does not include any prerogative of the firstborn.

Bibliography: M. Bloch, *Das mosaisch-talmudische Erbrecht* (1890), 12–14, nos. 16–20; R. Kirsch, *Der Erstgeborene nach mosaisch-talmudischem Recht,* 1 (1901); Gulak, Yesodei, 3 (1922), 10, 74–76, 78, 84f., 102, 131; Herzog, Instit, 1 (1936), 50; ET, 1 (1951³), 4f.; 3 (1951), 276–83; 11 (1965), 37–39; B.-Z. Schereschewsky, *Dinei Mishpaḥah* (1967²), 353–8; M. Elon, *Ha-Mishpat Ha-Ivri* (1973), I, 160ff, II, 279.

Ben-Zion Shereschewsky

MAMZER (Heb. ממזר), usually translated as "bastard."

Definition. "If she cannot contract a legally valid marriage to this man, but can contract a legally valid marriage to others, her offspring [from the former] is a *mamzer.* Such is the case when a man has sexual relations with any of the *ervot* ["forbidden"; see Incest] in the Torah" (Kid. 3:12; cf. Yev. 4:13). Thus, a *mamzer* is the issue of a couple whose sexual relationship is forbidden according to the Torah and punishable by *karet* or death. Because of this a marriage between them is void (Sh. Ar., EH 4:13), and thus, for example, the issue of a union between brother and sister or between a man and a woman validly married to another at the time is a *mamzer* (see Adultery; Yev. 45b; Maim. Yad, Issurei Bi'ah 15:1; Tur and *Beit Yosef,* EH 4; Sh. Ar., EH 4:13). On the other hand, in Jewish law – unlike in other systems of law – the mere fact that a child is born (or conceived) out of lawful wedlock does not make him a *mamzer* and he is not an illegitimate child, i.e., one whose status or rights are impaired. The parents of the *mamzer* are indeed unmarried – either in fact or since they are so considered in law because of an absolute legal bar to a marriage between them – but unlike a man and a woman who, from the legal point of view, can marry each other but do not want to, the parents of the *mamzer,* owing to the said legal bar, cannot marry each other even if they want to. If one parent is non-Jewish this fact alone does not make the child a *mamzer* (see Marriage; Yev. 45b; Maim. Yad, Issurei Bi'ah 15:3; Tur, EH 4; Sh. Ar., EH 4:19).

Consequences of the State of Mamzerut. These are twofold and relate to marriage and to personal status. (1) Marriage. The Bible lays down: "A *mamzer* shall not enter the congregation of the Lord" (Deut. 23:3), i.e., a marriage between a *mamzer* (male or female) and a legitimate Jew or Jewess is prohibited. If such a marriage is nevertheless contracted, it is legally valid but must be dissolved by divorce (see Marriage, Prohibited). A marriage between two *mamzerim* is permitted (Yev. 45b; Kid. 69a, 74a; Maim. Yad., Issurei Bi'ah 15:33; Sh. Ar., EH 4:24) and so also is a marriage between a *mamzer* and a proselyte (Yev. 79b; Kid. 67a and Rashi, 72b–73a; Maim. Yad, Issurei Bi'ah 15:7; Sh. Ar., EH 4:22). (2) Personal status. The offspring of a *mamzer* (whether male or female) and a legitimate Jew or Jewess are also *mamzerim,* since "*mamzerim* . . . are forbidden and forbidden for all time, whether they are males or females" (Yev. 8:3) and the rule is that in the case of a prohibited union the offspring follows the status of the "defective" parent (Kid. 3:12; see *Yuḥasin*). On the other hand, as the offspring of a union between a Jew and a gentile takes the status of the mother, a child born of a *mamzer* and a gentile mother will be gentile and not a *mamzer;* thus after proper conversion to Judaism, he will acquire the status of a legitimate proselyte and the fact that his father was a *mamzer* will be wholly irrelevant (Kid. 68b, Rashi; Maim. Yad, Issurei Bi'ah 15:3; Tur and *Beit Yosef,* EH 4; Sh. Ar., EH 4:20).

Except with regard to marriage, as stated above, the personal status of a *mamzer* does not prejudice him in any way. His rights of inheritance are equal to those of any other heir (Yev. 22b; Maim. Yad, Naḥalot, 1:7; Sh. Ar., ḤM 276:6). His birth releases his father's wife from the obligation of levirate marriage and *ḥalizah.* The *mamzer* is eligible to hold any public office, the highest (i.e., that of a king), for he remains "thy brother" and "from among thy brethren shalt thou set a king over thee" (Deut. 17:15; Tos. to Yev. 45b). Furthermore, according to the Mishnah, "a *mamzer* who is a scholar *[talmid ḥakham]* takes precedence over a high priest who is an ignoramous *[am ha-arez]*" (Hor. 3:8).

Asufi ("a Foundling"). Sometimes a doubt may arise whether a child is legitimate or not and therefore he has the status of "doubtful" *mamzer.* One such case is that of a foundling, i.e., a child found abandoned in a public place when the identity of neither parent is known; in this case it is unknown whether the parents are legitimate or *mamzerim* (Kid. 4:2; Maim., Issurei Bi'ah, 15:13; Tur, EH 4; Sh. Ar., EH 4:31). If such a child is found in or near a place inhabited by both Jews and gentiles, so that it is impossible to know even if he is of wholly Jewish parentage or not, he is considered both a "doubtful" *mamzer* and a "doubtful" gentile, so that if he later marries a Jewess and then afterward she wants to marry another man, she will require a divorce because of this latter doubt (Ket. 15b; Maim. *ibid.* 15:25; Tur, EH 4; Sh. Ar., EH 4:33). If, however, such a child is found in or near an exclusively Jewish place, he is assumed to be of wholly Jewish parentage; but as the identity and hence the status of such parents (whether *mamzer* or legitimate) is unknown, he is considered a "doubtful" *mamzer* (Kid. 74a; Maim., Issurei Bi'ah 15:21 Sh. Ar., EH 4:31–36). Thus, he cannot marry either a legitimate Jewess (because he may be a *mamzer*) or a female *mamzer* (because he may in fact be legitimate). However, the suspicion of *mamzerut* only attaches to him if the circumstances in which he was found were such as to cast doubt on the status of legitimacy of his parents; for instance if it was clear that they did not care for his survival. If there is any indication at all that he was abandoned out of necessity, such as hunger or in time of war, or if there are some signs of minimal concern for his welfare and future, such as his being circumcised, clothed, or abandoned in a place (like a synagogue) where he is likely to be comparatively safe from danger or any other place where people are more likely to find and take care of him, then it is assumed that his parents are of unimpeachable status and so is he. Therefore no suspicion of *mamzerut* will be attached to him (Kid. 73b; Maim. Yad, Issurei Bi'ah 15:31; Tur, EH 4; Sh. Ar., EH 4:31).

Shetuki (lit. "Undisclosed"). The other case where the status of "doubtful" *mamzer* may arise is that of a child known to be born of an unmarried Jewish mother who either refuses to disclose the identity of the father or claims not to know it (Kid. 69a; Maim. Yad, Issurei Bi'ah 15:12). Since the father's status is unknown, the child is likely to be considered a "doubtful" *mamzer* (Kid. 74a; Maim. *ibid.; Arukh ha-Shulḥan,* EH 4:47). However, if the majority of the inhabitants of the district and of those who habitually visit there are Jews of unimpeachable status, it will be presumed that the father was also of such unimpeachable status and therefore no suspicion of *mamzerut* will be cast on the child (Tur EH 6 *Beit Yosef, Baḥ* at the end); Sh. Ar., EH 6:17–18 and *Beit Shemu'el* n. 31; but cf. Maim., Issurei Bi'ah 18:13–15; *Arukh ha-Shulḥan,* EH 4:34). The mother can always avert the suspicion of *mamzerut* being cast on her child by declaring that the father was a legitimate Jew or a gentile. In the latter case the child takes its status from the mother (i.e., he is a Jew; Kid. 74a; Maim. Yad, Issurei Bi'ah 15:12, 14; Sh. Ar., EH 4:26; *Arukh ha-Shulḥan,* EH 4:30, 31, 56).

Karaites. Halakhic problems concerning a "doubtful" *mamzer* have arisen in connection with the Karaites because, while their form of *kiddushin* (*kiddushei-kesef* or *kiddushei bi'ah*) may be valid according to Jewish law (see Marriage[1]) their method of divorce does not accord with the *halakhah,* as their *get* (bill of divorce) is not in the form prescribed by the sages. Accordingly, a Karaite woman divorced by such a *get* is not properly divorced and remains a married woman *(eshet ish)* so that any child she bears to another man whom she marries on the strength of such a *get* is a *mamzer.* Since it is impossible to determine who, throughout the generations, remarried on the strength of such invalid divorce, Jewish law casts the suspicion of "doubtful" *mamzer* on all members of that community EH 4 *Beit Yosef* – end and *Darkhei Moshe,* n. 14; Rema, EH 4:37; *Turei Zahav,* n. 24, *Ba'er Heitev,* n. 49). Some *posekim,* however, did permit marriages between Karaites and Rabbanite Jews on varying halakhic grounds and such marriages were particularly prevalent in the 11th and 12 centuries. Especially noteworthy is the permission to contract such a marriage granted by David b. Solomon ibn Abi Zimra who based his decision on the grounds that the *kiddushin* of the Karaites are also invalid according to *halakhah,* as they are deemed to have taken place without witnesses, the witnesses of the *kiddushin* being disqualified according to *halakhah* (Resp. Radbaz, pt. 1, 73 and pt. 2, 796). Thus, according to him, no stigma of *mamzerut* is to be attached to a child of a woman who married, was divorced, and then married another man, all in accordance with Karaite rites only, since – in Jewish law – she is regarded as never having been married at all. On the strength of this argument and for some additional reasons arising out of the specific circumstances of the case, in 1966 a rabbinical court in the State of Israel permitted the marriage of a non-Karaite Jewess to a Karaite man by whom she had become pregnant (see also *Oẓar ha-Posekim,* EH 4, n. 175).

Bibliography: ET, 1 (1951³), 202; 2 (1949), 71–74; *Ha-Ma'or,* 12 (1961), issue 9, p. 28 (English numbering of the same: 11 (1961), issue 7); S. M. Pasmaneck, in: HUCA, 37 (1966), 121–45; B. Schereschewsky, *Dinei Mishpaḥah* (1967²), 345–51; M. Elon, *Ḥakikah Datit . . .* (1968), 178–81; idem, *Ha-Mishpat Ha-Ivri* (1973), II, 296ff., 351ff., 670, 814, III, 872ff., 1242.

Ben-Zion Schereschewsky

ORPHAN. The meaning of the word *yatom* ("orphan") as found in the traditional literature varies in accordance with the context in which it is found. If reference is being made to the social treatment of the orphan – the tragedy of his plight and his emotional vulnerability – no distinction is made whether the child has been orphaned of his father or of his mother (Maim. Yad, De'ot 6:10). If, however, reference is being made to the special privileges accorded the orphan by the civil code, then only the fatherless child is meant (Resp. Maharashdam, ḤM nos. 196, 454).

Social Background. The Bible is particularly concerned with the helplessness of the orphan. The command to render him justice and the prohibition against oppressing him are reiterated constantly. The great solicitude for his defenselessness is reflected in God's role as his protector: "A father of the fatherless, and a judge of the widows, is God in His holy habitation" (Ps. 68:6; cf. 10:14). In conjunction with the levite, the resident alien, and the widow, the orphan is frequently cited as the object of charity and the subject of social legislation (e.g., Deut. 16:11 and 14; 24:19–21; 26:12–13). The biblical admonitions with regard to the orphan and their specific modes of implementation as found throughout talmudic literature have been summarized by Maimonides as follows (Maim. Yad, De'ot 6:10):

A man ought to be especially heedful of his behavior toward widows and orphans, for their souls are exceedingly depressed and their spirits low. Even if they are wealthy, even if they are the widow and orphans of a king, we are specifically enjoined concerning them, as it is said, "Ye shall not afflict any widow or orphan" (Ex. 22:21). How are we to conduct ourselves toward them? One may not speak to them otherwise than tenderly. One must show them unvarying courtesy; not hurt them physically with hard toil, nor wound their feelings with hard speech. One must take greater care of their property than of one's own. Whoever irritates them, provokes them to anger, pains them, tyrannizes over them, or causes them loss of money, is guilty of a transgression, and all the more so if one beats them or curses them. Though no stripes are inflicted for this transgression, its punishment is explicitly set forth in the Torah [in the following terms], "My wrath shall wax hot, and I will slay you with the sword" (Ex. 22:23). He Who created the world by His word made a covenant with widows and orphans that, when they will cry out because of violence, they will be answered; as it is said, "If thou

1. page 356.

afflict them in any wise – for if they cry at all unto Me, I will surely hear their cry" (Ex. 22:22). The above only applies to cases where a person afflicts them for his own ends. But if a teacher punishes orphan children in order to teach them Torah or a trade, or lead them in the right way – this is permissible. And yet he should not treat them like others, but make a distinction in their favor. He should guide them gently, with the utmost tenderness and courtesy, as it is said, "For the Lord will plead their cause" (Prov. 23:11). [In all of these rules] there is no distinction between an orphan bereft of a father or one bereft of a mother. To what age are they to be regarded in these respects as orphans? Till they reach the age when they no longer need an adult on whom they depend to train them and care for them, and when each of them can provide for all his wants, like other grown-up persons.

Bringing Up. Taking an orphan into one's home and raising him are regarded in the Talmud as most praiseworthy: "Whoever brings up an orphan in his home, Scripture ascribes it to him as though he had begotten him" (Sanh. 19b). Such acts constitute uninterrupted *ẓedakah* ("charity"). "Happy are they that keep justice, that do righteousness at all times [Ps. 106:3] – Is it possible to do righteousness at all times? . . . This refers to a man who brings up an orphan boy or orphan girl in his house and enables them to marry" (Ket. 50a). For more particulars on this aspect see Adoption.

Maintenance and Succession. The Talmud shows great concern for the claims of minor children to support from their father's estate. Unlike Persian authorities, the rabbis recognized no legal differences between children of "privileged" or "secondary" wives, and extended protection even to a man's proved illegitimate offspring (see Maintenance, Parent and Child, *Yuḥasin*). They also extended the legal protection of orphan girls by seeing to it that each *ketubbah* should specifically pledge the bridegroom's estate for the support of his surviving minor daughters *(ketubbat benan nokevan)*, and, in the absence of his pledge, by construing the omission as an error. Ultimately, the right of female orphans to support came to overshadow the claims of all other heirs, and, if need be, the entire estate was used for this purpose (Ket. 4:11; 13:3; TJ, Git. 5:3–4, 46d; and commentaries; see Succession[1]). In the case of impoverished orphan children whose father left little or no property, the Talmud holds the community responsible for their support, for marrying them off, and for providing them with the means to live economically independent lives. Communal funds were to be used to rent and furnish a house for a young man and to fit out a girl with clothing and a minimum dowry. If the communal funds were low, the orphan girl was given priority over the boy. If the community chest could afford to do so, the provisions provided for the orphan were made in accordance with his social position and the former manner of life to which he had been accustomed (Ket. 6:5 and 67b).

Guardianship. "The court is the father of orphans"; if a man died without appointing a guardian for his minor children, the court must do so (Yad, Naḥalot 10:5; cf. BK 37a). For more particulars see *Apotropos*.

Exemptions from some Laws. Minor orphans and their property are exempt from the ordinary laws of overreaching (*ona'ah;* Sh. Ar., ḤM 109:4–5), usury (*ribbit de-Rabbanan;* YD 160:18), the seventh-year recession of debts (prosbul; ḤM 67:28), communal taxation for the charity fund (*ẓedakah*, with specified exceptions; BB 8a and Sh. Ar., YD 248:3). For further particulars see Taxation.[2]

Procedure and Litigation. Whenever orphans of any age are involved in litigation regarding their father's property or transactions, judicial practice is to enter on their behalf all pleas and all arguments that their father could have entered (BB 23a). See Pleas; Practice and Procedure.

See also Child Marriage; Execution (Civil).

Bibliography: M. Cohn, in: *Zeitschrift fuer vergleichende Rechtswissenschaft,* 37 (1919–20), 417–45; Gulak, Yesodei, 1 (1922), 37, 154 n. 11; 3 (1922), 147ff.; 4 (1922), 43, 140; L. M. Epstein, *The Jewish Marriage Contract* (1927), 121–43, 175–92; Herzog, Instit, 1 (1936), 173f.; Baron, Social², *2* (1952), 253, 271; 5 (1957), 321 n. 81; M. Elon, *Ha-Mishpat Ha-Ivri* (1973), II, 354, 461, 502, 514, 531ff., 649, 669ff., 730, 787ff.

Aaron Kirschenbaum

ADOPTION as a legal act changing the personal status of a child towards his natural parents and creating a legal relationship of personal status between the child and his adopter similar to that existing between natural parents and their children is not known as a legal institution in Jewish Law. According to *halakhah* the personal status of parent and child is based on the natural family relationship only and there is no recognized way of creating this status artificially by a legal act or fiction. However, Jewish law does provide for consequences essentially similar to those caused by adoption to be created by legal means.

These consequences are the right and obligation of a person to assume responsibility for (a) a child's physical and mental welfare and (b) his financial position, including matters of inheritance and maintenance. The legal means of achieving this result are: (1) by the appointment of the adopter as a "guardian" (see *Apotropos*) of the child, with exclusive authority to care for the latter's personal welfare, including his upbringing, education and determination of his place of abode; and (2) by entrusting the administration of the child's property to the adopter, the latter undertaking to be accountable to the child and, at his own expense and without any right of recourse, to assume all such financial obligations as are imposed by law on natural parents vis-a-vis their children. Thus, the child is for all practical purposes placed in the same position toward his adopters as he would otherwise be toward his natural parents, since all matters of education, maintenance, upbringing, and financial administration are taken care of (Ket. 101b; Maim., Yad, Ishut, 23:17–18; and Sh. Ar., EH 114 and Tur *ibid.*, Sh. Ar., ḤM 60:2–5, 207:20–21; PDR, 3 (n.d.), 109–125). On the death of the adopter, his heirs would be obliged to continue to maintain the "adopted" child out of the former's estate the said undertaking having created a legal debt to be satisfied as any other debt (Sh. Ar., ḤM 60:4).

Indeed, in principle neither the rights of the child toward his natural parents, nor their obligations toward him are in any way affected by the method of "adoption" described above; but in fact, the result approximated very closely to what is generally understood as adoption in the full sense of the word. The primary question in matters of adoption is the extent to which the natural parents are to be deprived of, and the adoptive parents vested with, the rights and obligations to look after the child's welfare. This is resolved in accordance with the rule that determined that in all matters concerning a child, his welfare and interests are the overriding considerations always to be regarded as decisive (Responsa Rashba, attributed to Naḥmanides, 38; Responsa Radbaz, 1:123; Responsa Samuel di Modena, EH 123; Sh. Ar., EH 82, *Pitḥei Teshuvah* 7).

Even without private adoption, the court, as the "father of all orphans," has the power to order the removal of a child from his parents' custody, if this is considered necessary for his welfare (see *Apotropos*). So far as his pecuniary rights are con-

1. page 449; 2. page 680.

cerned, the child, by virtue of his adopters' legal undertakings toward him, acquires an additional debtor, since his natural parents are not released from their own obligations imposed on them by law, i.e. until the age of six. Furthermore, the natural parents continue to be liable for the basic needs of their child from the age of six, to the extent that such needs are not or cannot be satisfied by the adopter; the continuation of this liability is based on *Dinei Ẓedakah* – the duty to give charity (see Parent and Child; PDR, 3 (n.d.), 170–6; 4 (n.d.), 3–8).

With regard to right of inheritance, which according to *halakhah* is recognized as existing between a child and his natural parents only, the matter can be dealt with by means of testamentary disposition, whereby the adopter makes provision in his will for such portion of his estate to devolve on the child as the latter would have got by law had the former been his natural parent (see Civil Case 85/49, in: *Pesakim shel Beit ha-Mishpat ha-Elyon u-Vattei ha-Mishpat ha-Meḥoziyyim be-Yisrael,* 1 (1948/49), 343–8). In accordance with the rule that "Scripture looks upon one who brings up an orphan as if he had begotten him" (Sanh. 19b; Meg. 13a), there is no halakhic objection to the adopter calling the "adopted" child his son and the latter calling the former his father (Sanh. *ibid.,* based on II Sam. 21:8). Hence, provisions in documents in which these appellations are used by either party, where the adopter has no natural children and/or the child has no natural parent, may be taken as intended by the one to favor the other, according to the general tenor of the document (Sh. Ar., EH 19, *Pitḥei Teshuvah*, 3; ḤM 42:15; Resp. Ḥatam Sofer, EH 76). Since the legal acts mentioned above bring about no actual change in personal status, they do not affect the laws of marriage and divorce, so far as they might concern any of the parties involved.

In the State of Israel adoption is governed by the Adoption of Children Law, 5720/1960, which empowers the district court and, with the consent of all the parties concerned, the rabbinical court, to grant an adoption order in respect of any person under the age of 18 years, provided that the prospective adopter is at least 18 years older than the prospective adoptee and the court is satisfied that the matter is in the best interests of the adoptee. Such an order has the effect of severing all family ties between the child and his natural parents. On the other hand, such a court order creates new family ties between the adopter and the child to the same extent as are legally recognized as existing between natural parents and their child – unless the order is restricted or conditional in some respect. Thus, an adoption order would generally confer rights of intestate succession on the adoptee, who would henceforth also bear his adopter's name. However, the order does not affect the consequences of the blood relationship between the adoptee and his natural parents, so that the prohibitions and permissions of marriage and divorce continue to apply. On the other hand, adoption as such does not create new such prohibitions or permissions between the adopted and the adoptive family. There is no legal adoption of persons over the age of 18 years.

Bibliography: J. Kister, *Sekirah al Immuẓ Yeladim . . .* (1953); G. Felder, Hakohen, in: *Sinai,* 48 (1961), 204ff; Findling, in: No'am, 4 (1961), 65ff., Ezraḥi, *ibid.*, 94ff., Rudner, *ibid.,* 61ff.; B. Schereschewsky, *Dinei Mishpaḥah* (1967²), 395 ff; M. Elon, *Ha-Mishpat Ha-Ivri* (1973), I, 83, II, 669ff.

Ben-Zion Schereschewsky

APOTROPOS ("Guardian").

The Concept. The term *apotropos* (Heb. אפוטרופוס , for guardianship in Jewish law is derived from the Greek ἀπότροπος and means the "father" of minors or the "guardian" or "custodian" of another's affair (see Maimonides to Mishnah, Bik. 1:5; Obadiah of Bertinoro, ad loc., and Git. 5:4). The need for an *apotropos* arises with persons who are unable to take care of their own affairs, such as minors and adults who are mentally defective or absentees (*ibid.; Sha'arei Uziel,* 1 (1944), 1, 2). Halakhic sources deal mainly with an *apotropos* charged with responsibility for the property of his ward, thus taking in activities that in modern times would be the function of the administrator of an estate (see Succession) or executor of a will, as well as the trusteeship of consecrated property (*ibid.;* PDR, 2:18, 25). In principle, however, there is nothing in the *halakhah* against appointing an *apotropos* also over the person of another (see PDR, 2:177 and 4:97, 108; Resp. Rosh 82:2; *Sha'arei Uziel,* 1 (1944), 126, 173–6). The halakhic justification for the appointment of an *apotropos* over a person who has not expressed an opinion in the matter and is unable to do so owing to his being an absentee or a minor or incompetent, i.e., legally speaking, absent, is based on the principle that "a benefit may be bestowed on a person in his absence," since the function of an *apotropos* is to act solely in the interests of his ward (PDR 2:181).

Guardianship Over Minors. The Identity of the Guardian. Some persons have the legal standing of guardians of others, even if not specifically appointed, such as a father with respect to his minor children (Resp. Rosh 87:1; 96:2; Isserles to Sh. Ar., ḤM 285:8; Resp. Maharashdam, ḤM 308; today the father is usually called natural guardian) or a person who undertakes responsibility for the care and welfare of minors who are dependent on him or who are members of his household, including small children and babes-in-arms (Git. 52a and Rashi, *ibid.; Maggid Mishneh* to Maim., Yad, Naḥalot 11:10; Resp. Rosh 87:1; Tur, ḤM 290:31; Sh. Ar., ḤM 290:24; PDR, 2:168–70, 172–3). Minors are boys under the age of 13 or girls under the age of 12 (PDR, 3:154, 156, 159). Guardianship over minors can also be established by an appointment by their fathers (Git., *loc. cit.;* Sh. Ar., ḤM 290:1) or if they have not done so, by the court, by virtue of its authority as the "father of orphans" (Git. 37a; Resp. Rosh 85:5, 6:87:1; Sh. Ar., ḤM 290:1–2).

A mother has not the legal standing of guardian of her children, unless she is specifically appointed or stands in the same relationship toward them as a householder toward orphans formally part of his household, as mentioned above (Sh. Ar., ḤM 290:1, 24; PDR 2:162, 173). The court is also obliged to appoint a guardian over them if their own father, or the guardian appointed by him, is incapable of taking proper care of the minors, or for any other reason that may be in the interests of the minors (BK 37a; Isserles to Sh. Ar., ḤM 285:8; 290:5; PDR 2:170, 171; 4:108).

Generally speaking, the court, if guided by the interests of the ward as the overriding consideration, is unrestricted in its choice of guardian. Therefore, the court will seek to appoint someone of personal integrity, who is competent in worldly affairs and able to handle the affairs of orphans (BM 70a; Ket. 109b; Tur and *Beit Yosef* to Tur, ḤM 290:4; Sh. Ar., ḤM 290:2, 6). All other factors being equal, a relative of the ward is preferred over a stranger, he being presumed to take care of the minor's affairs better than a stranger *(Beit Yosef* and Darkhei Moshe 3 to Tur, ḤM 285:13; Isserles to Sh. Ar., ḤM 285:8, *Sha'arei Uziel,* 1 (1944), 108–9; Resp. Maharashdam, ḤM 312). Talmudic law disapproved of entrusting the immovable property of a minor to the stewardship of a relative who was in line to inherit such property, lest at some future time, when it will be forgotten that the property came into his possession in his capacity as guardian only, he claim that it came to him by inheritance (i.e., by virtue of presumptive possession – see

Ḥazakah; BM 39a and Codes; Resp. Ribash 495), but modern systems of land registration, providing for registration of immovable property in the name of the real owner have rendered this fear groundless, and it is no longer considered a bar to the appointment of a relative as guardian (PDR, 2:364, 367–8; *Sha'arei Uziel, ibid.*).

Talmudic law was also opposed to appointing women as guardians, since they were not regarded as being sufficiently competent or experienced in business matters (Git. 52a and Rashi, *ibid.*, ad loc. Resp. Ribash 495; Sh. Ar., ḤM 290:2). However, some of the *posekim* express the opinion that there is no objection to the court appointing a woman who is experienced in business matters and accustomed to going about in public if the best interests of the minor would thereby be served (*Baḥ* to ḤM 290:3; Resp. Ribash 495; Sh. Ar., ḤM 285:9; *Sha'arei Uziel* 1 (1944), 109–11). All the authorities agree that the father may appoint a woman to serve as the guardian of his children (Sh. Ar., ḤM 290:1) and a woman may also hold the position of guardian, without being specifically appointed thereto, with respect to members of her household dependent upon her (see above) and, if necessary, such a woman may be appointed guardian expressly by the court (Resp. Ribash 495). These provisions apply particularly to a minor's mother (PDR, 2:172, 173, 177; Resp. Maharam, ḤM 236).

Two or more persons may be appointed to serve as coguardians over a minor, or with a division of functions and powers between them, e.g., separate guardians may be appointed over his person and property respectively, as the best interests of the minor may dictate (Resp. Rosh 82:2). Similarly the court may appoint a guardian to serve together with the minor's father, in a case where the latter is considered incapable of fully discharging his duties toward the child (Resp. Rosh, 82:2; PDR, *ibid.*, *Sha'arei Uziel,* 1 (1944), 126). In case of disagreement, the majority opinion may be followed and, when opinions are divided equally, the court will decide the issue (Resp. Maharashdam, ḤM 434). A person must not be appointed guardian except with his own consent (Rashi, Git. 52b; *Maggid Mishneh* to Maim. Yad, Naḥalot 11:5).

Powers and Functions. The functions of a guardian are generally defined on his appointment, and he is to be guided by the overriding consideration of the best interests of his ward according to the circumstances. When entrusted with guardianship over the person of his ward, he has the duty of directing the latter's upbringing and education, determining his place of abode, and generally taking care of him (Resp. Rosh, 82:2; Resp. Maharashdam, EH 123; PDR, 2:177; 4:108; *Sha'arei Uziel,* 1 (1944), 126, 173–6). Responsibility for the property of the ward entails careful investment thereof by the guardian i.e., "near to benefit and far from loss," so that the capital be preserved as far as possible and only the dividends used to defray the minor's current expenses, including his maintenance (Git., *loc. cit.;* Sh. Ar., ḤM 290:8–11, 13). Since the guardian has authority only to act for the benefit of his ward, he is generally not entitled to represent the latter as a defendant in judicial proceedings, lest the claimant succeed and the debt be recovered from the minor's property. But when it is clear that the creditor is entitled to recover his debt from the property of the minor – e.g., when the testator had admitted such indebtedness, or if delaying legal proceedings until such time as the latter attains majority would be to his detriment, e.g., in the case of an interest-bearing debt or when the creditor is prepared to waive part of his rights if he will not have to wait with his claim until the minor's majority or in any other case where it is clearly to the benefit of the minor to be represented, as defendant in the proceedings, the guardian will have authority to represent him (Git. 52a and Rashi, ad loc.; Ar. 22a–b; Maim. Yad, Naḥalot 11:7; Malveh ve-Loveh 11:7; Sh. Ar., ḤM 110; 290:12, *Sha'arei Uziel,* 1 (1944), 182–6; PDR, 3:155-160).

All guardians, including those who have the legal standing of guardians (see above) and including the father of a minor, are subject to supervision by the court (Git. 52a and Codes; *Sha'arei Uziel,* 1:170; PDR, 2:170–1), and the court may set aside any step taken by the guardian as not being in the best interests of his ward and therefore in excess of his powers (PDR, 2:181). In this event the guardian may be held personally liable for any damage suffered by his ward as a result of his actions (BK 39a and Tos. thereto; and Codes), a threat he may avert only by seeking the prior approval of the court to his proposed course of action (Tosef., BB 8:15; Nov. Rashba to Git. 52a; Isserles to Sh. Ar., ḤM 290:13; PDR, 2:180). At any rate, he has to obtain such approval when dealing with the minor's immovable property (Sh. Ar., and PDR, *ibid.*), or making gifts from the latter's property, or waiving any of his rights (Sh. Ar., ḤM 235:26), including also the effecting of any compromise on his behalf (Isserles to ḤM 110:11).

Guardians are not entitled to any remuneration for their services unless specifically provided for in advance, such services being considered as the fulfillment of a religious duty *(mitzvah)* and therefore presumed to have been undertaken as a *mitzvah* and not for reward (PDR, 5:87–88). No act performed during the subsistence of the guardianship and affecting the rights of a minor is of any legal validity unless undertaken by, or with the approval of, his guardian (Ket. 70a, and Codes).

Termination of Guardianship. A guardianship terminates automatically when the ward attains his majority, since guardians are generally appointed only over minors (BM 39a; Maim. Yad, Naḥalot, 10:8; Sh. Ar., ḤM 290:1, 26). If, however, the father has specifically appointed a guardian over his adult children, guardianship over them will come into force, but will terminate upon their demand (PDR, 3:154, 156–60). The guardian's appointment may also be terminated by his removal from office by the court, a step which will only be taken when deemed in the interests of the minor, e.g., if the guardian has dealt prejudicially with the property of his ward or if his conduct – even in regard to the handling of his own affairs – casts doubt on his personal integrity (Git. 52b, and Codes; PDR, 1:353, 359). It is pursuant to this power that the court may order the removal of a minor from his parents' house and appoint a guardian over his person or property (*Beit Yosef* to ḤM 290:6; Isserles to Sh. Ar., ḤM 285:8; Resp. Maharashdam, EH 123; PDR, 2:170, 171).

A guardianship may also be terminated on the strength of an application to the court by the guardian asking to be relieved of his appointment, since he cannot be compelled to serve against his will (*Beit Yosef*, to Tur, ḤM 290:22). But explicit discharge by the court is required, for once undertaken the task of a guardian cannot be abandoned unilaterally (Tosef., BB 8:12; Sh. Ar., ḤM 290:23). The court will not release the guardian from his duties until it has appointed another in his place, so as not to leave the minor or his property without supervision.

Upon the termination of his appointment, the guardian is required to hand over to his successor all the minor's property, to submit a report of his activities and, on the minor's demand, he will also have to take an oath that he has not retained any of the minor's assets (Git. 52a; *Beit Yosef,* ḤM 290:22; *Baḥ, ibid.*, 23; *Sha'arei Uziel,* 1:192–5). When the termination arises because the ward attains majority, he is entitled – even if he is a prodigal – to take possession of his property, unless there is an express instruction to the contrary from his father or the testator (BM 39a; Sh. Ar., ḤM 290:26). Being a prodigal is not sufficient reason for subjecting him to guardianship (Resp. Ribash 20); only if his conduct stems from mental illness will a guardian be appointed over him (see above).

Guardianship Over Adults. The court will appoint a guardian over an idiot who, because he is mentally defective or suffering from mental illness, is unable to manage his own affairs, a rule applying also to a deaf-mute. To such a guardianship apply, generally, the laws of guardianship in respect to minors (Ket. 48a; Maim. Yad, Mekhirah, 29:4; Naḥalot, 10:8; Sh. Ar., ḤM 235:20; ḤM 285:2; 290:27). Inability to take care of one's own affairs is also the basis for the court's authority to appoint a guardian (or custodian) over the property of an absentee person, i.e., one who has left his place of residence and whose whereabouts are unknown, if the court deem the appointment necessary for the preservation of his property (BM 39a–b; Maim. Yad, Naḥalot 7:4–10; Tur, *Beit Yosef* and *Baḥ*, ḤM 285; Sh. Ar., *ibid.; Sha'arei Uziel,* 1, 13–23). In this case, unlike that of a minor, the court is not obliged to concern itself with seeking a suitable candidate for the appointment, but has authority to appoint the applicant's nominee, if suitable, as the appointment of a guardian over an adult of full capacity is not in fulfillment of a *mitzvah* (*Maggid Mishneh* to Maim. Yad, Naḥalot 7:5; Isserles to Sh. Ar., ḤM 285:2). However, the court will not appoint a guardian over the assets of an absentee unless his absence is due to duress – e.g., if he is forced to abandon his assets while fleeing for his life. Therefore, a guardian will not be appointed over property voluntarily left, without supervision by its owner – since, had he wanted it, he could have made the appointment himself – except in respect of property which came to him after his departure and without his knowledge, e.g., by way of inheritance (BM 38a–b, 39a–b; Maim, Yad, Naḥalot, 7:4–8; Sh. Ar., ḤM 285:1–4 and Isserles, ad loc., 4; *Sha'arei Uziel,* 1, 13–23).

See also Succession and Wills with reference to guardianship from these aspects.

In the State of Israel, guardianship is mainly governed by the following laws: The Women's Equal Rights Law, 1951; The Capacity and Guardianship Law, 1962; The Administrator General Ordinance, No. 37 of 1944 (as amended); and The Succession Law, 1965. The first of the abovementioned laws (sec. 3) provides that "both parents are the natural guardians of their children; where one parent dies, the other shall be the natural guardian" and further, in conformity with Jewish law, that the said provision does not affect the inherent power of the competent court to "deal with matters of guardianship over the persons or property of children with the interest of the children as the paramount consideration." In the absence of any express provision to the contrary in any of the abovementioned laws, halakhic law is applied.

Bibliography: Bloch, *Vormundschaft nach mosaisch-talmudischem Recht* (1904); M. Cohn, in: *Zeitschrift fuer vergleichende Rechtswissenschaft,* 37 (1920), 435–45; Gulak, Yesodei, 3 (1922), 106, 146–54; Gulak, Oẓar, 140–8; Assaf, in: *Ha-Mishpat ha-Ivri,* 2 (1926/27), 75–81; ET, 2 (1949), 121–9; 3 (1951), 35–36, s.v. *Bore'aḥ;* M. Silberg, *Ha-Ma'amad ha-Ishi be-Yisrael* (1965[4]), index, and *Millu'im ve-Hashlamot* (1967), index; B. Schereschewsky, *Dinei Mispaḥah* (1967[2]), 403–25; Baker, *Legal System of Israel* (1968), index s.v. Guardianship; M. Elon, in: ILR, 4 (1969), 121–7; idem, *Ha-Mishpat Ha-Ivri* (1973), II, 480ff., 588ff.

Ben-Zion Schereschewsky

SUCCESSION, devolution of the deceased person's property on his legal heirs.

Order of Succession. The Pentateuchal source of the order of succession is "If a man die and have no son, then ye shall cause his inheritance to pass unto his daughter. And if he have no daughter, then ye shall give his inheritance unto his brethren. And if he have no brethren, then ye shall give his inheritance unto his father's brethren. And if his father have no brethren, then ye shall give his inheritance unto his kinsman that is next to him of his family and he shall possess it. And it shall be unto the children of Israel a statute of judgment, as the Lord commanded Moses" (Num. 27:8–11).

Scripture makes no mention of the father inheriting from his son but this is laid down in the Mishnah: "The father has precedence over all his offspring" (BB 8:2). An interpretation that son and daughter inherit like shares in their father's estate – and that Scripture merely indicates that daughters inherit all of the estate in the absence of sons – was raised and rejected in the Talmud (BB 110a–b) and it was confirmed that the daughter only inherits if there is no son (see below). A daughter succeeding to her father's estate was enjoined to marry "only into the family of the tribe of their father . . . So shall no inheritance of the children of Israel remove from tribe to tribe; for the children of Israel shall cleave everyone to the inheritance of the tribe of his fathers" (Num. 36:6–7; cf. also Philo, Spec. 2:126). In the Book of Tobit (6:10–11) two additional elements were attached to the above law: firstly, the enjoinder that the daughter marry "someone from a clan of her father's tribe" was interpreted as a duty imposed not only on a daughter upon her father's death, but also on the father – if he had no sons – to marry his daughter to one of his kinsmen; secondly, the father's violation of the enjoinder was treated as punishable by death, "according to the law of the Book of Moses" (*ibid.,* 6:13). The sages of the Talmud laid down that the duty of the daughter to marry as above mentioned was applicable only to the particular generation to whom the enjoinder was directed (BB 120a and Rashbam ad loc.).

Jewish law has the parentelic system of succession, conferring the right of inheritance on all the kin of the deceased in the agnate (paternal) line of descendancy and ascendancy. Precedence among the heirs is determined, firstly, according to the degree of kinship with the deceased: the first parentela includes the deceased's children and their descendants, to the end of the line; the second includes the deceased's father and his descendants; the third, the father's father and his descendants; and so on in an ascending order – "that the estate may ultimately find its way to Reuben (the eldest son of the Patriarch Jacob)" (BB 8:2; 115a–b). The nearer parentela takes precedence over and excludes more distant ones from the inheritance: "the lineal descendants of any one with a priority to succession take precedence" (BB 8:2).

The mother's family is not regarded as kin for the purposes of inheritance and therefore she does not inherit from her sons nor do her brothers or other relatives. Sons do, however, succeed to their mother's estate (BB 8:1). In post-talmudic times the mother too was recognized as a legal heir in a number of *takkanot* (see Gulak, Yesodei, 3 (1922), 94).

Relatives of the deceased, even if born out of wedlock or of an invalid marriage, are his kin and legal heirs for all purposes as if born of a valid marriage, except for the offspring of a bondswoman or a non-Jewess, who take the status of their mother and are not numbered among the father's family (Yev. 2:5; Sh. Ar., ḤM 276:6).

"Inheritance in the Grave" (Yerushah ba-Kever). According to this principle, the place of a son who predeceases his father is taken by his children in inheriting the portion which he, but for his death, would have inherited (BB 115a; Yad, Naḥalot, 1:3, 5).

If the deceased's sole survivors should be a daughter and a sons's daughter, the latter will inherit the whole estate since she takes the place of her father to the exclusion of his sister; the Sadducees, however, held the opinion that in such event the inheritance is shared between the deceased's daughter and his granddaughter (BB 115–116a). A son who predeceases his mother "does not inherit from his mother to transmit the [inheritance] to [his] brothers on his father's side" (BB 114b).

Primogeniture. The firstborn son of the father takes a double portion in his estate: "...he shall acknowledge the firstborn, ... by giving him a double portion of all that he hath; for he is the firstfruits of his strength; the right of the firstborn is his" (Deut. 21:16–17). The firstborn is entitled to the double portion even if he is a *mamzer.* On the other hand, the law of the firstborn does not apply to daughters who inherit in the absence of sons (Sif. Deut. 215). The firstborn only takes a double portion from the estate of his father and not from that of his mother or any other relative (Yad, Naḥalot, 2:8). If the firstborn predeceases his father, the double share which he would otherwise have inherited from his father's estate is taken by his heirs (Sh. Ar., ḤM 277:15). If the firstborn is born after his father's death (or in the case of twins) he does not receive a double portion (BB 142b).

The inheritance due to the firstborn equals the portions of two ordinary heirs. Thus if the deceased is survived by five sons including the firstborn, the latter takes a third, i.e., two-sixths of the estate, and the other four heirs take one-sixth each; if there are nine sons, the firstborn takes a fifth and each of the others takes one-tenth (Yad, Naḥalot, 2:1).

The portion of the birthright is fixed according to the state of the inheritance at the time of its devolution. Hence it is neither diminished by the birth of another son after the father's death, nor is it increased by the subsequent death of a son (BB 142b). The firstborn only receives a double portion out of the *muḥzakim,* i.e., estate assets already held by the deceased in his possession at the time of his death. With regard to *re'uyim,* i.e., assets contingent to come to the deceased but not held by him at the time of his death, the firstborn takes only the share of an ordinary heir. Hence the firstborn does not take a double portion of an inheritance that accrues to his father after the latter's death, nor of the unrecovered debts owing by others to the latter – whether verbal or witnessed by deed. The firstborn does, however, take a double portion of all such outstanding debts owing to his father as were secured by pledges held by the latter in his possession at the time of his death (Bek. 8:9; Sh. Ar., ḤM 278:7). Just as he takes a double portion, so the firstborn is obliged to defray a double portion of the outstanding debts owed by his deceased father (BB 124a). See also Firstborn.

The Husband as Heir to His Wife. The husband is heir to his wife and takes precedence over all her other heirs. Opinions are divided in the codes as to whether the husband's right to succeed to his wife's estate stems from the Pentateuchal or the rabbinical law (Yad, Naḥalot 1:8; Sh. Ar., EH 90:1 and *Beit Shemu'el,* n. 1) The husband is heir to his wife even if their marriage was a prohibited one – as for example between a priest and a divorcee (Yad, Naḥalot 1:8) – provided only that they were still married to each other at the time of her death (Tur, EH 90). It does not matter that the husband was planning to divorce his wife, but if he had claimed that his marriage was based on a mistake, for example if he had raised a plea of blemish or defect on the part of his wife, he forfeits his right of inheritance (*Teshuvot Maimoniyyot,* Ishut, no. 35). In explaining this *halakhah* the *aḥaronim* expressed the opinion that although mere admission by the husband concerning his wife's defect does not suffice to dissolve their marriage, yet for the purposes of inheritance the husband's admission is like the testimony of 100 witnesses and therefore upon the death of the wife her husband will not be regarded as one who is heir to his wife's estate (*Ḥelkat Meḥokek,* EH 90, n. 15). According to some scholars, even a *mored* (see Husband and Wife[1]) or a husband who has refused to cohabit with his wife due to his vow, forfeits his right to inherit her estate (Rema, EH 90:5). The husband only inherits the part of his wife's estate in her possession at the time of her death and he does not take her place in inheriting her contingent inheritance (Sh. Ar., EH 90:1). If she became entitled to an inheritance during her lifetime but she died before gaining possession thereof, the inheritance will nevertheless be deemed to have been held by her and it will pass to her husband (Resp. Maharashdam, EH n. 98).

The husband's right to inherit his wife's estate proved to be to the detriment of the wife's relatives and heirs since they received nothing at all from her estate. Various *takkanot* accordingly came to be made, aimed at defining the inheritance rights of the wife's heirs and limiting those of her husband. The first of these, dating from the mishnaic period, is known as the *ketubbat benin dikhrin* (i.e., *ketubbah* of male children). In terms thereof the husband inherited his wife's estate, but if the wife predeceased her husband leaving sons from the latter, these sons would upon their father's death inherit her *ketubbah* and dowry in addition to their portions in the estate of their father shared with his other sons. The object of the *takkanah* was "in order that all men might thereby be encouraged to give to a daughter as much as to a son" (Ket. 52b; Sh. Ar., EH 111), i.e., so that the father should not hesitate to give his daughter a large dowry since it would remain in the hands of his descendants and not with his daughter's husband. In geonic times the need for this *takkanah* fell away and it was abolished, since it had anyhow become customary for fathers to give more to their daughters (Tur, EH 111). Later many of the *posekim* sought to revive the validity of this *takkanah* but its abrogation was confirmed by Isserles (Rema, EH 111:16).

In the period of the *rishonim* various *takkanot* were made to limit the husband's right to inherit his wife's estate. In some communities, if the wife died without issue, it became customary for the whole of the dowry given to her upon marriage to be inherited by her father or his heirs, and in other communities for the dowry to be divided between the husband and the wife's heirs on the paternal side (Sh. Ar., EH 118:19; *Teshuvot Maimoniyyot,* Ishut no. 35).

In France and Germany one of the ordinances known as the *takkanat Shum* (שו"ם – Speyer, Worms, Mainz) came to be widely accepted. The effect thereof was to oblige the husband to return whatever remained of his wife's dowry – save for deduction of burial expenses – to the donor thereof or to her heirs, if she died childless within a year of her marriage; the second part of the ordinance laid down that upon the death of either husband or wife within the second year of their marriage, half of the dowry was to be returned to the heirs of the deceased if there were no surviving children (Rema, EH 53:3). In Spain similar *takkanot* were made. The most important of these, the *takkanah* of Toledo, laid down that if the wife was survived by her husband and any children of their marriage, her estate was to be shared equally between them; if there were no surviving children, her estate was to be divided between her husband and those who would have succeeded to her estate had she survived her husband. The object of the *takkanah* was to prevent the entire inheritance of the wife's family from going to her husband, and in this manner the scholars restricted the husband's rights as legal heir to his wife – in the opinion of some of the *posekim* even in accordance with the Pentateuchal law (see

1. page 381.

above) – and afforded him only one-half of her estate (Resp. Rosh, 55:1, 6; Rema, EH 118:8).

The Wife's Rights to Her Husband's Estate. The wife is not a legal heir to her husband's estate (BB 8:1) but has a number of rights which afford her a share therein and ensure provision for her sustenance and essential needs until her death or remarriage. The widow receives from the estate her husband's *ketubbah* obligations, the dowry increment, and her own property brought into the marriage and she is further entitled to maintenance from the husband's estate until her death or remarriage.

Important changes were introduced by the *takkanot* of Toledo and Molina with regard to the widow's rights to the estate of her deceased husband. These had the object of strengthening the hand of the husband's heirs against the widow's claims upon the estate, and laid down that if the husband was survived by any children the wife might claim no more than one-half of the total value of the estate toward payment of her dowry, *ketubbah,* and its increment. Thus the husband's heirs were afforded the option of settling the widow's claims in full – as was usually done when the total amount thereof did not exceed one-half of the estate – or settling her claims by paying her one-half of the value of the estate, even if less than due to her. If there were no children and the widow's claims were directed against the other heirs to her husband's estate, the latter would first return to her whatever remained – in specie, at the time of her husband's death – of the dowry she had brought him, and from the remainder of the estate she would recover her *ketubbah* and its increment in an amount not exceeding one-half of the value of the estate, the option as above mentioned again residing with the heirs (Resp. Rosh, 50:9; Sh. Ar., EH 118:1 and *Beit Shemu'el* ad loc. no. 1). In a *takkanah* of Castile it was laid down that a wife surviving her husband, without any children of their marriage, might take from the estate everything proved to have been brought by her as a dowry and remaining in specie at the time of her husband's death, and from the rest of the estate one-quarter, with three-quarters going to the husband's heirs (Resp. Rashba, vol. 3, no. 432).

Inheritance Rights of Daughters. Since by law sons exclude daughters as heirs (see above), it became necessary to make provision for the support of daughters after the father's death. This was achieved by the scholars through an obligation imposed on the heirs of the deceased to maintain his daughters and by way of giving daughters part of the estate as a dowry.

Maintenance of Daughters. The rule is: "If a man died and left sons and daughters, and the property was great, the sons inherit and the daughters receive maintenance; but if the property was small, the daughters receive maintenance and the sons go a-begging" (Ket. 4:6; 13:3). By mishnaic times this obligation had become part of the generally accepted law as a *tenai bet din* (i.e., a *takkanah* of the early scholars). Daughters are entitled to maintenance out of the estate of their deceased father until they reach the age of majority, or become betrothed (Ket. 4:11; 53b). Since the daughter's right to maintenance, as distinct from her right to a dowry, stems from the *ketubbah* deed (of her parents), any testamentary instruction of the deceased in deprivation of this right will have no legal validity (Ket. 68b; Sh. Ar., EH 112:10). Daughters only receive maintenance out of the estate of their deceased father if he is survived by sons as well; if the father is survived by daughters only, the latter share his estate – even though any of them be minors – and the question of their maintenance is no longer relevant (Sh. Ar., EH 112:18).

Dowry. Sons are obliged to give their deceased father's daughters part of his estate as a dowry, as if the father were alive. This obligation is known as *issur nekhasim* (i.e., giving the the daughter one-tenth of the estate), in terms whereof an assessment is made of what the father would have given his daughter as a dowry – according to his disposition, gathered from his friends and acquaintances, his transactions and standing – and if this cannot be established by the court, she is given one-tenth of the estate as the *parnasat ha-bat* (i.e., dowry; Sh. Ar., EH 113:1, based on Ket. 68a). According to some scholars, a daughter is also entitled to receive a dowry out of her deceased mother's estate, but this is disputed by other scholars (EH 113:1, Rema). The father may deprive his daughter of a dowry by testamentary instruction since the *parnasat ha-bat* is merely an assessment of the father's disposition (Ket. 68b) Although the daughter's dowry is recoverable at the time of her marriage, the court may earlier decide on what she should be given upon her marriage (*Beit Yosef* and *Darkhei Moshe,* EH 113).

The dowry is regarded as a charge in favor of the daughter on the estate of her father, as at the time of his death, and she may seize from third parties any of the estate assets sold or mortgaged by her brothers. However, debts incurred by the deceased himself, as well as the obligations for the *ketubbah* of his widow and maintenance for the latter and her daughters, take preference over the daughters' dowry (Ket. 69a; Sh. Ar., EH 113:5,6).

See also Dowry and Parent and Child.

Shetar Ḥaẓi Zakhar. In post-talmudic times it became customary in the Ashkenazi communities for a father to allot to his daughter one-half of a son's share in his estate, for which purpose there was evolved a special deed known as the *shetar ḥaẓi zakhar* ("deed for half of the male child's share"). The deed was written by the father – and sometimes by the mother too (*Naḥalot Shivah,* no. 21, n. 1) – in favor of the daughter or her husband. It was generally written at the time of the daughter's marriage, the father undertaking to pay his daughter a specified sum of money, generally a very high amount, to fall due for payment one hour before his death, with a condition exempting his sons liability for such debt after his death if they should give the daughter one-half of a son's share in his estate (Rema, ḤM 281:7). This development was an important step toward the regulation of the daughters' right of inheritance in Jewish law (for further details see Assaf, bibl.).

Proselytes as Heirs. A proselyte is regarded as a newborn person whose ties of kinship with his family have been severed for inheritance purposes. The scholars ruled, however, that a proselyte may accept an inheritance from his gentile father, lest the loss thereof tempt him to return to his former ways. A proselyte's estate is inherited by sons born after his conversion to the exclusion of his other sons, whether or not proselytized along with himself (Kid. 17b). The estate of a proselyte who dies without any legal heirs may be acquired in the same way as abandoned property, by the firstcomer, who is regarded as an heir for the purposes of estate liabilities in favor of third parties (Rema, ḤM 275:28).

Devolution of Inheritance and Renunciation. Upon death the estate passes automatically and immediately into the ownership of the heirs. Hence an heir cannot renounce his share by waiver thereof, since in Jewish law a person cannot waive something that already belongs to him but only that which is yet to come to him, and the heir can only transfer his share in the same way as any other property is transferred through one of the recognized modes for its assignment or alienation (see Acquisition). An exception to this rule is the birthright portion of the firstborn (see above), as distinguished from his ordinary share (Tur, ḤM 278; Sh. Ar., ḤM 278:10). An heir may, however, abandon his share in the same way as he abandons any of his own property (*Sma,* ḤM 278, no. 27) and a husband's renunciation of his right to his wife's estate is valid if made prior to their marriage, but not thereafter (Ket. 9:1, 83a).

Debts of the Deceased. It is a *mitzvah* for the heirs of the deceased to pay his debts. They will be compelled to do so if they inherit land and, according to a *takkanah* of the *geonim,* the creditor may recover from the heirs even when they inherit movable property. If they inherit both, the heirs prevail if they want payment to be made out of the land rather than the movable property as desired by the creditor (Sh. Ar., ḤM 107:1). For the purposes of her dowry (see above) a daughter takes only from the land left by the deceased, a rule that survived the above-mentioned *takkanah* of the *geonim* (Sh. Ar., EH 113:2).

Payment is always recovered from the poorest quality land (i.e., *zibburit,* Sh. Ar., ḤM 108:18). A stipulation by the creditor to recover payment out of the debtor's best *(iddit)* or medium *(beinonit)* land is not binding on the latter's heirs unless this was expressly provided for in the stipulation (*ibid.;* see also Execution). If the heirs of the deceased inherit nothing from him, they will not be obliged – not even morally – to defray his debts, since they do not have to do so out of their own property (Sh. Ar., ḤM 107:1). An heir is not heard if he should plead, "I do not take nor will I pay" (Rema, ḤM 107:1; and Sh. Ar., ḤM 278:10). The heirs are liable for debt of the deceased to the extent that these do not exceed the value of the assets held by the deceased at the time of devolution of the inheritance, his contingent assets *(re'uyim)* being excluded for this purpose (Rema, ḤM 104:16). However, a debt due to the deceased is considered part of the assets held by him at the time of his death. Some scholars have explained this special rule on the basis of the extensive development that took place with regard to credit transactions, with creditors coming to rely upon such as upon movable property rather than as contingent assets (Resp. Rosh, 36:3), and other scholars have regarded loans due to the deceased as property held by him upon death since the money of the loan had previously been in his possession (*Beit Shemu'el,* EH 100, no. 3).

The creditor recovers his debt from each of the heirs on a pro-rata basis (Tos. to BB 107a s.v. *u-va ba'al ḥov*). A field hypothecated (see Lien) by the deceased is recovered by the mortgagee from the heir who receives it as part of his share, and he may recoup from the remaining heirs (Sh. Ar., ḤM 175:4). Similarly, if a creditor should experience difficulty when seeking to recover a proportionate share of the debt from each of the heirs, he may recover the whole debt out of the share of any one of them, and that one may recoup from the others (Resp. Rosh, 79:7).

A verbal debt (see Obligations, Law of[1]) is not recoverable from the heirs of the debtor except in the following cases: the debtor had before his death and from his sickbed admitted such indebtedness; the loan was for a fixed period and not yet due for payment; or the debtor had refused to make payment notwithstanding a judgment of the court, maintaining his refusal until death. In each of these three cases the creditor recovers without swearing an oath (Sh. Ar., ḤM 108:11). A debt witnessed by deed is only recoverable after the creditor has sworn that the debt is still outstanding (Sh. Ar., ḤM 108:17). If the heir should plead that he was left no property by the deceased and the creditor plead with certainty that the deceased did leave property, the heir will be exempted from liability upon taking the equitable oath (*shevu'at hesset;* Sh. Ar., ḤM 107:2). A creditor holding a bond of indebtedness with a credency *(ne'emanut)* clause in his favor (see *Shetar*[2]) will not be exempted from delivering an oath when seeking to recover from the debtor's heirs unless he was so exempted expressly with reference to the debtor and his heirs (Sh. Ar., ḤM 71:14–17). In case of a similar clause in favor of the debtor with regard to a plea of payment of the bond, the creditor will not be entitled to recover from the former's heirs on such bond (Sh. Ar., ḤM 71:21).

Debts of the deceased are not recoverable from his heirs as long as they are minors, regardless of any clause whatever stipulated in the bond of indebtedness, lest contradictory evidence come to light (*ibid.,* 108:3). However, in the three events mentioned above in which a verbal debt of the deceased is recoverable from his heirs, his debts will be recoverable from the minor orphans too *(ibid.).* The court has the discretion to allow debts to be recovered from the minor orphans if this be to their advantage, e.g., because the creditor is prepared to waive part of the debt in return for recovering the balance forthwith (Rema, ḤM 110:1), and the minor heirs may also be recovered from when they are liable to a penalty for nonpayment on due date (*Siftei Kohen,* ḤM 110, no. 3). If some of the heirs are majors the creditor recovers from them pro-rata to their share in the estate. For the purpose of division of the estate the court will appoint a guardian for the minor (Sh. Ar., ḤM 110:1).

Commorientes. Where two persons die at or about the same time and it is unknown who died first, the rights of their heirs are determined in accordance with the following order of priority: If one of the claimants is a "certain" heir – i.e., whatever the sequence of the deaths – and the other a "doubtful" heir – i.e., only upon a particular sequence of death – the former claimant excludes the latter and takes all (Rashbam, BB 158b); if both claimants are doubtful heirs they take equal shares of the inheritance (Yev. 38a; Yad, Naḥalot 5:5); if one of the claimants is kin to the deceased himself and the other has become entitled through the death of a relative who is kin to the deceased, the former claimant takes all in both cases (Yad, Naḥalot 5:6), for the reason that the inheritance is not to be diverted from the kin of the deceased unless this is warranted by proof of a particular sequence of deaths (see M. Silberg, *Ha-Ma'amad ha-Ishi be-Yisrael* (1965), 314–22).

On the inheritance of public offices, see Public Authority,[3] on the inheritance rights of apostates, see Apostate.

In the State of Israel. Matters of inheritance are governed by the Succession Law, 5725–1965, the provisions whereof accord with Jewish law in a number of respects and digress therefrom in others. Thus, as in Jewish law, the law lays down, inter alia, that children born out of wedlock and even *mamzerim* are included among the heirs (sec. 3 (c)). The Jewish law principles with reference to commorientes (see above) were adopted virtually without change. On the other hand the law differs from the traditional approach in laying down that the line of succession ends with the grandparents and their descendants, whereafter the state succeeds, and that both husband and wife are in the line of succession to each other. So too the law recognizes no distinction between sons and daughters, between the paternal and maternal lines (sec. 10), nor does it mention the double portion of the firstborn. (On the question of the absorption of Jewish law in these matters, see Elon, bibl.). An important principle incorporated in the law is that of the widow's right to maintenance out of the estate; unlike Jewish law, this right is extended to other relatives of the deceased besides the widow and daughter, and is also wider in scope (secs. 57, 58).

See also Apotropos; Wills.

Bibliography: I. M. Hazan, *Successione per Israele* (1851); H. B. Fassel, *Das mosaisch-rabbinische Civilrecht,* 1 (1852), 274–320; A. Wolff, *Das juedische Erbrecht* (1888); M. Bloch, *Das mosaisch-talmudische Erbrecht* (1890); I. S. Zuri, *Mishpat ha-Talmud,* 3 (1921), 1–24; Gulak, Yesodei, 3 (1922), 71–112; Ch. Tchernowitz, in: *Jewish Studies . . . I. Abrahams* (1927), 402–15; S. Assaf, in: *Emet le-Ya'akov, Sefer Yovel . . . J. Freimann* (1937), 8–13 (Heb. section); Ch. Cohen, in: *Yavneh,* 3

1. page 244; 2. page 184; 3. page 650.

(1948/49), 80–83; J. D. Cohen, in: *Ha-Torah ve-ha-Medinah,* 2 (1949/50), 18–24; B. M. H. Ouziel, *ibid.*, 9–17; ET, 2 (1949), 16–20; 5 (1953), 152–6; 6 (1954), 279–82; 9 (1959), 536–42; A. Karlin, in: *Ha-Peraklit,* 9 (1952/53), 22–26; J. Hakohen, in: *Ha-Torah ve-ha-Medinah,* 5–6 (1952/54), 177–90; B. M. H. Ouziel, in: *Talpioth,* 5 (1952), 451–74; 6 (1953), 51–64; J. Herzog, *ibid.*, 6 (1953), 36–50; A. Karlin, *Divrei Mishpat,* 1 (1954) *(Dinei Yerushot ve-Ẓavva'ot);* S. D. Revital, in: *Sugyot Nivḥarot be-Mishpat* (1958), 442–69; E. J. Waldenburg, in: *Sefer Yovel le-Shimon Federbusch* (1960), 221–6; E. E. Urbach, in: *Divrei ha-Congress ha-Olami ha-Revi'i le-Madda'ei ha-Yahadut,* 1 (1967), 133–41; Engl. summary: *ibid.*, 263 (Eng. section); B. Schereschewsky, *Dinei Mishpahah* (1967²), 224–70; M. Elon, in: ILR, 4 (1969), 126–40; idem, Mafte'aḥ, 92–104; idem, *Ha-Mishpat Ha-Ivri* (1973), I, 81ff., 103ff., 145ff., 160ff., 220, II, 248ff., 373ff., 416ff., 465ff., 470–476, 487ff., 531ff., 538ff., 635ff., 650–654, 670ff., 676–686, 781ff., 783ff., III, 1239ff., 1249.

Shmuel Shilo

WILLS (Heb. צוואה). A will is a person's disposition of his property in favor of another in such manner that the testator retains the property or his rights to it until his death. There are three different forms of wills, each governed by different legal rules as regards their time of coming into effect and their scope and manner of execution. These are: *mattenat* (or *ẓavva'at*) *bari,* i.e., a (literally) gift by a healthy person; *mattenat* (or *ẓavva'at*) *shekhiv me-ra,* i.e., a gift by a person critically ill; and *meẓavveh meḥamat mitah,* i.e., a gift in contemplation of death. There are detailed biblical provisions regarding the legal order of succession (Num. 27:8–11; Deut. 21:16–17). However, save for isolated hints (see e.g., Job 42:15), there is no biblical provision regarding the possibility of a person determining the disposition of his property after his death in a manner not according with the rules laid down for the legal order of succession.

Mattenat Bari. A person who wishes to give his property to a person who is not his legal heir must divest himself of it during his lifetime so that the property shall not, on his death, automatically be dealt with in accordance with the laws of succession (Rashbam, BB 135b). He may, however, donate the body of the property by way of a gift taking immediate effect, while retaining for himself the usufruct of the property until his death (BB 8:7: "From today and after my death"). This is a *mattenat bari.* In form this disposition by will is identical to donation in the case of regular gift. Since the legator transfers his property to the legatee "from today," he may not afterward retract from the will, although the legatee only becomes entitled to the usufruct of the property after the legator's death (Sh. Ar., ḤM 257:6, 7). A will from which it may be inferred that the transfer (*kinyan;* see Acquisition) is "from today and after death," is regarded as one in which these words are expressly stated (BB 136a; Tur and Sh. Ar., ḤM 258). It is not possible for the legator to bequeath by way of *mattenat bari* any property except that which is then in his possession (Rema, ḤM 257:7; see also Contract). If the legator employs the words, "from today if I should not retract until after my death," or "from today if I do not retract during my lifetime," he is free to retract from the bequest (Tos. BM 19b; Sh. Ar., ḤM 257:7).

Mattenat Shekhiv me-Ra. A *shekhiv me-ra* is a person who is "ill and confined to bed." According to Maimonides, a *shekhiv me-ra* is "a sick man whose entire body has been weakened and whose strength has waned because of his sickness, so that he cannot walk outside and is confined to bed" (i.e., critically ill; Yad, Zekhiyyah 8:2). Unlike the *mattenat bari,* the provisions of a *mattenat shekhiv me-ra* come into effect on the death of the legator *(ibid.),* since the scholars enacted that the latter form of testacy should be regarded in law as a form of inheritance which comes into effect on the benefactor's death (BB 149a). The scholars enacted far-reaching alleviations with regard to the formalities of conveyance by *mattenat shekhiv me-ra,* dispensing with the need for a formal *kinyan* since "the instruction of a *shekhiv me-ra* has the same force as a document written and delivered" (Git. 13a) and because this was a *takkanah* of the scholars aimed at easing the mind of the sick person (Yad, Zekhiyyah 8:2). The wishes of the testator may be expressed orally or in writing, or by implication (BB 156b; Git. 15a; Sh. Ar., ḤM 250:7). The will may be an unwitnessed, handwritten deed, to be delivered to the beneficiary (Git. 71a; see Yad, Naḥalot 4:1).

If this form of will is formulated orally by a *shekhiv me-ra* before witnesses, the latter may reduce the terms of it to writing for delivery to the beneficiary. The delivery may take place during the testator's lifetime or after his death, since this instrument is written solely as a record of the testator's oral statements which immediately on recital take effect as the will (*Sma,* ḤM 253, n. 77).

The special validity which attaches to a *shekhiv me-ra* will is forfeited if the testator should employ one of the regular forms of *kinyan* for gift (Ket. 55b), since in so doing he manifests his intention to effect no more than a regular *mattenat bari.* This result would follow, for instance, if the benefactor should effect a *kinyan sudar* or *ḥazakah,* a lifting or pulling, or a gift *aggav karka* (incidental to land generally; Tos. BB 152a; Tur, ḤM 250:28; Yad, Zekhiyyah 8:10, 11; *Sma,* ḤM 250, n. 54), or, similarly, if he should draw up a deed, or declare his will and tell the witnesses to draw up a deed for delivery to the beneficiary (Yad, Zekhiyyah 8:12, 13). If the testator declares, orally or in writing, that his resort to a *kinyan* customary for a gift is meant to add rather than detract from his true purpose (a procedure known as *yippui ko'aḥ*), or if it should be apparent that he erroneously believed a *kinyan* was required to effect a *mattenat shekhiv me-ra,* the fact of the *kinyan* will not detract from the validity of the will as a *mattenat shekhiv me-ra* (*Taz,* ḤM 250:17).

The will of a *shekhiv me-ra* is valid only if the testator "gave all his property and left nothing [for himself]; but if he left a part it is like the *mattenat bari* which is only acquired by a formal *kinyan.*" The explanation for this is that a *shekhiv me-ra* who only disposes of part of his property does not do so in the expectation of his death – otherwise he would dispose of all his property; hence it is inferred that he intends to make a regular *mattenat bari,* which leaves no room for application of the rabbinical enactment that his instruction "has the same force as a document written and delivered" (Sh. Ar., ḤM 250:4; BB 151b). At the same time, even if a *shekhiv me-ra* leaves part of his property (for himself), his disposition will require no *kinyan* if it is made *meḥamat mitah* – that is, when it appears from his statements, explicitly or implicitly, that the disposition is made by him in the apprehension of death (Sh. Ar., ḤM 250:7; BB 151b). This is in fact the position in practically every case of a will made by a *shekhiv me-ra.* The will of a *shekhiv me-ra* may be retracted from by the testator (Yad, Zekhiyyah 9:15) by way of his oral or written expression of the wish to revoke the will (Rashbam, BB 152b). The revocation need not be express and will be implied if the testator makes another will relating to the same property (TJ, BB 8:7, 16b; BB 135b; Yad, loc. cit.). Revocation of part of a will is regarded as a revocation of the whole (BB 148b), and the same consequence follows if the testator should will his estate to several persons and afterward revoke his bequest to any one of them (Rema, ḤM 250:12). The will of a *shekhiv me-ra* is automatically revoked on the latter's recovery from his illness (Git. 72b), notwithstanding any prior express stipulation by him to the contrary. This is explained on the grounds of an enactment by the scholars that the expressed wishes of a *shekhiv me-ra* should be fulfilled out of apprehension for the mental agony which the latter might suffer if left in doubt about the fulfillment of his wishes; hence, on his recovery, the justification for the *takkanah* falls away, since he is once again in a position to make the disposition in any manner he desires (Resp. Rashba, vol. 1, no. 975).

Meẓavveh Meḥamat Mitah. The scholars widened the concept of a *shekhiv me-ra* in recognizing as equally valid the will of a "healthy" person if made *meḥamat mitah,* that is, in contemplation of death – *mortis causa.* A "healthy" person is regarded as having willed his property *meḥamat mitah* in one of the following circumstances: when he is seriously ill (even though he does not fall within the definition of a *shekhiv me-ra* – see above); when he is about to be executed under the law of the land; when he sets out with a caravan on a desert journey; and when he leaves on a sea voyage (Git. 65b, 66a and Rashi ad loc.). These four circumstances correspond to those in which it is incumbent to offer thanksgiving to the Almighty (Psalm 107; Ber. 54b). A disposition *meḥamat mitah* requires no formal *kinyan,* whether it relates to all or only a part of the testator's property (Yad, Zekhiyyah 8:24; Sh. Ar., ḤM 250:8). The manner of evolution of the law concerning a *meḥamat mitah* disposition is described in the language of the Mishnah, pertaining mainly to the laws of divorce but extended also to the laws of wills, as follows: "At first they used to say: If a man was led forth in chains and was about to be executed under the law of the land and said, 'Write out a bill of divorce for my wife,' they would write it out and deliver it [because being in a state of bewilderment he said only 'write out' and did not manage to say also 'deliver'] . . . Then they changed this and said, 'Also if a man went on a voyage or set out with a caravan.' R. Simeon Shezuri says, 'Also if a man was at the point of death' " (Git. 6:5). The *halakhah* was decided according to R. Simeon (TJ, Git. 6:7, 48a).

Some scholars held that it was only in the matter of granting a divorce that a valid *meḥamat mitah* disposition was constituted in any one of the four above-mentioned circumstances (*Piskei ha-Rosh,* BB 9:18; *Beit Yosef,* ḤM 250:13), and that any other *meḥamat mitah* disposition was only valid in the case of a person seriously ill or one about to be executed, but not in the other two cases. The scholars made this distinction on the basis that in the latter two cases the testator harbors the intention of returning to his home (Rosh, loc. cit.), or that death is not imminent (Nov. Rashba, BB 146b; *Maggid Mishneh,* Zekhiyyah 8:24). Other scholars (*Beit Yosef,* loc. cit., quoting Alfasi, Maimonides, and Naḥmanides) took the view that there was no reason for distinguishing between a divorce and the disposition of property by will for this purpose.

A "healthy" person whose will is not made within the framework of one of the above-mentioned circumstances is not regarded as a person willing his property *meḥamat mitah,* notwithstanding his express declaration that he is acting as such out of fear that he might die suddenly (Resp. Rashba, vol. 1, no. 975; vol 3, no. 118; Sh. Ar., ḤM 250:14). Hai Gaon was of the opinion that if a "healthy" person willed his property in the apprehension of sudden death and in fact died shortly thereafter, his will was to be regarded as one *meḥamat mitah* (Judah b. Barzillai, *Sefer ha-Shetarot,* no. 54; *Keneset ha-Gedolah,* ḤM 250, *Beit Yosef,* no. 131).

Undertaking and Acknowledgment or Admission (Odita, Hoda'ah). One of the telling limitations imposed by Jewish law on the different forms of testamentary disposition is the fact that the disposition is valid only in respect of property in the possession of the testator at the time the will is made (Yad, Mekhirah 22:1, 5). To overcome this limitation there evolved the use of a will formulated as an undertaking, since the law, although it precluded any possibility of a person transferring property not yet in existence or possessed by him (in his *reshut*), presented no obstacle to undertaking an obligation in respect of such property (Resp. Rashba, vol. 3, no. 118). Such an undertaking could be effected in writing or before witnesses, and also by way of an acknowledgment (of indebtedness) called *odita.* According to one view an *odita* may only be effected by a *shekhiv me-ra* (*Ittur,* s.v., *Hoda'ah; Or Zaru'a,* no. 722, 4).

If the aforesaid undertaking is made in writing and the instrument is delivered before witnesses, the beneficiary may recover it even from *nekhasim mesh'ubadim* (i.e., encumbered and alienated property; see Lien;[1] but if not so delivered, the beneficiary may only recover from *nekhasim benei ḥorin* ("free property"; *Maggid Mishneh,* Mekhirah 11:15; Sh. Ar., ḤM 40:1 and *Siftei Kohen* thereto, no. 3). In the case of an undertaking before witnesses, the benefactor declares, "Be witnesses unto me that I obligate myself," and the witnesses acquire from him (Yad and Sh. Ar., loc. cit.). The acknowledgment may also be made by the benefactor acknowledging indebtedness in writing or by declaring before witnesses: "Be witnesses unto me that I am indebted"; in this event the witnesses do not require a formal acquisition *(kinyan)* from the benefactor (*Sma* ḤM 40:1, and, *Netivot ha-Mishpat, Mishpat ha-Urim* n. 1, *Mishpat ha-Kohanim,* n. 3).

A testamentary disposition by undertaking or acknowledgment is irrevocable, whether effected by a *bari* or a *shekhiv me-ra,* and in the latter case the disposition is not revoked on the benefactor's death (R. Isaac, in Tos. BB 149a; Sh. Ar., ḤM 250:3). The usual time specified for fulfillment of the undertaking is an hour before the death of the benefactor so that the beneficiary should be unable to demand fulfillment during the benefactor's lifetime, since the due date of fulfillment is ascertainable only after the latter's death. However, it is essential that the due time of fulfillment be fixed at a date within the benefactor's lifetime, since an undertaking falling due for fulfillment after the promisor's death is void (Resp. Maharik, no. 89). Testamentary dispositions of this nature have been customary throughout the Diaspora in various forms and degrees of complexity. It is possible that the use of this form of will was adopted to avoid giving the appearance that the inheritance was being diverted from the legal heir – conduct of which the Mishnah says "The sages have no pleasure in him" (BB 8:5); it was therefore preferred through the means of such an undertaking to avoid a legal devolution of the estate. Widespread use of such an undertaking was made in the *shetar ḥaẓi zakhar,* a deed by means of which a father gave his daughter a share of the property equal to one-half of a son's portion (under the laws of succession). This deed, given to the daughter upon her marriage, may be regarded as a form of irrevocable will of the father (the deed being irrevocable in order to ensure the father's donation to his daughter and her husband). In this case, too, the time of fulfillment usually specified is one hour before the father's death. In order to overcome the difficulty of donating a specified portion of one's estate upon a daughter's marriage, at a time when the exact extent of the estate is still unknown, the following procedure was laid down: the father acknowledges that he owes his daughter a sum of money exceeding the estimated value of one-half of a son's share, adding a condition that the heir shall have the option either to pay this amount to

1. page 287.

the daughter of the deceased, or to give her a share of the estate equal to one-half of a son's portion (*Naḥalat Shivah,* no. 21; Rema, ḤM 281:7 and EH 108:3).

Mitzvah to Carry out the Wishes of the Deceased. Although a will may be invalid for one reason or another, it may still be recognized in certain circumstances in terms of the rule that "It is a *mitzvah* to carry out the wishes of the deceased" (Ket. 70a, Git. 14b). Thus it is the duty of the legal heirs to carry out the wishes of the testator, and this is a duty which the court will enforce. However, the above rule is not always to be applied as a strict legal duty, and when the duty is merely a moral one, the court will not compel compliance with the testator's directions (*Shevut Ya'akov,* vol. 1, no. 168). The rule applies to the bequest of both a *bari* and a *shekhiv me-ra* (Yad, Zekhiyyah 4:5; Sh. Ar., ḤM 252:2) whether made orally or in writing (Tos., BB 149a). The rule's scope of operation is a matter of scholarly dispute; there are three different views: (1) that it applies only in respect of property deposited with a trustee, at the time of the bequest, so that he should carry out the latter (Resp. Ritba, no. 54; Rema, ḤM 252:2); (2) that it applies even when the property is not deposited as mentioned above, provided that the legal heir of the deceased has been directed to carry out the bequest and does not object thereto (Resp. Ritba, loc. cit.; *Sha'arei Uziel,* 1 (1944), 227); (3) that it is applicable in every event, and even if the bequest has not been directed to any of the legal heirs, the latter are obliged to carry it out (*Haggahot Mordekhai,* BB no. 666). According to the aforementioned rule, ownership of the bequested property does not automatically pass to the beneficiary, but the duty is imposed on the legal heirs to transfer the said property to him (Rashi, Git. 14b; *Mordekhai,* BB, no. 630), from which derives an important distinction between a will taking effect by virtue of the above-mentioned rule and the wills of a *bari* and a *shekhiv me-ra,* namely: in the former case the beneficiary is not entitled to recover the bequested property from third-party purchasers (*Haggahot Mordekhai,* BB, no. 666), where he does have this right in the latter case (Resp. Rosh 86:5; Sh. Ar., ḤM 111:9 and 257:6).

Capacity to Bequeath. A person's legal capacity to make a bequest is generally coextensive with his capacity to make a regular gift, but there are a number of special rules relating to the former: (1) Although, according to some of the *posekim,* a minor generally requires his guardian's approval in order to make a gift (Yad, Mekhirah 29:7; Sh. Ar., ḤM 235:2), such approval is unnecessary as regards a *mattenat shekhiv me-ra.* The explanation for this apparently lies in the fact that a *mattenat shekhiv me-ra* falls due after the benefactor's death, whereas guardianship terminates on the minor's death, and also because the primary task of a guardian is to safeguard the minor's interests, a task which falls away on the minor's death (Resp. Maharam Alshekh, 101). (2) It is doubtful whether the tacit *shekhiv me-ra* bequest of a deaf-mute *(ḥeresh),* is valid, even though his tacit, regular gift is valid. The doubt arises from the fact that both the possibility of alienating by implication and a *mattenat shekhiv me-ra* derive from rabbinical enactment, and the rule is that "one does not add one *takkanah* to another" (BM 5b). On the other hand, it is possible that the rule, "the instruction of a *shekhiv me-ra* has the same force as a document written and delivered," applies also to the tacit acts of a deaf-mute – even with regard to his disposition of land and despite the fact that he cannot do so by way of a regular gift (*Kesef ha-Kedoshim,* 250:6). (3) A proselyte has no capacity to make a *shekhiv me-ra* bequest: "A *mattenat shekhiv me-ra* has been given the same force by the rabbis as an inheritance; therefore where there can be inheritance there can also be gift and where there cannot be inheritance there also cannot be gift" (BB 149a). Hence, in view of the fact that a proselyte who leaves no offspring conceived after his proselytization has no heirs (Tos. BB 149a), he cannot make a *mattenat shekhiv me-ra* (Sh. Ar., ḤM 256:1 and Rema thereto). According to some scholars, his capacity to bequeath is only limited as regards offspring conceived before his proselytization and who are not his legal heirs, but his *shekhiv me-ra* bequest made to any other person is valid (Sh. Ar., ḤM 256, *Sma* n. 3). Other scholars hold that the *shekhiv me-ra* bequest of a proselyte is of no effect, regardless of who the beneficiary may be (*Hassagot Rabad* on *Rif,* BB 149a, in the name of Hai Gaon; *Hassagot Rabad* on Yad, Zekhiyyah 9:7). According to another view, the rule that it is a *mitzvah* to carry out the wishes of the deceased does not apply to a proselyte (Tos., BB 149a; Tur, ḤM 256:7–9; Rema, ḤM 256:1).

Capacity to Benefit from a Bequest. A person's legal capacity to benefit from a bequest is generally coextensive with his capacity to receive a regular gift, but here, too, there exist a number of special rules: (1) According to some of the *posekim* a proselyte cannot receive a *mattenat shekhiv me-ra* (Rabad, quoted in *Shitah Mekubbeẓet,* BB 149a and *Tosefot Rid,* ad loc., end of no. 15). (2) Even the *posekim* who hold that a person cannot give a regular gift to his offspring as long as they are embryos, agree that it is acceptable for him to make them a *shekhiv me-ra* bequest (*Beit Yosef* and *Derishah,* ḤM 210:3; *Siftei Kohen,* ḤM 210, n. 1).

A person who lacks capacity to benefit from a bequest, may benefit from it if it is executed in the form of assignment to a third party on his behalf. This possibility also applies in the case of a *mattenat shekhiv me-ra,* and it is possible to benefit an embryo in this manner, even according to the *posekim* who reject the possibility of a *mattenat shekhiv me-ra* in favor of an embryo (Tur, ḤM 210:1).

Subject Matter of the Bequest. In general the restrictions placed on the possible subject matter of a regular gift are applicable also as regards the subject matter of a bequest. According to certain *posekim,* a person cannot make a *mattenat shekhiv me-ra* and retain for himself the usufruct of the property in question, even though this may be done in the case of a regular gift (Rabad, quoted in *Beit Yosef,* ḤM 209:10; opinion quoted by Rema, ḤM 209:7). The reason for this is that a *mattenat shekhiv me-ra* is acquired after the benefactor's death so that his retention of the usufruct is solely for the benefit of his legal heirs and not for himself. A bequest may be made of property in kind and also in the form of a fixed payment (Ta'an. 21a; Ket. 69b), or by establishing a fund, with the income from it designated for a particular purpose (*Pitḥei Teshuvah,* ḤM 246, n. 2). It is possible for the testator to nominate an executor *(apotropos)* of his estate (Rema ḤM 250:1). There is also an opinion that a *shekhiv me-ra* may entrust the executor with the actual decision as to division of the estate (*Mordekhai,* BB, no. 600).

At times wills have included charitable bequests. When such a bequest is made in a manner whereby the principal is established as a perpetual fund, while the income from it is dedicated to the charitable purpose, the estate – or the portion concerned – is known as a *keren kayyemet* (Resp. Rashba, vol. 3, no. 295; *Keneset ha-Gedolah,* YD 253. For the aspect of charities see *Hekdesh*).

Form and Wording of Wills. It is desirable that it be indicated in the will whether the testator is a *bari* or a *shekhiv me-ra,* although omission to do so does not affect the will's validity (Yad, Zekhiyyah 9:22; Tur, ḤM 251:3). In the case of a dispute between the legal heirs and the beneficiaries under the will, the burden of proof as to the testator's state of health devolves on the latter, since the legal heirs are deemed entitled *(muḥzakim)* to the estate's assets and "the burden of proof rests on the claimant" (Yad and Tur, loc. cit.; Sh. Ar., ḤM 251:2). The following are the customary versions, since talmudic times, to describe the testator's state of health: for a *mattenat bari,* "while he was walking on his feet in the market"; for a *mattenat shekhiv me-ra,* "while he was ill and confined to his bed"; and for a *shekhiv me-ra* will reduced to writing only after the testator's death, "and from his illness he died" (BB 153a, 154a), this version being essential since the disposition will be void if the testator should not die from the illness (BB *ibid.;* Sh. Ar., loc. cit.).

The testator must employ the phraseology which is effective for transfer of title in regular gifts. Thus it is necessary for the testator to use a verb denoting gift (*natan,* "gave," etc.; BB 148b; Sh. Ar., ḤM 253:2). A *shekhiv me-ra* testator who bequeathes in favor of his legal heir may employ a verb denoting inheritance (ḤM 281:3). The phraseology used by the testator must clearly show that the testator is alienating the asset concerned and not that he is promising to transfer title to it (Rashi, Git. 40b). Use of the past or present tense confers title but not use of the future tense (Yad, Zekhiyyah 4:11; Sh. Ar., ḤM 245:1) On the other hand, a *shekhiv me-ra* will couched in the future tense, is valid since in this case the testator speaks of a gift to take effect in the future – after his death. However, even a *shekhiv me-ra* will is invalid if phrased as a mere promise (*Beit Yosef,* EH 51, *Maggid Mishneh,* Yad, Mekhirah 2:8; *Baḥ,* ḤM 253:2). Language phrased in the form of a request to the testator's legal heirs to give specific assets to the beneficiaries under the wills is valid and effective (*Terumat Ha-Deshen* pt. 2 *(Pesakim u-Ketavim)* no. 99; Rema, ḤM 250:21).

As in all cases of gift, the will of both a healthy person and that of a *shekhiv me-ra* must be executed in public, and the testator must direct the witnesses to sign the will in like manner: "... Sit in the markets and public places and write for him openly and publicly a deed of gift" (Yad, Zekhiyyah 5:1, 4; BB 40b; Tur, ḤM 242:7). A *meḥamat mitah* testator is not required to direct that the disposition be made public (Yad, Zekhiyyah 9:2), but if he should expressly direct the witnesses to keep his will secret, it will be invalid (*Perisha,* ḤM 242:4).

Interpretation of Wills. Wills are generally subject to the same principles of interpretation as are all other documents (see Interpretation[1]). The process of *umedana* ("estimation") is of particular application to the interpretation of wills – that is the process of endeavoring to fathom the mind of the testator in order to understand his true intention – and the will itself is virtually the exclusive means to do this. The legal heirs of the deceased are deemed to be in possession of his property. Hence, a person claiming under the will is subject to the rule that "the holder of a deed is always at a disadvantage," for the reason that "the burden of proof rests with the claimant" (Bik. 2:10; Ket. 83b), and the beneficiary under the will accordingly has the burden of proving that the testator's intention was such that the will should be interpreted in his favor. The aforementioned rule only applies where doubt has arisen with regard to the interpretation of the will, and it does not operate in order to void the will entirely (Resp. Ribash, no. 145; Sh. Ar., ḤM 42:9).

The principle of estimation may serve to entirely invalidate a will. Thus in a case where a *shekhiv me-ra,* in the belief that his son is dead, bequeaths all his property to another, the disposition will be invalid if it should subsequently transpire that the son is alive – and in this event the latter will inherit from his father (BB 146b). Similarly, in certain circumstances a beneficiary under a will may become the mere custodian of the estate assets should it be so determined as an outcome of estimation that it was this that the testator intended (BB 131b; Sh. Ar., EH 107 and ḤM 246:4–12).

1. page 68.

Various rules were determined with regard to the interpretation of certain expressions in a will. Thus with reference to a *shekhiv me-ra* will, it was laid down that the term *banim* means "sons" and excludes daughters (TJ, Ket. 13:1, 35d) and that the intention of the testator who bequeaths all his property to his *banim,* when he has one son only and daughters, is to bequeath all to his son (BB 143b and see the biblical texts there cited; Yad, Zekhiyyah 11:1). Disputed in the Talmud is the intention of the testator who bequeaths to his *banim* when he has a single son and a grandson, and it was decided that in such a case it is not intended that the grandson be included *(ibid.).*

If a will contains contradictory directions which cannot possibly be reconciled with each other, the direction recorded last in the will prevails, on the assumption that the testator has repudiated the earlier direction (BB 10:2; Yad, Malveh 27:14; Sh. Ar., ḤM 42:5). However, when the contradiction emerges from the directions contained in one and the same passage of the will, the later reference is of no special import and the rule that "the holder of a deed is always at a disadvantage" applies *(ibid.).*

Authority to interpret documents is in general entrusted to the courts. With regard to a *shekhiv me-ra* will this authority is sometimes entrusted to the persons present at the time of its execution (BB 113b; Sh. Ar., ḤM 253:1). Thus if a *shekhiv me-ra* bequeathed his property in the presence of three persons, the latter may adjudge in the matter of the will and with reference to any doubt arising in connection with its interpretation (Rema, ḤM 253:1). However, if these persons were requested to be present as witnesses to the will, they will be disqualified from acting as judges in matters concerning the will (*Beit Yosef,* ḤM 7:6; Sh. Ar., ḤM 7:5). Another opinion that they will be disqualified even if they were not requested to serve as witnesses but intended to act as such (Rashbam, BB 113b) was rejected by a majority of the *posekim* (Tos. BB 114a; Sh. Ar., loc. cit.). Three persons present at the time of the testamentary disposition may only act as judges in connection with it when the will is made in the daytime, since the *halakhah* is that the adjudication shall not take place at night (see *Bet Din;* Sh. Ar., ḤM 5:2 and 253:1). If sums of money are bequeathed by a *shekhiv me-ra* to several persons, and it transpires that the latter's estate is lacking in funds, the position will depend on the way in which the bequest is worded. If the wording is, "give two hundred *zuz* to A, three hundred *zuz* to B, and four hundred *zuz* to C," each of the persons mentioned receives only his proportionate share of the available amount; if, however, the wording is, "give two hundred *zuz* to A, thereafter three hundred *zuz* to B and thereafter four hundred *zuz* to C," the parties will take precedence in turn in accordance with the order in which their names are mentioned (Yad, Zekhiyyah, 10:13, 14).

Accrual of Rights Under a Will. The beneficiary under a *mattenat bari* becomes entitled to the disposition in accordance with the terms of it, that is to the body of the property immediately and to its fruits upon the donor's death. In this case the beneficiary's right to the body of the donated property is a regular proprietary right, which he may, therefore, sell even during the donor's lifetime, and if the beneficiary should predecease the donor, the former's heirs become entitled to the donation (Sh. Ar., ḤM 257:4). The beneficiary under a *shekhiv me-ra* will becomes entitled to the bequeathed property upon the testator's death since a *shekhiv me-ra* will is subject to the same law as is succession according to law (see above). Therefore, if the beneficiary should predecease the testator, the former's heirs do not become entitled to anything at all (Sh. Ar., ḤM 125:9 and *Siftei Kohen* n. 36).

Renunciation of Rights Under a Will. In general, a person's refusal to accept property given to him as a gift will be effective if the refusal is made before the property comes into his possession, and in this event he does not become entitled to it (Ker. 24a). In the case of a gift or bequest made in the beneficiary's presence, the latter must at this very stage express his refusal of it (Sh. Ar., ḤM 245:10); if he should wish to renounce a gift or bequest not made in his presence, he must do so immediately on becoming aware of it (Rif, *Halakhot,* BB 138a; *Piskei ha-Rosh, ibid.;* Yad, Zekhiyyah 9:13). A renunciation made by a beneficiary who remains silent for a period after having become aware that the gift or bequest has been made is ineffective (Yad, Zekhiyyah 9:14; Sh. Ar., ḤM 245:10). The renunciation must be made in an unequivocal manner, and the beneficiary must clearly state that he has no intention at all of becoming entitled to the gift or bequest and that it is a nullity *ab initio* (Yad, Zekhiyyah 9:13; Sh. Ar., ḤM 245:7 and *Sma* n. 18).

Fideicommissary Bequests. The testator may direct that particular assets shall be given to the beneficiary for a limited period and that after this period these assets shall pass to another. A will is generally made in this form when the testator wishes to ensure that his property shall not, after the beneficiary's death, pass to the latter's heirs but shall go to some other person (Yad, Zekhiyyah 3:9; Sh. Ar., ḤM 241:6 and Rema, to 248:3). In principle there is no restriction on the possible order of successive beneficiaries which the testator may determine, but in practice this right is qualified by the requirement that all the beneficiaries must be alive at the time the gift or bequest is made (Resp. Rosh, no. 84:1 and 2). Each beneficiary under such a will in turn enjoys the usufruct of the bequeathed property and has the right to deal with the latter as with his own property – even to sell it.

A moral prohibition was imposed on the sale of such property by any one of the fideicommissaries – save for the last beneficiary mentioned in the will – since this was held to amount to a frustration of the testator's original intention; a sale effected by one of the fideicommissaries contrary to the above prohibition is nevertheless valid (BB 137a; Yad, Zekhiyyah 12:8, 9). A disposition of the bequeathed property by way of a *shekhiv me-ra* will on the part of a fideicommissary is ineffective, since the property only passes into the new beneficiary's possession after the death of the testator and at this time the property is no longer that of the latter but that of the fideicommissary next in line in terms of the original will (BB 137a; Yad, Zekhiyyah 12:10).

In the case where property is bequeathed to an unmarried woman, "to you and thereafter to A," and the woman subsequently marries, the property will not pass in turn to A but the woman's husband will become entitled to it (Ket. 95b); however, if a bequest of this nature is made to a married woman, the beneficiary next in line will in turn succeed to the property, since this will be assessed to have been the testator's true intention (Ket. loc. cit.; Yad, Zekhiyyah 12:12; Sh. Ar., EH 91:2 and ḤM 248:8).

Where property is bequeathed by a *shekhiv me-ra* will to a legal heir of the testator "to you and thereafter to A," the property will not upon the beneficiary's death pass to A but to the beneficiary's legal heirs (Yad, Zekhiyyah 12:7; Sh. Ar., ḤM 248:1; BB 129b and Rashbam, ad loc.). The explanation for this is as follows: since in a *shekhiv me-ra* will the property only passes to the beneficiary after the testator's death, and since the beneficiary is a legal heir of the testator, the former becomes entitled to the property by virtue of the law of the Torah and the testator may not stipulate that his property shall after the beneficiary's death pass to A and not to the beneficiary's legal heirs, for this is a stipulation contrary to the law of the Torah and therefore void; this rule is referred to in the Talmud as *yerushah ein lah hefsek* ("an inheritance cannot be terminated"; BB 129b, 133a).

Takkanot Concerning the Form and Execution of Wills. In many communities different *takkanot* were enacted with regard to various documents which, in particular, obliged those executing the documents to do so before a scribe or rabbi (Sh. Ar., ḤM 61:1), both as a protection against forgeries and in order to make the documents publicly known (*Baḥ,* ḤM 61:1). At times it was laid down that a document executed contrary to a particular *takkanah* was of no effect and a fine was even imposed on the person who executed it (S. Buber, *Anshei Shem* (1895), 225f.). In some cases it was necessary for certain deeds to be publicly announced in the synagogue (Resp. Ribash, no. 388; Resp. Rashba, vol. 3, no. 431). The manner of execution of wills was specially dealt with in a number of *takkanot.* Thus two years after the expulsion of the Jews from Spain, the *takkanot* of Fez were enacted which included, among others, this *takkanah:* "Whoever shall wish to make a gift or will, whether male or female, shall do so before the *ḥakham* or *dayyan* of the town, otherwise the gift or will shall be of no worth" (*Kerem Ḥamar,* vol. 2, no. 11). This *takkanah* was later extended (*ibid.,* no. 19) and a further *takkanah* prescribed that "any *shekhiv me-ra* will or gift which shall not be made before the *ḥakham* or *dayyan* of the town shall be null and void; that is, everything that a *shekhiv me-ra* shall do is void if not done before a *dayyan*" (*ibid.,* 36 a/b, *takkanot* pertaining to ḤM, no. 4). These *takkanot* were apparently enacted for two reasons: to ensure that the testator was of sound mind when making the will, and so that the scholar could stress before the testator the fact that the latter was transferring the inheritance from his legal heirs to someone else, a consequence looked upon with disfavor by the scholars (*Mishpatim Yesharim,* no. 2:161, and see above). Similar *takkanot* were enacted also in Jerusalem (Resp. Mabit, no. 2, pt. 2, no. 1).

Jerusalem Takkanot. It was the custom that the estate of a person who died in Jerusalem without leaving any heirs in Ereẓ Israel passed to the public, a custom apparently aimed at preventing the authorities from taking the estate. The public would administer the estate, and if the heirs of the deceased later came to claim the estate, it would be sought to influence them to leave part of it to the community chest. At a later stage a *takkanah* was enacted to the effect that the estate of a deceased person without any heirs in Ereẓ Israel actually passed to the public (see Rivlin, in bibl.). However, even after the enactment of this *takkanah* a person could still keep his estate from passing to the public by making a will. A deterioration in the position of Jerusalem Jewry led to the enactment of a number of further *takkanot* in this connection. Thus in 1730 there was a reinstatement of an ancient *takkanah* which laid down that a will had to be executed before communal representatives and that it was necessary that there be present a representative of the communal leadership of Constantinople, communal appointees, as well as a *parnas* and scribe of the community and, failing this, the will would have no validity. At the same time it was expressly laid down that a person could bequeath as he wished before the above-mentioned persons (*Sefer ha-Takkanot ve-Haskamot . . . Yerushalayim . . .* (1883[2]) 24b–26a). In 1737 a far-reaching *takkanah* was enacted which forbade a person without heirs in Erez Israel from making a will (*ibid.,* 18a/b). When this *takkanah* was circumvented by persons who made a *mattenat bari* abroad before coming to settle in Ereẓ Israel, there was enacted a *takkanah* in 1776 which rendered invalid various kinds of wills, including a *mattenat bari* "from today and after my death," whether executed in or outside of Ereẓ Israel (*ibid.,* 29a/b). In 1810 Ashkenazi Jews *(Perushim)* began to settle in Ereẓ Israel, and they objected to the above *takkanot.* For some years a dispute was waged in regard to these *takkanot,* and in the end they were not followed by the Askhenazi Jews (see Rivlin, in bibl., p. 619).

Takkanot Concerning Disposition of the Property of Spouses. The Toledo *takkanot* enacted in favor of the wife's family were aimed at preventing the entire assets contributed by the wife to her husband from passing to the latter on her death. These *takkanot* provided that the wife's relatives – who would normally inherit from her in the event that she survived her husband – should receive one-half of her estate. It was decided by Asher b. Jehiel that a wife could not dispose of her property by will so as to leave it all to her husband or some other person and thereby frustrate the object of the above *takkanot* (Resp. nos. 55:1 and 40:2). In consequence of the decision, *takkanot* were enacted in the communities of the Spanish exiles which expressly incorporated the import of the decision into the Toledo *takkanot.* The exiles of 1391 who settled in North Africa enacted – under the guidance of R. Simeon b. Ẓemah Duran – a series of *takkanot,* the third of which, among others, rendered it forbidden for a woman to make any form of will in which she purported to transfer one-half of her estate "to any person in the world save to any offspring she has by her husband who would be her nearest heir; and if she has done so, it shall henceforth be null and void" (*Tashbeẓ,* 2:292).

From the statements of the *posekim* of the Moroccan communities, it appears that despite the existence of various *takkanot* which followed those of Toledo, it still remained possible for a woman to make gifts to her husband or other persons (*Mishpat u-Ẓedakah be-Ya'akov,* pt. 2, no. 83; *Mishpatim Yesharim,* no. 2:211). On the other hand it was decided there that a *shekhiv me-ra* bequest made by a woman in which she gave a large part of her property to her husband was invalid (*Ner Ma'aravi,* no. 1:16). Another *takkanah* enacted in Fez imposed restrictions on the husband's freedom to make a testamentary disposition of his property by prescribing that if the wife objected to the *shekhiv me-ra* will of her husband, her share – or that of her heirs – in the estate would remain unaffected by the will. Another *takkanah* laid down that before distribution of the estate in accordance with the existing *takkanot,* there were to be recovered from it *mattenat bari* but not *shekhiv me-ra* bequests to which the wife of the deceased objected (*Kerem Ḥamar,* vol. 2, 34b, no. 6; the scholars were divided on the interpretation of this *takkanah* – see *Mishpatim Yesharim,* no. 2:268).

In consequence of the migrations of the Spanish exiles similar *takkanot* to those of Toledo were enacted in many communities of the Mediterranean countries. In some places a woman was expressly precluded from bequeathing part of her property to her husband; this was prescribed, for instance, in the *takkanot* of Arta (*Torat Ḥayyim,* EH 24), apparently enacted in 1597 (see Resp. Ranaḥ, no. 25)

In the State of Israel. In the Succession Law of 1965 the Knesset partly adopted and partly rejected different principles pertaining to testamentary dispositions in Jewish law. The *mattenat bari* and *shekhiv me-ra* forms of will were adopted both in formulation and content (sec. 23; M. Elon, in ILR, 4 (1969), 133f.). The Law – in reception of Jewish law principles and contrary to English law – empowers the court to give effect to a formally defective will when there is no doubt as to its genuineness (sec. 25).

Bibliography: L. Bodenheimer, *Das Testament unter Benennung einer . . . Erbschaft . . .* (1847); M. Bloch, *Das mosaisch-talmudische Ebrecht* (1890); M. W. Rapaport, in: *Zeitschrift fuer vergleichende Rechtswissenschaft,* 14 (1900), 1–148; Gulak, Yesodei, 3 (1922), 113–45; idem, Oẓar, 110–31; idem, in: *Tarbiz,* 4 (1933), 121–6; idem, *Das Urkundenwesen im Talmud* (1935), 125–36; Herzog, Instit, 1 (1936), 152–4; 2 (1939), 29f.; S. Assaf, in: *Emet le Ya'akov . . . Freimann* (1937), 8–13; E. Rivlin, *Azkarah . . . ha-Rav . . . Kook,* 3 Maḥlakah 5, Ereẓ Israel (1937), 559–619; Ḥ. Cohn, in: *Yavneh,* 3 (1949), 80–105; A. Friemann, *ibid.,* 106–10; ET, 1 (1951[3]), 86–88, 251–3, 255; 7 (1956), 114–34; A. Karlin, *Divrei Mishpat,* 1 (1954), 46–81; R. Yaron, *Gifts in Contemplation of Death in Jewish and Roman Law* (1960); A. Kimmelmann, *Ẓavva'at Bari ve-Ẓavva'at Shekhiv me-Ra be-Dinei Yisrael . . . (1963); idem, in: Sinai,* 55 (1964), 145–55; E. E. Urbach, in: *Divrei ha-Congress ha-Olami ha-Revi'i le-Madda'ei ha-Yahadut,* 1 (1967), 133–41; Elon, Mafte'aḥ, 139f., 168–73, 242–5; idem, in: ILR, 4 (1969), 126–40; idem, *Ha-Mishpat Ha-Ivri* (1973), I, 81ff., 103, II, 361ff., 364ff., 369ff., 476, 670ff., 680, 683ff., 783, III, 992.

Shmuel Shilo

VI. CRIMINAL LAW

Contents

PENAL LAW.

Principles of Legality. Under talmudic law, no act is a criminal offense and punishable as such unless laid down in express terms in the Bible (the Written Law). For this purpose, it is not sufficient that there should be a provision imposing a specified penalty in respect of any given act *(onesh)* – e.g., the murderer shall be killed (Num. 35:16–21), or the adulterers shall be killed (Lev. 20:10) – so long as the commission of the act has not first distinctly been prohibited *(azharah)* – e.g., you shall not murder (Ex. 20:13; Deut. 5:17), or you shall not commit adultery *(ibid.)*. Where such prohibition is lacking, even the availability of a penal provision will not warrant the imposition of the penalty provided (Zev. 106a–b, et al.); the penal provision is a *nuda lex,* which may be interpreted as a threat of divine punishment, in respect of which no prior prohibition is required (Mak. 13b).

All biblical injunctions are either positive *(mitzvot aseh)* or negative *(mitzvot lo ta'aseh),* i.e., either to do or to abstain from doing a certain thing. Any negative injunction qualifies as prohibition for the purposes of penal legislation (Maim. Comm. to Mishnah, Mak. 3:1). But no prohibition may be inferred, *e contrario,* from any positive injunction (Tem. 4a). The prohibitory provision is required not only for capital offenses (Sanh. 54a–b), but also for offenses punishable by flogging (Mak. 4b; Ket. 46a), and even for offenses punishable by fines (Sifra, Kedoshim, 2, 1). A prohibition may not be inferred, either by analogy or by any other form of logical deduction; from the prohibition on intercourse, for instance, with the daughter of one's father or of one's mother (Lev. 18:9), the prohibition on intercourse with one's full sister could not be inferred, but had to be stated expressly (Lev. 18:11).

Similarly, the penal provision must be explicit as applying to an offense constituted of certain factual elements, and may not be extended to cover other offenses, whether by way of analogy or by way of other logical deductions. Thus, for instance, malicious witnesses who commit perjury by testifying that an innocent man has committed a capital offense are to be executed only if the accused has not yet been executed himself: for it is written, "you shall do to him as he schemed to do to his fellow" (Deut. 19:19), and not as has been done already to his fellow, and the latter may not be inferred, *a fortiori,* from the former (Mak. 5b). The reason underlying this seemingly hairsplitting precaution has been said to be that if the punishment laid down by law were the right and proper one for the lesser crime or the lesser evil, it could not be the right and proper punishment for the graver one (Maharsha to Sanh. 64b), and the Divine Legislator having seen fit to penalize the lesser offense, no human legislator should presume to improve on or rectify His action, least of all by human logic *(Korban Aharon, Middot Aharon,* 2:13). This strict legality already gave rise to practical difficulties in talmudic times. "Not in order to contravene the law, but in order to make fences around the law" (Sanh. 46a; Yev. 90b; Yad, Sanh. 24:4), were the courts empowered to impose punishments even where the principle of legality could not be observed (see Extraordinary Remedies). Such extralegal sanctions were imposed not only at the discretion of the courts, but also by virtue of express penal legislation (see *Takkanot*[1]).

Parties to Offenses. As a general rule, only the actual perpetrator of an offense is criminally responsible in Jewish law. Thus no responsibility attaches to procurers, counsellors, inciters, and other such offenders who cause the offense to be committed by some other person (except, of course, where the incitement as such constitutes the offense, as, e.g., incitement to idolatry: Deut. 13:7–11).

Principals and Agents. Even where a person hires another to commit a crime, criminal responsibility attaches only to the agent who actually commits it, and not to the principal who made him commit it (Kid. 42b–43a; BK 51a, 79a; BM 10b; et al.). Where the commission of the offense entails some enjoyment, as the consumption of prohibited food or consummation of prohibited intercourse, it is clear that he who has the enjoyment pays the penalty (Kid. 43a); but even where the agent derives no enjoyment at all from the commission of the offense, it is he who is responsible, because as a person endowed with free will he has to obey God rather than men (Kid. 42b). There are several exceptions to this rule: first, where the agent is not capable of criminal responsibility, whether because he is a minor, or insane, or otherwise exempt from repsonsibility, his principal is responsible (BM 10b; Rema, ḤM 182:1, 348:8); or, where the actual perpetrator is an innocent agent, that is, ignorant of the fact that it is an offense he commits (Tos. to Kid. 42b s.v. *amai;* Tos. to BK 79a s.v. *natnu; Mordekhai,* BM 1, 237; and cf. Redak, II Sam. 12:9). Further exceptions apply to particular offenses and are derived from biblical exegesis, such as stealing trust money (Ex. 22:6), slaughtering and stealing oxen or sheep (Ex. 21:37), or trespass on sacred things (Lev. 5:15) – for all of which the principal and not the agent is criminally responsible (Kid. 42b–43a). However, the blameworthiness of the procurer did not escape the talmudic jurists: everybody agrees that he is liable to some punishment, lesser *(dina zuta)* or greater *(dina rabba;* Kid. 43a), and the view generally taken is that he will be visited with divine punishment (Kid. 43a; Yad, Roẓe'aḥ 2:2–3). The matter is very distinctly put apropos the biblical injunction that where a woman committed bestiality both she and the beast should be killed (Lev. 20:16): "The woman has sinned, but what sin did the beast commit? But because it caused mischief, it must be stoned – and if a beast which does not know any difference between good and evil is stoned because of the mischief it caused, *a fortiori* must a man who caused another to commit a capital offense be taken by God from this world" (Sifra, Kedoshim, 10:5). Maimonides goes even further, allowing not only for divine punishment but also for human capital punishment, whether by the king by virtue of his royal prerogative (see Extraordinary Remedies), or by the court in exercise of its emergency powers, wherever circumstances of time and place so require (Yad, Roẓe'aḥ 2:4); and indeed capital punishment was actually imposed on a father who had ordered his son to commit homicide (Ribash, Resp. no. 251). But short of capital punishment, courts are at any rate admonished to administer "very hard floggings" and impose severe imprisonment for long periods, so as to deter and threaten potential criminals that they may not think they can commit with impunity their crimes by the hands of others (Yad, Roẓe'aḥ 2:5). See also Agency.

Joint Offenders. As a general rule, a criminal offense is committed by a single person acting alone, and not by two or more acting together (Sifra, Va-Yikra, 7; Shab. 92b). Thus, where an offense is committed by joint offenders, all are liable only if the offense could not have been committed otherwise than by all of them together; if the offense could have been committed by any one (or more) of them, they are all entitled to the benefit of the doubt that none of them did actually complete the offense (Yad, Shab. 1:15–16). Where, therefore, a man is beaten to death by several people, none of them would be criminally liable (Sanh. 78a); but where the death was clearly caused by the last stroke, the man who struck last would be guilty of murder (Yad, Roẓe'aḥ 4:6–7). It might be otherwise where death could not have ensued unless by the combined action of all attackers together: in such a case they would all be liable (Rashba, Nov., BK 53b). Like accessories before and at the offense, so are accessories after the fact free from responsibility

1. page 78.

for the offense – except, again, in the case of incitement to idolatry, where the protection of the offender is made an offense (Deut. 13:9).

Attempts and Inchoate Offenses. From the foregoing it is already apparent that, as a rule, no offense is committed unless it is completed: he who completes the offense if guilty; he who commits only part of the offense, or does not achieve the criminal result, is not guilty (Sifra, Va-Yikra, 7, 9; Shab. 92b–93a). No criminal intent, however farreaching, suffices to render any act punishable which is not the completed offense defined by law (Kid. 39b; Ḥul. 142a). In exceptional cases, however, the attempt as such constitutes the completed offenses, e.g., malicious perjury (Deut. 19:16), where the false witnesses are liable only if the result intended by them had not yet been achieved (Mak. 1:6). But, again, the potential turpitude of the attempt to commit an offense has not escaped juridical notice: he who raises a hand against another, even without striking him, is not only wicked, but should (according at least to one great scholar) have his hand cut off, if he is prone to strike frequently (Sanh. 58b and Rashi). Extralegal punishments have indeed been inflicted time and again on attempts, especially of murder (e.g., Resp. Maharam of Rothenburg, ed. Prague, no. 383; and cf. *Darkhei Moshe,* ḤM 420, n. 7).

Criminal Responsibility. No person is criminally responsible for any act unless he did that act willfully (Av. Zar. 54a; BK 28b; Yad, Yesodei ha-Torah 5:4; Sanh. 20:2). Willfulness is excluded by duress *(ones),* a concept much wider in Jewish than in other systems of law. For the purpose of penal law, it can be roughly divided into five categories: (1) coercion; (2) threats of death, including governmental decrees threatening criminal prosecution; (3) torture; (4) *force majeure,* including sickness and other happenings beyond one's control; and (5) mistakes of fact and unconsciousness. As distinguished from duress for the purposes of civil law, generally no duress is recognized in criminal law which flows from any monetary cause, as, e.g., the necessity to save any property from perdition (*Beit Yosef,* ḤM 388; Rema, ḤM 388:2).

Duress by Coercion. The coercion by violence of a married woman to commit adultery (nowadays known as rape) exempts her from any criminal responsibility (Deut. 22:26). No such coercion is recognized in regard to the male adulterer, because he cannot physiologically be raped (Yev. 53b). Where the woman is an isolated spot ("in the open country": Deut. 22:25), or otherwise incapable of summoning help, she will be presumed to have been coerced against her will (Naḥmanides ad loc.; Sif. Deut. 243), even where she could have resisted by striking back, but failed to do so in the belief she was not allowed to, she is deemed to have been raped (Naḥmanides, *ibid.*). It is irrelevant that, after having been forced to submit, she eventually acquiesced: it is the duress of human urges and human nature that then compel her to surrender (Yad, Issurei Bi'ah 1:9).

Duress by Threats. There are three grave offenses of which it is said that a man must let himself be killed rather than commit any of them, namely, idolatry, adultery or incest *(gillui arayot),* and homicide (Sanh. 74a; Yad, Yesodei ha-Torah 5:2; Sh. Ar., YD 157:1). This rule has sometimes been wrongly interpreted as excluding the defense of duress by threats of death in the case of any of these offenses; as a matter of law, however, where the rule is disobeyed and any such offense is committed in order to escape death, the offender is not criminally responsible, however reprehensible he may be morally or religiously (Yad, *ibid.* 4). It is irrevocably presumed that where a man acts under threat of immediate death and in order to save his life, any criminal intent in respect of that act is excluded or superseded, and he cannot be criminally responsible for it.

In the Middle Ages, the threat of prosecution and death became a very effective inducement to denounce Judaism and outwardly embrace another religion. So long as a man did only what was really required to save his life, the transgression was recognized as being committed under duress; as soon as he did anything not so required, it was deemed to be done willfully, however strong the initial duress may have been (Rema, YD 124:9; Ribash, Resp. nos. 4, 11, 12).

Duress by Torture is closely related to the two foregoing categories; on the one hand, it entails physical force, and the sheer force applied may be sufficient to deprive the victim of his free will; on the other hand, it entails threats of death, or of ever more torture to come until death may ensue, and hence any criminal intent will be replaced or superseded by the wish to have the torture terminated (cf. Ket. 33b for an instance of torture to compel to idolatry).

Duress by Force Majeure, as an instance of duress, is well illustrated by the case of a man who fell ill, and his doctors prescribed for his cure the consumption of prohibited food; while partaking of such food is a criminal offense, the patient will not be liable to punishment, as his intent was not criminal but medical (Yad, *ibid.* 6). It is, however, made clear that this defense would not hold good for all offenses: thus, a man cannot be heard to say that for medical reasons and in order to save his life, he had to commit adultery (Yad, *ibid.* 9) or even a lesser indecency (Sanh. 75a). Other unforeseen circumstances which may make a man act unlawfully, contrary to his real intentions, are, e.g., attacks by wild beasts (cf. BM 7:9), or accidents such as fire (BM 47b, 49b) and other like dangers: the defense of duress in these cases is closely related to that of self-defense or self-help (see below). It is noteworthy that in English and Israel law, the commission of an offense in order to avoid grievous harm or injury which could not otherwise be avoided is excused by reason of "necessity" (Sec. 18, Criminal Code Ordinance, 1936).

Duress by Mistake or Unconsciousness. A lesser form of duress is the "duress of sleep" (cf. Ber. 4b): a man who has fallen asleep is not criminally (as distinguished from civilly; BK 2:6) responsible for anything he did while asleep, for the reason that he acted without any criminal (or other) intent. The same applies to acts of automatism or anything done in a state of unconsciousness, however induced. Jewish law – again, as distinguished from other systems of law – includes within this category, as a species of duress, also the common mistake of fact: it is regarded as the "duress of the heart" (Shev. 26a) if a man acts under a misapprehension of relevant facts, and any criminal intent may be excluded by such other intent as is warranted by the facts mistakenly believed to exist. If a man acts under such factual misapprehension, it is as if he acted outside the physical world as it really exists, hence the analogy with sleep and unconsciousness. Similarly, the forgetfulness of old age may constitute duress (Ber. 8b).

The Deaf and Dumb, Lunatics, Infants, and the Blind. Apart from these forms of duress, which are applicable to all persons, there are special categories of persons who are wholly exempt from criminal responsibility for reason of the duress inherent in their infirmity or deficiency, namely, the deaf and dumb, the insane, and infants – all regarded in law as devoid of reason (Yev. 99b; Ḥag. 2b; Git. 23a; et al.). Persons who are both deaf and dumb (Ter. 1:2) are equated with infants for all purposes of the law (cf. Tur, ḤM 235:19), and the law exempting infants from criminal responsibility is derived from scriptural exegesis (Mekh. Mishpatim 4; Sanh. 52b, 54a, 68b). It is not quite settled at what age infancy ends for purposes of criminal law: there are dicta to the effect that divine punishment is not imposed for sins committed before the age of 20 (TJ, Bik. 2:1, 64c: TJ, Sanh.

11:7, 30b; Shab. 89b; Tanḥ. B, Koraḥ 6), and it is said that where Heaven exempts from punishment, men ought not to punish (cf. Sanh. 82b); on the other hand, with the age of 13 for the male and 12 for the female, the age of reason is reached (Nid. 45b; Yad, Ishut 2:1, 10), and there would no longer be any rational cause for exemption from responsibility. Some scholars hold that while human beings are criminally responsible as from the age of 13 and 12 respectively, no capital punishment would be imposed unti they reached the age of 20. However that may be, we find exhortations to punish infants by flogging, even below the age of reason, not because of their responsibility, but only in order to deter them from further crime (Yad, Genevah 1:10). As far as sexual crimes are concerned, an infant girl is deemed to be so easily tempted as to deprive her of any willfulness (Yev. 33b, 61b; TJ, Sot. 1:2, 16c).

The insane is a person whose mind is permanently deranged (Yad, Edut 9:9). Monomaniacs who "go around alone at nights, stay overnight in cemeteries, tear their clothes, and lose everything they are given" (Ḥag. 3b; Tosef., Ter. 1:3), as well as idiots who are so retarded as to be unable to differentiate between contradictory matters (Yad, *ibid.* 10; ḤM 35:10), are presumed to be insane. They are not criminally responsible for any of their acts (BK 87a; cf. Git. 22b), and it is – in contradistinction to modern systems of law – irrelevant whether any causal connection can be established between the disease and the offense: once insanity is shown, criminal responsibility is excluded. Persons who suffer from transient attacks of insanity, such as epileptics, are criminally responsible only for acts committed during lucid intervals (cf. Yad, *ibid.* 9; ḤM 35:9). Apart from being devoid of reason, the insane are also devoid of will – hence any sexual offense committed by an insane woman is deemed to have been committed unwillfully (*Mishneh la-Melekh,* Ishut 11:8).

Opinions were divided among talmudic jurists in regard to the criminal responsibility of the blind (Bk 86b; Tosef., Mak. 2:9), but the rule eventually evolved that blindness does not affect such responsibility, any more than the obligation to obey all the laws; but a blind person who kills inadvertently is exempt from exile to a city of refuge, because his act is near to duress (Yad, Roze'ah 6:14). The blind man differs from the deaf and dumb in that he freely expresses himself, while with the latter one never knows whether he is in possession of his mental and volitive faculties or not, and Jewish law does not recognize any presumption of sanity.

Intoxication. Self-induced intoxication as such is not regarded as duress sufficient to exempt from criminal responsibility for acts committed while drunk (Tosef., Ter. 3:1), except where the intoxication amounts to the "drunkenness of Lot" (Gen. 19:33–35), that is to say, to virtual unconsciousness (Er. 65a).

Ignorance of Law. Talmudic law differs from most (if not all) other systems of law also in one further respect: namely, that ignorance of law is a good defense to any criminal charge. Not only is nobody punishable for an offense committed bona fide, i.e., in the mistaken belief that his act was lawful, but it is incumbent upon the prosecution to show that the accused was, immediately before the commission of the offense, expressly warned by two competent witnesses that it would be unlawful for him to commit it, and that if he committed it he would be liable to that specific penalty provided for it by law (Sanh. 8b; et al.; and see Evidence, Practice and Procedure). It is this antecedent warning that enables the court to distinguish between the intentional *(mezid)* and the unintentional *(shogeg)* offender (Yad, Sanhedrin 12:2 and Issurei Bi'ah 1:3), the latter category comprising not only those acting "with a claim of right" in ignorance of the law, but also those who by accident or misadventure achieved any criminal result without intending it (Yad, Roẓe'aḥ 6:1–9), or who achieved any result (however criminal) different from the criminal result they intended to achieve (*ibid.* 4:1). Within the category of unintentional offenders, a distinction is made between those nearer to duress and those nearer to criminality: the former acted without negligence, and their conduct was in no way blameworthy; the latter acted recklessly and in disregard of common standards of behavior (the most striking example is the man who maintained that it was perfectly lawful to kill). While neither is, as a matter of law, criminally responsible, the one nearer to criminality may not be entitled to resort to cities of refuge (Yad, *ibid.* 6:10) and is liable to be flogged and imprisoned for purposes of deterrence (Yad, *ibid.* 2:5 and Sanh. 24:4). Previous warning of illegality was held to be unnecessary where the nature of the offense or its planning rendered the warning impracticable, such as in cases of perjury (Ket. 32a) or burglary at night (Sanh. 72b), or where it was redundant, as in the case of the rebellious elder (Sanh. 88b) or of recidivists (Sanh. 81b; and cf. Maim. Yad, Sanhedrin 18: 5). Some scholars held the warning unnecessary also where the offender was a man learned in the law (Sanh. 8b).

Self-Defense and Rescue. Another important cause of exemption from criminal responsibility is the right and duty of defense against unlawful attack and of protection from danger; where any person (including an infant) pursues another with the manifest intent to kill him, everybody is under a duty to rescue the victim, even by killing the pursuer (Sanh. 8:7; Yad, Roẓe'aḥ 1:6). This general rule has been extended to cover the killing of an embryo endangering the life of the mother (Yad, *ibid.* 9; and see Abortion) and the killing of a rapist caught before completion of his offense, if he could not otherwise be induced to desist (Yad, *ibid.* 10). It would be as unlawful to kill the pursuer where the victim could be rescued by some other means (though even then the killer would not be guilty of murder (Yad, *ibid.* 13)), as it would be unlawful not to kill the pursuer if the victim could not otherwise be rescued (Yad, *ibid.* 14–16). Thus the nature of this defense is not just duress; here the criminal intent is superseded by the intent to fulfill a legal duty, and hence the defense is one of justification.

Justification. In the more technical sense of the term, justification exempts from criminal responsibility the following three categories of persons: officers of the court who kill or injure any person (or property) in the course of performing their official duties (cf. Mak. 3:14; Yad, Sanhedrin 16:12); any person lawfully engaged in the execution of convicts (Lev. 24:16; Deut. 13:10, 17:7, 21:21, 22:21, 24); and any person who acts upon the advice or instruction of the court as to what is the law (Sifra, Va-Yikra, 7, 1–2; Hor. 2b, 3b).

Bibliography: ET, 1 (1951), 162–72, 193–5, 303–5, 321–4; 11 (1965), 291–314; J.D. Michaelis, *Mosaisches Recht,* 6 vols. (1770–75); M. Duschak, *Das mosaisch-talmudische Strafrecht* (1869); H.B. Fassel, *Ve-Shaftu ve-Hiẓẓilu: Das mosaisch-rabbinische Strafgesetz und strafrechtliche Gerichts-Verfahren* (1870); S. Mayer, *Geschichte der Strafrechte* (1876); B. Berger, *Criminal Code of the Jews* (1880); S. Mendelsohn, *Criminal Jurisprudence of the Ancient Hebrews* (1891; repr. 1968); G. Foerster, *Das mosaische Strafrecht in seiner geschichtlichen Entwickelung* (1900); H. Vogelstein, in: MGWJ, 48 (1904), 513–33; J. Steinberg, in: *Zeitschrift fuer vergleichende Rechtswissenschaft,* 25 (1911), 140–97; I.S. Zuri, *Mishpat ha-Talmud,* 1 (1921); 6 (1921); S. Assaf, *Ha-Onshin Aḥarei Ḥatimat ha-Talmud* (1922); H. Cohen, in: *Jeschurun,* 9 (1922), 272–99; V. Aptowitzer, in: JQR, 15 (1924/25), 55–118; idem, in: HUCA, 3 (1926), 117–55; J. Manen, in: HHY, 10 (1926), 200–8; L. Kantor, *Beitraege zur Lehre von der strafrechtlichen*

Schuld im Talmud (1926); M. Higger, *Intention in Talmudic Law* (1927); P. Dykan, *Dinei Onshin*, 1 (1938; 1955²); 2 (1947; 1962²); 3 (1953); idem, in: *Sinai*, 60 (1966), 51–62; H.E. Goldin, *Hebrew Criminal Law and Procedure* (1952); J. Ginzberg, *Mishpatim le-Yisrael* (1956); M. Minkowitz, *Ha-Maḥashavah ha-Pelilit ba-Mishpat ha-Talmudi u-va-Mishpat ha-Mekubbal ha-Angli* (1961); D. Daube, *Collaboration with Tyranny in Rabbinic Law* (1965); M. Elon, in: ILR, 3 (1968), 94–97; idem, Mafte'aḥ, 219, 222; idem, *Ha-Mishpat Ha-Ivri* (1973), I, 8ff., 25ff., 44ff.; II, 290ff., 312, 421–425, 435ff., 496ff., 566–569, 647ff., 790ff., 808ff., III, 1136ff.

Haim H. Cohn

HOMICIDE. The shedding of blood *(shefikhut damim)* is the primeval sin (Gen. 4:8) and throughout the centuries ranks in Jewish law as the gravest and most reprehensible of all offenses (cf. Maim. *Guide*, 3:41, and Yad, Roẓe'aḥ 1:4); "violence" in Genesis 6:13 was murder (Gen. R. 31:6), and the "very wicked sinners" of Sodom (Gen. 13:13) were murderers (Sanh. 109a). Bloodshed is the subject of the first admonition of a criminal nature in the Bible: "Whoever sheds the blood of man by man shall his blood be shed; for in His image did God make men" (Gen. 9:6). God will require a reckoning for human life, of every man for that of his fellow man (Gen. 9:5). Blood unlawfully shed cries out to God from the ground (Gen. 4:10) and "pollutes the land, and the land can have no expiation for blood that is shed on it except by the blood of him who shed it" (Num. 35:33). Blood unlawfully shed is innocent blood *(dam naki)* (Deut. 19:10, 13; 21:8; 27:25; I Sam. 19:5; II Kings 21:16; 24:4; Isa. 59:7; Jer. 2:34; 7:6; 19:4; 22:3, 17; Joel 4:19; et al.), of the righteous (Ex. 23:7; II Sam. 4:11; I Kings 2:32; Lam. 4:13), or blood shed "without cause" *(dam ḥinnam)* (I Kings 2:31; I Sam. 25:31). "Blood" is also often used as a term indicating general lawlessness and criminality (Isa. 1:15; Prov. 1:16, 18), "men of blood" are lawless criminals (II Sam. 16:7–8; Prov. 29:10), and "cities of blood," places of corruption and wickedness (Nah. 3:1). Following the biblical reference to the image of God (Gen. 9:6), it is said that all bloodshed is a disparagement of God's own image (Tosef., Yev. 8:4; and caused God to turn away from the land, the Temple to be destroyed (Tosef., Yoma 1:12; Shab. 33a; Sif. Num. 161) and dispersion *(galut)* to come into the world (Avot 5:9; Num. R. 7:10).

Killing is prohibited as one of the Ten Commandments (Ex. 20:13; Deut. 5:17), but the death penalty is prescribed only for willful murder (Ex. 21:12, 14; Lev. 24:17, 21; Num. 35:16–21; Deut. 19:11), as distinguished from unpremeditated manslaughter or accidental killing (Ex. 21:13; Num. 35:22, 23; Deut. 19:4–6). In biblical law, willfulness or premeditation is established by showing either that a deadly instrument was used (Num. 25:16–18) or that the assailant harbored hatred or enmity toward the victim (Num. 35:20–21; Deut. 19:11). The willful murderer is executed, but the accidental killer finds asylum in a city of refuge. The following special cases of killing are mentioned in the Bible: Causing the death of a slave by excessive chastisement (Ex. 21:20–21) – the injunction "he shall surely be punished" *(ibid.)* was later interpreted to imply capital punishment (Sanh. 52b); Where a man surprises a burglar at night and kills him, there is no "bloodguilt" on him – it is otherwise if the killing is committed during daytime (Ex. 22:1–2); A man is liable to capital punishment where death is caused by his ox which he knew to be dangerous and failed to guard properly (Ex. 21:29) – but the death penalty may be compounded by ransom (Ex. 21:30); Where death ensues as a result of assaulting a man "with stone or fist," though without intent to kill, the killing is regarded as murder (Ex. 21:18 *e contrario;* cf. also Mekh. *Mishpatim,* 6); Where a man had been killed and the killer was unknown, a solemn ritual had to be performed in order that "the guilt for the blood of the innocent" should not remain among the people (Deut. 21:1–9).

Judicial murder was likewise regarded as "shedding the blood of the innocent" (Jer. 26:15; cf. Sus. 62) and hence (semble) as capital homicide (I Kings 21:19 as interpreted by Maim. Yad, Roẓe'aḥ, 4:9). Talmudic law greatly refined the distinctions between premeditated and unpremeditated homicide. Willful murder *(mezid)* was distinguished from "nearly willful" manslaughter *(shogeg karov la-mezid)*, and unpremeditated homicide was subdivided into killings that were negligent, accidental, "nearly unavoidable" *(shogeg karov le-ones)*, under duress *(ones)*, or justifiable (Maim. Yad, Roẓe'aḥ Chs. 3–6). (For details of gradations of criminal intent, duress, and justification, see Penal Law.)

"Justifiable" homicides include both those that are permissible, e.g., killing the burglar at night, and those that are obligatory, such as the participation in public executions (Lev. 20:2; 24:14; Deut. 17:7; 21:21; 22:21); killing a man in self-defense (Sanh. 72a), or to prevent a man from killing another or from committing rape (Sanh. 8:7); or the killing, in public, of persistent heretics and apostates (Maim. Yad, Roẓe'aḥ 4:10; Tur., ḤM 425). Failure to perform any such obligatory killing is regarded as a sin, but is not punishable (Maim. *ibid.* 1:15–16). Where heathens threaten to kill a whole group unless one of them is delivered up for being killed, they must rather all be killed and not deliver anyone; but if the demand is for a named individual, then he should be surrendered (TJ, Ter. 8:10, 46b; Tosef., Ter. 7:20). While killing may be justifiable in self-defense or in defense of another's life *(supra)*, the general rule is that the preservation of a man's own life does not justify the killing of another (Sanh. 74a).

Talmudic law also further extended the principle that premeditation in murder is to be determined either by the nature of the instrument used or by previous expressions of enmity. While there are deadly instruments, such as iron bars or knives, the use of which would afford conclusive evidence of premeditation (Maim. Yad, Roẓe'aḥ, 3:4), the court will in the majority of cases have to infer premeditation not only from the nature of the instrument used, but also from other circumstances, such as which part of the victim's body was hit or served the assailant as his target, or the distance from which he hit or threw stones at the victim, or the assailant's strength to attack and the victim's strength to resist (*ibid.* 3:2, 5,6). Thus, where a man is pushed from the roof of a house, or into water or fire, premeditation will be inferred only where in all the proven circumstances – height of the house, depth of the water, respective strengths of assailant and victim – death was the natural consequence of the act and must have been intended by the assailant (*ibid.* 3:9). There is, however, notwithstanding the presence of premeditation, no capital murder in Jewish law, unless death is caused by the direct physical act of the assailant. Thus, starving a man to death, or exposing him to heat or cold or wild beasts, or in any other way bringing about his death by the anticipated – and however certain – operation of a supervening cause, would not be capital murder (*ibid.* 3:10–13). The same applies to murder committed not by the instigator himself, but by his agent or servant (*ibid.* 2:2; as to accomplices see Penal Law).

As regards liability to capital punishment, it does not matter even that the victim was a newborn infant (Nid. 5:3; Maim., *ibid.* 2:6) though a premature child must be at least 30 days *(ibid.)*, nor that the victim was so old or sick as to be about to die anyhow (Sanh. 78a; Maim. *ibid.* 2:7); but where a man was *in extremis* from fatal wounds inflicted on him by others, it would not be capital murder to kill him *(ibid.).* The categories of capital murder were thus drastically cut down by talmudic law: only premeditated murder, at the hands of the accused himself, committed after previous warning by two witnesses (*hatra'ah*, see Evidence, Penal Law), was punishable by death. Execution was by the sword (Sanh. 9:1; see Capital Punishment). The other, noncapital, categories of homicide – excluding homicides under duress and justification – could still be punished by the death penalty, either at the hands of the king or, in situations of emergency, even by the court (Maim. *ibid.* 2:4; and see Extraordinary Remedies); failing this, in the language of Maimonides, "the court would be bound to administer floggings so grave as to approach the death penalty, to impose imprisonment on severest conditions for long periods, and to inflict all sorts of pain in order to deter and frighten other criminals" (*ibid.* 2:5). In this respect, homicide differs from all other capital offenses, for which either the prescribed capital punishment is inflicted or none at all; the reason is that homicide – as distinguished from other grave capital offenses, such as idolatry, incest, or the desecration of the Sabbath – "destroys the civilization of the world" (*ibid.* 4:9). In exceptional cases of excess of justification, as where the justificatory purpose could have been attained by means short of killing, or where the justificatory purpose allowed by law was exceeded, "He is deemed a shedder of blood and he deserves to be put to death. He may not, however, be put to death by the court" (Maim. Yad, Roẓe'aḥ, 1:13). In post-talmudic times, homicides within the Jewish communities were relatively rare, and even the justifiable – including the obligatory – classes of homicide fell into obsolescence. Opinions differed in the various periods and various places as to what the proper punishment was to be: some early scholars held that no murderer should be executed, but only flogged and ostracized (see *Ḥerem;* Natronai Gaon, quoted in Tur, ḤM 425; *Or Zaru'a*, pt. I, 112; *Sha'arei Ẓedek* 4:7, 39); others held that murderers should be executed, but not by the sword (*Zikhron Yehudah* 58; Resp. Ribash 251; Resp. Maharam of Lublin 138; et al.; cf. *Ḥokhmat Shelomo,* Sanh. 52b; and see Capital Punishment). On the law in the State of Israel see Capital Punishment.

Bibliography: S. Mayer, *Die Rechte der Israeliten, Athener und Roemer,* 3 (1876), 522–33; S. Mendelsohn, *Criminal Jurisprudence of the Ancient Hebrews* (1891), 58–77; H. Vogelstein, in: MGWJ, 48 (1904), 513–53; M. Sulzberger, *Ancient Hebrew Law of Homicide* (1915); J. Ziegler, in: *Festschrift Adolf Schwarz* (1917), 75–88; S. Assaf, *Ha-Onshin Aḥarei Ḥatimat ha-Talmud* (1922), 147 (index), s.v. *Roẓe'aḥ;* ET, 1 (1951^3), 162–8, 282f.; P. Dickstein (Daykan) *Dinei Onshin,* 3 (1953), 720–30; J. Ginzberg, *Mishpatim le-Yisrael* (1956), 378 (index), s.v. *Hereg,* etc.; M.Z. Neriyah, in: *Ha-Torah ve-ha-Medinah,* 11–13 (1956^2), 126–47; D. Daube, *Collaboration with Tyranny in Rabbinic Law* (1965); M. Elon, *Ha-Mishpat Ha-Ivri* (1973), II, 283, 290ff., 423ff., 790ff.; III, 845ff., 1103.

Haim H. Cohn

SUICIDE. "But for your own life-blood I will require a reckoning" (Gen. 9:5) – these are the suicides whose blood is claimed by God (Gen. R. 34:19; Yad, Roẓe'aḥ 2:3). The "reckoning" is, of course, God's only, but on earth the suicide is denied certain honors due to the dead, provided the surviving mourners are not aggrieved by such denials (Sem. 2:1; YD 345:1). The suggestion that words of scorn be exclaimed at this grave was met by R. Akiva with the rejoinder, "do not abase him and do not praise him" (Sem. 2:1). In order to be reprehensible, the suicide must be voluntary and premeditated (*me'abbed aẓmo la-da'at,* that is, he must knowingly destroy himself). A person destroying himself is presumed to do so without the necessary premeditation *(she-lo la-da'at)* – whether from pathological depression and not being in possession of his mental faculties (cf. Yad, Sanhedrin 18:6), or from "duress" (see Penal Law). Duress includes not only compulsion, such as the necessity to kill oneself rather than surrender to the enemy or violate God's laws (see below), but also the (subjectively) reasonable despair of life or the identification with a person who just died. Most of the suicides reported in Bible, Talmud, and Midrash fall into either of these categories, which may explain the fact that they are not adversely or deprecatingly commented upon (cf. the suicides of King Saul (I Sam. 31:4) and his armor-bearer (*ibid.* 5); of Achitophel (II Sam. 17:23) and of Zimri (I Kings 16:18) and of the servant of Judah ha-Nasi who killed himself when learning of his master's death (Ket. 103b), and of the pagan executioner who joined Ḥananiah (Ḥanina) b. Teradyon in the flames (Av. Zar. 18a)).

Duress is also present where the suicide amounts to self-inflicted punishment for real or imagined sinfulness: the apostate Yakum of Ẓerorot is said to have entered paradise after having taken his own life in a manner devised to combine all four modes of judicial execution (Mid. Ps. to 11:7); and Ḥiyya b. Ashi is said to have caused his own death in despair over an offense he intended to commit and thought he had committed, though in fact he had not committed it at all (Kid. 81b). Where a man chooses to die rather than surrender to the heathen, no question of duress arises, because his conduct is highly praiseworthy (Git. 57b); the most notable instances are those related in the Books of the Maccabees (e.g., II Macc. 14:37–46) and the reported mass suicide at Masada (which has recently given rise to some halakhic discussion). As for the violation of Divine law, while every man has to decide for himself whether he will kill himself rather than commit any such violation (Git. 57b), the law was settled to the effect that where he is required to commit idolatry, adultery *(gillui arayot),* or murder, he must kill himself or let himself be killed rather than commit any of those crimes (Sanh. 74a; Sh. Ar., YD 157).

The scope of duress being as wide as it is, the law will presume that a man found dead from his own hand took his life involuntarily and without premeditation (Sem. 2:3), until the contrary is proved from what the man himself had been heard to say before his death (Sem. 2:2). As far as minors are concerned, the presumption of duress appears to be irrebuttable (Sem. 2:4–5; YD 345:3). So long as the presumption is not rebutted, a suicide may not in any way be discriminated against (Yad, Evel 1:11). The law, however, has to take cognizance of attempted suicide: a person who does any act by which he endangers his own life is liable to disciplinary flogging (*makkat mardut;* Yad, Roẓe'aḥ 11:5). Opinions are divided whether a man may inflict nonfatal wounds on himself (BK 91b); and the law is that while he is not allowed to do so, he is not punishable if he does so (BK 8:6; ḤM 420:31); yet not only might he be punished at the hands of heaven (Tosef., BK 9:31), but the disciplinary flogging may always be imposed in lieu of punishment (Yad, Roẓe'aḥ 11:5; ḤM 427:10). If suicide attempts are epidemic or otherwise constitute a threat to national security, the court may exercise its emergency powers and impose not only floggings but also imprisonment (cf. Yad, Roẓe'aḥ 2:4–5).

Bibliography: S. Goren, in: *Maḥanayim,* 87 (1964), 7–12; L.I. Rabinowitz, in: *Sinai,* 55 (1964), 329–32; Ch. W. Reines, in: *Juda,* 10 (1961), 160–70; A. Roth, *Eine Studie ueber den Selbstmord, von juedischen Standpunkte* (1878); J. Ginzburg, *Mishpatim le-Yisra'el* (1956), 247–57, 307f.; J. Nedava, in: *Mishpat ve-Kalkalah,* 3 (1956/57), 87–99; Z. Rabinowicz, in:

Harofe Haivri, 34 (1961), 153–6; ET, 12 (1967), 68 lf; M. Elon, *Ha-Mishpat Ha-Ivri* (1973); III, 1156 n. 64.

Haim H. Cohn

ABDUCTION (or **Manstealing**; Heb. גנבת נפש, *genevat nefesh*), stealing of a human being for capital gain. According to the Bible, abduction is a capital offense. "He who kidnaps a man – whether he has sold him or is still holding him – shall be put to death" (Ex. 21:16); and, "If a man is found to have kidnapped a fellow Israelite, enslaving him or selling him, that kidnapper shall die" (Deut. 24:7). The first passage appears to prohibit the abduction of any person, while the latter is confined to Israelites only; the first appears to outlaw any abduction, however motivated (cf. *Codex Hammurapi,* 14), while the latter requires either enslavement or sale as an essential element to constitute the offense. Talmudic law, in order to reconcile these conflicting scriptural texts or to render prosecution for this capital offense more difficult (or for both purposes), made the detention, the enslavement, and the sale of the abducted person all necessary elements of the offense, giving the Hebrew "and" (which in the translation quoted above is rendered as "or") its cumulative meaning (Sanh. 85b, 86a). Thus, abduction without detention or enslavement or sale, like enslavement or sale or detention without abduction, however morally reprehensible, was not punishable (even by flogging), because none of these acts was in itself a completed offense. On the other hand, even the slightest, most harmless, and casual use of the abducted person would amount to "enslavement"; and as for the "sale," it does not matter that the sale of any human being (other than a slave) is legally void (BK 68b). In this context, any attempt at selling the person, by delivering him or her into the hands of a purchaser, would suffice. However, the attempted sale has to be proved in addition to the purchaser's custody, because giving away the abducted person as a gift would not be a "sale" even for this purpose (Rashba to BK 78b). The term rendered in the translation quoted above as "kidnap" is *ganov* ("steal"). The injunction of the Decalogue, "Thou shalt not steal" (Ex. 20:13), has been interpreted to refer to the stealing of persons rather than the stealing of chattels. The reason for this is both because the latter is proscribed elsewhere (Lev. 19:11), and because of the context of the command next to the interdictions of murder and adultery, both of which are capital offenses and offenses against the human person (Mekh. Mishpatim, 5). It has been said that this interpretation reflects the abhorrence with which the talmudic jurists viewed this particular crime; alternatively, it has been maintained that the reliance on the general words "Thou shalt not steal," made the interdiction of manstealing applicable also to non-Jews and hence amounted to a repudiation of slave trading, which in other legal systems of the period was considered wholly legitimate.

There is no recorded instance of any prosecution for abduction – not, presumably, because no abductions occurred, but because it proved difficult, if not impossible, to find the required groups of witnesses. These would have been required not only for each of the constituent elements of the offense, but also for the prescribed warnings that first had to be administered to the accused in respect of the abduction, the detention, the enslavement, and the sale, separately. The classical instance of abduction reported in the Bible is Joseph's sale into slavery (Gen. 37; cf. 40:15, "I was kidnapped from the land of the Hebrews"). In the Talmud there is a report from Alexandria that brides were abducted from under the canopy (BM 104a; Tosef. Ket. 4:9), not necessarily for enslavement or sale, but (as it appears from the context) for marriage to the abductors.

Bibliography: D. Daube, *Studies in Biblical Law* (1947); ET, 5 (1953), 386–93; S. Mendelsohn, *Criminal Jurisprudence of the Ancient Hebrews* (1968²), 52, 126; M. Elon, *Ha-Mishpat Ha-Ivri* (1973), II, 283, 351ff., 524, 687ff.

Haim. H. Cohn

ASSAULT, the infliction of any degree of violence on the body of another person, whether injury results or not. the biblical injunction, "he may be given up to forty lashes but not more" (Deut. 25:3), which applies to flogging by way of punishment, was interpreted as prohibiting, *a fortiori,* the nonauthorized flogging of an innocent person (Maim. Yad, Ḥovel u-Mazzik 5:1; Sh. Ar., ḤM 420:1). As it violated a negative biblical injunction for which no other penalty was prescribed, assault itself was punishable with flogging (Mak. 9a; Ket. 32b). Striking one's father or mother was an assault punishable with death (Ex. 21:15), but the capital offense was later restricted only to such blows as caused bodily injury (Sanh. 11:1). Criminal assaults, which result in any assessable injury and which also give rise to claims for damages, prompted the question of whether the civil or the criminal sanction was to prevail, it being common ground that for any one wrong not more than one sanction could be imposed (Mak. 4b; 13b). While as a general rule the lesser (civil) remedy would merge with the greater (criminal) remedy, so that the assailant would be liable to be flogged rather than held liable in damages, it was held that the sanction of payment of damages should prevail over the criminal sanction – for the practical reason (as distinguished from several hermeneutical ones) that having the assailant flogged would not relieve the victim's injury, and "the Torah has regard for the money of the injured" (Tos. to Ket. 32a). Thus, flogging came to be administered only where the assault had not caused any assessable injury (Ket. 32b; Maim. Yad, Ḥovel u-Mazzik 5:3; Sh. Ar., ḤM 420:2). This state of the law apparently failed to satisfy the rabbis, and in consequence they prescribed fines for assaults which were insulting, but which had not caused substantial damage. The amounts of the fines were fixed, varying in accordance with the severity of the assault (e.g., kicking, slapping, punching, spitting, hair pulling, etc.) – always leaving it to the discretion of the court to increase or reduce the fine in special circumstances (BK 8:6; Maim. Yad, Ḥovel u-Mazzik 3:8–11; Sh. Ar., ḤM 420:41–43).

While criminal liability depended on the availability of sufficient evidence of warning previously administered to the assailant and of the act of the assault itself, liability for damages could be established on the strength of the assailant's own admission or other simplified modes of proof (Maim. Yad, Ḥovel u-Mazzik 5:4–8). Damages were to be estimated and assessed by the court; the biblical law of talion (Ex. 21:23–25; Lev. 24:19–20) being replaced for this purpose by an elaborate system of assessing the value of injured limbs in terms of money (BK 83b–86a).

Another distinction between criminal and civil assaults is that the criminal assault is deemed to be spiteful and malicious (Maim. Yad, Ḥovel u-Mazzik 5:1), whereas the civil assault might be unintentional: the warning, "nor must you show pity," given in connection with talion (Deut. 19:21), was interpreted so as to render even the unintentional assailant liable in damages (Maim. Yad, Ḥovel u-Mazzik 1:4), apart from the rule that the civil responsibility of a man never depends on the willfulness of his acts (BK 2:6). The amount of damages, however, would be reduced in cases of unintended assaults (see Damages). Mutual or anticipated assaults, as in boxing or wrestling matches, even if they result in grievous injury, do not give rise to claims for damages (Resp. Rosh 101:6; Sh. Ar., ḤM 421:5); but where two men assault each other maliciously, the one who suffered the greater injury has a claim for the damage suffered in excess of the damage inflicted by him (BK 3:8).

Assaults may be intentional, though not spiteful: for instance, if an injury results from surgical treatment, the surgeon – provided he was duly qualified – is not liable for damages (Tosef., BK 9:11). The same rule applies to a father beating his son, a teacher his pupil, and the messenger of the court assaulting a person in the course of duty *(ibid.)*. In all those cases, liability may, however, be established by proving that the assailant exceeded the measure of violence necessary to achieve his legitimate purpose *(ibid.)*. Still, if only by way of exhortation, assailants of this kind are warned that while they go free under the laws of men, they may yet be judged by the laws of Heaven (Tosef., BK 6:17). The assailant can only cite the consent of the victim to being assaulted if the victim has expressly waived beforehand any claim to damages, and if no grave injury was caused, for no man seriously consents to be injured (BK 8:7; BK 93a). The injunction, "nor must you show pity," was applied also where the assailant was indigent: that being no ground for reducing the damages (Maim. Yad, Ḥovel u-Mazzik, 1:4). But, however generous the award might appear, where it was made according to the letter of the law, it was of no use when the victim could not collect the judgment debt, and, being practically unenforceable, did not provide any sanction against the assailant. Ways and means had to be found also to deter people who resorted to violence and against whom damages were no effective sanction: thus R. Huna is reported to have ordered the hand of one such recidivist to be cut off (Sanh. 58b) – a drastic measure which was sought to be justified by the extraordinary powers of the court to impose extralegal punishment in situations of emergency (Sanh. 46a), but also explained away as a mere curse which was not actually carried into effect (cf. Nid. 13b). The precedent of Huna was followed in Spain several centuries later, when an assailant who had attacked a rabbinical judge at night and wounded him badly, had both his hands cut off (Resp. *Zikhron Yehudah*, no. 58). Cutting off the hand that sinned is reminiscent of biblical law (Deut. 25:12), and it was used as a threat to a husband who habitually beat his wife and wounded her (Beit Yosef, Tur, EH 74, end). Huna, however, did not rely on the biblical law, but on the verse, "the high arm shall be broken" (Job 38:15), a precept which would scarcely warrant the hand being cut off. Indeed, in later sources the breaking of the hand is a punishment meted out to one who beat a rabbi with his fist (*Sefer Ḥasidim*, 631).

Jurisdiction in matters of personal injuries *(Dinei Ḥavalot)* is held not to have devolved on postexilic courts: these are regarded as "agents" of the ancient courts only in such common matters as contract and debt, but not in matters as rare and exceptional as personal injuries (BK 84a). This assumption of infrequency was disproved soon enough; and Jewish courts everywhere and at all times in effect assumed jurisdiction in personal injury cases, not only awarding discretionary damages, but also inflicting punishments, such as fines (e.g., Resp. Rosh 13:4; *Mordekhai*, Kid. 554), and floggings (*Sha'arei Ẓedek*, 4:7:39; *Halakhot Pesukot min ha-Ge'onim*, 89; *Teshuvot ha-Ge'onim, Sha'arei Teshuvah*, 181; Resp. Maharyu nos. 28, 87; et al.), as well as lesser penances such as fasting and beardshaving (*Or Zaru'a* BK 8, nos. 329 and 347). The legal basis for such punitive measures were normally *takkanot* or local custom (Resp. Rosh 101:1), but courts certainly followed also the precedents provided by the usage of earlier authorities. It is said that an ancient *herem* *("ḥerem kadmonim")* hangs over those who do violence to others (Rema and *Sma*, Sh. Ar., ḤM 420:1), and that, on the strength of that ban, they may not be admitted to communal worship or any matter of ritual, unless the *ḥerem* was first lifted from them by order of the court, after compliance with any judgment that may have been given against them (*Ḥatam Sofer*, ḤM no. 182). Notwithstanding this preexisting *ḥerem*, both the imposition of and the threatening with bans and excommunication was a common measure against violence (Resp. Maharam of Rothenburg, ed. Prague nos. 81, 927; et al.).

Bibliography: S.Assaf, *Ha-Onshin Aḥarei Ḥatimat ha-Talmud* (1922), index s.v. *Ḥovel ba-Ḥavero;* Finkelstein, Middle Ages, index; ET, 7 (1956), 376–82, s.v. *Dinei Kenasot;* 12 (1967), 679–746, s.v. *Hovel;* M. Elon, *Ha-Mishpat Ha-Ivri* (1973), I, 9ff., 26, II, 568, 637ff., 666.

Haim H. Cohn

ABORTION. Abortion is defined as the artificial termination of a woman's pregnancy.

In the Bible a monetary penalty is imposed for causing abortion of a woman's foetus in the course of a quarrel, and the penalty of death if the woman's own death results therefrom. "And if men strive together, and hurt a woman with child, so that her fruit depart, and yet no harm follow – he shall be surely fined, according as the woman's husband shall lay upon him; and he shall pay as the judges determine. But if any harm follow – then thou shalt give life for life" (Ex. 21:22–23). According to the Septuagint the term "harm" applied to the foetus and not to the woman, and a distinction is drawn between the abortion of a foetus which has not yet assumed complete shape – for which there is the monetary penalty – and the abortion of a foetus which has assumed complete shape – for which the penalty is "life for life." Philo (Spec. 3:108) specifically prescribes the imposition of the death penalty for causing an abortion, and the text is likewise construed in the Samaritan Targum and by a substantial number of Karaite commentators. A. Geiger deduces from this the existence of an ancient law according to which (contrary to talmudic *halakhah*) the penalty for aborting a foetus of completed shape was death (*Ha-Mikra ve-Targumav*, 280–1, 343–4). The talmudic scholars, however, maintained that the word "harm" refers to the woman and not to the foetus, since the scriptural injunction, "He that smiteth a man so that he dieth, shall surely be put to death" (Ex. 21:12), did not apply to the killing of a foetus (Mekh. SbY, ad loc.; also Mekh., Mishpatim, 8; Targ. Yer., Ex. 21:22–23; BK 42a). Similarly, Josephus states that a person who causes the abortion of a woman's foetus as a result of kicking her shall pay a fine for "diminishing the population," in addition to paying monetary compensation to the husband, and that such a person shall be put to death if the woman dies of the blow (Ant. 4:278). According to the laws of the ancient East (Sumer, Assyria, the Hittites), punishment for inflicting an aborting blow was monetary and sometimes even flagellation, but not death (except for one provision in Assyrian law concerning willful abortion, self-inflicted). In the Code of Hammurapi (no. 209, 210) there is a parallel to the construction of the two quoted passages: "If a man strikes a woman [with child] causing her fruit to depart, he shall pay ten shekalim for her loss of child. If the woman should die, he who struck the blow shall be put to death."

In talmudic times, as in ancient *halakhah*, abortion was not considered a transgression unless the foetus was viable (*ben keyama;* Mekh., Mishpatim, 4 and see Sanh. 84b and Nid. 44b; see Rashi Ex. 21:12), hence, even if an infant is only one day old, his killer is guilty of murder (Nid. 5:3). In the view of R. Ishmael, only a gentile, to whom some of the basic transgressions applied with greater stringency, incurred the death penalty for causing the loss of the foetus (Sanh. 57b). Thus abortion, although prohibited, does not constitute murder (Tos., Sanh. 59a, Ḥul. 33a). The scholars deduced the prohibition against abortion by an *a fortiori* argument from the laws concerning abstention from procreation, or onanism, or having sexual relations with one's wife when likely to harm the foetus in her womb – the perpetrator whereof being regarded as "a shedder of blood" (Yev. 63b; Nid. 13a and 31a; *Ḥavvat Ya'ir*, no. 31; *She'elat Yaveẓ*, 1:43; *Mishpetei Uziel*, 3:46). This is apparently also the meaning of Josephus' statement that "the Law has commanded to raise all the children and prohibited women from aborting or destroying seed; a woman who does so shall be judged a murderess of children for she has caused a soul to be lost and the family of man to be diminished" (Apion 2:202).

The Zohar explains that the basis of the prohibition against abortion is that "a person who kills the foetus in his wife's womb desecrates that which was built by the Holy One and His craftsmanship." Israel is praised because notwithstanding the decree, in Egypt, "every son that is born ye shall cast into the river" (Ex. 1:22), "there was found no single person to kill the foetus in the womb of the woman, much less after its birth. By virtue of this Israel went out of bondage" (Zohar, Ex., ed. Warsaw, 3b).

Abortion is permitted if the foetus endangers the mother's life. Thus, "if a woman travails to give birth [and it is feared she may die], one may sever the foetus from her womb and extract it, member by member, for her life takes precedence over his" (Oho. 7:6). This is the case only as long as the foetus has not emerged into the world, when it is not a life at all and "it may be killed and the mother saved" (Rashi and Meiri, Sanh. 72b). But, from the moment that the greater part of the foetus has emerged into the world – either its head only, or its greater part – it may not be touched, even if it endangers the mother's life *"ein doḥin nefesh mi-penei nefesh"* ("one may not reject one life to save another" – Oho. and Sanh. *ibid.*). Even though one is enjoined to save a person who is being pursued, if necessary by killing the pursuer (see Penal Law), the law distinguishes between a foetus which has emerged into the world and a "pursuer," since "she [the mother] is pursued from heaven" (Sanh. 72b) and moreover, "such is the way of the world" (Maim. Yad, Roẓe'aḥ, 1:9) and "one does not know whether the foetus is pursuing the mother, or the mother the foetus" (TJ, Sanh. 8:9, 26c). However, when the mother's life is endangered, she herself may destroy the foetus – even if its greater part has emerged – "for even if in the eyes of others the law of a foetus is not as the law of a pursuer, the mother may yet regard the foetus as pursuing her" (Meiri, *ibid.*).

Contrary to the rule that a person is always fully liable for damage *(mu'ad le-olam),* whether inadvertently or willfully caused (BK 2:6, see Penal Law, Torts), it was determined with regard to damage caused by abortion, that "he who with the leave of the *bet din* and does injury – is absolved if he does so inadvertently, but is liable if he does so willfully – this being for the good order of the world" (Tosef., Git. 4:7), for "if we do not absolve those who have acted inadvertently, they will refrain from carrying out the abortion and saving the mother" (*Tashbeẓ*, pt. 3, no. 82; Minḥat Bik., Tosef., Git. 4:7).

Some authorities permit abortion only when there is danger to the life of the mother deriving from the foetus "because it is pursuing to kill her" (Maim. *loc. cit.;* Sh. Ar., ḤM 425:2), but permission to "abort the foetus which has not emerged into the world should not be facilitated [in order] to save [the mother] from illness deriving from an inflammation not connected with the pregnancy, or a poisonous fever . . . in these cases the foetus is not [per se] the cause of her illness" *(Paḥad Yiẓḥak, s.v. Nefalim).* Contrary to these opinions, the majority of the later

authorities *(aḥaronim)* maintain that abortion should be permitted if it is necessary for the recuperation of the mother, even if there is no mortal danger attaching to the pregnancy and even if the mother's illness has not been directly caused by the foetus (Resp. *Maharit*, pt. I, no. 99). Jacob Emden permitted abortion "as long as the foetus has not emerged from the womb, even if not in order to save the mother's life, but only to save her from the harassment and great pain which the foetus causes her" *(She'elat Yaveẓ* 1:43). A similar view was adopted by Benzion Meir Ḥai Uziel, namely that abortion is prohibited if merely intended for its own sake, but permitted "if intended to serve the mother's needs . . . even if not vital"; and who accordingly decided that abortion was permissible to save the mother from the deafness which would result, according to medical opinion, from her continued pregnancy *(Mishpetei Uziel, loc. cit.).* In the Kovno ghetto, at the time of the Holocaust, the Germans decreed that every Jewish woman falling pregnant shall be killed together with her foetus. As a result, in 1942 Rabbi Ephraim Oshry decided that an abortion was permissible in order to save a pregnant woman from the consequences of the decree *(Mi-Ma'amakim,* no. 20).

The permissibility of abortion has also been discussed in relation to a pregnancy resulting from a prohibited (i.e., adulterous) union (see *Ḥavvat Ya'ir, ibid.*). Jacob Emden permitted abortion to a married woman made pregnant through her adultery, since the offspring would be a *mamzer* (see *Mamzer*), but not to an unmarried woman who becomes pregnant, since the taint of bastardy does not attach to her offspring *(She'elat Yaveẓ,* 1:43, see also *Yuḥasin).* In a later responsum it was decided that abortion was prohibited even in the former case *(Leḥem ha-Panim,* last *Kunteres,* no. 19), but this decision was reversed by Uziel, in deciding that in the case of bastardous offspring abortion was permissible at the hands of the mother herself *(Mishpetei Uziel,* 3, no. 47).

In recent years the question of the permissibility of an abortion has also been raised in cases where there is the fear that birth may be given to a child suffering from a mental or physical defect because of an illness, such as rubeola or measles, contracted by the mother or due to the aftereffects of drugs, such as thalidomide, taken by her. The general tendency is to uphold the prohibition against abortion in such cases, unless justified in the interests of the mother's health, which factor has, however, been deemed to extend to profound emotional or mental disturbance (see: Unterman, Zweig, in bibliography). An important factor in deciding whether or not an abortion should be permitted is the stage of the pregnancy: the shorter this period, the stronger are the considerations in favor of permitting abortion *(Ḥavvat Ya'ir* and *She'elat Yaveẓ, loc. cit.; Resp. Beit Shelomo* by Solomon of Skolo; ḤM 132).

In the State of Israel. Abortion and attempted abortion are prohibited in the Criminal Law Ordinance of 1936 (based on English law), on pain of imprisonment (sec. 175). An amendment in 1966 to the above ordinance relieved the mother of criminal responsibility for a self-inflicted abortion, formerly also punishable (sec. 176). Causing the death of a person in an attempt to perform an illegal abortion constitutes manslaughter, for which the maximum penalty is life imprisonment. An abortion performed in good faith and in order to save the mother's life, or to prevent her suffering serious physical or mental injury, is not a punishable offense. Terms such as "endangerment of life" and "grievous harm or injury" are given a wide and liberal interpretation, even by the prosecution in considering whether or not to put offenders on trial.

Bibliography: Aptowitzer, in: *Sinai,* 11 (1943), 9–32; P. Korngruen, *Ḥukkei ha-Mizraḥ ha-Kadmon* (1944), 200–26; J.

Ginzberg, *Mishpatim le-Yisrael* (1956), 223–32, 301–4; Unterman, in: *No'am,* 6 (1963), 1–11; Zweig, *ibid.*, 7 (1964), 36–56; Weinberg, *ibid.*, 9 (1966), 193–215; I. Jakobovits, *Jewish Medical Ethics* (1962), 182ff.; U. Cassuto, *Commentary on the Book of Exodus* (1967), 273–7; Rosner and Bleich, in: *Tradition,* vol. 10 no. 2 (1968), 48–120; D.M. Feldman, *Birth Control in Jewish Law* (1968), 251–94; M. Elon, in: ILR (1969), 467–478; idem, *Ha-Mishpat Ha-Ivri* (1973), II, 496.

Menachem Elon

SEXUAL OFFENSES. Although the technical term for sexual offenses in general is *gillui arayot* (lit. "the uncovering of nakedness"), the term is usually (though not always: cf. Ex. 20:26; Isa. 47:3, et al.) employed to denote carnal knowledge (Lev. 18:6–19). In the present context, however, the term "sexual offenses" includes offenses committed by prohibited sexual intercourse, offenses of unlawful sexual conduct short of intercourse, and related offenses presumably motivated by the sexual urge.

As well as acts of adultery and incest, the Bible also prohibits sodomy and homosexuality (18:22), denouncing such acts as "abhorrent" and making them capital offenses (20:13); having carnal relations with any beast is also made a capital offense (18:23; 20:15–16). These offenses were punishable by stoning to death (Sanh. 7:4; Maim. Yad, Issurei Bi'ah, 1:4), and the beast with which the offense had been committed was also destroyed (Lev. 20:15–16). A married girl (i.e., *me'orasah,* her legal status after *kiddushin,* but before *ḥuppah;* see Marriage) who was found not to have been a virgin (though claiming to be one upon her *kiddushin*) is liable to be stoned to death, "for she did a shameful thing in Israel" (Deut. 22:20–21). Both she and her seducer are thus punished if they had intercourse with each other by mutual consent (Deut. 22:23–24); but where the girl did not consent her seducer alone is liable to execution (Deut. 22:25–27).

It is noteworthy that apart from this particular case and cases of adulterous or incestuous intercourse, rape as such is not a criminal offense in Jewish law: the rapist will merely be held liable to pay the girl's father 50 shekels of silver by way of bride-price, "and she shall be his wife, because he has humbled her; and he may not put her away all his days" (Deut. 22:28–29). Under talmudic law, the rapist must also compensate the girl for the physical and psychological damage she sustained (Ket. 42a–43b). But if the girl refuses to marry him, he is not compelled to marry her (Ket. 39b). If a girl was raped by several men, she is given the choice of the one who is to marry her (TJ, Ket. 3:6, 27d; for further details see Rape).

It is an offense to have intercourse with a woman, including one's wife, "having her sickness," i.e., *niddah* during the period of her menstruation (Lev. 18:19 and 20:18). The penalty is *karet* (see Divine Punishment): "both of them shall be cut off from among their people" *(ibid.).* If they were warned beforehand and witnesses are available, they are liable to be flogged (Mak. 3:1).

It is an offense, punishable by flogging, to have sexual intercourse with a non-Jew, by way of purported or intended marriage (Yad, *ibid.*, 12:1). For other sexual intercourse with a non-Jew (which is not criminal), flogging may be administered by way of rebuke and admonition (*makkat mardut; ibid.* 12:2). The biblical story of Phinehas (Num. 25:6–8) gave rise to the rule that where intercourse between Jew and an idolatress takes place in public, any person present may kill them (Sanh. 9:6; Yad, Issurei Bi'ah 12:4). Failing such summary execution, the offender is liable to divine punishment and flogging (*ibid.* 12:6).

Marrying a person born of an adulterous or incestuous union (see *Mamzer*) and having sexual intercourse with him or her is a criminal offense punishable by flogging (*ibid.* 15:2). Marrying a person whose testes are crushed or whose member is cut off (Deut. 23:2), and having (or attempting to have) sexual intercourse with him, is also punishable by flogging (Yad, Issurei Bi'ah 16:1) – although the offense was qualified so as to apply only where the infirmity had not existed from birth but was acquired later by human act or accident (*ibid.* 16:9; Yev. 75b). It is similarly an offense punishable by flogging to castrate a person by causing injury to his sexual organs (Shab. 110b) – an offense which was extended even to the castration of animals (Tosef., Mak. 5:6; Yad, Issurei Bi'ah 16:10); but does not apply to females *(ibid.)* nor to castrations that do not cause injury to sexual organs (*ibid.* 16:12).

Some particular offenses apply to *kohanim* (priests) only: e.g., a *kohen* who marries a divorcee, a harlot (including a non-Jewess), or a woman born of a prohibited union with a priest (Lev. 21:7), and has sexual intercourse with her, is guilty of an offense and liable to be flogged (Yad, *ibid.* 17:2), and so is the woman partner (Yad, *ibid.* 17:5). The high priest who had sexual intercourse with a widow (Lev. 21:13–14) was also liable to be flogged (Yad, *ibid.* 17:3).

The only sexual offense short of intercourse is "approaching" (Lev. 18:6) any person with whom intercourse is prohibited under penalty of death (including divine punishment). Embracing and kissing such persons, and other such precoital activities, are offenses punishable by flogging (Yad, Issurei Bi'ah 21:1). But it is no offense – however reprehensible and "foolish" it may be in some cases – to embrace or kiss one's mother, daughter, sister, or aunt, or such other relatives who do not normally arouse the sexual urge (*ibid.* 21:6; see Incest). The prohibition against "cult prostitution" (Deut. 23:18) was interpreted as creating the offense of sexual intercourse with a harlot (cf. Lev. 19:29), both she and the man being liable to be flogged (Maim. Yad, Na'arah Betulah, 2:17). But however much prostitution may be condemned (cf. e.g., Jer. 3:1–3), it appears in biblical times to have been widespread (cf. Gen. 34:31; 38:15; Judg. 11:1; 16:1; Isa. 23:15–16; Prov. 7:9–22; et al.) and not punishable. In post-talmudic times, sexual licentiousness was punished as a matter of course (cf. e.g., *Halakhot Pesukot min ha-Ge'onim,* 94).

There are several prohibited acts which do not amount to punishable offenses, but which may render the perpetrator liable to flogging by way of admonition and rebuke: e.g., indecent gestures or suggestions to women with whom intercourse is prohibited (Yad, Issurei Bi'ah, 21:2); lesbian conduct among women (*ibid.* 21:8); sexual intercourse with one's wife in public (*ibid.* 21:14); being secluded with a woman with whom intercourse is prohibited – other than one's mother, daughter, or (menstruous) wife, and also except a woman married to another man (because, in the latter case, the flogging might bring her into disrepute; 22:3).

In the State of Israel, rape is punishable with up to 14 years' imprisonment; when committed in the presence of several accessories to the crime, the punishment is up to 20 years' imprisonment (Section 152, Criminal Code Ordinance, 1936, as amended in 1966). Constructive (statutory) rape (sexual intercourse with an infant girl) has been extended up to the girl's age of 17. Proven acts of sodomy (homosexuality), buggery (carnal knowledge *per anum*), and bestiality (carnal knowledge of animals) are felonies. The largest group of sexual offenses comes under the heading of "indecent acts" – for which the penalty may increase in gravity if they are committed by force, or upon children, or in public. The law relating to procuration for purposes of prostitution and the keeping of brothels was restated and made considerably more severe in the Penal Law Amendment (Prostitution Offenses) Law, 5722–1962.

Bibliography: Guttmann, Mafte'aḥ, 2 (1917), 122–8; S. Assaf, *Ha-Onshim Aḥarei Ḥatimat ha-Talmud* (1922), passim; ET, 1 (1951³), 168–72, 5 (1953), 295–300; 12 (1967), 49–74; G. Melber, *Averat Innus va-Averot Miniyyot Aḥerot ba-Mishpat ha-Ivri u-va-Mishpat ha-Angli* . . . (Diss. Jerusalem 1960), summary in Eng.; EH, 2 (1965), 935–7.

Haim H. Cohn

INCEST. The general prohibition against incest with one's "near of kin" (Lev. 18:6) has been held to be limited to the following degrees of consanguinity: parents (18:7); mother-in-law (20:14); stepmother (18:8); sister and half sister (18:9) but not a stepsister; granddaughter (18:10); father's and mother's sister (18:12–13); wife of father's brother (18:14); daughter-in-law (18:15); brother's wife (18:16); stepdaughter and stepgranddaughter (18:17); and wife's sister during the lifetime of the former (18:18). This list is exhaustive and may not be added to by analogies (Sifra, Aḥarei-Mot 13:15), since creation of any criminal offense requires the express pronouncement both of the conduct prohibited and the resulting punishment (see Penal Law; cf. Ker. 3a; Sanh. 74a). A list of another 20 degrees of consanguinity was later drawn up, however, by way of analogy – albeit not to create additional criminal offenses, but as additional prohibitions of intercourse and impediments to marriage (Yev. 21a; Maim. Yad, Ishut 1:6).

The punishment for the various offenses of incest varies – while biblical law prescribed death by burning for incest with one's mother-in-law (Lev. 20:14), it did not prescribe any particular mode of execution for other capital offenses of incest (Lev. 20:11, 12, 17, 19, 20, 21), some of which were clearly to be visited with divine punishment (*karet;* Lev. 20:17, 20, 21). In talmudic law, the offenses of incest were eventually classified as follows: (1) those punishable with death by stoning – incest with mother, stepmother, daughter-in-law (Sanh. 7:4); (2) those punishable with death by burning – incest with stepdaughter, stepgranddaughter, mother-in-law, grandmother-in-law, daughter, and granddaughter (Sanh. 9:1); and (3) all other offenses of incest to be punishable with *karet* or flogging (Maim. Yad, Issurei Bi'ah 1:4–7). As several of the offenses are threatened with both judicial and divine punishment (e.g., incest with mother and stepmother; Ker. 1:1), the rule was evolved that capital punishment would be imposed judicially only where the offense had been committed after previous warning that it was punishable and in the presence of witnesses; while divine punishment was deemed to apply where the offense had been committed without such previous warning and without witnesses being available (Yad, Issurei Bi'ah 1:2–3). Flogging came to be administered not only by way of punishment for such incestuous acts as had been made criminal offenses, but also by way of admonition and rebuke *(makkat mardut),* for incestuous acts which were not criminal (Maim. *ibid.* 1:8). Occasionally, capital offenses were reduced to offenses punishable with flogging, as in the case of incest with one's wife's near relations after her death (*ibid.* 2:8).

Incest is a capital offense only where sexual intercourse has taken place (Shab. 13a), although complete penetration is not a required element (Maim. *ibid.* 1:10); but the prohibition to come near anyone of one's "near of kin" was interpreted to render any bodily proximity, within the prohibited degrees of kinship, punishable with flogging (Maim. Yad, Issurei Bi'ah 21:1) – except kissing or embracing one's mother, daughter, sister, or aunt, or such other relatives who do not normally arouse the sexual urge (*ibid.* 21:6; and see Sexual Offenses). The offense of incest is committed by the female as well as by the male participant (Yev. 84b; TJ, Sanh. 7, 9, 25a; Ker. 2:4; Maim. Yad, Issurei Bi'ah 1:1); but where the offense is committed upon an infant or upon a person asleep or by a person unaware of the incestuous relationship, only the initiator of the act is punishable (Ker. 2:6).

Each single act of sexual intercourse amounts to a complete commission of the offense (Maim. *ibid.* 3:12). The turpitude of this kind of offense is stressed in the Bible by such epithets as "wickedness" (*zimmah,* Lev. 20:14; Ezek. 22, 11), "corruption" (*tevel,* Lev. 20:12), "shame" (*ḥesed,* Lev. 20:17), and "impurity" (*niddah,* Lev. 20:21). Incest is one of the three cardinal offenses (together with murder and idolatry) which a man may not commit even in order to save himself from certain death (Sanh. 74a; Yad, Yesodei ha-Torah 5:2); nor in order to save another person's life (Tosef. Shab. 15:17); nor can there be any justification for its commission on any medical grounds (TJ, Shab. 14:4, 14d; Pes. 25a). Opinions are divided among medieval scholars as to whether a woman, as well as a man, must choose to die rather than commit incest. Some hold that a woman, being the passive partner, may submit to incest rather than be killed (Rashi to Yoma 82a; Isserles, YD 157:1 and cf. Tos. to Av. Zar. 54a), while others maintain that she should prefer death (ET, 6 (1954), 110). It is also maintained that the female's enjoyment is tantamount to the male's action (Tos. BK 32a), constituting "an overt act" for which her punishment is flogging.

In the State of Israel there is no statutory prohibition against incest as such, but it is an offense, punishable with five years' imprisonment, for anyone to have sexual intercourse with an unmarried girl below the age of 21 who is his or his wife's descendant, or his ward, or who has been entrusted to him for education or supervision (Section 155, Criminal Code Ordinance, 1936). Apart from this particular provision, it would seem that sexual intercourse within the prohibited degrees of consanguinity described above is, indeed, left to divine punishment.

Bibliography: E. Neufeld, *Ancient Hebrew Marriage Laws* (1944), 191–212; D.R. Mace, *Hebrew Marriage* (1953), 20ff.; E.A. Speiser, in: A. Altmann (ed.), *Biblical and Other Studies* (1963), 62–81; Z. Falk, in: *Tarbiz,* 32 (1963), 19–34; M. Mielziner, *The Jewish Law of Marriage and Divorce* (1901²), 33–41; L. Blau, in: *Abhandlungen . . . Chajes* (1933), 6–21; ET, 1 (1951³), 204–11, 214, 321–4; 2 (1949), 23f., 257–61; 4 (1952), 745–52; 6 (1954), 106–15; M. Elon, *Ha-Mishpat Ha-Ivri* (1973), I, 184, 217, II, 248, 282ff., 312, 396, 456ff., 659, 808ff.

Haim H. Cohn

ADULTERY is the capital offense of sexual intercourse by a married woman with a man other than her husband (Lev. 20:10; Deut. 22:22). A man defiles himself by having carnal relations with another's wife (Lev. 18:20) and a wife who "goes astray," "breaks faith" with her husband (Num. 5:12). It is not a criminal offense for a man to have sexual intercourse with an unmarried woman, even though he be married.

It appears that originally it was the husband's right to punish his adulterous wife himself (cf. the story of Judah – ordering even his daughter-in-law to be burned: Gen. 38:24) and that he could take the law into his own hands even against the adulterer (cf. Prov. 6:34). It was only when adultery was elevated to the rank of a grave offense against God as well that the husband was required to resort to the priests or to the courts. Yet, so far as the adulterer was concerned, it is probable that he could always buy himself off by paying to the husband a sum of money by way of compensation: compounding was not prohibited for adultery (cf. Prov. 6:35) as it was for murder (Num. 35:31). Where sufficient evidence was available both of the act of adultery (Mak. 7a) and of the adulterer and the adulteress having first each been duly warned (Sanh. 41a), both would be liable to the death penalty. The trial reported in the apocryphal book of Susannah (37–41) was held without any evidence being adduced of a previous warning having been administered, either because the book predates the mishnaic law to this effect, or because the warning appeared irrelevant to the point of the story. No particular mode of execution is prescribed in the Bible, but talmudical law (Sifra, to Lev. 20:10) prescribed strangulation as being the most humane mode of capital punishment (Sanh. 52b, et al.). An older tradition appears to be that the punishment for adultery was stoning: the lighter offenses of the unvirginal bride (Deut. 22:21) and of the betrothed woman and her adulterer (Deut. 22:24) were punished by stoning, and the severer offense of adultery would certainly not have carried a lighter punishment. Stoning of adulteresses is moreover vouched for in prophetic allegories (e.g., Ezek. 16:38–40) and is described in the New Testament as commanded by the Law of Moses (John 8:5). In the aggravated case of adultery by a priest's daughter, the adulteress was burned (Lev. 21:9), while the adulterer remained liable to strangulation (Sifra to Lev. 21:9). Burning is provided for another similar offense (Lev. 20:14) and is also found in prophetic allegory (e.g., Ezek. 23:25; Nah. 3:15). Where the woman was a slave "designated" for another man, the punishment was not death (Lev. 19:20), but he had to bring a sacrifice (Lev. 19:7), while she was flogged (Ker. 11a). Where insufficient evidence was available (the nature of the offense being such as usually took place in secret: cf. Job 24:15), a husband was entitled to have his wife, whom he suspected of adultery, subjected to the ordeal of the waters of bitterness (Num 5:12–31). If found guilty, her punishment was a kind of talio, she being made to suffer with those organs of her body with which she had sinned (Sot. 1:7). One of the features of the ordeal was that the woman's hair was "loosened" (Num. 5:18), that is, disarranged (except, according to R. Judah, if her hair was very beautiful: Sot. 1:5). This disarrangement of the hair (usually covered and concealed) may be the origin of the later punishment of shaving a woman's head – more particularly in cases where lesser misconduct, and not the act of adultery, could be proved against her. Other punishments meted out to adulteresses in post-talmudic times included death, both by strangulation (hanging) and by burning, imprisonment, and commonly, public flogging.

Family Aspects. See Divorce; Husband and Wife; *Mamzer.*

Bibliography: M. Greenberg, in: *Sefer Y. Kaufmann* (1960), 5–28; idem, in: IDB, 1 (1962), 739; de Vaux, Anc Isr, 36–37; S. Loewenstamm, in: BM, 13 (1962), 55–59; 18–19 (1964), 77–78; M. Weinfeld, *ibid.*, 17 (1964), 58–63; E. Neufeld, *Ancient Hebrew Marriage Laws* (1944), 163–75; L. Epstein, *Sex Laws and Customs in Judaism* (1948), 194–215; G. Cohen, in: *The Samuel Freedland Lectures* (1966), 1–21; H.L. Ginsberg, in: *Sefer Y. Kaufmann* (1960), 58–65; J.J. Finkelstein, in: JAOS, 86 (1966), 355–72; Buechler, in: MGWJ, 5 (1911), 196–219; idem, in: WZKM, 19 (1905), 91–138; V. Aptowitzer, in: JQR, 15 (1924/25), 79–82; ET, 2 (1942), 290–3; 4 (1952), 759–64; Sh. M. Paul, *Studies in the Book of the Covenant in the Light of Cuneiform and Biblical Law* (Leiden, 1970), 96–98; M. Elon, *Ha-Mishpat Ha-Ivri* (1973), II, 287, 659, 842ff.

Haim H. Cohn

RAPE (Heb. אונס, *ones*), sexual intercourse with a woman against her will. Unless the contrary be proved by the testimony of witnesses, intercourse with a woman in a place where no one could have come to her aid even if she had cried out ("in the open country," Deut. 22:25,27) will be presumed to have occurred against her will. If, however, it happened in a place where she could have summoned help ("in the town," Deut. 22:23), but there are no witnesses to testify that she did so, she will be presumed to have been seduced, i.e., to have consented to intercourse (*ibid.* and Sif. Deut. 242 and commentaries; Yad, Na'arah Betulah 1:2 and *Hassagot Rabad* thereto). If intercourse took place while she was asleep and thus unaware, she is considered to have been raped because of the absence of her free will. Intercourse with a female minor is always regarded as rape since she has no will of her own (Yev. 33b, 61b; Sh. Ar., EH 178:3 and Beit Shemu'el n.3, thereto). If intercourse began as a forcible violation but terminated with the woman's consent, she will nevertheless be regarded as having been raped since in such circumstances her passions and nature have compelled her to acquiesce (Ket. 51b; Yad, Issurei Bi'ah 1:9).

Legal Consequences. In Civil Matters. A person who violates a virgin *na'arah* (between the ages of 12 years and one day and 12 years and six months) must pay a fine at the fixed amount of 50 shekels of silver (Deut. 22:28–29), as well as compensation for pain and suffering, shame, and blemish, which is to be assessed according to the circumstances in each case (Yad, Na'arah Betulah 2:1–6; see Damages). If the *na'arah* is seduced, the seducer is liable to pay the same fine and compensation, but in view of her consent is not liable for compensation for pain and suffering *(ẓa'ar; ibid.).* Since when laying down the liability for the fine the pentateuchal law speaks of a *na'arah* only, there is no liability for a fine upon the rape or seduction of a *bogeret* i.e., a girl above the age of 12 years and six months (Yad, *ibid.* 1:8), but compensation for pain and suffering, shame, and blemish is due if she was raped (Tur, EH 177, contrary to Yad, *ibid.* 2:10, 11). The seducer of a *bogeret* is exempt from all financial liability toward her since, having consented to the intercourse, she is presumed to have waived all such claims (Ket. 42a; Yad, *ibid.; Beit Yosef,* EH 177).

In Personal Law Matters. In addition to the financial liabilities mentioned above the violator of a *na'arah* is compelled to marry her, "She shall be his wife . . . he cannot put her away all his days" (Deut. 22:29), unless marriage between them is prohibited by the pentateuchal or rabbinic law (see Marriage, Prohibited). However, for the reasons set out above concerning the fine, this obligation does not apply if the victim is a *bogeret* (Ket. 39a; Yad, *ibid.* 1:3; 2:7; Resp. Radbaz, no. 63; *haggahot* of Akiva Eger to Sh. Ar., EH 177:2). The *na'arah* or her father may refuse her marriage to the violator, in which event the transgressor will be exempt from the obligation to marry her and be liable only for the fine and the other payments (Yad, *ibid.* 1:3; Sh. Ar., EH 177:3). A person who seduces a *na'arah* has no obligation to marry her (Yad, *ibid.*). A married woman who has been raped does not become prohibited to her husband unless he is a priest, in which case he must divorce her (Yev. 56b; Yad, Ishut 24:19, 21; Sh. Ar., EH 6:10, 11; see also Marriage, Prohibited). The outraged wife's pecuniary rights toward her husband, in particular her *ketubbah,* remain unaffected in both cases since there is no blameworthiness on her part (Yad, *ibid.* 24:22; Sh. Ar., EH 115:6).

In suits concerning matters of rape and seduction the court must be composed of three competent ordained judges *(mumḥim semukhim),* and, therefore, in strict law the fine (see above) is no longer recoverable since today there are no *semukhim* (see *Bet Din*); in various *takkanot,* however, the scholars have nevertheless regulated for recovery of the fine, "lest the sinner be rewarded" (Tur, EH 177; Sh. Ar., EH 177:2; Resp. Radbaz, no. 63; see also Fine).

In the State of Israel. Of practical significance is the *halakhah* concerning the effect of rape on the marital relationship between the victim and her husband, since this is a matter of personal law which for Jews is governed by Jewish law. The purely civil-law aspects, such as the question of compensation, are governed before the civil courts by the general law of the state, i.e., the Civil Wrongs Ordinance, 1946 (N.V. 1968). The provision that a person must marry the *na'arah* he has violated is rendered unenforceable by the provisions of the Marriage Age Law, 1950, as amended in 1960.

See also Sexual Offenses: Penal Law.

Bibliography: ET, 1 (1951[3]), 166–72; 2 (1949), 60–63, 295f.; B. Schereschewsky, *Dinei Mishpaḥah* (1967[2]), 49–51, 316; M. Elon, *Ha-Mishpat Ha-Ivri* (1973), I, 133, II, 287, 290 ff., 790 ff., III, 842 ff.

Ben-Zion Schereschewsky

REBELLIOUS SON. "If a man have a stubborn and rebellious son, that will not hearken to the voice of his father and [not "or"] the voice of his mother and though they chasten him, will not hearken unto them, then shall his father and his mother lay hold of him and bring him out unto the elders of his city . . . They shall say unto the elders of his city: This our son is stubborn and rebellious, he doth not hearken to our voice, he is a glutton and a drunkard. And all the men of his city shall stone him with stones that he die; so shalt thou put away the evil from the midst of thee; and all Israel shall hear, and fear" (Deut. 21:18–21).

It appears that this law was intended to limit the powers of the *pater familias:* the head of the household could no longer punish the defiant son himself, according to his own whim, but had to bring him before the elders (i.e., judges) for punishment. In earlier laws (e.g., Hammurapi Code, nos. 168, 169) only the father had to be defied; in biblical law it must be both father and mother, and the father cannot act without the mother's concurrence. If either was dead (Sif. Deut. 219) or refused to join in the prosecution, the son could not be indicted (Sanh. 8:4), but it was not necessary that father and mother should be validly married to each other (Sanh. 71a).

There is no record of a rebellious son ever having been executed, except for a dictum of R. Jonathan stating that he had once seen such a one and sat on his grave (Sanh. 71a). However, it is an old and probably valid tradition that there never had been, nor ever will be, a rebellious son, and that the law had been pronounced for educational and deterrent purposes only, so that parents be rewarded for bringing their children up properly (*ibid.;* Tosef. Sanh. 11:6).

Interpreting every single word of the biblical text restrictively, the talmudic jurists reduced the practicability of this law to nil. The "son" must be old enough to bear criminal responsibility, that is 13 years of age (see Penal Law), but must still be a "son" and not a man: as soon as a beard grows ("by which is meant the pubic hair, not that of the face, for the sages spoke euphemistically") he is no longer a "son" but a man (Sanh. 8:1). The period during which he may thus be indicted as a "son" is three months only (Sanh. 69a; Yad, Mamrim 7:6), or, according to another version, not more than six months (TJ, Sanh. 8:1,26a). The term "son" excludes a daughter (Sanh. 8:1; Sif. Deut. 218), though daughters are no less apt to be rebellious (Sanh. 69b–70a).

The offense is composed of two distinct elements: repeated (Sif. loc. cit.) disloyalty and defiance, consisting in repudiating and reviling the parents (Ex. 21:17), and being a "glutton and drunkard." This second element was held to involve the gluttonous eating of meat and drinking of wine (in which sense the same words occur in Prov. 23:20–21), not on a legitimate occasion (Sanh. 8:2), but in the company of loafers and criminals (Sanh. 70b; Yad, Mamrim 7:2) and in a ravenous manner (Yad, Mamrim 7:1). There are detailed provisions about the minimum quantities that must be devoured in order to qualify for the use of the term (cf. Yad, Mamrim 7:2–3). As no "son" can afford such extravagance, the law requires that he must have stolen money from his father and misappropriated it to buy drinks and food (Sanh. 8:3, 71a; Yad, Mamrim 7:2). "Who does not heed his father and mother" was interpreted as excluding one who does not heed God: thus, eating pork or other prohibited food, being an offense against God, would not qualify as gluttony in defiance of parents *(ibid.).* But it was also said that one who in his use of the stolen money performed a precept and thus heeded his Father in heaven could not be indicted (TJ, Sanh. *ibid.*).

As father and mother have to be "defied," to "take hold of him," to "say" to the elders, and to show them "this" is our son, neither of them may be deaf, dumb, blind, lame, or crippled, or else the son cannot be indicted as rebellious (Sanh. 8:4; Sif. Deut. 219). Either of them could condone the offense and withdraw the complaint at any time before conviction (Sif. Deut. 218; Sanh. 88b; TJ, Sanh. 8:6, 26b; Yad; Mamrim 7:8).

The son had first to be brought before a court of three judges (see *Bet Din*) where, when he was convicted, he would be flogged and warned that unless he desisted from his wanton conduct he would be indicted as a rebellious son and liable to be stoned; if he did not desist, he would be brought before a court of 23, including the three judges who had warned him(Sanh. 8:4; 71b; Mid. Tan. to 21:18; Yad, Mamrim 7:7). If he escaped before sentence was passed, and in the meantime his hair had grown, he had to be discharged; but if he escaped after sentence, he would be executed if caught (Sanh. 71b; Yad, Mamrim 7:9).

The sentence passed upon a rebellious son had to be published far and wide, so that "all Israel will hear and be afraid" (Sanh. 89a; Mid. Tan. to 21:21). According to one view, the sentence was to be passed and executed at Jerusalem, at the time of mass pilgrimages, when all the people would be there to see and to hear (Tosef. Sanh. 11:7). It is said that the rebellious son is executed, not because of what he has actually done, but because of what he was foreseen to be prone to do were he allowed to live. His conduct showed that eventually he would have ruined his parents and become a robber and murderer (Sanh. 72a; TJ, Sanh. 8:7,26b), so God considered it better for him to die innocent than to die guilty (Sanh. 8:5).

"In our times, we pay no attention to gluttonous and defiant sons, and everybody covers up the sins of his children; even where they might be liable to flogging or to capital punishment under the law, they are not even reprimanded. Many such children are leading purposeless lives and learn nothing – and we know that Jerusalem was destroyed because children loafed around and did not study" (Shab. 119b; Samuel Eliezer Edels, *Ḥiddushei Halakhot ve-Aggadot,* Sanh. 71a).

Bibliography: J.S. Zuri, *Mishpat ha-Talmud,* 6 (1921), 88; ET, 3 (1951), 362–7; A.Ch. Freimann, in: EM, 2 (1954), 160–2; M. Elon, *Ha-Mishpat Ha-Ivri* (1973), II, 305 ff.

Haim H. Cohn

THEFT AND ROBBERY (Heb. גנבה וגזלה). An object which is in the possession of a person without the consent of its owner or any other person having a right thereto, when that person knows

– or should know – that the latter does not consent, is considered to be stolen or robbed by him, regardless of whether the person holding it intends to restore it to the possession of the person entitled to it after a time or not at all (Sh. Ar., ḤM 348:1). The thief differs from the robber in the fact that the former steals furtively, when unobserved, whereas the robber takes openly and forcefully (BK 79b). This distinction is of practical significance for criminal law only; in dealing with civil cases the law relating to a robber applies equally to a thief and vice versa.

Civil Aspects. To establish that the object is in his possession, it is necessary for the thief or robber to perform an act of acquisition *(kinyan),* such as a "lifting up" or "pulling" thereof, in the same manner as a person who wishes to acquire ownership of ownerless property; without this the object does not enter his possession and no theft or robbery is committed (BK 79a and Tos. thereto). In terms of this definition, land is never robbed (Suk. 30b), as it remains in the possession of its owner and never of the robber because it cannot be carried away, and the owner, who can always restore it to his possession by judicial means (BM7a and Tos. to BM 61a), retains control thereof. On the other hand, a bailee who, without the owner's consent, overtly converts an object to his own use or denies the ownership of the bailor is thereby stealing it (Yad, Gezelah 3:11 and 14). This rule applies in the case of any person, such as a borrower or hirer, who has acquired possession of property with the owner's consent and thereafter refuses to return it (*Maggid Mishneh,* Gezalah 1:3). Many of the scholars of the Talmud are of the opinion that anyone who borrows a thing without the owner's consent is a robber (BB 88a). Moreover, some of them hold that anyone into whose hands a thing comes with the consent of its owner who afterward changes or departs from the use intended for it by the owner is a robber (BM 78a), for his possession thereof is contrary to the owner's wishes. Similarly, a man who finds a lost article and takes it with the purpose of keeping it is a robber (BM 26b), but a bailee who fails to return a thing, falsely pleading that it was stolen from him, is a thief and not a robber (BK 108b).

Certain things are not subject to the law of robbery because people do not mind their being taken; therefore a man who takes them without permission becomes entitled to them, as in the case of a tailor appropriating part of the thread with which he sews a suit, or a carpenter appropriating the sawdust from timber (BK 119a), or a son supported by his father who gives a morsel of food to a friend (Tosef., BK 11:4). In some cases the rabbis, for the sake of peace and order, regulated for the extension of the laws of robbery to property not legally subject thereto, because the ownership is not effective in law – as in the case of property found by a deaf-mute, idiot, or minor – as well as animals, birds, and fishes caught in certain snares set for them (Git. 59b).

Restitution. The thief or robber is obliged to restore the stolen property itself (in specie) to the owner. The obligation comes into being from the time that the robbery is committed and is not fulfilled until the stolen property is returned in such a manner as to enable the owner to know that it has been restored to his possession (BM 31a).

Shinnui. If the thing robbed is damaged while in the robber's possession, he is obliged to compensate the owner for the loss in accordance with the law applicable to a tort-feasor (see Rashba in: *Shitah Mekubbeẓet,* BK 97a); if improved while in the possession of the robber, it must be returned with all improvements, for which the robber is entitled to be compensated. If the thing is lost or destroyed while in the possession of the robber (cf. Sanh. 72a), or is changed to such an extent that it can no longer be put to its former use and is not fit for the owner's purpose (Rashba and Ramah in: *Shitah Mekubbeẓet,* BK 96a), the robber must pay the value of the thing robbed at the time of the robbery. The Talmud records disputing opinions on the law of *shinnui.* As indicated, *shinnui* ("transmutation," *"specificatio"*) is constituted when the stolen property has undergone a change, whether an improvement or deterioration, to the extent that it is no longer fit for its former use, such as wood converted into utensils, wool into clothes, stones which are cut (BK 93b), an animal which has grown old, a coin which has cracked and is not fit to be used, fruit which has rotted, and wine that has gone sour (BK 96b). An accepted criterion for testing whether the *shinnui* is such that the stolen property is rendered unfit for its former use is to examine whether it has undergone a change of name (BK 65b), for people customarily call something which has a specific use by a particular name, so that a change of name denotes a *shinnui.* Yet some scholars are of the opinion that *shinnui* is subject to no special law: the robber must restore the changed object itself; if it is damaged by the change, he must compensate for it; if improved, he is entitled to compensation. However, most scholars hold that the return of the changed stolen property does not serve to restore the owner to the position he held prior to the robbery, inasmuch as the thing is no longer fit to be used by the owner as before and is therefore as if lost to him; thus the robber has to compensate for the thing according to its value at the time of the robbery, thereby acquiring ownership of the changed article. A third opinion is that in law the robber must restore the changed thing itself, but the rabbis – in order to encourage contrition on the part of the robbers – regulated that stolen property, if improved, need not be returned and the robber must only pay compensation for it (BK 66a, 93b, 94a). Again, others are of the opinion that even when the possibility of restoring the thing to its prior use remains – and therefore by law the *shinnui* does not transfer title – still if the loss which the robber would sustain in restoring the thing to its former use exceeds the benefit which the owner would derive from it, then the rabbis regulated that the robber need not restore it. In such an event the robber need only compensate for its value. An example of such a case is where the robber would have to demolish a whole structure in order to return a stolen beam which he had built into it (BK 95a).

Any profits which the stolen property may yield while detained by the robber belong apparently to the robber and he is not required to account for them to the owner (see Rema, ḤM 354:1). Moreover, any loss suffered by the owner as a result of being deprived of the use of the stolen property while it was detained by the robber is an economic loss, for which the robber is not required to compensate him (ḤM 363:3 and *Sma* thereto). Similarly the robber does not pay for a sickness from which a beast recovers (ḤM 363:1).

Ye'ush. Apart from *shinnui* the robber may also acquire ownership of the stolen property and be required merely to pay compensation for it in the event of the owner's *ye'ush* ("despair"). Once the owner has lost all hope of the stolen property being restored to his possession, his ownership thereof is extinguished and title thereto is acquired by the robber, who is required only to pay its value at the time of the robbery. Opinions are divided in the Talmud on the question as to when exactly *ye'ush* is constituted and title conferred on the robber. Some scholars hold that *ye'ush* follows mere theft but not mere robbery; some hold the opposite view; and still others aver that *ye'ush* follows either (BK 114a–b). Another view is that despair alone does not suffice as it cannot be ascertained whether the owner has truly abandoned hope; to be recognized as real, *ye'ush* must therefore be accompanied by something more: either *ye'ush* with a change of possession, the stolen property having passed from the robber to a third person, or *ye'ush* accompanied by a change in the name by which the stolen article is called, i.e., when it has changed to such an extent, that people will incline to call it by another name even if it were possible to restore the article to its prior name. Mere *ye'ush* is nevertheless held by some scholars to suffice and to confer title to the stolen property on the robber (BK 66a–67a, 115a).

In strict law, when the thief delivers the stolen property into the possession of a third party prior to the owner's *ye'ush* the latter may recover possession of his property from the third party without payment, for he has remained owner thereof. This law, if unamended, would have caused hardship to a bona fide purchaser on the open market, who could never be certain that he would not be deprived of his purchase by its true owner; as a result, since they had no means of taking precautions, people would never be in a position to buy anything with certainty. The rabbis accordingly enacted the *takkanat ha-shuk* ("open market rule") to protect both the purchaser in good faith and the owner. It provided that a man who purchases and pays for an article in the market without being in a position to know that it was stolen, while obliged to return it to the owner, is also entitled to demand a refund of the price from the latter. The owner accordingly recovers his property without causing the purchaser any loss (BK 115a).

In a case where the robber has transferred the stolen property into the possession of a third party and it is consumed by the latter prior to the owner's *ye'ush,* the Talmud records a dispute over whether the owner may demand compensation from one or the other at his option or from the robber only (BK 111b). Again, opinions are divided on the question of whether the heirs (of the robber) are considered as strangers, in the same position as a third party into whose possession the stolen property has come, or whether their possession is as that of the robber from whom they inherited *(ibid.)*. In the post-talmudic period, the courts adopted the practice of restoring the stolen property itself to the owner even after *ye'ush* and a change of possession (Rema, HM 356:7).

Shalom Albeck

The Criminal Law. Stealing is repeatedly prohibited in the Bible. As the prohibition contained in the Decalogue (Ex. 20:13; Deut. 5:17) appears in the context of capital offenses, such as murder and adultery, it has been held to constitute the capital offense of man-stealing (see Abduction), while the prohibition of theft (Lev. 19:11) and robbery (Lev. 19:13), which appear in the context of fraudulent and oppressive dealings with men, were held to constitute the non-capital offense of larceny of money or chattels (Mekh. Yitro 8; Sanh. 86a; BM 61b). The differentiation between theft and robbery is the same as in civil law (see above): theft is committed clandestinely, robbery openly (Yad, Genevah 1:3). It does not matter whether or not the thief (or robber) intended to enrich himself, permanently or at all, or whether he committed the offense only to annoy the owner or as a practical joke, or with the intention of borrowing and returning the thing taken, or with the resolve to pay all damages and penalties (BM 61b; Tosef., BK 10:37; Sifra Kedoshim 2); and it is said that the prohibition extends also to stealing one's own from the thief (BK 27b; Tosef., BK 10:38).

Criminal misappropriations are classified as falling into seven categories: (1) Fraud, that is, "stealing another man's mind"; (2) stealing by way of falsifying weights and measures; (3) stealing things which are useless or the use of which is forbidden to their owner, which is not punishable; (4) misappropriating bills, lands, or consecrated property – for which only restitution has to be made; (5) stealing chattels, for which the penalty is double payment (Ex. 22:8); (6) stealing and selling or slaughtering oxen or sheep, for which the penalty is five or fourfold (Ex. 21:37); and (7) man-stealing for which the punishment is death (Mekh. Mishpatim 13; Tosef., BK 7:8–17).

Although stealing and robbery constitute violations of negative injunctions by overt acts, they are not punishable by flogging, because they entail monetary sanctions and one species of sanction always excludes all others (Yad, Genevah 3:1). But flogging was administered to a thief where the thing stolen had already been returned by him prior to his conviction and he has committed the theft for purposes other than self-enrichment (cf. *Minḥat Ḥinnukh,* no. 224); or where the offender (e.g., an infant or slave) was not capable of owning property from which reparation could be made (Yad, Genevah 1:10). Where the offense of stealing is merged in a graver offense, as for example where stealing is committed by slaughtering on the Sabbath an animal belonging to another, the capital punishment for the violation of the Sabbath absorbs and nullifies any monetary liability for stealing (Ket. 31a; Yad, Genevah 3:1–2); but where the offense is completed before the graver offense is commenced, as where pork is first stolen and then eaten, the monetary penalties for the theft are incurred in addition to the liability to be flogged for eating pork (Ket. 31b; Yad, loc. cit.).

The main difference between civil and criminal misappropriation is that while the civil remedy is restoration *in statu quo ante,* the criminal sanction is the payment of "double" (Ex. 22:8) or quadruple or quintuple (Ex. 21:37). While restitution may be ordered even where no witnesses are available to testify to the theft and to the previous warning administered to the thief (see Penal Law), as, for example, on the admission of the thief himself, the sanction of double, fourfold, or fivefold payment may not be imposed on him otherwise than upon judicial conviction (Ex. 22:8) on the strength of the testimony of witnesses (BK 64b; Yad, Genevah 1:4–5). The purpose of imposing the penalty of double restitution has been said to be that the thief should lose what he had intended his victim to lose (Yad, loc. cit.), and the reason for quadruple or quintuple that he who not only steals, but also sells or slaughters the animal stolen, has proved himself a persistent offender (Tosef., BK 7:2).

Payments recovered as penalties for theft are paid over to the victim ("he shall pay double unto his neighbor": Ex. 22:8). Execution is levied on the chattels of the thief first; if these are found insufficient, then execution proceeds to the best of his lands (Ex. 22:4; BK 7a–b). If he has neither movable nor real property, then the court orders that the thief be sold into slavery ("if he have nothing, then he shall be sold for his theft": Ex. 22:2) and the proceeds of the sale be paid out to the victim; but no such sale is ordered where only the penalties exceeding the value of the thing stolen are irrecoverable: once restitution has been made, the court waits for recovery of penalties until the thief attains the means to make the payments (Kid. 18a). Nor is a woman thief ever sold into slavery (Sot. 3:8). As the thief is sold "for his theft" only (Ex. 22:2), he may not be sold where his value exceeds that of the thing stolen; but where the value of the thing stolen exceeds the proceeds of the sale of the thief, he remains indebted for the balance, which may be recovered from him as a civil debt if and when, after his release (Ex. 21:2; and see Slavery), he acquires property of his own (Yad, Genevah 3:11–14). A thief sold for several thefts from different victims will be held in partnership by all of them, and the proceeds of his sale will be distributed among them *pro rata* (*ibid.* 3:16).

In later talmudic and post-talmudic times, the sale of thieves into slavery became, of course, obsolete. Already in the seventh and eighth centuries, convicted thieves were flogged (*Halakhot Pesukot min ha-Ge'onim,* no. 94), presumably because nothing could be recovered from them. Later, there are ever-increasing indications to the effect that thieves became a grave menace to society, not so much because of the monetary damage they caused within the community, but because of the ill-repute their misconduct brought upon the Jews at large: they were ostracized and expelled from their cities (see *Ḥerem*), and delivered to non-Jewish authorities for adjudication and punishment (cf. e.g., *Takkanot Medinat Mehrin,* no. 265; *Pinkas Hekhsherim shel Kehillat Pozna,* nos. 1614 and 1655) quite apart from such routine punishments as floggings, fines (*Takkanot Medinat Mehrin,* no. 263) and imprisonment (*Tashbeẓ* 3:168) administered to them.

Haim H. Cohn

Bibliography: Ch. Tchernowitz, in: *Zeitschrift fuer vergleichende Rechtswissenschaft,* 25 (1911), 443–58; idem, *Shi'urim be-Talmud,* 1 (1913), 63–121; I. S. Zuri, *Mishpat ha-Talmud,* 6 (1921), 50–58; S. Assaf, *Ha-Onshin Aḥarei Ḥatimat ha-Talmud* (1922), index; Gulak Yesodei, 2 (1922), 219–25; M. Jung, *Jewish Law of Theft* (1929); Herzog, Instit, 1 (1936), 101–5; ET, 5 (1953), 454–86, 517–29; 6 (1954), 199–225; EM, 2 (1954), 464f.; S. Loewenstamm, *ibid.,* 536f.; B.Z.M. Ouziel, in: *Berakhah li-Menaḥem Z. Eichenstein* (1955), 64f.; N. Rakover, in: *Sinai,* 49 (1961), 17–28, 296–307; B. Cohen, in: *Jewish and Roman Law,* 1 (1966), 159–78; 2 (1966), 472–537, 772–5, 786f.; S. Albeck, in: *Bar-Ilan,* 4–5 (1967), 117–31; M. Elon, *Ha-Mishpat Ha-Ivri* (1973), I, 57ff., 175ff., 184, 202ff., 217, II, 329ff., 490ff., 494, 512ff., 534ff., 564ff., 571ff., 618ff., 724, III, 950, 1002ff., 1078 n. 267, 1340ff.

OPPRESSION (Heb. עשק), an offense against property, standing midway between theft and robbery and fraud and often overlapping with either of them. The injunction, rendered in English as "Thou shalt not oppress thy neighbor" (Lev. 19:13), really means (like the injuction immediately following: "nor rob him") that you must not try to enrich yourself by, or derive any material benefit from, any violation of your neighbor's rights. The exact dividing line between oppression (coercion) and robbery gave rise to a discussion among talmudic scholars: where a man failed to restore property to its lawful owner, some held that it was oppression if he admitted the other's ownership, and robbery if he denied it; others held it to be oppression if he asserted that he had already returned it, and robbery if he refused to return it; a third opinion was that it was oppression if he denied that he had ever received the property, and robbery if he asserted that he had already returned it; a fourth scholar held that oppression and robbery were essentially identical terms (BM 111a). The proximity in the Bible of the offenses of stealing, deceit, perjury, oppression, and robbery (Lev. 19:11–13) led an ancient authority to observe that he who steals will eventually commit deceit, perjury, oppression, and robbery (Sifra Kedoshim 3:2); and it is in reliance on the same authority that oppression per se has been held by some to be limited to the crime of withholding a laborer's wages (*ibid.* 3:2; cf. Rashi to Lev. 19:13). The particular oppression of laborers, in witholding their wages, is the subject of a special prohibition, accompanied by a mandatory injunction that the payment of such wages may not be delayed even for one night (Deut. 24:14–15; see Labor Law). The definition of oppression, as it eventually emerged, is given by Maimonides in the following terms: "Oppression is the forceful withholding and not restoring of money which had been received with the owner's consent, as, for instance, where a man had taken a loan or hired a house and, on being asked to return the same, is so violent and hard that nothing can be got out of him" (Yad, Gezelah va-Avedah 1:4; and cf. ḤM 359:8). Although it is in the nature of a criminal offense, no punishment can be inflicted for such oppression, as the proper remedy is an order for the payment of the money due, and civil and criminal sanctions are mutually exclusive (see Flogging). But the guilt before God subsists even after payment, hence a sacrificial penalty is imposed on the oppressor (Lev. 5:23–26). Oppressors are also regarded as criminals so as to disqualify them as witnesses before the court (Sanh. 25b; Yad, Edut 10:4). As against strangers, the prohibition of oppression is extended to cover also intimidations and importunities (Ex. 22:20; 23:9), even where no violation of monetary rights is involved (BM 59b and Rashi *ibid.*). Monetary oppression has frequently been denounced as one of the most reprehensible of offenses (Jer. 21:12; 22:17; Ezek, 22:29; Zech. 7:10; Mal. 3:5; Ps. 62:11; 72:4–5; et al.), and its elimination as one of the conditions precedent to national and religious survival (Jer. 7:6).

In the State of Israel, the offense consists of taking advantage of the distress, the physical or mental weakness, or the inexperience or lightheadedness of another person in order to obtain something not legally due, or profiteering from services rendered or commodities sold (Sect. 13, Penal Law Amendment (Deceit, Blackmail and Extortion) Law, 5723–1963).

Haim H. Cohn

FRAUD, the prohibition against wronging another in selling or buying property (Lev. 25:14) is one of civil (see Ona'ah) rather than criminal law – although, since it is a negative injunction, its violation by any overt act may result in the punishment of flogging (Tos. and *Penei Yehoshu'a* to BM 61a; cf. Maim. Yad, Sanhedrin 18:1). Where reparation can be made by the payment of money, no such punishment may be inflicted in addition (cf. Yad, loc. cit., 2 and Mekhirah 12:1; Ket. 32a; Mak. 4b, 16a). The express repetition, "And ye shall not wrong one another, but thou shalt fear thy God" (Lev. 25:17), was interpreted to prohibit the "wronging" of another not only in commercial transactions but also in noncommercial intercourse: the prohibition extends to "wronging by words" as distinguished from wronging by fraudulent deeds and devices; and wronging by words includes pestering people in vain as well as offending or ridiculing them (BM 4:10). It is said that wronging by words is even more reprehensible than wronging by fraudulent deeds, because while the latter is an offense against property only and can be redressed by the payment of money, the former is an offense against the person and his reputation, for which money will not normally be an adequate compensation (BM 58b; Yad, Mekhirah 14:12–18; see Slander). However, though not constituting a cause of action for damages, wronging by words is not punishable by flogging either, because the mere utterance of words is not considered such an overt act of violation as may be punished in this way (cf. Yad, Sanhedrin 18:2). The admonition "but thou shalt fear thy God" (Lev. 25:17) is said to indicate that even though the offender may escape human punishment, divine retribution is certain to follow (Yad, Mekhirah 14:18; Ibn Ezra to Lev. 25:17).

The fact that fraud, even in the civil law meaning of the term, was in biblical times regarded as eminently criminal in character is well illustrated in Ezekiel's discourse on individual criminal responsibility: the same responsibility attaches for wronging the poor and needy, converting property, and not restoring pledges, as for murder, robbery, and adultery (Ezek. 18:10–13), and for all those misdeeds the same capital punishment is threatened *(ibid.).* Fraud and oppression are usually found in the same context as usury (Ex. 22:20, 24; Lev. 25:14, 17, 27; Deut. 23:17,

20; Ezek. 7–8, 12–13, 17). Fraud has also been held as tantamount to larceny (see Theft and Robbery; Tur, ḤM 227). As fraud and oppression go hand in hand, their victims are often the weak and the underprivileged; hence there are particular prohibitions on fraud against strangers (Ex. 22:20), widows and orphans (Ex. 22:21), and slaves (Deut. 23:17). Wronging widows and orphans is so repulsive in the eyes of God that "if they cry at all unto Me . . . My wrath shall wax hot and I will kill you with the sword, and your wives shall be widows and your children fatherless" (Ex. 22:22–23). Wronging and vexing the poor and the stranger draws forth God's wrath (Ezek. 22:29–31 et al.) and is a cause of national disaster (Jer. 22:3–6).

In post-talmudic times, fraudulent business practices often resulted in the courts barring or suspending the offender from carrying on business. While isolated instances of fraud would be dealt with as civil matters, repeated and notorious fraudulent business practices might be punished by the sequestration of the offender's business, depriving him of his livelihood (S. Assaf, *Ha-Onshin Aḥarei Ḥatimat ha-Talmud* (1922), 43). On other aspects of fraud see also *Gerama.*

In the State of Israel, the criminal law on fraud and kindred offenses has been reformed and expanded by the Penal Law Amendment (Deceit, Blackmail and Extortion) Law, 5723–1963. Fraud is there defined as any representation of fact – past, present, or future – made in writing, by word of mouth, or by conduct, which the maker knew to be false or did not believe to be true. It is made a criminal offense not only to obtain anything by such fraud, but also to obtain anything by any trick not amounting to fraud or by the exploitation of another's mistake or ignorance. Particular instances of fraud mentioned in the Act are pretenses of sorcery or fortune-telling; forgeries and unauthorized alterations of documents and the use or uttering of the same; the fraudulent suppression or concealment of any document or chattel, and the fraudulent incitement of others to make, alter, or conceal documents; as well as the issue of a check where the drawer knew that the banker on whom it was drawn was not bound to honor it.

Bibliography: ET, 1 (1951^3), 160f.; 2 (1949), 18f.; EM, 1 (1950), 149f.; M. Elon, *Ha-Mishpat Ha-Ivri* (1973), II, 526, 536ff., 576, 604ff., 687ff.

Haim H. Cohn

WEIGHTS AND MEASURES. The biblical injunction, "You shall not have in your pouch alternate weights, larger and smaller; you shall not have in your house alternate measures, a larger and a smaller; you must have completely honest weights and completely honest measures" (Deut. 25:13–15) was interpreted not as prohibiting any fraud by means of false weights and measures (which is dealt with in Lev. 19:35–36), but as applying to the manufacture or possession of any weights or measures, including utensils (such as pots or pitchers), which might be used for weighing or measuring and cause false weighing or measuring (BB 89b; Maim. Yad, Genevah 7:3; Sh. Ar., ḤM 231:3). While the manufacture of false weights and measures may be punishable with flogging, the mere possession thereof is not, the violation of a negative injunction being so punishable only where an act is committed, as distinguished from the omission to get rid of the prohibited utensils. In order effectively to enforce the prohibition, courts in talmudical times appointed market inspectors charged with the control of all weights and measures even in private houses (BB 89a). There are detailed provisions for the manner in and the materials with which weights and measures are to be manufactured or repaired so as to be and remain accurate (Maim. Yad, Genevah, 8:4–11; Sh. Ar., ḤM 231:4–11). It is said that the crime of false measures is graver than even those crimes (like incest) which are punishable with *karet* (Divine Punishment); the latter can be expiated by repentance and flogging, whereas in the case of the former repentance is of no avail, since neither the damage caused or the persons to whom restitution has to be made can be ascertained (BB 88b and Rashi ad loc., Maim. Yad, Genevah 7:12). See also *Hafka'at She'arim.*

Bibliography: ET, 1 (1951), 343, s.v. *Eifah ve-Eifah;* EM, (1950), 272f., s.v. *Eifah ve-Eifah;* 4 (1962), 846–78, s.v. *Middot u-Mishkalot;* M. Bloch, *Das mosaisch-talmudische Polizeirecht* (1879), 35ff. Y. Gilat, *Mishnato shel R. Eliezer b. Hyrcanus* (1968), 11–20; idem, in: *Tarbiz,* 28 (1958/59), 230ff.; Sperber, in: *Journal of the Economic and Social History of the Orient,* 8 (1965), 266–71.

Haim H. Cohn

USURY.

Biblical Law. Sources. "If thou lend money to any of My people, even to the poor with thee, thou shalt not be to him as a creditor *(nosheh),* neither shall ye lay upon him interest" (Ex. 22:24). "And if thy brother be waxen poor and his means fail with thee . . . Take no interest of him or increase; but fear thy God; that thy brother may live with thee. Thou shalt not give him thy money upon interest, nor give him thy victuals for increase" (Lev. 25:35–37). "Thou shalt not lend upon interest to thy brother: interest of money, interest of victuals, interest of anything that is lent upon interest. Unto a foreigner thou mayest lend upon interest; but unto thy brother thou shalt not lend upon interest; that the Lord thy God may bless thee in all that thou puttest thy hand unto . . ." (Deut. 23:20–21). The prohibition on taking interest in Exodus and Leviticus seems to be confined to the poor in straits and not to extend to moneylending in the normal course of business, but the deuteronomic prohibition clearly applies to all moneylending, excluding only business dealings with foreigners.

Definition. The biblical term for interest is *neshekh* (Ex. 22:24; Deut. 23:20), but in the levitical text it occurs alongside *tarbit* or *marbit* (25:36–37). In the Jewish Publication Society translation (1962) *neshekh* is rendered as "advance interest" and *tarbit* or *marbit* as "accrued interest" – the one being deducted in advance, the other being added at the time of repayment. This is only one of many interpretations which were made of the terms *neshekh* and *tarbit* from the time of the Mishnah (BM 5:1) onward and by no means the best one. One commentator regards *neshekh* as accumulating interest and *tarbit* as a fixed sum of interest which never increase (Ramban to Lev. 25:36). The most authoritative view is that of Rava, that there is no difference in meaning between *neshekh* and *tarbit* (BM 60b); but while Rava maintains that the Torah used two synonyms in order to make the prohibition of interest a twofold one *(ibid.),* the better explanation etymologically would be that *neshekh,* meaning bite, was the term used for the exaction of interest from the point of view of the debtor, and *tarbit* or *marbit,* meaning increase, was the term used for the recovery of interest by the creditor (Solomon Luntschitz, *Keli Yakar,* Be-Ḥukkotai, Lev. 25:36).

The prohibition on interest is not a prohibition on usury in the modern sense of the term, that is, excessive interest, but of all, even minimal, interest. There is no difference in law between various rates of interest, as all interest is prohibited.

Legal Character of Prohibition. It has been said that the prohibition on interest rests on two grounds: firstly, that the prosperous ought to help the indigent, if not by gifts, then at least by free loans; and secondly, that interest (or excessive interest) was seen to lie at the root of social ruin and was therefore to be outlawed in toto. Both these considerations would apply only internally: there could be no obligation to help foreigners, nor was public policy concerned with their well-being. Moreover, moneylending transactions with foreigners were motivated solely by the legitimate desire to make profits, while the internal economy was eminently agrarian and had no money markets of any importance. It follows from the charitable nature of the prohibition on interest that its violation was not regarded as a criminal offense to which any penal sanctions attached, but rather as a moral transgression; in other words, while taking interest would not entail any punishment, granting free loans and refraining from taking interest would lead to God's rewards and blessings (Deut. 23:21 and Ramban thereto). It was only in the prophecies of Ezekiel that usury came to be identified with the gravest of crimes: it is mentioned in the context of larceny, adultery, homicide, and other such "abominations" which are worthy of death (18:11–13). The threat of death for usury was later interpreted as the divine sanction against irrecoverable and illegitimate self-enrichment (BM 61b). "He that augmenteth his substance by interest and increase" is listed among the "evil men" (Prov. 28:8); while "He that putteth not out his money on interest" is among the upright and righteous (Ps. 15:5).

Implementation. The prohibition on taking interest does not appear to have been generally observed in biblical times. The creditor *(nosheh),* far from giving free loans, is often described as exacting and implacable (cf. I Sam. 22:2; II Kings 4:1; Isa. 50:1; et al.); and the prophet decries those who have "taken interest and increase" and forgotten God (Ezek. 22:12). Nehemiah had to rebuke the noble and the rich for exacting interest, "every one to his brother" (Neh. 5:7); and he had formally and solemnly to adjure them to abstain from levying execution (12–13). From the Elephantine papyri it appears that among the Jews in Egypt in the fifth century b.c.e. it was a matter of course that interest would be charged on loans: not only did they disregard the biblical injunctions as far as the taking of interest was concerned, but they made no recourse to any legal fictions in order to evade the prohibition (R. Yaron, *Mishpat shel Mismekhei Yev* (1961) 136).

Talmudic Law. Extension of Prohibition. It is not only the creditor who takes interest who is violating the biblical prohibition, but also the debtor who agrees to pay interest, the guarantor who guarantees the debt which bears interest, the witnesses who attest the creation of an interest-bearing debt, and even the scribe who writes out the deed (BM 5:11; BM 75b; Yad, Malveh 4:2). This is one of the very rare cases in which accessories to the offense are held responsible (see Penal Law). "Although the creditor and debtor transgress these biblical prohibitions, there is no flogging for it, as the interest must be repaid" (Yad, Malveh 4:3). The *Ḥinnukh* (no. 74) says further that none of the accessories is flogged "for since even the creditor is not flogged . . . it would not be right that those who are mere accessories should be liable for flogging."

The most far-reaching extensions of the prohibition relate, however, to the nature of the "interest" prohibited. Interest is no longer only the lending of four dinars for five, or of one bushel of wheat for two (BM 5:1), but is extended to all benefits which smack of interest or might look like it. Thus, the borrower may not allow the lender to live on his premises without payment of rent or at a reduced rent (BM 5:2), and if he had resided there without paying rent before lending the money, he must now be charged rent (BM 64b). The prohibition of lending one bushel of wheat for two was also extended to the lending of one bushel of wheat for one, since it was possible that the value of the wheat might increase between the date of the loan and the date of the return, and such increase in value would amount to prohibited interest (BM 5:9; TJ, BM 5:7, 10d); but the rule does not apply where seeds are lent for sowing and not for consumption (BM 5:8), and where the borrower possesses even the smallest quantity of the same species, he may borrow any quantity (BM 75a; Yad, Malveh 10:1–5). Where two men agree to do work for each other in turn, they may agree only on the same kind of work for each, as otherwise the work of one might be more valuable than that of the other and thus amount to prohibited interest (BM 5:10; Yad, Malveh 7:11). Gifts that one man may send to another in view of a forthcoming request for a loan, or in gratitude for a loan granted and returned, fall within the prohibition on interest – as are also "words," conveying to the lender, for instance, any valuable information (BM 5:10), or even greetings, where they would not otherwise have been exchanged (BM 75b; Tosef., BM 6:17). A mortgagee, even if he is in possession of the mortgaged property, is not allowed to take its produce; if he has taken it, he must either return it or set it off against the capital debt (BM 67a–b; Yad, Malveh 6:1–8; see also Lien; Pledge).

Interest in the guise of sale was also prohibited. Fruit and other agricultural produce may not be sold unless and until its market price is established (BM 5:7), for otherwise the purchaser might, by paying in advance a price below the eventual market value, receive interest on his money; such advance purchase amounted in effect to financing the farmers, and were thus in the nature of loans rather than sales. But there is nothing to prevent the farmer from selling below the market value, once that value has been established: this would no longer be a disguised loan but a genuine if ill-advised sale (BM 63b; Yad, Malveh 9:1), subject always to the seller's remedies for *ona'ah* (BM 4:4). Sales of products without current market values would be recognized as such, and not be invalidated as disguised loans, only where the goods sold were actually in the hands of the seller at the time of the sale (Tosef., BM 6:2–5), or, where they had to be processed or manufactured, were almost completed at the time of the sale (BM 74a; Yad, Malveh 9:2).

Any payment is prohibited interest which compensates a party to any transaction for money being left, for any length of time, in the hands of the other party, although it should, according to law or custom, have already been paid over (BM 63b). Thus, as rent is legally due only at the end of the period of lease, a discount may be given for rent paid in advance (see Lease and Hire); but as the purchase price for goods or land sold is payable at the time of the sale, any price increase for later payment would amount to prohibited interest (BM 5:2; BM 65a; Yad, Malveh 8:1).

A further notable extension of the prohibition on interest relates to contracts of partnership. An arrangement by which one partner finances a business and the other manages it, and losses are borne by the managing partner only while the profits are shared between them is illegal, for it comes within the prohibition on interest (BM 70a; BM 5:6; Yad, Malveh 8:12). Where the financing partner bears or shares the losses, such an arrangement is valid only if the managing partner is being paid a salary for his work instead of, or in addition to, a share in the profits (BM 5:4; Yad, Malveh 5:9).

All these talmudic extensions of the prohibitions on interest are known as *avak ribbit,* i.e., the dust of interest, as distinguished from *ribbit keẓuẓah,* i.e., interest proper in an amount or at a rate agreed upon between lender and borrower (BM 61b, 67a, et al.). The difference in law between *avak ribbit* and *ribbit keẓuẓah* is that the latter, if it has been paid by the borrower to the lender, is recoverable from the lender, while the former, once paid, is not recoverable, though a contract tainted with the dust of interest will not be enforced (BM 61b; Yad, Malveh 4:6; Sh. Ar., YD 161:1–2; see also Contract).

Evasion of Prohibition. It has been said that the evasion of the prohibitions on interest reflects the conflict between law and life (Globus, see bibl., p. 39). It is remarkable how the talmudic jurists extended the prohibition on interest so as to cover, and invalidate, transactions far removed from the loans to which the biblical prohibition had attached, and at the same time sought ways and means to validate transactions clearly or conceivably falling within that prohibition. This phenomenon can only be explained by the change of economic conditions: it was in the amoraic period in Babylonia that the prohibitory laws against interest proved to be no longer compatible with the economic needs of the community; and ever since the necessity of finding legal subterfuges to evade those laws has persisted. The prohibition of price increase for payment which is made after a time lapse was practically abolished by the provision that any price may be agreed upon and recovered so long as the increase involved is not expressly but only tacitly stipulated (BM 65a; YD 173:1). The mishnaic rule that a managing partner must be paid a salary in order to validate the partnership agreement was set at nought in practice by the provision that such a salary need be nominal only (BM 68b). Profit-sharing partnerships were validated by regarding the investment of the financing partner as half loan and half deposit. While the borrower is responsible for the loan, the bailee is not responsible for the loss of the deposit; thus, the financing partner (as bailor) will also bear his share in the losses, and the partnership is legal (BM 104b). Even where the financing partner's share in the profits is redeemed in advance by a down payment, the agreement is upheld, provided that the business could reasonably be expected to be profitable (TJ, BM 5:8, 10c); and, later, deeds were formulated in which a pre-estimate of the expected profits was stipulated in advance as a fixed sum (BM 68a).

A farmer who had received a loan was allowed to make a formal conveyance of his lands (or part of them) to his creditor and still remain on his lands as his creditor's tenant; the creditor would be entitled to the produce of the land, not as interest on the loan but as income from his property (BM 68a). One jurist even held that is was permissible to let money on hire, like chattels, against payment of rent, as distinguished from giving a loan against payment of interest (BM 69b). A vendor may sell goods on credit at a price of 100 units payable at a future date, and immediately repurchase the goods at the price of 90 units payable cash down: each of the two contracts of sale would be valid (BM 62b).

Another form of evasion was to lend money on interest to a non-Jew, in order that the non-Jew might relend the money to the intended Jewish debtor; both lending transactions are valid (BM 61b).

Some of these forms of evasion, though practiced in talmudic times, were not accepted as the *halakhah* (BM 68a per Rava; Yad, Malveh 5:8; 5:16; 6:4–5); others, though recognized as legally valid and feasible, were deprecated as reprehensible and forbidden (BM 61b–62b; Yad, Malveh 5:15) because of the stratagem involved in the device *(ha'aramah)*.

Sanctions. Originally, courts appear to have been empowered to fine the creditor for taking interest by refraining from enforcing even his claim for the repayment of the capital (Tosef., BM 5:22), but the rule evolved that taking interest did not affect the creditor's enforceable right to have his capital debt repaid (BM 72a; Yad, Malveh 4:6). Where a bill, however, includes both capital and interest without differentiating between them, the bill is not enforceable (YD 161:11; Sh. Ar., ḤM 52:1), and "whoever finds a bill which includes interest, shall tear it up" (Tosef., BM 5:23; see also Contract). Moneylenders who take interest are disqualified as witnesses and are not administered oaths (Sanh. 3:3), and even the borrower who pays interest is disqualified (Sanh. 25a). In their moral turpitude, moneylenders who take interest are likened to apostates who deny God (Tosef., BM 6:17) and to shedders of blood (BM 61b); and they have no share in the world to come (Mekh. Mishpatim 19). They are doomed to lose all their property and go bankrupt (BM 71a; Sh. Ar., YD 160:2).

Legality of Interest. While biblical law allowed the taking of interest from foreigners, excluding alien residents (Lev. 25:35), talmudic law extended the exemption: "One may borrow from them [foreigners] and lend them on interest; similarly in the case of an alien resident" (BM 5:6,70b–71a). However lawful interest transactions with foreigners were, they were looked upon with disapproval: some jurists held that they were permissible only when no other means of subsistence was available (BM 70b); others would allow them only to persons learned in the law, as the uneducated might fall into the error of believing that interest is permissible in general (BM 71a). The psalmist's praise of the man who would not lend his money on interest (Ps. 15:5) was interpreted to apply to the man who would not take interest from a foreigner (Mak. 24a).

Post-Talmudic Law. Transactions Among Jews. The talmudic evasions of the prohibition against interest served as precedents for the legalization of transactions involving interest. Thus it was deduced from the evasions reported in the Talmud that it would be permissible for a lender to lend 100 units to a businessman for him to use in his business; when it had increased to 200, the lender would be entitled to the 200, provided that he had paid the borrower some salary in consideration of his work (*Piskei ha-Rosh* BM 5:23; *Mordekhai* BM 319). Rashi is reported to have ruled that you may send your friend to take a loan on interest from another for you, or you may send your friend to give your money on interest to another; for interest is prohibited only as between lender and borrower, but not as between their respective agents. The general rule that a man's agent is like himself (see Agency) would not apply here, as the taking of interest is a criminal offense, and in criminal matters no man can be made responsible for the deed of another (see Penal Law; *Mordekhai* BM 338).

In time, a standard form of legalization of interest was established, known as *hetter iskah,* meaning the permission to form a partnership. A deed, known as *shetar iskah,* was drawn up and attested by two witnesses, stipulating that the lender would supply a certain sum of money to the borrower for a joint venture; the borrower alone would manage the business and he would guarantee the lender's investment against all loss; he would also guarantee to the lender a fixed amount of minimum profit. The deed would also contain a stipulation that the borrower would be paid a nominal sum as a salary, as well as an agreement on the part of the lender to share the losses. In order to render this loss-sharing agreement nugatory, provision would normally be made for such loss to be proved by particular, mostly unobtainable, evidence (*Naḥalat Shivah,* no. 40; cf. *Terumat ha-Deshen,* Resp. no. 302). The amount of the capital loan plus the guaranteed minimum profit would be recoverable on the deed at the stipulated time it matured.

In the course of the centuries this form of legalizing interest has become so well established that nowadays all interest transactions are freely carried out, even in compliance with Jewish law, by simply adding to the note or contract concerned the words *al-pi hetter iskah.* The prohibition on interest has lost all practical significance in business transactions, and is now relegated to the realm of friendly and charitable loans where, indeed, it had originated.

Transactions with non-Jews. In 1179 the Church decreed that the taking of interest was forbidden by Scripture as well as by the laws of nature, and that all Christian usurers would be liable to excommunication. As canon law did not apply to Jews, this decree did not prevent them from lending money on interest, and moneylending soon became a typically Jewish business. The Jews were practically forced into it by the severe restrictions placed upon them in the pursuit of any other trade or profession in most countries of Europe. From the point of view of Jewish law, the taking of interest from non-Jews was permitted; and the talmudic restriction that it should not be done unless there were no other means of subsistence was duly held to be compiled with: "If we nowadays allow interest to be taken from non-Jews, it is because there is no end to the yoke and the burden king and ministers impose on us, and everything we take in the minimum for our subsistence, and anyhow we are condemned to live in the midst of the nations and cannot earn our living in any other manner except by money dealings with them; therefore the taking of interest is not to be prohibited" (Tos. to BM 70b s.v. *tashikh*). With the renewed change in circumstances, the prohibition on taking interest would apply to Jews and non-Jews alike (YD 159:1).

See also *Hekdesh;* Lien; Partnership; Pledge; and *Takkanot.*

Bibliography: J. Marcuse, *Das biblisch-talmudische Zinsenrecht* (1895); E. Cohn, in: *Zeitschrift fuer vergleichende Rechtswissenschaft,* 18 (1905), 37–72; J. Hejcl, *Das alttestamentliche Zinsverbot im Lichte der ethnologischen Jurisprudenz sowie des altorientalischen Zinswesens* (1907); H. L. Strack, in: *Realencyklopaedie fuer protestantische Theologie und Ḳirche,* 21 (1908[3]), 518–21; I. S. Zuri, *Mishpat ha-Talmud,* 5 (1921), 63f., 134–9; Gulak, Yesodei, 2 (1922), 72, 107, 172–6; I. Bernfeld, *Das Zinsverbot bei den Juden nach talmudisch-rabbinischen Recht* (1924); S. Rosenbaum, in: *Ha-Mishpat ha-Ivri,* 2 (1926), 27, 191–4; E. L. Globus, in: *Ha-Mishpat,* 2 (1927), 23–43; E. S. Rappaport, in: *Zeitschrift fuer vergleichende Rechtswissenschaft,* 47 (1932/33), 256–378; A. Gulak, *Toledot ha-Mishpat be Yisrael bi-Tekufat ha-Talmud,* 1 (*Ha-Ḥiyyuv ve-Shi'budav,* 1939), 45, 117f., 145; Herzog, Instit, 2 (1939), 135; S. J. Rabinowitz, in: *Yavneh,* 3 (1949), 165–74; R. Katzenelboigen, *ibid.,* 175–9; B. N. Nelson, *The Idea of Usury, from Tribal Brotherhood to Universal Otherhood* (1949); ET, 1 (1951[3]), 46f.; 2 (1949), 51; 4 (1952), 111; 7 (1956), 394; 9 (1959), 714–22; 10 (1961), 102f., 108; J. Rosenthal, in: *Talpioth,* 5 (1951/52), 475–92; 6 (1952/53), 130–52; T. Be'eri, in: *Ha-Torah ve-ha-Medinah,* 5–6 (1952/54), 296–301; J. Segal, *ibid.,* 9–10 (1957/59), 451–90; E. Neufeld, in: JQR, 44 (1953/54), 194–204; idem, in: HUCA, 26 (1955), 355–412; S. Stein, in: JSS, 1 (1956), 141–64; B. Rabinowitz-Te'omim, in: *Ha-Torah ve-ha-Medinah,* 11–13 (1959–62), 16–45; J. T. Noonan, *The Scholastic Analysis of Usury* (1957); N. N. Lemberger, in: *No'am,* 2 (1958/59), 33–37; J. Wassermann, *ibid.,* 3 (1959/60), 195–203; M. N. Lemberger, *ibid.,* 4 (1960/61), 251–7; Z. Domb, *ibid.,* 258–65; B. Cohen, *Jewish and Roman Law,* 2 (1966), 433–56, 784f.; S. E. Loewenstamm, in: EM, 5 (1968), 929f.; M. Elon, Mafte'aḥ, 302–7; idem, in: *Ḥok u-Mishpat,* 1 (1955), issue 22, pp. 6–8; idem, *Ha-Mishpat Ha-Ivri* (1973), I, 163ff., 206ff., II, 489, 660, 730, 787ff., III, 1069, 1073.

Haim H. Cohn

FORGERY. Forgery of documents is not, either in biblical or in talmudic law, a criminal offense: it may be an instrument for the perpetration of fraud and come within the general prohibition of fraudulent acts (Lev. 19:35; Deut. 25:13–16) or fraudulent words (Lev. 25:14). Nevertheless, it is a recognized evil which the law is called upon to prevent, and there are detailed provisions in the Talmud for the making of legally binding documents in such a manner that they cannot be forged: thus, documents must be written on and with material that cannot be effaced (Git. 19a et al.) and is enduring (Git. 22b, 23a); precautions must be taken that no space be left between the text of the document and the signatures, so that nothing could be inserted after signing (BB 162–7). The rule evolved that a document *(Shetar)* was valid only if it be executed in the manner of unforgeable bills *(Ke-Tikkun Shitrei Yisrael she-Einan Yekholin le-Hizdayyef)* to which nothing at all could be added and from which nothing could be erased (Maim. Yad, Malveh ve-Loveh 27:1).

Where a document appeared on the face of it to have been tampered with or added to, so that a suspicion of forgery arose in the eyes of the court, recourse was had to compulsory measures in order to induce the plaintiff to confess that he was suing on a false document (BB 167a). It is not clear what these compulsory measures were: literally translated, the reports say that the plaintiff was "bound, and then admitted the document to be false" (the word used for "binding" is the same as that used for the binding of a person to be flogged (cf. Mak. 3:12), as distinguished from and preliminary to the flogging itself (Mak. 3:13); or for the functions of non-judicial officers attached to the courts, who "bind and flog people on orders of the court"; Rashi to Deut. 1:15). The binding *(koftin)* was later interpreted to mean compelling (*kofin;* Meir ha-Levi Abulafia, quoted in *Beit Yosef,* ḤM 42 n. 3–5), and the compulsion was authorized to be carried out by floggings (Tur and Sh. Ar., ḤM 42:3). It is, however, to be noted that these floggings – or any other compulsory measures – were not sanctions or punishments imposed for forging the documents, but only means to extort confessions of forgery: when a forgery was admitted or proved, the only sanction was that the claim based upon any such forged document was dismissed. It was only in much later times that forgers were punished by the courts, or more often – presumably because of the private law character of forgery in Jewish law – delivered for trial and punishment to the gentile courts (Assaf, *Ha-Onshin* 144). Even the notion that forgers of documents could be disqualified on that account from testifying or taking an oath was dismissed as unwarranted (*Ḥatam Sofer,* ḤM 39; *Pitḥei Teshuvah,* ḤM 34:7, n. 17).

In order to have a claim based on a document dismissed, it was not always necessary to prove that it was false – in certain circumstances it sufficed that it was reputed to be false (Ket. 36b; Maim. Yad, Edut 22:5). On the other hand, even the admitted forgery of a document would not necessarily vitiate a claim, as where a true document had been in existence and lost (BB 32b; Yad, To'en ve-Nitan 15:9). A man ought not to lend out his seal, so as not to tempt others to use it without his authority (BM 27b; Yev. 120b); his seal appearing (e.g., on a barrel of wine), it is presumed not to have been tampered with (Av. Zar. 69b). In the State of Israel, the Criminal Law Amendment (Offenses of Fraud, Extraction and Exploitation) Law 5723–1963 replaced the Criminal Code Ordinance 1936 mitigating the previous penalties for forgery (other than forgery of bank notes).

Bibliography: M. Bloch, *Das mosaisch-talmudische Polizeirecht* (1879), 39, no. 20; Gulak, Yesodei, 2 (1922), 134–6; 4 (1922), 165–7; S. Assaf, *Ha-Onshin Aḥarei Ḥatimat ha-Talmud* (1922), passim; A. Gulak, *Urkundenwesen im Talmud* (1935), passim; M. Elon, *Ha-Mishpat Ha-Ivri* (1973), II, 642.

Haim H. Cohn

INFORMER (Heb. מוסר or מסור) is a Jew who denounces a fellow-Jew to a non-Jew, and more particularly to non-Jewish authorities, thereby causing actual or potential damage. The damage may be caused or apprehended either to the person denounced and his property, or to the community at large, or to some specified or unspecified group of persons.

A distinction is made between the denunciation (*mesirah,* "delivery") of money and the denunciation of persons, but the prohibition of informing applies to both classes in the same manner. It is no defense to a charge of informing that the person denounced is a sinner and wicked, or has caused the informer grief or harm – no informer will ever have a share in the world to come (Maim. Yad, Ḥovel u-Mazzik 8:9). The only exception seems to be that a Jew may inform on another Jew who had informed against him – for as the informer is liable to be killed, he must *a fortiori* be liable to be informed against (Rema ḤM 388:9). Similarly, a man may save himself from violence by denouncing his attacker if he has no other means of escape (*Darkhei Moshe* ḤM 388; *Yam shel Shelomo* BK 8:42).

Talmudic Law. Instances of informing reported in the Talmud are scarce. A judge who had been denounced to the authorities for having unlawfully exercised jurisdiction sentenced the informer to death (Ber. 58a). A death sentence was likewise passed on a litigant who repeatedly threatened to denounce his adversary, the court apparently being satisfied that he would indeed do so and that irreparable damage might ensue (BK 117a). The underlying rationale has been held to be that when a man is going to kill you, you may kill him first (Ber. 58a), and an impending denunciation was held to be tantamount to an immediate threat of killing. The threat is no less immediate and substantial for the reason that only so long as nobody was actually killed there must always remain a doubt as to whether anybody would indeed be killed – the probability that that would be the result of the denunciation suffices to warrant drastic counteraction (Rashba, Resp., vol. 1, no. 181). In order to save property from the reach of informers, false vows and oaths are permissible to prove its alienation (Ned. 3:4).

Like apostates, informers ought not to be saved from danger, even of their lives (Av. Zar. 26b); it has been said that "it is a good deed to let them perish and bring them down into the pit of destruction" (Maim., Akkum ve-Ḥukkoteihem 10:1).

Medieval Law. Historical Background. Denunciations have rightly been described as the canker of Jewish medieval society (I. Abrahams, *Jewish Life in the Middle Ages* (1932[2]); Kaufmann, in JQR, 8 (1896), 227). Obadiah of Bertinoro relates a report of the Jewish community of Palermo which may be valid for many other communities of the time: "Among the Jews there are many informers who have no sense of right or wrong and who continually betray one another shamelessly. If one Jew hates another, he conjures up some false accusation against him that is absolutely without foundation" (Transl. in: J. R. Marcus, *The Jew in the Medieval World* (1960), 394f.). Jewish courts saw themselves called upon to combat this mischief as best they could.

Denunciations always fell on all-too-willing ears, both ecclesiastical and secular authorities being anyway hopelessly prejudiced against Jews. The informers not only wrought easy vengeance on whoever had wronged them, but they not unreasonably hoped to render themselves useful and important in the eyes of the authorities by volunteering such information. The testimony of these informers, presumably well-informed Jews themselves, was generally quite sufficient to warrant massacres or expulsions and plunder.

Penal Law. The law was laid down by Maimonides as follows: "It is lawful to kill the informer anywhere, even at this time when capital jurisdiction has ceased. It is lawful to kill him before he has informed: when he says, I am going to deliver [i.e., denounce] the person or the money – regardless of the amount involved – of X into their hands, he has rendered himself liable to death; if, on being warned not to commit the crime, he dares to insist on informing, the court is bound to have him killed. But when he [is indicted after having] already denounced the other person, it seems to me that he may not any longer be killed, unless it is reasonably apprehended that he might continue and inform on others. And it is a frequent occurrence in the cities of the Maghrib (see English translation of Book of Torts, H. Klein, Yale University (1954)) either to kill informers who must be feared to make denunciations, or to deliver them into the hands of the non-Jews [i.e., non-Jewish courts] to have them killed, flogged, or imprisoned as their guilt requires. So may a man who causes grief or damage to the community be delivered into the hands of non-Jews to have him flogged, imprisoned, or fined – but not a man who causes grief or damage to an individual. Nor may the property of an informer be confiscated, for although his person is liable to perish, his property ought to go to his heirs" (Maim., Ḥovel u-Mazzik 8:10–11).

Sentencing informers to death was regarded as a duty (a *mitzvah*) of the court (Maim., Ḥovel u-Mazzik 8:10–11; Ribash, Resp. no. 79), as it had to be assumed that, unless the informer was eliminated in time, the disaster likely to be caused by him could not be prevented. Thus it has been said that a court refraining from having the informer killed will be responsible and be punished for anything that may happen as if the court itself had been the informer (*Zikhron Yehudah,* no. 75). There it is reported that Joseph ibn Migash had an informer executed on the Day of Atonement which fell on a Sabbath at the hour of *ne'ilah* – which shows how sacred a duty the elimination of informers was conceived by great judges. The differentiation between an informer who had to be eliminated before doing his misdeed and was therefore liable to death, and an informer who had already done his misdeed and was therefore no longer liable to death (unless he was likely to repeat it), would indicate that the death penalty for the informer was in the nature of a preventive rather than of a punitive measure, a supposition corroborated by the special procedural provisions set out below.

Notwithstanding the duty of having informers killed, the death penalty was not generally regarded as compulsory and obligatory but rather as the maximum penalty. In many instances there were bodily mutilations, such as cutting out the tongue or gouging out the eyes (Rosh, Resp. no. 17:8; Maharam of Rothenburg, Resp., ed. Prague, no 485; Rema ḤM 388:10) or cutting off hands and feet (*Takkanot Maehren,* ed. by I. Halpern, 124 no. 374), so as to render the informer incapable of carrying out his evil designs. On the other hand, such mutilations were decried as ineffective and unsuited to replace the death penalty (*Yam shel Shelomo* Yev. 10:20; Maharam of Lublin, Resp. no. 138). In cases in which monetary damage only was caused or apprehended, the usual sanction was the *ḥerem* (BK 117a; *Tashbeẓ* 3:158), often accompanied by excommunication and exile. There were many communities in which annual general bans were pronounced against people who knew of informers or their plans and failed to bring them to the notice of the court (*Takkanot Va'ad Arba Araẓot,* quoted by Assaf, *Ha-Onshin . . .,*), and against anybody who would have resort to non-Jewish authorities and thereby cause damage to any Jew (*Takkanot Rabbenu Tam,* quoted in Maharam of Rothenburg, Resp., ed. Cremona, no. 78, *Takkanot* of the Portuguese community in Hamburg, quoted by Assaf, *Ha-Onshin . . .* no. 92).

A good example of a scale of penalties according to the gravity of the offense is provided by *takkanot* made in Castile in

1432: an informer who has denounced another without causing actual damage is fined 100 ducats and imprisoned for ten days; if actual damage was caused, he must also make good the damage. If the denunciation was to non-Jewish authorities and no damage was caused, he is fined 200 ducats and imprisoned for 20 days; if monetary damage was caused, he must also make good the damage and is ostracized for ten days; if physical injury (including arrest) was caused, the punishment is at the free discretion of the court. Denunciations other than of individual persons are punished, on a first conviction, with 100 lashes and expulsion from the town; on the second conviction, the penalty is increased; on a third conviction, the penalty will be death (Assaf, *Ha-Onshin . . .*, no. 92; Baer, Spain, 2 (1961), 264f., Elon, *Ha-Mishpat Ha-Ivri,* II, 647ff.). Where the evidence was not sufficient for a conviction – e.g., where there was one single witness only – but the court considered the suspect a security risk for the community, the Castilian *takkanot* provided that a mark should be set on his forehead by burning it with a hot iron *(ibid.)*. All informers and suspected informers were disqualified as witness and would not be allowed to take an oath (Maim., Ḥovel u-Mazzik 8:8; ḤM 388:8; Resp. Radbaz, pt. I no. 348; Maharashdam, Resp. ḤM no. 355).

Procedure and Evidence. Isaac b. Sheshet – who was himself, together with two other great scholars of his time, Nissim Gerondi and Ḥasdai Crescas, the victim of a denunciation in about 1375, in pursuance of which he was arrested and later released on bail (Ribash, Resp. nos. 373, 376) – laid down five special rules of evidence and procedure applying to trials of informers only: (1) they may be interrogated, and if they confess, may be convicted on their own confessions; (2) attorneys may be appointed to defend them only after their interrogation has been completed; (3) they must be detained pending trial and may not be released on bail; (4) the testimony of the witnesses for the prosecution may be taken in their absence (to the same effect: Rosh, Resp. 17:1); (5) the fact that the complainant who laid the charge against the informer may be incompetent as a witness does not affect the validity of the charge (Ribash, Resp. nos. 234–9). Further procedural and evidentiary facilities had already been allowed much earlier by Solomon b. Abraham Adret; namely, that in trials of informers it would not matter that the court might not be properly constituted, and that informers need no previous warning that what they were going to do was punishable by law (see Penal Law, Evidence); in general, all the procedural and evidentiary safeguards prescribed in capital cases did not apply to informers, so long as you "go after the ascertainment of the truth and the prevention of damage . . . " (*Iggeret ha-Rashba,* published by D. Kaufmann, in: JQR, 8 (1896), 228ff.).

Jurisdiction and Costs. Instead of trying informers themselves, many Jewish courts preferred to hand them over to the royal courts for trial if a charge could only be made out against them under the law of the land (Ribash, Resp. nos. 79 and 239; Rashbash, Resp. no. 177). However, as the informers were, as a rule, welcome instruments in the hands of the authorities, if only as a means of extorting money from the Jewish community, their courts could rarely be counted on to mete out justice to them. In many countries Jewish courts tried, and sometimes succeeded, to obtain the royal assent to their own exercise of capital jurisdiction. It appears that the non-Jewish (royal or lower) authorities often had to be brided into allowing or suffering such jurisdiction, or for helping the court to execute judgments of expulsion. Kings are reported to have demanded monetary compensation for the loss of taxpayers before allowing judgments of expulsion to be executed. That the costs involved in prosecuting and punishing informers must therefore have been very substantial is also shown by rulings to the effect that the whole community must bear these costs, and each individual member is taxed with his share thereof (Rosh, Resp. no. 6:22; Ribash, Resp. no. 79).

See also Taxation.

Bibliography: D. Kaufmann, in: JQR, 8 (1896), 217–38; M. Frank, *Kehillot Ashkenaz u-Vattei Dineihen* (1937), index, s.v. *Dinei Mesirah;* Baer, Urkunden, 1 (1929), index, s.v. *Malsin,* 2 (1936), index; s.v. *Denunzianten;* Baer, Spain, index; Baron, Community, index, Dinur, Golah, 2 (1966), 402–9; H. H. Ben-Sasson (ed.), *Toledot Am Yisrael,* 3 (1969), index, s.v. *Malshinut;* I. Halpern (ed.), *Takkanot Medinat Mehrin* (1951), index, s.v. *Massur;* idem, *Pinkas Va'ad Arba Arazot* (1945), index, s.v. *Malshinut;* B. D. Weinryb, *Texts and Studies in the Communal History of Polish Jewry* (1950), 53ff.; S. Dubnow, *Pinkas ha-Medinah O Va'ad ha-Kehillot ha-Rashiyyot bi-Medinat Lita* (1925), index, s.v. *Moser;* Dubnow, Hist. Russ., 1 (1916), 337–78; 2 (1918), 84–85; J. Levitats, *Jewish Community in Russia 1772–1844* (1943), index; S. Ginsberg, *Historishe Verk,* 1 (1937), 238–65; (1937), 178–87; Heb. trans. in his: *Ketavim Historiyyim* (1944), 152–78; M. Kayserling, in: *Jahrbuch fuer die Geschichte der Juden und des Judentums,* 4 (1869), 263–334; I. Loeb, in: REJ, 13 (1886), 187–216; S. Assaf, *Ha-Onshin, Aḥarei Ḥatimat ha-Talmud* (1922); Finkelstein, Middle Ages; I. Epstein, *The Responsa of Rabbi Solomon ben Adreth of Barcelona . . .* (1925), 49–52; idem, *The Responsa of Rabbi Simon ben Ẓemaḥ Duran . . .* (1930), 46, 65–69; A. M. Hershman, *Rabbi Isaac ben Sheshet Perfet and his Times* (1943), 88–90; G. Horowitz, *The Spirit of Jewish Law* (1953), 228–30, 621–3; I. Szczepanski, in: *Sefer Yovel Federbusch* (1960), 343–51; M. Elon, *Ha-Mishpat Ha-Ivri* (1973), I, 9, 11, II, 435ff., 635ff., 644ff., 647ff.

Haim H. Cohn

BRIBERY, making a gift to a person in authority, especially a judge. The injunction not to take bribes is several times repeated in the Bible, twice with the reason given that "bribes blind the clear-sighted and upset the pleas of the just" (Ex. 23:8; Deut. 16:19). This was later interpreted to mean not only that a corrupt judge tends to identify the interests of the donor with his own and is thus blind to the rights of the other party (Ket. 105b, Shab. 119a), but also that such a judge would not grow old without becoming physically blind (Pe'ah 8:9). The warning is also sounded that the taking of bribes might lead to the shedding of innocent blood (Deut. 27:25). God is praised as being unreceptive to bribes (Deut. 10:17, et al.), and as human judges are generally exhorted to imitate divine qualities (Shab. 133b; Mekh., Shirah 3) so they are urged to be impartial, and not susceptible to bribes (II Chron. 19:7) and reminded that judicial services should be given free (Bek. 29a). There is no penalty and no non-penal sanction prescribed in the Bible for taking bribes. The donor of bribes is blamed as a tempter or accomplice of the taker (Maim. Yad, Sanhedrin 23:2; Sh. Ar., ḤM 9:1), transgressing the injunction "you shall not place a stumbling block before the blind" (Lev. 19:14). Bribery seems to have been rather widespread (cf. I. Sam. 8:3), or else the prophets would hardly have denounced it so vehemently (Isa. 1:23; 5:23; 33:15; Ezek. 22:12; Amos 5:12; Micah 7:3), but it was in the nature of unethical misconduct rather than of a criminal offense.

Under talmudic law, where no penalty was prescribed in the Bible for the violation of a negative injunction, the transgressor was liable to be flogged (Mak. 16a; Tosef., Mak. 5:16; see *Minḥat Bikkurim* for reading). In the case of bribery this provision was largely academic, as the requisite witnesses would not normally be available – the act being always committed in secret (cf. Ibn Ezra to Deut. 27:14). The rule was therefore evolved that taking a bribe invalidates the judge's decision, and this was extended even to the taking of fees (Bek. 4:6). The invalidation of the proceeding was regarded as a quasi-penalty *(kenas)* imposed on the judge for taking bribes or fees (Tos. to Kid. 58b top; *Sma,* ḤM 9:5), and it may have counted toward the judge's liability to pay damages where a party had already acted on his judgment. The prohibition against a judge taking fees was mitigated by a renowned jurist, Karna, who allowed both parties to reimburse him in equal shares for the loss he had actually suffered by sitting in court instead of earning his wages as a winetaster (Ket. 105a). This precedent was not applied to a judge who took a fee for the loss of his time without proving actual loss of money: while his decisions remained unaffected he was called "ugly" *(ibid.).* Other talmudic jurists carried the rule against bribery to extremes by refusing to sit in judgment over any person who had shown them the slightest courtesy, such as helping them to alight from a boat *(ibid.).*

Originally, judges were remunerated from Temple revenues *(ibid.),* which furnished the legal basis for their remuneration, in later periods, from communal funds. As all members were required to contribute to the communal funds, so were litigants later – as today in the rabbinical courts in Israel – required to pay court fees, not to any particular judge but into a general fund out of which all court expenses were defrayed. There are, nevertheless, occasional instances of judges demanding exorbitant fees for their services (e.g., the incident reported by Obadiah of Bertinoro to Bek. 4:6).

Bribing non-Jewish rulers, officials, and judges was regarded as legitimate at all times. In view of their bias against Jews it is not difficult to understand such an attitude. Not only was it quite usual to bribe kings (I Kings 15:19; II Kings 16:8; Ber. 28b; et al.), but expenses involved in bribing judges and sheriffs were often expressly included in the expenses recoverable from debtors (cf. Gulak, Oẓar, 237, no. 249).

In the State of Israel the taker and the donor of bribes are equally punishable. Demanding a bribe is tantamount to taking it, and offering or promising one to giving it. Even the intermediary between the donor and the taker (or the intended taker) bears the same criminal responsibility. No extraneous evidence being normally available, the taker is a competent witness against the donor, and vice versa, and though they are accomplices their evidence need not be corroborated (Penal Law Revision (Bribery Offenses) Act, 5712–1952).

Bibliography: ET, 1 (1951[3]), 266; 3 (1951), 173f.; M. Elon, in: ILR, 4 (1969), 99f.; *ibid. Ha-Mishpat Ha-Ivri* (1973), I, p. 32 n. 106, 103, II, 669, 688ff.

Haim H. Cohn

GAMBLING. It is said that people who play games of dice are the sinners "in whose hands is craftiness" (Ps. 26, 10), calculating with their left hand and covering with their right, and defrauding and robbing each other (Mid. Ps. to 26:7). Dice are variously named in the Talmud as *kubbiyyah* (RH 1:8; Sanh. 3:3; et al.), *pesipas* (Sanh. 25b), or *tipas* (Tosef., Sanh. 5:2), apparently all words of Greek origin denoting small, wooden, mostly painted cubes. The player is sometimes called *kubiustos,* and it is said of him that he is afraid of daylight (Ḥul. 91b). Slaves are said to be notorious gamblers – which is the reason given for the rule that the sale of a slave could not be rescinded where it turned out that he was a *kubiustos* (BB 92b–93a and Rashbam *ibid.*).

However sinful and reprehensible gambling may be, it was not regarded as a criminal offense in talmudic law. A gambler who had no other trade but lived by gambling was disqualified as a judge and as a witness (RH 1:8; Sanh. 3:3), and in order to have his disqualification removed, had first to pay back (or to distribute to charities) all the money he had earned from his gambling (Sanh. 25b; *Piskei ha-Rosh,* Sanh. 3:10). For the purpose of such disqualification, moreover, the concept of gambling was expressly extended to include betting on animal races and the flights of pigeons and other birds (Sanh. 25a–b). Opinions differ as to the reason for such disqualification: some hold that taking money from another by way of game or sport, without giving valuable consideration in return, is like larceny; others hold that wasting time and money in gambling, instead of engaging in studies or in a trade or profession, amounts to ignoring the "general welfare of the world" *(yishuvo shel olam)*; both schools conclude that gamblers cannot, therefore, be reliable (*ibid.;* and Yad, Gezelah Va-Avedah 6:10–11 and Edut 10:4). The rule did not apply to occasional gamblers who earned their livelihood by an honest trade (Sanh. 3:3; Rema, ḤM 370:3; *Mordekhai,* Sanh. 690; *Kesef Mishneh,* Edut 10:4; et al.). A vow not to earn money was understood to mean not to win money by gambling (TJ, Ned. 5:4, 39b). As gambling easily grows into an irresistible obsession, vows and oaths to abstain from it in the future were frequently taken, and the question arose whether such vows were irrevocable: those who held that they were regarded gambling as offensive and prohibited anyway (cf. e.g. TJ, Ned. *ibid.* and *Korban Edah* and *Penei Moshe ibid.*; Resp. Rashba, vol. 1, no. 755; Resp. Radbaz pt. 1: 214; Resp. Maharashdam, YD 84; et al.); others also considered the psychological aspect and held such vows to be impossible to maintain (Resp. Ribash 281, 432; et al.). But so long as the vow had not been lawfully revoked, any gambling in contravention of it would be punished with flogging and heavy fines (Resp. Rosh 11:8).

In the Middle Ages, the playing of games of chance came to be recognized in many communities as a criminal offense: with the impoverishment of ghetto populations, the public danger of gambling and the necessity to suppress it called for drastic measures. The following is an example of a communal law *(takkanah)* on gambling: "Nobody may play at cards or dice or any other games whatsoever that the mouth could speak or the heart think, even on Rosh-Ḥodesh, Ḥanukkah, Purim, *ḥol ha-mo'ed,* and other days on which no *Taḥanun* is said, and even at the bed of a woman confined in childbirth or at a sickbed – and everybody whoever it may be, including boys and girls, manservants and maidservants, shall be punished if they should (God forbid) contravene and play; if the offender is well-to-do, he shall pay for every occasion two silver coins, one for the *talmud torah* and one for the poor of Jerusalem; and if he is poor so that he cannot be punished by fine, he shall be punished by imprisonment and tortured by iron chains as befits such offenders – always according to his blameworthiness and the exigencies of the day; and in any case shall his shame be made public, by announcing that this man has contravened this law" (*Takkanot Medinat Mehrin,* ed. I. Halpern, 92f.; Elon, *Ha-Mishpat Ha-Ivri* II, 664ff.).

The modern distinction between games of skill (which are lawful) and games of chance (which are prohibited) was already made in Jewish medieval sources: some scholars held that games of skill were allowed and games of chance prohibited on a Sabbath (*Shiltei ha-Gibborim,* Er. 104a); some doubted the validity of the distinction and held that all games, even chess, were prohibited on Sabbath (several responsa on the subject are printed in full in *Paḥad Yiẓḥak* (by Isaac Lampronti) s.v. *Shevu'ah she-Lo Lisḥok*). Games of skill, such as chess, were never made a criminal offense, though disapproved of as a waste of time which should properly be devoted to study; and domestic gambling, even for money, became customary during the night of Christmas.

The Israel Penal Law Amendment (Prohibited Games; Lottery and Betting) Law, 5724–1964, provides for the punishment, with imprisonment up to one year and a fine of up to 5,000 pounds, of professional gamblers (and much lighter punishment for occasional gamblers); the prohibition attaches to games in which money or other material benefits can be won, and the results of which depend more on chance than on understanding or skill, or – as in the case of bets – depend purely on guesswork.

Bibliography: L. Loew, *Die Lebensalter in der juedischen Literatur* (1875), 323–37; V. Kurrein, in: MGWJ, 66 (1922), 203–11; I. Rivkind, in: *Tarbiz,* 4 (1932/33), 366–76; idem, in: *Horeb,* 1 (1934), 82–91; idem, *Der Kamf kegen Azartshpilen bay Yidn* (1946); I. Jakobovits, *Jewish Law Faces Modern Problems* (1965), 109–12; L. Landman, in: JQR, 57 (1966/67), 298–318; 58 (1967/68), 34–62; idem, in: *Tradition,* 10 no. 1 (1968/69), 75–86; I. Abrahams, *Jewish Life in the Middle Ages* (1932[2]), 397–422; ET, 2 (1949), 113; 5 (1953), 520–2; J. Bazak, in: *Ha-Peraklit,* 16 (1960), 47–60; idem, in: *Sinai,* 48 (1961), 111–27; M. Elon, *Ha-Mishpat Ha-Ivri* (1973), I, 202ff., II, 636, 658ff., 664ff.

Haim H. Cohn

SLANDER. The only instance of defamation in biblical law for which a penalty is prescribed is that of the virgin (Deut. 22:19) – and that defamation is in the nature of a matrimonial stratagem (cf. Deut. 22:16–17) rather than of a specifically defamatory offense. Still, in order to invest the prohibition of defamation with the greatest possible weight, talmudic jurists interpreted the biblical injunction, "Thou shalt surely rebuke thy neighbor, and not bear sin because of him" (Lev. 19:17), as meaning that you may reprove your neighbor so long as you do not insult him; but if you make him blush or turn pale from shame or fury, then you have incurred guilt because of him (Sifra, Kedoshim 4:8; Ar. 16b). Other biblical exhortations – like "Thou shalt not go up and down as a tale bearer" (Lev. 19:16), or "Thou shalt not utter a false report" (Ex. 23:1), or "Thou shalt not hate thy brother in thy heart" (Lev. 19:17), "Thou shalt not take vengeance, nor bear any grudge" (*ibid.,* 18), and "Love thy neighbor as thyself" *(ibid.)* – have all been summoned to help invest the prohibition of slander with biblical authority (Israel Meir ha-Kohen of Radin, *Ḥafeẓ Ḥayyim, Petiḥah*). Particular prohibitions of insult, such as "Thou shalt not curse the deaf" (Lev. 19:14), or "Thou shalt not put a curse upon a ruler of thy people" (Ex. 22:27), were interpreted as particular instances of a general prohibition against insulting (Sifra, Kedoshim 2:13; Mekh., Mishpatim 19; Shev. 36a).

Though regarded as the violation of express biblical negative injunctions, slander is not punishable even by flogging, because mere talk does not amount to an overt act, and only such acts are punishable (Yad, Sanhedrin 18:2). More severe are the moral and religious admonitions against slanderers: "even though the slanderer is not flogged, his sin is very great indeed, and the sages have said that he who makes another's face turn pale in public, has no share in the world to come" (Avot 3:11). "Therefore everybody must be very careful not to abase another man in public, not to call him a name which puts him to shame, nor to say anything that might embarrass him" (Yad, De'ot 6:8). Some scholars went so far as to compare the slanderer to a murderer, because both "shed blood" (BM 58b); and all slanderers are characterized as wicked and stupid (Yad, Hovel u-Mazzik 3:7).

It would appear that mere moral exhortations were found insufficient to curb the mischief. A later source provides specific sanctions as follows: A person calling another a slave, shall be placed under a ban (*niddui;* see *ḥerem*); a person calling another a bastard *(mamzer)* shall be liable to 40 stripes; and if a person calls another wicked, the other may interfere with his livelihood (Kid. 28a). Attempts were made to interpret these particular sanctions as talionic (cf. Tos. and *Beit ha-Beḥirah,* Kid. 28a); but it is not impossible that they simply reflect decisions taken in cases which had actually occurred. The sanction of *niddui* for calling a man a slave has been codified (Yad, Talmud Torah 6:14; Sh. Ar., YD 334:43); and as for the administration of disciplinary floggings *(makkat mardut),* the rule was eventually held to be subject to local customs: where customary local regulations provided for different sanctions for slander, the customary rule prevailed (Resp. Rosh, 101:1; Rema, ḤM 420:41). In fact, disciplinary floggings appear to have remained in most places the most common punishment, at least for graver cases of slander (see e.g., Resp. Maharshal, nos. 11, 28, and 59; *Yam shel Shelomo* BK 8:34, 48, and 49). In other places, and in lighter cases, fines were imposed – and we often find fines substituted for *niddui* or for floggings at the option of the insulted person who had first to be appeased (Tur, ḤM 420:33 and *Beit Yosef* thereto).

A particular instance of punishable slander is insulting a scholar. A person convicted of having insulted a scholar is liable to *niddui* as well as to a fine of one litra of gold awarded to the aggrieved scholar (Yad, Talmud Torah 6:12). This preferential treatment of scholars left its traces also in the civil law: while a person is not liable in damages for mischief done by word of mouth only (BK 91a; Yad, Ḥovel 3:5; ḤM 420:39), where a scholar was put to shame, he is awarded 35 gold dinars by way of fine (TJ, BK 8:6, 6c; Yad, Ḥovel 3:5; Resp. Rashba, vol. 1 no. 475; Resp. Ribash, nos. 27, 216, and 220). The civil and criminal remedies are, of course, overlapping and identical. The insulted scholar may always forego the fine (Yad, Ḥovel 3:6). The remedy allowed to "scholars" was soon extended to all pious people (Resp. Rosh, 15:10; Tur, ḤM 420:32), and eventually became obsolete when remedies for slanders were no longer confined to particular classes of persons.

Another particular instance of slander is that of widows and orphans. "Mistreating" widows and orphans means, literally, causing them distress; if you cause them distress by insulting them, God will heed their outcry as soon as they cry out to Him; His anger will blaze forth and He will put you to the sword, and your wives shall become widows and your children orphans (Ex. 22:21–23). This is a typical instance of Divine punishment: for though the court will not impose flogging for this offense (see above), still the punishment therefore is expressly prescribed in the Torah: "and a covenant was concluded between them and the Creator of the World, that whenever they cry, He hears them and acts" (Yad, De'ot 6:10). Slandering the dead is also regarded as a great sin, to be expiated by fasting and prayers; and the court may punish it by fine (*Mordekhai,* BK 81–82; Rema, ḤM 420:38). While there are dicta to the effect that speaking the truth cannot constitute slander (Rema, ḤM 420:38), the better view seems to be that it is irrelevant whether the slanderous words were true or not (Israel Meir ha-Kohen of Radin, *Ḥafeẓ Ḥayyim* 1:1). In the State of Israel, the Knesset enacted "The Prohibition of Defamation Law 5725–1965" (as amended in 1967).

About Jewish legal principles in this law, see Elon, in ILR 4.

Bibliography: D. Daube, in: *Essays in Honor of J. H. Hertz* (1942), 111–29; ET, 1 (1951[3]), 160f.; 3 (1951), 49f.; 9 (1959), 207–14; N. Rakover, in: *Sinai,* 51 (1962), 197–209, 326–45;

T. D. Rosenthal, *ibid.*, 53 (1963), 59–66; M. Elon, in: ILR, 4 (1969), 100–2; idem, *Ha-Mishpat Ha-Ivri* (1973), I, 9ff., III, 841.

Haim H. Cohn

SORCERY. First and foremost among the "abhorrent practices of the nations" mentioned in the Bible are the various forms of sorcery: "let no one be found among you who . . . is an augur, a soothsayer, a diviner, a sorcerer, one who casts spells, one who consults ghosts or familiar spirits, or one who inquires of the dead. For anyone who does such things is abhorrent to the Lord" (Deut. 18:9–14). Divination and soothsaying (Lev. 19:26) and the turning to ghosts and spirits (Lev. 19:31 and 20:27) had been proscribed separately before, and witchcraft in general is outlawed with the lapidary "Thou shalt not suffer a witch to live" (Ex. 22:17). It was to be the characteristic of Judaism that nothing would be achieved by magic, but everything by the will and spirit of God: hence the confrontations of Joseph and the magicians of Egypt (Gen. 41), of Moses and Aaron and Egyptian sorcerers (Ex. 7), of Daniel and the Babylonian astrologers (Dan. 2), etc., and hence also the classification of crimes of sorcery as tantamount to idolatrous crimes of human sacrifices (Deut. 18:10) and to idolatrous sacrifices in general (Ex. 22:19) and its visitation, just as idolatry itself, with death by stoning (Lev. 20:27; see Capital Punishment). In a God-fearing Israel, there is no room for augury and sorcery (Num. 23:23; Isa. 8:19), and the presence of astrologers (Isa. 47:13) and fortune-tellers is an indication of godlessness (Naḥ. 3:4; Ezek. 13:20–23; et al.). Nonetheless, magic practices remained widespread throughout, and not only with idolaters (see, e.g., I Sam. 28:4–20; II Kings 18:4; II Chron. 33:6).

Talmudic law differentiated between capital and non-capital sorcery, retaining the death penalty only for those species for which the Bible expressly enjoined it, namely witchcraft (*kishuf;* Ex. 22:17) and conjuring a death (*ov* and *yidoni;* Lev. 20:27; Sanh. 7:4). *Kishuf* is nowhere exactly defined, but a distinction is drawn between actual witchcraft, committed by some overt and consummate act which resulted in mischief, and then punishable, and the mere pretense at witchcraft which, however unlawful and prohibited, is not punishable (Sanh. 7:11 and 67b). Witchcraft appears to have been widespread among women (cf. Avot 2:7), and Simeon b. Shetaḥ is reported to have ordered the execution of 80 witches in Ashkelon on a single day as an emergency measure (Sanh. 6:4 and Maimonides in his commentary thereto). It is witchcraft that makes for the devastation of the world (Sot. 9:13). All other species of sorcery are painstakingly defined in talmudic sources, apparently upon patterns of contemporary pagan usage. Thus, *ov* conjures the dead to speak through his armpit, while *yidoni* makes them speak through his mouth (Sanh. 7:7), both using bones of the dead in the process (Sanh. 65b). The aggravating circumstance, deserving of capital punishment, obviously is the use of human remains for purposes of sorcery, for he who simply communicates with the dead (in cemeteries or elsewhere) and serves as their mouthpiece *(doresh el ha-metim)* is punishable with flogging only (Yad, Avodat Kokhavim 11:13) – and this would, presumably, apply also to modern spiritualism (*Da'at Kohen,* no. 69). Other offenses punishable with flogging (both for committing and soliciting them) are: *niḥush,* defined as superstitions based on certain happenings or circumstances (Sanh. 65b; Yad, Avodat Kokhavim 11:4); *kesem,* being fortune-telling from sands, stones, and the like (Maim., loc. cit. 11:6); *onanut* (done by the *me'onen*), being astrological forecasts of fortunes (R. Akiva in Sanh. 65b; Maim. loc. cit. 11:8); and *ḥever,* the incantation of magic and unintelligible formulae for purposes of healing or of casting spells (Maim. loc. cit. 11:10). It is presumably because these practices were so widespread that it was postulated that judges must have a thorough knowledge of magic and astrology (Sanh. 17a; Maim. Yad, Sanhedrin 2:1; and see Bet Din).

While there is no information about the measure of law enforcement in this field in talmudic and pre-talmudic times, it seems certain that this branch of the law fell into disuse in the Middle Ages. Superstitions of all kinds not only flourished and were tolerated, but found their way even into the positive law (see YD 179, passim, for at least eight instances). What became known as "practical Kabbalah" is, legally speaking, sorcery at its worst. The penal provisions relating to sorcery are a living illustration of the unenforceability of criminal law (whether divine or human) which is out of tune with the practices and concepts of the people. In modern Israel law, witchcraft and related practices are instances of unlawful false pretenses for obtaining money or credit (Penal Law Amendment (Deceit, Blackmail, and Extortion), Law, 5723–1963).

Bibliography: A. Lods, *La croyance à la vie future et le culte des morts dans l'antiquité Israélite* (Thesis, Paris, 1906); L. Blau, *Das altjuedische Zauberwesen* (1914²); I. S. Zuri, *Mishpat ha-Talmud,* 6 (1921), 91; M. Gaster, *Studies and Texts in Folklore, Magic, Medieval Romance, Hebrew Apocrypha and Samaritan Archaeology,* 3 vols. (1925–28); A. Berliner, *Aus dem Leben der Juden Deutschlands im Mittelalter* (1937), 72–83; EM, 1 (1950), 135–7; 2 (1954), 710f.; 4 (1962), 348–65; ET, 1 (1951³), 113–6; 7 (1956), 245–8; M. Elon, *Ha-Mishpat Ha-Ivri* (1973), II, 424 n. 104, III, 987 n. 39.

Haim H. Cohn

PERJURY. Witnesses are guilty of perjury if it is proved, by the evidence of at least two other competent and consistent witnesses, that they had not been present at the time and at the place where they had testified to have been when the event in issue had happened (Mak. 1:4). Such false witnesses are known as *edim zomemim* (lit. conspiring witnesses). It is not sufficient that anything to which those witnesses had testified is contradicted by new witnesses, to the effect that what they had testified was untrue (as for "contradictions," see Witness): such contradictions are only the starting point of the evidence required to convict those witnesses of perjury (Maim. Yad, Edut 18:4), namely, that they could not possibly have witnessed the facts to which they had testified (*ibid.*, 18:2). Even though the evidence of the first set of witnesses had been accepted by the court as truthful, it is the evidence of the latter set of witnesses, testifying to the "alibi" of the first, that is to be accepted as conclusive (Mak. 5b; Yad, Edut 18:3) irrespective of the actual number of witnesses in each set. The latter set of witnesses must testify in the presence of the first set. Should this not be possible, e.g., if the first set are dead, this constitutes a "contradiction" and both testimonies will be discarded (cf. Yad, Edut 18:5). Where no evidence of perjury in the technical sense was available, but the evidence had conclusively been contradicted (e.g., where the murdered man appeared in court alive), the court would inflict disciplinary lashes (*Makkat Mardut* – see Flogging; Yad, Edut 18:6; *Sha'arei Ẓedek* 4:7, 24 and 45; Resp. Rosh, 58:4; et al.).

The punishment for perjury is laid down in the Bible: "you shall do to him as he schemed to do his fellow . . . Nor must you show pity: life for life, eye for eye, tooth for tooth, hand for hand, foot for foot" (Deut. 19:19–21). The Sadducees interpreted this law literally: the false witness would not forfeit his life, unless and until the man against whom he had testified had been executed; but the Pharisean interpretation, which is the source of the law as it was eventually established, was that the witness must be made to suffer what he had schemed to do, but not what he had actually caused to occur, to his fellow (Sif. Deut. 190; Mak. 1:6) – so that the biblical law was held to be applicable only where a man had been sentenced on the strength of false testimony, but before he was executed; the witnesses who had testified against him were then formally tried and convicted of perjury (Yad, Edut 20:2). This was a highly improbable contingency, as there was hardly an interval between sentence and execution (see Practice and Procedure). The enunciation of this rule is followed in the Talmud by the objection that it could not be right to take the life of the witness when the life of the person he had schemed to kill had not in fact been taken; or, if the Bible really required that to be the law, then *a fortiori* must the life of the witness be taken after that person had been executed: if a man is liable to die because of having intended to kill, surely he must be liable to die if he had actually killed. The objection was dismissed in reliance on the rule (see Penal Law) that no criminal offense can be created by analogy or logical deduction (Mak. 5b; and cf. Sanh. 74a and 76a; et al.).

Later commentators theorized that God's presence in the court (cf. Deut. 19:17) would sufficiently enlighten the minds of the judges to detect the falsehood of the testimony in time, before execution, for it is written, "do not bring death on the righteous and innocent, for I will not acquit the wrongdoer" (Ex. 23:7): it follows that the offense of perjury can have been committed only where the accused had not yet been executed for the alleged crime, for a man who was executed could not have been other than rightly convicted (Naḥmanides, commentary, Deut. 19:19).

The rule was, however, limited to capital cases only. Perjured witnesses were given the same non-capital punishments as had already been inflicted on those against whom they had testified (Yad, Edut 20:2), and where the defendant in a civil case had paid the judgment debt, the amount so paid was recovered from the witnesses (Tur, ḤM 38:2). Where the sanction imposed on the strength of their testimony could not be imposed on them (e.g., where an alleged manslayer had been banished to a city of refuge, or where a priest had been suspended from office), they would be flogged (Yad, Edut 20:8–9; Tur, ḤM 38:3). To be convicted of perjury, no previous warning had to be given to false witnesses (Ket. 33a; Yad, Edut 18:4; Tur, ḤM 38:9). No single witness could be convicted of perjury: the conviction had always to be in respect of both (or all) the witnesses who had testified falsely together (Mak. 1:7); and when once one false witness had alone been convicted, it was said that innocent blood had been shed (Mak. 5b). As perjured witnesses are disqualified from being admitted as a witness in future, all convictions of perjury must be given wide publicity (Sanh. 89a; Maim. Yad, Edut 18:7), to fulfill the biblical command that "all others will hear and be afraid" (Deut. 19:20).

Bibliography: D. Hoffmann, in MWJ, 5 (1878), 1–14; O. Baehr, *Das Gesetz ueber falsche Zeugen nach Bibel und Talmud* (1882); J. Horovitz, in: *Festschrift . . . David Hoffmann* (1914), 139–61; idem, *Untersuchungen zur rabbinischen Lehre von den falschen Zeugen* (1914); J. S. Zuri, *Mishpat ha-Talmud,* 7 (1921), 46; Gulak, Yesodei, 4 (1922), 161–3; ET, 8 (1957), 609–23; L. Finkelstein, *The Pharisees,* 1 (1962[3]), 142–4; 2 (1962[3]), 696–8; Z. Dor, in: *Sefer ha-Shanah Bar-Ilan,* 2 (1964), 107–24; P. Daykan, in; *Sinai,* 56 (1964/65), 295–302; S. Schmida, *Li-Ve'ayat Edei Sheker* (Diss. 1965); M. Elon, *Ha-Mishpat Ha-Ivri* (1973), II, 331ff.

Haim H. Cohn

CONTEMPT OF COURT. According to the Talmud cursing a judge is a scriptural prohibition. The verse "You shall not revile God" (Ex. 22:27) is interpreted as referring to human judges (Mekh. *ibid.;* Sanh. 66a; Maim. Yad, Sanhedrin 26:1) as is a preceding verse " . . . the case of both parties shall come before God: he whom God declares guilty shall pay double to the other" (*ibid.,* 22:8). In both these verses the word *Elohim* is used and was taken to mean "judges." Cursing any person is an offense punishable with flogging (see Slander), cursing a judge, by virtue of the extra prohibition, is punished by a double flogging (Maim. *ibid.,* 2). As in every other offense punishable with flogging, so in contempt of court the offender must have been warned beforehand; however, insulting a judge or the court may be punished with anathema (see *Ḥerem*) or with admonitory lashes *(makkot mardut)* even though spontaneous and not punishable by law (Maim. *ibid.,* 5). The court may, however, at its discretion, condone such an unpremeditated insult and abstain from taking action on it, whereas a premeditated curse must be punished according to law and no apology can be accepted (Maim. *ibid.,* 6).

It appears that in talmudic times the administrative, and not the judicial, officers of the court were the main target of contempt of court – demonstrated both in words and violence – and detailed rules were worked out to facilitate the perilous tasks of court messengers assigned to serve summonses and to execute judgments (BK 112b–113a; Maim. *ibid.,* 25:5–11; ḤM 11). The standard punishment for contempt of court messengers is anathema *(niddui),* after three prior warnings *(ibid.);* but admonitory lashes were also administered not only for insulting process-servers (Kid. 12b, 70b), but especially for failure to pay judgment debts (Ket. 86a–b). The source for the authority to proclaim anathema was taken to be Deborah's curse on those who did not come to the help of the Lord (Judg. 5:23). One scholar, invoking the wide authority given to Ezra by the Persian king for the punishment of offenders (Ezra 7:26), went so far as to authorize the infliction of imprisonment, shackling, and confiscation of goods (MK 16a), but in practice no such severe measures appear ever to have been adopted. No witnesses were required to prove such contempt: the complaint of the court official was accepted as conclusive – and expressly excluded from the applicability of the rules against slander (*ibid.,* and Maim., and ḤM *ibid.*).

In post-talmudic times, obedience to the courts had to be enforced by more rigorous means: both admonitory lashes (cf. e.g., Resp. Rosh 8:2 and 11:4) and imprisonment (cf. e.g., Rema and ḤM 97:15; Resp. Ribash 484) were widely used against persons who wilfully persisted in disobeying the court. However, such extreme sanctions were resorted to only where previous public admonitions (cf. e.g., Resp. Maharam Minz 38, 39, 101), the exclusion from religious and civic honors, the disqualification from suing and testifying, and similar measures (including the anathema) had been of no avail (S. Assaf, *Battei Din . . .* (1924), 118 and passim). It has been maintained that all these sanctions were not punitive in nature but solely designed to execute the judgment of the court or make the adjudged debtor pay his debt (Elon) – a modern distinction which in most cases is rather academic. The talmudic formula, "he shall be beaten until his soul departs" (Ket. 86b et al.), has an unmistakably punitive undertone: compelling the debtor to pay coincides with punishing him for his contempt.

See Imprisonment.

Bibliography: M. Bloch, *Civilprozess-Ordnung nach mosaisch-rabbinischem Rechte* (1882), 24–27, nos. 35–42; S. Assaf, *Ha-Onshin Aḥarei Ḥatimat ha-Talmud* (1922), passim; M. Elon, in: *Sefer Yovel le-Finḥas Rosen* (1962), 171–201; idem,

Ḥerut ha-Perat be-Darkhei Geviyyat Ḥov ba-Mishpat ha-Ivri (1964), 136, 256; idem, *Ha-Mishpat Ha-Ivri* (1973), I, 11ff., 156ff., III, 1077; ET, 3 (1951), 172; 8 (1957), 656–9, no. 6; 12 (1967), 119–28.

Haim H. Cohn

POLICE OFFENSES, offenses arising in connection with the prevention of public mischief and for the maintenance of public security, as laid down in the Bible, that have formed the basis for elaborate regulations in later periods of Jewish law. Thus, the biblical injunction against false weights and measures (Deut. 25:13–15) led to the appointment of special inspectors who were authorized not only to enter shops and ascertain the accuracy of weights and measures in use, but also to impose penalties, e.g., floggings or fines. Similarly, the biblical injunction against fraud (Lev. 25:14, 17) and oppression (Lev. 19:13) led to the prohibition of profiteering and to the appointment of special officers charged with the supervision of prices (cf. Yoma 9a); and profiteers too were liable to be flogged. Gambling and betting were prohibited as if they were species of larceny, and so were such potentially injurious acts as hunting in populated areas or taking animals already captured in the trap of another (Yad, Gezelah 6:8–12). The biblical injunctions for the protection of animals (Deut. 22:4, 6–7; Ex. 23:5) gave rise to the prohibition against hurting any living creature (BM 32a, b), and led to the elaboration of rules for the prevention of collisions between loaded animals in the street and hence also between ships and vehicles (Yad, Roẓe'aḥ 13:11–12).

The injuction that you shall not bring bloodguilt on your house (Deut. 22:8) was interpreted as not limited to the traditional requirement of providing a parapet for the roof lest anyone should fall from it, but as extending to any act or omission likely to endanger human life (Yad, *ibid.*, 11:4). It is no excuse for a man to say that his conduct endangers himself too; even if he chooses to disregard his own safety, he cannot disregard that of others and he is liable to be flogged if he does. Thus the supply or consumption of unclean or noxious food or water is prohibited (*ibid.*, 11:7–16) and so is the creation of any danger to the public (BK 27a–30a). There are also express provisions for the annual inspection of streets and thoroughfares by officers of the court to make sure they are not damaged by rain and are safe for traffic (Tosef. Shek 1:1). Where particular roads or journeys were dangerous, the court would appoint officers to accompany travelers and guard their safety; if they failed in watchfulness, the officers were regarded as if they had shed innocent blood (Yad, Evel 14:3). Where there were dangers of overcrowding or public licentiousness, court officers would mingle among the crowds to maintain law and order (Yad, Yom Tov 6:21).

The biblical prohibition against a woman putting on a man's clothing and vice versa (Deut. 22:5) may have served as the authority and pattern for later regulations governing dress and appearance. As dressing in the clothing of the opposite sex was regarded as conduct conducive to sexual perversion, so was dressing in the gentile fashion regarded as a first step toward assimilation. Sumptuary laws against extravagance and luxury became increasingly frequent, not only to prevent the following of the practices of gentiles (cf. Lev. 20:23), but also to ensure humility in walking before God (cf. Micah 6:8). Penalties were imposed mostly as fines, but we find also public denunciations (see *Ḥerem*). In some places, regulations were also laid down to make certain dresses or robes obligatory, e.g., for judges and notables (*Takkanot Mehrin*, 530). Generally, the biblical injunction to appoint executive officers in addition to judges (Deut. 16:18) was interpreted as imposing a duty to attach to each court "men with sticks and rods, standing at the service of the judges, to patrol markets and streets, inspect shops, rectify prices and measures, and redress all injury: they act only on the orders of the court, and when they detect a breach of law, they bring it before the court for adjudication" (Yad, Sanhedrin 1:1). It appears that until the destruction of the Temple, petty offenses were not, in Jerusalem, brought before the ordinary criminal courts, but before two or three police courts (*dayyanei gezerot*, Ket. 13:1), who were sitting full time and therefore (in contradistinction to judges) entitled to remuneration (Ket. 105a).

Bibliography: M. Block, *Das mosaisch-talmudische Polizeirecht* (1879); Frankel, Mishnah; C. Roth, in: JQR, 18 (1927/28), 357–83; ET, 3 (1951), 163f.; J. R. Marcus, *The Jew in the Medieval World* (1960), 193–7; M. Elon, *Ha-Mishpat Ha-Ivri* (1973), II, 636, 642, 649ff., 654, 659, 663, III, 995, 1102ff.

Haim H. Cohn

PUNISHMENT. While there is no modern theory of punishment that cannot, in some form or other, be traced back to biblical concepts, the original and foremost purpose of punishment in biblical law was the appeasement of God. God abhors the criminal ways of other nations (Lev. 20:23) whose practices the Israelites must not follow *(ibid.)* and from whose abominations they must not learn (Deut. 20:18); by violating His laws, His name is profaned (Lev. 22:31–32); and not only are criminals abhorrent to God (Deut. 18:12; 22:5; 25:16; 27:15), as well as crimes (Lev. 18:27–29), but God's own holiness obliges man to be holy like Him (Lev. 19:2). By taking "impassioned action" (Num. 25:13) to punish violators of His laws, expiation is made to God and God's "fierce anger" (Deut. 13:18) turned away from Israel (Num. 25:4). Closely related to the appeasement of God is another expiatory purpose of punishment: a crime, and more particularly the shedding of blood, pollutes the land – "and no expiation can be made for the land for the blood that is shed therein but by the blood of him that shed it" (Num. 35:33). Excrement must be covered because the land being holy demands that "thy camp be holy, . . ." (Deut. 23:15), so that God would "see no unseemly thing" occurring there *(ibid.)*.

Still another aspect is reflected in the talionic punishment of death for homicide, as originally formulated: "Whoso sheddeth man's blood, by man shall his blood be shed; for in the image of God made He man" (Gen. 9:6). Man being created in the image of God, it is an affront to God to kill him and killing the killer is the only acceptable expiation to God. Similarly, purging Israel of the blood of the innocent (Deut. 19:13) by killing the killer appears to be necessary in order to avoid blood guilt attaching to the land and to the people forever (cf. Deut. 21:9; 19:10); and it is for this reason that a murderer must be taken even from God's very altar to be put to death (Ex. 21:14).

All talionic punishment as such reflects its underlying purpose, namely the apparent restitution of the *status quo ante* by inflicting on the offender the injury inflicted by him (Lev. 24:20) and by doing to him what he had done to another (Lev. 24:19). This sort of sanction (see Talion), where the character and measure of punishment is precisely commensurate with those of the crime, is intended to represent exact justice. It was, indeed, by proving that this kind of "exact justice" necessarily involved unavoidable injustice, that some talmudical jurists justified the abolition of talionic punishment except for murder (BK 84a). And while they did not abolish it for murder, whether by reason of the many express biblical injunctions that murderers must be killed (especially Num. 35:31), or in order to retain the deterrent effect of the death penalty, many of them held that judges must do everything in their power to avoid passing death sentences (cf. Mak. 1:10), e.g., by rigorously cross-examining the witnesses long enough to have them contradict themselves or each other in some particular (Mak. 7a) and thus render their evidence unreliable (see Evidence, Witness). The warning was already sounded then that any reticence in imposing capital punishment would result in an increase of crime and bloodshed (Mak. 1:10). Maimonides comments on the talmudical discussion, that while it was true that the courts must always satisfy themselves that the incriminating evidence was credible and admissible, once they were so satisfied, they ought to order the execution even of a thousand men, day after day, if that is what the law (the Torah) prescribes (his commentary to the Mishnah, Mak. 1:10).

The most common purpose of punishment, as found in the Bible, is "to put away the evil from the midst of thee" (Deut. 17:7, 12; 19:19; 21:21; 22:24; 24:7). While such "putting away" is applied in the Bible to capital punishment only (which indeed constitutes the only effective total elimination), the principle underlying the elimination of evil, as distinguished from that of the evildoer (cf. Ps. 104:35 and Ber. 10a), provides a theory of punishment of universal validity and applicable to all criminal sanctions. It means that the act of punishment is not so much directed against the individual offender – who is, however, unavoidably its victim – as it is a demonstration of resentment and disapproval of that particular mode of conduct. By branding that conduct as worthy of, and necessitating, judicial punishment, it is outlawed and ostracized. Similarly, punishment is inflicted on the offender not so much for his own sake as for the deterrence of others: that all people should hear and be afraid (Deut. 17:13 – rebellious elder; 19:20 – perjury; 21:21 – rebellious son). From the point of view of criminal law enforcement policies, the deterrent aspect of punishment in Jewish law is already the most important of all: people who hear and see a man heavily punished for his offense are supposed to be deterred from committing the offense and incurring the risk of such punishment (they "will do no more presumptuously" – Deut. 19:20). Hence the particular injunction to have the offender hanged on a stake after having been put to death (Deut. 21:22), so as to publicize the execution as widely and impressively as possible; but note that the corpse must be taken off the gibbet before nightfall, "for he that is hanged is a reproach to God" and defiles the land (Deut. 21:23) – and no concession made to policies of law enforcement can derogate from the affront to God involved in killing and hanging a human being.

It is not only the principle known in modern criminology as "general prevention," the deterrence of the general public, but also that of "special prevention," the prevention of the individual offender from committing further crimes, that is reflected in Jewish law. It has been said that the imposition of capital punishment on such offenders as the rebellious son (Deut. 21:18–21), the rebellious elder (Deut. 17:12), the abductor (Ex. 21:16), and the burglar (Ex. 22:1) is justified on the ground that these are all potential murderers (cf. Maim., Guide 3:41); and rather than let them take innocent human lives, they should themselves be eliminated. That the deterrent effect of punishment on the offender himself was a consideration which weighed heavily with the talmudical jurists is illustrated also by the rule that where punishment had proved to have had no beneficial deterrent effect on the offender and he has committed the same or some similar offenses over and over again, he would be liable to be imprisoned and "fed on barley until his belly bursts" (Sanh. 9:5).

The talmudical law reformers also achieved the substitution for the ever-threatening divine punishment by the judicial punishment of flogging, making it clear that whoever underwent judicial punishment would not be visited with any further divine punishment (Mak. 3:15). They went so far as to lay down that even though God had Himself expressly proclaimed that a criminal would not be "guiltless" and escape divine wrath (Ex. 20:7; Deut. 5:11), the judicial authorities in imposing the flogging were authorized by the Torah itself to clear him: if God would never clear him, a court of justice could (Shevu. 21a). The measure of punishment must always conform to the gravity of the offense on the one hand, and the blameworthiness of the individual offender on the other: "according to the measure of his wickedness" (Deut. 25:2). Even here the talmudical law reformers found cause for some mitigatory improvement: they interpreted "wickedness" as the yardstick for the measure of punishment, as including also the physical capacity of the offender to undergo and suffer punishment (cf. Maim., Comm. Mak. 3:10 and Yad, Sanhedrin 17:1). In several instances, the particular turpitude of the offense is expressly stressed as reason for heavy penalties (e.g., "because she hath wrought a wanton deed in Israel" – Deut. 22:21, "it is wickedness" – Lev. 20:14); and in post-talmudic times, the imposition of severe punishments (such as capital punishment) was always justified by stressing the severity of the particular offense and the public danger of mischief thereby caused.

Maimonides laid down that the gravity and measure of punishment are to be determined, first, by the gravity of the offense: the greater the mischief caused, the heavier must be the penalty; second, by the frequency of the offense: the more widespread and epidemic the offense, the heavier must the penalty be; third, the temptation prompting the offense: the more easily a man is tempted to commit it, and the more difficult it is for him to resist the temptation, the heavier must the penalty be; and fourth, the secrecy of the offense: the more difficult it is to detect the offense and catch the offender, the more necessary is it to deter potential offenders by heavy penalties (Maim., Guide 3:41).

See also Penal Law.

Bibliography: E. Goitein, *Das Vergeltungsprincip im biblischen und talmudischen Strafrecht* (1893); S. Gronemann, in: *Zeitschrift fuer vergleichende Rechswissenschaft,* 13 (1899), 415–50; J. Wohlgemuth, *Das juedische Strafrecht und die positive Strafrechtsschule* (1903); J. Herrmann, *Die Idee der Suehne im Alten Testament* (1905); I. S. Zuri, *Mishpat ha-Talmud,* 6 (1921), 1–27; A. Pomeranz, in: *Ha-Mishpat,* 3 (1928), 23–27; A. Buechler, *Studies in Sin and Atonement in the Rabbinic Literature* (1928); J. Lipkin, in: *Haolam,* 16 (1928), 281–3; T. Ostersetzer, in: *Sefer ha-Shanah li-Yhudei Polanyah,* 1 (1938), 35–60; H. H. Cohn, in: ILR, 5 (1970), 53–74; S. Assaf, *Ha-Onshin Aḥarei Ḥatimat ha-Talmud* (1922); Dubnow, Hist. Russ., index, s.v. *Kahal Courts;* I. Levitas, *Jewish Community in Russia* (1943), 198–217; Baron, Community, index; Baer, Spain, index, s.v. *Criminal Jurisdiction of Jewish Community*; M. Elon, *Ha-Mishpat Ha-Ivri* (1973), I, 44ff., 57ff., II, 421–425, 566–569.

Haim H. Cohn

DIVINE PUNISHMENT. In a system of law based on divine revelation all punishment originally and ultimately derives from God. Even though human agencies may be entrusted with authority to inflict punishments in certain prescribed cases, God's own overriding punishing power remains unaffected, and the ways and means of divine punishment are as numerous and varied as they are of catastrophic unpredictability (cf. the punishments threatened for "rejecting God's laws and spurning His rules" in Lev. 26:14–43 and Deut. 28:15–68). God punishes whole peoples (the Flood: Gen. 6; Sodom and Gomorrah: Gen. 18; Egypt: Ex. 14:27–28; et al.) as well as individuals (Cain: Gen. 4:10–15; Aaron's sons: Lev. 10:1–2; Miriam: Num. 12:6–10; Korah and his company: Num. 16:28–35; et al.); and visits "the guilt of the fathers upon the children, upon the third and upon the fourth generations of those who reject" Him (Ex. 20:5; Deut. 5:9). The fear of God is inculcated in those tending to be cruel or callous (Ex. 22:26; Lev. 19:14, 32), and specific retaliatory punishments will be inflicted by God for mistreating widows and orphans (Ex. 22:21–23).

Originally, divine punishment was independent of and additional to judicial punishment: there are several biblical instances in which capital punishment is prescribed for a particular offense and yet the threat of divine punishment is superadded (e.g., Ex. 31:14). In one instance, the law explicitly states that where the prescribed capital punishment is not carried out, God will himself set His face "against that man and his kin and will cut off from among their people both him and all who follow him in going astray after Molech" (Lev. 20:2–5). This juxtaposition of divine and judicial punishments appears conclusively to disprove the view that *karet* ("cutting off") was not a divine punishment of death, but rather a judicial punishment of excommunication. While, in the nature of things, all judicial punishment is uncertain, depending on the offender being caught, evidence against him being available, and the "people of the land not hiding their eyes" from him (Lev. 20:4), divine punishment is certain and inescapable, and thus a much more effective deterrent: the omniscient God will not suffer His laws to be disobeyed with impunity (cf. Deut. 32:41). The fundamental injustice underlying the ideas of inherited guilt and deferred punishment and unbounded wrath is, from the point of view of penal policy, a lesser evil than God's failure to mete out deserved punishment.

For a good many offenses, the divine *karet* is the only punishment prescribed. It has been suggested that they are such offenses as are committed in private, for which eyewitnesses will not usually be available; such as, for instance, the eating of fat or blood (Lev. 7:25–27; 17:10, 14) or various sexual offenses (Lev. 20:17–18; 18:29), or the nonobservance of the Day of Atonement (Lev. 23:29–30) or of Passover (Ex. 12:15, 19). Others maintain that these offenses are mostly of a religious or sacerdotal character, such as failure to circumcise (Gen. 17:14) or to bring certain sacrifices (Num. 9:13), as well as the nonobservance of the religious festivals already mentioned; and that for such religious sins any judicial punishment was thought inappropriate (cf. Sifra 1:19). There are, however, some offenses, punishable by *karet* only, that do not fit into either of these categories as, for instance, public blasphemy (Num. 15:30–31). This fact – together with the gravity of some of the sexual offenses so punishable – led some scholars to assume that *karet*, even though a threat of divine punishment, was at the same time an authorization of judicial capital punishment (cf. Ibn Ezra, Lev. 18:29). This theory is strengthened by the fact that some of the offenses punishable with *karet* are stated to be also judicially punishable (Ex. 31:14; Lev. 20:6).

Apart from *karet*, divine punishment is expressed in terms of simple death (e.g., Num. 18:7) as well as of "bearing one's iniquity" or guilt (e.g., Lev. 5:1; 7:18; 17:16; 20:19; 24:15; Num. 5:31). Sometimes "he shall bear his guilt" is followed by "and he shall die" (Ex. 28:43; Num. 18:32); sometimes it is combined with the threat of *karet* (Lev. 19:8), and sometimes joined with the threat of childlessness (Lev. 20:20). It has therefore been suggested that where the "bearing of guilt" stands alone, it is meant only as imposing the duty to bring a sacrifice to God (Tosef., Shevu. 3:1).

With the development of jurisprudence, it was sought to purge divine punishment from apparent injustice (Jer. 31:28–29; Ezek. 18:2–29), and it was later relegated altogether to the realm of homiletics: people were warned that premature death (at the age of 50), or death without leaving issues, were signs of the divine *karet* (Sem. 3:8; MK 28a; Rashi and Tos., Shab. 25a–b), and that every undetected murderer would meet with "accidental" death at the hands of God (Mak. 10b). By talmudic law, *karet*, though interpreted as divine capital punishment, was absolved by the human judicial punishment of flogging (Mak. 13a–b; Yad, Sanhedrin 19:1): having been flogged, the offender is no longer liable to *karet* (Mak. 3:15). This substitution of flogging for divine punishment was in legal theory founded on the notion that God would forgive offenders who had repented, and in His mercy refrain from punishing them; undergoing the flogging was regarded as tantamount to repentance. By being flogged, the offender could avoid divine punishment since he cannot be punished twice for the same offense (Mak. 13b). The recidivist, who after having twice been flogged again committed the same offense, was given up – presumably because the supposed repentance could not have been genuine – and was imprisoned and kept on a diet of barley until his belly burst (Sanh. 9:5; Yad, Sanhedrin 18:4).

Where a lesser penalty, such as a fine, is merged in the larger penalty for the same offense and will not therefore be recoverable, it is sometimes held that in order to satisfy divine law as well as human law *(Dinei Shamayim)* and not be liable to future divine retribution, one should pay also the lesser penalty, especially where it is payable to the victim (cf. BM 91a; Tos. to BK 70b–71a; Tos. to Ḥul. 130b).

Bibliography: Rothschild, in: MGWJ, 25 (1876), 89–91; J. Lipkin, in: *Ha-Mishpat*, 3 (1928), 9–16; A. Buechler, *Studies in Sin and Atonement*... (1928); ET, 7 (1956), 392–5; EM, 4 (1962), 330–2; B. Cohen, *Jewish and Roman Law*, 2 (1966), 740–4, 801; M. Elon, *Ha-Mishpat Ha-Ivri* (1973), II, 496, 815ff.

Haim H. Cohn

ORDEAL, the generic term for the various ways and means by which divine judgment would be ascertained. The most common form of ordeal, which survived long into the Middle Ages and beyond, was entirely unknown to biblical as well as to later Jewish law: namely, the exposing of an accused person to physical dangers which were supposed to be harmless to him if he were innocent but which were considered conclusive proof of divine condemnation if he suffered harm. The only remnant of this kind of ordeal may be found in the Ordeal of Jealousy. It is an early talmudic tradition (Sot. 9:9) that these "waters of bitterness" ceased to be effective when adulterers proliferated. Traces of a similar ordeal by water may be found in the water that Moses made the Israelites drink after he had sprinkled it with powder ground from the golden calf (Ex. 32:20), the talmudic tradition being that this was the method used to detect the guilty. Another widespread method of ascertaining God's judgment was the curse. A written curse had first to be erased into the "water of bitterness" to be swallowed by the woman suspected of adultery (Num. 5:23), so that either the curse or the water or both could be instrumental in the ordeal. The curse is interchangeable with, and a forerunner of, the oath: he who takes the oath before God (cf. Ex. 22:7–8, 10) brings God's curse on himself if he perjures himself (cf. II Chron. 6:22–23). On hearing the oath sworn at His altar, God judges – condemning the wicked and justifying the righteous (see also Zech.

5:3–4; et al.). There is a statement that when atonement was made for general sinfulness (Lev. 16:21–22), God would, by changing red into white, reveal His forgiveness or by not changing the color indicate unforgiveness (Yoma 6:8; 67a). In many instances, God's judgment was, of course, executed directly, manifesting itself in the very act of divine punishment (e.g., Num. 16:5–7, 31–35; Deut. 11:6; I Kings 18:38).

Bibliography: J. Kohler, in: *Zeitschrift fuer vergleichende Rechtswissenschaft,* 5 (1884), 368–76; J. G. Frazer, *Folklore in the Old Testament,* 3 (1919), 304–414; J. Morgenstern, in: *HUCA Jubilee Volume 1875–1925* (1925), 113–43; R. Press, in: ZAW, 51 (1933), 121–40, 227–55; ET (1951³), 182–5; EM, 1 (1950), 179–83; 5 (1968), 1003f.

Haim H. Cohn

TALION, a concept of punishment whereby the prescribed penalty is identical with, or equivalent to, the offense. Identical (or "true") talions are death for homicide ("Whosoever sheddeth man's blood, by man shall his blood be shed": Gen. 9:6), wounding for wounding ("an eye for an eye": Ex. 21:23–25; Lev. 24:19–20), and doing to the false witness "as he had purposed to do unto his fellow" (Deut. 19:19). Equivalent talions conform to some feature characteristic of the offense, but not to its essence or degree: the hand that sinned shall be cut off (Deut. 25:12) – not a hand for a hand, but the hand for what it had done. In the case of the adulteress, it is that part of her body with which she is suspected of having sinned that will be visited with divine punishment if she is guilty (Num. 5:21 as interpreted in Sot. 8b–9a, and see Adultery). (For further biblical equivalent punishments see Ex. 32:20; Judg. 1:7; II Sam. 4:12; II Kings 9:26; Dan. 6:25.) While most identical talions were abolished by talmudic law (see below), equivalent talions survived through talmudic times (cf. Sanh. 58b; Nid. 13b) into the Middle Ages (cf. Resp. Rosh, 17:8 and 18:13; *Zikhron Yehudah* no. 58; et al.), and traces can even be found in modern law (e.g., the confiscation, mostly as an additional punishment, of firearms, vehicles, or other objects by means of which an offense was committed, or of smuggled goods; or the suspension of trading or driving licenses for trading or driving offenses).

True talionic punishments were undoubtedly practiced in biblical and post-biblical times. To retaliate measure for measure is God's own way of meting out justice (cf. Isa. 3:11; Jer. 17:10; 50:15; Ezek. 7:8; Obad. 15; et al.), and is defended by Philo as the only just method of punishment (Spec. 3:181–2). The account of the talion in Josephus (Ant. 4:280) supports the theory that, as in ancient Rome (Tabula 8:2), the victim had the choice of either accepting monetary compensation or insisting on talion (cf. Ex. 21:30 for an analogous case). Even in the talmudic discussion on the talion, one prominent dissenter consistently maintained that "an eye for an eye" meant the actual physical extraction of the offender's eye for that of the victim (BK 83b–84a). The majority, however, settled the law to the effect that talion for wounding was virtually abolished and replaced by the payment of damages (BK 8:1), primarily because the justice of the talion is more apparent than real: after all, one man's eye may be larger, smaller, sharper, or weaker than another's, and by taking one for the other, you take something equal in name only, but not in substance. Not only is the ratio of talion thus frustrated, but the biblical injunction that there should be one standard of law for all, would also be violated (Lev. 24:22). Also if a blind man takes another's eye, what kind of eye could be taken from him? or a cripple without legs who did injury to another's leg, what injury can be done to his? Nor can an eye or any other organ be extracted from a living man's body without causing further incidental injury, such as making him lose vast amounts of blood or even endangering his life; "and the Torah said, an eye for an eye, and not an eye and a soul for an eye" (BK 83b–84a). The very risk, unavoidable as it is, of exceeding the prescribed measure, is enough to render talion indefensible and impracticable (Saadiah Gaon, quoted by Ibn Ezra in his commentary on Ex. 21:24).

The monetary compensation replacing talion was not wholly in the nature of civil damages, however, but had a distinctly punitive element. This is clear from the rule that the penalty for inflicting injuries not resulting in pecuniary damage was flogging (Ket. 32b; Sanh. 85a; Mak. 9a). The only reason why flogging could not be administered where any damages were payable was that two sanctions could never be imposed for any one offense (Ket. 37a; Mak. 13b; et al.).

While talionic practice was effectively outlawed, the talionic principle, as one of natural justice, was held in the Talmud: the measure by which a man measures is the measure by which he will be measured (Sot. 1:7; Tosef. Sot. 3:1 as to punishments and 4:1 as to rewards). The famous precept of Hillel's, said to embody the whole of the Torah, that you should not do to another what you would not like to have done to you (Shab. 31a) is derived from the same principle.

Bibliography: E. Goitein, *Das Vergeltungsprincip im biblischen und talmudischen Strafrecht* (1893); D.W. Amram, in: JQR, 2 (1911/12), 191–211; J. Horovitz, in: *Festschrift . . . Hermann Cohen* (1912), 609–58; J. Weismann, in: *Festschrift . . . Adolf Wach* (1913), 100–99; E. Merz, *Die Blutrache bei den Israeliten* (1916); S. Kaatz, in: *Jeschurun,* 13 (1926), 43–50 (Germ.); J. Norden, *Auge um Auge, Zahn um Zahn* (1916); J.K. Miklisanski, in: JBL, 66 (1947), 295–303; ET, 12 (1967), 693–5.

Haim H. Cohn

CAPITAL PUNISHMENT, the standard penalty for crime in all ancient civilizations.

In the Bible. Many of the crimes for which any biblical punishment is prescribed carry the death penalty. The three methods of executing criminals found in the Bible are stoning, burning, and hanging.

Stoning was the instinctive, violent expression of popular wrath (Ex. 17:4, 8:22; Num. 14:10; I Sam. 30:6; I Kings 12:18; II Chron. 10:18), and is often expressly prescribed as a mode of execution (Lev. 20:2, 27; 24:16; Num. 15:35; Deut. 13:11, 17:5, 21:21, 22:21, et al.). As the survival of *vindicta publica,* it was and remained characterized by the active participation of the whole populace (Lev. 24:16; Num. 15:35; Deut. 17:7; et al.) – all the people had to pelt the guilty one with stones until he died. Stonings were presumably the standard form of judicial execution in biblical times (Lev. 24:23; Num. 15:36; I Kings 21:13; II Chron. 24:21).

Burning is mentioned as a pre-Sinaitic punishment (Gen. 38:24). As a mode of judicial execution it is prescribed in respect of two offenses only (Lev. 20:14, 21:9), but it may have been used to aggravate the punishment of stoning, the corpse being burned after execution (Josh. 7:25). It is also reported as a non-Jewish (Babylonian) punishment (Dan. 3:6). There is no biblical record to indicate whether and how judicial executions were ever carried out by burning.

Hanging is reported in the Bible only as either a mode of execution of non-Jews who presumably acted in accordance with their own laws (e.g., Egyptians: Gen. 40:22; II Sam. 21:6–12: Philistines; and Persians: Esth. 7:9), or as a non-Jewish law imported to or to be applied in Israel (Ezra 6:11), or as an extralegal or extra-judicial measure (Josh. 8:29). However, biblical law prescribes hanging after execution: every person found guilty of a capital offense and put to death had to be hanged on a stake (Deut. 21:22); but the body had to be taken down the same day and buried before nightfall, "for a hanged body is an affront to God" (*ibid.*, 23).

Talmudic Law distinguished four methods of judicial execution *(arba mitot bet din):* stoning, burning, slaying, and strangling. In no area can the genius of the talmudic law reformers better be demonstrated than in that of capital punishment. Two general theories were propounded which, though dated from a period too late to have ever stood the test of practical application, reflect old traditions and well-established ways of thinking: namely, first, that "love your neighbor as yourself" (Lev. 19:17) was to be interpreted as applying even to the condemned criminal – you love him by giving him the most humane ("the most beautiful") death possible (Sanh. 45a, 52a et al.), secondly, that judicial execution should resemble the taking of life by God: as the body remains externally unchanged when God takes the life, so in judicial executions the body should not be destroyed or mutilated (Sanh. 52a; Sifra Kedoshim 9:11).

Stoning was not only confined to the 18 offenses for which the Bible had expressly prescribed it (Maim., Yad, Sanhedrin 15:10), but instead of having all the people kill the convicted person by pelting stones at him a "stoning place" was designed from which he was to be pushed down to death (Sanh. 6:4). This must not be too high, so that the body should not be mutilated falling down (Rashi, Sanh. 45a), and not too low, so that death would be instantaneous. One of the hermeneutical reasons given for this change of the law was the scriptural rule that "the hands of the witnesses shall be first upon him to put him to death" (Deut. 17:7); it is true that "the hand of all the people [should be on him] afterward" *(ibid.),* but it is the hand of the witness which is to put him to death. A mode of "stoning" had therefore to be devised in which the witness would not only be assured of the first chance to lay hands on the convicted person, but also of the certainty of thereby putting him to death (Sanh. 6:4). Talmudic jurists may have been influenced by Roman law (Saxum Tarpeium of the Twelve Tables 8:13f., 8:23) or by Syrian or Greek laws (cf. II Macc. 6:10), or perhaps by a single biblical precedent with prisoners of war (II Chron. 25:12) – what they attained was a more humane substitute for the biblical stoning, by which the danger of mutilation was considerably reduced and death accelerated. Maimonides justifies the talmudic method with the reflection that it really made no difference whether stones were thrown at one or one was thrown on the stones (Maimonides, Comment. to Sanh. 6:4). A great penal reform was achieved with the exclusion of the general public from the execution of death sentences and the elimination therefrom of all traces of *vindicta publica.* The participation of witnesses – and perhaps also the blood avenger – was not eliminated because they were regarded as a lesser evil in comparison with professional executioners.

Burning remained confined to the adultery of a priest's daughter and to certain forms of incest (Sanh. 9:1; Maim. Yad, Sanhedrin 15:11). Here again the question arose of how to execute by burning without destroying the body: an old tradition has it that when Aaron's sons were consumed by divine fire (Lev. 10:2) only their souls were burnt, their bodies remaining intact (Sanh. 52a); in accordance with this, a mode of burning which would leave the body intact had to be devised. The man to be burnt was to be immersed in mud up to his knees (so that he should not fall); two kerchiefs were then to be bound round his neck, each to be held in the hands of one witness and drawn in opposite directions until he opened his mouth, and then a burning wick was to be thrown into his mouth "which would go down into his bowels" (Sanh. 7:2). As will be seen, this mode of execution is almost identical with that of strangling, it being reasonable to suppose that the wick will no longer burn when it arrives in the bowels, but suffocation will already have supervened. The Talmud explains that hot lead or zinc is meant by the mishnaic wick taking the wick to be a metallic substance (Sanh. 52a), insisting that as little pain as possible should be inflicted (see Maim. Comment. to Sanh. 7:2). There is no record that this method of burning was ever practiced. There is a report that a priest's daughter was burnt for adultery by being bound with bundles of grapevine which were then ignited (Sanh. *ibid.*). The explanation there given was that this may have been the method employed by a Sadducean court, leading some scholars to conclude that that had been the original biblical mode of burning, the Sadducees rejecting later oral law modifications. The same older method of burning is reported to have been adopted by a later Babylonian scholar, Ḥama b. Tobiah, who was rebuked for it (Sanh. 52b). That burnings may also have taken place at the stake appears from midrashic sources (cf. Gen. R. 65:22; Mid. Ps. 11:7). Josephus reports that Herod ordered men who had incited others to desecrate the Temple to be burnt alive and their accomplices to be killed by the sword (Wars, 1:655).

Slaying by the sword was the mode of executing murderers and the inhabitants of the subverted town (Sanh. 9:1). As for the subverted town, it is the biblical prescript that its inhabitants be "put to the sword" (Deut. 13:16); and as for murderers, a slave murdered by his master must be "avenged" (Ex. 21:20), and as God is said to "avenge" by the sword (Lev. 26:25), the murderer of the slave, and *a fortiori* of the free man, is to be executed by the sword (Sanh. 52b). Slaying consisted in decapitating with a sword, "in the way practiced by the [Roman] government" (Sanh. 7:3). There ensued a discussion, which continued for centuries (cf. Tos. to Sanh. 52b), whether this would not contravene the injunction, "neither shall ye walk in their statutes" (Lev. 18:3). One scholar thought it would be less cruel or mutilating, and less Roman-like, to have the convict lay his head on a block and decapitate him with a hatchet, but the majority held that to be worse (Sanh. 7:3). While there was no particular mode of execution for murder prescribed in the Bible, it is probable that originally such executions were by way of talion: in the same manner in which the victim had been murdered, his murderer would be executed (cf. Philo 3:182, Spec., 314–317; Jub. 5:31; Jos., Ant., 4:279). If that be so the talmudic reform would equalize the law and have death made instantaneous in all cases. There are no reports of murderers having been judicially executed by the sword, but kings are reported to have used this mode of execution, not necessarily for murderers (cf. Jos., Ant., 14:450, 464; Acts 12:2). It became the law that the king, who may order the execution of rebels and of offenders against his majesty even without judicial conviction, always executes with the sword (Maim., Yad, Melakhim 3:8, Sanhedrin 14:2). Indeed, God, too, kills by the sword (Num. 14:16; Lam. 2:21).

Strangling is the residuary capital punishment; where no other mode of execution is prescribed, the death penalty is carried out by strangulation (Sanh. 52b, 84b, 89a), supposed not only to be the most humane but also the least mutilating (Sanh. 52b). The mishnaic procedure resembles that for burning. The convicted man is immersed in mud up to his knees, two kerchiefs are bound round his neck and then drawn in opposite directions by the two witnesses until he suffocates (Sanh. 7:3). Strangling is applied in six capital offenses (Sanh. 11:1, Yad, Sanhedrin 15:13). There is no report of this mode of execution ever having been carried out. (For strangulations by hanging, see Extraordinary Remedies.) *Post mortem* hangings were restricted by talmudic law, some holding that only executions by way of stoning should be followed by a *post mortem* hanging, and the majority view being that these hangings should be limited to the two offenses of blasphemy and idolatry only (Sanh. 6:4).

Though in strict law the competence to inflict capital punishment ceased with the destruction of the Temple (Sanh. 37b, Ket. 30a; cf. Sanh. 41a, 40 years earlier), Jewish courts continued, wherever they had the power (e.g., in Muslim Spain), to pass and execute death sentences – not even necessarily for capital offenses as defined in the law, but also for offenses considered, in the circumstances prevailing at the time, as particularly dangerous or obnoxious (e.g., informers: Yad, Ḥovel u-Mazzik 8:11), or even for such offenses alone as distinguished from those originally punishable under the law (cf. Resp. Rosh 17:1). In order not to give the appearance of exercising sanhedrical jurisdiction, they would also normally refrain from using any of the four legal modes of execution (Resp. Maharam of Lublin, 138); but isolated instances are found of stoning (*Zikhron Yehudah,* 75), slaying (*ibid.,* 58; Resp. Rosh, 17:2), and strangling (*Zeka Aharon* 95), along with such newly devised or imitated modes of execution as starvation in a subterranean pit (Resp. Rosh, 32:4), drowning, bleeding, or delivering into the hands of official executioners (S. Assaf, *Ha-Onshin Aḥarei Hatimat ha-Talmud,* no. 28). In most cases, however, the manner in which the death sentences were to be executed was probably left to the discretion of the persons who were authorized or assigned by the court to carry them out (cf. Resp. Rema, 11 & 17).

In Israel. The rule that with the destruction of the Temple the competence to impose capital punishment ceased gave rise to objections to capital punishment being retained under the laws of the new State of Israel. During the first murder trial to be held after the state was established, the two chief rabbis of Israel cabled the minister of justice urging the immediate abolition of the death penalty and warning the court that pronouncing a capital sentence would be incompatible with, and a sin against, Jewish law. While death sentences for murder were pronounced in Israel until the coming into force of the Penal Law Revision (Abolition of the Death Penalty for Murder) Law 5714–1954, no such sentence was ever executed. The death penalty remained in force in Israel for offenses under the Crime of Genocide (Prevention and Punishment) Law, 5710–1950, and for treason which is committed in times of actual warfare under the Penal Law Revision (State Security) Law, 5717–1957. The mode of execution under Israel law is hanging for civilians and shooting for soldiers (Sect. 493, Military Justice Law, 5715–1955).

See also Extraordinary Remedies and Punishment.

Bibliography: S. Mendelsohn, *Criminal Jurisprudence of the Ancient Hebrews* (1891), 256f. index, s.v.; S. Gronemann, in: *Zeitschrift fuer vergleichende Rechtswissenschaft,* 13 (1899), 415–50; A.Buechler, in: MGWJ, 50 (1906), 539–62, 664–706; D. de Sola Pool, *Capital Punishment among the Jews* (1916); V. Aptowitzer, in: JQR, 15 (1924/25), 55–118; S. Katz, *Die Strafe im talmudischen Recht* (1936), 44–52; ET, 2 (1949), 163f.; 10 (1961), 587–92; S. Ch. Cook, in: *Ha-Torah ve-ha-Medinah,* 3 (1950/51), 163f.; J.M. Tikoczinsky, *ibid.,* 4 (1951/52), 33–44; B. Rabinowitz-Teomim, *ibid.,* 45–81; S. Israeli, *ibid.,* 82–89; Ch. Z. Reines, in: *Sinai,* 39 (1955/56), 162–8; J.M. Ginzberg, *Mishpatim le-Yisrael* (1957), 381 index, s.v. *Mitat Beit Din;* G.J. Blidstein, in: *Judaism,* 14 (1965), 159–71; E.M. Good, in: *Stanford Law Review,* 19 (1966/67), 947–77; H. Freedman, in: *The Bridge* (Sydney), 3 (1967), no. 2, p. 4–8; H. Cohen, in: ILR, 5 (1970), 62–63; M. Elon, *Ha-Mishpat Ha-Ivri* (1973), I, 7, 9, 11, 45 n. 140, 194 n. 86, II, 283, 421ff., 435, 647ff., 790ff., 808 ff., III, 842 ff., 845 ff., 1103.

Haim H. Cohn

BLOOD-AVENGER. A person who is authorized by law, or who is duty-bound to kill a murderer is called *go'el ha-dam* – usually translated as an avenger of blood, but more accurately to be rendered as a redeemer of blood (cf. Lev. 25:25; Ruth 3:12; I Kings 16:11). By putting the murderer to death (Num. 35:19, 21), the avenger expiates the blood shed on the polluted land (Num. 35:33). Originally private revenge was customary in Israel, as in other ancient civilizations, not only for homicide but also for mayhem (cf. Gen. 4:23–24) and rape (Gen. 34:25–26); and the restrictions of the avenger's rights and their legal regulation mark the beginnings of a system of criminal law (see B. Cohen in bibl.). It was laid down that only murder with malice aforethought (Num. 35:20–21; Deut. 19:11–13) or committed with a murderous instrument (Num. 35:16–18; for further examples, see Maim., Yad, Roẓe'aḥ u-Shemirat Nefesh 6:6–9), gave rise to the avenger's right (see Mak. 12a, Sanh. 45b); the unintentional manslayer was entitled to refuge from the avenger (Num. 35:12, 15; Deut. 19:4–6) and was liable to be killed by him only when he prematurely left the city of refuge (Num. 35:26–28). It may be considered a concession to human nature that avenging was not wholly prohibited, but only restricted and regulated: the natural "hot anger" (Deut. 19:6) of the victim's next of kin is left at least some legal outlet.

The avenger's rights were further restricted by being made subject to and dependent on the prior judicial conviction of the murderer – whether the murder was premeditated or not was a question not for the avenger but for the court to decide (Maim. loc. cit. 1:5, following Num. 35:12; "the manslayer may not die unless he has stood trial before the assembly"; but cf. Yad, loc. cit. 5:7–10). Opinions of later jurists were divided as to what the avenger's real function was; some held that he initiated the proceedings, searching for the murderer and bringing him to court for trial (Ran, Nov., Sanh. 45b; *Beit ha-Beḥirah* ad loc.); some thought he appeared before the court and participated in the proceedings as a prosecutor (Nissim Gerondi, basing himself on the Targum pseudo-Jonathan who renders *go'el ha-dam* as "claimant of blood"); others relegated the avenger to the role of an executioner, it being his right and privilege to execute the death penalty pronounced by the court (Yad, loc. cit. 1:2; Ritba, Nov., Mak. 10b). That the avenger had a *locus standi* in court appears probable from the scriptural injunction that the court "shall decide between the slayer and the blood-avenger" (Num. 35:24). While the slayer would protest his innocence or, alternatively, his lack of malice, the avenger would plead premeditation (cf. *Malbim* ad loc.); by finding a lack of malice, the court is said to "protect the manslayer from the blood-avenger" (Num. 35:25). Where an alleged murderer stood trial but was not convicted (either because of lack of sufficient evidence or because the verdict had not yet been given) and the avenger killed him, most jurists held that while the killing was unlawful the avenger was not guilty of murder (*Beit ha-Beḥirah,* Sanh. 45b) – the proferred reason being that the avenger had a better right to kill than even the unintentional manslayer (Yad, loc. cit. 6:5), or that Scripture itself recognized the avenger's "hot anger" (Deut. 19:6) as negating premeditation (Redak to II Sam. 14:7). However, if the avenger killed the murderer within the walls of the city of refuge, it was murder pure and simple (Tosef., Mak. 3:6).

Any next of kin entitled to inherit the deceased's estate qualified as an avenger (Yad, loc. cit. 1:2). Some later authorities even include maternal relatives although they are not in line for inheritance (*Or Same'aḥ* to Yad, loc. cit., against Maimonides). Women also qualify as avengers (Yad, loc. cit. 1:3). There are biblical instances of a father (II Sam. 13:31–38), a son (II Kings 14:5–6), brothers (Judg. 8:4–21; II Sam. 2:22–23), and also the king (I Kings 2:29–34) as avengers. It was later laid down that where no next of kin was available or came forward, an avenger was to be appointed by the court (Sanh. 45b).

There is little doubt that legally the rights (and duties) of the blood-avenger became obsolete (*Ḥavvat Ya'ir* 146), though the killing by the avenger of a murderer is even today legally regarded by some scholars as no more than unintentional manslaughter (e.g. *Keẓot ha-Ḥoshen* ḤM 2). Apart from the law, the right and duty of avenging the blood of one's nearest is still deeply imprinted on the mind and religious conviction of most Oriental (including many Jewish) communities; notwithstanding repeated efforts from various quarters, blood-vengeance is not, however, recognized in Israel law even as a mitigating circumstance.

Bibliography: M. Duschak, *Mosaisch-Talmudisches Strafrecht* (1869), 19f.; S. Mayer, *Rechte der Israeliten, Athener, und Roemer,* 3 (1876), 36–47; E. Goitein, *Vergeltungsprincip im biblischen und talmudischen Strafrecht* (1891); G. Foerster, *Das mosaische Strafrecht . . .* (1900), 9ff.; J. Weismann, *Talion und oeffentliche Strafe im mosaischen Rechte* (1913); E. Merz, *Blutrache bei den Israeliten* (1916); ET, 5 (1953), 220–33; J.M. Ginzburg, *Mishpatim le-Yisra'el* (1956), 356–74; EM, 2 (1965), 392–4; B. Cohen, *Jewish and Roman Law,* 2 (1966), 624–7; addenda 793f.

Haim H. Cohn

CITY OF REFUGE (Heb. עיר מקלט), Moses assigned six cities (Num. 35:13, Deut. 19:9) to which "shall flee thither and live whoso killeth his neighbor unawares and hated him not in time past." Moses himself set aside three of these cities (Bezer, Ramoth, and Golan) in Transjordan (Deut. 4:43), while Joshua "sanctified" the other three (Kedesh, Shechem, and Hebron) west of the Jordan after the conquest (Josh. 20:7). These cities were all populated towns in which the manslayer would be immune from persecution by the blood avenger (Num. 35:12) and where he could lead a normal life and earn his livelihood – the words "and live" (Deut. 4:42; 19:5) being interpreted to mean that he was entitled to all normal amenities of life: if he was a scholar he was even entitled to take his school with him; if a pupil he was entitled to have his teacher brought to him (Mak. 10a). But in order to discourage avengers from frequenting these cities, certain trades – believed to increase commercial intercourse – were banned to them, such as the manufacture of textiles, ropes, and glassware (Tosef., Mak. 3:9), and the sale of arms and hunting tools (Mak. 10a). According to a later tradition, it was not only the six cities of refuge proper (which were all levitical cities: Num. 35:6), but also the additional 42 cities allotted to the levites (Josh. 21; I Chron. 6:39ff.) which provided a refuge to manslayers (Mak. 13a; Maim. Yad, Roẓe'aḥ 8:9) – the difference between the six cities and the other levitical cities being that in the former one was automatically immune from persecution, whereas in the latter asylum had to be expressly requested (*ibid.*, 8:10). Moreover, in the former one could claim housing as of right (Tosef., Mak. 3:6), whereas in the latter one had to pay rent (Mak. 13a).

The procedure – which talmudic scholars reconstructed from biblical accounts – was that the manslayer fled to the nearest city of refuge: in order to facilitate his escape, road signs had to be put up on all crossings showing the way to the refuge (Mak. 10b; Tosef., Mak. 3:5), and all roads leading to a city of refuge had to be straight and level and always kept in good repair (Yad, loc. cit., 8:5). On arrival, the man had to present himself at the city gate before the elders of the city, who would give him accommodation (Josh. 20:4). Afterward he would be taken to court, which provided an escort to protect him from any encounter with the avenger on the way from the city to the court or back (Mak. 2:5–6). Should the court find him guilty of premeditated murder, he would be executed; if found guilty of unpremeditated manslaughter, he would be returned to the city of refuge to stay there until the death of the then officiating high priest; if no high priest was alive or officiated at the time of the verdict, or if it was a high priest who killed or was killed, the killer would have to stay there for life (Maim. loc. cit., 7:10). It is reported that mothers of the priests would have food and clothing sent to the refugees, so as to persuade them to pray for a long life for the priests, notwithstanding their exile (Mak. 2:6). During their stay they were not allowed to leave the city precincts, not even in order to testify in court where a man's life depended on their testimony (Mak. 2:7; Maim. loc. cit., 7:8); for if they left the city, the avengers were free to kill them (Num. 35:27). They were allowed to occupy places of honor in the cities of refuge, provided that they first disclosed to the people honoring them that they had come there as refugees (Mak. 2:8; Tosef., Mak. 3:8). On his release from the city of refuge, the refugee returned to normal life wherever he pleased, and if the avenger killed him he was guilty of murder (Maim. loc. cit., 7:13). Opinions were divided as to whether positions of trust and honor were restored to him or whether he had forfeited them (Mak. 2:8) because of the misfortune he had brought into the world (Maim. loc. cit., 7:14). Exile to a city of refuge was tantamount to punishment for unintentional homicide, and, like punishment for murder, could not be compounded (see Compounding Offenses) by the payment of blood money (Num. 35:32).

A more ancient type of asylum was the altar: as a murderer with malice aforethought is to be taken from God's very altar "that he may die" (Ex. 21:14), so may the unintentional manslayer seek refuge at the altar to escape punishment (Mak. 12a; Maim. loc. cit., 5:12); and if he does, he is led away from the altar and escorted into a city of refuge (*ibid.*, 5:14). Several instances of manslayers seeking refuge at the altar are reported in the Bible (I Kings 1:50; 2:28–30).

Bibliography: S. Baeck, in: MGWJ, 18 (1869), 307–12, 565–72; A.P. Bissel, *The Law of Asylum in Israel* (1884); S. Ohlenburg, *Die biblischen Asyle im talmudischen Gewande* (1895); N.M. Nicolsky, in: ZAW, 48 (1930), 146–75; M. Loehr, *Asylwesen im Alten Testament* (1930); ET, 6 (1954), 122–35; 7 (1956), 672, no. 6; Greenberg, in: JBL, 78 (1959), 125–32; Weinberg, in: *Hadorom,* 14 (1961), 3–13; Sorozkin, in: *Sefer ha-Yovel . . . Jung* (1962), 47–54; M. Elon, *Ha-Mishpat Ha-Ivri* (1973), I, 187 ff.

Haim H. Cohn

FLOGGING, punishment by beating or whipping. This at all times has been the instinctive way to inflict disciplinary punishment: a parent "disciplines" his son by beating him (cf. Deut. 8:5; 21:18; Prov. 19:18; 23:13–14; 29:17) as does a master his slave (Ex. 21:20, 26). More than any other punishment, flogging is a means of correction rather than retribution, and, being a substitute for the capital punishment which, in a rabbinic view, every violator of God's word properly deserves, it reflects God's infinite mercy (cf. Sanh. 10a, Rashi *ibid.*).

In Biblical Law. It appears that, where no other punishment was expressly prescribed, flogging was in biblical law the standard punishment for all offenses (Deut. 25:2). The exegetical difficulties which arose in view of the preceding verse (25:1) gave rise to such restrictive interpretations as that the law of flogging applied only in limited cases of assault (Ibn Ezra, *ibid.*) or perjury (cf. Mak. 2b); but there need not necessarily be any connection between the two verses – the former being construed as a self-contained exhortation to do justice in civil cases as well as in cases of mutual criminal accusations (cf. Mid. Tan. to 25:1). It is noteworthy that flogging is the only punishment mentioned in the Bible as a general rule, and not in relation to any particular offense (but cf. Deut. 21:22 regarding post-mortem hangings; see also Capital Punishment), the only exception being the flogging prescribed, in addition to a fine, for the slanderer of a virgin (Deut. 22:18).

The maximum number of strokes to be administered in any one case is 40 (Deut. 25:3), "lest being flogged further, to excess, your brother is degraded before your eyes" (*ibid.*). While this number was later understood as the standard, fixed number of strokes to be administered in each case (less one), there is no valid reason to assume that it was not in fact intended and regarded as a maximum limit – the preceding words, "as his guilt warrants" (25:2) indicating that the number of strokes was to be determined in each individual case according to the gravity of the offense, provided only they did not exceed the prescribed maximum. The scriptural intention to prevent any "degradation" of the human person is served by the fact that no discretion was allowed to the judges, who may tend to harshness or cruelty (Ibn Ezra, *ibid.*). There is no record of the manner in which floggings were administered in biblical times. Various instruments of beating are mentioned in the Bible (Judg. 8:7, 16; Prov. 10:13; 26:3; I Kings 12:11, 14; et al.), but any conclusion that they (or any of them) were the instruments used in judicial floggings is unwarranted.

In Talmudic Law. Talmudic law not only made detailed provision for the manner in which floggings were to be carried out, but also altered the concept of the biblical punishment; the maximum of 40 lashes was reduced to 39 (Mak. 3:10), so as to avoid the danger of exceeding 40 even by mistake; and the offenses which carried the punishment of flogging were exactly defined, depriving it of its character as a residuary and omnibus punishment. The number of 39 lashes became the standard rather than the maximum number; but in order to prevent death by flogging – which would amount to a violation of the biblical injunction of "not more" than flogging – the person to be flogged was first physically examined in order to determine the number of lashes that could safely be administered to him (Mak. 3:11). Where, as a result of such examination, less than 39 lashes were administered, and it then turned out that the offender could well bear more, the previous estimate would be allowed to stand and the offender discharged (Maim. Yad, Sanhedrin 17:2). But the offender would also be discharged where physical symptoms manifested themselves during the course of the flogging, so that he would not be able to stand any more lashes, even though on previous examination he had been found fit to stand more (*ibid.* 17:5). It also happened that as a result of such examination, floggings were postponed for another day or later, until the offender was fit to undergo them (*ibid.* 17:3).

Offenses Punishable by this Method. The offenses carrying the punishment of flogging are, firstly, all those for which the divine punishment of *karet* is prescribed; secondly, all violations by overt act of negative biblical injunctions (*ibid.* 18:1). However speech is not, as such, considered an overt act: thus, a person insulting the deaf or going about as a talebearer among the people in violation of express negative injunctions (Lev. 19:14–16) would not be liable to be flogged (Yad, loc. cit.). It is only when speech is tantamount to an act, as in vows substituting another animal for a sacred animal (Lev. 27:10), that flogging is inflicted (Tem. 3b); as it is also for swearing falsely by, or taking in vain, the name of God – "for the Lord will not clear one who swears falsely by His name" (Ex. 20:7; Deut. 5:11), but the court will, by flogging him (Tem. 3a). Flogging is also prescribed for cursing, i.e., wickedly using the name of God – because failure "to revere this honored and awesome Name" is expressly given as the cause of the infliction of *makkot,* a term meaning lashes as well as plagues (Deut. 28:58–59). Even though the offense is committed not just by speech but also by an overt act, it does not always result in a flogging: thus, where reparation must be made by money, as for the crime of stealing (Ex. 20:13; Deut. 5:17), the payment of damages and fines is preferred to flogging; and as two punishments may not be inflicted for the same offense, the rule is that he who pays is not flogged (Mak. 1:2; 4b; Ket. 32a). For the same reason, no flogging can be inflicted where the offense carries capital (as distinguished from divine) punishment (Tosef., Mak. 5:17). Where the negative injunction is coupled with a positive one, as for instance: "thou shalt not take the dam with the young, thou shalt let the dam go, but the young thou mayest take" (Deut. 22:6–7), liability to be flogged only ensues if the negative injunction is violated and the positive disobeyed as well (Mak. 3:4; Ḥul. 12:4).

Floggings were administered with a whip made of calfskin on the bare upper body of the offender – one third of the lashes being given on the breast and the other two thirds on the back. The offender stood in a bowed position with the one administering the beating on a stone above him and the blows were accompanied by the recital of admonitory and consolatory verses from Scripture (Mak. 3:12–14; Yad, loc. cit. 16:8–11). If death ensued, even though the flogging was administered according to law, the executioner was not liable; but if the law had not been faithfully observed by him, he would be obliged to resort to a city of refuge as in the case of any other accidental homicide (Yad, loc. cit. 16:12).

Disciplinary Floggings. There are reports in the Talmud of several extralegal floggings being prescribed (see Extraordinary Remedies), for example, for having marital intercourse in public (Yev. 90b). In many cases, the flogging appears to have been sanctioned as a legal punishment, even though not falling within the categories set out above; for example, where a man and a woman seclude themselves (Kid. 81a), or for taking unreasonable vows (TJ, Suk. 5:2, 55b), or for falling asleep during watch duty in the Temple (Mid. 1:2); but these cases may also be regarded as instances of disciplinary rather than punitive measures. Disciplinary flogging *(makkat mardut)* was an innovation of the talmudic jurists. While the violation of a negative injunction calls for punishment, the act of violation being a matter of the past, the failure to obey a positive command calls for coercive measures calculated to enforce such obedience. Accordingly, while punitive floggings may (indeed, must) be restricted to a maximum number of blows, disciplinary floggings must be unrestricted – to be continued until the offender performs his duty. The maximum number of 40 lashes applies only where there has been a violation of a negative injunction, but in the case of positive commands, "as when they say to him: build a *sukkah* – and he refuses or: take a *lulav* – and he refuses – he is flogged until his soul departs" (Ket. 86a–b). In the case of payment of a civil debt, which is also a positive command imposed by law, the question arose whether such payment could be enforced by a disciplinary flogging *(ibid.);* the better opinion appears to be that it could not, at any rate for so long as the debtor had any property attachable in execution proceedings or if he claimed to have no property only when he was attempting to avoid payment (*Piskei ha-Rosh,* Ket. 9:13).

Disciplinary floggings were also resorted to where an offender was not liable to punishment for formal reasons, for example for lack of previous warning (Yad, loc. cit., 18:5). It was this innovation of the idea of a disciplinary flogging that enabled the courts, in post-talmudic times, to make use of the penalty of flogging for the maintenance of law and order and for the observance of religion. It is found to have been applied in an unlimited variety of cases and in different modes of execution. The flogging was mostly carried out in public, so as to have a deterrent effect: sometimes in the courthouse (Hai Gaon, comm. to Kelim 22:3, s.v. *safsal*), sometimes in the synagogue (*Yam shel Shelomo,* BK 8:48, and Resp. Maharshal 28; Resp. Maharam of Lublin 46), and sometimes in the square outside the synagogue or in other public thoroughfares (Resp. Ribash 351). Although because of jurisdictional doubts (see *Bet Din*), the application of a disciplinary, as opposed to that of punitive, flogging was preferred, the courts did not normally adopt the rule that disciplinary floggings ought not to be restricted, but ordered floggings to be limited to a certain amount of lashes – some holding that the biblical maximum applied *a fortiori (Yam shel Shelomo, ibid.),* some leaving the extent of the flogging in each individual case to the discretion of the court (*Sha'arei Ẓedek* 4:7, 39; *Halakhot Pesukot min ha-Ge'onim* 89; *Sha'arei Teshuvah* 181). The argument that such discretionary floggings constituted a much severer punishment for many much lighter offenses than the biblical flogging was countered with the assertion that the execution of the flogging should be so humane as to counterbalance the increased measure of strokes (Resp. Ribash 90). Indeed, it appears that the lashes were not normally inflicted on the bare body, nor with a leather whip, nor on the breast or back, but rather on less vulnerable parts. Following a talmudic dictum that a flogging is to be administered where an offense is reported but not proved (*malkin al lo tovah ha-shemu'ah:* Kid. 81a), post-talmudic courts introduced the punishment of flogging where an offense was threatened or commenced but not completed (Resp. Maharam of Rothenburg, ed. Prague 383; and cf. *Darkhei Moshe,* ḤM 421 n. 7); but mere suspicion alone was held insufficient to warrant flogging (*Halakhot Pesukot min ha-Ge'onim* 94), unless substantiated by at least one witness or by common repute (*Sha'arei Ẓedek* 3:6, 38). In many places, notables were exempt from floggings, and people were normally allowed to pay a fine instead (cf. *Yam shel Shelomo,* BK 8:49). Corporal punishment was abolished in Israel by the Punishment of Whipping (Abolition) Law 5710–1950.

Bibliography: S. Mendelsohn, *Criminal Jurisprudence of the Ancient Hebrews* (1891), 39f. (no. 21), 171f. (nos. 138, 139); S. Assaf, *Ha-Onshin Aḥarei Ḥatimat ha-Talmud* (1922), 146 index, s.v. *Makkat Mardut* and *Malkot;* Jacob, in: MGWJ, 68 (1924), 276–81; Aptowitzer, in: *Ha-Mishpat ha-Ivri,* 5 (1935/36), 33–104; S. Katz, *Die Strafe im Talmudischen Recht* (1936), 63f.; ET, 1 (1951^3), 136; J.M. Ginzburg, *Mishpatim le-Yisrael* (1956), 381 index, s.v. *Makkat, Malkot;* EM, 4 (1962), 1160f., s.v. *Malkot;* M. Elon, *Ḥerut ha-Perat be-Darkhei Geviyyat Ḥov ha-Mishpat ha-Ivri* (1964), 22–26, 207f.; idem, *Ha-Mishpat Ha-Ivri* (1973), I, 10, 150 n. 44, 189, II, 421 ff., 437 ff., 499 ff., 568 ff., 648 ff., 692 ff., 720, III, 841.

Haim H. Cohn

IMPRISONMENT, the act of depriving a person of his liberty by restricting his freedom of movement and confining him within a particular defined locality, where he is under the direct and constant supervision of the confining authority. This form of restraint on individual liberty is sometimes referred to as arrest or detention *(ma'aẓar)* and sometimes as imprisonment *(ma'asar).* The most frequent cases of imprisonment are: (1) arrest of a person suspected of having committed a criminal offense in order to ensure his arraignment and presence at the trial or to prevent him from interfering with the course of inquiries; (2) detention of a person convicted and sentenced to death or banishment – pending execution of the sentence; (3) imprisonment without trial by virtue of an administrative order of the government, issued against a political background; (4) imprisonment aimed at compelling compliance with the instruction of a judicial tribunal; (5) imprisonment imposed as a punishment for the commission of an offense.

The first four categories of imprisonment were known in most ancient legal systems; punitive imprisonment, however, was apparently unknown in the legal systems of the Ancient East or in Greek and Roman law – in keeping with the dictum of Ulpian: *"carcer enim ad continendos homines, non ad puniendos habari debet"* ("prison is intended for the confinement, and not punishment, of people"). Most European legal systems only came to give general recognition to imprisonment as a punitive measure from the commencement of the 14th century onward (see W. Mittermaier, *Gefaengniskunde* (1954), 2–3, 3–17; Von Hentig, *Die Strafe,* 2 (1955), 159–83; see also Imprisonment for Debt).

IN THE BIBLE

Biblical references to imprisonment within the context of Jewish law (the imprisonment of Joseph in Egypt (Gen. 39:20; 40:3–4, 7; 42:16–19) and of Samson by the Philistines (Judg. 16:21) were not within that context) are made in the cases of detaining a transgressor until delivery and execution of the judgment (Lev. 24:12; Num. 15:34) and as an administrative measure (I Kings 22:27; II Chron. 16:10; Jer. 37:15–16; 38:4–14); at the close of the biblical period imprisonment is mentioned as one of the means entrusted to the court, presumably for the purpose of compelling compliance with its instructions (Ezra 7:25–26).

IN THE TALMUDIC PERIOD

In the Talmud there are *halakhot* relating to a person detained in prison (with reference to the laws of Sotah – Sot. 4:5), a person promised his release from imprisonment (with reference to the laws of the paschal lamb – Pes. 8:6), and a person released from prison (with reference to the laws of Festivals – MK 3:1). During this period there were Jewish and gentile prisons for imprisonment at the hands of Jews and gentiles respectively (Pes. 91a; TJ, Pes. 8:6, 36a, and MK 3:1, 81c). Mention is made of a building inhabited by the warder of the prison in Maḥoza, a Babylonian city, the majority of whose residents were Jewish (Yoma 11a; see also TJ, Kid. 4:12, 66d).

Detention of a suspect pending completion of the judicial proceedings against him continued to be the most common form of imprisonment in this period (Mekh., Nezikin, 6; Ket. 33b); his detention was forbidden, however, unless it was possible to point to evidence tending to prove commission of the offense (TJ, Sanh. 7:10, 25a). It was also customary to detain a person who had been convicted and sentenced to death pending execution of the sentence (Sif. Num., 114; Sanh. 11:4). The sages interpreted the passage from the Book of Ezra (7:25–26) as authority for the court to imprison a person refusing to comply with its instructions (MK 16a), and to this end severe conditions of detention were sometimes imposed (*Oẓar ha-Ge'onim,* ed. by B.M. Lewin, Mashkin, p. 68).

Imprisonment as punishment for an offense is known for the first time during the talmudic period (referred to as *hakhnasah la-kippah,* i.e., confinement in a "cell" – Sanh. 9:5; Tosef., Sanh. 12:7–8). This punishment was imposed in two cases: after the offender had committed an offense for which the punishment was *karet* (Divine Punishment) three or more times; and for the offense of murder (see Homicide) whenever the court was unable – on account of procedural and formal defects – to convict the accused but was convinced that he had murdered the deceased. Conditions of imprisonment in the "cell" were particularly severe (Sanh. 81b). The sages found a hint for punitive imprisonment in a biblical passage; it was, however, apparently a rabbinical enactment (*takkanah*) made by virtue of the sages' authority to impose punishment for criminal offenses – even beyond the framework of the pentateuchal law – whenever rendered necessary by the existing exigencies (see *Takkanot*[1] and Yad, Roẓe'aḥ, 4:8–9).

IN THE POST-TALMUDIC PERIOD

In the post-talmudic times increasing recourse was had to imprisonment within the Jewish legal system and, along with pretrial detention and imprisonment to compel compliance with the instructions of the court, punitive imprisonment – imposed in respect of various types of offenses – became a common phenomenon in Jewish law, particularly from the early 14th century onward.

This phenomenon was linked to the problem of Jewish judicial autonomy in the various centers of Jewish life. This autonomy related primarily to the field of civil law, but in most Jewish centers it extended also to criminal law, although varying in scope from center to center (see Introduction). One of its manifestations in the field of criminal law was the existence of Jewish prisons in various centers, as is evident from numerous halakhic and historical sources; in particular, much material on this subject is available regarding the situation in Poland and neighboring territories, covering details such as the names of some of the prisons and their Jewish warders, their salaries, etc. (see Elon, in *Sefer Yovel,* pp. 178–84). Imprisonment, within its various categories, was imposed by the *bet-din* even in centers where there were no prisons under Jewish supervision, execution thereof being entrusted to the governmental authorities (Elon, *ibid.,* 184f.).

Arrest and Detention. In the ninth century, the Babylonian *gaon* Paltoi decided that it was permissible to arrest an offender on the Sabbath if knowledge about him first came to light on this day (*Halakhot Pesukot min ha-Ge'onim* no. 135); later, a contrary decision was given by Sherira Gaon (*Shibbolei ha-Leket* no. 60) and the problem was discussed over a long period in the Codes (Rema, OḤ 339:4). In Spain various *halakhot* were fixed concerning the arrest of a person, particularly with reference to his release on guarantee or bail (Resp. Rosh, 13:3; Resp. Ribash, 234–9, 508). Detention was also employed as a means of preventing someone from taking flight in circumstances calculated to cause great hardship to another, e.g., if the husband sought to place his wife in the position of an *agunah;* in this event it was decided that arrest was permissible even on the Sabbath (*Shevut Ya'akov,* vol. 1, no. 14).

Imprisonment to Compel Compliance with the Court (Ma'asar Kefiyyah). Imprisonment was used by the court as a means of compelling a husband to grant a bill of divorce *(get)* to a wife with whom marriage was prohibited (Rashi, Pes. 91a; Resp. Ribash, 348), as well as in all other cases where it is permitted to compel the husband to grant a *get* (Rashba, vol. 2, resp. 276) and also as a means of compelling the levir to grant *ḥaliẓah* (Resp. Rosh 52:8; see Levirate Marriage, and Divorce, and compare the legal position in the State of Israel in this respect).

Contempt of Court. Imprisonment was also used as a sanction for noncompliance with various instructions of the court (Resp. Rif. 146; Resp. Ritba, 159; *Takkanot Medinat Mehrin* (Moravia), no. 247; *Pinkas ha-Medinah [Lita],* no. 546). Imprisonment was mentioned by some of the *posekim* as a sanction available to the court (Maim. Yad, Sanhedrin 24:9; Tur, ḤM 2); other *posekim* made no mention thereof in this context (Sh. Ar. and Rema, ḤM 2), but in the later Codes this possibility was again acknowledged (*Levush, Ir Shushan, Sema, Urim ve-Tummim,* and *Netivot ha-Mishpat,* ḤM 2).

Punitive Imprisonment. Serious Crimes. The talmudic law of *hakhnasah la-kippah* (see above) became an analogy for the imposition of similar punitive imprisonment in certain cases of murder, when the possibility of carrying out the capital sentence was excluded according to the original law (Yad, Roẓe'aḥ 4:8–9). Punitive imprisonment was likewise prescribed in cases of homicide not carrying liability, according to the original law, for the death sentence (Yad, Roẓe'aḥ 2:2–5) in a case of murder involving doubt as to whether the death resulted directly from the murderer's act (Resp. Ribash no. 251), or if there was one witness only (i.e., if he proved to be reliable and delivered convincing testimony – *Yam shel Shelomo,* BK 8:6). Sentence of death was imposed on a Jew who committed, for the third time, the offense of informing on and denouncing a fellow Jew to the gentiles, and other forms of punishment, including imprisonment, were imposed for a first or second offense of this nature (see Elon, *Ha-Mishpat Ha-Ivri,* II, pp. 647 ff. and Informer).

Commencing in the 14th century imprisonment became accepted in Jewish law, under the influence of the surrounding legal systems (see above) as a regular mode of punishment in respect of numerous other offenses. It became one of the most common and effective sanctions to be adopted by the Jewish courts and in various *takkanot,* in answer to the circumstances and conditions of Jewish life in different periods.

Offenses Against Morality and the Family Laws. The penalty of imprisonment was imposed upon commission of offenses such as having sexual relations with a non-Jew (*Zikhron Yehudah* no. 91), adultery (i.e. in cases of sexual relations with a married woman – Resp. Ribash, no. 351), sodomy (Mabit, vol. 1; resp. no. 22), and prostitution; and, in some localities, it was imposed "against certain youths who harass girls and women in the streets at nighttime" (see Elon, in bibl., p. 193). Imprisonment was also imposed as a punishment for marrying in a ceremony attended by less than a *minyan* – aimed at avoiding various kinds of secret marriages (Resp. Ribash, no. 232; see also Takkanot; Marriage).

Offenses Against Property. Imprisonment was an accepted sanction for theft (see Theft and Robbery; Resp. Ritba, no. 159; *Divrei Rivot* no. 232; see also Elon, p. 194) and was imposed even when commission of the offense could not be proved by the testimony of two witnesses, but the court was persuaded of the theft on the strength of the circumstantial evidence (*Tashbeẓ* 3:168). Not only the thief was imprisoned, but also any person knowingly undermining the inquiry into the theft (Elon, p. 194).

Assault and Insult. Imprisonment was prescribed as the punishment for assault, and in certain places a monetary fine was imposed – nonpayment whereof rendered the offender liable to imprisonment (*Zikhron Yehudah* no. 36; Elon, p. 195). Defamation (see Slander) was also punished with imprisonment *(ibid.).*

Gambling. Playing games of chance, a common phenomenon in the Middle Ages, was combated by the Jewish communal leaders and courts by the adoption of various stringent measures (see Gambling), including imprisonment imposed on both male and female participants and on the owner permitting gambling to

1. page 78.

take place on his premises. In terms of a *takkanah* enacted in the Cracow community in the middle of the 17th century, a woman sentenced to imprisonment was to be detained *in nayen Dudik* ("in the new 'Dudik' " – the name of a jail possibly intended for female prisoners only), for the period "from completion of the *Shaḥarit* service until completion of the *Arvit* service in the Synagogue" (see Elon, p. 196) – so that she was enabled to return home in the evening without spending the night in jail.

Sundry Offenses. Imprisonment was also imposed in respect of offenses of a religious nature, e.g., in the case of a person who threatened to become an apostate unless his request be met for the performance of a ceremony of marriage between himself and a woman prohibited to him by law (Resp. Ritba, no. 179); it was also used against the followers of Shabbetai Ẓevi, and even against the followers of Ḥasidism in its early controversial stages. It was likewise imposed for delivering false testimony, smuggling, and other offenses. In *takkanot* of the Cracow community, enacted at the end of the 16th century, the poor were prohibited, on pain of imprisonment, from begging for alms in the streets – the beadle of the synagogue being entrusted with the duty of collecting contributions and distributing them among the poor; this was justified on the ground that almsgiving in the streets was "tantamount to robbing the respectable poor," since such poor people were ashamed to beg for alms and turned solely to the communal charity box (Elon, pp. 196–7).

The Pillory and House Arrest. Putting offenders in the "Kuna," as the pillory was known in Poland and Lithuania, was a form of punishment meted out in these countries in the late Middle Ages, by Jews as well as gentiles. In some places the "Kuna" consisted of a chain attached to the wall of a synagogue, near the entrance, to which the offender was tied by his neck and hands for a number of hours and was aimed at submitting the offender to shame and ignominy. This form of punishment was commonly found in Catholic churches and on feudal estates and was sometimes imposed in the Jewish community as a punishment for defamation, informing, and like offenses (Elon, pp. 197–8). In the late 17th century, in the Hamburg congregation of Portuguese Jews, house arrest was a form of punishment imposed in respect of certain offenses (Elon, *ibid.*).

Treatment of Prisoners. It is apparent that punitive imprisonment was introduced into the Jewish legal system under the influence of legal systems surrounding the centers of Jewish life. This may be concluded from the use of the "Kuna" (see above) and from the fact that Jewish law, like other legal systems, only introduced imprisonment as a mode of punishment from the 14th century onward. In the process, Jewish law nevertheless stopped short of absorbing some of the accompanying features of imprisonment, such as the cruelty displayed toward prisoners and the inhuman conditions of their detention that prevailed in various countries until the 19th century. In various *takkanot* and responsa it was laid down, e.g., that prisoners awaiting trial were to be kept under different conditions of detention than those to which convicted prisoners were subject, and that the latter too were to be provided with food, clean quarters, and – separate therefrom – sanitary facilities (Elon, pp. 199–201).

Bibliography: S. Assaf, *Ha-Onshin Aḥarei Ḥatimat ha-Talmud* (1922), passim; M. Shlapoverski, in: *Ha-Torah ve-ha-Medinah,* 5–6 (1952/54), 302–5; M. Elon, in: *Sefer Yovel le-Pinḥas Rosen* (1962), 171–201; idem, *Ha-Mishpat Ha-Ivri* (1973), I, 9ff., 25ff., II, 647, 649, 653, 664 ff., 704 ff.

Menachem Elon

ḤEREM (Heb. חרם) has two distinct connotations: the (apparently original) one is the proscription of a man or thing for immediate or ultimate destruction, whether by way of punishment (Ex. 22:19 – for sacrificing to alien gods; Deut. 13:16–17 – for the subversion of a town) or warlike conquest (Deut. 7:2), to please God (Num. 21:2–3) or to prevent mischief (Deut. 20: 17–18); the other (apparently derivative) is the proscription of a man or thing for consecration to God (Lev. 27:28; Num. 18:14; Josh. 6:17; Ezek. 44:29). Proscribed things were taboo, reserved for the exclusive use of God and priests, and any conversion thereof, during war, to one's own use was a capital offense (Josh. 7:15). Proscribed men – a proscription permissable only (it seems) in respect of enemies in war (Naḥmanides to Lev. 27:29) – were put to death (Lev. 27:29); although in earlier times such proscriptions might have occurred (as in other civilizations) also in respect of members of one's household (cf. Judg. 11:30–31 and see Naḥmanides, *ibid.*). The confiscation of property, threatened in Ezra 10:8 as a sanction for non-obedience to princes and elders, was, qua *ḥerem,* intended as a consecration to God; but it is accompanied by the warning that the offender will, in addition, himself be isolated from the congregation *(ibid.)* – a first indication of a *ḥerem* operating by way of excommunication. Indeed, the criminal jurisdiction vested in Ezra included a power to root out "banishment" (*sheroshu:* JPS "banishment": Ezra 7:26) which was interpreted in the Talmud to mean persecution *(hardafah)* by *niddui* and *ḥerem* (MK 16a).

Niddui is the term employed in tannaitic literature for the punishment of an offender by his isolation from, and his being held in enforced contempt by, the community at large. A precedent for such punitive isolation and contempt is found in the Bible (Num. 12:14) and was described as *niddui* (Sif. Num. 104). Some hold that the tannaitic *niddui* was the expulsion of a member from the order of the Pharisees: "if he failed to maintain the standards required," he would be expelled from the order and "declared *menuddeh*" ("defiled"), and his former comrades would withdraw from his company "lest he defile them" (see bibl., Finkelstein, vol. I, p. 77). This theory is based mainly on the records of infliction of *niddui* on renowned scholars for non-compliance with the rules of the majority (Eduy. 5:6; BM 59b), but it takes no account of the fact that *niddui* was, even during the tannaitic period, inflicted or threatened also on laymen (e.g., a hunter: Shab. 130a, Kid. 72a) and for offenses or misconduct unconnected with any rules of the Pharisees (Ta'an. 3:8; Pes. 53a). While *niddui* may well have implied expulsion from scholarly or holy orders, the sanction as such was a general one, applicable at the discretion of the courts or of the heads of academies. As it was a criminal punishment, a great scholar who was threatened with *niddui* rightly protested that before he could be so punished it had first to be clearly established on whom might *niddui* be inflicted, in what measure, and for what offenses (TJ, MK 3:1, 81c). Later talmudic law reintroduced the *ḥerem* as an aggravated form of *niddui* (MK 16a): first a *niddui* was pronounced, and when it had not (on the application of the *menuddeh:* Maim. Yad, Talmud Torah 7:6) been lifted after 30 days, it was extended for another 30 days; after the 60 days had expired, a *ḥerem* was imposed (MK 16a; Maim. loc. cit.; Sh. Ar., YD 334: 1, 13). Another innovation was the *nezifah* ("reprimand") which was to last for seven days (MK 16a): the commentators were not quite certain about the implications of the *nezifah,* and surmised that while *niddui* and *ḥerem* implied compulsory isolation, the seven days' isolation inherent in the *nezifah* was rather a voluntary one, dictated by shame and remorse; and while *niddui* and *ḥerem* had to be lifted by the court and unless so lifted would last forever (Rema, Sh. Ar., YD 334, 24), *nezifah* expired automatically after seven days (*Piskei ha-Rosh* MK 3:7).

Niddui differed from *ḥerem* mainly in that with the *menuddeh* social intercourse was allowed for purposes of study and of business, whereas the *muḥram* had to study alone (so as not to forget what he had learned) and find his livelihood from a small shop he was permitted to maintain (MK 15a; Maim. *ibid.* 7:4–5; Sh. Ar., YD 334:2). Otherwise the restrictions imposed on the *muḥram* were *(a fortiori)* those imposed on the *menuddeh,* namely: he had to conduct himself as if he were in a state of mourning, not being allowed to have his hair cut or his laundry washed or to wear shoes (except for out-of-town walks). He was even forbidden to wash, except for his face, hands, and feet; but he was not obliged to rend his clothes (notwithstanding the contrary report in BM 59b) nor to lower his bedstead (MK 15a–b; Sem. 5:10–13; *Piskei ha-Rosh* MK 3:4); and he had to live in confinement with his family only, no outsider being allowed to come near him, eat and drink with him, greet him, or give him any enjoyment (*ibid.;* Sh. Ar., YD 334:2). He could not be counted as one of the three required for the special grace after meals formula nor as one of the ten *(minyan)* required for communal prayers (Maim. *ibid.* 7:4; Sh. Ar. YD loc. cit.); and after his death his coffin would be stoned, if only symbolically by placing a single stone on it (Eduy. 5:6; MK 15a; Maim. loc. cit.).

Both *niddui* and *ḥerem* appear in the Talmud at times in the Aramaic form *shamta* – a term which, by being retransliterated into Hebrew, was interpreted as indicating the civil death (*sham mitah*) or the utter loneliness *(shemamah)* involved in this punishment (MK 17a). Notwithstanding its potential severity, however, *niddui* was apparently regarded as a relatively light penalty, reserved mainly for minor offenses, perhaps because it could so easily be lifted and terminated. Talmudic scholars counted 24 offenses for which *niddui* was prescribed (Ber. 19a), listed by Maimonides as follows (loc. cit. 6:14):

(1) Insulting a scholar, even after his death; (2) contempt of an officer of the court; (3) calling any man a slave; (4) disobedience to a court summons; (5) disregarding any rabbinic prescription (such as the washing of hands (Eduy. 5:6)); (6) nonpayment of judgment debts; (7) keeping dangerous dogs or other dangerous things without properly guarding them; (8) selling land to a gentile in disregard of a neighbor's right of preemption (see *Maẓranut*); (9) recovering money on the judgment of a gentile court, where the money was not due under Jewish law; (10) failure by a priest to give other priests their dues; (11) nonobservance of the second festival day customarily observed abroad; (12) doing work in the afternoon of Passover Eve; (13) mentioning God's name in speech or oath in trifling matters; (14) causing the public to profane God's name (*ḥillul ha-Shem*); (15) causing the public to eat sacrificial meals outside the Temple; (16) establishing the calendar, i.e., fixing the lengths of months and years, outside the Land of Israel; (17) placing any stumbling-block before the blind (Lev. 19:14); (18) obstructing the public in the performance of any precept; (19) negligence in ritual slaughtering; (20) failure to have knives used for ritual slaughter periodically inspected; (21) willful sexual self-stimulation; (22) such business relations with one's divorced wife as might lead to intimacy; (23) connections or activities of a scholar which bring him into disrepute; and (24) imposing a *niddui* without sufficient cause. The list is not exhaustive (Rabad ad loc.), and was supplemented in the Shulḥan Arukh by additional offenses among which are the following:

(1) Breaking a vow; (2) doing work while a corpse lies unburied in town; (3) disobedience to Torah precepts on the strength of spurious analogies or arguments; (4) demanding the performance of the impossible; (5) insisting on minority views overruled by the majority; (6) usurpation by a disciple of his teacher's functions; and (7) applying to the king or a leader with a view to evading or circumventing the authority of the competent court (YD 334:44). (The *niddui* for disobedience to law on spurious analogies or arguments might be identical with the ban referred to in John 9:22, 12:42.)

The existence of an offense of imposing a *niddui* without sufficient cause indicates that, under talmudic law, the *niddui* could be imposed not only by the court but also by individual scholars and even by laymen: for instance, creditors used to impose a *niddui* on delinquent debtors (MK 16a), and in later periods we find debtors agreeing in writing beforehand to be placed under *niddui* by the creditor in the event of non-payment (e.g., *Maḥzor Vitry* 567). Individual scholars used to impose a *niddui* for their own vindication from insults (MK 16a), a practice which persisted throughout the ages (cf. e.g., Resp. Joseph Kolon 168–9; Resp. Maharyu 163), although deprecated in no uncertain terms (Maim. *ibid.* 7:13; Tur, YD 334; Sh. Ar., YD 243:9; and cf. Kid. 32a; Meg. 28a). There is a strong opinion to the effect that this power of individual scholars is now obsolete (Rema, Sh. Ar., YD 243:8); it was never recognized for any purpose other than as a punishment for insults, and the scholar was forbidden to use it for his business purposes (TJ, MK 3:1, 81d; YD 334:19).

Normally, *niddui* would be pronounced by the court; it is only by order of a court that a man is regarded as a *menuddeh;* non-judicial *niddui* renders him only "half-*menuddeh*" (*menuddeh la-ḥaẓa'in*) from whom the public at large need not dissociate itself (Sh. Ar., YD 334:12). Where the offense charged was civil disobedience or nonpayment of debts, the court would first warn the delinquent that unless he obeyed or paid a *niddui* would be pronounced against him, but no warning was required where the offense was of a religious nature (MK 16a and Rashi ad loc.). The *niddui* and its causes had to be publicly announced (*ibid.* interpreting Judg. 5:23), but could be pronounced in the absence of the accused (Maim. loc. cit. 7:2, 13; Sh. Ar., YD 334:29). No formal procedure nor any adduction of evidence was required: the court could act on its own knowledge or on evidence that would be otherwise inadmissible (Rema YD 334:43). The formulae used for the pronouncement as well as for lifting of the *niddui* could be very short (Maim. loc. cit. 7:2–3; Sh. Ar., YD 334:23); but it would be enlarged and embellished with curses and imprecations when a *ḥerem* was imposed (*ibid.;* Shev. 36a). The ban could be lifted by any court, not necessarily the court which had imposed it (Maim. loc. cit. 7:9), but a *niddui* imposed by an individual had to be lifted by that same person or – where he was unknown or unavailable – by the *nasi* or leader of the community (MK 17a; TJ, MK 3:1, 81d; Maim. loc. cit. 7:10). The delinquent had a claim as of right to have the ban against him lifted as soon as he had done the act or rectified the omission of which he had been accused, or ceased to do that which he had been accused of doing (Maim. loc. cit. 9) – hence *niddui* was a coercive as well as a punitive measure.

Courts were urged not to pronounce *niddui* against judges (*Takkanat Usha,* MK 17a), scholars (Resh Lakish, *ibid.*), or notables (*zaken;* TJ, MK 3:1, 81d), but rather to ask them to stay at home; only if they persisted in and repeated their offenses was *niddui* pronounced against them to prevent *ḥillul ha-Shem* (by insinuations of discriminations and privileges; *ibid.*). Flogging is considered a more suitable punishment for judges and scholars than *niddui* (MK 17a and Rashi *ibid.*); but where a scholar's misconduct is due to a failure of his memory by reason of old age or sickness, he should rather be treated as if he were "the Holy Ark holding fragments of the broken tablets" (TJ, MK 3:1, 81d and *Korban ha-Edah, ibid.*).

In Post-Talmudic Law. The distinction between the punitive and coercive functions of *niddui* and *ḥerem* became more clearly marked: on the one hand they grew into the most deterrent, and often very cruel, punishment for past misdeed or past misconduct; on the other they were invoked for purposes of future law enforcement, either by warning potential individual offenders of imminent excommunication, or by attaching the threat of excommunication to secure general acceptance of and obedience to a newly created law: several such laws have thus become known by the name of *ḥerem* (e.g., *ḥerem de-Rabbenu Gershom;* see Bigamy[1]).

From the geonic period and throughout the Middle Ages until recent times, courts added further and greater hardships to the living conditions of the *menuddeh* as laid down in the Talmud – the talmudic provisions being regarded as a minimum which the court could increase according to the severity of the individual case (Sh. Ar., YD 334:10; Rema YD 334:6). Among such additional hardships were prohibitions against performing circumcision of the *menuddeh's* children or their marriages; expulsions of his children from school and of his wife from synagogue; and prohibitions against burial of the *menuddeh* and according him any honor due to the dead (Rema, *ibid.*). He was to be treated as a non-Jew, his bread and wine were forbidden like those of a heathen, his books were regarded as magicians' trash, his *ẓiẓit* were to be cut off and the *mezuzah* removed from his door (e.g., *Sha'arei Ẓedek* 4:5, 14). Treating a Jew as if he were a non-Jew amounted, within the closed Jewish community, to civil death; and indeed it is said that a man on whom a *ḥerem* lies can be regarded as dead (cf. also the precept in the Karaite "Book of Precepts" by Anan b. David, after describing the ban to be imposed for capital offenses: "In short, we must treat him as if he were dead": L. Nemoy, *Karaite Anthology* (1952), 13).

The constant growth and increasing frequency of the *ḥerem* as punishment was in no small degree due to the predominant role excommunication played as a punishment in the Church: some features of the later penances inflicted on excommunicated Jews were even borrowed from practices of the Church (see bibliography, Abrahams p. 66f.). It happened also that the ecclesiastical or secular gentile authorities enjoined Jewish courts from imposing or enforcing a *ḥerem,* as for instance where it had been imposed for having recourse to non-Jewish courts: in such cases the law was laid down that in monetary matters the Jewish court would have to give in, whereas in religious matters the Jewish court had to insist on its authority even at the risk of incurring punishment for disobedience (Israel Isserlin, *Terumat ha-Deshen* 276; and cf. YD 334:44, 48). Visiting the guilt of the *menuddeh* on his innocent wife and children and making life in general unbearable for him, shocked the conscience of many a great rabbi (cf., e.g., Resp. Ribash 173, 185; *Yam Shel Shelomo* BK 10:13). Not only did they and many others try to mitigate the hardships of the *ḥerem* when they had to impose it, but they endeavored to abstain from imposing it at all. Thus, Asher b. Jehiel says that he never imposed a *ḥerem* without the previous consent of the congregation (Resp. Rosh 43:9); Jacob Levi Moellin imposed only one single *ḥerem* during his lifetime (*Minhagei Maharil,* quoted Assaf. Onshin (see bibliography), p. 34); and Israel Bruna relates his father's last will enjoining him from ever imposing a *ḥerem* (Resp. 189).

The severity and cruelty of total *niddui* or *ḥerem* led to the creation of lighter punishments, involving only partial excommunication and not inhibiting the offender in his daily life – such as permanent or temporary expulsion from town or province, expulsion from the synagogue, change of the synagogue seat for an inferior one, and public denunciations and reprimands. Application of graver or lighter punishments was left entirely to the discretion of the courts (cf. Resp. Rashba, vol. 5 no. 238; *Zikharon Yehudah* 63; et al.); and the same or similar offenses are found punished at one place or time with *niddui* and another place or time with floggings, expulsions, or reprimands. Among the many and varied offenses for which *niddui* was imposed, mention may be made of a husband's refusal to divorce his wife though ordered to do so (*Or Zaru'a* BK 161; Resp. Maharam of Rothenburg, ed. Prague, 927, and see Divorce), and of a bridegroom's refusal to marry his bride (Resp. Maharam of Rothenburg, ed. Prague, 250) – as well as property offenses ranging from theft and receiving stolen property to bankruptcy, fraud, and forgery (cf. e.g., *Takkanot Medinat Mehrin,* ed. I. Halpern, p. 161). On the other hand, assaults (including wife-beating) and offenses against morality were more often visited with the lighter expulsions (many illustrations in Assaf, *Onshin* (see bibliography), passim). So it was laid down that the straying disciple who is found in possession of profane books and frequents theatrical and musical entertainment should be flogged rather than excommunicated (Tur., YD 334).

The Procedure of Pronouncing a Ḥerem. The minor forms of the *ḥerem, nezifah,* and *niddui,* were pronounced by the head of the rabbinic court. A severe *ḥerem* was pronounced in the synagogue either before the open Ark or while holding a Torah scroll. The proclamation was made with the sounding of the *shofar,* while those present held wax candles which were symbolically extinguished after the excommunication was declared. The person was anathematized, excommunicated, and several biblical curses were evoked upon him. The proclamation contained a public warning not to associate with the anathematized and concluded with a plea for the welfare of the congregation of the faithful.

In Later Centuries. *Ḥerem* and *niddui* became so common in later centuries that they no longer made any impression and lost their force. They became the standard rabbinic reaction to all forms of deviation or non-conformity considered incompatible with or dangerous to Orthodoxy. As such, they are sometimes imposed by extreme Orthodox authorities at the present day, but as neither the persons afflicted nor the public at large regard themselves as bound by them, they have ceased to be a terror or have much effect. (It is arguable that the imposition of *niddui* or *ḥerem* by persons acting in unison – e.g., a court of three – amounts to a criminal conspiracy to cause injury to a person or the reputation of a person and to injure him in his trade or profession, which in Israel is punishable with two years' imprisonment: Section 36, Criminal Code Ordinance, 1936.)

Bibliography: Naḥmanides, *Mishpetei ha-Ḥerem* (1515), also printed as annex to *Sefer Kol Bo;* J. Wiesner, *Der Bann in seiner geschichtlichen Entwicklungen* . . . (1864); D. Friedmann, *Emek Berakhah* (1881); M. Aron, *Histoire de l'excommunication juive* (1882); S. Mandl, *Der Bann* (1898); E. Schulmann, in: *Ha-Goren,* 3 (1902), 90–97; Gulak, Yesodei, 2 (1922), 16f., 35, 52–56, 64, 216ff.; 3 (1922), 17ff.; 4 (1922), 60, 83–85, 89–91, 112, 129, 132ff.; S. Assaf, *Ha-Onshin Aḥarei Ḥatimat ha-Talmud* (1922), 146 index, s.v.; idem, *Battei Din ve-Sidreihem* . . . (1924), 32–34; L. Finkelstein, Middle Ages, 387 index, s.v.; I. Abrahams, *Jewish Life in the Middle Ages* (1932[2]); Gulak, Oẓar xlf., 160, 195, 298ff., 333f., 360; M. Frank, *Kehillot Ashkenaz u-Vattei Dineihen* (1937), 163 index s.v.; Baron, Community, 3 (1942), 429 index, s.v.; J. Katz, *Tradition and Crisis* (1961), index, s.v. *Excommunication;* I. Agus, *Urban Civilization in Pre-Crusade Europe,* 2 (1965), index; M. Elon, *Ha-Mishpat Ha-Ivri* (1973), I, 11ff., 65, 203ff., II, 399 n.47, 415ff., 535ff., 548ff., 564ff., 591ff., 647ff., III, 875ff.

Haim H. Cohn

1. page 367.

FINES (Heb. קְנָסוֹת, *kenasot*) are distinguishable from damages in that they are not commensurate with the actual amount of damage suffered, whether such damage has been sustained by tortious act or by breach of contract or by an offense (see also Obligations, Law of; Torts) as where for a particular tort only half of the sustained damage is recoverable, or where the law prescribes more than the full damage to be paid (e.g., in case of theft: Ex. 21:37), such payment is classified as a fine (Maim. Yad, Nizkei Mamon 2:7–8). Of the four instances of fines prescribed in biblical law, three are liquidated amounts (30 shekels of silver: Ex. 21:32; 100 shekels of silver: Deut. 22:19; 50 shekels of silver: Deut. 22:29), and one is unliquidated ("silver in proportion to the bride price for virgins": Ex. 22:16). The Talmud asserts that while the payment of damages commensurate to the damage caused is rational by law *(min ha-din)* the imposition of fines was something novel *(ḥadash)* decreed by heaven (Ket. 38a, Rashi *ibid.*), so that fines are not to be regarded as law proper but rather as royal (divine) commands *(ibid.)*. Not being the normal compensation for the actual damage suffered, fines have a quasi-penal character ("penalties"), and hence can only be recovered on the evidence of two witnesses, and not on the admission or confession of the defendant (Ket. 42b–43a; Shev. 38b; Yad, loc. cit. and Genevah 3:8). Another consequence of the quasi-penal character of the fine is that it is merged in any graver penalty prescribed for the same act since not more than one penalty can be inflicted for the same offense; where capital punishment or flogging are prescribed for any offense, these alone will be inflicted and no fine imposed (Mak. 4b; Ket. 32b, 37a; BK 83b). The only exception to this rule is the case of wounding, where the payment of a fine and damages is to be preferred to any other punishment (Yad, Ḥovel u-Mazzik 4:9).

In talmudic law, the sanction of fines was introduced for a multitude of causes: e.g., where the damage is not visible to the eye (as where A ritually defiled B's food) and is not liable according to the law of the Torah (Git. 53a; Yad, loc. cit. 7:1–3); where it is doubtful which of several claimants is entitled to stolen goods (Yev. 118b; Yad, Gezelah ve-Avedah 4:9); for the alienation of immovables which cannot be the subject of theft (TJ, BK 10:6, 7c); for selling slaves or cattle to heathens (Git. 44a); for slander (BK 91a; Yad, Ḥovel u-Mazzik 3:5–7); where a tortfeasor is not liable in damages because of a supervening act of a third party (TJ, Kil. 7:3, 31a; see *Gerama and Garme*); et al. In some cases, the amount of the fine is fixed by law (e.g., in certain cases of slander and assault: TJ, BK 8:8, 6c; BK 8:6; for rape: Deut. 22:29); in most cases, however, it is left to the discretion of the court in the exercise of its expropriatory powers (see confiscation; MK 16a; Yad, Sanhedrin, 24:6; ḤM 2:1 and Rema ad loc.). Even where the amount had been fixed by law, instances are recorded in which the courts imposed heavier fines, e.g., on recidivists (BK 96b). Fixed tariffs have the advantage of assuring equality before the law (Ket. 3:7); and even where the amount of the fine was to be assessed according to the dignity and standing of the person injured, a great jurist held that all persons were to be presumed to be of equal rank and status (BK 8:6).

Contractual fines (see Contract) which a person undertook to forfeit in the event of his default were enforceable unless tainted by *asmakhta* (BB 168a). While formal jurisdiction for the imposition of fines ceased with the destruction of the Temple (see *Bet Din*), it was in post-talmudic law that fines became the standard sanction for minor (i.e., most) criminal offenses. Opinions are divided as to whether the present jurisdiction extends only to fines not fixed in the Bible or in the Talmud (Hagra to ḤM 1:5) or whether fines fixed in the Talmud are included in this jurisdiction (*Piskei ha-Rosh* to Git. 4:41; Rema to ḤM 1:5); but there is general consensus that in matters not covered by biblical and talmudic law, courts have an unfettered discretion to impose fines (cf. Resp. Rosh 101:1) – a talmudic authority being invoked to the effect that fines may be imposed not only by virtue of law but also by virtue of custom (TJ, Pes. 4:3, 30d).

A few examples of the many newly created offenses for which fines were imposed are: resisting rabbinical authority (Resp. Rosh 21:8–9); accepting a bribe for changing one's testimony (*ibid.* 58:4); refusing to let others use one's books (*ibid.* 93:3); instituting proceedings in non-Jewish courts (Resp. Maharam of Rothenburg quoted in *Mordekhai,* BK 195); frequenting theaters and other places of public entertainment, as well as gambling (S. Assaf, *Ha-Onshin Aḥarei Ḥatimat ha-Talmud,* 116 no. 126); taking a dog into a synagogue (*ibid.*, 95, no. 12); and many similar contraventions. But fines were also imposed for receiving stolen goods (*ibid.*, 137, no. 163), fraudulent business transactions (*ibid.*, 133 no. 157), and unfair competition (*ibid.*, 127, no. 141). Fines were also the alternative punishment for floggings, where these could not be imposed or executed (Rema to ḤM 2:1; *Darkhei Moshe* ad loc., n. 5; Resp. *Ḥatam Sofer* ḤM 181), as, conversely, flogging was imposed where a fine could not be recovered – although the standard sanction for the nonpayment of fines was imprisonment (*Zikhron Yehudah* 36).

The greatest reform in post-talmudic law in respect of fines however concerned the nature of the payee. While both in biblical and talmudic law it was the person injured (or, in the case of a minor girl, her father) who was entitled to the fine and no fines were payable into any public fund, later courts ordered fines to be paid to the injured person only where he insisted (*Yam shel Shelomo* BK 8:49), but normally would order fines to be paid to public charities, at times giving the injured person a choice of the particular charity to be benefited (Resp. Maharyu 147). More often than not, the charity was left undefined, and the fine was then recovered from the debtor by the community treasurers in charge of collecting for general charities (cf. YD 256:1). But there are also instances of fines being imposed for named charities, such as the study of the Torah (Resp. Rosh 13:4); the maintenance of Torah students (*haspakah; Takkanot Medinat Mehrin,* 46 (no. 139), 47 (no. 140)); the poor of Jerusalem or of the Holy Land (*ibid.* 39, no. 117). A frequent destination of part of all fines recovered was the governor or government of the city or country in which the Jewish court was sitting. In many such cities or countries, the privilege of internal jurisdiction was granted to Jewish courts only on condition that part of all fines recovered would be paid into the official treasury (*ibid.* 39, no. 117; Resp. Rosh, 21:8–9). Whatever the destination was, however, it was the strict rule that the courts or judges were not allowed to appropriate any fines to themselves (Assaf. loc. cit., p. 43); and there are detailed provisions for accounts to be kept and published of the disposition of all fines imposed, recovered, and distributed (*Takkanot Medinat Mehrin,* 25 no. 80). Whether or not the fine was paid to the injured person, the court always insisted that the defendant do everything in his power to pacify him – even to the extent of proclaiming a *ḥerem* on him until he did so (Rif, *Halakhot* BK 84b, *Piskei ha-Rosh* BK 1:20; Yad, Sanhedrin 5:17; *Sha'arei Ẓedek* 4:1, 19). This rule applied even where the fine was irrecoverable owing to lack of jurisdiction; and where a man had possessed himself of a fine he could not recover in the courts, he was held entitled to retain it (BK 15b).

See also Extraordinary Remedies.

Bibliography: M.W. Rapaport, *Der Talmud und sein Recht*

(1912), 2–69 (third pagination); S. Assaf, *Ha-Onshin Aḥarei Ḥatimat ha-Talmud* (1922), index, s.v. *Kenasot Mamon;* Gulak, Yesodei, 2 (1922), 15–17; J.M. Ginzburg, *Mishpatim le-Yisrael* (1956), 378 index, s.v. *Dinei Kenasot;* ET, 1 (1951³), 168–72; 2 (1949), 168–74; 3 (1951), 49–50, 162; 7 (1956), 376–82; 10 (1961), 98, 106f.; 12 (1967), 733f., 740; Finkelstein, Middle Ages, index, s.v. *Fines;* Neuman, Spain, 1 (1942), 126–9; Baer, Spain, passim; Halpern, Pinkas, passim; idem, *Takkanot Medinat Mehrin* (1952), passim; Baron, Community, index; J. Marcus, *Communal Sick-Care in the German Ghetto* (1947), index; I. Levitats, *Jewish Community in Russia* (1943), index; M. Wischnitzer, *History of Jewish Crafts and Guilds* (1965), 215, 271; M. Elon, *Ha-Mishpat Ha-Ivri* (1973), I, 10, 149 n. 42, 175 ff., II, 332 n. 417, 498 ff., 566 ff., 579ff., 646ff., 659, 665ff., 687ff., III, 885, see also Index, *Kenas.*

Haim H. Cohn

COMPOUNDING OFFENSES. The injunction: "Ye shall take no ransom for the life of a murderer . . . And ye shall accept no ransom for him that is fled to his city of refuge" (Num. 35:31–32), was interpreted as an exception to the general rule that for all other offenses you may accept a "ransom" *(kofer),* except only for the offense of homicide (BK 83b; Rashbam to Num. 35:31). It seems that the capital offense of adultery was compounded in this way (Prov. 6:35). The rule that even the worst examples of personal injury (such as blinding or mutilating) were not to be punished by way of talion (as prescribed in the Bible, Ex. 21:24–25; Lev. 24:19–20), but were to be compensated for by the payment of damages, was based on the principle that as offenses short of homicide they were compoundable by money (BK 83b, 84a). The fact that the "ransom" was in these cases translated into "damages" (cf. Maim. Yad, Ḥovel u-Mazzik 1:3), caused some confusion and overlapping between civil and criminal law in this field. By the payment of damages the offender is relieved from criminal responsibility (see Assault), the damages operating as "expiation money" (cf. Ex. 30:12, 15, and 16) in lieu of the otherwise expiating punishment. In the same way the owner of the ox that is a habitual gorer, who, though forewarned, fails to guard it so that it kills a man or a woman is liable to "be put to death," but may "redeem his life" by paying such ransom as "is laid upon him" (Ex. 21:29–30). The dispute between the *tannaim* as to whether the ransom is to be assessed according to the value of the killed man or of the owner of the ox (Mekh. Mishpatim 10; BK 40a), as well as the parallel dispute as to whether the ransom is in the nature of damages *(mamon)* or of expiation (BK 40a), reflect the underlying difference between purely civil and additionally criminal remedies. This distinction is not affected by the talmudic interpretation of the liability of the ox-owner to be put to death, as this relates only to the law of heaven (*bi-ydei shamayim*), the theory of expiation by payment of the ransom applying to divine punishment as well (Sanh. 15b; Maim. Yad, Nizkei Mamon 10:4).

It is because the ransom underwent this transformation into damages that the injunction not to accept a ransom in cases of homicide was interpreted as addressed to the court (*ibid.,* Roẓe'aḥ 1:4). In fact, it was not only the court but more particularly such interested persons as blood-avengers that were enjoined from compounding homicides – as was pointed out by later authorities (e.g., *Minḥat Ḥinnukh* 412). However it appears that such compounding had already been practiced by judges in biblical times and led to accusations of corruption (cf. Amos 5:12; and contrast I Sam. 12:3) – perhaps not so much because the judges corruptly enriched themselves (See Bribery), but because of the inequality thereby created between rich offenders, who could afford to ransom themselves, and indigent offenders who could not (cf. Prov. 13:8; cf. Job 36:18). The elimination of this inequality in cases of homicide may have made it appear even more reprehensible in other cases, at least from the point of view of judicial ethics. In later periods courts allowed offenders to compound offenses for which previous courts had imposed severe punishments (such as flogging) by making payments to the injured person or to the poor (cf. e.g., Resp. *Eitan ha-Ezraḥi 7; Yam shel Shelomo* BK 8:49; Resp. Maharshal 28).

Bibliography: J.M. Ginzberg, *Mishpatim le-Yisrael* (1956), 143f., 221–3; M. Greenberg, in: *Yeḥezkel Kaufmann Jubilee Volume* (1960), 5–28.

Haim H. Cohn

CONFISCATION, EXPROPRIATION, FORFEITURE.

Confiscation is mentioned once in the Bible as a quasi-criminal sanction against disobedience to lawful orders (Ezra 10:8). Relying on this precedent the rule was enunciated that courts are empowered to expropriate (*hefker bet din;* Git. 36b, Yev. 89b); and the power of the courts to impose pecuniary penalties – apart from fines, the amounts of which are already prescribed (e.g., Ex. 21:32; Deut. 22:19, 29) – is derived from this general power of expropriation (MK 16a). This power was regarded as necessary, as the authority given to Ezra and his courts to impose pecuniary punishments (Ezra 7:26 – rendered in the AV as punishment of "confiscation of goods") is presumed to have derived from Persian and not from Jewish law. Thus, even legally prescribed penalties were already increased by talmudic courts in severe cases, e.g., for recidivists (BK 96b); and in post-talmudic times ample use was made of this expropriatory power in the judicial campaign against lawlessness and violence (Maim. Yad, Sanhedrin 24:6; ḤM 2). A talmudic source seems to indicate that semi-confiscatory powers for punitive purposes could also be vested in non-judicial authorities, e.g., a Temple inspector who found a guard asleep on duty was authorized to burn his clothing (Mid. 1:2), an authority said to be derived from the expropriatory powers of the courts (*Piskei ha-Rosh, ibid.*). In later times it was held by some scholars that the townsfolk *(benei ha-ir)* or the seven notables *(shivah tuvei ha-ir),* exercising both legislative and quasi-judicial functions in the prevention of and fight against crime, were by virtue of this expropriatory power also customarily authorized to impose pecuniary sanctions (Rema ḤM 2).

Judicial expropriations were not, however, confined to criminal or qausi-criminal sanctions. They were also used for public utility purposes on the authority of Joshua and the elders of his time who redistributed the land among the tribes and families (Josh. 19:51). Such redistribution presupposed not only the power to divest an owner of some of his property, but also the power to vest that property in someone else – while punitive confiscations need not, according to some scholars, result in the confiscated property being vested in anybody else (*Yam shel Shelomo,* Yev. 10:19). But while punitive confiscation presupposes some guilt or blameworthiness on the part of the owner (Tos. to Yev. 90a), public utility expropriations could also lawfully deprive innocent persons of their property (Resp. Akiva Eger 105). In the perspective of legal history, the most important use made of the expropriatory powers of the court was quasi-legislative. This use is best illustrated by some examples: thus, the legal rule that a lost chattel is to be returned to the claimant although he cannot formally prove his ownership, provided he satisfies the finder as to his bona fides by means of tokens (distinctive marks, *simanim*), was explained as an expropriation by the court of any rights in the chattel in favor of the claimant (BM 27b and Rashi *ibid.*). Also, a disposition by a son of his father's property before the latter's death, in payment of his father's debts or other responsibilities, was validated as an authorized disposition of money expropriated by the court for these purposes (BM 16a). Dispositions by infants of property in their hands were – if they were to their benefit – validated as authorized dispositions of expropriated property vested in the court, where the infants were legally incapable of disposing of their own property (Git. 59a and Tos. to Git. 40b s.v. וכתב). Hillel's famous law reform, the Prosbul, which made all debts recoverable notwithstanding their remission under biblical law (Deut. 15:2), was later sought to be explained and justified by the expropriatory powers of the court (Git. 36–37). In all these (and many similar) cases the expropriatory powers of the court were invoked in theory only, by way of legal fiction, and mostly *ex post facto:* the rules were not established by their actual exercise by any given court but were explained and justified by the mere existence of those powers, which, had they actually been exercised in any particular case calling for the application of the rules, could have brought about the desired result (see also *Takkanot*).

These powers were also used to do justice in particular and individual cases: for instance, by purporting to expropriate an amount of money from a defendant and vesting it in a plaintiff the court exercised a jurisdiction based on law, even where there was no law under which the plaintiff could have claimed that money (cf. Maim. Yad, Sanhedrin 24:6). Or, marriages lawfully contracted which could not (but should) otherwise be dissolved – as, for example, the marriage of a girl abducted from under her canopy (see Abduction) – were invalidated by retroactively expropriating from the bridegroom the money (the ring) with which he had married the bride (Yev. 110a, cf. Yev. 90b). Similarly it was sought to validate the will of a wife, if she bequeathed her estate to a third party, by retroactively expropriating the husband's right to inherit from his wife (Resp. Rosh 55:10). A judgment already enforced, though founded on an error, was upheld because of the special circumstances of that case, on the strength of the expropriatory powers of the court (*Tummim* 25). The same consideration may have led the court to leave a widow in undisturbed possession of her husband's estate, which she had unlawfully but in good faith appropriated to herself (TJ, Ket. 9:3, 33a and Kid. 1:3, 159d).

Finally, there are expropriatory powers vested in the king (or other head of the state; cf. Ezek. 46:18). According to biblical law, these powers appear to have been unlimited (cf. Eccles. 2:4 and 8; I Sam. 8:14), whereas under talmudic law they were limited to the king's military and road-building requirements, although the king alone decided what these requirements were (Sanh. 2:4). The story that Ahab could not buy Naboth's vineyard without the owner's consent and had to have recourse to unlawful means to attain it (I Kings 21) is explained by the king's desire to purchase the land which he could not do unilaterally and he thereupon confiscated it, which he had the right to do (*Haggahot Maimoniyyot* to Melakhim 4:6). Nevertheless, the claim of the king to the vineyard after Naboth's death could not be based on the royal right to forfeiture of lands and goods of persons executed by royal decree, because Naboth was executed by judicial process and as such his lawful heirs inherited (Sanh. 48b). The claim of Ahab is therefore made to depend on the fact that as a nephew of Naboth he was in fact such an heir (Tosef., Sanh. 4:6). The law was eventually codified to the effect that the king was not allowed to confiscate money or goods (and, *a fortiori,* lands) without paying compensation for them, and if he did confiscate without this it was sheer plunder (Maim. Yad, Melakhim 3:8); for everything that he expropriated he had to pay fair compensation (*ibid.*, 4:3, 6).

In modern legal terminology, "confiscation" and "forfeiture" usually indicate expropriations without compensation (such as of smuggled goods), while the term "expropriation" is normally reserved for acquisitions for public purposes against payment of compensation.

See also Public Authority; Takkanot.

Bibliography: S. Assaf, *Ha-Onshin Aḥarei Ḥatimat ha-Talmud* (1922), nos. 141, 150, 157, 163; S. Zeitlin, in: JQR, 39 (1948/49), 6f.; ET, 3 (1951), 173; 8 (1957), 343; 10 (1961), 95–110; J.M. Ginzberg, *Mishpatim le-Yisrael* (1956), 39f., 85–87; H. Cohn, in: *Essays in Jurisprudence in Honor of Roscoe Pound* (1962), 65–68, 77f.; idem, in: *Divrei ha-Congress ha-Olami ha-Revi'i le-Madda'ei ha-Yahadut,* 1 (1967), 185–8, English abstract 267; M. Elon, *Ha-Mishpat Ha-Ivri* (1973), Index, *hafkaot rekhush.*

Haim H. Cohn

EXTRAORDINARY REMEDIES.

Extrajudicial Remedies. As in other ancient civilizations, the earliest method of vindicating violated rights under biblical law was self-redress. A burglar at night may be killed on the spot (Ex. 22:1), life may be taken for life (see Blood-Avenger) and limb for limb (see Talion). Even when another man's rights were violated, one was exhorted not to stand idly by, but to interfere actively to vindicate them (Lev. 19:16; and cf. Ex. 23:4–5; Deut. 22:1–4). Again, as in other systems of law, self-redress was largely superseded by judicial redress – firstly because of unavoidable excesses on the part of avengers, secondly because the effectiveness of self-redress always depended upon the injured party being stronger than the wrongdoer and the weak victim was in the danger of being left without a remedy, and thirdly because an injured party ought not to be the judge in his own cause. The right to self-help survived in the criminal law mainly in the form of self-defense or the defense of others; but in civil law self-redress is in talmudic law much more in evidence than in most other systems, and was a well-established legal remedy.

The biblical license to kill the nocturnal burglar (Ex. 22:1) is retained in talmudic law for the reason that such a burglar presumably knows beforehand that, if caught, he might be killed by the irate landlord and is therefore presumed to come with the intention to kill the landlord first, and: "whoever comes to kill you, better forestall him and kill him first" (Yoma 85b; Maim. Yad, Genevah, 9:7–9). There is no restriction in law as to the mode of killing such a burglar: "you may kill him in whatever way you can" (Sanh. 72b). But if the thief is caught alive, no harm may be done to him; nor may the landlord lay hands on him if he knows that the thief comes for money only and has no murderous designs, or where there are people around who would hinder him (*ibid.;* Maim. *ibid.*, 10–12). Similarly, the biblical allusion to the duty of saving the girl in danger (Deut. 22:27) led to the rule that a man was allowed to kill the persecutor in order to save the persecuted girl from death or rape (Maim. Yad, Roẓe'aḥ u-Shemirat Nefesh, 1:10). While efforts must be made to avert the danger by means other than killing, a man is not to be charged with culpable homicide if he did kill even though the danger could have been averted by other means (*ibid.*, 13). A person is under a duty to save another from death or rape even by killing the offender, and his failure to do so, while not a punishable offense (*ibid.*, 15–16), is considered a grave sin (Lev. 19:16).

The general right of self-redress in civil cases has been stated by Maimonides as follows: "A man may take the law into his own hands, if he had the power to do so, since he acts in conformity with the law and he is not obliged to take the trouble and go to court, even though he would lose nothing by the delay involved in court proceedings; and where his adversary complained and brought him to court, and the court found that he had acted lawfully and had judged for himself truthfully according to law, his act cannot be challenged" (Yad, Sanhedrin, 2:12). This final rule was preceded by a dispute between talmudic jurists, some of whom held that a man may take the law into his own hands only where otherwise, i.e., by going to court, he would suffer monetary damage (BK 27b). This view was rejected because there could be nothing wrong in doing what the law had laid down as right in the first place (*Piskei ha-Rosh* BK 3:3). The party taking the law into his own hands only took the risk that the court might, on the complaint of the other party, overrule him; so that in cases of any doubt it was always safer to go to court at the outset.

There were, however, cases of doubt as to what the law actually was, and as to where the respective rights of the parties lay – in which instance the court would uphold the title of that party who took the law into his own hands and put the court, so to speak, before a fait accompli (*kol de-allim gavar:* BB 34b). The reason for this rule – "a very startling phenomenon indeed" (Herzog) – is stated by Asheri to be that it would be unreasonable to leave the parties quarreling all the time – one trying to outwit the other – so it was laid down that once one of them had possessed himself of the chose in action, he was to prevail; the presumption being that the better and truer one's right is, the better and more unrelenting effort one will make to vindicate it, while a man with a doubtful right will not go to the trouble of vindicating it at the risk of being again deprived of it in court (*Piskei ha-Rosh* BB 3:22). This reasoning appears to be both legally and psychologically unsatisfactory; a better explanation might be that where the other party did not establish any better title to the chose in action, he could not succeed as against the party in possession, such possession being for this purpose recognized as accompanied by a claim of right (see Evidence).

The rule applied not only to land but also to movables and money. Although courts are no longer competent to award fines, where a person entitled in law to a fine has taken it from the wrongdoer, *tefisah,* he may retain it (BK 15b; Sh. Ar., ḤM 1:5); and where he had taken more than was due to him, the wrongdoer may sue only for the return of the balance (Tur and Rema, *ibid.*). A wife who had succeeded in collecting her *ketubbah* from her husband is allowed to retain it notwithstanding the husband's contention that only half of it is due to her (Ket. 16b). The holder of a bill which was unenforceable because of formal defects may retain the amount of the bill if he succeeded in collecting it (the numerous and rather complicated rules of *tefisah* were compiled by Jacob Lissa and are appended to ch. 25 of the standard editions of Sh. Ar., ḤM). But there is a notable exception to this rule; namely, no creditor may enter the debtor's house against his will, for it is written, "Thou shalt stand without" (Deut. 24:11); nor the debtor's property be attached or sold in satisfaction of a debt otherwise than by process of the court (BM 9:13). Even where the debtor had agreed, by contract in writing, that the creditor may satisfy himself by seizing the debtor's property in case of default, the creditor was not allowed to do so except where no court was available to award him a legal judgment (Sh. Ar., ḤM 61:6, see Execution; Pledge).

Two instances of extrajudicial authority inflicting punishments for crime may be mentioned. One is the prerogative of the king to kill any person disobeying or slandering him (Maim. Yad, Melakhim, 3:8) – not only is the king not bound by the rules of law and procedure, but he may lawfully execute murderers acquitted for lack of evidence or other formal grounds if he considers it necessary for the public good (*ibid.,* 10). The other is the right of zealots (*kanna'im*) to kill thieves of Temple utensils, idolatrous blasphemers, and men cohabiting with idolatresses, without legal process, if they are caught *in flagrante delicto* (Sanh. 9:6): this rule derives its justification from the praise God heaped on Phinehas for his impassioned act in stabbing the man whom he found cohabiting with the Midianite woman (Num. 25:6–13).

Extralegal Remedies. Instances are already reported in the Bible of punishments being inflicted, mostly drastic and wholesale, and sometimes at the express command of God, but outside the framework of the law and without legal process (e.g., Gen. 34:25–29; Ex. 32:27–28; Judg. 20:13). With the elaboration of talmudic criminal law and procedure and rules of evidence, and the consequential complication of the criminal process, the necessity soon arose for extraordinary procedures in cases of emergency *(Hora'at Sha'ah):* it was in such an emergency that Simeon b. Shetaḥ is reported to have sentenced and executed 80 witches in Ashkelon on one day (Sanh. 6:4). Extralegal punishments such as these were stated to be justified or even mandatory whenever the court considered their infliction necessary for upholding the authority and enforcing the observance of the law (Yev. 90b; TJ, Hag. 2:2, 78a). With the lapse of capital jurisdiction (see *Bet Din*) – but not previously, as some scholars wrongly hold – this emergency power was called in aid to enable courts to administer the criminal law and uphold law and order generally, the lapsing of the jurisdiction created the "emergency" which necessitated the recourse to such emergency powers. Thus, courts were empowered to inflict corporal and even capital punishment on offenders who were not, under the law, liable to be so punished (Maim. Yad, Sanhedrin, 24:4); and there are instances already in talmudic times of illegal punishments being administered – such as cutting off the hand of a recidivist offender (Sanh. 58b), or burning an adulteress alive (Sanh. 52b; the Talmud *(ibid.),* however, adds: "That was done because the *bet din* at that time was not learned in the law."), or piercing the eyes of a murderer (Sanh. 27a). In post-talmudic times, new forms of capital punishment were advisedly introduced, not only for penological reasons but also to demonstrate that these courts were not administering the regular law. Justification for such innovations was found in the biblical reference to "the judges that shall be in those days" (Deut. 17:9), the nature and content of the *Hora'at Sha'ah,* as the term indicates, depending on the circumstances and requirements of the time (*Bet ha-Beḥirah* Sanh. 52b; Resp. Rashba vol. 5, no. 238). The same considerations led to a general dispensation with formal requirements of the law of evidence and procedure (Resp. Rashba vol. 4, no. 311). Conversely, prior deviations from such law, as, e.g., executions on the strength of confessions only, were retrospectively explained as exceptional emergencies (Maim., loc. cit. 18:6).

A peculiar instance of an extralegal remedy is the rule that where a litigant has a dangerously violent man for his adversary, he may be allowed to sue him in non-Jewish courts under non-Jewish law (Maim. *ibid.,* 26:7; Resp. Rosh 6:27; Tur, ḤM 2; see Introduction). In civil cases, courts are vested with proprietary powers so as to be able to do justice and grant remedies even contrary to the letter of the law (Maim. loc. cit., 24:6; and see Confiscation, Expropriation, Forfeiture; *Takkanot*).

Bibliography: Vogelstein, in: MGWJ, 48 (1904), 513–53; H. Cohen, in: *Jeschurun,* 9 (1922), 272–99; S. Assaf, *Ha-Onshin Aḥarei Ḥatimat ha-Talmud* (1922), passim; Gulak, Yesodei, 1

(1922), 171; 2 (1922), 17, 18; A. Gulak, *Toledot ha-Mishpat be-Yisrael,* 1 (1939), *Ha-Ḥiyyuv ve-Shi'budav,* 112 n. 41, 113–6; Herzog, Instit, 1 (1936), 226–8, 264f., 272f.; B. Cohen, *Jewish and Roman Law,* 2 (1966), 624–50, addenda 793–6; ET, 2 (1949), 11–13, 7 (1956), 385f.; 8 (1957), 512–27; Z. Wahrhaftig, *Ha-Ḥazakah ba-Mishpat ha-Ivri* (1964), 51–77; M. Elon, *Ha-Mishpat Ha-Ivri* (1973), I, 15ff., 42ff., 71ff., 119 n. 167, II, 421 ff., 436ff.

Haim H. Cohn

VII. JURISDICTION, PROCEDURE, EVIDENCE AND EXECUTION

Contents

For Extraordinary Remedies and *Ḥerem* see the section on Criminal Law.

BET DIN (Heb. בית דין, lit. "house of judgment"). The Bible records that Moses sat as a magistrate among the people (Ex. 18:13) and, either on the advice of Jethro, his father-in-law (Ex. 18:17–23), or on the advice of the people (Deut. 1:9–14), he later delegated his judicial powers to appointed "chiefs of thousands, hundreds, fifties, and tens" (Ex. 18:21; Deut. 1:15) – reserving to himself jurisdiction in only the most difficult, major disputes (Ex. 18:22 and 26; Deut. 1:17). It is therefore probable that Israel was one of those civilizations in which the judicature preceded the law, and that some of the later, codified law may have originated in judicial precedents. The earliest reports of such legal decisions already indicate a high standard of judicial practice and qualifications. Judges had to be "able men, such as fear God, men of truth, hating unjust gain" (Ex. 18:21) and "wise men, and understanding and full of knowledge" (Deut. 1:13). They were charged to "hear the causes between your brethren and judge righteously between a man and his brother and a stranger," not be "partial in judgment," but to "hear the small and the great alike; fear no man, for judgment is God's" (Deut. 1:16–17). When the children of Israel settled in their land, the allocation of jurisdiction on a purely numerical basis ("thousands, hundreds, fifties, tens") was to be replaced by allocation on a local basis, i.e., that judges were to be appointed in every town within the various tribes (Deut. 16:18 and Sif. Deut. 144; Sanh. 16b). It is disputed whether this injunction to establish courts in every town applied only in the land of Israel or also in the Diaspora. Some hold that outside the land of Israel courts ought to be established in every district, but need not be established in every town (Mak. 7a); whereas others hold that the injunction applies only in Israel, viz. "in all the settlements that the Lord your God is giving you," but not "in foreign countries in which He has dispersed you" (Maim. Yad, Sanhedrin, 1:2). However, later authorities regard as obligatory the establishment of a court in every community (cf., e.g., *Arukh ha-Shulḥan* ḤM 1:18). In towns with less than 120 inhabitants, there was only a court of three judges – three being the minimum number – so that where opinions were divided, a majority could prevail (Sanh. 3b; Yad, Sanhedrin, 1:4). In towns with 120 inhabitants or more, the court should have 23 judges and be designated as a "Sanhedrin Ketannah" (Sanh. 1:6; Yad, Sanhedrin, 1:10). Courts of 23 judges also sat in the Temple precincts in Jerusalem (Sanh. 11:2; Yad, Sanhedrin, 1:3). The highest court was the "Sanhedrin Gedolah" of 71 judges which sat in the Temple *(Lishkat ha-Gazit)* in Jerusalem (Mid. 5:4; Sanh. 11:2; Yad, Sanhedrin, 1:3 and 14:12), corresponding to the 70 elders and officers who took their place with Moses to "share the burden of the people" (Num. 11:16–17).

The jurisdiction of the various courts was as follows.

(1) Courts of three judges exercised jurisdiction in civil matters generally (Sanh. 1:1), including those which might involve the imposition of fines (Sanh. 1:1; Sanh. 3a). They also had jurisdiction in matters of divorce (Git. 5b) and *ḥaliẓah* (Yev. 12:1). A court of three judges was required for the conversion of non-Jews (Yev. 46b); for absolution from vows (Ned. 78a; TJ, Ḥag. 1:8, 76c and Ned. 10:8, 42b); for the circumvention of the law annulling debts in the Sabbatical year ("prosbul"; Shev. 10:4; Git. 32b); for the non-release of slaves after six years (Ex. 21:6; Mekh. Mishpatim 2; Yad, Avadim 3:9); for the enslavement of one who commits a theft and does not have the means to pay for the principal (Ex. 22:2; Yad, Genevah 3:11); and also for the taking of any evidence, even in noncontroversial cases (Yev. 87b; Resp. *Ha-Meyuḥasot la-Ramban* 113; Resp. Rashba vol. 1, no. 749). Compulsory orders in matters of ritual would also require the concurrence of three judges in order to be valid (Ket. 86a; Ḥul. 132b), as would the imposition of any sanction for disobedience (*Mordekhai* Git. 384).

(2) Courts of 23 judges exercised jurisdiction in criminal matters generally, including capital cases (Sanh. 1:4). They also exercised jurisdiction in quasi-criminal cases, in which the destruction of animals might be involved (e.g., Lev. 20:15–16; Ex. 21:28–29; Sanh. 1:4). Where a case was originally of a civil nature, such as slander, but might in due course give rise to criminal sanctions, such as slander of unchastity (Deut. 22:14), it was brought before a court of 23 (Sanh. 1:1); if the slander was found to be groundless, the matter would be referred to a court of three for civil judgment (Maim. Yad, Sanhedrin, 5:3). According to one view, the imposition of the penalty of flogging required a court of 23 (Sanh. 1:2), but the prevailing view is that a court of three is sufficient (Sanh. 1:2; Yad, Sanhedrin, 5:4), as it is really a penalty that is not necessarily for criminal offenses (see Contempt of Court), as well as being the accepted method of judicial admonition *(makkot mardut)*.

(3) The court of 71 judges had practically unlimited judicial, legislative, and administrative powers but certain judicial and administrative functions were reserved to it alone. Thus, the high priest (Sanh. 1:5), the head of a tribe (Sanh. 16a), and presumably also the president of the Sanhedrin *(nasi)*, could, if accused of a crime, only be tried by the court of 71. Certain crimes were also reserved to its jurisdiction, such as the uttering of false prophecy (Sanh. 1:5), rebellious teaching by an elder (*"zaken mamre"*; Sanh. 11:2; see Majority Rule), and the subversion of a whole town or tribe (Sanh. 1:5); and certain death penalties had to be confirmed by it before being carried out (such as of the rebellious son, the enticer to idolatry, and false witnesses; Tosef., Sanh. 11:7). The ordeal of a woman suspected of adultery took place in the Great Court at Jerusalem only (Sot. 1:4).

Among the administrative functions reserved to the Great Sanhedrin were the appointment of courts of 23 (Sanh. 1:5; Maim. Yad, Sanhedrin 5:1); the election of kings (Yad, loc. cit. and Melakhim 1:3) and of high priests (Yad, Kelei ha-Mikdash 4:15); the expansion of the limits of the city of Jerusalem and of the Temple precincts (Sanh. 1:5), and the partition of the country among the tribes (Sanh. 16a); the declaration of war (Sanh. 1:5); the offering of a sacrifice for the sin of the whole community (Lev. 4:13–15; Sanh. 13b); and the appointment and control of priests serving in the Temple (Mid. 5:4; Tosef., Ḥag. 2:9). The legislative functions of the Great Sanhedrin cannot easily be enumerated. It has been authoritatively said that the Great Court of Jerusalem was the essential source of all Oral Law (Yad, Mamrim 1:1). The law as laid down (or as interpreted) by the Great Sanhedrin is binding on everybody, and any person contravening or repudiating it was liable to the death penalty (Deut. 17:12; Sif. Deut. 155; Yad, Mamrim 1:2), even where the law as laid down (or interpreted) by the court might appear misconceived: "even though they show you as right what in your eyes is left or as left what is right – you must obey them" (Sif. Deut. 154; but cf. Hor. 1:1 and TJ, Hor. 1:1, 45d; and see Authority, Rabbinical[1]). As a corollary of their legislative powers, the Great Sanhedrin also exercised advisory functions: wherever in any court any question of law was in doubt, the final and binding opinion of the Great Court at Jerusalem would have to be taken (Sanh. 88b; Yad, Mamrim 1:4). For the question of appeals see Practice and Procedure.

(4) Apart from the regular courts mentioned above, there sat in the Temple a special court of priests charged with the supervision of the Temple ritual and with civil matters concerning the priests (cf. Ket. 1:5). Mention is also made of a special court of levites, presumably with similar functions (cf. Tosef., Sanh. 4:7). Originally, the priests performed general judicial

1. page 54.

functions: they were the sole competent interpreters of God's judgment (Ex. 28:15, 30, 43; Num. 27:21; Deut. 33:8–10); later, they adjudicated matters together or alternately with the judges (Deut. 17:9; 19:17; 21:5), and it seems that the litigants had the choice of applying to the priest for the dictum of God or to the judges for judgment according to law; eventually, the judicial functions of the priests were reduced to their simply being allotted some seats in the Great Sanhedrin (Sif. Deut. 153).

(5) While no regular court could consist of less than three judges (Sanh. 3b), recognized experts in the law *("mumḥeh la-rabbim")* were already in talmudical times admitted as single judges (Sanh. 5a), albeit in civil cases only and not without express reservations and disapproval – there being no true single judge other than God alone (Avot 4:8; Yad, Sanhedrin 2:11). No litigant could be compelled to submit to the jurisdiction of a single judge (Sh. Ar., ḤM 3:2).

Appointment of Judges. The appointment of judges presupposed the *"semikhah"* ("laying of hands") by the appointer upon the appointee, as Moses laid his hands upon Joshua (Num. 27:23) thereby making him leader and supreme judge in succession to himself. The tradition is that throughout the ages judges received their authority from their immediate predecessors who "laid their hands" upon them; so it came about that in law the president of the Great Sanhedrin would be the authority conferring judicial powers on graduating judges (Sanh. 5a), in a formal procedure before a court of three in which he participated or which he appointed (Yad, Sanhedrin 4:5). But judges were also appointed by kings (e.g., II Chron. 19:5–6), a power which appears to have eventually devolved on the exilarch in Babylonia (Yad, Sanhedrin 4:13), but was superseded even there by the overriding authority of the heads of the academies (*rashei yeshivot;* cf. A. Harkavy (ed.), *Zikhron la-Rishonim,* 80f., no. 180). Courts need not be composed of authorized judges only: any duly authorized judge could form a court by co-opting to himself the necessary number of laymen (Yad, Sanhedrin 4:11).

The original practice of *semikhah* ceased about the middle of the fourth century and at the present time *battei din* exercise their judicial functions only as agents of, and by virtue of, an implied authority from the Ancients (Git. 88b; BK 84b; Yad, Sanhedrin 5:8). This "agency" does not extend to capital cases; even for cases involving fines nonauthorized judges would not be qualified (Sh. Ar., ḤM 1:1). It is only because of force of circumstances that the scope of jurisdiction was in practice never restricted, but extended to whatever causes local conditions required (cf. *Netivot ha-Mishpat,* Mishpat ha-Urim, ḤM 1:1; Nov. Ramban Yev. 46b).

One of the consequences of the cessation of the traditional authorization of judges was the adoption in many (mostly Western European) communities of a system of election of judges: in Spain, the judges were elected every year, along with all other officers of the community (cf. Resp. Ribash 214). The leading rabbinical authorities of the period were time and again consulted about election procedures (cf., e.g., Resp. Rashba vol. 3, nos. 417, 422–5; vol. 5, no. 284), so as to ensure that the best and most impartial candidates would be elected. It seems that, when elected, they could not refuse to serve, even though they had not put up their candidature (cf. Rema ḤM 25:3; see Introduction).

In the State of Israel today, the procedure for appointing rabbinical judges is similar to that for appointing secular judges (*Dayyanim* Act, 5715–1955), but while the qualifications of secular judges are laid down in the law, those of rabbinical judges are in each individual case to be attested to by the chief rabbis on the strength of examinations.

No authorization *(semikhah)* and no appointment of a judge will be valid where the appointee did not possess the necessary qualifications (Maim. Yad, Sanhedrin 4:15); and the sin of appointing unqualified judges is said to be tantamount to erecting an *asherah* beside the altar of the Lord (Sanh. 7b); and where the man was appointed because he was rich, it was like making gods of silver or gods of gold *(ibid.)*, not only causing miscarriages of justice but idolatry (Maim. loc. cit., 3:8); and it is reported that judges appointed because of their money were treated with open contempt (TJ, Bik. 3:3, 65d). "The Sages have said that from the Great Court messengers were sent out all over the country of Israel, and they looked for judges who were wise and feared sin and were humble and clearsighted and of good appearance and good manners, and first they made them judges in their towns, and then they brought them to the gates of the Temple, and finally they would elevate them to the Great Court" (Maim. loc. cit., 2:8).

Qualifications. The judicial qualifications have been enumerated by Maimonides as follows: judges must be wise and sensible, learned in the law and full of knowledge, and also acquainted to some extent with other subjects such as medicine, arithmetic, astronomy and astrology, and the ways of sorcerers and magicians and the absurdities of idolatry and suchlike matters (so as to know how to judge them); a judge must not be too old, nor may he be a eunuch or a childless man; and as he must be pure in mind, so must he be pure from bodily defects, but as well a man of stature and imposing appearance; and he should be conversant in many languages so as not to stand in need of interpreters. The seven fundamental qualities of a judge are wisdom, humility, fear of God, disdain of money, love of truth, love of people, and a good reputation. A judge must have a good eye, a humble soul, must be pleasant in company, and speak kindly to people; he must be very strict with himself and conquer lustful impulses; he must have a courageous heart to save the oppressed from the oppressor's hate, cruelty, and persecution, and eschew wrong and injustice (Yad, Sanhedrin 2:1–7). Playing cards for money or other games of chance and lending money on interest also disqualify a person from judicial functions (Sanh. 3:3). A judge who is a relative of one of the litigants, or has any other personal relationship toward him ("loves him or hates him"), must disqualify himself from sitting in judgment over him (Sanh. 3:4–5). A judge should not engage in manual work, so as not to expose himself to popular contempt (Kid. 70a).

Principles of Judicial Conduct. A judge must show patience, indulgence, humility, and respect for persons when sitting in court (Yad, Sanhedrin 25:1; Sh. Ar., ḤM 8:2–5); he must always hear both parties to the case (Sanh. 7b; Shev. 31a; and Codes); he may not in any way discriminate between the parties (Lev. 19:15; Shev. 30a–31a; Yad, Sanhedrin 21:1–2; 20:5–7; Sh. Ar., ḤM 17:1 and commentaries ad loc.); nor may he act under the possible pressures of any undue influence, including bribery by money or by words (Deut. 16:19; Sanh. 3:5; Shab. 119a; Ket. 105b; and Codes); he must, on the one hand, proceed with deliberation and care, and reconsider again and again before finally pronouncing his verdict (Avot 1:1; Sanh. 35a; Sif. Deut. 16 and Codes), but may not, on the other hand, unduly delay justice (Yad, Sanhedrin 14:10 and 20:6); and he must so conduct himself that justice is not only done but is also manifestly seen to be done (Yoma 38a; Shek. 3:2) and readily understood by the litigants (ḤM 14:4). Before joining a court, a judge must satisfy himself that the judges sitting with him are properly qualified (Yad, Sanhedrin 2:14); and no judge should sit together with another judge whom he hates or despises (Sh. Ar., ḤM 7:8). Nor may a judge – especially in criminal cases – instead of considering and deciding the issue before him on his own, rely on the opinion of greater judges in the court and try thus to disburden himself of his judicial responsibility (Tosef., Sanh. 3:8; Yad, Sanhedrin 10:1).

For further details of Courts and Jurisdiction see also Introduction; Arbitration; *Takkanot.*

Bibliography: D. Hoffmann, *Der Oberste Gerichtshof in der Stadt des Heiligthums* (1878); J. Jelsky, *Die innere Einrichtung des Grossen Synedrions zu Jerusalem und ihre Fortsetzung im spaeteren palaestinensischen Lehrhause* . . . (1894); A. Buechler, *Das Synedrion in Jerusalem und das Grosse Beth-Din in der Quaderkammer des Jerusalemischen Tempels* (1902); Schuerer, Gesch, 4 (1911[4]), index, s.v. *Gerichtswesen;* Gulak, Yesodei, 4 (1922), index; S. Assaf, *Battei ha-Din ve-Sidreihem Aḥarei Ḥatimat ha-Talmud* (1924); idem, in: *Ha-Mishpat ha-Ivri,* 1 (1925/26), 105–20; A. Feldman, in: *Juridical Review,* 41 (1929); D. M. Shohet, *The Jewish Court in the Middle Ages* (1931); A. A. Neuman, *The Jews in Spain,* 2 (1942), index, s.v. *Courts, Jewish;* H. Albeck, in: *Zion,* 8 (1942/43), 85–93; I. Levitats, *Jewish Community in Russia 1772–1844* (1943), 198–217; A. Weiss, in: *Sefer ha-Yovel . . . Ginzburg* (1946), 189–216; Albright, in: *A. Marx Jubilee Volume* (1950), 61–82; Gershoni, in: *Ha-Torah ve-ha-Medinah,* 2 (1950), 72–75; ET, 1 (1951[3]), 117–9; 2 (1949), 253; 3 (1951), 150–74, 174–80, 181; 8 (1957), 510–2; S. B. Hoenig, *The Great Sanhedrin* (1953); H. Mantel, *Studies in the History of the Sanhedrin* (1961); Silberg, in: *Molad,* 23 (1965/66), 265–74; Baron, Social[2], index, s.v. *Courts, Jewish;* M. Elon, *Ha-Mishpat Ha-Ivri* (1973), I, 6–35, 42ff., 65ff., 83ff., 171ff., 224ff., 231ff., II, 291ff., 455ff., 496, 529ff., 561ff., 569ff., 598, 667ff., 740ff., 776ff., 800ff., III, 863n. 68, 871ff., 1077, 1087ff., 1218ff., 1224ff; and index – *Bet Din, Dayyan, Sanhedrin.*

Haim H. Cohn

ARBITRATION, method of settling disputes by their submission, voluntarily and with the mutual consent of all parties, for adjudication by a person or institution.

Function of Arbitration. In ancient Greek and Roman law – up to the middle of the third century c.e. – the adjudication of disputes was primarily dealt with by arbitration. But in Jewish law such adjudication from the beginning was based on a system of regular courts, empowered to enforce their judgments on the parties. This is ordained in the Pentateuch (Ex. 18:25–26, and more specifically Deut. 16:18 and 17:8–13). Reference is made to a system of established courts in the time of King Jehoshaphat in the eighth century b.c.e. (II Chron. 19:5–11), and talmudic tradition ascribes to Ezra, in the middle of the fifth century b.c.e., an enactment that courts *(battei dinin)* be held on Mondays and Thursdays (Ket. 1:1; BK 82a) to judge the people whether they wish it or not (Sif. Deut. 144 – contrary to the opinion of B. Cohen, *Jewish and Roman Law,* 2 (1966), 657ff., and Baron, Social[2], 2 (1952), 266f., that arbitration preceded a system of presiding courts in Jewish law as well; see bibliography below: Gulak, Assaf). See also Bet Din.

The beginnings of the arbitral institutions are traceable to the middle of the second century c.e., in the period of Hadrian's decrees or even, it has been suggested, to the time of Rabban Gamaliel of Jabneh (first to the second century; see G. Alon, below, and Elon, *Ha-Mishpat Ha-Ivri* I, p. 18). This was one of the low periods in the history of Jewish judicial autonomy, in which judicial authority was restricted, even in the field of civil law, i.e., *dinei mamonot,* as opposed to criminal law (TJ, Sanh. 7:2, 24b), and the prohibition against ordination *(semikhah)* was decreed (Sanh. 14a). To ensure the continued existence of Jewish judicial authority, therefore, the institution of arbitration was resorted to, and Jews turned to it of their own free will, prompted by their religio-national feelings. The laws of arbitration are first discussed by R. Meir and other scholars of that period (Sanh. 3:1) and the institution was known and employed mainly in Ereẓ Israel and not in Babylonia, where the Jews enjoyed wide judicial autonomy. For this reason too, the original meaning of the mishnaic term *shetarei berurin* ("deeds of arbitration," MK 3:3; BM 1:8; BB 10:4) was forgotten and it was interpreted as meaning the statements of the parties, claims, or pleadings (BB 168a), whereas the *amoraim* of Ereẓ Israel adhered to the original meaning of the term, i.e., "*Compromisin,* this one chooses one [arbitrator] and this one chooses another" (TJ, MK 3:3, 82a). The existence in practice of the situation as described, and the background to the creation of arbitration as an institution of Jewish judicial authority, find expression in an order of Honorius in 398 c.e., according to which Jews were rendered subject to Roman law and the regular courts, but permitted, in civil law matters and by mutual consent of the parties, to resort to their own arbitration proceedings, enforceable at the hands of the provincial judges (*Codex Theodosianus,* 2:2, 10; also quoted, with slight changes, in *Codex Justinianus,* 1:9, 8).

At various times and in different countries of the Diaspora, arbitration continued to serve as a substitute for judicial autonomy, in particular where such autonomy had been weakened. But it also fulfilled important functions even where there was autonomy, which was general in the countries of the Diaspora. Thus, it aided in relieving the burden on the regular courts and in speeding up legal proceedings (see e.g., *Or Zaru'a,* BK 10:436) or was employed when the regular court was disqualified from hearing a suit because of its own interest in it (see S. Dubnow (ed.), *Pinkas ha-Medinah* (1925), 6, no. 13 and 307, no. 12) or for other reasons (*Shevut Ya'akov,* vol. 2, no. 143).

Composition. Ordinarily, in Jewish law, the arbitral tribunal is composed of three arbitrators. The Mishnah (Sanh. 3:1) records a dispute between R. Meir and other scholars, the former stating that each party chooses one arbitrator and both choose the third, while the other scholars hold that the two arbitrators choose the third. Gulak correctly points out that the scholars sought to lend to arbitration proceedings (at least externally, although the matter is of substantive importance too: see below) the appearance of a Jewish court, composed generally of three judges, in contrast with the single arbiter customary under Roman law. The plain meaning of R. Meir's statement seems to be that the third arbitrator is chosen by the two parties only (so too, TJ, Sanh. 3:1, 21a), but the interpretation of the Babylonian *amoraim* was that all agreed that the consent of the two (arbitrators) is required for the appointment of the third and that R. Meir merely added that the consent of the parties to the third (arbitrator) is also required. The *halakhah* was decided accordingly (Sh. Ar., ḤM 13:1; Maim. Yad, Sanhedrin 7:1 gives conflicting interpretations). However, the opinion has been expressed that where the arbitrators are empowered to decide not only according to strict law, but also to effect a compromise *(pesharah),* the two arbitrators may not appoint a third without the consent of the two parties (*Arukh ha-Shulḥan,* ḤM 13:1).

When the two arbitrators are unable to agree on the appointment of the third, the appointment is made by the elders of the city – whose status in various matters is as that of the court (see *Takkanot ha-Kahal;*[1] and cf. *Piskei ha-Rosh,* Sanh. 3:2; Sh. Ar., ḤM 13:1, Isserles *ibid.*) and it was often customary for the rabbi of the city to be the third arbitrator (the *"shalish"*; I. Halperin (ed.), *Pinkas Va'ad Arba Araẓot* (1945), 111–2, no. 270; 142–3, no. 335; Dubnow, op. cit., 246, no. 932; *Shevut Ya'akov,* vol. 2, no. 143; *He-Avar,* 2 (1918), 73, no. 16). In the Vilna community, where, as in other communities, arbitration

1. page 655.

was customary despite the existence of regular *battei din,* it was the practice to stipulate in the rabbi's letter of appointment that he would not be required to serve as a third or fifth arbitrator etc., as the case might be (*He-Avar,* 2 (1918), 66, no. 11). The parties to arbitration may agree to a smaller or to a larger number than three (Sh. Ar., ḤM 3:1; Resp. Rosh, 56:1 and 56:7; Resp. Rashba vol. 2, no. 83; Resp. Jacob Weill 11; Naḥmanides, to Deut. 1:12; Isserles to Sh. Ar., 13:1), a rule carried out in practice (Halperin, op. cit., p. 85, 309; Dubnow, op. cit., 225, no. 843; 232, no. 888), and in one case cited, ten arbitrators were appointed (Resp. Ritba 85). A party is not heard, however, if an increase in the number of arbitrators is requested as a subterfuge (*Arukh ha-Shulḥan,* ḤM 13:5). When four arbitrators are appointed, the fifth is again chosen by them and not by the parties (*Noda bi-Yhudah, Mahadura Kamma,* ḤM 2).

R. Meir's statement would allow for either party to reject the other's arbitrator, even if the latter be competent to judge in accordance with the *halakhah* (TJ, Sanh. 3:2, 21a). The Babylonian Talmud, however, interpreted R. Meir as conceding that an expert *(mumḥeh)* could not be so rejected (Sanh. 23a). The opinion of the scholars who differ from R. Meir is that one party cannot reject the other's arbitrator in the absence of evidence that the latter is a relative of the litigants (or of the other arbitrators: Resp. Rema 104) or not competent to serve as a judge (as detailed in the Mishnah, Sanh. 3:3–4). A bond of friendship between a party and his arbitrator does not of itself entitle the other party to disqualify him (Resp. Maharik 16), but if a defendant wishes to appoint an arbitrator whose integrity is in question, the former is not heard and he is compelled to appear before the regular court. Similarly, the defendant need not appear at arbitration proceedings until the claimant has appointed an honest arbitrator (*Piskei ha-Rosh,* Sanh. 3:2; Sh. Ar., ḤM 13:1). An arbitrator cannot be disqualified merely because he is not "godfearing" (Resp. RiMigash 114).

Status and Functions of Arbitrators. The talmudic sages saw a particular advantage in arbitration, in that each party could nominate an arbitrator of his own choice who represented the interests of the party choosing him and therefore a just decision was ensured (Sanh. 23a and Rashi, *ibid.,* cf. TJ, Sanh. 3:1, 21a). In the 13th century, Asher b. Jehiel pointed out that it was wrong to interpret the above passages as justifying the arbitrator's blind support of the party by whom he was chosen when they should rather be read as meaning that the arbitrators appointed by both parties would thoroughly investigate the facts objectively and negotiate on the respective merits of the litigants' claims – the third arbitrator listening to them and then deciding between them (*Piskei ha-Rosh,* Sanh. 3:2, see also *Darkhei Moshe* ḤM 13:3 and Resp. Maharik 16).

The status of arbitrators has been described as equivalent in every way to that of *dayyanim* (*Panim Me'irot,* vol. 2, no. 159), and hence an arbitrator is precluded from hearing the contentions of the party appointing him in the absence of the other party, unless this is agreed upon or is local custom (*Arukh ha-Shulḥan,* ḤM 13:4). Arbitrators' fees are payable to the arbitrators chosen by each party, regardless of the outcome, lest the arbitrator be unduly influenced because of his interest in recovering his fees *(ibid.).* To ensure the maximum integrity of the arbitrators, an opinion was expressed that these fees be defrayed from a communal fund especially set up for this purpose and that a ban *(ḥerem)* be imposed on both the donor and recipient of any gift beyond the allocation from this fund *(Panim Me'irot, ibid.),* but this far-reaching proposal was apparently not adopted (S. Assaf, *Battei Din . . .* (1924), 57).

On the other hand, formal legal requirements are relaxed in arbitration proceedings (see e.g., *Resp. Rashba,* vol. 2, no. 64). From the procedural point of view, too, arbitrators act as *dayyanim* and in various places special rules of procedure in arbitration proceedings are provided for. Thus in Cracow, in the 17th century, it was determined that arbitrators were required to commence their hearing within 24 hours of their appointment and to give their decision within three days of the hearing, a limit of nine days being provided for when the issue was complicated (Balaban, in: JJLG, 10 (1912), 333–4).

Agreement to, and the Subject Matter of Arbitration. The Talmud does not deal specifically with the question as to when an agreement to resort to arbitration is considered irrevocable. The problem is touched upon in connection with a case where the parties accepted a relative or other person legally incompetent to act as judge or witness, when it was held that, if accompanied by an act of *kinyan* (see Acquisition), such acceptance could not be revoked; if there was no such *kinyan,* either party may revoke its acceptance at any time up to the completion of the litigation, but not thereafter (Sanh. 24a–b). *A fortiori,* where legally competent arbitrators are appointed, there can be no withdrawal from the submission to arbitration if agreed upon by way of a *kinyan,* nor after the conclusion of the proceedings (*Beit ha-Beḥirah,* Sanh. p. 83–84; Isserles to Sh. Ar., ḤM 13:2).

However, additional ways were sought to enhance the institution of arbitration and to prevent a party's withdrawal of its submission thereto. One such way was the drawing up of a deed of arbitration, referred to already in the Mishnah (above), which can be written only on the decision of both parties, both of whom pay the scribe's fees (BB 10:4 and Codes). The Mishnah also mentions a deed of arbitration as one of the documents permitted to be written on *ḥol ha-mo'ed* ("the intermediate days of a festival"; MK 3:3). Rashi's opinion is that the purpose of a deed of arbitration is to render submission to arbitration irrevocable (BM 20a), since the writing of a document has the same legal effect as a *kinyan* (Nov. Ramban, BM 20a; see also *Nimmukei Yosef,* MK 3:3). Support for the fact that writing a deed is regarded as a *kinyan* is to be found also in the case of providing surety for which *kinyan* is required (Sh. Ar., ḤM 129:4–6; see also Ket. 102a), a view supported in most of the Codes. Other scholars express the view that a deed of arbitration is written "so that the arbitrators should not forget" (cited in *Beit ha-Beḥirah,* Sanh. p. 84; cf. Maim. Yad, Yom Tov, 7:12) and its mere reduction to writing does not preclude the parties' revocation of the arbitration agreement. Yet another opinion is that the deed is an undertaking by the arbitrators to hear the matter, which they cannot later deny (*Or Zaru'a,* BB 10:232).

A further opinion, accepted in most of the Codes, is that once the parties have commenced their pleas before the arbitrators, they (the parties) can no longer withdraw from the arbitration (*Ha-Ittur,* vol. 1, s.v. *Berurin; Beit ha-Beḥirah,* loc. cit; *Nimmukei Yosef,* BM 20a. Their reliance on TJ, Sanh. 3:4, 21a and on BK 112b may, however, be considered as not being within the plain meaning of these texts). This view is also quoted by Isserles (to Sh. Ar., ḤM 13:2), who holds that it is generally agreed that where it is not customary for a deed of arbitration to be written, the parties may not withdraw after the commencement of their pleas. Two extreme and contradictory opinions are: firstly, that once the names of the arbitrators have been determined the parties may no longer withdraw, even if no deed has been written and the parties have not yet commenced their pleas (*Or Zaru'a,* Sanh. 3:8), and secondly, that even where there are legally competent arbitrators the parties may withdraw at any time before the proceedings have been concluded, except where the agreement to arbitrate was effected by an act of *kinyan* (Ibn Migash, quoted in *Ha-Ittur,* loc. cit.).

There is a complete consensus of opinion that where the arbitrators are empowered to adjudicate on the basis of a compromise, the parties may withdraw, provided that they had not already performed a *kinyan* or undertaken in writing to observe any such compromise, as the absence of a *kinyan* gives rise to the suspicion of a mistaken release (see *Meḥilah*), or *asmakhta* (Sh. Ar., ḤM 12:7 and Isserles ad loc.). It was customary for most arbitration deeds to be effected with the aid of a *kinyan*, apparently also because the arbitrators were generally empowered to adjudicate both on a strictly legal ruling and by way of compromise (see forms of arbitration deeds in Gulak, Oẓar, 281–6). Similarly it was customary to provide therein for payment of a fixed penalty upon withdrawal, or to deter such withdrawal by the imposition of an oath or ban *(ibid.)*.

The subject matter of an arbitration may be an existing dispute between the parties, or one that is likely to arise between them as a result of a particular transaction (as, unlike in the case of real acquisition, a man may obligate himself in respect of something which is not yet in existence, or not quantified (see Contract;[1] *Leḥem Rav* 82 and see Warhaftig, pp. 516–7)). Similarly, in the opinion of Nissim Gerondi, the issue for arbitration may relate to matters of both civil and criminal law, e.g., "robbery *(gezelot)* and assaults" (Nov. Ran, Sanh. 23a), contrary to the view of Warhaftig, pp. 518–9, that Jewish law permits arbitration in civil cases only. The reason therefore would seem to be that at times the regular courts, required to be composed of expert and professional judges, were themselves obliged to resort to the principle of arbitration, but in practice it was customary only for civil law cases to be referred to arbitration (see e.g., S. Dubnow (ed.), *Pinkas ha-Medinah* (1925), 145, no. 609). An important detail, frequently prescribed in deeds of arbitration, was that the proceedings had to be concluded within a stated period, the arbitrators themselves sometimes being given authority to extend such period at their discretion (Gulak, Oẓar, loc. cit; see also above).

Decision of the Arbitral Body. As in the case of the regular court, the decision of the majority prevailed, unless they were authorized to impose a compromise, for which a unanimous decision was required (Sh. Ar., ḤM 12:18). According to talmudic *halakhah,* a party may require the regular court to submit written reasons for its judgment (Sanh. 31b and Codes), but an arbitral body is not obliged to do so, even upon request (Tos. and *Yad Ramah* to Sanh. 31b and *Beit ha-Beḥirah,* Sanh. p. 138, *Piskei ha-Rosh,* BM 5:45, Sh. Ar., ḤM 14:4, Isserles). Sometimes however, it is considered desirable to make known the reasons for a judgment – as was hald by M. M. Krochmal in the 17th century, in a suit by members of the community of Vienna against the leaders for the return of money allegedly misappropriated, so that "you shall be blameless in the eyes of God and of the people" (see his *Ẓemaḥ Ẓedek* 37).

A decision on a matter not included in the issues submitted to the arbitrators for decision, renders their decision void *pro tanto* (Resp. Rosh 85:5–6, see also Resp. Jacob Berab 27; Resp. Maharashdam, ḤM 4; *Divrei Rivot* no. 155; *Leḥem Rav* 85). A compromise imposed by the arbitrators, when they were not authorized to do so in the deed of arbitration, is also a void decision (Resp. Be-Rab 27). Similarly, their decision is voidable in the event of improper conduct on their part, e.g., if it appears that any one of them was acting for his own benefit (Resp. Maharashdam, ḤM 4) or that they gave their decision without hearing both parties (*Leḥem Rav* 87) or that it was given after the period prescribed in the deed of arbitration had expired (Resp. Rashba vol. 3, no. 209. See also Resp. Ribash 300; Resp. Radbaz 953 (518)). The right of appeal against the arbitrator's decision is coextensive with the right of appeal against judgments of the regular courts (OPD 71ff.), but the parties may stipulate, at the time of the arbitration agreement, that they shall not appeal against or object to the arbitral decision but accept it as final (Resp. Radbaz 953; Gulak, Oẓar, 284–5, no. 306; *Takkanot Moshe Zacuto;* see Assaf, p. 78).

In Modern Israel. In the years 1909 to 1910 there was founded in Palestine the *Mishpat ha-Shalom ha-Ivri,* an institution designed to serve the Jewish *yishuv* as a forum for the adjudication of all disputes of a civil law nature, and thus to revive the jurisdiction of Jewish law. From the point of view of the general law of the land, this institution functioned as an arbitral body, reaching the peak of its activities in the years 1920–30. Its presiding arbitrators adjudicated mainly in accordance with general principles of justice, equity, and public order. The rabbinical courts too – whose jurisdiction from the general law viewpoint is confined to matters of personal status only – have had a certain proportion of matters of a civil law nature referred to them for adjudication when sitting in effect as arbitral bodies. This tendency has to a certain extent been intensified in recent years and decisions of this nature of the rabbinical courts carry with them an element of laying down guiding principles with reference to new problems arising in all fields of civil law (see Introduction).

Arbitration in the State of Israel is governed by the Arbitration Law, 5728/1968, based on the recommendations of an advisory committee in 1965. The law deals in detail *(inter alia)* with the manner of appointing arbitrators and their removal from office, their powers and the auxiliary powers of the regular courts, and with the rules of procedure in arbitrations and the manner of confirming or setting aside decisions. The provisions of a common form of agreement between the parties to submit to arbitration, appearing in a schedule to the law, is binding upon them unless they have otherwise agreed. These provisions deal with the composition of the arbitral tribunal, the manner in which it is to be conducted, and its powers vis-à-vis the parties. Several of the provisions of the above law are based on Jewish law.

Bibliography: Gulak, Yesodei, 4 (1922), 23–32; Gulak, Oẓar, 281–6; S. Assaf, *Battei Din . . .* (1924), 54–57; Warhaftig, in: *Mazkeret . . . Herzog* (1952), 507–29; Alon, Toledot, 1 (1958[3]), 137ff.; Alon, Meḥkarim, 2 (1958), 30ff., 44ff.; ET, 11 (1965), 684–97; B. Cohen, *Jewish and Roman Law*, 2 (1966), 651–709, 796ff., Elon, in: ILR, 2 (1967), 528ff.; 3 (1968), 421ff., 434ff.; idem, *Ha-Mishpat Ha-Ivri* (1973), I, 17ff., 68ff., 77ff., 84ff., 115ff., II, 668ff.

Menachem Elon

COMPROMISE (Heb. פשרה, *pesharah;* apparently derived from the term *pesher,* "solution," Eccles. 8:1), deciding a civil law dispute *(dinei mamonot)* by the court or an arbitral body, through the exercise of their discretion and not according to the laws governing the dispute. In Jewish law, compromise is allied to arbitration both with regard to the way it evolved and in some of its rules and trends (the two are treated contiguously in the Tur and *Shulḥan Arukh* ḤM 12 and 13).

Pesharah and Bizzu'a. In talmudic sources the term *bizẓu'a* is synonymous with and equivalent to the term *pesharah.* (In Scripture *bizẓu'a* was used to mean divide or cut: Amos 9:1, and to execute or carry out: Zech. 4:9). Gulak makes the interesting conjecture – based partly on the fact that several talmudic sources indicate that *pesharah* and *bizẓu'a* were two distinct matters – that there was a difference of principle between the two. *Pesharah* was carried out by the court itself and in the opinion of all the scholars, was something permitted, and even

1. page 248..

desirable, for restoring peace between the litigants. On the other hand the court before which the matter was brought in the case of *biẓẓu'a* would refer investigation to other persons – knowledgeable and expert in the field of that particular matter – for its disposal by way of a compromise between the parties. Referral of a matter by the court in this way was customary in ancient law and when the Romans abrogated Jewish judicial autonomy after the Bar Kokhba War (132–135 c.e.), some scholars refrained from adjudicating according to strict law, preferring a compromise between the parties to be effected by others who were knowledgeable in the matter (TJ, Sanh. 1:1, 18b; Mekh. Yitro, 2; see also Introduction). Consequently there were scholars who came to regard *biẓẓu'a* as forbidden, since they looked with disfavor on the fact that the court evaded making its own decision in the matter. (Gulak stresses that a prohibition against compromising is always expressed in terms of *biẓẓu'a* and not *pesharah,* since the latter, effected by the *dayyan* himself, is a *mitzvah.*) In the course of time the difference between *pesharah* and *biẓẓu'a* came to be forgotten, as in both cases the object was to compromise between the parties and the rules laid down for the one came equally to govern the other. In this article the principles of compromise are treated in a like manner; i.e., the terms are regarded as applying to the same concept, as is the case in halakhic literature.

Desirability of Compromise. Three different opinions on the subject of compromise are found in the Talmud, all originating from the middle of the second century when the weakening of Jewish judicial autonomy encouraged a movement toward finding a replacement by way of arbitration and compromise. Joshua b. Korḥah based his opinion that *"biẓẓu'a* is a *mitzvah"* on the scriptural injunction: "Execute the judgment of truth and peace in your gates" (Zech. 8:16), commenting that justice which involved both peace and charity was to be found in *biẓẓu'a* (Sif. Deut. 17; Tosef., Sanh. 1:2–3; Sanh. 6b; TJ, Sanh. 1:1, 18b). A contrary opinion was expressed by R. Eliezer, the son of Yose the Galilean, who stated that "*biẓẓu'a* is forbidden and the *boẓe'a* ["arbitrator"] an offender . . . but let the law cut through the mountain, as it is written 'For the judgment is God's' " (Deut. 1:17; Tosef., Sanh. 1:2; Sanh. 6b). The third opinion, that of Simeon b. Menasya, was that compromise was neither a *mitzvah* nor prohibited, but simply permissible (Sanh. 6b). The *halakhah* was decided to the effect that it is a *mitzvah* to ascertain from the litigants beforehand whether they want their dispute resolved according to law or by compromise and that their decision must be abided by; moreover, "it is praiseworthy if a court always effects a compromise" (Maim. Yad, Sanhedrin 22:4; Tur and Sh. Ar., ḤM 12:2). It remains a *mitzvah* for the court to effect a compromise even after it has heard the pleas of the parties and knows in whose favor the suit is weighted, but once its decision has been given the court may no longer effect a compromise and "let the law cut through the mountain" (Tosef., Sanh. 1:2–3; Sanh. 6b; TJ, Sanh. 1:1, 18b; Yad, Sanhedrin 22:4; Tur and Sh. Ar., ḤM 12:2).

In the geonic period it was determined that even after judgment had been given a compromise could still be effected, at the hands of someone other than a judge and elsewhere than at the place where the court was situated (L. Ginzberg, *Ginzei Schechter,* 2 (1929), 126; Sh. Ar., ḤM 12:2). Similarly, it is permissible for the court to compromise between the parties, even after giving judgment if either of them is liable in law to take an oath, in order that the need for this be obviated by virtue of the compromise (Sh. Ar., ḤM 12:2). Since the equitable oath *(shevu'at hesset)* is imposed on one of the parties in practically all legal suits, great efforts were made to induce the parties to a compromise and thus avoid the gravity of the oath (see also Sh. Ar., ḤM 12:17). Compromise was permitted to the court even if this involved some waiver of the rights of orphans "so as to shelter them from disputes" (Sh. Ar., ḤM 12:3).

The scholars extended the discussion on the merits and demerits of compromise in monetary disputes between man and his fellow to the precepts governing man's relationship with God and man's conduct in general. Thus the statement of Eliezer b. Jacob – that a man who steals wheat and then, when making bread with it, says the blessing on separating the *ḥallah,* is actually blaspheming God (quoted in connection with the meaning of the word *boẓe'a;* Sanh. 6b) – was explained by Simeon Kayyara (ninth century) as an example of a defective compromise: "since he compromised with the precepts of God, acting as if robbery were permitted but that he was in duty bound to separate the *ḥallah;* this is a *mitzvah* performed as the result of a transgression, something God hates" (*Halakhot Gedolot,* ed. Warsaw, Berakhot, p. 10a). Judah's compromise in rescuing Joseph from the pit and selling him to the Ishmaelites (Gen. 37:26–28) has been interpreted as unworthy conduct: "since he should have said 'Let us return him to our father' " (Rashi to Sanh. 6b), and as worthy conduct: since this compromise was imperative in the circumstances (Maharsha, Sanh. 6b).

Nature of Compromise. Compromise is comparable to a judicial decision and must therefore be made after weighty deliberation. Thus, "compromise too requires an application of the mind to the decision" (*hekhre'a ha-da'at;* TJ, Sanh. 1:1, 18b); "the *dayyan* must take as much care with compromise as with a legal decision" (*Leḥem Rav* 87); "just as the law should not be perverted, so it is warned that a compromise should not lean more to the one than the other" (Sh. Ar., ḤM 12:2). Some scholars interpreted the injunction, "Justice, justice shalt thou follow" (Deut. 16:20) as meaning, "Justice, once for the law and once for compromise" (Sanh. 32b and Rashi ad loc.). Other scholars interpreted the verse, "In righteousness shalt thou judge thy neighbor" (Lev. 19:15) as referring to a judgment based on the law, and Deuteronomy 16:20 as relating entirely to compromise, since in compromise there is a two-fold need for justice as the arbitrator cannot have recourse to the governing law and therefore has to exercise great care and discretion "to see who of them is telling the truth and who deserves to be treated with greater severity" (*Yad Ramah* and *Beit ha-Beḥirah,* Sanh. 32b).

The Making of a Compromise and its Validity. Compromise is generally effected by a court of three, but the parties may consent to two judges or even a single one. The court is not authorized to compromise between the parties unless they have previously consented to the court's taking this course rather than judging in accordance with the applicable law. In special cases, when the court is satisfied that there is no means of evaluating a matter on the strength of the evidence, it may give "a judgment in the nature of a compromise . . . and decide as it may deem fit according to its own estimate." This is so since the court is forbidden to let a dispute pass out of its hands without having given a decision on it, as "this will increase conflict and the imposition of peace in the world is the duty of the court" (Resp. Rosh, 107:6; Sh. Ar., ḤM 12:5). Unlike a judgment of the court or of arbitrators – which is given by majority decision – compromise must be unanimously arrived at by all the judges (Sh. Ar., ḤM 12:18). The parties may retract from the compromise – even if they had previously authorized the court to adopt this course – as long as a *kinyan* (see Acquisition) has not been performed by them and provided that they did not undertake in writing to abide by the compromise. However, once execution of the compromise decision has been begun (Sanh. 6a; Sh. Ar., ḤM 12:7), the parties may no longer withdraw.

For additional details on the laws of compromise, see Arbitration.

Bibliography: Gulak, Yesodei, 4 (1922), 177f.; Gulak, Oẓar, 281–6; idem, in: *Yavneh,* 3 (1941/42), 19–34; Herzog, Instit, 2 (1939), 33–35; M. Elon, *Ha Mishpat Ha-Ivri* (1973), I, 111, II, 513 n.16, 613 n.24, 636. For further bibliography see Arbitration.

Menachem Elon

ATTORNEY. Biblical law requires that "the two parties to the dispute shall appear before the Lord, before the priests or magistrates" (Deut. 19:17), i.e., in person and not by proxy. It was considered essential that the court should hear all pleadings and arguments, as well as all testimony, directly from the mouths of litigants or witnesses; even interpreters were not to be admitted (Mak. 1:9; Maim. Yad, Sanhedrin, 21:8). While legal and economical developments subsequently necessitated changes in the practice of the courts, the prejudice against proxies could never be eradicated, and the courts which admitted advocates did so only by way of accommodation to a necessary evil (Resp. Maharam of Rothenburg, no. 357). This prejudice was enhanced by the fact that those who acted as spokesmen for litigants were often found to be sly and untruthful (Resp. Ribash 235). The Talmud applies the verse "oppressors and robbers who did that which is not good among his people" (Ezek. 18:18) to attorneys (Shevu. 31a). Furthermore, there were legal difficulties to contend with: e.g., a debtor was presumed never to be impertinent enough to prevaricate in the presence of his creditor (BK 107a, et al.), but there could not be any such presumption in the face of the creditor's attorney; or a party may have to take an oath, which could not be administered to his proxy. The general rule that "a man's agent is as himself" (Kid. 42a) was not applied to agents for litigants – an anomaly which it has been found difficult to justify but which can be explained only by the overriding desire "to discourage litigation by outsiders" (Herzog, Instit, 1 (1936), 203ff.).

However, ways had to be found to enable plaintiffs to be represented if injustice was to be avoided – e.g., where the plaintiff himself was absent, or where he was weak and timid and the defendant violent and powerful (Tos. to Shevu. 31a; Tur. ḤM 123:16 and Beit Yosef *ibid.*). Nevertheless, talmudic jurists still would not accept a power of attorney in favor of another, unless the plaintiff had therein transferred his rights in the chose in action to the attorney, so that the attorney in effect claimed in his own right (BK 70a) – not unlike the *mandatum in res suam* of Roman law. This rule resulted in the past that a defendant was unable to appoint an attorney on his behalf, as he had no chose in action to transfer (*Piskei ha-Rosh* Shevu. 4:2; Sh. Ar., ḤM 124). Gulak has shown that the rule is of Babylonian origin and influenced by Babylonian laws; but it became Jewish law (Sh. Ar., ḤM 122–23). The requirements for such a transfer to be inserted in powers of attorney were in the course of time radically mitigated and Maimonides expressed regret at reforms by which purely fictitious transfers were admitted to validate powers of attorney (Maim. Yad, Sheluḥin ve-Shutafin 3:7). While transfers continued to be inserted in all powers of attorney, they were nearly always fictitious: anything the attorney recovered by virtue thereof, although ostensibly for himself, would have to be accounted for immediately to his principal (*ibid.* 3:1). See also Assignment of Debt.

With regard to the representation of defendants, there is a tradition in the Jerusalem Talmud that the high priest, when sued in court, could appoint an attorney *(entelar)* to represent him (TJ, Sanh. 2:1, 19d). Whether it was this tradition or the pressure of changing conditions, attorneys for defendants were soon admitted into the courts, and instead of powers of attorney containing the formal transfer, even oral authorization of the attorney by the defendant before the court was accepted as sufficient (Menahem b. Solomon ha-Me'iri, *Beit ha-Beḥirah* to Sanh. 18a). Where the parties were present in person and the court could, if necessary, administer oaths directly to them and perceive their bearing and demeanor, their being assisted by skilled pleaders was not considered too reprehensible and could even be useful (cf. *Urim ve-Tummim* and *Arukh ha-Shulḥan* to ḤM 124). The rule then evolved that a plaintiff, by presenting his claim, submitted to the court's jurisdiction and thus also by implication submitted to its procedure, including any customary or equitable admission of defendants' attorneys (cf. Siftei Kohen, Sh. Ar., ḤM 124). But apart from custom (and equity), the purely legal position has never been resolved (see *Shittah Mekubbeẓet* to BK 70a).

The stipulation of fees was regarded as an assurance of the attorney's good faith (Resp. Rif, no. 157; *Be'er Heitev* to Sh. Ar., ḤM 123:10, 11) eliminating the suspicion that he might engage in champerty or unlawful enrichment. Such stipulations were usually very generously enforced by the courts (Resp. Rashba 2, no. 393; 3, no. 141; 5, no. 287.)

See also Agency; for defenders in criminal cases, see Practice and Procedure, penal.

Bibliography: Rav Ẓa'ir (Tchernowitz), in: *Ha-Shilo'aḥ,* 3 (1898), 418–22; Gulak, Yesodei, 4 (1922), 54–64; idem., Oẓar, 272–9; idem, *Das Urkundenwesen im Talmud* (1935), 137–47; S. Assaf, *Battei ha-Din ve-Sidreihem Aḥarei Ḥatimat ha-Talmud* (1924), 95–99; Herzog, Instit, 1 (1936), 202–11; Lipkin, in: *Sinai,* 30 (1951/52), 46–61; 31 (1951/52), 265–83; ET, 4 (1952), 101–4 s.v. *Ba'al Din;* 11 (1965), 44–48 s.v. *Harsha'ah;* N. Rakower, *Ha-Sheliḥut ve-ha-Harsha'ah Ba-Mishpat Ha-Ivri* (1972), p. 308 ff.; M. Elon, *Ha-Mishpat Ha-Ivri* (1973), II, 533 ff., 617, III, 1254 ff., 1260.

Haim H. Cohn

PRACTICE AND PROCEDURE.

Civil. Court Sessions. The courts of three (judges) exercising jurisdiction in civil matters (see *bet din*) held their sessions during the day, but – following Jethro's advice to Moses that judges should be available "at all times" (Ex. 18:22) – they would continue sitting at night to complete any proceedings commenced during the day (Sanh. 4:1). The session started early in the morning, with the judges robing themselves – they had special robes "wrapped around them," so that they would not look around too much (*Sma,* ḤM 5 n. 16) – and usually continued for six hours until mealtime (Shab. 10a). While originally the session was not interrupted even for prayers, the law was later revised so that in this case it may be interrupted (ḤM 5:4). No court was held on the Sabbath or holidays, lest any writing was done. On the eves of the Sabbath or holidays the courts would sit only in exceptionally urgent cases (Rema, ḤM 5:2), but a party summoned was not punished for failing to appear on such a day (ḤM 5:2). The court may sit on the intermediate days of a festival (*Ḥol ha-Mo'ed,* MK 14b).

Parties. Any person, male or female (Sif. Deut. 190), may sue and be sued, except minors, deaf-mutes, and lunatics. Actions brought by or against guardians on behalf of such incapacitated persons may be heard by the court, but any judgment rendered is binding only if in their favor (Git. 52a). Non-Jews who sue or are sued in a Jewish court may demand that their own non-Jewish law be applied to them (Yad, Melakhim 10:12); a Jew litigating with a non-Jew was originally entitled to claim any benefit of non-Jewish law, but this discrimination was later abolished (cf. *Beit ha-Beḥirah*, BK 113a).

The rule is that parties must litigate in person and may not be represented; and even when and where representation is allowed, the parties are required to attend in person so as to enable the court to form a direct opinion of them (*Sma*, ḤM 13n. 12, 17 n. 14). An exception was made in favor of women defendants: if such women were accustomed to stay at home and not to be seen in public they were allowed to make their statements to a scribe of the court in their own homes (Tos. to Shevu. 30a). When suing for his own usufruct in his wife's property, a husband may also sue for the principal without special authorization, but not otherwise (Git. 48b; ḤM 122:8).

Joint claimants may sue jointly or separately (Ket. 94a; ḤM 77:9, 122:9), but in an action by one of them, the others will normally be included by order of the court. In cases of joint liabilities each defendant can be sued only for his share of the debt, unless he expressly or by implication guaranteed the whole debt (ḤM 77:1); such a guarantee is implied in the debts of partners, joint contractors, and joint tort-feasors *(ibid.)*.

Venue. The plaintiff "follows the defendant." i.e., the claim has to be lodged in the court of the place where the defendant resides (Rema, ḤM 14:1); but if the plaintiff finds the defendant at a place where there is a court in session, he may sue him there and then (Resp. Maharik no. 14). The ancient rule that a party had the right to insist on trial by the Great Court at Jerusalem (Yad, Sanhedrin 6:7), though obsolete (*ibid.* 9), has been interpreted in many countries as enabling the plaintiff to compel the defendant to stand trial outside his place of residence in a court of higher repute or authority (Sanh. 31b; Tur ḤM 14; ḤM 14:1 and Rema thereto). The debtor's property may be attached by order of the court sitting at the place where the property is situated (Rema, ḤM 73:10).

Summonses. On the plaintiff's application a summons is issued to the defendant to appear in court on a day named in the summons (MK 16a; ḤM 11:1). A plaintiff need not disclose particulars of his claim before the defendant stands in court to answer the summons (BB 31a), and, if he does, he is not bound by any such particulars unless he repeats them in court (ḤM 80:1). This rule was devised in order that the defendant should not have time, before coming into court, to fabricate a defense (Rashbam, BB 31a); but later jurists held this purpose to be outweighed by the more desirable opportunity of an out-of-court settlement if the claim was disclosed in advance (*Siftei Kohen*, ḤM 11, n.1).

The issue of a summons requires an order of the full court (Sanh. 8a), but one judge may make the order if the others are present in court. The summons is delivered by the officer of the court, either orally or by a written notice endorsed by the court (ḤM 11:6). It must specify not only the exact time the defendant is required to appear in court, but also the name of the plaintiff suing him (Nov. Ritba MK 16a). It may specify alternative dates of hearing (MK 16a), so that if the defendant fails to appear at one date, he must appear at the next specified date (Rashi thereto). Originally, such alternative summonses were issued for the next following Monday, Thursday, and Monday (Yad, Sanhedrin 25:8), these being the fixed court days in talmudic times (Ket. 3a). If not drawn up as alternative summonses, they could be issued subsequently one after the other in case of nonappearance (Rashi, BK 113a).

The court has discretion on whether or not to issue a summons; it may refuse to summon scholars of great eminence (Kid. 70a), practicing rabbis, and women who live in seclusion (ḤM 124). Each summons contained a warning that, failing his appearance in court on the date (or one of the dates) specified, the defendant was liable to be declared under a ban (see Rashba, BK 113a). A defendant who had to go on a journey or was otherwise prevented from attending court had to send an apology and request an adjournment (ḤM 11:1 and Rema thereto). Failing both appearance and apology, the court would issue a bill of attainder (*petiḥah)* to be served on the defaulter, and a ban would be imposed on him, unless he appeared in court within one week, paid the expenses of the *petiḥah,* and produced it to be torn up (BK 112b–113a). A less rigorous mode of enforcing court summonses was the attachment of the defaulter's property (Resp. Rosh 73:1, 97:4).

Default Procedure. It is forbidden to adjudicate the plaintiff's case in the absence of the defendant (though duly summoned) except where the plaintiff's claim is *prima facie* valid, e.g., where it is based on a bill signed by the defendant and confirmed by witnesses (BK 112b; Tur ḤM 106 and *Beit Yosef* thereto), or where the defendant is abroad more than 30 days' journey away (Yad, Malveh 13:1; ḤM 106). The reason for this deviation from the general rule that there shall be no adjudication unless both parties stand before the court (cf. Deut. 19:17), is said by Maimonides to be "that not everybody should take the money of other people and then go and settle abroad, with the result that borrowers will find all doors closed to them" (Yad, Malveh 13:1). Judgments in civil cases may always be given in the absence of the parties (ḤM 18:6).

Cause List. Hearing "out high and low alike," and fearing no man (Deut. 1:17) was interpreted as prohibiting any preference of major over minor cases (Sanh. 8a; Yad, Sanhedrin 20:10): the case that came in first must be heard first, whatever its relative importance (Rashi, Sanh. 8a; ḤM 15:1). There are several exceptions to this rule: the case of a scholar is given preference, so that he should not be kept too long from his studies (Ned. 62a); orphans and widows are given preference even over scholars, for it is by judging them that justice is done (Isa. 1:17); and cases in which one of the parties is a woman are advanced so as not to keep her waiting in court (Yev. 100a).

Subject Matter. The court will not entertain a claim for anything of less than minimal value (BM 55a; Yad, Sanh. 20:11). Opinions were divided on whether the court, once seized of a claim for *shaveh perutah,* could proceed to deal with other (ideal and non-valuable) matters between the same parties; the leading view is that it could (BM 55b; Yad, loc. cit.; ḤM 6:1).

Settlement. When the parties stand before the court, they must first be advised to settle their dispute by a friendly compromise (Sanh. 6b), which is the "judgment of peace" alluded to by the prophet (Zech. 8:16). Failing such compromise, the court will ask them whether they insist on adjudication according to law, or whether they would not rather empower the court to adjudicate between them by way of fair compromise (Yad, Sanhedrin 22:4; ḤM 12:2); and courts were admonished to do everything in their power to dissuade parties from insisting on adjudication according to law (ḤM 12:20). However, so long as a compromise had not actually been implemented by *kinyan* (see Acquisition) or by performance, the parties might go back on their agreement and resort to law (ḤM 12:7, 19).

Court Decorum. The parties are required to stand up before the court (cf. Deut. 19:17), and so are the witnesses (Shev. 30a), and they may not sit down except with the court's permission (Yad, Sanhedrin 21:3; ḤM 17:1). Maimonides comments sadly upon the fact that the post-talmudic courts always allow parties and witnesses to be seated – there being no longer sufficient strength in us to conduct ourselves according to the law (loc. cit. 21:5; ḤM 17:3). Permission to be seated may not be given to one party unless it is also given to the other (Tosef., Sanh. 6:2; TJ, Sanh. 3:10, 21c). Even where a scholar is permitted to be seated out of respect for him, his opponent must be given the same permission, and it is up to him whether he avails himself of it or not (Shev. 30b; Yad, Sanhedrin 21:4; ḤM 17:2).

There is no rule requiring parties (or attorneys) to be dressed in any particular manner; but where one party is more richly dressed than the other, he will be ordered to dress in the same manner as the other before being allowed to address the court (Shev. 31a). This rule has been said to be now obsolete, because differences in dress are no longer so ostentatious (*Siftei Kohen,* ḤM 17 n. 2); others have held that instead of ordering the party to change his dress, the court should rather assure the other party that his adversary's showy appearance makes no impression on it (Maharshal, quoted in *Baḥ.,* ḤM 17:1 and in *Be'er ha-Golah,* ḤM 17, n. 4).

Equality of Parties. The injunction: "Judge your neighbor fairly" (Lev. 19:15) was interpreted as prescribing equal treatment by the court for all parties before it (Shev. 30a; Yad, Sanhedrin 21:1; ḤM 17:1). In particular, the parties must all be given the same opportunity and the same time of audience *(ibid.);* no party may be heard in the absence of the other (Shevu. 31a; Sanh. 7b; Yad, loc. cit. 21:7; ḤM 17:5). Where one party desires to be represented or to be accompanied by friends, relatives, or partners, the other party may be so represented or accompanied too, and will be heard to oppose such representation or escort through lack of equal facilities (ḤM 17:4 and *Pithei Teshuvah,* ḤM 17 n. 7). Where there are several plaintiffs and one defendant (or vice versa), they will be asked to choose one of them to argue for all, so as to keep the proportions even (*Sma,* ḤM 17 n. 8).

The injunction not to favor the poor or to show deference to the rich (Lev. 19:15; cf. Ex. 23:3) was elaborated as follows:

No judge should have compassion for the poor and say, this man is destitute and his adversary is rich – why should he not support him? I will give judgment for the poor man and thus cause him to be honorably provided for; nor should a judge favor the rich: when there are before him a wealthy notable and a poor ignorant man, he should not greet the notable and show him any respect, lest the other may be embarrassed; nor should he say to himself, how can I decide against him and cause him disgrace? I will rather send him away now and tell him in private later that he ought to satisfy the other party – but he must give true judgment forthwith. And when there are before him two men, one good and one evil, he may not say, the one is a criminal and probably lies, and the other is virtuous and will stick to the truth – but he must regard both as if they were potential evildoers who might lie in order to strengthen their own case, and he must judge them according to his best conscience; and, having so judged them, he should then regard them both as perfectly in order (ḤM 17:10).

Pleadings. The rule is that the parties must plead for themselves (see Attorney), orally, but if both so agree, they may be allowed to put their arguments into writing, either by dictating them to the scribe of the court or by filing written briefs (Rema, ḤM 13:3); in the latter case, they cannot be allowed to go back on anything they have written *(ibid.),* and it appears that the courts have resorted to written pleading so as to prevent parties from changing their positions every now and then (cf. Rema, ḤM 80, n. 2). The costs of all such written records are borne equally by both parties (BB 10:4; 168a).

The court may not put any argument in a party's mouth or teach him how to argue his case (Avot 1:8; Yad, Sanhedrin 21:10; ḤM 17:8), nor may the court express an opinion presupposing a hypothetical argument ("if A would plead this way, judgment might be given for him"; Rema, ḤM 17:5). On the other hand, the court is admonished to open the mouth of the dumb for him (Prov. 31:8), i.e., to help a litigant who is intellectually or emotionally unable to express himself to formulate his argument (Yad, Sanhedrin 21:11, ḤM 17:9). This rule applies especially to orphans and imbeciles (cf. *Baḥ.,* ḤM 17, n. 12).

The plaintiff pleads his case first (BK 46b; ḤM 24), but he may be allowed by the court to postpone his pleading in whole or in part if he so desires (Rema, ḤM 24). There is a curious exception to the rule: if by hearing the plaintiff first, the property of the defendant may depreciate (e.g., by rumors in the market that the title is disputed), the defendant is heard first (ḤM 24 and *Siftei Kohen* thereto, n. 1). When the plaintiff has stated his case, the defendant is bound to reply forthwith, but the court may, in a suitable case, give him time to think and prepare his defense (Rema, ḤM 16:2). For the various pleadings open to litigants and their respective effects, see Pleas.

Evidence. Where a case cannot be disposed of on the pleadings and has to be proved by evidence, the parties must be ready with their witnesses and documents on the day of the pleading, but the court may allow them up to 30 days' grace to produce their witnesses or documents (Sanh. 3:8; BK 112b; ḤM 16:1). Opinions were divided on what should happen if they failed to do so within this time limit (Sanh. 3:8), and the law was eventually settled to the effect that while the court would not extend the time limit (except where the witnesses are known to reside at a distance of more than 30 days' journey; ḤM 16:1), any judgment given on the pleadings was subject to review, and could be annulled, if and when warranted by any further evidence being adduced (ḤM 20:1). Where a party had declared in court that there were no witnesses or documents available to prove his case, he would not afterward be allowed to adduce such evidence, the suspicion being that it would be fabricated (Yad, Sanhedrin 7:7–8; ḤM 20:1); but where a party declared that there were witnesses or documents in existence but he could not trace them, the court would make a public announcement threatening a *ḥerem* on any person who withheld evidence (ḤM 16:3); such an announcement would even be initiated by the court where evidence was lacking to prove claims or defenses by representatives of estates (ḤM 71:8). Before testifying, witnesses were warned by the court of the consequences of perjury and the moral turpitude this involved (Yad, Edut 17:2; ḤM 28:7).

For the burden of adducing evidence, and presumptions in lieu of evidence, see Evidence.

Deliberations. Having heard the parties and their witnesses, the judges confer with each other. According to ancient Jerusalem custom, the conference is conducted in private (Yad, Sanhedrin 22:9; ḤM 18:1); but while the parties always had to be excluded, primarily because they ought not to know how each judge voted (Maim. *Comm. to Mishnah,* Sanh. 3:7), it appears that some courts allowed the general public to be present while they conferred (*Baḥ.,* ḤM 18:1); and there is a talmudic tradition that the judges' students were allowed not only to be present but also to participate in the discussions (Sanh. 33b, and Rashi thereto). Witnesses who testified in the case could express their opinion on the merits of the case while giving testimony, but could not be heard during the judges' conference, because "no witness is made a judge" (Yad, Edut 5:8).

The conference starts with the oldest (or presiding) judge stating his opinion (Sanh. 4:2, Yad, Sanhedrin 11:6); but the view was expressed that, as in criminal cases, it should rather be the youngest member of the court who states his opinion first, the same reasons applying in civil cases as well (Rema, ḤM 18:1; see also below). Any judge may, in the course of deliberations, change any opinion he previously expressed (Sanh. 4:1). If a judge cannot make up his mind, he must say so, and need not apologize or give reasons for saying so (Yad, Sanhedrin 8:3).

Two more judges will then be added to the court (Sanh. 3:6), as the judge unable to form an opinion is regarded as being absent and the remaining two judges, even if of one mind, are not regarded as a court (Rashi, Sanh. 29a). The augmented court (of five) will start deliberations anew, but need not hear the case once more (ḤM 18:1).

Judgment. At the close of the deliberations, the parties are called back into court and asked to stand up (Shevu. 30b; Yad, Sanhedrin 21:3; ḤM 17:1); the presiding judge announces the decision, without disclosing whether or not the judgment is unanimous, or how each judge voted. If the judgment is unanimous, so much the better; if not, the majority prevails (Sanh. 3:6, Sanh. 3b; et al.). If (owing to the judges being unable to form an opinion) the court has been increased time and again up to the maximum of 71 members and is still almost equally divided, judgment will be given for the defendant as the plaintiff has not established his case to the satisfaction of a clear majority (Yad, loc. cit. 8:2; ḤM 18:2).

Any party may ask the court for a record of the judgment in writing (Sanh. 30a; Yad, loc. cit. 22:8, ḤM 19:2) and for a written statement of the reasons behind it (BM 69b and Tos. thereto; Sanh. 31b; Tur, ḤM 14 and *Beit Yosef* thereto), if only for the purposes of appeal to the Great Court (Yad, Sanhedrin 6:6). The written judgment (and the reasons for it) must be signed by all the judges, including the dissenter (R. Johanan in TJ, Sanh. 3:12, 21d). While judgment is given on the day the case was heard (Sanh. 4:1; Maim. *Comm. to Mishnah,* Avot. 5:8; ḤM 17:11), and any delay of justice is regarded as a violation of "Ye shall do no unrighteousness in judgment" (Lev. 19:15), the written record of the judgment and the reasons for it may be given whenever a party applies for it, without any time limit (Rema, ḤM 14:4). Where the judgment has not been put into writing, the fitness of the judges to say what judgment they gave ceases when the parties no longer stand before them (Kid. 74a; ḤM 23:1), i.e., when they are no longer associated with the case (Tosef., BM 1:12). This rule apparently caused great hardship and was later restricted, first to discretionary judgments given without pleadings and without evidence, and then to judgments given by a single judge (ḤM 23:1; Resp. Rosh 6:15, 56:3; *Mordekhai* Kid. 541), and was thus virtually abolished.

The judgment may not exceed the amount of the claim (Rema ḤM 17:12); but where the court is satisfied that the plaintiff was genuinely ignorant of the real extent of his rights, it may impose fines and other sanctions on the defendant to compel him to satisfy the plaintiff even beyond his claim (*Sma,* ḤM 17:26; *Baḥ* ḤM 17).

For the effect of judgments *inter partes* and *inter alios,* see *Ma'aseh.*

Revision. A judgment is always subject to revision, normally by the court that made it in the first place, if new evidence has come to light disproving the facts on which the judgment was based, providing the party seeking to adduce such new evidence is not debarred from so doing (see above; Sanh. 3:8; Yad, Sanhedrin 7:6; ḤM 20:1). Every judgment is also subject to revision for errors of law. Originally the rule appears to have been general and to have applied in all civil cases, whatever the quality of the error (Sanh. 4:1); later it was confined to erroneous judgments of nonprofessional and non-expert judges (Bek. 4:4); finally, the rule was confined to errors of mishnaic (i.e., clear and undisputed) law, as distinguished from "errors of discretion" (Sanh. 6a, 33a; Ket. 84b, 100a). While "discretion" was originally understood in its wide literal sense (cf. Sanh. 29b; TJ, Sanh. 1:1, 18a), it was eventually confined to matters on which there were different views in the Talmud and the *halakhah* had not been decided; whatever view the judge followed, his judgment would not (for that reason alone) be subject to revision. It might be otherwise where the court followed one opinion in ignorance or disregard of the fact that another opinion had been accepted and put into practice "throughout the world" (Yad, Sanhedrin 6:2; ḤM 25:2). The revisable error could (in certain well-defined circumstances) be of great moment to the judge personally, as he might find himself saddled with the obligation to pay out of his own pocket any irrecoverable damage caused by his error (Yad, loc. cit., 6:3; ḤM 25:3).

Apart from revisable error, unwarranted assumption of judicial authority (whether it resulted in error or not) is a cause for having the judgment set aside, but it stands until set aside (Yad, loc. cit., 6:4; ḤM 25:4). The finding of unwarranted assumption of judicial authority is tantamount to a finding of a trespass, and counts in damages *(ibid.).* In many countries, the revision of judgments of errors of law was reserved to courts of appeal, i.e., mostly courts presided over by the leading scholars of the community.

Modern Law. While the procedure in Israel civil courts is mainly based on English law, the procedure in the rabbinical courts is governed by the *Takkanot ha-Diyyun* which were enacted by the chief rabbinate of Israel in 1960 (revising earlier *takkanot* of 1943). They purport to reflect talmudic and post-talmudic law, but actually deviate from it and follow modern procedural concepts in many important particulars; for example, the requirement of written statements of claim, representation by attorneys, cross-examination of parties (in addition to witnesses), reduction of judgments into writing before delivery, and discretion in the matter of costs.

Penal. For the composition of courts competent to adjudicate in criminal cases, see *Bet din.* The composition of the court and certain matters of procedure differ in capital and non-capital cases. While the following account deals with capital cases (unless otherwise indicated), practice and procedure were modeled on them as far as possible (cf. Maim., Yad, Sanhedrin 16:1–4).

Court Sessions. In criminal cases, the court sits only during the day and adjourns at sunset (Sanh. 4:1; Yad, Sanhedrin 11:1). If the proceedings have been concluded during the day, a judgment of acquittal will be announced forthwith, but a judgment of conviction and sentence may not be announced until the following day (*ibid.*), since there is a chance that the judges may change their minds during the night (Rashi, Sanh. 32a). No criminal sessions may therefore be held on the eves of the Sabbath and holidays (Sanh. 4:1; Yad, Sanhedrin 11:2); and either because a trial is regarded as potentially a first step in an execution, which may not take place on a Sabbath (TJ, Sanh. 4:7, 22b), or because the trial involves writing prohibited on the Sabbath (Tos. to Beẓeh 36b and Sanh. 35a), no criminal trials may be held on the Sabbath or holidays.

In the Temple precincts (see *Bet din*), criminal sessions started after the morning sacrifices and ended with the late afternoon sacrifice (Sanh. 88b); otherwise the time of court sessions is the same in criminal as in civil cases. The following is a mishnaic account of the manner in which courts of 23 held criminal trials:

The court sat in the form of a half-circle, so that the judges could all see one another. The two court scribes stood before them, one at the right and one at the left, and recorded the words of the judges – one the words of those in favor of conviction, and the other the words of those in favor of acquittal. Three rows of learned disciples sat before them, each knowing his place; when the seat of a judge became vacant, his place would be filled with the first sitting in the first row (Sanh. 4:3–4 – according to Maim., Yad, Sanhedrin 1:9; but Rashi (to

Mishnah, Sanh. 36b) states that the two scribes write the words both of those in favor and those against, so that if one scribe errs the other can correct him).

The public and the disciples would be already in court when the judges entered – the presiding judge last – and everyone present would rise and remain standing until the presiding judge gave them leave to sit down (Tosef., Sanh. 7:8).

Duplicity of Trials. Only one capital case may be tried on any one day in any one court (Sanh. 6:4; Tosef., Sanh. 7:2). An exception was made where there were several participants in one crime, provided they were all liable to the same penalty (Sanh. 46a). However, where participants in one crime were liable to execution by different methods, as, e.g., in adultery where the male adulterer was liable to strangulation and the female adulteress, if a priest's daughter, to burning, they had to be tried separately on different days (Yad, Sanhedrin 14:10).

Arrest. The arrest and detention of persons awaiting trial is reported in the Bible (Lev. 24:12; Num. 15:34), and the appointment of judges presupposed the concomitant appointment of police officers (*shoterim:* Deut. 16:18). Maimonides describes *shoterim* as officers equipped with sticks and whips who would patrol streets and marketplaces, and bring any criminals they caught before the court; these officers would also be dispatched by the court to arrest any person against whom a complaint had been brought ("they act upon the judges' orders in every matter": Yad, Sanhedrin 1:1). In capital cases the accused would be detained pending trial (Sif. Num. 114; Yad, Sanhedrin 11:2), if he was caught *in flagranti delicto* or there was at least some *prima facie* evidence against him (TJ, Sanh. 7:8, 25a). However, the fact that the available evidence was as yet insufficient to put a man on trial was no reason not to detain him until sufficient evidence was available (Sanh. 81b). Or, where death had not yet ensued but the victim was dangerously wounded, the assailant would be detained until the degree of his offense could be determined (Sanh. 78b; Ket. 33b). The accused would always be held in custody (Yad, Sanhedrin 12:3). Opinions were divided on whether an arrest could be made on the Sabbath.

Bail. The release of an accused person on bail pending trial is already mentioned in early sources (Mekh. Nezikin 6). The rule evolved that in capital cases no bail should be allowed (*ibid.;* and Resp. Ribash no. 236, quoted in *Beit Yosef,* ḤM 388:12, n. 5), from which it may be inferred that in non-capital cases bail would be granted as a matter of course.

Default Proceedings. No criminal proceeding may be conducted in the absence of the accused (Sanh. 79b; Yad, Roẓe'aḥ 4:7, Sanhedrin 14:7).

Prosecution. There is good authority for the proposition that in cases of homicide the blood-avenger acted as prosecutor (Nov. Ran; Sanh. 45a). Where no blood-avenger was forthcoming, the court would appoint one for this purpose (Sanh. 45b). By analogy, it may be assumed that in cases other than homicide the victim of the offense acted as complainant and prosecutor. In offenses of a public nature, the court initiated the proceedings and dispensed with prosecutors. Such proceedings were normally prompted by witnesses who came forward and notified the court that an offense had been committed; if they could identify and name the accused and satisfy the court that a *prima facie* case could be made out against him, the court would take action (Yad, Sanhedrin 12:1).

Defense. In criminal matters, any person who wished to plead in favor of the accused was allowed and even encouraged to do so (Sanh. 4:1). If a disciple of the judges wished to plead for the accused, he was raised to the bench and allowed to stay there until the end of the day (Sanh. 5:4), clearly a potent encouragement. There are records in post-talmudic times of defense attorneys having been appointed by the court (e.g., Ribash Resp. no. 235).

Evidence. Unlike civil trials, criminal trials started with the interrogation of the witnesses. Before this, each witness had to be warned separately by the court in the following terms:

If you are going to tell us anything which you only believe or opine, or anything you may have heard from any other person, however trustworthy he may seem to you, or anything you know from rumors – or if you are not aware that this court is going to examine you by a probing cross-examination – you had better know that a criminal trial is not like a civil trial; in a civil case, a false witness pays money to the man he has wronged and will then be discharged; but in a criminal case, his blood and the blood of his children will be on him until the end of the world. Man was created single in this world, to show you that whoever causes one single soul to perish from this world is regarded as if he had caused the whole world to perish; and he who keeps one single soul alive in this world is regarded as having kept the whole world alive. Are not all men created in the form of Adam, the first man, and still the form of each man is different from that of anybody else? Therefore can each and everybody say, it is for me that the world was created. And do not say, why should we bring this calamity upon ourselves? for it is written, whoever is able to testify from what he has seen or known, and does not do so, will be punished [Lev. 5:1]; nor may you say, it is more convenient for us to incur punishment for our silence, than to bring upon ourselves the blood of that criminal; for it is written, there is rejoicing when the wicked perish (Sanh. 4:5; Yad, Sanhedrin 12:3).

The evidence of at least two witnesses (Deut. 17:6) is required to prove not only that the accused was seen to have committed the act constituting the offense (Ket. 26b; Sanh. 30a; Git. 33b), but also that, immediately before committing it, he had been warned of its unlawfulness and of the exact penalty he would incur (Yad, Sanhedrin 12:2). No circumstantial evidence is ever sufficient to support a conviction (Sanh. 37b; Tosef., Sanh. 8:3; see Evidence; Penal law). The accused must be present during the examination of the witnesses, but opinions are divided on whether he must stand up or may be seated. The judges, are of course, seated when hearing evidence (ḤM 28:6), while the witnesses stand (Shevu. 30a; ḤM 28:5).

For the methods of examination of witness, see Witness.

Deliberations. It is only if and when the evidence of all the witnesses heard is first found consistent, i.e., if it is established to the satisfaction of the court that the witnesses do not contradict themselves or each other in any material particular, that the deliberations (in the technical sense) start (Sanh. 5:4; Yad, Sanhedrin 12:3). If the evidence is found to be inconsistent, the accused is acquitted and discharged there and then. The rule is that the youngest member of the court has the first say in the deliberations (Sanh. 4:2; Yad, Sanhedrin 11:6), in case the junior members be unduly impressed and influenced by what their elders have to say (Yad, Sanhedrin 10:6; Rashi to Ex. 23:2 and to Sanh. 36a); but this rule yields to another that the deliberations must always start with a view propounded in favor of the accused (Sanh. 4:1, 5:4; Yad, Sanhedrin 11:1, 12:3). Talmudic scholars wondered how anything could be said in favor of the accused once the evidence against him had been found to be consistent, and they solved the problem by suggesting that "opening in favor of the accused" really meant asking the accused whether he could adduce any evidence in rebuttal (Sanh. 32b; TJ, Sanh. 4:1, 22a), or reassuring the accused that if he was innocent he had nothing to fear from the evidence adduced against him (*ibid.;* Yad, Sanhedrin 10:7). Deliberations were thus held in the presence of the accused, and it would appear that at this stage he was given the opportunity of saying anything he wished in his defense: "If he says, I wish to plead in favor of myself, he is heard, provided there is some substance in his words" (Sanh. 5:4). According to Maimonides, he is even raised to the bench for this purpose (Yad, Sanhedrin 10:8). However, he is not allowed to say anything to his detriment, and as soon as he opens his mouth to admit his guilt of otherwise prejudice himself, he is silenced and reprimanded by the court (Tosef., Sanh. 9:4). Where the accused is not capable of speaking for himself, the court or a judge will do so for him (Sanh. 29a).

It appears that the credibility and weight of the evidence, even though it was found consistent (and hence admissible), was an open issue for the deliberation of the judges, as was the legal question whether the act committed by the accused constituted a punishable offense (Yad, Sanhedrin 10:9). Having once expressed his view in favor of an acquittal, a judge is not allowed to change his view during the deliberations (Sanh. 4:1, 5:5, 34a; Yad, Sanhedrin 10:2); but having expressed his opinion condemning the accused, a judge may change his mind even during the deliberations (*ibid.;* Yad, Sanhedrin 11:1). Judges ought not to follow the opinion of other, greater judges, especially in criminal cases, but must decide solely according to their own knowledge and personal conviction (Tosef., Sanh. 3:8; Yad, Sanhedrin 10:1).

If, at the end of the day, a majority for an acquittal has been reached, the accused is acquitted forthwith; if no such majority has emerged, the case is adjourned to the next day (see above), the judges conferring, in groups of two, throughout the night, abstaining from too much food and from all alcohol. The next morning, back in court, the scribes checked the judges' views with those they had expressed the day before, so that the number of those arguing in favor of an acquittal could meanwhile only have increased (Sanh. 5:5, Yad, Sanhedrin 12:3). If a clear majority for conviction has eventually been reached, judgment will be pronounced accordingly; but a "clear majority" presupposes some minority and accordingly, where the whole court is unanimous that the accused be convicted, proceedings are adjourned and deliberations continued until at least one judge changes his view and votes for an acquittal (Sanh. 17a; Yad, Sanhedrin 9:1). It is believed that this rule applied only to the Great Sanhedrin of 71 (Maim., Yad, *ibid.,* speaks of the "Sanhedrin" as distinguished from the "Small Sanhedrin" in the immediately following paragraph), while in courts of 23 and of three unanimity was as good as, or even better than, a majority.

Judgment. The sentence pronounces the accused guilty and specifies the punishment to be inflicted on him; it is not reasoned. Unlike in civil cases (see above), the accused knows which of the judges were in the majority and which in the minority, and what were the reasons which prompted each judge in his voting, since he had been present at their deliberations.

Once a capital sentence is pronounced, the accused is in law deemed to be dead (Sanh. 71b), and a person killing him would not be guilty of homicide (Yad, Mamrim 7, 9), nor would a person wounding him be guilty of any offense or liable for damages (Tosef., BK 9:15). The theory was propounded that it is this legal fiction which enables the court and the executioners to execute capital sentences without incurring liability as murderers.

On the other hand, as long as the sentence has not been carried out, the judgment is subject to revision: on the way from the court to the place of execution, a herald announces that *A* son of *B* is going to be executed for having committed the offense *C,* and witnesses *D* and *E* have testified against him; whoever has anything to say in his defense should come forward to say it (Sanh. 6:1). The case is returned to court for a retrial not only if any such person is forthcoming but even if the accused himself wishes to plead again in his own defense – provided there is some substance in what he says *(ibid.).* In order to find out whether or not there is some substance in what the accused wishes to say, two men learned in the law are seconded to accompany him on his way to the place of execution (Yad, Sanhedrin 13:1), and if they are satisfied that there is some such substance, they will have him brought back into court even two and three times *(ibid.).* If, on retrial or redeliberation, the accused is acquitted, the sentence is deemed to be annulled *ex tunc,* as if it had never been passed.

Where the accused escapes after sentence and before execution and then is caught and brought before the court which had sentenced him, his trial is not reopened, but the sentence stands (Mak. 1:10). It might be different if he were brought before a court in Ereẓ Israel, and the court which had sentenced him had sat outside Ereẓ Israel (Yad, Sanhedrin 13:8). For the purpose of establishing that sentence had duly been pronounced against him, two witnesses must testify that in their presence sentence had been passed on this particular accused and they had also heard the evidence given against him by two named witnesses (Mak. 1:10; Yad, Sanhedrin 13:7). Before the sentence is finally executed, the accused is asked to confess in order that he may have a share in the world to come (Sanh. 6:2). If he does not know how to make confession, he is asked to repeat the words, "may my death expiate all my sins" *(ibid.).*

For the various modes of execution, see Capital Punishment.

Bibliography: Civil: H.B. Fassel, *Das mosaisch-rabbinische Gerichts-Verfahren in civilrechtlichen Sachen* (1859); M. Bloch, *Die Civilprocess-Ordung nach mosaisch-rabbinischem Rechte* (1882); J. Kohler, in: *Zeitschrift fuer vergleichende Rechtswissenschaft,* 20 (1907), 247–64; Juster, Juifs, 2 (1914), 93–126; T.S. Zuri, *Mishpat ha-Talmud,* 7 (1921); Gulak, Yesodei, 4 (1922); S. Assaf, *Battei ha-Din ve-Sidreihem Aḥarei Ḥatimat ha-Talmud* (1924); idem, in: *Ha-Mishpat ha-Ivri,* 1 (1925/26), 105–20; M. Frank, *Kehillot Ashkenaz u-Vattei Dineihem* (1937); N. Kirsch, in: *Yavneh,* 3 (1948/49), 128–36; B.M. Rakover, in: *Sinai,* 38 (1955/56), 312–20; A. Weiss, *Seder ha-Diyyun* (1957); Elon, Mafte'aḥ, 190–9; idem, in: ILR, 3 (1968), 426–8, 437f.; 4 (1969), 103f. idem. *Ha-Mishpat Ha-Ivri* (1973), I, 83ff., II, 321ff., 428ff., 497ff., 504ff., 533ff., 602ff., 617ff., 639ff., 646ff., 667ff., 715 n. 8, 800 ff., 810 ff., 816ff., III, 1254ff. Penal: H.B. Fassel, *Das mosaisch-rabbinische Strafgesetz und strafrechtliche Gerichts-Verfahren* (1870); J. Fuerst, *Das peinliche Rechtsverfahren im juedischen Alterthume* (1870); M. Bloch, *Das mosaisch-talmudische Strafgerichtverfahren* (1901), Juster, Juifs, 2 (1914), 127–214; T.S. Zuri, *Mishpat ha-Talmud,* 7 (1921); H.E. Goldin, *Hebrew Criminal Law and Procedure* (1952); A. Weiss, *Seder ha-Diyyun* (1957); J. Ostrow, in: JQR, 48 (1957/58), 352–70; N. Rakover, in: *Ha-Peraklit,* 18 (1961/62), 264–72, 306–30; Elon, Mafte'aḥ, 190–9; idem, *Ha-Mishpat Ha-Ivri* (1973), II, 247ff., 428 ff., 497 ff., 566ff., 639ff., 646ff., 816ff., III, 856; Mendelsohn, *The Criminal Jurisprudence of the Ancient Hebrews* (1968²); H.E. Baker, *Legal System of Israel* (1968), 197–231.

Haim H. Cohn

PLEAS.

Nature of Pleas. Talmudic law developed certain well-defined forms of pleading in civil cases (not unlike the *actio, formula,* and *exceptio* in Roman law). These forms of pleading constitute a catalog of causes of actions and defenses which could be applied in, and adapted to, all kinds of civil litigations. Unlike

Roman law, pleas were not reduced to abstract terms, but expressed in direct language: for instance, the action of debt is rendered as the plea of "I have money in your hands"; the defense of payment is rendered as the plea of "I have paid." The law of pleas thus comprises the catalog of the various pleas and the provisions governing the applicability and effect of each particular one. However, in the sources there is no systematic differentiation between the two, and they will be considered together below. It often happens that not only the burden of proof (see Evidence) or of taking the oath will depend on the pleas chosen by the party but also the immediate outcome of the action, where in the circumstances a given plea is considered conclusive.

Pleas of the Plaintiff. Plaintiff's pleas, or causes of action, can be roughly divided into three classes: debt – "I have money in your hands"; or "I have a loan in your hands"; or "I have wages with you"; chattels – "I have a deposit in your hands": or "I have deposited this or that chattel with you"; or "you have stolen this chattel from me"; and oath – where the cause of action depends on accounts to be rendered and the defendant (e.g., an agent, executor, or guardian) is sued to verify his accounts on oath.

In order to be valid and to require a plea (or an oath) in reply, the plaintiff's plea must be such as to disclose a legally valid cause of action. Where a plaintiff would not be entitled to judgment, even though his plea be proved or admitted, no defense is called for. Thus, the plea "you promised to lend me money" – which is a promise unenforceable in law – or the plea "you insulted me" – which, if proved or admitted, could not bear weight in a case of damages – would be rejected as irrelevant from the outset.

Pleas of the Defendant. Whenever a cause of action has been pleaded by the plaintiff, "it is not a proper reply for the defendant to say, I owe you nothing, or you have nothing in my hands, or you are lying; but the court will tell the defendant to reply specifically to the plaintiff's plea and be as explicit in his defense as the plaintiff was in his claim: have you or have you not taken a loan from him?; has he or has he not made this deposit with you?; have you or have you not stolen his chattel?; have you or have you not hired him?; and in the same way with all other pleas. The reason is that a defendant may err [in law] . . . and believe that he is not liable to the plaintiff; therefore he is told: how can you say 'I owe him nothing'? maybe the law renders you liable to him and you do not know; you must submit to the judges explicit statements of fact, and they will advise you whether you are or are not liable. Even a great scholar is told: you do not lose anything by replying to his plea and explaining to us how it is that you are not liable to him; is it because 'the thing has never happened' or although 'it happened, it is because you already made restitution to him' "(Yad, To'en 6:1).

Defendant's pleas may roughly be divided into admissions and denials.

Admissions are of three kinds:

(1) full and express admission of the whole claim – such an admission establishes the claim "like a hundred witnesses";

(2) partial admission and partial denial, with the result that the oath will be administered to the defendant;

(3) implied admission – plea of "I have not borrowed" is, on proof of the loan, taken as an admission that the defendant has not repaid the loan; or, a plea of "I have repaid" is, on proof of non-repayment, taken as an admission that a loan had been made (BB 6a; Shevu. 41b; Yad, To'en 6:3). For pleas of "feigning" or "satiation" to revoke out-of-court admissions, and for the effect of admissions in general, see Admission.

Denials are also of three kinds: "no such thing has ever happened" – i.e., a total denial of the fact (the loan, the contract, the tort) underlying the cause of action: "I have paid" – i.e., an assertion that any liability which may have existed has already been fully satisfied; and "you have renounced the debt," or "the money you gave me was in repayment of a debt which you owed me, or was a gift" (Yad, To'en 6:2) – i.e., in the nature of a plea of confession and avoidance.

The general rules that the burden of proving his case rests upon the plaintiff (see Evidence) and that, in the absence of such proof, the defendant has to take the oath to verify his denial, apply to all these pleas of denial. The presumption that a debtor will not lie in the face of his creditor was in the course of time superseded by the presumption that the plaintiff will not lodge a claim unless he has a cause of action. While by virtue of the former presumption the defendant would be believed on his oath, by virtue of the latter he was required to take the oath to disprove the plaintiff's claim (Shevu. 40b).

Plea of Repayment. In the case of the plea of repayment, the following special provisions should be noted:

Where the defendant pleaded repayment, it was not sufficient for the plaintiff to prove that he had given the defendant a loan, because a loan given before witnesses need not necessarily be repaid before witnesses (Shevu. 41b), and the claim would be dismissed on the defendant's oath verifying his plea. The same rule applied to claims on bills: where the signature of the defendant on the bill was proved or admitted, his defense of repayment would be accepted on his taking the oath (BB 176a; Yad, Malveh 11:3; Sh. Ar., ḤM 69:2); but some later jurists held that the plea of repayment was not available against a bill which was in the hands of the plaintiff, as it would normally have been returned or destroyed on payment (Rema, ḤM 69:2 and the references given there). The matter appears to be left to the discretion of the court in each particular case (Resp. Ribash, no. 454; *Siftei Kohen;* ḤM 69, n. 14). Where the plea of repayment is inadmissible in law, e.g., where the loan or bill was made with formal *kinyan* (see Acquisition, ḤM 39:3), the plaintiff will recover on the bill on taking the oath that it is still unpaid (Shevu. 41a; Yad, Malveh 14:2). Where a debt is repayable at a certain date, the defendant will not be heard to plead that he repaid it before that date because of the presumption that no debtor pays a debt before it matures (see Evidence). The plaintiff will be entitled to recover without oath, on proof of the debt and of the time stipulated for repayment (BB 5a–b; ḤM 78:1).

In order to forestall pleas of repayment and their all too easy verification by oath, it became customary to stipulate beforehand either that repayment must be made in the presence of witnesses – in which case the plaintiff could recover without oath unless the defendant produced witnesses of repayment (Shevu. 6:2; Yad, Malveh 15:1; ḤM 70:3) – or that the plea of repayment should not be available to the defendant and that the plaintiff should be entitled to recover on his assertion that he had not been paid (Yad, Malveh 15:3; ḤM 71:1).

Plea of Insolvency. Originally the law was that a debtor who pleaded that he was unable to pay was not required to take the oath, but the burden was on the creditor to discover property of the debtor on which execution could be levied (Yad, Malveh 2:1). However, when "defrauders increased and borrowers found lenders' doors closed," it was laid down that the debtor should take the oath that he possessed nothing and concealed nothing and that he would disclose any property coming into his hands (Yad, Malveh 2:2; ḤM 99:1). There are two noteworthy exceptions to this rule: a man reputed to be poor and honest will not be required to take the oath if the court suspects the creditor of desiring to annoy or embarrass him; and a man reputed to be a cheat and swindler will not be allowed to verify his plea on oath even though he volunteers to do so (Yad, Malveh 2:4; ḤM 99:4–5; see also Execution, Civil[1]).

Plea of Counterclaim. Where a plaintiff sues on a bill, it is no defense for the defendant to plead that the plaintiff is indebted to him on another bill: each sues and recovers on his own bill separately (Ket. 13:9; Yad, Malveh 24:10; Sh. Ar., ḤM 85:3). But where the defendant denies the bill sued upon by the plaintiff, his plea prevails that the plaintiff would not have made a later bill in favor of the defendant had he really been indebted to him (Sh. Ar., loc. cit.; but see Yad, loc. cit. and *Siftei Kohen* to Sh. Ar., ḤM 85, n.7). Where the defendant pleads that the plaintiff already "has mine in his hands," the plaintiff is entitled to have his claim judged first, and the defendant's claim for restitution or to have one claim offset by the other will be adjudicated separately (BK 46b; Rashi and Tosef. thereto; Tur, ḤM 24:1; Rema, ḤM 24:1).

Identical Pleas. Where in respect of a certain sum of money or of a chattel, both parties plead "this is mine," and both are in possession of it (i.e., each holds it with his hand), and none can prove previous or present title, both will have to take the oath that they are entitled to at least one-half of it, and then one-half will be judged to belong to each (BM 1:1; Yad, To'en 9:7; ḤM 138:1). Where the mutual "this is mine" is pleaded in respect of land, or in respect of a chattel not in the possession of either, the party who first succeeds in taking possession, even by force, cannot be ousted unless the other can prove that he has a better title to it (BB 34b–35a; Yad, To'en 15:4; ḤM 139:4). For this rule, which in effect legitimizes seizing by force, the Solomonic reason was given that it would only be the true owner who would go to the length of using force and facing the ensuing lawsuit (Resp. Rosh 77:1; *Beit Yosef,* ḤM 139, n. 1; see also Extraordinary Remedies).

Pleas of Law. As a general rule, pleas are assertions or denials of fact only; but there are some exceptions to the rule, two of which are noteworthy: (1) the plea of "I do not want this legal privilege." Wherever the law confers a benefit on the class of persons to which the pleader belongs, he will be heard if he waives that benefit (Ket. 83a). Thus, the rule that a husband must maintain his wife in consideration of her handiwork for him was established in favor of his wife, and she may plead, "I will not claim maintenance and I will not work" (Ket. 58b). Or, where a plaintiff is allowed by law to recover on taking the oath, he may plead, "I do not want the privilege of taking the oath," and have the oath shifted to the defendant (Yad, To'en 1:4; ḤM 87:12); and (2) the plea of "I rely on the other view." Where the authorities are divided on a given question of law the defendant is entitled to plead that the opinion most favorable to him should be adopted (*Keneset ha-Gedolah,* ḤM 25, *Beit Yosef*). This post-talmudic rule is based on the premise that the benefit of any possible doubt on what the law is must accrue to the defendant, the burden of establishing his case always being on the plaintiff (see also Codification of the Law).

Weight of Pleas. Even where no evidence is available or forthcoming to substantiate a plea and even before such evidence is called for, the court will accept a plea as valid and conclusive in the following cases:

(1) Where the plea is fortified by a legal presumption (see Evidence and Ḥazakah[2]) or by generally recognized standards or patterns of conduct. For instance, the plea, "I have not been paid" is accepted as conclusive if fortified by the presumption that no debtor pays a debt before maturity (BB 5b).

(2) Where the plea is eminently reasonable *(sevarah).* The reasonableness cannot generally be determined from the particular circumstances of the case at issue, but rather from legal rules evolved for this purpose. Thus, a man's plea is not believed if by that plea he accuses himself of wrongdoing (Ket. 18b), unless he can adduce a good reason *(amatla)* for so doing. Where, by his own mouth, a man has taken upon himself a certain status or obligation which could not otherwise be proved against him, he is believed on his plea that the status has come to an end or that obligation has been performed, for "the mouth that obligated is the mouth that discharged" (Ket. 2:5). For instance, a woman who cannot otherwise be proved to have been married is believed on her plea that her marriage has been dissolved (Ket. 2:5; Yad, Gerushin 12:1; Sh. Ar., EH 152:6).

Witnesses whose attestation to a deed cannot be proved other than by their own testimony are believed on their plea that they were incompetent or coerced to attest (Ket. 2:3; Ket. 18b; Yad, Edut 3:6; ḤM 46:37), provided they did not plead that their incompetency was due to criminal conduct (Yad, Edut 3:7; ḤM 46:37). Opinions are divided on whether a defendant who admitted that a bill, which could not otherwise be proved, had been authorized by him, would be believed on his plea that he had paid the bill (BM 7a; Ket. 19a; BB 154b); the better opinion seems to be that as long as the bill is in the hands of the plaintiff it is presumed to be unpaid (Tur, ḤM 82:3), and the defendant's unsworn plea of repayment is not sufficient to discharge him (see above; and Rashi, Ket. 19a, s.v. *Ein ha-Malveh*). Similarly, a plea is believed if it was "in the hands" of the pleader to execute it by his own act (Sanh. 30a; ḤM 255:8).

(3) A particular brand of reasonableness is known as *miggo,* meaning something like "inasmuch": inasmuch as you could have succeeded by some other more far-reaching plea, the lesser plea, by which you likewise succeed, can be accepted as credible. "If A makes a certain statement which does not appear probable on the face of it, this fact will not tend to weaken his case, if he could have made another statement which would have appeared probable. If that other statement would have been acceptable to the court, the one that he actually makes must also be accepted, for had he wished to tell an untruth he would have rather made that other statement" (Herzog, Instit, 1 (1936), 250ff.). In the much shorter and clearer words of Shabbetai b. Meir ha-Kohen (*Shakh*) in his "Rules of *Miggo*" (appended to his commentary *Siftei Kohen* to ḤM 82, hereinafter referred to as Rules), "he is known to speak the truth, for if he had wanted to lie, a better plea would have been open to him" (Rule 26). *Miggo* is the amoraic version and elaboration of the mishnaic "the mouth that obligated is the mouth that discharged" (cf. Ket. 2:2, 16a; the different problems of *miggo* are dealt with in the *Shakh* at the end of ḤM 82).

Miggo is, generally speaking, available in respect of pleas of defendants only (Rules 1, 14, 15); *miggo* is of no use against witnesses (Rules 5, 12); *miggo* is of use against a written deed (Rule 11); where the taking of an oath is prescribed (other than the post-mishnaic oath), *miggo* is not available in lieu of it, nor will it be allowed where the more far-reaching plea could have resulted in a Pentateuchal or mishnaic oath being imposed, for the actual plea may have been put forward only for the purpose of evading the oath (Rules 25, 28); *miggo* does not apply where it would contradict local custom in matters of commerce (Rule 2); both the more far-reaching and the actual plea must relate to the same subject matter (Rule 13); *miggo* does not operate retroactively (Rule 8); where the more far-reaching plea would obviously have been a lie, it cannot operate as *miggo* on the actual plea; nor will *miggo* be of any avail to strengthen a plea which is manifestly false (Rule 9); whether the *miggo* is of avail against presumptions of fact is discussed (Rules 10, 16); *miggo* is of no avail against any possessory title *(ibid.); miggo* is not allowed

1. page 632; 2. page 595.

where the more far-reaching plea would have been "I do not know" (Rule 3); *miggo* is allowed only in respect of pleas which are outspoken and unambiguous (Rule 7); there are differences of opinion on whether *miggo* would be allowed where the pleader could have remained silent instead of pleading, and by remaining silent would have attained the same or a better result (Rules 19, 21); whether *miggo* is available where the more far-reaching plea would have been unreasonable or unusual, or would have been an affront or an impertinence to the creditor is discussed (Rules 6, 22); *miggo* is not available where the more far-reaching plea would have incriminated the pleader (Rule 24); *miggo* is applied only to the plea of a single pleader: where the same plea is put forward by more than one, none can avail himself of *miggo* (Rule 4); *miggo* is allowed in respect of pleas of fact only, and not in respect of pleas of law (Rule 31); and where there recommends itself to the court a reasoning *(sevarah)* which appears (however slightly) better than *miggo* in the particular case before it, *miggo* may be discarded at the discretion of the court (Rule 32).

Rejection of Pleas. Untrustworthiness. Once a defendant has denied having taken a loan and the fact that he has is proved by witnesses, he will not be allowed to plead that he has repaid the loan (BM 17a; Yad, To'en 6:1; ḤM 79:5), provided the denial has been made in court (Yad, To'en 6:2; ḤM 79:9). The denial which proved untrue renders the pleader, insofar as the same subject matter is concerned, a "potential denier," *huḥzak,* whose pleas will no longer be accepted as trustworthy. The same rule applies where a debtor had admitted the debt and, when sued in court, denied it (ḤM 79:10), provided the previous admission could not be explained away as unintentional (Sanh. 29b; Yad, To'en 6:6).

Inconsistency. No alternative or inconsistent pleas are allowed (BB 31a; ḤM 80:1). While pleading in court, however, the pleader may rectify his plea and explain it or even substitute another plea for it, as long as his original plea has not been proved or disproved by evidence (Yad, To'en 7:7–8; Tur, ḤM 80:4). Statements made out of court are not regarded as "pleas" and may freely be contradicted by pleas in court (Sh. Ar., ḤM 79:9, 80:1).

Public Policy. Pleas which may otherwise be perfectly legitimate sometimes cannot be raised because their acceptance might lead to undesirable results from a moral, humanitarian, or economic point of view. Examples of purposes for which such pleas are rejected are: that a wrongdoer should not reap a reward (Ket. 11a, 39b; et al.); that the lenders' doors not be closed in the face of borrowers (Ket. 88a; Git. 49b–50a; BK 7b–8a; et al.); for the protection of open markets (BK 115a); that it be not too easy for a husband to divorce his wife (Ket. 39b); and that equity and generosity may prevail over strict law (BM 83a; 108a; Ket. 97a; et al.).

Suggestion of Pleas. Where the defendant (or, in exceptional cases such as widows and orphans, the plaintiff) appears unable or unfit to formulate the plea which is open to him in the circumstances, the court will "open the mouth of the dumb for him" (Prov. 31:8) and enter the plea for the defendant of its own accord (Ket. 36a; Git. 37b; BB 41a; *Piskei ha-Rosh;* BK 1:3). The court will not, however, of its own accord enter for the defendant a plea to the effect that any admission made by him out of court was false or unintended (Yad, To'en 6:8; ḤM 81:21; but see Rema, ḤM 81:14).

Bibliography: Gulak, Yesodei, 4 (1922), passim: Herzog, Instit, 1 (1936), 57f., 241, 250–5, 268; 2 (1939), 108, 117f.; ET, 1 (1951[3]), 140, 224–6, 253f., 255–7, 263–6, 267f.; 2 (1949), 52–55, 70f.; 3 (1951), 106–10; 4 (1952), 199–208; 5 (1953), 524–7; 6 (1954), 200; 7 (1956), 290–5, 321–8, 733–8; 8 (1957), 404–35, 722–43; 9 (1959), 451–9, 722–46; B. de Vries, in: *Tarbiz,* 36 (1966/67), 229–38; Z. Frankel. *Der gerichtliche Beweis nach mosaisch-talmudischen Rechte* (1846); H.B. Fassel, *Das mosaisch-rabbinische Gerichtsverfahren in civilrechtlichen Sachen* (1859); Z. Freudenthal, in: MGWJ, 9 (1860), 161–75; M. Bloch, *Die Civilprocess-Ordnung nach mosaisch-rabbinischen Rechte* (1882); D. Fink, *Miggo als Rechtsbeweis im babylonischen Talmud* (1891); T.S. Zuri, *Mishpat ha-Talmud,* 7 (1921); Elon, Mafte'aḥ, 84–88; idem, in: ILR, 3 (1968), 437f.; idem, *Ha-Mishpat Ha-Ivri* (1973) – see Bibliography to Practice and Procedure.

Haim H. Cohn

ḤAZAKAH (Heb. חזקה ; lit. "possession," "taking possession"), a term of expressing three main concepts in Jewish law: (1) a mode of acquiring ownership; (2) a means of proving ownership or rights in property; (3) a factual-legal presumption *(praesumptio juris)* as to the existence of a particular fact or state of affairs. In its first connotation *ḥazakah* creates a new legal reality, unlike the latter two cases where it is merely instrumental in proving or presuming an existing one. For *ḥazakah* in its connotation of possession see also Evidence, Ownership, Property. For (1) see Acquisition.

ḤAZAKAH AS PROOF OF OWNERSHIP

Immovable Property. Possession per se of immovable property (*karka* or *mekarke'in,* lit. "land," as opposed to *metaltelin,* "movable property") known to have belonged to another does not displace the title of the legal owner (*mara kamma,* "first owner") thereto, for "land is never stolen" (*karka einah nigzelet;* BK 95a; TJ, BK 10:6, 7c) and "is always in the possession of its owner" (BM 102b). The possessor is accordingly required to prove that he acquired the property in a legally recognized way. If, however, he has held undisturbed possession in the manner of an owner for a period of three consecutive years, without protest from the previous owner, the possessor's plea that he purchased the property or received it as a gift (from the first owner or his father) and that the deed thereto has been lost, is believed. Where his possession is not accompanied by such a claim of right *(she-ein immah ta'anah)* but merely with the contention that "no one ever said anything to me," the *ḥazakah* is not established (BB 3:3). Where the property is purchased or inherited from another, the holder's mere plea (some scholars require proof on his part) that the deceased or seller held possession of the property in the manner of an owner, for even one day, will validate the occupier's *ḥazakah,* for "he cannot be expected to know how his father came by the property" (Rashbam, BB 41a). For this reason the court would "plead the cause " of the heir or purchaser (BB 23a), to the effect that he came by the property in lawful manner.

In Jewish law *ḥazakah* is part of procedural law only (as "mere evidence," *Yad Ramah,* BB 170a; for this reason the laws of *ḥazakah* are treated by Maimonides in *hilkhot To'en ve-Nitan* and not in the book on *Kinyan*), in contrast with the Roman law *usucapio* of the Twelve Tables, which is a matter of the substantive law whereby ownership is created by virtue of possession for a period of two years. The *ḥazakah* of Jewish law is somewhat akin to the possession in the Roman *praescriptio longi temporis* of the end of the second century c.e., according to which possession of property for ten or 20 years effectively established title, if accompanied by *iusta causa.* There, however, possession is equally effective even if it transpires that ownership was acquired in a defective manner *ab initio,* in contrast with the Jewish law, where "he who possesses a field by virtue of a deed which is found to be defective, his *ḥazakah* is not established" (Tosef., BB 2:2; BB 32b; cf. TJ, Shevu. 6:2, 37a, where a contrary opinion is expressed).

Period of Possession. According to some *tannaim* (BB 36b and BB 3:1; *Tanna Kamma*) *ḥazakah* always requires possession for a period of three full years (this period is mentioned already in the Hammurapi code, sec. 30–31). Rava, a Babylonian *amora* of the first half of the fourth century, explains the length of this period on the ground that it is not customary for a purchaser to preserve his title deed for longer than three years, and that thereafter the first owner is not entitled to demand production of the purchaser's deed (BB 29a). In the case of a field producing one annual crop only, the period is 18 months according to R. Ishmael and 14 months according to R. Akiva, i.e., a period sufficient for the cultivation and enjoyment of three crops; a period covering the production of three crops – even if enjoyed in one year – is sufficient, according to Ishmael, in the case of a field of diverse trees whose fruits are harvested in different seasons (BB 3:1). According to Judah, a *tanna* of the second century, the period of three years applies in the case of an absent (abroad, "in Spain") owner (BB 3:2), but one year suffices where both the first owner and the occupier are present in the same country (Tosef., BB 2:1; according to BB 41 a *ḥazakah* is immediately effective in the latter case). An analogous distinction is made in the Roman *praescriptio longi temporis,* between possession *inter absentes* (20 years) and *inter praesentes* (10 years). Some scholars (Gulak, Karl) are of the opinion (based on BB 3:2) that in ancient *halakhah* the law of *ḥazakah* was applicable only when both parties were in the same country; at the commencement of the amoraic period, this *halakhah* was interpreted as having been instituted because of "conditions of emergency" (BB 38a–b), whereby there was no means of travel between various districts within Ereẓ Israel; in times of peace, however, *ḥazakah* is effective even in the absence of the first owner. However, the question of the operation of *ḥazakah* between parties in different countries remained a disputed one even during the early amoraic period (TJ, BB 3:3, 14a).

Manner of Exercising Possession. Possession must be held "in the manner in which people normally use the particular property" (Yad, To'en ve-Nitan 11:2); it must therefore be held for an uninterrupted period, unless it is local custom to cultivate the field one year and leave it fallow the next (BB 29a). It is a requirement that the possessor not only cultivate the field, but that he also enjoy its fruits, "for the essence of *ḥazakah* is the gathering of fruit . . . , " without which evidence of all his other activities on the land will not avail (TJ, BB 3:3, 14a; BB 36b).

Protest. Protest on the part of the first owner within the period of three years interrupts the occupier's *ḥazakah,* because it has the effect of warning the occupier to preserve his title deed as proof of ownership. In ancient *halakhah* this protest (variously called ערר or ערער *(arar;* Tosef., BB 2:4; TJ, BB 3:3, 14a; BB 39b) and מחאה *(meḥa'ah;* BB 29a, 39a et al.) by the *amoraim* of Ereẓ Israel and Babylonia respectively), served the procedural function of commencing litigation (analogous to the Roman *litis contestatio*) and was accordingly required to be made before the court. Doubt was already cast on this requirement by the *amoraim* of Ereẓ Israel (TJ, BB 3:3, 14a), and according to the Babylonian *amoraim* protest requires no more than that it should be made known to the public *(gillui milta le-rabbim)* by the first owner, or that he make a statement before witnesses that he maintains his interest in the property (BB 39b). In the fourth century the Babylonian *amoraim* prescribed a formula for the protest: "*Peloni* is a robber who occupies my land by robbery and on the morrow I shall bring suit against him," but an unqualified statement: "*Peloni* is a robber" is not an effective protest (BB 38b–39a), lest the occupier plead that "he merely insulted me and therefore I did not look to my deed" (Yad, To'en 11:7). Protest before two witnesses – not necessarily in the presence of the occupier – suffices, for the fact thereof is bound to come to the occupier's notice one way or another (BB 38b, 39b; Yad, To'en 11:5).

Any reasonable explanation for the lack of protest is a bar to effective *ḥazakah.* For this reason *ḥazakah* does not operate between husband and wife or parent and child, each in respect of the other's property, for in these cases the one party is not fastidious about the other's use of the property (BB 3:3; *Teshuvot ha-Rashba ha-Meyuḥasot le-ha-Ramban,* no. 93). In suits between other related parties, the issue of *ḥazakah* is decided by the court on the merits of the evidence in each case, depending on "whether one brother relied on the other in the running of his affairs," etc. (Resp. Rashba, pt. 1, no. 950; Tur and Sh. Ar., ḤM 149:6–8). Nor is *ḥazakah* gained by artisans (building contractors), partners, metayers אריסין – tenants receiving a share of the crop; see Lease and Hire) and guardians (see Apotropos; BB 3:3), for they occupy by license (*reshut;* BB 42b; TJ, BB 3:5, 14a) and there is therefore no purpose in making protest against them. Possession will also not lead to *ḥazakah* when the first owner is unable to make protest, whether for lack of communication with the occupier because of emergency conditions (BB 38a–b; see above) or because the occupier came on the property by the use of force, "like those of a certain family who are prepared to commit murder for monetary gain" (BB 47a). The exilarchs ("of that time") were also barred from gaining *ḥazakah* because the property owners "stood in awe of them" (i.e., of making protest; Yad, To'en 13:2; BB 36a; Rashbam ad loc.; Joseph b. Samuel Tov Elem, *Teshuvot Ge'onim Kadmonim* no. 48, ascribes the lack of protest to the pleasure derived by the owners from the exilarch's use of their property). Nor could others gain *ḥazakah* over the property of the exilarchs, for the latter did not "hasten" to protest, because they were able to take forcible possession of their property or because they were not particular, on account of their wealth, about others using their property (BB 36a and Rashbam *ibid.; Ge'onim Kadmonim,* no. 48; *Bet ha-Beḥirah,* BB 36a). A non-Jew who acquires forcible possession and a Jew who derives his title through him do not gain *ḥazakah* over the property of a Jew (BB 35b), though in the time of R. Joseph, in Babylonia, it was decided otherwise, for there was a "judicial system which permitted no person to exercise duress against any other person" (*Bet ha-Beḥirah,* BB 35b and Git. 58b).

Plurality of Occupiers and Successive Owners. *Ḥazakah* may be gained through someone occupying on behalf of the person claiming *ḥazakah,* as in the case of the tenant to whom the claimant lets the dwelling (BB 29a); and possession by one partner on behalf of another is similarly effective if each of them has occupied the property for part of the three-year period, provided that this partnership arrangement between them was publicly known (BB 29b; *Bet ha-Beḥirah,* BB 29b; Yad, To'en 12:5 – "since they are partners, they are as one"). The required period for *ḥazakah* is cumulative both as against successive "first owners" and in favor of successive possessors, who respectively derive title from their predecessors (Tosef., BB 2:7–8). At the commencement of the amoraic period, Rav determined that the combined period for which possession was held by both the seller and the purchaser would only be cumulative in the case of a sale by deed, as in this manner the matter would become public and the "first owner" aware that a cumulative *ḥazakah* was challenging his ownership.

Aspects of Ḥazakah in Post-Talmudic Times. Aspects of *ḥazakah* were discussed by the *posekim* against the prevailing social and communal background. One matter discussed was the application of *ḥazakah* to a permanent seating place in the synagogue, which became an asset capable of being alienated and inherited (Sh. Ar., ḤM 162:7; Rema and *Pitḥei Teshuvah* ad loc.). Some of the scholars recognized the application of *ḥazakah* thereto (Meir ha-Levi Abulafia and others), but stress was laid on the difficulty of establishing uninterrupted synagogue attendance at all appointed services for three years – a requirement for effective *ḥazakah* (*Shitah Mekubbeẓet* and Nov. Ritba to BB 29b). Some scholars excused absence on account of illness or mourning (*Bet ha-Beḥirah* BB 29a) and even occasional absence for pressing business reasons (Responsa Rashba pt. 1, no. 943; Tur, ḤM 140:16; *Bet ha-Beḥirah* BB 29a differs), and the latter view prevailed (*Beit Yosef* ḤM 141:2; Rema ḤM 140:8). On the other hand, *ḥazakah* was generally not recognized as extending to public and communal property such as consecrated property, *talmud torahs,* charitable institutions, and the like, for "who shall make protest?" (Rashba, pt. 1 no. 642), and when recognized, *ḥazakah* was held to be effective only under special circumstances and in respect of property in the care of appointed officials or seven representative citizens (Tur and Sh. Ar., ḤM 149 end).

Many of the discussions of this period centered around relationships between Jews of different social status and between Jews and their gentile neighbors. The talmudic *halakhah* precluding others from gaining *ḥazakah* of the property of exilarchs and vice versa was discussed by Solomon b. Abraham Adret and Asher b. Jehiel in relation to the property of Jews who held official positions and exercised authority. Both decided that the cases were not analogous, for the exilarchs functioned as "quasi-royalty" and ". . . in these generations a Jew who should find favor with the king does not impose such awe . . . " as would deter the owner of property from protesting (Resp. Rosh 18:17; Resp. Rashba, pt. 1, no. 941; Tur, ḤM 149: 13; *Sma* ḤM 149, no. 18; *Siftei Kohen* ḤM 149, n. 12). The question of *ḥazakah* in relation to a non-Jew or a Jew deriving title through him was frequently treated and the decision made dependent on the prevailing attitude of the central government toward the particular Jewish community: "in a case where the Jew can bring the non-Jew before the court of the land, a Jew deriving title through a non-Jew has *ḥazakah*" (Ravyah, quoted in *Mordekhai* BB 3:553; Raḥ quoted in the Nov. Ritba, BB 35b and see there Ha-Ittur's dissenting opinion; cf. also Tur and Sh. Ar., ḤM 149:14 and 236:9; BB 55a and commentators ad loc.). Some of the *halakhot* of *ḥazakah* relating to immovable property were applied also in the matter of *Ḥezkat ha-Yishuv* ("the right of domicile").

Movable Property. Contrary to the rule in the case of immovable property, "movables" are in the *ḥazakah* of the person having the physical possession thereof even if the plaintiff brings witnesses that the movables are known to belong to him, and the former's plea that he acquired them according to law is accepted (Yad, To'en 8:1; Tur, ḤM 133:1; source of the rule: BB 3:3; Tosef., BB 2:6; only "the launderer has no *ḥazakah*"), except when the chattels are known to be stolen property (BK 68b, 94b; Sh. Ar., ḤM 354:2). The authorities were in dispute on the requirement of a plea of right on the part of the possessor in the case of movables (*Shitah Mekubbeẓet* BB 28b). *Ḥazakah* of movables is gained forthwith, possession for a period of two or three days and sometimes even one hour – depending upon the subject matter – being sufficient (BB 36a and Rabbenu Gershom ad loc.; also Rashbam BB 42a). However, not every *tefisah* ("taking of possession," "seizure") establishes valid *ḥazakah,* thus ". . . if they saw him hiding articles under his garments and he came out and said 'these are mine' he is not believed," unless there is a reasonable explanation for this type of behavior, as in the case of articles which are habitually concealed and the like (Shevu. 46a–b).

The rule excluding the operation of *ḥazakah* as between "first owners" and possessors standing in a special relationship toward each other (see above) applies also to movables, e.g., in the case of the artisan, the bailee, etc. (BB 3:3; Tosef., BB 2:5–6). Similarly it does not operate in respect of "articles which are made to be given on loan or hire" (Shevu. 46a–b), where the first owner may account for the fact that movables of this type are found in the hands of the possessor on these grounds. On the other hand, the first owner's claim that these movables were stolen from him is not believed, for this is an admission that they were not lent and "we do not presume a man to be a thief" (Shevu. 46b; Rosh and Ran ad loc.). Most commentators include in the category of "articles which are made to be given on loan or hire," all chattels "which are likely to be lent by their owners" (Rif and Ran to Shevu. 46b). According to this view, only chattels which their owners fear may be damaged, such as certain types of books (Rashi to Shevu. 46b), or those which are particularly valuable, such as articles of silver and gold (*Terumat ha-Deshen,* no. 335), are not to be considered as made to be given on loan or hire. This view is opposed by Maimonides, who holds that such a view in effect invalidates in respect of most movables – the principle that a thing must be considered to be the property of the person in whose possession it is found. Maimonides distinguishes between articles which are "likely to be given on loan or hire" – in which category he places all movables – and things which are "made to be given on loan or hire," defined by him as articles which in a particular locality are specifically made with a view to their being borrowed or hired for a fee and not for sale or home use, such as "large copper kettles for cooking at celebrations," etc., *ḥazakah* applying to the latter case only (Yad, To'en 8:9); other articles may also come within the latter category but only where their owner has witnesses to prove that he has constantly lent or hired them out and that he holds them for such purpose (To'en 8:9 and 10 and Rabad's stricture thereon).

Special Categories of Movables. In the case of slaves, a period of three years is required for effective *ḥazakah* (BB 3:1). Animals (livestock) were apparently deemed to be like other movables in the tannaitic period, i.e., *ḥazakah* was effective immediately; this may be deduced from the existence of a special ruling precluding shepherds from acquiring *ḥazakah,* as in the case of the artisan and bailee (Tosef., BB 2:5). At the commencement of the amoraic period, Simeon b. Lakish determined that the normal rule of *ḥazakah* did not apply in respect of livestock (BB 36a), for they "stray from place to place" (TJ, BB 3:1. 13d) and therefore "the fact of detaining it under his hand does not constitute proof, for it went of its own accord into his *reshut*" (i.e., domain; Yad, To'en 10:1). Differing opinions were expressed with regard to establishing *ḥazakah* in respect of chattels not falling within the normal rule, e.g., articles made to be given on loan or hire and livestock; some of the *posekim* expressed the opinion that in these cases *ḥazakah* is never established; others held that it is established after a period of three years; and some held that there is no fixed period for effective *ḥazakah,* the court having the discretion to decide the matter in each case (*Yad Ramah* BB 36a; Rashbam BB 36a; Nov. Ritba BB 36a; Nov. Rashba BB 46a; Tur, ḤM 133:10 and 135:1–2; Resp. Maharam of Rothenburg, ed. Prague, no. 180).

See also Limitation of Actions and Hassagat Gevul. For *ḥazakah* in relation to servitudes *(ḥezkat tashmishim)* and torts see Servitudes.

ḤAZAKAH AS A LEGAL-FACTUAL PRESUMPTION

This occurs in a number of forms:

(1) A legal presumption of the continued existence of a once-ascertained state of affairs, until the contrary be proved – "an object is presumed to possess its usual status" (Nid. 2a), e.g., that the flesh of an animal is presumed to be forbidden as having been cut from a living animal until it is ascertained that it was ritually slaughtered; once slaughtered, the animal's flesh is presumed to be permitted unless the manner in which it became *terefah* becomes known (Ḥul. 9a); that the husband is alive at the time that the bill of divorce is handed to the wife, even though he was old or ill when the agent or *shali'aḥ* left him (Git. 3:3); similarly the presumptions of normal health and fitness, referred to variously as *ḥezkat ha-guf* (Ket. 75b), *ḥezkat bari* (Kid. 79b; BB 153b), and *ḥezkat kashrut* (BB 31b).

(2) A legal presumption of the existence of a fixed and accepted custom or of the psychological nature of man, such as the following: that an agent fulfills his mandate (Er. 31b); that a woman does not have the impudence to declare (falsely) in her husband's presence that he has divorced her (Yev. 116a) and she is therefore believed; that a debtor does not settle his debt before due date, therefore his plea (without proof) that he repaid the debt before due date is not believed (BB 5a–b); that a *ḥaver* does not allow anything which is untithed to leave his hands and therefore if he dies leaving a silo full of produce, this is presumed to have been tithed (Pes. 9a); that no man affixes his signature to a document unless he knows the contents thereof, and he cannot therefore plead that he did not read or understand its contents (PDR 1:293–5).

(3) Legal presumptions permitting a conclusion of fact to be inferred from particular surrounding circumstances. Presumptions of this kind were relied upon even in cases of capital punishment, as if the conclusion had been proved by the evidence of witnesses: "we flog . . . stone and burn on the strength of presumption" (Kid. 80a, and examples there quoted), "even where there is no testimony on the matter" (Rashi ad loc.). Similarly, in certain circumstances a woman reputed to be married to a particular man was held to be his wife (Yad, Issurei Bi'ah, 1:21, as per TJ, Kid. 4:10, 66b).

Support for the validity of the latter presumptions was found in the law of the Torah that the penalty for "one who curses or smites his father" is death: "how do we know for sure that he is his father? Only by way of presumption" (Yad and TJ, loc. cit.; in Ḥul. 11b, the aforesaid *halakhah* concerning "one who smites his father" serves as a basis for deduction of the majority rule.

Bibliography: Z. Frankel, *Der gerichtliche Beweis nach mosaisch-talmudischem Rechte* (1846), 437–74; M. Bloch, *Das mosaisch-talmudische Besitzrecht* (1897), 13–48; J. Lewin, in: *Zeitschrift fuer vergleichende Rechtswissenschaft,* 29 (1913), 151–298; J. Kohler, *ibid.,* 31 (1914), 312–5; J.S. Zuri, *Mishpat ha-Talmud,* 4 (1921), 19–28; Gulak, Yesodei, 1 (1922), 16f., 168–75; 4 (1922), 99f., 105, 114–28; A. Gulak, *Le-Ḥeker Toledot ha-Mishpat ha-Ivri bi-Tekufat ha-Talmud,* 1 (1929) *(Dinei Karka'ot),* 95–108; J.L. Kroch, *Ḥazakah Rabbah* (1927–63); Z. Karl, in: *Ha-Mishpat ha-Ivri,* 4 (1932/33), 93–112; Herzog, Instit, 1 (1936), 225–73; A. Karlin, in: *Sinai,* 22 (1947/48), 223–34; J.N. Epstein, *Mevo'ot le-Sifrut ha-Amora'im* (1962), 246–8; ET, 1 (1951[3]), passim (articles beginning with *"Ein Adam . . . "*); J. Unterman, in: *Sinai,* 54 (1964), 4–10; Z. Warhaftig, *Ha-Ḥazakah ba-Mishpat ha-Ivri* (1964); J. Algazi, *Kehillat Ya'akov,* 2 (1898), 64a–87b *("Kunteres Middot Hakhamim"),* M. Elon, *Ha-Mishpat Ha-Ivri* (1973), I, 132ff., II, 304ff., 383ff., 432, 502, 509 n. 306, 604ff., 721 n. 41, 733ff., 735ff., 754ff., 810ff., 812ff., 822ff., III, 881, 993, 1062ff., 1107ff., 1110ff.

Menachem Elon

LIMITATION OF ACTIONS. The Concept and its Substance. In the talmudic period, Jewish law generally did not recognize the principle that the right to bring an action could be affected by the passage of time (i.e., extinctive prescription); in the post-talmudic period, it came to be recognized as a principle that there was a limit to the claimant's right of instituting action on account of the passing of time, without extinction of the underlying right itself. In Jewish law, the principle of limitation of actions is grounded on the reasoning that delay in instituting action serves to cast doubt on the reliability of the claimant's evidence. Consequently, prescription serves to deprive the plaintiff of a remedial action only if the defendant denies the existence of the right forming the subject matter of the action, but not if he admits its existence.

In the Talmudic Period. In the Talmud, the principle of limitation of actions – apart from two exceptional cases – was wholly unrecognized: "a creditor may recover his debt at any time, even if it has not been mentioned" (Tosef., Ket. 12:3; cf. the version in TJ, Ket. 12:4, 35b and TB, Ket. 104a).

The Widow's Claim for her Ketubbah. One exception to the general rule is the claim of a widow for her *ketubbah,* which becomes prescribed under certain circumstances. In a dispute with R. Meir, the scholars held that "a widow, as long as she lives in her husband's house, may recover her *ketubbah* at any time; when, however, she lives in her father's house [and not with the heirs, and is therefore not inhibited from claiming her *ketubbah* from them], she may recover her *ketubbah* within 25 years only" (from the date of her husband's death; Ket. 12:4). Thereafter, her right to recover the *ketubbah* is extinguished, on the assumption that she has waived it, taking into account the great delay in instituting action and the fact that the *ketubbah* "is not like a loan and therefore she has not suffered any loss" (Ket. 104a and Rashi ad loc.). R. Meir expressed the contrary opinion that as long as she lives in her father's house she may recover her *ketubbah* at any time, but as long as she lives in her husband's house, she may only recover her *ketubbah* within 25 years, for "25 years suffices for her to extend favors in exhaustion of her *ketubbah*" (as it may be assumed that during this period she made use of the assets of the estate to render favors (gifts) to her neighbors in an amount corresponding to the value of her *ketubbah:* Ket. 12:4 and Rashi ad loc.). In the opinion of R. Ishmael, the period is three years only (Tosef., Ket. 12:3). The *halakhah* was determined according to the first view (Yad, Ishut, 16:21–24; Sh. Ar., EH 101:1–4). In talmudic times, this limitation of action in the case of a widow seeking to recover her *ketubbah* after the lapse of 25 years from the date of her husband's death already applied only where she was not in possession of the *ketubbah* deed; there was no limitation of action if she was in possession of such a deed at the time her claim was brought. Similarly, her right of action for recovery of the *ketubbah* remained intact even though she lived in her parents' home after her husband's death, provided that the attitude of the heirs toward her was particularly favorable ("delivering her maintenance to her on their shoulders"), on the presumption that the nature of this relationship had served to inhibit her from demanding her *ketubbah* from them (Ket. 12:4; 104b). On the widow's death her heirs too could recover her *ketubbah* only within 25 years (Ket. 12:4), commencing, according to some of the *posekim,* from the date of their succeeding to her right, i.e., on her death (Tur and Sh. Ar., EH 101:1), and according to others, from the date that the cause of action arose, i.e., on the death of the husband (Rashi and R. Hananel, Shevu. 48a; *Bet ha-Beḥira,* Ket. 104b).

The Widow's Claim for Maintenance. Another exception to the general rule is to be found in a halakhic ruling from amoraic times stating that a delay of two years on the part of a poor widow – or three years on the part of a rich one – in claiming maintenance from the estate of the deceased husband, barred her from recovering maintenance for the period which had elapsed (Ket. 96a; TJ, Ket. 11:2, 34b has two or three months respectively). The reasoning behind this quasi-limitation of action is likewise based on the assumption that the widow, by virtue of her delay, has waived her claim for maintenance (Rashi Ket. 96a; *Bet ha-Beḥirah ibid.;* Yad, Ishut, 18:26; Tur and Sh. Ar., EH 93:14). If, during the aforesaid period, the widow has borrowed for her maintenance or if she has been in possession of a pledge, she cannot be presumed to have waived her claim for maintenance and it does not become prescribed (TJ, loc. cit.).

Roman Law. Roman law of that period also did not recognize the principle of limitation of actions, although there were the *actiones temporales,* which had to be brought within a fixed period, mostly within one year (the *annus utilis*). However, the reason for the limitation of those actions lay in the fact that they were founded on a right "granted" by the praetor who limited in advance the period within which an action could be brought for enforcement. Consequently, once this period had elapsed, the remedial action as well as the underlying right itself became extinguished. In contradistinction to this, actions based on civil law *(actiones civiles),* as well as those praetorian rights in respect of which the praetor had not determined any fixed period for instituting action, were numbered among the *actiones perpetuae,* which could be brought at any time (save for a number of exceptions). It was only in 424 c.e., in a law of Honorius and Theodosius, that the principle of prescription was recognized in respect of all actions. The general period of prescription was fixed at 30 years and, in certain exceptional cases, at 40 years (R. Sohm, Institutionen (1949[7]), 709–15).

In the Post-Talmudic Period. From the beginning of the 13th century, Jewish law began to give limited recognition to the principle of limitation of actions. While the principle was preserved that limitation of the right of action could not extinguish the underlying right itself, the doctrine evolved that delay in bringing an action served to cast doubt on the credibility of the evidence adduced in proof of the claim.

Effect of Delay of Credibility of Claimant's Evidence. Thus at the end of the 13th century Asher b. Jehiel, dealing with a claim based on old deeds, expressed the fear that an unduly long silence might serve as a subterfuge to enable deceit to go unnoticed or to be forgotten; he accordingly demanded that a suit of this nature be thoroughly investigated if the defendant should plead that he paid the debt or deny its very existence and, "if I assess as a strong probability *(umdenah de-mukhaḥ)* that the suit is a fraudulent one and unfounded, I say that no *dayyan* in Israel should grant relief in this suit, and this I write and sign for delivery into the hands of the defendant" (Resp. Rosh, 68:20, 85:10). However, this view was not generally accepted at once and in the 14th century Isaac b. Sheshet of Spain and North Africa gave his opinion that a plea by a defendant based on the plaintiff's long delay in bringing his action was "an idle plea, lacking in substance, and served neither to prove nor disprove the existence of the debt" (Resp. Ribash no. 404). In time, however, Asher b. Jehiel's view on the effect of delay in bringing an action came to be generally accepted, and even supplemented by various further details. In the 15th century, Joseph Colon (of northern Italy) decided that overlong delay carried with it a suspicion of fraud, which obliged a careful investigation of the matter, even if it was written (in the deed) that the defendant would "raise no plea against the deed and took this upon himself on ban and oath" (Resp. Maharik No. 190; *Darkhei Moshe* ḤM 61, n. 5; Rema ḤM 61:9. The *halakhah* was decided accordingly by Joseph Caro and Moses Isserles (Sh. Ar., ḤM 98:1–2). In the 16th century Samuel di Medina (of the Balkan countries and Turkey) decided that where no reasonable justification could be found to account for the delay, the court should endeavor to effect a compromise between the parties (Resp. Maharashdam, ḤM 367), while Isaac Adarbi, Medina's contemporary and compatriot, charged the court with compelling the parties to a compromise in a suit based on a long-delayed claim (*Divrei Rivot* no. 109). Until this time, i.e., the beginning of the 17th century, no fixed period of prescription had been determined and the court would investigate and determine each case on its merits.

Fixed Periods for Limitation of Actions. From the beginning of the 17th century, the need became increasingly felt for precise legal directions concerning the period within which a defendant could expect a particular action to be brought against him. Jewish law accordingly came to recognize the principle – by way of *takkanah* and custom (see *minhag*) – that the mere lapse of time sufficed to impugn the credibility of the evidence in support of the claim, without the need for any particular investigation by the court. Consequently, if the defendant denied the existence of the debt, he was absolved from liability when he delivered an oath as to the truth of his plea. At the same time the substantive principle, basic to prescription in Jewish law, that the lapse of time did not operate to extinguish the underlying right itself, was preserved, so that a debtor who did not deny the existence of the debt – and certainly one who admitted it – was obliged to make repayment notwithstanding prescription of the right of action. The period of prescription was determined in advance – generally three years and in certain cases six (*Pinkas ha-Medinah, Lita,* ed. by S. Dubnow (1925), *Takkanah* 205 of 1628; Benjamin Ze'ev Wolf, *Misgeret ha-Shulḥan,* 61, n. 16; Ẓevi Hirsch b. Azriel, *Ateret Ẓevi,* to Sh. Ar., *ibid.;* Jacob Lorbeerbaum, *Netivot ha-Mishpat, Mishpat ha-Kohanim,* n. 18). Once more, this new development with regard to the law of prescription was not immediately accepted by all the halakhic scholars. Thus Abraham Ankawa (19th century, Morocco), in commenting on this development in Polish and Lithuanian Jewish centers, remarked that it was "a great innovation, and presumably a *takkanah* they enacted for themselves, although contrary to the law, for whatever reason they had at the time" (*Kerem Ḥamar* ḤM no. 33). So too, at the beginning of the 18th century, Jacob Reicher (Galicia) had decided in accordance with the principles laid down in the Shulḥan Arukh, in a matter concerning an old deed (*Shevut Ya'akov,* vol. 3, no. 182). His younger contemporary, Jonathan Eybeschuetz expressed the opinion that "at this time much scrutiny is required, to keep the court from giving effect [in the case of an old deed] to a fraudulent suit" (*Urim* ḤM 61, n. 18). In the course of time, however, this development came to be accepted as part of the law of prescription, and was even refined and supplemented by certain additional rules, namely: if the debt cannot be recovered from the debtor on account of his impoverishment, prescription is interrupted for the period of his impoverishment; prescription does not apply during the period in which either the plaintiff or defendant is a minor; prescription does not bar the institution of an action if the debtor has waived such a plea in writing, in clear and unequivocal terms, even after completion of the period of prescription (*Kesef ha-Kedoshim* 61:9).

In the State of Israel. A substantial number of the various provisions of the Prescription Law, 5718/1958, accord with the principles of prescription in Jewish law, including the principle that "prescription shall not per se void the right itself" (sec. 2). On the other hand, this Law includes the provision that an admission by the defendant of the plaintiff's right shall only have the effect of nullifying the period of prescription already accrued if the admission is not "accompanied by a plea of prescription" (sec. 9). This provision is at variance with the Jewish law principle that the defendant – if he has admitted the existence of the plaintiff's right – is not entitled to void the claim by pleading that the period within which the action may be instituted has lapsed.

For prescription with regard to immovable property, see *Ḥazakah.*

Bibliography: I.S. Zuri, *Mishpat ha-Talmud,* 7 (1921), 15f.; M. Elon, in: *Ha-Peraklit,* 14 (1957/58), 179–89, 243–79; idem, in: ILR, 4 (1969), 108–11; idem, *Ha-Mishpat Ha-Ivri* (1973), I, 110ff., II, 827; Z. Warhaftig, *Ha-Ḥazakah ba-Mishpat ha-Ivri* (1964), 263–85.

Menachem Elon

EVIDENCE.

Non-evidentiary Proceedings in Biblical Law. The revelation of divine law is found not only in legislation but also in adjudication in particular cases (cf. Lev. 24:12–14; Num. 15:32–34; 27:1–8; Deut. 1–17), whether through Moses or judges or priests (Ex. 28:30; Num. 27:21; Deut. 17:9–12; 21:5; 33:8–10). Adjudications without evidence survived in judicial, nondivine proceedings as demonstrated by the report of the trial held by King Solomon between the two women each claiming the same child (I Kings 3:24–25) and by contemporaneous trial reports from other civilizations. Judges appear to have devised their own tests of credibility.

Evidentiary Proceedings in Biblical Law. The existence and availability of human witnesses and other modes of proof seem from earliest times to have been part of judicial proceedings (cf. Ex. 22:9, 12). Witnesses appear to have testified to the facts prior to God being asked to pronounce the law (Num. 15:32–35); and eventually it came about that a person "able to testify, as one who has either seen or known of the matter," was guilty of an offense if he failed to come forward and testify (Lev. 5:1).

Evidence in Criminal Cases. Proof of Guilt. Biblical law had already established that in criminal cases the evidence of at least two witnesses is a *sine qua non* of any conviction and punishment (Deut. 17:6; 19:15). This rule appears to have applied both in judicial and in priestly adjudications (cf. Deut. 19:17), and was interpreted as prescribing a minimum burden of proof, from which no later legal development could in any way derogate. Post-biblical law thus concentrated on devising measures to assure the greatest possible reliability of witnesses' testimony: they were cautioned by the court that they would be rigorously cross-examined, that they must not rely on hearsay or on opinions, and that they must be conscious of their grave responsibility – since a human life was at stake (Sanh. 4:5). They were in fact subjected to cross-examination by the court – each witness separately – and their evidence would not be accepted unless their respective testimonies were found to be consistent with each other in all relevant particulars (Sanh. 5:1–4; Maim. Yad, Sanhedrin 12:1–3; for particulars of the cross-examination of witnesses and their qualifications, see Witness).

The further rule was evolved that it was not sufficient for witnesses to testify to the commission of the offense by the accused: they also had to testify that the accused had been warned by them beforehand against committing that particular offense *(hatra'ah)* – that is, that the accused knew that in committing the act he was violating the law (Tosef. Sanh. 11:1; Sanh. 8b; et al.). Elaborate rules were laid down for the identification of the accused by the witnesses, and where the court was not satisfied beyond any doubt as to such identification, the accused was discharged even before the witnesses were examined on the merits of the case (Maim. *ibid.*). According to some scholars, he was also thus discharged where the victim of the offense had not been identified by the witnesses to the satisfaction of the court (see *Leḥem Mishneh, ibid.*).

Evidence in Defense. Whereas a witness testifying in a criminal case was not allowed to raise a point in defense of or against the accused (Maim. Yad, Edut 5:8) – a witness being disqualified from performing the function of a judge – when the evidence of the prosecuting witnesses had been found admissible and *prima facie* conclusive, public announcements had to be made inviting any person able to raise a point in favor *(zekhut)* of the accused, to come forward and speak (Sanh. 6:1). While the charge against the accused could be proved only by the *viva voce* evidence of witnesses, any shred of evidence from which a defense could be inferred would be used in his favor (Rashi, Sanh. 42b). For this purpose, a favorable point is not necessarily a rebuttal of the testimony of the prosecuting witnesses, but merely any fact or circumstance likely to arouse in the mind of the court a doubt as to the guilt of the accused; hence such points did not automatically result in an acquittal, but they were sufficient justification for the case to be remitted to the court for reconsideration – even four or five times. There is no explicit presumption of innocence in Jewish law; the requirements of proof of guilt are, however, so stringent and rigorous, and the possibilities of establishing a valid defense so wide and flexible, that a conviction is much more difficult and an acquittal much easier to obtain than under a rebuttable presumption of innocence.

Changes in Standard of Proof. In talmudic law the standards of proof required, even in criminal cases, were largely reduced where the jurisdiction rested on considerations of "emergency" (*hora'at sha'ah;* see Extraordinary Remedies). After the virtual cessation of jurisdiction in capital cases (see Capital Punishment), and particularly in post-talmudic law, all criminal jurisdiction rested on considerations of "emergency" to which the provisions relating to the dispensation from the normal rules of evidence and procedure were held to apply. The rules of evidence prevailing in the Sanhedrin were held inapplicable in the courts of the Diaspora, when they were called upon to enforce public order by the imposition of fines or flogging (Resp. Rashba, vol. 4, no. 311).

Evidence in Civil Cases. Burden of Proof. It was in the law of evidence in civil cases in which the genius of the talmudic jurists, unfettered by scriptural restrictions, could develop fully. The obstacle that there was to be "one manner of law" (Lev. 24:22) in criminal and civil cases alike (Sanh. 4:1) was overcome with the assertion that the Torah takes pity on the money (property) of the people of Israel, and if the standards of proof in civil cases were as strict and rigorous as in criminal cases, nobody would lend his neighbor any money anymore, for fear the borrower would deny his debt or the memory of a witness would fail him (TJ, Sanh. 4:1, 22a). Accordingly, a balance had to be struck between the exigencies of formal justice which required the burden of proof to be on the initiator of the proceedings (Sif. Deut. 16; BK 46b) and commercial and judicial convenience which required the greatest possible elasticity in handling and discharging that burden.

Presumption of Rightful Possession. The fundamental rule that the plaintiff has the burden of proving his claim (*(ha-moẓi mi-ḥavero alav ha-re'ayah)* is based on the presumption *(ḥazakah)* of the rightful possession by the defendant of the chose in action – i.e., the thing (or money) claimed *(ḥezkat mamon)*: so long as the defendant's possession was not proved to be unrightful, it will not be disturbed – hence a defendant in possession is always in a better position that the plaintiff (Shevu. 46a; Maim. Yad, To'en ve-Nitan, 8:1; Sh. Ar., ḤM 133:1). But in order to raise the presumption of title, the possession must be accompanied by a claim of right (BB 3:3 and Codes); where the defendant in possession does not claim a specific right thereto, the burden is shifted to him to prove a right to retain the chose in action. Or where a claim is made according to custom, and the defense (that is, the possession) is contrary to custom, such as in a claim for workmen's wages (TJ, BM 7:1, 11b), the presumption of rightfulness operates in favor of the plaintiff and shifts the burden of proof onto the defendant. In an action between heirs, where the defendant has seized part of the estate, his claim of right is not any better than that of the plaintiff, and he will have to prove that his possession is rightful (Yev. 37b and Tos. *ibid.*). Where a man was seen to take a chattel out of a house, it was held to be on him to prove that he took it rightfully (BB 33b; Hai Gaon, *Sefer ha-Mikkaḥ ve-ha-Mimkar,* ch. 40), presumably because his possession was too recent to give rise to any presumption to that effect. Conversely, past possession which had meanwhile ceased *(ḥezkat mara kamma)* would give rise to a presumption of title only where the other party was not in possession either (BM 100a). These rules do not apply to possession of land and houses but only of money and chattels – for lands and other immovables there must be an uninterrupted possession of three years (BB 3:1), coupled with a claim of right (BB 3:3), in order to give rise to a presumption of title.

Presumptions and Quasi-Presumptions of Conduct. In order to mitigate the burden of proof and to simplify the judicial process, the sages have, presumably from their own accumulated judicial experience, established a vast number of quasi-presumptions, rooted in the psychology of human conduct, which apply to every litigant before the court, unless and until the contrary is proved. To give a few examples: a man does not waste his words or his money in vain without good cause (Ket. 58b, 10a); nor will he stand by inactive when his money is taken or his property endangered (Shab. 117b, 120b, 153a; Sanh. 72b) or when a wrong is being done or threatened to him (BB 60a). A man does not pay a debt before it falls due (BB 5a–b); nor does a man tolerate defects in a thing sold to him (Ket. 75b–76a). On the other hand, no man buys a chattel without having first seen and examined it *(ibid.)*. A debtor will not easily lie in the face of his creditor (BM 3a), nor a wife in the face of her husband (Ket. 22b), nor anybody in the face of a man who must know the truth (Tos. Ket. 18a; BK 107a). A man is not expected to remember things which do not concern him (Shevu. 34b). A man will not leave his house empty and his household unprovided for (Ket. 107a). However, he is apt to understate his fortune so as not to appear rich (BB 174b–175a), and will rather have one ounce of his own than nine ounces of his neighbor's (BM 38a); nor will he sell and dispose of any goods unless he has to (BB 47b). No man commits a wrong unless for his own benefit (BM 5b) and the purpose of an act is its normal consequence ("everybody knows why the bride gets married"; Shab. 33a). No person is lighthearted in the hour of his death (BB 175a), or defrauds the Temple treasury *(hekdesh;* Shevu. 42b; Ar. 23a). Apart from such general presumptions, there are special ones relating to particular contracts or offices, as for example the presumption that an agent has duly performed the duties of his agency (Git. 64a), or that a priest has duly performed the duties of his office (TJ, Shek. 7:2, 50c). See also Ḥazakah.

Presumptions of Credibility *(ne'emanut)*. Much stronger than these general and special presumptions of conduct are two further categories of presumptions, which are – theoretically at least – irrebuttable (comparable to, but not identical with, the Roman *praesumptiones iuris et de iure*). One is the presumption of credibility (*ne'emanut*) and the other is the presumption of common sense *(umdana mukhaḥat)*.

The presumption of credibility is primarily based on the notion that the party or witness concerned has an intimate knowledge of the matter in issue and has no reason to distort it. Thus, where a man says he has divorced his wife, his word is taken as conclusive for the court to permit her remarriage – because the matter is within his own knowledge, and he has no reason to distort it, as he could even now divorce her any time (BB 134b–135a, but see Maim. Gerushin 12:5; Sh. Ar., EH 152:1; see also Divorce). Or, a woman is believed when she says that her first husband has divorced her – because the matter is within her own knowledge and she need not have disclosed her previous marriage at all *(ha-peh she-asar hu ha-peh she-hittir;* Ket. 2:5). Or, an action will not lie for land which the defendant had told the plaintiff he had bought from the plaintiff's father, although the defendant could not prove the purchase: he will be believed that he bought it, because he need not have disclosed that it had ever belonged to the plaintiff's father in the first place (Ket. 2:2). The law would be different where the ownership of the plaintiff's father could be proved by witnesses *(ibid.)*.

Some of these irrebuttable presumptions of credibility are based on Scripture, e.g., where a father says he has given his daughter in marriage (Deut. 22:16: "I gave this man my daughter to wife"; Ket. 22a), or a father's nomination of his firstborn son (BB 127b, following Deut. 21:17). There are, however, also presumptions of credibility which rank in weight with the rebuttable presumptions of conduct – that is, they are capable of being displaced by express evidence to the contrary. A man is presumed not to lie about matters which are easily ascertainable (Yev. 115a); and a man is presumed to remember matters which are extraordinary and astonishing (Ḥul. 75b). Conversely, a man whose words were proved false on one point, will no longer be believed on other points in the same case; notwithstanding any presumption in his favor, he will be required to adduce express proof for the other points (BM 17a; Maim. Yad, Gerushin 13:1). Credibility is also presumed for statements made for purposes unconnected with the litigation (*mesi'aḥ lefi tummo:* Git. 28b; cf. BK 114f.). A man is believed where his statement (e.g., that he had become a convert on his own, without a *bet din*) disqualifies him (Yev. 47a), but no such statement is accepted as proof of disqualification of anybody else, even his wife or children *(ibid.)*.

Presumptions of Common Sense *(umdana mukhaḥat)*. The presumption of common sense applies to bring acts or conduct into conformity with reason or propriety: the presumption is that a person acts reasonably and properly, notwithstanding any outward appearance to the contrary; and his acts will therefore be judged not according to appearances, but according to what, in reason and propriety, they ought to have been. Thus, a man is presumed not to give away the whole of his property during his lifetime; hence where a dying person disposed of all his property and then recovered, his act will not be enforced by the courts, and he is regarded as having acted in the mistaken belief that he was going to die (BB 146b). The same applies to transactions made for an ulterior motive; where a woman had given away her property in order to deprive her future husband of his legal rights thereto, and on divorce reclaimed the property, the court is reported to have torn the deed of gift into pieces (Ket. 78b;

Maim. *Zekhiyyah u-Mattanah* 6:12). A husband giving his property to his wife is irrebuttably presumed to have made her only his trustee and not to have deprived himself and his children of all his property (BB 131b; for a list of these presumptions see *Piskei ha-Rosh* Ket. 11:9.).

Presumptions of Conditions *(umdana be-gillui da'at).* While these presumptions apply whether or not the mistake or motive was expressed or admitted, there are other cases in which these or similar presumptions apply only where such mistake or motive can be inferred from express statements made at the time of the transaction (*umdanot be-gillui da'at*). Thus, where a man disposed of his property, mentioning that he had decided to emigrate, and then he did not in fact emigrate, he will be presumed to have disposed of his property only conditional on his emigration (Kid. 49b). Or, where a man had made a will bequeathing his property to strangers, because he had heard that his sons had died, and then it appeared that they had not died, his will was set aside as having been made by mistake (BB 132a). Even where a vendor had stated, at the time of the sale, that he sold in order to have the money for a certain purpose, and that purpose could not afterward be effected, he was held entitled to have the sale set aside (Ket. 97a). It has been said that reservations giving rise to such presumptions must, however, always be reasonable: the man desiring to emigrate, for instance, could have the sale or gift of his landed properties set aside if the emigration did not transpire, but not the sale of his personal effects which he would be assumed to take with him on his emigration (Tos., Ket. 97a).

Judicial Notice *(anan sahadei).* All these presumptions and quasi-presumptions are being taken notice of by the court *ex officio* (*anan sahadei;* Resp. Rosh 34:1, 81:1), and in this respect they are similar to matters of custom and usage (cf. TJ, Pe'ah 7:6, 20b). Not unlike the concept of "judicial notice" in modern law, they replace formal evidence which would otherwise have to be adduced by the party on whom the burden of proof lies: in the language of the Mishnah, the disputant of a presumption of credibility in a given case would say, "we do not live from his mouth," but he has to adduce proof to verify his words (cf. Ket. 1:6–9). In some cases, especially those involving marital status, courts will take notice also of common repute or rumor (*kol;* Git. 89a; Ket. 36b; et al.; on presumptions see also *Hazakah*).

Modes of Proof. Where neither presumption nor custom avails the party on whom the burden of proof lies, he may discharge it by adducing evidence, either in the form of an oath, or in the form of a *shetar,* or in the form of the testimony of witnesses.

Evaluation of Evidence. Notwithstanding the formal and apparent sufficiency of the evidence adduced, however, the court is not bound by it, but has to weigh its reliability and satisfy itself of its truth before deciding the case in accordance therewith: it is a matter for the mind and heart of the individual judge, and no hard-and-fast rules can be laid down (Maim. Yad, Sanhedrin 24:1–2).

Fraud on the Court. Where the judge has gained the impression that the case before him, though duly proven, is a fraud *(din merummeh),* Maimonides holds that he ought to disqualify himself and leave the case to be decided by some other judge (*ibid.* 3); but the better opinion appears to be that he ought to dismiss the case there and then (Resp. Rosh 68:20; ḤM 15:3). Where it was the defendant who had deceived the court, judgment would be given in favor of the plaintiff, so as not to let "the sinner reap the fruits of his sin" (Resp. Rosh 107:6). The same rule would apply where a party sought to prevent the court from discovering the whole truth, whether by refusing to submit to cross-examination, or by suppressing evidence, or by any other means *(ibid.).*

Additional Evidence. Even though a case has been duly proved and decided, any party claiming that new evidence has been discovered, which might change the outcome of the proceedings, is entitled to have the case reopened (Sanh. 4:1). The only exceptions to this rule are, first, where the court has fixed a time limit for the adducing of additional evidence and that time has expired; and second, where the party has expressly declared in court that there is no additional evidence available to him (Sanh. 3:8) – in these cases it is apprehended that the additional evidence might have been fabricated (Rashi Sanh. 31a).

Call for Evidence *(hakhrazah, ḥerem).* As in criminal cases, so in certain civil cases the court may call for evidence by public announcements *(hakhrazah).* These cases mainly concern unknown owners of found chattels (BM 2:2–6). In later times, the courts would pronounce a *ḥerem* ("ban") upon anybody who could testify or produce evidence on a matter in issue and did not in fact do so (ḤM 16:3).

Formal Evidence *(gillui milta be-alma).* It is not only by vesting a wide discretion in the judge but also by legislatively relaxing the rules of evidence in proper cases that the law seeks to avoid any possible hardships which may arise from the objective difficulties of obtaining evidence. Such legislative relaxations are to be found particularly in respect of routine matters. Thus no formal evidence is required for the identification of litigants who identify themselves; even a relative or a minor can identify a brother-in-law for the purpose of *ḥaliẓah* (Yev. 39b; Yad, Yibum, 4:31; Sh. Ar., EH 169:8; see Levirate Marriage) or the evidence of one witness (who would nowadays be called a "formal" witness) is sufficient to establish matters of physical examination, such as the appearance of signs of puberty or the symptoms of a disease – matters which have to be proved, not because they can be seriously contested but in order "that judgment may be rendered without a stammer" (Rashi, Ket. 28a).

Legislative Relaxation of Rules of Evidence. In matters of marital status, there are many situations where the law contents itself with the evidence of a disqualified or a single witness, or hearsay, or other generally inadmissible modes of proof, because, in the language of Maimonides, these are generally matters which can be verified by other means and on which a man will not normally lie, as e.g., the death of another man; "and while the Torah insists on the testimony of two witnesses and all the other rules of evidence in cases which cannot be proved otherwise, as e.g., whether A killed B or A lent money to B, in these matters in which it is unlikely that any witness would lie, have the sages seen fit to relax the rules and to accept the evidence of bondswomen, and in writing, and without cross-examination, so that the daughters of Israel may not lose their remedy" (Yad, Gerushin 13, 29).

See also Agunah.

Bibliography: Z. Frankel, *Der gerichtliche Beweis nach mosaisch-talmudischem Rechte* (1846); J. Freudenthal, in: MGWJ, 9 (1860), 161–75; N. Hirsch, in: *Jeschurun,* 12 (Ger., 1865/66), 80–88, 109–22, 147–65, 249–58, 328–94; J. Klein, *Das Gesetz ueber das gerichtliche Beweisverfahren nach mosaisch-thalmudischem Rechte* (1885); Gulak, Yesodei, 4 (1922), passim; S. Assaf, *Battei Din ve-Sidreihem* (1924), 102ff.; S. Rosenbaum, in: *Ha-Mishpat,* 1 (1927), 280–90; S. Kaatz, in: *Jeschurun,* 15 (Ger., 1928), 89–98, 179–87; Z. Karl, in: *Ha-Mishpat ha-Ivri,* 3 (1928), 89–127; A. Gulak, *Le-Ḥeker Toledot ha-Mishpat ha-Ivri bi-Tekufat ha-Talmud,* 1 (*Dinei Karka'ot,* 1929), 66f.; D.M. Shohet, *The Jewish Court in the Middle Ages* (1931), 171–85 (contains bibliography); P. Dickstein, in: *Ha-*

Mishpat ha-Ivri, 4 (1932/33), 212–20; Herzog, Institutions, 1 (1936), 233, 255ff., 367ff.; 2 (1939), 185–8; ET, 1 (1951[3]), 137–41; 2 (1949), 70f.; 3 (1951); 106–10; 4 (1952), 199–208; 6 (1954), 85, 106, 705–14; 7 (1956), 290–5; 8 (1957), 404–44, 609–23, 722–43; 9 (1959), 64–103, 156–7, 448–9, 722–46; 12 (1967), 307–13; A. Karlin, in: *Ha-Peraklit,* 11 (1954/55), 49–57, 154–61, 247–54; 12 (1955/56), 185–91; J. Ginzberg, *Mishpatim le-Yisrael* (1956), passim; S. Fischer, in: *No'am,* 2 (1959), 211–22; E.E. Urbach, in: *Mazkeret . . . Herzog* (1962), 395–7, 402–8; Jaeger, in: *Recueils de la Société Jean Bodin,* 16 (1965); Ch. S. Hefez, in: *Mishpatim,* 1 (1969), 67ff.; Elon, Mafte'aḥ, 279–302; idem, *Ha-Mishpat Ha-Ivri* (1973), I, 166 n. 126, II, 255ff., 275ff., 298ff., 321ff., 346ff., 358ff. 383, 423ff., 428ff., 497ff., 568ff., 602ff., 622ff., 649, 735ff., 753, 810ff., III, 1001, 1062ff.; J.S.Zuri, *Mishpat ha-Talmud* (1921), 38–64.

Haim H. Cohn

WITNESS

Definition. Jewish law distinguishes between attesting and testifying witnesses. The former are required to be present at, and then and there attest, formal legal acts which failing such attestation, are normally invalid; the latter are required to testify in court, either to an act previously attested by them or to any fact they have witnessed. The rules on competency (see below) apply to testifying witnesses only. A document duly attested by at least two attesting witnesses and confirmed by the court (see Sh. Ar., ḤM 46:7–8) is admitted as evidence and equivalent to oral testimony in civil cases, and need not be proved by testifying witnesses (Sh. Ar., ḤM 28:12).

The distinction between testifying and attesting witnesses has practical significance also for purposes of modern Israel law. While the validity of an act governed by Jewish law (e.g., marriage or divorce) may depend on the competency under Jewish law of the attesting witnesses, which will have to be determined according to Jewish law, the competency of testifying witnesses, even concerning acts governed by Jewish law, will always be determined by the law of the court *(lex fori)* in which the evidence is taken.

The Two-Witnesses Rule. As a general rule, no single witness alone is competent to attest or testify: there must always be at least two (Deut. 19:15; Sif. Deut. 188; Sot. 2b; Sanh. 30a; Yad, Edut 5:1). The following are some of several exceptions to the general rule: whenever two testifying witnesses would be sufficient to prove a claim, one is sufficient to require the defendant to take an oath that the claim is unfounded (Shev. 40a; Ket. 87b; BM 3b–4a; Yad, To'en 1:1); thus, in the case of widow claiming on her *ketubbah* or the holder of a bill claiming on it, where a single witness has testified that the claim had already been settled, the interested party will be required to take the oath before being allowed to recover (Ket. 9:7; Sh. Ar., ḤM 84:5). Conversely, a party who has partly admitted a claim will be excused from taking the oath if he is corroborated by at least a single witness (Rema ḤM 87:6; *Beit Yosef* ḤM 75 n. 3); and the testimony of a single depositary who still held the deposit was considered sufficient to prove which of the rival claims to a deposit was valid (Git. 64a; Sh. Ar., ḤM 56:1). A woman is allowed to remarry on the testimony of a single witness that her husband is dead (Yev. 16:7; Eduy. 6:1, 8:5; Ber. 27a; Ket. 22b–23a); and the testimony of a single witness is normally sufficient in matters of ritual (Git. 2b–3a; Yad, Edut 11:7). In criminal cases, both witnesses must have witnessed the whole event together (cf. Mak. 1:9), but in civil cases, testimonies of various witnesses to particular facts, as well as a witness and a document, may be combined to satisfy the two-witnesses rule (Sh. Ar., ḤM 30:6).

Competency. Maimonides lists ten classes of persons who are not competent to attest or testify, namely: women, slaves, minors, lunatics, the deaf, the blind, the wicked, the contemptible, relatives, and the interested parties (Yad, Edut 9:1).

(1) *Women.* By the method of *gezerah shavah* (see Interpretation), it is derived from Scripture that only men can be competent witnesses. Maimonides gives as the reason for the disqualification of women the fact that the Bible uses the masculine form when speaking of witnesses (Sif. Deut. 190; Shev. 30a; Sh. Ar., ḤM 35:14; Yad, Edut 9:2), but Joseph Caro questioned the validity of this derivation in view of the fact that "the whole Torah always uses the masculine form" (*Kesef Mishneh* to Yad, Edut 9:2). Another reason was suggested in the Talmud: that the place of a woman was in her home and not in court (Shev. 30a; cf. Git. 46a), as the honor of the king's daughter was within the house (Ps. 45:14. It is perhaps noteworthy that the Tur (ḤM 35) omits women from the list of incompetent witnesses). Women are admitted as competent witnesses in matters within their particular knowledge, for example, on customs or events in places frequented only by women (Rema ḤM 35:14; *Darkhei Moshe* ḤM 35, n. 3; *Beit Yosef, ibid.*, n. 15; *Terumat ha-Deshen* Resp. no. 353); in matters of their own and other women's purity (Ket. 72a; Ket 2:6); for purposes of identification, especially of other women (Yev. 39b); or in matters outside the realm of strict law (BK 114b). In post-talmudic times, the evidence of women was often admitted where there were no other witnesses available (cf. e.g., Resp. Maharam of Rothenburg, ed. Prague, no. 920; Resp. Maharik no. 179). In Israel, the disqualification of women as witnesses was abolished by the Equality of Women's Rights Act, 5711–1951.

(2) *Slaves.* Witnesses must be free Jewish citizens (*Benei Ḥorin u-Venei Berit;* BK 1:3), excluding both slaves and non-Jews (BK 15a; Yad, Edut 9:4; Sh. Ar., ḤM 34:19). The evidence of non-Jews is admitted if secular law so requires (*Maggid Mishneh,* Malveh 27:1), as well as to attest or identify documents made in non-Jewish courts, or whenever the court sees no reason to doubt their objectivity (*Tashbeẓ* 1:78; *Beit Yosef* ḤM 34:32; *Baḥ* ḤM 34:32; *Keẓot ha-Ḥoshen* 68, n. 1; Tos. to Git. 9b).

(3) *Minors.* A person is incompetent as a witness until he reaches the age of 13. Between the ages of 13 and 20, he is competent as a witness with regard to movable property, but in respect of immovable property he is competent only if he is found to have the necessary understanding and experience (BB 155b; Yad, Edut. 9:8; Sh. Ar., ḤM 35:3). From the age of 20, all disqualification by reason of age is removed.

(4) *Lunatics.* In this category are included not only insane persons (for definitions see Penal Law), but also idiots and epileptics (Yad, Edut 9:9–10; Sh. Ar., ḤM 35:8–10).

(5) *The Deaf.* Both the deaf and the dumb are included in this category. "Despite the fact that their vision may be excellent and their intelligence perfect, they must testify by word of their mouth, or must hear the warning which the court administers to them" (see Practice and Procedure), and as they cannot speak or hear, they cannot testify (Yad, Edut 9:11; Sh. Ar., ḤM 35:11).

(6) *The Blind.* "Despite the fact that they may be able to recognize voices and thus identify people, they are by Scripture disqualified as witnesses, for it is written, (whether he hath seen or known) [Lev. 5:1]– only one who can see can testify" (Yad, Edut 9:12; Sh. Ar., ḤM 35:12).

(7) *The Wicked.* According to the Bible, "the wicked" or "the guilty" are unjust witnesses (Ex. 23:1), therefore they are *a*

priori disqualified. They may be divided into five groups: criminals, swindlers, perjurers, illiterates, and informers. "Wicked" or "guilty" are epithets attributed to persons who have committed capital offenses (Num. 35:31) or who are liable to be flogged (Deut. 25:2), hence these are incompetent witnesses (Yad, Edut 10:2; Sh. Ar., ḤM 34:2). A person who has committed any other offense or who is liable to any other punishment is also deemed incompetent as a witness, although not in the Bible (Rema ḤM 34:2). Into the category of swindlers fall thieves and robbers (Sh. Ar., ḤM 34:7); usurers (*ibid.*, 34:10); tricksters, gamblers, and gamesters (Sanh. 3:3; Sh. Ar., ḤM 34:16), as well as idlers and vagabonds who are suspected of spending their leisure in criminal activities (Yad, Edut 10:4; Sh. Ar., ḤM 34:16). Tax collectors who do not work for a fixed salary, but receive as remuneration a portion of the moneys collected, are suspected of appropriating more than is due to them, and therefore are incompetent witnesses (Yad, loc. cit.; Sh. Ar., ḤM 34:14); another reason for their disqualification was said to be that they were suspected of undue preferences and discriminations in assessing tax liabilities (Rema ḤM 34:14). Once a witness was found guilty of perjury, he would no longer be a competent witness, even after he had made good any damage caused by his false testimony (Sanh. 27a; Yad, loc. cit.; Sh. Ar., ḤM 34:8). A man who has no inkling of Bible and Mishnah, nor of civilized standards of conduct *(derekh ereẓ)*, is presumed to be idle and disorderly (Kid. 1:10) and therefore incompetent as a witness (Kid. 40b; Yad, Edut 11:1; Sh. Ar., ḤM 34:17). This presumption is rebuttable by evidence that, notwithstanding the man's illiteracy, his conduct is irreproachable (Yad, Edut 11:2–4; Sh. Ar., loc. cit.). *A fortiori,* agnostics *(eppikoresim)* and heretics, including those who transgress law or ritual from conviction or malice, are wholly and irrevocably disqualified (Yad, Edut 11:10; Sh. Ar., ḤM 34:22). Though not technically transgressors of the law, informers are considered worse than criminals and hence incompetent (Yad, loc. cit.; Sh. Ar., loc. cit.).

(8) *The Contemptible.* It is presumed that people who do not conform to the conventions of society, for example, by eating in the streets (Kid. 40b), or walking around naked while working (BK 86b), or accepting alms from non-Jews in public (Sanh. 26b), would not shrink from perjuring themselves, and therefore are incompetent witnesses (Yad, Edut 11:5; Sh. Ar., ḤM 34:18).

(9) *Relatives.* The biblical injunction that parents shall not be put to death "for" their children, nor children "for" their parents (Deut. 24:16), was interpreted as prohibiting the testimony of parents against children and of children against parents (Sif. Deut. 280; Sanh. 27b), and served as the source for the disqualification of relatives in general (Yad, Edut 13:1). The Mishnah lists as disqualified relatives: father, brother, uncle, brother-in-law, stepfather, father-in-law, and their sons and sons-in-law (Sanh. 3:4); the rule was extended to cover nephews and first cousins (Yad, Edut 13:3; Sh. Ar., ḤM 33:2). Where the relationship is to a woman, the disqualification extends to her husband (Yad, Edut 13:6; Sh. Ar., ḤM 33:3). The fact that a disqualified kinsman does not maintain any connection with the party concerned is irrelevant (Yad, Edut 13:15; Sh. Ar., ḤM 33:10). Witnesses who are related to one another are incompetent to attest or testify together (Mak. 6a); similarly witnesses related to any of the judges are incompetent (Sh. Ar., ḤM 33:17). As relatives are incompetent to testify for or against the party to whom they are related, *a fortiori* the party himself is incompetent to testify for or against himself, for "a man is related to himself" (Sanh. 9b–10a; Yev. 25b). But while the incompetency of the relatives results only in their testimony being inadmissible as evidence, there can be no "testimony" of a party at all (*Piskei ha-Rosh* Mak. 1:13–14; Resp. Rosh, no. 60:1; Nov. Ramban Mak. 6b; Nov. Ran Sanh. 9b; Resp. Ribash 195), and everything he says in court is properly classified as pleading.

(10) *The Interested Party.* A witness is disqualified where any benefit may accrue to him from his testimony (BB 43a; Yad, Edut 15:1), as where he has some stake in the outcome of the proceedings (Sh. Ar., ḤM 37:1; Yad, Edut 15:4). However, the benefit must be present and immediate and not speculative only (Sh. Ar., ḤM 37:10). The question whether some such direct or indirect benefit may accrue to a witness is often puzzling: "these things depend on the discretion of the judge and the depth of his understanding as to what is the gist of the case at issue" (Yad, Edut 16:4; Sh. Ar., ḤM 37:21). It is a "well-established custom" that where local usages or regulations are in issue townspeople are competent witnesses, even though they may, as local residents, have some interest in the matter (Resp. Rosh, 5:4; Sh. Ar., ḤM 37:22). The same "custom" would appear to apply to attesting witnesses who were appointed as such by authority (cf. Sh. Ar., ḤM 33:18). In criminal cases, there is no disqualifying "interest"; thus, the kinsmen of the murdered man are competent witnesses against the murderer, those of the assaulted against the assailant, and the victim of an offense against the accused (Rema ḤM 33:16; *Siftei Kohen* ḤM 33 n. 16).

Disqualification. No witness may say that he is (or was) wicked so as to disqualify himself from attesting or testifying (Sanh. 9b; Yad, Edut 12:2; Sh. Ar., ḤM 34:25). A party who wishes to disqualify witnesses of the other party has to prove their incompetency by the evidence of at least two other competent witnesses (Sanh. 3:1; Yad, Edut 12:1; Sh. Ar., ḤM 34:25). Disqualification as a witness is not regarded as a penalty, and hence no previous warning is required; but in cases of improper or contemptible conduct and minor transgressions, it has been suggested that a person should not be disqualified as a witness unless previously warned that this would happen if he persisted in his conduct (Yad, loc. cit.; Sh. Ar., ḤM 34:24).

Where a witness attested an act or a document, he cannot testify that he was incompetent to do so (Ket. 18b & 19b; Yad, Edut 3:7; Sh. Ar., ḤM 46:37). It might be otherwise if his signature could be identified only by his own testimony: if he could be heard to deny his signature, he ought also to be heard to say that his signature was worthless (Ket. 2:3; Sh. Ar., ḤM loc. cit.) – always provided he did not incriminate himself.

Where the court has reason to suspect that a person offered as a witness is incompetent, it may decline to admit his testimony (Rema ḤM 34:25; Yad, To'en 2:3), and ought to turn him down as an attesting witness (Sh. Ar., ḤM 92:5 and *Siftei Kohen* ad loc.). Where a witness has given evidence, and it subsequently transpires that he was incompetent, his evidence will be regarded as wrongly admitted and the case be reopened only if the incompetence was derived from Scripture or had been announced by public proclamation (Sanh. 26b; Yad, Edut 11:6; Sh. Ar., ḤM 34:23). A person called to attest or testify together with another person whom he knows to be incompetent as a witness must decline to attest or testify, even though the incompetence of the other is not yet known or proved to the court (Yad, Edut 10:1; Sh. Ar., ḤM 34:1). The rationale of this rule appears to be that since the incompetence of any one witness invalidates the evidence of the whole group of witnesses to which he belongs (Mak. 1:8; Yad, Edut 5:3; Sh. Ar., ḤM 36:1), if the first man attested or testified notwithstanding the other's incompetence, the evidence would be nullified (cf. *Siftei Kohen* ḤM 34, n. 3). In civil cases, parties may stipulate that, notwithstanding any incompetence, the evidence of witnesses named shall be accepted and acted upon by the court (Sanh. 3:2; Yad, Sanhedrin 7:2; Sh. Ar., ḤM 22:1).

Disqualification no longer holds: in the case of criminals, after their punishment is completed (Yad, Edut 12:4; Sh. Ar., ḤM 34:29); in the case of wicked persons not liable to punishment, when it is proved to the satisfaction of the court that they have repented and that their conduct is now irreproachable *(ibid.)* – there are detailed provisions as to what acts constitute sufficient proof of repentance (Yad, Edut 12:5–10; Sh. Ar., ḤM 34:29–35); and in the case of relatives, after the relationship or affinity has come to an end (Yad, Edut 14:1; Sh. Ar., ḤM 33:12).

Remuneration. As a financial interest in the testimony disqualifies the witness, the stipulation or acceptance of remuneration for testifying invalidates the evidence (Bek. 4:6). However, where the witness has returned the fee he received before testifying, his evidence is admissible; the acceptance of remuneration in itself is not a cause of incompetence, but is visited with the sanction of invalidating the evidence as a deterrent only (Rema ḤM 34:18). The rule prohibiting remuneration is confined to testifying witnesses only; attesting witnesses may always be remunerated *(ibid.)* and there are express provisions for the remuneration of witnesses attesting divorces (Sh. Ar., EH 130:21). A man suspected of accepting money for giving evidence is not a credible witness and should never be believed (Tosef. Bek. 3:8). A man who hires false witnesses to testify for him is answerable to Heaven, though not himself criminally responsible (see Penal Law; Yad, Edut 17:7; Sh. Ar., ḤM 32:2; Rema ad loc.).

Duty to Testify. Any person able to testify as one who has seen or learned of the matter who does not come forward to testify is liable to punishment (Lev. 5:1), but the punishment will be meted out to him by God only (see Divine Punishment; BK 55b–56a). While in criminal cases the witness is under obligation to come forward and testify of his own accord, in civil cases the duty to testify arises only when the man is summoned to do so (Yad, Edut 1:1; Sh. Ar., ḤM 28:1). Kings are exempt from the duty to testify (Sanh. 2:2; Yad, Edut 11:9) and though high priests are generally exempt, they must testify for the king (Yad, Edut 1:3). The duty relates only to matters which the witness has seen himself, or which he has heard from the mouth of the accused or a party to the action; a man may not testify to things of which he has no personal knowledge (Rema ḤM 28:1), nor may he testify on what he has heard other people telling him, however true and trustworthy it may appear to him (Yad, Edut 17:1, 5), and any such testimony is regarded as false *(ibid.)*.

Persons who were planted and hidden on the premises to overlook a certain act or overhear certain words are not admitted as witnesses (Yad, Edut 17:3), except in the case of prosecution against inciters to idolatry (Sanh. 7:10; Sanh. 29a, 67a). A witness whose memory is defective may be allowed to refresh it by looking at what he had written at the time, or even by listening to the evidence of other witnesses (Ket. 20b; Yad, Edut 8:2; Sh. Ar., ḤM 28:14; *Beit Yosef* ḤM 28, n. 13–14), but not by what the party tells him, unless that party is a scholar and not suspected of using undue influence (Yad, Edut 8:3). Yet the fact that the witness recognizes some contemporary handwriting as his own does not render the writing admissible in evidence if he does not remember the facts to which that writing relates (Sh. Ar., ḤM 28:13; cf. Yad, Edut 8:1). There is no presumption that the passage of time adversely affects any witness's memory (Sh. Ar., *ibid.*).

Examination. The biblical injunction, "thou shalt then inquire and make search and ask diligently" (Deut. 13:15), was literally interpreted to require testifying witnesses to be subjected to three different kinds of examination: enquiry *(ḥakirah)*, investigation *(derishah)*, and interrogation (*bedikah;* Sanh. 40a). Originally, the rule was held to apply in all cases, both civil and criminal (Sanh. 4:1), but it was later relaxed to apply in criminal cases only, and possibly in cases of tort, so as not to render the recovery of debts too cumbersome and thus "shut the doors before borrowers" (Sanh. 3a, 32a; Yev. 122b; Yad, Edut 3:1; Sh. Ar., ḤM 30:1). It is the duty of the court, Maimonides says: "to interrogate the witnesses and examine them and question them extensively and probe into their accuracy and refer them back to previous questions so as to make them desist from or change their testimony if it was in any way faulty; but the court must be very careful lest, by such examination, 'the witness might learn to lie' " (Yad, Edut 1:4 based on Sanh. 32b). The purpose of the examination is, of course, to find out if the witnesses are truthful and consistent; even though all potentially untruthful witnesses have already been sifted and excluded by disqualification, further precautionary rules were deemed necessary to make sure of the witness's veracity.

Ḥakirah is the examination relating to the time and place at which the event at issue occurred (Sanh. 5:1; Sanh. 40b). Every examination starts with questions of this kind, which are indispensable (Nov. Ran. Sanh. 40a). The particular legal importance of this part of the examination is due to its function as sole cause for allegations of perjury (Yad, Edut 1:5).

Derishah is the examination relating to the substance of the facts at issue: who did it? what did he do? how did he do it? did you warn him beforehand? etc. (Sanh. 5:1, 40b). Or, in civil cases, how do you know the defendant is liable to the plaintiff? (Sanh. 3:6). As this line of examination is likewise indispensable, it is regarded in law as part of the *ḥakirah* (Yad, Edut 1:4).

Bedikah is a sort of cross-examination relating to accompanying and surrounding circumstances and not directly touching upon the facts in issue (Yad, Edut 1:6). The more a judge conducts examinations of this kind the better (Sanh. 5:2), because it leads to the true facts being established (Deut. 13:15; Sif. Deut. 93, 149; Sanh. 41a). On the other hand, questioning of this kind is dispensable, and judgment may be given on the testimony of witnesses who have not been so cross-examined (Nov. Ran Sanh. 40a). The conduct and amount of cross-examinations is at the discretion of the judges; they ought to insist on it whenever there is the least suspicion of an attempt to mislead or deceive the court (*din merummeh;* Shev. 30b–31a; Yad, Sanhedrin 24:3 and Edut 3:2; Sh. Ar., ḤM 15:3). Such suspicion may arise, for instance, where several witnesses testify in exactly the same words – which would not normally happen unless they had learned their testimony by heart (TJ, Sanh. 3:8, 21c; *Piskei ha-Rosh,* Sanh. 3:32; Sh. Ar., ḤM 28:10). In these cases, cross-examination should concentrate on points on which suspicion arose and not be allowed to spread boundlessly (Nov. Ran, Sanh. 32b; Ribash, Resp. no. 266; Rema ḤM 15:3). Notwithstanding all cross-examination, the witnesses stick consistently to their story but the judge is not satisfied that they are telling the truth, he should disqualify himself and let another judge take his place (Shevu. 30b–31a; Sanh. 32b; Yad, Sanhedrin 24:3; Sh. Ar., ḤM 15:3), or he might even, if satisfied that there had been an attempt to mislead the court, furnish the innocent party with a certificate in writing to the effect that no other judge should entertain the suit against him (Resp. Rosh, No. 68:20).

Disproof. Where two sets of witnesses contradict each other on a matter material to the issue, i.e., under either *ḥakirah* or *derishah* as distinguished from *bedikah* (Yad, Edut 2:1), the evidence of either set is insufficient in law to establish the facts at issue. The reason is that there is no knowing which of the two groups of witnesses is testifying to the truth and which is lying (Yad, Edut 18:2, 22:1; Sh. Ar., ḤM 31:1). Where, however, there are inconsistencies or contradictions within the evidence of one set of witnesses and none within the other, the evidence of the consistent group will have to be accepted – the other being dismissed as untruthful because inconsistent. After a fact has been established judicially on the strength of the testimony of two (or more) consistent witnesses, the findings of fact will not necessarily be affected by contradictory witnesses coming forward after judgment (TJ, Yev. 15:5, 15a), but the court may always reopen a case where fresh evidence becomes available (see Practice and Procedure).

Contradictions on matters not material to the issue will not normally affect the admissibility of the testimony (Sanh. 41a; Nov. Ran ad loc.), though the court may reject the testimony as unreliable because of contradictions on immaterial points (Yad, Edut 2:2). It seems that in civil cases, contradictions must always relate to matters material to the issue in order to warrant their rejection as insufficient (Sanh. 30b; Yad, Edut 3:2; Sh. Ar., ḤM 30:2). Where one witness positively testifies to a fact material to the issue, and the other testifies that the fact is unknown to him, the testimony of the former is deemed to be contradicted; where the fact testified to is not material to the issue, the ignorance of the second witness does not amount to contradiction (Yad, Edut 2:1). As there is no knowing whether the contradicting or contradicted evidence is true, neither will be regarded as perjury. While evidence of perjury must be given in the presence of the perjured witnesses, evidence contradicting previously given testimony may be given in the absence of the former witnesses (Ket. 19b–20a; Yad, Edut 18:5).

Where the evidence of witnesses to the effect that a man is "wicked" and hence incompetent to testify is contradicted by other evidence, even though the first evidence is insufficient in law to disqualify him, the man will not be admitted as a witness because of the doubts arising on his credibility (Yad, Edut 12:3); but there is a strong dissent holding that every man is to be presumed competent until proven otherwise by valid and conclusive evidence (Tos. to Ket. 26b s.v. *Anan; Shitah Mekubbeẓet* Ket. 26b).

See also *Agunah; Takkanot; Takkanot ha-Kahal;* Evidence; Perjury.

Bibliography: Z. Frankel, *Der gerichtliche Beweis nach mosaisch-talmudischem Rechte* (1846); N. Hirsch, in: *Jeschurun,* 12 (1865/66), 80–88, 109–22, 147–65, 249–58; 382–94 (Germ.); I. Tonelis Handl, *Die Zulaessigkeit zur Zeugenaussage und zur Eidesablegung nach mosaisch-rabbinischem Rechte* (1866; Hebr. and Germ.); L. Loew, in: *Ben Chananja,* 9 (1866), Suppl.; repr. in his: *Gesammelte Schriften,* 3 (1893), 335–45; M. Bloch, *Die Civilprocess-Ordnung nach mosaisch-rabbinischem Rechte* (1882), 43–53; I.S. Zuri, *Mishpat ha-Talmud,* 7 (1921), 43–53; Gulak, Yesodei, 2 (1922), 28, 30, 134ff.; 4 (1922), 150–63; idem, Oẓar, 305–11; S. Kaatz, in: *Jeschurun,* 15 (1928), 89–98, 179–87 (Germ.); Z. Karl, in: *Ha-Mishpat ha-Ivri,* 3 (1928), 89–127; A. Gulak, in: *Tarbiz,* 12 (1940/41), 181–9; Z. Karl, in: *Ha-Peraklit,* 5 (1948), 81–85; ET, 1 (1951[3]), 88–90, 117–9, 225f.; 2 (1949), 14f., 60, 65, 137, 247, 252f., 300f.; 3 (1951), 160f., 378f.; 5 (1953), 46–51, 337–43, 381–5, 517–22, 528f.; 6 (1954), 199f.; 7 (1956), 290–5, 383–5, 638–64; 8 (1957), 352f., 429–31; 9 (1959), 64–103, 729–46; 11 (1965), 242; A. Weiss, *Seder ha-Diyyun* (1957), 86–124, 206–54; J. Cohen, in: *Ha-Torah ve-ha-Medinah,* 11–13 (1959/62), 517–40; S. Atlas, in: *Sefer Yovel . . . Abraham Weiss* (1964), 73–90; H. Jaeger, in: *Recueils de la Société Jean Bodin,* 16 (1965), 415–594; G. Holzer, in: *Sinai,* 67 (1970), 94–112; Elon, Mafte'aḥ, 206–18; idem, *Ha-Mishpat Ha-Ivri* (1973), I, 85ff., 107ff., 115 n. 158, II, 243 ff., 275 n. 136, 298ff., 307ff., 428ff., 497ff., 501ff., 568, 596ff., 600ff., 816ff., 828.

Haim H. Cohn

ADMISSION, legal concept applying both to debts and facts. Formal admission by a defendant is regarded as equal to "the evidence of a hundred witnesses" (*hodaat baal din kemeya edim dami;* BM 3b). This admission had to be a formal one, before duly appointed witnesses, or before the court, or in writing. When the denial of having received a loan is proved to be false, this is regarded as tantamount to an admission that it has not been repaid. Admissions were originally regarded as irrevocable, but in order to alleviate hardships caused by hasty admissions, the Talmud evolved two causes for their revocation; a plea that the person making the admission had not been serious, or that he had had a special reason for making the admission. When partial admission has been made, the admission is accepted and he is bound to take an oath with regard to the remainder. Admissions can also apply to procedural matters; e.g., on the part of a party to an action that he has no witnesses, in which case he cannot subsequently call one.

The formal admission of a debt, or of facts from which any liability may be inferred, is in civil cases the best evidence of such liability (Git. 40b, 64a; Kid. 65b). The requirements of formality may be met: (1) by making the admission before two competent witnesses, expressly requested to hear and witness the admission (Sanh. 29a); (2) by way of pleading before the court, whether as plaintiff or defendant (Sh. Ar., ḤM 81:22); (3) in writing (*ibid.,* 17); (4) through any of the recognized modes of *kinyan* ("acquisition" *ibid.*); (5) on oath or the "symbolic shaking of hands by the two parties . . . which is the equivalent of an oath" (*ibid.,* 28; Herzog, Instit, 2 (1939), 103).

While generally the admission must be explicit, in an action for the recovery of a loan, the denial of the loan would amount to an admission of nonpayment which is implicit in the denial (BB 6a; Shevu; 38b); on proof of the loan, the defendant will then be bound by his admission that he has not repaid it. Conversely, where a plaintiff claims that the defendant owes him a certain species of goods without reserving his right to claim also some other species, he is deemed to have admitted that the defendant owes him only the species claimed and no other, and any admission by the defendant that he does owe another species than that claimed, will not avail the plaintiff (BK 35b). The general rule in a conflict between two contradictory admissions is that the explicit prevails over the implicit and the negative (e.g., "I have not acquired property") over the positive (e.g., "I have transferred my property"; Tosef., BB 10:1; Git. 40b).

As formal admissions were irrevocable, they were widely used as a means of creating new liabilities, as distinguished from the mere acknowledgment of already existing ones. Even though recognized as factually false admissions, they were held to bind the person making them (BB 149a), whether by way of gratuitously incurring a new and enforceable obligation (Ket. 101b–102b; Maim. Yad, Mekhirah, 11:15), or by way of transfer *(kinyan).* The property concerned thus passes from the owner to the person now admitted by him to have acquired it from him, the concurrence of the beneficiary not being required as he was only benefiting by the admission (Git. 40b; Maim. Yad, Zekhiyyah, 4:12). Admissions of this nonprocedural variety are also termed *udita* or *odaita.*

With a view to alleviating hardships caused by precipitate admissions, talmudic jurists evolved two pleas for having them revoked: the plea of feigning *(hashta'ah)* and the plea of satiation *(hasba'ah).* Where a man, not of his own accord but in reply to a question or demand, made an admission, and on being sued maintained that he had not been serious about it and that the admission was not true, an oath would be administered to him to the effect that he had not intended to admit the debt and that he did not in fact owe it (Sanh. 29a). Similarly, a statement of a person that he had admitted debts owed by him, only for the purpose of ostensibly reducing his assets so as not to appear rich was accepted (Sanh. 29b). Neither plea is valid against admissions made in court, or in writing, or by *kinyan,* or on oath (Sh. Ar., ḤM 81). As to admissions made in writing, some scholars hold that so long as the deed has not been delivered to the creditor, the admittor may plead that he was not serious or that he wrote it in order to appear poor (Sh. Ar., ḤM 65:22 and Isserles to Sh. Ar., ḤM 81:17). A dying man is presumed not to be frivolous on his deathbed, and his admissions are irrevocable (Sanh. 29b), so are admissions made by his debtors in his favor and presence while he is dying (Isserles *ibid.,* 81:2). The public (the community) must be presumed neither to make rash admissions nor to be interested in appearing without means, hence none of the pleas is available against admissions made by or on behalf of the public (Isserles *ibid.,* 81:1). Where only part of a claim is admitted, the admittor will be adjudged to the extent of his admission and be required to take the oath that he does not owe the remainder (Shevu. 7:1). This rule is based on the presumption that no debtor has the temerity to deny his debt falsely in the face of his creditor (Shevu. 42b; BM 3a), a presumption which, curiously enough, does not necessarily apply to a debtor denying the whole (as distinguished from a part) of the debt. Where the whole is denied, the oath is administered to the defendant upon the presumption that a plaintiff will not normally abuse the process of the court (Shevu. 40b). Where the defendant satisfies the admitted portion of the claim without adjudication, the claim is deemed to be for the nonadmitted portion only and to be denied in whole (BM 4a, 4b). While a part admission must fit the subject matter of the claim (Shevu. 38b), it need not necessarily fit the cause of action; thus, the admission of a deposit might fit the claim on a loan (Sh. Ar., ḤM 88:19). The claim of the whole must precede the admission of the part, the admittor who is not yet a defendant being regarded as a volunteer returning a lost object (Sh. Ar., ḤM 75:3). An admission is not allowed to prejudice the admittor's creditors: the holder of a bill may not be heard to admit that he has no claim on it, or the possessor of chattel that they belong to somebody else, so as to deprive his creditors of an attachable asset (Kid. 65b; Ket. 19a). Admissions need not relate to substantive liabilities, but may be procedural in nature: thus a party may admit that he has no witnesses to prove a particular fact, and he will not then be allowed to call a witness to prove it, lest the witness be suborned (Sanh. 31a); or, having once admitted a particular witness to be untrustworthy, he will not later be able to rely on his testimony (Ket. 44a). Admissions could be accepted for one purpose and rejected for another, e.g., the admission of a wrongful act would be inadmissible as a confession in criminal or quasi-criminal proceedings, but could afford the basis for awarding damages in a civil suit. This rule is found to have been applied to larceny (BM 37a), to the seduction of women (Ket. 41a; see Rape), to arson (Resp. Rashba 2:231), to usury *(ibid.),* to embezzlement (see Theft and Robbery), and to breach of trust (Isserles to Sh. Ar., ḤM 388:8; Nov. Ritba Ket. 72a); a wife admitting her adultery was held to lose, on the strength of her admission, any claim to maintenance or other monetary benefits, but not her status as a married woman, thus incurring no liability to be divorced or punished (Maim. Yad, Ishut, 24:18). An early authority posed the question whether the injunction, "you shall have one standard of law" (Lev. 24:22), should not be read to prohibit any distinction between civil and criminal law with regard to admissions and answers in the negative, (Tosef. Shevu. 3:8). Concerning the concept *hoda'ah* as a declaration of tax liability, see Taxation.[1]

Bibliography: Z. Frankel, *Der gerichtliche Beweis nach mosaisch-talmudischem Rechte* (1846), 127–30, 336–58; M. Bloch, *Die Civilprocess-Ordnung nach mosaisch-rabbinischem Rechte* (1882), 41–43; Gulak, Yesodei, 2 (1922), 44–47; 4 (1922), 78–84; Gulak, Oẓar, 211–3; Karl, in: *Ha-Mishpat ha-Ivri,* 3 (1927/28), 95–98; Herzog, Instit, 1 (1936), 196–200, 268; 2 (1939), 42, 44, 94–97; ET, 1 (1951³), 116–7, 253–4, 267–8; 8 (1957), 404–31; M. Elon, *Ha-Mishpat Ha-Ivri* (1973), II, 498ff., 505ff., 535 n. 29, 811ff.

Haim H. Cohn

CONFESSION. Along with admissions of fact from which any criminal responsibility may be inferred, confessions are not admissible as evidence in criminal or quasi-criminal proceedings, for "no man may call himself a wrongdoer" (Sanh. 9b). This rule against self-incrimination developed from the rule that a wrongdoer is incompetent as a witness, being presumed to be unjust and untruthful (cf. Ex. 23:1). Since some people might admit to misconduct in order to disqualify themselves from testifying, to cure this mischief the rule was laid down that no man can be heard to say of himself that he is so guilty as to be an incompetent witness (Sanh. 25a; BK 72b). The rule was originally derived from the principle that no man is competent to testify in his own favor (Ket. 27a) – his confession being intended to confer the benefit of not being required to testify.

The rule against self-incrimination dates only from talmudic times. Several instances of confessions are recorded in the Bible (e.g., Josh. 7:19–20; II Sam. 1:16; cf. I Sam. 14:43), but these are dismissed by talmudic scholars either as confessions after trial and conviction, made for the sole purpose of expiating the sin before God (Sanh. 43b), or as exceptions to the general rule (*hora'at Sha'ah;* cf. Maim. comm. to the Mishnah, Sanh. 6:2; Ralbag to II Sam. 1:14). As all instances recorded in the Bible related to proceedings before kings or rulers, it may be that they did not consider themselves bound to observe regular court procedures (cf. Maim. Yad, Melakhim 3:10). Confessions are inadmissible not only in capital cases, but also in cases involving only flogging, fines (Rashi to Yev. 25b), or quasi-punishments (*ibid.;* cf. Resp. Rosh 11:5). Opinions are divided on whether a *ḥerem* and public admonitions could be administered on the strength of a confession only.

Varying reasons were given for the rule against self-incrimination: the earliest and commonest is that the biblical requirement of the evidence of at least two witnesses for the condemnation of any man (Deut. 17:6, 19:15) implicitly excludes any other mode of proof (Tosef., Sanh. 11:1, 5). Maimonides adds that melancholy and depressed persons must be prevented from confessing to crimes which they have not committed so as to be put to death (Yad, Sanhedrin 18:6). Another theory was based on the prophet's words that all souls are God's (Ezek. 18:4), hence no man may be allowed to forfeit his life (as distinguished from his property) by his own admission, his life not being his own to dispose of but God's (David b. Solomon ibn Abi Zimra); still another scholar held that if confessions were accorded any probative value at all, courts might be inclined to overrate them, as King David did (II Sam. 1:16), and be guilty of a dereliction of their own fact-finding task (Joseph ibn Migash). A 19th-century jurist (Mordechai Epstein) pointed out that the real difference between civil admissions and criminal confessions was

1. page 685.

that by an admission an obligation was created which had only to be enforced by the court, whereas in a criminal conviction it is the court which creates the accused's liability to punishment. While it is nowhere expressed, the reason for the exclusion of confessions may well have been the desire to prevent their being elicited by torture or other violent means: it is a fact that – unlike most contemporaneous law books – neither Bible nor Talmud provide for any interrogation of the accused as part of the criminal trial, so that there was no room for attempts to extort confessions.

See also Practice and Procedure, Criminal.

Bibliography: ET, 1 (1951), 88–90, 225–7, 266; 7 (1956), 372; 8 (1957), 432–5; H. Cohn, in: *Journal of Criminal Law, Criminology and Police Science,* 51 (1960–61), 175–8; H.E. Baker, *Legal System of Israel* (1968), 226; M. Elon in ILR 4 (1969), 473; idem, *Ha-Mishpat Ha-Ivri* (1973), II, 568 ff.

Haim H. Cohn

OATH.

BIBLICAL LAW.

Classes of Oaths.

God makes His own solemn promises either in the form of a covenant (Gen. 9:11, 15; 15:18; Ex. 6:4; et al.) or in the form of an oath (e.g., Gen. 22:16–17; Ex. 32:13; Deut. 1:34–35; 4:21; Is. 62:8; Jer. 22:5 and 44:26; Amos 4:2 and 6:8; Ps. 110:4). The oath is thus God's own expression of ultimate truth, and is in common usage whenever a statement is intended to convey a truthful purpose, or relate true facts, in solemn form.

The following classes of oaths may be distinguished, viz.:

(1) Oaths of Covenant: To reinforce covenants and pacts, either mutual (e.g., Gen. 21:23–32; 26:28–31; I Sam. 20:3, 16–17, 42; Ezra 10:3–5) or unilateral (Gen. 31:53, 25:33; et al.) oaths were taken. Once an oath was taken to confirm a pact, it would not be broken even though induced by fraud (Jos. 9:15–20).

(2) Oaths of Adjuration: Oaths sworn (usually in the form of curses uttered) to warn against evildoing are mostly addressed to the general public, either in respect of violation of the law in general (e.g., Deut. 27:26; 28:15) or in respect of any particular offense (e.g., Deut. 27:15–25; 29:18–19; Jos. 6:26; I Sam. 14:24–28). A good example is the "public imprecation" against potential witnesses not to withhold testimony (Lev. 5:1), which was presumably made in particular cases presently before the court. The oath of adjuration is also administered to the suspected adulteress in the course of ordeal proceedings (Num. 5:19).

(3) Oaths of Promise: To reinforce a promise for future conduct, the oath is mostly tendered by the promisee (e.g., Gen. 24:3; 50:25; Jos. 2:12; I Kings 22:16; II Kings 11:4, 25:24; Neh. 5:12) and then taken by the promisor (Gen. 47:31; 24:9; Jos. 2:17–20). Unilateral oaths of promise usually take the form of vows (e.g., Num. 30:11, 14; Lev. 5:4).

(4) Oaths of Loyalty: Apart from the oaths of covenant between God and His people, we find also instances of declarations which could be classified as oaths of loyalty in the modern sense (Jos. 22:21–29; II Chron. 15:14) as well as prophecies of oaths of loyalty to God (Is. 19:18; 45:23; Zeph. 1:5; et al.).

(5) Oaths of Judicial Proof: "The oath before the Lord" (Ex. 22:10) decides between litigants where no other proof is available. Thus, where property entrusted for safekeeping was stolen and the thief was not caught, the bailed "deposes before God" that he has not laid hands on the property (Ex. 22:7, 10) and is discharged. If it afterwards appears that he has sworn falsely, he must restore the property plus one-fifth of the value thereof and bring a sacrifice for the expiation of his sin (Lev. 5:21–26). The causes enumerated for administering oaths are allegations of misappropriation of deposits or investments, wrongful conversion of lost and found articles, and forceful acquisition of property (*ibid.* 21–22). There is no biblical record of any case in which the judicial oath was actually administered.

Forms of Oaths.

(1) Normally the oath is taken by invoking God and swearing in His name (Gen. 21:23; 24:2; Deut. 6:13; Judg. 21:7; I Sam. 20:42; II Sam. 19:8; I Kings 1:17; Is. 48:1; Jer. 12:16; Ps. 63:12; et al.) – as indeed God Himself swears by Himself (Gen. 22:16; Is. 45:23; Jer. 22:5) or by His right hand and the arm of His strength (Is. 62:8) or by His great name (Jer. 44:26) or by His holiness (Amos 4:2). God is at times circumscribed, e.g., as the everliving one (Dan. 12:7) and often the oath is taken by the life of God (Jer. 5:2; 38:16; I Sam. 14:39, 45, 28:10; I Kings 18:10; et al.).

(2) Swearing without invoking the name of God was not infrequent: e.g., Jacob's oath by "the fear of his father Isaac" (Gen. 31:53), or the oaths by "my life" or "your life" or the life of my or your soul (e.g., I Sam. 1:26; 17:55; II Sam. 14:19) or by the life of the king (Gen. 42:15). But "swearing without God" (Jer. 5:7) means false swearing or swearing by false gods, which is tantamount to worshiping them (cf. Deut. 6:13; Jos. 23:7; Jer. 12:16),

(3) Especially in cases of adjuration, the oath is often recited to the deponent who then swears by saying "Amen" or repeating "Amen, Amen" (Num. 5:22; Deut. 27:15–26; Jer. 11:3–5). The God by whom one swears is also called the God of Amen (Is. 65:16).

(4) The oath is also taken by lifting up one's hand to God (Gen. 14:22). God Himself swears by raising His hand (Ex. 6:8; Deut. 32:40; Ezek. 20:5).

(5) An ancient form of taking the oath is putting one's hand under the thigh of the adjurer (Gen. 24:9; 47:29) – the thigh being an euphemism for the procreative organ (cf. Gen. 46:26; Judg. 8:30; et al.; describing the offspring as coming out of the thighs or loins) – a form of oath found also in other ancient civilizations.

(6) Oaths of covenant appear also to have been taken by cutting an animal or animals into pieces and passing between them (Jer. 34:18; and cf. Gen. 15:9–10); similar rites are known from ancient Greece. Or, oaths of covenant were sworn on stones and cairns (Gen. 31:51–52), as were oaths of promise (Gen. 28:18–22) – again, a rite found also in other ancient civilizations.

False and Vain Oaths.

False or useless swearing by God is one of the grave sins prescribed in the Decalogue (Ex. 20:7; Deut. 5:11) and a criminal offense (Lev. 19:12). Only he who has never sworn deceitfully is worthy to ascend to the hill of God and to stand in His holy place (Ps. 24:3–4). In the wisdom literature, swearing in general is discouraged, the taker of oaths being compared to the sinner and the man who abstains from swearing to the righteous (Ecc. 9:2; and see Ben Sira 23:9; et al. Cf. Matthew 5:33–37). The desecration of God's name for false swearing (Jer. 5:2) is at the root of Jerusalem's ruin and destruction, and it is when truth prevails and false swearing is no longer "loved" that Jerusalem will be redeemed (Zech. 8:15–17).

TALMUDIC LAW

General Rules.

(1) The oath, as here understood, is a mode of judicial proof. It is applicable only in civil and not in criminal cases.

(2) The oath is a residuary proof only: it is admitted only

where no sufficient evidence is available (Shevu. 45a, 48b). Where an oath had been taken and judgment pronounced, and then witnesses came forward and testified that the oath had been false, the judgment is quashed and any money recovered thereon restituted (BK 106a; Yad, To'en ve-Nitan 2:11).

(3) The oath is a party oath, originally administered as purgatory oath to the defendant, but later admitted in special cases also as confirmatory oath of the plaintiff (Shevu. 7:1). (For witnesses' oaths, see below under Post-Talmudical Law.)

(4) The oath is admissible to deny, or confirm, a liquidated and valid claim only: where (or insofar as) the claim does not disclose a cause of action and could be dismissed *in limine,* no oath may be administered (BM 4b–5a; Yad, loc. cit. 1:15). An exception to this rule is made in respect of unliquidated claims for accounts against trustees, partners, and agents (Shevu. 7:8).

(5) The oath need not be confined to one particular cause of action: once the oath is administered to a defendant, he may be required to incorporate in it any number of additional claims in respect of other debts allegedly due from him to the same plaintiff (*"Gilgul Shevu'ah";* Shevu. 7:8; Kid. 28a; Yad, loc. cit., 1:13; Sh. Ar., ḤM 94, passim).

(6) No oath is administered to suspected liars, such as gamblers, gamesters, usurers, and the like, or to people who have once perjured themselves (Shevu. 7:4; Yad, loc. cit., 2:1–2; ḤM 92:2–3), or who are otherwise disqualified as witnesses for their wickedness (Yad, loc. cit.; ḤM 92:3).

(7) Not only is no oath administered to minors, or to the deaf and dumb, or insane persons (Yad, loc. cit., 5:12; ḤM 96:5), but originally none would be administered even to rebut the claim of any such person (Shevu. 6:4; Yad, loc. cit., 5:9; ḤM 96:1), until the law was reformed to allow such claims to be presented and require them to be rebutted by an oath (Yad, loc. cit., 5:10; ḤM 96:2).

(8) Originally, oaths were admitted to rebut, or confirm, claims in respect of movable property only, excluding lands, slaves, and written deeds (Shevu. 6:5; BM 56b); but the law was later extended to allow, and require, the administration of oaths also in claims for immovables and deeds (Yad, loc. cit., 5:1; ḤM 95:1).

(9) The right to have an oath administered to one's debtor is enforceable in a separate action (BM 17a; Yad, loc. cit., 7:5). The right may, however, be contracted out (Ket. 9:5). Opinions are divided whether this right devolves to one's heirs (Shevu. 48a; Yad, Sheluḥin. 9:3). Like all other enforceable debts, the liability to take an oath lapses in the seventh year of remission (Deut. 15:1; Shevu. 7:8).

(10) The duty to take an oath is personal and does not devolve on the debtor's heirs: if the debtor died after the death of the creditor, the crditor's heirs inherit the chose in action and may recover on taking the oath that the claim is still unsatisfied; but where the creditor died after the debtor's death, the claim is extinguished if it cannot be enforced otherwise than by tendering the oath (Sh. Ar., ḤM 108:11).

Classes of Oaths. The Talmud classifies the judicial oaths chronologically, the classes varying in sanctity and gravity in descending order – the earlier the severer.

The Pentateuchal Oath (Shevu'at ha-Torah).

(1) the oath of bailees: where property was entrusted to the defendant for bailment, safekeeping, or other custody, and the defendant claimed that it was lost or stolen, or that it depreciated without his fault, the oath is imposed on him to verify his defense (Shevu. 5 and 8, BK 107b; BM 93a; Yad, Shevu'ot 11:5 and She'elah u-Fikkadon, 4:1; Sh. Ar., ḤM 87:7; see also Bailment).

(2) Where the defendant admits part of the claim, he will be adjudicated to pay the amount admitted and to take an oath that he does not owe more (Shevu. 6:1; BM 3a; Yad, Shevu'ot 11:5, and To'en ve-Nitan, 1:1; Sh. Ar., ḤM 87:1; see also Admission).

(3) Where the defendant denies the claim in whole, and the plaintiff could adduce only one witness to prove his claim (for the two-witnesses-rule, see Witness), the defendant will have to take the oath that he owes nothing (Shevu. 40a; Yad, Shevu'ot 11:5, To'en ve-Nitan, 1:1 and 3:6; Sh. Ar., ḤM 87:1 and 7).

The Mishnaic Oath (Shevu'ah mi-Divrei Soferim). The following are plaintiff's oaths ("they swear and take"):

(1) The laborer's oath: On a claim for wages, the plaintiff is entitled to judgment on taking the oath as to the amount due to him (Shevu. 7:1), provided the contract of employment is uncontested or has first been duly proved, and provided the claim is made promptly (Shevu. 45b; Yad, Seḥirut, 1:6; Sh. Ar., ḤM 89:1–3). See also Labor Law.

(2) The shopkeeper's oath: Where the plaintiff claims to have advanced money or goods to a third party upon the defendant's request, and the request is uncontested or has first been duly proved, the plaintiff may recover on taking the oath as to the amount so advanced and due to him (Shevu. 7:5; Yad, Malveh ve-Loveh, 16:5; Sh. Ar., ḤM 91:1). The fact that a debt was entered in the shopkeeper's books was not originally sufficient in itself to entitle him to recover even on taking the oath (Yad, loc. cit., 16:6); later the rule was established that where a merchant kept regular books on account, his oath would be accepted to verify his books (Resp. Rosh, nos. 86:1 and 103:2; Sh. Ar., ḤM 91:4–5).

(3) The landlord's oath: Where it was duly proved, or admitted, that the defendant entered the plaintiff's house empty-handed and left it with chattels in his hands, the plaintiff may recover upon his oath as to what it was the defendant had taken away (Shevu. 7:2 and 46a; Yad, Gezelah va-Avedah, 4:1–2; Sh. Ar., ḤM 90:1). In the absence of the landlord himself, his wife or any other person in charge of the premises could take the oath (Shevu. 46b; Yad, loc. cit., 4:6; Sh. Ar., ḤM 90:4; *Sefer Teshuvot ha-Rashba ha-Meyuḥasot le-ha-Ramban,* no. 89). The oath was later extended to all cases where it was proved, or admitted, that some monetary damage had been caused by the defendant, for instance, where he had been seen to throw the plaintiff's purse into the water or into fire: the plaintiff would be entitled to recover damages on taking the oath as to what had been the contents of the purse, provided the claim did not exceed what would normally be kept in a purse (BK 62a; Yad, Ḥovel u-Mazzik, 7:17; Sh. Ar., ḤM 388:1).

(4) The injured's oath: Where it was duly proved, or admitted, that the plaintiff had been whole and sound when encountering the defendant, and when he left him he was found injured, the plaintiff is entitled to recover damages on taking the oath that it was the defendant who had injured him (Shevu. 7:3; Yad, loc. cit., 5:4; Sh. Ar., ḤM 90:16). Where the injury could have been neither self-inflicted nor caused by a third party, however, the plaintiff was allowed to recover without taking the oath (Shevu. 46b; Yad, loc. cit., 5:5; Sh. Ar., ḤM 90:16; see also Damages).

(5) The billholder's oath: While a bill duly proved to have been made by the defendant is normally sufficient evidence of the debt (see *Shetar*), where the plaintiff "detracts" from the bill by admitting to have received part of the debt evidenced by it, he has to take the oath that the balance is still due to him (Tosef., Shevu. 6:5; Shevu. 41a; Yad, Malveh ve-Loveh, 14:1; Sh. Ar., ḤM 84:1). The same rule applies to the widow's claim on her *ketubbah* (Ket. 9:7); but the widow's oath was later required even where she did not expressly admit any part payment, so as

to establish that she had not received anything on account of her *ketubbah* during her husband's lifetime (Git. 4:3; Sh. Ar., EH 96:1).

(6) The shifted oath: Where the defendant is a suspected liar and cannot therefore be sworn (see above), the oath is shifted to the plaintiff to verify his claim (Shevu. 7:4; Yad, To'en ve-Nitan, 2:4; Sh. Ar., ḤM 92:7). If the plaintiff is a suspected liar, too, the liability to take the oath reverts to the defendant, but as he will not be allowed to take it, judgment will anyhow be entered against him *(ibid.)*. This highly unsatisfactory result was sought to be avoided by applying the general rule that the burden of proving his claim always rested on the plaintiff (see Evidence), and as the plaintiff would not be allowed to take the shifted oath, his claim ought to be dismissed (cf. Rema Sh. Ar., ḤM 92:7), the more so where the plaintiff had known that the defendant was a suspected liar and ought therefore to have abstained from doing business with him (Resp. Rosh, n. 11:1).

The following is a defendant's oath ("they swear and do not pay"): (7) The Pentateuchal oath of the bailees was in the Mishnah extended to partners, tenant farmers, guardians, married women (in their capacity as agents of their husbands), and self-appointed administrators of estates (Shevu. 7:8; Yad, Sheluḥin ve-Shuttafin, 9:1; ḤM 93:1). The same oath is imposed by the husband on his wife in respect of any business carried on by her (Ket. 9:4).

The Post-Mishnaic Oath (Shevu'at Hesset). The presumption has been raised that plaintiffs will not put forward unfounded and vexatious claims; and the rule evolved (in the third century) that a plaintiff who could not otherwise prove his claim, was entitled to have an oath administered to the defendant that he did not owe anything (Shevu. 40b; Yad, To'en ve-Nitan, 1:3; Sh. Ar., ḤM 87:1). A defendant unwilling to take this oath but still persisting in his denial of indebtedness, had the right to shift the oath to the plaintiff who, upon taking it, would be entitled to recover (Shevu. 41a; Yad, loc. cit., 1:6; Sh. Ar., ḤM 87:11); but the Pentateuchal and mishnaic oaths could not be so shifted except as set out above (see the shifted oath). In the event of the plaintiff's refusing to take the shifted oath, the claim will be dismissed (Sh. Ar., ḤM 87:12). For obligations confirmed by way of oath, see Elon, *Ha-Mishpat Ha-Ivri* I, p. 158.

Administration of Oaths. The Pentateuchal and mishnaic oaths are taken by holding the Scroll of the Torah in one's hand and swearing by God (Shevu. 38b; Yad, Shevu'ot, 11:8; ḤM 87:15). God need not be mentioned by name but may be described by one of His attributes. The oath is taken standing up (Shevu. 4:13; Sh. Ar., ḤM 87:16, 17). The post-mishnaic oath is taken without holding the Scroll and without mentioning God (Sh. Ar., ḤM 87:18; a contrary rule is given by Yad, Shevu'ot, 11:13, to the effect that the Scroll should at least be held out to the deponent so as to instill fear into him). The oath is pronounced either by the person taking it or by the court administering it; in the latter case, the deponent responds with "Amen" (Yad, Shevu'ot 11:10). There was a rule to the effect that oaths must always be taken in Hebrew (Yad, Shevu'ot 11:8), but it was later mitigated so as to allow the oath to be taken in the language best understood by the deponent (*ibid.*, 11:14; Sh. Ar., ḤM 87:20).

Before administering the oath, the court warns the deponent of the gravity of the oath and the inescapability of divine punishment for any false oath. This warning is not required for the post-mishnaic oath (Shevu. 39a; Yad, Shevu'ot 11:15, 16; Sh. Ar., ḤM 87:20–21). The court also warns the party at whose instance the oath is administered, that he should abstain if his case was wrong so as not to have the oath administered unnecessarily, whereupon that party has to say "Amen" to confirm his own good faith (Yad, To'en ve-Nitan, 1:11; Sh. Ar., ḤM 87:22).

Sanctions. (1) Where a defendant was by law required to take the Pentateuchal oath and refused, judgment would be entered against him and execution be levied against his property forthwith (Shevu. 41a; Yad, loc. cit., 1:4; Sh. Ar., ḤM 87:9).

(2) Where a plaintiff was by law allowed to take the mishnaic oath and obtain judgment, he could forego his privilege and have the post-mishnaic oath administered to the defendant (Yad, loc. cit., 1:4; Sh. Ar., ḤM 87:12). However, the defendant would then shift the post-mishnaic oath back to the plaintiff (see above), and if the plaintiff still refused to take the oath, his claim would be dismissed (Sh. Ar., ḤM 87:12); but it must be borne in mind that the refusal or reticence to take the much severer mishnaic oath did not necessarily entail such refusal or reticence in respect of the much lighter post-mishnaic oath.

(3) Where a defendant refused to take the mishnaic or post-mishnaic oath, a *ḥerem* (ban) lasting 30 days would be pronounced against him (Yad, loc. cit., 1:5; Sh. Ar., ḤM 87:9); for refusal to take the oath, he would also be liable to flogging (Yad, loc. cit., 1:5); but judgment would not be entered against him so as to authorize execution upon his goods or lands (Shevu. 41a; Yad, loc. cit.; Sh. Ar., ḤM 87:9).

For other functions of the oath apart from its use as a proof see Elon, *Ha-Mishpat Ha-Ivri;* index *shevuah.*

POST-TALMUDIC LAW

To the classes another class was added at a much later period (as from the 14th century), namely, the testimonial oath. Originally, potential witnesses could be sworn only to the effect that they were, or were not, able to testify on a given matter (Shevu. 4:3) – the purpose of such "oath of the witnesses" was solely to avoid suppression of testimony. It was an innovation to have witnesses, who were prepared and about to give evidence, swear first that they would testify to the truth; but the swearing in of witnesses became a widespread practice (Ribash, Resp. no. 170; Tashbeẓ 3:15), though not a binding rule of law (Resp. *Ḥatam Sofer,* ḤM no. 207). It is not practiced in the rabbinical courts of today. The rule appears to be that it is in the free discretion of each particular court to administer the testimonial oath whenever in its opinion circumstances so require (cf. *Beit Yosef* ḤM 28:1; Rema Sh. Ar., ḤM 28:2; *Urim ve-Tummim* ḤM 28:2; and *Sma,* Sh. Ar., ḤM 28 n. 16); but it has been said justifiably that a witness who cannot be believed without being first sworn, cannot be believed at all (Tos. to Kid. 43b s.v. *Hashta*).

JURAMENTUM JUDAEORUM OR MORE JUDAICO (THE JEWRY OATH)

As from the fifth century and throughout the Middle Ages, Jews testifying in non-Jewish (Christian) courts were required to take an oath which was invariably so formulated as to be binding upon them under Jewish law. Its essential elements were the solemn invocation of God; the enumeration of certain miraculous events from biblical history in which God's omnipotence was especially manifest; and curses to discourage perjury (Kisch, Germany, 275). Most medieval lawbooks and statutes contain elaborate provisions and formulae for the Jewry Oath. Many provided for concomitant degradations and insults, such as having Jews take their oaths while standing on a pigskin (*ibid.*, 278 et al.).

Bibliography: J. Pedersen, *Der Eid bei den Semiten* (1914); M.H. Segal, in: *Leshonenu,* 1 (1929), 215–27; S. Blank, in: HUCA, 23 (1950/51), 73–95; N.H. Tur-Sinai, *Ha-Lashon ve-ha-Sefer,* 3 (1957), 177–86; M. Greenberg, in: JBL, 76 (1957), 34–39; H. Silving, in: *Yale Law Journal,* 68 (1959), 1329–48; M. R. Lehman, in: ZAW, 81 (1969), 74–91; J. Seldenus,

Dissertatio de Juramentis (Excerptio ex eius libro secundo de Synedriis) (1618); K.F. Goeschel, *Der Eid*... (1837); Z. Frankel, *Die Eidesleistung der Juden in theologischer und historischer Beziehung* (1847[2]); L. Zunz, *Die Vorschriften ueber Eidesleistung der Juden* (1859); L. Loew, in: *Ben Chananja*, 9 (1866), suppl., 17–25, reprinted in his *Gesammelte Schriften*, 3 (1893), 335–45; T. Tonelis Handl, *Die Zulaessigkeit zur Zeugenaussage und zur Eidesablegung nach mosaich-rabbinischem Rechte* (1866; Ger., and Heb. *Edut le-Yisrael*); J. Blumenstein, *Die verschiedenen Eidesarten nach mosaisch-talmudischem Rechte und die Faelle ihrer Anwendung* (1883); R. Hirzel, *Der Eid* (1902); F. Thudichum, *Geschichte des Eides* (1911); D. Hoffmann, in: *Jeschurun*, 1 (1914), 186–97 (Ger.); J. Pedersen, *Der Eid bei den Semiten* (1914); Gulak, Yesodei, 4 (1922), 129–49; H. Tykocinsky, *Die gaonaeischen Verordnungen* (1929), 67–99; T. Bernfeld, *Eid und Geluebde nach Talmud und Schulchan Aruch* (1930[3]); S. Rosenblatt, in: PAAJR, 7 (1935/36), 229–43; Herzog, Instit, 1 (1936), 11–13; Kisch, Germany, 275–87, 506–15; idem, in: HUCA, 14 (1939), 431–56 (Ger.); Z. Warhaftig, in: *Yavneh*, 3 (1949), 147–51; ET, 1 (1951[3]), 267f.; 5 (1953), 522–4, 528; 6 (1954), 37–61; 8 (1957), 741–3; B. Cohen, in: HJ, 7 (1945), 51–74, reprinted in his *Jewish and Roman Law*, 2 (1966), 710–33, and addenda 797–800; idem, in: *Goldziher Memorial Volume*, 2 (1958), 50–70, reprinted op. cit., 734–54 and addenda 801; Elon, Mafte'aḥ, 310–26; idem, in: ILR, 4 (1969), 106–8; idem, *Ha-Mishpat Ha-Ivri* (1973), I, 107ff., 175ff., II, 276ff., 490ff., 504ff., 535ff., 570ff., 579, 604ff., 617ff., 646, 816ff., III, 842, 1001ff., 1340ff.

Haim H. Cohn

EXECUTION (Civil), laws concerning methods of recovering a debt.

Definition and Substance of the Concept. In Jewish law, a debt or obligation *(ḥiyyuv)* creates in favor of the creditor not only a personal right of action against the debtor, but also a right *in rem* in the form of a lien over the latter's property (termed *aḥarayut nekhasim;* see Lien; Obligations, Law of). Hence, many of the laws concerning the methods of satisfying a debt out of the debtor's property also apply to the recovery of a debt with the consent of the debtor, and not merely to recovery of a debt by court action; e.g., such matters as the distinction between the different categories of assets out of which the debt must be satisfied, the distinction between free and "encumbered and alienated assets" *(nekhasim benei ḥorin* and *meshu'badim*, respectively), or the matter of preferential rights as between several creditors, etc.

Recovery of debt will here be dealt with from two main aspects: (1) methods of recovery involving the exercise of constraint against the person or liberty of the debtor; and (2) methods of recovery from the debtor's assets.

Execution in Jewish Law and in Other Legal Systems – Fundamental Principles. There are detailed instructions under biblical law governing the relationship between the lender (creditor) and borrower (debtor; Ex. 22:24–26; Deut. 24:6, 10–13), the essence of which is to enjoin the creditor not to prejudice the debtor's basic necessities of life or his personal honor and freedom. This is in contrast to the right given the creditor in the laws of Hammurapi to enslave the debtor as well as the debtor's wife, children, and slaves (secs. 114–6, 151–2, also 117–9) and in further contrast with similar provisions in the laws of Assyria, Ashnunna, Sumer, etc. (see Elon, *Ḥerut ha-Perat* 3–8). In biblical law the institution of slavery is limited to two cases only: (1) the thief who does not have the means to make restitution and is "sold for his theft" (Ex. 22:2); and (2) the person who voluntarily "sells himself" because of his extreme poverty (Lev. 25:39). Scriptural references indicate, however, that in practice bondage for debt was customary at times (II Kings 4:1; Isa. 50:1 and see I Sam. 22:2) – presumably under the influence of the surrounding legal systems; but the practice was strongly criticized by the prophets (Amos 2:6, 8:4–6; Micah 2:1–2) and after Nehemiah's sharp condemnation of the "nobles and rulers" for indulging in this practice (Neh. 5:1–13) bondage for debt was abolished in practice as well as in theory. The Bible makes no mention of imprisonment for debt and, indeed, Jewish law has given only the most limited recognition to imprisonment, even in the field of criminal law (see Imprisonment).

Accordingly, methods of execution in Jewish law were in direct contradistinction to execution procedures under the Roman Twelve Tables. By the *legis actio per manus iniectionem*, the creditor was entitled – on the expiration of the 30 days' grace given the debtor to repay his debt and a further 60 days within which someone could redeem him from imprisonment and pay the debt on his behalf – to put the debtor to death or to sell him *"trans tiberim"*; if there were several creditors, each was entitled to a share of the debtor's corpse. The underlying motive of execution in Roman law was not only to satisfy the creditor's legitimate and material claim, but also to extract vengeance and to punish the debtor for not fulfilling his obligation (see H.F. Jolowicz, *Historical Introduction to the Study of Roman Law* (1952[2]), 192; Elon, *Ḥerut ha-Perat* 11f.). In the course of time the harshness of these provisions were modified and the creditor's right to sell or to put the debtor to death was abolished by the *Lex Poetelia* in 313 (326?) b.c.e., but it still remained possible to imprison the debtor until he repaid the debt or made adequate compensation for it by his own labor (Elon, *ibid.*). The basic attitude toward the creditor-debtor relationship as laid down in biblical law, with the later further requirement that the debtor make repayment by the due date, has, throughout the ages, remained at the root of the rules of execution in Jewish law (see Yad, Malveh, chs. 1 and 2; Tur and Sh. Ar., ḤM 97–98), although certain changes and modifications were, at various times, introduced in keeping with the social and ethical realities prevailing in the different centers of Jewish life (see below).

Distinguishing between a Pauper and a Man of Means. The biblical passages mentioned above already delineated the basic concept of protecting the poor against the obduracy of their creditors. Talmudic scholars emphasized the distinction in unequivocal terms: "To the poor of your people you shall not be as a creditor, but to the rich" (Mekh., Mishpatim; 19, p. 316), and "You shall not be as a creditor to him – do not harass and demand from him when you know he has no means" (Mekh. SbY to 22:24; BM 75b and Codes). In post-talmudic times the distinction acquired a particular significance, especially in relation to imprisonment for debt.

Entry into the Debtor's Home. Entering the home of the debtor, in order to remove his assets in satisfaction of a debt, was prohibited in the Torah (Deut. 24:10–11). According to one opinion, entry for this purpose was forbidden to both the creditor and the debtor – so that the former might not remove assets of the best kind and so that the latter might not take out assets of the worst kind – only the officer of the court being permitted to enter in order to remove assets of a median kind (see below TJ, BM 9:14, 12b). The majority of the scholars, however, interpreted the prohibition as directed only against the creditor, to prevent him from violating the borrower's private domain and conspiring against his person or property (TJ, BM

9:14, 12b; Git. 50a and Codes). To avoid the danger of this happening to even the slightest degree, some of the scholars were of the opinion that it was also forbidden for the creditor forcibly to seize a pledge from the debtor, even if it was found outside his home and even if the court had sanctioned a distraint on him. According to these scholars it was only permissible for the officer of the court forcibly to extract from the debtor security for his debt (Sif. Deut. 276; Tosef., BM 10:8; BM 31b; 113 a–b). Some scholars expressed the opinion that, in principle, the prohibition against entering the debtor's home only applied to the creditor personally and that the officer of the court was even permitted to enter the debtor's home for the purpose of recovering assets in satisfaction of the debt; other scholars also prohibited the officer of the court from entering the debtor's house and the *halakhah* was so decided (BM 113b and Codes). Similarly, a further dispute between the scholars as to whether the prohibition against entry applied in respect of all debts or only to debts arising from loans, was decided in accordance with the latter view (Sif. Deut. 276; BM 115a and Codes).

The prohibition against entering the debtor's home hindered the effective recovery of a debt if the debtor pleaded that he had no assets and if no assets were found outside his home, since it was impossible to search his home so as to ascertain the truth of his plea. The post-talmudic scholars sought to overcome this difficulty in various ways. For example, Alfasi decided that entry is permissible if the debtor is "given to violent and evil ways and is arrogant" (i.e., in refusing to pay – quoted in *Sefer ha-Terumot,* 1:3), but Maimonides did not accept this view and regarded any permission to enter the debtor's home as against biblical law (Yad, Malveh, 2:2), and other scholars also rejected any permit of this nature (*Sefer ha-Terumot,* 1:3; Resp. Rashba, vol. 1, no. 909; vol. 2, no. 225). Some scholars sought to overcome the problem by giving a restricted interpretation to the biblical prohibition. Thus, for example, Meir ha-Levi Abulafia argued that the officer of the court is only prohibited from entering the debtor's home when the debt can be recovered from other assets outside his home; if no such other assets are found and the creditor contends – even doubtfully – that the debtor has assets inside his home, the court officer may enter the latter's home and seek assets on which to levy execution (quoted in Tur, ḤM 97:26). Jacob b. Meir Tam and Asher b. Jehiel offered a solution based on the following reasoning: the biblical prohibition refers only to the case of the creditor attempting to take a pledge from the debtor's property as security for repayment of the loan at some time after the debt was created; but not to the case of the creditor seeking entry in order to collect payment of the debt, after the lapse of the due date (see also Pledge). It follows therefore that entry into the debtor's home in the latter circumstances had never in fact been prohibited and was permissible (*Sefer ha-Yashar,* Nov. no. 602; *Piskei ha-Rosh,* BM 9:46–47), and this distinction was accepted by the majority of the *posekim* (Sh. Ar., ḤM 97:6, 15 and standard commentaries); but such entry was nevertheless still restricted to the court officer (Tur, ḤM 97:26; Sh. Ar., ḤM 97:6, 15; *Keẓot ha-Ḥoshen,* ḤM 97, n. 2; Elon, *Ḥerut ha-Perat* (60, n. 35)). When it is clear that the debtor is impoverished and has no property, entry into his home is prohibited since "this can only cause him shame and suffering" (*Sma,* ḤM 99 n. 13).

Compulsory Labor. The possibility of compelling satisfaction of a debt by means of the debtor's own labor was recognized in various legal systems during the Middle Ages. This form of compulsion represented a temporizing with the institution of enslavement for debt – all the recognized characteristics of this sometimes being manifest, while at other times and places the debtor was merely required to cover the principal and interest of the debt with his own labor (see Elon, *Ḥerut ha-Perat* 68ff.).

There was in Jewish law no trace of this kind of compulsion until the 11th century (except for the contents of one of the *aggadot* concerning the destruction of the Temple: Git. 58a). From this time onward, however, the question was discussed in the light of the surrounding legal realities and the need for more efficient methods of debt collection. On the one hand, the halakhic scholars regarded compulsory labor as prejudicial to the debtor's personal liberty – particularly in view of the general attitude of Jewish law toward any kind of labor-hire as a restraint on personal freedom, for which reason it has afforded the laborer special privileges, such as the right of retracting, etc. (BM 10a, 77a; see also Labor Law). On the other hand, compulsory labor involved no actual deprivation of the debtor's liberty – such as resulted from a sale into slavery – if its object was merely to give the creditor due satisfaction for his debt. Alfasi, and other scholars following him, decided that the debtor should labor-hire himself in order to repay his debt (quoted in Resp. Maharam of Rothenburg, ed. Cremona, no. 146). Some scholars distinguished between different kinds of obligations, and thus, for example, it was decided that in the case of a debt arising from the debtor's obligation to maintain his wife, he could be compelled to work in order to maintain her, since he expressly undertook to do so in the *ketubbah* – a factor not present in any other obligation and thus precluding compulsory labor (Elijah of Paris, Tos., Ket. 63a). Other scholars were of the opinion that compulsory labor was precluded in all cases, including even that of a wife's maintenance (Jacob Tam quoted in *Haggahot Maimoniyyot;* Yad, Ishut, 12:s.s. 8), and this view was accepted by the majority of the *posekim* (Resp. Rosh, no. 78:2; Tur, EH, 70; Tur, ḤM 97:28–30, 99:18–19; Sh. Ar., EH 70:3, 154:3; ḤM 97:15), although some of the latter did recognize the exception in respect of a wife's maintenance (Rema, EH 70:3; *Ḥelkat Meḥokek, Beit Shemu'el* and *Yeshu'ot Ya'akov, ibid.*). A further opinion that compulsory labor could be imposed in respect of other obligations, if the debtor was accustomed to labor and to hiring himself (the opinion of Radbaz, quoted in *Erekh Leḥem,* ḤM 97:15), was later rejected by most of the scholars (*Tal Orot, Parashat Kedoshim; Mishkenot ha-Ro'im.* "Beth," no. 39).

Imprisonment for Debt. In talmudic times and for a long time afterward, Jewish law completely excluded the possibility of imprisonment for debt. In the course of time, however, and because of the surrounding legal realities as well as internal social and economic changes, the question of imprisonment for debt came to the surface in Jewish law, and a number of basic halakhic rules were laid down on this subject. For greater detail see Imprisonment for Debt.

Execution Procedure. Execution procedure in Jewish law is based upon talmudic and post-talmudic sources and may be briefly summarized as follows: when it is sought to execute a judgment of the court ("if the borrower fails to give of his own accord, payment is levied through the court": Yad, Malveh 18:1), the court will grant a stay of execution – if so requested by the debtor in order to give him the chance of raising money to repay the debt – for a period of 30 days; during this period the debtor is not obliged to provide any pledge or surety, unless the court sees grounds for suspecting that he will place his assets beyond reach or in some other manner evade payment of the debt (Sh. Ar., ḤM 100:1; Resp. Maharik, sec. 14); the period of the stay may be increased or reduced by the court, depending on the circumstances (Tur ḤM 100:1; Rema ḤM 100:1), but no stay will be granted in respect of certain debts arising from tort (Yad, Ḥovel u-Mazzik, 2:20; see also Sh. Ar., ḤM 420:27; for further details concerning the stay, see *Arukh ha-Shulḥan,* ḤM

100:2). No stay of execution will be granted when an appeal is lodged against the judgment, unless so warranted by special circumstances (Rema ḤM 14:4; *Baḥ* ḤM 14:4; see also *Takkanot ha-Diyyun be-Vattei ha-Din ha-Rabbaniyyim be-Yisrael,* 5720–1959/60, Rule 132, and Taxation[1]). The creditor may also demand that the court impose a general ban on anyone who has money or chattels and refuses, without reasonable cause, to repay a debt (Yad, Malveh, 22:1; Sh. Ar., ḤM 100:1). Upon the debtor's failure to repay within the period of the stay, the court will issue a writ of *adrakhta* (see below, Yad, *ibid.;* ḤM 100:3), which is followed by various other procedural steps until the actual sale of the debtor's property or the creditor's "going down" to the property *(horadat ba'al ḥov la-nekhasim),* in satisfaction of the debt. If a stay of execution is not sought by the debtor and he declares that he will not pay the debt, the writ of *adrakhta* is issued forthwith (BK 112b; Yad and Sh. Ar., *ibid.*). If the debtor is found to have no property he is "warned" by the court three times – on a consecutive Monday, Thursday, and Monday – and then the lesser ban *(niddui)* is pronounced against him until he pays the debt or pleads that he has no means of doing so and delivers a solemn oath accordingly (the oath of *ein li;* see below). If he suffers the ban for 30 days without seeking its retraction, it will be extended for a further 30 days and thereafter the full ban (*ḥerem,* "excommunication") is pronounced against him (ḤM, *ibid.*).

Adrakhta and Tirpa. The word *adrakhta* means "to pursue and overtake" (cf. Judg. 20:43; Ket. 60b), hence it is the term used for a document empowering a creditor to "pursue" his debtor's property and levy payment thereon, wherever found (Rashi to BM 16b and 35b). Other scholars gave the term the meaning of the word *dorekh* ("treading upon"), i.e., by virtue of the writ of *adrakhta,* the creditor becomes master over and "treads upon" the debtor's property for the purpose of recovering the debt therefrom (Rashbam to BB 169a and see *Yad Ramah, ibid.*). The writ is issued for the recovery of payment out of both the free property, and the "encumbered and alienated" property (*nekhasim benei ḥorin* and *meshu'badim;* see Lien). The *adrakhta* in respect of free property is written as follows: "X was adjudged to be indebted to Y in such and such an amount and, he not having paid voluntarily, we have written out this *adrakhta* on such and such a field of his." Thereupon the bond of indebtedness is torn up, and according to one opinion, this fact must be stated in the writ of *adrakhta* to prevent any possibility of the creditor recovering a second time on the same bond (Yad, Malveh, 22:13; Sh. Ar., ḤM 98:9–10; Meiri, in: *Shitah Mekubbeẓet* BK 111b).

If the debtor has no free property, the *adrakhta* on the "encumbered and alienated" property is written thus: "X was adjudged to be indebted to Y in such and such an amount by virtue of a bond in the latter's hands; since he has not paid the debt and whereas we have not found any free property of his and have already torn up Y's bond, we therefore give Y the power to investigate and seek out and lay hands on all the property of X that he can find, including all the lands sold by X from such and such a time on, and Y is hereby authorized to recover the debt and levy payment on all such property" (Yad, Malveh, 22:6; Sh. Ar., ḤM 98:9; for the *adrakhta* version as to orphans' property, see Yad, Malveh, 12:9; ḤM 109:2). If the creditor finds any encumbered property which he is entitled to seize for the purpose of recovering payment, he will do so and thereupon the *adrakhta* is torn up (for the same reasons as the bond is torn up) and a writ of *tirpa* ("tearing apart," seizure) is issued (in which the tearing up of the *adrakhta* is recited: for the text see Yad, Malveh, 22:8; Sh. Ar., ḤM 98:9; for a different order of procedure concerning the *adrakhta* and *tirpa,* see commentaries to BK and BB, *ibid.*). A creditor executing a *tirpa* against encumbered property is required to take a solemn oath that he has not yet recovered payment of the debt, nor granted a release from or sold his claim (Shevu. 45a; Yad, Malveh, 22:10; ḤM 114:4).

Appraisement and Related Procedures. After the creditor finds free property of the debtor and also in the case of recovering payment from encumbered property, following upon a writ of *tirpa,* an appraisement (*shuma*) of the property is made (at the instance of the court) by three persons possessing the necessary expertise (Codes, *ibid.;* according to some scholars the appraisement is made before the *adrakhta* or *tirpa* is written, *Yad Ramah,* BB 169a). The appraisement is made according to the value for which the property can be sold at the particular time and place, without any need for the creditor to sell it somewhere else or wait until the price might rise (ḤM 101:9). If the appraisers disagree, the majority opinion is accepted and if each gives a different estimate, the average of the three estimates is taken (ḤM 103:1–3). The appraisement document is headed by the words *iggeret shum* ("letter of appraisement"), by which name it is known (MK 3:3, BM 1:8; for other interpretations of the term *iggeret shum* see commentaries on BM 20a and MK 18b).

After the appraisement has been approved by the court, there is a public announcement or advertisement *(hakhrazah)* in which the judges announce: "whoever wishes to buy may come and do so," in order to find the highest bidder. In origin, the law of *hakhrazah* applied in respect of consecrated property and the property of orphans (Ar. 21b and Codes), but was extended also to property sold in execution (Ket. 100b; Tos. to Ar. 21b and Codes). The scholars disputed the question whether the sale of orphans' property should be so advertised for 30 or 60 days and the *halakhah* was decided that the period should be 30 days where the announcement is made daily and 60 days where it is made on Mondays and Thursdays only (Ar. 21b and Codes.). According to some of the *posekim,* an announcement for 30 days is made even in matters not concerned with orphans' property (Rema ḤM 103:1), but another opinion is that in the case of recovering payment out of free property, an announcement is made "as may be deemed necessary, until there are no higher bids" *(ibid.).*

The announcement is made in the morning and evening, when the "workmen set out and return home," and is only made for the sale of land, not for the sale of chattels, nor is it made if the sale is for urgent purposes, such as maintenance, funeral expenses, or poll tax (Ket. 100b and Codes). The property is sold to the person paying the highest price beyond the appraised value or – if there be no one to raise the price – to the person paying the appraised value. The purchaser is given a *shetar hakhrazah* or *iggeret bikkoret* ("letter of examination," Ket. 99b and see Rashi ad loc.; cf. also *Tosefot Yom Tov,* Ket. 11:5; for the text see *Sefer ha-Terumot,* 3:2; *Beit Yosef* ḤM 103:17; cf. also other interpretations in *Arukh ha-Shalem,* s.v. *iggeret bikkoret*). The creditor is given a preferential right of acquiring the property for himself if no one offers more than the appraised value or if he equals any other offers (Sh. Ar., ḤM 103:1). In this event the creditor is given a *shetar horadah* (i.e., he "goes down" to the property, it is "appraised" to him; for the text see Tur ḤM 103:17 where it is called a *shetar shuma;* cf. BM 16b, where it is called a *shetar aḥaletata;* Yad, Malveh, 22:10–11, where it is also called a *shetar horadah* but a different version of the text is given; see also the standard commentaries and Gulak, *Oẓar ha-Shetarot* p. 314ff.).

One opinion is that once the *adrakhta* has reached the hands of the creditor, he may also enjoy the fruits of the property, but

1. page 690.

another opinion is that he may do so only after the appraisement and the announcement (BM 35b) – the *halakhah* was decided in accordance with the latter view (Malveh, 22:12). The execution proceedings are completed when the property is sold and the proceeds paid to the creditor or the property itself transferred to him.

Restoration of Property Transferred to the Creditor. In strict law the creditor to whom the debtor's land is transferred is not thereafter obliged to return the land if the debtor subsequently acquired the means to repay the debt in cash; but the scholars enacted, in a *takkanah* referred to in the Talmud as *shuma hadar* (BM 16b and Codes; cf. Gulak, *Ha-Ḥiyyuv ve-Shi'budav,* 125, on the use of the term *shuma* in this connection), that this should be done for the sake of "Do what is right and good in the sight of the Lord" (Deut. 6:18 and see Takkanot[1]). Chattels recovered by the creditor, however, are not returnable to the debtor (Rema ḤM 103:9). According to one view, land is returnable to the debtor if he repays the debt within 12 months but the *halakhah* was decided according to the view that land is always returnable to the debtor (i.e., upon repayment of the debt, BM 16b, and 35a, and Codes). Land recovered by the creditor and then sold by him, or given in gift, or inherited upon his death, is however not returnable to the debtor *(ibid.)*. According to some scholars, the land must always be returned to a debtor, even if given by him voluntarily in satisfaction of the debt and not as a result of execution proceedings; but other scholars hold that his voluntary surrender of the land is a bar to its ever being returned to him against payment of the debt *(ibid.)*. Similarly, a stipulation between the creditor and debtor and effected by way of a formal *kinyan* (see Acquisition), to the effect that the former shall not be obliged to return the land to the latter, holds good even when the land is turned over to the creditor as a result of execution proceedings (Sh. Ar., ḤM 103:9).

Categories of Assets for Recovery of Debt. If the debtor owns cash (coins), chattels, and land, he must pay in cash and cannot refer the creditor to other property (Sh. Ar., ḤM 101:1); if the debtor wishes to pay in cash but the creditor wants land or chattels, some scholars give the creditor the right to choose, but the *halakhah* was decided according to the view that the choice is the debtor's (Tur and Sh. Ar., ḤM 101:3). If the debtor owns land only, the creditor may refuse to accept it and choose to wait until the debtor is able to pay him in cash (ḤM 101:4). If the debtor has chattels and land but no cash, the creditor recovers payment out of the chattels, but the debtor has the right to choose the chattels for this purpose (ḤM 101:2); the creditor cannot demand land if the debtor offers chattels in payment.

If the debtor has no chattels or such chattels do not satisfy the debt, payment is extracted from his land (Yad, Malveh 1:4 and ḤM 101:10) and – when such land consists of fields of different quality – in this order: a debt arising from tort is satisfied from the *iddit* or best land; a wife's jointure *(Ketubbah)* from the *zibburit* (the poorest or worst land); and all other obligations from the *beinonit* or land of medium quality (Git. 48b; Yad, Malveh 19:1; ḤM 102:1). In strict law, according to some scholars, all obligations except those in tort can be satisfied from the *zibburit,* but the scholars prescribed that all obligations except for the wife's jointure should be satisfied from the *beinonit* so as not to close the door before a borrower; other scholars hold the opinion that in strict law, all obligations except those in tort and the wife's jointure must be satisfied from the *beinonit* (Git. 49b and Codes; TJ, Git. 5:1, 46c; and see above, entry into the debtor's home; on the question of levying payment on chattels or land sold by the debtor to a third party see Lien).

In many places it was customarily stipulated in bond agreements that the debtor had to pay the debt in cash, without putting the creditor to the trouble of execution proceedings and for this purpose the debtor was obliged personally to deal with the sale of his property and to pay the creditor in cash (Resp. Rashba, quoted in *Beit Yosef* on ḤM 101:10).

"Arrangement" for the Benefit of Impoverished Debtors *(siddur le-ba'al ḥov)*. The Pentateuch lays down various provisions concerning the taking of a pledge from a borrower and the duty to restore it in case the borrower is impoverished and requires the pledge for the elementary necessities of life. The scholars have interpreted these laws as applying to the taking of a pledge other than at the time of the loan and for purposes of securing the loan, but not when it is taken in satisfaction of the loan (see Pledge). The scholars laid down that when the creditor seeks to levy on the debtor's property – i.e., after due date of payment and in satisfaction of the debt – certain property serving the debtor's elementary needs is to be entirely beyond the reach of the levy. This exclusion of a part of the debtor's property from the creditor's grasp is termed *mesaderin le-va'al ḥov;* i.e., an assessment is made of how much to leave the debtor for his vital necessities (Rashi, BM 113b), or an "arrangement" is made for his necessities, as laid down by the scholars (Rashi to Ned. 65b); the version of some scholars is *mesaredin le-va'al ḥov,* from the word שריד = a remnant, i.e., leaving the debtor a shred or remnant (Rashi, BM 113b).

The basic idea of an "arrangement" is found in a *baraita* which lays down that a creditor may demand that an expensive suit of clothing belonging to the debtor be sold in satisfaction of the debt, but the latter must be left with some other ordinary clothing. In the opinion of R. Ishmael and R. Akiva, "all Israelites are entitled to the same robe," and even an expensive suit must be left to the debtor (BM 113b). However, the detailed laws of "arrangement" laid down by Judah ha-Nasi in the Mishnah (Ar. 6:3), relate only to *arakhin* obligations (to the Temple) and not ordinary debts and only in the *baraita* cited is mention made of "arrangement" in relation to all debts (BM 113b). According to some of the *amoraim,* no "arrangement" of this nature is ever made (BM 114a) and this view is followed by some of the *posekim* (*Sefer ha-Yashar,* Nov. no. 602), but the majority of the *posekim* confirm the institution (Yad, Malveh, 1:7, 2:1–2; Sh. Ar., ḤM 97:6ff., 23). There is also an opinion that "arrangement" is only made in the case of a debt originating from loan (and not, for example, from hire; ḤM 97:29; *Arukh ha-Shulḥan* 97:35).

Within the framework of the arrangement the debtor is left with the following: food for a period of 30 days – according to the normal requirements of the average townsman, even though the debtor may have lived as a pauper; clothing for a period of 12 months ("he does not require to wear silken apparel or a head-covering of gold – these shall be taken from him and he shall be given what is due to him"; see above); a bed and other requirements for sleeping; essential home furniture, such as a table and chair (*Arukh ha-Shulḥan* 97:26); his shoes; an artisan is left with two of each kind of tool used by him (Yad, Malveh 1:7 and ḤM 97:23); according to R. Eliezer a farmer is left with a pair of working animals, and the owner of an ass or a boat is left with the ass or boat respectively, but the majority opinion of the scholars, according to which the *halakhah* was decided, is that these are regular assets and not artisans' utensils (Ar. 23b; and Codes). The debtor retains his *tefillin* but not his books *(ibid.)*, but some scholars say that if the debtor is a *talmid hakham,* his books are not taken from him (the opinion of Judah Barzillai, quoted in *Sefer ha-Terumot* 1:1, 8). An interesting innovation is the decision of Moses Sofer (at the beginning of the 19th century)

.1. page 83.

that a shopkeeper's stock of goods is not to be sold in execution, "since in these times the essence of their livelihood is to buy and sell on credit, it would amount to taking their lives in pledge (Deut. 24:6) if their stock is taken from their shops; therefore the practice is to take payment in instalments at fixed times . . . so that the shopkeeper shall not fail completely" (Nov. Ḥatam Sofer ḤM 97).

The laws of the "arrangement" are not concerned with the needs of the debtor's wife and children, even though they are the debtor's responsibility (Ar. 6:3f., and Codes). Hai Gaon held the view, however, that the debtor's needs for his household and children, for whose maintenance he is responsible, come within the arrangement – and this was the practice in Kairouan (see Elon, *Ḥerut ha-Perat* 47, n. 43). The creditor does not, however – but for an entirely different reason – levy payment on the clothing of the debtor's wife and children, even if it was bought by the debtor with his own money. In the opinion of some of the *posekim,* this includes their Sabbath and festival garments, even if they are very expensive. The reason is that it is presumed that such garments are given by the debtor to his wife and children with the intention that the garments become their own property and the law precludes the creditor from levying payment on chattels that have passed out of the debtor's ownership (Yad, Malveh, 1:5; ḤM 97:25, 26 and Isserles ad loc; and see Lien). Some scholars hold, on the strength of this view, that a wife's jewelry given to her by her husband, the debtor, is also excluded from the creditor's levy (and see *Sma,* ḤM 97 n. 62). Garments or jewelry owned by the debtor's wife prior to their marriage or acquired thereafter with her own private funds, as well as garments or jewelry expressly purchased by the husband for his wife, are clearly excluded from the levy (ḤM 97:26 and *Sma* n. 63).

Plurality of Creditors – Preferential Rights. In the case of a written obligation (*shetar* or deed), the creditor in whose favor the obligation was first established takes preference in levying payment on the debtor's land, whether still in the latter's possession (i.e., the free property) or whether already acquired from the debtor by a third party (i.e., "encumbered and alienated" property; Ket. 94a; Yad, Malveh, 20:1; Sh. Ar., ḤM 104:1). This preferential right upon recovery of a debt is the result of an attitude of Jewish law which gives the creditor, upon the creation of the debt, over and above his personal right of recourse against the debtor, a lien on the latter's land. This lien, which is in the nature of a real right, takes precedence over any similar right acquired by a subsequent creditor. If a later creditor forestalls an earlier one in levying on the debtor's land, some scholars hold that what he succeeds in recovering cannot be taken from him by an earlier creditor despite the right of a creditor by deed to seize a debtor's "encumbered and alienated" assets – since a later creditor still takes precedence over a regular purchaser, so that "the door shall not be bolted before a borrower" (Ket. 94a and Tos. to *ibid.*). Other scholars *(ibid.),* followed by the majority of the *posekim* (Alfasi and Asheri to Ket. 94a; and Codes), hold that in these circumstances the levy of the later creditor is not valid and the earlier creditor may seize from the later one whatever the later may have recovered. However, if the later creditor forestalls the earlier one and levies on the *beinonit* land, but leaves the debtor with *zibburit,* the levy will be valid since the earlier creditor is still able to recover his debt from the *zibburit* (Sh. Ar., ḤM 104:1).

So far as the debtor's chattels are concerned, the earlier creditor takes no precedence in recovering his debt from such chattels, since there is no lien over movable property. In the case of two creditors simultaneously claiming the debtor's chattels, some scholars hold that the earlier creditor takes precedence but the majority opinion of the *posekim* is that there is no preferential right and the debtor's assets are shared between the two creditors (see below; Ket. 94a; and Codes). Even in respect of land there is no preferential right unless the land was in the debtor's possession prior to establishment of the debt; and if the debtor, at the time the debt was established, charges in favor of two or more creditors any land which he may acquire in the future (see Lien), the earlier creditor will have no preferential right in respect of such land, since when the debtor acquires the land it is automatically charged in favor of both creditors (BB 157b; and Codes).

In the case of a mere oral obligation there is no preferential right between creditors, neither over land nor chattels, and two creditors seeking to levy payment at the same time must share the debtor's property (Rif. Resp. no. 197; see also *Sma* to Sh. Ar., ḤM 104 no. 3 and 31). According to some scholars, however, there is an order of preference in respect of land in the debtor's possession (ḤM 104:13 and *Sma*), even in the case of oral debt.

The *posekim* dispute the method of dividing the debtor's property amongst his creditors when there is no preferential right. One opinion is that each creditor takes a share of the property in proportion to the size of his debt, since it would be inequitable to divide the property equally in proportion to the number of creditors (Rabennu Hananel, in Tur ḤM 104:11; Yad, Malveh 20:4 quoting the Geonim); whereas others hold that the debtor's property is shared equally amongst the creditors according to their number, provided that no creditor receives more than the due amount of his debt, since the small creditor is thereby afforded greater protection (Ket. 94a; Alfasi and Rashi ad loc.; and Codes).

Preferential Rights and Insolvency. A consequence of the law of preference as described above is that Jewish law does not recognize some of the laws of insolvency customary in other legal systems. Thus, it does not recognize a concurrence with regard to division of an insolvent estate, whereby all the debtor's assets – save for those specifically charged in favor of a particular creditor or creditors – are divided among his creditors on a concurrent basis in proportion to the size of each creditor's claim. Because of the lien over the debtor's land afforded in Jewish law to each of the creditors, the order of precedence in recovering a debt follows the order of the establishment of the various liens, in similar manner to the order of preference in other legal systems regarding specifically charged assets. Even in cases where there is no prescribed order of preference, for example, in respect of the debtor's chattels or land acquired by him after the establishment of the debt, the assets are distributed amongst the creditors in proportion to the number of creditors and not to the size of each claim.

In post-talmudic times the law was supplemented, within the above-mentioned framework, by a number of rules very similar to the familiar insolvency laws. Some of these rules were aimed at protecting all the creditors. Thus, for example, it was laid down that in cases where the law afforded no preferential right, a proportional share of the debtor's estate had to be reserved for those creditors who had not yet claimed repayment and even for those creditors holding claims that were not yet due for payment. (*Teshuvot Maimoniyyot,* Mishp. no. 41; Resp. Rashba, vol. 1, no. 1111; *Keẓot ha-Ḥoshen* ḤM 104, s.s. 2). It also became customary to announce in public that anyone failing to lodge his claim against a particular insolvent within a specified period would lose his right (Resp. Rashba, vol. 1, no. 893).

In different periods, when economic crises led to an increase in cases of insolvency, various *takkanot* were enacted to deal with the situation (see Elon, *Ḥerut ha-Perat* 172ff.). These provided for the appointment of a trustee *(ne'eman)* over the property of an insolvent (a *bore'aḥ* or "fugitive" as he is called in the halakhic literature and *takkanot* of Poland, Germany, and Lithuania in the 17th and 18th centuries: see Elon, *Ḥerut ha-Perat* 180, no. 265). The trustee's task was to collect and receive all the debtor's property – which thus became vested in him – and to sell the same and distribute the proceeds amongst the creditors; the *takkanot* prescribed a punishment of a year's imprisonment for a debtor who willfully squandered his property, and could not pay his debts (Halpern, Pinkas Takk. 112, 128; Elon, *Ḥerut ha-Perat* 180–3).

Execution in the Absence of the Debtor. The scholars of the Talmud express conflicting opinions on the question of levying payment on the debtor's property when he is absent and there is no reasonable prospect of reaching him. One opinion is that in these circumstances, payment is not levied, even if the creditor should take an oath that the debt has not yet been paid; another opinion is that a debt is not recovered in the debtor's absence except with regard to a debt on which interest is payable; a third opinion is that payment is not levied unless the debtor had faced trial and thereafter taken flight; a further view is that payment is levied in the debtor's absence and the possibility that he may have paid the debt and received a release from his bond is disregarded, in order that "a person shall not take his neighbor's money and then go and sit abroad, which would cause the door to be bolted before borrowers" (Ket. 88a, TJ, Ket. 9:9, 33b, 8). Some of the *posekim* follow the third of these opinions (Hai Gaon, quoted in *Sefer ha-Terumot,* 15:1; Rabbenu Ḥananel, quoted by Alfasi, Asheri, and in Tos. to Ket. 88a); the majority of the *posekim,* however, hold the opinion that payment is levied in the debtor's absence, on both his land and chattels, after the creditor has presented his bond of indebtedness and taken an oath that the debt had not yet been paid (Alfasi and Asheri, Ket. 88a; Yad, Malveh, 13:1; Sh. Ar., ḤM 106:1). In the event that the debtor goes abroad before the debt falls due for payment, some scholars hold that by virtue of the presumption that no person pays a debt before its due date, the creditor may levy payment without taking the oath of non-payment – even though the debt may meanwhile have fallen due – since the fact that the creditor holds the bond of indebtedness obviates the fear that the debtor may meanwhile have paid the debt through an agent. Other scholars hold that in these circumstances the creditor is required to take the prescribed oath just because of the fear that the debtor may have paid the debt through an agent (*Sefer ha-Terumot,* 15:1; Tur, ḤM 106:3).

At no time is payment levied in the debtor's absence, unless the latter cannot be reached by an agent in a return journey lasting not more than 30 days (some scholars fix a longer and others a shorter period); if the debtor is somewhere where he can be reached in less than the stated period, the court will dispatch an agent to notify the debtor of the proposed levy on his assets. The expenses involved are paid by the creditor, but these may be recovered in turn from the debtor (Yad, Malveh, 13:1 and ḤM 106:1); expenses incurred by the creditor for his own benefit, such as those connected with the issue of a writ of *adrakhta,* etc. are not recoverable from the debtor (*Sma* n. 2 and *Siftei Kohen* ḤM 106). Execution in the debtor's absence is conditional upon the prior fulfillment of three requirements by the creditor: (1) probate of the bond of indebtedness held by him; (2) proof that the debtor is abroad and is not available to face trial; and (3) proof that the assets on which it is sought to levy payment belong to the debtor (Malveh 13:2; ḤM 106:2). In order to obviate the difficulties attending an execution in the debtor's absence, the creditor may request the court to restrain the debtor from leaving the country unless he provides a surety for the payment of the debt (Sh. Ar., ḤM 73:10; see also Elon, *Ḥerut ha-Perat* 218, n. 409; PDR 2:65ff.).

Impoverished Debtors and the Plea of Ein li. "It is the law of the Torah that when the lender comes to recover payment of the debt, and it is found that the borrower has property, then an assessment ["arrangement"] for his vital needs is made and the remainder is given to his creditor . . . ; if it is found that the debtor has no property, or that he only has objects which fall within the assessment – the debtor is allowed to go his way and he is not imprisoned, neither is he asked to produce evidence that he is a pauper, nor is an oath taken from him in the manner that an idolator is adjudged, as it is written: 'you shall not be as a creditor unto him.' " (Yad, Malveh, 2:1). This was the law as it prevailed until geonic times. The advent of the geonic period was accompanied by material changes in the economic life of Babylonian Jewry. Commerce, extending to the North African and other countries, came increasingly to replace agriculture and the crafts as the mainstay of Jewish existence. Whereas formerly loans were taken primarily for the borrower's daily needs, they now came to be employed mainly for profit-making purposes, and the growing capital flow and development of external trade made it difficult to keep a check on the assets of a debtor, all of which encouraged the phenomenon of concealing assets. In the course of time this led to the adoption of far-reaching changes in the means of recovering a debt (see above; and also Imprisonment for Debt.). These changes only partially asserted themselves in the geonic period, but two developments from this period may be mentioned, both aimed at a more effective process of debt recovery from a debtor pleading a lack of means.

One development was to place the debtor under a strict ban for a predetermined period, as a means of compelling payment. Thus it was decided by Hai Gaon, the first to mention this practice, that because of the adoption of various subterfuges by people of means seeking to evade payment of their debts – including those falsely swearing to their lack of means – any debtor pleading a lack of means to pay a debt shall have the ban imposed on him for a period of 90 days, during which time he is "severed" from Israel – so as to induce the disclosure of his assets and payment of the debt. Upon the expiry of this period he is made to take an oath that he has no means (for the terms of the oath, see below). Only a debtor who is reputed to be a pauper and known as such by the people is exempt from the ban when pleading no means of paying his debt (see A. Harkavy, *Zikkaron la-Rishonim,* no. 182). The ban for 90 days is also mentioned in the Talmud (BK 112b), but there it is imposed on a debtor who has means and pleads in court that the bond of indebtedness is a forgery; if, after being given a respite in order to prove his plea, he fails to appear in court, the ban will be imposed on him for 90 days and thereafter an *adrakhta* issued on his assets. This drastic innovation was not generally accepted as part of Jewish law. It was rejected by Alfasi and Raviah as contrary to the law (their statements quoted by way of the Mordecai in *Baḥ* ḤM 99:5) and it is not mentioned at all by later *posekim.* Only in the 16th and 17th centuries is it mentioned again – in various communal *takkanot* – as the imposition of a ban for a period of three days, thirty days, etc., with reference to a debtor pleading that he has no means (see Elon, *Ḥerut ha-Perat* 44, n. 25).

A second development in the geonic period toward more efficient debt collection was a *takkanah* providing for the administration of the oath of *ein li* ("I have no means") or *shevu'at ha-ḥashad* (oath taken when "suspected" of having means) to a debtor pleading a lack of means to repay his debt: "After the redaction of the *Gemara,* when the early geonim saw the swindlers increase in number and the door bolted before a borrower, they regulated that a solemn oath – having the stringency of biblical law – be taken from a borrower to the effect that he has nothing beyond the assessment that is made for him and that he has not concealed anything with others and has given no returnable gifts; the oath shall include that whatever he may earn or that may come into his hand or possession, in any manner whatever, shall not be used at all to feed or clothe either his wife or children or be given to anyone as a gift, save that he shall take from it sustenance for 30 days and raiment for 12 months – such as is due to him; neither the sustenance of gluttons nor of the nobility nor the raiment of high officials, but such as he has been accustomed to – and the remainder he shall give to his creditors, in due order of preference, until the whole of his debt is collected" (Yad, Malveh, 2:2). Unlike the case of the ban imposed for 90 days, the pauper was also subjected to this oath, but was later exempted from it by Maimonides, on the grounds that the oath was designed "to deal with swindlers and not with those generally accepted to be paupers" (Yad, Malveh, 2:4). The administration of this oath, as qualified by Maimonides, was accepted by the *posekim* (Tur and Sh. Ar., ḤM 99:4).

A similar oath can be traced in the legal systems of various European countries, commencing from the 12th century onward; thus for example, in the *Offenbarungseid* of German and Austrian law, the debtor is also committed to make all his future earnings available to his creditor (see Elon, *Ḥerut ha-Perat* 49, n. 52).

The underlying purport of the Jewish laws of execution is to ensure the existence of an effective debt-collection procedure, so as not to "bolt the door before a borrower," while maintaining adequate safeguards against the violation of a debtor's personal freedom and dignity. The pursuit of this twofold objective has ensured that the laws of execution at all times recognize a material distinction between a genuinely impoverished debtor and a debtor of means seeking to evade fulfilment of his obligations towards the creditor, a distinction lucidly enunciated in the statements of Maimonides already cited.

In the State of Israel. The Execution Law, passed by the Knesset in 1967, sets out in detail the law in regard to matters such as execution procedure, the order of recovery out of the debtor's property, attachment of chattels and land, property exempted from execution, receiving and realization of the debtor's property, specific performance according to judgment, inquiry into the debtor's financial position, imprisonment, etc. The trend of this law conforms to that of the rules of execution in Jewish law, on which a substantial number of its provisions are based.

Bibliography: M. Bloch, *Die Civilprocess-Ordnung nach mosaisch-rabbinischen Rechte* (1882), 90–106; Gulak, Yesodei, 2 (1922), 107–9; 4 (1922), 184–96; Gulak, Oẓar, 314–36; idem, *Toledot ha-Mishpat be-Yisrael bi-Tekufat ha-Talmud,* 1 (1939) *(Ha-Ḥiyyuv ve-Shi'budav),* 118–40; Herzog, Instit, 1 (1936), 4f; 386; S. J. Zevin, in: *Sinai,* 3 (1938), 55–71, 246; ET, 5 (1953), 92–132; 9 (1959), 143–55; B. Cohen, in: *Louis Ginzberg Jubilee Volume* (1945), 113–32, republished in his *Jewish and Roman Law* (1966), 159–78; addenda *ibid.* 772–5; M. Elon, *Ḥerut ha-Perat be-Darkhei Geviyyat Ḥov ba-Mishpat ha-Ivri* (1964); idem, in: ILR, 3 (1968), 103–7; idem, *Ha-Mishpat Ha-Ivri* (1973), I, 11ff., 65, 202ff., II, 257ff., 264ff., 331ff., 482ff., 514ff., 531ff., 535ff., 575ff., 601ff., 617ff., 647ff., 673ff., III, 839, 885ff., 1281.

Menachem Elon

IMPRISONMENT FOR DEBT, the imprisonment of a debtor who fails to pay his debt on or before the date due.

Prevalence in Other Legal Systems. Influenced by Roman law (see Execution (Civil)), imprisonment for debt was the most common means of personal coercion found in the debt collection procedures of various medieval legal systems. It developed from the institution of slavery for debt, as practiced in ancient legal systems, but was aimed at restraining the debtor's personal freedom rather than exploiting his labor potential. Imprisonment was imposed both on the debtor of means, who concealed his assets and thus attempted to evade payment of the debt, and on an impoverished debtor who owned no property at all. In certain periods debtors were incarcerated in "private" prisons, where they were subjected to various hardships at the creditor's behest, while elsewhere incarceration in public prisons only was allowed. Imprisoned debtors languished under difficult conditions and the discussion of imprisonment procedures and conditions occupies a prominent part of the legal and general literature of the Middle Ages (see J. Kohler, *Shakespeare vor dem Forum der Jurisprudenz* (1919^2), 1–160).

Modern legal systems have introduced far-reaching changes into the institution of imprisonment for debt. In most continental systems it has been completely, or almost completely, abolished; in England and in many states in the U.S. imprisonment for debt is still practiced, but is only imposed in the case of a debtor of means who evades payment of the debt, and the period of imprisonment is limited and prescribed (see H.S.G. Halsbury, *Laws of England,* 2 (1953^3), 638ff.; E. Pfiffner, *Schuldverhaft und Personalarrest im Vollstreckungsverfahren,* 1957).

Biblical and Talmudic Sources. Originally, Jewish law absolutely rejected the concept of imprisonment for debt. Biblical law prohibits the creditor from prejudicing the debtor's basic necessities of life. The creditor is enjoined to "stand outside" and not to enter the debtor's home in order to collect his pledge (Ex. 22:24–26; Deut. 24:6, 10–12), *a fortiori,* therefore, it is forbidden to imprison the debtor (see also Execution, Civil). It is noteworthy that at that time Jewish law in general gave only the most limited recognition to the use of imprisonment, even in the field of criminal law (see Imprisonment). This absolute prohibition was maintained in talmudic times and for a considerable time thereafter. Thus, Maimonides laid down: "but if the debtor is found to have no assets or only such as form part of the "arrangement" (see Execution, Civil) that is made for the debtor, then the debtor is allowed to go his way and he is not imprisoned" (Yad, Malveh 2:1).

The Post-Talmudic Period. This attitude of Jewish law underwent a substantive change in the 14th century, the beginnings of such change being already traceable to the 13th century. In the latter half of the 13th century a vigorous halakhic debate ensued regarding the continued validity of the accepted rule against imprisonment for nonpayment of a debt. These doubts were strongly motivated by socioeconomic factors of the time. The development of commercial life and the practice of credit facilities on the one hand, and the prevalence of concealment and fraudulent disposition by debtors of their assets to evade their obligations on the other hand, obliged creditors – and eventually even the borrowers as well – to seek more effective means of debt collection than those hitherto available under Jewish law. The prevalence of evasion of debt and concealment of assets on the part of debtors – by way of a fictitious assignment or alienation thereof to a wife or minor children, or by way of fictitious admission of indebtedness to a relative, thus giving the latter a preferential right to recover out of the debtor's property – is widely referred to in the responsa literature of contemporary scholars (see, e.g., Resp. Rashba, vol. 2, nos. 225, 283, 312, 360; vol. 4, no. 158; Resp. Rosh, nos. 78:1 and 2).

Although these halakhic scholars employed various measures to render such fraudulent dispositions invalid (*ibid.*, and Resp. Rosh, no. 78:3), they remained adamently opposed to the sanction of imprisonment of debtors. It became customary, however, as was the practice in the surrounding legal systems, for the parties themselves to stipulate expressly in the bond of indebtedness that the creditor would have the right to imprison the debtor upon his failure to pay the debt. Nevertheless, it is recorded that Solomon b. Adret held that a debtor could not be imprisoned on the strength of such a condition, even though he had been concealing his assets in the particular case (Resp. Rashba, vol. 1, no. 1069). Similarly, Asher b. Jehiel rejected the possibility of the debtor's imprisonment in two other cases, on the ground that the Bible permitted the deprivation of an individual's liberty only in the case of a thief who lacks the means of making restitution and is sold for his theft (Ex. 22:2; see also Execution, Civil), but not for any other kind of debt; he added that even an express condition between the parties providing for the debtor's imprisonment is void and unenforceable, since it is a condition relating to one's person *(tenai she-ba-guf),* and not one concerning a monetary matter *(tenai she-ba-ma-mon)* and there is no freedom of contract in respect of the former (see Contract[1]), which is in the nature of a *Jus Cogens,* rather than a *Jus Dispositivum* (Resp. Rosh, 68:10; 18:4). This opinion was still followed by the author of the Tur and by other scholars of this period (Tur, ḤM 97:31; *Maggid Mishneh* and *Migdal Oz,* Malveh 25:14).

Certain scholars of this period, however, already acknowledged a substantive change in the law concerning the imprisonment of a debtor. It was first mentioned in Germany by Alexander Suslin ha-Kohen, who decided – on the basis of a liberal interpretation of a talmudic statement used as a peg for his opinion rather than as proof – that "a person who has the means and fails to pay shall be imprisoned" (*Sefer ha-Aguddah,* Shab., no. 150). A more detailed account of the socioeconomic background to, and the evolution of, the relevant change in the law, is to be found in the responsa of Isaac b. Sheshet Perfet (Ribash). Bar Sheshet was asked to decide on the validity of an agreement between a creditor and his debtor providing for the latter's imprisonment upon his failure to pay the debt (an agreement current among the Jews at this time – see Elon, *Ḥerut ha-Perat . . .,* 137–40). He delivered a reply comprised of three parts (Resp. Ribash, no. 484). In the first, he gave a detailed exposition of the halakhic reasons for opposing the imprisonment of the debtor, despite an express condition to this effect: since regarding the creditor-debtor relationship the Torah stresses that the debtor shall not be deprived of his basic necessities for survival, his personal imprisonment is certainly prohibited: and since even an ordinary laborer may retract from a work contract (see Labor Law), it therefore follows that a debtor may not be imprisoned and deprived of his personal freedom in such a drastic manner; that a condition of the abovementioned kind is a *tenai she-ba-guf* (see above) in respect whereof there is no freedom of contract; and in deciding against imprisonment for debt, Asher b. Jehiel had already established a precedent in the matter (see above). In the second part of his responsum, Bar Sheshet described the current position in the Saragossa community, of which he was spiritual leader, and noted the existence of a *takkanah* enacted by the local community (see *Takkanot ha-Kahal*) whereby the judges used to imprison a debtor who had agreed to submit to such action upon his failure to repay the debt; a debtor could be imprisoned even in the absence of such a condition if he was unable to provide sureties for payment of the debt. Bar Sheshet added that when he wished to object to the *takkanah* as being contrary to biblical law, he was answered that this was a regulation in the interest of trade *(takkanat ha-shuk),* aimed at swindlers and intended so as not to have "the door bolted before borrowers," which persuaded him not to interfere with the practice. In the third part of his responsum, Bar Sheshet explained the halakhic basis for his decision, in the course of which he introduced a new approach to the question of imprisonment for debt in Jewish law, an approach founded on two basic premises: first, the doctrine that "payment of a debt is a *mitzvah,* the upholding whereof shall be compelled" (Ket. 86a; see also Obligations, Law of), which Bar Sheshet interprets liberally, allowing for imprisonment to be included as one of the means of compulsion; secondly, that compulsion by imprisonment is only permissible in circumstances which warrant the inference that the debtor is a man of means deliberately concealing his property from the creditor, but when the debtor is a pauper without any means of payment it is clear, Bar Sheshet holds, that his imprisonment is forbidden – notwithstanding his own express consent thereto – since in this case the injunction "You shall not be a creditor unto him" (Ex. 22:24) applies.

This innovation, which distinguishes, for the purposes of imprisonment, between a debtor of means evading payment and an impoverished debtor, was not lightly accepted in the Jewish legal system. In the following century Israel Isserlein vigorously opposed imprisonment for debt under any circumstances whatsoever (*Leket Yosher,* YD, pp. 79f.), and it was likewise opposed by Joseph Caro (Sh. Ar., ḤM 97:15) and Isaac Adarbi (*Divrei Rivot,* no. 302). The innovation was accepted, however, by such scholars as Samuel de Medina (Resp. Maharashdam, ḤM no. 390), Elijah b. Ḥayyim (Resp. Ranaḥ, no. 58), and Moses Isserles (Rema, ḤM 97:15) and thereafter it became accepted in Jewish law (see e.g., *Yam shel Shelomo,* BK 8:65; *Levush, Ir Shushan* 97:15; *Sma,* ḤM 107, n. 10; see also Elon, *Ḥerut ha-Perat . . .,* 172ff.) In a series of additional directives, special conditions of imprisonment were laid down, to be applicable even where the imprisonment of the debtor was considered permissible. Thus, for example, it was prescribed that a lenient form of imprisonment should be imposed (*Takkanot Megorashei Castilia be-Fez* (1545), quoted in *Kerem Ḥamar,* 2:4a, *takkanah* 22), and only in a "dignified prison," i.e., one with proper standards of cleanliness, sanitation, and hygiene (Resp. *Ḥikekei Lev,* ḤM no. 5).

Tax Debts. The halakhic scholars took a different and more stringent attitude toward the evasion of tax payments. The various governments under whose protection the Jews resided in post-talmudic times imposed heavy taxes, as "toleration money," on their respective Jewish communities and any delay in payment put the Jews in danger of persecution and expulsion. Communal leaders and halakhic scholars also attached much importance to taxes levied on individual members for the upkeep of communal services, a source of revenue on which organized communal life was largely dependent (see Taxation[2]). Accordingly, even in times when the scholars were absolutely opposed to imprisonment for debt, it was nevertheless permitted in respect of a tax debt. (It is possible that Rashi to Pes. 91a and *Hassagot Rabad,* Malveh 24:14, favoring imprisonment for debt, were intended to refer to a tax debt, since in their time imprisonment for an ordinary debt had not yet been permitted.) Asher b. Jehiel, who was strongly opposed to imprisonment for debt, noted that the prohibition applied to a debt between a man and his neighbor and that in respect of "the king's tax" it was customary for the communities to imprison a defaulter because "the law of the land is law" (see *Dina De-Malkhuta Dina;* Resp. Rosh 68:10). Elsewhere (Resp. Rosh 7:11) he added the important detail that it was customary in communities of the

1. page 251; 2. page 666, 697.

Diaspora to imprison debtors for failure to pay a communal tax, such debtors not being brought before the court but adjudged by the city elders in accordance with local custom (see also *Zikhron Yehudah* no. 79).

Notwithstanding this stringent attitude of the scholars toward a tax debt, it would seem that even in this case it was customary to distinguish between a debtor of means and a pauper, although there are indications that in later times imprisonment for a tax debt was imposed without distinction (see Elon, *Ḥerut-ha-Perat* . . . , 207 n. 365). An equally stringent approach was customarily adopted by communal leaders in the case of imprisonment for the nonpayment of a fine (see below; see also Taxation).

Takkanot Ha-Kahal Concerning Imprisonment for Debt. One of the legal sources for the continued development of Jewish law has been the *takkanot* enacted in all fields of the law throughout the ages. Legislation of this kind was mostly instituted by the halakhic scholars, but a substantial part – particularly from the tenth century onward – stems from *takkanot* enacted by the community through its leaders. A great deal of enactment of this kind was directed toward the problem of imprisonment for debt, because of its close connection with the social and economic conditions in the community. The *takkanot* mentioned by Bar Sheshet and Asher b. Jehiel (see above) are early illustrations of such enactments on the subject of imprisonment for debt and many instances of these can be found in the *takkanot ha-kahal* of Poland, Lithuania, and Germany, dating from the end of the 16th century onward. The end of the 16th century until the middle of the 17th century was a period of severe economic crisis for the Jews of these countries, giving rise to an increase in cases of nonpayment of debt and bankruptcy (see Elon, *Ḥerut ha-Perat* . . . , 172ff.). Numerous communal *takkanot* from this period deal with *boreḥim* (a term originally applied to runaway debtors or bankrupts and later to all defaulting debtors), with much attention being paid to the question of imprisoning the debtor. These *takkanot* often permitted imprisonment of the debtor if only for a short period though he might be a pauper without means of making payment, a fact that evoked strong criticism from the halakhic scholars.

In *takkanot* of the Cracow community (1595), a precise procedure was laid down for the recovery of a debt from a debtor pleading the lack of means to make payment: first, the pronouncement of a ban for three days, followed – in default of payment – by imprisonment of the debtor for eight days in the communal prison (the *"dudik"*; see Imprisonment[1]); thereafter an investigation for a period up to 30 days, to ascertain the truth or otherwise of the debtor's plea. The automatic eight-day imprisonment of the debtor, even when he is likely to be a pauper (except when he is known to be the victim of accident, fire, or robbery) was justified by the initiators of the *takkanah* because of the increase in the number of swindlers and their evil ways (see M. Balaban, in JJLG, 10 (1912), 335). Nine years later it was laid down in another Cracow *takkanah* that, "on account of the existing situation," any debtor pleading a lack of means to repay a debt exceeding "200 Polish gold coins," would be liable to imprisonment for a period not exceeding three months, unless "it is known that he has suffered some loss as a result of fire or robbery, etc." and provided that the debtor be released for one month after each month of imprisonment (see P.H. Wettstein, in *Oẓar ha-Sifrut* (1891–92), 600f.). These *takkanot* prescribed imprisonment not only in respect of a debt arising from a loan, but also for debts arising from tort, nonpayment of a teacher's salary, and taxes (M. Balaban, in: JJLG, 11 (1916), 99f.). In the case of a tax debt, imprisonment was prescribed "until the tax and expenses be paid," such exceptional severity being justified at the time on the grounds that many considered themselves at liberty to ignore tax payments without considering that this amounted to "robbing the public," for which reasons the public was to be carefully warned about the matter (M. Balaban, 10 (1912)., 356).

This general trend, at times increased by additional stringent measures, is reflected in a long series of communal *takkanot* from the 17th and 18th centuries. The *takkanot* of the Council of Four Lands of 1624 provided that a debtor pleading a lack of means was rendered liable to imprisonment for a period of one month (except in the clear case of an "act of God") and that a debtor known to have willfully squandered his money could be imprisoned for one year. Similar provisions are to be found in the *takkanot* of the Council of Lithuania (1623–52) and the Council of Moravia (1650–59) and in the *takkanot* of the communities of Posen (1642), Nikolsburg, and Tiktin (in the first half of the 18th century). The main difference between the various *takkanot* lay in the period of imprisonment laid down in each case, the fact of imprisonment being recurringly justified as an emergency measure, specifically designed to cope with the ever-increasing number of swindlers (for details, see Elon, *Ḥerut ha-Perat* . . . ,180–225).

An instructive *takkanah,* illustrative of Jewish law's humane approach toward the debtor – despite its far-reaching sanction of the use of imprisonment – is one enacted in 1637 by the Council of Lithuania, which obliged a creditor who demanded the debtor's imprisonment to provide for the latter's sustenance as determined by the court, but gave the creditor the right to recover the cost of this together with the debt (S. Dubnow (ed.), *Pinkas ha-Medinah [Lita]*, p. 70 no. 333); fulfillment of this requirement by the creditor was a precondition to the imprisonment of the debtor. This *takkanah* marks a significant divergence from the prevailing trend in other legal systems of that time, in which no consideration was given to the needs of the debtor during his imprisonment.

The provisions of the *takkanot ha-kahal* regarding the automatic imprisonment – even if only for a very short period – of any debtor failing to make payment, represented a deviation from the fundamental principle of Jewish law against prejudicing an impoverished debtor in any manner or form, and consequently evoked strong criticism from halakhic scholars. It must be borne in mind that such authority as Jewish law confers on communal leaders to enact *takkanot,* even though they may be contrary to a particular rule of Jewish law, is confined to the fields of the civil and criminal law, and does not apply to matters of ritual law *(issur ve-hetter).* The question of imprisoning an impoverished debtor was looked upon as a matter falling within the sphere of ritual law, by which it was forbidden. Thus R. Joel Sirkes (first half of the 17th century) stated: "those imprisoning even someone who has no means to pay, in terms of communal *takkanot,* have no authority to rely on and it was also written by Ribash that it is forbidden to seize the [debtor's] person; and the community has no power to make such an enactment in contravention of an *issur*" ("prohibition"; *Bah,* ḤM 97:28). Similarly, 100 years later Jonathan Eybeschuetz states: "in our time it is the custom simply to imprison a debtor who has no means to pay and no protest is made; perhaps all this is done on the premise that everyone is concealing his assets; the matter requires reflection, for they have no authority to rely on" (*Tummim* ḤM 97, n. 13). It is clear that Eybeschuetz was not quite reconciled to the attempt to justify the indiscriminate imprisonment of debtors on the grounds of the existing social and economic realities, nor to the presumption that seemingly called for every debtor to be suspected in advance of concealing his assets. Indeed, eventually these *takkanot ha-kahal* which

1. page 539.

sanctioned even the imprisonment of impoverished debtors – if only for a short and fixed period – came to be rejected by the Jewish legal system, since they amounted to a direct and material contradiction of the fundamental principle of Jewish law that imprisonment is not to serve as a punitive measure, but as a means of recovering a debt when the debtor is able to pay but conceals his assets and evades payments (see also Taxation).

In the State of Israel. The problem of imprisonment for debt engaged the attention of the Knesset for a period of ten years. In 1957 a bill was introduced which proposed the complete abolition of imprisonment for debt, a proposal which was, however, rejected by a majority of the members on the grounds that it did away with an important means of debt recovery in the case of stubborn debtors. In the Knesset debates on this and other related bills introduced from time to time, the attitude of Jewish law toward the problem was frequently cited – those who favored imprisonment for debt stressing the change in the course of time from its complete prohibition to its eventual permissability in the light of changed economic and social circumstances – with reference to a stubborn debtor of means. This attitude of Jewish law was finally accepted by the Knesset and embodied in the Execution Law, 5727–1967. Under this law (secs. 67–74), an inquiry is made by the chief execution officer into a debtor's financial position, in order to ascertain his ability to comply with the judgment; thereafter the debtor may be ordered to pay the debt in a lump sum or in installments, and upon his failure to do so within the period prescribed by the chief execution officer, he may be imprisoned for a period not exceeding 21 days, if no other means exist of compelling his compliance with the judgment. It is further provided that a debtor who has served the term of imprisonment ordered against him may not be imprisoned again in respect of the same debt or installment. In the case of a judgment for a debt deriving from maintenance for a wife, children, or parents, an imprisonment order may be issued without prior inquiry into the debtor's financial position.

Bibliography: P. Dickstein, in: *Ha-Mishpat Ha-Ivri,* I (1917/18), 29–76; M. Elon, *Ḥerut ha-Perat be-Darkhei Geviyyat Ḥov* ... (1964), 111–237, 255–69; idem, in: ILR, 3 (1968), 107–19; 4 (1969), 111–3; idem, *Ha-Mishpat Ha-Ivri* (1973) II, 483ff., 535ff., III, 1281; B. Cohen, in: *Louis Ginzberg Jubilee Volume* (1945), 113–32, republished in his *Jewish and Roman Law* (1966), 159–78; addenda *ibid.* 772–5.

Menachem Elon

VIII. PUBLIC AND ADMINISTRATIVE LAW; CONFLICT OF LAWS

Contents

PUBLIC AUTHORITY AND ADMINISTRATIVE LAW.

Jewish Public and Administrative Law
Qualifications, Duties, and Standing of Communal Leaders
The Public Authority and Laws of Property and Obligation
The Public Authority and the Exercise of its Own Discretion
The Public Authority as an Employer
Election of Public Officeholders
In the State of Israel

Jewish Public and Administrative Law. Public law during the early periods of Jewish law is concerned *inter alia* with the legal relationship between the individual head of the people – the king, nasi, or exilarch – and the public. (For details see subsection The King's Law in the Introduction; Elon, *Ha-Mishpat Ha-Ivri,* I, 42 ff., II, 399, III, 837 ff., see also Extraordinary Remedies). The special power and place of the Jewish community from the tenth century on led to the development of a very varied system of public and administrative law concerning the legal relationship between the collective leadership, whether appointed or elected, and the public. It has been stated that "the foundations of the community, as they remained in existence until the modern Enlightenment, were laid mainly in the first generation of the Second Temple period" (Y. Baer, in: *Zion,* 15 (1950), 1). Attributable to this early period are a number of tannaitic sources incorporating *halakhot* concerning the "townspeople" (*benei ha-ir* or *anshei ha-ir,* Shek. 2:1; BB 1:5), as well as certain *beraitot* concerning the authority of the townspeople to compel each other toward the satisfaction of public needs in various fields (Tosef., BM 11:23ff; BB 8a). At the head of such public authority stood the "seven good [elder] citizens" (*tovei ha-ir,* Jos., Ant., 4:214; TJ, Meg. 3:2, 74a; Meg. 26a). However, it was only with the rise of the Jewish community in various parts of the Diaspora from the tenth century onward that Jewish law came to experience its main development in the field of the laws concerning a public authority as a body composed of representatives of the public. It is a public authority entrusted with the duty and power to arrange matters of common concern to the public in this latter sense that is dealt with.

The representative and elective institutions of local Jewish government and intercommunal organizations were built up on the principles of Jewish law, and the halakhic scholars, as well as the communal leaders, were called upon to resolve (the latter by way of communal enactments) the numerous problems arising in the field of administrative law. These related among others: to the legal standing, composition, and powers of the public authority; to the determination of relations between the individual and the public authority and between the latter and its servants; to the composition of the communal institutions and the methods of election and appointment to the latter and to other public positions; to the legislative institutions of the community, the modes of legislation, and the related administration of the law (see *Takkanot ha-Kahal*); to the legal aspects and administration of its institutions (see *Hekdesh*); to the imposition and collection of taxes (see Taxation[1]); and to many additional problems concerning economic and fiscal relations in the community. This wide range of problems was dealt with in a very large number of responsa and communal enactments, in the course of which the halakhic scholars and public leaders developed a new and complete system of public law within the framework of the *halakhah.*

Qualifications, Duties, and Standing of Communal Leaders. The qualifications and duties of public representatives are discussed in the Bible and in the Talmud, mainly from the social, moral, and ideological aspects. The ways of the Patriarchs and other leading Jewish figures – such as Moses, Aaron, Samuel, and David – in dealings with the people serve as a basic source of guidance for the relationship between the people and their leaders, between the citizen and the public authority. It has been stated that appointment of "a good public leader *[parnas tov]* is one of the three things proclaimed by the Almighty Himself" (Ber. 55a; Kal. R. 8); that the Almighty had already shown to Adam "every generation with its leaders" (*dor dor u-farnasav,* Av. Zar. 5a), and to Moses, "all the leaders destined to serve Israel from the day of its leaving behind the wilderness until the time of the resurrection of the dead" (Sif. Num. 139); that in time to come, "when the Almighty shall renew His world, He shall stand Himself and arrange the leaders of the generation" (Yal., Isa. 454).

The requirements demanded of the leader representing the public are many and stringent: "In the past you acted only on your own behalf, from now on [i.e., upon appointment] you are bound in the service of the public" (Yal., Deut. 802); "a leader who domineers over the public" is one of those "whom the mind does not tolerate" (Pes. 113b) and over whom "the Almighty weeps every day" (Ḥag. 5b). It is not only forbidden for a leader to impose undue awe on the community if not intended "for the sake of Heaven" (*le-shem shamayim;* RH 17a), but he must himself stand in awe of the public (Sot. 40a). The scholars described in various ways the mutual interdependence between the citizen and the public authority: "A leader shall not be imposed on the public unless the latter is first consulted" (Ber. 55a), but once appointed, "even the most ordinary . . . is like the mightiest of the mighty" (RH 25b), to whom the public owes obedience and honor. This interdependence is illustrated in the difference of opinion between Judah Nesi'ah (grandson of Judah ha-Nasi) and other scholars as to whether the stature of a leader follows that of his generation – *parnas le-fi doro* – or whether the generation is influenced by its leaders – *dor le-fi parnas.*

These, and other similar concepts scattered in halakhic and aggadic literature, guided the halakhic scholars in their determination of the principles of Jewish administrative law. A person engaged in public affairs is as one studying the Torah (TJ, Ber. 5:1, 8d). Moreover, "If he be engaged in studying the Torah and the time comes for recital of the *Shema* ["morning prayers"], he shall leave off studying and recite the *Shema* . . . if he be engaged in the affairs of the public, he shall not leave off but complete this work, and recite the *Shema* if there remain time to do so" (Yad., Keri'at Shema 2:5; Sh. Ar., OḤ 70:4; based on Tosef., Ber. 1:4, 2:6; see also Lieberman, *Tosefta ki-Feshutah,* Berakhot, p. 3). Hence it followed that it was not merely a privilege to represent the public but also a duty. Thus in a case where a member of the community was elected to public office, contrary to his own declared wishes in the matter (namely, appointment as a tax assessor; see Taxation[2]), it was decided that "no person is free to exempt himself . . . since every individual is bound in the service of the public in his town . . . and therefore anyone who has sought to exclude himself from the consensus has done nothing and is bound to fulfill the duties of his office because the community has not agreed that he be excluded" (Resp. Rashba, vol. 3, no. 417; cf. also vol. 1, no. 769; vol. 7, no. 490; *Tashbeẓ,* 2:98).

In post-talmudic times the legal standing of a public authority was given precise definition based on the central legal doctrine accepted by the scholars of this period as the source of the community's standing and authority to make enactments; namely, that the standing of the communal leadership is assimilated to that of a court (*bet din;* see *Takkanot ha-Kahal*). In a certain case a person sought appointment to a public office; he had previously sworn a false oath with regard to his tax declaration, was fined for so doing, and came to an arrangement with the community concerning this tax payment. It was held by

1. page 666; 2. page 686.

Israel Isserlein (15th-century scholar of Vienna) that since such a person was unfit for appointment as a *dayyan,* he was also unfit to be numbered among the leaders of the community: "the leaders of the community fulfill the role of a court when they sit in supervision over the affairs of the public and private individuals" (*Pesakim u-Khetavim,* no. 214). This principle set a guide standard for the qualifications required of commmunal leaders (see, e.g., *Terumat ha-Deshen,* Resp. no. 344): "communal leaders appointed to attend to the needs of the public or private individuals are like *dayyanim,* and it is forbidden to include among them anyone who is disqualified from adjudicating on account of his own bad conduct" (Rema, ḤM 37:22). A further reason given by the scholars for assimilating the standing of communal leaders to that of *dayyanim* is that the duties of the former are largely concerned with providing for the social needs of the community, determination of the measure of support and relief for each being a task of a judicial nature (BB 8b and Rashi thereto; Sh. Ar., YD 256:3; *Mishpetei Uziel,* ḤM no. 4).

The assimilation of the communal leader's standing to that of a *dayyan* is naturally limited to such powers as he enjoys in his official capacity only. Hence communal leaders who have been empowered to elect a body to supervise public affairs must do so themselves, since they have no power to delegate this authority to others (see below), even though an ordinary court has authority to appoint an agent and entrust him with the execution of certain tasks (Resp. Ribash no. 228).

The Public Authority and Laws of Property and Obligation. The aforementioned assimilation facilitated the solution of a number of problems arising in Jewish law with regard to legal relations between the public authority and the individual. Thus, for instance, the general requirement in Jewish law of a formal act of *kinyan* (see Acquisition; Contract) in order to lend a transaction legal effect would normally have constituted a serious obstacle to the efficient administration of a public authority's multiple affairs. However, beginning in the 13th century, the new legal principle of the validity of any legal transaction effected by a public authority, even without a *kinyan,* came to be recognized. Apparently this was first laid down by Meir b. Baruch of Rothenburg in a case concerning the hire of a teacher by the community (quoted in *Mordekhai,* BM 457.8). Normally the parties would have been entitled to retract, since no formal *kinyan* had been effected and the teacher had not yet commenced his work (see Labor Law), but Meir of Rothenburg decided that there could be no retraction from the contract of hire "because a matter done by the public requires no *kinyan* – although this would be required in the case of an individual." He based this innovation on a wide construction of a number of talmudic rulings from which it may be inferred that the public has to be regarded differently from the individual, even though these contain no suggestion whatever that a *kinyan* might be dispensed with in a transaction effected by a public body (Meg. 26a; Git. 36a); in addition he compared the case of a transaction effected by a public body to that of a small gift, where withdrawal from the transaction is prohibited as amounting to a breach of faith and not because the transaction has full legal validity (i.e., when effected without a formal *kinyan;* BM 49a; Yad, Mekhirah 7:9; Sh. Ar., ḤM 204:8; see also Contract). He further decided that a suretyship for the fulfillment of the contract of employment between the community and the teacher was valid, even though it had been undertaken without a *kinyan* and in a manner in which the suretyship would otherwise be of no legal effect *(ibid.).* This decision is also given as the source of the rule that a gift by a public body is fully valid even if it is made without a formal *kinyan* (Sh. Ar., ḤM 204:9, and see also *Ha-Gra* thereto, n. 11). The law was similarly decided in regard to other legal matters affecting the public (see, e.g., Resp. Ribash no. 476; Rema, ḤM 81:1). This principle took root in the Diaspora: "The custom is widespread that whatever the communal leaders decide to do is valid and effective . . . and neither *kinyan* nor deed is required" (Resp. Rosh 6:19 and 21); similarly, in Constantinople in the 15th century it was held: "The widely accepted *halakhah* is that all matters of the public and anything that is done by or before the public is valid, even without *kinyan,* nor do the laws of alienation and acquisition *[hakna'ah]* apply in respect of such transactions" (*Mayim Amukkim,* no. 63); it was likewise decided by Isserles that "All matters of the public require no *kinyan*" (Rema, ḤM 163:6).

Other fundamental requirements of the law of *kinyan* were also relaxed with reference to a public authority. It was thus laid down, e.g., that the public may validly acquire something not yet in existence and alienate to someone not yet in existence (*Mayim Amukkim,* no. 63; see also Acquisition, Contract); and also that in a public matter *asmakhta* constitutes no defect (Resp. *Mabit,* vol. 2, pt. 2, no. 228). One of the explanations given for this fundamental innovation was that it had to be assumed that in any transaction with which the public was connected the parties would make up their minds absolutely *(gemirut ha-da'at),* even without a *kinyan* and notwithstanding the fact of *asmakhta* and so on (see, e.g., Resp. Ribash no. 476; Rema, ḤM 81:1; *Sma,* ḤM 204, n. 14); however, the main explanation given for this innovation is the fact that the legal standing of a public authority has to be assimilated to that of a court, that is "because it is influenced by the rule of *hefker bet din* . . . and a public authority, in its dealings with the public, is as a court for the whole world" (Resp. Rashbash no. 566, also no. 112; cf. the statement of Meir of Rothenburg quoted in *Mordekhai,* BM 457–8; idem, Resp., ed. Prague, no. 38). For the same reason it was held that a public body might not plead that it had not seriously intended a particular transaction, nor that it had erred and not properly understood the nature thereof (Rashbash, loc. cit.).

Relaxation of the requirements of the law of *kinyan,* of the rule of *asmakhta,* and so on, in the case of public matters naturally extended not only to the public body but also to the individual transacting with that body, so that he too was not free to withdraw from the transaction, even if it was effected without a *kinyan,* etc. (Resp. Rashbash no. 112; *She'ot de-Rabbanan,* no. 14; *Ba'ei Ḥayyei* ḤM, no. 81; PDR 6: 172f., 180f.).

The Public Authority and the Exercise of its Own Discretion. A basic question of administrative law concerning the power of a public authority to delegate authority in a matter requiring the exercise of its own discretion was extensively dealt with in a responsum of Isaac b. Sheshet Perfet (Resp. Ribash no. 228). A certain Catalonian community was granted a royal privilege in terms of which three communal trustees, together with the court, were authorized to nominate 30 persons to supervise the affairs of the community, particularly tax matters. The trustees and the court were unable to reach agreement on the execution of their task and instead agreed to elect two persons and delegate to them authority to appoint the 30 communal leaders. When this was done, a section of the community objected on the ground that authority could not be delegated by a body required to exercise its own discretion. In upholding this objection Isaac b. Sheshet held that even if in general an agent could delegate his authority to another – in circumstances where it could be assumed that the principal was not particular about the matter (see Agency, Law of) – this was not so in the case of a public authority, even though the latter is in a sense an agent of the public. The explanation offered is that no express power to delegate authority was given in the royal privilege, and the matter was of great importance since all the affairs of the community depended on selection of its 30 leaders, and those responsible for their selection had to choose leaders possessing suitable qualities; wise, just, and peace-loving persons, knowledgeable in the affairs of the community: "it is not the intention of the community that those who have to select them [the 30] shall be able to appoint others to act in their own place, even if these others equal them in wisdom and standing"; if, however, the responsible parties had been given express authority to delegate their powers, "then it would be as if the community itself had chosen these two."

In the same matter Isaac b. Sheshet went on to give an important ruling concerning resort to the law of the land in the interpretation of the royal privilege. In his opinion, even if it were to be said that the privilege had been given with the intention that it be construed "only according to the law of the land," and even if according to this "anyone entrusted with a matter may in turn entrust this matter to anyone he chooses," yet in the case under consideration the delegation of authority remained invalid, because the rules of administrative law, so far as the Jewish community was concerned, derived their authority from Jewish law also, which did not allow for the delegation of authority in the case at hand. This ruling also involved no conflict with the law of the land in accordance with which the privilege had been given, since the general authorities were not concerned if the Jewish public failed to avail itself of the powers given under the law of the land, but were only concerned when the Jewish collective interpreted the privilege in such a manner as to lend itself wider authority than was available under this law: "the king is only particular about an extension of authority, not about a narrowing of it"*(ibid.)*.

The Public Authority as an Employer. The great development of Jewish public law that followed on the rise of the Jewish community also made itself felt in the field of master and servant, in relation to employment by a public body. Special requirements relating to a public-service contract had already been emphasized in talmudic law. Thus, it was laid down that if a public-bath attendant, barber, or baker was the only one available and a festival was approaching, he could be restrained from leaving his employment until he provided a replacement (Tosef., BM 11:27; see also Contract). In addition, in order to avoid harm to the public, it was laid down that an individual fulfilling his duties to the public in a negligent manner might be dismissed immediately, as in the case of a public gardener, butcher, or bloodletter, a scribe, a teacher of young children, "as well as other like artisans who may cause irretrievable harm, may be dismissed without warning, since they are appointed by the public for as long as they carry out their duties in a proper manner" (Yad, Sekhirut 10:7, based on BM 109a and BB 21b). The majority of the *rishonim* interpret the rule of the *Gemara* as also extending to a private servant, considering that he too may be dismissed during the duration of his service contract if he has caused irretrievable damage (*Hassagot Rabad,* Sekhirut 10:7; *Beit ha-Beḥirah,* BM 109a; Tur and Sh. Ar., ḤM 306:8; Rema thereto; *Sma* thereto, n. 19). It was, however, laid down that a servant might not be dismissed without proper warning unless he was continually guilty of slackness in his work, and it must also be proved in the presence of the worker that he was indeed failing in his duties (Rema loc. cit.; *Maggid Mishneh,* Sekhirut 10:7; *Nimmukei Yosef,* BM 109a; see also below).

In post-talmudic times the halakhic scholars had to contend with the converse question: namely, whether it was permissible for a public authority to dismiss its servant without justifiable reason, on expiry of the agreed period of service, in the same way as could a private employer, who is free to refrain from renewing his servant's employment. (In modern times Jewish law has come to recognize the master's duty to pay severance pay to his servant on his dismissal: see *Ha'anakah.*[1]) The talmudic rule that the high priest may not be dismissed from his office (TJ, Sanh. 2:1, 19d) did not serve as an analogy for public servants in general (see Assaf, *Mi-Sifrut ha-Ge'onim,* 73f.; *Sha'arei Teshuvah,* nos. 50, 51). From the 12th century, Jewish law consistently tended toward recognition of the principle that a public servant may not be dismissed from his employment except for justifiable reason. Maimonides laid down the general rule: "a person is not removed from a public position in Israel unless he has offended" (Yad, Kelei ha-Mikdash 4:21); also that "it is not proper to dismiss any officeholder from office on account of mere rumors concerning him; this cannot be done even if he has no enemies, all the less so if there are people in the town who are his enemies and have ulterior motives" (his Resp. (ed. Blau) no. 111; this was also the view of Meir ha-Levi and R. Yom Tov b. Abraham Ishbil (Ritba), see Nov. Ritba to Mak. 13a). This principle was explained on the ground of "avoiding suspicion," that is, termination of the servant's employment with the public may arouse suspicion that the servant is being dismissed on account of his improper conduct (Resp. Rashba, vol. 5, no. 283; quoted also in *Beit Yosef,* OḤ 53, conclusion).

At the same time, it is held to be permissible to dismiss a public servant whenever it is customary "to appoint people in charge of public matters for a fixed period," so that at the end of it these men depart and are replaced by others, whether they be appointed in charge of food supplies, the charity fund, tax, or any other public service, and whether or not they receive any remuneration for their service; "even if no fixed period of service be stipulated for them, the terms of their appointment shall be similarly in accordance with the custom . . . because of their practice to replace [officials], the suspicion mentioned above is eliminated" (Rashba loc. cit.). In his responsum Solomon ibn Adret confirmed that such was in fact the custom in his time: "that the competent in each generation carry out tasks on behalf of the public, and thereafter depart to be replaced by others." The statement of this twofold principle – that a public servant may not be dismissed without justifiable cause except when it is the custom to hold office for a fixed period only – was accepted as *halakhah* in the Shulḥan Arukh (OḤ 53:25–26) and was applied in the different centers of Jewish life in respect of all persons employed by a public authority (*keneset ha-gedolah,* OḤ 53, *Beit Yosef; Arukh Ha-Shulḥan,* OḤ 53:26; *Mishnah Berurah,* OḤ 53, no. 73ff.; *Even ha-Ezel to Yad,* Sekhirut 10:7). In modern times attempts have been made to distinguish between different categories of public servants, although there is no apparent justification for this in the halakhic sources (see PDR 3:94ff.).

The discussions concerning dismissal of a public servant also embraced the related and more far-reaching proposition that a public office be transmitted from father to son by way of inheritance. In this respect too there was already the tannaitic rule, on the analogy of a king succeeded by his son (Deut. 17:20), that "all the leaders *[parnasim]* of Israel have their places taken by their sons" (Sif. Deut. 162; cf. Sifra Ẓav 5). Also Maimonides laid down that "Not only the kingship, but all offices and appointments in Israel are an inheritance from father to son for all time" (Yad, Melakhim, 1:7; Kelei ha-Mikdash, 4:20). In later times a trend toward restriction of this widely stated rule asserted itself. Thus, some scholars held that the rabbinate too was an office that could be passed by inheritance (Resp. Ribash no. 271; Rema, YD 245:22). Others disagreed, taking the view that "the crown of Torah is not an inheritance" (Resp.

1. page 317.

Maharashdam, YD, no. 85; Shneur Zalman of Lyady, Sh. Ar., OḤ 53:33, et al.). This was also Moses Sofer's original opinion, which he later reversed (Resp. Ḥatam Sofer, OḤ 12 and 13). It was laid down that local custom concerning inheritance of an office was to be followed (Rema loc. cit.). A son can in no event inherit a public office unless he is qualified for it and worthy of doing so (Sifra, loc. cit.; Maim. Yad, Melakhim, 1:7; Rema, Sh. Ar., YD 245:22; Ḥatam Sofer loc. cit.; for further details see OPD 46, 112; PDR 4:211; see also Labor Law).

Election of Public Officeholders. Questions such as the nomination of candidates, their number, their manner of election, etc., are extensively dealt with in post-talmudic halakhic literature (see *Takkanot ha-Kahal;* Taxation[1]). In modern times, with the renewal of Jewish autonomy in Ereẓ Israel and the establishment of the State of Israel, halakhic discussion has been resumed in relation to various problems arising in connection with the election of officeholders to representative state and municipal bodies. The primary sources relied upon in this discussion are found in the post-talmudic halakhic literature dealing with the leadership and administration of the community and its institutions; sometimes, when these sources do not deal specifically with the subject discussed by modern scholars, a conclusion is reached by way of analogy.

Majority and Minority. The principle of electing a public representative by majority vote was based by the scholars on the doctrine of *Aḥarei rabbim le-hattot* ("to follow a multitude": Ex. 23:2; see Majority Rule), which was interpreted to mean "that in all matters to which the community consents the majority is followed" (Resp. Rosh 6:5; in talmudic *halakhah* the doctrine was interpreted as pertaining to a majority of the court in giving its decision, or to the concept of majority as a legal presumption; see *Takkanot ha-Kahal;*[2] *Ḥazakah*[3]). At various times extensive discussions and sharp disputes centered around the question of the weight to be attached to the vote of individual members of the community. Many scholars objected to a scale graded in accordance with social and economic standing: "and it makes no difference whether this majority was composed of rich or poor, of scholars or the common people" (Resp. Re'em no. 53). An illiterate person was held to be eligible even for certain public appointments (Resp. Rashba, vol. 3, no. 399).

An informative description of some such disputes is to be found in a responsum of Menahem Mendel Krochmal (mid-17th-century leader of Moravian Jewry; *Ẓemaḥ Ẓedek* no. 2). It had been the custom in a certain community for all taxpayers, regardless of their financial standing or education, to participate in the election of communal leaders and the appointment of public officials. Some of the "respected citizens" sought to depart from this custom and to have it laid down that only a person paying tax in excess of a certain rate, or a *talmid ḥakham* ("at least qualified as a *ḥaver*"), could participate in the elections. Krochmal mentions that the "respected citizens" supported their demand with the argument that "most of the needs and affairs of the public involve the expenditure of money; how is it likely that the opinion of a poor man shall be as weighty as that of a rich man, or the opinion of an *am ha-areẓ* who is not wealthy be considered in the same way as that of a *ḥaver.*" They further contended that what they were seeking was anyhow customary in "large and important communities." The rest of the community objected to such a change in the system: "the poor, the masses of the people cry out against the derogation of their rights, since they also pay tax and contribute their share, and even if the rich pay more, the poor at any rate find the little they pay to be a greater burden than do the rich in paying much more."

In his decision Krochmal strongly condemned the discriminatory nature of the proposed change in the election system and held that – at the very least – "the little of the poor is balanced against the much of the rich." He nevertheless upheld the custom prevailing in most of the communities of striking a balance between a majority based on the number of souls and a majority based on financial contribution. He also rejected the proposition that those lacking in knowledge of the Torah be deprived of their vote, "lest they separate themselves from the public . . . which will lead to increased strife in Israel." A change involving discrimination against any section of the public was forbidden except with the unanimous consent of all members of the community, and, added Krochmal, in communities where there was such discrimination it had to be assumed that this had been instituted with the unanimous approval of the entire community. In recent times halakhic scholars have accepted as binding the view that every vote is to carry equal weight (see, e.g., *Mishpetei Uziel,* ḤM no. 3).

Eligible Age. The question of the age at which the right to elect and be elected to public office is acquired has in recent times come to be discussed by analogy with the criterion of age in other fields of the law. The general view is that the usual age of legal capacity – namely 13 years and one day for a man and 12 years and a day for a woman – is not to be relied upon as decisive with regard to the right to participate in elections, since in Jewish law the age of legal capacity is dependent on the specific nature of the legal act involved (see Elon, ILR, 1969, p. 121ff.) and exercise of the voting right carries with it legal consequences affecting the public as a whole – a factor calling for greater maturity on the part of the voter. According to one view, the active right to elect is acquired at 18 years: at this age a person has legal capacity to adjudicate in matters of civil law (*dinei mamonot;* Sh. Ar., ḤM 7:3) and to perform public religious duties, for instance as a ritual slaughterer (Rema, YD 1:5). Another view is that the right to vote is acquired from the age of 20, paralleling the biblical military age (Ex. 30:14; Num. 1:3) and the age of full majority, for instance for the purpose of the sale of paternal land which has been inherited (Yad, Mekhirah, 29:13; Sh. Ar., ḤM 235:9).

In the case of the passive right to be elected, the general view is that the minimal age is 20 years and over. At this age a person has the right to adjudicate in matters of criminal law (*dinei nefashot;* TJ, Sanh. 4:7, 22b) and even – for the purpose of permanent appointment as a *dayyan* – in matters of civil law (*Pitḥei Teshuvah,* ḤM 7, n. 4). Other scholars arrive at this age (20) following the minimal age for permanent appointment as a cantor (Sh. Ar., OḤ 53:8) or as an *apotropos* (cf. Resp. Ribash no. 20). There is also an opinion that distinguishes between a person elected to a state body, such as the Knesset (by virtue of whose far-reaching substantive powers the function of its representatives is held to be analogous to that of a *dayyan* adjudicating in matters of the criminal law), and a person elected to a municipal body (whose function is held to be analogous to that of the *dayyan* adjudicating in matters of the civil law, and who is therefore eligible from the age of 18 years).

Women. A woman's right to elect and be elected to public office has been the subject of much halakhic discussion in recent times. In particular a great deal of opposition has been expressed to granting women the passive right to be elected, such opposition being based on tannaitic and amoraic law (Sif. Deut., 157 and Ber. 49a, respectively): "A woman is not appointed to the kingship, as it is said, 'set a king over thee' (Deut. 17:15) and not a queen; similarly for all offices in Israel none but men are appointed" (Yad, Malakhim 1:5). Some scholars took a different view, basing themselves on the fact that Deborah "judged Israel" (Judg. 4:4), i.e., that she functioned not only as a judge

pages 657, 686; 2. page 595; 3. page 656.

but was also the leader of the people. The *rishonim* had already commented on the contradiction between the fact of Deborah's leadership and the rule excluding women from public office, a contradiction they sought to reconcile by the qualification that the objection to a woman's leadership is eliminated when she is accepted by the will of the people (Nov. Rashba and Ran, Shevu. 30a; cf. also Tos. to BK 15a and Nid. 40a). On this basis some latter-day scholars have decided that a woman is entitled to elect and be elected (see, e.g., *Mishpetei Uziel,* ḤM no. 6), their conclusion being influenced by the consideration that under existing social conditions "men and women meet daily in business transactions" *(ibid.).* Although at the time he gave this decision (in the 1940s) R. Uziel wrote that it was of a purely theoretical nature and was not to be applied in practice (*ibid.* and see p. 292), it has nevertheless been accepted in practice in the State of Israel by the decisive majority of religious Jewry so far as concerns Knesset and municipal elections.

Period of Residence. The period of residence qualifying a person to elect and be elected has generally followed the period laid down for tax liability (see Taxation;[1] see also Resp. Maharit, vol. 1, no. 69; *Mishpetei Uziel,* ḤM no. 3).

Proportional Representation. In detailed decisions, scholars such as Rabbi Kook, Jacob Meir, and Ḥayyim Brody expressed the opinion that the system of elections on a proportional basis answers the requirements of Jewish law, one of their main reasons being that in this way representation in the government of the state and its institutions is offered to all sections of the people (see *Sinai,* 14 (1943/44), 100–14).

In the State of Israel. In the Supreme Court. A number of Jewish law principles, concerning the legal standing of a public body and the relationship between the latter and its employees, have been considered and relied upon in decisions of the Supreme Court of Israel. In one case a municipal employee who had been dismissed on a charge of improper conduct applied to the Supreme Court – sitting as a high court of justice – to have his dismissal set aside on the ground that he had been given no opportunity to make himself heard and to answer the charge against himself prior to his dismissal. The court rejected the municipality's plea that in terms of the municipalities ordinance it had been under no obligation to hear the employee prior to his dismissal and upheld the employee's application, relying mainly on the following principles of Jewish law: (1) a person appointed to a public office, or holding a position with a public institution, may not be dismissed without a reasonable cause; (2) municipal councillors are as judges and therefore may not act arbitrarily but must consider a case on its merits; (3) since the councillors are like judges they have to follow a procedure that accords with natural justice, and a basic principle of Jewish law is that a person subjected to an inquiry must be enabled to appear and state his case (see PD 20, pt. 1 (1966), 29; cf. Resp. Rema no. 108). In another case the court applied the Jewish law principle that – for the good of the public – there is an obligation to dismiss a public servant who is proved to have neglected his duties after he has been given due warning (see PD 20, pt. 1 (1966), 41). In another instance the court, relying on the principle that a member of a public body is as a judge, concluded that no fault was to be found with a publicly elected official for not always following the opinions of those by whom he had been elected, since he has to act as a judge seeking the truth of a matter (PD 21, pt. 1 (1967), 59), provided only that he does so upon mature consideration and does not irresponsibly and often change his views (PD 20, pt. 1 (1966),651). Another principle of Jewish law which the court has applied precludes a judge from adjudging a matter from which he stands to derive personal benefit, and in terms of this the court set aside the decision of a local council which had been taken with the participation of a councillor who had a personal interest in the matter (*ibid.,* 103; see also PD 19, pt. 3 (1965), 393).

In the Rabbinical Courts. There is among others a decision of the rabbinical court on a basic problem that has arisen in recent years, touching on the above-mentioned rules of Jewish administrative law (the court in this instance sitting as an arbitral body since its jurisdictional authority is confined to matters of personal status; see Introduction). Three political parties entered the municipal elections under a joint list, having agreed that if only two of their candidates were elected then the second one on the list resign in favor of the next candidate on the list; only two candidates were elected and the second one refused to resign as agreed. It was contended before the court that the agreement was invalid because it had not been effected by means of a *kinyan,* because it related to something not yet in existence (the agreement having been concluded prior to the elections), and because it was defective on account of *asmakhta* (i.e., since the parties had been confident that more than two of their candidates would be elected, there had been no *gemirut ha-da'at*). The court rejected all these contentions and upheld the validity of the agreement, relying on the principles discussed above governing a public authority. The court emphasized that these principles applied not only to a public authority administering municipal affairs, but also to the public constituting a political party: "If it is the rule that in public matters there is no need for a *kinyan,* and the power of the public in its doings is so great that it is not restricted by the limitations imposed on the legal act of an individual – for instance as regards something that is not yet in existence, *asmakhta,* etc. – then there is no matter that is more eminently of a public nature than the matter under consideration, namely the composition of the public leadership" (PDR 6:176). It was accordingly held that the second one of the elected representatives was obliged to resign, as undertaken in the agreement. The decision was confirmed on appeal (*ibid.* 178ff.) and in addition the following guiding principle in the field of Jewish administrative law was laid down: "We have to add and say to the litigants that public leaders should not, in the course of their public duties, avail themselves of the plea that they are not bound by their own undertakings because of their questionable legal validity. Statements and undertakings, particularly in public affairs, are sacred matters which have to be observed and fulfilled wholeheartedly, in letter and spirit . . . for the public is always bound by its statements and may not retract" *(ibid.).*

Bibliography: J.S. Zuri, *Mishpat ha-Talmud,* 8 (1922), 52–60; idem, *Toledot ha-Mishpat ha-Ẓibburi ha-Ivri,* 1 (1931), 301ff.; E.J. Waldenberg, *Ẓiẓ Eli'ezer,* 2 (1947), no. 24; Z. Warhaftig, in: *Sinai,* 23 (1948), 24–49; M. Findling, in: *Yavneh,* 3 (1949), 50–56, 63; A. Karlin, in: *Ha-Torah ve-ha-Medinah,* 1 (1949), 58–66; J. Pilz, *ibid.,* 2 (1950), 55–58; J.H. Asafi, *ibid.,* 4 (1951), 241–3; N.Z. Friedmann, *ibid.,* 7–8 (1954/57), 63–71; T.A. Agus, in: JQR, 43 (1952/53), 153–76; M. Feinstein, in: *Ha-Ma'or,* 12 (1960), issue 2 (English numbering: 10 (1960), issue 10), 4–7; M. Amsel, *ibid.,* 7–10; M. Vogelmann, in: *Sinai,* 48 (1960/61), 196–203; M. Elon, in: *Meḥkerei Mishpat le-Zekher Avraham Rosenthal* (1964), 1–54; idem, in: *Fifth World Congress of Jewish Studies,* 3 (1969), 90f. (Eng. Abstract); idem, *Ha-Mishpat Ha-Ivri* (1973), I, 131, II, 569ff., 587ff., 613ff., 645ff., 789ff., III, 1252.

Menachem Elon

TAKKANOT HA-KAHAL (Heb. תקנות הקהל). This article is arranged according to the following outline:

1. page 675.

The Concept. The *Takkanot ha-Kahal* embrace that part of legislation in Jewish law which is enacted by the public or its representatives in contradistinction to the *takkanot* enacted by a halakhic authority, i.e., by the court and halakhic scholars (see *Takkanot*). The enactment of legislation by the public is already to be found in ancient *halakhah*. Thus it was stated that the *benei ha-ir* ("townspeople") have authority to pass enactments obliging all residents of their town in matters such as the prices of commodities, weights and measures, and laborer's wages, and to impose fines on those transgressing their enactments (Tosef. BM 11:23; BB 8b). The same sources (Tosef. BM 11:24–26) disclose that legislative authority was entrusted also to more restricted bodies, such as various artisans' and traders' associations within the town, such regulations obliging only the members of the particular association.

For as long as a single Jewish center – first Ereẓ Israel and later the Babylonian Jewish center – exercised hegemony over the entire Diaspora, there was little legislative activity of a local nature, both from the aspect of quantity and in the degree of authority carried. The great impetus to legislation by the public came at the end of the tenth century with the emerging stature of the Jewish community. The community enjoyed a substantial degree of autonomy. It had its own internal governing bodies, saw to the social and educational needs of its members, maintained a *bet din* possessing jurisdiction in the areas of civil, administrative, and ritual law, and to some extent also criminal jurisdiction. It also imposed and collected taxes, both to satisfy the fiscal demands of the ruling power and to finance communal services. The legal order governing the fulfillment of these manifold tasks was in large measure derived through the enactment of *takkanot* by the community. To ensure that the communal enactments be capable of fulfilling their envisaged objectives, the halakhic scholars saw the need to found these *takkanot* on principles belonging to the sphere of the public law and, from the aspect of their legal validity, to free them from the requirements and restrictions found in the private law. In consequence the scholars evolved basic principles in the area of Jewish public law constituting an impressive part of their wide legal creativity in this field, against the background of the social and economic realities of Jewish autonomy (see *Introduction;* Public Authority and Administrative Law; *Takkanot;* Taxation; *Hekdesh*).

Source of Authority. The earliest manifestations of non-halakhic legislative authority are to be found in the powers vested in the king (see Introduction) and in the already mentioned *benei ha-ir.* The authority of the community to make enactments was substantiated by the scholars thus: "In respect of each and every public the position is that the individuals are subject to the majority, and according to the latter they must conduct themselves in all their affairs; and they [i.e., the majority] stand in the same relationship to the people of their town as the people of Israel to the great *bet din* or the king" (Resp. Rashba, vol. 3, no. 411; also vol. 1, no. 729; vol. 5, no. 126, et al.). It was held that just as the court is competent to enact *takkanot* in the area of civil and criminal law, even though their content contradict a particular rule of the *halakhah,* so the community too is competent to make enactments in these areas, even though contrary to existing law (Resp. R. Gershom Me'or ha-Golah, ed. Eidelberg, no. 67; Responsum of Joseph Tov Elem quoted in Resp. Maharam of Rothenburg, ed. Lemberg, no. 423; idem, ed. Berlin, no. 220, p. 37; Resp. Rashba, vol. 4, no. 311; Resp. Rosh, 101:1; Resp. *Yakhin u-Vo'az,* pt. 2, no. 20). Sometimes the scholars are found to have employed the expression *hefker ẓibbur hefker,* as an alternative parallel to the rule of *hefker bet din hefker,* in terms whereof legislative authority is conferred on the courts and halakhic scholars (see *Takkanot;*[1] Resp. Rashba, vol. 4, no. 142; Resp. Ribash, no. 399). This parallel between the public and the court was not, however, meant to have application to legislative authority in matters of ritual prohibitions and permissions. In this area the community has no authority to enact a *takkanah* contradicting the *halakhah* (Resp. Rashba, vol. 3, no. 411; *Tashbeẓ,* 2:132 and 239). Here the community was likened to the individual. Just as the individual may contract out of the law of the Torah in matters of the civil law *(mamon)* but not in those of ritual prohibition (see Contract[2]), so the community cannot make an enactment which is contrary to the law of the Torah on a matter of ritual prohibition, legislative authority on matters of the latter kind being entrusted to the halakhic scholars alone (Resp. Ribash, no. 305).

Majority and Minority. From 11th-century responsa it may be gathered that at that time communal enactments were passed by the majority of the community, thereupon binding also the minority opposed to their passage (Resp. Rif, ed. Leiter, no. 13; idem, ed. Biadnowitz, no. 85; Responsum of Joseph Tov Elem, quoted in Resp. Maharam of Rothenburg, ed. Lemberg, no. 423). In the 12th century Rabbenu Tam held that the majority was not empowered to impose a *takkanah* on the minority opposed thereto and only after the latter's acceptance of it – expressly or by implication – could the majority compel the individual by fine and punishment to compliance therewith (*Mordekhai,* BK no. 179 and BB no. 480; Resp. Maharam of Rothenburg, ed. Cremona, no. 230; *Teshuvot Maimuniyyot,* Shofetim, no. 10). This view was not accepted by the majority of the scholars (Resp. Ḥayyim Or Zaru'a, no. 222; *Mordekhai,* BB no. 482; Resp. Rashba, vol. 2, no. 279; vol. 5, nos. 270, 242; Resp. Re'em, no. 57). Some of the scholars distinguished between *takkanot* of the community enacted by majority opinion and the *takkanot* of professional associations, for which the consent of all members was required. This distinction was explained on the ground that the latter associations involved only a restricted public not having the responsibility of a community, and because of the serious likelihood that the professional interests of the minority might be prejudiced by the majority (Nov. Ramban, BB 9a; *Beit Yosef,* Tur ḤM 231:30; Sh. Ar., ḤM 231:28; *Leḥem Rav,* no. 216). The doctrine that the majority prevails derives from the exegesis of the words *aḥarei rabbim lehattot* ("to follow a multitude") in Exodus 23:2 (see Majority Rule). In talmudic *halakhah* the above passage is interpreted in relation both to a majority judgment of the court (Sanh. 2a–3b) and to a majority as a matter of legal presumption (Ḥul. 11a). From neither case can it be deduced that the majority of the public may impose its enactment on the opposing minority. The scholars did, however, conclude that "in respect of a matter concerning the public the Torah enjoined to follow a multitude and in any matter assented to by the public the majority is followed and the individuals must uphold all that is assented to by the majority" (Resp. Rosh, 6:5). This wide interpretation was held to be a matter of practical necessity "because if it were not so and the minority had the power to set aside the assent of the majority, the community would never agree on anything . . . for

1. page 77; 2. page 251.

when would the community ever be in unanimous agreement?" (Resp. Rosh, 6:5, 7; see also *Kol Bo,* no. 142). It was similarly decided by a majority of the scholars that a *takkanah* enacted by majority opinion also binds the minority, even though it has not participated in the enactment of the *takkanah,* since those absent at the time thereof are deemed to have implicitly consented to it and because such is the accepted custom (Resp. *Mabit* 1:264; *Mishpat Shalom,* no. 231, letter *Vav* and references there quoted). Here again the explanation was given that "they must perforce bow to the majority and bear the burden of its enactment, for otherwise no room would be left for applying the rule, to follow a multitude, if those who dissent were to absent themselves [at the time of enactment of the *takkanah*] . . . a possibility that reason rejects" (Resp. Abraham Alegre, ḤM no. 5; see also Resp. Ribash, no. 249; Resp. Ḥatam Sofer, ḤM no. 116).

The Role of the Communal Representatives. The Jewish community was headed by its duly appointed or elected representatives, called by various names such as *tovei ha-ir* (lit. "good citizens"), *parnasim,* and so on, and sometimes also *shivah tovei ha-ir* (lit. "seven good citizens") – a concept already known in talmudic times (Meg. 26a; see also Jos., Ant., 4:214) – although their number varied from time to time. The *tovei ha-ir* were required to be " . . . persons chosen not on account of wisdom, wealth or honor, but simply . . . persons sent by the public to be in charge of public matters" (Resp. Rashba, vol. 1, no. 617; see also Public Authority; Taxation). Some scholars held it necessary that the enactment of *takkanot* by the *tovei ha-ir* take place in the presence of the public as the only means of ensuring their enactment with the consent of a majority of the local public (*Mordekhai,* BB no. 480). However, the majority of the scholars took the view that public representatives chosen to be in charge of all public matters are deemed to represent a majority of the public, "by virtue of being sent by the majority of the public which has elected them," and therefore may enact *takkanot* in the public absence (Rashba, loc. cit.; Resp. *Mabit,* 1:84); but representatives chosen for limited purposes only cannot always be said to represent the majority and their enactments must be made in the public presence.

Scope of the Takkanot. A problem facing the halakhic scholars was how to invest the communal enactments with the legal efficacy to bind also the classes of persons incapacitated by the rules of the private law from being party to a legal obligation – such as minors and those yet to be born – efficacy without which the *takkanot* would have little practical value. The solution was found through an assimilation of the *takkanot* to the case of customs on various matters instituted by past generations (e.g., concerning festivals, fasts, etc.) – te observance whereof is enjoined also on sons, i.e., succeeding generations (Pes. 50b) since "the fathers are the source of their children" (Resp. Rashba, vol. 3, no. 411; Resp. Ribash, no. 399). The matter was also substantiated with the aid of other analogies from the laws of the oath, and so on (Rashba and Ribash, loc. cit.; see also Resp. Maharam Alashkar, no. 49; *Tashbez* 2:132). At the root of these analogies lay the conviction that the orderly operation of communal enactments demanded their general applicability and continuity, "for if not so . . . it would become necessary to renew them daily since every day there are minors who reach their majority, and that is an unacceptable matter" (Ribash, loc. cit.). So too it was held that those taking up residence in a particular community are subject to all its existing communal enactments, since "they are deemed to have expressly taken upon themselves all the enactments of that town . . . when coming to live there, hence they are the same as the other townspeople and embraced by their *takkanot*" (Ribash, loc. cit.). The stated three factors – the rule that in enacting a *takkanah* the majority also binds the minority opposed thereto, investment of the communal representatives with legislative authority, and investment of the communal enactments with validity even in relation to persons lacking in legal capacity – jointly operated to confer fully on the communal enactments the standing of norms of the public law just as legislation is part of the public law in other legal systems. Consequently the validity of the communal enactments was not measured by the standards and requirements applying to a matter of the private law.

Halakhah and the Takkanot ha-Kahal. The communal enactments share the general objective of all other *takkanot* – to add a directive in answer to a problem which finds no solution in the *halakhah,* or to sanction a departure from the *halakhah* when dictated by the needs of the hour (see *Takkanot*). The halakhic scholars endowed communal enactments with full legal sanction, whether these added to existing *halakhah* or provided contrary thereto. Reference to the halakhic sources, particularly the responsa literature, will reveal a most extensive range of directives on matters of the civil as well as criminal law, laid down in communal enactment, and accepted even when contrary to the *halakhah* on such matters. The following are a few examples (others are mentioned above, s.v. under the heading Source of Authority).

In matters affecting communal property, or other public matters, such as taxation, charitable endowment, and so on, communal enactments made provision, contrary to talmudic *halakhah,* for admitting also the testimony of witnesses residing within the community concerned. This applied notwithstanding the fact of their own pecuniary interest in the matter since, for instance, the tax exemption of one member of the community served to increase the burden on his fellows, and despite the frequent fact of their kinship with the litigants, on account of communal intermarriage (Resp. Rashba, vol. 5, nos. 184 and 286; vol. 6, no. 7; Resp. Rosh, 5:4). This legal situation was accepted as *halakhah* in the codes (Sh. Ar., ḤM 7:12, 37:22; see also Taxation).

In different communities *takkanot* were enacted whereby the signature of the town scribe on various kinds of deeds was granted the same efficacy as the signature of two competent witnesses. Such enactments were designed to prevent a number of possible complications, among others the impossibility of verifying deeds on account of the death, or absence abroad, of the witnesses thereto. Deeds signed by the town scribe were held fully valid, since "the public is entitled to assent [i.e., enact] in any wise on a matter pertaining to the civil law *[mamon]*, and it is accepted and valid as if it were an absolute law, for the duly given assent of the public on a matter renders it law" (*Sefer Teshuvot ha-Rashba ha-Meyuḥasot le-ha-Ramban,* no. 65; Resp. Rashba, vol. 3, no. 438). The possibility of illiteracy on the part of a witness was the background to communal enactments which laid down that the town scribe could sign in the name of a witness, on the latter's instructions (Resp. Rashba, vol. 2, no. 111; see also vol. 4, no. 199).

Another communal enactment made provision for the court to proclaim a specified period within which any interested party could submit his claims in respect of a particular asset put up for sale, failing which he would forfeit his rights to such property. This *takkanah* was required to ensure the more efficient transaction of business. Although amounting to a departure from the law – since no support is found in the *halakhah* for the proposition that a person should forfeit his rights on account of failure to lodge his claims thereto within a specified period (see Limitation of Actions) – it was nevertheless held valid because "an enactment of the community sets aside the *halakhah,* for the townspeople are entitled to stipulate among themselves as they please" (Resp. Rashba, vol. 4, no. 260). Many examples of communal enactments of this kind are to be found in the area of tax law (see Taxation), and the laws concerning the legal standing of a public authority and its relationships with its employees and the community in general (see Public Authority). They are also found in the laws pertaining to the administration of consecrated and other public property (see *Hekdesh*). These legal branches developed particularly from the tenth century onward in the different Jewish centers, and communal enactments provided the answer to many of the legal problems arising in connection therewith.

Takkanot ha-Kahal and Halakhic Authority. That communal enactments whose contents contradicted the *halakhah* could be laid down with a large measure of independence, as already described, held out the possibility that these enactments might become divorced from the living body of the *halakhah*. On the surface, there existed the likelihood that the legal directives originating from communal enactments might, if uncontrolled, evolve into a legal system parallel to the halakhic legal system, leading inevitably to the exclusion of the former directives from the regular framework of the halakhic system. This threat was countered through the development in Jewish law of a number of safeguards serving to link the communal enactments to halakhic authority. These safeguards were not calculated to prejudice the community's legislative independence as regards the possibility that its enactments might conflict with one or other rule of the *halakhah*, yet they served to subjugate such enactments to the spirit and objective of the overall halakhic system. There were three such safeguards, each of which is outlined below, one functioning prior to the enactment of a *takkanah* and the other two thereafter.

Approval by "a Distinguished Person." The first safeguard, accepted by the majority of the halakhic scholars, was the need for a *takkanah* to be approved – prior to its enactment – by "a distinguished person" *(adam ḥashuv)* residing within the community concerned. The need for such approval was designed to ensure the halakhic scholars some measure of control, even if qualified, over the communal enactments (see below). Support for the need for a distinguished person's approval was found in the talmudic law pertaining to the enactment of a *takkanah* by a professional association. The butchers of a certain town made a *takkanah* to regulate their workdays in a particular manner, enforceable by imposition of a fine in the form of tearing the hide of the animal slaughtered by the offending butcher. In a case where this punishment was carried out, the offending butcher instituted an action against his fellows to recover compensation for the damages resulting therefrom. His claim was upheld by Rava on the ground that there was present a distinguished person in that town but no approval of the regulation had been obtained from him, and it was therefore invalid (BB 9a). Some of the scholars held the need for the aforesaid approval, apparently innovated by the *amoraim*, to exist only with reference to a *takkanah* enacted by a restricted section of the public, such as a professional association, this for the reason of preventing the adoption of resolutions calculated to cause loss to the consumer public, and so on (Nov. Ramban, BB 9a; Nov. Ran, BB loc. cit., Resp. Ribash, no. 399; Resp. Maharam Alashkar, no. 49). However, the majority of the scholars took the view that the stated approval must be also obtained in respect of communal enactments, since the fact of such approval would serve to stress the link between the *takkanah* and halakhic authority, and the *halakhah* was decided accordingly (Resp. Rashba, vol. 1, no. 1206; vol. 4, no. 185; *Piskei ha-Rosh*, BB 1:33; Sh. Ar., ḤM 231:28 – Rema, *Sma* and *Siftei Kohen*, ad loc.). Presumably this safeguard was actually practised in the different Jewish communities, and sometimes a special directive on the matter is to be found in the body of a *takkanot* collection (see, e.g., J. Halpern (ed.), *Takkanot Medinat Mehrin*, nos. 176, 286, 335). There are, however, also references to the fact that certain communities (see, e.g., Resp. Maharalbaḥ, no. 99), and even a representative body such as the Council of Four Lands (see Resp. Baḥ Ḥadashot, no. 43), did not consistently observe the need to obtain the approval of a distinguished person to their *takkanot*. The halakhic scholars were at pains to convince the communal leaders of this need (see Resp. Maharalbaḥ, no. 99 and Resp. Baḥ Ḥadashot, no. 43). Yet at the commencement of the 19th century it was still held by Moses Sofer that the stated approval was a requirement not of the strict law but of the custom followed by the communities (Resp. Ḥatam Sofer, ḤM 116).

Different opinions were expressed as regards the attributes of "a distinguished person" from whom approval of a *takkanah* must be obtained. One opinion held that he may be either a *talmid ḥakham* ("scholar") or a *parnas* appointed by the community, and the presence of either in the town serves to withhold validity from a *takkanah* until his approval thereof can be obtained (Resp. Rashba, vol. 4, no. 185, et al.). According to another opinion, "a distinguished person" is "a *talmid ḥakham* who is also in charge of the public" (opinion of Ibn Migash, quoted in *Shitah Mekubbeẓet*, BB 9a and in Resp. Rashba, vol. 5, no. 125) – i.e., a person who combined in himself the qualities both of being a learned scholar and of having been accepted as a leader of the public. This opinion was accepted by a majority of the halakhic scholars who interpreted "a distinguished person" thus: "a distinguished scholar able to order the affairs of the community concerned and help its inhabitants to prosper in their ways" (Yad, Mekhirah 14:11); "a learned scholar and leader" responsible for public affairs (*Piskei ha-Rosh*, BB 1:33; Tur ḤM 231:30; Sh. Ar., ḤM 231:28). Thus if locally there be present no person blessed with both these qualities, then the communal enactment should be fully valid even without the approval of a distinguished person (*Yad Ramah*, BB 9b, no. 103; *Maggid Mishneh*, Mekhirah 14:11).

Principles of Justice and Equity. The decisive factor in the integration of communal enactments within the overall framework of Jewish law has been the supervisory authority exercised by the halakhic scholars so as to ensure that the enactments, even when contradicting the contents of a specific halakhic directive, should not depart from the general principles of justice and equity underlying the entire Jewish legal system. These substantive principles served as the common basis of the *halakhah* and of the communal enactments, the zealous preservation of these principles ensuring that the latter become an integral part of the overall Jewish legal system.

These principles find expression in various ways. Thus, for instance, Solomon b. Abraham Adret stated with reference to a particular communal enactment, "if it is a matter which makes no fence to the law and brings no real good, then even if it was instituted by the representatives and leaders of the public – the public will not need to act in accordance with their wishes" (Resp. vol. 7, no. 108; also vol. 5, no. 287 and vol. 7, no. 340). In another case the communal leaders enacted a *takkanah* serving to enjoin a member of the community from obtaining the ruling power's permission to continue his duties of supervising against the commission of various offenses; a sector of the public objected to the *takkanah* as opening the door to moral laxity on the part of the public. In his responsum on the matter, Adret held that the *takkanah* would have been valid if it had made provision for the position itself to remain but prescribed its entrustment to someone else; however, since the *takkanah* purported to abolish entirely a position of such vital nature, it had to be regarded as of no effect; "and even if the *takkanah* was enacted by the people responsible for most of the needs of the public, yet the fact is that they have to make enactments which enable the community to uphold and not breach the law, and they may not breach the fences of the Torah" (Resp., vol. 2, no. 279). Just as it is forbidden that a *takkanah* should contain anything tending to encourage moral laxity on the part of the public, so it is forbidden that a *takkanah* should be unduly onerous – even though it serves a laudable purpose and remedies a particular situation; hence, according to Adret, in the same way as there had been laid down the principle that a *takkanah* of the halakhic scholars must not be imposed on the public unless the majority is able to abide thereby (Av. Zar. 36a; see *Takkanot*[1]), so too the community may not enact a *takkanah* by which the majority of its members is unable to abide (loc. cit.; also vol. 7, no. 108).

A material principle guarded by the halakhic scholars with the utmost care was that ensuring the right of the minority in general, and of the individual in particular, not to be prejudiced by the majority in an arbitrary manner and without justifiable cause. In several centers it happened that the community sought to enact a *takkanah* purporting to impose tax on a local resident in respect of his property situated elsewhere, thereby rendering him liable for double taxation since he was also liable for tax at the place of situation of his property. In this regard it was held by Adret that it was not within the power of the community to make an enactment – notwithstanding the consent thereto of the majority – imposing an obligation that involved a "robbing" *(gezel)* of the individual, which would be the inevitable but unacceptable result of the individual having to pay tax twice on the same property (Resp., vol. 1, no. 788; vol. 5, no. 178; Resp. Maharam of Rothenburg, ed. Prague, no. 106; see in detail under Taxation[2]). A like conclusion was stated by Isserles in unambiguous manner: "It is an accepted matter that the *tovei ha-ir* are not authorized to deal high-handedly with the individuals, nor may the majority forcefully dispossess [lit. "rob"] the individual . . . since the townspeople have no power to make enactments except as conferred on them by law; but to do as they please, that is something that never was nor ever will be!" (Resp. Rema, no. 73). There was also applied to communal enactments the principle that they must apply equally to all and not single out particular persons (*Sha'arei Ẓedek* pt. 4 sec. 4 no. 16). The rule was formulated that a *takkanah* is valid when two conditions are fulfilled: it must be "a *takkanah* [i.e., to mend matters] for the public, and it must apply equally to all" (Nov. Ritba, Av. Zar. 36b; cf. the principle of equality before the law in relation to the doctrine of *dina de-malkhuta dina;* see Introduction).

The requirement that legislation accord with the principles of justice and equity led to the observance of the further rule that the provisions of communal enactments should only be made to take effect from the time of their enactment onward, and not retroactively to any earlier period. There was frequent application of this rule in relation to tax laws (see, e.g., Resp. Ribash, no. 477; see also Taxation), and also in other legal fields (see, e.g., *Zikhron Yehudah,* no. 78).

Interpretation of Takkanot ha-Kahal. The third factor which safeguarded the integration of communal enactments into the overall Jewish legal system was the fact that the authoritative interpretation of these enactments was usually entrusted to the same body or persons who interpreted the rules of the *halakhah* in general, namely the competent halakhic scholars. In their interpretative activities the latter relied on the different Jewish law rules of interpretation, and examined the content and formulation of a *takkanah* before them by analogy to the talmudic *halakhah* and codificatory literature. In consequence the integration of the communal enactments into Jewish law was affected not only as regards subject matter but also from the literary aspect, as expressed in the responsa literature. For particulars, see Interpretation.[3]

Takkanot ha-Kahal and the Jewish Legal System. The phenomenon of a community enacting a *takkanah* which remained subject to halakhic scrutiny and became integrated with the *halakhah,* even though it did not always accord with one or another rule of the *halakhah* itself, is understandable and in keeping with the image of Jewish society until the coming of the Emancipation at the end of the 18th century. Both the community and the bearers of the *halakhah* acknowledged the existence of a single ultimate and guiding value – the authority of the Torah and the *halakhah.* The communal leaders never regarded their enactments as a means of undermining or evading in any way the sanctity of the *halakhah.* On the contrary, they saw their enactment as a special means – adapted to the needs of their time and place – toward modeling public and private life in their community on the principles, objectives, and spirit of Jewish law. These enactments not only constituted a means of ordering – within the wider framework of the *halakhah* – special legal problems arising from particular social and economic trends in the different periods and centers of the Jewish dispersion. They also served toward the evolution of basic principles pertaining to the modes of legislation by a Jewish public in accordance with Jewish law, and toward the development and crystallization of principles of justice and equity, of safeguarding minority rights, and equality before the law, as well as other principles to which the communal enactments were required to conform. For further general details see *Takkanot.* For details of various *takkanot* arranged according to centers and periods see Elon, *Ha-Mishpat Ha-Ivri* II, 631–712.

Bibliography: Baron, Community; L.J. Rabbinowitz, *The Ḥerem Hayyishub* (1945); A. Karlin, in: *Ha-Torah ve-ha-Medinah,* 1 (1949), 58–66; B. Lipkin, *ibid.,* 2 (1950), 41–54; idem, in: *Sinai* 25 (1949), 233–53; J. Baer, in: *Zion,* 15 (1949/50), 1–41; ET, 3 (1951), 180, 376–8; J.A. Agus, in: JQR, 43 (1952/53), 153–76; S. Albeck, in: *Zion,* 19 (1953/54), 128–36; 25 (1959/60), 85–121; A.H. Freimann, in: *Yavneh,* 2 (1947/48), 1–6; M. Elon, in: *Meḥkarei Mishpat le-Zekher Avraham Rosenthal* (1964), 1–54; idem, Mafte'aḥ, 251–67, 413–24; idem, *Ha-Mishpat Ha-Ivri* (1973), II, 367–390, 547–712, III, 1278ff. See also bibliography of *Takkanot.*

Menachem Elon

TAXATION. This article is arranged according to the following outline:

1. page 80; 2. page 676; 3. page 71.

Ethics of Tax Payment
Halakhic Compilations of Tax Law
In the State of Israel

The Concept. Tax is a compulsory payment, in currency or in specie, exacted by a public authority, for the purpose of satisfying the latter's own needs or those of the public, or part of the public. In certain periods tax or tribute involved not only a payment but also personal service, such as labor.

The Biblical Period. Although no detailed description has come down of the taxation system practiced during this period, various particulars of it can be gathered from a number of scriptural references to the subject. Thus the prerogatives enumerated in I Samuel 8:11–17 give an indication of the servitudes, levies, and obligations which the king was entitled to impose on the population, including the following: a tenth of the yield of the field and of the vineyard and the flock, a levy on the vineyard and the olive grove, and compulsory personal service. The biblical description reflects the fiscal system in operation in the Canaanite city kingdoms. The First Book of Kings (4:7–15) tells of King Solomon's division of the kingdom into 12 administrative units, each under the charge of an officer responsible for providing the king and his household with victuals for one month in the year.

Terminology. Matters of taxation are mentioned in the Bible under a variety of terms, a number of which continued to be in use in later times. One of these, *mekhes* (Num. 31:28, 37–41), is mentioned in connection with the tribute paid to the priests from the spoil of the war with the Midianites. The like term in Akkadian, *miksu,* described both a tribute from the yield of the fields and a toll levied on travelers and their goods (EM, 4 (1962), 964f.), and in the latter sense the term *mekhes* was employed by the sages of the Talmud (see, e.g., Kil. 9:2; Shab. 8:2, Sem. 2:9) and is still in use in modern Hebrew in the State of Israel. It is clear that a toll of this kind was levied by the kings of Israel on goods imported from abroad or those in transit (cf. I Kings 10:15). In the Bible the term *mas* (mod. Heb. for "tax") occurs in the sense of compulsory labor in the king's service (Ex. 1:11; II Sam. 20:24; I Kings 4:6 and 5:27), and is synonymous with the term *mas oved* (JPS, "taskwork"). The main taxes imposed for the benefit of the Persian kingdom were the *mindeh, belo,* and *halakh,* which are mentioned in the letter of the Persian king to the scribe Ezra, exempting all the priests, levites, and other servants of the "house of God" from their payment (Ezra 7:24). The *mindeh* was a general tax payable in money, the *belo* a tax in specie, and the *halakh* apparently a tax on land. Besides the regular taxes, the king apparently from time to time imposed taxes on the people for special purposes, such as those exacted by Menahem and Jehoiakim for payment to the conquerors (II Kings 15:19–20 and 23:35); the former a fixed sum and the latter on a proportional basis.

Some of the tax alleviations mentioned in the Bible include exemptions given to "the father's house" in reward for a person's act of special bravery (I. Sam. 17:25), the general release granted in celebration of a special occasion – as in the case of Queen Esther's coronation (Esth. 2:18) – and the exemption given to the servants of the Temple. At times the tax burden weighed heavily on the people and the oppressive fiscal policy followed in the time of King Solomon was a cause of the rebellion against his son Rehoboam (I Kings 12) and led to the killing of Adoram, the officer in charge of the levy. In a sense the concept of tax, as an imposed duty to contribute toward the needs of an individual, or of the public, is reflected also in the laws relating to matters of *terumah* ("heave offering"); *ma'aser* ("tithe"); *leket, shikhḥah,* and *pe'ah* ("gleanings," "the forgotten sheaf," and "the corner of the fields," respectively); *ẓedakah* ("charity"), the half-and third-*shekel; shemittah* ("the year of the release"); and *yovel* ("Jubilee").

The Talmudic Period. The Talmud discusses both those taxes imposed by the Jewish local authorities on the Jewish town residents and those imposed by the central governmental authority on the Jewish public. The material on the laws of taxation during this period is scant, but the laws discussed nevertheless formed the basis of a number of post-talmudic tax rules.

Jewish Municipal Taxes. "The resident of a town may be compelled to contribute to the building of a [town] wall, doors, and a crossbar" (BB 1:5), and to the building of a prayer house, to the purchase of the Scrolls of the Law and of the Prophets (Tosef., BM 11:23), and to the hire of the town guards (BB 8a). Similarly, he may be compelled to contribute toward the cost of the town's water supply and drainage system, an expense which must also be borne by a person who owns a dwelling in the town even though he is not resident there (Tosef., BM 11:17 according to the Vienna MS; see also Yad, Shekhenim 6:3; Resp. Maharam of Rothenburg quoted in *Mordekhai,* BB 475; Sh. Ar., ḤM 163:2). In the same way the townsmen have to contribute toward the cost of providing the poor with food and clothing and toward the communal charity box and *ma'ot ḥittin* (money for the poor to buy wheat on Passover; BB *ibid.;* TJ, BB 1:4, 12d). For the purpose of liability for some of these taxes – namely for repair of the wall or *ma'ot ḥittin* – a person is regarded in the Talmud (TJ and TB, *ibid.*) as a resident if he has lived in a town for 12 months; if he has bought a dwelling there he immediately becomes liable; as regards certain contributions, e.g., to the charity box, he becomes liable upon shorter periods of residence (*ibid.,* see also Domicile; with regard to *ma'ot ḥittin* on Passover, see further *Or Zaru'a,* Hilkhot Pesaḥim, no. 255).

The *amoraim* of Ereẓ Israel discussed the principle of yardsticks for determining the rate of such taxes, deliberating whether a tax should be levied as a poll tax (according to the number of persons in the family), or according to financial means, or "according to the proximity of the dwelling" (that is according to the measure of benefit the taxpayer derived from his relative proximity to the wall), the first method being rejected in favor of one of the other two (BB 7b). The majority of the *posekim* held that these two yardsticks should be combined in such a manner that the rate of contribution would first be apportioned according to the financial means of each resident and then according to the measure of benefit derived from his relative proximity to the wall, so that "a poor man nearer the wall shall pay more than one further away; a rich man nearer the wall shall pay more than one further away, but a rich man further from the wall shall pay more than a poor man nearer the wall" (Tos. to BB 7b; Tur and Sh. Ar., ḤM 163:3; for a different opinion, see Yad, Shekhenim 6:4 and R. Hananel, BB *ibid.*). A similar problem is discussed in the Talmud in connection with a caravan in the wilderness threatened by a band of robbers and it is stated that: "the contribution to be paid by each [for buying them off] shall be apportioned in accordance with the amount of money which each has and not in accordance with the number of persons there"; but if they hire a guide to go in front of them, the calculation will have to be made "also according to the number of souls" in the caravan since a misstep could involve danger to life (Tosef., BM 7:13; BK 116b; in the TJ, BM 6:4, 11a the word "also" is omitted before the words "according to the number of souls"); however all this only applies if the manner of apportionment of the contribution is not determined by local custom, since this always prevails (BK 116b; see also Tosef., BK, and TJ, loc. cit.).

Taxes of the Central Government. The tannaitic and amoraic sources mention various kinds of taxes imposed by the general government. Some of those imposed by the Roman authorities in Ereẓ Israel included the *tributum soli,* a land tax, the *tributum capitis* or poll tax, *arnona,* and a customs toll on the transit of goods, as well as a toll on highways and bridges (see Alon, bibl.). Among the taxes levied by the Persian authorities were the *taska,* a land tax, and the *karga,* a poll tax (see J. Newman, bibl.).

The Persian Government in Babylonia. The Babylonian halakhic scholars upheld the various taxes imposed by the governmental authorities, in reliance on the rule of *dina de-malkhuta dina* ("the law of the land is law," BB 55a, et al.), even giving effect to certain acts which were valid under general law but not in Jewish law. Thus under Persian law a person's land became charged in the king's favor for payment of the *taska* and if it was not paid the land could be sold by the royal officials to anyone paying the tax in the landowner's stead. The *amora* Samuel upheld the validity of such a sale on the basis of the above-mentioned rule (BB 55a; see also BM 73b). Similarly upheld was the rule of Persian law that not only the king could enslave a person who failed to pay the *karga* but anyone else paying the tax in the debtor's stead (Yev. 46a; BM 73b) – except that in Jewish law "he shall not treat him as a slave" (Yad, Gezelah, 5:16; Sh. Ar., YD 267:16).

The Roman Government in Ereẓ Israel. The scholars of Ereẓ Israel, however, looked upon the Romans as foreign conquerors whose rule should be rebelled against and whose taxes were an instrument of robbery and extortion leveled against the Jews. Hence tax evasion was customary in Ereẓ Israel (Ned. 3:4; BB 127b, R. Johanan) and there the *tannaim* discussed the question of whether or not it was permissible to avoid paying customs in certain circumstances (BK 113a). A certain change of attitude is manifest at the time of R. Judah na-Nasi, who, like some other men, instructed his sons not to elude customs (lest they be detected and the authorities confiscate everything they had; Pes. 112b; but cf. TJ, Ket. 12:3, 34d). Regarded in a similarly unfavorable light were the *gabba'im* and *mokhesim* – Jewish officials and publicans who collected taxes and imposts on behalf of the Roman authorities – who were looked upon as robbers and disqualified from being witnesses or judges (Sanh. 25b), whose money could not be taken for charitable purposes (BK 10:1), and who were not acceptable as *ḥaverim* (Tosef., Dem. 3:4; TJ, Dem. 2:3, 23a). At a later time the opposition to Roman rule became less intense and the *halakhot* permitting customs evasion came to be interpreted as applying to customs dues imposed without any specified limit or those imposed without the authority of the ruling power (but by the customs collector himself) – in which case it was held that the rule of *dina de-malkhuta dina* did not apply (BK 113a; Ned. 28a). Customs evasion eventually became strictly prohibited: "a person who evades customs is as one who has shed blood – and not only shed blood, but also worshiped idols, committed acts of unchastity, and profaned the Sabbath" (Sem. 2:9). Similarly, it was laid down in the codes: "If the king fixes a tax of, say, a third or a quarter or another fixed measure and appoints to collect it on his behalf an Israelite known to be a trustworthy person who would not add to what was ordered by the king, this collector is not presumed to be a robber, for the king's decree has the force of law. Moreover, one who avoids paying such a tax is a transgressor, for he steals the king's property, whether the king be a gentile or an Israelite" (Yad, Gezelah, 5:11; cf. Sanh. 25b).

Tax Immunity. Just as the Persian rulers exempted priests, levites, and other servants of the Temple from the payment of taxes, so the sages of the Talmud laid down that *talmidei ḥakhamim* should be exempted from contributing toward the upkeep of the town guard – for the reason that they did not need any protection since the Torah was their guard (Ned. 62b; BB 7b, ff.). However, some of the sages did not exempt rabbinical scholars from such imposts (R. Judah ha-Nasi and R. Naḥman b. Ḥisda, BB *ibid.*) and the fact that there were scholars who paid these is confirmed in several talmudic sources (see e.g., Yev. 17a; Sanh. 27a/b; Yoma 77a – expunged by the censorship and quoted in *Ein Ya'akov* and *Dikdukei Soferim,* Yoma 77a). Exemption of scholars from tax payments was known in other contemporary legal systems (see S. Lieberman, in: JQR, 36 (1945/46), 360–4) and was also a practice in later times (see below). It was laid down that rabbinical scholars must pay taxes levied for the upkeep of roads and streets (BB 8a; Yad, Shekhenim, 6:6; Sh. Ar., YD 243:2, and ḤM 163:4). Orphans (whose liabilities are lightened in a number of respects in Jewish law) must contribute taxes for the purposes of the town guard, the digging of a well, the supply of water to the town and fields, and toward all other matters from which they derive benefit; if the expenditure fails to bring about the desired result, the orphans will be entitled to a refund of whatever they paid, since in the absence of a benefit such payment amounts to a waiver of their money, an act beyond their legal capacity (BB loc. cit. and Rashi thereto; Yad, and Sh. Ar., loc. cit.). In the case of an unemployed person who has no income (a *pardakht*) the town residents may approach the government tax collector to release him from his tax contribution; sometimes he is held liable like all other residents and sometimes released (BB 55a; see also Rashbam, Tos., *Bet ha-Beḥirah* and *Shitah Mekkubbeẓet* thereto; Kohut, Arukh, s.v. "אנדיסק" and supplement thereto s.v. "פרדכש"; M. Beer, bibl., pp. 250f.).

The Post-Talmudic Period in General. The main development of Jewish tax law came in the post-talmudic period, both as regards the determination of general principles and detailed rules and as regards the volume and compass of the material. At the same time this development was an important factor in the evolution of Jewish public law and a number of basic principles in this field evolved from the discussions on the laws of taxation. Therefore a comprehensive discussion of the laws of taxation offers some insight into the evolution of Jewish public and administrative law (see also Public Authority).

In the post-talmudic period the distinction between Jewish municipal taxes and those imposed by the government was maintained as the basis for discussion of the laws of taxation, and the great development in this branch of the law is mainly to be ascribed to two historical factors affecting the Jewish people, one internal, the other external. From the close of the geonic period onward, Jewish autonomy found its main expression in the various Jewish communal organizations or in a roof organization embracing a number of communities. Starting from this time Jewish life was molded by the new historical reality that hegemony was no longer exercised over the whole Jewish dispersion by a single center – as previously in Ereẓ Israel and Babylonia – and different centers, functioning alongside or in succession to one another, came into existence in Spain, Germany, North Africa, the Balkan countries, Poland, Western Europe, and so on. The result was the strengthening of the individual community and the development of its organizations, and this led in turn to great development in the fields of administrative law and communal enactment (see *Takkanot ha-Kahal*), and to the creation of a proliferous collection of decisions concerning relations between the citizen and the public. The community provided various social services and maintained religious, educational, and judicial institutions, as well as its own administrative and governing bodies, all of which had to be financed through various methods of taxation.

The decisive external factor was that the central governments of the various countries of Jewish settlement in the Middle Ages imposed heavy taxes on the Jews (as "toleration money") in return for their right to live in these countries, and the halakhic scholars stressed their factual purpose so far as the Jewish community was concerned: "the various taxes are for the purposes of protection and they guard us amid the nations; for what reason would the nations have to protect us and to settle us in their midst if not for the benefit they derive by exacting taxes and imposts from the Jews?" (Resp. Ran, no. 2; *Piskei ha-Rosh,* BB 1:29). These taxes were not imposed on the individual directly, but collectively on all the communities in a particular area or on a specific community, and the authorities held the communal leaders responsible for payment of the overall amount. Thus "in all matters of taxation each community has been obliged to make a partnership of its members . . . since the king makes a general demand and not from the individual" (Resp. Rashba, vol. 5, no. 270). Normally the central authority periodically imposed a "fixed tax" of a comparatively reasonable amount. Sometimes however – on account of special circumstances such as war – an "unlimited tax" of a very large sum of money was imposed, and in these cases the scholars laid down different rules from those governing the regular tax (see illustrations below; on the two types of taxes, see, e.g., *Terumat ha-Deshen,* beginning of Resp. no. 341 and conclusion of no. 342). The fact that taxes were collected by the community both for its own purposes and on behalf of the central authority was instrumental in the development of a refined tax law system governing matters such as determination of the rate of contribution to the tax and tax classification, assessment adjudication and collection, and determination of tax alleviations and exemptions, a system which was evolved in close cooperation between the halakhic scholars and communal leaders.

Legal Foundations of the Tax Law System. In part, the tax law of this period was based on the legal principles determined by the scholars in talmudic times, but in the main it was derived from additional legal sources.

Dina de-Malkhuta Dina. This doctrine was relied upon and its application extended to meet the new and changing needs of the time. Thus, for instance, many scholars found it necessary to decide – contrary to the rule in the Talmud that the doctrine of *dina de-malkhuta dina* does not apply to an unlimited tax – that a tax exacted for the waging of war and "other costly needs" should be heeded even if it was an unlimited tax (R. Isaac the Elder, quoted in *Haggahot Mordekhai,* BB no. 659 end, and in *Teshuvot Maimuniyyot,* Gezelah, no. 9). This change resulted from the strong hand displayed by the ruling power, particularly in the case of German Jewry: "even if our taxes at the present time have no fixed rate but are imposed at the will of the ruler, it is necessary that they be paid and whoever fails to do so is liable to suffer punishment of death, plunder, or imprisonment . . . for in these times these are all called taxes" (*Mordekhai,* BK no. 190, in the name of Meir of Rothenburg; see also Resp. Ḥayyim Or Zaru'a, no. 253, and cf. his criticism, no. 110; Resp. Maharil, no. 71; Resp. Maharyu (Jacob Weil), no. 38). In Spain too, in the 14th century, a similar opinion was expressed although in a different context: "all government decrees concerning Jews, even as regards a monetary fine, are a matter of *pikku'aḥ nefesh*" (Resp. Ribash, no. 460). From the legal standpoint this approach was justified by the scholars on the grounds that since it was known that the ruling power behaved in the manner described and that with that knowledge "we establish residence under them and take upon ourselves the hardships and burdens they impose, all of these shall henceforth fall under the rule of *dina de-malkhuta dina*" (*Terumat ha-Deshen,* Resp. no. 341; see also Resp. Maharam Mintz, no. 1; Resp. Maharik, no. 4; for further illustrations see below).

Tax Rules from the Talmudic Period. The principle that the town residents must contribute toward the costs of their security needs, the provision of social and religious services, sanitation, and so on, was applied and extended in post-talmudic times to the payment of various other taxes (Meir of Rothenburg, quoted in *Mordekhai,* BB, 478) and generally to "any matter of the town's needs" (*Mordekhai,* loc. cit.; Resp. Rosh, 6:22) so as to cover the whole spectrum of the community's requirements (Sh. Ar., ḤM 163:1, and see below).

The Community as a Partnership. In addition, the post-talmudic scholars applied to the legal relationship between different members of the community the law of partnership, and by virtue of this deduced a number of conclusions pertaining to the field of tax law. Thus, for instance, they based the legal right to oblige a community member to swear that his declaration of taxable assets was correct (see below) on the rule that one partner may oblige his fellow to swear an oath even in the case of a "doubtful" plea (*ta'anat shema; Terumat ha-Deshen,* Resp. no. 341). The rule that a community member might not secure a personal tax waiver except through the mediation of the community was justified likewise on the principle of partnership law restricting a partner's right to enjoy personally a benefit which should be enjoyed by the whole partnership without the consent of his partners (Resp. Maharam of Rothenburg, ed. Prague, no. 918, 932). Similarly, the scholars followed the rule that partners are jointly liable for the whole of a partnership debt in laying down that all members of the community bore collective responsibility for the whole amount of the tax imposed (Resp. Rosh 5:9; for further illustration see, e.g., *Mordekhai,* Ket. no. 239; Rema, ḤM 163:3, 6 and 176:25; *Noda bi-Yhudah,* Mahadura Tinyana, ḤM no. 40, and see below).

Communal Enactments (Takkanot ha-Kahal) and Custom. The scholars found the methods outlined above insufficient to overcome the wide array of tax law problems with which they and the communal leaders were confronted. Application of the private law rules of partnership offered no comprehensive basis for solving the myriad tax law problems that arose and belonged, by their very nature, to the field of the public law – not only because partnership law offered no analogy for the overwhelming majority of tax law matters but also because a legal arrangement governing relationships between two or three partners was often unsuited to regulating the legal relationships between all the different units comprising the community. They found the way to settling most of the laws of taxation through using the authority vested in the public to make enactments (see *Takkanot ha-Kahal*), and by means of the legal source of custom (see *Minhag*). A certain initial hesitation over the binding nature of a custom when it was contrary to "an established and known *halakhah*" of the Talmud on a matter of tax law (see the statement of R. Baruch of Mainz in the 13th century, quoted in *Mordekhai,* BB no. 477) was overcome, and every rule and usage deriving from communal enactment or custom was given full legal recognition. The fact that these two legal sources were instrumental in the development of most of the post-talmudic tax laws accounts, therefore, for the great diversity found in Jewish tax law, which reflects the *takkanot* and customs of the various Jewish communities.

The existence of this fact was constantly stressed by the halakhic scholars of all communities. Thus Solomon b. Abraham Adret, leader of Spanish Jewry in the 13th century and one of the main formulators of Jewish public law, stated: "Nowhere are the tax laws founded on talmudic sanctity and everywhere there are to be found variations of such laws deriving from local usage and the consent of earlier scholars who 'set the landmarks'; and the town residents are entitled to establish fixed *takkanot* and uphold recognized customs as they please even if they do not accord with the *halakhah,* this being a matter of the civil law. Therefore if in this matter they have a known custom it should be followed, since custom overrides the *halakhah* in matters of this kind" (Resp. Rashba, vol. 4, nos. 260, 177; vol. 3, nos. 398, 436; vol. 5, nos. 180, 363, 270; vol. 1, no. 664, et al.). A similar view was expressed by R. Meir b. Baruch of Rothenburg, a contemporary of Adret and leader of German Jewry: "tax matters are dependent neither on analogy from nor on express talmudic law, but on the custom of the land . . . since tax laws are part of the law of the land . . . and the product of many different customs" (Resp. Maharam of Rothenburg, ed. Prague, nos. 106, 995; see also the statements of R. Avigdor Kohen Ẓedek, quoted in *Mordekhai,* BB, 477). R. Israel Isserlein added the following explicit remarks: "In all matters affecting the public, their custom shall be followed in accordance with the order they set for themselves, as dictated by their needs and the matter under consideration – for if they be required to follow the strict law in every matter, there will always be strife among themselves; furthermore, at the outset they allow each other to waive the strict law and make up their minds to follow the imperatives of their own custom" (*Terumat ha-Deshen,* Resp. no. 342). This idea was restated in a responsum of the 16th-century Greek halakhist, Benjamin Ze'ev (*Binyamin Ze'ev,* 293), who added: "a custom of the town residents overrides [a decision of] a court of talmudic scholars, even though it has relied on Scripture, and not merely the custom of scholars but also the custom of ass drivers is to be relied upon" (see also Resp. Maharashdam, ḤM nos. 369 and 404; *Noda bi-Yehudah,* Mahadura Tinyana, ḤM no. 40).

In the context of tax law, important principles pertaining to custom in general were laid down. These included the stipulation that a custom must be established and widespread: "that the town residents practiced the custom at least three times, for often the public reaches a conclusion according to need without intending to establish a custom at all" (*Terumat ha-Deshen,* Resp. no. 342). Similarly, it was decided that the established existence of a custom need not be proved in the formal ways prescribed by the laws of evidence: "although it is necessary to inquire whether a custom is established or not, the inquiry itself need not be overly formal and hearsay evidence as well as the evidence of disqualified witnesses is admissible" *(ibid.).* These principles were accepted as decided law (*Darkhei Moshe,* ḤM 163, n. 7; Rema, ḤM 163:3). (For validity of a "bad custom" in the tax law field, see *Minhag.*[1]).

An exaggerated proliferation of local *takkanot* and customs was prevented by the fact that these were usually enacted for or adopted by all the communities in a particular region. Thus Solomon b. Abraham Adret relates that the Jewish community of Barcelona and its environs enacted uniform *takkanot* in the matter of taxes, their assessment and collection – "one chest and one pocket for us all" – and he describes how the community of Barcelona proper, the largest in the region, first consulted with all the surrounding communities on the *takkanot* to be enacted, although in other areas the main community sometimes neglected such prior consultation (Resp. Rashba, vol. 3, no. 412). Other regional enactments of this kind are evidenced in the *takkanot* of Vallidolid (of 1432) and those of the German communities (see Finkelstein, bibl.; also Halpern, Pinkas; *Takkanot Medinat Mehrin; Pinkas ha-Medinah,* bibl.; see further Resp. Maharam of Rothenburg, ed., Prague, no. 241; *Massa Melekh,* 5:1, 1–3).

Integration of Tax Law into the Jewish Legal System. The creation of tax laws in this manner carried with it the danger that the link between this branch of the law and the overall system of Jewish law, which was based on the talmudic *halakhah* and its evolution, might become weakened. This aspect was stressed by the halakhic scholars, and Solomon b. Abraham Adret, for instance, pointed out the diversity in tax laws and noted that this was because the communal enactments were not based on binding talmudic law, "for if so there would be one measure for all the communities, as there is in regard to all other laws of the Torah" (Resp. Rashba, vol. 5, no. 270; and see also vol. 3, no. 412). The scholars and communal leaders nevertheless succeeded in preserving the proliferous body of the tax laws that developed in the Diaspora during this period as an integral part of the Jewish legal system, mainly through adherence to the principles enumerated below.

Reliance on Halakhic Sources. The halakhic scholars were understandably anxious to establish a link between the various *takkanot* and customs and the strict law: "even though it has been said . . . that in tax matters custom overrides the law, it is at any rate desirable and proper to examine carefully whether we can reconcile all the customs with the strict law, and even if not entirely so it is yet preferable that we find support in the teachings of the scholars and substantiate them with the aid of reason and logic" (*Terumat ha-Deshen,* Resp. no. 342). Thus, for example, support in the form of several talmudic references, was found for the widely accepted custom that a person appealing against a tax assessment has first to pay as assessed before the legal hearing could take place, even though this custom was in contradiction to the Jewish law principle that the burden of proof is on the claimant (see below). Similarly, a *takkanah* aimed at extending the creditor's lien to cover also a tax debtor's money in the hands of a third party even when it was no longer held in specie – and contrary to a rule of the Talmud – was justified by R. Nissim by way of an interpretation which lent a specific legal character to a tax debt (see below). An interesting expression of this general trend is found in two responsa of the 17th-century German halakhic scholar, Jair Ḥayyim Bacharach (Resp. *Ḥavvot Ya'ir,* nos. 57, 58), who was consulted in both cases by the communal leaders on the procedure to be followed upon their discovery that the taxpayer's assets in fact far exceeded the amount on which he had been assessed. After giving a detailed exposition of the talmudic law and existing custom concerning tax assessment, Bacharach went on to describe his approach to the question of integrating law and *takkanot* in the field of taxation: "although certainly in assessment and related matters the community has authority to act as it thinks proper, and it is not necessary to hearken to the voice of a person who seeks to find the original approach of the law [on these matters], yet you should endeavor to examine the reasoning of our scholars and call it to your aid . . . and thereafter do as you see fit, keeping close to the law of the Torah." Having dealt with the attitude of the *halakhah* and with the existing *takkanot* and customs, Bacharach concluded by stating: "So my humble opinion tends to be like the decisions which are given by lay tribunals [*piskei ba'alei battim;* see Introduction] together with some measure of application of the strict law."

Legal Interpretation by the Halakhic Scholars. Another reason for the orderly integration of tax enactments and customs into the Jewish legal system was the fact that in most cases the problems and disputes arising from them were brought before the halakhic scholars. In answering these problems and in their interpretation of the various *takkanot* and customs, the scholars applied the accepted rules of interpretation as well as the general principles of Jewish law normally applied in the courts (see below) and a problem that fell outside the purview of an existing custom or *takkanah* was dealt with according to talmudic law and the codes (see, e.g., Resp. Rashba, vol. 4, no. 260; Resp. Maharam of Rothenburg, loc. cit., and further illustration

1. page 107.

below), since "in all matters that have not been explicitly stated [in communal enactments] we are obliged to adhere as close as possible to the law of the Torah" (Resp. Rama da Fano, no. 43; Resp. Maharashdam, ḤM no. 442).

Principles of Equity and Justice. Also instrumental in the maintenance of an organic link between tax laws and the general system of Jewish law was the scholars' practice of scrutinizing customs and enactments and invalidating them when they were contrary to Jewish law principles of equity and justice. Thus a *takkanah* aimed at rendering the taxpayer liable for double taxation on the same property – both at his place of residence and at the place where the property was situated – was rendered null since "this is nothing but robbery, and it is not possible to stipulate contrary to the law of robbery" (Resp. Rashba, vol. 5, no. 178; vol. 1, no. 788; see also Resp. Maharam of Rothenburg, ed. Prague, no. 106). On the strength of the said principles the scholars also invalidated another *takkanah* which purported to lend a tax obligation retroactive effect, and further, excluded the possibility of combining two methods of tax assessment in a manner drastically increasing the taxpayer's burden (see below). Similarly, a tax custom whose purpose was "to extract vengeance from an individual or individuals" was held to be of no force and effect (*Massa Melekh, Ne'ilat She'arim, Minhagei Mamon;* see also *Takkanot ha-Kahal*).

Accumulation of Tax Takkanot and Customs in Halakhic Literature. Another reason for the close link between the tax law and the general halakhic system is to be found in the fact that a very substantial part of tax customs and *takkanot* were quoted, often in full, and discussed in the vast responsa literature and other compilations of the halakhic scholars (see below).

Yardsticks of Tax Assessment. The problem of the yardstick to be applied in the assessment of an individual's tax liability continued to occupy the attention of the post-talmudic halakhic scholars.

Poll Tax. This tax, apparently imposed throughout the post-talmudic period, was "a fixed per capita allocation" (Resp. Rashba, vol. 5, no. 220) and was often referred to during this period by its talmudic name, *karga* (Resp. Rashba, vol. 5, no. 178, et al.).

Assessment According to Financial Means. Generally, most taxes were levied in accordance with the taxpayer's means, a principle the scholars regarded as fundamental to Jewish law. Thus it was decided that the individual members of the community should contribute according to their means toward a specified sum required for their own security needs, contrary to the practice in the case of an amount collected by the central authority: "and if at first, when the gentiles were appointed to be in charge of the guards, they departed from Jewish law in equating the poor with the rich, yet now that they entrusted this matter to ourselves we should not change the law of the Torah that in matters dependent on money the calculation must be made according to means . . . and it may not be said . . . that the rich shall not make increase, nor the poor decrease" (*Mordekhai,* BB no. 475 in the name of Maharam of Rothenburg, and no. 497). This approach was fortified by a legal explanation with an interesting historical background: "whatever new decrees and afflictions the gentiles may impose on Israel, even if they should be minded to afflict us by having us refrain from food and drink, yet all is collected according to financial means, for their main concern is the money" (*Piskei ha-Rosh,* BB 1:22; cf. also *takkanot* of the Saragossa community, in Dinur, Golah, 2, pt. 2 (1966^2), 366f.).

Assessment in Accordance with the Tax Purpose. Some scholars held that individual tax liability should be assessed in accordance with the purpose for which the tax was imposed. Thus if the purpose was to raise a specific sum in order to bribe the authorities to prevent riots against the Jews on the eve of their festivals, "the law holds that they should pay [tax] according to means as well as souls, since on these days both persons and property are endangered – all this in accordance with the need of the hour and the local situation." In the case of regular taxes imposed by the authorities, means alone was to be the criterion: "for the kings and governments only impose taxes on people with means, and they protect their means by payment of the taxes." If a specified sum was to be raised for the purpose of bribing the authorities not to forbid ritual slaughter or the sale of bread to Jews, assessment was to be according to souls alone, since in this case rich and poor would suffer equal harm. All these distinctions, however, were to remain subject to local custom and enactment (Resp. Rashba, vol. 3, no. 401). All were not consistently observed, and in another responsum Solomon b. Abraham Adret himself (*ibid.,* no. 381) laid down that the cantor's emolument was to be paid out of the community chest; although he fulfills the duty for rich and poor alike the poor cannot afford as much as the rich, and in all matters of the public weal which are dependent on money the contribution must be made according to means. On the other hand, in a later period the opinion was expressed that in the case of the cantor's emolument, the assessment required a combination of two methods – one-half according to souls – for although the poor had as much need of the cantor as did the rich, yet the rich were prepared to pay more to a cantor with a better voice, and "therefore they made this compromise" (Sh. Ar., OḤ, 53:23 and *Taz, ibid.,* no. 14). As a result of the multiplication of possible distinctions of this nature, it was laid down that these matters had to be decided "on the merits of each case, as the judges see fit" (Rema, ḤM 163:3); "since these matters are not clearly dealt with in the *halakhah* as found in books only, but must be dealt with by the judges . . . in taking account of the abnormal and emergency situation and the decrees of the authorities" (*Terumat ha-Deshen,* Resp. no. 345). It was held that liability for tax existed even when the taxpayer had no need for the services financed thereby and therefore could not expect any return consideration. Thus it was decided that the cost of educating children – if this was beyond their fathers' means – should be borne by the whole community, each member contributing according to his means (Resp. Ramah, no. 241; Sh. Ar., loc. cit.); moreover, it was held to be the rule that all the needs of the town must be financed by the whole community, even if some were not in need of certain services, such as a wedding hall or ritual bath, and so on (Resp. Mahari Mintz, no. 7; Sh. Ar., loc. cit.). At different times when the rich sought to evade their tax duty, the halakhic scholars responded in various ways (see, e.g., Dinur, Golah, 2, pt. 2 (1966), 393–5).

Tax Purposes. The purposes for which taxes were levied during the post-talmudic period embraced a wide spectrum of municipal needs – such as maintaining the town guard, providing health, educational, and religious services, and for judicial and civil execution institutions, funds for combating informers, funds for charity to the poor, for hospitality, and for *ma'ot ḥittin* on Passover – in addition to various taxes, fixed or otherwise, imposed by the central authorities on the Jewish community and collected by the communal authorities from its members (see illustrations cited and see also Tur, Sh. Ar., ḤM 163, and standard commentaries). These taxes were known by various names, some corresponding to those mentioned in the Talmud, and other taxes were called by the names customary in the various countries of Jewish settlement.

Taxable Property. Taxes were mainly direct and based on income from property, movable or immovable: "for property which cannot be utilized and earned from is not properly taxable" (Resp. Ran, no. 2:21). Non income-bearing property was subject to tax reduction in the case of a special property tax or a non-recurrent "unprescribed" tax imposed in a very large amount in the event of a special false accusation or other emergency. The increasingly severe fiscal burden imposed by the ruling power, particularly in the case of German Jewry, fostered the tendency toward imposing taxes on non income-bearing property also, as will be detailed below.

Land. "It was accepted in ancient times that taxes should not be imposed on land, for tax derives only from a business transaction" (Maharam of Rothenburg, quoted in *Mordekhai,* BB no. 481), and this continued to be the practice in 13th-century Germany although unsuccessful efforts had been made to bring about a change *(ibid.).* A land tax, in Meir b. Baruch's opinion *(ibid.),* could exist only in the event that "the land itself is tax-burdened," that is if the tax was expressly imposed as a property tax on land, or if the tax was imposed in a time of emergency when there was reason to fear "the plunder of courtyards and land, and the burning and destruction of houses" (Sh. Ar., ḤM 163:3). Similarly, in the case of a person buying and selling land, "it is the universal custom that tax is payable on everything that a person may wish to sell, whether household articles or land . . . for anything that is for sale is like merchandise" (Resp. Maharyu, no. 84, and see below).

Houses. In the case of houses it was decided that local custom should be followed, and when there was no such custom the issue depended on the nature of the tax: if imposed to finance the expenses of the town guard the tax would extend also to houses, i.e., to owners of houses in the town even if they did not reside there (see below); however, if the tax "be like all other fixed taxes payable annually – to the ruling power or municipal authorities – on account of the income earned in the town, houses will not be subject to tax; yet if a person should own two or three houses, he must pay tax on them for this is no different to any other income, but he shall not pay tax on his own dwelling, save in the case of a tax in a large amount or when the ruler has determined that they shall pay tax on everything they own" (Maharam of Rothenburg, quoted in *Mordekhai,* BB no. 475 and see Resp. Maharyu, no 84).

In certain areas of Spain in the 13th century, tax was payable on land even independently of its sale (Resp. Rashba, vol. 5, no. 182). In one case it was decided that on land and all else from which no income was derived, tax was payable at one-quarter of the regular rate (*Teshuvot ha-Rashba ha-Meyuḥasot le-ha-Ramban,* no. 184); this was apparently a property tax expressly imposed as such. On houses, however, no tax was imposed (Resp. Rashba, vol. 5, no. 179, 182).

Vineyards and Fields. The rule was established that even income-bearing movable property from which a loss could more commonly be anticipated than a profit – such as the yield from a field or vineyard – should not be taxable. Hence it was decided as early as the 11th century that a tax which the town residents sought to impose on a woman's vineyard was contrary to law because the great effort and expense involved in the vineyard's cultivation did not necessarily assure an income and it was wrong that an asset should be consumed by the tax levied on it (Resp. Joseph Tov Elem (Bonfils), quoted in Resp. Maharam of Rothenburg, ed. Prague, no. 941 and in *Mordekhai,* BB no. 481; see also *Takkanot Rashi,* quoted in Resp. Maharam of Rothenburg, ed. Berlin, no. 866 and in Finkelstein, bibl., p. 149). However, in 15th-century Germany there was a change in the profitability of vineyards: "in these countries, in the main the people sustain themselves by their vineyards and derive their wealth from them." Thus a situation arose in which there was no possibility of exempting vineyards entirely from taxation yet frequent heavy losses from such property could nevertheless be anticipated. It was decided, therefore, that tax was to be assessed on one-half of the value of the property, but that no exemption was to be granted in the case of a "very large and exaggerated" emergency tax (*Terumat ha-Deshen,* Resp. no. 342). In Salonika, in the 17th century, tax was payable on the full value (*Massa Melekh,* 3:2, 1).

Money Loaned on Interest. This was an obvious category of taxable property: "there is no more convenient class of merchandise; since the lender holds his pledge and his money grows, he benefits without effort or strain, or any need to supervise, nor does he have any expense . . . " (R. Yom Tov Elem, quoted in Resp. Maharam of Rothenburg, ed. Prague, no. 941). In the course of time, when it became increasingly likely that money loaned to non-Jewish borrowers would never be repaid, it was decided that the interest was not to be taxed (as in the case of vineyards), except that exemption was not to be granted on the whole amount of the loan, for since "in our time we mostly earn our livelihood from lending money on interest, what other source of taxation is there?" If interest was reflected as capital and compounded thereon, the interest was to be regarded as capital and taxable (*Terumat ha-Deshen,* Resp. no. 342). A person was held to be liable for tax on income derived not only from his own property but also from the property of others held in his possession (*Mordekhai,* BB no. 481; Nimmukei Menahem of Merseburg, Din. 5; see also various opinions in *Terumat ha-Deshen,* Resp. no. 342 and Rema, ḤM 163:3). It was held that a debt which the creditor despaired of recovering might be excluded from his list of taxable property provided that he assigned his right in the matter to the communal trustee; if the debt was recovered by the community, two-thirds of it had to go to the community and the remainder to the creditor (*Terumat ha-Deshen,* loc. cit.; for a different ratio, see Resp. Maharyu, nos. 84 and 133). In another *takkanah* debts were declared completely tax-free (Resp. Rama da Fano, no. 43).

Money in Deposit or Trust. It was Hai Gaon's opinion (quoted in *Terumat ha-Deshen,* Resp. no. 342) that money deposited with a trustee was not taxable, since no profit was derived from it by its owner. From the 13th century onward, the majority of the German *posekim* came to hold the converse opinion (Resp. Ḥayyim Or Zaru'a, no. 253; *Terumat ha-Deshen,* loc. cit.; Resp. Maharyu, no. 133; cf. the contrary opinion in Nimmukei Menahem of Merseburg, Dinim 10, 18), and it was stated: "Our custom is that a person is liable on all that he owns, whether openly or concealed" (Resp. Maharil, no. 121). In a special *takkanah* of the Mantua community in the 16th century, even a "hidden portion *[maneh kavur]* earning no income" was declared taxable. It was necessary to decide that no tax was payable for the period of the theft on a sum of money stolen and later returned to its owner, since the particularly stringent nature of the rule which – contrary to the general law and custom – rendered taxable such money "from which its owner certainly derives no income," required that it be narrowly interpreted and its operation confined to the case of an asset "guarded in the owner's possession" (Resp. Rama da Fano, no. 43; see also Rema, ḤM 163:3).

Rights and Obligations. Some scholars held that a property right recoverable by action, such as a right to payment of a dowry, was taxable (Resp. Maharyu, no. 82), but not a right which its owner was uncertain of recovering; nor were the unpaid wages of a teacher, laborer, or employee taxable – even if already due – until they were actually paid (*Terumat ha-Deshen,* Resp. no. 342). A debt was held to be deductible from the amount of a person's taxable assets (Resp. Rashba, vol. 1, no. 1074, et al.), and apparently the deduction was allowed only after the debt had matured, although in 15th-century Germany it was allowed even before maturity of the debt (*Terumat ha-Deshen* and Rema, loc. cit.).

Jewelry, Gold, and other Valuable Articles. It was deduced from the statements of "some of the *geonim*" (quoted in *Terumat ha-Deshen,* loc. cit.) that no tax was payable on property of this kind since no profit was derived from it; an 11th-century *takkanah* nevertheless records the assessment of such articles at half value for tax purposes (*Takkanot Rashi,* quoted in Resp. Maharam of Rothenburg, ed. Berlin, no. 866), and in the 15th century it was the practice to assess these articles at their full value on account of the "swindlers" who used to invest the money they earned in precious stones and jewels in order to gain tax exemption (*Terumat ha-Deshen,* loc. cit.).

Books. Solomon b. Abraham Adret ruled that book manuscripts which were of very great value, were taxable at one-quarter of their value, i.e., at the same rate as land, even though they were not income producing (*Teshuvot ha-Rashba ha-Meyuhasot le-ha-Ramban,* no. 184); however, the majority of the scholars exempted them entirely – both because books were not income producing and "lest in future people refrain from hiring scribes to write books" (*Terumat ha-Deshen,* loc. cit.).

Meat and Wine. A tax on the purchase and sale of wine and meat is mentioned in various medieval *takkanot* and responsa (Resp. Rashba, vol. 2, no. 213; Resp. Rosh, nos. 6:14, 102:6; Resp. Ritba, no. 44; *Takkanot Castile,* in Finkelstein, bibl., p. 371).

Tax Ceiling. At first it was considered that there was no ceiling on the amount of a person's tax liability: "it has been the custom since ancient times . . . that a person is liable for tax, however high the amount, on all of his business transactions" (Resp. Maharam of Rothenburg, ed. Berlin, p. 204 no. 127). Later, in certain areas, such a ceiling was provided for, but was only applied in respect of regular taxes and not of those specially imposed in times of emergency or in other special circumstances (*Massa Ḥayyim, Missim ve-Arnoniyyot,* nos. 37, 61).

Consecrated Property. Property dedicated to the needs of the poor, or to religious and educational needs, and the like (see *Hekdesh*) was regarded as exempt from tax on various grounds: since consecrated property was deemed to belong to the community it was not logical for the community to tax its own assets (Resp. Ran, no. 2); such property was not intended for profit-making purposes – a precondition to taxation *(ibid.);* and in order to encourage the consecration of property (to strengthen the hands of those "who perform a *mitzvah*" (*ibid., Terumat ha-Deshen,* Resp. no. 342). It was decided that the exemption only applied in respect of property that had already been dedicated and set aside at a particular place, but not otherwise, in order to discourage fraudulent acts (Resp. Rashba, vol. 5, nos. 142 and 141, 143; vol. 2, no. 57; Resp. Rosh, 13:6; Sh. Ar., ḤM 163:3; for further particulars, see *Massa Melekh,* pt. 3).

Place of Residence, Business, or Situation of Property. It was laid down that tax was payable at the place where the taxpayer was resident. In general, a person was regarded as a resident of the town in which he had lived for a period of 12 months or more; a lesser period entailed the duty to contribute toward some of the town's needs, and a person immediately became the resident of a town in which he purchased a dwelling (see above). In the 12th century the *posekim* disagreed on the criteria of residence for purposes of tax liability. According to one view, "even if he has rented a house he is not to be likened to one who has purchased a dwelling there [in the town], since in the latter case the *kinyan* proves that he has made up his mind to settle, but if a dwelling is rented it may not be his intention to settle and he should not be held liable"; another opinion was that "a person who comes to dwell and settle there is like one who purchases a dwelling there" (opinions quoted in *Mordekhai,* BB no. 477 and in Resp. Maharyu, no. 124), and this latter became the accepted opinion (*Terumat ha-Deshen,* Resp. no. 342; Resp. Maharik, no. 17). It was held that at all events a fixed local custom to impose tax liability, even upon residence in the town for a period of less than 12 months, was to be followed (*Mordekhai,* loc. cit.), and in various places other periods were prescribed (see e.g., *takkanot* of the Saragossa community, 1331, in Dinur, Golah, 2, pt. 2 (1966^2), 345f.; Resp. Rashba, vol. 3, no. 397; see also Sh. Ar., ḤM 163:2; for further particulars, see *Massa Melekh,* pt. 1).

Situation of Property. A property tax was regarded as payable at the place where the property was situated regardless of the owner's place of residence (Resp. Rashba, vol. 5, 178; Resp. Ritba, no. 157). This principle was deduced from the talmudic rule that a person owning property (a *ḥazer*) in a town of which he is not a resident must contribute toward the costs of the town's water supply (Maharam of Rothenburg, quoted in *Mordekhai,* BB no. 475, on the authority of Tosef., BM 11:18). Meir of Rothenburg's reasoning in this matter is interesting. Starting from the mishnaic *halakhah* that "the [upkeep of the] water channel, the city wall, and the towers thereof and all the city's needs . . . were provided from the residue of the shekel-chamber" (i.e., from the money of all Israel; Shek. 4:2), he poses the question, "and why shall the city not be built by the Jerusalemites themselves, on their own?" His answer is "because no tribal division was made of Jerusalem and it is a dwelling place for all the house of Israel, therefore the funds come from the residue of the shekel-chamber, contributed by all Israel" (*ibid.*).

Place of Business Transaction. Tax on profits derived from a business transaction was likewise held to be payable at the place where the business was transacted and the profit made (Resp. Rashba, vol. 5, no. 263), for the reason of *dina de-malkhuta dina,* since according to the general law of the land the king may "decree that no person shall carry on business in his country unless he pay so-and-so much" (Resp. Rashba, vol. 3, no. 440; vol. 1, no. 664; vol. 5, nos. 263, 286); even talmudic law entitled the residents of a town to call upon a person not to carry on his business there "in order not to diminish their profit" unless he paid them tax on his profits, and his refusal to do so gave the townspeople authority to restrain him from carrying on business in their community (Resp. Rashba, vol. 5, no. 270; see also Resp. Ritba, no. 157). The community was at all events held to be entitled to enact a *takkanah* that anyone carrying on business in their town should pay them tax on this, since "on this matter all communities have rules and *takkanot* not derived from talmudic law" (Resp. Rashba, vol. 3, no. 397). Moreover, even people coming to a particular town in circumstances of *ones*, for instance when fleeing from the enemy, with the intention of returning to their own town once the danger had passed, could be liable to contribute toward the taxes of that town after they had sojourned there for more than 12 months and transacted business like the townspeople, although perhaps not at the same rate as the permanent residents of the town (*Binyamin Ze'ev,* no. 293, with detailed discussion and quotation of different opinions; for further particulars, see *Massa Melekh,* 1:2, 1–2).

Double Taxation. It was held to be clear that a person who was not resident in the town where he transacted business could only be taxed by that community on business transacted locally and not on business transacted in the town of his residence or on property he owned there (Resp. Rashba, vol. 3, no. 440). Furthermore, even the community where he lived could not tax him on business transacted in another community, "for if this be permitted an injustice will be done in that he is made to pay twice" (*ibid.*), and it was an important principle that "the same asset cannot be taxed in two different places" (Resp. Rashba, vol. 5, no. 270). In one instance the leaders of a certain community sought to enact that a resident of the local community was to be taxed also on his property situated in the area of another community because "the community has authority to make enactments and rules so that no one shall escape liability." Notwithstanding the right of a community to make enactments in tax matters even if they were contrary to a rule of the *halakhah,* Solomon b. Abraham Adret rejected the validity of this *takkanah* because it was "nothing less than robbery and it is not possible to contract out of the laws of robbery . . . for the community has no right to rob an individual of his money and take it for itself" (Resp. Rashba, vol.5, no. 178). This decision of principle led to the enactment, in certain communities, of *takkanot* aimed one and the same time at avoiding double taxation while minimizing , as far as possible, loss of tax income to the community in which the taxpayer resided. Thus the *takkanah* of a certain community rendered local residents liable for tax even on their property situated elsewhere, but as they were allowed first to deduct from their tax assessment the tax payable to the other community and the balance went to the local community, the *takkanah* apparently brought little benefit to the local community (Resp. Rashba, vol.5, no. 282, also no. 178). This distinction between property situated at the taxpayer's place of residence and property situated elsewhere naturally also influenced the laws concerning the declaration of assets for purposes of tax payment. Thus it was laid down that a taxpayer owning property in another country where he also had a creditor was to deduct the debt in question from the property declaration he submitted to the foreign country and not from the declaration he submitted to the authorities at his place of residence (Resp. Rashba, vol. 1, no. 1074).

The objection in principle to double taxation was apparently not always generally accepted in the Jewish community in Germany. In the 14th century it was stated: "some hold that money which is retained by a person outside the town of his residence . . . is tax exempt . . . and others say that a person who has money outside his town, even abroad, must pay tax on all his money, and must also pay tax in the other place on the same money, even if the money has never come into his hands, and this is the custom of the majority of the people" (Menahem of Merseburg, quoted in Resp. Maharyu, no. 133). This was still the case in the 15th century: "It is the custom in all these countries that taxes and impositions are payable also on property that has always remained outside the country, and I am accustomed to dealing accordingly" (*ibid.*).

Date of Accrual of Liability. The halakhic scholars were much occupied with the question of whether liability for a tax obligation accrued on the date when the basis for its existence came into being or on the date when the tax payment became due for collection. The difference related mainly to two events of common occurrence in daily life: firstly, when a resident left or joined a community after imposition but before collection of the tax; secondly, when the taxpayer's financial position changed between the time of imposition of the tax and the time of its collection.

Leaving or Joining the Community. *Leaving the Community.* A minority opinion held a person to be exempt from paying tax to the community which he left after the imposition but before the collection of such a tax (R. Tam, quoted in *Mordekhai,* BB nos. 475–476 and in Resp. Maharik, no. 2; see also *Massa Melekh,* 1:2; 3:2). However, the majority of the *posekim* disputed this view: "It seems to me to be as a law of the Torah that when the king has called for a tax . . . everything that one possesses becomes charged in the king's favor, and, even if one should run away before collection of the tax, everything is already so charged – for the law of the land is law and even the measure that is within the jar becomes charged in favor of the *karga*" (Isaac the Elder, quoted in *Mordekhai,* BB no. 476 and in *Teshuvot Maimuniyyot,* Gezelah, no. 9; Judah of Paris, quoted in *Mordekhai,* BB no. 659); similarly, "the *geonim* of France decided that when a man leaves his city, he must pay the tax imposed on him" and, in any event, "such is the custom in all the communities that a person cannot, upon leaving the city, gain exemption from a tax for which he has already become liable" (see *Mordekhai,* BB nos. 656 and 476).

This question was also disputed in Spain in the community of Solomon b. Abraham Adret and there the matter was decided in accordance with the above-mentioned principle, after "they investigated and inquired from other communities and ascertained from all the communities and their leaders that they follow the opinion of those who exempt persons who come into the community [after imposition of the tax] and hold liable those who leave the community; since then the dispute has become resolved and in accordance with this we apply the law in all the communities in our area" (Resp. Rashba, vol. 5, no. 179). In other places *takkanot* were enacted to the express effect that anyone intending to leave the city had first to pay all the taxes for which liability had already accrued (*ibid.,* vol. 3, no. 406; see also vol. 3, no. 405 and vol. 4, no. 260) and the *halakhah* was thus decided in all later periods: "The law obliges him to pay in full, on all his property, the taxes that have already been imposed, along with all the expenses involved, since he has already become liable for them as one of the taxpayers and he cannot rid himself of them by departing from the city" (Resp. Ritba, no. 157). A similar decision was given by Joseph Colon in Italy in the 15th century: "The prevailing *halakhah* among the Jewish people is that those who run away after imposition of a tax are not thereby exempt from paying their share of the tax" (Resp. Maharik, no. 2); moreover, "anyone escaping from the tax so as not to contribute along with his neighbor will not in the long run, if he returns to the country, derive any reward from his action" (*Leket Yosher,* OḤ p. 139; see also Sh. Ar., ḤM 163:2). Since a person leaving a city was liable for the payment of his share of the tax, it was held, in a certain case where the authorities refunded part of the tax collected to residents of the community that such person was also entitled to claim his share of the amount refunded by the authorities (Resp. Rashba, vol. 3, no. 405).

In the German community the scope of tax liability of a departing resident was even extended. It was laid down that the tax liability existed not only if the amount payable had been finally determined at the time of the resident's departure, but it sufficed if it had been known that a tax was going to be imposed, even though the amount had not yet been settled between the community and the authorities (Resp. Ḥayyim Or Zaru'a, no. 80). In the 15th century the matter was more precisely defined: "A person leaving the city or the country to settle in another country must share equally with the residents of his former place of domicile the burden of any new tax imposed on them within 30 days of his departure" (*Terumat ha-Deshen,* Resp. no. 342); this was because it had to be assumed that the tax had been "under preparation" for some time prior to its imposition, at which time the departing resident was included in the reckoning, and also that the tax was under discussion in the community for some time prior to its imposition; therefore to exempt from such a tax any person leaving the city a few days before the imposition of the tax would amount to encouraging many to evade taxes by leaving the city and returning there in due course (*ibid.*; see also Rema, ḤM 163:3; *Massa Melekh*, 1:2, 3–4).

Joining the Community. The natural corollary of this rule was to exempt a person from liability for a tax imposed before he had joined the community even though the tax fell due for collection after his arrival, "since it is not possible to burn the candle at both ends by holding newcomers liable at the time when the tax is collected and departing residents liable at the time when the tax obligation is created" (Resp. Rashba, vol. 5, no. 179). This was also the custom followed in various other communities ("the custom of the community in Crete is not to reduce the tax for the departing resident nor to exact it from the newcomer," quoted in *Mordekhai,* BB no. 656). It was further decided that a community could not demand that a newcomer contribute toward the payment of any particular tax imposed for a reason clearly connected with an event preceding his arrival–as in the case of a tax imposed by one authority because the community had made a similar tax payment before to another authority, at a time when the newcomer was not yet a resident of the community (Resp. Rashba, vol. 4, no. 260).

Retroactive Tax Liability. The majority of the halakhic scholars held that the imposition of retroactive tax liability – that is imposition of liability on a person not resident in the community at the time of creation of the underlying tax obligation – was invalid even though it was sanctioned by custom or express *takkanah.* In a certain case it was held that a tax imposed by the community for the purpose of repaying an existing loan could not be exacted from a person who came to live in that community after the loan had been taken, even though he came there before the imposition of the tax: "for why should he repay that which he has not borrowed and how shall he restore that which he has not himself taken ['robbed']?" (Rashba, quoted in Resp. Ribash, no. 477). Moreover, this principle could not be set aside even by an express communal enactment, since "the community cannot make any law or *takkanah* to the detriment of an individual member and contrary to the accepted law, except with the latter's consent, because the community cannot stipulate to 'rob' others" (Ribash, *ibid.;* see also Resp. Rashba, vol. 3, no. 412). On the other hand, the German scholars regarded as valid "a *takkanah* that anyone coming to live with us in the city within a given year shall pay retroactively the tax paid by the others at the beginning of that year" (Resp. Ḥayyim Or Zaru'a, no. 226; in this particular case the individual concerned was exempted because he came to live not in the city itself but in a nearby village; cf. however Resp. Rashba, vol. 4, no. 260 where the validity of an express *takkanah* of the type mentioned above was apparently recognized in certain cases).

Change in the Taxpayers' Financial Position. In principle, the date of creation of the underlying tax obligation was recognized as the crucial time for the purpose of determining the measure of individual liability for the tax. Hence the taxpayer had to be assessed according to his financial position at that time, regardless of any change in his financial position at the time of collection of the tax. The halakhic scholars justified this rule by likening the residents of the community to partners, who remain liable for repayment of the debt according to the rate of individual participation in the original obligation and not according to their respective financial positions at the time of repayment. However, while the community had no authority to determine by *takkanah* that the time of the collection of the tax and not the time of its imposition was to be deemed the crucial date for purposes of the essential liability for the tax obligation, it was held that so far as the measure of individual contribution toward the tax was concerned the community was entitled to enact by *takkanah* that the individual taxpayer be assessed according to his financial position at the time of collection, and this was the practice followed (Rashba, quoted in Resp. Ribash, no. 477). This *takkanah* was explained on the basis of the difference between the rules of private law concerning a loan taken by individual partners and the rules of public law concerning a loan taken by the community: "for the community that borrows for communal purposes is not like those who borrow for themselves personally, but it borrows for the community chest" (*tevat ha-kahal;* for particulars of this concept, see Resp. Rashba, vol.3, no. 411; vol. 4, no. 309 and other references to it in this article), "and this debt it has to repay from whatever is available in the chest at the time of payment; such is the custom all over, and neither the poor who have become rich nor the rich who have become poor . . . pay except according to their means at the time of payment; this is also our practice and in any event it is impossible to do otherwise" (Resp. Rashba, vol. 3, no. 412; for particulars of this development from private to public law, see Public Authority; *Takkanot ha-Kahal*). However, it was pointed out that this explanation lacked validity in the case of a person who was not a resident of the city at the time when the loan was taken, since he could in no way be said to have borrowed "for the community chest" (Rashba and Ribash, loc.cit.).

Other scholars determined the crucial date for purposes of tax liability according to the substantive nature of the tax in question. This is the case of a tax of the kind that was regularly imposed from year to year by the authorities, it was held that a person coming to live in the community in the middle of the tax year should be liable for payment of a share pro rata to the remainder of the tax period, since for the duration of that period he would benefit on account of the tax imposed; hence there was all the more reason why a resident who became rich in the course of the tax period had to contribute in accordance with his current means. However, in the case of a nonrecurring tax only those who were resident in the city at the time it was imposed had to contribute (Resp. Rosh 6:12; see also Rema, ḤM 163:3).

Tax Relief and Immunity. Tax relief on a personal basis is recognized in Jewish law, sometimes for financial reasons and sometimes for social or demographic reasons.

Persons of Limited Means. It was held that the poor had no obligation whatsoever to pay tax (Resp. Rosh, 6:4, 12), neither on their income from business transactions nor in the form of a poll tax (see *takkanot* of the Saragossa community in Dinur, Golah, 2, pt. 2 (1966^2), 366f.). Elsewhere it was laid down that widows, unmarried orphans, and the disabled were not to be taxed unless their property exceeded a certain amount, and then on the excess only (*Takkanot* Castile (Finkelstein, bibl. p. 371)). A 15th-century German *takkanah* exempted from tax all persons who owned less than a certain amount, but rendered those who owned more than the specified amount liable for tax on all their property (*Terumat ha-Deshen,* Resp. no. 342). In 13th century Germany it had been the practice to exempt orphans until their majority and marriage (Or Zaru'a, quoted in *Terumat ha-Deshen,* loc. cit.), but in the time of Israel Isserlein orphans also were taxed in accordance with their financial means, on account of the increased tax burden and because tax payment was a matter of safeguarding the security of the community, an obligation regarded as devolving on orphans also *(ibid.);* however, it was laid down that orphans were exempt from the duty of contributing toward the building of a synagogue (Rema, ḤM 163:4).

In cases where persons of limited means were held liable for tax, the communal leaders and halakhic scholars sought legal ways to ease their burden (see, e.g., Resp. Rashba, vol. 5, no. 220). An interesting illustration of this can be found in the *takkanot* of the Huesca community of 1340. These prescribed a detailed and onerous list of diverse taxes, apparently aimed at financing communal services as well as raising the amount levied by the crown. The list included poll tax; property tax on houses, vineyards, fields, and gardens; a business and profits tax on wine and various other commodities; and taxes on leases and loans, on gold and silver jewelry, expensive garments, and the like. At the same time, "50 Jews who do not today own property to the value of 50 solidos" were exempted from the poll tax; also exempted were "those who study day and night and have no other occupation" (Dinur, loc. cit., pp. 349–53, and see below with reference to exemptions granted to scholars). On the other hand, the scholars were opposed to exempting a person from tax liability on the grounds of alleged straitened financial circumstances when in fact there was no more at stake than the interests of a man of means under whose patronage such a person was working. Thus Isserlein mentions that in Germany in the 15th century "some of the *ba'alei battim* ['householders'] have to some extent been forcing the custom of having their servants made exempt even though they have money on which they earn, because they eat at the table of the *ba'alei battim.*" Criticizing this custom, he declared "that it ought not to be followed" (*Terumat ha-Deshen,* Resp. no. 342; for further particulars, see *Massa Melekh,* 4:4; as regards tax liability and exemption of "an idle person transacting no business in the city," see Tur and Sh. Ar., ḤM 163:6 and standard commentaries; *Massa Melekh,* 1:1,4; this case was one that had become of little practical importance, "to be in the position of an idler is something that is not so common – I have skimmed over it" (loc. cit.)).

Encouraging Settlement in Ereẓ Israel. In Germany in the 12th century it was decided that a person remained liable for a tax imposed before he left his place of residence, even though he intended to settle in Ereẓ Israel, since "the upholding of life *(pikku'aḥ nefesh)* is a more important *mitzvah* than settling in Ereẓ Israel . . . and the tax for which he is liable should not be imposed on the public for the sake of the *mitzvah* of settling in Ereẓ Israel" (quoted in *Mordekhai,* BB no. 656). It is possible that in this case the tax was required in circumstances of special urgency. On the other hand, it is mentioned that in the Turkish countries in the 16th century – the period following the expulsion from Spain and the mass immigration to and consolidation of the Jewish settlement in Ereẓ Israel – it had been the fixed custom for many years in the city that "anyone migrating to Israel to take up residence there had his property exempted from all kinds of taxes, even if it was left behind in that city" (quoted in *Paḥad Yiẓḥak,* s.v. *Missim zeh Yammim*). In one case the residents of the city sought to abrogate the custom in question by an express *takkanah,* but it was decided that they had no authority to do so "especially because by enacting such a *takkanah* they would deter the public from fulfilling the *mitzvah* of living in Ereẓ Israel" (*Paḥad Yiẓḥak,* loc. cit.; *Massa Melekh,* 1:2:3, 4; 5:2, 6; see also *Massa Ḥayyim, Missim ve-Aroniyyot,* no. 2).

Large Families. Another kind of tax exemption was that granted to "a person who has 12 children" (quoted in *Paḥad Yiẓḥak* s.v. *Missim, Mi she-Hayu Lo*). In a certain case in Italy it was decided that the father of such a large family was to be entirely exempted from tax payment and that the tax collected from him had to be returned, "since this is not something decreed by the king contrary to law, but it is the law of the land" (*ibid.).* This exemption apparently had its roots in the general law of taxation in Italy.

Talmidei Ḥakhamim (Halakhic scholars). The circumstances of a scholar's immunity from taxation, based on the talmudic *halakhah* (see above), remained a subject of much discussion in post-talmudic times. As in talmudic times, there continued to be a measure of reciprocity on this subject between Jewish law and the surrounding legal systems. Influenced by Roman law, tax immunity was customary in the case of scholars and the Catholic clergy and such immunity was also extended in the Muslim countries, although in a more restricted manner (See Baron, Social[2] 5 (1957), 76; idem, Community, 2 (1942), 14f., 274; cf. *Tashbeẓ* 3:254).

Reservations. In the geonic period it was laid down that rabbis were to be exempted from taxes imposed on the community by the king and his ministers (*Zikkaron la-Rishonim . . .* 1, pt. 4 (1887), ed. Harkavy, no. 537), an exemption which apparently extended to all kinds of taxes. Starting from the tenth century, some of the scholars greatly reduced the scope of this exemption in holding that it should apply only in the case of an inclusive tax imposed on the community as a whole; a tax imposed on an individual basis was to be borne by halakhic scholars also and the community had no obligation to pay for them (R. Hananel, quoted in Nov. Ramban, BB 8a; *Beit Yosef,* ḤM 163:11). Notwithstanding his earlier ruling, which ran counter to the view prevailing in his day that a scholar was forbidden to seek sustenance from the public in order to devote himself to study (as this amounted to a profanation of God's Name), Maimonides decided that in the matter of taxation, "the Torah has exempted all *talmidei ḥakhamim* from all governmental dues, such as a levy, *arnona,* or special personal tax . . . which must be paid for them by the community, including [a tax for] the building of a wall and the like; and even if the *talmid ḥakham* be a man of great financial means he is not to be held liable for any of these" (Comm. Avot 4:5). To exact a tax payment from a *talmid ḥakham* would amount to "robbing" him (idem, Resp. (ed. Blau) no. 325; cf. Yad, Talmud Torah, 6:10). Many of the scholars followed the opinion of R. Hananel (Nov. Ramban, *Bet ha-Beḥirah* and Nov. Ran, BB 8a), but others accepted Maimonides' view (*Yad Ramah,* BB 8a; *Sefer ha-Ḥinnukh,* no. 222), as did the majority of the *posekim* (Resp. Rosh 15:7–8; Tur and Sh. Ar., YD 243:2–3; ḤM 163:4–6; R. Jeroham, *Sefer Meisharim* 32:2). Asher b. Jehiel averred: "In these generations I see the need, *a foritiori,* to apply this rule; in the time of the talmudic sages, *talmidei ḥakhamim* – of whom there were thousands – were exempt from various burdens and taxes; all the more reason in these generations – when it is hard to find one in a city and two in the same family – to exempt them from such burdens" (Resp. Rosh, loc.cit.). This was indeed the practice followed and even where the most onerous tax burden was imposed, "those who study day and night and have no other occupation" (*Takkanot* Huesca of 1340, in Dinur, loc. cit. p. 349) were exempted even from poll tax. In the Castilian *takkanot* of 1432 the widows of certain scholars and communal leaders were also exempted from tax, a concession partly based on the rule that "the wife of a *ḥaver* is as a *ḥaver* himself" (Av. Zar. 39a), and because the widow of a *ḥaver* remained entitled to some of the rights formerly enjoyed by her husband (Finkelstein, see bibl. p. 369).

"The Torah is his Occupation" (Torato Omanuto). In the Talmud the term *rabbanan,* in the context of tax exemption, is employed without qualification, but the *geonim* established the requirement of *"torato omanuto"* (quoted in *Terumat ha-Deshen,* Resp. no. 342). Differing opinions were expressed on the interpretation of this phrase. One view was that it meant, "they fulfill *ve-hagita bo yomam va-laylah* with all their strength and ability, and do not leave off studying the Torah except to fulfill a *mitzvah,* to seek a livelihood and sustenance for themselves and their families" (Responsum of Meir ha-Levi in: *Sefer Kol Bo,* 108d; see also Naḥmanides and *Piskei ha-Rosh,* BB 1:26; *Terumat ha-Deshen,* Resp. no. 341; Resp. Israel of Bruna, no. 102). Other scholars held it to be a precondition of the

exemption of a *talmid ḥakham* that "he is not occupied at all with worldly needs" (*Bet ha-Beḥirah*, BB 8a; *Sefer Ḥasidim*, no. 1493; see also *takkanot* Huesca, above).

The Role of Custom. It was decided that although the law concerning a *talmid ḥakham* was no longer practiced with regard to certain matters (e.g., the special fine imposed on a person who shamed him), it still remained in effect as regards his exemption from taxation (*Terumat ha-Deshen*, Resp. no. 341). The exemption was taken to apply not only to a scholar holding office as a rabbi or head of a yeshivah, but also, as appeared from the talmudic source from which the exemption was derived, to scholars who " 'trudge from city to city and from country to country' . . . those are scholars who go from yeshiva to yeshivah, because it is not customary for one who is qualified to be at the head to trudge from city to city" (*Terumat ha-Deshen,* Resp. no. 342; Resp. Maharit, vol. 2, ḤM no. 59 et al.). However, by the 15th century there were places where no scholars except those serving as the heads of yeshivot were exempt from taxation (*Terumat ha-Deshen,* loc. cit.) and, in consequence, the *halakhah* was decided that "there are places where it has been the practice to exempt *talmidei ḥakhamim* from taxation and other places where the practice has been not to exempt them" (Sh. Ar., YD 243:2).

Cantor of the Synagogue. Differences of opinion were also expressed concerning the position of a synagogue cantor, who usually also served as teacher of the children and therefore could be regarded, to some extent, as a scholar. Isaac b. Sheshet Perfet held that he was exempt from tax but other scholars disagreed (Resp. Ribash, nos. 475-7); Isserlein testifies that "in no community have I found them to hold their cantor liable for tax, even if he should have some means, and this is a worthy and proper custom" (*Terumat ha-Deshen*, loc. cit.; see also Rema, ḤM 163:5).

In the State of Israel. The tax liability of a *talmid ḥakham* has been discussed under existing circumstances in the State of Israel. It was held that since rabbis and heads of yeshivot receive full salaries and a substantial proportion of the taxes of the state went toward the provision of various services to which *talmidei ḥakhamim* also had to contribute, and since tax exemption was a matter of custom, it was necessary that "the custom be upheld to exact tax, at the appointed rate, from rabbis, heads of yeshivot, and *talmidei ḥakhamim* who earn salaries" (see K. P. Tekhorsh, bibl., p. 279. For further particulars concerning taxation of scholars, see *Massa Melekh,* 4:1–3;5:2,5).

Governmental or Communal Exemption. A common problem in post-talmudic Jewish life was that which arose when individuals, generally those who were influential in governmental circles, gained for themselves a personal tax immunity from the authorities. The halakhic scholars and communal leaders fought against this phenomenon although German and Spanish Jewry differed in their approaches to the matter.

Governmental Exemption in Germany. As early as the 11th century a German *takkanah* decreed, on pain of ban, that "no local male or female resident shall be entitled to secure his/her exemption from the public burden" (*Takkanot Rashi,* quoted in Resp. Maharam of Rothenburg, ed. Berlin, no. 866). A 13th century *takkanah* laid down that "no person shall secure exemption from the tax because he moves in the royal court" (Finkelstein, bibl., p. 226). In one of his responsa, R. Simḥah of Speyer – after discussing the tannaitic *halakhah* concerning a customs waiver granted to partners (Tosef., BM 8:25–26) – laid down that as far as the community was concerned any governmental exemption had to be shared equally between all its members (as was the custom followed by his uncle, Kalonymus b. Meir), since "all Israelites are sureties for each other to accept the burden of their exile and will share with each other in their comfort and redemption" (quoted in *Or Zaru'ah,* BK no. 460, and in Resp. Maharam of Rothenburg, ed. Prague, no. 932). Similarly, the case was cited of "R. Eliakim, who was close to the royal court and shared with the community any exemption given him by the king" (Resp. Maharam of Rothenburg, ed. Prague, no. 930).

Meir of Rothenburg strongly criticized those who secured any form of tax relief without sharing the benefit of this with the community. In a case where a person acted on his own initiative and came to an arrangement with the authorities "to pay tax independently [of the community]" he laid down that all members of the community had to be regarded as partners for all tax purposes, and a partner could not enjoy personally a benefit due to the whole partnership without the approval of his other partners even if this was not the law of the Torah, "since it has been the custom in the whole kingdom for them to be partners, they are not entitled to act separately, for if everyone were to do so it would lead to evil consequences because everyone would throw off the burden from himself and impose it on his neighbor and endless quarrels shall come about . . . therefore it is necessary to protest againt Reuben who saw fit to act separately" (Resp. Maharam of Rothenburg, ed. Lemberg, no. 108). In a similar case he added that the consent of the authorities was of no effect because "it is not *dina de-malkhuta* but *gezelah de-malkhuta,* like a tax collector exacting a tax in an unspecified amount . . . since it is the custom in the city for all the Jews to participate in the tax"; he held that the person who made the separate arrangement was to return to the authorities and explain that it was the law of the Jews not to act separately but to carry the burden jointly, that all his fellow-Jews were quarreling with him on this account, and that he no longer wished to pay tax independently. In R. Meir's opinion it was necessary to take a more stringent approach in such matters, even if there was no support for this in the Talmud (Resp. Maharam of Rothenburg, ed. Cremona, no. 222; idem, ed. Prague, no. 915). At the same time he ruled that the prohibition was only to apply when the individual was granted an exemption prior to the final determination of the amount of the tax imposed on the community, for in this case it could be assumed that the reduction granted to the individual would have to be made up by the community in general; if, however, an individual exemption was granted after the final determination and it was known that this fact had in no way increased the amount of the tax for others, the individual concerned could not be required to participate with the others (Resp., ed. Prague, no. 134; ed. Lemberg, no. 358; *Mordekhai,* BK no. 177; *Teshuvot Maimuniyyot,* Kinyan, no. 1). This distinction of principle was accepted, with slight modifications, by the majority of the *posekim* (Resp. Ḥayyim Or Zaru'a, nos. 80 and 206; Resp. Ribash, no. 132; Resp. Maharil, no. 71; Resp. Maharyu, no. 38; *Terumat ha-Deshen,* Resp. no. 341 and *ibid., Pesakim u-Khetavim,* no. 144).

Governmental Exemption in Spain. The Spanish halakhic scholars apparently took a less stringent view of personal exemption from taxation. In one case Solomon b. Abraham Adret dealt with the scope of a tax exemption granted to an individual by the authorities and concluded that it did not extend to taxes connected with the protection and security of the Jewish public; on the question of individual tax exemption itself, he stated: "I do not put myself forward in the matter – this has been and remains a disputed topic – until the court asks for my opinion" (Resp. Rashba, vol. 5, no. 183; vol. 1, no. 644; but cf. vol. 5, nos. 279, 281). A 14th-century *takkanah* of the Alcolea community ruled that a ban of one year could be imposed on any person seeking from the authorities exemption or relief from taxation, and this was also applicable to a person availing himself of such a privilege which had been arranged by a friend, "even without his knowledge" (Resp. Ribash, no. 460; see also Rema, ḤM 163:6; for further particulars, see *Massa Melekh,* pt. 2; 4:8).

Exemption by the Community. Clearly, the reasons for objecting to a personal tax privilege granted by the authorities had no relevance in the case of a personal exemption granted by the community itself. The scope of this kind of exemption, however, was discussed in a number of instances (see, e.g., Resp. Rashba, vol. 1, no. 967; vol. 5, no. 281; Resp. Rosh, 6:19). In these cases the problem of the legal validity attaching to the act of waiver arose and it was ruled that the matter depended on local tax usage (Resp. Rashba, vol. 5, no. 180). It was decided that since a waiver of this kind was effected by the public, it had to be regarded as fully valid: "all matters agreed to by the community or its duly appointed representatives require no *kinyan* or deed, but the statements of the former are regarded as written and delivered" (Resp. Rosh, 6:21; see also Rema, ḤM 163:6; Public Authority;[1] *Takkanot ha-Kahal;* for further particulars, see *Massa Melekh,* 5:1, 4–8).

Methods of Tax Assessment. The halakhic scholars were greatly preoccupied with the problem of the method of assessing the taxpayers' assets, which formed the subject matter of many communal *takkanot.* Two principal methods were followed: the first based on a declaration of assets submitted by the taxpayer, called a *hoda'ah,* and the second on an evaluation of assets by communal assessors or trustees, which was called a *pesak,* the assessors being referred to as *posekim* (for a comparison, see, e.g., Resp. Rashba, vol. 3, no. 411, and Resp. Ribash, no. 457). These two methods had much in common and other variations were also in use (Ribash, loc. cit.).

Declaration by the Taxpayer (Hoda'ah). Detailed descriptions of this method of assessment are to be found in a number of responsa. In Spain a date was fixed for submission of the declaration to the trustees (*ne'emanim;* for particulars of this office see below), as well as a later date for submission of a supplementary declaration (Resp. Ritba, no. 114). In another Spanish responsum it is indicated that the community used to appoint 12 persons to determine procedure and supervise submission of the declaration. Among their tasks was determining the date, place, and person to whom the declaration had to be submitted, and in what language it should be made. These 12 persons were given authority to make occasional changes in the details concerning completion and submission of the declaration, but not to change the essential method itself: "they may not change from the method of the *hoda'ah* to that of the *pesak* or to any other method" (Resp. Ribash, no. 457, also nos. 458, 459). The taxpayers *(pore'ei ha-mas)* were required to set out in the declaration full details of their property, business transactions, debts, pledges, and the like (Resp. Rashba, vol. 3, nos. 383, 396, 399, 408; Resp. Ribash, loc. cit.).

It was required that a reasonable and uniform period be prescribed for completion and submission of the declaration, "since some may arrange this in a day and some need ten days or more" (Resp. Ribash, nos. 458 and 459). The taxpayer would bring his declaration form *(pinkas hoda'ato)* to the trustees for them to examine its contents in his presence and then to record the total amount declared in the communal register (*pinkas ha-kahal);* they then returned to the taxpayer "a token of his declaration" (*mazkeret hoda'ato;* Resp. Rashba, vol. 1, no. 1074; vol. 3, no. 383). The amount that each individual had to contribute toward the tax could be ascertained from the communal register; the names of those who did not have to pay were followed by a blank space and no mention of any amount (Resp. Rosh, 5:9; 6:4). From time to time a new declaration of property had to be submitted and, in case of increase, tax had to be paid on the increment (Resp. Rashba, vol. 3, no. 407); in the event that there was a large decrease as compared with the amount previously declared, the trustees would inquire into the matter, which often led to acrimonious dispute (Resp. Ritba, no. 114).

Evaluation of Assets by Tax Assessors. There is early testimony that the community appointed trustees for the purpose of faithfully assessing each member of the community, so as to avoid complaints of an unjust apportionment of the tax (Yom Tov Elem, quoted in Resp. Maharam of Rothenburg, ed. Lemberg, no. 423). These had to be "knowledgeable in the tax" so as to assess each individual according to his assets (*Teshuvot Ge'onei Mizraḥ u-Ma'arav,* no. 205). Sometimes the city elders and judges who were knowledgeable in all local transactions would prepare a "deed of comparison" *(shetar hashvayah)* so as to "compare between them and see how much tax or charity each would have to pay and thereby avoid dispute among the taxpayers" (*Sefer ha-Shetarot* of Judah b. Barzillai, ed. by S.J. Halberstam, p. 137f.). After assessment of the tax a *shetar pesika* would be written to the effect that the communal leaders had determined that X was to pay so-and-so much tax each year and that no one, not even the court or the communal leaders, should have the authority to vary such a determination (*ibid.,* p. 75).

In various responsa of a later period details are given of the functions of these assessors *(posekim)* and of the *pinkas ha-pesika* they kept (see, e.g., Resp. Rashba, vol. 5, no. 279, 281). The assessors recorded the assessed amount of each taxpayer – based on their estimate – in the communal register (*pinkas ha-kahal;* Resp. Rosh, 6:4). Without doubt this assessment too was based on various particulars available to the assessors, although at times they erred grossly in their estimates (Resp. Rosh, 6:4) and on occasion their assessment was followed by protracted argument with the taxpayer which occasionally ended in a very substantial correction of the original assessment (e.g., from 800 *zehuvim* to 150: Resp. Maharyu, no. 124). When a person was assessed as having no taxable assets, a blank space was left beside his name in the communal register (Resp. Rosh, 6:4).

The Trustees. The number of tax assessors (called trustees and by several other names) varied from place to place (the responsa collections of various scholars mention the figure of three, four, ten, and so on) and they were generally chosen by lot from a number of candidates (Resp. Rashba, vol. 3, no. 417). They were required to have expert knowledge of the tax system and to perform their duties faithfully: "and it is the custom in the communities that they appoint the shrewd . . . they examine minutely to impose justly on everyone, according to the efforts and activities of each, and they must judge others as they would themselves as it has been said (Shab. 31a) 'do not unto your neighbor that which is hateful to you' "(Joseph Tov Elem, quoted in Resp. Maharam of Rothenburg, ed. Prague, no. 941). Those who assessed the tax liability of each according to evaluation of his assets were warned "to guard against favoring one who is liked or dealing onerously with one who is disliked, in order not to be disqualified from testimony or the oath" (Or Zaru'a, quoted in Resp. Maharashdam, ḤM 442).

Generally, such an appointment was looked upon as an honorable one: "all families in the city would like one of their members to be appointed, for the honor of the family alone" (Resp. Rashba, vol. 3, no. 399), but there is no doubt that such an appointment also served personal economic interests. In a case where the wealthy families insisted that their interests be represented by two of the five appointees, Israel Isserlein saw fit to accede to their request since the other three would still

1. pages 647, 655.

compose an impartial majority; also, letting the rich have their representatives would show them that their contentions were being taken into account and they would therefore refrain from strictures and appeals; this was possible, however, only if the two men chosen by the rich were "men of truth, certainly not those reputed to be swindlers and cunning men" (*Terumat ha-Deshen,* Resp. no. 342). Sometimes a candidate for election would give notice of his unwillingness to accept the position, and in a case where such a person was nevertheless elected, Solomon b. Abraham Adret held that "his withdrawal from the assent is of no effect, and he is obliged to take up his trusteeship since the community has seen fit to disregard his wishes" (Resp. Rashba, vol. 3, no. 417; see also vol. 4, no. 309). At times an appointee sought to be released from his position after having served for a period (Resp. Ribash, no. 461).

This dual attitude toward appointment as a trustee found legal recognition in the determination that the trustee's liability for any damage he himself caused had to be equated with that of a gratuitous bailee and not a bailee for reward (see Bailment; Resp. Rashba, vol. 5, no. 101). Cases of refusal to accept appointment as a trustee are mentioned in particular in circumstances where the central authorities imposed special emergency taxes on the community – e.g., for the purpose of waging war – and the latter found itself unable to bear the burden of the tax and the means employed for its collection (as in the case of the tax imposed in Prague in 1751: see Elon, *Ḥerut ha-Peraṭ,* pp. 221f.).

In a case where one of the three trustees was unable to read the contents of the declarations, he was nevertheless held to be fit for his position on the ground that the other two could read the contents to him and that they could be trusted to do so without distortion; since the main task of the trustees was to apply the same standards to all, it was held that the trustees who could not read remained as competent as the other two, and sometimes more so, as far as expertise in matters of collection, payment, loans, and the accumulation of other related knowledge was concerned (Resp. Rashba, vol. 3, no. 399). This was an expression of Solomon b. Abraham Adret's general objective of involving all members of the public in communal administration; elsewhere he added: "in many places individuals are not so literate, yet they are appointed along with those who are knowledgeable" (a similar view was taken with regard to signature by the town scribe in place of a witness who could not sign his own name: Resp. Rashba, vol. 2, no. 111; the same held good even for the appointment of a judge from among the residents of a village where "there is no one who knows even one letter" if the man was accepted by the public: *ibid.,* no. 290). The trustees were enjoined to observe total secrecy concerning details which came to their knowledge in the execution of their duties (*Avodat Massa,* no. 1:2). Apparently this office led to the emergence, in the course of time, of special experts in tax matters. Thus in one of his responsa Asher b. Jehiel mentions that he was asked to give his decision "after consulting with tax specialists" and that he saw fit to do so and to uphold their conclusion (Resp. Rosh, 6:4). This phenomenon is probably to be attributed to the fact that the tax laws were based largely on the various *takkanot* and customs in this field, an area in which the experts had gradually acquired special knowledge.

Documentary Evidence. In various *takkanot* provision was made concerning the right or otherwise of the assessors to demand documents from the taxpayer. In one instance it was laid down that the ten trustees were sworn "to act faithfully and truthfully to the best of their knowledge and not to seize the records *(kitvei zikhronot)* of any individual" unless it was agreed by a majority of the ten "to inquire into the affairs of such an individual and to punish him" (Resp. Rashba, vol. 5, no. 126; vol. 3, no. 411).

Erroneous Assessment. Asher b. Jehiel held that in the case of error, even gross error, made by the assessors in the taxpayer's favor – for instance "if they taxed Reuben on 1,000 *zehuvim,* . . . and later ascertained that he had 10,000 *zehuvim*" – the taxpayer was to benefit from the erroneous assessment and did not have to add to it since he had paid according to the estimate and "had divine assistance" (Resp. Rosh, 6:4). Samuel di Medina, the 16th-century scholar of Salonika, found this decision difficult to comprehend but followed it nevertheless, out of high regard for his predecessor (Resp. Maharashdam, ḤM 442). Around 100 years later a different decision was given in Germany in a case where an assessment of property had been made for tax purposes, and on the taxpayer's death two years later "many times this amount was found in his estate" (Resp. *Ḥavvot Ya'ir,* no. 57). The question that arose was whether to deal with the matter in a manner favoring the assessed party "and say that during the two years in question he had prospered greatly or had an unexpected windfall," or to hold that he had "deceived" for purposes of the assessment and therefore additional tax had to be exacted from him. In his decision Jair Ḥayyim Bacharach reviewed at length the *halakhah* and contemporary customs concerning tax assessment and laid down that the decision in a matter of this kind had to take into account a number of factors, such as the nature of the business carried on by the assessed (that is, whether or not it allowed for the possibility of such sudden enrichment), his previous conduct in tax matters, and the general position as regards the prevalence of tax fraud and concealment. (The same approach was followed in another case, *ibid.,* no. 58.)

Information under Oath and Ban. In order to ensure the veracity of the taxpayer's declaration, it was customary in many places to impose a ban on a person filing an inaccurate declaration, or to require the taxpayer to take an oath on the truth of his declaration. Solomon b. Abraham Adret decided that in strict law an individual could not be compelled to swear to the truth of his declaration: "as in the case of a debtor pleading a lack of means to pay his creditor, when the court cannot, in law, ban or compel him to take an oath, and instead tells the claimant: 'go seek him out and recover from him'!" However, in the same way as it had been ordinated that a ban could be imposed on a debtor pleading a lack of means (*ein li:* see Execution (Civil); Yad, Malveh, 2:2), in this case too "the ban may be imposed without any qualification . . . so that everyone who has some means shall pay his proportional share to the community chest." Since the *geonim* had ruled that a debtor pleading a lack of means could be made to take a solemn oath to this effect, "it is possible that in this matter too [i.e., the taxpayer's declaration] the same may be done on the basis of a *takkanah*" (Resp. Rashba, vol. 3, no. 392).

The practice of swearing such an oath in accordance with various *takkanot* came to be expressly recognized by Solomon b. Abraham Adret (see, e.g., *ibid.,* no. 408). Asher b. Jehiel was opposed to an individual's swearing an oath of this kind in tax matters, distinguishing between such an oath and that which one partner could require from his fellow partner even in the case of *ta'anat shema* ("doubtful plea"; see Oath); he was only prepared to recognize the custom whereby in communal enactments of this kind, "they impose a ban on the whole community to observe them, but do not require an oath from each individual" (Resp. Rosh, 6:13). This ban was imposed in general terms in the presence of all persons above the age of 15 who were called upon to make payment honestly (Resp. Rashba, vol. 5, no. 222). However, Asher b. Jehiel's opinion was not accepted and in the 15th century Isserlein based the community's right to require an individual to swear an oath to the truth of his tax declaration on the premise that the members of a community were comparable to partners and one partner could require an oath from his fellow even on a *ta'anat shema* (Terumat ha-Deshen, Resp. no. 343 and see below). This was also the decision of Isserles (Rema, ḤM 163:3) and of later *posekim* (see e.g., *Noda bi-Yhudah,* Mahadura Tinyana, ḤM no. 40). Bacharach expressed the opinion that after the conduct of the taxpayer and the general position as regards honesty in tax payment were taken into account, it was in the absolute discretion of the community "to prevent one from taking an oath even if he should wish to do so, and to require an oath, according to their discretion, from one who should wish to do so; and no explanation is called for, provided only that their hearts shall be turned toward heaven" (Resp. *Ḥavvot Ya'ir,* no. 57 and see particulars cited there of cases in which the oath was taken).

Alternating Between Different Tax Methods. It was held that where it was customary for the whole community to follow the self-assessment method (i.e., by way of a declaration) an individual had to be refused a request that his liability be assessed by assessors: "impose on me as you see fit, and I shall do as you wish" even if he made his request because "I am afraid I shall not on my own be able to do as required by law." The reason for this was that an individual was not entitled to choose his own method but had to follow the one agreed upon by the public (Resp. Rashba, vol. 3, no. 392). The trustees too were held to have no power "to change from the method of declaration to that of assessment *pesak* or to any other method" (Resp. Ribash, no. 457); only the community itself could do so (*Terumat ha-Deshen,* Resp. no. 343, and see below; Rema, ḤM 163:3) and sometimes it exercised this power. This fact is illustrated, for instance, in the extant records of the tax system practiced in the Mantua community from the end of the 16th century until the beginning of the 18th. The tax code of this community, the "order of assessment" *(seder ha-ha'arakhah),* dating from the end of the 16th century, deals in detail with the various kinds of taxable property and income, and sets out the order of assessment of property and tax by the assessors, the manner of their election, and so on. Yet it appears that from the end of the 18th century this community practiced the *casella* system – named after the case or box into which the tax payment was deposited – which introduced many changes into the tax collection procedure, mainly a changeover to the method of individual self-assessment (see Simonsohn, bibl. vol. 1, pp. 272–301).

The community, however, was not entitled, when it varied the tax method, to adopt indiscriminately the stringencies of different methods in determining the taxpayer's liability: "so far as concerns the wish of his community to do something that is new and completely unheard of, namely to combine the stringencies of two systems by both assessing and imposing a ban, and then not allowing him any reduction in the assessed amount while obliging him to pay the difference (if he be under-assessed at a time when he himself knows that he owns more than the assessed amount) this is robbery and extortion, and a person is not put to death in two ways . . . we must not innovate further stringencies and once they have made their assessment they cannot any more impose a ban on him and there is no substance in the statements of those who would insist on combining the stringences of both systems" (*Noda bi-Yhudah*, loc. cit.). This is one more illustration of a restriction on the community against departing from the general principles of equality and justice (see above).

Tax Methods and Socio-Economic Class Dispute. To a large extent both the choice of tax method and the desire to change from one to the other were an outcome of communal dispute of a social and economic nature, and it was no easy task for the halakhic scholars to conciliate between the conflicting class interests. Isserlein, who in a certain case saw fit to uphold the demand of the wealthy that two out of the five trustees be their own representatives (see above), gives a further interesting description of the manner in which the actual tax method was determined (*Terumat ha-Deshen,* Resp. no. 343).

A "heavy tax" had been imposed on the community; for the purpose of its collection, the community prescribed the method of individual self-assessment, by declaration, the latter to be affirmed under oath. A wealthy section of the community *(ba'alei kissin)* objected to this method and demanded that the assets and tax liability of each be determined by assessors, "as has been the custom for some years." Alternatively, they demanded that even if the declaration method was applied the taxpayer should not be required to detail all particulars of his assets in the declaration: "out of concern for the fact that this might cause them harm in a number of ways"; instead the taxpayer should merely have to specify the general amount at which he assessed his assets and affirm under oath that he had no more. This time Isserlein rejected the demands of the wealthy. As regards the first, he held that the community members had to be regarded as partners and since each partner had the right to require an oath from his fellow partner even on a doubtful plea (because otherwise a partner would permit himself to depart from the truth by reason of his activity on behalf of the partnership business), therefore there certainly existed grounds for the same reasoning in respect of the wealthy members of the community, who were likely to permit themselves an untruthful declaration because they were active on behalf of the community and represented it before the authorities, and because each of them would assume that none of the others submitted a truthful declaration. Furthermore, if assessment were to be made by assessors without the oath of the taxpayer, it would be impossible to ascertain the true state of affairs: "human beings are not prophets who are able to know what the next man has in his money-box . . . a person may become rich unbeknown to anyone else . . and people are likely to conceal their assets so as to avoid being regarded as having reached satiety." So far as the alternative demand was concerned, Isserlein held that it was indeed proper according to talmudic law, but that it had already been laid down by the *geonim* and later scholars that a person taking any oath was required to give details of the matter sworn to, so as to avoid error or deceit; this was all the more so in tax matters, when "people are in the habit of employing all kinds of strategems to evade payment." Therefore if the taxpayer were allowed a general oath without providing details, it would open the way to error and abuse: "hence it is necessary to set out in detail and explain clearly all the assets, their quality and substance . . . and this has been the practice since long ago in all our borders."

It may be noted that this reasoning provided a basis not only for the determination of a method of tax assessment where none had previously existed, but also for the variation of a method of tax collection practiced for some time (this was also the conclusion of Rema, ḤM 163:3. For further particulars of tax assessment methods, see *Massa Melekh,* 5:2).

Tax Appeals. The communal fiscal system allowed for the taxpayer to appeal against his assessment to a higher instance, on both the amount and questions of law. In many communities there were special tribunals for this purpose (e.g., in the Mantua community: see Simonsohn, bibl., vol. 1, pp. 274, 283f.) and often appeals of this nature would be aired before the halakhic scholars, who dealt with the matter at issue according to the *halakhah* and the pertinent customs and *takkanot.*

Presumption of Possession (Din Muhzak) in Favor of the Community. In this connection a fundamental problem with an important bearing on the relationship between the community and the individual in Jewish law was discussed. A *takkanah* attributed to R. Gershom b. Judah laid down that a person could not object before the courts in respect of a tax imposed on him, "until he pays what was imposed on him, either in cash or in pledges." This rule was equated with the general rule applicable to all appeals against a judgment, namely that payment is not to be delayed until the appeal is heard (*Binyamin Ze'ev,* no. 295; cf. *Takkanot Medinat Mehrin,* no. 214). It was laid down that only in the event that the city elders agreed with the individual that the tax imposed on him was unlawful would the legal hearing have to be disposed of first (*takkanah* quoted in Resp. Maharik, no. 17 (cf. also nos. 1, 2) and in *Binyamin Ze'ev,* no. 295). Meir of Rothenburg thought that this presumption in favor of the community had no talmudic basis, but on further consideration he concluded that this was "a custom according with the Law of the Torah." On the basis of the doctrine of *dina de-malkhuta dina* (BM 73b; and see above), he held that the king was "presumed to be in possession of *[muhzak]* the tax [demanded] of each individual" and therefore "also the community wishes to be presumed in possession, to be defendants and not plaintiffs . . . with regard to the rule that the burden of proof is on the person who seeks to recover from another . . . for thus it will at all times have the upper hand" (Resp. Maharam of Rothenburg, ed. Prague, nos. 106, 915; ed. Lemberg, no. 371). He also held that his reasoning contributed to the good order of the public, "for if we were to hold otherwise, everyone would reply to the community, saying: 'I am exempt from the law' or 'I have already paid my tax' . . . everyone would do wrong and think in his heart 'who shall sue me?' . . . since a shared pot is neither hot nor cold" (see BB 24b). In his opinion this additional substantiation could also be based on various analogies from the talmudic law (idem, ed. Prague, no. 106; *Mordekhai,* BB no. 522). However, the presumption only operated in the community's favor in case of doubt about the true legal position; if *prima facie* it appeared that the law was against the community, the individual would not have to comply except after conclusion of the legal hearing: "justice shall not be perverted against the individual for the sake of the public, nor is robbery permissible because it is committed by the public" (Maharam, loc. cit., and cf. BB 100a). Therefore, if the individual pleads, "this is the law of the community and this has been their practice until now," while the community contends otherwise, and the matter is uncertain, "then why should the community be in a stronger position? And the position of the claimants is not worsened even if they are not many, since they are representative of the community" (*Nimmukei Menahem* of Menahem Merseburg, Din 37).

Solomon b. Abraham Adret reached the same conclusion, except that he emphasized that in law the principle which placed the burden of proof on the claimant was also applicable between the community and the individual; however, "it is an ordinance for the sake of good public order, that it shall not be possible for every person to say, 'I shall not pay until adjucation of my plea that I am not liable,' otherwise everyone shall do so with the result that the tax will never be collected, and only the swindlers shall be encouraged. We here [in Barcelona] have also ruled that any person who denies liability must first make payment before the matter can be adjudicated upon." In such a case it did not suffice for the individual to provide a surety for the amount in dispute (Resp. Rashba, vol. 3, nos. 398 and 406).

Presumption and the Rights of the Individual. Later the scholars became concerned that this presumption, which was necessary as an effective deterrent against tax evasion, should not prejudice the rights of the individual in disputes with the community. Thus, for example, it was decided that in a case where there were two differing halakhic opinions, one rendering the individual liable for tax and the other exempting him from it, the law had to be applied in favor of the community which is presumed to be in possession – as is the law in any other case of actual possession (see Extraordinary Remedies; also Codification of Law, s.v. the plea of *kim li;* Resp. Maharyu, no. 133). Similarly, it was decided that in a dispute between the individual and the tax trustees concerning the statements made by the former in his deliberations with them, the trustees had to be believed because they were representatives of the community, "and the community is [presumed to be] in possession . . . and because of this they are believed" (Resp. Maharyu, no. 124). Concern that the operation of the presumption might prejudice the rights of the individual was particularly real because, theoretically, the justification for affording the community a favored status in this respect was capable of being applied in every case of dispute between the community and the individual and not necessarily in tax matters only, as in fact could be deduced from the talmudic sources quoted as an analogy for the presumption (see *Terumat ha-Deshen,* Resp. no. 341).

Limiting the Scope of the Presumption. As a way of safeguarding the rights of the "defenseless" individual in disputes with the "powerful" community, the scholars laid down several material reservations, by means of which the presumption that the community was in possession was restricted. First was that the presumption only operated in favor of the community in respect of a tax imposed by the ruling power and "all other payments for governmental purposes" embraced within the rule of *dina de-malkhuta dina,* so far as "all other public matters and needs" was concerned the presumption did not apply. With a view to safeguarding the interests of the public, it was held to be sufficient if the individual gave a pledge for the amount in dispute, "so that he shall be the plaintiff and the one in pursuit of justice, and the public not be occasioned loss." It was also laid down that the presumption could not be held to operate in favor of the public with regard to the plea of *kim li* (see above; *Terumat ha-Deshen,* loc. cit.). Secondly, since the explanation for the presumption in favor of the community was based on the theory that the king was presumed to be in possession of the tax by virtue of the rule of *dina de-malkhuta dina*, (the community being the agent of the king), therefore if the community had already paid the tax to the government and then sought to collect the tax from individual members of the community, it could no longer rely on the operation of the presumptions in its favor, since on making payment to the king it had ceased to be his agent (*Nimmukei Menahem* of Merseburg, Din 37). On the basis of this distinction Joseph b. Ezra, the 16th-century scholar from Salonika, concluded: "accordingly we learn at this time, when the communities do not distinguish between the king's taxes and other taxes, that there is no room for presuming in favor of the public unless there is a custom to this effect and such custom is not called into question" (*Massa Melekh,* pt. 6, 3rd *Tenai*). Thirdly, if there was still time for it the individual was entitled to have the legal hearing take place prior to the due date of the tax payment and in this event no pledge was to be taken from him (*Massa Melekh,* pt. 6, 3rd *Tenai;* see also *Terumat ha-Deshen*; Resp. no. 341). Fourthly, in the 16th century it was concluded, from the thesis that the community acted as the agent of the government, that in circumstances where it could be assumed that the community made its plea in order to safeguard its own interests and because it acted as the agent of the government, the presumption would not avail the community: "and there is no distinction between the kings' due and other public needs – they [the community] are the ones who claim and seek to cover payment and the burden of proof is theirs." The only difference between the community and the individual, in case of a dispute between them, lay in the fact that the former could demand a pledge from the individual in order to ensure a legal hearing of their dispute (Resp. Menahem da Fano, no. 43; already in R. Gershom's *takkanah* the matter of taking a pledge was mentioned, although apparently in satisfaction of the debt and not only for the purpose of securing its repayment; see also Pledge. For further particulars see *Massa Melekh,* pt. 6).

Adjudication and Evidence. The special circumstances which formed the background to the development of the tax law system led to the appearance of *takkanot* and customs which introduced into this field of the law far-reaching changes that also affected matters of adjudication and the laws of evidence. Apart from the fact that special tax courts, composed of communal leaders adjudicating "in accordance with their own custom" (Resp. Rosh, 7:11; and see below), existed in many places, significant changes were introduced into the *halakhah* concerning *dayyanim* and witnesses even in the courts presided over by the halakhic scholars.

Disqualification of Witnesses and Judges. Jewish law lays down stringent requirements governing the competency of witnesses, and disqualifies relatives of the litigants as well as other interested parties from acting as witnesses in a suit (Tur and Sh. Ar., ḤM 33 and 37 and standard commentaries; see also Witness). Hence in strict law the testimony of a member of the community was inadmissible in any matter connected with local taxes, since any tax ruling for or against an individual member of the community inevitably affected the tax rate for the rest of the community also. According to talmudic law, a town resident was disqualified from testifying in a matter concerning the property common to the residents in his town, such as the public baths, unless he renounced all benefit from the particular property (BB 43a; Sh. Ar., ḤM 37:18ff.). In post-talmudic times, however, the existing realities of Jewish life made the strict observance of this rule impossible, certainly as regards a number of public matters (see *Takkanot ha-Kahal*[1]), particularly the adjudication of tax disputes. As late as the 12th and 13th centuries it was still decided in Germany that the testimony of communal leaders to the effect that a person had made a declaration before them in regard to a tax matter was not to be admitted, "as long as they [the communal leaders] have not paid their share of the tax," in view of their interest in the matter (*Mordekhai,* BB no. 483, in the name of Avi ha-Ezri and of Meir of Rothenburg). In one instance Asher b. Jehiel decided that a member of the community was not competent to testify unless he "genuinely" renounced all personal benefit in the matter concerned (Resp. 58:1, 3), and in another case he went to the extent of holding that so far as tax was concerned, it was quite inconceivable for a member of the community to renounce effectively (or exclude himself from) all benefit deriving from his testimony: "for this matter of tax payment will ever be customary, and it is impossible for them to effect a renunciation in such manner as never to benefit from the tax that will be paid" (*ibid.,* 6:15, also 6:21). In addition, the question of the disqualification of witnesses on the grounds of their kinship with one or other of the parties, or with the judges, often presented problems, since members of the community intermarried and created ties of affinity with each other. For all these reasons judges themselves were often in a similar position of being disqualified by law from hearing a matter (BB loc. cit.; Tur and Sh. Ar., ḤM 7:12; *Beit Yosef* and other standard commentaries).

Abrogation of Disqualifications. The problems outlined above were overcome by means of communal enactments which expressly qualified members of the community as witnesses and judges in matters concerning their fellow-residents. The question of the validity of a *takkanah* of this kind was raised before Solomon b. Abraham Adret, and answered in the affirmative: "This too is clear, that the enactment of the community is conclusive; in tax matters it has been the practice of all the communities to adjudge the town residents and to gather testimony from them, even though they be relatives of the judges or the litigants; moreover, it may be that the interests of the court and of the witnesses are at stake in their judgment and testimony, but they nevertheless testify for themselves; all this derives from the law of communal enactment" (Resp. Rashba, vol. 6, no. 7). He held that a *takkanah* of this kind was vital for the proper administration of justice in tax matters in particular and in matters of the public domain in general, "for otherwise you annul all communal enactments, yet the custom of the communities is law and in all matters of this kind it must be held that custom overrides the *halakhah*" (*ibid.,* vol. 5, no. 286); furthermore, *takkanot* of this nature were common "and no community has ever called this matter into question" (*ibid.,* no. 184; cf. the like opinion in Resp. Rosh, 6:15).

The impact of these *takkanot* became part of the fixed law: "Tax matters are not dealt with by the local judges, since they and their relatives have an interest therein . . . but if they have made a *takkanah* or the local custom is that the local judges deal also with tax matters . . . then this is the law" (Sh. Ar., ḤM 7:12); likewise as regards witnesses: "in these times it has been the practice to accept witnesses from among members of the [local] community . . . in regard to all their matters, and they are competent even in matters involving their relatives, for the reason that they [the communities] have accepted this for themselves" (ḤM 37:22). This *halakhah* became so widely accepted that at the beginning of the 20th century it was stated: "In our time we have never seen or heard that a matter affecting the community shall not be adjudged by the local *dayyanim* . . . and the local *dayyanim* are competent to deal with all matters of the community" (*Arukh ha-Shulḥan,* ḤM 7:22. For further particulars see *Minhag; Takkanot ha-Kahal; Massa Melekh,* pt. 7.).

Principles of Interpretation. The fact that a substantial part of the Jewish tax law system became based on written *takkanot* enacted in the various communities, contributed toward great creativity in the field of the interpretation of laws. In tax disputes between the individual and the community, and between different communities, the halakhic scholars were frequently called upon to interpret these *takkanot* and in so doing they not only decided the concrete matter before them, but also established guiding principles of interpretation of importance to Jewish law in general (see Interpretation[2]). It may be noted that the scholars based the principles they applied in the interpretation of the communal enactments on a wide discussion of and reliance on various analogies from talmudic law, as can be seen from the responsa mentioned below.

Interpretation of Communal Enactments. Interpretation of the communal enactments was, in the main, the task of the halakhic scholars before whom a particular matter was brought, and very many of the responsa concerning tax matters include detailed discussions on such interpretations (see, e.g., Resp. Rashba, vol. 5, nos. 277, 279; Resp. Ritba, nos. 114, 120; Resp. Maharyu, no. 84; and see illustrations below). Sometimes, however, a *takkanah* included an express provision that any doubt concerning the meaning of a matter mentioned in it was to be resolved by the interpretation of the incumbent communal leaders (called *muqaddimūn* or *berurim*), and the scholars

1. page 658; 2. page 71.

decided that in this event the interpretative authority was entrusted to the aforesaid leaders (Resp. Rashba, vol. 3, no. 409; vol. 5, no. 221). Notwithstanding such an express provision there remained the possibility that in certain cases the issue had to be left to the decision of the halakhic scholars. This happened, for instance, in a case (Resp. Ritba, no. 134) which arose from a *takkanah* laying down that a person giving in marriage "a daughter or sister" to someone who did not pay tax in that community was liable, in certain circumstances, to pay tax on the amount given as a dowry. A resident of the community gave his granddaughter in marriage and the community demanded tax from him, contending that this case too was covered by the *takkanah* since "grandchildren are as children." The grandfather challenged this demand, pleading that such a construction was valid "in the language of the Torah" (see, e.g., Yev. 62b with reference to the *mitzvah* of procreation), "... but in human parlance and dealings, grandchildren are not called children," and therefore when a person bequeathed his property to his "children" his grandchildren were not included in the bequest (BB 143b). The communal leaders rejected this plea and, on the basis of the provision that anything in the *takkanah* whose meaning was doubtful must be interpreted as the communal leaders saw fit, contended that their own interpretation was binding. In his responsum Yom Tov b. Abraham Ishbili (Ritba) proved from talmudic law that in all matters concerning business transactions, vows, and communal enactments, the standards of "human parlance" had to be applied, and by these standards grandchildren were not to be equated with children (cf. also Yad, Nedarim, 9:23; Sh. Ar.; YD 217:46). On this basis he held that there was no further room for the communal leaders to interpret the term under dispute, "since the language used is not doubtful but clear" and the communal leaders' interpretative authority was confined solely to a case where doubt existed about the meaning of a particular term.

Ambiguity in Tax Enactments. In a case of conflicting provisions in a *takkanah* dealing with tax liability, it was held that the *takkanah* in question had to be interpreted in favor of the taxpayer (Resp. Rashba, vol. 5, no. 281) and so too if the text of the relevant provision allowed for alternative interpretations. The basis for this statement was as follows: since the *takkanah* purported to impose on the individual a payment for which he would not otherwise be liable, therefore "everything that falls outside the ambit of the strict law cannot be made to apply to him except when this is clearly justified, and until this is so talmudic law has to be applied ... because the burden of proof is on the plaintiff" (Resp. Rashba, vol. 3, no. 397; Ritba, no. 157). For the same reason an ambiguity in the text operated to the disadvantage of the individual if in strict law he was liable for the tax. In a case where the community had agreed to grant one of its members a tax exemption without specifying the period of its duration, Asher b. Jehiel rejected the member's plea that his had been an exemption for life and held that the law was in favor of the community if it pleaded that the exemption had been intended for one year only: "since he is obliged to pay along with the others but seeks to escape liability on the plea that he was granted an exemption, therefore he is at a disadvantage ... and since he was given an undefined exemption, we have to interpret this exemption as restricted to the minimum that we have to adjudge him" (Resp. Rosh, 6:19).

Language of the Takkanah and Intention. It was held to be a basic principle that a *takkanah* must be interpreted in accordance with the knowledge and understanding of those who had authority to do so – the halakhic scholars or the communal leader *(muqaddimūn)*, as the case might be – and not according to "the intention of those who enact the *takkanah*" (Resp. Rashba, vol. 3, no. 409; in this particular case authority was entrusted to the *muqaddimūn*). However, exaggerated adherence to this principle was to be avoided, since "at all events there are times when the intention is common knowledge and is like a stake that cannot be uprooted, so that all know that a certain condition or matter was instituted, beyond any doubt, with a specific intention, even though the language allows for a contrary interpretation" *(ibid.)*. This rule was illustrated in a dispute involving the interpretation of a *takkanah* stating that tax declarations had to be brought to the synagogue on a particular day of the week. In actual fact, however, the tax trustees sat in the courtyard *(ḥaẓer)* in front of the synagogue and on one of the upper floors *(aliyah)* but not inside the synagogue itself. Therefore it was averred that this was not in keeping with the language of the *takkanah* since places such as the *ḥaẓer, aliyah, azarah,* and so on had their own separate names and identities. This contention was rejected out of hand by Solomon b. Abraham Adret, for the reason that the relevant text had to be interpreted, in each case, in its own substantive context; thus if the *takkanah* in question had been concerned with prayer, the intention would have been to refer to the synagogue itself, that is the place where the congregation was led in prayer, but in a *takkanah* concerned with the submission of tax declarations, "the intention was not that they should actually be inside [the synagogue], for what need is there for them to be inside? On the contrary, no more was intended than that they should be in one of its areas, so as to be available to all" (Resp. Rashba, vol. 5, no. 222).

Various kinds of formalistic sophistry in interpreting the text were rejected. A certain *takkanah* stated: "If at the time of accounting it shall be found that a person shows an increase in his capital and money and all his property, beyond what was shown at the time of accounting in the previous year, he shall pay so-and-so much on such increase." A member of the community who showed an increase in respect of some items but not in respect of "all his property" therefore contended that his case fell outside the ambit of the *takkanah*. Again Solomon b. Abraham Adret rejected this as "an idle plea ... devoid of all reason or substance," since the meaning of the *takkanah* was not that the taxpayer had to show an increase in everything actually mentioned, but merely in one or other part of his assets, "and it is the way of the world to speak in this manner ... the intention is plain, that everyone shall every year supplement his account with the increase over the previous year" (Resp. Rashba, vol. 3, no. 407). In the case of another *takkanah*, enforced by ban, it was provided that the taxpayer had to submit an annual declaration affirmed under oath, "and he shall not add thereto nor detract therefrom in any event whatever," until submission of the next annual return. A member of the community discovered in the middle of the year that he had forgotten to declare a certain asset but voiced his fear of rectifying the matter in view of the ban accompanying the stated provision. Solomon b. Abraham Adret replied that it was inconceivable for a person to escape tax liability on account of his own forgetfulness: "this is something which the ear, the heart, and reason all reject," hence the said condition could not reasonably be given its plain meaning, namely that nothing at all could be added to the declaration: "how does it matter to them [the community] that he shall not add when he wishes to do so?" There was no choice, he held, but to say that principally it was intended that there should be no detraction, and that the words "he shall not add thereto," represented no more than a routine and customary form of expression (loc. cit., no. 408).

Tax Collection Procedure. Securing and Recovering a Tax Debt. It was laid down that a tax debt, "from the moment of its assessment by the trustees," must be regarded in the same way as a debt "by deed" and was to be recovered out of the debtor's "free" property *(nekhasim benei ḥorin),* and failing this from his "alienated and encumbered property *(nekhasim meshu'badim),* that is from property which the debtor had transferred to a third party after becoming liable for the tax (see Lien; Resp. Rashba, vol. 5, no. 136; vol. 4, nos. 64, 65). The free property included all the property, movable or immovable, in the debtor's possession, except that he had to be left with his basic needs for survival (Resp. Rashba, loc. cit.; see also Execution (Civil)) and except as otherwise provided in any *takkanah.* An instance is recorded in which the community enacted that a debtor's seat in the synagogue could not be attached in payment of a debt, not even a tax debt; later a special *takkanah* was enacted in connection with an extraordinary tax imposed by the central authorities, to the effect that even a synagogue seat could be taken in satisfaction of such an unpaid tax debt (Resp. Rosh, 5:4; at that time a synagogue seat entailed a proprietary right: see *Ḥazakah*[1]).

For the purposes of recovering a tax debt, the concept of *nekhasim meshu'badim* had a wider scope than in the case of a regular debt. Thus it was held: "It has been the custom of all the communities . . . that when a person's money is subject to a debt owed to the community and this money is given to another, then the party becoming entitled to it takes the place of the first owner"; therefore the tax could be exacted from such money – even though this was not the law in case of any other debt – since "the tax obligation is imposed on the money, and all money which is so obligated and acquired by the second owner is still subject to the obligation of the first owner" (Resp. Ran, no. 10). It was also the practice to oblige the tax debtor to provide a surety or pledge for repayment of the debt (see, e.g., Resp. Rashba, vol. 3, no. 398; Resp. Rosh, 6:29;7:11).

Fine, Ban, or Imprisonment. The customary means of coercion in post-talmudic times, a fine or ban (*niddui* or *ḥerem*), were also adopted against errant taxpayers (see, e.g., Resp. Ramah, no. 250; Resp. Rosh, 6:29, 28:4). Another means of enforcing a tax debt was imprisonment. Originally, in Jewish law imprisonment was not employed as a means of enforcing repayment of a debt, no matter what kind, since this was looked upon as prejudicial to the debtor's personal freedom and inimical to the fundamental principles of Jewish law governing the creditor-debtor relationship. It was only from the 14th century onward – in consequence of changed socio-economic conditions and influenced by the surrounding legal systems – that the Jewish communities came to adopt imprisonment for debt, and then with material reservations designed to protect an impoverished debtor (see Imprisonment for Debt). However, in the case of a tax debt, imprisonment as a means of coercion had come into practice at an earlier date, apparently as early as the 11th century (see Rashi to Pes. 91a and Elon, *Ḥerut ha-Perat* . . ., p. 113). At any rate, it is recorded that in the 13th century it was "the custom of the communities to imprison any person who failed to pay the king's tax because the law of the land is law" (Resp. Rosh, 68:10). Some scholars explained this law on the basis that since the tax in question went to the government and since the general law of the land required that the debtor be imprisoned until he paid the tax, it followed that the community had to do likewise as "the king's agents" (Resp. Ranaḥ, no. 58; cf. the same concept above). However, as regards a tax debt, imprisonment was customary, not only in respect of "the king's tax," but also in respect of a communal tax: "The custom is widespread, in all countries of the Diaspora, that a person who owes [and fails to pay] tax to the community is incarcerated in prison; he is not brought before the court, but the communal leaders adjudge him in accordance with their custom, and he is not set free until he pays or until he provides a surety or binds himself by deed . . . for such is the tax law" (Resp. Rosh, 7:11). This continued to be the practice in the following century (see, e.g., *Zikhron Yehudah,* no. 79; see also the charter of rights for Majorcan Jewry, of 1315, in Dinur, loc. cit., vol. 2, pt. 2, p. 354).

After imprisonment had become an accepted means of enforcement in the case of regular unpaid debts, that is from the 14th century, it continued to be used, sometimes with increased severity, in respect of tax debts. Joseph Colon, the 15th century Italian halakhic scholar, stated that it was permissible to have a recalcitrant tax debtor imprisoned and compelled to pay his debt, even through intervention of the gentiles; this he explained on the basis that a Jew who refused to submit to the internal Jewish government was as one who refused to be adjudged before a Jewish court and whom it was permissible to sue in the civil courts, and under the general law of the land it was the practice for debtors to be imprisoned (Resp. Maharik, no. 17; here this rule was attributed to R. Gershom b. Judah; see also Rema, ḤM 163:1). Even in such a case, however, it was forbidden for all of the debtor's property to be handed to the civil authorities in a manner that caused him loss far beyond the measure of his tax liability (Resp. Maharik, no. 127); furthermore, it was forbidden to coerce, through the general authorities, any individual who was not a resident of the community claiming the tax from him, since such an individual was not subject to the jurisdiction of that community: "shall robbery be permitted because it is committed by the public?" (Resp. Maharik, loc. cit.). From the end of the 16th century onward, there are instances of particular severity in the enforcement of tax collection methods. Tax evasion had become a severe hindrance to the effective organization of autonomous Jewish life and to the maintenance of proper relations with the central government. Thus, for example, the following procedure was adopted: if a tax debt remained unpaid for three days, the debtor was declared "obdurate" *(sarvan);* if he persisted in his refusal, a ban was imposed, with various degrees of severity (see *Ḥerem*); if thereafter the debt remained unpaid for a specific period of time, the debtor was imprisoned until the debt and the expenses involved were paid. This procedure was justified thus: "therefore we have taken such a stringent approach as concerns the tax *takkanah* because we see that many stumble in this respect and permit themselves latitude in tax matters, without taking to heart that this amounts to robbery of the public; hence we very carefully warn the public about this matter" (see *takkanot* of the Cracow community and of Moravia in the 17th century in Elon, *Ḥerut ha-Perat . . .,* pp.178–80, 195f.). In another *takkanah* provision was even made for various sanctions, including imprisonment, to be adopted against communal leaders in the event of their failure to transfer the tax monies *("Toleranzgelder")* to the proper destination in time, so as to avoid "great wrath" on the part of the government (Elon, *ibid.,* p. 221). A similar detailed description has come down of the onerous tax collection procedures which, in the middle of the 18th century, the leaders of the Prague community were compelled by the government to adopt in order to raise the amount the latter prescribed for financing a war (see Elon, *ibid.,* pp. 221 f.).

Ethics of Tax Payment. At all times the halakhic scholars sought to educate members of the public toward genuine payment of their taxes, and emphasized the basic premise that anyone who evaded payment of his share of the tax increased the burden of the remaining members of the community by obliging them to pay more than their due share, and that this was the case whether the tax went to the government or toward

1. page 593.

financing the various services provided by the community. Hence it was held that tax evasion entailed not only ordinary robbery, but also "robbery of the public" *(gezel ha-rabbim)*, which had to be most severely punished (see BB 35b, 88b). This transgression is repeatedly warned against (see, e.g., *Sefer Ḥasidim*, nos. 671, 1386, 1451), and not only the offender was held to be subject to punishment but also the communal leaders (even when they had paid their own due share of the tax) who failed to enact suitable *takkanot* designed to discourage others from tax evasion (loc. cit., no. 671). Samuel di Medina concluded that tax evasion rendered a person "a robber and disqualified as a witness and profit gained in consequence is to be weighed against the loss of the world to come" (Resp. Maharashdam, ḤM no. 442).

The multiple exhortations against tax evasion were aimed at counteracting a common human weakness to justify such conduct on a variety of grounds (see e.g., *Terumat ha-Deshen*, Resp. no. 343). Hence in various *takkanot* a strict ban was imposed on all persons evading tax payment or aiding and abetting the evasion (see, e.g., *takkanot* of Valladolid of 1432, in Finkelstein, loc. cit., p. 371). Indeed, many were most careful to meet their tax liability in full, and often, after having submitted declarations of their taxable property, they returned to advise the trustees of any particulars they had forgotten to mention, in order to fulfill "the duty toward Heaven" and pay the true amount that was due (Resp. Rashba, vol. 3, no. 408). However, there were also instances where means of special severity had to be adopted to cope with tax evasion: "In these times fraud is prevalent and it is right to act with great severity so as not to encourage those who practice it" (Resp. Maharil, no. 121 and see above). A detailed and instructive illustration of the demand for integrity in tax payment is to be found in the "order of assessment" of the Mantua community of 1695. After it is stressed that the individual must faithfully render his tax "report" in all its details – lest he commit "robbery of the public" and his transgression be "beyond bearing" – it is stated (ch. 15): "for he shall not permit himself to do so and think that others too do not submit their report honestly and justly, and therefore he may act like them and withhold for himself . . . it is forbidden to do so for two reasons: firstly, this is simply a vain answer and an unfounded judgment, for how can he have clear information about the others . . . and secondly if it were true as he thinks, I would be surprised to know who permitted the robbery of those of good and upright heart because of someome who acts dishonestly, or who permitted a man to forfeit his right in the world to come because of that sinner or sinners?" (see further *Massa Ḥayyim, Missim ve-Arnoniyyot*, no. 16).

Halakhic Compilations of Tax Law. The special development that took place in the field of tax law also left its mark on the literary sources of Jewish law. The fact that this development took place mainly in the 12th and 13th centuries can be clearly deduced from a review of the classic halakhic compilations of Jewish law. Thus, for example, there is very little mention of tax law in Alfasi's *Sefer ha-Halakhot* or in Maimonides' *Mishneh Torah* (11th and 12th centuries respectively). The subject is discussed more widely in Jacob b. Asher's *Turim* (ḤM 163) from the 14th century, and the scope of the discussion is progressively wider in Joseph Caro's *Beit Yosef* and Shulḥan Arukh, in Moses Isserles' *Darkhei Moshe* and glosses (ḤM 163) from the 16th century in Ereẓ Israel and Poland respectively, and in Ḥayyim Benveniste's *Keneset ha-Gedolah* to the *Tur* and *Beit Yosef* in the 17th century in Turkey. In the responsa collections also, particularly those dating from the 13th century onward, whole sections are devoted to tax law, which provide a great deal of informative material on this field of Jewish law (see indexes to the responsa collections; for particulars of all the above-mentioned works, see Codification of Law).

The emergence of compilations specially devoted to the subject of tax law is of interest. As early as the 11th century a small work of this kind was compiled by Joseph Tov Elem (quoted in Resp. Maharam of Rothenburg, ed. Prague, nos. 940, 941). In the 14th century some 50 tax *halakhot*, in summary form, were quoted in the Nimmukim of Menahem of Merseburg (printed as an addendum to Resp. Maharyu). The most comprehensive and interesting compilation of this nature is the *Massa Melekh*, written by the 16th century scholar from Salonika, Joseph b. Isaac ibn Ezra. Divided into seven parts, the work is a comprehensive review of tax law, titled and subtitled according to subject matter. At the end of these seven parts the author added a concluding section, *Ne'ilat She'arim*, containing a detailed exposition of the laws of custom with the author's explanation that tax law was based, first and foremost, on the legal source of custom. An interesting literary feature is the author's condensation of his own detailed discussions within the body of his work, into brief summarized *halakhot*, each containing the conclusion drawn from the preceding discussion (see summaries of the seven parts, pp. 65, 1–70, 2 and of the *Ne'ilat She'arim*, pp. 70, 2–72, 4). This method corresponded to that adopted by Joseph Caro, whose Shulḥan Arukh contains the summarized conclusions of the discussions in his *Beit Yosef*. Another such compilation is the *Avodat Massa*, written by the 19th century scholar from Izmir, Joshua Abraham Judah. His book is composed of 24 sections subdivided into paragraphs and contains collections of tax *takkanot* and customs from Joseph Escapa, a rabbi of Izmir in the 17th century, and subsequent scholars. Some time later a work called *Massa Ḥayyim* was compiled by Ḥayyim Palaggi, also of Izmir. It is divided into three parts, the first containing a very large collection of diverse *takkanot* and customs, particularly in the tax law field, the second dealing with various laws concerning tax matters, and the last part with the law of custom in general; each part is arranged in alphabetical order. In addition, tax laws are dealt with in detail in the *takkanot* collections of the various communities (see bibl.).

In the State of Israel. For a discussion of the sources and details of the tax laws in the State of Israel see Witkon and Ne'eman (bibl:). It may be noted that terms such as *mas, mekhes, belo,* and *arnona* are still current in the State in the context of tax matters, although they generally have a different meaning from that attributed to them in the course of this article (see Witkon-Ne'eman, pp. 4–8, et al.). In 1964 a tax museum was established in Jerusalem for the preservation of historical material relating to Jewish tax law and all matters touching on taxation in Ereẓ Israel in its earlier and later periods and in the State of Israel. In addition to various research projects, a periodical, *Rivon le-Inyenei Missim*, devoted to tax matters, is published regularly under the auspices of the museum.

Bibliography: *Seder ha-Ha'arakhah li-Kehillat Mantovah* (1695, reprint 1963); Finkelstein, Middle Ages, index s.v. *Taxes; Pinkas ha-Medinah . . . Lita . . .*, ed. by S. Dubnow (1925), s.v. *Missim;* Gulak, Oẓar, 337–44; idem, in: *Sefer Magnes* (1938), 97–104; idem, in: *Tarbiz*, 11 (1939/40), 119–22; J. Newman, *Agricultural Life of the Jews in Babylonia* (1932), s.v. *Taxation;* B. D. Weinryb, in: HUCA, 16 (1941), 187–214 (Germ.); Baron, Community, 2 (1942), 246–89, and index (in vol. 3) s.v. *Taxes and Taxpayers;* Neuman, Spain, 1 (1942), 60–111; 2 (1942), index s.v. *Taxation; Takkanot Kandia ve-Zikhronoteha*, ed. by E. S. Artom (=Hartom) and U. M. D. Cassuto, 1 (1943); Halpern, Pinkas, s.v. *Missim;* M. Benayahu, in: *Kobez al Jad*, 4 (14;1946),

193–228; ET, 2 (1949), 194–6; 5 (1953), 46–51; *Takkanot Medinat Mehrin,* ed. by J. Halpern (1951), index s.v. *Missim;* I. M. Horn, *Meḥkarim* (1951), 73–91; K. P. Tekhorsh, in: *Ha-Torah ve-ha-Medinah,* 5–6 (1952/54), 233–82; M. Beer, in: *Tarbiz,* 33 (1953/54), 247–58; S. Baron, *Historyah Ḥevratit ve-Datit shel Am Yisrael* 1, pt. 3 (1957), 50f.; 2, pt. 4 (1965), 138–45; J. Katz, *Masoret u-Mashber* (1958), s.v. *Missim;* Alon, Toledot, indexes s.v. *Missim* in both vols.; B.Z. Benedikt in: *Ha-Torah ve-ha-Medinah,* 11–13 (1959/62), 590–8; D. J. Kohen, in: *Sefer Yovel le-Y.Baer* (1960), 364–8; Baer, Spain, index in vol. 2 s.v. *Taxation;* S. Simonsohn, *Toledot ha-Yehudim be-Dukkasut Mantovah,* 2 vols. (1962–64), index s.v. *Mas;* J. Bazak, *Hilkhot Missim ba-Mekorot ha-Ivriyyim* (1964); EM, 5 (1968), 13, 51–55; *Toledot Am Yisrael,* ed. by H. H. Ben-Sasson, 3 vols. (1969), index in vol. 3 s.v. *Mas;* A. Witkon and J. Ne'eman, *Dinei Missim* (1969[4]); M. Elon, *Ḥerut ha-Perat be-Darkhei Geviyyat Ḥov . . .* (1964), 15–17, 75, 81, 85, 113f., 127–31, 136, 152, 164, 178–80, 195f., 221f.; idem, Mafte'aḥ, 132–8, 649; idem, *Ha-Mishpat Ha-Ivri* (1973), I, 8, 10ff., 25ff., 32ff., 36, 43, 52ff., 119, II, 330, 347–349, 368, 372ff., 379ff., 389ff., 528, 550, 566ff., 570ff., 585ff., 596–598, 602–607, 617–630, 642, 649, 658ff., 746–749, 752ff., 764ff., III, 1204–1207.

Menachem Elon

HEKDESH (Heb. הקדש), consecrated property, property dedicated to the needs of the Temple; in post-talmudic times the term *hekdesh* without qualification *(setam hekdesh)* came to mean property set aside for charitable purposes or for the fulfillment of any other *mitzvah.*

Consecration for the Temple Needs. The consecration of property was the means of providing for the upkeep of the Temple and the sacrificial services as detailed in Scripture (Lev. 27; II Kings 12:5–17, et al.). In the Temple period a person could consecrate property to either (1) the Temple treasury *(hekdesh bedek ha-Bayit)* that was utilized for maintaining and repairing the Temple buildings; or (2) the altar (*hekdesh Mizbe'aḥ)* for the purchase of sacrifices, namely the animals, and meal-and drink-offerings brought to the Temple altar. If a man simply consecrated his property without specifying which of these two purposes he intended and such property included animals fit for sacrifice at the altar, the animals would be sold for sacrifice and the proceeds allocated to the Temple treasury; i.e., "simple consecration to the Temple treasury" (Tem. 7:2; Shek. 4:7, opinion of R. Eliezer; Maim. Yad, Arakhin 5:7).

Irredeemable and Redeemable Consecration (Kedushat ha-Guf and Kedushat Damim). Property could be consecrated with different degrees of sanctity: i.e., intrinsic sancitity *(kedushat ha-guf)*, embracing all objects consecrated to the altar and fit for sacrificial purposes, such as animals, doves and pigeons, flour, incense, wine and oil; or monetary sanctity *(kedushat damim),* embracing objects consecrated to the Temple treasury, as well as objects consecrated to the altar that were not fit for sacrifice or disqualified because of blemish from use at the altar. Consecrated property of the former kind could not be redeemed, whereas the latter could and the redemption money applied to the purpose for which the property was consecrated. Redeemed property ceased to be sacred and was relegated to its former secular status; but objects fit for the altar could be redeemed solely for the purpose of sacrifice there, since "anything which is fit for the altar, is never released from the altar" (Men. 101a; Maim. Yad, Arakhin 5:7).

Creation of Consecrated Property. Contrary to the general principle of Jewish law that the transfer of ownership cannot be effected in a merely oral manner but requires the performance of a symbolic act such as *mesirah, meshikhah,* or *ḥazakah* (see Acquisition), the rule is that simply an oral statement suffices to transfer the ownership of property from the common man *(hedyot)* to *hekdesh* ("Dedication to the Temple by word of mouth is equal to the act of delivery to a common person even if the property is situated at the world's end": Kid. 1:6 and 28b–29a). This reference introduces the concept that consecrated property is in the ownership of God *(bi-reshut Gavoha),* and therefore can be transferred to Him by mere oral declaration, since "His is the earth and the fulness thereof" and "the earth is as a courtyard which acquires for Him" (TJ, Kid. 1:6, 61a; *Bet ha-Beḥirah*, Kid. 28b).

Legal Implications of Consecrated Property. The principle that consecrated property is *bi-reshut Gavoha* and not in the ownership of a neighbor or the common man (*bi-reshut re'ehu* or *hedyot*) had the effect of placing such property to a large extent beyond customary legal relationships. Thus neither the law of *ona'ah* was applicable to it: "even if a man sold a thousand dinars' worth for one dinar or one dinar's worth for a thousand" (BM 4:9; Tosef. BK 4:3; Maim. Yad, Mekhirah, 13:8; Tur and Sh. Ar., ḤM 227:29), nor the prohibition against usury (BM 57b; Tur, YD 160). Similarly, no compensation was recoverable in tort under any of the recognized heads of tort (see *Avot Nezikin*), in respect of damage caused by or to consecrated property – in terms of the rule that "there is tort in respect of the common man, but not in respect of consecrated property" (i.e., *Gavoha:* BK 4:3 and 37b; Tosef. BK 4:1; TJ, Git. 5:1, 46c; Rashi and Tos. BK 6b; Maim., Yad, Nizkei Mamon 8:1). Furthermore a man who stole consecrated property was not liable to pay double compensation and whoever slaughtered or sold it was only required to make good the capital value and was exempted from the four-or five-fold penalty (BM 4:9; Maim. Yad, Genevah 2:1; see also Theft and Robbery).

So, too, the law on the different degrees of liability for damage or loss attaching to the four categories of bailees (see Bailment) did not apply to consecrated property, a bailee being exempted from taking the judicial oath or from paying compensation in respect of such property (BM 4:9; Shev.6:5; Maim. Yad, Sekhirut, 2:1; Tur and Sh. Ar., ḤM 301:1). In strict law *(din Torah)* a man was exempt from the need to take the different forms of oath (BM 4:9, Shev. 6:5; Maim. Yad, To'en 5:1; Tur and Sh. Ar., ḤM 95:1), but the scholars (BM 58a) prescribed that the oath, including the bailees' oath, was required even in respect of consecrated property in order that such property should not be lightly dealt with; the rabbinical *takkanah* on taking the oath had to be regarded – according to some of the *posekim* – as having the severity of biblical law (Maim. Yad, To'en 5:1). Consecrated property was also distinguished from other property in relation to its modes of acquisition. Thus, *hekdesh* could acquire from the common man and the common man from *hekdesh* by way of money *(kinyan kesef),* whereas one person could only acquire from another in one of the prescribed manners, such as by way of the formality of "drawing" (*meshikhah;* Kid. 1:6; Tosef. Kid. 1:9).

The institution of *hekdesh* bears a certain resemblance to the concept of a legal *"persona"* found in other legal systems. The two are nevertheless distinguishable because of the notion that consecrated property is in the ownership of God and does not belong to any legally created *persona,* as well as by the fact that to a large extent such property is not circumscribed by or subject to the customary legal relationships. R. Ishmael's opinion that *hekdesh* funds could be used to purchase wines, oils, and flours, in order that these could be sold to those requiring them for sacrificial purposes and the profits set aside for the sacred funds, was disputed by R. Akiva, who stated that there could be no trading for profit with the sacred funds (Shek. 4:3) – since "there must be no poverty where there is wealth" (Ket. 106b; see also Rashi *(mahadura kamma) Shitah Mekubbezet,* Ket. 106b and "lest loss be caused to the sanctuary" (Maim. Com., Ar. 6:5)). The custodian of *hekdesh* was the treasurer of the temple *(gizbar).* It was his task to collect all consecrated property, supervise it, buy and sell according to the needs of the sacred funds, represent *hekdesh* at law, and "all *Melekhet ha-Kodesh* was done by him" (Tosef. Shek. 2:15; Maim. Yad, Kelei ha-Mikdash 4:18).

Consecration as a Mitzvah. Although it was considered a *mitzvah* for a man to contribute part of his assets for *hekdesh* purposes "in order to subdue his inclination to be parsimonious" (Maim. Yad, Arakhin 8:12, with ref. to Prov. 3:9), failure to do so involved no blame, in accordance with the biblical injunction, "But, if thou shalt forbear to vow, it shall be no sin in thee" (Deut. 23:23; Yad, Arakhin 8:12). Moreover, according to Maimonides, it was forbidden for a man to consecrate all his property, and "whoever did so acted contrary to the requirements of the law and committed a foolish rather than a pious act . . . placing himself at the mercy of his fellow beings . . ." (Yad, Arakhin 8:13). If a person nevertheless did so, the clothing of his wife and children would be excluded by law from the effect of his consecration (Ar. 6:5; Yad, Arakhin 3:14). Similarly, it was a *mitzvah* to fulfill an undertaking to consecrate by not later than the first festival after such an undertaking had been given and failure to do so after three festivals had passed was a transgression against the negative precept of "thou shalt not be slack to pay it" (Deut. 23:22; Yad, Ma'aseh ha-Korbanot 14:13).

Misappropriation of Consecrated Property (i.e., Sacrilege, Me'ilah be-Hekdesh). Deriving a benefit from consecrated property – of either degree of sanctity – was forbidden for as long as it retained its sanctity, the enjoyment of such benefit being considered sacrilege (*me'ilah;* Me'il. 15a; Yad, Me'ilah 1:1). The inadvertent misappropriation of consecrated property of "monetary" sanctity (see above) by the transfer of it to another as *hullin* ("secular property") put an end to its sanctity and rendered it *hullin;* consecrated property of "intrinsic" sanctity (see above) retained its sanctity, however, and did not become secular (Kid. 55a; Me'il. 20a; Maim. Yad, *Me'ilah,* ch. 6).

Hekdesh after the Destruction of the Temple. After the destruction of the Temple the *tannaim* laid down that a man must no longer consecrate his property as this could give rise to complications if someone were to derive benefit from it, resulting in *me'ilah.* If a man did this, however, the property would be duly consecrated, but certain precautions would be taken: "if an animal – the door should be locked before it, so that it die of itself; if fruits, garments, or vessels – they should be left to rot; if coins or metal vessels – they should be thrown into the Dead Sea or the ocean so as to lose them" (Av. Zar. 13a and Rashi *ibid.;* Yad, Arakhin, 8:8). The Talmud records an incident from amoraic times where people ceased to frequent a bathhouse that had been consecrated, for fear of committing possible *me'ilah* (BM 6a–b).

Consecration for the Poor, or for the Purpose of any Other Mitzvah. In post-talmudic times the term *hekdesh* was principally used, theoretically and in practice, to signify the dedication of property for a charitable purpose or for the fulfillment of some other *mitzvah:* "since we no longer have the Temple, the unqualified consecration of property means consecration for synagogues or the poor" (Nov. Ri Migash, BB 102b; see also Resp. Rashba vol. 5 no. 135; *Sefer ha-Terumot,* 46:4 and 8; *Bet ha-Behirah* Av. Zar. 13b); ". . . even if he said 'consecration to heaven,' his intention is for charity" (Resp. Rashbash, no. 361). Only if a person stated that he intended consecration proper to the altar or the Temple funds would the sanctity of *hekdesh* apply to the property concerned, as well as the prohibition against benefiting from it (Nov. Ri Migash, BB 102b; Rema, YD 258:1). Other scholars expressed the opinion that even in the post-Temple period the law was that if a man simply stated that he was consecrating property, without specifying for what purpose, the sanctity of *hekdesh* with the prohibition against deriving any benefit it would still be applicable – even if such a person in his heart envisaged an appropriation for the needs of *talmud torah* and the like. In the 13th century the example was quoted of a book found in Russia bearing the inscription that it had been given to *hekdesh* by a certain individual, and therefore studying from it was prohibited lest a benefit be derived from consecrated property (*Or Zaru'a,* Av. Zar., nos. 128 and 129). It was held that the proper way to overcome the prohibition was to approach a scholar with a request for the property to be "released" from its consecration on the grounds that the consecrator had repented of his undertaking – as in the case of a vow (see Sh. Ar., YD, 258:1).

Comparison between Consecration for the Temple Needs and Consecration for the Poor. The special rules laid down for consecration for the needs of the Temple did not generally apply to consecration for the poor or for the purposes of some other *mitzvah;* the latter were subject to the same laws as those governing the property of the common man (Tur HM, 95, in the name of R. Isaiah; see also Resp. Rosh 13:1) and "certainly there can be no question" of the law of *me'ilah* applying to consecration for the poor (Resp. Maharashdam, YD 208). In certain matters, however, the law of consecration for the Temple needs was extended to consecrations of the other kind. In the opinion of most halakhic scholars, the rule that "a mere declaration to the sanctuary is equivalent to transfer to the common man," was applicable also to *zedakah* and "whoever states 'I give such and such an object to charity' . . . may not retract" (Rif, *Halakhot,* BK 36b; Ran. Nov. Ned. 29b; Resp. Radbaz, pt. I, no. 802; Sh. Ar., YD 258:13). Similarly, the laws of *zedakah* were applied in the case of consecration for the poor or for some other *mitzvah,* and in several respects these laws are similar to those of *hekdesh;* for example, the negative precept, "thou shalt not be slack to pay it" applies also to *zedakah,* with certain variations (RH 6a and Codes). It was also decided that the act of consecration would be effective even if couched in the language of *asmakhta* – since "the law of *asmakhta* does not apply to vows and consecrations" (Resp. Rif, ed. Leiter, no. 247; *Teshuvot ha-Rashba ha-Meyuhasot le-ha-Ramban,* no. 183; see also Sh. Ar., YD 258:10).

Loans at Interest from Hekdesh Funds. The analogy between consecration for charitable purposes and consecration for the Temple needs – despite their substantial difference – provided the halakhic scholars with a solution to the problem of the permissibility of deriving profit from *hekdesh* monies *(ma'ot);* namely, the consecration (by endowment) of a capital fund whose income was to be set aside for the consecratory purpose. The customary and virtually the only means of deriving income from such monies, was by their loan against interest; however, if this was permissible with regard to consecration for the Temple, funds consecrated for the poor (i.e., *zedakah*) were regarded as property of the "common man" (see e.g., BK 93a) and could not therefore be lent at interest (Raviah, quoted in *Or Zaru'a,* Hilkhot Zedakah, sec. 30 and in Resp. Maharam of Rothenburg, ed. Lemberg, no. 478). At the beginning of the 14th century Isaac b. Moses of Vienna, pupil of Eliezer b. Joel ha-Levi (Ravyah) decided that only such *zedakah* money as had already been allocated for distribution to a particular individual fell within the prohibition since thereafter it was as if the money already belonged to this individual; until such allocation, however, "the law of *hekdesh* applies [to *ẓedakah*] and there is no prohibition against earning interest. Accordingly, when people contribute money and stipulate that the capital is to be preserved but the income distributed to the poor, the law of *hekdesh* certainly applies to such capital and it may be lent against fixed interest which is prohibited by biblical law *[ribbit keẓuẓah de-oraita]* since it is not about to be distributed . . . " (*Or Zaru'a, ibid.*: the author at first states that this was his opinion prior to knowing that Ravyah had laid down a prohibition on the same matter, but he gives no hint at all that he subsequently retracted). This problem, a vexatious one for medieval scholars and communal leaders, was also resolved by Solomon b. Abraham Adret along similar lines, but on the basis of a different halakhic distinction. In reply to the question whether it was permissible to "lend at interest money contributed for the poor and held by treasurers" – which was customary at that time (Resp. Rashba, vol. 1, no. 669) – Solomon b. Abraham Adret replied that "the Law has only prohibited interest coming directly from the borrower to the lender," and here there is no lender since these monies have no specific owners and there is no specific share that any poor individual may recover from the treasurers, who distribute as they see fit – much, little, or none at all; hence lending at interest was prohibited only in respect of money consecrated for the specified poor, but "in the consecrations customary in our areas the poor are not specified and interest is permissible" (*Teshuvot ha-Rashba ha-Meyuḥasot le-ha-Ramban* no. 222). Solomon b. Abraham Adret added, however, that he instructed thus in theory only but not in practice, and "it is not desirable that this be done, lest the fence be breached" (*ibid.;* but cf. idem, Resp. Rashba vol. 5, no. 249).

The far-reaching innovation contained in the two abovementioned decisions was not accepted by other scholars. Meir of Rothenburg took the view that the lending of *ẓedakah* money at fixed interest was a *mitzvah* stemming from a transgression, but in view of the prevailing custom he refrained from instructing the *hekdesh* trustee to act in any other way: "by reason of our sins, the matter has spread to become permissible throughout the kingdom, and the *gabba'im* sin but not for their own sake, because it is the sin of the whole community; I have not the power to protest and it is better that it be done by them inadvertently and not intentionally" (Resp. Maharam of Rothenburg, ed. Lemberg, no. 478). However, he wrote to questioners that thenceforth they were to refrain from the practice (cf. *ibid.*, 234 and 425) and in his opinion money consecrated for the poor could only be lent at interest when the prohibition stemmed solely from rabbinical law, as was the law with regard to orphan money (*ibid.*, see also BM 70a). The same opinion was expressed by the latter's pupil, Asher b. Jehiel, who added that this was "plain law requiring no proof" (Rosh 13:17, and 8 and also 10). This view was also accepted as the law in the Tur and Shulḥan Arukh (YD 160:18). It may be surmised that after the rabbis had prescribed a *hetter iska,* i.e., permission to take interest on loans of money given from any source whatever (see *"Shetar Iska"* in: Usury, *Naḥalat Shivah,* no. 40; see also Usury), this general permission reduced the need for the special permission innovated by Isaac b. Moses and Solomon b. Abraham Adret in respect of funds for the poor.

Purposes of Hekdesh Funds. From the geonic period onward, the term *hekdesh* came to be widely used to denote the dedication of property for public or communal needs, for the benefit of the poor or the fulfillment of other *mitzvot.* The purposes for which such funds were endowed were many and diverse, as can be gathered from the responsa of the *geonim* and later scholars, and included such beneficiaries as: "the poor in general" (as early as the time of the *geonim,* Hai and Sherira, see S. Assaf, *Teshuvot ha-Ge'onim* (1927), 69, no. 59); "the poor relatives of the donor"; "synagogal needs" (Scrolls of Law, cantor's salary, etc.); "the ransom of captives" (e.g., Resp. Rif, ed. Leiter, no. 6); *"talmud torah"* and "those who cling to *Torat ha-Shem*" (presumably the same, Resp. Rashba, vol. 1, no. 1100); "the burial of the dead"; "dowries for orphans about to be married"; and many others. In various places it was laid down in *takkanot* that a portion of the fine imposed on a person convicted of a criminal offense was to go to *hekdesh* (see e.g., *Zikhron Yehudah,* 36). Many funds took their names from their particular localities, such as *Hekdesh Kahal Tortosa* (Resp. Rashba, vol. 1 no. 656), *Hekdesh le-Aniyyei Saragosa* (*ibid.* 617), *Hekdesh Ashkelona* (Resp. Rosh 3:13), etc. Testamentary bequests were also commonly expressed in wills in terms of *hekdesh.* The term was further used to describe particular institutions which served as *talmudei torah,* homes for the poor or the aged, hospitals, hospices for travelers, etc. (see e.g., Resp. Ranaḥ, no. 84, giving a detailed description of such *hekdesh* institutions in Constantinople). Halakhic literature, *takkanot* collections, and Jewish communal documents of the Middle Ages are richly studded with varied references to matters of *hekdesh* and its different purposes, offering material of much historical interest.

Changing the Purpose of Hekdesh Funds. A frequent question concerned the permissibility of changing the original purpose for which the *hekdesh* funds and the fruits thereof were designated. With regard to *ẓedakah* monies it was laid down that "the townsmen may convert the soup kitchen to a charity box and vice versa, and to divert their use to any purpose they think fit" (BB 8b, and Codes); in the opinion of Jacob b. Meir Tam, the townsmen were at liberty to divert the funds even toward a purpose that was permissible but not obligatory *(devar ha-reshut)* such as the maintenance of the town guard (Tos. to BB 8b). On the other hand, it was decided that funds explicitly contributed for a specified purpose could not be diverted (Resp. Rambam, ed. Blau, no. 206; Resp. Ritba no. 206); a standing local custom relied on by the communal leaders for the diversion of funds from their stated purpose justified the assumption that a contribution was given subject to the said custom (S. Assaf, *Teshuvot ha-Ge'onim* (1927), 69, no. 59; *Teshuvot ha-Rashba ha-Meyuḥasot le-ha-Ramban*, no. 268), unless the contrary had been expressly stipulated (Resp. Rambam ed. Blau no. 206; Rema YD 259:2). In the discussions on this question, the nature of the charitable purpose played an important role and the principle was accepted that there could only be a change in charitable object from a less to a more important one: e.g., funds for the synagogue or cemetery could be applied to the needs of a house of study or those of *talmud torah,* but not vice versa (Sh. Ar., YD 259:2). The same principle applied in the case of a field contributed for the purpose of the annual distribution of its produce to the poor, even when seven prominent townsmen agreed to a change of purpose, since the contributor had declared his intention that the field be used for this particular purpose only and any change would amount to "robbing the poor" (Resp. Rashba, vol. 5, no. 269; in this case the change was prohibited even for the purpose of *talmud torah,* Sh. Ar., YD 259:2; see also PDR 1:359f.). However, diverting funds was held to be permissible even of those destined for *talmud torah* or the support of the poor, for the purpose of redeeming captives, since this amounted to saving life and took precedence over all other charitable purposes (Sh. Ar., YD 251:14, 252:1).

Administration and Legal Procedure. *Hekdesh* is administered by an *apotropos* ("guardian" or "trustee") or *gizbar* ("treasurer") appointed by the benefactor or the court; the court is the higher guardian of *hekdesh* and in the administration the *apotropos* is subject to the court's supervision (*Sha'arei Uziel,* 1 (1944), 108–15; PDR, 2:34). The trustee must be godfearing, trustworthy, and experienced in negotiating transactions (Resp. Rambam ed. Blau, no. 54), his task being to guard the *hekdesh* assets from all loss and to administer them faithfully in accordance with the purposes for which they were endowed and the instructions of the court (PDR 1:359f.) If there is a strong suspicion concerning the good faith of his administration of the assets, the court is obliged to dismiss him from his position (PDR *ibid.*) but if he was appointed by the benefactor himself, he cannot be dismissed unless proved to have been derelict in his duties (PDR 2:27ff.). In many places it was customary to appoint special supervisors, called *avi yetomim* ("father of orphans"), as a board of control over trustees, and this had been considered appropriate also for *hekdesh* assets (*Taz* to Sh. Ar., YD, 258:5; PDR loc. cit.).

Contrary to the rule evolved from talmudic law, that a three-year period of undisputed possession does not confer the title of *ḥazakah* ("presumptive ownership") in respect of *hekdesh* for public needs – because there is no one to protest on its behalf – it was decided by Solomon b. Abraham Adret that in his time *hekdesh* assets were so organized as to make it possible for them to be acquired by *ḥazakah,* "since here there are known owners and appointed treasurers, who have a part in such property and buy, sell, and barter with the knowledge of the *ḥavurah*" (i.e., society or corporate body; Resp. Rashba, quoted in *Beit Yosef,* ḤM 149, n. 37). It was also thus decided in respect of all *hekdesh* property supervised by treasurers (Sh. Ar., ḤM 149:31 and see Rema thereto). On the question of the extent to which a charitable fund of such kind could be regarded as having a separate legal identity, see Legal Person.

Evidence in Matters of Hekdesh. In the post-talmudic period *hekdesh* was associated with an interesting development in the rules of evidence in Jewish law. In talmudic times the law was that persons connected with or having an interest in the matter under dispute were disqualified from testifying in regard to it (see Witness) and a townsman could not therefore testify in a matter concerning the property of his town, unless he had renounced all benefit from such property (BB 43a and Codes). In terms of this halakhic ruling it was decided, as late as the beginning of the 11th century, that those who worshiped in a particular synagogue were disqualified from testifying in regard to *hekdesh* contributed for the benefit of that synagogue (Resp. Rif, ed. Leiter, nos. 163 and 247). With the proliferation of public institutions and particularly as far as the community was concerned, the observance of the prohibition in matters involving the interests of such bodies represented an ever-increasing burden, with the result that new customs and *takkanot* established and confirmed the competency of such witnesses, "in all public matters, including *hekdeshot*, for if it were not to be so, who would there be to testify? . . there would be no remedy where public needs are concerned . . . if competent witnesses have to be brought from outside . . . there would be found but one in a thousand" (Resp. Rashba, vol. 1, no 680). This custom became the decided law enshrined in the Shulḥan Arukh (ḤM, 37:22; see also *Takkanot Ha-kahal;* Taxation[1]).

The concept of *hekdesh* in its later meaning was a creation of the post-talmudic historico-social situation, and was accompanied by a number of legal developments corresponding to the changes in the social fabric of Jewish life. The phenomenon of a term bearing two different meanings, of which *hekdesh* is an interesting example, offers evidence of one of the paths along which Jewish law has developed. Adherence to a common appellation for a concept with alternative meanings – despite the substantial difference between them – permitted the application of laws pertaining to the concept within one of its meanings – *hekdesh* or consecration for the Temple needs – to the concept within its alternative meaning – *hekdesh* or endowment for charitable purposes – for the purpose of solving certain problems arising from the changing realities of daily life.

In the State of Israel. In Israel *hekdesh* exists in two forms. First is the endowment of property as approved by a religious court and administered in terms of religious law. Originally, Muslim law was applied, even in respect of non-Muslim endowments of this kind. In terms of the Palestine Order-in-Council, 1922, the Jewish community, as well as several Christian communities, were empowered to found *Wakf* or religious endowments and to administer them according to the religious law of the community in question. The second is the endowment of property for charitable purposes according to the civil, as opposed to the religious law, namely in terms of the "Charitable Trusts Ordinance." The ordinance subjects the charitable trust and the trustee administering it to the supervision of the courts and defines "charitable trusts" as "including all purposes for the benefit of the public or any section of the public within or without Palestine [now to be read "the State of Israel"], of any of the following categories: (1) for the relief of poverty; (2) for the advancement of education or knowledge; (3) for the advancement of religion or the maintenance of religious rites or practices; (4) for any other purpose beneficial, or of interest to mankind."

Bibliography: J. Lampronti, *Paḥad Yiẓḥak,* s.v. *Hekdesh* and *Beit Hekdesh;* Gulak, Yesodei, 1 (1922), 50–54, 98f.; Gulak, Oẓar, 112, 128–31, 347f.; Herzog, Instit, 1 (1936), 288–91, 295; 2 (1939), 17, 30, 68 n. 1, 189; B.Z.M.Ḥ. Ouziel, *Sha'arei Uziel,* 1 (1944), 93–107; ET, 2 (1949), 40–42, 201f.; 5 (1953), 51–65; 10 (1961), 352–442; M. Elon, *Ha-Mishpat Ha-Ivri* (1973), II, 327ff., 338, 596ff., 730 n. 14.

Menachem Elon

NOACHIDE LAWS. Legal norms which according to Jewish Law are binding upon non-Jews. The Talmudic list of seven such norms includes: 1. a requirement of the establishment of a system of civil law, and prohibitions against, 2. blasphemy, 3. idolatry, 4. murder, 5. robbery, 6. sexual immorality, and 7. the eating of flesh torn from a living animal (Tosef. Av. Zar. 8:4; Sanh. 56a).

While in the amoraic period the above-mentioned list of seven precepts is clearly accepted as the framework of the Noachide Laws, a variety of tannaitic sources indicate lack of complete agreement as to the number of such laws, as well as to the specific norms to be included. The Tosefta (Av. Zar. 8:6) records four possible additional prohibitions against (1) drinking the blood of a living animal; (2) emasculation; (3) sorcery; and (4) all magical practices listed in Deuteronomy 18:10–11. The Talmud records a position which would add prohibitions against crossbreeding of animals of different species, and grafting trees of different kinds (Sanh. 56b). Nonrabbinic sources of the tannaitic period indicate even greater divergence. The Book of Jubilees (7:20ff.) records a substantially different list of six commandments given by Noah to his sons: (1) to observe righteousness; (2) to cover the shame of their flesh; (3) to bless their creator; (4) to honor parents; (5) to love their neighbor; and (6) to guard against fornication, uncleanness, and all iniquity (see L. Finkelstein, bibl.). Acts (15:20) refers to four commandments addressed to non-Jews, " . . . that they abstain from pollutions of idols, from fornication, from things strangled, and

1. pages 658, 693.

from blood." This latter list is the only one that bears any systematic relationship to the set of religious laws which the Pentateuch makes obligatory upon resident aliens (the *ger ha-gar* and *ezraḥ*).

Nature and Purpose. There are indications that even during the talmudic period itself there was divergence of opinion as to whether the Noachide Laws constituted a formulation of natural law or were intended solely to govern the behavior of the non-Jewish resident living under Jewish jurisdiction. The natural law position is expressed most clearly by the assertion, as to five of the seven laws, that they would have been made mandatory even had they not been revealed (Yoma 67b; Sifra *Aḥarei Mot,* 13:10). Similarly, the rabbinic insistence that six of the seven Noachide Laws were actually revealed to Adam partakes of a clearly universalistic thrust (Gen. R. 16:6, 24:5). The seventh law, against the eating of flesh torn from a living animal, could have been revealed at the earliest to Noah, since prior to the flood the eating of flesh was prohibited altogether. The very fact that these laws were denominated as the "seven laws of the sons of Noah" constitutes further indication of this trend since the term "sons of Noah" is, in rabbinic usage, a technical term including all human beings except those whom Jewish law defines as being Jews. Nor was there a lack of technical terminology available specifically to describe the resident alien. On the other hand, the entire context of the talmudic discussion of the Noachide Laws is that of actual enforcement by rabbinic courts. To that end, not only is the punishment for each crime enumerated, but standards of procedure and evidence are discussed as well (Sanh. 56a–59a). This presumption of the jurisdiction of Jewish courts is most comprehensible if the laws themselves are intended to apply to non-Jews resident in areas of Jewish sovereignty. Of a similar nature is the position of Yose that the parameters of the proscription against magical practices by Noachides is the verse in Deuternonomy (18:10) which begins, "There shall not be found among you . . . " (Sanh. 56b). The attempt of Finkelstein (op. cit.) to date the formulation of the seven Noachide commandments during the Hasmonean era would also suggest a rabbinic concern with the actual legal status of the non-Jew in a sovereign Jewish state. It might even be the case that the substitution by the *tanna* of the school of Manasseh of emasculation and forbidden mixtures of plants for the establishment of a judicial system and blasphemy (Sanh. 56b), itself reflects a concern with the regulation of the life of the resident alien already under the jurisdiction of Jewish courts. Of course, the seven commandments themselves are subject to either interpretation; e.g., the establishment of courts of justice can mean either an independent non-Jewish judiciary and legal system or can simply bring the non-Jew under the rubric of Jewish civil law and its judicial system.

The Basis of Authority. A question related to the above is that of the basis of authority of these laws over the non-Jew. Talmudic texts seem constantly to alternate between two terms, reflecting contradictory assumptions as to the basis of authority, namely seven precepts "which were commanded" *(she-niẓtavvu)* to the Noachides, and seven precepts "which the Noachides accepted upon themselves" (*she-kibbelu aleihem;* BK 38a; TJ, Av. Zar. 2:1, 40c; Ḥul. 92ab; Sanh. 56b). This disparity between authority based on revelation as opposed to consent reaches a climax when Maimonides asserts that the only proper basis for acceptance of the Noachide laws by a non-Jew is divine authority and revelation to Moses, and that " . . . if he observed them due to intellectual conviction [i.e., consent] such a one is not a resident alien, nor of the righteous of the nations of the world, nor of their wise men" (Yad, Melakhim 8:11; the possibility that the final *"ve-lo"* ("nor") is a scribal error for *"ella"* ("but rather") while very appealing, is not borne out by any manuscript evidence). Of course, this same conflict between revelation and consent as basis of authority appears with regard to the binding authority of Torah over the Jew, in the form of "we will do and obey" (Ex. 24:7) as opposed to "He (God) suspended the mountain upon them like a cask, and said to them, "If ye accept the Torah, 'tis well; if not, there shall be your burial' " (Shab. 88a).

Noachide Laws and Pre-Sinaitic Laws. The *amoraim,* having received a clear tradition of seven Noachide Laws, had difficulty in explaining why other pre-Sinaitic laws were not included, such as procreation, circumcision, and the law of the sinew. They propounded two somewhat strained principles to explain the anomalies. The absence of circumcision and the sinew is explained through the assertion that any pre-Sinaitic law which was not repeated at Sinai was thenceforth applicable solely to Israelites (Sanh. 59a), whence procreation, while indeed obligatory on non-Jews according to Johanan (Yev. 62a) would nevertheless not be listed (cf. Tos. to Yev. 62a s.v. *benei;* Tos. to Ḥag. 2b s.v. *lo*).

Liability for Violation of the Laws. While committed to the principle that "There is nothing permitted to an Israelite yet forbidden to a heathen" (Sanh. 59a), the seven Noachide Laws were not as extensive as the parallel prohibitions applicable to Jews, and there are indeed situations in which a non-Jew would be liable for committing an act for which a Jew would not be liable. As to the latter point, as a general rule, the Noachide is criminally liable for violation of any of his seven laws even though technical definitional limitations would prevent liability by a Jew performing the same act. Thus a non-Jew is liable for blasphemy – even if only with one of the divine attributes; murder – even of a foetus (see Embryo); robbery – even of less than a *perutah;* and the eating of flesh torn from a living animal – even of a quantity less than the size of an olive. In all these cases a Jew would not be liable (Sanh. 56a–59b; Yad, Melakhim, ch. 9, 10). One additional element of greater severity is that violation of any one of the seven laws subjects the Noachide to capital punishment by decapitation (Sanh. 57a).

Bibliography: S. Krauss, in: REJ, 47 (1903), 32–40; L. Finkelstein, in: JBL, 49 (1930), 21–25; L. Blau, in: *Abhandlungen . . . Chajes* (1933), 6–21; P.L. Biberfeld, *Das noachidische Urrecht* (1937); ET, 3 (1951), 348–62; R. Loewe, in: *Studies in Memory of Leon Roth* (1966), 125–31, 136–44; M. Elon, *Ha-Mishpat Ha-Ivri* (1973), I, p. 183ff., 216ff.

Saul Berman

DINA DE-MALKHUTA DINA (Aram. דינא דמלכותא דינא), the halakhic rule that the law of the country is binding, and, in certain cases, is to be preferred to Jewish law. The problem of *dina de-malkhuta dina* is similar to – but not identical with – the problem of conflict of laws in other legal systems.

The Historical Background. The original significance of this rule, which was laid down by the *amora,* Samuel, can be deduced from the historical events of that era. The conquest of Babylon from the Parthians by Ardashir I, king of the Sassanids in 226 C.E., brought an end to the period of tranquility from which the Jews in Babylonia had benefited. Losing their political and religious autonomy, they had to adapt themselves to the powerful and centralized rule of the Sassanids. In 241 Shapur I, son of Ardashir, succeeded to the throne and granted the minorities under his rule cultural and religious autonomy which also applied to the Jews. Samuel, their leader at that time, imbued Babylonian Jewry with the consciousness that they must become reconciled to the new government, and a personal friendship was apparently established between Samuel and Shapur (Neusner, Babylonia, vol. 2; 16, 27, 30, 45, 71). Consequently Samuel's rule had important political significance, since it recognized the new Sassanid kingdom as a civilized rule possessing good and equitable laws which Jews were bound to obey, as they were to pay the taxes it imposed (*ibid.*, 69, 95).

The Principle in the Talmud. Samuel's principle is cited only four times in the Talmud (Ned. 28a; Git. 10b; BK 113a; BB 54b and 55a). Three *halakhot* that are cited by Rabbah (according to another reading by Rava, fourth generation of Babylonian *amoraim*), in the name of the exilarch Ukvan b. Nehemiah, and are attributed to Samuel deal with the relationship of Jews to the Persian government and with the relationship of Jewish to gentile law. These *halakhot* establish that the Persian law of the presumptive ownership of land is to be recognzied even if it is opposed to Jewish law (see Ḥazakah); that the sale of land confiscated by the government for non-payment of tax on the land is valid, but only if the sale is because of non-payment of the land tax and not because of non-payment of the poll tax (BB 55a; et cf. BK 113b). Additional *halakhot* adopted in consequence of *dina de-malkhuta dina* are: recognition of the Persian rules for the transfer of land even if they are not in accordance with Jewish law (BB 54b and 55a); the right of the king to sell a person into slavery for evading payment of the poll tax and the option of a Jew to buy him from the government executive officers and to enslave him (Yev. 46a; BM 73b); a prohibition against cheating tax collectors and concealing assets from them, unless the taxes are illegal for the reasons mentioned in the Talmud (Ned. 28a; BK 113a); and the recognition of bills executed by, or endorsed by, non-Jewish courts despite their being invalid according to Jewish law. The Talmud records a dispute as to the scope of the last *halakhah.* One opinion is that every type of document is to be recognized except for bills of divorce and manumission; according to another view the recognition is granted only to declaratory bills serving as evidence, such as bills of debt, but not to constructive bills such as benefactions (Git. 10b). It may be assumed that the definite but restricted recognition of the government's right to punish wrongdoers was based in part on Samuel's principle, although this is not stated explicitly in the talmudic sources. His principle was accepted as definitive *halakhah,* in the talmudic era and later. In spite of the permissiveness of the *halakhah* in adopting a foreign statute, Jewish law remained dominant in Jewish society, as is amply testified by the great legal creativity of Babylonian Jewry in the talmudic era.

The Legal Basis of the Principle. No legal basis for Samuel's principle is given by the Talmud; nor, apparently, did this problem engage the attention of the *geonim.* In one responsum of the geonic period an effort was made to establish the principle for practical religious reasons. The responder, having regard to the realities before him – Jews under a foreign government – states that it is the will of God that Jews should obey the laws of their rulers, a verse from the book of Nehemiah (9:37) being quoted in support of this view (S. Assaf (ed.), *Teshuvot ha-Ge'onim* (1942), no. 66). Later a number of legal explanations were suggested for Samuel's principle. According to one, Jewish law is able in certain cases to accept non-Jewish law because non-Jews are commanded to enact laws to preserve orderly social life (see Noachide Laws; Rashi, Git. 9b). According to another view the reason is contractual; i.e., the inhabitants have accepted the king's statutes or the king himself: "For all the citizens accept the king's statutes and laws of their own free will" (Rashbam BB 54b), or "For the inhabitants of that country have accepted him [the king] and take it for granted that he is their master and they are servants to him" (Maim. Yad, Gezelah 5:18). A third view that has been adopted, especially by later authorities, bases the rule *dina de-malkhuta dina* on the right of the court to expropriate a person's property (*hefker bet din hefker,* see *Bet Din*[1] and *Takkanot*[2]); namely, that the halakhic scholars, by virtue of their authority to enact *takkanot* in monetary matters, even in opposition to the laws of the Torah, have in certain matters recognized the customs of the kingdom and its statutes (*Teshuvot Ba'alei ha-Tosafot* no. 12; *Devar Avraham,* vol. 1, no. 1). Some scholars have compared the right of non-Jewish kings to the power of a king of Israel (Nov. Ritba, BB 55a). Others take the view that the legality of the king's statutes derives from the simple fact that the land belongs to the king, who lays down the conditions of residence, and if Jews wish to dwell in his land they are obliged to obey his directions (Ran, Ned. 28a; *Or Zaru'a,* BK, no. 447; for an additional reason, similar but not identical, see *Or Zaru'a, ibid.* and *Devar Avraham,* vol. 1 no. 1). Still others see the halakhic validity of custom as the basis of *dina-de-malkhuta dina* (*Aliyyot de-Rabbenu Yonah,* BB 55a). Most of these views reflect the sociopolitical outlook of the Middle Ages.

In recent times halakhic scholars have been occupied by the problem of whether the principle *dina de-malkhuta dina* derives from rabbinic or biblical law. The accepted view is that it is of biblical authority and thus those consequences in the field of *halakhah* that derive from this conclusion must be applied to it (see *ibid.; Resp. Ḥatam Sofer,* YD, nos. 127 and 314; *Avnei Millu'im,* 28:2; *Devar Avraham,* vol. 1, no. 1).

The Nature of the Government and the Statute. The halakhic authorities did not accept every law and every kingdom for the purpose of applying the principle *dina de-malkhuta dina* and a series of conditions and qualifications were established.

(1) The Recognized Government. There were scholars who held that the principle applied only where there existed a monarchist form of government (*Oraḥ la-Ẓaddik,* ḤM, no. 1). Others, however, were of the opinion that Samuel's rule included other types of authority. With changes in the forms of government and the increase of non-monarchic states, the second view gained acceptance (*Keneset ha-Gedolah,* Tur, ḤM 369).

(2) Dina de-Malkhuta Dina and the Kingdom of Israel. Another problem is whether the principle applies to Jewish kings in the land of Israel. From talmudic sources it follows that a distinction must be made between the laws of Jewish kings and those of non-Jewish kings as far as *dina de-malkhuta dina* is concerned; this was also the opinion of most early halakhists (*Teshuvot Ba'alei ha-Tosafot* no. 12; Nov. Rashba, Ned. 28a). According to Solomon b. Abraham Adret, those who believe that *dina de-malkhuta dina* does not apply to Jewish kings admit that it does apply to them if they rule outside Israel (Resp. Rashba, vol. 2, no. 134). This opinion corresponds with one of the reasons given for the principle not applying to Jewish kings in Israel: "But the laws of Jewish kings are not valid because Israel was divided among [is the inheritance of] every individual Israelite and does not belong to the king, while in the case of non-Jews their law is that the whole land belongs to the king" (*Or Zaru'a,* BK, no. 447). In the course of time the school that held that Samuel's principle was to be applied to a Jewish government in Israel grew stronger (*Tashbeẓ,* pt. 4, section 1, no. 14).

(3) The Principle of Equality. All agree that the law of the kingdom must apply equally to all its citizens (Maim. Yad, Gezelah, 5:14; Sh. Ar., ḤM 369:8). Resulting from the conditions of Jewish life in exile, the principle of equality was so interpreted that certain types of discrimination were recognized as valid. In one case it was decided that it is sufficient if the law does not discriminate between Jew and Jew despite the fact that

1. page 77; 2. page 561.

Jews as a whole are adversely discriminated against (Resp. Maharik, no. 194). An additional loophole is: the king is permitted to enact special laws for "strangers, not of his own country" (*Ḥokhmat Shelomo* ḤM, 369:8).

The Scope of Laws Included in Dina de-Malkhuta Dina. (1) Issur ("religious prohibitions") and Monetary Law. All agree that the principle does not apply to religious or ritual observances *(issur ve-hetter)*. This was so certain that it was not particularly stressed and is mentioned only in a few sources (*Tashbeẓ*, pt. 1, no. 158).

(2) The King's Interests. Some scholars limited the application of *dina da-malkhuta dina* to such matters only as were the king's interests; namely, the needs of the kingdom and not matters of purely private law (*Sefer ha-Terumot*, 46:8); but most scholars believed that the principle is applicable even in matters of pure private law (*ibid.; Maggid Mishneh*, Yad, Malveh ve-Loveh 27:1; Resp. Rashba, vol. 1, no. 895).

(3) "Non-Jewish Ways" and New Laws of the King. Some halakhists affirm that the laws of the kingdom must be recognized but not "non-Jewish ways." This concept is somewhat obscure; in medieval times when it was first discussed, it apparently meant laws that were based on local customs whose source was not the laws of the kingdom but popular usage; these had no validity since the principle is that "the law of the king is binding but the laws of his people are not binding for us" (Resp. Rashba, vol. 6, no. 149; *Bet ha-Beḥirah*, BK 113b). On the other hand most medieval halakhists held that Samuel's rule does not apply to laws introduced by the kings themselves that were not previously the law of the land (*Teshuvot Ba'alei ha-Tosafot* no. 12; Nov. Ritba, BB 55a; Nov. Rashba, BB 55a). This was under the influence of the point of view prevailing in general medieval jurisprudence, which only recognized the validity of ancient laws. Despite the fact that most of the early halakhists held this view, since Maimonides and Asher b. Jehiel apparently disagreed with it (Alfasi does not discuss it at all), Joseph Caro decided the law in conformity with their opinion (see Codification of Law), and in the Shulḥan Arukh he makes no mention of the restriction of *dina de-malkhuta dina* to ancient law. Joseph Caro's decision served in the following generations as the basis for the extension of Samuel's principle, an imperative necessity when medieval views on the static quality of law underwent sweeping changes and the main laws of the country were no longer based upon ancient statutes but on current legislation (Sh. Ar., ḤM 369:8–10).

(4) State Laws in Opposition to Torah Law. According to some halakhists the law of the state is binding only when it does not oppose Torah law; i.e., only when it relates to matters not explicitly dealt with in the Torah (A. Sofer (ed.), *Teshuvot Ḥakhmei Provinẓyah* (1967), ḤM, no. 49; *Siftei Kohen*, ḤM 73, no. 39, *Ḥatam Sofer*, Resp. ḤM no. 44). This distinction is not sufficiently clear, since it is difficult to find the dividing line between what is available in Torah law and what constitutes a lacuna since, according to the point of view of halakhists, the solution of every problem is to be found in the *halakhah* itself.

Taxes. The king's right to collect taxes was already recognized in the Talmud, and was strengthened by all halakhists in the post-talmudic period. Evading payment of tax is considered robbery (Tashbeẓ, pt. 3 no. 46). The authorities, however, continued to differentiate between justified taxes and confiscations and those without justification (Sh. Ar., ḤM 369:6–11). In practice the way this distinction operated was decided in every individual case, in accordance with the conditions at the actual place and with the substance of the tax. According to the talmudic *halakhah* an unlimited tax is not to be recognized, but later it was declared valid by the *posekim* if it was for "great needs," such as financing a war (*Haggahot Mordekhai*, BB no. 659). Even taxes which were "wicked and cruel" were, from sheer necessity, at times recognized as legal. Thus it was decided that the rule that taxes which have no limit are not to be recognized is to be interpreted as referring to current constant taxes whose sum is at this time greater and beyond the usual amount; when the tax was *ab initio* not fixed, the king may place an arbitrary burden upon the community (*Terumat ha-Deshen*, no. 341).

Bills Executed in Non-Jewish Courts. Beginning with the period of the *geonim* and until the 13th century the aim of limiting the acceptance of bills executed by non-Jewish courts prevailed (S. Assaf (ed.), *Teshuvot ha-Ge'onim* (1942), no. 66; Maim. Yad, Malveh ve-Loveh 27:1), but after this period most halakhists extended acceptance of these documents (Ramban, Nov., BB 55a, Rashba, Nov., Git. 10b). This approach may be inferred from the communal *takkanot*. Communities which undertook to rule in all matters according to Maimonides' *Mishneh Torah* stipulated that in three *halakhot* his ruling was not to be followed, one of the three being Maimonides' *halakhah* that benefactions executed by non-Jewish courts were invalid (A. H. Hershman, *Rabbi Isaac ben Sheshet Perfet* (Eng., 1943), 88f.). Because of this tendency it was decided – in opposition to the *halakhah* of the geonic period that permitted the collection of bills executed by non-Jewish courts from free assets only (S. Assaf (ed.), *Teshuvot ha-Ge'onim* (1927), no. 123) – that such a bill is to be treated like any normal bill and can be collected also from property transferred by the debtor (see Lien;[1] Resp. Rashba, vol. 3, no. 69; *Piskei ha-Rosh*, Git. 1:10, 11). Likewise there was an extension of recognition of non-Jewish courts in which the bills were executed. The need to establish the honesty of the courts, mentioned by the early authorities (Rif. *Halakhot* Git. 10a; Maim. Yad, Malveh ve-Loveh 27:1), was to all intents and purposes no longer demanded, the tendency being to assume the uprightness of the courts until the contrary was proved (*Piskei ha-Rosh*, Git 1:10, 11). Not only were the judges recognized but also administrative officers like notaries (Resp. Ramban, in *Sifran shel Rishonim*, ed. Asaf (1935) no. 46), and among late authorities all kinds of documents issued by those authorities were recognized (*Be'er Yiẓḥak*, EH, 5:4; *Sho'el u-Meshiv* pt. 1, no. 10). See also Shetar.

Changes in the Value of the Coinage. Another problem frequently dealt with in connection with *dina de-malkhuta dina* is that of changes in the value of the coinage. Thus it was laid down that if the government decided that a debt is to be paid in a certain way this could be done despite the possibility of being involved in a breach of the prohibitions against usury or theft (*Sefer ha-Terumot*, 46:5; *Meisharim* 6:1; *Ḥatam Sofer*, Resp., ḤM, no. 58).

Appointments to Religious and Juridical Office by the Government. The question of *dina de-malkhuta dina* was also raised in connection with appointments by the government to juridical and religious office in the Jewish community. Some held that the principle applied to such appointments. The opinion that was accepted is that though indeed there is basis for the principle even in these cases, it is the duty of one so appointed not to accept the appointment if it is against the will of the members of the Jewish community (Resp. Ribash, no. 271; Rema, ḤM 3:4; *Tashbeẓ*, pt. 1 nos. 158, 162; Rema, Resp. no. 123; *Ḥatam Sofer*, Resp. ḤM no. 19).

Bibliography: A Rodriguez, *She'elot u-Teshuvot Oraḥ la-Ẓaddik* (1785), 586–74a; D. Hoffmann, *Mar Samuel, Rector der juedischen Akademie zu Nehardea in Babylonien* (1873); J. Newman, *Agricultural Life of the Jews in Babylonia between the Years 20 c.e. and 500 c.e.* (1932); J. Horovitz, in: MGWJ, 80

1. page 137.

(1936), 215–31; A. Roth, in: *Ha-Soker,* 5 (1937–38), 110–25; F. Kern, *Kingship and Law in the Middle Ages* (1939); P. Biberfeld, *Dina de-Malkhuta Dina* (Schriftenreihe des Bundes Juedischer Akademiker, vol. 2, n.d.); T. Leibowitz, in: *Ha-Peraklit,* 4 (1947), 230–8; I.M. Horon, *Meḥkarim* (1951), 41–134; ET, 7 (1956), 295–308; S. Bendov, in: *Talpioth,* 7 (1960), 395–405; 8 (1963), 79–84, 526–30; 9 (1964), 230–7; S. Lieberman and Y. Kutscher, in: *Leshonenu,* 27 (1963), 34–39; S. Safrai, in: JJS, 14 (1963), 67–70; M. Beer, in: *Tarbiz,* 33 (1963/64), 247–58; S. Albeck, in: *Sefer Yovel . . . Abraham Weiss* (1964), 109–25; D. Daube, *Collaboration with Tyranny in Rabbinic Law* (1965); Neusner, Babylonia, 2 (1966); L. Landman, *Jewish Law in the Diaspora; Confrontation and Accomodation* (1968); M. Elon, *Ha-Mishpat Ha-Ivri* (1973), I, 14, 51–59, 71, 116, 167–171, II, 565 n. 32, 570 n. 53, 602ff., 670ff., 746ff., III, 901 n. 64.

Shmuel Shilo

CONFLICT OF LAWS (also called Private International Law), is a branch of the law dealing with the adjudication of a matter which involves some foreign element, for instance the fact that one of the parties is a foreign citizen, or that the matter in issue arose, wholly or in part, in another country – as in the case of a contract signed in one country and breached in another – and the like. Where there is a conflict of laws, two main questions arise: does the forum in question have jurisdiction to deal with the matter; if it has jurisdiction, what law shall be chosen to apply to the matter? The choice of laws available to the forum include the following main possibilities: (1) The personal law *(lex personalis)* by which the plaintiff or defendant is governed; the personal law may be determined either by the law of the party's place of domicile *(lex domicilii)* or by his national law *(lex ligeantiae);* (2) the law of the place where obligation was established, for instance the place where the contract was concluded *(lex actus; lex loci contractus);* (3) the law of the place where the legal act is to be carried out, for instance the fulfillment of a contract *(lex loci solutionis);* (4) the law of the place of situation of the property forming the subject matter of the dispute *(lex situs);* (5) the law of the place of situation of the forum seized of the dispute *(lex fori).* (See A.V. Dicey and J.H.C. Morris, 1967[8].)

This entry is arranged according to the following outline:

In Jewish Law
Multiplicity of Legal Rules
  Concerning the Laws of Marriage
  Concerning the Laws of Divorce
  Concerning Labor Law
  Concerning the Laws of Partnership, Land Tenancy, etc.
Conflict of a Factual-Legal Nature
  Concerning Bonds of Indebtedness
  Concerning the *Ketubbah*
Jewish and Non-Jewish Parties to the Same Suit
Conflict of Laws; Principles Where the Foreign Law Is Applicable
  Distinguishing between Material and Procedural Law
  Lex Domicilii as Opposed to *Lex Situs*

In Jewish Law. The subject of the conflict of laws is not a defined branch of Jewish law. This is attributable to a substantive quality of Jewish law, namely that it is a personal law purporting to apply to each and every Jew, wherever he may be – even if outside the territorial bounds of Jewish sovereignty or autonomy. For this reason the mere fact that a contract is concluded in one country but is to be fulfilled in another is of no consequence in Jewish law. Moreover, Jewish law – for the substantially greater part of its history – has functioned as a legal system generally enjoying Jewish judicial autonomy but not Jewish political sovereignty (see Introduction[1]); the result has been that in suits before the Jewish courts both parties have usually been Jews, with little occasion for questions of conflict of laws to arise in relation to the personalities of the litigants (although there are isolated *halakhot* in this regard; see below).

Nevertheless, the fundamental problems that arise in the field of the conflict of laws occur also in Jewish law, in which they derive from two material phenomena of this legal system. One is the multiplicity of diverse customs in regard to the same subject, a fact expressed in the doctrine, "all is in accordance with the custom of the country" *(ha-kol lefi minhag ha-medinah;* see below). This multiplicity was already in evidence in talmudic times and became increasingly pronounced from the tenth century onward, when in the different centers of Jewish life hegemony was no longer exercised by a single center over the whole Diaspora, thus leading to the enactment of numerous local ordinances (see *Takkanot,* especially *Takkanot ha-Kahal*), to the spread of new customs (see *Minhag*), and to much local decision (see Introduction). The natural outcome of this phenomenon was the problem of choosing between the different laws, for instance when the matter in issue arose partly in one place and partly in another, not between Jewish law and other law, but between diverse customs and *takkanot* within the Jewish legal system. The second phenomenon which brought about the problem of conflict of laws in Jewish law has been the contact between Jewish law and secular law; from this contact there evolved the doctrine of *dina de-malkhuta dina* ("the law of the land is law"), and in pursuance thereof the creation of a number of rules pertaining to the field of the conflict of laws.

Multiplicity of Legal Rules. The existence of varying rules deriving from different customs and *takkanot* on a particular legal subject is to be found in various fields of the law. Wherever this reality exists and the various stages of a legal obligation have to be fulfilled in different places where varying rules are practiced in regard to such obligation, the question arises whether to apply to the obligation, the law that is customary at the place and time of its establishment, or that which is customary at the place and time of its fulfillment, or any other law.

Concerning the Laws of Marriage. Even in ancient times varying local customs had evolved and were practiced concerning the pecuniary relations between spouses. As regards the amount of the dowry, R. Simeon b. Gamaliel adopted the rule of "all in accordance with the custom of the country" (Ket. 6:4), and the *halakhah,* with reference to both the *ketubbah* and the dowry, was determined as follows: "a marriage without condition is transacted in accordance with the custom of the country; also the wife who has agreed to contribute (i.e., a dowry to her husband) must do so in accordance with the custom of the country, and when she comes to recover her *ketubbah* she recovers what is contained therein in accordance with the custom of the country; in all these and similar matters the custom of the country is an important principle and must be followed, but such custom must be widespread throughout the country" (Yad, Ishut 23:12; Sh. Ar., EH 66:11). Thus there were different customs concerning a widow's right to lodging and maintenance from the estate; the custom in Jerusalem and Galilee was to make the continuation of this right a matter of the widow's choice, and only if she preferred to claim her *ketubbah* would her right to maintenance and lodging become forfeited; in Judea the custom was to leave the choice with the deceased's heirs, and if they offered to pay the widow's *ketubbah,* she would forfeit the right to maintenance and lodging (Ket. 4:12); the people of Babylonia and environs followed the

1. page 18.

custom of the Judeans, and those of Nehardea and environs followed the custom of the Jerusalemites and Galileans (Ket. 54a).

This diversity of custom created problems relating to the conflict of laws. In the case of a woman of Maḥoza (in Babylonia) who was married to a man from the area of Nehardea, it was decided that she was governed by the law as customary in Nehardea, i.e., that the deceased's heirs could not deprive her of her rights by paying her *ketubbah* as mentioned (Ket. 54a). In a case in the 13th century, husband and wife were from separate towns and married in a third town; in each of the three places different customs prevailed concerning the financial obligations between spouses. Since the latter had not themselves defined these in the *ketubbah,* Solomon b. Abraham Adret decided that the custom to be followed in their case was that of the place of celebration of the marriage, if that was where they intended to live, otherwise the custom of the place where they intended to live; if they had not decided on the place of residence, the custom at the place where the husband was resident was to be followed, since in law the husband determines the place of residence (Tosef., Ket. 13:2; Ket. 110a–b) – "for he marries in accordance with the conditions at his own place of residence, whereto he takes her" (Resp. Rashba, vol. 1, no. 662 and cf. vol. 3, no. 433). The same conclusion was reached by other scholars on the basis of the talmudic rule concerning the woman of Maḥoza who married a man from Nehardea (Nov. Ritba, Ket. 54a; see also *Beit Yosef* EH 66, toward the concl.; Resp. Maharashdam, ḤM no. 327) and thus the *halakhah* was decided – "if a person married a woman from a certain place with the intention that she live with him at his place, the custom of his place is to be followed" (Rema to EH 66:12). In a 17th century decision it was laid down that since the amount of the *ketubbah* was 500 gold coins in Lithuania and 400 gold coins in Poland, "the custom of the place of marriage is not followed but only that of the place of domicile" (*Ḥelkat Meḥokek* 66, n. 46 and *Beit Shemu'el* 66, n. 27); moreover, the customary law of their chosen domicile was held to be applicable to the parties even if they had agreed that they would settle there two or three years after their marriage (*ibid.,* 66, n. 46), and opinions were divided on the question whether to follow the custom of the place of marriage or that of the place of intended domicile in the event that the husband die before their having settled in the latter place (*ibid.; Beit Shemu'el,* 66, n. 27).

Some scholars held the opinion that the customary law of the place of celebration of the marriage governs the financial obligations between spouses: "a matter must be dealt with only according to [the law of] the place where the *ketubbah* was written, the husband having only undertaken liability therefore in accordance with the law of such place" (Resp. Ribash, no. 105). It was similarly decided as regards differing customs deriving from the different communal *takkanot* relating to heritage of the dowry on the wife's death: "in all places local custom is followed, and even if they did not stipulate at the time of marriage, they are considered to have done so, for everyone who marries does so in accordance with the custom; even if he went to a place where the custom of the communities is not practiced, the law of the place where he married her is followed" (Rema to EH 118:19, based on Resp. Ribash, no. 105). Clearly, if the parties expressly stipulated that the custom of the husband's place of residence be followed, their position would be governed accordingly (see *Ḥelkat Meḥokek* to EH 118:19 and *Beit Shemu'el,* 118 n. 26, in which manner the apparent contradiction between Isserles' statements, here and in EH 66:12, is reconciled).

A dispute waged between prominent 16th-century scholars centered around the claim of Hannah Gracia Mendes – one of the *anusim* (Marranos) from Portugal who had reached Turkey, where they openly reembraced Judaism – for half of her husband's estate, in accordance with the custom in Portugal, the place of celebration of the marriage. The dispute concerned the validity of an undertaking made at the time of marriage which was not celebrated in accordance with Jewish law; otherwise, however, all agreed that she was entitled to succeed in her claim in accordance with the law in practice in Portugal even if this was not the law in Turkey where the hearing took place (*Avkat Rokhel,* nos. 80–81; Resp. Maharashdam, ḤM no. 327; Resp. Maharibal 2:23; see also Civil Appeal 100/49, in *Pesakim shel Beit ha-Mishpat ha-Elyon,* 6 (1951/52), 140ff.). In Israel the rabbinical court has accepted the opinion of the scholars who held that the law of the place of celebration of the marriage must be applied – even if on the basis of *halakhah* the marriage be invalid. In the case of a Jewish couple who had immigrated from Russia, having been married in Russia in a civil marriage ceremony only, in 1942, and were seeking a divorce before the above court, it decided that their common property should be divided in accordance with the law in practice in Russia in 1942 regarding the division of property between separated spouses (PDR 5:124ff.; see M. Elon, *Ḥakikah Datit* (1968), 169–72).

Some of the scholars dealing with the Mendes matter (see above) determined, as a matter of principle, that all contracts and acquisitions of property (*kinyanim;* see Contract and Acquisition), made among the Marranos themselves, in accordance with the general law of their land, were to have legal validity, even after the Marranos' open return to Judaism. One of the reasons advanced for this far-reaching determination was the fact of the Marranos' interest, for the sake of proper order in business matters, in ensuring that all their commercial and economic transactions have full legal validity – "and this is as a fixed custom among them, overriding the *halakhah*" (*Mabit,* in *Avkat Rokhel,* no. 80; see also *Minhag*). Of particular interest is a reason advanced by Samuel de Modena, paralleling one of the general principles in the field of the conflict of laws: "for if it were otherwise, none of the *anusim* who came from there [from Portugal and Spain to Turkey] would be able to live if the transactions they had with each other there in accordance with local custom but not according to the law of the Torah, were now reopened; this is plainly inconceivable; as regards everything that was done there, we must say: what is done is done, from now on a new reckoning" (Resp. Maharashdam, ḤM no. 327).

Concerning the Laws of Divorce. An illustration of the conflict of laws in the above field, arising in Spain in the 13th century in regard to a *takkanah* prohibiting the divorce of a wife against her will, is to be found in the responsa collection of Solomon b. Adret (vol. 4, no. 186). At that time this *takkanah* was not followed everywhere in Spain. The question arose whether a wife could be divorced against her will in the event that the *takkanah* was in force at the place of celebration of their marriage but not at the place to which they later moved – where the divorce proceedings were taking place – Solomon b. Adret replied: "for anyone marrying at a place where a wife cannot be divorced except with her consent is so bound, and he marries her in the knowledge that he cannot divorce her except with her consent . . . and even if he takes her away from the place of their marriage . . . to another place, he may not divorce her except in accordance with the custom of the place of their marriage."

Concerning Labor Law. In this field, too, there evolved different local customs, and the rule, "all in accordance with the custom of the country" (BM 7:1) was applied with particular reliance on the principle that "custom overrides the *halakhah*"

(TJ, BM 7:1; see also *Minhag*). This diversity naturally led to cases of conflicting laws. The Mishnah records that there were places where it was customary for laborers to go to work early in the morning and return late in the evening, while in other places they did not set out so early or return so late (BM 7:1, 11b). In the Jerusalem Talmud it is stated that it was not customary for the people of Tiberias to start early and finish late, but this was the case with the people of Beth-Maon; it was laid down that residents of Tiberias hired as laborers in Beth-Maon must act in accordance with the custom in Beth-Maon and laborers from Beth-Maon hired in Tiberias must act in accordance with the custom in Tiberias – i.e., that the determining law is the law of the place of fulfillment of the obligation; nevertheless, if an employer from Tiberias should hire in Beth-Maon laborers to work in Tiberias, they must start early and finish late according to the custom in Beth-Maon because the fact that the employer does not hire laborers in Tiberias, but comes specially to Beth-Maon for this purpose, proves his intention to find laborers who will start early and finish late, and it is as if he expressly stipulated to such effect (TJ, BM 7:1, 11b).

Concerning the Laws of Partnership, Land Tenancy (Arisut), etc. Instances of differing and conflicting customs are mentioned also in fields of the civil law such as partnership (BB 1:1, 2), lease and land tenancy in return for a share of the crop (*arisut;* BM 9:1), etc. (see Lease and Hire). In these cases too it was laid down that the custom of the place where the obligation is established must be followed (Resp. Rashba, vol. 1, no. 662). Of interest is the conflict of laws principle laid down in a responsum of Simeon b. Ẓemaḥ Duran, 14th-century scholar of North Africa, in relation to a business partnership (*Tashbeẓ* 2:226). A dispute between one partner and the others concerning distribution of the partnership profits was brought before "a certain merchant who adjudicated between them," i.e., a lay judge adjudicating in accordance with the trade custom and not Jewish law. In an appeal before Duran against this decision, Duran held that the merchant's judgment did not conform with that required to be given in accordance with Jewish law; the contention of the partners who succeeded in the first instance, that the matter was originally brought before a merchant-judge in accordance with the local trade custom and that his decision was binding on the parties, was answered by Duran to this effect: the custom in question, although followed in the locality where the partners then found themselves, was not in existence at the place where the partnership was established, hence the local custom of the former place, i.e., the place of operation of the partnership, was not to be applied to their case, but the matter had to be dealt with in accordance with the custom at the place of establishment of the partnership.

Conflict of a Factual-Legal Nature. A conflict of laws, in the wider sense of the term, may arise not only when there are in operation divergent legal methods at the various stages of an obligation, but also when there exists, at these various stages, a divergence of legal facts.

Concerning Bonds of Indebtedness. When a bond specifies a particular currency which is in circulation in two countries, but the value thereof is greater in one country than in the other, the rule is that the amount stated is payable in accordance with the value of the currency in the country where the bond was drawn up and not its value in the country where the bond is presented for payment: "When a person seeks to recover payment of a bond from his neighbor, then, if it is recorded as having been written in Babylonia – he recovers in Babylonian currency; if in Ereẓ Israel, he recovers in the currency of Ereẓ Israel; if there is no qualification in the bond, then, if he seeks to recover in Babylonia – he recovers in Babylonian currency, and if he seeks to recover in Ereẓ Israel – he recovers in the currency of Ereẓ Israel" (Tosef., Ket. 13 (12):3 and BB 11:3; according to the version in Ket. 110b; Yad, Malveh 17:9; Sh. Ar., ḤM 42:14). The *posekim* were divided on the reason for the second part of the above rule; some of them expressed the opinion that the bond is recovered according to the currency value at the place where the bond is presented for payment, because it is presumed that the bond was drawn up at the place where it is presented for payment; but if the presumption be rebutted, by proof that the bond was drawn up elsewhere, it will be payable according to the currency value at the latter place (Yad and Sh. Ar., loc. cit.; *Sefer ha-Terumot* 54:1); other *posekim* explained the rule on the basis that in the circumstances in question, the parties intentionally omit any mention in the bond of the place where it is drawn up in order that the amount be payable according to the currency value at the place where the bond shall be presented for payment, and, according to this explanation, the currency value will always be as determined at the place of presentation of the bond for payment (Ran to Alfasi, end of Ketubbot; pupils of R. Jonah, in *Shitah Mekubbeẓet,* Ket. 110b; Nov. Ritba Ket. 110b; see also *Kesef Mishneh*, Malveh 17:9; Rema ḤM 42:14 and *Siftei Kohen* thereto, n. 34).

Concerning the Ketubbah. A similar problem was discussed in relation to payment of the amount specified in the *ketubbah,* in a case where the parties had married in Ereẓ Israel and were being divorced in Cappadocia (a country in Asia Minor which was famous for its coin mint – see S. Lieberman, *Tosefta ke-Feshutta,* 6 (1967), 389), and the same currency was in circulation in both countries, although at different values (Ket. 13:11; see also Tos., Ket. 110b and BB 11:3). The scholars who differed from R. Simeon b. Gamaliel were of the opinion that the *ketubbah* and a bond of indebtedness were subject to different rules (Ket. 13:11). As regards the substance of the difference, the opinions stated in the Jerusalem Talmud differ from those in the Babylonian Talmud. According to the former, the value of the currency was higher in Ereẓ Israel than in Cappadocia, and in respect of the *ketubbah* – a right of the wife flowing from the Torah, according to these scholars – the scholars were always careful to see that it was received by the wife according to the higher value, i.e., according to the value in Ereẓ Israel, even if the marriage took place in Cappadocia (TJ, Ket. 13:11). In the Babylonian Talmud it is held that the currency value was lower in Ereẓ Israel than in Cappadocia, and as far as concerned the *ketubbah* – in the opinion of these scholars a right given the wife by rabbinic enactment (see Takkanot) – it was more leniently regarded by the scholars than any other bond of indebtedness, and therefore it was held to be payable in accordance with the currency in Erez Israel, i.e., according to the lower value, even if the marriage took place in Cappadocia (Ket. 110b). R. Simeon's opinion, according to both Talmuds, was that the *ketubbah* was subject to the same law as any other bond of indebtedness (according to the Babylonian Talmud because in his view the *ketubbah* was an obligation of biblical law; according to the Jerusalem Talmud because it was an obligation of rabbinical law), and it was always necessary to pay according to the currency value at the place of establishment of the obligation, i.e., the place where the marriage took place.

It may be noted that the same problem was discussed in principle in relation to other halakhic matters. Thus it was laid down that a person transporting – other than in Jerusalem – second tithe fruits from a cheaper to a more expensive area, or vice versa, had to redeem the fruits according to their value at the place of redemption and not as valued at the place from which they were brought (Ma'as. Sh. 4:1; see also Ned. 8:4 in TB and TJ; see also Domicile). For the validity of documents drawn up in non-Jewish courts see Shetar.

Jewish and Non-Jewish Parties to the Same Suit. According to a *baraita* of the talmudic law, if in a suit between a Jew and a gentile, before a Jewish court, there exists the possibility of favoring the Jew either according to the general law or according to the Jewish law, then this should be done by the court (BK 113a; cf. Sif. Deut. 16; Yad, Malakhim 10:12). This *halakhah* is quoted in the Talmud in the context of heavy and arbitrary tax quotas imposed on the Jews (see Taxation[1]); it is also to be understood as a reciprocal measure, i.e., as a reaction to the unequal treatment afforded Jews in the gentile courts (in like manner to the *halakhah* in BK 4:3, see BK 38a – "because they did not take upon themselves the seven Noachian laws"; see also Albeck and other commentators to the Mishnah and *Gemara,* loc. cit.). Thus in the 13th century it was laid down that "at any rate this [the foregoing] was not said in regard to those who follow a defined religious faith; if they come before us to be adjudged, their way shall not be barred in the slightest manner, but the law shall cleave the mountain, whether in his favor or against him" (i.e. whether in favor of the Jewish or gentile party – *Bet ha-Beḥirah* BK 38a; and this is also the interpretation given in other similar cases: *Bet ha-Beḥirah* BK 37b–38a and Av. Zar., 3a, 6b, 22a, 26a). This talmudic *halakhah* is still quoted in Maimonides' *Mishneh Torah* but in the later Codes, such as the *Arba'ah Turim* and the Shulḥan Arukh it is not mentioned at all. The very discussion of this *halakhah* ceased to be of any practical significance since the non-Jewish party was not subject to the jurisdiction of the Jewish courts and acted in accordance with the general law (in many places the central government would appoint a special judge to deal with suits between Jews and non-Jews; see, Bibliography, Elon, *Ha-Mishpat Ha-Ivri* I, p. 34 n. 109.

From various talmudic *halakhot* it may be deduced that in a legal transaction involving both a Jewish and a non-Jewish party, the latter acted in accordance with the foreign law – a fact that was calculated, in certain cases, to influence the manner in which the issue was decided. Thus the following problem is discussed in the Talmud: the debtor dies leaving orphans (see Orphan); thereupon the surety pays the creditor before notifying the orphans of the fact of payment and then seeks to recoup this payment from the orphans (see Suretyship). The surety's haste in paying the debt without prior approach to the orphans arouses suspicion of a conspiracy, i.e., the possibility that the debtor had paid the debt before he died in order to avoid a claim against the orphans, and that the surety and creditor conspired to recover the debt a second time, from the orphans, so as to share the money (BB 174b). In the course of the talmudic discussion the opinion is expressed that the above-mentioned suspicion only arises in the event that the creditor is a Jew, for the reason that in Jewish law the creditor must first have recourse to the debtor – hence the debtor's fear that the creditor might have recourse to the orphans and his decision to forestall this possibility by paying the debt; however, in the case of a non-Jewish creditor, there would be no reason to suspect that the debtor paid the debt during his lifetime, since according to Persian law, to which the creditor was subject, the latter might have direct recourse to the surety, and the debtor would know that the creditor was going to do so and not have recourse to the orphans (BB 174b; the contrary opinion expressed here also takes cognizance of the fact that in Persian law the creditor may claim directly from the surety). Hence it was decided, in Spain in the 14th century, that when the law applicable to the non-Jewish creditor is identical with Jewish law, the case of the latter will be no different from that of a Jewish creditor (*Maggid Mishneh* Malveh 26:6). Also recorded is the case of a non-Jew who hypothecated his courtyard to a Jew, which he then sold to a Jew (see BM 73b; Yad, Malveh 7:6; Sh. Ar., YD 172:5).

Conflict of Laws; Principles Where the Foreign Law Is Applicable. From application of the doctrine of *dina de-malkhuta dina,* rules are often derived (see above) which may serve as guiding principles in the field of the conflict of laws, of which the following two examples may be noted.

Distinguishing Between Material and Procedural Law. Elijah b. Ḥayyim, head of the Constantinople rabbis at the end of the 16th century, laid down that even in the case where Jewish law is subject, by virtue of the doctrine of *dina-de-malkhuta dina,* to the foreign law, it is subject only to the material and not the procedural part of such law; hence the laws of evidence are always to be applied in accordance with Jewish law – i.e., the *lex fori,* which is the intrinsic law absorbing the foreign law. The case under discussion (Resp. Ranaḥ no. 58) concerned the question of imprisonment for debt. Elijah b. Ḥayyim held that even on the assumption that the doctrine of *dina de malkhuta dina* was applicable (according to the accepted view this could not have been the case since the question of personal freedom is a matter of the ritual law *(issur ve-hetter)* to which the doctrine is not applicable), only the material provision of the law of the land was to be applied, i.e., the provision that a defaulting debtor was to be imprisoned if he had the means to pay, but not otherwise; however, the mode of inquiry into, and proof of, the debtor's financial position had to accord with Jewish law. Hence Elijah b. Ḥayyim concluded that in a case where it was not satisfactorily proved, in accordance with the foreign law, that the debtor lacked the means of paying this debt, but according to the rules of evidence in Jewish law, there was adequate proof of the debtor's lack of means to make payment, then the debtor was to be treated as such and could not be imprisoned (see M. Elon, *Ḥerut ha-Perat* (1964), 164 n. 200).

Lex Domicilii as Opposed to Lex Situs. The validity of a will executed by a Marrano Jew in Majorca was the subject of a dispute between two 14th century halakhic scholars, Isaac b. Sheshet Perfet and Simeon b. Ẓemaḥ Duran (Resp. Ribash nos. 46–52; *Tashbeẓ* 1:58–61). The testator bequeathed his estate to his daughters on condition that the estate pass to his wife on their death. When the daughters died, the civil court decided that the estate was to pass to the testator's widow in accordance with the will, and called on all persons holding estate assets to restore such to the widow. The heirs of the daughters challenged the will on the ground that in Jewish law, in such circumstances, the estate belonged to the natural heirs of the deceased beneficiary ("Inheritance has no interruption" – BB 129b; Sh. Ar., ḤM 248:1) and called for restoration of the estate assets to themselves. Bar Sheshet held it to be correct that the heirs of the daughters would succeed to the estate if the will "had been executed amongst Jews at a place where they judged according to Jewish law"; however, he added, "the testator was living in Majorca presumably as a gentile and the wife claiming under the will, as well as those claiming to inherit by virtue of kinship are also presumed to be living there as gentiles, and even as Jews they have been required to be adjudged in accordance with the law of the gentiles; for this has always been their practice of their own will; how then shall one of the parties go to a far place to be adjudged in accordance with Jewish law? Let them come before their own judge in Majorca, namely the bailus *(gizbar),* and whoever shall succeed and be held by the bailus to be entitled to the testator's property shall be the heir." Thus Bar Sheshet regarded the *lex domicilii* as the law which was intended by the testator to apply to the will and all concerned therewith, so that none of the possible heirs, or beneficiaries under the will,

1. page 665.

were entitled to demand that the validity of the will be judged according to any other law.

Duran took a different approach, determining at the outset that Jewish law continued to apply to all the parties, even though they had been Marranos (for the opinions of Mabit and Maharashdam in the matter of Gracia Mendes see above). He added, however, that even if the doctrine of *dina de-malkhuta dina* was applicable to the case, the fact remained that "the rulers of the land are concerned only with the property in such land"; and as regards property outside of Majorca (i.e., North Africa in this case) "on the contrary, we must say that the same law is not to be applied on account of this very doctrine in order that the government of the land in which the property in issue is situated shall not be particular – when there are in such land those who have a claim of right – about the fact that the latter lose their right because of the opposing law of another land." In his opinion therefore the *lex situs,* the law of the place of situation of the property, was the proper law applicable to assets in a foreign country, and not the law of the place of domicile of the testator and beneficiaries, and since at the place of situation of the property there were those who claimed it in accordance with Jewish law, this law, being the *lex situs,* as well as the *lex fori,* was to be applied (see also Public Authority; as regards the interpretation of privilege granted by the central government to the Jewish community, see Resp. Ribash no. 228).

Bibliography: M. Elon, *Ha-Mishpat Ha-Ivri* (1973), I, 10 n. 20, 36ff., 131ff., 198ff., II, 556ff., 700ff., 760, 822 n. 65, III, 876 n. 134, 1088, 1239ff.

Menachem Elon

ABBREVIATIONS*

*With regard to further bibliographical data see M. Elon, *Ha-Mishpat Ha-Ivri,* Vol. 3, indices of Sources, Personal Names and Subject Matter.

Adderet Eliyahu, Karaite treatise by Elijah b. Moses Bashyazi.
Admat Kodesh, Resp. by Nissim Ḥayyim Moses b. Joseph Mizraḥi.
Aguddah, Sefer ha-, Nov. by Alexander Suslin ha-Kohen.
Ahavat Ḥesed, compilation by Israel Meir ha-Kohen.
Aliyyot de-Rabbenu Yonah, Nov. by Jonah b. Abraham Gerondi.
Alon, Mehkarim, G. Alon, *Meḥkarim be-Toledot Yisrael bi-Ymei Bayit Sheni u-vi-Tekufat ha-Mishnah ve-ha-Talmud,* 2 vols. (1957–58).
Alon, Toledot, G. Alon, *Toledot ha-Yehudim be-Ereẓ Yisrael bi-Tekufat ha-Mishnah ve-ha-Talmud,* 1(1958^3), 2(1961^2).
Ant., Josephus, *Jewish Antiquities* (Loeb Classics ed.).
Apion, Josephus, *Against Apion* (Loeb Classics ed.).
Ar., *Arakhin* (talmudic tractate).
Arist., Letter of Aristeas (Pseudepigrapha).
ARN^1, *Avot de-Rabbi Nathan,* version (1) ed. Schechter, 1887.
ARN^2, *Avot de-Rabbi Nathan,* version (2) ed. Schechter, 1945^2.
Arukh ha-Shulḥan, codification by Jehiel Michel Epstein.
Asayin (= positive precepts), subdivision of: (1) Maimonides, *Sefer ha-Mitzvot;* (2) Moses b. Jacob of Coucy, *Semag.*
Asefat Dinim, subdivision of *Sedei Ḥemed* by Ḥayyim Hezekiah Medini, an encyclopaedia of precepts and responsa.
Asheri = Asher b. Jehiel.
Assaf, Ge'onim, S. Assaf, *Tekufat ha-Ge'onim ve-Sifrutah* (1955). (1955).
Assaf, Mekorot, S. Assaf, *Mekorot le-Toledot ha-Ḥinnukh be-Yisrael,* 4 vols. (1925–43).
Ateret Ḥakhamim, by Baruch Frankel-Teomim; pt. 1: Resp. to Sh. Ar.; pt. 2: Nov. to Talmud.
Ateret Zahav, subdivision of the *Levush,* a codification by Mordecai b. Abraham (Levush) Jaffe; *Ateret Zahav* parallels Tur, YD.
Ateret Ẓevi, Comm. to Sh. Ar. by Ẓevi Hirsch b. Azriel.
AV, Authorized Version of the Bible.
Avad., *Avadim* (post-talmudic tractate).
Avir Ya'akov, Resp. by Jacob Avigdor.
Avkat Rokhel, Resp. by Joseph b. Ephraim Caro.
Avnei Millu'im, Comm. to Sh. Ar., EH, by Aryeh Loeb b. Joseph ha-Kohen.
Avnei Nezer, Resp. on Sh. Ar. by Abraham b. Ze'ev Nahum Bornstein of Sochaczew.
Avodat Massa, Compilation of Tax Law by Yoasha Abraham Judah.
Avot, *Avot* (talmudic tractate).
Av. Zar., *Avodah Zarah* (talmudic tractate).
Aẓei ha-Levanon, Resp. by Judah Leib Zirelson.
Azulai, Ḥ.Y.D. Azulai, *Shem ha-Gedolim,* ed. by I.E. Benjacob, 2 pts. (1852) (and other editions).
Ba'al ha-Tanya = Shneur Zalman of Lyady.
Bacher, Bab Amor, W. Bacher, *Agada der babylonischen Amoraeer* (1913^2).
Bacher, Pal Amor, W. Bacher, *Agada der palaestinensischen Amoraeer* (Heb. ed. *Aggadat Amora'ei Ereẓ Yisrael*), 2 vols. (1892–99).
Bacher, Tann, W. Bacher, *Agada der Tannaiten* (Heb. ed. *Aggadot ha-Tanna'im*), vol. 1, pt. 1 and 2 (1903); vol. 2 (1890).
Bacher, Trad, W. Bacher, *Tradition und Tradenten in den Schulen Palaestinas und Babyloniens* (1914).
Ba'ei Ḥayyei, Resp. by Ḥayyim b. Israel Benveniste.
Baer, Spain, Yitzhak (Fritz) Baer, History of the Jews in Christian Spain, 2 vols. (1961–66).
Baer, Studien, Yitzhak (Fritz) Baer, *Studien zur Geschichte der Juden im Koenigreich Aragonien waehrend des 13. und 14. Jahrhunderts* (1913).
Baer, Toledot, Yitzhak (Fritz) Baer, *Toledot ha-Yehudim bi-Sefarad ha-Nozerit mi-Tehillatan shel ha-Kehillot ad ha-Gerush,* 2 vols. (1959^2).
Baer, Urkunden, Yitzhak (Fritz) Baer, *Die Juden im christlichen Spanien,* 2 vols. (1929–36).
Ba'er Heitev, Comm. to Sh. Ar. The parts on OḤ and EH are by Judah b. Simeon Ashkenazi, the parts on YD and ḤM by Zechariah Mendel b. Aryeh Leib. Printed in most editions of Sh. Ar.
Baḥ, usual abbreviation for *Bayit Ḥadash,* a commentary on Tur by Joel Sirkes; printed in most editions of Tur.
I Bar., I Baruch (Apocrypha).
II Bar., II Baruch (Pseudepigrapha).
III Bar., III Baruch (Pseudepigrapha).
Baron, Community, S. W. Baron, *The Jewish Community, its History and Structure in the American Revolution,* 3 vols. (1942).
Baron, Social, S. W. Baron, *Social and Religious History of the Jews,* 3 vols. (1937); enlarged, 1–2 (1952^2), 3–14 (1957–69).
Bayit Ḥadash, see *Baḥ.*
BB, *Bava Batra* (talmudic tractate).
Bek., *Bekhorot* (talmudic tractate).
Benjacob, Ozar, I. E. Benjacob, *Oẓar ha-Sefarim* (1880; repr. 1956).
Ben Sira, see Ecclus.
Ben-Yehuda, Millon, E. Ben-Yehuda, *Millon ha-Lashon ha-Ivrit,* 16 vols. (1908–59; repr. in 8 vols. 1959).
Ber., *Berakhot* (talmudic tractate).
Berab = Jacob Berab, also called Ri Berav.
Bedek ha-Bayit, by Joseph b. Ephraim Caro, additions to his *Beit Yosef* (a comm. to Tur). Printed sometimes inside *Beit Yosef,* in smaller type. Appears in most editions of Tur.
Be'er ha-Golah, Commentary to Sh. Ar. by Moses b. Naphtali Hirsch Rivkes; printed in most editions of Sh. Ar.
Be'er Mayim, Resp. by Raphael b. Abraham Manasseh Jacob.
Be'er Mayim Ḥayyim, Resp. by Samuel b. Ḥayyim Vital.
Be'er Yiẓḥak, Resp. by Isaac Elhanan Spector.
Beit ha-Beḥirah, Comm. to Talmud by Menahem b. Solomon Meiri.
Beit Me'ir, Nov. on Sh. Ar. by Meir b. Judah Leib Posner.
Beit Shelomo, Resp. by Solomon b. Aaron Ḥason (the younger).
Beit Shemu'el, Comm. to Sh. Ar., EH, by Samuel b. Uri Shraga Phoebus.
Beit Ya'akov, by Jacob b. Jacob Moses Lorberbaum; pt. 1: Nov. to Ket.; pt. 2: Comm. to EH.
Beit Yisrael, collective name for the commentaries *Derishah, Perishah,* and *Be'urim* by Joshua b. Alexander ha-Kohen Falk. See under the names of the commentaries.
Beit Yiẓḥak, Resp. by Isaac Schmelkes.
Beit Yosef: (1) Comm. on Tur by Joseph b. Ephraim Caro; printed in most editions of Tur; (2) Resp. by the same.
Ben Yehudah, Resp. by Abraham b. Judah Litsch Rosenbaum.
Bertinoro, Standard commentary to Mishnah Obadiah Bertinoro. Printed in most editios of the Mishnah.
[Be'urei] Ha-Gra, Comm. to Bible, Talmud, and Sh. Ar. by Elijah b. Solomon Zalman (Gaon of Vilna); printed in major editions of the mentioned works.
Be'urim, Glosses to Isserles' *Darkhei Moshe* (a comm. on Tur) by Joshua b. Alexander ha-Kohen Falk; printed in many editions of Tur.
Beẓah, *Beẓah* (talmudic tractate).
Bik., *Bikkurim* (talmudic tractate).
Binyamin Ze'ev, Resp. by Benjamin Ze'ev b. Mattathias of Arta.
Birkei Yosef, Nov. by Ḥayyim Joseph David Azulai.

BK, *Bava Kamma* (talmudic tractate).
BM, *Bava Meẓia* (talmudic tractate).
Bruell, Jahrbuecher, *Jahrbuecher fuer juedische Geschichte und Litteratur,* ed. by N. Bruell, Frankfort (1874–90).
Ha-Buẓ ve-ha-Argaman, subdivision of the *Levush* (a codification by Mordecai b. Abraham (Levush) Jaffe); *Ha-Buẓ ve-ha-Argaman* parallels Tur. EH.
Charles, Apocrypha, R. H. Charles, *Apocrypha and Pseudepigrapha . . . ,* 2 vols. (1913; repr. 1963–66).
Cher., Philo, *De Cherubim.*
I (or II) Chron., Chronicles, books I and II (Bible).
CIG, *Corpus Inscriptionum Graecarum.*
CIJ, *Corpus Inscriptionum Judaicarum,* 2 vols. (1936–52).
CIL, *Corpus Inscriptionum Latinarum.*
CIS, *Corpus Inscriptionum Semiticarum* (1881 ff.).
Cod. Just., Codex Justinianus.
Cod. Theod., Codex Theodosianus.
Comm. = Commentary
Conf., Philo, *De Confusione Linguarum.*
Conforte, Kore, D. Conforte, *Kore ha-Dorot* (1846^2).
Cong., Philo, *De Congressu Quaerendae Eruditionis Gratia.*
Cont., Philo, *De Vita Contemplativa.*
Cowley, Aramaic, A. Cowley, *Aramaic Papyri of the Fifth Century B.C.* (1923).
Cowley, Cat, A. E. Cowley, *A Concise Catalogue of the Hebrew Printed Books in the Bodleian Library* (1929).
Da'at Kohen, Resp. by Abraham Isaac ha-Kohen Kook.
Daiches, Jews, S. Daiches, *Jews in Babylonia* (1910).
Dan., Daniel (Bible)
Darkhei Moshe, Comm. on Tur by Moses b. Israel Isserles; printed in most editions of Tur.
Darkhei No'am, Resp. by Mordecai b. Judah ha-Levi,.
Darkhei Teshuvah, Nov. by Ẓevi Shapiro; printed in the major editions of Sh. Ar.
De'ah ve-Haskel, Resp. by Obadiah Hadaya (see *Yaskil Avdi*).
Decal, Philo, *De Decalogo.*
Dem., *Demai* (talmudic tractate).
DER, *Derekh Ereẓ Rabbah* (post-talmudic tractate).
Derashot Ran, Sermons by Nissim b. Reuben Gerondi.
Derekh Ḥayyim, Comm. to *Avot* by Judah Loew (Lob, Liwa) b. Bezalel (Maharal) of Prague.
Derishah, by Joshua b. Alexander ha-Kohen Falk; additions to his *Perishah* (comm. on Tur); printed in many editions of Tur.
Derushei ha-Ẓelah, Sermons by Ezekiel b. Judah Halevi Landau.
Det., Philo, *Quod deterius potiori insidiari solet.*
Deus., Philo, *Quod Deus immutabilis sit.*
Deut., Deuteronomy (Bible)
Deut. R., *Deuteronomy Rabbah.*
Devar Avraham, Resp. by Abraham Shapira.
Devar Shemu'el, Resp. by Samuel Aboab.
Devar Yehoshu'a, Resp. by Joshua Menahem b. Isaac Aryeh Ehrenberg.
DEZ, *Derekh Ereẓ Zuta* (post-talmudic tractate).
Dikdukei Soferim, variae lectiones of the talmudic text by Raphael Nathan Rabbinowicz.
Dinur, Golah, B. Dinur (Dinaburg), *Yisrael ba-Golah,* 2 vols. in 7 (1959–68) = vols. 5 and 6 of his *Toledot Yisrael,* second series.
Divrei Emet, Resp. by Isaac Bekhor David.
Divrei Ge'onim, Digest of responsa by Ḥayyim Aryeh b. Jeḥiel Ẓevi Kahana.
Divrei Ḥamudot, Comm. on *Piskei ha-Rosh* by Yom Tov Lipmann b. Nathan ha-Levi Heller; printed in major editions of the Talmud.

Divrei Ḥayyim, several works by Ḥayyim Halberstamm; if quoted alone refers to his Responsa.
Divrei Malkhi'el, Resp. by Malchiel Tenenbaum.
Divrei Rivot, Resp. by Isaac b. Samuel Adarbi.
Divrei Shemu'el, Resp. by Samuel Raphael Arditi.
Dubnow, Divrei, S. Dubnow, *Divrei Yemei Am Olam,* 11 vols. (1923–38 and further editions).
Dubnow, Hist., S. Dubnow, *History of the Jews* (1967).
Dubnow, Outline, S. Dubnow, *An Outline of Jewish History,* 3 vols. (1925–29).
Ebr., Philo, *De Ebrietate.*
Eccles., Ecclesiastes (Bible)
Eccles. R., *Ecclesiastes Rabbah.*
Ecclus., Ecclesiasticus or Wisdom of Ben Sira (or Sirach; Apocrypha).
Edut be-Ya'akov, Resp. by Jacob b. Abraham Boton.
Edut bi-Yhosef, Resp. by Joseph b. Isaac Almosnino.
Eduy., *Eduyyot* (mishnaic tractate).
EH, *Even ha-Ezer.*
Ein Ya'akov, Digest of talmudic *aggadot* by Jacob (ibn) Ḥabib.
Ein Yiẓḥak, Resp. by Isaac Elhanan Spector.
EIS^3, *Encyclopaedia of Islam,* New Edition (1960 ff.).
Eisenstein, Dinim, J. D. Eisenstein, *Oẓar Dinim u-Minhagim* (1917; several reprints).
Eisenstein, Yisrael, J. D. Eisenstein, *Oẓar Yisrael,* 10 vols. (1907–13; repr. with additions 1951).
EIV, *Enziklopedyah Ivrit* (1949 ff.).
EJ, *Encyclopaedia Judaica* (German, A–L only), 10 vols. (1928–34).
Elon, Ha-Mishpat ha-Ivri, M. Elon, *Ha-Mishpat Ha-Ivri, Toldotav, Mekorotav, Ekronotav,* 3 vols. (1973).
Elon, Mafte'ah, M. Elon (ed.), *Mafte'ah ha-She'elot ve-ha-Tsehuvot, She'elot u-Teshuvot ha-Rosh* (1965).
EM, *Enziklopedyah Mikra'it* (1950 ff.).
I (or II) En., I and II Enoch (Pseudepigrapha).
Ep., Jer., Epistle of Jeremy (Apocrypha).
Ephraim of Lentshitz = Solomon Luntschitz.
Epstein, Amora'im, J.N. Epstein, *Mevo'ot le-Sifrut ha-Amora'im* (1962).
Epstein, Marriage, L.M. Epstein, *Marriage Laws in the Bible and the Talmud* (1942).
Epstein, Mishnah, J.N. Epstein, *Mavo le-Nusaḥ ha-Mishnah,* 2 vols. (1964^2).
Epstein, Tanna'im, J.N. Epstein, *Mevo'ot le-Sifrut ha-Tannai'im* (1947).
Er., *Eruvim* (talmudic tractate).
Erekh Leḥem, Nov. and glosses to Sh. Ar. by Jacob b. Abraham Castro.
I Esd., I Esdras (Apocrypha) (= III Ezra).
II Esd., II Esdras (Apocrypha) (= IV Ezra)
Eshkol, Sefer ha-, Digest of *halakhot* by Abraham b. Isaac of Narbonne.
ESS, *Encyclopaedia of the Social Sciences,* 15 vols. (1930–35); reprinted in 8 vols. (1948–49).
Esth., Esther (Bible).
Est. R., *Esther Rabbah.*
ET, *Enziklopedyah Talmudit* (1947 ff.).
Et Sofer, Treatise on Law Court documents by Abraham b. Mordecai Ankawa, in the 2nd vol. of his Resp. *Kerem Ḥamar.*
Etan ha-Ezraḥi, Resp. by Abraham b. Israel Jehiel (Shrenzl) Rapaport.
Even ha-Ezel, Nov. to Maimonides' *Yad Ḥazakah* by Isser Zalman Meltzer.
Even ha-Ezer, also called *Raban* or *Ẓafenat Pa'ne'aḥ,* rabbinical work with varied contents by Eliezer b. Nathan of Mainz; not

identical with the subdivision of Tur, Shulḥan Arukh, etc.
Ex., Exodus (Bible)
Ex. R., *Exodus Rabbah.*
Exs., Philo, *De Exzecrationibus.*
Ezek., Ezekiel (Bible).
Ezra, Ezra (Bible).
III Ezra, III Ezra (Pseudepigrapha).
IV Ezra, IV Ezra (Pseudepigrapha).
Ezrat Yehudah, Resp. by Issar Judah b. Nehemiah of Brisk.
Finkelstein, Middle, L. Finkelstein, *Jewish Self-Government in the Middle Ages* (1924).
Frankel, Mevo, Z. Frankel, *Mevo ha-Yerushalmi* (1870; reprint 1967).
Frankel, Mishnah, Z. Frankel, *Darkhei ha-Mishnah* (1923²; reprint 1959²)
Frey, Corpus, J.-B. Frey, *Corpus Inscriptionum Judaicarum,* 2 vols. (1936–52).
Frunkin-Rivlin, A.L. Frumkin and E. Rivlin, *Toledot Ḥakhmei Yerushalayim,* 3 vols. (1928–30), Supplement vol. (1930).
Fuerst, Karaeertum, J. Fuerst, *Geschichte des Karaeertums,* 3 vols. (1862–69).
Fug., Philo, *De Fuga et Inventione.*
Gan Eden, Karaite treatise by Aaron b. Elijah of Nicomedia.
Geiger, Mikra, A. Geiger, *Ha-Mikra ve-Targumav,* tr. by J.L. Baruch (1949).
Gen., Genesis (Bible).
Gen. R., *Genesis Rabbah.*
Ger., *Gerim* (post-talmudic tractate).
Germ. Jud., M. Brann, I. Elbogen, A. Freimann, and H. Tykocinski (eds.) *Germania Judaica,* vol. 1 (1917; repr. 1934 and 1963); vol. 2, in 2 pts. (1917–68), ed. by Z. Avneri.
Gersonides = Levi b. Gershom, also called Leo Hebraeus, or Ralbag.
Ghirondi-Neppi, M.S. Ghirondi and G.H. Neppi, *Toledot Gedolei Yisrael u-Ge'onei Italyah . . . u-Ve'urim al Sefer Zekher Ẓaddikim li-Verakhah . . .* (1853), index in ZHB, 17 (1914), 171–83.
Gig., Philo, *De Gigantibus.*
Ginnat Veradim, Resp. by Abraham b. Mordecai ha-Levi.
Ginzberg, Legends, L. Ginzberg, *Legends of the Jews,* 7 vols. (1909–38; and reprints).
Git., *Gittin* (talmudic tractate).
Graetz-Rabbinowitz, H. Graetz, *Divrei Yemei Yisrael,* tr. by S.P. Rabbinowitz (1928–29²).
Gross, Gal Jud, H. Gross, *Gallia Judaica* (1897; repr. with add. 1969).
Guide, Maimonides, *Guide of the Perplexed.*
Gulak, Ozar, A. Gulak, *Oẓar ha-Shetarot ha-Nehugim be-Yisrael* (1926).
Gulak, Yesodei, A. Gulak, *Yesodei ha-Mishpat ha-Ivri, Seder Dinei Mamonot be-Yisrael, al pi Mekorot ha-Talmud ve-ha-Posekim,* 4 vols. (1922; repr. 1967).
Guttmann, Mafte'ah, M. Guttmann, *Mafte'aḥ ha-Talmud,* 3 vols. (1906–30).
Hab., Habakkuk (Bible).
Ḥag., *Ḥagigah* (talmudic tractate).
Haggahot, another name for *Rema.*
Haggahot Asheri, glosses to *Piskei ha-Rosh* by Israel of Krems; printed in most Talmud editions.
Haggahot Maimuniyyot, Comm. to Maimonides' *Yad Ḥazakah* by Meir ha-Kohen; printed in most eds. of Yad.
Haggahot Mordekhai, glosses to *Mordekhai* by Samuel Schlettstadt; printed in most editions of the Talmud after *Mordekhai.*
Haggahot ha-Rashash, annotations of Samuel Strashun on the Talmud, Rashi and Tosafot (printed in major editions of the Talmud).

Haggai, Haggai (Bible).
Ha-Gra = Elijah b. Solomon Zalman (Gaon of Vilna).
Ha-Gra, Commentaries on Bible, Talmud, and Sh. Ar. respectively, by Elijah b. Solomon Zalman (Gaon of Vilna); printed in major editions of the mentioned works.
Ḥakham Ẓevi, Resp. by Ẓevi Hirsch b. Jacob Ashkenazi.
Ḥal., *Ḥallah* (talmudic tractate).
Halakhot = Rif, *Halakhot.* Compilation and abstract of the Talmud by Isaac b. Jacob ha-Kohen Alfasi; printed in most editions of the Talmud.
Halakhot Gedolot, compilation of *halakhot* from the Geonic period, arranged acc. to the Talmud. Here cited acc. to ed. Warsaw (1874). Author probably Simeon Kayyara of Basra.
Halakhot Pesukot le-Rav Yehudai Ga'on, compilation of *halakhot.*
Halakhot Pesukot min ha-Ge'onim, Compilation of *halakhot* from the geonic period by different authors.
Halevy, Dorot, I. Halevy, *Dorot ha-Rishonim,* 6 vols. (1897–1939).
Halpern, Pinkas, I. Halpern (Halperin), *Pinkas Va'ad Arba Araẓot* (1945).
Ḥananel, Comm. to Talmud by Ḥananel b. Ḥushi'el; printed in some editions of the Talmud.
Harei Besamim, Resp. by Aryeh Leib b. Isaac Horowitz.
Ḥassidim, Sefer, Ethical maxims by Judah b. Samuel he-Ḥasid.
Hassagot Rabad on Rif, Glosses on Rif, *Halakhot,* by Abraham b. David of Posquières.
Hassagot Rabad [on Yad], Glosses on Maimonides, *Yad Ḥazakah,* by Abraham b. David of Posquières.
Hassagot Ramban, Glosses by Naḥmanides on Maimonides' *Sefer ha-Mitzvot;* usually printed together with *Sefer ha-Mitzvot.*
Ḥatam Sofer = Moses Sofer
Ḥavvot Ya'ir, Resp. and varia by Jair Ḥayyim Bacharach
Ḥayyim Or Zaru'a = Ḥayyim (Eliezer) b. Isaac.
Ḥazon Ish, Nov. by Abraham Isaiah Karelitz.
Ḥedvat Ya'akov, Resp. by Aryeh Judah Jacob b. David Dov Meisels.
Heikhal Yiẓḥak, Resp. by Isaac ha-Levi Herzog.
Heilprin, Dorot, J. Heilprin (Heilperin), *Seder ha-Dorot,* 3 vols. (1882; repr. 1956).
Ḥelkat Meḥokek, Comm. to Sh. Ar., EH, by Moses b. Isaac Judah Lima.
Ḥelkat Ya'akov, Resp. by Mordecai Jacob Breisch.
Ḥemdah Genuzah, Resp. from the geonic period by different authors.
Ḥemdat Shelomo, Resp. by Solomon Zalman Lipschitz.
Her., Philo, *Quis Rerum Divinarum Heres.*
Herzog, Instit., I. Herzog, *The Main Institutions of Jewish Law,* 2 vols. (1936–39; repr. 1967).
HḤY, *Ha-Zofeh le-Ḥokhmat Yisrael* (first four volumes under the title *Ha-Zofeh me-Ereẓ Hagar*) (1910/11–13).
Ḥida = Ḥayyim Joseph David Azulai.
Ḥiddushei Halakhot ve-Aggadot, Nov. by Samuel Eliezer b. Judah ha-Levi Edels.
Ḥikekei Lev, Resp. by Ḥayyim Palaggi.
Ḥikrei Lev, Nov. to Sh. Ar. by Joseph Raphael b. Ḥayyim Joseph Ḥazzan
Hil. = Hilkhot . . . (e.g., *Hilkhot Shabbat*).
Ḥinnukh, Sefer, ha-, List and explanation of precepts attributed (probably erroneously) to Aaron ha-Levi of Barcelona.
Hirschberg, Afrikah, H.Z. Hirschberg, *Toledot ha-Yehudim be-Afrikah ha-Ẓefonit,* 2 vols. (1965).
HJ, *Historia Judaica* (1938–61).

ḤM, *Ḥoshen Mishpat.*
Ḥok Ya'akov, Comm. to Hil. Pesaḥ in Sh. Ar., OH, by Jacob b. Joseph Reicher.
Ḥokhmat Shelomo (1), Glosses to Talmud, *Rashi* and Tosafot by Solomon b. Jehiel ("Maharshal") Luria; printed in many editions of the Talmud.
Ḥokhmat Shelomo (2), Glosses and Nov. to Sh. Ar. by Solomon b. Judah Aaron Kluger; printed in many editions of Sh. Ar.
Hor., *Horayot* (talmudic tractate).
Hos., Hosea (Bible).
HUCA, *Hebrew Union College Annual* (1904; 1924ff.)
Ḥul., *Ḥullin* (talmudic tractate).
Hur, subdivision of the *Levush*, a codification by Mordecai b. Abraham (Levush) Jaffe; *Ḥur* (or *Levush ha-Ḥur*) parallels Tur, OḤ, 242–269.
Ḥut ha-Meshullash, fourth part of the *Tashbeẓ* (Resp.), by Simeon b. Ẓemah Duran.
Hyman, Toledot, A. Hyman, *Toledot Tanna'im ve-Amora'im* (1910; repr. 1964).
Ibn Daud, Tradition, Abraham Ibn Daud, *Sefer ha-Qabbalah – The Book of Tradition*, ed. and tr. by G. D. Cohen (1967).
Ibn Ezra, Comm. to the Bible by Abraham Ibn Ezra; printed in the major editions of the Bible *("Mikra'ot Gedolot")*.
ILR, Israel Law Review (1966ff.).
Imrei Yosher, Resp. by Meir B. Aaron Judah Arik.
Ios., Philo, *De Iosepho.*
Ir Shushan, Subdivision of the *Levush*, a codification by Mordecai b. Abraham (Levush) Jaffe; *Ir Shushan* parallels Tur, ḤM.
Isa., Isaiah (Bible).
Israel of Bruna = Israel b. Ḥayyim Bruna.
Ittur, compilation of *halakhot* by Isaac b. Abba Mari of Marseilles.
Jacob Be Rab = Be Rab.
Jacob b. Jacob Moses of Lissa = Jacob b. Jacob Moses Lorberbaum.
Jastrow, Dict., M. Jastrow, *Dictionary of the Targumim, the Talmud Babli and Yerushalmi, and the Midrashic literature*, 2 vols. (1886–1902 and reprints).
JE, *Jewish Encyclopedia*, 12 vols. (1901–05; several reprints).
Jer., Jeremiah (Bible).
JJGL, *Jahrbuch fuer juedische Geschichte und Literatur* (Berlin) (1898–1938).
JJLG, *Jahrbuch der juedisch-literarischen Gesellschaft* (Frankfort) (1903–32).
JJS, Journal of Jewish Studies (1948ff.).
JL, *Juedisches Lexikon*, 5 vols. (1927–30).
Job, Job (Bible).
Joel, Joel (Bible).
Jos. Ant., Josephus, *Antiquities* (Loeb Classics ed.).
Jos., Apion, Josephus, *Against Apion* (Loeb Classics ed.).
Jos., index, *Josephus' Works*, Loeb Classics ed., index of names.
Jos., Life, Josephus, *Life* (ed. Loeb Classics).
Jos., Wars, Josephus, *The Jewish War* (Loeb Classics ed.).
Josh., Joshua (Bible).
JPS, Jewish Publication Society of America, *The Torah* (1962, 1967^2); *The Holy Scriptures* (1917).
JQR, *Jewish Quarterly Review* (1889ff.).
JTSA, Jewish Theological Seminary of America (also abbreviated as JTS).
Jub., Jubilees (Pseudepigrapha).
Judah B. Simeon = Judah b. Simeon Ashkenazi.
Judah Minz = Judah b. Eliezer ha-Levi Minz.
Judg., Judges (Bible).
Judith, Book of Judith (Apocrypha).
JYB, *Jewish Year Book* (1896ff.).
JZWL, *Juedische Zeitschrift fuer Wissenschaft und Leben* (1862-75).
Kal., *Kallah* (post-talmudic tractate).
Kal. R., *Kallah Rabbati* (post-talmudic tractate).
Kappei Aharon, Resp. by Aaron Azriel.
Kaufmann, Schriften, D, Kaufmann, *Gesammelte Schriften*, 3 vols. (1908–15).
Kaufmann, Y., Y. Kaufmann, *Toledot ha-Emunah ha-Yisre'elit*, 4 vols. (1937–57).
Kehillat Ya'akov, Talmudic methodology, definitions etc. by Israel Jacob b. Yom Tov Algazi.
Kelei Ḥemdah, Nov. and *pilpulim* by Meir Dan Plotzki of Ostrova, arranged acc. to the Torah.
Keli Yakar, Annotations to the Torah by Solomon Luntschitz.
Kelim, *Kelim* (mishnaic tractate).
Keneh Ḥokhmah, Sermons by Judah Loeb Pochwitzer.
Keneset ha-Gedolah, Digest of *halakhot* by Ḥayyim b. Israel Benveniste; subdivided into annotations to *Beit Yosef* and annotations to Tur.
Kenset Yisrael, Resp. by Ezekiel b. Abraham Katzenellenbogen.
Ker., *Keritot* (talmudic tractate).
Kerem Ḥamar, Resp. and varia by Abraham b. Mordecai Ankawa.
Kerem Shelomo, Resp. by Solomon b. Joseph Amarillo.
Keritut, [Sefer], Methodology of the Talmud by Samson b. Isaac of Chinon.
Kesef ha-Kedoshim, Comm. to Sh. Ar., ḤM, by Abraham Wahrmann; printed in major editions of Ah. Ar.
Kesef Mishneh, Comm. to Maimonides, *Yad Ḥazakah*, by Joseph b. Ephraim Caro; printed in most editions of *Yad Ḥazakah*.
Ket., *Ketubbot* (talmudic tractate).
Keẓot ha-Ḥoshen, Comm. to Sh. Ar., HM, by Aryeh Loeb b. Joseph ha-Kohen; printed in major editions of Sh. Ar.
Kid., *Kiddushin* (talmudic tractate).
Kil., *Kilayim* (talmudic tractate (T.J.)).
Kin., *Kinnim* (mishnaic tractate).
Kisch, Germany, G. Kisch, *Jews in Medieval Germany* (1949).
Klausner, Bayit Sheni, J. Klausner, *Historyah shel ha-Bayit ha-Sheni*, 5 vols. ($1950/51^2$).
Klein, Corpus, S. Klein (ed.), *Juedisch-palaestinisches Corpus Inscriptionum* (1920).
Kohut, Arukh, H.J.A. Kohut (ed.), *Sefer he-Arukh ha-Shalem*, by Nathan b. Jehiel of Rome, 8 vols. (1876–92; Supplement by S. Krauss et al., 1936; repr. 1955).
Kol Bo, [Sefer], Anonymous collection of ritual rules; also called *Sefer ha-Likkutim*.
Kol Mevasser, Resp. by Meshullam Rath.
Korban Aharon, Comm. to *Sifra* by Aaron b. Abraham ibn Ḥayyim; pt. 1 is called: *Middot Aharon*.
Korban Edah, Comm. to Jer. Talmud by David Frankel, with additions: Shiyyurei Korban; printed in most editions of Jer. Talmud.
Krauss, Tal Arch, S. Krauss, *Talmudische Archaeologie*, 3 vols. (1910–12; repr. 1966).
KS, *Kirjath Sepher* (1923/4ff.).
Kunteres ha-Kelalim, subdivision of *Sedei Ḥemed*, an encyclopaedia of precepts and responsa by Ḥayyim Hezekiah Medini.
Kunteres ha-Semikhah, a treatise by Levi b. Ḥabib; printed at the end of his responsa.
Kunteres Tikkun Olam, part of *Mishpat Shalom* (Nov. by Shalom Mordecai b. Moses Schwadron).
Kut., *Kuttim* (post talmudic tractate).
L.A., Philo, *Legum Allegoriae.*
Lam., Lamentations (Bible).

Lam. R., *Lamentations Rabbah.*

Landshuth, Ammudei, L. Landshuth, *Ammudei ha-Avodah* (1857–62; repr. with index, 1965).

Lavin (negative precepts), subdivision of: (1) Maimonides, *Sefer ha-Mitzvot;* (2) Moses b. Jacob of Coucy, *Semag.*

Legat., Philo, *De Legatione ad Caium.*

Leḥem Mishneh, Comm. to Maimonides, *Yad Ḥazakah,* by Abraham [Ḥiyya] b. Moses Boton; printed in most editions of *Yad Hazakah.*

Leḥem Rav, Resp. by Abraham [Hiyya] b. Moses Boton.

Leket Yosher, Resp. and varia by Israel b. Pethahiah Isserlein, collected by Joseph (Joselein) b. Moses.

Leo Hebraeus = Levi b. Gershom, also called Ralbag or Gersonides.

Lev., Leviticus (Bible).

Lev. R., *Leviticus Rabbah.*

Levush [*Malkhut*], Codification by Mordecai b. Abraham (Levush) Jaffe, with subdivisions: [*Levush ha-*] *Tekhelet* (parallels Tur OḤ 1–241); [*Levush ha-*] *Ḥur* (parallels Tur OḤ 242–697); [*Levush*] *Ateret Zahav* (parallels Tur YD); [*Levush*] *ha-Buẓ ve-ha-Argaman* (parallels Tur EH); [*Levush*] *Ir Shushan* (parallels Tur ḤM); under the name *Levush* the author wrote also other works.

Levy J., Chald Targ., J. Levy, *Chaldaeisches Woerterbuch ueber die Targumim,* 2 vols. (1867–68; repr. 1959).

Levy, J., Neuhebr Tal., J. Levy, *Neuhebraeisches und chaldaeisches Woerterbuch ueber die Talmudim . . .,* 4 vols. (1875–89; repr. 1963).

Lewin, Ozar, B. M. Lewin, *Oẓar ha-Ge'onim,* 12 vols. (1928–43).

Lewysohn, Zool, L. Lewysohn, *Zoologie des Talmuds* (1858).

Life, Josephus, *Life* (Loeb Classics ed.).

Li-Leshonot ha-Rambam, fifth part (nos. 1374–1700) of the Resp. by David b. Solomon ibn Abi Zimra (Radbaz).

Likkutim, Sefer ha-, another name for [*Sefer*] *Kol Bo.*

Loew, Flora, I. Loew, *Die Flora der Juden,* 4 vols. (1924–34; repr. 1967).

LSI, *Laws of the State of Israel* (1958ff.).

LXX, Septuagint (Greek translation of the Bible).

Ma'adanei Yom Tov, Comm. on *Piskei ha-Rosh* by Yom Tov Lipmann b. Nathan ha-Levi Heller; printed in many editions of the Talmud.

Ma'as., *Ma'aserot* (talmudic tractate).

Ma'as. Sh., *Ma'aser Sheni* (talmudic tractate).

Mabit = Moses b. Joseph Trani.

I, II, III, and IV, Maccabees, I, II, III (Apocrypha), IV (Pseudepigrapha).

Magen Avot, Comm. to *Avot* by Simeon b. Ẓemah Duran.

Magen Avraham, Comm. to Sh. Ar., OḤ, by Abraham Abele b. Ḥayyim ha-Levi Gombiner; printed in most editions of Sh. Ar., OḤ.

Maggid Mishneh, Comm. to Maimonides, *Yad Ḥazakah,* by Vidal Yom Tov of Tolosa; printed in most editions of the *Yad Ḥazakah.*

Maḥaneh Efrayim, Resp. and Nov., arranged acc. to Maimonides' *Yad Ḥazakah,* by Ephraim b. Aaron Navon.

Maharai = Israel b. Pethahiah Isserlein.

Maharal of Prague = Judah Loew (Lob, Liwa), b. Bezalel.

Maharalbaḥ = Levi b. Ḥabib.

Maharam Alashkar = Moses b. Isaac Alashkar.

Maharam Alshekh = Moses b. Ḥayyim Alshekh.

Maharam Mintz = Moses Mintz.

Maharam of Lublin = Meir b. Gedaliah of Lublin.

Maharam of Padua = Meir Katzenellenbogen.

Maharam of Rothenburg = Meir b. Baruch of Rothenburg.

Maharam Shik = Moses b. Joseph Schick.

Maharash Engel = Samuel b. Ze'ev Wolf Engel.

Maharashdam = Samuel b. Moses Medina.

Maharḥash = Ḥayyim (ben) Shabbetai.

Mahari Basan = Jehiel b. Ḥayyim Basan.

Mahari b. Lev = Joseph ibn Lev.

Mahari'az = Jekuthiel Asher Zalman Ensil Zusmir.

Maharibal = Joseph ibn Lev.

Mahariḥ = Jacob (Israel) Ḥagiz.

Maharik = Joseph b. Solomon Colon.

Maharikash = Jacob b. Abraham Castro.

Maharil = Jacob b. Moses Moellin.

Maharimat = Joseph b. Moses di Trani (not identical with the Maharit).

Maharit = Joseph b. Moses Trani.

Maharitaẓ = Yom Tov b. Akiva Ẓahalon.

Maharsha = Samuel Eliezer b. Judah ha-Levi Edels.

Maharshag = Simeon b. Judah Gruenfeld.

Maharshak = Samson b. Isaac of Chinon.

Maharshakh = Solomon b. Abraham.

Maharshal = Solomon b. Jeḥiel Luria.

Maharsham = Shalom Mordecai b. Moses Schwadron.

Maharyu = Jacob b. Judah Weil.

Maḥazeh Avraham, Resp. by Abraham Menahem b. Meir ha-Levi Steinberg.

Maḥazik Berakhah, Nov. by Ḥayyim Joseph David Azulai.

Maimonides = Moses b. Maimon, or Rambam.

Maimonides, Guide, Maimonides, *Guide of the Perplexed.*

Maim., Yad, Maimonides, *Mishneh Torah (Yad Ḥazakah).*

Mak., *Makkot* (talmudic tractate)..

Makhsh., *Makhshirin* (mishnaic tractate).

Mal., Malachi (Bible).

Malbim = Meir Loeb b. Jehiel Michael.

Malbim = Malbim's comm. to the Bible; printed in the major editions.

Malbushei Yom Tov, Nov. on *Levush,* OḤ by Yom Tov Lipmann b. Nathan ha-Levi Heller.

Mann, Egypt, J. Mann, *Jews in Egypt and in Palestine under the Fatmid Caliphs,* 2 vols. (1920–22).

Mann, Texts, J. Mann, *Texts and Studies,* 2 vols. (1931–35).

Mappah, another name for *Rema.*

Mareh ha-Panim, Comm. to Jer. Talmud by Moses b. Simeon Margolies; printed in most editions of Jer. Talmud.

Margalioth, Gedolei, M. Margalioth, *Enziklopedyah le-Toledot Gedolei Yisrael,* 4 vols. (1946–50).

Margalioth, Hakhmei, M. Margolioth, *Enziklopedyah le-Hakhmei ha-Talmud ve-ha-Ge'onim,* 2 vols. (1945).

Margaliyyot ha-Yam, Nov. by Reuben Margoliot.

Mart. Isa., Martyrdom of Isaiah (Pseudepigrapha).

Mas., Masorah.

Masat Binyamin, Resp. by Benjamin Aaron b. Abraham Slonik Ha-Mashbir = Joseph Samuel b. Isaac Rodi.

Massa Ḥayyim, Tax *halakhot* by Ḥayyim Palaggi, with the subdivisions *Missim ve-Arnoniyyot* and *Torat ha-Minhagot.*

Massa Melekh, Compilation of Tax Law by Joseph b. Isaac Ibn Ezra with concluding part *Ne'ilat She'arim.*

Matteh Asher, Resp. by Asher b. Emanuel Shalem.

Matteh Shimon, Digest of Resp. and Nov. to Tur and *Beit Yosef,* ḤM, by Mordecai Simeon b. Solomon.

Matteh Yosef, Resp. by Joseph b. Moses ha-Levi Nazir.

Mayim Amukkim, Resp. by Elijah b. Abraham Mizraḥi.

Mayim Ḥayyim, Resp. by Ḥayyim b. Dov Beresh Rapaport.

Mayim Rabbim, Resp. by Raphael Meldola.

Me-Emek ha-Bakha, Resp. by Simeon b. Jekuthiel Ephrati.

Meg., *Megillah* (talmudic tractate).

Meg. Ta'an., *Megillat Ta'anit* (in HUCA, 8–9 (1931–32), 318–51).

Me'il., *Me'ilah* (mishnaic tractate).

Me'irat Einayim, usual abbreviation: *Sma* (from: *Sefer Me'irat Einayim*); comm. to Sh. Ar. by Joshua b. Alexander ha-Kohen Falk; printed in most editions of the Sh. Ar.

Mekh., *Mekhilta de-R. Ishmael.*

Mekh. Sby., *Mekhlita de-R. Simeon bar Yoḥai.*

Melammed le-Ho'il, Resp. by David Ẓevi Hoffmann.

Melsharim, [*Sefer*], compilation of *halakhot* by Jeroham b. Meshullam.

Men., *Menaḥot* (talmudic tractate).

Meshiv Davar, Resp. by Naphtali Ẓevi Judah Berlin.

Mez., *Mezuzah* (post-talmudic tractate).

MGWJ, *Monatsschrift fuer Geschichte und Wissenschaft des Judentums* (1851–1939).

Mi-Gei ha-Haregah, Resp. by Simeon b. Jekuthiel Ephrati.

Mi-Ma'amakim, Resp. by Ephraim Oshry.

Michael, Or, H. H. Michael, *Or ha-Ḥayyim: Ḥakhmei Yisrael ve-Sifreihem*, ed. by S. Z. H. Halberstam and N. Ben-Menahem (1965²).

Mid., *Middot* (mishnaic tractate).

Mid. Ag., *Midrash Aggadah.*

Mid. Hag., *Midrash ha-Gadol.*

Mid. Job, *Midrash Job.*

Mid. Jonah, *Midrash Jonah.*

Mid. Lek. Tov, *Midrash Lekaḥ Tov.*

Mid. Prov., *Midrash Proverbs.*

Mid. Ps., *Midrash Tehillim* (Eng. tr. *The Midrash on Psalms* (JPS, 1959)).

Mid. Sam., *Midrash Samuel.*

Mid. Song, *Midrash Shir ha-Shirim.*

Mid. Tan., *Midrash Tanna'im* on Deuteronomy.

Middot Aharon, first part of *Korban Aharon*, a comm. to *Sifra* by Aaron b. Abraham Ibn Ḥayyim.

Mig., Philo, *De Migratione Abrahami.*

Mik., *Mikva'ot* (mishnaic tractate).

Migdal Oz, Comm. to Maimonides, *Yad Ḥazakah*, by Ibn Gaon Shem Tov b. Abraham; printed in most editions of the *Yad Ḥazakah.*

Mikhtam le-David, Resp. by David Samuel b. Jacob Pardo.

Mikkaḥ ve-ha-Mimkar, Sefer ha-, Rabbinical treatise by Hai Gaon.

Milano, Iralia, A. Milano, *Storia degli Ebrei in Italia* (1963).

Milḥamot ha-Shem, Glosses to Rif, *Halakhot*, by Naḥmanides.

Minḥat Ḥinnukh, Comm. to *Sefer ha-Ḥinnukh*, by Joseph b. Moses Babad.

Minḥat Yiẓḥak, Resp. by Isaac Jacob b. Joseph Judah Weiss.

Misgeret ha-Shulḥan, Comm. to Sh. Ar., ḤM, by Benjamin Ze'ev Wolf b. Shabbetai; printed in most editions of Sh. Ar.

Mish., Mishnah.

Mishkenot ha-Ro'im, *Halakhot* in alphabetical order by Uzziel Alshekh.

Mishnah Berurah, Comm. to Sh. Ar., OḤ by Israel Meir ha-Kohen.

Mishneh le-Melekh, Comm. to Maimonides, *Yad Ḥazakah*, by Judah Rosanes; printed in most editions of *Yad Ḥazakah.*

Mishpat ha-Kohanim, Nov. to Sh. Ar., ḤM, by Jacob Moses Lorberbaum, part of his *Netivot ha-Mishpat;* printed in major editions of Sh. Ar.

Mishpat Kohen, Resp. by Abraham Isaac ha-Kohen Kook.

Mishpat Shalom, Nov. by Shalom Mordecai b. Moses Schwadron; contains: *Kunteres Tikkun Olam.*

Mishpat u-Ẓedakah be-Ya'akov, Resp. by Jacob b. Reuben Ibn Ẓur.

Mishpat ha-Urim, Comm. to Sh. Ar., ḤM, by Jacob b. Jacob Moses Lorberbaum, part of his *Netivot ha-Mishpat;* printed in major editions of Sh. Ar.

Mishpat Ẓedek, Resp. by Melammed Meir b. Shem Tov.

Mishpatim Yesharim, Resp. by Raphael b. Mordecai Berdugo.

Mishpetei Shemu'el, Resp. by Samuel b. Moses Kalai (Kal'i).

Mishpetei ha-Tanna'im, Kunteres, Nov. on *Levush*, OḤ by Yom Tov Lipmann b. Nathan ha-Levi Heller.

Mishpetei Uzzi'el (Uziel), Resp. by Ben-Zion Meir Ḥai *Ouziel.

Missim ve-Arnoniyyot, Tax *halakhot* by Ḥayyim Palaggi, a subdivision of his work *Massa Ḥayyim* on the same subject.

Mitzvot, Sefer ha-, Elucidation of precepts by Maimonides; subdivided into *Lavin* (negative precepts) and *Asayin* (postive precepts).

Mitzvot Gadol, Sefer, Elucidation of precepts by Moses b. Jacob of Coucy, subdivided into *Lavin* (negative precepts) and *Asayin* (positive precepts); the usual abbreviation is *Semag.*

Mitzvot Katan, Sefer, Elucidation of precepts by Isaac b. Joseph of Corbeil; the usual abbreviation is *Semak.*

MJC, see Neubauer, Chronicles.

MK, *Mo'ed Katan* (talmudic tractate).

Mo'adim u-Zemannim, Rabbinical treatises by Moses Sternbuch.

Modigliano, Joseph Samuel = Joseph Samuel b. Isaac, Rodi (Ha-Mashbir).

Mordekhai (Mordecai), halakhic compilation by Mordecai b. Hillel; printed in most editions of the Talmud after the texts.

Mos., Philo, *De Vita Mosis.*

Moses b. Maimon = Maimonides, also called Rambam.

Moses b. Naḥman = Naḥmanides, also called Ramban.

MT, Masoretic Text of the Bible.

Muram = Isaiah Menahem b. Isaac (from: Morenu R. Mendel).

Mut., Philo, *De Mutatione Nominum.*

Nah., Nahum (Bible).

Naḥal Yiẓḥak, Comm. on Sh. Ar., ḤM, by Isaac Elhanan Spector.

Naḥalah li-Yhoshu'a, Resp. by Joshua Ẓunẓin.

Naḥalat Shivah, collection of legal forms by Samuel b. David Moses ha-Levi.

Naḥmanides = Moses b. Naḥman, also called Ramban.

Naz., *Nazir* (talmudic tractate).

Naẓiv = Naphtali Ẓevi Judah Berlin.

Ned., *Nedarim* (talmudic tractate).

Ne'eman Shemu'el, Resp. by Samuel Isaac Modigliano.

Neg., *Nega'im* (mishnaic tractate).

Neh., Nehemiah (Bible).

Ne'ilat She'arim, concluding part of *Massa Melekh* (a work on Tax Law) by Joseph b. Isaac Ibn Ezra, containing an exposition of customary law and subdivided into *Minhagei Issur* and *Minhagei Mamon.*

Ner Ma'aravi, Resp. by Jacob b. Malka.

Netivot ha-Mishpat, by Jacob Moses Lorberbaum; subdivided into *Mishpat ha-Kohanim*, Nov. to Sh. Ar., ḤM and *Mishpat ha-Urim*, a comm. on the same; printed in major editions of Sh. Ar.

Netivot Olam, Sayings of the Sages by Judah Loew (Lob, Liwa) b. Bezalel.

Neubauer, Cat., A. Neubauer, *Catalogue of the Hebrew Manuscripts in the Bodleian Library* . . ., 2 vols. (1886–1906).

Neubauer, Chronicles, A. Neubauer, *Mediaeval Jewish Chronicles*, 2 vols. (Heb., 1887–95; repr. 1965), Eng. title of *Seder ha-Ḥakhamim ve-Korot ha-Yamim.*

Neuman, Spain, A. A. Neuman, *The Jews in Spain, their Social, Political, and Cultural Life During the Middle Ages*, 2 vols. (1942).

Neusner, Babylonia, J. Neusner, *History of the Jews in Babylonia*, 5 vols. (1965–70, 2nd revised printing 1969ff.).

Nid., *Niddah* (talmudic tractate).
Nimmukei Menahem of Merseburg, Tax *halakhot* by the same, printed at the end of Resp. Maharyu
Nimmukei Yosef, Comm. to Rif, *Halakhot,* by Joseph Habib (Habiba); printed in many editions of the Talmud.
Noah, Fragment of Book of Noah (Pseudepigrapha).
Noda bi-Yhudah, Resp. by Ezekiel b. Judah ha-Levi Landau; there is a first collection *(Mahadura Kamma)* and a second collection *(Mahadura Tinyana).*
Nov. = Novellae, Hiddushim.
Num., Numbers (Bible).
Num. R., *Numbers Rabbah.*
Obad., Obadiah (Bible).
OH, *Orah Hayyim.*
Ohel Moshe (1), Notes to Talmud, *Midrash Rabbah,* Yad, *Sifrei* and to several Resp., by Eleazar Horowitz.
Ohel Moshe (2), Resp. by Moses Jonah Zweig.
Oho., *Oholot* (mishnaic tractate).
Oholei Tam, Resp. by Tam ibn Yahya Jacob b. David; printed in the rabbinical collection *Tummat Yesharim.*
Oholei Ya'akov, Resp. by Jacob de Castro.
Op., Philo, *De Opificio Mundi.*
OPD, *Osef Piskei Din shel ha-Rabbanut ha-Rashit le-Erez Yisrael, Bet ha-Din ha-Gadol le-Irurim* (1950).
Or., *Orlah* (talmudic tractate).
Or ha-Me'ir, Resp. by Judah Meir b. Jacob Samson Shapiro.
Or Same'ah, Comm. to Maimonides, *Yad Hazakah,* by Meir Simhah ha-Kohen of Dvinsk; printed in many editions of the *Yad Hazakah.*
Or. Sibyll., Sibylline Oracles (Pseudepigrapha).
Or Zaru'a, Nov. and compilation of *halakhot* by Isaac b. Moses of Vienna.
Orah, Sefer ha-, Compilation of ritual precepts by Rashi.
Orah la-Zaddik, Resp. by Abraham Hayyim Rodrigues.
Ozar ha-Posekim, Digest of Responsa.

PAAJR, *Proceedings of the American Academy for Jewish Research* (1930ff.).
Pahad Yizhak, Rabbinical encyclopaedia by Isaac Lampronti.
Panim Me'irot, Resp. by Meir b. Isaac Eisenstadt.
Par., *Parah* (mishnaic tractate).
Parashat Mordekhai, Resp. by Mordecai b. Abraham Naphtali Banet.
Pauly-Wissowa, A.F. Pauly, *Realencyklopaedie* der Klassischen *Altertum-wissenschaft,* ed. by G. Wissowa et al. (1894ff.).
PD, *Piskei Din shel Bet ha-Mishpat ha-Elyon le-Yisrael* (1948ff.).
PDR, *Piskei Din shel Battei ha-Din ha-Rabbaniyyim be-Yisrael.*
PdRE, *Pirkei de-R. Eliezer* (Eng. tr. 1916, 1965^2).
PdRK, *Pesikta de-Rav Kahana.*
Pe'ah, *Pe'ah* (talmudic tractate).
Pe'at ha-Sadeh la-Dinim and *Pe'at ha-Sadeh la-Kelalim,* subdivisions of the *Sedei Hemed,* an encyclopaedia of precepts and responsa, by Hayyim Hezekiah Medini.
Penei Moshe (1), Resp. by Moses Benveniste.
Penei Moshe (2), Comm. to Jer. Talmud by Moses b. Simeon Margolies; printed in most editions of the Jer. Talmud.
Penei Moshe (3), Comm. on the aggadic passages of 18 treatises of the Bab. and Jer. Talmud, by Moses b. Isaiah Katz.
Penei Yehoshu'a, Nov. by Jacob Joshua b. Zevi Hirsch Falk.
Peri Hadash, Comm. on Sh. Ar. by Hezekiah da Silva.
Perishah, Comm. on Tur by Joshua b. Alexander ha-Kohen Falk; printed in major edition of Tur; forms together with *Derishah* and *Be'urim* (by the same author) the *Beit Yisrael.*
Perles, Beitraege, J. Perles, *Beitraege zur rabbinischen Sprach- und Alterthumskunde* (1893).

Pes., *Pesahim* (talmudic tractate).
Pesakim u-Khetavim, 2nd part of the *Terumat ha-Deshen* by Israel b. Pethahiah Isserlein; also called *Piskei Maharai.*
Pesh., Peshitta (Syriac translation of the Bible).
Pesher Hab., Commentary to Habakkuk from Qumran; see IQp Hab.
PIASH, *Proceedings of the Israel Academy of Sciences and Humanities* (1963/4ff.).
Pilpula Harifta, Comm. to *Piskei ha-Rosh, Seder Nezikin,* by Yom Tov Lipmann b. Nathan ha-Levi Heller; printed in major editions of the Talmud.
Piskei Maharai, see *Terumat ha-Deshen,* 2nd part; also called *Pesakim u-Khetavim.*
Piskei ha-Rosh, a compilation of *halakhot,* arranged on the Talmud, by Asher b. Jehiel (Rosh); printed in major Talmud editions.
Pithei Teshuvah, Comm. to Sh. Ar. by Abraham Hirsch b. Jacob Eisenstadt; printed in major editions of the Sh. Ar.
PR, *Pesikta Rabbati.*
Praem., Philo, *De Praemis et Poenis.*
Prawer, Zalbanim, J. Prawer, *Toledot Mamlekhet ha-Zalbanim be-Erez Yisrael,* 2 vols. (1963).
Prichard, Texts, J. B. Pritchard (ed.), *Ancient Near Eastern Texts . . .* (1970^3).
Pr. Man., Prayer of Manasses (Apocrypha).
Prob., Philo, *Quod Omnis Probus Liber Sit.*
Prov., Proverbs (Bible).
Ps., Psalms (Bible).
Ps. of Sol., Psalms of Solomon (Pseudepigrapha).

Rabad = Abraham b. David of Posquières (Rabad III.).
Raban = Eliezer b. Nathan of Mainz.
Raban, also called *Zafenat Pa'ne'ah* or *Even ha-Ezer,* see under the last name.
Rabi ( ) = Abraham b. Isaac of Narbonne.
Rabinovitz, Dik Sof, see Dik. Sof.
Radad = David Dov b. Aryeh Judah Jacob Meisels.
Radam = Dov Berush b. Isaac Meisels.
Radbaz = David b. Solomon ibn Abi Zimra.
Radbaz, Comm. to Maimonides, *Yad Hazakah,* by David b. Solomon ibn Abi Zimra.
Ralbag = Levi b. Gershom, also called Gersonides, or Leo Hebraeus.
Ralbag, Bible comm. by Levi b. Gershon
Rama [da Fano] = Menahem Azariah Fano.
Ramah = Meir b. Todros [ha-Levi]Abulafia.
Ramam = Menahem of Merseburg.
Rambam = Maimonides; real name: Moses b. Maimon.
Ramban = Nahmanides; real name: Moses b. Nahman.
Ramban, Comm. to Torah by Nahmanides; printed in major editions ("Mikra'ot Gedolot").
Ran = Nissim b. Reuben Gerondi.
Ran on Rif, Comm. on Rif, *Halakhot,* by Nissim b. Reuben Gerondi.
Ranah = Elijah b. Hayyim.
Rash = Samson b. Abraham of Sens.
Rash, Comm. to Mishnah, by Samson b. Abraham of Sens; printed in major Talmud editions.
Rashash = Samuel Strashun.
Rashba = Solomon b. Abraham Adret.
Rashba, Resp., see also: *Sefer Teshuvot ha-Rashba ha-Meyuhasot le-ha--Ramban,* by Solomon b. Abraham Adret.
Rashbad = Samuel b. David.
Rashbam = Samuel b. Meir.
Rashbam = Comm. on Bible and Talmud by Samuel b. Meir;

printed in major editions of Bible and most editions of Talmud.
Rashbash = Solomon b. Simeon Duran.
Rashi = Solomon b. Isaac of Troyes.
Rashi, Comm. on Bible and Talmud by Rashi; printed in almost all Bible and Talmud editions.
Raviah = Eliezer b. Joel ha-Levi.
Redak = David Kimḥi.
Redak, Comm. to Bible by David Kimchi.
Redakh = David b. Ḥayyim ha-Kohen of Corfu.
Re'em = Elijah b. Abraham Mizraḥi.
Rema = Moses b. Israel Isserles.
Rema, Glosses to Sh. Ar. by Moses b. Israel Isserles; printed in almost all editions of the Sh. Ar. inside the text in Rashi type; also called *Mappah* or *Haggahot.*
Remak = Moses Kimḥi.
Remakh = Moses ha-Kohen mi-Lunel.
Reshakh = Solomon b. Abraham; also called Maharshakh.
Resp. = Responsa, *She'elot u-Teshuvot.*
RH, *Rosh Ha-Shanah* (talmudic tractate).
Ri Berav = Berab.
Ri Escapa = Joseph b. Saul Escapa.
Ri Migash = Joseph b. Meir ha-Levi ibn Migash.
Riba = Isaac b. Asher ha-Levi; Riba II (Riba ha-Baḥur) = his grandson with the same name.
Ribam = Isaac b. Mordecai (or: Isaac b. Meir).
Ribash = Isaac b. Sheshet Perfet (or: Barfat).
Rid = Isaiah b. Mali di Trani the Elder.
Ridbaz = Jacob David b. Ze'ev Willowski.
Rif = Isaac b. Jacob ha-Kohen Alfasi.
Rif, *Halakhot,* Compilation and abstract of the Talmud by Isaac b. Jacob ha-Kohen Alfasi.
Ritba = Yom Tov b. Abraham Ishbili.
Riẓbam = Isaac b. Mordecai.
Rosanes, Togarmah, S. A. Rosanes, *Divrei Yemei Yisrael be-Togarmah,* 6 vols. (1907–45), and in 3 vols. (1930–38²).
Rosh = Asher b. Jehiel, also called Asheri.
Rosh Mashbir, Resp. by Joseph Samuel b. Isaac, Rodi.
Roth, England, C. Roth, *History of the Jews in England* (1964³).
Roth, Italy, C. Roth, *History of the Jews in Italy* (1946).
Roth, Marranos, C. Roth, *History of the Marranos* (2nd rev. ed. 1959; reprint 1966).
Ruth, Ruth (Bible).
Ruth R., *Ruth Rabbah.*
Sac., Philo, *De Sacrificiis Abelis et Caini.*
I and II Sam., Samuel, books I and II (Bible).
Sanh., *Sanhedrin* (talmudic tractate).
Scholem, Mysticism, G. Scholem, *Major Trends in Jewish Mysticism* (rev. ed., 1946; paperback ed. with additional bibliography 1961).
Sedei Ḥemed, Encyclopaedia of precepts and responsa by Ḥayyim Hezekiah Medini; subdivisions: *Asefat Dinim, Kunteres ha-Kelalim, Pe'at ha-Sadeh la-Dinim, Pe'at ha-Sadeh la-Kelalim.*
Sef. T., *Sefer Torah* (post-talmudic tractate).
Sem., *Semahot* (post-talmudic tractate).
Semag, Usual abbreviation of *Sefer Mitzvot Gadol,* elucidation of precepts by Moses b. Jacob of Coucy; subdivided into *Lavin* (negative precepts) and *Asayin* (positive precepts).
Semak, Usual abbreviation of *Sefer Mitzvot Katan,* elucidation of precepts by Isaac b. Joseph of Corbeil.
SER, *Seder Eliyahu Rabbah.*
SEZ, *Seder Eliyahu Zuta.*
Shab., *Shabbat* (talmudic tractate).
Sh. Ar., J. Caro, Shulḥan Arukh.
OḤ – *Oraḥ Ḥayyim*
YD – *Yoreh De'ah*
EH – *Even ha-Ezer*
ḤM – *Ḥoshen Mishpat.*
Sha'ar Mishpat, Comm. to Sh. Ar., ḤM, by Israel Isser b. Ze'ev Wolf.
Sha'arei Shevu'ot, Treatise on the law of oaths by David b. Saadiah; usually printed together with Rif, *Halakhot;* also called: *She'arim of R. Alfasi.*
Sha'arei Teshuvah, Collection of resp. from Geonic period, by different authors.
Sha'arei Uzzi'el, Rabbinical treatise by Ben-Zion Meir Hai Ouziel.
Sha'arei Ẓedek, Collection of resp. from Geonic period, by different authors.
Shadal [or Shedal] = Samuel David Luzzatto.
Shai la-Moreh, Resp. by Shabbetai Jonah.
Shakh, Usual abbreviation of *Siftei Kohen,* a comm. to Sh. Ar., YD and ḤM, by Shabbetai b. Meir ha-Kohen; printed in most editions of Sh. Ar.
Sha'ot-de-Rabbanan, Resp. by Solomon b. Judah ha-Kohen.
She'arim of R. Alfasi, see *Sha'arei Shevu'ot.*
Shedal, see Shadal.
She'elot u-Teshuvot ha-Ge'onim, Collection of resp. by different authors.
She'erit Yisrael, Resp. by Israel Ze'ev Mintzberg.
She'erit Yosef, Resp. by Joseph b. Mordecai Gershon ha-Kohen.
She'ilat Yaveẓ, Resp. by Jacob Emden (Yaveẓ).
She'iltot, Compilation arranged acc. to the Torah by Aḥa (Aḥai) of Shabha.
Shek., *Shekalim* (talmudic tractate).
Shem Aryeh, Resp. by Aryeh Leib Lipschutz.
Shemesh Ẓedakah, Resp. by Samson Morpurgo.
Shenei ha-Me'orot ha-Gedolim, Resp. by Elijah Covo.
Shetarot, Sefer ha-, Collection of legal forms by Judah b. Barzillai al-Bargeloni.
Shev., *Shevi'it* (talmudic tractate).
Shevu., *Shevu'ot* (talmudic tractate).
Shevut Ya'akov, Resp. by Jacob b. Joseph Reicher.
Shibbolei ha-Leket, Compilation on ritual by Zedekiah b. Abraham Anav.
Shiltei Gibborim, Comm. to Rif, *Halakhot,* by Joshua Boaz b. Simeon; printed in major editions of the Talmud.
Shittah Mekubbeẓet, Compilation of talmudical commentaries by Bezalel Ashkenazi.
Shivat Ẓiyyon, Resp. by Samuel b. Ezekiel Landau.
Shiyyurei Korban, by David Fraenkel; additions to his comm. to Jer. Talmud *Korban Edah,* both printed in most editions of Jer. Talmud.
Sho'el u-Meshiv, Resp. by Joseph Saul ha-Levi Nathanson.
Sh[*ulḥan*] *Ar*[ukh] [of Ba'al ha-Tanyal], Code by Shneur Zalman of Lyady; not identical with the code by Joseph Caro.
Shunami, Bibl., S. Shunami, *Bibliography of Jewish Bibliographies* (1965²).
Sif. Deut., *Sifrei Deuteronomy.*
Sif. Num., *Sifrei Numbers.*
Sifra, *Sifra* on Leviticus.
Siftei Kohen, Comm. to Sh. Ar., YD and ḤM by Shabbetai b. Meir ha-Kohen; printed in most editions of Sh. Ar.; usual abbreviation: *Shakh.*
Sif. Zut., *Sifrei Zuta.*
Simḥat Yom Tov, Resp. by Yom Tov b. Jacob Algazi.
Simlah Ḥadashah, Treatise on *Sheḥitah* by Alexander Sender b.

Ephraim Zalman Schor; see also *Tevu'ot Shor.*
Simeon b. Ẓemah = Simeon b. Ẓemaḥ Duran.
Sma, Comm. to Sh. Ar. by Joshua b. Alexander ha-Kohen Falk; the full title is: *Sefer Me'irat Einayim;* printed in most editions of Sh. Ar.
Sob., Philo, *De Sobrietate.*
Sof., *Soferim* (post-talmudic tractate).
Solomon b. Isaac ha-Levi = Solomon b. Isaac Levy.
Solomon b. Isaac of Troyes = Rashi.
Som., Philo, *De Somniis.*
Song, Song of Songs (Bible).
Song Ch., Song of the Three Children (Apocrypha).
Song R., *Song of Songs Rabbah.*
SOR, *Seder Olam Rabbah.*
Sot., *Sotah* (talmudic tractate).
SOZ, *Seder Olam Zuta.*
Spec., Philo, *De Specialibus Legibus.*
Steinschneider, Cat., M. Steinschneider, *Catalogus Librorum Hebraeorum in Bibliotheca Bodleiana,* 3 vols. (1852–60; reprints 1931 and 1964).
Suk., *Sukkah* (talmudic tractate).
Sus., Susanna (Apocrypha).
Ta'an., *Ta'anit* (talmudic tractate).
Tal Orot, Rabbinical work with various contents, by Joseph ibn Gioia.
Tam., *Tamid* (mishnaic tractate).
Tam, Rabbenu = Tam Jacob b. Meir.
Tanḥ., *Tanḥuma.*
Tanḥ. B., *Tanḥuma,* Buber ed. (1885).
Targ. Jon., Targum Jonathan (Aramaic version of the Prophets).
Targ. Onk., Targum Onkelos (Aramaic version of the Pentateuch).
Targ. Yer., Targum Yerushalmi.
Tashbaẓ = Samson b. Ẓadok.
Tashbeẓ = Simeon b. Ẓemah Duran, sometimes also abbreviation for Samson b. Ẓadok, usually known as Tashbaẓ.
Tashbeẓ [Sefer ha-], Resp. by Simeon b. Ẓemaḥ Duran; the fourth part of this work is called: *Ḥut ha-Meshullash.*
Taz, Usual abbreviation of *Turei Zahav,* comm. to Sh. Ar. by David b. Samuel ha-Levi; printed in most editions of Sh. Ar.
TB, Babylonian Talmud or Talmud Bavli.
Tcherikover, Corpus, V. Tcherikover, A. Fuks, and M. Stern, *Corpus Papyrorum Judaicorum,* 3 vols. (1957–60).
Tef., *Tefillin* (post-talmudic tractate).
(Ha)-Tekhelet, subdivision of the *Levush* (a codification by Mordecai b. Abraham (Levush) Jaffe); *Ha-Tekhelet* parallels Tur, OḤ 1–241.
Tem., *Temurah* (mishnaic tractate).
Ter., *Terumah* (talmudic tractate).
Terumat ha-Deshen, by Israel b. Pethahiah Isserlein; subdivided into a part containing responsa, and a second part called *Pesakim u-Khetavim* or *Piskei Maharai.*
Terumot, Sefer ha-, Compilation of *halakhot* by Samuel b.Isaac Sardi.
Teshuvot Ba'alei ha-Tosafot, Collection of responsa by the Tosafists.
Teshuvot Ge'onei Mizraḥ u-Ma'arav, Collection of responsa.
Teshuvot ha-Geonim, Collection of responsa from Geonic period.
Teshuvot Ḥakhmei Provinẓyah, Collection of responsa by different Provencal authors.
Teshuvot Ḥakhmei Ẓarefat ve-Loter, Collection of responsa by different French authors.
Teshuvot Maimuniyyot, Resp. pertaining to Maimonides' *Yad Ḥazakah;* printed in major editions of this work after the text; authorship, see *Haggahot Maimuniyyot.*
Test. Patr., Testament of the twelve Patriarchs (Pseudepigrapha).
Ash. – Asher
Ben. – Benjamin
Dan – Dan
Gad – Gad
Iss. – Issachar
Joseph – Joseph
Judah – Judah
Levi – Levi
Naph. – Naphtali
Reu. – Reuben
Sim – Simeon
Zeb. – Zebulun.
Tevu'ot Shor, by Alexander Sender b. Ephraim Zalman Schor, a comm. to his *Simlah Ḥadashah,* a work on *Sheḥitah.*
Tiferet Ẓevi, Resp. by Ẓevi Hirsch of the "AHW" Communities (Altona, Hamburg, Wandsbeck).
Tiktin, Judah b. Simeon = Judah b. Simeon Ashkenazi.
TJ, Jerusalem Talmud or Talmud Yerushalmi.
Tob., Tobit (Apocrypha).
Toh., *Tohorot* (mishnaic tractate).
Toledot Adam ve-Ḥavvah, Codification by Jeroham b. Meshullam.
Torat Emet, Resp. by Aaron b. Joseph Sasson.
Torat Ḥayyim, Resp. by Ḥayyim (ben) Shabbetai.
Torat ha-Minhagot, subdivision of the *Massa Ḥayyim* (a work on tax law) by Ḥayyim Palaggi, containing an exposition of customary law.
Tos., *Tosafot.*
Tosafot Rid, Explanations to the Talmud and decisions by Isaiah b. Mali di Trani the Elder
Tosef., Tosefta.
Tosefot Yom Tov, comm. to Mishnah by Yom Tov Lipmann b. Nathan ha-Levi Heller; printed in most editions of the Mishnah.
Tummim, subdivision of the comm. to Sh. Ar., ḤM, *Urim ve-Tummim by* Jonathan Eybeschuetz; printed in the major editions of Sh. Ar.
Tur, usual abbreviation for the *Arba'ah Turim* of Jacob b. Asher.
Turei Zahav, Comm. to Sh. Ar. by David b. Samuel ha-Levi; printed in most editions of Sh. Ar.; usual abbreviation: *Taz.*
TY, *Tevul Yom* (mishnaic tractate).
UJE, *Universal Jewish Encyclopedia,* 10 vols. (1939–43).
Uk., *Ukzin* (mishnaic tractate).
Urbach, Tosafot, E. E. Urbach, *Ba'alei ha-Tosafot* (1957^2).
Urim, subdivision of the following.
Urim ve-Tummim, Comm. to Sh. Ar., ḤM, by Jonathan Eybeschuetz; printed in the major editions of the Sh. Ar.; subdivided in places into *Urim* and *Tummim.*
Vikku'aḥ Mayim Ḥayyim, Polemics against Isserles and Caro by Ḥayyim b. Bezalel.
Virt., Philo, *De Virtutibus.*
Vulg., Vulgate (Latin translation of the Bible).
Wars, Josephus, *The Jewish War.*
Weiss, Dor, I. H. Weiss, *Dor, Dor ve-Dorshav,* 5 vols. (1904^4).
Wisd., Wisdom of Solomon (Apocrypha).
Yad, Maimonides, *Mishneh Torah (Yad Ḥazakah).*
Yad., *Yadayim* (mishnaic tractate).
Yad Malakhi, Methodological treatise by Malachi b. Jacob ha-Kohen.
Yad Ramah, Nov. by Meir b. Todros [ha-Levi] Abulafia.
Yakhin u-Vo'az, Resp. by Ẓemaḥ b. Solomon Duran.
Yal., *Yalkut Shimoni.*
Yal. Mak., *Yalkut Makhiri.*

Yal. Reub., *Yalkut Reubeni.*

Yam ha-Gadol, Resp. by Jacob Moses Toledano.

Yam shel Shelomo, Compilation arranged acc. to Talmud by Solomon b. Jehiel (Maharshal) Luria.

Yashar, Sefer ha-, by Tam, Jacob b. Meir (Rabbenu Tam); 1st pt.: Resp.; 2nd pt.: Nov.

Yaskil Avdi, Resp. by Obadiah Hadaya (printed together with his Resp. *De'ah ve-Haskel*).

Yaveẓ = Jacob Emden.

YD, *Yoreh De'ah.*

Yehudah Ya'aleh, Resp. by Judah b. Israel Aszod.

Yekar Tiferet, Comm. to Maimonides' *Yad Ḥazakah,* by David b. Solomon ibn Zimra, printed in most editions of *Yad Ḥazakah.*

Yere'im [ha-Shalem], [Sefer], Treatise on precepts by Eliezer b. Samuel of Metz.

Yeshu'ot Ya'akov, Resp. by Jacob Meshullam b. Mordecai Ze'ev Ornstein.

Yev., *Yevamot* (talmudic tractate).

Yiẓḥak Rei'aḥ, Resp. by Isaac b. Samuel Abendanan.

YMMY, *Yedi'ot ha-Makhon le-Madda'ei ha-Yahadut* (1924/25ff.).

Yoma, *Yoma* (talmudic tractate).

Ẓafenat Pa'ne'aḥ (1), also called *Raban* or *Even ha-Ezer,* see under the last name.

Ẓafenat Pa'ne'aḥ (2), Resp. by Joseph Rozin.

Zav., *Zavim* (mishnaic tractate).

Zayit Ra'anan, Resp. by Moses Judah Leib b. Benjamin Silberberg.

Zech., Zechariah (Bible).

Ẓeidah la-Derekh, Codification by Menahem b. Aaron ibn Zerah.

Zedakah u-Mishpat, Resp. by Ẓedakah b. Saadiah Huẓin.

Zekan Aharon, Resp. by Elijah b. Benjamin ha-Levi.

Zekher Ẓaddik, Sermons by Eliezer Katzenellenbogen.

Ẓemaḥ Ẓedek (1), Resp. by Menahem Mendel Krochmal.

Ẓemaḥ Ẓedek, (2), Resp. by Menahem Mendel Shneersohn.

Zeph., Zephaniah (Bible).

Zera Avraham, Resp. by Abraham b. David Yiẓḥaki.

Zera Emet, Resp. by Ishmael b. Abraham Isaac ha-Kohen.

Zev., *Zevaḥim* (talmudic tractate).

Ẓevi la-Ẓaddik, Resp. by Ẓevi Elimelech b. David Shapira.

Zikhron Yehudah, Resp. by Judah b. Asher.

Zikhron Yosef, Resp. by Joseph b. Menahem Steinhardt.

Zikhronot, Sefer ha-, Sermons on several precepts by Samuel Aboab.

Zikkaron la-Rishonim . . ., by Albert (Abraham Elijah) Harkavy; contains in vol. 1 pt. 4 (1887) a collection of Geonic responsa.

Ẓiẓ., *Ẓiẓit* (post-talmudic tractate).

Ẓiẓ Eliezer, Resp. by Eliezer Judah b. Jacob Gedaliah Waldenberg.

Zunz-Albeck, Derashot, L. Zunz, *Ha-Derashot be-Yisrael,* Heb. tr. of Zunz, Vortraege by H. Albeck (1954^2).

INDEX

A

B

C

D

E

F

G

H

I

J

K

L

M

N

O

P

Pain, *see Za'ar*
Pardakht (unemployed person) 666
PARENT AND CHILD 424
– abortion 482
– adoption 440
– apostate mother's child 378
– *apotropos* 442
– assault 480, 595
– child marriage 363ff
– circumcision of *menuddeh*'s children 543
– disciplinary punishment 532
– divorce agreement 414ff
– education 672
– embracing 486
– embryo 433
– father entitled to fine 546
– firstborn 434, 602
– foundling 436
– *hazakah* 592
– homicide 470
– honoring parents 708
– incest prohibition 487ff
– levirate marriage 403ff
– maintenance 6, 68, 379, 394ff, 640
– orphan 438
– payment of debts 549
– presumptions of credibility 602
– public office 650
– raped girl's marriage 490
– rapist's payment to girl's father 485
– rebellious son 67, 491
– robbery 493
– *shetuki* 437
– slavery 232ff
– succession 383, 445ff
– *takkanot* 37
– tax exemption for large family 681
– testimony prohibition 607
– widow's rights 401
– will 456, 695, 722
– *yuhasin* 429
Parnasat ha-bat, see **DOWRY**
Parnasim 22, 646, 650, 657, 660
Parshanut, see **INTERPRETATION**
PARTNERSHIP 275
– business documents 186
– community 161
– conflict of laws 719
– contract 247
– corporation 160ff
– court procedure 575
– criminal offenses 470ff
– *hazakah* 592
– lease and hire 270
– legal maxims 158
– *mazranut* 230
– *mehilah* 307
– *minhag* 102ff, 109
– oaths 617, 619
– oral agreement custom 251
– overreaching 218
– property 197
– *shetar iska* 187
– slavery 235, 496
– surety 286
– taxation 667ff, 679, 684
– torts 323
– usury 502
Passover
– divine punishment 523
– *herem* 541
– investment in companies and *hamez* 162
– lien 291
– *ma'ot hittin* 664, 672
– refraining from labor on eve of 106
– searching for leaven 273
– slaves 232
Pater-familias 167, 491
Paternity 430ff
Patria potestas 42, 231
Paupers, *see* Poverty
Pedigree, *see* **YUHASIN**
PENAL LAW 469
– admissions 613
– agency 167
– compounding offenses 547
– confession 614
– court procedure 580ff
– death penalty 526
– development 29
– evidence 599ff
– false oaths 616
– homicide 475ff
– illegal contracts 252
– legal capacity to adjudicate 652
– majority rule 164
– *sevarah* 118
– slavery 231
– *takkanot* 78
– *Takkanot ha-Kahal* 655ff
– taxation 667
– terminology 5
– witnesses 605ff
– *see also:* under individual crimes
Penalty, *see* **FINES; PUNISHMENT**
Penalty meal 355
Pentateuch
– as source of law 12
– halakhic interpretation 53
– homiletical discussions 126
– *ketubbah* 388
– king's law 30
– law and morality 153

R

S

– property 197ff
– *sefer ha-Miknah* 183
– servitudes 204
– *Shi'buda de-Rabbi Nathan* 303
– slaves 231ff
– stolen property 495ff
– *Takkanot ha-Kahal* 658ff
– taxation 673ff
– usury 502
Sanhedrin
– courts 561ff, 583
– evidence rules 600
– power of decision 123
– *takkanot* 82
Sanhedrin Gedolah 561ff, 575, 579, 583
Sanhedrin Ketannah 561ff
Sarsur, see Brokerage
Sarvan (obdurate) 698
Satiation 613
Savoraim 17
Scholars law, *see De-Rabbanan* law
Secular property, *see Ḥullin*
Security for loan, *see* **SURETYSHIP**
Seder ha-ha'arakhah (order of assessment) 689
Seduction
– admission 613
– obligations, law of 242
– rape 181, 490
– sexual offenses 485
Sefer Asheri, see Piskei ha-Rosh
Sefer Gezerata (Sadducean code) 123
Sefer ha-Halakhot 127, 128, 699
Sefer ha-Mitzvot 133
Sefer ha-She'iltot 125
Sefer ha-Terumot 133
Sefer Me'irat Einayim 143
Sefer Mitzvot Gadol 133
Sefer Mitzvot Katan 133
Sefer Torah 619
Sekhirut, see **LEASE AND HIRE**
Self-defense
– criminal responsibility exemption 474
– extraordinary remedies 550
– justifiable homicide 476
– maritime law 335
– *ones* 472
– taxation 667
Self-incrimination, *see* **CONFESSION**
SeMaG, *see Sefer Mitzvot Gadol*
SeMaK, *see Sefer Mitzvot Katan*
Semikhah
– appointment of judges 563ff
– prohibition against 565
Semikhat da'at 172ff
Separation, Marital 395
SERVITUDES 203
– acquisition 205
– nuisance 329ff
– property 198
– *shetar ḥov* 186
Setam hekdesh 701
SEVARAH 117
– authority, rabbinical 55
– bailee's liability 258
– criminal offenses 517
– interpretation 63
– legal source of Jewish law 14
– logical interpretation of Bible 66
– pleas 587, 589
Severance pay, *see* **HA'ANAKAH**
Sex, *see* Cohabitation
SEXUAL OFFENSES 485
– admissions 613
– adultery 488ff
– capital punishment 527
– criminal responsibility of minors 473
– divine punishment 523
– extraordinary remedies 552
– flogging 534
– *ḥerem* 541
– imprisonment 538
– incest 487ff
– levir and *yevamah*'s kin 404
– marriage, prohibited 360ff
– Noachide Laws 708
– penal law 469
– rape 181, 489
– wearing clothes of opposite sex 519
Shali'aḥ, see **AGENCY**
SHALISH 260
– admission 613
– oath 616ff
– pleas 585
– taxation 674
– witness 605
Shame, *see Boshet*
Shamta, see **ḤEREM**
She'elot u-teshuvot, see Responsa
Shefikhut damim, see **HOMICIDE**
Sheḥitah
– *ḥazakah* 595
– *ḥerem* 541
– legal capacity 652
– tax assessment 672
Shekhiv me-ra (sick person)
– admissions 613
– presumptions of common sense 602
– will 433, 453ff
Shema 113
Shemittah, see Sabbatical Year and Jubilee
Shen (tooth)
– *avot nezikin* 324ff
– torts 319ff
Shenei ketuvim ha-makhḥishim zeh et zeh (hermeneutical rule) 64
SHETAR 183
– acquisition 208
– acquisition of slave 233ff

T

U

V

W

Y

Z

CONTRIBUTORS

Elon, Menachem, Dr. Jur., Advocate, Rabbi; Professor of Jewish Law and Director of the Institute for Research in Jewish Law, the Hebrew University of Jerusalem.

Introduction
Abortion
Arbitration
Authority, Rabbinical
Codification of Law
Compromise
Conflict of Laws
Contract
Execution (Civil)
Ha'anakah
Hafka'at She'arim
Hassagat Gevul
Ḥazakah
Hekdesh
Imprisonment
Imprisonment for Debt
Interpretation
Levirate Marriage and Ḥaliẓah
Lien
Limitation of Actions
Ma'aseh (Case and Precedent)
Minhag (Custom)
Obligations, Law of
Pledge
Public Authority & Administrative Law
Sevarah (Legal Logic)
Suretyship
Takkanot (Legislation)
Takkanot Ha-Kahal
Taxation

Albeck, Shalom, Ph. D., Professor of Talmud and Law, Bar-Ilan University, Ramat Gan.

Acquisition
Assignment
Avot Nezikin
Damages
Gerama and Garme
Gift
Hefker
Lost Property
Maritime Law
Maẓranut
Mistake
Nuisance
Ownership
Property
Sale
Servitude
Theft and Robbery (Civil aspects)
Torts
Ye'ush

Berman, Saul, M.A., M.H.L., Rabbi; Brookline, Massachusetts.

Law and Morality
Noachide Laws

Cohn, Haim H., Justice of the Supreme Court of Israel, Jerusalem; Visiting Professor of Law, the Hebrew University of Jerusalem.

Abduction
Admission
Adultery
Assault
Attorney
Bet Din
Blood-Avenger
Bribery
Capital Punishment
City of Refuge
Compounding Offenses
Confession
Confiscation, Expropriation and Forfeiture
Contempt of Court
Divine Punishment
Evidence
Extraordinary Remedies
Fines
Flogging
Forgery
Fraud
Gambling
Ḥerem
Homicide
Incest
Informers
Oath
Oppression
Ordeal
Penal Law
Perjury
Pleas
Police Offenses
Practice and Procedure
Punishment
Rebellious Son
Sexual Offenses
Slander
Slavery
Sorcery
Suicide
Talion
Theft and Robbery (Criminal Law)
Usury
Weights and Measures
Witness

Ehrman, A. Zvi, Dr. Jur., F.J.C., Rabbi, Ramat Gan.

Antichresis
Asmakhta
Conditions

Fuss, Abraham, M., Ph. D., J.D.; Advocate, Jerusalem – New York.

Shetar

Kirschenbaum, Aaron, Ph. D., Rabbi; Associate Professor of Jewish Law, Tel Aviv University.

Domicile
Legal Maxims
Legal Person
Meḥilah
Orphan
Shi'buda De-Rabbi Nathan

Rakover, Nahum, Dr. Jur., Rabbi; Ministry of Justice, Jerusalem.

Agency
Bailment
Lease and Hire
Shalish

Revital, Shmuel D., Dr. Jur., State Comptroller's Office, Jerusalem.

Partnership

Rottenberg, Yechezkel, M. Jur., Instructor in Jewish Law, the Hebrew University of Jerusalem.

Unjust Enrichment

Schereschewsky, Ben-Zion, Dr. Jur.; President of the District Court, Jerusalem.

Adoption
Agunah
Apostate
Apotropos
Betrothal
Bigamy and Polygamy
Child Marriage
Civil Marriage
Mamzer
Marriage
Marriage, Prohibited
Mixed Marriage; Intermarriage
Concubine
Divorce
Dowry
Embryo
Firstborn
Husband and Wife
Ketubbah
Maintenance
Parent and Child
Rape
Widow
Yuḥasin

Shilo, Shmuel, Dr. Jur., Rabbi; Lecturer in Jewish Law, the Hebrew University of Jerusalem.

Dina De-Malkhuta Dina
Loan
Majority Rule
Ona'ah
Ones
Succession
Wills

Warhaftig, Shillem, Dr. Jur.; Ministry of Justice, Jerusalem.

Labor Law